First Philosophy

First Philosophy

Fundamental Problems and Readings in Philosophy

SECOND EDITION

General Editor

ANDREW BAILEY

Contributing Editor

ROBERT M. MARTIN

broadview press

Library and Archives Canada Cataloguing in Publication

First philosophy : fundamental problems and readings in philosophy / general editor Andrew Bailey ; contributing editor Robert M. Martin. — 2nd ed.

Includes bibliographical references.
ISBN 978-1-55111-971-7

1. Philosophy—Textbooks. I. Bailey, Andrew, 1969- II. Martin, Robert M.

B29.F57 2011   100   C2011-900758-4

Broadview Press is an independent, international publishing house, incorporated in 1985.

We welcome comments and suggestions regarding any aspect of our publications—please feel free to contact us at the addresses below or at broadview@broadviewpress.com.

North America	PO Box 1243, Peterborough, Ontario, Canada K9J 7H5
	2215 Kenmore Ave., Buffalo, New York, USA 14207
	Tel: (705) 743-8990; Fax: (705) 743-8353
	email: customerservice@broadviewpress.com
UK, Europe, Central Asia,	Eurospan Group, 3 Henrietta St., London WC2E 8LU, UK
Middle East, Africa, India,	Tel: 44 (0) 1767 604972; Fax: 44 (0) 1767 601640
and Southeast Asia	email: eurospan@turpin-distribution.com
Australia and New Zealand	NewSouth Books, c/o TL Distribution
	15-23 Helles Ave., Moorebank, NSW, Australia 2170
	Tel: (02) 8778 9999; Fax: (02) 8778 9944
	email: orders@tldistribution.com.au

www.broadviewpress.com

Broadview Press acknowledges the financial support of the Government of Canada through the Canada Book Fund for our publishing activities.

PRINTED IN CANADA

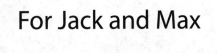

For Jack and Max

CONTENTS

Chapter 4: Philosophy of Science—When, if Ever, Are Scientific Inferences Justified?

Chapter 5: Philosophy of Mind—What Is the Place of Mind in the Physical World?

HOW TO USE THIS BOOK

This book is an introduction to philosophy. It is intended to be a reasonably representative—though very far from exhaustive—sampling of important philosophical questions, major philosophers and their most important works, periods of philosophical history, and styles of philosophical thought.[1] More than half of the included readings, however, were published since 1950, and another important aim of the book is to provide some background for *current* philosophical debates, to give the interested reader a springboard for the plunge into the exciting world of contemporary philosophy (debates about the nature of consciousness, say, or quantum theories of free will, or feminist ethics, or the status of scientific knowledge, or welfarist vs. libertarian accounts of social justice, or …).

The aim of this book is to introduce philosophy through philosophy itself: it is not a book *about* philosophy but a book *of* philosophy, in which more than forty great philosophers speak for themselves. Each of the readings is prefaced by a set of notes, but these notes make no attempt to explain or summarize the reading. Instead, the goal of the notes is to provide *background information* helpful for understanding the reading—to remove as many of the unnecessary barriers to comprehension as possible, and to encourage a deeper and more sophisticated encounter with great pieces of philosophy. The notes to selections, therefore, do not stand alone and *certainly* are not a substitute for the reading itself: they are meant to be consulted in combination with the reading. (The philosophical selections are also quite heavily annotated throughout by the editor, again in an effort to get merely contingent difficulties for comprehension out of the way and allow the reader to devote all his or her effort to understanding the philosophy itself.)

The reader can of course take or leave these notes as they choose, and read them (or not) in any order. One good way of proceeding, however, would be the following. First, read the selection (so that nothing said in the notes inadvertently taints your first impression of the piece). Then, go back and read some of the notes—the biographical sketch, information on the author's philosophical project, structural and background information—and with these things in mind read the selection again. Spend some time *thinking* about the reading: ask yourself if you really feel you have a good grasp on what the author is trying to say, and then—no less importantly—ask yourself whether the author gives good reasons to believe that their position is *true*. (Chapter 1 tries to give some helpful suggestions for this process of critical reflection.) After this, it should be worthwhile going back to the notes, checking your impressions against any 'common misconceptions,' and then running through at least some of the suggestions for critical reflection. Finally, you might want to go on and read more material by the philosopher in question, or examine what other philosophers have said about his or her ideas: the suggestions for further reading will point you in the right direction.

A word of explanation about the 'Suggestions for Critical Reflection' section: although the notes to the readings contain no philosophical critique of the selection, the questions in this section are largely intended to help the reader generate his or her own critique. As such, they are supposed to be thought-provoking, rather than straightforwardly easy to answer. They try to suggest fruitful avenues for critical thought (though they do not cover every possible angle of questioning, or even all the important ones),

---

1   There are two major exceptions to this. First, this book focuses exclusively on 'Western' philosophy—that is, roughly, on the philosophical traditions of Europe and of the descendents of European settlers in North America and Australasia. In particular, it does not attempt to encompass the rich philosophical heritage of Asia or Africa. Second, this collection generally ignores an important strain of twentieth-century philosophy, so-called 'Continental' philosophy, which includes thinkers such as Husserl, Heidegger, Sartre, Foucault, Derrida, and Habermas, and is characterized by such movements as existentialism, hermeneutics, structuralism, and deconstructionism.

and only very rarely is there some particular 'right answer' to the question. Thus, these questions should not be considered a kind of 'self-test' to see if you understand the material: even people with a very good grasp of the material will typically be puzzled by the questions—because they are *supposed* to be puzzling questions.

The readings and their accompanying notes are designed to be 'modular'; that is, in general, one reading can be understood without the benefit of having read any of the other selections. This means that the selections can be read in any order. The current arrangement of the readings groups them by topic, and then orders them so that they follow a reasonably natural progression through a particular philosophical problem. However, quite different courses of study could be plotted through this book, emphasizing, say, philosophers grouped by nationality, by historical period, by philosophical approach, and so on. Furthermore, often readings from one section can quite naturally be brought into another (e.g., Descartes' *Meditations* into the Philosophy of Mind section, or Plato's *Republic* into the section on justice). One natural way of doing the readings is chronologically; here is a list of the contents of the book arranged according to the date of the first 'publication' of the work in its original language:

The readings in this anthology are, so far as is practicable, 'complete': that is, they are entire articles, chapters, or sections of books. The editors feel it is important for students to be able to see an argument in the context in which it was originally presented; also, the fact that the readings are not edited to include only what is relevant to one particular philosophical concern means that they can be used in a variety of different ways following a variety of different lines of thought across the ages. Some instructors will wish to assign for their students shorter excerpts of some of these readings, rather than having them read all of the work included: the fact that complete, or almost complete, pieces of philosophy are included in this anthology gives the instructor the freedom to pick the excerpts that best fit their pedagogical aims. We have also included an alternative table of contents giving suggestions for abridgement corresponding to the shortened pieces most commonly found in other introductory philosophy anthologies.

The notes to the readings in this anthology are almost entirely a work of synthesis, and a large number of books and articles were consulted in their preparation; it is impossible—without adding an immense apparatus of notes and references—to acknowledge them in detail, but all my main sources have been included as suggestions for further reading. This is, I believe, appropriate for a textbook, but it is not intended to model good referencing practices for student essays. All the material and annotations accompanying the readings were written by the editors, and none of it (unless otherwise noted) was cop-ied from other sources. Typically, the notes for each reading amalgamate information from a dozen or so sources; in a few instances, especially for biographical information on still-living philosophers, the notes rely heavily on a smaller number of sources (and I tried to indicate this in the text when it occurred). These sources are not footnoted in the body of the text, as they should be in a student (or professional) essay. However, citations are provided at the back of the book for all direct quotations. All of the books, articles and websites that I referred to and found useful are also listed in bibliographies: Chapter 1 lists general works of reference, and the introductory material for each selection includes suggestions for further reading which include the works I looked at (when I found them helpful).

Students should make sure they are aware of the citation system that their instructor prefers them to use in their class work.

Thanks to Alan Belk, Lance Hickey, Peter Loptson, and Mark Migotti for pointing out errors and omissions in the first edition. In case of a third edition but also, more importantly, for the general good of his soul, the editor would warmly welcome further corrections or suggestions for improvement:

Andrew Bailey
Department of Philosophy
The University of Guelph
Guelph, Ontario N1G 2W1
Canada
abailey@uoguelph.ca

This book has a companion website containing additional readings, review quizzes, and tips for reading and writing philosophy:

http://sites.broadviewpress.com/firstphilosophy

A companion website for instructors is also available, and contains quizzes for each of the book's readings as well as teaching notes. If you are an instructor and would like access to this site, please email customerservice@broadviewpress.com.

SUGGESTIONS FOR ABRIDGEMENT

The following version of the table of contents identifies shorter excerpts of the readings—often those selections most frequently reprinted in other introductory philosophy anthologies—as suggestions for instructors who wish to assign briefer readings for their students.

CHAPTER 1

Philosophy

WHAT IS PHILOSOPHY?

Philosophy, at least according to the origin of the word in classical Greek, is the "love of wisdom"—philosophers are lovers of wisdom. The first philosophers of the Western tradition lived on the shores of the Mediterranean in the sixth century BCE (that is, more than 2,500 years ago);[1] thinkers such as Thales, Xenophanes, Pythagoras, Heraclitus, and Protagoras tried systematically to answer questions about the ultimate nature of the universe, the standards of knowledge, the objectivity of moral claims, and the existence and nature of God. Questions like these are still at the core of the discipline today.

So what is philosophy? It can be characterized either as a particular sort of *method*, or in terms of its *subject matter*, or as a kind of intellectual *attitude*.

Philosophy as a Method

One view is that philosophy studies the same things—the same world—as, for example, scientists do, but that they do so in a different, and complementary, way. In particular, it is often claimed that while scientists draw conclusions from empirical *observations* of the world, philosophers use *rational arguments* to justify claims about the world. For instance, both scientists and philosophers are involved in contemporary studies of the human mind. Neuroscientists and psychologists are busily mapping out correlations between brain states and mental states—finding which parts of the visual

cortex play a role in dreaming, for example—and building computer models of intelligent information processing (such as chess-playing programs). Philosophers are also involved in cognitive science, trying to discover just what would *count* as discovering that dreaming is really nothing more than certain electro-chemical events in the brain, or would count as building a computer which feels pain or genuinely has beliefs. These second kinds of questions are crucial to the whole project of cognitive science, but they are not empirical, scientific questions: there simply is no fact about the brain that a scientist could observe to answer them. And so these questions—which are part of cognitive science—are dealt with by philosophers.

Here are two more examples. Economists study the distribution of wealth in society, and develop theories about how wealth and other goods can come to be distributed one way rather than another (e.g., concentrated in a small proportion of the population, as in Brazil, or spread more evenly across society, as in Sweden). However, questions about which kind of distribution is more *just*, which kind of society is best to live in, are not answered within economic theory—these are philosophical questions. Medical professionals are concerned with facts about sickness and death, and often have to make decisions about the severity of an illness or weigh the risk of death from a certain procedure. Philosophers also examine the phenomenon of death, but ask different questions: for example, they ask whether people can survive their own deaths (i.e., if there is a soul), whether death is really a harm for the person who dies, under what conditions—if any—we should assist people in committing suicide, and so on.

---

1   In the East, Lao-Tzu, the founder of Taoism, probably lived at about the same time in China. Buddha and Confucius were born a few decades later. In India, an oral literature called the *Veda* had been asking philosophical questions since at least 1500 BCE.

One reason why philosophers deal differently with phenomena than scientists do is that philosophers are using different techniques of investigation. The core of the philosophical method is the application of *rational thought* to problems. There are (arguably) two main aspects to this: the use of conceptual or linguistic *analysis* to clarify ideas and questions; and the use of formal or informal *logic* to argue for certain answers to those questions.

For example, questions about the morality of abortion often pivot on the following question: is a foetus a *person* or not? A person is, roughly, someone who has similar moral status to a normal adult human being. Being a person is not simply *the same thing* as being a member of the human species, however, since it is at least possible that some human beings are not persons (brain-dead individuals in permanent comas, for example?) and some persons might not be human beings (intelligent life from other planets, or gorillas, perhaps?). If it turns out that a foetus *is* a person, abortion will be morally problematic—it may even be a kind of murder. On the other hand, if a foetus is no more a person than, say, one of my kidneys, abortion may be as morally permissible as a transplant. So *is* a foetus a person? How would one even go about discovering the answer to this question? Philosophers proceed by using *conceptual analysis*. What we need to find out, first of all, is what makes something a person—what the essential difference is between persons and non-persons—and then we can apply this general account to human foetuses to see if they satisfy the definition. Put another way, we need to discover precisely what the word "person" means.

Since different conceptual analyses will provide importantly different answers to questions about the morality of abortion, we need to *justify* our definition: we need to give reasons to believe that one particular analysis of personhood is correct. This is where logic comes in: logic is the study of arguments, and its techniques are designed to distinguish between good arguments—by which we should be persuaded—and bad arguments, which we should not find persuasive. (The next main section of this chapter will tell you a little more about logic.)

Philosophy as a Subject Matter

Another way of understanding philosophy is to say that philosophers study a special set of issues, and that it is this subject matter which defines the subject. Philosophical questions fit three major characteristics:

1. They are of deep and lasting interest to human beings;
2. They have answers, but the answers have not yet been settled on;
3. The answers cannot be decided by science, faith or common sense.

Philosophers try to give the best possible answers to such questions. That is, they seek the one answer which is more justified than any other possible answer. There are lots of questions which count as philosophical, according to these criteria. All can be classified as versions of one of three basic philosophical questions.

The first foundational philosophical question is *What exists?* For example: Does God exist? Are quarks really real, or are they just fictional postulates of a particular scientific theory? Are numbers real? Do persons exist, and what is the difference between a person and her physical body, or between a person and a 'mere animal'? The various questions of existence are studied by the branch of philosophy called Metaphysics, and by its various sub-fields such as Philosophy of Mind and Philosophy of Religion.

The second fundamental philosophical question is *What do we know?* For example, can we be sure that a scientific theory is actually true, or is it merely the currently dominant simplification of reality? The world appears to us to be full of colors and smells, but can we ever find out whether it really is colored or smelly (i.e., even if no one is perceiving it)? Everyone believes that 5+6=11, but what makes us so sure of this—could we be wrong, and if not, why not? The branch of philosophy which deals with these kinds of questions is called Epistemology. Philosophy of Science examines the special claims to knowledge made by the natural sciences, and Logic is the study of the nature of rational justification.

The third major philosophical question is *What should we do?* If I make a million dollars selling widgets or playing basketball, is it okay for me to keep all of that money and do what I want with it, or do I have some kind of moral obligation to give a portion of my income to the less well off? If I could get out of trouble by telling a lie, and no one else will really be harmed by my lie, is it alright to do so? Is Mozart's *Requiem* more or less artistically valuable than The Beatles' *Sergeant Pepper's Lonely Hearts Club Band*? Questions like these are addressed by Value Theory, which includes such philosophical areas as Ethics, Aesthetics, Political Philosophy, and Philosophy of Law.

Philosophy as an Attitude

A third view is that philosophy is a state of being—a kind of intellectual independence. Philosophy is a reflective activity, an attitude of critical and systematic thoughtfulness. To be philosophical is to continue to question the assumptions behind every claim until we come to our most basic beliefs about reality, and then to critically examine those beliefs. For example, most of us assume that criminals are responsible for their actions, and that this is at least partly why we punish them. But *are* they responsible for what they do? We know that social pressures are very powerful in affecting our behavior. Is it unfair to make individuals entirely responsible for society's effects on them when those effects are negative? How much of our personal identity is bound up with the kind of community we belong to, and how far are we free to choose our own personalities and values? Furthermore, it is common to believe that the brain is the physical cause of all our behavior, that the brain is an entirely physical organ, and that all physical objects are subject to deterministic causal laws. If all of this is right, then presumably all human behavior is just the result of complex causal laws affecting our brain and body, and we could no more choose our actions than a falling rock could choose to take a different route down the mountainside. If this is true, then can we even make sense of the notion of moral responsibility? If it is not true, then where does free will come from and how (if at all) does it allow us to escape the laws of physics? Here, a questioning attitude towards our assumptions about criminals has shown that we might not have properly considered the bases of our assumptions. This ultimately leads us to fundamental questions about the place of human beings in the world.

Here are three quotes from famous philosophers which give the flavor of this view of philosophy as a critical attitude:

Socrates, one of the earliest Western philosophers, who lived in Greece around 400 BCE, is said to have declared that "it is the greatest good for a man to discuss virtue every day and those other things about which you hear me conversing and testing myself and others, for the unexamined life is not worth living."

Immanuel Kant—the most important thinker of the late eighteenth century—called this philosophical state of being "Enlightenment."

> Enlightenment is the emergence of man from the immaturity for which he is himself responsible. Immaturity is the inability to use one's understanding without the guidance of another. Man is responsible for his own immaturity, when it is caused, by lack not of understanding, but of the resolution and the courage to use it without the guidance of another. *Sapere aude!* Have the courage to use your own reason! is the slogan of Enlightenment.

Finally, in the twentieth century, Bertrand Russell wrote the following assessment of the value of philosophy:

> Philosophy is to be studied, not for the sake of any definite answers to its questions, since no definite answers can, as a rule, be known to be true, but rather for the sake of the questions themselves; because these questions enlarge our conception of what is possible, enrich our intellectual imagination and diminish the dogmatic assurance which closes the mind against speculation; but above all because, through the greatness of the universe which philosophy contemplates, the mind also is rendered great, and becomes capable of that union with the universe which constitutes its highest good.

Questions for Further Thought:

1. Here are some more examples of phenomena which are studied by both scientists and philosophers: color, sense perception, medical practices like abortion and euthanasia, human languages, mathematics, quantum mechanics,

the evolution of species, democracy, taxation. What contribution (if any) might philosophers make to the study of these topics?

2. How well does *mathematics* fit into the division between science and philosophy described above? How does *religion* fit into this classification?

3. Here are a few simple candidate definitions of "person": a person is anything which is capable of making rational decisions; a person is any creature who can feel pain; a person is any creature with a soul; a person is any creature which has the appropriate place in a human community. Which of these, if any, do you think are plausible? What are the consequences of these definitions for moral issues like abortion or vegetarianism? Try to come up with a more sophisticated conceptual analysis of personhood.

4. Do you think criminals are responsible for their actions?

5. Should society support philosophy, and to what degree (e.g., should tax dollars be spent paying philosophers to teach at public universities? Why (not)?)?

Suggestions for Further Reading

As a general rule, it is far better to read philosophy than to read *about* philosophy. A brief but moving work often anthologized in the "what is philosophy" section of introductory textbooks is Plato's *Apology*, which features a speech by Socrates defending the practice of philosophy in the face of his fourth-century BCE Athenian contemporaries, who are about to condemn him to death for it. Two more modern works, which are introductions to philosophy but also significant pieces of philosophy in their own right, are Bertrand Russell's *The Problems of Philosophy* (Oxford University Press, 1912) and *The Central Questions of Philosophy* by A.J. Ayer (Penguin, 1973).

Two aging, slightly idiosyncratic, but nevertheless well-respected histories of western philosophy are Bertrand Russell's *A History of Western Philosophy* (George Allen & Unwin, 1961) and the massive *History of Philosophy* by Frederick Copleston, originally published between 1946 and 1968 and recently re-issued in nine garish volumes by Image Books. Two shorter and more recent histories are *A Brief History of Western Philosophy* by Anthony Kenny (Blackwell, 1998) and *The Oxford Illustrated History of Western Philosophy*, edited by Anthony Kenny (Oxford University Press, 1994).

Finally, there are a number of useful philosophical reference works. The major encyclopedia of philosophy is now the ten-volume *Routledge Encyclopedia of Philosophy*, published in 1998. This replaced the old standby—which is still a useful work, consisting of eight volumes—*The Encyclopedia of Philosophy* edited by Paul Edwards (Macmillan, 1967). Shorter philosophy reference works include *The Concise Routledge Encyclopedia of Philosophy* (Routledge, 2000); *The Cambridge Dictionary of Philosophy*, edited by Robert Audi (Cambridge University Press, 1999); the *Oxford Dictionary of Philosophy*, by Simon Blackburn (Oxford University Press, 1996); *The Blackwell Companion to Philosophy*, edited by Nicholas Bunnin and E.P. Tsui-James (Blackwell, 1996); *The Oxford Companion to Philosophy*, edited by Ted Honderich (Oxford University Press, 1995); *The Philosopher's Dictionary*, by Robert Martin (Broadview, 1994); and the *Penguin Dictionary of Philosophy*, edited by Thomas Mautner (Penguin, 1997). Online philosophy is not always very reliable and should be treated with caution, but two websites which are dependable and likely to be around for a while are the *Stanford Encyclopedia of Philosophy* (http://plato.stanford.edu/) and *The Internet Encyclopedia of Philosophy* (http://www. utm. edu/research/iep/).

A BRIEF INTRODUCTION TO ARGUMENTS

Evaluating Arguments

The main tool of philosophy is the *argument*. An argument is any sequence of statements intended to establish—or at least to make plausible—some particular claim. For example, if I say that Vancouver is a better place to live than Toronto because it has a beautiful setting between the mountains and the ocean, is less congested, and has a lower cost of living, then I am making an argument. The claim which is being defended is called the *conclusion*, and the statements which together are supposed to show that the conclusion is (likely to be) true are called the *premises*. Often arguments will be strung together in a sequence, with the conclusions of earlier arguments featuring as premises of the later ones. For example, I might go on to argue that since Vancouver is a better place to live than Toronto, and since one's living conditions are a big part of what determines one's happiness, then the people who live in Vancouver must, in general, be happier than those living in Toronto. Usually, a piece of philosophy is primarily made up of chains of argumentation: good philosophy consists of good arguments; bad philosophy contains bad arguments.

What makes the difference between a good and a bad argument? It's important to notice, first of all, that the difference is *not* that good arguments have true conclusions and bad arguments have false ones. A perfectly good argument might, unluckily, happen to have a conclusion that is false. For example, you might argue that you know this rope will bear my weight because you know that the rope's rating is greater than my weight, you know that the rope's manufacturer is a reliable one, you have a good understanding of the safety standards which are imposed on rope makers and vendors, and you have carefully inspected this rope for flaws. Nevertheless, it still might be the case that this rope is the one in 50 million which has a hidden defect causing it to snap. If so, that makes me unlucky, but it doesn't suddenly make your argument a bad one—we were still being quite reasonable when we trusted the rope. On the other hand, it is very easy to give appallingly bad arguments for true conclusions: Every sentence beginning with the letter "c" is true; "Chickens lay eggs" begins with the letter "c"; Therefore, chickens lay eggs.

But there is a deeper reason why the evaluation of arguments doesn't begin by assessing the truth of the conclusion. The whole point of making arguments is to establish *whether or not* some particular claim is true or false. An argument works by starting from some claims which, ideally, everyone is willing to accept as true—the premises—and then showing that something interesting—something *new*—follows from them: i.e., an argument tells you that *if* you believe these premises, *then* you should also believe this conclusion. In general, it would be unfair, therefore, to simply reject the conclusion and suppose that the argument must be a bad one—in fact, it would often be intellectually dishonest. If the argument *were* a good one, then it would show you that you might be *wrong* in supposing its conclusion to be false; and to refuse to accept this is not to respond to the argument but simply to ignore it.[2]

It follows that there are exactly two reasonable ways to criticize an argument: the first is to question the truth of the *premises*; and the second is to question the claim that if the premises are true then the conclusion is true as well—that is, one can critique the *strength* of the argument. Querying the truth of

---

2   Of course, occasionally, you might legitimately know *for sure* that the conclusion is false, and then you could safely ignore arguments which try to show it is true: for example, *after* the rope breaks, I could dismiss your argument that it is safe (again, though, this would not show that your argument was *bad*, just that I need not be persuaded that the conclusion is true). However, this will not do for philosophical arguments: all interesting philosophy deals with issues where, though we may have firm opinions, we cannot just insist that we know all the answers and can therefore afford to ignore relevant arguments.

the premises (i.e., asking whether it's really true that Vancouver is less congested or cheaper than Toronto) is fairly straightforward. The thing to bear in mind is that you will usually be working backwards down a chain of argumentation: that is, each premise of a philosopher's main argument will often be supported by sub-arguments, and the controversial premises in these sub-arguments might be defended by further arguments, and so on. Normally it is not enough to merely demand to know whether some particular premise is true: one must look for *why* the arguer thinks it is true, and then engage with *that* argument.

Understanding and critiquing the strength of an argument (either your own or someone else's) is somewhat more complex. In fact, this is the main subject of most books and courses in introductory logic. When dealing with the strength of an argument, it is usual to divide arguments into two classes: *deductive* arguments and *inductive* arguments. Good deductive arguments are the strongest possible kind of argument: if their premises are true, then their conclusion *must necessarily* be true. For example, if all bandicoots are rat-like marsupials, and if Billy is a bandicoot, then it cannot possibly be false that Billy is a rat-like marsupial. On the other hand, good inductive arguments establish that, if the premises are true, then the conclusion is *highly likely* (but not absolutely certain) to be true as well. For example, I may notice that the first bandicoot I see is rat-like, and the second one is, and the third, and so on; eventually, I might reasonably conclude that all bandicoots are rat-like. This is a good argument for a probable conclusion, but nevertheless the conclusion can never be shown to be *necessarily* true. Perhaps a non-rat-like bandicoot once existed before I was born, or perhaps there is one living now in an obscure corner of New Guinea, or perhaps no bandicoot so far has ever been non-rat-like but at some point, in the future, a mutant bandicoot will be born that in no way resembles a rat, and so on.

Deductive Arguments and Validity

The strength of deductive arguments is an on/off affair, rather than a matter of degree. Either these arguments are such that if the premises are true

then the conclusion necessarily must be, or they are not. Strong deductive arguments are called *valid*; otherwise, they are called *invalid*. The main thing to notice about validity is that its definition is an *if… then…* statement: *if* the premises *were* true, then the conclusion *would* be. For example, an argument can be valid even if its premises and its conclusion are not true: all that matters is that if the premises *had* been true, the conclusion necessarily would have been as well. This is an example of a valid argument:

1. Either bees are rodents or they are birds.
2. Bees are not birds.
3. Therefore bees are rodents.

If the first premise were true, then (since the second premise is already true), the conclusion would *have* to be true—that's what makes this argument valid. This example makes it clear that validity, though a highly desirable property in an argument, is not enough all by itself to make a good argument: good deductive arguments are both valid *and* have true premises. When arguments are good in this way they are called *sound*: sound arguments have the attractive feature that they necessarily have true conclusions. To show that an argument is unsound, it is enough to show that it is either invalid or has a false premise.

It bears emphasizing that even arguments which have true premises and a true conclusion can be unsound. For example:

1. Only US citizens can become the President of America.
2. George W. Bush is a US citizen.
3. Therefore, George W. Bush was elected President of America.

This argument is not valid, and therefore it should not convince anyone who does not already believe the conclusion to start believing it. It is not valid because the conclusion could have been false even though the premises were true: Bush could have lost to Gore in 2000, for example. The question to ask, in thinking about the validity of arguments is this: Is there a coherent possible world, which I can even *imagine*, in which the premises are true and the conclusion false? If there is, then the argument is invalid.

When assessing the deductive arguments that you encounter in philosophical work, it is often useful to try to lay out, as clearly as possible, their *structure*. A standard and fairly simple way to do this is simply to pull out the logical connecting phrases and to replace, with letters, the sentences they connect. Five of the most common and important 'logical operators' are *and, or, it is not the case that, if … then …*, and *if and only if*…. For example, consider the following argument: "If God is perfectly powerful (omnipotent) and perfectly good, then no evil would exist. But evil does exist. Therefore, God cannot be both omnipotent and perfectly good, so either God is not all-powerful or he is not perfectly good." The structure of this argument could be laid bare as follows:

1. If (O and G) then not-E.
2. E.
3. Therefore not-(O and G).
4. Therefore either not-O or not-G.

Revealing the structure in this way can make it easier to see whether or not the argument is valid. And in this case, it is valid. In fact, no matter what O, G, and E stand for—no matter how we fill in the blanks—*any* argument of this form must be valid. You could try it yourself—invent random sentences to fill in for O, G, and E, and no matter how hard you try, you will never produce an argument with all true premises and a false conclusion.[3] What this shows is that validity is often a property of the *form* or structure of an argument. (This is why deductive logic is known as "formal logic." It is not formal in the sense that it is stiff and ceremonious, but because it has to do with argument forms.)

Using this kind of shorthand, therefore, it is possible to describe certain general argument forms which are *invariably* valid and which—since they are often used in philosophical writing—it can be handy to look out for. For example, a very common and valuable form of argument looks like this: if P then Q; P; therefore Q. This form is often called *modus ponens*. Another—

which appears in the previous argument about God and evil—is *modus tollens*: if P then Q; not-Q; therefore not-P. A *disjunctive syllogism* works as follows: either P or Q; not-P; therefore Q. A *hypothetical syllogism* has the structure: if P then Q; if Q then R; therefore if P then R. Finally, a slightly more complicated but still common argument structure is sometimes called a *constructive dilemma*: either P or Q; if P then R; if Q then R; therefore R.

Inductive Arguments and Inductive Strength

I noted above that the validity of deductive arguments is a yes/no affair—that a deductive argument is either extremely strong or it is hopelessly weak. This is not true for inductive arguments. The strength of an inductive argument—the amount of support the premises give to the conclusion—is a matter of degree, and there is no clear dividing line between the 'strong' inductive arguments and the 'weak' ones. Nevertheless, some inductive arguments are obviously much stronger than others, and it is useful to think a little bit about what factors make a difference.

There are lots of different types and structures of inductive arguments; here I will briefly describe four which are fairly representative and commonly encountered in philosophy. The first is *inductive generalization*. This type of argument is the prototype inductive argument—indeed, it is often what people mean when they use the term "induction"—and it has the following form:

1. *x* per cent of observed Fs are G.
2. Therefore *x* per cent of all Fs are G.

That is, inductive generalizations work by inferring a claim about an entire *population* of objects from data about a *sample* of those objects. For example:

(a) Every swan I have ever seen is white, so all swans (in the past and future, and on every part of the planet) are white.

(b) Every swan I have ever seen is white, so probably all the swans around here are white.

(c) 800 of the 1,000 rocks we have taken from the Moon contain silicon, so probably around 80% of the Moon's surface contains silicon.

---

3   Since the argument about God and evil is valid, then we are left with only two possibilities. Either all its premises are true, and then it is sound and its conclusion *must* inescapably be true. Or one of its premises is false, in which case the conclusion *might* be false (though we would still not have shown that it *is* false). The only way to effectively critique this argument, therefore, is to argue against one of the claims 1 and 2.

(d) We have tested two very pure samples of copper in the lab and found that each sample has a boiling point of 2,567°C; we conclude that 2,567°C is the boiling point for copper.

(e) Every intricate system I have seen created (such as houses and watches) has been the product of intelligent design, so therefore all intricate systems (including, for example, frogs and volcanoes) must be the product of intelligent design.

The two main considerations when assessing the strength of inductive generalizations are the following. First, ask how *representative* is the sample? How likely is it that whatever is true of the sample will also be true of the population as a whole? For instance, although the sample size in argument (c) is much larger than that in argument (d), it is much more likely to be biased: we know that pure copper is very uniform, so a small sample will do; but the surface of the Moon might well be highly variable, and so data about the areas around moon landings may not be representative of the surface as a whole. Second, it is important to gauge how cautious and *accurate* the conclusion is, given the data—how far beyond the evidence does it go? The conclusion to argument (a) is a much more radical inference from the data than that in argument (b); consequently, though less exciting, the conclusion of argument (b) is much better supported by the premise.

A second type of inductive argument is an *argument from analogy*. It most commonly has the following form:

1. Object (or objects) A and object (or objects) B are alike in having features F, G, H, …
2. B has feature X.
3. Therefore A has feature X as well.

These examples illustrate arguments from analogy:

(a) Human brains and dolphin brains are large, compared to body size. Humans are capable of planning for the future. So, dolphins must also be capable of planning for the future.

(b) Humans and dolphins are both mammals and often grow to more than five feet long. Humans are capable of planning for the future. So, dolphins must also be capable of planning for the future.

(c) Eagles and robins are alike in having wings, feathers, claws, and beaks. Eagles kill and eat sheep. Therefore, robins kill and eat sheep.

(d) Anselm's ontological argument has the same argumentative form as Gaunilo's "perfect island" argument. But Gaunilo's argument is a patently bad argument. So there must be something wrong with the ontological argument.

(e) An eye and a watch are both complex systems in which all of the parts are inter-dependent and where any small mis-adjustment could lead to a complete failure of the whole. A watch is the product of intelligent design. Therefore, the eye must also be the product of intelligent design (i.e., God exists).

The strength of an argument from analogy depends mostly on two things: first, the degree of *positive relevance* that the noted similarities (F, G, H …) have to the target property X; and second, the absence of *relevant dissimilarities*—properties which A has but B does not, which make it *less* likely that A is X. For example, the similarity (brain size) between humans and dolphins cited in argument (a) is much more relevant to the target property (planning) than are the similarities cited in argument (b). This, of course, makes (a) a much stronger argument than (b). The primary problem with argument (c), on the other hand, is that we know that robins are much smaller and weaker than eagles and this dissimilarity makes it far less likely that they kill sheep.

A third form of inductive argument is often called *inference to the best explanation* or sometimes *abduction*. This kind of argument works in the following way. Suppose we have a certain quantity of data to explain (such as the behavior of light in various media, or facts about the complexity of biological organisms, or a set of ethical claims). Suppose also that we have a number of theories which account for this data in different ways (e.g., the theory that light is a particle, or the theory that light is a wave, or the theory that it is somehow both). One way of arguing for the truth of one of these theories, over the others, is to show that one theory provides a much *better explanation* of the data than the others. What counts as making a theory a better explanation can be a bit tricky, but some basic criteria would be:

1. The theory predicts all the data we know to be true.
2. The theory explains all this data in the most economical and theoretically satisfying way (scientists and mathematicians often call this the most *beautiful* theory).
3. The theory predicts some *new* phenomena which turn out to exist and which would be a big surprise if one of the competing theories were true. (For example, one of the clinchers for Einstein's theory of relativity was the observation that starlight is bent by the sun's gravity. This would have been a big surprise under the older Newtonian theory, but was predicted by Einstein's theory.)

Here are some examples of inferences to the best explanation:

(a) When I inter-breed my pea plants, I observe certain patterns in the properties of the plants produced (e.g., in the proportion of tall plants, or of plants which produce wrinkled peas). If the properties of pea plants were generated randomly, these patterns would be highly surprising. However, if plants pass on packets of information (genes) to their offspring, the patterns I have observed would be neatly explained. Therefore, genes exist.

(b) The biological world is a highly complex and inter-dependent system. It is highly unlikely that such a system would have come about (and would continue to hang together) from the purely random motions of particles. It would be much less surprising if it were the result of conscious design from a super-intelligent creator. Therefore, the biological world was deliberately created (and therefore, God exists).

(c) The biological world is a highly complex and inter-dependent system. It is highly unlikely that such a system would have come about (and would continue to hang together) from the purely random motions of particles. It would be much less surprising if it were the result of an evolutionary process of natural selection which mechanically preserves order and eliminates randomness, and which (if it existed) would produce a world much like the one we see

around us. Therefore, the theory of evolution is true.

The final type of inductive argument that I want to mention here is usually called *reductio ad absurdum*, which means "reduction to absurdity." It is always a negative argument, and has this structure:

1. Suppose (for the sake of argument) that position *p* were true.
2. If *p* were true then something else, *q*, would also have to be true.
3. However *q* is absurd—it can't possibly be true.
4. Therefore *p* can't be true either.

In fact, this argument style can be either inductive or deductive, depending on how rigorous the premises 2 and 3 are. If *p* logically implies *q*, and if *q* is a logical contradiction, then it is deductively certain that *p* can't be true (at least, assuming the classical laws of logic). On the other hand, if *q* is merely absurd but not literally *impossible*, then the argument is inductive: it makes it highly likely that *p* is false, but does not prove it beyond all doubt.

Here are a few examples of *reductio* arguments:

(a) Suppose that gun control were a good idea. That would mean it's a good idea for the government to gather information on anything we own which, in the wrong hands could be a lethal weapon, such as kitchen knives and baseball bats. But that would be ridiculous. This shows gun control cannot be a good idea.

(b) If you think that foetuses have a right to life because they have hearts and fingers and toes, then you must believe that *anything* with a heart, fingers, and toes has a right to life. But that would be absurd. Therefore, a claim like this about foetuses cannot be a good argument against abortion.

(c) Suppose, for the sake of argument, that this is not the best possible world. But that would mean God had either deliberately chosen to create a sub-standard world or had failed to notice that this was not the best of all possible worlds, and either of these options is absurd. Therefore, it must be true that this is the best of all possible worlds.

(d) "The anti-vitalist says that there is no such thing as vital spirit. But this claim is self-refuting. The speaker can be taken seriously only if his claim cannot. For if the claim is true, then the speaker does not have vital spirit and must be *dead*. But if he is dead, then his statement is a meaningless string of noises, devoid of reason and truth." (If you want more information, see Paul Churchland's "Eliminative Materialism and the Propositional Attitudes," *Journal of Philosophy* 78 [1981].)

The critical questions to ask about *reductio* arguments are simply: *Does* the supposedly absurd consequence follow from the position being attacked? and Is it *really* absurd?

A Few Common Fallacies

Just as it can be useful to look for common patterns of reasoning in philosophical writing, it can also be helpful to be on guard for a few recurring fallacies—and, equally importantly, to take care not to commit them in your own philosophical writing. Here are four common ones:

Begging the question does not mean, as the media would have us believe, stimulating one to ask a further question; instead, it means to assume as true (as one of your premises) the very same thing which you are supposedly attempting to prove. This fallacy is sometimes called *circular reasoning* or even (the old Latin name) *petitio principii*. To argue, for example, that God exists because (a) it says in the Bible that God exists, (b) God wrote the Bible, and (c) God would not lie, is to commit a blatant case of begging the question. In this case, of course, one would have no reason to accept the premises as true unless one *already* believed the conclusion. Usually, however, arguments that beg the question are a little more disguised. For example, "Adultery is immoral, since sexual relations outside marriage violate ethical principles," or "Terrorism is bad, because it encourages further acts of terrorism," are both instances of circular reasoning.

Arguing *ad hominem* means attacking or rejecting a position not because the arguments for it are poor, but because the person presenting those arguments is unattractive in some way: i.e., an attack is directed at the person (*ad hominem*) rather than at their argu-

ment. The following are implicit *ad hominem* arguments: "You say you want to close down the church? Well, Hitler and Stalin would agree with you!" and "We shouldn't trust the claim, by philosophers such as Anselm, Aquinas, and Leibniz, that God exists, since they were all Christian philosophers and so of course they were biased." Such attacks are fallacious because they have nothing at all to do with how reasonable a claim is: even if the claim is false, *ad hominem* attacks do nothing to show this.

Straw man arguments are particularly devious, and this fallacy can be hard to spot (or to avoid committing) unless great care is taken. The *straw man* fallacy consists in misrepresenting someone else's position so that it can be more easily criticized. It is like attacking a dummy stuffed with straw instead of a real opponent. For example, it's not uncommon to see attacks on "pro-choice" activists for thinking that abortion is a good thing. However, whatever the merits of either position, this objection is clearly unfair—no serious abortion advocates think it is a positively *good thing* to have an abortion; at most they claim that (at least in some circumstances) it is a lesser evil than the alternative. Here's an even more familiar example, containing two straw men, one after the other: "We should clean out the closets. They're getting a bit messy." "Why, we just went through those closets last year. Do we have to clean them out every day?" "I never said anything about cleaning them out every day. You just want to keep all your junk forever, which is simply ridiculous."

Arguments from ignorance, finally, are based on the assumption that lack of evidence *for* something is evidence that it is false, or that lack of evidence *against* something is evidence for its truth. Generally, neither of these assumptions are reliable. For example, even if we could find no good proof to show that God exists, this would not, all by itself, suffice to show that God does *not* exist: it would still be possible, for example, that God exists but transcends our limited human reason. Consider the following 'argument' by Senator Joseph McCarthy, about some poor official in the State Department: "I do not have much information on this except the general statement of the agency that there is nothing in the files to disprove his Communist connections."

Suggestions for Critical Reflection

1. Suppose some deductive argument has a premise which is necessarily false. Is it a valid argument?

2. Suppose some deductive argument has a conclusion which is necessarily true. Is it a valid argument? From this information alone, can you tell whether it is sound?

3. Is the following argument form valid: if P then Q; Q; therefore P? How about: if P then Q; not-P; so not-Q?

4. No inductive argument is strong enough to *prove* that its conclusion is true: the best it can do is to show that the conclusion is highly probable. Does this make inductive arguments bad or less useful? Why don't we restrict ourselves to using only deductive arguments?

5. Formal logic provides mechanical and reliable methods for assessing the validity of deductive arguments. Do you think there might be some similar system for evaluating the strength of inductive arguments?

6. I have listed four important fallacies; can you identify any other common patterns of poor reasoning?

Suggestions for Further Reading

An entertaining, thought-provoking and brief introduction to logic can be found in Graham Priest's *Logic: A Very Short Introduction* (Oxford University Press, 2000); an equally brief but highly practical primer on arguing is Anthony Weston's *A Rulebook for Arguments* (Hackett, 2001). There are many books which competently lay out the nuts and bolts of formal logic: Richard Jeffrey's *Formal Logic: Its Scope and Limits* (McGraw-Hill, 1991) is short but rigorous and clear; *The Logic Book* by Bergmann, Moor, and Nelson (McGraw-Hill, 1998), on the other hand, is rather painstaking but is one of the most complete texts. An interesting book which explains not only classical formal logic but also makes accessible some more recently developed logical languages, such as modal logic and intuitionistic logic, is Bell, DeVidi, and Solomon's *Logical Options* (Broadview Press, 2001). Two somewhat older texts, which were used to teach many of the current generation of professional philosophers and are still much used today, are Wilfrid Hodges's *Logic* (Penguin, 1977) and E.J. Lemmon's *Beginning Logic* (Hackett, 1978).

One of the best introductory texts on inductive logic is Brian Skyrms's *Choice & Chance* (Wadsworth, 2000). Other good texts include Copi and Burgess-Jackson's *Informal Logic* (Prentice Hall, 1995), Fogelin and Sinnott-Armstrong's *Understanding Arguments* (Harcourt, 2001), and Douglas Walton's *Informal Logic: A Handbook for Critical Argumentation* (Cambridge University Press, 1989). Quite a good book on fallacies is *Attacking Faulty Reasoning* by T. Edward Damer (Wadsworth, 2000), while Darrell Huff's *How to Lie with Statistics* (W.W. Norton, 1954) is an entertaining guide to the tricks that can be played with bad inductive arguments in, for example, advertising.

INTRODUCTORY TIPS ON READING AND WRITING PHILOSOPHY

Reading Philosophy

As you will soon find out, if you haven't already, it is not easy to read philosophy. It can be exhilarating, stimulating, life-changing, or even annoying, but it isn't easy. There are no real shortcuts for engaging with philosophy (though the notes accompanying the readings in this book are intended to remove a few of the more unnecessary barriers); however, there are two things to remember which will help you get the most out of reading philosophy—*read it several times*, and *read it actively*.

Philosophical writing is not like a novel, a historical narrative, or even a textbook: it is typically dense, compressed, and written to contribute to an ongoing debate with which you may not yet be fully familiar. This means, no matter how smart you are, it is highly unlikely that you will get an adequate understanding of any halfway interesting piece of philosophy the first time through, and it may even take two or three more readings before it really becomes clear. Furthermore, even after that point, repeated readings of good philosophy will usually reveal new and interesting nuances to the writer's position, and occasionally you will notice some small point that seems to open a mental door and show you what the author is trying to say in a whole new way. As they say, if a piece of philosophy isn't worth reading at least twice, it isn't worth reading once. Every selection in this book, I guarantee, is well worth reading once.

As you go through a piece of philosophy, it is very important to engage with it: instead of just letting the words wash over you, you should make a positive effort, first, to understand and then, to critically assess the ideas you encounter. On your first read-through it is a good idea to try to formulate a high-level understanding of what the philosopher is attempting: What are the main claims? What is the overall structure of the arguments behind them? At this stage, it can be useful to pay explicit attention to section headings and introductory paragraphs.

Ideally during a second reading, you should try to reconstruct the author's arguments and sub-arguments in more detail. To help yourself understand them, consider jotting down their outlines on a sheet of paper. At this point, it can be extremely fruitful to pay attention to special definitions or distinctions used by the author in the arguments. It is also helpful to consider the historical context in which the philosopher wrote, and to look for connections to ideas found in other philosophical works.

Finally, on third and subsequent readings, it is valuable to expressly look for *objections* to the writer's argument (Are the premises true? Is the argument strong?), *unclarities* in position statements, or *assumptions* they depend upon, but do not argue for. I make these suggestions partly because the process of critical assessment is helpful in coming to understand a philosopher's work; but more importantly for the reason that—perhaps contrary to popular opinion—philosophers are typically playing for very high stakes. When philosophers write about whether God exists, whether science is a rational enterprise, or whether unfettered capitalism creates a just society, they are seriously interested in discovering the *answers* to these questions. The arguments they make, if they are good enough, will be strong reasons to believe one thing rather than another. If you are reading philosophy properly, you must sincerely join the debate and be honestly prepared to be persuaded—but it is also important not to let yourself be persuaded too easily.

Writing Philosophy

Writing philosophy consists, in roughly equal measures, of *thinking* about philosophy and then of trying to express your ideas *clearly and precisely*. This makes it somewhat unlike other writing: the point of writing philosophy is not, alas, to entertain, nor to explain some chunk of knowledge, nor to trick or cajole the reader into accepting a certain thesis. The point of philosophical writing is, really, to *do* philosophy.

This means that, since philosophy is based on arguments, most philosophical essays will have the underlying structure of an argument. They will seek to defend some particular philosophical claim by developing one or more good arguments for that claim.[4]

There is no particular template to follow for philosophical writing (there are lots of different kinds of good philosophical writing—lots of different ways of arguing well), but here are seven suggestions you might find useful:

1. Take your time. Spend time thinking, and then leave yourself enough time to get the writing right.

2. After you've thought for a while, begin by making an outline of the points you want to make (rather than immediately launching into prose). Then write several drafts, preferably allowing some cooling-off time between drafts so you can come back refreshed and with a more objective eye. Be prepared for the fact that writing a second draft doesn't mean merely tinkering with what you've already got, but starting at the beginning and writing it again.

3. Strive to be clear. Avoid unnecessary jargon, and use plain, simple words whenever possible; concrete examples can be extremely useful in explaining what you mean. It's also worth remembering that the clarity of a piece of writing has a lot to do with its structure. Ideally, the argumentative structure of your essay should be obvious to the reader, and it is a good idea to use your introduction to give the reader a 'road map' of the argument to follow.

4. Aim for precision. Make sure the *thesis* of your essay is spelled out in sufficient detail that the reader is left in no doubt about what you are arguing for (and therefore, what the implications will be, if your arguments are strong ones). Also, take care to define important terms so the reader knows exactly what you mean by them. Terms should normally be defined under any of the following three conditions: (a) the word is a technical term which a layperson probably won't know the meaning of (e.g., "intrinsic value"); (b) it is an ordinary word whose meaning is not sufficiently clear or precise for philosophical purposes (e.g., "abortion"); or (c) it is an ordinary word that you are going to use to mean something other than what it normally means (e.g., "person").

5. Focus. Everything you write should directly contribute to establishing your thesis. Anything which is unnecessary for your arguments should be eliminated. Make every word count. Also, don't be over-ambitious; properly done, philosophy moves at a fairly slow pace—it is unlikely that anyone could show adequately that, for example, there is no such thing as matter in three or fewer pages.

6. Argue as well and as carefully as you can. Defend your position using reason and not rhetoric; critically assess the strength of your arguments, and consider the plausibility of your premises. It's important to consider alternatives to your own position and possible counter-arguments; don't be afraid to raise and attempt to reply to objections to your position. (If you make a serious objection, one which you cannot answer, perhaps you should change your position.)

7. When you think you are finished, read the essay out loud and/or give it to someone else to read—at a minimum, this is a good way of checking for ease of reading, and it may reveal problems with your essay or argument that hadn't previously occurred to you.

---

4   The conclusion of a philosophical essay, however, need not always be something like: "God exists," or "Physical objects are not colored." It could just as legitimately be something like: "Philosopher A's third argument is flawed," or "When the arguments of philosopher A and those of philosopher B are compared, B wins," or "No one has yet given a good argument to show either P or not-P," or even "Philosopher A's argument is not, as is widely thought, X but instead it is Y." Though these kinds of claims are, perhaps, less immediately exciting than the first two examples, they are still philosophical claims, they still need to be argued for, and they can be extremely important in an overall debate about, say, the existence of God.

Suggestions for Further Reading

There are several short books devoted to helping students do well in philosophy courses. Perhaps the best of the bunch is Jay Rosenberg's *The Practice of Philosophy: A Handbook for Beginners* (Prentice Hall, 1995); A.P. Martinich's *Philosophical Writing* (Black-well, 1996) is also very good. Also useful are: Anne M. Edwards, *Writing to Learn: An Introduction to Writing Philosophical Essays* (McGraw-Hill, 1999); Graybosch, Scott, and Garrison, *The Philosophy Student Writer's Manual* (Prentice Hall, 1998); and Zachery Seech, *Writing Philosophy Papers* (third edition, Wadsworth, 2000).

CHAPTER 2

Philosophy of Religion —Does God Exist?

INTRODUCTION TO THE QUESTION

The philosophy of religion is the sub-field of philosophy concerned with the rational evaluation of the truth of religious claims; in particular, the philosophy of religion deals most centrally with claims about the existence, nature and activities of God. For example, one might ask, is it coherent to say that God is absolutely all-powerful?[1] Can God be *both* all-knowing and unchanging?[2] If God is all-knowing—and so knows everything that I am going to do—then in what sense can human beings really be said to have free will? Does God exist eternally, or instead is God somehow 'outside' of time altogether? Does God listen to and answer prayers? Does God ever cause miracles to occur? Does God punish sinners, and if so then what counts as sin and how does the deity punish it? How can a deity consign souls to eternal damnation and yet still be considered benevolent? Could God command us to torture little children for fun, and if he did so would this be a moral duty? If God is inexpressibly mysterious, as some religious creeds assert,

then how does one know what one believes in if one believes in God? And so on.

The religious proposition singled out for philosophical evaluation in this chapter is something like the following: that there exists one, and exactly one, deity who is eternal, immaterial, all-powerful, all-knowing, and perfectly morally good, and who created the universe and all its inhabitants. The first five readings in this chapter introduce (and evaluate) the three main arguments in favor of the existence of such an entity and the most important argument against its existence.

One of the earliest philosophical arguments for the existence of God comes from Saint Anselm in the eleventh century, and is called the *ontological argument*. The ontological argument tries to show that God *necessarily* exists since God's existence is logically entailed by the concept of God. This argument, a version of which also appears in Descartes' *Meditations* in Chapter Three, is criticized by a monk called Gaunilo in the Anselm reading, and also in the selections in this chapter from Aquinas and Hume.

The second main type of argument for the existence of God is what is called the *cosmological argument*. Arguments of this type start from observations about the world (the 'cosmos'), such as that every event has a cause or that all natural things depend for their existence on something else, and infer from this that there must be some entity—a creator and a sustainer—which necessarily exists and upon which everything else depends for its existence. Aquinas presents three cosmological arguments, the first three of his 'Five Ways.'

---

1   Consider, for instance, this old quandary: can God make a stone so heavy that even God cannot lift it? Whichever way this question is answered, it seems that there must be at least one thing which God cannot do.

2   After all, as the world changes over time, so must the facts which God knows to be true at that time. What God knew to be true ten seconds ago will differ from what he knows to be true now, which will be different again from what will be true in ten seconds, and so on. So (it appears) God's beliefs must be constantly changing if they are to remain true, so God cannot be eternally unchanging.

Finally, the third main variety of argument for God is the so-called *teleological argument*, often known as the *argument from design*. These arguments begin from the premise that the natural world shows signs of intelligent design or purpose (the Greek for purpose is *telos*) and from this draw the conclusion that the universe must have had an intelligent designer—God. The fifth of Aquinas's arguments for God is a member of this species, and the argument from design is also presented, but then roundly criticized, by Hume.

Perhaps the most important argument *against* the existence of God is known as the *problem of evil*. This argument essentially claims that the existence of evil is incompatible with the existence of a powerful and benevolent God; since evil clearly does exist, God cannot. The problem of evil is addressed briefly by Aquinas, but turned into a serious difficulty for the existence of God by Hume in Parts X and XI of his *Dialogues Concerning Natural Religion*. Leibniz provides a classic defense of theism against the problem of evil (a 'theodicy'), but a modern philosopher, J.L. Mackie, argues that the problem of evil is logically unbeatable.

The final two readings in this chapter, William James's "The Will to Believe" and Alvin Plantinga's "Is Belief in God Properly Basic?" ask what we should do if it turns out that there *is* no rational reason to believe in God, or if there is no good evidence for God's exis-

tence beyond the belief itself. James argues that, even if we can have no good intellectual reasons for faith, we nevertheless have the right to choose to believe in God for emotional or "passional" reasons instead, while Plantinga argues that belief in God may be a "basic" belief that requires no further justification.

If you want to explore this area of philosophy in more depth, there are many books available which discuss the philosophy of religion. Some of the more philosophically informed ones are: Brian Davies, *An Introduction to the Philosophy of Religion* (Oxford University Press, 2004); Anthony Flew, *God, Freedom and Immortality* (Prometheus Books, 1984); John Hick, *Arguments for the Existence of God* (Macmillan, 1970); John Hick, *Philosophy of Religion* (Prentice-Hall, 1990); Anthony Kenny, *The God of the Philosophers* (Oxford University Press, 1979); Alvin Plantinga, *God and Other Minds* (Cornell University Press, 1967); William Rowe, *Philosophy of Religion* (Wadsworth, 2006); Bertrand Russell, *Why I Am Not a Christian* (Simon and Schuster, 1957); Richard Swinburne, *The Existence of God* (Oxford University Press, 1979); and Charles Taliaferro, *An Introduction to Contemporary Philosophy of Religion* (Blackwell, 1997). Two useful reference texts are *A Companion to Philosophy of Religion*, edited by Philip Quinn and Charles Taliaferro (Blackwell, 1999), and William Wainwright (ed.), *The Oxford Handbook of Philosophy of Religion* (Oxford University Press, 2007).

ST. ANSELM OF CANTERBURY
Proslogion

Who Was St. Anselm of Canterbury?

Anselm was born in 1033 to a noble family in Aosta, Italy, but after his mother's death (when he was 23) he repudiated his inherited wealth and the political career for which his father had prepared him and took up the life of a wandering scholar. In 1060 he became a monk at the Benedictine abbey of Bec in Normandy, rose rapidly through various positions of authority, and was elected Abbot in 1078. He was highly successful as Abbot, attracting monks from all over Europe and confirming Bec in its position as one of the main centers of learning of the time; during this time he became internationally known as a leading intellectual and established himself as a spiritual counsellor to kings from Ireland to Jerusalem. In 1093, much against his will, he succeeded his old teacher Lanfranc as Archbishop of Canterbury—the head of the church in England. He died there in 1109, at the age of 76. His tenure as Archbishop was stormy in the extreme: the king of England at the time, William Rufus, "seems to have combined the virtues of an American gangster with those of a South American dictator,"[1] and was determined to make the wealthy and powerful church subservient to royal authority. Anselm, by contrast, considered himself effectively co-ruler of England on the Pope's behalf, and he resisted William's encroachments fiercely and bravely. Anselm was exiled from England twice (for a total of more than five years), but eventually reached a compromise with William's

brother and successor, Henry I, after the Pope threatened the king's excommunication.[2]

Anselm is probably the most impressive philosopher and theologian of the early Middle Ages (i.e., between about 500 and 1100 CE). His major philosophical works are *Monologion* (which means "soliloquy"), *Proslogion* (Latin for "allocution," a formal speech or address), and a series of dialogues: *On the Grammarian*, *On Truth*, and *On Free Will*. His most important theological writing is *Cur Deus Homo*, or "Why God Became Man." In his final, unfinished work he tried to unravel the mystery of how a soul could come into existence. When he was told that he was soon to die, he is supposed to have replied, characteristically, "If it is His will I shall gladly obey, but if He should prefer me to stay with you just long enough to solve the question of the origin of the soul which I have been turning over in my mind, I would gratefully accept the chance, for I doubt whether anybody else will solve it when I am gone."

What Was Anselm's Overall Philosophical Project?

The original title of Anselm's *Proslogion* was *Faith Seeking Understanding*, and this encapsulates Anselm's

---

1   Max Charlesworth, from his introduction to *St. Anselm's Proslogion* (Clarendon Press, 1965), p. 17.

2   To excommunicate someone is to ban them from membership in the church and so, in the Catholic tradition, to exclude them from all the sacraments such as attending mass and receiving absolution for sins. Since it was believed that this would prevent those excommunicated from entering heaven, it was considered an extremely serious punishment.

consuming theological interest: he wanted to apply the tools of reason in order to better understand some (though not all) of what he already believed on the basis of faith. In fact, Anselm is often credited with being the first major thinker in the medieval Christian tradition to place great importance on the rational justification of theology, not because faith by itself is inadequate but because rational proofs can improve our grasp of the nature of God. Anselm thought of the search for religious truth as not so much accumulating facts about God but as coming to a better personal *acquaintance* with God, as one might come to know more about a friend over time. Since we clearly cannot sit down with God over a cup of coffee and chat, this process of finding out more about God depends to a large degree on careful, rational thought about God's nature.

Anselm is best remembered for originating one of the most stimulating and controversial of the arguments for the existence of God, the so-called Ontological Argument. ("Ontological" means "concerning what exists"; in this context, the idea is that we can come to know about God's 'pure' existence, without any sensory contact with God or his effects.) The Ontological Argument, if it works, not only proves as a matter of logic that God exists but also proves that God has a certain nature—that he is wise, good, infinite, powerful, and so on. The selection from Anselm given here is his presentation of this argument from the *Proslogion*, then a critique of the argument from Gaunilo, a monk from the Abbey of Marmoutiers near Tours, and finally Anselm's response to that criticism. (Although Anselm's response to Gaunilo can be challenging reading, coming to grips with his compressed arguments is exhilarating, and important for better understanding his argument in the *Proslogion*.)

What Is the Structure of This Reading?

After a preface, in which he explains how the idea for the Ontological Argument came to him, Anselm lays out the Ontological Argument in Chapters 2 and 3 of the *Proslogion*. His argument has three parts:
(a) That something-than-which-nothing-greater-can-be-thought must really exist (Chapter 2).

(b) That furthermore it must necessarily exist: that is, it exists in such a way that it cannot be conceived by the human mind as not existing (first part of Chapter 3).
(c) That the entity described in (a) and (b) must be God (second part of Chapter 3).

In Chapter 4 Anselm responds to a possible objection to part (b) of the argument. In Chapter 5 he briefly draws some consequences about the nature of God.

In the next section Gaunilo of Marmoutiers responds "on behalf of the Fool." Gaunilo's most important objections are:
(a) That God cannot be meaningfully thought about by human beings (Paragraph 4). Anselm responds to this in parts of Replies 1, 2, 8, and 9.
(b) That even if we could think about God, thinking about things doesn't show all by itself that they exist (Paragraphs 2 and 5). Anselm deals with this in Replies 1, 2, and 6.
(c) That if the Ontological Argument establishes the existence of God it ought also to establish the existence of the "Lost Island," which is absurd (Paragraph 6). Anselm's response—which, rightly or wrongly, doesn't take the objection very seriously—is at the start of Reply 3.
(d) That that-than-which-a-greater-cannot-be-thought can be thought not to exist (Para. 7). Anselm answers in Replies 1, 3, and 9.

Some Useful Background Information

1. The Ontological Argument is an '*a priori*' argument: that is, it purports to prove the existence of God on the basis of reason alone, independently of sense experience (e.g., independently of the results of empirical science). Anselm wants to show that the *idea* of God (all by itself) proves that God must exist.
2. Anselm makes use of various distinctions that it is useful to be aware of. The first is between two kinds of existence: existence in the mind (in Latin, "in intellectu") and existence in actual reality ("in re"). Something can exist in the mind but not in reality: for example, I can imagine a gold dinosaur and this dinosaur exists only *in intellectu* but not *in re*. Or something can exist

in reality but not in anyone's mind: for example, a particular rock no one has ever seen, on the dark side of the Moon. Or something can exist in *both* the mind and reality: the Eiffel Tower, for instance, is both *in re* and *in intellectu* since it is both in Paris and in our thoughts. Finally, some unreal thing no one has ever thought of would be neither *in re* nor *in intellectu*.

3. Then there is a distinction between two ways of thinking about an idea: this is the difference between merely thinking the words that express an idea and actually thinking about the thing itself. As Anselm puts it, "in one sense a thing is thought when the word signifying it is thought; in another sense when the very object which the thing is is understood." For example, the Fool might think to himself, "God does not exist," but if he does not really know what God is, then for him only "the sound of the letters or syllables" exists *in intellectu* and not actually God himself. This is sometimes explained in terms of the meaning of words or ideas: some of the ideas you think about really are meaningful to you (such as "Paris"), but some only *seem* meaningful when all you are really doing is silently mouthing the words (such as, perhaps, "crapulous"). Notice that, on this way of talking, ideas can be meaningful for us even if we do not know *everything* about their objects. For example, I don't need to have ever visited Paris to think meaningfully about that city; similarly, Anselm held that we can think about God even though God might be unimaginably greater than any picture we can form in our minds.

4. Finally, a third distinction is raised by Gaunilo and talked about by Anselm in his reply. This is the technical distinction between *thinking* (in Latin, "cogitare") and *understanding* ("intelligere"). For Anselm and Gaunilo, to think or conceive is to entertain possibilities—it's to consider things that may not actually be true and treat them (perhaps only temporarily) as if they were. For example, although I know I currently exist I could perhaps conceive of myself as not existing; although it may turn out to be false that extraterrestrials will visit the Earth within fifty years, I can certainly think that they will. By contrast, "understanding" is what philosophers today would call a 'success term': by definition, you cannot *understand* something to be true (or real) if it is in fact false (or unreal). Thus, according to Gaunilo, we could, strictly speaking, only understand the phrase "God exists" if in fact God does exist.

One important question we can now ask is the following: can we think meaningfully about things that are *not* possible? For example, can we think about square circles or married bachelors? According to Anselm, the answer to this question is no: we can, as it were, think the *words* "square circle," but we can't really think about the things themselves. What this means, significantly, is that for Anselm anything we can properly think about must really be possible.

Some Common Misconceptions

1. Anselm is not just claiming that we can prove something exists by simply *thinking* of it existing: he realizes that not every concept which includes the idea of existence is actually exemplified. He thinks that the concept of God (that is, that-than-which-a-greater-cannot-be-thought) is a *uniquely special* concept in this respect; God, according to Anselm, has a unique kind of reality.

2. The unwary sometimes suppose that Anselm argues in the following way: God exists in our minds (*in intellectu*); our minds exist in the world (*in re*); therefore God must also exist in the world. This, however, is not his argument. (If it were, it would merely establish that the *concept* of God exists, while Anselm wants to show that God *himself* exists. Furthermore, when Anselm says things exist *in intellectu* it's not at all clear that he literally wants to say they are *located inside our heads*; the Eiffel Tower which is the object of our thoughts is the very same one as that which is located in Paris.)

3. Anselm (perhaps contrary to what Aquinas says about him in the next reading) does not think that the existence of God is simply self-evident:

that is, he doesn't think either (a) that we all already know that God exists, or (b) that merely to say "God does not exist" is to say something obviously self-contradictory (like saying "triangles have four sides"). What he does think is that *after* hearing his argument, it becomes obvious that God must exist. Similarly, he does not claim that everyone already has the concept of God (e.g., that we are born with the knowledge of God); his claim is rather that everyone can grasp that concept if it is explained to them.

How Important and Influential Is This Passage?

Rejected as mere verbal trickery by many subsequent philosophers (including St. Thomas Aquinas, in the next selection; the influential nineteenth-century philosopher Arthur Schopenhauer called it a "charming joke"), the Ontological Argument was nevertheless popular throughout the Middle Ages, was revived by René Descartes and Gottfried Leibniz in the seventeenth and eighteenth centuries, was influentially used by G.W.F. Hegel in the nineteenth century, and is still attractive to some philosophers today. Many more contemporary philosophers think it fallacious, but it has proved frustratingly difficult to uncontroversially pin down precisely what is wrong with this 'many-faced' argument. Early in the twentieth century developments in the logic of predicates (predicates are 'describing phrases' like "... is green" or "... is taller than ...") bolstered Immanuel Kant's objection that "existence is not a predicate" (see question 5 below). However more recent developments in the logic of possibility and necessity (called modal logic) have apparently given the argument a new lease on life.

Suggestions for Critical Reflection

1. If Anselm's argument is sound, what if anything does it tell us about God (in addition to the fact that he exists)?
2. The concepts 'bachelor' or 'unicorn' do not entail that such things exist. Why does Anselm think that the concept 'God' is importantly different? Is he right? What about the concept of 'an integer between 10 and 12': do you think this concept might commit us to the existence of the number 11? Does this show that not all existence claims are empirical?
3. What do you think about Anselm's distinction between two kinds of existence (*in re* and *in intellectu*)? Do you agree that being thought about is a kind of existence?
4. Does Gaunilo's example of the "Lost Island" show that Anselm has made a mistake? If so, does it show *what* mistake (or mistakes) has been made?
5. The famous eighteenth-century German philosopher Immanuel Kant argued that the flaw in the Ontological Argument is that it mistakenly treats existence as a property. When we say that leopards are spotted we are ascribing a property (being covered in spots) to leopards; however, Kant would argue, when we say that leopards exist, we are not pointing to all the leopards and saying that they have the property of existence. Instead, we are saying something not about actual leopards but about the concept 'leopard': we are saying that something in the actual world fits that concept. If we say that Boy Scouts are honest, we might go on to talk about some Boy Scout who is *perfectly* honest—who possesses the property of honesty to perfection. However, if we say that Boy Scouts exist, it is incoherent to try to point to the perfectly existing Boy Scout. Existence, therefore, is not a property, and so (according to Kant's argument) we have no reason to believe that a being which possesses all the properties of the most perfect thing—i.e., which is that-than-which-a-greater-cannot-be-thought—must exist. What do you think of this objection to the Ontological Argument? Is it decisive?
6. Suppose we agree with Anselm (against Kant) that existence *is* a perfection. Does this mean that an actual serial killer is more perfect than a merely fictional one?
7. Another objection to the Ontological Argument is the following: we may (as human beings) be able to *think* of an absolutely perfect

being, but (contrary to Anselm's assumption) it does not follow from this that an absolutely perfect being is actually *possible*. That is, although we are unable to see what is logically impossible in the idea of a perfect being, it might nevertheless still *be* logically impossible; and since we can't rule this out, we can't show *a priori* that God exists. What do you think of this objection? If it works, what implications does it have for our knowledge of possibility?

8. Finally, a third possible objection to Anselm's Ontological Argument: Even if Anselm succeeds in showing that the being-than-which-nothing-greater-can-be-thought must be *thought of* as existing, it still doesn't follow that it actually *does* exist. To conceive of something as being a certain way, the argument goes, does not mean that it actually *is* that way, or even that one must *believe* that it is that way: for example, one can conceive of the sky as being bright green, even though it isn't. So, for God, we can and perhaps must conceive of God as existing, but it doesn't follow that God does exist (or even that we must believe that God exists). What do you think of this objection? How do you think Anselm might respond to it?

Suggestions for Further Reading

The best biography of Anselm was written by his friend and contemporary Eadmer (*The Life of St. Anselm by Eadmer*, ed. R.W. Southern, Oxford University Press, 1962). Nearly all of Anselm's writings are collected in *Anselm of Canterbury: The Major Works* (ed. Brian Davis and G.R. Evans) from Oxford University Press, 1998. M.J. Charlesworth's edition of the *Proslogion* (Clarendon Press, 1965, re-printed by the University of Notre Dame Press in 1979) contains the Latin text, a translation, and a detailed philosophical commentary. There is also *A Companion to the Study of St. Anselm* written by Jasper Hopkins (University of Minnesota Press, 1972). Two books specifically about the Ontological Argument are Jonathan Barnes, *The Ontological Argument* (Macmillan, 1972) and Charles Hartshorne, *Anselm's Discovery* (Open Court, 1965). Two useful anthologies of papers about the Onto-

logical Argument are Alvin Plantinga (ed.), *The Ontological Argument* (Doubleday, 1965) and John Hick and Arthur McGill (eds.), *The Many-Faced Argument* (Macmillan, 1967). Kant's objection to the Ontological Argument is in his *Critique of Pure Reason* (Second Division, Book II, Chapter III, Section 4), and his argument is criticized by Jerome Shaffer, "Existence, Predication and the Ontological Argument," *Mind* 71 (1962). A version of the objection that we can't know *a priori* that a perfect being exists is developed by W.L. Rowe in "The Ontological Argument and Question-Begging," *International Journal for Philosophy of Religion* 7 (1976).

Proslogion
Preface and Chapters 2–5[3]

Preface

After I had published, at the pressing entreaties of several of my brethren, a certain short tract[4] as an example of meditation on the meaning of faith from the point of view of one seeking, through silent reasoning within himself, things he knows not—reflecting that this was made up of a connected chain of many arguments, I began to wonder if perhaps it might be possible to find one single argument that for its proof required no other save itself, and that by itself would suffice to prove that God really exists, that He is the supreme good needing no other and is He whom all things have need of for their being and well-being, and also to prove whatever we believe about the Divine Being. But as often and as diligently as I turned my thoughts to this, sometimes it seemed to me that I

---

3   The *Proslogion* was written between 1077 and 1078. Gaunilo's reply was written shortly after it appeared, and Anselm's response quickly after that. The translation reprinted here, of all three works, is by M.J. Charlesworth and appears in *Anselm of Canterbury: The Major Works*, edited by Brian Davies and G.R. Evans (Oxford World's Classics, 1998). By permission of Oxford University Press.

4   The *Monologion*, probably written one year before the *Proslogion*.

had almost reached what I was seeking, sometimes it eluded my acutest thinking completely, so that finally, in desperation, I was about to give up what I was looking for as something impossible to find. However, when I had decided to put aside this idea altogether, lest by uselessly occupying my mind it might prevent other ideas with which I could make some progress, then, in spite of my unwillingness and my resistance to it, it began to force itself upon me more and more pressingly. So it was that one day when I was quite worn out with resisting its importunacy, there came to me, in the very conflict of my thoughts, what I had despaired of finding, so that I eagerly grasped the notion which in my distraction I had been rejecting.

Judging, then, that what had given me such joy to discover would afford pleasure, if it were written down, to anyone who might read it, I have written the following short tract dealing with this question as well as several others, from the point of view of one trying to raise his mind to contemplate God and seeking to understand what he believes. In my opinion, neither this tract nor the other I mentioned before deserves to be called a book or to carry its author's name, and yet I did not think they should be sent forth without some title (by which, so to speak, they might invite those into whose hands they should come, to read them); so I have given to each its title, the first being called *An Example of Meditation on the Meaning of Faith*, and the sequel *Faith in Quest of Understanding*.

However, as both of them, under these titles, had already been copied out by several readers, a number of people (above all the reverend Archbishop of Lyons, Hugh, apostolic delegate to Gaul, who commanded me by his apostolic authority) have urged me to put my name to them. For the sake of greater convenience I have named the first book *Monologion*, that is, a soliloquy; and the other *Proslogion*, that is, an allocution.

…

Chapter 2. That God truly exists

Well then, Lord, You who give understanding to faith, grant me that I may understand, as much as You see fit, that You exist as we believe You to exist, and that You are what we believe You to be. Now we believe that You are something than which nothing greater can be

thought. Or can it be that a thing of such a nature does not exist, since 'the Fool has said in his heart, there is no God'?[5] But surely, when this same Fool hears what I am speaking about, namely, 'something-than-which-nothing-greater-can-be-thought', he understands what he hears, and what he understands is in his mind, even if he does not understand that it actually exists. For it is one thing for an object to exist in the mind, and another thing to understand that an object actually exists. Thus, when a painter plans beforehand what he is going to execute, he has [the picture] in his mind, but he does not yet think that it actually exists because he has not yet executed it. However, when he has actually painted it, then he both has it in his mind and understands that it exists because he has now made it. Even the Fool, then, is forced to agree that something-than-which-nothing-greater-can-be-thought exists in the mind, since he understands this when he hears it, and whatever is understood is in the mind. And surely that-than-which-a-greater-cannot-be-thought cannot exist in the mind alone. For if it exists solely in the mind, it can be thought to exist in reality also, which is greater. If then that-than-which-a-greater-cannot-be-thought exists in the mind alone, this same that-than-which-a-greater-*cannot*-be-thought is that-than-which-a-greater-*can*-be-thought. But this is obviously impossible. Therefore there is absolutely no doubt that something-than-which-a-greater-cannot-be-thought exists both in the mind and in reality.

Chapter 3. That God cannot be thought not to exist

And certainly this being so truly exists that it cannot be even thought not to exist. For something can be thought to exist that cannot be thought not to exist, and this is greater than that which can be thought not to exist. Hence, if that-than-which-a-greater-cannot-be-thought can be thought not to exist, then that-than-which-a-greater-cannot-be-thought is not the same as that-than-which-a-greater-cannot-be-thought, which is absurd. Something-than-which-a-greater-cannot-

---

5   This quotation is from the first line of Psalms 13 and 52 in the Vulgate version of the Bible, 14 and 53 in the King James version. Later citations in this reading also refer to the Vulgate.

be-thought exists so truly then, that it cannot be even thought not to exist.

And You, Lord our God, are this being. You exist so truly, Lord my God, that You cannot even be thought not to exist. And this is as it should be, for if some intelligence could think of something better than You, the creature would be above its Creator and would judge its Creator—and that is completely absurd. In fact, everything else there is, except You alone, can be thought of as not existing. You alone, then, of all things most truly exist and therefore of all things possess existence to the highest degree; for anything else does not exist as truly, and so possesses existence to a lesser degree. Why then did 'the Fool say in his heart, there is no God' when it is so evident to any rational mind that You of all things exist to the highest degree? Why indeed, unless because he was stupid and a fool?

Chapter 4. How 'the Fool said in his heart' what cannot be thought

How indeed has he 'said in his heart' what he could not think; or how could he not think what he 'said in his heart', since to 'say in one's heart' and to 'think' are the same? But if he really (indeed, since he really) both thought because he 'said in his heart' and did not 'say in his heart' because he could not think, there is not only one sense in which something is 'said in one's heart' or thought. For in one sense a thing is thought when the word signifying it is thought; in another sense when the very object which the thing is is understood. In the first sense, then, God can be thought not to exist, but not at all in the second sense. No one, indeed, understanding what God is can think that God does not exist, even though he may say these words in his heart either without any [objective] signification or with some peculiar signification. For God is that-than-which-nothing-greater-can-be-thought. Whoever really understands this understands clearly that this same being so exists that not even in thought can it not exist. Thus whoever understands that God exists in such a way cannot think of Him as not existing.

I give thanks, good Lord, I give thanks to You, since what I believed before through Your free gift I now so understand through Your illumination, that if I did not want to *believe* that You existed, I should nevertheless be unable not to *understand* it.

Chapter 5. That God is whatever it is better to be than not to be and that, existing through Himself alone, He makes all other beings from nothing

What then are You, Lord God, You than whom nothing greater can be thought? But what are You save that supreme being, existing through Yourself alone, who made everything else from nothing? For whatever is not this is less than that which can be thought of; but this cannot be thought about You. What goodness, then, could be wanting to the supreme good, through which every good exists? Thus You are just, truthful, happy, and whatever it is better to be than not to be—for it is better to be just rather than unjust, and happy rather than unhappy.

Pro Insipiente

("On Behalf of the Fool"), by Gaunilo of Marmoutiers

Paragraph 1

To one doubting whether there is, or denying that there is, something of such a nature than which nothing greater can be thought, it is said here [in the *Proslogion*] that its existence is proved, first because the very one who denies or doubts it already has it in his mind, since when he hears it spoken of he understands what is said; and further, because what he understands is necessarily such that it exists not only in the mind but also in reality. And this is proved by the fact that it is greater to exist both in the mind and in reality than in the mind alone. For if this same being exists in the mind alone, anything that existed also in reality would be greater than this being, and thus that which is greater than everything would be less than some thing and would not be greater than everything, which is obviously contradictory. Therefore, it is necessarily the case that that which is greater than everything, being already proved to exist in the mind, should exist not only in the mind but also in reality, since otherwise it would not be greater than everything.

Paragraph 2

But he [the Fool] can perhaps reply that this thing is said already to exist in the mind only in the sense that I understand what is said. For could I not say that all kinds of unreal things, not existing in themselves in any way at all, are equally in the mind since if anyone speaks about them I understand whatever he says? Unless perhaps it is manifest that this being is such that it can be entertained in the mind in a different way from unreal or doubtfully real things, so that I am not said to think of or have in thought what is heard, but to understand and have it in mind, in that I cannot really think of this being in any other way save by understanding it, that is to say, by grasping by certain knowledge that the thing itself actually exists. But if this is the case, first, there will be no difference between having an object in mind (taken as preceding in time), and understanding that the object actually exists (taken as following in time), as in the case of the picture which exists first in the mind of the painter and then in the completed work. And thus it would be scarcely conceivable that, when this object had been spoken of and heard, it could not be thought not to exist in the same way in which God can [be thought] not to exist. For if He cannot, why put forward this whole argument against anyone denying or doubting that there is something of this kind? Finally, that it is such a thing that, as soon as it is thought of, it cannot but be certainly perceived by the mind as indubitably existing, must be proved to me by some indisputable argument and not by that proposed, namely, that it must already be in my mind when I understand what I hear. For this is in my view like [arguing that] any things doubtfully real or even unreal are capable of existing if these things are mentioned by someone whose spoken words I might understand, and, even more, that [they exist] if, though deceived about them as often happens, I should believe them [to exist]—which argument I still do not believe!

Paragraph 3

Hence, the example of the painter having the picture he is about to make already in his mind cannot support this argument. For this picture, before it is actually made, is contained in the very art of the painter and such a thing in the art of any artist is nothing but a certain part of his very understanding, since as St. Augustine says,[6] 'when the artisan is about actually to make a box he has it beforehand in his art. The box which is actually made is not a living thing, but the box which is in his art is a living thing since the soul of the artist, in which these things exist before their actual realization, is a living thing'. Now how are these things living in the living soul of the artist unless they are identical with the knowledge or understanding of the soul itself? But, apart from those things which are known to belong to the very nature of the mind itself, in the case of any truth perceived by the mind by being either heard or understood, then it cannot be doubted that this truth is one thing and that the understanding which grasps it is another. Therefore even if it were true that there was something than which nothing greater could be thought, this thing, heard and understood, would not, however, be the same as the not-yet-made picture is in the mind of the painter.

Paragraph 4

To this we may add something that has already been mentioned, namely, that upon hearing it spoken of I can so little think of or entertain in my mind this being (that which is greater than all those others that are able to be thought of, and which it is said can be none other than God Himself) in terms of an object known to me either by species or genus, as I can think of God Himself, whom indeed for this very reason I can even think does not exist. For neither do I know the reality itself, nor can I form an idea from some other things like it since, as you say yourself, it is such that nothing could be like it. For if I heard something said about a man who was completely unknown to me so that I did not even know whether he existed, I could nevertheless think about him in his very reality as a man by means of that specific or generic notion by which I know what a man is or men are. However, it could happen that, because of a falsehood on the part of the speaker, the man I thought of did not actually exist, although I thought of him nevertheless as a truly

---

6   St. Augustine, a north African bishop who lived from 354 until 430, was the most important early Christian theologian and Anselm's major intellectual influence. This quote is from his *Treatises on the Gospel of John*.

existing object—not this particular man but any man in general. It is not, then, in the way that I have this unreal thing in thought or in mind that I can have that object in my mind when I hear 'God' or 'something greater than everything' spoken of. For while I was able to think of the former in terms of a truly existing thing which was known to me, I know nothing at all of the latter save for the verbal formula, and on the basis of this alone one can scarcely or never think of any truth. For when one thinks in this way, one thinks not so much of the word itself, which is indeed a real thing (that is to say, the sound of the letters or syllables), as of the meaning of the word which is heard. However, it [that which is greater than everything] is not thought of in the way of one who knows what is meant by that expression—thought of, that is, in terms of the thing [signified] or as true in thought alone. It is rather in the way of one who does not really know this object but thinks of it in terms of an affection of his mind produced by hearing the spoken words, and who tries to imagine what the words he has heard might mean. However, it would be astonishing if he could ever [attain to] the truth of the thing. Therefore, when I hear and understand someone saying that there is something greater than everything that can be thought of, it is agreed that it is in this latter sense that it is in my mind and not in any other sense. So much for the claim that that supreme nature exists already in my mind.

Paragraph 5

That, however, [this nature] necessarily exists in reality is demonstrated to me from the fact that, unless it existed, whatever exists in reality would be greater than it and consequently it would not be that which is greater than everything that undoubtedly had already been proved to exist in the mind. To this I reply as follows: if something that cannot even be thought in the true and real sense must be said to exist in the mind, then I do not deny that this also exists in my mind in the same way. But since from this one cannot in any way conclude that it exists also in reality, I certainly do not yet concede that it actually exists, until this is proved to me by an indubitable argument. For he who claims that it actually exists because otherwise it would not be that which is greater than everything

does not consider carefully enough whom he is addressing. For I certainly do not yet admit this greater [than everything] to be any truly existing thing; indeed I doubt or even deny it. And I do not concede that it exists in a different way from that—if one ought to speak of 'existence' here—when the mind tries to imagine a completely unknown thing on the basis of the spoken words alone. How then can it be proved to me on that basis that that which is greater than everything truly exists in reality (because it is evident that it is greater than all others) if I keep on denying and also doubting that this is evident and do not admit that this greater [than everything] is either in my mind or thought, not even in the sense in which many doubtfully real and unreal things are? It must first of all be proved to me then that this same greater than everything truly exists in reality somewhere, and then only will the fact that it is greater than everything make it clear that it also subsists in itself.

Paragraph 6

For example: they say that there is in the ocean somewhere an island which, because of the difficulty (or rather the impossibility) of finding that which does not exist, some have called the 'Lost Island'. And the story goes that it is blessed with all manner of priceless riches and delights in abundance, much more even than the Happy Isles,[7] and, having no owner or inhabitant, it is superior everywhere in abundance of riches to all those other lands that men inhabit. Now, if anyone tell me that it is like this, I shall easily understand what is said, since nothing is difficult about it. But if he should then go on to say, as though it were a logical consequence of this: You cannot any more doubt that this island that is more excellent than all other lands truly exists somewhere in reality than you can doubt that it is in your mind; and since it is more excellent to exist not only in the mind alone but also in reality, therefore it must needs be that it exists. For if it did not exist, any other land existing in reality would be more excellent than it, and so this island, already conceived by you to be more

---

7   The mythical land—often located where the sun sets in the West—where people in classical times believed the souls of heroes lived in bliss.

excellent than others, will not be more excellent. If, I say, someone wishes thus to persuade me that this island really exists beyond all doubt, I should either think that he was joking, or I should find it hard to decide which of us I ought to judge the bigger fool—I, if I agreed with him, or he, if he thought that he had proved the existence of this island with any certainty, unless he had first convinced me that its very excellence exists in my mind precisely as a thing existing truly and indubitably and not just as something unreal or doubtfully real.

Paragraph 7

Thus first of all might the Fool reply to objections. And if then someone should assert that this greater [than everything] is such that it cannot be thought not to exist (again without any other proof than that otherwise it would not be greater than everything), then he could make this same reply and say: When have I said that there truly existed some being that is 'greater than everything', such that from this it could be proved to me that this same being really existed to such a degree that it could not be thought not to exist? That is why it must first be conclusively proved by argument that there is some higher nature, namely that which is greater and better than all the things that are, so that from this we can also infer everything else which necessarily cannot be wanting to what is greater and better than everything. When, however, it is said that this supreme being cannot be *thought* not to exist, it would perhaps be better to say that it cannot be *understood* not to exist nor even to be able not to exist. For, strictly speaking, unreal things cannot be *understood*, though certainly they can be *thought* of in the same way as the Fool *thought* that God does not exist. I know with complete certainty that I exist, but I also know at the same time nevertheless that I can not-exist. And I *understand* without any doubt that that which exists to the highest degree, namely God, both exists and cannot not exist. I do not know, however, whether I can *think* of myself as not existing while I know with absolute certainty that I do exist; but if I can, why cannot [I do the same] with regard to anything else I know with the same certainty? If however I cannot, this will not be the distinguishing characteristic of God [namely, to be such that He cannot be thought not to exist].

Paragraph 8

The other parts of this tract[8] are argued so truly, so brilliantly and so splendidly, and are also of so much worth and instinct with so fragrant a perfume of devout and holy feeling, that in no way should they be rejected because of those things at the beginning (rightly intuited, but less surely argued out). Rather the latter should be demonstrated more firmly and so everything received with very great respect and praise.

Anselm's *Reply to Gaunilo*

Since it is not the Fool, against whom I spoke in my tract, who takes me up, but one who, though speaking on the Fool's behalf, is an orthodox Christian and no fool, it will suffice if I reply to the Christian.

Reply 1

You say then—you, whoever you are, who claim that the Fool can say these things—that the being than-which-a-greater-cannot-be-thought is not in the mind except as what cannot be thought of, in the true sense, at all. And [you claim], moreover, that what I say does not follow, namely, that 'that-than-which-a-greater-cannot-be-thought' exists in reality from the fact that it exists in the mind, any more than that the Lost Island most certainly exists from the fact that, when it is described in words, he who hears it described has no doubt that it exists in his mind. I reply as follows: If 'that-than-which-a-greater-cannot-be-thought' is neither understood nor thought of, and is neither in the mind nor in thought, then it is evident that *either* God is not that-than-which-a-greater-cannot-be-thought *or* is not understood nor thought of, and is not in the mind nor in thought. Now my strongest argument that this is false is to appeal to your faith and to your conscience. Therefore 'that-than-which-a-greater-cannot-be-thought' is truly understood and thought and is in the mind and in thought. For this reason, [the arguments] by which you attempt to prove the contrary are either

---

8   The *Proslogion* has 26 chapters, of which only chapters two to five—those which contain the ontological argument about which Gaunilo has complaints—are reprinted here.

not true, or what you believe follows from them does not in fact follow.

Moreover, you maintain that, from the fact that that-than-which-a-greater-cannot-be-thought is understood, it does not follow that it is in the mind, nor that, if it is in the mind, it therefore exists in reality. I insist, however, that simply if it can be thought it is necessary that it exists. For 'that-than-which-a-greater-cannot-be-thought' cannot be thought save as being without a beginning. But whatever can be thought as existing and does not actually exist can be thought as having a beginning of its existence. Consequently, 'that-than-which-a-greater-cannot-be-thought' cannot be thought as existing and yet not actually exist. If, therefore, it can be thought as existing, it exists of necessity.

Further: even if it can be thought of, then certainly it necessarily exists. For no one who denies or doubts that there is something-than-which-a-greater-cannot-be-thought, denies or doubts that, if this being were to exist, it would not be capable of not-existing either actually or in the mind—otherwise it would not be that-than-which-a-greater-cannot-be-thought. But, whatever can be thought as existing and does not actually exist, could, if it were to exist, possibly not exist either actually or in the mind. For this reason, if it can merely be thought, 'that-than-which-a-greater-cannot-be-thought' cannot not exist. However, let us suppose that it does not exist even though it can be thought. Now, whatever can be thought and does not actually exist would not be, if it should exist, 'that-than-which-a-greater-cannot-be-thought'. If, therefore, it were 'that-than-which-a-greater-cannot-be-thought' it would not be that-than-which-a-greater-cannot-be-thought, which is completely absurd. It is, then, false that something-than-which-a-greater-cannot-be-thought does not exist if it can merely be thought; and it is all the more false if it can be understood and be in the mind.

I will go further: It cannot be doubted that whatever does not exist in any one place or at any one time, even though it does exist in some place or at some time, can however be thought to exist at no place and at no time, just as it does not exist in some place or at some time. For what did not exist yesterday and today exists can thus, as it is understood not to have existed yesterday, be supposed not to exist at any time. And

that which does not exist here in this place, and does exist elsewhere can, in the same way as it does not exist here, be thought not to exist anywhere. Similarly with a thing some of whose particular parts do not exist in the place and at the time its other parts exist—all of its parts, and therefore the whole thing itself, can be thought to exist at no time and in no place. For even if it be said that time always exists and that the world is everywhere, the former does not, however, always exist as a whole, nor is the other as a whole everywhere; and as certain particular parts of time do not exist when other parts do exist, therefore they can be even thought not to exist at any time. Again, as certain particular parts of the world do not exist in the same place where other parts do exist, they can thus be supposed not to exist anywhere. Moreover, what is made up of parts can be broken up in thought and can possibly not exist. Thus it is that whatever does not exist as a whole at a certain place and time can be thought not to exist, even if it does actually exist. But 'that-than-which-a-greater-cannot-be-thought' cannot be thought not to exist if it does actually exist, otherwise, if it exists it is not that-than-which-a-greater-cannot-be-thought, which is absurd. In no way, then, does this being not exist as a whole in any particular place or at any particular time; but it exists as a whole at every time and in every place.

Do you not consider then that that about which we understand these things can to some extent be thought or understood, or can exist in thought or in the mind? For if it cannot, we could not understand these things about it. And if you say that, because it is not completely understood, it cannot be understood at all and cannot be in the mind, then you must say [equally] that one who cannot see the purest light of the sun directly does not see daylight, which is the same thing as the light of the sun. Surely then 'that-than-which-a-greater-cannot-be-thought' is understood and is in the mind to the extent that we understand these things about it.

Reply 2

I said, then, in the argument that you criticize, that when the Fool hears 'that-than-which-a-greater-cannot-be-thought' spoken of he understands what he hears. Obviously if it is spoken of in a known language and he does not understand it, then either he has no intelligence at all, or a completely obtuse one.

Next I said that, if it is understood it is in the mind; or does what has been proved to exist necessarily in actual reality not exist in any mind? But you will say that, even if it is in the mind, yet it does not follow that it is understood. Observe then that, from the fact that it is understood, it does follow that it is in the mind. For, just as what is thought is thought by means of a thought, and what is thought by a thought is thus, as thought, *in* thought, so also, what is understood is understood by the mind, and what is understood by the mind is thus, as understood, *in* the mind. What could be more obvious than this?

I said further that if a thing exists even in the mind alone, it can be thought to exist also in reality, which is greater. If, then, it (namely, 'that-than-which-a-greater-cannot-be-thought') exists in the mind alone, it is something than which a greater *can* be thought. What, I ask you, could be more logical? For if it exists even in the mind alone, cannot it be thought to exist also in reality? And if it can [be so thought], is it not the case that he who thinks this thinks of something greater than it, if it exists in the mind alone? What, then, could follow more logically than that, if 'that-than-which-a-greater-cannot-be-thought' exists in the mind alone, it is the same as that-than-which-a-greater-*can*-be-thought? But surely 'that-than-which-a-greater-*can*-be-thought' is not for any mind [the same as] 'that-than-which-a-greater-*cannot*-be-thought'. Does it not follow, then, that 'that-than-which-a-greater-*cannot*-be-thought', if it exists in anyone's mind, does not exist in the mind alone? For if it exists in the mind alone, it is that-than-which-a-greater-*can*-be-thought, which is absurd.

Reply 3

You claim, however, that this is as though someone asserted that it cannot be doubted that a certain island in the ocean (which is more fertile than all other lands and which, because of the difficulty or even the impossibility of discovering what does not exist, is called the 'Lost Island') truly exists in reality since anyone easily understands it when it is described in words. Now, I truly promise that if anyone should discover for me something existing either in reality or in the mind alone—except 'that-than-which-a-greater-cannot-be-thought'—to which the logic of my argument would apply, then I shall find that Lost Island and give it, never more to be lost, to that person. It has already been clearly seen, however, that 'that-than-which-a-greater-cannot-be-thought' cannot be thought not to exist, because it exists as a matter of such certain truth. Otherwise it would not exist at all. In short, if anyone says that he thinks that this being does not exist, I reply that, when he thinks of this, either he thinks of something than which a greater cannot be thought, or he does not think of it. If he does not think of it, then he does not think that what he does not think of does not exist. If, however, he does think of it, then indeed he thinks of something which cannot be even thought not to exist. For if it could be thought not to exist, it could be thought to have a beginning and an end—but this cannot be. Thus, he who thinks of it thinks of something that cannot be thought not to exist; indeed, he who thinks of this does not think of it as not existing, otherwise he would think what cannot be thought. Therefore 'that-than-which-a-greater-cannot-be-thought' cannot be thought not to exist.

Reply 4

You say, moreover, that when it is said that this supreme reality cannot be *thought* not to exist, it would perhaps be better to say that it cannot be *understood* not to exist or even to be able not to exist. However, it must rather be said that it cannot be *thought*. For if I had said that the thing in question could not be *understood* not to exist, perhaps you yourself (who claim that we cannot understand—if this word is to be taken strictly—things that are unreal) would object that nothing that exists can be understood not to exist. For it is false [to say that] what exists does not exist, so that it is not the distinguishing characteristic of God not to be able to be understood not to exist. But, if any of those things which exist with absolute certainty can be understood not to exist, in the same way other things that certainly exist can be understood not to exist. But, if the matter is carefully considered, this objection cannot be made apropos[9] [the term] 'thought'. For even if none of those things that exist

---

9   With respect to, concerning.

can be *understood* not to exist, all however can be *thought* as not existing, save that which exists to a supreme degree. For in fact all those things (and they alone) that have a beginning or end or are made up of parts and, as I have already said, all those things that do not exist as a whole in a particular place or at a particular time can be thought as not existing. Only that being in which there is neither beginning nor end nor conjunction of parts, and that thought does not discern save as a whole in every place and at every time, cannot be thought as not existing.

Know then that you can think of yourself as not existing while yet you are absolutely sure that you exist. I am astonished that you have said that you do not know this. For we think of many things that we know to exist, as not existing; and [we think of] many things that we know not to exist, as existing—not judging that it is really as we think but imagining it to be so. We *can*, in fact, think of something as not existing while knowing that it does exist, since we can [think of] the one and know the other at the same time. And we *cannot* think of something as not existing if yet we know that it does exist, since we cannot think of it as existing and not existing at the same time. He, therefore, who distinguishes these two senses of this assertion will understand that [in one sense] nothing can be thought as not existing while yet it is known to exist, and that [in another sense] whatever exists, save that-than-which-a-greater-cannot-be-thought, can be thought of as not existing even when we know that it does exist. Thus it is that, on the one hand, it is the distinguishing characteristic of God that He cannot be thought of as not existing, and that, on the other hand, many things, the while they do exist, cannot be thought of as not existing. In what sense, however, one can say that God can be thought of as not existing I think I have adequately explained in my tract.

Reply 5

As for the other objections you make against me on behalf of the Fool, it is quite easy to meet them, even for one weak in the head, and so I considered it a waste of time to show this. But since I hear that they appear to certain readers to have some force against me, I will deal briefly with them.

First, you often reiterate that I say that that which is greater than everything exists in the mind, and that if it is in the mind, it exists also in reality, for otherwise that which is greater than everything would not be that which is greater than everything. However, nowhere in all that I have said will you find such an argument. For 'that which is greater than everything' and 'that-than-which-a-greater-cannot-be-thought' are not equivalent for the purpose of proving the real existence of the thing spoken of. Thus, if anyone should say that 'that-than-which-a-greater-cannot-be-thought' is not something that actually exists, or that it can possibly not exist, or even can be thought of as not existing, he can easily be refuted. For what does not exist can possibly not exist, and what can not exist can be thought of as not existing. However, whatever can be thought of as not existing, if it actually exists, is not that-than-which-a-greater-cannot-be-thought. But if it does not exist, indeed even if it should exist, it would not be that-than-which-a-greater-cannot-be-thought. But it cannot be asserted that 'that-than-which-a-greater-cannot-be-thought' is not, if it exists, that-than-which-a-greater-cannot-be-thought, or that, if it should exist, it would not be that-than-which-a-greater-cannot-be-thought. It is evident, then, that it neither does not exist nor can not exist or be thought of as not existing. For if it does exist in another way it is not what it is said to be, and if it should exist [in another way] it would not be [what it was said to be].

However it seems that it is not as easy to prove this in respect of what is said to be greater than everything. For it is not as evident that that which can be thought of as not existing is not that which is greater than everything, as that it is not that-than-which-a-greater-cannot-be-thought. And, in the same way, neither is it indubitable that, if there is something which is 'greater than everything', it is identical with 'that-than-which-a-greater-cannot-be-thought'; nor, if there were [such a being], that no other like it might exist—as this is certain in respect of what is said to be 'that-than-which-a-greater-cannot-be-thought'. For what if someone should say that something that is greater than everything actually exists, and yet that this same being can be thought of as not existing, and that something greater than it can be thought, even if this does not exist? In this case can it be inferred as evidently that [this being] is therefore not that which is greater than everything, as it would quite evidently be said in the other case that it is therefore not that-than-which-a-greater-cannot-be-thought? The former [inference] needs, in fact, a premiss in addition to this which is said to be 'greater than everything'; but the latter needs nothing save this utterance itself, namely, 'that-than-which-a-greater-cannot-be-thought'. Therefore, if what 'that-than-which-a-greater-cannot-be-thought' of itself proves concerning itself cannot be proved in the same way in respect of what is said to be 'greater than everything', you criticize me unjustly for having said what I did not say, since it differs so much from what I did say.

If, however, it can [be proved] by means of another argument, you should not have criticized me for having asserted what can be proved. Whether it can [be proved], however, is easily appreciated by one who understands that it can [in respect of] 'that-than-which-a-greater-cannot-be-thought'. For one cannot in any way understand 'that-than-which-a-greater-cannot-be-thought' without [understanding that it is] that which alone is greater than everything. As, therefore, 'that-than-which-a-greater-cannot-be-thought' is understood and is in the mind, and is consequently judged to exist in true reality, so also that which is greater than everything is said to be understood and to exist in the mind, and so is necessarily inferred to exist in reality itself. You see, then, how right you were to compare me with that stupid person who wished to maintain that the Lost Island existed from the sole fact that being described it was understood.

Reply 6

You object, moreover, that any unreal or doubtfully real things at all can equally be understood and exist in the mind in the same way as the being I was speaking of. I am astonished that you urge this [objection] against me, for I was concerned to prove something which was in doubt, and for me it was sufficient that I should first show that it was understood and existed in the mind *in some way or other*, leaving it to be determined subsequently whether it was in the mind alone as unreal things are, or in reality also as true things are. For, if unreal or doubtfully real things are understood and exist in the mind in the sense that,

when they are spoken of, he who hears them understands what the speaker means, nothing prevents what I have spoken of being understood and existing in the mind. But how are these [assertions] consistent, that is, when you assert that if someone speaks of unreal things you would understand whatever he says, and that, in the case of a thing which is not entertained in thought in the same way as even unreal things are, you do not say that you think of it or have it in thought upon hearing it spoken of, but rather that you understand it and have it in mind since, precisely, you cannot think of it save by understanding it, that is, knowing certainly that the thing exists in reality itself? How, I say, are both [assertions] consistent, namely that unreal things are understood, and that 'to understand' means knowing with certainty that something actually exists? You should have seen that nothing [of this applies] to me. But if unreal things are, in a sense, understood (this definition applying not to every kind of understanding but to a certain kind) then I ought not to be criticized for having said that 'that-than-which-a-greater-cannot-be-thought' is understood and is in the mind, even before it was certain that it existed in reality itself.

Reply 7

Next, you say that it can hardly be believed that when this [that-than-which-a-greater-cannot-be-thought] has been spoken of and heard, it cannot be thought not to exist, as even it can be thought that God does not exist. Now those who have attained even a little expertise in disputation and argument could reply to that on my behalf. For is it reasonable that someone should therefore deny what he understands because it is said to be [the same as] that which he denies since he does not understand it? Or if that is denied [to exist] which is understood only to some extent and is the same as what is not understood at all, is not what is in doubt more easily proved from the fact that it is in some mind than from the fact that it is in no mind at all? For this reason it cannot be believed that anyone should deny 'that-than-which-a-greater-cannot-be-thought' (which, being heard, he understands to some extent), on the ground that he denies God whose meaning he does not think of in any way at all. On the other hand, if it is denied on the ground that it is not understood completely, even so is not that which is understood in some way easier to prove than that which is not understood in any way? It was therefore not wholly without reason that, to prove against the Fool that God exists, I proposed 'that-than-which-a-greater-cannot-be-thought', since he would understand this in some way, [whereas] he would understand the former [God] in no way at all.

Reply 8

In fact, your painstaking argument that 'that-than-which-a-greater-cannot-be-thought' is not like the not-yet-realized painting in the mind of the painter is beside the point. For I did not propose [the example] of the foreknown picture because I wanted to assert that what was at issue was in the same case, but rather that so I could show that something not understood as existing exists in the mind.

Again, you say that upon hearing of 'that-than-which-a-greater-cannot-be-thought' you cannot think of it as a real object known either generically or specifically or have it in your mind, on the grounds that you neither know the thing itself nor can you form an idea of it from other things similar to it. But obviously this is not so. For since everything that is less good is similar in so far as it is good to that which is more good, it is evident to every rational mind that, mounting from the less good to the more good we can from those things than which something greater can be thought conjecture a great deal about that-than-which-a-greater-cannot-be-thought. Who, for example, cannot think of this (even if he does not believe that what he thinks of actually exists) namely, that if something that has a beginning and end is good, that which, although it has had a beginning, does not, however, have an end, is much better? And just as this latter is better than the former, so also that which has neither beginning nor end is better again than this, even if it passes always from the past through the present to the future. Again, whether something of this kind actually exists or not, that which does not lack anything at all, nor is forced to change or move, is very much better still. Cannot this be thought? Or can we think of something greater than this? Or is not this precisely to form an idea of that-than-which-a-greater-cannot-be-thought from those things than which a greater can be thought? There is, then, a way by which one can form an idea of

'that-than-which-a-greater-cannot-be-thought'. In this way, therefore, the Fool who does not accept the sacred authority [of Revelation] can easily be refuted if he denies that he can form an idea from other things of 'that-than-which-a-greater-cannot-be-thought'. But if any orthodox Christian should deny this let him remember that "the invisible things of God from the creation of the world are clearly seen through the things that have been made, even his eternal power and Godhead."[10]

Reply 9

But even if it were true that [the object] that-than-which-a-greater-cannot-be-thought cannot be thought of nor understood, it would not, however, be false that [the formula] 'that-than-which-a-greater-cannot-be-thought' could be thought of and understood. For just as nothing prevents one from saying 'ineffable'[11] although one cannot specify what is said to be ineffable; and just as one can think of the inconceivable—although one cannot think of what 'inconceivable' applies to—so also, when 'that-than-which-a-greater-cannot-be-thought' is spoken of, there is no doubt at all that what is heard can be thought of and understood even if the thing itself cannot be thought of and understood. For if someone is so witless as to say that there is not something than-which-a-greater-cannot-be-thought, yet he will not be so shameless as to say that he is not able to understand and think of what he was speaking about. Or if such a one is to be found, not only should his assertion be condemned, but he himself condemned. Whoever, then, denies that there is something than-which-a-greater-cannot-be-thought, at any rate understands and thinks of the denial he makes, and this denial cannot be understood and thought about apart from its elements. Now, one element [of the denial] is 'that-than-which-a-greater-cannot-be-thought'. Whoever, therefore, denies this understands and thinks of 'that-than-which-a-greater-cannot-be-thought'. It is evident, moreover, that in the same way one can think of and understand that which cannot not exist. And one who thinks of this

---

10 A biblical quote, from St. Paul's Epistle to the Romans (1:20).

11 "Ineffable" means unutterable or indescribable—incapable of being expressed.

thinks of something greater than one who thinks of what can not exist. When, therefore, one thinks of that-than-which-a-greater-cannot-be-thought, if one thinks of what can not exist, one does not think of that-than-which-a-greater-cannot-be-thought. Now the same thing cannot at the same time be thought of and not thought of. For this reason he who thinks of that-than-which-a-greater-cannot-be-thought does not think of something that can not exist but something that cannot not exist. Therefore what he thinks of exists necessarily, since whatever can not exist is not what he thinks of.

Reply 10

I think now that I have shown that I have proved in the above tract, not by a weak argumentation but by a sufficiently necessary one, that something-than-which-a-greater-cannot-be-thought exists in reality itself, and that this proof has not been weakened by the force of any objection. For the import of this proof is in itself of such force that what is spoken of is proved (as a necessary consequence of the fact that it is understood or thought of) both to exist in actual reality and to be itself whatever must be believed about the Divine Being. For we believe of the Divine Being whatever it can, absolutely speaking, be thought better to be than not to be. For example, it is better to be eternal than not eternal, good than not good, indeed goodness itself than not goodness-itself. However, nothing of this kind cannot but be that-than-which-a-greater-cannot-be-thought. It is, then, necessary that 'that-than-which-a-greater-cannot-be-thought' should be whatever must be believed about the Divine Nature.

I thank you for your kindness both in criticizing and praising my tract. For since you praised so fulsomely those parts that appeared to you to be worthy of acceptance, it is quite clear that you have criticized those parts that seemed to you to be weak, not from any malice but from good will.

ST. THOMAS AQUINAS
Summa Theologiae

Who Was St. Thomas Aquinas?

Saint Thomas was born in 1225 in Roccasecca in southern Italy, the son of the count of Aquino. At the age of five he was sent to be educated at the great Benedictine abbey of Monte Casino, and at 14 he went to university in Naples. His father expected him to join the respectable and wealthy Benedictine order of monks. However, when he was 19 Aquinas instead joined the recently formed Dominican order of celibate, mendicant (begging) friars. These monks had adopted a life of complete poverty and traveled Europe studying and teaching the gospel. Thomas's father was outraged, and—according to legend—he locked Aquinas in the family castle for a year and of-fered him bribes, including a beautiful prostitute, to join the Benedictines instead. Aquinas is said to have grabbed a burning brand from the fire and chased away the prostitute; his family eventually allowed him to leave and travel to Paris. He went on to study Greek and Islamic philosophy, natural science, and theology in Paris and Cologne under Albertus Magnus ("Albert the Great"), a Dominican who was famed for his vast learning. His colleagues in Cologne nicknamed Aquinas "the dumb ox," because of his reserved personality and large size; Albertus is said to have responded that Thomas's bellowing would be heard throughout the world. In 1256 Aquinas was made a regent master (professor) at the University of Paris. He taught in Paris and Naples until, on December 6, 1273, he had a deeply religious experience after which he stopped writing. "All that I have written seems to me like straw compared to what has now been revealed to me," he said. He died four months later.

Aquinas became known to later ages as the Angelic Doctor, and was canonized in 1323. In fact, starting shortly after his death, miraculous powers (such as healing the blind) were attributed to Aquinas' corpse, and the Cistercian monks who possessed the body became concerned that members of the Dominican order would steal their treasure: as a safeguard, they "exhumed the corpse of Brother Thomas from its resting place, cut off the head and placed it in a hiding place in a corner of the chapel," so that even if the body were stolen they would still have the skull. His sister was given one of his hands.

Aquinas wrote voluminously— over eight million words of closely reasoned prose, especially amazing considering he was less than 50 when he died. He is said to have committed the entire Bible to memory, and was able to dictate to six or seven secretaries at one time. (His own handwriting was so unintelligible it has been dubbed the *litera inintelligibilis*.) His two major works, both written in Latin, are *Summa contra Gentiles* and *Summa Theologiae*. The first (written between 1259 and 1264) defends Christianity against a large number of objections, without assuming in advance that Christianity is true—it was reputedly written as a handbook for missionaries seeking to convert Muslims and others to Catholicism. The second (written between 1265 and 1273) attempts to summarize Catholic doctrine in such a way that it is consistent with rational philosophy and the natural science of the day.

What Was Aquinas' Overall Philosophical Project?

Aquinas was the most important philosopher of the Middle Ages. His great achievement was that he brought together Christian theology with the insights of classical Greek philosophy—especially the work of Aristotle—and created a formidably systematic and powerful body of thought. Much of this system, as part of the medieval tradition called "scholasticism," became the standard intellectual world view for Christian Europe for hundreds of years: it formed the basis of European science and philosophy until the intellectual Renaissance of the sixteenth century, and still underpins much Catholic theology.[1] In 1879 Pope Leo XIII recognized the philosophical system of Aquinas as the official doctrine of the Catholic Church.

The writings of the classical philosophers like Plato and Aristotle were lost to Western Europe for centuries after the fall of the Roman empire, but they were preserved by Jewish, Byzantine, and Islamic scholars on the Eastern and Southern shores of the Mediterranean. Starting in the sixth century CE these writings, translated into Latin, trickled back into non-Arabic Europe and by the thirteenth century, when Aquinas was writing, most of the texts of Plato and Aristotle were again available to Western thinkers. In particular, in the second half of the twelfth century, Aristotle's writings on physics and metaphysics came to light. This triggered a deep intellectual conflict in Western Europe. Christian theology is ultimately based on *faith* or scriptural revelation, while the conclusions of Plato and Aristotle are supported by *reason*. When theology and philosophy disagree—and in particular, when philosophers provide us with a rationally compelling argument against a theological claim—which are we to believe? Many conservative Christian theologians at the time viewed classical philosophy as a pagan threat to Christian dogma, but Aquinas

---

1   Although Aquinas' work is usually considered the keystone of scholasticism, he didn't create the tradition single-handedly. Other prominent scholastics—who did not all agree with Aquinas—were Peter Abelard (France, 1079–1142), John Duns Scotus (Scotland, c. 1266–1308), William of Occam (England, c. 1285–1349), and Jean Buridan (France, c. 1295–1358).

was deeply impressed by the work of Aristotle—he considered him the greatest of all philosophers, often referring to him in his writings as simply "*The* Philosopher"—and set out to reconcile Aristotle's writings with Catholic doctrine. He did this, it is important to note, not because he wanted to remove any threat to Christianity from pagan science, but because he thought a lot of what Aristotle had to say was *demonstrably true*.

Aquinas' reconciliation project had two prongs. First, he tried to show whenever possible that Aristotelian thought did not conflict with Christianity but actually supported it: thus faith could be conjoined with reason—religion could be combined with science—by showing how the human powers of reason allowed us to *better understand* the revealed truths of Catholicism.

Second, Aquinas argued that when Aristotle's conclusions did conflict with revealed truth, his arguments were not rationally compelling—but that neither were there any rationally compelling arguments on the other side. For example, Aristotle argued that the universe is eternal and uncreated; Christianity holds that the universe was created a finite amount of time ago by God. Aquinas tried to show that *neither* position is provable. In situations like this, Aquinas argued, we discover that reason falls short and some truths can only be known on the basis of faith.

Together, these two kinds of argument were intended to show that there is no conflict between reason and faith and in fact, rational argument, properly carried out, can only strengthen faith, either by further supporting points of doctrine and making them comprehensible to the rational mind, or by revealing the limits of reason. Importantly, this only works when we reason rigorously and *well*. The foolish, according to Aquinas, might be led into error by arguments which are only apparently persuasive, and one important solution to this problem is not to suppress reason but to *encourage* trained, critical, rational reflection on such arguments. (Of course, this solution, Aquinas realized, was not appropriate for the poor and uneducated; the peasants should instead be urged to rely upon their faith.)

Aquinas distinguished sharply between philosophy and theology. He held that theology begins from faith in God and interprets all things as creatures of God, while philosophy moves in the other direction: it starts with the concrete objects of sense perception—such as animals, rocks, and trees—and reasons towards more general conceptions, eventually making its way to God. In our selection from *Summa Theologiae* Aquinas is doing philosophy, and so all five of the proofs for the existence of God given in the Third Article are based upon Aristotelian science—that is, each proof starts from what intellectuals in the thirteenth century thought was a properly rational understanding of ordinary objects, and shows that this scientific understanding leads us to God. Properly understood, according to Aristotle, the natural phenomena appealed to in all of the "five ways" can only be ultimately explained—even *within* a completed science—by bringing in God.

What Is the Structure of This Reading?

This reading is a good example of the medieval 'scholastic' method of doing philosophy. Aquinas begins by dividing up his subject matter—which is the knowledge of God—into a sequence of more precise questions. Question 2 of Part I of the *Summa Theologiae*, he tells us, is about God's essence, and in particular about whether God exists. He breaks down this question into three parts, and in each part—called an 'Article'—Aquinas first considers objections to his position, then lays out his view, and then answers the objections. The First Article considers whether God's existence is *self-evident*: that is, whether it is simply obvious to everyone who considers the matter that God must exist. Aquinas claims that it is not self-evident (except to the learned), and so some kind of argument will be needed to convince the unbeliever. In this section Aquinas argues against the Ontological Argument for the existence of God (see the previous section on Anselm's *Proslogion*). The Second Article discusses whether God's existence can be rationally demonstrated at all, or whether it is something that must be merely accepted on faith: Aquinas argues that God's existence can be proven. Finally, the Third Article (after considering two quite powerful objections to the existence of God) proceeds to lay out this proof; in fact, Aquinas thinks there are no fewer than *five* good arguments for the existence of God (his famous "five ways").

Some Useful Background Information

1. Some of Aquinas' terminology comes from Aristotelian logic. The basic argument form in this logic is called a 'syllogism,' and one of the most important types of syllogism is one called a 'categorical' syllogism. Such arguments, according to Aristotle, always have two premises and a conclusion and always make use of exactly three 'terms.' For example, one might argue thus: All human beings are mortal; All Canadians are human beings; Therefore, all Canadians are mortal. This has the following structure: (1) All M are P; (2) All S are M; therefore, (3) all S are P. In this argument *mortal* (P) is called the 'major term' and *Canadian* (S) is the 'minor term'—they are the predicate and subject of the conclusion, respectively. The 'middle term' is *human being* (M), and it appears in each premise but not the conclusion.

2. All five of Aquinas' arguments for the existence of God have the same basic form. They all move from some familiar empirical fact about the world to the conclusion that there must be some 'transcendent cause' upon which these facts depend. A 'transcendent cause' is a cause which transcends—lies beyond—the natural world; that is, it is a cause which is not itself *part* of the ever-changing physical universe but which *explains* the existence and nature of that universe.

3. In his first argument for the existence of God Aquinas uses the word "motion" in a somewhat technical sense. Aquinas is not just talking about a change of position but about *all* change in the physical world: the motion of the tides, the growth of a plant, the erosion of a mountain range, or someone baking a cake. Furthermore, in Aristotelian science, all motion or change is a transformation from a state of 'potentiality' to a state of 'actuality.' For example, imagine a row of dominoes standing next to each other. Each domino is *actually* standing up, but it is

potentially falling down. When one domino is knocked down, it bumps into the next domino in the series and converts that potentiality into actuality—it makes the domino fall down. For Aristotle and Aquinas *all* change is this kind of movement, from being only potentially X into being actually X.

One important thing to notice about the domino example is that a domino cannot be toppled by something only *potentially* falling down—the domino next to it must be *actually* falling to have any effect. In other words, mere potentiality cannot make anything happen at all—or, to put it yet another way, a domino cannot knock *itself* over. This last claim is crucial for Aquinas' argument in the First Way to work.

4. The Aristotelian notion of an 'efficient cause' plays a key role in Aquinas' Second Way. The 'efficient cause' of something, according to Aristotle, is simply the agent (the object or substance) which brings it about: for example, the 'efficient cause' of tides is the moon's gravity. It's worth noticing that, sometimes, the continuing presence of an effect requires the continuation of the cause. If the moon's gravity went away, ocean tides would also subside; if the force causing the moon to orbit the Earth disappeared, according to Aristotelian science, the moon would stop moving.[2] Thus, if God is ultimately the 'efficient cause' of, say, the movements of the tides, God must still be presently acting as that cause.

5. When Aquinas talks about 'merely possible' being in the Third Way he again does not use this phrase in quite the modern sense. For modern philosophers, something is 'merely possible' if it might not have existed—for example, the book you are holding has 'merely possible' (or contingent) being, in this modern sense, because under other circumstances it might never have

---

2 Notice that this is importantly different from modern science. Today, we know that motions like planetary orbits, once started, simply continue forever unless some force stops them—this is Newton's first law of motion.

been written at all. By contrast, many modern philosophers would agree that mathematical objects, like the number two, have necessary existence—there are no possible circumstances in which the number two could fail to exist. But this is not quite what Aquinas means by 'possible' and 'necessary': for him, something has 'merely possible' being if it is *generated* and *corruptible*. Something is generated if there was a time at which it didn't exist—a time at which it came into being. Something is corruptible if there will be a time at which it ceases to exist. Since things can't come into existence for no reason at all (according to Aquinas), all non-necessary beings must have been generated by *something else*. For example, this book was generated by me, I was generated by my parents, and so on.

6. Aquinas also distinguishes between two different sorts of necessary (i.e., eternal) being. Some entities have necessary being but were nevertheless created by something else (God). For example, suppose that angels are non-corruptible, eternal beings; nevertheless, they have this nature only because God has created them in that way, so their necessary being is derivative of the necessary being of God. God himself, by contrast, is eternal and uncreated—the necessity of his being is, so to speak, built-in, rather than derived from some other source; God is necessarily necessary.

7. In the Fifth Way, the empirical fact from which Aquinas begins is this: different kinds of things, like water and air and plants, co-operate with each other in such a way that a stable order of nature is produced and maintained. They seem to act 'for an end,' which is to say, for a particular *purpose*. For example, heat causes water to evaporate; this water then condenses as clouds and falls as rain; as it falls it nourishes plants and animals, and finally runs back into lakes and oceans where it once again evaporates; and so on. This co-operative cycle is stable and self-perpetuating, but the entities that make it up—the water, plants, and so on—do not *intend* for this to happen: they just, as a matter of fact, act in a way that preserves the system.

Some Common Misconceptions

1. Aquinas does not say that *everything* must have a cause, or that all creation involves a change in the creator. If he did say that, he would have to admit that God must himself have a cause, or that God must himself be moved. When Aquinas asserts that God is the 'first' element of a series, he means that God is importantly different than the other members of that series: God is not a changeable thing, for example, but is instead an Unmoved Mover who brings into existence even the phenomenon of change itself.

2. Although Aquinas thinks that the world in fact began a finite amount of time ago, he does not argue that the notion of an infinite time is rationally incoherent: "By faith alone do we hold, and by no demonstration can it be proved, that the world did not always exist," he says in *Summa Theologiae* (Part I, Question 46, Article 2). But this is not inconsistent with Aquinas' attempt to rationally demonstrate that there must have been a first cause. He thinks he can prove that the world must have been created by God—i.e., that God is the ultimate or underlying cause of the world—but, he argues in a treatise called *On the Eternity of the World*, no one can demonstrate that God's on-going creation of the world might not be spread over an infinitely long period of time. (Analogously, we might loosely say that the curvature of space causes gravitational effects and the curvature of space could conceivably continue for ever.) Aquinas, that is, thought of God not just as a temporally first cause of the universe, back at the beginning of time like a supernatural Big Bang, but as the most fundamental cause of everything that happens in the natural world throughout time.

3. When Aquinas says that God is a necessary being, he means (roughly) that God's existence does not depend on the existence of anything else. He does not mean that God's existence is what modern philosophers would call "logically necessary." If God were logically necessary, then

it would be impossible for God not to exist—it would be self-contradictory to assert that God does not exist, like saying that some bachelors are married. Aquinas does not think that it is self-contradictory to say that God does not exist, just that it is demonstrably false.

4. Aquinas was well aware that his Five Ways, even if they are sound, only prove the *existence* of God and, by themselves, fail to establish important positive conclusions about the nature of God (e.g., his moral goodness). In the section of the *Summa Theologiae* which comes after our selection, he goes on to give arguments about God's nature. Furthermore, Aquinas was aware he had not yet proved that there can be only one God, and he goes on to try to show—on the basis of philosophical arguments—that any entity whose necessary being is essential rather than derived must be simple, perfect, infinite, immutable, eternal, and one—i.e., if there is a God at all, there can be only one God (*Summa Theologiae* Part I, Questions 3 to 11).

5. Although Aquinas appeals to empirical facts as the premises of his arguments for God, he does not think his *conclusion* that God exists is a merely empirical hypothesis. For example, he does not think any amount of future scientific research could ever cast doubt on his arguments. Contrast that with, for example, the claim that electrons are the unseen cause of the pictures that appear on our television sets. It might be that future scientific advances could call into question our present sub-atomic theory, and so cast doubt on the existence of electrons: maybe all the phenomena we explain by talking about electrons can be better explained by talking about some other kind of invisible particle, or about some other category of thing altogether. By contrast, according to Aquinas, our proofs of the existence of God do not depend on the truth of some particular scientific theory; they follow from the mere existence of change, causation, contingent beings, or whatever, *however* these things are ultimately explained by science.

How Important and Influential Is This Passage?

Aquinas thought that, although the existence of God is not self-evident, reason is capable of proving to the careful thinker that God exists. The "five ways" he lists in this passage include versions of many of the most important arguments for God's existence, and—as a convenient, short, and very capable outline of the main arguments—this section from Aquinas' *Summa Theologiae* has been at the center of debate about the existence of God for hundreds of years.

Suggestions for Critical Reflection

1. Do any of Aquinas' five arguments actually prove that God exists? If none of them work, does this show that God does *not* exist?

2. Do Aquinas' five arguments establish the existence of a *personal* God—of a God who resembles the Christian conception of him? Does Aquinas show that there can be only *one* God, or are his arguments compatible with the existence of numerous gods?

3. Aquinas claims that there cannot be an infinite hierarchy of causes. Is he right about this? Do you think he gives compelling arguments for his claim? We are quite familiar with infinite sequences, such as the succession of integers (… -3, -2, -1, 1, 2, 3 …). Should Aquinas be worried about such infinite series? Why or why not?

4. Aquinas asserts that if everything were merely possible (and not necessary), then there would have to be some time in the past at which nothing at all existed. Does this follow? What might Aquinas have had in mind when he made this move?

5. For Aquinas, could anything have *both* possible and necessary being? Does this fit with your intuitions about possibility and necessity? What, if anything, is the connection between something being eternal and it having necessary being—for example, in your view, could something necessarily exist, but only for a finite amount of time, or could something that might not have existed at all be eternal?

6. Aquinas asserts that we must have an idea of *the best*, before we can judge anything to be *better than* something else. Do you agree with this claim? Support your answer with examples.

7. To what extent do you think that Aquinas' arguments depend on specifically Aristotelian science? How much does the fact that Aristotelian science has now been discredited in favor of post-Newtonian science cast doubt on his arguments?

Suggestions for Further Reading

A standard introductory collection of Aquinas' writings is *Basic Writings of St. Thomas Aquinas*, edited by Anton Pegis (Random House, 1945). It's worth comparing the selection given here with Aquinas' other discussion of the arguments for the existence of God in *Summa contra Gentiles*, Book I, Chapters 9–14; this can be found in Aquinas' *Selected Writings*, ed. Ralph McInerny (Penguin, 1998). A useful history of philosophy of the period (including Anselm) is Frederick Copleston's *A History of Philosophy*, Volume II (Doubleday, 1950). Some good shorter books about Aquinas' thought are F.C. Copleston's *Aquinas* (Penguin, 1955), Brian Davies's *The Thought of Thomas Aquinas* (Oxford University Press, 1992), and Anthony Kenny's *Aquinas* (Oxford University Press, 1980). A book specifically about Aquinas' arguments for God is Kenny's *The Five Ways* (Routledge & Kegan Paul, 1969). Two useful collections of articles are Anthony Kenny (ed.), *Aquinas: A Collection of Critical Essays* (Anchor Doubleday, 1969) and Norman Kretzmann and Eleanor Stump (eds.), *The Cambridge Companion to Aquinas* (Cambridge University Press, 1993).

Summa Theologiae
Part I, Question 2, The Existence of God (In Three Articles)[3]

Because the chief aim of sacred doctrine is to teach the knowledge of God not only as He is in Himself, but also as He is the beginning of things and their last end, and especially of rational creatures, as is clear from what has been already said, therefore, in our endeavor to expound this science, we shall treat: (1) of God; (2) of the rational creature's movement towards God; (3) of Christ Who as man is our way to God.

In treating of God there will be a threefold division:—

For we shall consider (1) whatever concerns the divine essence. (2) Whatever concerns the distinctions of Persons. (3) Whatever concerns the procession of creatures from Him.

Concerning the divine essence, we must consider:—

(1) Whether God exists? (2) The manner of His existence, or, rather, what is *not* the manner of His existence. (3) Whatever concerns His operations—namely, His knowledge, will, power.

Concerning the first, there are three points of inquiry:—

(1) Whether the proposition *God exists* is self-evident? (2) Whether it is demonstrable? (3) Whether God exists?

First Article: Whether the existence of God is self-evident?

We proceed thus to the First Article:—

Objection 1. It seems that the existence of God is self-evident. For those things are said to be self-evident to us the knowledge of which exists naturally in us, as we can see in regard to first principles. But as

---

3   This part of the *Summa Theologiae* was written around 1265. The translation used here, by Anton C. Pegis, is taken from *Basic Writings of Saint Thomas Aquinas*, Volume I, Hackett Publishing Company, 1997; pp. 18-24. Reprinted by permission of Hackett Publishing Company, Inc. All rights reserved.

Damascene[4] says, *the knowledge of God is naturally implanted in all*. Therefore the existence of God is self-evident.

Objection 2. Further, those things are said to be self-evident which are known as soon as the terms are known, which the Philosopher[5] says is true of the first principles of demonstration. Thus, when the nature of a whole and of a part is known, it is at once recognized that every whole is greater than its part. But as soon as the signification of the name *God* is understood, it is at once seen that God exists. For by this name is signified that thing than which nothing greater can be conceived. But that which exists actually and mentally is greater than that which exists only mentally. Therefore, since as soon as the name *God* is understood it exists mentally, it also follows that it exists actually. Therefore the proposition *God exists* is self-evident.

Objection 3. Further, the existence of truth is self-evident. For whoever denies the existence of truth grants that truth does not exist: and, if truth does not exist, then the proposition *Truth does not exist* is true: and if there is anything true, there must be truth. But God is truth itself: *I am the way, the truth, and the life* (John xiv.6). Therefore *God exists* is self-evident.

On the contrary, No one can mentally admit the opposite of what is self-evident, as the Philosopher states concerning the first principles of demonstration. But the opposite of the proposition *God is* can be mentally admitted: *The fool said in his heart, There is no God* (Psalms lii.1[6]). Therefore, that God exists is not self-evident.

I answer that, A thing can be self-evident in either of two ways: on the one hand, self-evident in itself, though not to us; on the other, self-evident in itself, and to us. A proposition is self-evident because the predicate is included in the essence of the subject: e.g., *Man is an animal*, for animal is contained in the essence of man. If, therefore, the essence of the predicate and subject be known to all, the proposition will be self-evident to all; as is clear with regard to the first principles of demonstration, the terms of which are certain common notions that no one is ignorant of, such as being and non-being, whole and part, and the like. If, however, there are some to whom the essence of the predicate and subject is unknown, the proposition will be self-evident in itself, but not to those who do not know the meaning of the predicate and subject of the proposition. Therefore, it happens, as Boethius[7] says, that there are some notions of the mind which are common and self-evident only to the learned, as that incorporeal substances are not in space. Therefore I say that this proposition, *God exists*, of itself is self-evident, for the predicate is the same as the subject, because God is His own existence as will be hereafter shown. Now because we do not know the essence of God, the proposition is not self-evident to us, but needs to be demonstrated by things that are more known to us, though less known in their nature—namely, by His effects.

Reply to Objection 1. To know that God exists in a general and confused way is implanted in us by nature, inasmuch as God is man's beatitude.[8] For man naturally desires happiness, and what is naturally desired by man is naturally known by him. This, however, is not to know absolutely that God exists; just as to know that someone is approaching is not the same as to know that Peter is approaching, even though it is Peter who is approaching; for there are many who imagine that man's perfect good, which is happiness, consists in riches, and others in pleasures, and others in something else.

---

4   St. John Damascene, an eighth-century monk in Jerusalem who wrote a book called *De Fide Orthodoxa* (On the Orthodox Faith), from which this quote is taken.

5   Aristotle. This reference is to Aristotle's *Posterior Analytics*.

6   Aquinas is referring to the first line of the fifty-second psalm in the Latin "Vulgate" version of the Bible, still used by the Catholic Church. Many English translations, such as the "King James" version, number the psalms differently. The quote is found in psalms 14 and 53 in the King James.

7   An aristocratic Christian Roman from the early sixth century, Boethius translated Aristotle's logical writings and wrote several theological treatises.

8   Supreme blessedness or happiness.

Reply to Objection 2. Perhaps not everyone who hears this name *God* understands it to signify something than which nothing greater can be thought, seeing that some have believed God to be a body. Yet, granted that everyone understands that by this name *God* is signified something than which nothing greater can be thought, nevertheless, it does not therefore follow that he understands that what the name signifies exists actually, but only that it exists mentally. Nor can it be argued that it actually exists, unless it be admitted that there actually exists something than which nothing greater can be thought; and this precisely is not admitted by those who hold that God does not exist.

Reply to Objection 3. The existence of truth in general is self-evident, but the existence of a Primal Truth is not self-evident to us.

Second Article: Whether it can be demonstrated that God exists?

We proceed thus to the Second Article:—

Objection 1. It seems that the existence of God cannot be demonstrated. For it is an article of faith that God exists. But what is of faith cannot be demonstrated, because a demonstration produces scientific knowledge, whereas faith is of the unseen, as is clear from the Apostle[9] (Hebrews xi.1). Therefore it cannot be demonstrated that God exists.

Objection 2. Further, essence is the middle term of demonstration. But we cannot know in what God's essence consists, but solely in what it does not consist, as Damascene says. Therefore we cannot demonstrate that God exists.

Objection 3. Further, if the existence of God were demonstrated, this could only be from His effects. But His effects are not proportioned to Him, since He is infinite and His effects are finite, and between the finite and infinite there is no proportion. Therefore,

since a cause cannot be demonstrated by an effect not proportioned to it, it seems that the existence of God cannot be demonstrated.

On the contrary, The Apostle says: *The invisible things of Him are clearly seen, being understood by the things that are made* (Romans i.20). But this would not be unless the existence of God could be demonstrated through the things that are made; for the first thing we must know of anything is, whether it exists.

I answer that, Demonstration can be made in two ways: One is through the cause, and is called *propter quid*, and this is to argue from what is prior absolutely. The other is through the effect, and is called a demonstration *quia*; this is to argue from what is prior relatively only to us. When an effect is better known to us than its cause, from the effect we proceed to the knowledge of the cause. And from every effect the existence of its proper cause can be demonstrated, so long as its effects are better known to us; because, since every effect depends upon its cause, if the effect exists, the cause must pre-exist. Hence the existence of God, in so far as it is not self-evident to us, can be demonstrated from those of His effects which are known to us.

Reply to Objection 1. The existence of God and other like truths about God, which can be known by natural reason, are not articles of faith, but are preambles to the articles; for faith presupposes natural knowledge, even as grace[10] presupposes nature and perfection the perfectible. Nevertheless, there is nothing to prevent a man, who cannot grasp a proof, from accepting, as a matter of faith, something which in itself is capable of being scientifically known and demonstrated.

Reply to Objection 2. When the existence of a cause is demonstrated from an effect, this effect takes the place of the definition of the cause in proving the cause's existence. This is especially the case in regard to God, because, in order to prove the existence of anything, it is necessary to accept as a middle term the meaning of the name, and not its essence, for the question of its essence follows on the question of its existence. Now the names given to God are derived

---

9   Aquinas means St. Paul, a Jewish Roman citizen who lived in Jerusalem in the first century CE and who became an important missionary and the most significant founder of the church after his conversion to Christianity on the road to Damascus. He is often considered to be something like the second founder of Christianity. (However, it is now thought that St. Paul probably did not in fact write the *Epistle to the Hebrews*.)

10   The unmerited favor or protection of God.

from His effects, as will be later shown. Consequently, in demonstrating the existence of God from His effects, we may take for the middle term the meaning of the name *God*.

Reply to Objection 3. From effects not proportioned to the cause no perfect knowledge of that cause can be obtained. Yet from every effect the existence of the cause can be clearly demonstrated, and so we can demonstrate the existence of God from His effects; though from them we cannot know God perfectly as He is in His essence.

Third Article: Whether God exists?

We proceed thus to the Third Article:—

Objection 1. It seems that God does not exist; because if one of two contraries[11] be infinite, the other would be altogether destroyed. But the name *God* means that He is infinite goodness. If, therefore, God existed, there would be no evil discoverable; but there is evil in the world. Therefore God does not exist.

Objection 2. Further, it is superfluous to suppose that what can be accounted for by a few principles has been produced by many. But it seems that everything we see in the world can be accounted for by other principles, supposing God did not exist. For all natural things can be reduced to one principle, which is nature; and all voluntary things can be reduced to one principle, which is human reason, or will. Therefore there is no need to suppose God's existence.

On the contrary, It is said in the person of God: *I am Who am* (Exodus iii.14).

I answer that, The existence of God can be proved in five ways.

The first and more manifest way is the argument from motion. It is certain, and evident to our senses, that in the world some things are in motion. Now whatever is moved is moved by another, for nothing can be moved except it is in potentiality to that towards which it is moved; whereas a thing moves inasmuch as it is in act. For motion is nothing else than the reduction of something from potentiality to

---

11   Contraries are properties which cannot both apply to a thing at the same time, though they can both fail to apply, e.g., being red all over and green all over, or being ugly and beautiful, or being wise and stupid.

actuality. But nothing can be reduced from potentiality to actuality, except by something in a state of actuality. Thus that which is actually hot, as fire, makes wood, which is potentially hot, to be actually hot, and thereby moves and changes it. Now it is not possible that the same thing should be at once in actuality and potentiality in the same respect, but only in different respects. For what is actually hot cannot simultaneously be potentially hot; but it is simultaneously potentially cold. It is therefore impossible that in the same respect and in the same way a thing should be both mover and moved, *i.e.*, that it should move itself. Therefore, whatever is moved must be moved by another. If that by which it is moved be itself moved, then this also must needs be moved by another, and that by another again. But this cannot go on to infinity, because then there would be no first mover, and, consequently, no other mover, seeing that subsequent movers move only inasmuch as they are moved by the first mover; as the staff moves only because it is moved by the hand. Therefore it is necessary to arrive at a first mover, moved by no other; and this everyone understands to be God.

The second way is from the nature of efficient cause. In the world of sensible things we find there is an order of efficient causes. There is no case known (neither is it, indeed, possible) in which a thing is found to be the efficient cause of itself; for so it would be prior to itself, which is impossible. Now in efficient causes it is not possible to go on to infinity, because in all efficient causes following in order, the first is the cause of the intermediate cause, and the intermediate is the cause of the ultimate cause, whether the intermediate cause be several, or one only. Now to take away the cause is to take away the effect. Therefore, if there be no first cause among efficient causes, there will be no ultimate, nor any intermediate, cause. But if in efficient causes it is possible to go on to infinity, there will be no first efficient cause, neither will there be an ultimate effect, nor any intermediate efficient causes; all of which is plainly false. Therefore it is necessary to admit a first efficient cause, to which everyone gives the name of God.

The third way is taken from possibility and necessity, and runs thus. We find in nature things that are possible to be and not to be, since they are found to be generated, and to be corrupted, and consequently, it is possible for them to be and not to be. But it is impossible for these always to exist, for that which can not-be at some time is not. Therefore, if everything can not-be, then at one time there was nothing in existence. Now if this were true, even now there would be nothing in existence, because that which does not exist begins to exist only through something already existing. Therefore, if at one time nothing was in existence, it would have been impossible for anything to have begun to exist; and thus even now nothing would be in existence—which is absurd. Therefore, not all beings are merely possible, but there must exist something the existence of which is necessary. But every necessary thing either has its necessity caused by another, or not. Now it is impossible to go on to infinity in necessary things which have their necessity caused by another, as has been already proved in regard to efficient causes. Therefore we cannot but admit the existence of some being having of itself its own necessity, and not receiving it from another but rather causing in others their necessity. This all men speak of as God.

The fourth way is taken from the gradation to be found in things. Among beings there are some more and some less good, true, noble, and the like. But *more* and *less* are predicated of different things according as they resemble in their different ways something which is the maximum, as a thing is said to be hotter according as it more nearly resembles that which is hottest; so that there is something which is truest, something best, something noblest, and, consequently, something which is most being, for those things that are greatest in truth are greatest in being, as it is writ-ten in *Metaphysics* ii.[12] Now the maximum in any genus is the cause of all in that genus, as fire, which is the maximum of heat, is the cause of all hot things, as is said in the same book. Therefore there must also be something which is to all beings the cause of their being, goodness, and every other perfection; and this we call God.

The fifth way is taken from the governance of the world. We see that things which lack knowledge, such as natural bodies, act for an end, and this is evident from their acting always, or nearly always, in the same way, so as to obtain the best result. Hence it is plain that they achieve their end, not fortuitously, but designedly. Now whatever lacks knowledge cannot move towards an end, unless it be directed by some being endowed with knowledge and intelligence; as the arrow is directed by the archer. Therefore some intelligent being exists by whom all natural things are directed to their end; and this being we call God.

Reply to Objection 1. As Augustine[13] says: *Since God is the highest good, He would not allow any evil to exist in His works, unless His omnipotence and goodness were such as to bring good even out of evil.* This is part of the infinite goodness of God, that He should allow evil to exist, and out of it produce good.

Reply to Objection 2. Since nature works for a determinate end under the direction of a higher agent, whatever is done by nature must be traced back to God as to its first cause. So likewise whatever is done voluntarily must be traced back to some higher cause other than human reason and will, since these can change and fail; for all things that are changeable and capable of defect must be traced back to an immovable and self-necessary first principle, as has been shown.

---

12   The second volume of a book by Aristotle.

13   St. Augustine, a north African bishop who lived from 354 until 430, was the most important early Christian theologian and philosopher. This quote is from his *Enchiridion* ("Handbook").

DAVID HUME
Dialogues Concerning Natural Religion

Who Was David Hume?

David Hume has been called the most important philosopher ever to have written in English. He was born to a strict Calvinist family in Edinburgh, Scotland's capital, in 1711, and spent his youth there and in Ninewells, his family's small land-holding near the border with England. Little is known of Hume's early childhood. His father, Joseph, died when he was two, and was educated by his mother Katherine—who never re-married—from an early age. He was a precociously intelligent and well-read child,[1] and by the age of 16 he had begun composing his first philosophical masterwork, *A Treatise of Human Nature*, on which he was to work, more or less continuously, for the next ten years.

Hume spent the years between 1723 and 1726 (i.e., between the ages of 12 and 15) studying a wide range of subjects at the University of Edinburgh but, like many students of that era, did not take a degree. His father and grandfather had both been lawyers, and his family expected him also to go into law, but, Hume later wrote, he found the law "nauseous" and discovered in himself "an unsurmountable aversion to every thing but the pursuits of philosophy and general learning."

Hume continued to read and write and, as a result of his feverish intellectual activity—motivated by his belief that he had made a major philosophical discovery—he suffered a nervous breakdown in 1734. He was forced to put philosophy aside for several months (during which time he attempted life as a businessman at Bristol, in the employ of a Portsmouth merchant, but found that it didn't suit him) and then left Britain for France. There, in the following three years, living frugally in the countryside in Anjou (and using up all his savings), he completed most of his book.

Hume's *A Treatise of Human Nature* was published anonymously when he was 27. Hume later wrote, it "fell *dead-born from the press*, without reaching such distinction as even to excite a murmur among the zealots." Hume's career as an intellectual and man of letters seemed to have ended before it had begun, and Hume blamed not the substance of his work but its style. "I was carry'd away by the Heat of Youth & Invention to publish too precipitately. So vast an Undertaking, plan'd before I was one and twenty, & compos'd before twenty-five, must necessarily be very defective. I have repented my Haste a hundred, & a hundred times." Hume returned to Scotland to live with his mother, and began to re-cast the material of the *Treatise* into two new books, which have become philosophical classics in their own right: *An Enquiry Concerning Human Understanding* (1748), and *An Enquiry Concerning the Principles of Morals* (1751). However both these books—though more successful than the *Treatise*—were slow to become influential during Hume's own lifetime.

---

1   As his mother put it, in her Scottish dialect: "Our Davie's a fine good-natured crater, but uncommon wake-minded."

Needing money, Hume got his first real job at the age of 34 and spent a well-paid year as tutor to a mad nobleman (the Marquess of Annandale). In 1746 Hume accepted a position as secretary to General St. Clair's military expedition to Canada (which never reached Canada and ended, oddly enough, with a brief attack on the French coast), and for two years after that was part of a secret diplomatic and military embassy by St. Clair to the courts of Vienna and Turin. During this period Hume was twice refused academic appointments at Scottish universities—first Edinburgh, then Glasgow—because of his reputation as a religious skeptic. Shortly afterwards, between 1755 and 1757, unsuccessful attempts were made in Edinburgh to have Hume excommunicated from the Church of Scotland.

In 1752 Hume was offered the Keepership of the Advocates' Library at Edinburgh and there, poorly paid but surrounded by books, he wrote the colossal six-volume *History of England*, which (though unpopular at first) eventually became his first major literary success. At this time he also published a controversial *Natural History of Religion*.

In 1763 Hume was made secretary of the English embassy at Paris, where he found himself very much in fashion and seems to have enjoyed the experience. There he fell in love with, but failed to win the hand of, the Comtesse de Boufflers, the mistress of a prominent French noble. (Some unkindly suggest this might have been partly because at the time, when Hume was in his fifties, he had come to resemble "a fat well-fed Bernardine monk.") In 1767, back in Scotland and now a fairly wealthy man, Hume was appointed an Under-Secretary of State, a senior position in the British civil service.

By the time Hume died in 1776, of cancer of the bowel, he had become respected as one of Europe's leading men of letters and a principal architect of the Enlightenment. His death gave him the reputation of something of a secular saint, as he faced his incurable condition with cheerfulness and resignation and refused to abandon his religious skepticism. In a short autobiography, written just before he died, Hume described his own character.

> I was ... a man of mild dispositions, of command of temper, of an open, social, and cheerful humour, capable of attachment, but little susceptible of enmity, and of great moderation in all my passions. Even my love of literary fame, my ruling passion, never soured my temper, notwithstanding my frequent disappointments. My company was not unacceptable to the young and careless, as well as to the studious and literary; and as I took a particular pleasure in the company of modest women, I had no reason to be displeased with the reception I met from them.... I cannot say there is no vanity in making this funeral oration of myself, but I hope it is not a misplaced one; and this is a matter of fact which is easily cleared and ascertained.

What Was Hume's Overall Philosophical Project?

Hume can be called the first 'post-skeptical' modern philosopher. He was wholly convinced (by, among others, the writings of his predecessors Descartes, Locke, and Berkeley, who appear elsewhere in this volume) that no knowledge that goes beyond the mere data of our own minds has anything like secure and reliable foundations: that is, he believed, we have no certain knowledge of the inner workings of the physical world and its laws, or of God, or of absolute moral 'truth,' or even of our own 'real selves.' All we have secure knowledge of is our own mental states and their relations: our sensory impressions, our ideas, our emotions, and so on.

Despite all this, Hume's philosophical project was a positive one: he wanted to develop a new, constructive science of human nature that would provide a defensible foundation for all the sciences, including ethics, physics and politics. Where Hume's predecessors tried in vain to argue against philosophical skepticism, Hume assumed that a certain kind of skepticism was actually true and tried to go beyond it, to say something positive about how we are to get on with our lives (including our lives as scientists and philosophers).

Much of Hume's philosophical writing, therefore, begins by showing the unstoppable power of skepticism in some domain—such as skepticism about causation or objective ethical truths—and then goes on to show how we can still talk sensibly about causation or ethics after all. The selection from *An Enquiry Concerning Human Understanding* which appears in Chapter Four follows this pattern. The structure of Hume's *Dialogues*, however, is more complex. Exactly what Hume's own religious views were remains a matter of some controversy, but a strong case can be made that Hume felt substantial conclusions about the existence and nature of God cannot be founded in experience and therefore cannot be made sense of at all. Hume may, in other words, have been unremittingly skeptical about religion.

One of the central aspects of both Hume's skeptical and his constructive philosophy is his strictly empirical methodology—a development of what was called in Hume's day 'the experimental method.' His science of human nature is based firmly on the experimental methods of the natural sciences, which emphasize the data of experience and observation, sometimes combined with mathematical or logical reasoning. Any other method of investigation—such as an appeal to 'innate intuition,' for example—is illegitimate. As Hume put it:

> If we take in our hand any volume; of divinity or school metaphysics, for instance; let us ask, *Does it contain any abstract reasoning concerning quantity or number?* No. *Does it contain any experimental reasoning concerning matter of fact and existence?* No. Commit it then to the flames: for it can contain nothing but sophistry and illusion. [This is the final paragraph of his *Enquiry Concerning Human Understanding*.]

This assumption that all human knowledge is either a "matter of fact" or a matter of "relations of ideas"—the product of experience or of reason—is often known as 'Hume's Fork.' You can find more about this in the Hume reading in Chapter Four.

This general philosophical attitude is also applied to religion. Hume's two main writings on religion are the *Dialogues Concerning Natural Religion* (which was published only after Hume's death, due to its controversial religious skepticism) and *The Natural History of Religion*. The former examines the rational basis for belief in God; the latter is a historical study of religion's origins in human nature and society: that is, Hume studies both the *reasons* for religious belief,

and the *causes* of religious belief. In the *Dialogues*, written in the 1750s, Hume raises powerful doubts about whether we could ever have good reasons for believing in God—all religion, if Hume is right, may be no more than "mere superstition." Why then is religious belief so common? In *The Natural History of Religion*, published in 1757, Hume argues that the causes of religious belief are independent of rationality and are instead based on human fear of the unpredictable and uncontrollable influences in our lives—such as the forces of nature—which we try to propitiate through worship. Furthermore, Hume suggests, religious belief is more harmful than it is beneficial. Even apart from the suffering and strife which they have historically caused, religions invent spurious sins (like suicide) which Hume argued are not really harmful, and create "frivolous merits" not grounded in any genuine good (such as attending certain ceremonies and abstaining from particular foods).

In his *Enquiry Concerning the Principles of Morals* Hume develops a secular alternative to religiously-based morality; the theory of moral life he develops there is based entirely upon an analysis of human nature and human needs and is completely independent of religion. (Hume is often thought of as the original founder of the moral doctrine called "utilitarianism"; that important moral theory is represented in this book by J.S. Mill's *Utilitarianism* in Chapter 7.)

What Is the Structure of This Reading?

There are three speakers in this dialogue: Cleanthes, who advocates the argument from design; Demea, who defends both mysticism and, occasionally, a kind of cosmological argument; and Philo, who plays the role of a skeptical critic of both of the others. The dialogue contains twelve sections: the first, sixth, and twelfth have been omitted here.

[PART I. Introductory discussion of the relationship between religion and philosophy.]

PART II. Demea and Philo claim that the nature of God is inaccessible, since it goes beyond human experience. Cleanthes presents the argument from design (to show that experience can give results about God), but Philo objects to the argument as being weak, even for an empirical argument. Cleanthes defends the analogy between a house and the universe and Philo re-presents the design argument for Demea's benefit, but then presents several objections to it.

PART III. Cleanthes defends the argument against Philo's objections, and Demea responds.

PART IV. The three discuss the question of whether the nature of God's mind is at all similar to ours (e.g., in containing a set of ideas), and thus whether we can intelligibly speak of God as a designer. Philo suggests that to say the universe is created by a mind like ours invites us to ask what caused the ordered ideas that make up that mind (ideas don't just appear and fall into a certain pattern all by themselves, any more than matter does), and then we have an infinite regress. Cleanthes responds to this argument, and Philo replies.

PART V. Philo goes on to reconsider the principle "like effects prove like causes," and to suggest what consequences this would have for our idea of God as a cause "proportioned to the effect."

[PART VI. Philo next suggests that reasoning very like the argument from design will show that God is not the cause of the universe, but its mind or soul, and the material universe is God's body—his point is that, if this conclusion is unacceptable, something must be wrong with the arguments for both conclusions. Cleanthes responds, arguing (in part) that the universe cannot have been infinite and so cannot be God, and Philo in turn argues for its infinity.]

PART VII. Philo next objects that reasoning very like the argument from design will show that a more plausible cause for the universe is not a human-like designer, but the kind of "generation or vegetation" which we observe giving rise to plants and animals. We have no good evidence, he argues, to think that reason—thought—is the only creative power in the universe.

PART VIII. Here Philo hypothesizes that more or less random motions of matter, over an endless duration of time, would eventually produce a complex world just like ours, and once formed this world would persist for some time. Cleanthes objects that this is implausible. Philo agrees, but asserts that it is no more implausible than any other hypothesis and so "a total suspension of judgment is here our only reasonable resource."

PART IX. Faced with the failure of the argument from design ("the argument *a posteriori*"), Demea urges a return to cosmological and ontological arguments (which he calls "the argument *a priori*"). His argument is rejected by Cleanthes.

PART X. The speakers discuss the problem of evil. Why would a good and powerful God allow pain, hardship, and misery to exist in the world? And does not the existence of evil in the world cast doubt upon our inference from the apparent design of the world to a benevolent designer?

PART XI. The three continue the discussion of the problem of evil. They examine four sources of evil, but it is suggested that at best they may establish the compatibility of evil with God and that they block any inference from a world containing evil to an infinitely good God. On the contrary, Philo suggests, the existence of evil means that we should infer an amoral origin of the universe.

[PART XII. After Demea's departure Philo completely reverses himself and admits that the argument from design does indeed show the existence of God; he claims, however, that it nevertheless tells us little about God's nature or about how human beings should behave.]

Some Useful Background Information

1. Probably, none of the three speakers in the dialogue fully and uniquely represents Hume's own views. Philo certainly comes closest to Hume's own position, but all three of the characters have philosophically important points to make. At the end of the *Dialogues* Hume offers no decisive verdict, but instead leaves his readers to grapple with the questions he raises. Furthermore, Hume's writing is often ironic, or intended to protect himself from charges of atheism: for example, claims by the various speakers that God's nature and existence is obvious to any rational thinker should be taken with a pinch of salt.

   It's important for the modern reader to understand that Hume had good reason to fear becoming known as an atheist. As recently as 1619 atheists were executed in Europe by having their tongues pulled out and then being burnt to death, and even in the eighteenth century there were stiff legal penalties in Britain for impiety: for example, in 1763, 70-year-old Peter Annet was sentenced to a year of hard labor for questioning the accounts of miracles in the Old Testament. At a minimum, a reputation for atheism could easily lead to social and professional isolation and, despite his caution, Hume himself felt some of these sorts of effects (such as twice being denied university posts).

2. In his *Dialogues* Hume is operating with certain distinctions that it is useful to be aware of. *Natural religion* (or natural theology) is religious belief that can be proven on the basis of public evidence, available to believer and unbeliever alike (such as facts about causation, or the concept of God). This is contrasted with *revealed religion* (or revelation), which is based on privileged information given only to believers (such as scripture).

Theism is the belief in a unique, all-powerful God who created the universe, and who remains active—sustaining the universe, answering prayers, granting revelations, and so on. Typically, evidence for the existence of God the creator is thought to be part of natural religion, while claims about the continuing activity of God (often called God's "immanence" or "providence") are more often based on revelation. *Deism* is a philosophical view that accepts rational arguments for the existence of God—accepts natural theology—but is skeptical of revelation and so denies the Christian (or Judaic or Islamic) revelation of an immanent God.

Deism was a fairly influential view during Hume's lifetime, and Hume always vigorously denied that he himself was a deist. In fact, his arguments in the *Dialogues* are much more focussed on deism than on theism, since what he is attacking is natural religion. Elsewhere in his writings, however, Hume levels a brief but seminal criticism at revealed religion, and

especially at the idea that miracles can be evidence of the existence and nature of God (Section X of *An Enquiry Concerning Human Understanding*). Many modern commentators (but by no means all of them) believe that Hume was in fact some kind of 'attenuated deist': that is, he may have thought that rational argument—and especially the argument from design—did make it at least somewhat likely that God exists, but it can tell us little about God's nature.

Anthropomorphism, by contrast, is a view which not only says that we can understand God but that we can appropriately describe God in language that draws its meaning from human activities and qualities, using such adjectives as "beautiful," "merciful," "fatherly," or "wise." ("Anthropomorphism" is from Greek words meaning "having the shape of a man.") This is a view Hume portrays Demea and Philo as rejecting.

3. Within natural religion, Hume (like other eighteenth-century thinkers) distinguishes between two types of argument, which he calls "the argument *a priori*" and "the argument *a posteriori*." The argument *a priori*, for Hume, is usually the cosmological argument for a First Cause. The argument *a posteriori* is the argument from design. See the introduction to this chapter on philosophy of religion for a little more information on these types of argument.

A Common Misconception

The *Dialogues* are deliberately written to be somewhat "literary" and philosophically ambiguous. Thus, for example, though many of the arguments he raises for and against are clear and compelling, it is not a clear-cut matter whether Hume himself would totally reject the argument from design, or tentatively endorse it, or whether he thinks the problem of evil conclusively eliminates the possibility of a morally benevolent Deity or not. It is left up to the reader to make these kinds of final judgments, on the basis of the arguments he or she has encountered in reading the *Dialogues*.

How Important and Influential Is This Passage?

In one of his last letters Hume wrote of the *Dialogues*: "Some of my Friends flatter me, that it is the best thing I ever wrote." After his death the skeptical ideas developed by Hume were gradually transmitted to the main flow of European culture (via thinkers such as Immanuel Kant, Baron d'Holbach, and the poet Percy Shelley), and by the nineteenth century Hume and others were considered to have so thoroughly overthrown the rational basis for belief in God that important religious philosophers such as Friedrich Schleiermacher (1768–1834) and Søren Kierkegaard (1813–1855) began to try to place religion less on a foundation of evidence and argument than on subjective experience and faith. Hume's own writings on religion, however, were neglected by philosophers and theologians until the 1930s (when interest in Hume was stimulated by changes in philosophical fashion, and especially the rise of a kind of radical empiricism called "logical positivism"). Since the 1960s the *Dialogues* have been widely considered the single most formidable attack on the rationality of belief in God ever mounted by a philosopher.

Suggestions for Critical Reflection

1. Do you think that Hume was an atheist, or a skeptic about God? What's the difference?
2. How close is the analogy between a machine and the universe? How about between an animal or plant and the universe? Do differences or similarities between the two things compared—e.g., between machines and the world—suggest important differences or similarities between their (alleged) designers?
3. Do you agree with Hume that "like effects prove like causes" (i.e., that similar effects demonstrate similar causes)?
4. Does the existence of order in nature *need* to be explained (or, for example, might it just be the result of random chance)? If it does require an explanation, can it only be explained by an appeal to an intelligent Designer? If we explain the order of nature by postulating a Designer, must we then go on to explain the Designer (and then explain the explanation of that Designer, and so on)?
5. Do you think that the existence of suffering makes it impossible to believe in an omnipotent and benevolent God? Do you think that the existence of suffering makes it impossible to infer the existence of an omnipotent and benevolent God from the evidence of design that we observe in the world? Are these two different questions?
6. What do you think of Hume's claim (in Part IX) that: "Whatever we conceive as existent, we can also conceive as non-existent"? If correct, how would this principle affect *a priori* attempts to prove the existence of God?

Suggestions for Further Reading

The most complete selection of Hume's writings on religion is *David Hume: Writings on Religion*, ed. Anthony Flew (Open Court, 1992). It includes the *Dialogues*, the *Natural History of Religion*, the essays "On Suicide" and "On the Immortality of the Soul" (neither of which were published during Hume's lifetime), and some other relevant material. The editions of the *Dialogues* edited by Norman Kemp Smith (Bobbs-Merrill, 1947) and by Nelson Pike (Bobbs-Merrill, 1970), both contain valuable commentary. A well-known attack by Hume on miracles is in his *Enquiry Concerning Human Understanding* (Clarendon Press, 1975), and the following section, section XI, is a precursor to the arguments in the *Dialogues*.

The standard modern biography of Hume is Ernest Campbell Mossner's *The Life of David Hume,* 2nd ed., (Oxford University Press, 1980).

J.C.A. Gaskin's *Hume's Philosophy of Religion,* 2nd ed., (Macmillan, 1988) is a useful secondary text, while Keith E. Yandell's *Hume's "Inexplicable Mystery": His Views on Religion* (Temple University Press, 1990) is somewhat more critical of Hume. There is also a commentary specifically on the *Dialogues*—Stanley Tweyman, *Scepticism and Belief in Hume's Dialogues Concerning Natural Religion* (Martinus Nijhoff, 1986)—and a book about Hume's attack on the argument from design: *Hume, Newton, and the Design Argument* by Robert H. Hurlbutt III, rev. ed., (University of Nebraska Press, 1985). Finally, Terence Penelhum's *God and Skepticism* (Reidel, 1983) is a very good general discussion of the issues Hume is thinking about.

Some useful articles are: John Bricke, "On the Interpretation of Hume's *Dialogues*," *Religious Studies* 11 (1975); Gary Doore, "The Argument from Design: Some Better Reasons for Agreeing with Hume," *Religious Studies* 16 (1980); J.C.A. Gaskin, "God, Hume, and Natural Belief," *Philosophy* 49 (1974); J. Noxon, "Hume's Agnosticism," *Philosophical Review* 73 (1964); Terence Penelhum, "Natural Belief and Religious Belief in Hume's Philosophy," *Philosophical Quarterly* 33 (1983); and Richard G. Swinburne, "The Argument from Design—A Defence," *Religious Studies* 11 (1972).

A significant modern attempt to revivify natural theology after Hume's critique is Richard Swinburne's *The Existence of God* (Clarendon Press, 1979). Finally, good places to start in thinking about how post-Humean scientific developments affect the argument from design are Richard Dawkins, *The Blind Watchmaker* (Longman, 1986) and John Leslie (ed.), *Physical Cosmology and Philosophy* (Macmillan, 1990).

from *Dialogues Concerning Natural Religion*[2]

Part II

I must own,[3] Cleanthes, said Demea, that nothing can more surprise me, than the light in which you have all along put this argument. By the whole tenor of your discourse, one would imagine that you were maintaining the being of a God, against the cavils of atheists and infidels; and were necessitated to become a champion for that fundamental principle of all religion. But this, I hope, is not by any means a question among us. No man, no man at least of common sense, I am persuaded, ever entertained a serious doubt with regard

to a truth so certain and self-evident. The question is not concerning the being, but the nature of God. This, I affirm, from the infirmities of human understanding, to be altogether incomprehensible and unknown to us. The essence of that supreme mind, his attributes, the manner of his existence, the very nature of his duration; these, and every particular which regards so divine a Being, are mysterious to men. Finite, weak, and blind creatures, we ought to humble ourselves in his august presence; and, conscious of our frailties, adore in silence his infinite perfections, which eye hath not seen, ear hath not heard, neither hath it entered into the heart of man to conceive.[4] They are covered in a deep cloud from human curiosity. It is profaneness to attempt penetrating through these sacred obscurities. And, next to the impiety of denying his existence, is the temerity[5] of prying into his nature and essence, decrees and attributes.

But lest you should think that my piety has here got the better of my philosophy, I shall support my opinion, if it needs any support, by a very great authority. I might cite all the divines,[6] almost, from the foundation of Christianity, who have ever treated of this or any other theological subject: But I shall confine myself, at present, to one equally celebrated for piety and philosophy. It is Father Malebranche,[7] who, I remember, thus expresses himself. "One ought not so much," says he, "to call God a spirit, in order to express positively what he is, as in order to signify that he is not matter. He is a Being infinitely perfect: of this we cannot doubt. But in the same manner as we ought not to imagine, even supposing him corporeal, that he is clothed with a human body, as the Anthropomorphites[8] asserted, under colour that that figure was the most perfect of any; so, neither ought we to imagine that the spirit of God has human ideas, or bears any resemblance to our spirit, under colour that

2 Hume's *Dialogues* were first published, three years after Hume's death, in 1779. This is a reprint of that edition, with some modernized spelling and capitalization.

3 I must admit.

4 This is paraphrased from the Bible: 1 Corinthians 2:9.

5 Audacity or impudence, rashness.

6 Priests or theologians.

7 Malebranche was an important French philosopher and follower of Descartes; his main work was *On the Search for the Truth* (1675), and it is from this that Philo is quoting.

8 See the background information, above.

we know nothing more perfect than a human mind. We ought rather to believe, that as he comprehends[9] the perfections of matter without being material … he comprehends also the perfections of created spirits without being spirit, in the manner we conceive spirit: That his true name is, He that is; or, in other words, Being without restriction, All Being, the Being infinite and universal."

After so great an authority, Demea, replied Philo, as that which you have produced, and a thousand more which you might produce, it would appear ridiculous in me to add my sentiment, or express my approbation[10] of your doctrine. But surely, where reasonable men treat these subjects, the question can never be concerning the being, but only the nature, of the Deity. The former truth, as you well observe, is unquestionable and self-evident. Nothing exists without a cause; and the original cause of this universe (whatever it be) we call God; and piously ascribe to him every species of perfection. Whoever scruples[11] this fundamental truth, deserves every punishment which can be inflicted among philosophers, to wit,[12] the greatest ridicule, contempt, and disapprobation. But as all perfection is entirely relative, we ought never to imagine that we comprehend the attributes of this divine Being, or to suppose that his perfections have any analogy or likeness to the perfections of a human creature. Wisdom, thought, design, knowledge; these we justly ascribe to him; because these words are honourable among men, and we have no other language or other conceptions by which we can express our adoration of him. But let us beware, lest we think that our ideas anywise correspond to his perfections, or that his attributes have any resemblance to these qualities among men. He is infinitely superior to our limited view and comprehension; and is more the object of worship in the temple, than of disputation in the schools.

In reality, Cleanthes, continued he, there is no need of having recourse to that affected scepticism so displeasing to you, in order to come at this determination. Our ideas reach no further than our experience. We

have no experience of divine attributes and operations. I need not conclude my syllogism. You can draw the inference yourself. And it is a pleasure to me (and I hope to you too) that just reasoning and sound piety here concur in the same conclusion, and both of them establish the adorably mysterious and incomprehensible nature of the supreme Being.

Not to lose any time in circumlocutions,[13] said Cleanthes, addressing himself to Demea, much less in replying to the pious declamations of Philo; I shall briefly explain how I conceive this matter. Look round the world: contemplate the whole and every part of it: you will find it to be nothing but one great machine, subdivided into an infinite number of lesser machines, which again admit of subdivisions to a degree beyond what human senses and faculties can trace and explain. All these various machines, and even their most minute parts, are adjusted to each other with an accuracy which ravishes into admiration all men who have ever contemplated them. The curious adapting of means to ends, throughout all nature, resembles exactly, though it much exceeds, the productions of human contrivance; of human designs, thought, wisdom, and intelligence. Since, therefore, the effects resemble each other, we are led to infer, by all the rules of analogy, that the causes also resemble; and that the Author of nature is somewhat similar to the mind of man, though possessed of much larger faculties, proportioned to the grandeur of the work which he has executed. By this argument *a posteriori*, and by this argument alone, do we prove at once the existence of a Deity, and his similarity to human mind and intelligence.

I shall be so free, Cleanthes, said Demea, as to tell you, that from the beginning, I could not approve of your conclusion concerning the similarity of the Deity to men; still less can I approve of the mediums by which you endeavour to establish it. What! No demonstration of the being of God! No abstract arguments! No proofs *a priori*! Are these, which have hitherto been so much insisted on by philosophers, all fallacy, all sophism?[14] Can we reach no further in this subject than experience and probability? I will

---

9   Includes.

10   Approval.

11   To scruple is to feel doubt or hesitation.

12   "To wit" is a phrase meaning "that is to say."

13   Unnecessarily wordy or roundabout language.

14   A sophism is a clever but misleading argument.

not say that this is betraying the cause of a Deity: But surely, by this affected candour, you give advantages to atheists, which they never could obtain by the mere dint of argument and reasoning.

What I chiefly scruple in this subject, said Philo, is not so much that all religious arguments are by Cleanthes reduced to experience, as that they appear not to be even the most certain and irrefragable[15] of that inferior kind. That a stone will fall, that fire will burn, that the earth has solidity, we have observed a thousand and a thousand times; and when any new instance of this nature is presented, we draw without hesitation the accustomed inference. The exact similarity of the cases gives us a perfect assurance of a similar event; and a stronger evidence is never desired nor sought after. But wherever you depart, in the least, from the similarity of the cases, you diminish proportionably the evidence; and may at last bring it to a very weak analogy, which is confessedly liable to error and uncertainty. After having experienced the circulation of the blood in human creatures, we make no doubt that it takes place in Titius and Mævius:[16] but from its circulation in frogs and fishes, it is only a presumption, though a strong one, from analogy, that it takes place in men and other animals. The analogical reasoning is much weaker, when we infer the circulation of the sap in vegetables from our experience that the blood circulates in animals; and those, who hastily followed that imperfect analogy, are found, by more accurate experiments, to have been mistaken.

If we see a house, Cleanthes, we conclude, with the greatest certainty, that it had an architect or builder; because this is precisely that species of effect which we have experienced to proceed from that species of cause. But surely you will not affirm, that the universe bears such a resemblance to a house, that we can with the same certainty infer a similar cause, or that the analogy is here entire and perfect. The dissimilitude is so striking, that the utmost you can here pretend to is a guess, a conjecture, a presumption concerning a similar cause; and how that pretension will be received in the world, I leave you to consider.

It would surely be very ill received, replied Cleanthes; and I should be deservedly blamed and detested, did I allow, that the proofs of a Deity amounted to no more than a guess or conjecture. But is the whole adjustment of means to ends in a house and in the universe so slight a resemblance? The economy of final causes?[17] The order, proportion, and arrangement of every part? Steps of a stair are plainly contrived, that human legs may use them in mounting; and this inference is certain and infallible. Human legs are also contrived for walking and mounting; and this inference, I allow, is not altogether so certain, because of the dissimilarity which you remark; but does it, therefore, deserve the name only of presumption or conjecture?

Good God! cried Demea, interrupting him, where are we? Zealous defenders of religion allow, that the proofs of a Deity fall short of perfect evidence! And you, Philo, on whose assistance I depended in proving the adorable mysteriousness of the divine nature, do you assent to all these extravagant[18] opinions of Cleanthes? For what other name can I give them? or, why spare my censure, when such principles are advanced, supported by such an authority, before so young a man as Pamphilus?[19]

You seem not to apprehend, replied Philo, that I argue with Cleanthes in his own way; and, by showing him the dangerous consequences of his tenets,[20] hope at last to reduce him to our opinion. But what sticks most with you, I observe, is the representation which

---

15 Unanswerable, undeniable.

16 That is, randomly chosen, generic human beings: John or Jane Doe.

17 Hume uses the word "economy" in its now somewhat archaic sense to mean an orderly arrangement or system (of any type, not necessarily a financial system nor necessarily one characterized by frugality). "Final causes" are one of the four types of causation (material, formal, efficient, final) identified by Aristotle: final causes are, roughly, the *reasons* for things, the *purposes* that explain them. For example, the structure of a can opener can be explained in terms of its purpose: it has a sharp pointy bit, for instance, *because* it is supposed to bite into the metal top of a can.

18 Excessive, unreasonable.

19 The character who is supposed to be listening to this dialogue and later writing it down.

20 Opinions or doctrines.

Cleanthes has made of the argument a posteriori; and finding that that argument is likely to escape your hold and vanish into air, you think it so disguised, that you can scarcely believe it to be set in its true light. Now, however much I may dissent, in other respects, from the dangerous principles of Cleanthes, I must allow that he has fairly represented that argument; and I shall endeavour so to state the matter to you, that you will entertain no further scruples with regard to it.

Were a man to abstract from every thing which he knows or has seen, he would be altogether incapable, merely from his own ideas, to determine what kind of scene the universe must be, or to give the preference to one state or situation of things above another. For as nothing which he clearly conceives could be esteemed impossible or implying a contradiction, every chimera of his fancy would be upon an equal footing; nor could he assign any just reason why he adheres to one idea or system, and rejects the others which are equally possible.

Again; after he opens his eyes, and contemplates the world as it really is, it would be impossible for him at first to assign the cause of any one event, much less of the whole of things, or of the universe. He might set his fancy a rambling; and she might bring him in an infinite variety of reports and representations. These would all be possible; but being all equally possible, he would never of himself give a satisfactory account for his preferring one of them to the rest. Experience alone can point out to him the true cause of any phenomenon.

Now, according to this method of reasoning, Demea, it follows, (and is, indeed, tacitly allowed by Cleanthes himself,) that order, arrangement, or the adjustment of final causes, is not of itself any proof of design; but only so far as it has been experienced to proceed from that principle. For aught[21] we can know *a priori*, matter may contain the source or spring of order originally within itself, as well as mind does; and there is no more difficulty in conceiving, that the several elements, from an internal unknown cause, may fall into the most exquisite arrangement, than to conceive that their ideas, in the great universal mind, from a like internal unknown cause, fall into

that arrangement. The equal possibility of both these suppositions is allowed. But, by experience, we find (according to Cleanthes) that there is a difference between them. Throw several pieces of steel together, without shape or form; they will never arrange themselves so as to compose a watch: stone, and mortar, and wood, without an architect, never erect a house. But the ideas in a human mind, we see, by an unknown, inexplicable economy, arrange themselves so as to form the plan of a watch or house. Experience, therefore, proves, that there is an original principle of order in mind, not in matter. From similar effects we infer similar causes. The adjustment of means to ends is alike in the universe, as in a machine of human contrivance. The causes, therefore, must be resembling.

I was from the beginning scandalized, I must own, with this resemblance, which is asserted, between the Deity and human creatures; and must conceive it to imply such a degradation of the supreme Being as no sound theist could endure. With your assistance, therefore, Demea, I shall endeavour to defend what you justly call the adorable mysteriousness of the divine Nature, and shall refute this reasoning of Cleanthes, provided he allows that I have made a fair representation of it.

When Cleanthes had assented, Philo, after a short pause, proceeded in the following manner.

That all inferences, Cleanthes, concerning fact, are founded on experience; and that all experimental reasonings are founded on the supposition that similar causes prove similar effects, and similar effects similar causes; I shall not at present much dispute with you. But observe, I entreat you, with what extreme caution all just reasoners proceed in the transferring of experiments to similar cases. Unless the cases be exactly similar, they repose no perfect confidence in applying their past observation to any particular phenomenon. Every alteration of circumstances occasions a doubt concerning the event; and it requires new experiments to prove certainly, that the new circumstances are of no moment or importance. A change in bulk, situation, arrangement, age, disposition of the air, or surrounding bodies; any of these particulars may be attended with the most unexpected consequences: and unless the objects be quite familiar to us, it is the highest temerity to expect with assurance,

---

21   For all, for anything.

after any of these changes, an event similar to that which before fell under our observation. The slow and deliberate steps of philosophers here, if any where, are distinguished from the precipitate march of the vulgar,[22] who, hurried on by the smallest similitude, are incapable of all discernment or consideration.

But can you think, Cleanthes, that your usual phlegm[23] and philosophy have been preserved in so wide a step as you have taken, when you compared to the universe houses, ships, furniture, machines, and, from their similarity in some circumstances, inferred a similarity in their causes? Thought, design, intelligence, such as we discover in men and other animals, is no more than one of the springs and principles of the universe, as well as heat or cold, attraction or repulsion, and a hundred others, which fall under daily observation. It is an active cause, by which some particular parts of nature, we find, produce alterations on other parts. But can a conclusion, with any propriety, be transferred from parts to the whole? Does not the great disproportion bar all comparison and inference? From observing the growth of a hair, can we learn any thing concerning the generation of a man? Would the manner of a leaf's blowing,[24] even though perfectly known, afford us any instruction concerning the vegetation of a tree?

But, allowing that we were to take the operations of one part of nature upon another, for the foundation of our judgement concerning the origin of the whole (which never can be admitted); yet why select so minute, so weak, so bounded a principle, as the reason and design of animals is found to be upon this planet? What peculiar privilege has this little agitation of the brain which we call thought, that we must thus make it the model of the whole universe? Our partiality[25] in our own favour does indeed present it on all occasions; but sound philosophy ought carefully to guard against so natural an illusion.

So far from admitting, continued Philo, that the operations of a part can afford us any just conclusion concerning the origin of the whole, I will not allow any one part to form a rule for another part, if the latter be very remote from the former. Is there any reasonable ground to conclude, that the inhabitants of other planets possess thought, intelligence, reason, or any thing similar to these faculties in men? When nature has so extremely diversified her manner of operation in this small globe, can we imagine that she incessantly copies herself throughout so immense a universe? And if thought, as we may well suppose, be confined merely to this narrow corner, and has even there so limited a sphere of action, with what propriety can we assign it for the original cause of all things? The narrow views of a peasant, who makes his domestic economy the rule for the government of kingdoms, is in comparison a pardonable sophism.

But were we ever so much assured, that a thought and reason, resembling the human, were to be found throughout the whole universe, and were its activity elsewhere vastly greater and more commanding than it appears in this globe; yet I cannot see, why the operations of a world constituted, arranged, adjusted, can with any propriety be extended to a world which is in its embryo state, and is advancing towards that constitution and arrangement. By observation, we know somewhat of the economy, action, and nourishment of a finished animal; but we must transfer with great caution that observation to the growth of a foetus in the womb, and still more to the formation of an animalcule[26] in the loins of its male parent. Nature, we find, even from our limited experience, possesses an infinite number of springs and principles, which incessantly discover[27] themselves on every change of her position and situation. And what new and unknown principles would actuate her in so new and unknown a situation as that of the formation of a universe, we cannot, without the utmost temerity, pretend to determine.

A very small part of this great system, during a very short time, is very imperfectly discovered to us;

---

22 The common people (from the Latin for "the common people," *vulgus*).

23 Calmness or coolness.

24 Blooming: i.e., growing from a bud into a fully formed leaf.

25 Bias.

26 A sperm cell. It was thought at the time that these were tiny animals.

27 Reveal, disclose, exhibit.

and do we thence pronounce decisively concerning the origin of the whole?

Admirable conclusion! Stone, wood, brick, iron, brass, have not, at this time, in this minute globe of earth, an order or arrangement without human art and contrivance; therefore the universe could not originally attain its order and arrangement, without something similar to human art. But is a part of nature a rule for another part very wide of the former? Is it a rule for the whole? Is a very small part a rule for the universe? Is nature in one situation, a certain rule for nature in another situation vastly different from the former?

And can you blame me, Cleanthes, if I here imitate the prudent reserve of Simonides, who, according to the noted story,[28] being asked by Hiero, What God was? desired a day to think of it, and then two days more; and after that manner continually prolonged the term, without ever bringing in his definition or description? Could you even blame me, if I had answered at first, that I did not know, and was sensible[29] that this subject lay vastly beyond the reach of my faculties? You might cry out sceptic and railler,[30] as much as you pleased: but having found, in so many other subjects much more familiar, the imperfections and even contradictions of human reason, I never should expect any success from its feeble conjectures, in a subject so sublime, and so remote from the sphere of our observation. When two species of objects have always been observed to be conjoined together, I can infer, by custom, the existence of one wherever I see the existence of the other; and this I call an argument from experience. But how this argument can have place, where the objects, as in the present case, are single, individual, without parallel, or specific resemblance, may be difficult to explain. And will any man tell me with a serious countenance, that an orderly universe must arise from some thought and art like the human, because we have experience of it? To ascertain this reasoning, it were requisite that we

had experience of the origin of worlds; and it is not sufficient, surely, that we have seen ships and cities arise from human art and contrivance....

Philo was proceeding in this vehement manner, somewhat between jest and earnest, as it appeared to me, when he observed some signs of impatience in Cleanthes, and then immediately stopped short. What I had to suggest, said Cleanthes, is only that you would not abuse terms, or make use of popular expressions to subvert philosophical reasonings. You know, that the vulgar often distinguish reason from experience, even where the question relates only to matter of fact and existence; though it is found, where that reason is properly analysed, that it is nothing but a species of experience. To prove by experience the origin of the universe from mind, is not more contrary to common speech, than to prove the motion of the earth from the same principle. And a caviller[31] might raise all the same objections to the Copernican system,[32] which you have urged against my reasonings. Have you other earths, might he say, which you have seen to move? Have....

Yes! cried Philo, interrupting him, we have other earths. Is not the moon another earth, which we see to turn round its centre? Is not Venus another earth, where we observe the same phenomenon? Are not the revolutions of the sun also a confirmation, from analogy, of the same theory? All the planets, are they not earths, which revolve about the sun? Are not the satellites moons, which move round Jupiter and Saturn, and along with these primary planets round the sun? These analogies and resemblances, with others which I have not mentioned, are the sole proofs of the Copernican system; and to you it belongs to consider, whether you have any analogies of the same kind to support your theory.

In reality, Cleanthes, continued he, the modern system of astronomy is now so much received by all inquirers, and has become so essential a part even of

28   Cicero, *De Natura Deorum* ("On the Nature of the Gods").

29   Aware or conscious.

30   A "railler" is one who rails: complains vehemently or bitterly.

31   One who cavils, i.e., finds fault or makes petty criticisms.

32   The model of the solar system introduced by Polish astronomer Nicolaus Copernicus (1473–1543) in which the planets move in circular orbits around the sun (rather than orbiting the Earth, as in the older theory).

our earliest education, that we are not commonly very scrupulous in examining the reasons upon which it is founded. It is now become a matter of mere curiosity to study the first writers on that subject, who had the full force of prejudice to encounter, and were obliged to turn their arguments on every side in order to render them popular and convincing. But if we peruse Galileo's famous Dialogues concerning the system of the world,[33] we shall find, that that great genius, one of the sublimest that ever existed, first bent all his endeavours to prove, that there was no foundation for the distinction commonly made between elementary and celestial substances.[34] The schools,[35] proceeding from the illusions of sense, had carried this distinction very far; and had established the latter substances to be ingenerable, incorruptible, unalterable, impassable; and had assigned all the opposite qualities to the former. But Galileo, beginning with the moon, proved its similarity in every particular to the earth; its convex figure, its natural darkness when not illuminated, its density, its distinction into solid and liquid, the variations of its phases, the mutual illuminations of the earth and moon, their mutual eclipses, the inequalities of the lunar surface, &c. After many instances of this kind, with regard to all the planets, men plainly saw that these bodies became proper objects of experience; and that the similarity of their nature enabled us to extend the same arguments and phenomena from one to the other.

In this cautious proceeding of the astronomers, you may read your own condemnation, Cleanthes; or rather may see, that the subject in which you are engaged exceeds all human reason and inquiry. Can you pretend to show any such similarity between the fabric of a house, and the generation of a universe? Have you ever seen nature in any such situation as resembles the first arrangement of the elements? Have

worlds ever been formed under your eye; and have you had leisure to observe the whole progress of the phenomenon, from the first appearance of order to its final consummation? If you have, then cite your experience, and deliver your theory.

Part III

How the most absurd argument, replied Cleanthes, in the hands of a man of ingenuity and invention, may acquire an air of probability! Are you not aware, Philo, that it became necessary for Copernicus and his first disciples to prove the similarity of the terrestrial and celestial matter; because several philosophers, blinded by old systems, and supported by some sensible[36] appearances, had denied this similarity? But that it is by no means necessary, that theists should prove the similarity of the works of nature to those of art; because this similarity is self-evident and undeniable? The same matter, a like form; what more is requisite to show an analogy between their causes, and to ascertain the origin of all things from a divine purpose and intention? Your objections, I must freely tell you, are no better than the abstruse[37] cavils of those philosophers who denied motion;[38] and ought to be refuted in the same manner, by illustrations, examples, and instances, rather than by serious argument and philosophy.

Suppose, therefore, that an articulate voice were heard in the clouds, much louder and more melodious than any which human art could ever reach: Suppose, that this voice were extended in the same instant over all nations, and spoke to each nation in its own language and dialect: suppose, that the words delivered not only contain a just sense and meaning, but convey some instruction altogether worthy of a benevolent Being, superior to mankind: Could you possibly hesitate a moment concerning the cause of this voice? And must you not instantly ascribe it to some design or purpose? Yet I cannot see but all

33 *Dialogue Concerning the Two Chief World Systems* (1632).

34 Between the material of which earthly things are made and the stuff of which the "celestial bodies" (stars and planets) are made.

35 The medieval philosophical system called "scholasticism"—see the notes to the Aquinas reading in this chapter for more information.

36 Perceptual—appearances that can be sensed or experienced.

37 Difficult to understand, obscure.

38 For example, the Greek philosopher Zeno of Elea (born in about 490 BCE), the originator of the so-called "Zeno's paradoxes" about motion.

the same objections (if they merit that appellation[39]) which lie against the system of theism, may also be produced against this inference.

Might you not say, that all conclusions concerning fact were founded on experience: that when we hear an articulate voice in the dark, and thence infer a man, it is only the resemblance of the effects which leads us to conclude that there is a like resemblance in the cause: but that this extraordinary voice, by its loudness, extent, and flexibility to all languages, bears so little analogy to any human voice, that we have no reason to suppose any analogy in their causes: and consequently, that a rational, wise, coherent speech proceeded, you know not whence, from some accidental whistling of the winds, not from any divine reason or intelligence? You see clearly your own objections in these cavils, and I hope too you see clearly, that they cannot possibly have more force in the one case than in the other.

But to bring the case still nearer the present one of the universe, I shall make two suppositions, which imply not any absurdity or impossibility. Suppose that there is a natural, universal, invariable language, common to every individual of human race; and that books are natural productions, which perpetuate themselves in the same manner with animals and vegetables, by descent and propagation.[40] Several expressions of our passions contain a universal language: all brute animals have a natural speech, which, however limited, is very intelligible to their own species. And as there are infinitely fewer parts and less contrivance in the finest composition of eloquence, than in the coarsest organised body, the propagation of an *Iliad* or *Æneid*[41] is an easier supposition than that of any plant or animal.

Suppose, therefore, that you enter into your library, thus peopled by natural volumes, containing the most refined reason and most exquisite beauty; could you possibly open one of them, and doubt, that its original cause bore the strongest analogy to mind and intelligence? When it reasons and discourses; when it expostulates, argues, and enforces its views and topics; when it applies sometimes to the pure intellect, sometimes to the affections; when it collects, disposes, and adorns every consideration suited to the subject; could you persist in asserting, that all this, at the bottom, had really no meaning; and that the first formation of this volume in the loins of its original parent proceeded not from thought and design? Your obstinacy, I know, reaches not that degree of firmness: even your sceptical play and wantonness would be abashed at so glaring an absurdity.

But if there be any difference, Philo, between this supposed case and the real one of the universe, it is all to the advantage of the latter. The anatomy of an animal affords many stronger instances of design than the perusal of Livy or Tacitus;[42] and any objection which you start in the former case, by carrying me back to so unusual and extraordinary a scene as the first formation of worlds, the same objection has place on the supposition of our vegetating library. Choose, then, your party, Philo, without ambiguity or evasion; assert either that a rational volume is no proof of a rational cause, or admit of a similar cause to all the works of nature.

Let me here observe too, continued Cleanthes, that this religious argument, instead of being weakened by that scepticism so much affected by you, rather acquires force from it, and becomes more firm and undisputed. To exclude all argument or reasoning of every kind, is either affectation or madness. The declared profession of every reasonable sceptic is only to reject abstruse, remote, and refined arguments; to adhere to common sense and the plain instincts of nature; and to assent, wherever any reasons strike him with so full a force that he cannot, without the greatest violence, prevent it. Now the arguments for natural religion are plainly of this kind; and nothing but the most perverse, obstinate metaphysics can reject them. Consider, anatomise the eye; survey its structure and

---

39   Name.

40   By (biological) reproduction.

41   Two well-known works of classical literature, the former written by Homer and the latter by Virgil.

42   Two Roman historians. Livy (59 BCE–17 CE) wrote a 142-volume history of Rome (of which only 35 volumes survive) from its foundation to his own time, while Tacitus (55–120 CE) wrote about the period of Roman history from 14 to 96 CE.

contrivance;[43] and tell me, from your own feeling, if the idea of a contriver does not immediately flow in upon you with a force like that of sensation. The most obvious conclusion, surely, is in favour of design; and it requires time, reflection, and study, to summon up those frivolous, though abstruse objections, which can support infidelity. Who can behold the male and female of each species, the correspondence of their parts and instincts, their passions, and whole course of life before and after generation, but must be sensible, that the propagation of the species is intended by nature? Millions and millions of such instances present themselves through every part of the universe; and no language can convey a more intelligible irresistible meaning, than the curious adjustment of final causes. To what degree, therefore, of blind dogmatism must one have attained, to reject such natural and such convincing arguments?

Some beauties in writing we may meet with, which seem contrary to rules, and which gain the affections, and animate the imagination, in opposition to all the precepts of criticism, and to the authority of the established masters of art. And if the argument for theism be, as you pretend, contradictory to the principles of logic; its universal, its irresistible influence proves clearly, that there may be arguments of a like irregular nature. Whatever cavils may be urged, an orderly world, as well as a coherent, articulate speech, will still be received as an incontestable proof of design and intention.

It sometimes happens, I own, that the religious arguments have not their due influence on an ignorant savage and barbarian; not because they are obscure and difficult, but because he never asks himself any question with regard to them. Whence arises the curious structure of an animal? From the copulation of its parents. And these whence? From their parents? A few removes set the objects at such a distance, that to him they are lost in darkness and confusion; nor is he actuated by any curiosity to trace them further. But this is neither dogmatism nor scepticism, but stupidity: a state of mind very different from your sifting, inquisitive disposition, my ingenious friend. You can trace causes from effects: you can compare the most distant and remote objects: and your greatest errors proceed not from barrenness of thought and invention, but from too luxuriant a fertility, which suppresses your natural good sense, by a profusion of unnecessary scruples and objections.

Here I could observe, Hermippus,[44] that Philo was a little embarrassed and confounded: But while he hesitated in delivering an answer, luckily for him, Demea broke in upon the discourse, and saved his countenance.

Your instance, Cleanthes, said he, drawn from books and language, being familiar, has, I confess, so much more force on that account: but is there not some danger too in this very circumstance; and may it not render us presumptuous, by making us imagine we comprehend the Deity, and have some adequate idea of his nature and attributes? When I read a volume, I enter into the mind and intention of the author: I become him, in a manner, for the instant; and have an immediate feeling and conception of those ideas which revolved in his imagination while employed in that composition. But so near an approach we never surely can make to the Deity. His ways are not our ways. His attributes are perfect, but incomprehensible. And this volume of nature contains a great and inexplicable riddle, more than any intelligible discourse or reasoning.

The ancient Platonists,[45] you know, were the most religious and devout of all the pagan philosophers; yet many of them, particularly Plotinus,[46] expressly declare, that intellect or understanding is not to be ascribed to the Deity; and that our most perfect worship of him consists, not in acts of veneration, reverence, gratitude, or love; but in a certain mysterious self-annihilation, or total extinction of all our faculties. These ideas are, perhaps, too far stretched; but still it must be acknowledged, that, by representing the Deity as so intelligible and comprehensible, and so similar to a human mind, we are guilty of the grossest and

---

43 Plan or design.

44 The character to whom Pamphilus, the narrator, is supposed to be sending his written record of the dialogue.

45 Followers of the philosophy of Plato.

46 An Egyptian philosopher, founder of a movement today called Neoplatonism, who lived from 205 to 270 CE. His main work is called *The Enneads*.

most narrow partiality, and make ourselves the model of the whole universe.

All the sentiments of the human mind, gratitude, resentment, love, friendship, approbation, blame, pity, emulation, envy, have a plain reference to the state and situation of man, and are calculated for preserving the existence and promoting the activity of such a being in such circumstances. It seems, therefore, unreasonable to transfer such sentiments to a supreme existence, or to suppose him actuated by them; and the phenomena besides of the universe will not support us in such a theory. All our ideas, derived from the senses, are confessedly false and illusive; and cannot therefore be supposed to have place in a supreme intelligence: and as the ideas of internal sentiment, added to those of the external senses, compose the whole furniture of human understanding, we may conclude, that none of the materials of thought are in any respect similar in the human and in the divine intelligence. Now, as to the manner of thinking; how can we make any comparison between them, or suppose them any wise resembling? Our thought is fluctuating, uncertain, fleeting, successive, and compounded; and were we to remove these circumstances, we absolutely annihilate its essence, and it would in such a case be an abuse of terms to apply to it the name of thought or reason. At least if it appear more pious and respectful (as it really is) still to retain these terms, when we mention the supreme Being, we ought to acknowledge, that their meaning, in that case, is totally incomprehensible; and that the infirmities of our nature do not permit us to reach any ideas which in the least correspond to the ineffable sublimity of the Divine attributes.

Part IV

It seems strange to me, said Cleanthes, that you, Demea, who are so sincere in the cause of religion, should still maintain the mysterious, incomprehensible nature of the Deity, and should insist so strenuously that he has no manner of likeness or resemblance to human creatures. The Deity, I can readily allow, possesses many powers and attributes of which we can have no comprehension: But if our ideas, so far as they go, be not just, and adequate, and correspondent to his real nature, I know not what there is in this subject worth insisting on. Is the name, without any meaning,

of such mighty importance? Or how do you mystics, who maintain the absolute incomprehensibility of the Deity, differ from sceptics or atheists, who assert, that the first cause of all is unknown and unintelligible? Their temerity must be very great, if, after rejecting the production by a mind, I mean a mind resembling the human (for I know of no other), they pretend to assign, with certainty, any other specific intelligible cause: and their conscience must be very scrupulous indeed, if they refuse to call the universal unknown cause a God or Deity; and to bestow on him as many sublime eulogies and unmeaning epithets as you shall please to require of them.

Who could imagine, replied Demea, that Cleanthes, the calm philosophical Cleanthes, would attempt to refute his antagonists by affixing a nickname to them; and, like the common bigots and inquisitors of the age, have recourse to invective and declamation, instead of reasoning? Or does he not perceive, that these topics are easily retorted, and that anthropomorphite is an appellation as invidious,[47] and implies as dangerous consequences, as the epithet of mystic, with which he has honoured us? In reality, Cleanthes, consider what it is you assert when you represent the Deity as similar to a human mind and understanding. What is the soul of man? A composition of various faculties, passions, sentiments, ideas; united, indeed, into one self or person, but still distinct from each other. When it reasons, the ideas, which are the parts of its discourse, arrange themselves in a certain form or order; which is not preserved entire for a moment, but immediately gives place to another arrangement. New opinions, new passions, new affections, new feelings arise, which continually diversify the mental scene, and produce in it the greatest variety and most rapid succession imaginable. How is this compatible with that perfect immutability and simplicity which all true theists ascribe to the Deity? By the same act, say they, he sees past, present, and future: His love and hatred, his mercy and justice, are one individual operation: He is entire in every point of space; and complete in every instant of duration. No succession, no change, no acquisition, no diminution. What he is implies not in it any shadow of distinction or diversity.

---

47   Likely to arouse ill will.

And what he is this moment he ever has been, and ever will be, without any new judgement, sentiment, or operation. He stands fixed in one simple, perfect state: nor can you ever say, with any propriety, that this act of his is different from that other; or that this judgement or idea has been lately formed, and will give place, by succession, to any different judgement or idea.

I can readily allow, said Cleanthes, that those who maintain the perfect simplicity of the supreme Being, to the extent in which you have explained it, are complete mystics, and chargeable with all the consequences which I have drawn from their opinion. They are, in a word, atheists, without knowing it. For though it be allowed, that the Deity possesses attributes of which we have no comprehension, yet ought we never to ascribe to him any attributes which are absolutely incompatible with that intelligent nature essential to him. A mind, whose acts and sentiments and ideas are not distinct and successive; one, that is wholly simple, and totally immutable, is a mind which has no thought, no reason, no will, no sentiment, no love, no hatred; or, in a word, is no mind at all. It is an abuse of terms to give it that appellation; and we may as well speak of limited extension without figure, or of number without composition.[48]

Pray consider, said Philo, whom you are at present inveighing against. You are honouring with the appellation of atheist all the sound, orthodox divines, almost, who have treated of this subject; and you will at last be, yourself, found, according to your reckoning, the only sound theist in the world. But if idolaters be atheists, as, I think, may justly be asserted, and Christian theologians the same, what becomes of the argument, so much celebrated, derived from the universal consent of mankind?[49]

But because I know you are not much swayed by names and authorities, I shall endeavour to show you, a little more distinctly, the inconveniences of that anthropomorphism, which you have embraced; and shall prove, that there is no ground to suppose a plan of the world to be formed in the divine mind, consisting of distinct ideas, differently arranged, in the same manner as an architect forms in his head the plan of a house which he intends to execute.

It is not easy, I own, to see what is gained by this supposition, whether we judge of the matter by reason or by experience. We are still obliged to mount higher, in order to find the cause of this cause, which you had assigned as satisfactory and conclusive.

If reason (I mean abstract reason, derived from inquiries *a priori*) be not alike mute with regard to all questions concerning cause and effect, this sentence at least it will venture to pronounce, That a mental world, or universe of ideas, requires a cause as much as does a material world, or universe of objects; and, if similar in its arrangement, must require a similar cause. For what is there in this subject, which should occasion a different conclusion or inference? In an abstract view, they are entirely alike; and no difficulty attends the one supposition, which is not common to both of them.

Again, when we will needs force experience to pronounce some sentence, even on these subjects which lie beyond her sphere, neither can she perceive any material difference in this particular, between these two kinds of worlds; but finds them to be governed by similar principles, and to depend upon an equal variety of causes in their operations. We have specimens in miniature of both of them. Our own mind resembles the one; a vegetable or animal body the other. Let experience, therefore, judge from these samples. Nothing seems more delicate, with regard to its causes, than thought; and as these causes never operate in two persons after the same manner, so we never find two persons who think exactly alike. Nor indeed does the same person think exactly alike at any two different periods of time. A difference of age, of the disposition of his body, of weather, of food, of company, of books, of passions; any of these particulars, or others more minute, are sufficient to alter the curious machinery of thought, and communicate to it very different movements and operations. As far as we can judge, vegetables and animal bodies are not

48 Of finite extension in three dimensions without shape, or plurality without component parts.

49 This is the argument for the existence of a deity from the (presumed) fact of almost universal belief in some sort of divinity. It appears, for example, in writings by Cicero (who lived in the first century BCE) and Sextus Empiricus (second century CE).

more delicate in their motions, nor depend upon a greater variety or more curious adjustment of springs and principles.

How, therefore, shall we satisfy ourselves concerning the cause of that Being whom you suppose the Author of nature, or, according to your system of anthropomorphism, the ideal world,[50] into which you trace the material? Have we not the same reason to trace that ideal world into another ideal world, or new intelligent principle? But if we stop, and go no further; why go so far? Why not stop at the material world? How can we satisfy ourselves without going on in infinitum?[51] And, after all, what satisfaction is there in that infinite progression? Let us remember the story of the Indian philosopher and his elephant.[52] It was never more applicable than to the present subject. If the material world rests upon a similar ideal world, this ideal world must rest upon some other; and so on, without end. It were better, therefore, never to look beyond the present material world. By supposing it to contain the principle of its order within itself, we really assert it to be God; and the sooner we arrive at that divine Being, so much the better. When you go one step beyond the mundane system, you only excite an inquisitive humour[53] which it is impossible ever to satisfy.

To say, that the different ideas which compose the reason of the supreme Being, fall into order of themselves, and by their own nature, is really to talk without any precise meaning. If it has a meaning, I would fain[54] know, why it is not as good sense to say, that the parts of the material world fall into order of themselves and by their own nature. Can the one opinion be intelligible, while the other is not so?

We have, indeed, experience of ideas which fall into order of themselves, and without any known cause. But, I am sure, we have a much larger experience of matter which does the same; as, in all instances of generation and vegetation,[55] where the accurate analysis of the cause exceeds all human comprehension. We have also experience of particular systems of thought and of matter which have no order; of the first in madness, of the second in corruption.[56] Why, then, should we think, that order is more essential to one than the other? And if it requires a cause in both, what do we gain by your system, in tracing the universe of objects into a similar universe of ideas? The first step which we make leads us on for ever. It were, therefore, wise in us to limit all our inquiries to the present world, without looking further. No satisfaction can ever be attained by these speculations, which so far exceed the narrow bounds of human understanding.

It was usual with the Peripatetics,[57] you know, Cleanthes, when the cause of any phenomenon was demanded, to have recourse to their faculties or occult qualities; and to say, for instance, that bread nourished by its nutritive faculty, and senna[58] purged by its purgative. But it has been discovered, that this subterfuge was nothing but the disguise of ignorance; and that these philosophers, though less ingenuous,[59] really said the same thing with the sceptics or the vulgar, who fairly confessed that they knew not the cause of these phenomena. In like manner, when it is asked, what cause produces order in the ideas of the supreme Being; can any other reason be assigned by you, anthropomorphites, than that it is a rational faculty, and that such is the nature of the Deity? But why a similar answer will not be equally satisfactory in accounting for the order of the world, without having recourse to any such intelligent Creator as you

---

50   World of ideas.

51   Forever, without limit.

52   This story, as it happens, appears in the reading from John Locke in Chapter 3. In brief, there is a myth that certain East Indian philosophers held that the world rests on the back of a giant elephant, which in turn is supported by an enormous tortoise. The problem, however, is this: What is the tortoise standing on?

53   In this context, a humour is a state of mind or disposition.

54   Willingly, gladly.

55   Animal procreation or plant growth.

56   Decay.

57   The philosophical followers of Aristotle in the third century BCE. (They were supposedly named after the *peripatos*, or covered walk, in a garden where Aristotle lectured.)

58   A laxative prepared from dried pods of the cassia tree.

59   Innocent, open.

insist on, may be difficult to determine. It is only to say, that such is the nature of material objects, and that they are all originally possessed of a faculty of order and proportion. These are only more learned and elaborate ways of confessing our ignorance; nor has the one hypothesis any real advantage above the other, except in its greater conformity to vulgar prejudices.

You have displayed this argument with great emphasis, replied Cleanthes: You seem not sensible how easy it is to answer it. Even in common life, if I assign a cause for any event, is it any objection, Philo, that I cannot assign the cause of that cause, and answer every new question which may incessantly be started? And what philosophers could possibly submit to so rigid a rule? Philosophers, who confess ultimate causes to be totally unknown; and are sensible, that the most refined principles into which they trace the phenomena, are still to them as inexplicable as these phenomena themselves are to the vulgar. The order and arrangement of nature, the curious adjustment of final causes, the plain use and intention of every part and organ; all these bespeak in the clearest language an intelligent cause or author. The heavens and the earth join in the same testimony: the whole chorus of nature raises one hymn to the praises of its Creator. You alone, or almost alone, disturb this general harmony. You start abstruse doubts, cavils, and objections: you ask me, what is the cause of this cause? I know not; I care not; that concerns not me. I have found a Deity; and here I stop my inquiry. Let those go further, who are wiser or more enterprising.

I pretend to be neither, replied Philo: And for that very reason, I should never perhaps have attempted to go so far; especially when I am sensible, that I must at last be contented to sit down with the same answer, which, without further trouble, might have satisfied me from the beginning. If I am still to remain in utter ignorance of causes, and can absolutely give an explication of nothing, I shall never esteem it any advantage to shove off for a moment a difficulty, which, you acknowledge, must immediately, in its full force, recur upon me. Naturalists indeed very justly explain particular effects by more general causes, though these general causes themselves should remain in the end totally inexplicable; but they never surely thought it satisfactory to explain a particular effect by

a particular cause, which was no more to be accounted for than the effect itself. An ideal system, arranged of itself, without a precedent design, is not a whit more explicable than a material one, which attains its order in a like manner; nor is there any more difficulty in the latter supposition than in the former.

Part V

But to show you still more inconveniences, continued Philo, in your anthropomorphism, please to take a new survey of your principles. Like effects prove like causes. This is the experimental argument; and this, you say too, is the sole theological argument. Now, it is certain, that the liker[60] the effects are which are seen, and the liker the causes which are inferred, the stronger is the argument. Every departure on either side diminishes the probability, and renders the experiment less conclusive. You cannot doubt of the principle; neither ought you to reject its consequences.

All the new discoveries in astronomy, which prove the immense grandeur and magnificence of the works of nature, are so many additional arguments for a Deity, according to the true system of theism; but, according to your hypothesis of experimental theism, they become so many objections, by removing the effect still further from all resemblance to the effects of human art and contrivance. For, if Lucretius, even following the old system of the world, could exclaim,

Quis regere immensi summam, quis habere profundi
Indu manu validas potis est moderanter habenas?
Quis pariter cœlos omnes convertere? et omnes
Ignibus ætheriis terras suffire feraces?
Omnibus inve locis esse omni tempore præsto?[61]

---

60 The more similar.

61 Lucretius (c. 99–55 BCE) was a Roman poet whose massive poem *De Rerum Natura* ("On the Nature of Things") is the most extensive account of the atomism of the Greek philosopher Epicurus that has survived. The quotation reads:

Who hath the power (I ask), who hath the power
To rule the sum of the immeasurable,
To hold with steady hand the giant reins
Of the unfathomed deep? Who hath the power
At once to rule a multitude of skies,

If Tully esteemed this reasoning so natural, as to put it into the mouth of his Epicurean: *Quibus enim oculis animi intueri potuit vester Plato fabricam illam tanti operis, qua construi a Deo atque ædificari mundum facit? quæ molitio? quæ ferramenta? qui vectes? quæ machinæ? qui ministri tanti muneris fuerunt? quemadmodum autem obedire et parere voluntati architecti aer, ignis, aqua, terra potuerunt?*[62] If this argument, I say, had any force in former ages, how much greater must it have at present, when the bounds of nature are so infinitely enlarged, and such a magnificent scene is opened to us? It is still more unreasonable to form our idea of so unlimited a cause from our experience of the narrow productions of human design and invention.

The discoveries by microscopes, as they open a new universe in miniature, are still objections, according to you, arguments, according to me. The further we push our researches of this kind, we are still led to infer the universal cause of all to be vastly different from mankind, or from any object of human experience and observation.

And what say you to the discoveries in anatomy, chemistry, botany? … These surely are no objections, replied Cleanthes; they only discover new instances of art and contrivance. It is still the image of mind reflected on us from innumerable objects. Add, a mind

---

At once to heat with fires ethereal all
The fruitful lands of multitudes of worlds,
To be at all times in all places near?
(Trans. W.E. Leonard)

62   Tully is the name usually used in the eighteenth century for the Roman orator and statesman Marcus Tullius Cicero (106–46 BCE). The structure of Hume's *Dialogues* is based on Cicero's "On the Nature of the Gods." The quotation given here, taken from that work, can be translated as follows: "What power of mental vision enabled your master Plato to discern the vast and elaborate architectural process which, as he makes out, the deity adopted in building the structure of the universe? What method of engineering was employed? What tools and levers and machines? What agents carried out so vast an undertaking? And how were air, fire, water and earth enabled to obey and execute the will of the architect?"

like the human, said Philo. I know of no other, replied Cleanthes. And the liker the better, insisted Philo. To be sure, said Cleanthes.

Now, Cleanthes, said Philo, with an air of alacrity and triumph, mark the consequences. *First,* by this method of reasoning, you renounce all claim to infinity in any of the attributes of the Deity. For, as the cause ought only to be proportioned to the effect, and the effect, so far as it falls under our cognisance, is not infinite; what pretensions have we, upon your suppositions, to ascribe that attribute to the divine Being? You will still insist, that, by removing him so much from all similarity to human creatures, we give in to the most arbitrary hypothesis, and at the same time weaken all proofs of his existence.

Secondly, you have no reason, on your theory, for ascribing perfection to the Deity, even in his finite capacity, or for supposing him free from every error, mistake, or incoherence, in his undertakings. There are many inexplicable difficulties in the works of nature, which, if we allow a perfect Author to be proved *a priori*, are easily solved, and become only seeming difficulties, from the narrow capacity of man, who cannot trace infinite relations. But according to your method of reasoning, these difficulties become all real; and perhaps will be insisted on, as new instances of likeness to human art and contrivance. At least, you must acknowledge, that it is impossible for us to tell, from our limited views, whether this system contains any great faults, or deserves any considerable praise, if compared to other possible, and even real systems. Could a peasant, if the *Æneid*[63] were read to him, pronounce that poem to be absolutely faultless, or even assign to it its proper rank among the productions of human wit, he, who had never seen any other production?

But were this world ever so perfect a production, it must still remain uncertain, whether all the excellences of the work can justly be ascribed to the workman. If we survey a ship, what an exalted idea must we form of the ingenuity of the carpenter

63   An epic poem written in Latin by Virgil (70–19 BCE), describing the wanderings of the hero Aeneas for the seven years between his escape of the destruction of Troy and his settling in Italy.

who framed so complicated, useful, and beautiful a machine? And what surprise must we feel, when we find him a stupid mechanic, who imitated others, and copied an art, which, through a long succession of ages, after multiplied trials, mistakes, corrections, deliberations, and controversies, had been gradually improving? Many worlds might have been botched and bungled, throughout an eternity, ere this system was struck out; much labour lost, many fruitless trials made; and a slow, but continued improvement carried on during infinite ages in the art of world-making. In such subjects, who can determine, where the truth; nay, who can conjecture where the probability, lies; amidst a great number of hypotheses which may be proposed, and a still greater which may be imagined?

And what shadow of an argument, continued Philo, can you produce, from your hypothesis, to prove the unity of the Deity? A great number of men join in building a house or ship, in rearing a city, in framing a commonwealth; why may not several deities combine in contriving and framing a world? This is only so much greater similarity to human affairs. By sharing the work among several, we may so much further limit the attributes of each, and get rid of that extensive power and knowledge, which must be supposed in one deity, and which, according to you, can only serve to weaken the proof of his existence. And if such foolish, such vicious creatures as man, can yet often unite in framing and executing one plan, how much more those deities or dæmons,[64] whom we may suppose several degrees more perfect?

To multiply causes without necessity, is indeed contrary to true philosophy: but this principle applies not to the present case. Were one deity antecedently proved by your theory, who were possessed of every attribute requisite to the production of the universe; it would be needless, I own (though not absurd) to suppose any other deity existent. But while it is still a question, whether all these attributes are united in one subject, or dispersed among several independent beings, by what phenomena in nature can we pretend to decide the controversy? Where we see a body raised in a scale, we are sure that there is in the opposite scale, however concealed from sight, some counterpoising weight equal to it; but it is still allowed to doubt, whether that weight be an aggregate of several distinct bodies, or one uniform united mass. And if the weight requisite very much exceeds any thing which we have ever seen conjoined in any single body, the former supposition becomes still more probable and natural. An intelligent being of such vast power and capacity as is necessary to produce the universe, or, to speak in the language of ancient philosophy, so prodigious an animal exceeds all analogy, and even comprehension.

But farther, Cleanthes: men are mortal, and renew their species by generation; and this is common to all living creatures. The two great sexes of male and female, says Milton,[65] animate the world. Why must this circumstance, so universal, so essential, be excluded from those numerous and limited deities? Behold, then, the theogony[66] of ancient times brought back upon us.

And why not become a perfect anthro-pomorphite? Why not assert the deity or deities to be corporeal, and to have eyes, a nose, mouth, ears, &c.? Epicurus[67] maintained, that no man had ever seen reason but in a human figure; therefore the gods must have a human figure. And this argument, which is deservedly so much ridiculed by Cicero, becomes, according to you, solid and philosophical.

In a word, Cleanthes, a man who follows your hypothesis is able perhaps to assert, or conjecture, that the universe, sometime, arose from something like design: but beyond that position he cannot ascertain one single circumstance; and is left afterwards to fix every point of his theology by the utmost license of fancy and hypothesis. This world, for aught he knows, is very faulty and imperfect, compared to a superior standard; and was only the first rude essay[68] of some

---

64 Demigods.

65 English poet John Milton (1608–1674), best known for his epic poem *Paradise Lost*.

66 An account of the genealogy of the gods: the theory of their family tree, so to speak.

67 A Greek philosopher (341–270 BCE) best known for defending an atomistic view of the world that sees it as built up entirely from an infinite number of tiny indestructible particles.

68 "Rude essay" means a rough attempt or primitive effort.

infant deity, who afterwards abandoned it, ashamed of his lame performance: it is the work only of some dependent, inferior deity; and is the object of derision to his superiors: it is the production of old age and dotage in some superannuated deity; and ever since his death, has run on at adventures,[69] from the first impulse and active force which it received from him.... You justly give signs of horror, Demea, at these strange suppositions; but these, and a thousand more of the same kind, are Cleanthes's suppositions, not mine. From the moment the attributes of the Deity are supposed finite, all these have place. And I cannot, for my part, think that so wild and unsettled a system of theology is, in any respect, preferable to none at all.

These suppositions I absolutely disown, cried Cleanthes: they strike me, however, with no horror, especially when proposed in that rambling way in which they drop from you. On the contrary, they give me pleasure, when I see, that, by the utmost indulgence of your imagination, you never get rid of the hypothesis of design in the universe, but are obliged at every turn to have recourse to it. To this concession I adhere steadily; and this I regard as a sufficient foundation for religion.

…

Part VII

But here, continued Philo, in examining the ancient system of the soul of the world, there strikes me, all on a sudden, a new idea, which, if just, must go near to subvert all your reasoning, and destroy even your first inferences, on which you repose such confidence. If the universe bears a greater likeness to animal bodies and to vegetables, than to the works of human art, it is more probable that its cause resembles the cause of the former than that of the latter, and its origin ought rather to be ascribed to generation or vegetation, than to reason or design. Your conclusion, even according to your own principles, is therefore lame and defective.

Pray open up this argument a little further, said Demea, for I do not rightly apprehend it in that concise manner in which you have expressed it.

Our friend Cleanthes, replied Philo, as you have heard, asserts, that since no question of fact can be proved otherwise than by experience, the existence of a Deity admits not of proof from any other medium. The world, says he, resembles the works of human contrivance; therefore its cause must also resemble that of the other. Here we may remark, that the operation of one very small part of nature, to wit man, upon another very small part, to wit that inanimate matter lying within his reach, is the rule by which Cleanthes judges of the origin of the whole; and he measures objects, so widely disproportioned, by the same individual standard. But to waive all objections drawn from this topic, I affirm, that there are other parts of the universe (besides the machines of human invention) which bear still a greater resemblance to the fabric of the world, and which, therefore, afford a better conjecture concerning the universal origin of this system. These parts are animals and vegetables. The world plainly resembles more an animal or a vegetable, than it does a watch or a knitting-loom. Its cause, therefore, it is more probable, resembles the cause of the former. The cause of the former is generation or vegetation. The cause, therefore, of the world, we may infer to be something similar or analogous to generation or vegetation.

But how is it conceivable, said Demea, that the world can arise from any thing similar to vegetation or generation?

Very easily, replied Philo. In like manner as a tree sheds its seed into the neighbouring fields, and produces other trees; so the great vegetable, the world, or this planetary system, produces within itself certain seeds, which, being scattered into the surrounding chaos, vegetate into new worlds. A comet, for instance, is the seed of a world; and after it has been fully ripened, by passing from sun to sun, and star to star, it is at last tossed into the unformed elements which everywhere surround this universe, and immediately sprouts up into a new system.

Or if, for the sake of variety (for I see no other advantage), we should suppose this world to be an animal; a comet is the egg of this animal: and in like manner as an ostrich lays its egg in the sand, which, without any further care, hatches the egg, and produces a new animal; so....

---

69   By chance.

I understand you, says Demea: But what wild, arbitrary suppositions are these! What *data* have you for such extraordinary conclusions? And is the slight, imaginary resemblance of the world to a vegetable or an animal sufficient to establish the same inference with regard to both? Objects, which are in general so widely different, ought they to be a standard for each other?

Right, cries Philo: This is the topic on which I have all along insisted. I have still asserted, that we have no data to establish any system of cosmogony.[70] Our experience, so imperfect in itself, and so limited both in extent and duration, can afford us no probable conjecture concerning the whole of things. But if we must needs fix on some hypothesis; by what rule, pray, ought we to determine our choice? Is there any other rule than the greater similarity of the objects compared? And does not a plant or an animal, which springs from vegetation or generation, bear a stronger resemblance to the world, than does any artificial machine, which arises from reason and design?

But what is this vegetation and generation of which you talk? said Demea. Can you explain their operations, and anatomise that fine internal structure on which they depend?

As much, at least, replied Philo, as Cleanthes can explain the operations of reason, or anatomise that internal structure on which it depends. But without any such elaborate disquisitions,[71] when I see an animal, I infer, that it sprang from generation; and that with as great certainty as you conclude a house to have been reared by design. These words, *generation*, *reason*, mark only certain powers and energies in nature, whose effects are known, but whose essence is incomprehensible; and one of these principles, more than the other, has no privilege for being made a standard to the whole of nature.

In reality, Demea, it may reasonably be expected, that the larger the views are which we take of things, the better will they conduct us in our conclusions concerning such extraordinary and such magnificent subjects. In this little corner of the world alone, there are four principles, *reason*, *instinct*, *generation*, *vegetation*, which are similar to each other, and are the causes of similar effects. What a number of other principles may we naturally suppose in the immense extent and variety of the universe, could we travel from planet to planet, and from system to system, in order to examine each part of this mighty fabric? Any one of these four principles above mentioned (and a hundred others which lie open to our conjecture) may afford us a theory by which to judge of the origin of the world; and it is a palpable and egregious partiality to confine our view entirely to that principle by which our own minds operate. Were this principle more intelligible on that account, such a partiality might be somewhat excusable: but reason, in its internal fabric and structure, is really as little known to us as instinct or vegetation; and, perhaps, even that vague, indeterminate word, nature, to which the vulgar refer every thing, is not at the bottom more inexplicable. The effects of these principles are all known to us from experience; but the principles themselves, and their manner of operation, are totally unknown; nor is it less intelligible, or less conformable to experience, to say, that the world arose by vegetation, from a seed shed by another world, than to say that it arose from a divine reason or contrivance, according to the sense in which Cleanthes understands it.

But methinks, said Demea, if the world had a vegetative quality, and could sow the seeds of new worlds into the infinite chaos, this power would be still an additional argument for design in its Author. For whence could arise so wonderful a faculty but from design? Or how can order spring from any thing which perceives not that order which it bestows?

You need only look around you, replied Philo, to satisfy yourself with regard to this question. A tree bestows order and organisation on that tree which springs from it, without knowing the order; an animal in the same manner on its offspring; a bird on its nest; and instances of this kind are even more frequent in the world than those of order, which arise from reason and contrivance. To say, that all this order in animals and vegetables proceeds ultimately from design, is begging the question;[72] nor can that great point be

---

70 The creation or origin of the universe.

71 Long explanations or speeches.

72 Arguing in a circle; assuming what is at issue in the argument.

ascertained otherwise than by proving, *a priori*, both that order is, from its nature, inseparably attached to thought; and that it can never of itself, or from original unknown principles, belong to matter.

But further, Demea; this objection which you urge can never be made use of by Cleanthes, without renouncing a defence which he has already made against one of my objections. When I inquired concerning the cause of that supreme reason and intelligence into which he resolves every thing; he told me, that the impossibility of satisfying such inquiries could never be admitted as an objection in any species of philosophy. *We must stop somewhere, says he; nor is it ever within the reach of human capacity to explain ultimate causes, or show the last connections of any objects. It is sufficient, if any steps, so far as we go, are supported by experience and observation.* Now, that vegetation and generation, as well as reason, are experienced to be principles of order in nature, is undeniable. If I rest my system of cosmogony on the former, preferably to the latter, it is at my choice. The matter seems entirely arbitrary. And when Cleanthes asks me what is the cause of my great vegetative or generative faculty, I am equally entitled to ask him the cause of his great reasoning principle. These questions we have agreed to forbear on both sides; and it is chiefly his interest on the present occasion to stick to this agreement. Judging by our limited and imperfect experience, generation has some privileges above reason: for we see every day the latter arise from the former, never the former from the latter.

Compare, I beseech you, the consequences on both sides. The world, say I, resembles an animal; therefore it is an animal, therefore it arose from generation. The steps, I confess, are wide; yet there is some small appearance of analogy in each step. The world, says Cleanthes, resembles a machine; therefore it is a machine, therefore it arose from design. The steps are here equally wide, and the analogy less striking. And if he pretends to carry on my hypothesis a step further, and to infer design or reason from the great principle of generation, on which I insist; I may, with better authority, use the same freedom to push further his hypothesis, and infer a divine generation or theogony from his principle of reason. I have at least some faint shadow of experience, which is the utmost that can

ever be attained in the present subject. Reason, in innumerable instances, is observed to arise from the principle of generation, and never to arise from any other principle.

Hesiod,[73] and all the ancient mythologists, were so struck with this analogy, that they universally explained the origin of nature from an animal birth, and copulation. Plato too, so far as he is intelligible, seems to have adopted some such notion in his *Timæus*.

The Brahmins[74] assert, that the world arose from an infinite spider, who spun this whole complicated mass from his bowels, and annihilates afterwards the whole or any part of it, by absorbing it again, and resolving it into his own essence. Here is a species of cosmogony, which appears to us ridiculous; because a spider is a little contemptible animal, whose operations we are never likely to take for a model of the whole universe. But still here is a new species of analogy, even in our globe. And were there a planet wholly inhabited by spiders (which is very possible), this inference would there appear as natural and irrefragable as that which in our planet ascribes the origin of all things to design and intelligence, as explained by Cleanthes. Why an orderly system may not be spun from the belly as well as from the brain, it will be difficult for him to give a satisfactory reason.

I must confess, Philo, replied Cleanthes, that of all men living, the task which you have undertaken, of raising doubts and objections, suits you best, and seems, in a manner, natural and unavoidable to you. So great is your fertility of invention, that I am not ashamed to acknowledge myself unable, on a sudden, to solve regularly such out-of-the-way difficulties as you incessantly start upon me: though I clearly see, in general, their fallacy and error. And I question not, but you are yourself, at present, in the same case, and have not the solution so ready as the objection: while you must be sensible, that common sense and reason are entirely against you; and that such whimsies as you have delivered, may puzzle, but never can convince us.

---

73   Hesiod was a Greek poet of the eighth century BCE who wrote a poem called *Theogony*, which seeks to explain natural phenomena in terms of a family of gods.

74   The priestly or intellectual caste in classical Hinduism.

Part VIII

What you ascribe to the fertility of my invention, replied Philo, is entirely owing to the nature of the subject. In subjects adapted to the narrow compass of human reason, there is commonly but one determination, which carries probability or conviction with it; and to a man of sound judgement, all other suppositions, but that one, appear entirely absurd and chimerical. But in such questions as the present, a hundred contradictory views may preserve a kind of imperfect analogy; and invention has here full scope to exert itself. Without any great effort of thought, I believe that I could, in an instant, propose other systems of cosmogony, which would have some faint appearance of truth, though it is a thousand, a million to one, if either yours or any one of mine be the true system.

For instance, what if I should revive the old Epicurean hypothesis? This is commonly, and I believe justly, esteemed the most absurd system that has yet been proposed; yet I know not whether, with a few alterations, it might not be brought to bear a faint appearance of probability. Instead of supposing matter infinite, as Epicurus did, let us suppose it finite. A finite number of particles is only susceptible of finite transpositions: and it must happen, in an eternal duration, that every possible order or position must be tried an infinite number of times. This world, therefore, with all its events, even the most minute, has before been produced and destroyed, and will again be produced and destroyed, without any bounds and limitations. No one, who has a conception of the powers of infinite, in comparison of finite, will ever scruple this determination.

But this supposes, said Demea, that matter can acquire motion, without any voluntary agent or first mover.

And where is the difficulty, replied Philo, of that supposition? Every event, before experience, is equally difficult and incomprehensible; and every event, after experience, is equally easy and intelligible. Motion, in many instances, from gravity, from elasticity, from electricity, begins in matter, without any known voluntary agent: and to suppose always, in these cases, an unknown voluntary agent, is mere hypothesis; and hypothesis attended with no advantages. The beginning of motion in matter itself is as conceivable *a priori* as its communication from mind and intelligence.

Besides, why may not motion have been propagated by impulse through all eternity, and the same stock of it, or nearly the same, be still upheld in the universe? As much is lost by the composition of motion, as much is gained by its resolution. And whatever the causes are, the fact is certain, that matter is, and always has been, in continual agitation, as far as human experience or tradition reaches. There is not probably, at present, in the whole universe, one particle of matter at absolute rest.

And this very consideration too, continued Philo, which we have stumbled on in the course of the argument, suggests a new hypothesis of cosmogony, that is not absolutely absurd and improbable. Is there a system, an order, an economy of things, by which matter can preserve that perpetual agitation which seems essential to it, and yet maintain a constancy in the forms which it produces? There certainly is such an economy; for this is actually the case with the present world. The continual motion of matter, therefore, in less than infinite transpositions, must produce this economy or order; and by its very nature, that order, when once established, supports itself, for many ages, if not to eternity. But wherever matter is so poised, arranged, and adjusted, as to continue in perpetual motion, and yet preserve a constancy in the forms, its situation must, of necessity, have all the same appearance of art and contrivance which we observe at present. All the parts of each form must have a relation to each other, and to the whole; and the whole itself must have a relation to the other parts of the universe; to the element in which the form subsists; to the materials with which it repairs its waste and decay; and to every other form which is hostile or friendly. A defect in any of these particulars destroys the form; and the matter of which it is composed is again set loose, and is thrown into irregular motions and fermentations, till it unite itself to some other regular form. If no such form be prepared to receive it, and if there be a great quantity of this corrupted matter in the universe, the universe itself is entirely disordered; whether it be the feeble embryo of a world in its first beginnings that is thus destroyed, or the rotten carcass of one languishing in old age and infirmity. In either case, a chaos ensues; till finite, though innumerable revolutions produce at last some forms, whose parts and organs are so adjusted as to support the forms amidst a continued succession of matter.

Suppose (for we shall endeavour to vary the expression), that matter were thrown into any position, by a blind, unguided force; it is evident that this first position must, in all probability, be the most confused and most disorderly imaginable, without any resemblance to those works of human contrivance, which, along with a symmetry of parts, discover an adjustment of means to ends, and a tendency to self-preservation. If the actuating force cease after this operation, matter must remain for ever in disorder, and continue an immense chaos, without any proportion or activity. But suppose that the actuating force, whatever it be, still continues in matter, this first position will immediately give place to a second, which will likewise in all probability be as disorderly as the first, and so on through many successions of changes and revolutions. No particular order or position ever continues a moment unaltered. The original force, still remaining in activity, gives a perpetual restlessness to matter. Every possible situation is produced, and instantly destroyed. If a glimpse or dawn of order appears for a moment, it is instantly hurried away, and confounded, by that never-ceasing force which actuates every part of matter.

Thus the universe goes on for many ages in a continued succession of chaos and disorder. But is it not possible that it may settle at last, so as not to lose its motion and active force (for that we have supposed inherent in it), yet so as to preserve an uniformity of appearance, amidst the continual motion and fluctuation of its parts? This we find to be the case with the universe at present. Every individual is perpetually changing, and every part of every individual; and yet the whole remains, in appearance, the same. May we not hope for such a position, or rather be assured of it, from the eternal revolutions of unguided matter; and may not this account for all the appearing wisdom and contrivance which is in the universe? Let us contemplate the subject a little, and we shall find, that this adjustment, if attained by matter of a seeming stability in the forms, with a real and perpetual revolution or motion of parts, affords a plausible, if not a true solution of the difficulty.

It is in vain, therefore, to insist upon the uses of the parts in animals or vegetables, and their curious adjustment to each other. I would fain know, how an animal could subsist, unless its parts were so adjusted? Do we not find, that it immediately perishes whenever this adjustment ceases, and that its matter corrupting tries some new form? It happens indeed, that the parts of the world are so well adjusted, that some regular form immediately lays claim to this corrupted matter: and if it were not so, could the world subsist? Must it not dissolve as well as the animal, and pass through new positions and situations, till in great, but finite succession, it falls at last into the present or some such order?

It is well, replied Cleanthes, you told us, that this hypothesis was suggested on a sudden, in the course of the argument. Had you had leisure to examine it, you would soon have perceived the insuperable[75] objections to which it is exposed. No form, you say, can subsist, unless it possess those powers and organs requisite for its subsistence: some new order or economy must be tried, and so on, without intermission; till at last some order, which can support and maintain itself, is fallen upon. But according to this hypothesis, whence arise the many conveniences and advantages which men and all animals possess? Two eyes, two ears, are not absolutely necessary for the subsistence of the species. Human race might have been propagated and preserved, without horses, dogs, cows, sheep, and those innumerable fruits and products which serve to our satisfaction and enjoyment. If no camels had been created for the use of man in the sandy deserts of Africa and Arabia, would the world have been dissolved? If no lodestone[76] had been framed to give that wonderful and useful direction to the needle, would human society and the human kind have been immediately extinguished? Though the maxims of nature be in general very frugal, yet instances of this kind are far from being rare; and any one of them is a sufficient proof of design, and of a

---

75   Impossible to overcome.

76   Magnetite: a naturally magnetic iron oxide.

benevolent design, which gave rise to the order and arrangement of the universe.

At least, you may safely infer, said Philo, that the foregoing hypothesis is so far incomplete and imperfect, which I shall not scruple to allow. But can we ever reasonably expect greater success in any attempts of this nature? Or can we ever hope to erect a system of cosmogony, that will be liable to no exceptions, and will contain no circumstance repugnant to our limited and imperfect experience of the analogy of nature? Your theory itself cannot surely pretend to any such advantage, even though you have run into *anthropomorphism*, the better to preserve a conformity to common experience. Let us once more put it to trial. In all instances which we have ever seen, ideas are copied from real objects, and are ectypal,[77] not archetypal, to express myself in learned terms: You reverse this order, and give thought the precedence. In all instances which we have ever seen, thought has no influence upon matter, except where that matter is so conjoined with it as to have an equal reciprocal influence upon it. No animal can move immediately any thing but the members of its own body; and indeed, the equality of action and reaction seems to be an universal law of nature: But your theory implies a contradiction to this experience. These instances, with many more, which it were easy to collect (particularly the supposition of a mind or system of thought that is eternal, or, in other words, an animal ingenerable and immortal); these instances, I say, may teach all of us sobriety in condemning each other, and let us see, that as no system of this kind ought ever to be received from a slight analogy, so neither ought any to be rejected on account of a small incongruity. For that is an inconvenience from which we can justly pronounce no one to be exempted.

All religious systems, it is confessed, are subject to great and insuperable difficulties. Each disputant triumphs in his turn; while he carries on an offensive war, and exposes the absurdities, barbarities, and pernicious tenets of his antagonist. But all of them, on the whole, prepare a complete triumph for the sceptic; who tells them, that no system ought ever to be embraced with regard to such subjects: for this plain reason, that no absurdity ought ever to be assented to with regard to any subject. A total suspense of judgement is here our only reasonable resource. And if every attack, as is commonly observed, and no defence, among theologians, is successful; how complete must be *his* victory, who remains always, with all mankind, on the offensive, and has himself no fixed station or abiding city, which he is ever, on any occasion, obliged to defend?

Part IX

But if so many difficulties attend the argument *a posteriori*, said Demea, had we not better adhere to that simple and sublime argument *a priori*, which, by offering to us infallible demonstration, cuts off at once all doubt and difficulty? By this argument, too, we may prove the infinity of the divine attributes, which, I am afraid, can never be ascertained with certainty from any other topic. For how can an effect, which either is finite, or, for aught we know, may be so; how can such an effect, I say, prove an infinite cause? The unity too of the divine nature, it is very difficult, if not absolutely impossible, to deduce merely from contemplating the works of nature; nor will the uniformity alone of the plan, even were it allowed, give us any assurance of that attribute. Whereas the argument *a priori*....

You seem to reason, Demea, interposed Cleanthes, as if those advantages and conveniences in the abstract argument were full proofs of its solidity. But it is first proper, in my opinion, to determine what argument of this nature you choose to insist on; and we shall afterwards, from itself, better than from its useful consequences, endeavour to determine what value we ought to put upon it.

The argument, replied Demea, which I would insist on, is the common one.[78] Whatever exists must have a cause or reason of its existence; it being absolutely impossible for any thing to produce itself, or be the cause of its own existence. In mounting up, therefore, from effects to causes, we must either go on in

---

77 Of the nature of a copy rather than of a prototype.

78 Hume takes this argument primarily from Samuel Clarke's *A Discourse Concerning the Being and Attributes of God* (1705), which was very influential in its time.

tracing an infinite succession, without any ultimate cause at all; or must at last have recourse to some ultimate cause, that is *necessarily* existent: now, that the first supposition is absurd, may be thus proved. In the infinite chain or succession of causes and effects, each single effect is determined to exist by the power and efficacy of that cause which immediately preceded; but the whole eternal chain or succession, taken together, is not determined or caused by any thing; and yet it is evident that it requires a cause or reason, as much as any particular object which begins to exist in time. The question is still reasonable, why this particular succession of causes existed from eternity, and not any other succession, or no succession at all. If there be no necessarily existent being, any supposition which can be formed is equally possible; nor is there any more absurdity in nothing's having existed from eternity, than there is in that succession of causes which constitutes the universe. What was it, then, which determined something to exist rather than nothing, and bestowed being on a particular possibility, exclusive of the rest? *External* causes, there are supposed to be none. *Chance* is a word without a meaning. Was it *nothing*? But that can never produce any thing. We must, therefore, have recourse to a necessarily existent Being, who carries the *reason* of his existence in himself, and who cannot be supposed not to exist, without an express contradiction. There is, consequently, such a Being; that is, there is a Deity.

I shall not leave it to Philo, said Cleanthes, though I know that the starting[79] objections is his chief delight, to point out the weakness of this metaphysical reasoning. It seems to me so obviously ill-grounded, and at the same time of so little consequence to the cause of true piety and religion, that I shall myself venture to show the fallacy of it.

I shall begin with observing, that there is an evident absurdity in pretending to demonstrate a matter of fact, or to prove it by any arguments *a priori*. Nothing is demonstrable, unless the contrary implies a contradiction. Nothing, that is distinctly conceivable, implies a contradiction. Whatever we conceive as existent, we can also conceive as non-existent. There is no being, therefore, whose non-existence implies a contradiction. Consequently there is no being, whose existence is demonstrable. I propose this argument as entirely decisive, and am willing to rest the whole controversy upon it.

It is pretended that the Deity is a necessarily existent Being; and this necessity of his existence is attempted to be explained by asserting, that if we knew his whole essence or nature, we should perceive it to be as impossible for him not to exist, as for twice two not to be four. But it is evident that this can never happen, while our faculties remain the same as at present. It will still be possible for us, at any time, to conceive the non-existence of what we formerly conceived to exist; nor can the mind ever lie under a necessity of supposing any object to remain always in being; in the same manner as we lie under a necessity of always conceiving twice two to be four. The words, therefore, *necessary existence*, have no meaning; or, which is the same thing, none that is consistent.

But further, why may not the material universe be the necessarily existent Being, according to this pretended explication of necessity? We dare not affirm that we know all the qualities of matter; and for aught we can determine, it may contain some qualities, which, were they known, would make its non-existence appear as great a contradiction as that twice two is five. I find only one argument employed to prove, that the material world is not the necessarily existent Being: and this argument is derived from the contingency both of the matter and the form of the world. "Any particle of matter," it is said, "may be *conceived* to be annihilated; and any form may be *conceived* to be altered. Such an annihilation or alteration, therefore, is not impossible."[80] But it seems a great partiality not to perceive, that the same argument extends equally to the Deity, so far as we have any conception of him; and that the mind can at least imagine him to be non-existent, or his attributes to be altered. It must be some unknown, inconceivable qualities, which can make his non-existence appear impossible, or his attributes unalterable: and no reason can be assigned, why these qualities may not belong to matter. As they are altogether unknown and

---

79 A hunting metaphor: to start game (such as birds) is to startle them out of their hiding place.

80 This paraphrases an argument to be found in Clarke.

inconceivable, they can never be proved incompatible with it.

Add to this, that in tracing an eternal succession of objects, it seems absurd to inquire for a general cause or first Author. How can any thing, that exists from eternity, have a cause, since that relation implies *a priori*ty in time, and a beginning of existence?

In such a chain, too, or succession of objects, each part is caused by that which preceded it, and causes that which succeeds it. Where then is the difficulty? But the whole, you say, wants[81] a cause. I answer, that the uniting of these parts into a whole, like the uniting of several distinct countries into one kingdom, or several distinct members into one body, is performed merely by an arbitrary act of the mind, and has no influence on the nature of things. Did I show you the particular causes of each individual in a collection of twenty particles of matter, I should think it very unreasonable, should you afterwards ask me, what was the cause of the whole twenty. This is sufficiently explained in explaining the cause of the parts.

Though the reasonings which you have urged, Cleanthes, may well excuse me, said Philo, from starting any further difficulties, yet I cannot forbear insisting still upon another topic. It is observed by arithmeticians, that the products of 9[82] compose always either 9, or some lesser product of 9, if you add together all the characters of which any of the former products is composed. Thus, of 18, 27, 36, which are products of 9, you make 9 by adding 1 to 8, 2 to 7, 3 to 6. Thus, 369 is a product also of 9; and if you add 3, 6, and 9, you make 18, a lesser product of 9. To a superficial observer, so wonderful a regularity may be admired as the effect either of chance or design: but a skilful algebraist immediately concludes it to be the work of necessity, and demonstrates, that it must for ever result from the nature of these numbers. Is it not probable, I ask, that the whole economy of the universe is conducted by a like necessity, though no human algebra can furnish a key which solves the difficulty? And instead of admiring the order of natural beings, may it not happen, that, could we penetrate

into the intimate nature of bodies, we should clearly see why it was absolutely impossible they could ever admit of any other disposition? So dangerous is it to introduce this idea of necessity into the present question! And so naturally does it afford an inference directly opposite to the religious hypothesis!

But dropping all these abstractions, continued Philo, and confining ourselves to more familiar topics, I shall venture to add an observation, that the argument *a priori* has seldom been found very convincing, except to people of a metaphysical head, who have accustomed themselves to abstract reasoning, and who, finding from mathematics, that the understanding frequently leads to truth through obscurity, and, contrary to first appearances, have transferred the same habit of thinking to subjects where it ought not to have place. Other people, even of good sense and the best inclined to religion, feel always some deficiency in such arguments, though they are not perhaps able to explain distinctly where it lies; a certain proof that men ever did, and ever will derive their religion from other sources than from this species of reasoning.

Part X

It is my opinion, I own, replied Demea, that each man feels, in a manner, the truth of religion within his own breast, and, from a consciousness of his imbecility and misery, rather than from any reasoning, is led to seek protection from that Being, on whom he and all nature is dependent. So anxious or so tedious are even the best scenes of life, that futurity[83] is still the object of all our hopes and fears. We incessantly look forward, and endeavour, by prayers, adoration, and sacrifice, to appease those unknown powers, whom we find, by experience, so able to afflict and oppress us. Wretched creatures that we are! What resource for us amidst the innumerable ills of life, did not religion suggest some methods of atonement, and appease those terrors with which we are incessantly agitated and tormented?

I am indeed persuaded, said Philo, that the best, and indeed the only method of bringing every one to a due sense of religion, is by just representations of the misery and wickedness of men. And for that purpose a talent of eloquence and strong imagery is

---

81 Lacks.

82 Numbers generated by multiplying 9 together with some other number: e.g., $9 \times 1 = 9$, $9 \times 2 = 18$, etc.

---

83 Existence after death.

more requisite than that of reasoning and argument. For is it necessary to prove what every one feels within himself? It is only necessary to make us feel it, if possible, more intimately and sensibly.

The people, indeed, replied Demea, are sufficiently convinced of this great and melancholy truth. The miseries of life; the unhappiness of man; the general corruptions of our nature; the unsatisfactory enjoyment of pleasures, riches, honours; these phrases have become almost proverbial in all languages. And who can doubt of what all men declare from their own immediate feeling and experience?

In this point, said Philo, the learned are perfectly agreed with the vulgar; and in all letters,[84] *sacred* and *profane*, the topic of human misery has been insisted on with the most pathetic[85] eloquence that sorrow and melancholy could inspire. The poets, who speak from sentiment, without a system, and whose testimony has therefore the more authority, abound in images of this nature. From Homer down to Dr. Young,[86] the whole inspired tribe have ever been sensible, that no other representation of things would suit the feeling and observation of each individual.

As to authorities, replied Demea, you need not seek them. Look round this library of Cleanthes. I shall venture to affirm, that, except authors of particular sciences, such as chemistry or botany, who have no occasion to treat of human life, there is scarce one of those innumerable writers, from whom the sense of human misery has not, in some passage or other, extorted a complaint and confession of it. At least, the chance is entirely on that side; and no one author has ever, so far as I can recollect, been so extravagant as to deny it.

There you must excuse me, said Philo: Leibniz has denied it;[87] and is perhaps the first who ventured upon so bold and paradoxical an opinion; at least, the first who made it essential to his philosophical system.

---

84   Literature.

85   Emotional.

86   Edward Young (1683–1765), the author of *Night Thoughts* (of which Dr. Johnson remarked "The excellence of this work is not exactness but copiousness").

87   In *Theodicy*: see the next reading.

And by being the first, replied Demea, might he not have been sensible of his error? For is this a subject in which philosophers can propose to make discoveries especially in so late an age? And can any man hope by a simple denial (for the subject scarcely admits of reasoning), to bear down the united testimony of mankind, founded on sense and consciousness?

And why should man, added he, pretend to an exemption from the lot of all other animals? The whole earth, believe me, Philo, is cursed and polluted. A perpetual war is kindled amongst all living creatures. Necessity, hunger, want, stimulate the strong and courageous: fear, anxiety, terror, agitate the weak and infirm. The first entrance into life gives anguish to the new-born infant and to its wretched parent: weakness, impotence, distress, attend each stage of that life: and it is at last finished in agony and horror.

Observe too, says Philo, the curious artifices of nature, in order to embitter the life of every living being. The stronger prey upon the weaker, and keep them in perpetual terror and anxiety. The weaker too, in their turn, often prey upon the stronger, and vex and molest them without relaxation. Consider that innumerable race of insects, which either are bred on the body of each animal, or, flying about, infix their stings in him. These insects have others still less than themselves, which torment them. And thus on each hand, before and behind, above and below, every animal is surrounded with enemies, which incessantly seek his misery and destruction.

Man alone, said Demea, seems to be, in part, an exception to this rule. For by combination in society, he can easily master lions, tigers, and bears, whose greater strength and agility naturally enable them to prey upon him.

On the contrary, it is here chiefly, cried Philo, that the uniform and equal maxims of nature are most apparent. Man, it is true, can, by combination, surmount all his real enemies, and become master of the whole animal creation: but does he not immediately raise up to himself imaginary enemies, the dæmons of his fancy, who haunt him with superstitious terrors, and blast every enjoyment of life? His pleasure, as he imagines, becomes, in their eyes, a crime: his food and repose give them umbrage and offence: his very sleep and dreams furnish new materials to anxious fear: and even death, his refuge from every other ill, presents only the dread of endless and innumerable woes. Nor does the wolf molest more the timid flock, than superstition does the anxious breast of wretched mortals.

Besides, consider, Demea: This very society, by which we surmount those wild beasts, our natural enemies; what new enemies does it not raise to us? What woe and misery does it not occasion? Man is the greatest enemy of man. Oppression, injustice, contempt, contumely,[88] violence, sedition, war, calumny,[89] treachery, fraud; by these they mutually torment each other; and they would soon dissolve that society which they had formed, were it not for the dread of still greater ills, which must attend their separation.

But though these external insults, said Demea, from animals, from men, from all the elements, which assault us, form a frightful catalogue of woes, they are nothing in comparison of those which arise within ourselves, from the distempered condition of our mind and body. How many lie under the lingering torment of diseases? Hear the pathetic enumeration of the great poet.

> Intestine stone and ulcer, colic-pangs,
> Dæmoniac frenzy, moping melancholy,
> And moon-struck madness, pining atrophy,
> Marasmus, and wide-wasting pestilence.
> Dire was the tossing, deep the groans: Despair
> Tended the sick, busiest from couch to couch.
> And over them triumphant Death his dart
> Shook: but delay'd to strike, though oft invok'd
> With vows, as their chief good and final hope.[90]

The disorders of the mind, continued Demea, though more secret, are not perhaps less dismal and vexatious. Remorse, shame, anguish, rage, disappointment, anxiety, fear, dejection, despair; who has ever passed through life without cruel inroads from these tormentors? How many have scarcely ever felt any better sensations? Labour and poverty, so abhorred by every one, are the certain lot of the far greater number; and those few privileged persons, who enjoy ease and opulence, never reach contentment or true felicity. All the goods of life united would not make a very happy man; but all the ills united would make a wretch indeed; and any one of them almost (and who can be free from every one?) nay often the absence of one good (and who can possess all?) is sufficient to render life ineligible.[91]

Were a stranger to drop on a sudden into this world, I would show him, as a specimen of its ills, a hospital full of diseases, a prison crowded with malefactors and debtors, a field of battle strewed with carcasses, a fleet foundering in the ocean, a nation languishing under tyranny, famine, or pestilence. To turn the gay[92] side of life to him, and give him a notion of its pleasures; whither should I conduct him? To a ball, to an opera, to court? He might justly think, that I was only showing him a diversity of distress and sorrow.

There is no evading such striking instances, said Philo, but by apologies, which still further aggravate the charge. Why have all men, I ask, in all ages, complained incessantly of the miseries of life? … They have no just reason, says one: these complaints proceed only from their discontented, repining, anxious disposition.… And can there possibly, I reply, be a more certain foundation of misery, than such a wretched temper?

But if they were really as unhappy as they pretend, says my antagonist, why do they remain in life? … "Not satisfied with life, afraid of death."[93] This is the secret chain, say I, that holds us. We are terrified, not bribed to the continuance of our existence.

It is only a false delicacy, he may insist, which a few refined spirits indulge, and which has spread these complaints among the whole race of mankind.… And what is this delicacy, I ask, which you blame? Is it any thing but a greater sensibility to all the pleasures and pains of life? And if the man of a delicate, refined temper, by being so much more alive than the rest of the world, is only so much more unhappy, what judgement must we form in general of human life?

---

88 Disgrace or insult.

89 Slander.

90 Milton, from *Paradise Lost*.

91 Unworthy of being chosen, undesirable.

92 Happy and carefree.

93 This and the following are probably references to Lucretius' Epicureanism, which includes arguments against fearing death.

Let men remain at rest, says our adversary, and they will be easy. They are willing artificers of their own misery.... No! reply I: an anxious languor[94] follows their repose; disappointment, vexation, trouble, their activity and ambition.

I can observe something like what you mention in some others, replied Cleanthes: but I confess I feel little or nothing of it in myself, and hope that it is not so common as you represent it.

If you feel not human misery yourself, cried Demea, I congratulate you on so happy a singularity. Others, seemingly the most prosperous, have not been ashamed to vent their complaints in the most melancholy strains. Let us attend to the great, the fortunate emperor, Charles V,[95] when, tired with human grandeur, he resigned all his extensive dominions into the hands of his son. In the last harangue which he made on that memorable occasion, he publicly avowed, *that the greatest prosperities which he had ever enjoyed, had been mixed with so many adversities, that he might truly say he had never enjoyed any satisfaction or contentment.* But did the retired life, in which he sought for shelter, afford him any greater happiness? If we may credit his son's account, his repentance commenced the very day of his resignation.

Cicero's fortune, from small beginnings, rose to the greatest lustre and renown; yet what pathetic complaints of the ills of life do his familiar letters, as well as philosophical discourses, contain? And suitably to his own experience, he introduces Cato,[96] the great, the fortunate Cato, protesting in his old age, that had he a new life in his offer, he would reject the present.

Ask yourself, ask any of your acquaintance, whether they would live over again the last ten or twenty years of their life. No! But the next twenty, they say, will be better:

And from the dregs of life, hope to receive
What the first sprightly running could not give.[97]

---

94 Faintness, laziness, fatigue.
95 King of Spain and Holy Roman Emperor (1519–1556).
96 A Roman statesman (234–149 BCE), known for his rigorous social and moral reforming.
97 From a play called *Aureng-zebe*, by the English dramatist and poet John Dryden (1631–1700).

Thus at last they find (such is the greatness of human misery, it reconciles even contradictions), that they complain at once of the shortness of life, and of its vanity and sorrow.

And is it possible, Cleanthes, said Philo, that after all these reflections, and infinitely more, which might be suggested, you can still persevere in your anthropomorphism, and assert the moral attributes of the Deity, his justice, benevolence, mercy, and rectitude, to be of the same nature with these virtues in human creatures? His power we allow is infinite: whatever he wills is executed: but neither man nor any other animal is happy: therefore he does not will their happiness. His wisdom is infinite: He is never mistaken in choosing the means to any end: but the course of nature tends not to human or animal felicity:[98] therefore it is not established for that purpose. Through the whole compass of human knowledge, there are no inferences more certain and infallible than these. In what respect, then, do his benevolence and mercy resemble the benevolence and mercy of men?

Epicurus's old questions are yet unanswered. Is he willing to prevent evil, but not able? Then is he impotent. Is he able, but not willing? Then is he malevolent. Is he both able and willing? Whence then is evil?

You ascribe, Cleanthes (and I believe justly), a purpose and intention to nature. But what, I beseech you, is the object of that curious artifice and machinery, which she has displayed in all animals? The preservation alone of individuals, and propagation of the species. It seems enough for her purpose, if such a rank[99] be barely upheld in the universe, without any care or concern for the happiness of the members that compose it. No resource for this purpose: no machinery, in order merely to give pleasure or ease: no fund of pure joy and contentment: no indulgence, without some want or necessity accompanying it. At least, the few phenomena of this nature are overbalanced by opposite phenomena of still greater importance.

Our sense of music, harmony, and indeed beauty of all kinds, gives satisfaction, without being absolutely necessary to the preservation and propagation of the species. But what racking pains, on the other hand,

---

98 Happiness.
99 Class, group.

arise from gouts, gravels,[100] megrims,[101] toothaches, rheumatisms, where the injury to the animal machinery is either small or incurable? Mirth, laughter, play, frolic, seem gratuitous satisfactions, which have no further tendency: spleen,[102] melancholy, discontent, superstition, are pains of the same nature. How then does the divine benevolence display itself, in the sense of you anthropomorphites? None but we mystics, as you were pleased to call us, can account for this strange mixture of phenomena, by deriving it from attributes, infinitely perfect, but incomprehensible.

And have you at last, said Cleanthes smiling, betrayed your intentions, Philo? Your long agreement with Demea did indeed a little surprise me; but I find you were all the while erecting a concealed battery against me. And I must confess, that you have now fallen upon a subject worthy of your noble spirit of opposition and controversy. If you can make out the present point, and prove mankind to be unhappy or corrupted, there is an end at once of all religion. For to what purpose establish the natural attributes of the Deity, while the moral are still doubtful and uncertain?[103]

You take umbrage very easily, replied Demea, at opinions the most innocent, and the most generally received, even amongst the religious and devout themselves: and nothing can be more surprising than to find a topic like this, concerning the wickedness and misery of man, charged with no less than atheism and profaneness. Have not all pious divines and preachers, who have indulged their rhetoric on so fertile a subject; have they not easily, I say, given a solution of any difficulties which may attend it? This world is but a point in comparison of the universe; this life but a moment in comparison of eternity. The present evil phenomena, therefore, are rectified in other regions, and in some future period of existence. And the eyes of men, being then opened to larger views of things, see the whole connection of general laws; and trace

with adoration, the benevolence and rectitude of the Deity, through all the mazes and intricacies of his providence.[104]

No! Replied Cleanthes, No! These arbitrary suppositions can never be admitted, contrary to matter of fact, visible and uncontroverted. Whence can any cause be known but from its known effects? Whence can any hypothesis be proved but from the apparent phenomena? To establish one hypothesis upon another, is building entirely in the air; and the utmost we ever attain, by these conjectures and fictions, is to ascertain the bare possibility of our opinion; but never can we, upon such terms, establish its reality.

The only method of supporting divine benevolence, and it is what I willingly embrace, is to deny absolutely the misery and wickedness of man. Your representations are exaggerated; your melancholy views mostly fictitious; your inferences contrary to fact and experience. Health is more common than sickness; pleasure than pain; happiness than misery. And for one vexation which we meet with, we attain, upon computation, a hundred enjoyments.

Admitting your position, replied Philo, which yet is extremely doubtful, you must at the same time allow, that if pain be less frequent than pleasure, it is infinitely more violent and durable. One hour of it is often able to outweigh a day, a week, a month of our common insipid enjoyments; and how many days, weeks, and months, are passed by several in the most acute torments? Pleasure, scarcely in one instance, is ever able to reach ecstasy and rapture; and in no one instance can it continue for any time at its highest pitch and altitude. The spirits evaporate, the nerves relax, the fabric is disordered, and the enjoyment quickly degenerates into fatigue and uneasiness. But pain often, good God, how often! rises to torture and agony; and the longer it continues, it becomes still more genuine agony and torture. Patience is exhausted, courage languishes, melancholy seizes us, and nothing terminates our misery but the removal of its cause, or another event,[105] which is the sole cure of

---

100 Painful aggregations of crystals in the urinary tract, e.g., kidney stones.

101 Migraines.

102 Ill-temper.

103 Why worry about God's being the cause of the universe, or intelligent, or omnipotent, while leaving it uncertain whether God is morally good?

---

104 Providence is God's loving intervention in, and direction of, the world.

105 Such as death.

all evil, but which, from our natural folly, we regard with still greater horror and consternation.

But not to insist upon these topics, continued Philo, though most obvious, certain, and important; I must use the freedom to admonish you, Cleanthes, that you have put the controversy upon a most dangerous issue, and are unawares introducing a total scepticism into the most essential articles of natural and revealed theology. What! no method of fixing a just foundation for religion, unless we allow the happiness of human life, and maintain a continued existence even in this world, with all our present pains, infirmities, vexations, and follies, to be eligible and desirable! But this is contrary to every one's feeling and experience: it is contrary to an authority so established as nothing can subvert. No decisive proofs can ever be produced against this authority; nor is it possible for you to compute, estimate, and compare, all the pains and all the pleasures in the lives of all men and of all animals: and thus, by your resting the whole system of religion on a point, which, from its very nature, must for ever be uncertain, you tacitly confess, that that system is equally uncertain.

But allowing you what never will be believed, at least what you never possibly can prove, that animal, or at least human happiness, in this life, exceeds its misery, you have yet done nothing: for this is not, by any means, what we expect from infinite power, infinite wisdom, and infinite goodness. Why is there any misery at all in the world? Not by chance surely. From some cause then. Is it from the intention of the Deity? But he is perfectly benevolent. Is it contrary to his intention? But he is almighty. Nothing can shake the solidity of this reasoning, so short, so clear, so decisive; except we assert, that these subjects exceed all human capacity, and that our common measures of truth and falsehood are not applicable to them; a topic which I have all along insisted on, but which you have, from the beginning, rejected with scorn and indignation.

But I will be contented to retire still from this entrenchment, for I deny that you can ever force me in it. I will allow, that pain or misery in man is compatible with infinite power and goodness in the Deity, even in your sense of these attributes: what are you advanced by all these concessions? A mere possible compatibility is not sufficient. You must prove these pure, unmixed, and uncontrollable attributes from the present mixed and confused phenomena, and from these alone. A hopeful undertaking! Were the phenomena ever so pure and unmixed, yet being finite, they would be insufficient for that purpose. How much more, where they are also so jarring and discordant!

Here, Cleanthes, I find myself at ease in my argument. Here I triumph. Formerly, when we argued concerning the natural attributes of intelligence and design, I needed all my sceptical and metaphysical subtlety to elude your grasp. In many views of the universe, and of its parts, particularly the latter, the beauty and fitness of final causes strike us with such irresistible force, that all objections appear (what I believe they really are) mere cavils and sophisms; nor can we then imagine how it was ever possible for us to repose any weight on them. But there is no view of human life, or of the condition of mankind, from which, without the greatest violence, we can infer the moral attributes, or learn that infinite benevolence, conjoined with infinite power and infinite wisdom, which we must discover by the eyes of faith alone. It is your turn now to tug the labouring oar, and to support your philosophical subtleties against the dictates of plain reason and experience.

Part XI

I scruple not to allow, said Cleanthes, that I have been apt to suspect the frequent repetition of the word *infinite*, which we meet with in all theological writers, to savour more of panegyric[106] than of philosophy; and that any purposes of reasoning, and even of religion, would be better served, were we to rest contented with more accurate and more moderate expressions. The terms, *admirable, excellent, superlatively great, wise*, and *holy*; these sufficiently fill the imaginations of men; and any thing beyond, besides that it leads into absurdities, has no influence on the affections or sentiments. Thus, in the present subject, if we abandon all human analogy, as seems your intention, Demea, I am afraid we abandon all religion, and retain no conception of the great object of our adoration. If we preserve human analogy, we must for ever find

_____

106 A formal or elaborate speech of praise.

it impossible to reconcile any mixture of evil in the universe with infinite attributes; much less can we ever prove the latter from the former. But supposing the Author of nature to be finitely perfect, though far exceeding mankind, a satisfactory account may then be given of natural and moral evil,[107] and every untoward phenomenon be explained and adjusted. A less evil may then be chosen, in order to avoid a greater; inconveniences be submitted to, in order to reach a desirable end; and in a word, benevolence, regulated by wisdom, and limited by necessity, may produce just such a world as the present. You, Philo, who are so prompt at starting views, and reflections, and analogies, I would gladly hear, at length, without interruption, your opinion of this new theory; and if it deserve our attention, we may afterwards, at more leisure, reduce it into form.

My sentiments, replied Philo, are not worth being made a mystery of; and therefore, without any ceremony, I shall deliver what occurs to me with regard to the present subject. It must, I think, be allowed, that if a very limited intelligence, whom we shall suppose utterly unacquainted with the universe, were assured, that it were the production of a very good, wise, and powerful Being, however finite, he would, from his conjectures, form *beforehand* a different notion of it from what we find it to be by experience; nor would he ever imagine, merely from these attributes of the cause, of which he is informed, that the effect could be so full of vice and misery and disorder, as it appears in this life. Supposing now, that this person were brought into the world, still assured that it was the workmanship of such a sublime and benevolent Being; he might, perhaps, be surprised at the disappointment; but would never retract his former belief, if founded on any very solid argument; since such a limited intelligence must be sensible of his own blindness and ignorance, and must allow, that there may be many solutions of those phenomena, which will for ever escape his comprehension. But supposing, which is the real case with regard to man, that this creature is not antecedently convinced of a supreme intelligence,

benevolent, and powerful, but is left to gather such a belief from the appearances of things; this entirely alters the case, nor will he ever find any reason for such a conclusion. He may be fully convinced of the narrow limits of his understanding; but this will not help him in forming an inference concerning the goodness of superior powers, since he must form that inference from what he knows, not from what he is ignorant of. The more you exaggerate his weakness and ignorance, the more diffident you render him, and give him the greater suspicion that such subjects are beyond the reach of his faculties. You are obliged, therefore, to reason with him merely from the known phenomena, and to drop every arbitrary supposition or conjecture.

Did I show you a house or palace, where there was not one apartment convenient or agreeable; where the windows, doors, fires, passages, stairs, and the whole economy of the building, were the source of noise, confusion, fatigue, darkness, and the extremes of heat and cold; you would certainly blame the contrivance, without any further examination. The architect would in vain display his subtlety, and prove to you, that if this door or that window were altered, greater ills would ensue. What he says may be strictly true: the alteration of one particular, while the other parts of the building remain, may only augment the inconveniences. But still you would assert in general, that, if the architect had had skill and good intentions, he might have formed such a plan of the whole, and might have adjusted the parts in such a manner, as would have remedied all or most of these inconveniences. His ignorance, or even your own ignorance of such a plan, will never convince you of the impossibility of it. If you find any inconveniences and deformities in the building, you will always, without entering into any detail, condemn the architect.

In short, I repeat the question: Is the world, considered in general, and as it appears to us in this life, different from what a man, or such a limited being, would, *beforehand*, expect from a very powerful, wise, and benevolent Deity? It must be strange prejudice to assert the contrary. And from thence I conclude, that however consistent the world may be, allowing certain suppositions and conjectures, with the idea of such a Deity, it can never afford us an

---

107 Natural evil is badness in nature (e.g., mosquitoes, volcanoes) while moral evil is badness caused by the free actions of human beings (e.g., traffic jams, rape).

inference concerning his existence. The consistence is not absolutely denied, only the inference. Conjectures, especially where infinity is excluded from the Divine attributes, may perhaps be sufficient to prove a consistence, but can never be foundations for any inference.

There seem to be *four* circumstances, on which depend all, or the greatest part of the ills, that molest sensible creatures; and it is not impossible but all these circumstances may be necessary and unavoidable. We know so little beyond common life, or even of common life, that, with regard to the economy of a universe, there is no conjecture, however wild, which may not be just; nor any one, however plausible, which may not be erroneous. All that belongs to human understanding, in this deep ignorance and obscurity, is to be sceptical, or at least cautious, and not to admit of any hypothesis whatever, much less of any which is supported by no appearance of probability. Now, this I assert to be the case with regard to all the causes of evil, and the circumstances on which it depends. None of them appear to human reason in the least degree necessary or unavoidable; nor can we suppose them such, without the utmost license of imagination.

The *first* circumstance which introduces evil, is that contrivance or economy of the animal creation, by which pains, as well as pleasures, are employed to excite all creatures to action, and make them vigilant in the great work of self-preservation. Now pleasure alone, in its various degrees, seems to human understanding sufficient for this purpose. All animals might be constantly in a state of enjoyment: but when urged by any of the necessities of nature, such as thirst, hunger, weariness; instead of pain, they might feel a diminution of pleasure, by which they might be prompted to seek that object which is necessary to their subsistence. Men pursue pleasure as eagerly as they avoid pain; at least they might have been so constituted. It seems, therefore, plainly possible to carry on the business of life without any pain. Why then is any animal ever rendered susceptible of such a sensation? If animals can be free from it an hour, they might enjoy a perpetual exemption from it; and it required as particular a contrivance of their organs to produce that feeling, as to endow them with sight,

hearing, or any of the senses. Shall we conjecture, that such a contrivance was necessary, without any appearance of reason? And shall we build on that conjecture as on the most certain truth?

But a capacity of pain would not alone produce pain, were it not for the *second* circumstance, viz. the conducting of the world by general laws; and this seems nowise necessary to a very perfect Being. It is true, if everything were conducted by particular volitions,[108] the course of nature would be perpetually broken, and no man could employ his reason in the conduct of life. But might not other particular volitions remedy this inconvenience? In short, might not the Deity exterminate all ill, wherever it were to be found; and produce all good, without any preparation, or long progress of causes and effects?

Besides, we must consider, that, according to the present economy of the world, the course of nature, though supposed exactly regular, yet to us appears not so, and many events are uncertain, and many disappoint our expectations. Health and sickness, calm and tempest, with an infinite number of other accidents,[109] whose causes are unknown and variable, have a great influence both on the fortunes of particular persons and on the prosperity of public societies; and indeed all human life, in a manner, depends on such accidents. A being, therefore, who knows the secret springs of the universe, might easily, by particular volitions, turn all these accidents to the good of mankind, and render the whole world happy, without discovering himself in any operation. A fleet, whose purposes were salutary to society, might always meet with a fair wind. Good princes enjoy sound health and long life. Persons born to power and authority, be framed with good tempers and virtuous dispositions. A few such events as these, regularly and wisely conducted, would change the face of the world; and yet would no more seem to disturb the course of nature, or confound human conduct, than the present economy of things, where the causes are secret, and variable, and compounded. Some small touches given to Caligula's brain in his infancy, might have converted him into a

---

108 By a sequence of individual decisions (by God) for each particular case.

109 (Seemingly) random occurrences.

Trajan.[110] One wave, a little higher than the rest, by burying Cæsar[111] and his fortune in the bottom of the ocean, might have restored liberty to a considerable part of mankind. There may, for aught we know, be good reasons why providence interposes not in this manner; but they are unknown to us; and though the mere supposition, that such reasons exist, may be sufficient to save the conclusion concerning the Divine attributes, yet surely it can never be sufficient to *establish* that conclusion.

If every thing in the universe be conducted by general laws, and if animals be rendered susceptible of pain, it scarcely seems possible but some ill must arise in the various shocks of matter, and the various concurrence and opposition of general laws; but this ill would be very rare, were it not for the *third* circumstance, which I proposed to mention, viz. the great frugality with which all powers and faculties are distributed to every particular being. So well adjusted are the organs and capacities of all animals, and so well fitted to their preservation, that, as far as history or tradition reaches, there appears not to be any single species which has yet been extinguished in the universe. Every animal has the requisite endowments; but these endowments are bestowed with so scrupulous an economy, that any considerable diminution must entirely destroy the creature. Wherever one power is increased, there is a proportional abatement in the others. Animals which excel in swiftness are commonly defective in force. Those which possess both are either imperfect in some of their senses, or are oppressed with the most craving wants. The human species, whose chief excellency is reason and sagacity, is of all others the most necessitous, and the most deficient in bodily advantages; without clothes, without arms, without food, without lodging, without any convenience of life, except what they owe to

their own skill and industry. In short, nature seems to have formed an exact calculation of the necessities of her creatures; and, like a *rigid master*, has afforded them little more powers or endowments than what are strictly sufficient to supply those necessities. An *indulgent parent* would have bestowed a large stock, in order to guard against accidents, and secure the happiness and welfare of the creature in the most unfortunate concurrence of circumstances. Every course of life would not have been so surrounded with precipices, that the least departure from the true path, by mistake or necessity, must involve us in misery and ruin. Some reserve, some fund, would have been provided to ensure happiness; nor would the powers and the necessities have been adjusted with so rigid an economy. The Author of nature is inconceivably powerful: his force is supposed great, if not altogether inexhaustible: nor is there any reason, as far as we can judge, to make him observe this strict frugality in his dealings with his creatures. It would have been better, were his power extremely limited, to have created fewer animals, and to have endowed these with more faculties for their happiness and preservation. A builder is never esteemed prudent, who undertakes a plan beyond what his stock will enable him to finish.

In order to cure most of the ills of human life, I require not that man should have the wings of the eagle, the swiftness of the stag, the force of the ox, the arms of the lion, the scales of the crocodile or rhinoceros; much less do I demand the sagacity of an angel or cherubim. I am contented to take an increase in one single power or faculty of his soul. Let him be endowed with a greater propensity to industry and labour; a more vigorous spring and activity of mind; a more constant bent to business and application. Let the whole species possess naturally an equal diligence with that which many individuals are able to attain by habit and reflection; and the most beneficial consequences, without any allay of ill, is the immediate and necessary result of this endowment. Almost all the moral, as well as natural evils of human life, arise from idleness; and were our species, by the original constitution of their frame, exempt from this vice or infirmity, the perfect cultivation of land, the improvement of arts and manufactures, the exact execution of every office and duty, immediately follow; and men at

---

110 Caligula was a Roman emperor (37–41 CE), noted for his tyrannical excesses, and assassinated at the age of 29. Trajan's reign as emperor (98–117 CE) was known for its many public works.

111 Julius Cæsar (100–44 BCE), the Roman general who conquered Gaul (France) and the southern part of Britain, made himself dictator of the Roman empire in 46 BCE.

once may fully reach that state of society, which is so imperfectly attained by the best regulated government. But as industry is a power, and the most valuable of any, nature seems determined, suitably to her usual maxims, to bestow it on men with a very sparing hand; and rather to punish him severely for his deficiency in it, than to reward him for his attainments. She has so contrived his frame, that nothing but the most violent necessity can oblige him to labour; and she employs all his other wants to overcome, at least in part, the want of diligence, and to endow him with some share of a faculty of which she has thought fit naturally to bereave him. Here our demands may be allowed very humble, and therefore the more reasonable. If we required the endowments of superior penetration and judgement, of a more delicate taste of beauty, of a nicer sensibility to benevolence and friendship; we might be told, that we impiously pretend to break the order of nature; that we want to exalt ourselves into a higher rank of being; that the presents which we require, not being suitable to our state and condition, would only be pernicious to us. But it is hard; I dare to repeat it, it is hard, that being placed in a world so full of wants and necessities, where almost every being and element is either our foe or refuses its assistance … we should also have our own temper to struggle with, and should be deprived of that faculty which can alone fence against these multiplied evils.

The *fourth* circumstance, whence arises the misery and ill of the universe, is the inaccurate workmanship of all the springs and principles of the great machine of nature. It must be acknowledged, that there are few parts of the universe, which seem not to serve some purpose, and whose removal would not produce a visible defect and disorder in the whole. The parts hang all together; nor can one be touched without affecting the rest, in a greater or less degree. But at the same time, it must be observed, that none of these parts or principles, however useful, are so accurately adjusted, as to keep precisely within those bounds in which their utility consists; but they are, all of them, apt, on every occasion, to run into the one extreme or the other. One would imagine, that this grand production had not received the last hand of the maker; so little finished is every part, and so coarse are the strokes with which it is executed. Thus, the winds are

requisite to convey the vapours along the surface of the globe, and to assist men in navigation: but how oft, rising up to tempests and hurricanes, do they become pernicious? Rains are necessary to nourish all the plants and animals of the earth: but how often are they defective? How often excessive? Heat is requisite to all life and vegetation; but is not always found in the due proportion. On the mixture and secretion of the humours and juices of the body depend the health and prosperity of the animal: but the parts perform not regularly their proper function. What more useful than all the passions of the mind, ambition, vanity, love, anger? But how oft do they break their bounds, and cause the greatest convulsions in society? There is nothing so advantageous in the universe, but what frequently becomes pernicious, by its excess or defect; nor has nature guarded, with the requisite accuracy, against all disorder or confusion. The irregularity is never perhaps so great as to destroy any species; but is often sufficient to involve the individuals in ruin and misery.

On the concurrence, then, of these *four* circumstances, does all or the greatest part of natural evil depend. Were all living creatures incapable of pain, or were the world administered by particular volitions, evil never could have found access into the universe: and were animals endowed with a large stock of powers and faculties, beyond what strict necessity requires; or were the several springs and principles of the universe so accurately framed as to preserve always the just temperament and medium; there must have been very little ill in comparison of what we feel at present. What then shall we pronounce on this occasion? Shall we say that these circumstances are not necessary, and that they might easily have been altered in the contrivance of the universe? This decision seems too presumptuous for creatures so blind and ignorant. Let us be more modest in our conclusions. Let us allow, that, if the goodness of the Deity (I mean a goodness like the human) could be established on any tolerable reasons *a priori*, these phenomena, however untoward, would not be sufficient to subvert that principle; but might easily, in some unknown manner, be reconcilable to it. But let us still assert, that as this goodness is not antecedently established, but must be inferred from the phenomena, there can be no grounds for such an inference, while there are so many ills in the universe, and while these ills might so easily have been remedied, as far as human understanding can be allowed to judge on such a subject. I am sceptic enough to allow, that the bad appearances, notwithstanding all my reasonings, may be compatible with such attributes as you suppose; but surely they can never prove these attributes. Such a conclusion cannot result from scepticism, but must arise from the phenomena, and from our confidence in the reasonings which we deduce from these phenomena.

Look round this universe. What an immense profusion of beings, animated and organised, sensible and active! You admire this prodigious variety and fecundity. But inspect a little more narrowly these living existences, the only beings worth regarding. How hostile and destructive to each other! How insufficient all of them for their own happiness! How contemptible or odious to the spectator! The whole presents nothing but the idea of a blind nature, impregnated by a great vivifying principle, and pouring forth from her lap, without discernment or parental care, her maimed and abortive children!

Here the Manichæan system[112] occurs as a proper hypothesis to solve the difficulty: and no doubt, in some respects, it is very specious,[113] and has more probability than the common hypothesis, by giving a plausible account of the strange mixture of good and ill which appears in life. But if we consider, on the other hand, the perfect uniformity and agreement of the parts of the universe, we shall not discover in it any marks of the combat of a malevolent with a benevolent Being. There is indeed an opposition of pains and pleasures in the feelings of sensible creatures: but are not all the operations of nature carried on by an opposition of principles, of hot and cold, moist and dry, light and heavy? The true conclusion is, that the original source of all things is entirely indifferent to all these principles; and has no more regard to good

above ill, than to heat above cold, or to drought above moisture, or to light above heavy.

There may *four* hypotheses be framed concerning the first causes of the universe: *that* they are endowed with perfect goodness; *that* they have perfect malice; *that* they are opposite, and have both goodness and malice; *that* they have neither goodness nor malice. Mixed phenomena can never prove the two former unmixed principles; and the uniformity and steadiness of general laws seem to oppose the third. The fourth, therefore, seems by far the most probable.

What I have said concerning natural evil will apply to moral, with little or no variation; and we have no more reason to infer, that the rectitude of the supreme Being resembles human rectitude, than that his benevolence resembles the human. Nay, it will be thought, that we have still greater cause to exclude from him moral sentiments, such as we feel them; since moral evil, in the opinion of many, is much more predominant above moral good than natural evil above natural good.

But even though this should not be allowed, and though the virtue which is in mankind should be acknowledged much superior to the vice, yet so long as there is any vice at all in the universe, it will very much puzzle you anthropomorphites, how to account for it. You must assign a cause for it, without having recourse to the first cause. But as every effect must have a cause, and that cause another, you must either carry on the progression *in infinitum*, or rest on that original principle, who is the ultimate cause of all things....

Hold! Hold! cried Demea: Whither does your imagination hurry you? I joined in alliance with you, in order to prove the incomprehensible nature of the divine Being, and refute the principles of Cleanthes, who would measure every thing by human rule and standard. But I now find you running into all the topics of the greatest libertines and infidels, and betraying that holy cause which you seemingly espoused. Are you secretly, then, a more dangerous enemy than Cleanthes himself?

And are you so late in perceiving it? replied Cleanthes. Believe me, Demea, your friend Philo, from the beginning, has been amusing himself at both our expense; and it must be confessed, that the injudicious

---

112 An adaptation, by the Parthian prophet Mani (216–277 CE), who lived in what is now Iran, of the Zoroastrian belief that opposing good and evil deities (God and Satan) rule the world.

113 Having the ring of truth (but actually false).

reasoning of our vulgar theology has given him but too just a handle of ridicule. The total infirmity of human reason, the absolute incomprehensibility of the divine nature, the great and universal misery, and still greater wickedness of men; these are strange topics, surely, to be so fondly cherished by orthodox divines and doctors. In ages of stupidity and ignorance, indeed, these principles may safely be espoused; and perhaps no views of things are more proper to promote superstition, than such as encourage the blind amazement, the diffidence, and melancholy of mankind. But at present....

Blame not so much, interposed Philo, the ignorance of these reverend gentlemen. They know how to change their style with the times. Formerly it was a most popular theological topic to maintain, that human life was vanity and misery, and to exaggerate all the ills and pains which are incident to men. But of late years, divines, we find, begin to retract this position; and maintain, though still with some hesitation, that there are more goods than evils, more pleasures than pains, even in this life. When religion stood entirely upon temper and education, it was thought proper to encourage melancholy; as indeed mankind never have recourse to superior powers so readily as in that disposition. But as men have now learned to form principles, and to draw consequences, it is necessary to change the batteries,[114] and to make use of such arguments as will endure at least some scrutiny and examination. This variation is the same (and from the same causes) with that which I formerly remarked with regard to scepticism.

Thus Philo continued to the last his spirit of opposition, and his censure of established opinions. But I could observe that Demea did not at all relish the latter part of the discourse; and he took occasion soon after, on some pretence or other, to leave the company.

---

114 A military metaphor: to adjust one's fortifications or one's armaments.

GOTTFRIED LEIBNIZ
Theodicy

Who Was Gottfried Leibniz?

Gottfried Wilhelm Leibniz was born in 1646 in Leipzig (a major city in Saxony, the east-central region of what is now Germany). His father Friedrich, a professor of moral philosophy at the University of Leipzig, died when he was six, but the young Gottfried had already been infected with a love of learning. He taught himself Latin at the age of seven or eight, and he read widely in his late father's large library. He went to the University of Leipzig at the age of 14, and then at 20 moved on to the University of Altdorf near Nuremberg, graduating with degrees in law and philosophy. However, he had no intention of pursuing an academic career, and after turning down a position as professor of law at the University of Altdorf, he got employment with the Elector of Mainz[1] in 1667 as part of a project to recodify and systematize the laws of Germany.

In 1672 Leibniz was sent to Paris, the leader of a devious political embassy trying to persuade the French king Louis XIV to invade Egypt and expel the Turks (and thus weaken the French economy and turn their attention away from Germany). Leibniz never got to present this idea to the French court, but he spent four years in Paris—at that time the intellectual capital of Europe—studying mathematics and philosophy

---

1   The political leader and archbishop of the region of Mainz, in Germany. Some German rulers were called "Electors" as they had the right to elect their overall ruler, the Holy Roman Emperor.

and encountering, for more or less the first time, the "mechanical philosophy" of Galileo, Bacon, Descartes, Gassendi, Hobbes, and others (see the Descartes reading in Chapter 3 for more details). Intoxicated with the philosophical excitement of the time, Leibniz plunged into the new philosophy and began the development of his own philosophical and scientific system. His early work was relatively amateurish, and he was very disappointed to be refused a research position with the Paris Academy of Sciences. However, it was during this period that Leibniz independently discovered the differential calculus (the mathematics of the variation of a function with respect to changes in independent variables, a tool crucial to the development of the new Newtonian science because it allowed the formal representation of rates of change); he was later to feud bitterly and publicly with Isaac Newton over who was the first to invent it.

Leibniz returned to Germany in 1676 and became Court Councillor and Librarian to the Duke of Brunswick in Hanover, where he lived until his death in 1714. During this period he took on a wide variety of jobs— including geologist, mining engineer (unsuccessfully supervising the draining of the silver mines in the Harz mountains), diplomat, linguist, and historian— but all the while continued with his philosophical work in a series of letters, essays, and two books. He never married (though at age 50 he made a marriage proposal that he quickly thought better of). He spent months at a time without leaving his study, eating at irregular hours, falling asleep over a book at one or two in the morning and waking at seven or eight to continue his reading. He was quick to anger and resented criticism, but he was also swift to regain his good humor. In his old age he was, unfortunately, a figure of ridicule at the Court of Hanover, an irascible old fossil in a huge black wig, wearing old-fashioned, overly ornate clothes (he was also, ironically, disliked by the townspeople because it was rumored he was an atheist). When he died only one mourner attended his funeral, even though by then he was widely recognized in Europe as an important scholar and original thinker.

Leibniz was a man who sought synthesis and reconciliation between opposing points of view wherever possible. He believed, as he put it in the last year of his life, that "the majority of the philosophical sects are right in the greater part of what they affirm, but not so much in what they deny." Perhaps because his childhood years were a time of great unrest in Europe—the aftermath of the Thirty Years War between the Holy Roman Empire, France, Sweden, and Spain (1618–1648)—Leibniz was, throughout his life, interested in political and religious reconciliation; for example, he had an ambitious scheme to reunite the Catholic and Protestant churches in Germany. Part of his plan to promote peace was a project to develop an ideal, universal language, which would promote communication and understanding between divided peoples. In his physics and philosophy he generally aimed to bring together the old Aristotelian-Scholastic tradition, which he learned as a student, with the new mechanical philosophy he encountered in France.

What Was Leibniz's Overall Philosophical Project?

Leibniz the philosopher was, first and foremost, a metaphysician. Metaphysics, in this sense, can be thought of as the study of 'ultimate reality'—that is, of the essential nature of the fundamental substances that make up the world (such as, perhaps, matter and spirit). Leibniz placed a particular weight on this understanding of substance as "the key to philosophy":

he believed that his own theory of substance was "so rich, that there follow from it most of the most important truths about God, the soul, and the nature of body, which are generally either unknown or unproved."

A good way to begin to understand his account of substance is to think about the following disagreement, which Leibniz had with the influential French philosopher René Descartes, who lived in the generation just prior to Leibniz. Descartes held that matter was a substance, but he thought of it as a *single*, continuous, extended lump of stuff. For Descartes, the whole material universe is fundamentally one single thing, spread out across all of space. In other words, there is only one material substance. On the other hand, Descartes believed that there are many mental substances (though they all belong to the same *category* of substance, i.e., they are all minds): God is one (infinite, uncreated, etc.) mental substance, and each finite human mind is another. My mind is a different individual substance from your mind, for example, but according to Descartes our bodies are both part of the same substance.

It is Descartes' view of material substance with which Leibniz disagreed. He firmly rejected the notion that a single substance can 'include' a large number of separable bits, and insisted that reality must consist of a large number of discrete individual things rather than of a continuous expanse of 'stuff.' As it is sometimes put, for Leibniz "substantiality requires individuality"—i.e., substances are indivisible, complete beings which have a special kind of 'substantial unity.' The whole of material reality simply could not be a single substance, according to Leibniz, because it blatantly fails to have the right kind of unity. For example, a pile of stones or flock of sheep is not a substance since its unity (as a single heap or flock) is only *accidental*; on the other hand, a human being is a substance, according to Leibniz, because that unity is not accidental but is, so to speak, "built in" to one's personhood: it is what he called a unity *per se*, a unity "in itself."

The importance of all this for Leibniz's philosophical system is that he took very seriously the idea that reality is fundamentally made up of a collection of indivisible substances—which Leibniz calls "substantial forms"—each of which possesses substantial unity and so is complete in itself. At least by the time of his later philosophy, Leibniz held that all of reality is made up of a large collection of immaterial substances (roughly, minds or souls) which he called *monads*: the material world is an "appearance" that somehow "results" from the activities of purely immaterial minds. Furthermore, since these monads are complete in themselves, their "substantial form" encompasses their whole nature—their parts and structure, their causal powers and activities, their whole life-cycle of changing states are all derived from their substantial forms. Hence, to fully know the form of a human soul, for example, would be to know everything about its nature, according to Leibniz: one would be able to predict and understand each and every activity of that soul, throughout its entire history.

Another consequence of Leibniz's metaphysics is that it presents *physics* in an important new light. Leibniz was writing during the heyday of the "new" or "mechanical" philosophy—typified by Descartes' philosophy and Newton's physics—which sought to explain all the phenomena of the material world, not in terms of mysterious forces or essences, but solely in terms of the complex collisions between bits of matter. Leibniz was part of this "new philosophy" movement—he agreed, in general terms, with the view that physics should be thought of as the study of matter in motion. Where he disagreed with many of his contemporaries, however, was over the concept of *physical force*—over the mechanism by which motion is transferred from one body to another (or conserved in a single moving body, like a planet). This was a matter of great interest and controversy in the seventeenth century, and was a far from trivial question. If a car rear-ends another vehicle waiting in neutral at a stop light, for example, it will cause the front car to roll forward. What philosophers of Leibniz's time were puzzled by was just exactly *what* is this invisible power which is transmitted from the first car to the second, and furthermore what keeps the second car moving when it is no longer being pushed by the first? In short, the movement of three-dimensional bodies through space was thought to be well understood, but what makes the bodies move in the first place was much more mysterious.

A natural response to this problem, at the time, was to turn to God as an explanation of this mystery. One such theory was called "occasionalism," and its most famous supporter was a French philosopher called Nicolas Malebranche (1638–1715). According to occasionalism, God is the true cause of all physical motion: God watches over the world and, when one body is hit by another moving body, this is the occasion for God to step in and cause the first body to move; similarly, God is constantly acting to keep moving bodies (like the Moon) in motion—without his intervention they would immediately halt. Leibniz, however, held that this role was beneath the dignity of God. It is far more worthy of God to have produced entities capable of initiating their own movements. And Leibniz's metaphysical framework allowed him, he thought, to explain how God has done this: reality consists in substantial forms, and these forms are active in their very nature—their movement is, once again, 'built in' to the individuals in the world at the moment of their creation, so God does not have to intervene 'from the outside' to bring about natural phenomena.

Interestingly, on this view, the fundamental individuals in the world (monads) do not really *interact* with each other; rather, they each independently run through the sequence of activities 'pre-programmed' by their forms, and God has designed the world—by creating the substantial forms in a certain way—so that all these activities mesh together. Leibniz called this "the system of pre-established harmony." For example, if I see a cat in the room, this perception is *not* caused in me by the cat, according to Leibniz, but arises in me "spontaneously from [my] own nature"; meanwhile, however, God has so arranged things so that what I see corresponds to reality—that is, there really is a cat in the room.

What Is the Structure of This Reading?

This reading is broken down into eight different "objections": each objection is an argument against the traditional conception of God (that God is an infinitely good, wise, and powerful being) premised either on the presence of evil in the world or on Leibniz's own theory that this is the greatest of all possible worlds. The first objection is in the form of the traditional

"problem of evil," but then there follow arguments to show that God is unjust in punishing sin, or culpable for the existence of sin, or insufficiently caring for his creation, or unfree to choose what kind of world he will create. Leibniz responds to each of these objections, trying to show that his philosophical system can answer all of them: in other words, he tries to defend the *possibility* of a God that is omniscient, omnipotent, and perfectly benevolent.

Some Useful Background Information

1. The title of Leibniz's book, *Theodicy*, is a word meaning "the vindication of God's power and goodness despite the existence of evil." That is, a theodicy is an attempt to respond to the problem of evil.

2. This reading is structured as a set of syllogisms, plus Leibniz's responses to them. A syllogism is an argument, and usually one of a particular form: it consists of two premises and a conclusion. Many of the arguments considered by Leibniz are a type of "categorical syllogism" and have the following form (known, believe it or not, by the medieval nickname "Barbara"):

   > All *M* is *P*.
   > All *S* is *M*.
   > Therefore all *S* is *P*.

   In arguments of this form, the first line is called the "major premise" (since it includes *P*, the predicate of the conclusion) and the second line is the "minor premise" (since it includes *S*, the subject of the conclusion). "Prosyllogisms" are syllogisms which have as their conclusion one of the premises of another syllogism—that is, they are what would often be called today "sub-arguments."

3. According to Leibniz there are "two great principles" on which "our reasonings are founded." They are the "principle of contradiction" and the "principle of sufficient reason." It is the principle of contradiction "in virtue of which we judge as false anything that involves contradiction, and as true whatever is opposed or contradictory to what is false" (*Monadology*, section 31). For example, suppose that, if some claim *P* were true,

then it would follow logically that some other claim (*Q*) would have to be both true and false. To say that *Q* is both true and false is to express a contradiction: "*Q* and not-*Q*." Since (arguably) no proposition can be both true and false at the same time (i.e., no contradictions are true), this shows as a matter of logic that *P* could not possibly be true, and hence (according to Leibniz) *P* must be false or, to put the same thing another way, not-*P* must be true.

The principle of sufficient reason says "no fact could ever be true or existent ... unless there were a sufficient reason why it was thus and not otherwise," as Leibniz puts it in the *Monadology*. In the case of necessary truths, they must be true because of the principle of contradiction—because their opposites must be false. In the case of contingent truths, their "sufficient reason," according to Leibniz, is "the principle of the best": that is, God could only have created the best possible world, and that is why the world is the way it is.

4. Although Leibniz probably did not invent the notion of a "possible world" (the concept can also be found in the work of his contemporary, Nicolas Malebranche, as early as 1674), he is generally thought of as the main developer of this way of talking prior to the twentieth century. The language of possible worlds is fairly straightforward, but has proved to be a powerful tool for thinking clearly and precisely about possibility, contingency, and necessity. In this way of talking, a "world" is a complete state of affairs: it is not just, say, a planet, but an entire universe, extended throughout space and time. A world is "possible" if it is logically consistent: that is, if it does not involve a contradiction. One way to think of this is to say that a possible world is a way the actual universe *might have been*. For example, the cover of this book might have been plaid, or the Vietnam War might never have taken place, or cats might have turned out to be robotic spies from outer space, or the laws of physics might have been different; and so there are possible worlds in which all these things are the case. (The actual world, of course, is also a possible world, since it too is a way the actual world could have been!) On the other hand, there are some differences from the actual world that are *not* possible (i.e., which appear in no possible universe). For example, two plus two must always equal four, oculists must (by definition) always be eye doctors, and the sky could never be red all over and blue all over at the same time. The 'space' of possible worlds can therefore be said to be exactly the set of all the universes that are possible. According to Leibniz, God necessarily and eternally has in his mind the ideas of each of these infinitely many possible worlds, and he has chosen just one of them—the best one—to make actual through an act of creation.

5. When Leibniz says that the actual world is the best of all possible worlds, he means this in both of two different ways. First, he means that it is "metaphysically" the best possible world: God has designed it in such a way that the maximum amount of variety and richness in the natural world is produced using the simplest and most efficient possible set of natural laws. Second, he means that it is "morally" the best possible world: it has been designed with the happiness of human beings as its primary aim.

Some Common Misconceptions

1. In Voltaire's novel *Candide* (1759), Leibniz is lampooned, in the person of the character Dr. Pangloss, for his thesis that this is the best of all possible worlds: Voltaire makes it seem that Leibniz's optimism is a foolish and wickedly complacent response to the evils of our world. However, Leibniz does not deny the existence of evil: he is perfectly aware that sometimes "bad things happen to good people." Nor does Leibniz claim that the existence of evil is necessary: he thinks that God could have made a world that did not contain evil, or could have chosen not to create any world at all. What Leibniz does think is that God *could not have made any world which is better than this one*: that is,

any possible world that contains less evil than the actual world is, nevertheless, for some reason, a less good world than the actual one. Thus, precisely the amount of evil which does exist—no more and no less—is necessary for this world to be the best of all possible worlds.

2. Leibniz does not think it is incumbent upon him to prove that this actually is the best of all possible worlds. In order to counter the problem of evil, Leibniz merely has to show that the existence of evil is *consistent* with the existence of a benevolent, all-powerful God—that is, he just has to show that this *might* be the best of all possible worlds even though it contains evil. (Nevertheless, "in order to make the matter clearer," Leibniz does his best to show that "this universe must be in reality better than every other possible universe.")

3. Leibniz does not think that whatever is true is true by absolute necessity. Although this is the best of all possible worlds and the only one which God, given his nature, could have made actual, there are nevertheless a huge number of non-actual but possible worlds, that God in some sense could have created but did not.

How Important and Influential Is This Passage?

This particular passage is not an especially influential and important piece of philosophy, nor is Leibniz's *Theodicy* today thought to be a central part of his writings (although it was the only philosophical book he published during his lifetime). On the other hand, Leibniz's idea that this is the best of all possible worlds—his defense of which is summarized in this selection, but which can be found spelled out in more detail in several places in his writings—is perhaps one of the most notorious ideas in all of philosophy. The idea of possible worlds, which Leibniz developed as part of his theodicy, has also been of great influence on twentieth-century philosophy, as a useful tool for thinking about possibility and necessity. (For example, when philosophers today want to say that something is necessarily true they will often assert that it is "true in all possible worlds.")

Suggestions for Critical Reflection

1. Leibniz asserts "the best plan is not always that which seeks to avoid evil." This may be true for human beings, such as military leaders who need to risk casualties in order to win battles, but how plausible a claim is it for an omnipotent deity—for a being whose actions are not constrained by the behavior of opponents or competitors, or even by the laws of physics?

2. Where do you think human free will enters into Leibniz's picture? Is it compatible with, or even entailed by, this being the best of all possible worlds? Why do you think that Leibniz says it would be "unfitting" for God to interfere with human freedom in order to hinder sin?

3. Where does *God's* freedom fit into a theory like Leibniz's? If God could only have created the best possible world (i.e., this world), then in what sense can we say that God is free? What do you think of Leibniz's response to this problem?

4. What do you think of Leibniz's claim that "every reality purely positive or absolute is a perfection; and that imperfection comes from limitation, that is, from the privative"? Do you agree that all evil consists in the *absence* of something that could have made things better, rather than the presence of something that is positively bad?

5. It sometimes appears that Leibniz argues in the following way: this must be the best of all possible worlds because a perfect God made it, and therefore it is possible that a perfect God exists. Do you think Leibniz does make this argument, and if so, does this strike you as a good argument? If it's a bad argument, how serious a problem is this for Leibniz's theodicy?

6. Do you think that there is a "universal harmony," and if so, does it make sense of all the evil in the world? Does it make sense of it by showing that the evil is necessary for some "higher purpose," or alternatively by showing that it is not *really* evil in the first place?

Suggestions for Further Reading

Currently the only English translation of Leibniz's *Theodicy* in print is that by E.M. Huggard, published by Open Court in 1985. The three classic philosophical works by Leibniz are the *Discourse on Metaphysics* (written in 1686), the *New System of the Nature of Substances and their Communication* (published in 1695), and the *Monadology* (written in 1714). Each of these works are fairly short, and can be found collected in, for example, *G.W. Leibniz: Philosophical Texts*, translated by R.S. Woolhouse and Richard Francks (Oxford University Press, 1998). Another important work by Leibniz, his response to John Locke's *Essay Concerning Human Understanding* (see Chapter 3), is *New Essays on Human Understanding*, translated by Peter Remnant and Jonathan Bennett and published by Cambridge University Press in 1996.

Leibniz presents four arguments for the existence of God at different places in his work: an "ontological" argument (in his *Discourse on Metaphysics*, section 23, and in *New Essays on Human Understanding*, Book IV, Chapter X); a "cosmological" argument (in *Monadology*); an "argument from eternal truths" (also in *Monadology*); and an "argument from pre-established harmony" (in the *New System*, section 16).

A detailed, recent biography of Leibniz is E.J. Aiton's *Leibniz*, published by Adam Hilger in 1985. Useful books on Leibniz's philosophy as a whole include Robert Merrihew Adams's *Leibniz: Determinist, Theist, Idealist* (Oxford University Press, 1994), C.D. Broad's *Leibniz: An Introduction* (Cambridge University Press, 1975), Stuart Brown's *Leibniz* (Harvester Press, 1984), Nicholas Rescher's *Leibniz: An Introduction to his Philosophy* (University Press of America, 1979), and Bertrand Russell's *A Critical Exposition of the Philosophy of Leibniz* (Allen and Unwin, 1937). A good collection of specially-written papers on Leibniz's philosophy is *The Cambridge Companion to Leibniz*, edited by Nicholas Jolley (Cambridge University Press, 1995).

Discussion of Leibniz's response to the problem of evil can be found in the following articles: David Blumenfeld's "Is the Best Possible World Possible?" *Philosophical Review* 84 (1975); Gregory Brown, "Compossibility, Harmony, and Perfection in Leibniz," *Philosophical Review* 96 (1987); Leroy Howe, "Leibniz on Evil," *Sophia* 10 (1971); Oliver Johnson, "Human Freedom in the Best of all Possible Worlds" *Philosophical Quarterly* 4 (1954); Michael Latzer, "Leibniz's Conception of Metaphysical Evil," *Journal of the History of Ideas* 55 (1994); Lawrence Resnik, "God and the Best Possible World," *American Philosophical Quarterly* 10 (1973); and Catherine Wilson, "Leibnizian Optimism," *Journal of Philosophy* 80 (1983).

Theodicy
Abridgement of the Argument Reduced to Syllogistic Form[2]

Some intelligent persons have desired that this supplement be made, and I have the more readily yielded to their wishes as in this way I have an opportunity again to remove certain difficulties and to make some observations which were not sufficiently emphasized in the work itself.

Objection I

i.   Whoever does not choose the best is lacking in power, or in knowledge, or in goodness.
ii. God did not choose the best in creating this world.
iii. Therefore, God has been lacking in power, or in knowledge, or in goodness.

Answer

I deny the minor, that is, the second premise of this syllogism; and our opponent proves it by this:

Prosyllogism

i.   Whoever makes things in which there is evil, which could have been made without any evil, or the making of which could have been omitted, does not choose the best.

---

2   The *Theodicy* was first published in 1710. This translation from the original French was made by George M. Duncan and comes from *The Philosophical Works of Leibnitz*, published in 1890 by Tuttle, Morehouse & Taylor. I have added the numbering of the premises of the various syllogisms.

ii.   God has made a world in which there is evil, a world, I say, which could have been made without any evil, or the making of which could have been omitted altogether.

iii.   Therefore, God has not chosen the best.

Answer

I grant the minor of this prosyllogism; for it must be confessed that there is evil in this world which God has made, and that it was possible to make a world without evil, or even not to create a world at all, for its creation has depended on the free will of God; but I deny the major, that is, the first of the two premises of the prosyllogism, and I might content myself with simply demanding its proof; but in order to make the matter clearer, I have wished to justify this denial by showing that the best plan is not always that which seeks to avoid evil, since it may happen that *the evil is accompanied by a greater good*. For example, a general of an army will prefer a great victory with a slight wound to a condition without wound and without victory. We have proved this more fully in the large work by making it clear, by instances taken from mathematics and elsewhere, that an imperfection in the part may be required for a greater perfection in the whole. In this I have followed the opinion of St. Augustine,[3] who has said a hundred times, that God has permitted evil in order to bring about good, that is, a greater good; and that of Thomas Aquinas (in libr. II. *sent. dist.* 32, qu. I, art. 1),[4] that the permitting of evil

tends to the good of the universe. I have shown that the ancients called Adam's fall[5] *felix culpa*, a happy sin, because it had been retrieved with immense advantage by the incarnation of the Son of God, who has given to the universe something nobler than anything that ever would have been among creatures except for it. For the sake of a clearer understanding, I have added, following many good authors, that it was in accordance with order and the general good that God allowed to certain creatures the opportunity of exercising their liberty, even when he foresaw that they would turn to evil, but which he could so well rectify; because it was not fitting that, in order to hinder sin, God should always act in an extraordinary manner. To overthrow this objection, therefore, it is sufficient to show that a world with evil might be better than a world without evil; but I have gone even farther, in the work, and have even proved that this universe must be in reality better than every other possible universe.

Objection II

i.   If there is more evil than good in intelligent creatures, then there is more evil than good in the whole work of God.

ii.   Now, there is more evil than good in intelligent creatures.

iii.   Therefore, there is more evil than good in the whole work of God.

Answer

I deny the major and the minor of this conditional syllogism. As to the major, I do not admit it at all, because this pretended deduction from a part to the whole, from intelligent creatures to all creatures, supposes tacitly and without proof that creatures destitute of reason cannot enter into comparison nor into account with those which possess it. But why may it not be that the surplus of good in the non-intelligent creatures which fill the world, compensates for, and even incomparably surpasses, the surplus of evil in

---

3   Augustine, a north African bishop who lived in the early fifth century, was a highly important early Christian theologian and philosopher. Some of his influential writings on the problem of evil appear in his book *Enchiridion* (which means "handbook"); his other important works include *City of God* and the autobiographical *Confessions*.

4   Leibniz is here referring to St. Thomas Aquinas' commentary on a work called the *Sentences* by Peter Lombard (specifically, to the first article of the first question of part 32 of Book II of the commentary). Lombard was bishop of Paris between 1150 and 1152, and his *Sentences* became a standard textbook for thirteenth-century students of theology.

---

5   According to the Old Testament Book of Genesis, the expulsion of Adam and Eve from the Garden of Eden for disobedience to God, and the consequent lapse of the human race into the human condition of suffering and "original sin."

the rational creatures? It is true that the value of the latter is greater; but, in compensation, the others are beyond comparison the more numerous, and it may be that the proportion of number and quantity surpasses that of value and of quality.

As to the minor, that is no more to be admitted; that is, it is not at all to be admitted that there is more evil than good in the intelligent creatures. There is no need even of granting that there is more evil than good in the human race, because it is possible, and in fact very probable, that the glory and the perfection of the blessed are incomparably greater than the misery and the imperfection of the damned, and that here the excellence of the total good in the smaller number exceeds the total evil in the greater number. The blessed approach the Divinity, by means of a Divine Mediator, as near as may suit these creatures,[6] and make such progress in good as is impossible for the damned to make in evil, approach as nearly as they may to the nature of demons. God is infinite, and the devil is limited; the good may and does go to infinity, while evil has its bounds. It is therefore possible, and is credible, that in the comparison of the blessed and the damned, the contrary of that which I have said might happen in the comparison of intelligent and non-intelligent creatures, takes place; namely, it is possible that in the comparison of the happy and the unhappy, the proportion of degree exceeds that of number, and that in the comparison of intelligent and non-intelligent creatures, the proportion of number is greater than that of value. I have the right to suppose that a thing is possible so long as its impossibility is not proved; and indeed that which I have here advanced is more than a supposition.

But in the second place, if I should admit that there is more evil than good in the human race, I have still good grounds for not admitting that there is more evil than good in all intelligent creatures. For there is an inconceivable number of genii,[7] and perhaps of other

rational creatures. And an opponent could not prove that in all the City of God, composed as well of genii as of rational animals without number and of an infinity of kinds, evil exceeds good. And although in order to answer an objection, there is no need of proving that a thing is, when its mere possibility suffices; yet, in this work, I have not omitted to show that it is a consequence of the supreme perfection of the Sovereign of the universe, that the kingdom of God is the most perfect of all possible states or governments, and that consequently the little evil there is, is required for the consummation of the immense good which is found there.

Objection III

i.   If it is always impossible not to sin, it is always unjust to punish.

ii. Now, it is always impossible not to sin; or, in other words, every sin is necessary.

iii. Therefore, it is always unjust to punish.

The minor of this is proved thus:

First Prosyllogism

i.   All that is predetermined[8] is necessary.

ii. Every event is predetermined.

iii. Therefore, every event (and consequently sin also) is necessary.

Again this second minor is proved thus:

Second Prosyllogism

i.   That which is future, that which is foreseen, that which is involved in the causes, is predetermined.

ii. Every event is such.

iii. Therefore, every event is predetermined.

Answer

I admit in a certain sense the conclusion of the second prosyllogism, which is the minor of the first; but I shall deny the major of the first prosyllogism, namely, that every thing predetermined is necessary; understanding by the necessity of sinning, for example, or by the impossibility of not sinning, or of not

---

6   Good and religious people, with the assistance of divine entities like the Virgin Mary, can become as much like God (in goodness) as is possible for mere created beings.

7   Supernatural spirits, such as the various types of angels.

8   Predetermined means "fixed in advance." See Chapter 6 for more discussion.

performing any action, the necessity with which we are here concerned, that is, that which is essential and absolute, and which destroys the morality of an action and the justice of punishments. For if anyone understood another necessity or impossibility, namely, a necessity which should be only moral, or which was only hypothetical (as will be explained shortly); it is clear that I should deny the major of the objection itself. I might content myself with this answer and demand the proof of the proposition denied; but I have again desired to explain my procedure in this work, in order to better elucidate the matter and to throw more light on the whole subject, by explaining the necessity which ought to be rejected and the determination which must take place. That *necessity* which is contrary to morality and which ought to be rejected, and which would render punishment unjust, is an insurmountable necessity which would make all opposition useless, even if we should wish with all our heart to avoid the necessary action, and should make all possible efforts to that end. Now, it is manifest that this is not applicable to voluntary actions, because we would not perform them if we did not choose to. Also their prevision[9] and predetermination are not absolute, but presuppose the will: if it is certain that we shall perform them, it is not less certain that we shall choose to perform them. These voluntary actions and their consequences will not take place no matter what we do or whether we wish them or not; but, *through* that which we shall do and through that which we shall wish to do, which leads to them. And this is involved in prevision and in predetermination, and even constitutes their ground. And the necessity of such an event is called conditional or hypothetical, or the necessity of consequence, because it supposes the will, and the other *requisites*; whereas the necessity which destroys morality and renders punishment unjust and reward useless, exists in things which will be whatever we may do or whatever we may wish to do, and, in a word, is in that which is essential; and this is what is called an absolute necessity. Thus it is to no purpose, as regards what is absolutely necessary, to make prohibitions or commands, to propose pen-

alties or prizes, to praise or to blame; it will be none the less. On the other hand, in voluntary actions and in that which depends upon them, precepts[10] armed with power to punish and to recompense are very often of use and are included in the order of causes which make an action exist. And it is for this reason that not only cares and labours but also prayers are useful; God having had these prayers in view before he regulated things and having had that consideration for them which was proper. This is why the precept which says *ora et labora* (pray and work), holds altogether good; and not only those who (under the vain pretext of the necessity of events) pretend that the care which business demands may be neglected, but also those who reason against prayer, fall into what the ancients even then called the *lazy sophism*.[11] Thus the predetermination of events by causes is just what contributes to morality instead of destroying it, and causes incline the will, without compelling it. This is why the *determination* in question is not a necessitation—it is certain (to him who knows all) that the effect will follow this inclination; but this effect does not follow by a necessary consequence, that is, one the contrary of which implies contradiction. It is also by an internal inclination such as this that the will is determined, without there being any necessity. Suppose that one has the greatest passion in the world (a great thirst, for example), you will admit to me that the soul can find some reason for resisting it, if it were only that of showing its power. Thus, although one may never be in a perfect indifference of equilibrium and there may be always a preponderance of inclination for the side taken, it, nevertheless, never renders the resolution taken absolutely necessary.

---

9 Being seen (by God) before they happened.

10 Laws or principles.

11 The 'lazy sophism' was an argument for fatalism, proposed by the Stoic philosopher Chrysippus (280–208 BCE) and strongly criticized by the Roman poet and philosopher Cicero (106–43 BCE). It runs roughly as follows: Whatever will be, will be; Therefore nothing you can do will change things; Therefore any action to try to influence events is pointless—you might just as well do nothing.

Objection IV

i.   Whoever can prevent the sin of another and does not do so but rather contributes to it although he is well informed of it, is accessory to it.

ii.   God can prevent the sin of intelligent creatures; but he does not do so, and rather contributes to it by his concurrence[12] and by the opportunities which he brings about, although he has a perfect knowledge of it.

iii. Hence, etc.

Answer

I deny the major of this syllogism. For it is possible that one could prevent sin, but ought not, because he could not do it without himself committing a sin, or (when God is in question) without performing an unreasonable action. Examples have been given and the application to God himself has been made. It is possible also that we contribute to evil and that sometimes we even open the road to it, in doing things which we are obliged to do; and, when we do our duty or (in speaking of God) when, after thorough consideration, we do that which reason demands, we are not responsible for the results, even when we foresee them. We do not desire these evils; but we are willing to permit them for the sake of a greater good which we cannot reasonably help preferring to other considerations. And this is a *consequent* will, which results from *antecedent* wills by which we will the good. I know that some persons, in speaking of the antecedent and consequent will of God, have understood by the *antecedent* that which wills that all men should be saved; and by the *consequent*, that which wills, in consequence of persistent sin, that some should be damned. But these are merely illustrations of a more general idea, and it may be said for the same reason that God, by his antecedent will, wills that men should not sin; and by his consequent or final and decreeing will (that which is always followed by its effect), he wills to permit them to sin, this permission being the result of superior reasons. And we have the right to say in general that the antecedent will of God tends to the production of good and the prevention of evil, each taken in itself and as if alone (*particulariter et secundum quid*, Thom. I, qu. 19, art. 6),[13] according to the measure of the degree of each good and of each evil; but that the divine consequent or final or total will tends toward the production of as many goods as may be put together, the combination of which becomes in this way determined, and includes also the permission of some evils and the exclusion of some goods, as the best possible plan for the universe demands. Arminius,[14] in his *Anti-perkinsus*, has very well explained that the will of God may be called consequent, not only in relation to the action of the creature considered beforehand in the divine understanding, but also in relation to other anterior[15] divine acts of will. But this consideration of the passage cited from Thomas Aquinas, and that from Scotus (I. dist. 46, qu. XI),[16] is enough to show that they make this distinction as I have done here. Nevertheless, if anyone objects to this use of terms let him substitute *deliberating* will, in place of antecedent, and final or decreeing will, in place of consequent. For I do not wish to dispute over words.

Objection V

i.   Whoever produces all that is real in a thing, is its cause.

ii.   God produces all that is real in sin.

iii. Hence, God is the cause of sin.

---

12 God's maintaining things in existence by a kind of continuous divine act of will.

13 This is a reference to Part I, Question 19, article 6 of St. Thomas Aquinas' *Summa Theologiae*.

14 Jacob Arminius (1560–1609) was a Protestant Dutch theologian who rejected the doctrine of predestination—i.e., he denied that God has already decided who will be damned and who will be saved, even before they are born.

15 Earlier.

16 The Scottish philosopher and theologian John Duns (c. 1266–1308), who is usually referred to as Duns Scotus ("Duns the Scot"). The reference is to section 46 of the first part of Scotus' commentary on the *Sentences* by Peter Lombard.

Answer

I might content myself with denying the major or the minor, since the term *real* admits of interpretations which would render these propositions false. But in order to explain more clearly, I will make a distinction. *Real* signifies either that which is positive only, or, it includes also privative[17] beings: in the first case, I deny the major and admit the minor; in the second case, I do the contrary. I might have limited myself to this, but I have chosen to proceed still farther and give the reason for this distinction. I have been very glad therefore to draw attention to the fact that every reality purely positive or absolute is a perfection; and that imperfection comes from limitation, that is, from the privative: for to limit is to refuse progress, or the greatest possible progress. Now God is the cause of all perfections and consequently of all realities considered as purely positive. But limitations or privations result from the original imperfection of creatures, which limits their receptivity. And it is with them as with a loaded vessel, which the river causes to move more or less slowly according to the weight which it carries: thus its speed depends upon the river, but the retardation which limits this speed comes from the load. Thus in the *Theodicy*, we have shown how the creature, in causing sin, is a defective cause;[18] how errors and evil inclinations are born of privation; and how privation is accidentally efficient;[19] and I have

justified the opinion of St. Augustine (lib. I. *ad Simpl.* qu. 2)[20] who explains, for example, how God makes the soul obdurate,[21] not by giving it something evil, but because the effect of his good impression is limited by the soul's resistance and by the circumstances which contribute to this resistance, so that he does not give it all the good which would overcome its evil. *Nec* (inquit) *ab illo erogatur aliquid quo homo fit deterior, sed tantum quo fit melior non erogatur.*[22] But if God had wished to do more, he would have had to make either other natures for creatures or other miracles to change their natures, things which the best plan could not admit. It is as if the current of the river must be more rapid than its fall admitted or that the boats should be loaded more lightly, if it were necessary to make them move more quickly. And the original limitation or imperfection of creatures requires that even the best plan of the universe could not receive more good, and could not be exempt from certain evils, which, however, are to result in a greater good. There are certain disorders in the parts which marvellously enhance the beauty of the whole; just as certain dissonances, when properly used, render harmony more beautiful. But this depends on what has already been said in answer to the first objection.

Objection VI

i.   Whoever punishes those who have done as well as it was in their power to do, is unjust.
ii.   God does so.
iii. Hence, etc.

Answer

I deny the minor of this argument. And I believe that God always gives sufficient aid and grace to those

---

17   A privation is an absence, or lack, or some quality or attribute. In medieval terminology, "privation" was the name of the state in which matter was supposed to exist *before* the process of generation begins, which gives it some form or other—i.e., before the "stuff" of matter became stars, or rocks, or trees, or anything at all.

18   Caused by some defect or limitation, rather than by some "positive" quality of the creature.

19   Privation, or limitation, doesn't necessarily cause anything at all—it does not have an essential power to have effects (be 'efficient'). Instead, privation can 'accidentally' have certain effects due to the surrounding circumstances. (By analogy, a hole in the ground doesn't normally, by its nature, suck surrounding objects into it; but in certain circumstances—e.g., when combined with somebody who isn't looking where they're going—the hole can be a partial cause of an

object falling into it.)

20   A reference to question 2 of Book I of Augustine's work *To Simplicianus, On Seven Different Questions*, written in about 395 CE.

21   Stubbornly wicked.

22   "Nor (he says) is man provided by him [God] with anything by which he becomes worse, but it is only that there is not furnished that by which he becomes better."

who have a good will, that is, to those who do not reject this grace by new sin. Thus I do not admit the damnation of infants who have died without baptism or outside of the church; nor the damnation of adults who have acted according to the light which God has given them. And I believe that *if any one has followed the light which has been given him,* he will undoubtedly receive greater light when he has need of it, as the late M. Hulseman, a profound and celebrated theologian at Leipzig, has somewhere remarked; and if such a man has failed to receive it during his lifetime he will at least receive it when at the point of death.

Objection VII

i.   Whoever gives only to some, and not to all, the means which produces in them effectively a good will and salutary final faith, has not sufficient goodness.
ii.   God does this.
iii. Hence, etc.

Answer

I deny the major of this. It is true that God could overcome the greatest resistance of the human heart; and does it, too, sometimes, either by internal grace, or by external circumstances which have a great effect on souls; but he does not always do this. Whence comes this distinction? it may be asked, and why does his goodness seem limited? It is because, as I have already said in answering the first objection, it would not have been in order always to act in an extraordinary manner, and to reverse the connection of things. The reasons of this connection, by means of which one is placed in more favourable circumstances than another, are hidden in the depths of the wisdom of God: they depend upon the universal harmony. The best plan of the universe, which God could not fail to choose, made it so. We judge from the event itself; since God has made it, it was not possible to do better. Far from being true that this conduct is contrary to goodness, it is supreme goodness which led him to it. This objection with its solution might have been drawn from what was said in regard to the first objection; but it seemed useful to touch upon it separately.

Objection VIII

i.   Whoever cannot fail to choose the best, is not free.
ii.   God cannot fail to choose the best.
iii. Hence, God is not free.

Answer

I deny the major of this argument; it is rather true liberty, and the most perfect, to be able to use one's free will for the best, and to always exercise this power, without ever being turned aside either by external force or by internal passions, the first of which causes slavery of the body, the second, slavery of the soul. There is nothing less servile, and nothing more in accordance with the highest degree of freedom, than to be always led toward the good, and always by one's own inclination, without any constraint and without any displeasure. And to object therefore that God had need of external things, is only a sophism.[23] He created them freely; but having proposed to himself an end, which is to exercise his goodness, wisdom has determined him to choose the means best fitted to attain this end. To call this a need, is to take that term in an unusual sense which frees it from all imperfection, just as when we speak of the wrath of God.

Seneca[24] has somewhere said that God commanded but once but that he obeys always, because he obeys laws which he willed to prescribe to himself: *semel jussit, semper paret.*[25] But he might better have said that God always commands and that he is always obeyed; for in willing, he always follows the inclination of his own nature, and all other things always follow his will. And as this will is always the same, it cannot be said that he obeys only that will which he formerly had. Nevertheless, although his will is always infallible and always tends toward the best, the evil, or the lesser good, which he rejects, does not

---

23 An argument which seems valid on the surface but which actually isn't.

24 A Roman playwright, philosopher, and statesman, who lived from about 5 BCE to 65 CE. He was widely known for his ethical writings, and his death by suicide was taken as a model of Stoic virtuous action.

25 "He commanded once, but obeys always."

cease to be possible in itself; otherwise the necessity of the good would be geometrical[26] (so to speak), or metaphysical, and altogether absolute; the contingency of things would be destroyed, and there would be no choice. But this sort of necessity, which does not destroy the possibility of the contrary, has this name only by analogy; it becomes effective, not by the pure essence of things, but by that which is outside of them, above them, namely, by the will of God. This necessity is called moral, because, to the sage, *necessity* and *what ought to be* are equivalent things; and when it always has its effect, as it really has in the perfect sage, that is, in God, it may be said that it is a happy necessity. The nearer creatures approach to it, the nearer they approach to perfect happiness. Also this kind of necessity is not that which we try to avoid and which destroys morality, rewards and praise. For that which it brings, does not happen whatever we may do or will, but because we will it so. And a will to which it is natural to choose well, merits praise so much the more; also it carries its reward with it, which is sovereign happiness. And as this constitution of the divine nature gives entire satisfaction to him who possesses it, it is also the best and the most desirable for the creatures who are all dependent on God. If the will of God did not have for a rule the principle of the best, it would either tend toward evil, which would be the worst; or it would be in some way indifferent to good and to evil, and would be guided by chance: but a will which would allow itself always to act by chance, would not be worth more for the government of the universe than the fortuitous concourse[27] of atoms, without there being any divinity therein. And even if God should abandon himself to chance only in some cases and in a certain way (as he would do, if he did not always work entirely for the best and if he were capable of preferring a lesser work to a greater, that is, an evil to a good, since that which prevents a greater good is an evil), he would be imperfect, as well as the object of his choice; he would not merit entire confidence; he would act without reason in such a case, and the government of the universe would be like certain games, equally divided between reason and chance. All this proves that this objection which is made against the choice of the best, perverts the notions of the free and of the necessary, and represents to us the best even as evil: which is either malicious or ridiculous.

---

26 Mathematical.

27 "Fortuitous concourse" means "coming and moving together by chance."

J.L. MACKIE

"Evil and Omnipotence"

Who Was J.L. Mackie?

John Leslie Mackie was born in Sydney, Australia, in 1917 and educated at Sydney University and Oriel College, Oxford. After serving in the Australian army during the Second World War, he taught at Sydney University from 1946 to 1954 and then at Otago University in Dunedin, New Zealand. In 1963 he moved permanently to England, and from 1967 until his death in 1981 he was a Fellow of University College, Oxford. He wrote six books and many philosophical papers, mostly on topics in metaphysics, ethics, the history of philosophy, and the philosophy of religion.

Mackie is probably best known for his 'error theory' of moral values. This holds that:

(a)   There are no objective moral values.

(b)   All ordinary moral judgments include a claim to objectivity, and so,

(c)   All ordinary moral judgments are false.

Mackie therefore argued that morality is not discovered but is *created* by human beings. We should scrap traditional moral theory, he said, and, instead of treating moral theory as descriptive of moral facts, we should reinvent morality as a device for encouraging empathy with the points of view of others.

Mackie's work, like most Australian analytical philosophy of this century, is notable for its dislike of obfuscation and obscurantism, and for its careful attempts at clarity and precision. "Evil and Omnipotence" is well known as probably the best short modern defense of an argument called 'the problem of evil.'

What Is the Structure of This Reading?

Mackie begins by introducing an argument against the existence of God (or, at least, of God as traditionally conceived) called 'the problem of evil.' He lays out its logical form (as a paradox), and tries to make clear its theological importance. He briefly discusses a kind of response to this paradox which he does think is adequate, but claims that such a response would be unacceptable to those who believe in God. Believers must thus attempt to give other solutions to the paradox, but Mackie argues that all of these attempts fail (and, he suggests, typically only seem as plausible as they do because of their vagueness and lack of clarity).

First, there are "half-hearted" responses which, Mackie says, really fail to address the problem. Then there are four more serious responses: (1) good cannot exist without evil; (2) evil is necessary as a means to good; (3) the universe is better with some evil in it;

(4) evil is due to human free will. (These responses fall naturally into two groups: 1 and 2, and 3 and 4.) Mackie argues carefully that all four of these responses to the problem of evil are fallacious.

In the course of his attack on the free-will response to the problem of evil, Mackie develops a further argument which he calls "the Paradox of Omnipotence." He argues that this paradox shows it is *logically impossible* that any (temporal) being could exist which had absolutely unlimited power.

The upshot of all this, Mackie concludes, is that God (as he is described by, say, Christianity) cannot possibly exist.

Some Useful Background Information

When Mackie talks about 'evil' in this article, he follows normal philosophical usage in this context. In everyday language the word "evil" tends to suggest an especially wicked kind of moral badness; however, the 'problem of evil,' though it certainly includes extreme ethical badness, is much broader in its scope than that. It's important to realize that, according to the argument from evil, any kind of 'sub-optimality' can be a problem for the existence of God. Therefore examples of 'evil' range along the spectrum from such mild harms as a nasty pimple, a job that does not give 100% satisfaction, or a mountain that would be just a little more beautiful if it were a slightly different shape, right up to major earthquakes, epidemics, and oil spills in the Alaskan wilderness. Moral 'evils' can be as minor as breaking a trivial promise or making a slightly cutting remark, or as serious as rape, torture, and genocide.

A Common Misconception

Mackie is not arguing that God does not exist: he is arguing that nothing like the *theistic conception* of

God can exist. That is, although some sort of God—perhaps an extremely powerful but somehow limited being, like say the classical Greek god Zeus—can escape the problem of evil, the sort of God envisaged by the main monotheistic religions such as Christianity, Judaism, and Islam cannot possibly be real. For many if not most of the people who believe in God, this is not a trivial conclusion: if it is a sound argument, the problem of evil shows that God, if he exists at all, must be either limited in his power, or limited in his knowledge, or not entirely morally good.

Suggestions for Critical Reflection

1. Why do responses like "Evil is something to be faced and overcome, not to be merely discussed" or "God works in mysterious ways, but I have faith" fail to deal rationally with the problem of evil (if they do)?

2. What do you think goodness is? Do you think evil is merely the absence of goodness (or vice versa) or, can something be neither good nor evil (nor both)?

3. Is the universe better with some evil in it than it would be without any? (For example, do you think a life of successful struggle against adversity is more valuable than one of uninterrupted pleasure? If so, why?) What do you make of Mackie's arguments against this claim?

4. Could all evil be due to human free will? If even some of it is, should God have given us free will (if he did)? Is it coherent to think that God could have made us so that we have free will but nevertheless always choose some particular option (the best one) on every occasion?

5. Do you agree that the notion of omnipotence must have some limits? For example, could God have made the number two smaller than the number one, or created things that are neither rocks nor non-rocks, or made violent rape a moral duty? If even an "omnipotent" deity must be restricted in these ways, how serious a problem is this for the traditional picture of God? How much does Mackie's "paradox of omnipotence" add to these worries?

Suggestions for Further Reading

Mackie's main book on philosophy of religion is *The Miracle of Theism* (1982), where he considers and rejects the main arguments for the existence of God. His two best-known books in other areas of philosophy are *The Cement of the Universe* (Oxford University Press, 1974), which is about causation, and *Ethics: Inventing Right and Wrong* (Penguin, 1977), which develops his "error theory" of morality.

There are several recent books on the problem of evil, including Michael Peterson, *God and Evil: An Introduction to the Issues* (Westview Press, 1998), Alvin Plantinga *God, Freedom and Evil* (William B. Eerdmans, 1978), and Richard Swinburne, *Providence and the Problem of Evil* (Oxford University Press, 1998). Three useful collections of readings are Mark Larrimore (ed.), *The Problem of Evil: A Reader* (Blackwell, 2000), M.M. Adams and R.M. Adams (eds.), *The Problem of Evil* (Oxford University Press, 1990), and Michael Petersen (ed.), *The Problem of Evil: Selected Readings* (University of Notre Dame Press, 1992).

"Evil and Omnipotence"[1]

The traditional arguments for the existence of God have been fairly thoroughly criticised by philosophers. But the theologian can, if he wishes, accept this criticism. He can admit that no rational proof of God's existence is possible. And he can still retain all that is essential to his position, by holding that God's existence is known in some other, non-rational way. I think, however, that a more telling criticism can be made by way of the traditional problem of evil. Here it can be shown, not that religious beliefs lack rational support, but that they are positively irrational, that the several parts of the essential theological doctrine are inconsistent with one another, so that the theologian can maintain his position as a whole only by a much more extreme rejection of reason than in the former

---

1   This article was originally published in 1955 in the journal *Mind* (New Series, Vol. 64, Issue 254, April 1955, pp. 200–212). By permission of Oxford University Press.

case. He must now be prepared to believe, not merely what cannot be proved, but what can be *disproved* from other beliefs that he also holds.

The problem of evil, in the sense in which I shall be using the phrase, is a problem only for someone who believes that there is a God who is both omnipotent[2] and wholly good. And it is a logical problem, the problem of clarifying and reconciling a number of beliefs: it is not a scientific problem that might be solved by further observations, or a practical problem that might be solved by a decision or an action. These points are obvious; I mention them only because they are sometimes ignored by theologians, who sometimes parry a statement of the problem with such remarks as "Well, can you solve the problem yourself?" or "This is a mystery which may be revealed to us later," or "Evil is something to be faced and overcome, not to be merely discussed."

In its simplest form the problem is this: God is omnipotent; God is wholly good; and yet evil exists. There seems to be some contradiction between these three propositions, so that if any two of them were true the third would be false. But at the same time all three are essential parts of most theological positions: the theologian, it seems, at once *must* adhere and *cannot consistently* adhere to all three. (The problem does not arise only for theists,[3] but I shall discuss it in the form in which it presents itself for ordinary theism.)

However, the contradiction does not arise immediately; to show it we need some additional premises, or perhaps some quasi-logical rules connecting the terms 'good', 'evil', and 'omnipotent'. These additional principles are that good is opposed to evil, in such a way that a good thing always eliminates evil as far as it can, and that there are no limits to what an omnipotent thing can do. From these it follows that a good omnipotent thing eliminates evil completely, and then the propositions that a good omnipotent thing exists, and that evil exists, are incompatible.

A. Adequate Solutions

Now once the problem is fully stated it is clear that it can be solved, in the sense that the problem will not arise if one gives up at least one of the propositions that constitute it. If you are prepared to say that God is not wholly good, or not quite omnipotent, or that evil does not exist, or that good is not opposed to the kind of evil that exists, or that there are limits to what an omnipotent thing can do, then the problem of evil will not arise for you.

There are, then, quite a number of adequate solutions of the problem of evil, and some of these have been adopted, or almost adopted, by various thinkers. For example, a few have been prepared to deny God's omnipotence, and rather more have been prepared to keep the term 'omnipotence' but severely to restrict its meaning, recording quite a number of things that an omnipotent being cannot do. Some have said that evil is an illusion, perhaps because they held that the whole world of temporal, changing things is an illusion, and that what we call evil belongs only to this world, or perhaps because they held that although temporal things are much as we see them, those that we call evil are not really evil. Some have said that what we call evil is merely the privation of good, that evil in a positive sense, evil that would really be opposed to good, does not exist. Many have agreed with Pope[4] that disorder is harmony not understood, and that partial evil is universal good. Whether any of these views is true is, of course, another question. But each of them gives an adequate solution of the problem of evil in the sense that if you accept it this problem does not arise for you, though you may, of course, have *other* problems to face.

---

2   "Omnipotent" means all-powerful; able to do anything at all. (Or at least anything that is not logically incoherent: God could make pigs fly, but even God, perhaps, could not make a male vixen or create a leaf that is—at the same time—both entirely green and not entirely green. This issue is discussed later in the article.)

3   For those who believe in one, powerful, benevolent God who created and watches over the universe.

4   Alexander Pope (1688–1744), an English writer best known for his mock-epic poems such as *The Rape of the Lock*. This quotation comes from Pope's *Essay on Man*, Epistle I: "All nature is but art, unknown to thee; All chance, direction, which thou canst not see; All discord, harmony, not understood; All partial evil, universal good: And, spite of pride, in erring reason's spite, One truth is clear, Whatever is, is right."

But often enough these adequate solutions are only *almost* adopted. The thinkers who restrict God's power, but keep the term 'omnipotence', may reasonably be suspected of thinking, in other contexts, that his power is really unlimited. Those who say that evil is an illusion may also be thinking, inconsistently, that this illusion is itself an evil. Those who say that "evil" is merely privation of good may also be thinking, inconsistently, that privation of good is an evil. (The fallacy here is akin to some forms of the "naturalistic fallacy" in ethics,[5] where some think, for example, that "good" is just what contributes to evolutionary progress, and that evolutionary progress is itself good.) If Pope meant what he said in the first line of his couplet, that "disorder" is only harmony not understood, the "partial evil" of the second line must, for consistency, mean "that which, taken in isolation, falsely appears to be evil", but it would more naturally mean "that which, in isolation, really is evil". The second line, in fact, hesitates between two views, that "partial evil" isn't really evil, since only the universal quality is real, and that "partial evil" is really an evil, but only a little one.

In addition, therefore, to adequate solutions, we must recognise unsatisfactory inconsistent solutions, in which there is only a half-hearted or temporary rejection of one of the propositions which together constitute the problem. In these, one of the constituent propositions is explicitly rejected, but it is covertly re-asserted or assumed elsewhere in the system.

B. Fallacious Solutions

Besides these half-hearted solutions, which explicitly reject but implicitly assert one of the constituent propositions, there are definitely fallacious solutions which explicitly maintain all the constituent propositions, but implicitly reject at least one of them in the course of the argument that explains away the problem of evil.

There are, in fact, many so-called solutions which purport to remove the contradiction without abandoning any of its constituent propositions. These must

---

5   This is the alleged fallacy of identifying an ethical concept with a "natural" (i.e., non-moral) notion, such as analyzing moral goodness as evolutionary fitness or the sensation of pleasure.

be fallacious, as we can see from the very statement of the problem, but it is not so easy to see in each case precisely where the fallacy lies. I suggest that in all cases the fallacy has the general form suggested above: in order to solve the problem one (or perhaps more) of its constituent propositions is given up, but in such a way that it appears to have been retained, and can therefore be asserted without qualification in other contexts. Sometimes there is a further complication: the supposed solution moves to and fro between, say, two of the constituent propositions, at one point asserting the first of these but covertly abandoning the second, at another point asserting the second but covertly abandoning the first. These fallacious solutions often turn upon some equivocation with the words 'good' and 'evil', or upon some vagueness about the way in which good and evil are opposed to one another, or about how much is meant by 'omnipotence'. I propose to examine some of these so-called solutions, and to exhibit their fallacies in detail. Incidentally, I shall also be considering whether an adequate solution could be reached by a minor modification of one or more of the constituent propositions, which would, however, still satisfy all the essential requirements of ordinary theism.

1. "Good cannot exist without evil" or "Evil is necessary as a counterpart to good."

It is sometimes suggested that evil is necessary as a counterpart to good, that if there were no evil there could be no good either, and that this solves the problem of evil. It is true that it points to an answer to the question "Why should there be evil?" But it does so only by qualifying some of the propositions that constitute the problem.

First, it sets a limit to what God can do, saying that God cannot create good without simultaneously creating evil, and this means either that God is not omnipotent or that there are some limits to what an omnipotent thing can do. It may be replied that these limits are always presupposed, that omnipotence has never meant the power to do what is logically impossible, and on the present view the existence of good without evil would be a logical impossibility. This interpretation of omnipotence may, indeed, be accepted as a modification of our original account which does not reject anything that is essential to theism, and I shall in general assume it in the subsequent discussion. It is, perhaps, the most common theistic view, but I think that some theists at least have maintained that God can do what is logically impossible. Many theists, at any rate, have held that logic itself is created or laid down by God, that logic is the way in which God arbitrarily chooses to think. (This is, of course, parallel to the ethical view that morally right actions are those which God arbitrarily chooses to command, and the two views encounter similar difficulties.[6]) And *this* account of logic is clearly inconsistent with the view that God is bound by logical necessities—unless it is possible for an omnipotent being to bind himself, an issue which we shall consider later, when we come to the Paradox of Omnipotence. This solution of the problem of evil cannot, therefore, be consistently adopted along with the view that logic is itself created by God.

But, secondly, this solution denies that evil is opposed to good in our original sense. If good and evil are counterparts, a good thing will not "eliminate evil as far as it can." Indeed, this view suggests that good and evil are not strictly qualities of things at all. Perhaps the suggestion is that good and evil are related in much the same way as great and small. Certainly, when the term 'great' is used relatively as a condensation of 'greater than so-and-so', and 'small' is used correspondingly, greatness and smallness are counterparts and cannot exist without each other. But in this sense greatness is not a quality, not an intrinsic feature of anything; and it would be absurd to think of a movement in favour of greatness and against smallness in this sense. Such a movement would be self-defeating, since relative greatness can be promoted only by a simultaneous promotion of relative smallness. I feel sure that no theists would be content to regard God's goodness as analogous to this—as if what he supports were not the *good* but the *better*, and as if he had the paradoxical aim that all things should be better than other things.

This point is obscured by the fact that 'great' and 'small' seem to have an absolute as well as a relative

sense. I cannot discuss here whether there is absolute magnitude or not, but if there is, there could be an absolute sense for 'great', it could mean of at least a certain size, and it would make sense to speak of all things getting bigger, of a universe that was expanding all over, and therefore it would make sense to speak of promoting greatness. But in *this* sense great and small are not logically necessary counterparts: either quality could exist without the other. There would be no logical impossibility in everything's being small or in everything's being great.

Neither in the absolute nor in the relative sense, then, of 'great' and 'small' do these terms provide an analogy of the sort that would be needed to support this solution of the problem of evil. In neither case are greatness and smallness both necessary counterparts and mutually opposed forces or possible objects for support and attack.

It may be replied that good and evil are necessary counterparts in the same way as any quality and its logical opposite: redness can occur, it is suggested, only if non-redness also occurs. But unless evil is merely the privation of good, they are not logical opposites, and some further argument would be needed to show that they are counterparts in the same way as genuine logical opposites. Let us assume that this could be given. There is still doubt of the correctness of the metaphysical principle that a quality must have a real opposite: I suggest that it is not really impossible that everything should be, say, red, that the truth is merely that if everything were red we should not notice redness, and so we should have no word 'red'; we observe and give names to qualities only if they have real opposites. If so, the principle that a term must have an opposite would belong only to our language or to our thought, and would not be an ontological principle,[7] and, correspondingly, the rule that good cannot exist without evil would not state a logical necessity of a sort that God would just have to put up with. God might have made everything good, though we should not have noticed it if he had.

But, finally, even if we concede that this is an ontological principle, it will provide a solution for the problem of evil only if one is prepared to say,

---

6   This ethical view is often called Divine Command Theory, and the usual label for its main problem is "the Euthyphro Dilemma" (from a dialogue by Plato in which the problem is first raised).

---

7   That is, not a principle constraining what exists.

"Evil exists, but only just enough evil to serve as the counterpart of good." I doubt whether any theist will accept this. After all, the *ontological* requirement that non-redness should occur would be satisfied even if all the universe, except for a minute speck, were red, and, if there were a corresponding requirement for evil as a counterpart to good, a minute dose of evil would presumably do. But theists are not usually willing to say, in all contexts, that all the evil that occurs is a minute and necessary dose.

2. "Evil is necessary as a means to good."

It is sometimes suggested that evil is necessary for good not as a counterpart but as a means. In its simple form this has little plausibility as a solution of the problem of evil, since it obviously implies a severe restriction of God's power. It would be a causal law that you cannot have a certain end without a certain means, so that if God has to introduce evil as a means to good, he must be subject to at least some causal laws. This certainly conflicts with what a theist normally means by omnipotence. This view of God as limited by causal laws also conflicts with the view that causal laws are themselves made by God, which is more widely held than the corresponding view about the laws of logic. This conflict would, indeed; be resolved if it were possible for an omnipotent being to bind himself, and this possibility has still to be considered. Unless a favourable answer can be given to this question, the suggestion that evil is necessary as a means to good solves the problem of evil only by denying one of its constituent propositions, either that God is omnipotent or that 'omnipotent' means what it says.

3. "The universe is better with some evil in it than it could be if there were no evil."

Much more important is a solution which at first seems to be a mere variant of the previous one, that evil may contribute to the goodness of a whole in which it is found, so that the universe as a whole is better as it is, with some evil in it, than it would be if there were no evil. This solution may be developed in either of two ways. It may be supported by an aesthetic analogy, by the fact that contrasts heighten beauty, that in a musical work, for example, there may occur discords which somehow add to the beauty of the work as a whole. Alternatively, it may be worked out in connexion with the notion of progress, that the best possible organisation of the universe will not be static, but progressive, that the gradual overcoming of evil by good is really a finer thing than would be the eternal unchallenged supremacy of good.

In either case, this solution usually starts from the assumption that the evil whose existence gives rise to the problem of evil is primarily what is called physical evil, that is to say, pain. In Hume's rather half-hearted presentation of the problem of evil, the evils that he stresses are pain and disease, and those who reply to him argue that the existence of pain and disease makes possible the existence of sympathy, benevolence, heroism, and the gradually successful struggle of doctors and reformers to overcome these evils. In fact, theists often seize the opportunity to accuse those who stress the problem of evil of taking a low, materialistic view of good and evil, equating these with pleasure and pain, and of ignoring the more spiritual goods which can arise in the struggle against evils.

But let us see exactly what is being done here. Let us call pain and misery 'first order evil' or 'evil (1)'. What contrasts with this, namely, pleasure and happiness, will be called 'first order good' or 'good (1)'. Distinct from this is 'second order good' or 'good (2)' which somehow emerges in a complex situation in which evil (1) is a necessary component—logically, not merely causally, necessary. (Exactly *how* it emerges does not matter: in the crudest version of this solution good (2) is simply the heightening of happiness by the contrast with misery, in other versions it includes sympathy with suffering, heroism in facing danger, and the gradual decrease of first order evil and increase of first order good.) It is also being assumed that second order good is more important than first order good or evil, in particular that it more than outweighs the first order evil it involves.

Now this is a particularly subtle attempt to solve the problem of evil. It defends God's goodness and omnipotence on the ground that (on a sufficiently long view) this is the best of all logically possible worlds, because it includes the important second order goods, and yet it admits that real evils, namely first order evils, exist. But does it still hold that good and evil are opposed? Not, clearly, in the sense that we set out originally: good does not tend to eliminate evil in general. Instead, we have a modified, a more complex pattern. First order good (e.g., happiness) *contrasts with* first order evil (e.g., misery): these two are opposed in a fairly mechanical way; some second order goods (e.g., benevolence) try to maximise first order good and minimise first order evil; but God's goodness is not this, it is rather the will to maximise *second* order good. We might, therefore, call God's goodness an example of a third order goodness, or good (3). While this account is different from our original one, it might well be held to be an improvement on it, to give a more accurate description of the way in which good is opposed to evil, and to be consistent with the essential theist position.

There might, however, be several objections to this solution. First, some might argue that such qualities as benevolence—and *a fortiori*[8] the third order goodness which promotes benevolence—have a merely derivative value, that they are not higher sorts of good, but merely means to good (1), that is, to happiness, so that it would be absurd for God to keep misery in existence in order to make possible the virtues of benevolence, heroism, etc. The theist who adopts the present solution must, of course, deny this, but he can do so with some plausibility, so I should not press this objection.

Secondly, it follows from this solution that God is not in our sense benevolent or sympathetic: he is not concerned to minimise evil (1), but only to promote good (2); and this might be a disturbing conclusion for some theists.

But, thirdly, the fatal objection is this. Our analysis shows clearly the possibility of the existence of a *second* order evil, an evil (2) contrasting with good (2) as evil (1) contrasts with good (1). This would include malevolence, cruelty, callousness, cowardice, and states in which good (1) is decreasing and evil (1) increasing. And just as good (2) is held to be the important kind of good, the kind that God is concerned to promote, so evil (2) will, by analogy, be the important kind of evil, the kind which God, if he were wholly good and omnipotent, would eliminate. And yet evil (2) plainly exists, and indeed most theists (in other contexts) stress its existence more than that of evil

(1). We should, therefore, state the problem of evil in terms of second order evil, and against this form of the problem the present solution is useless.

An attempt might be made to use this solution again, at a higher level, to explain the occurrence of evil (2): indeed the next main solution that we shall examine does just this, with the help of some new notions. Without any fresh notions, such a solution would have little plausibility: for example, we could hardly say that the really important good was a good (3), such as the increase of benevolence in proportion to cruelty, which logically required for its occurrence the occurrence of some second order evil. But even if evil (2) could be explained in this way, it is fairly clear that there would be third order evils contrasting with this third order good: and we should be well on the way to an infinite regress, where the solution of a problem of evil, stated in terms of evil (n), indicated the existence of an evil (n + 1), and a further problem to be solved.

4. "Evil is due to human freewill."

Perhaps the most important proposed solution of the problem of evil is that evil is not to be ascribed to God at all, but to the independent actions of human beings, supposed to have been endowed by God with freedom of the will. This solution may be combined with the preceding one: first order evil (e.g., pain) may be justified as a logically necessary component in second order good (e.g., sympathy) while second order evil (e.g., cruelty) is not *justified*, but is so ascribed to human beings that God cannot be held responsible for it. This combination evades my third criticism of the preceding solution.

The freewill solution also involves the preceding solution at a higher level. To explain why a wholly good God gave men freewill although it would lead to some important evils, it must be argued that it is better on the whole that men should act freely, and sometimes err, than that they should be innocent automata, acting rightly in a wholly determined way. Freedom, that is to say, is now treated as a third order good, and as being more valuable than second order goods (such as sympathy and heroism) would be if they were deterministically produced, and it is being assumed that second order evils, such as cruelty, are logically necessary accompaniments of freedom,

---

8   All the more, for an even stronger reason.

just as pain is a logically necessary pre-condition of sympathy.

I think that this solution is unsatisfactory primarily because of the incoherence of the notion of freedom of the will: but I cannot discuss this topic adequately here, although some of my criticisms will touch upon it.

First I should query the assumption that second order evils are logically necessary accompaniments of freedom. I should ask this: if God has made men such that in their free choices they sometimes prefer what is good and sometimes what is evil, why could he not have made men such that they always freely choose the good? If there is no logical impossibility in a man's freely choosing the good on one, or on several, occasions, there cannot be a logical impossibility in his freely choosing the good on every occasion. God was not, then, faced with a choice between making innocent automata and making beings who, in acting freely, would sometimes go wrong: there was open to him the obviously better possibility of making beings who would act freely but always go right. Clearly, his failure to avail himself of this possibility is inconsistent with his being both omnipotent and wholly good.

If it is replied that this objection is absurd, that the making of some wrong choices is logically necessary for freedom, it would seem that 'freedom' must here mean complete randomness or indeterminacy, including randomness with regard to the alternatives good and evil, in other words that men's choices and consequent actions can be "free" only if they are not determined by their characters. Only on this assumption can God escape the responsibility for men's actions; for if he made them as they are, but did not determine their wrong choices, this can only be because the wrong choices are not determined by men as they are. But then if freedom is randomness, how can it be a characteristic of *will*? And, still more, how can it be the most important good? What value or merit would there be in free choices if these were random actions which were not determined by the nature of the agent?

I conclude that to make this solution plausible two different senses of 'freedom' must be confused, one sense which will justify the view that freedom is a third order good, more valuable than other goods

would be without it, and another sense, sheer randomness, to prevent us from ascribing to God a decision to make men such that they sometimes go wrong when he might have made them such that they would always freely go right.

This criticism is sufficient to dispose of this solution. But besides this there is a fundamental difficulty in the notion of an omnipotent God creating men with free will, for if men's wills are really free this must mean that even God cannot control them, that is, that God is no longer omnipotent. It may be objected that God's gift of freedom to men does not mean that he cannot control their wills, but that he always *refrains* from controlling their wills. But why, we may ask, should God refrain from controlling evil wills? Why should he not leave men free to will rightly, but intervene when he sees them beginning to will wrongly? If God could do this, but does not, and if he is wholly good, the only explanation could be that even a wrong free act of will is not really evil, that its freedom is a value which outweighs its wrongness, so that there would be a loss of value if God took away the wrongness and the freedom together. But this is utterly opposed to what theists say about sin in other contexts. The present solution of the problem of evil, then, can be maintained only in the form that God has made men so free that he *cannot* control their wills.

This leads us to what I call the Paradox of Omnipotence: can an omnipotent being make things which he cannot subsequently control? Or, what is practically equivalent to this, can an omnipotent being make rules which then bind himself? (These are practically equivalent because any such rules could be regarded as setting certain things beyond his control, and *vice versa*.) The second of these formulations is relevant to the suggestions that we have already met, that an omnipotent God creates the rules of logic or causal laws, and is then bound by them.

It is clear that this is a paradox: the questions cannot be answered satisfactorily either in the affirmative or in the negative. If we answer "Yes", it follows that if God actually makes things which he cannot control, or makes rules which bind himself, he is not omnipotent once he has made them: there are *then* things which he cannot do. But if we answer "No", we are immediately asserting that there are things which he cannot do, that is to say that he is already not omnipotent.

It cannot be replied that the question which sets this paradox is not a proper question. It would make perfectly good sense to say that a human mechanic has made a machine which he cannot control: if there is any difficulty about the question it lies in the notion of omnipotence itself.

This, incidentally, shows that although we have approached this paradox from the free will theory, it is equally a problem for a theological determinist. No one thinks that machines have free will, yet they may well be beyond the control of their makers. The determinist might reply that anyone who makes anything determines its ways of acting, and so determines its subsequent behaviour: even the human mechanic does this by his *choice* of materials and structure for his machine, though he does not know all about either of these: the mechanic thus determines, though he may not foresee, his machine's actions. And since God is omniscient, and since his creation of things is total, he both determines and foresees the ways in which his creatures will act. We may grant this, but it is beside the point. The question is not whether God *originally* determined the future actions of his creatures, but whether he can *subsequently* control their actions, or whether he was able in his original creation to put things beyond his subsequent control. Even on determinist principles the answers "Yes" and "No" are equally irreconcilable with God's omnipotence.

Before suggesting a solution of this paradox, I would point out that there is a parallel Paradox of Sovereignty. Can a legal sovereign[9] make a law restricting its own future legislative power? For example, could the British parliament make a law forbidding any future parliament to socialise banking, and also forbidding the future repeal of this law itself? Or could the British parliament, which was legally sovereign in Australia in, say, 1899, pass a valid law, or series of laws, which made it no longer sovereign in 1933? Again, neither the affirmative nor the negative answer is really satisfactory. If we were to answer "Yes", we

should be admitting the validity of a law which, if it were actually made, would mean that parliament was, no longer sovereign. If we were to answer "No", we should be admitting that there is a law, not logically absurd, which parliament cannot validly make, that is, that parliament is not now a legal sovereign. This paradox can be solved in the following way. We should distinguish between first order laws, that is laws governing the actions of individuals and bodies other than the legislature, and second order laws, that is laws about laws, laws governing the actions of the legislature itself. Correspondingly, we should distinguish two orders of sovereignty, first order sovereignty (sovereignty (1)) which is unlimited authority to make first order laws, and second order sovereignty (sovereignty (2)) which is unlimited authority to make second order laws. If we say that parliament is sovereign we might mean that any parliament at any time has sovereignty (1), or we might mean that parliament has both sovereignty (1) and sovereignty (2) at present, but we cannot without contradiction mean both that the present parliament has sovereignty (2) and that every parliament at every time has sovereignty (1), for if the present parliament has sovereignty (2) it may use it to take away the sovereignty (1) of later parliaments. What the paradox shows is that we cannot ascribe to any continuing institution legal sovereignty in an inclusive sense.

The analogy between omnipotence and sovereignty shows that the paradox of omnipotence can be solved in a similar way. We must distinguish between first order omnipotence (omnipotence (1)), that is unlimited power to act, and second order omnipotence (omnipotence (2)), that is unlimited power to determine what powers to act things shall have. Then we could consistently say that God all the time has omnipotence (1), but if so no beings at any time have powers to act independently of God. Or we could say that God at one time had omnipotence (2), and used it to assign independent powers to act to certain things, so that God thereafter did not have omnipotence (1). But what the paradox shows is that we cannot consistently ascribe to any continuing being omnipotence in an inclusive sense.

An alternative solution of this paradox would be simply to deny that God is a continuing being, that any

---

9   To be sovereign is to exercise supreme, permanent authority.

times can be assigned to his actions at all. But on this assumption (which also has difficulties of its own) no meaning can be given to the assertion that God made men with wills so free that he could not control them. The paradox of omnipotence can be avoided by putting God outside time, but the freewill solution of the problem of evil cannot be saved in this way, and equally it remains impossible to hold that an omnipotent God *binds himself* by causal or logical laws.

Conclusion

Of the proposed solutions of the problem of evil which we have examined, none has stood up to criticism.

There may be other solutions which require examination, but this study strongly suggests that there is no valid solution of the problem which does not modify at least one of the constituent propositions in a way which would seriously affect the essential core of the theistic position.

Quite apart from the problem of evil, the paradox of omnipotence has shown that God's omnipotence must in any case be restricted in one way or another, that unqualified omnipotence cannot be ascribed to any being that continues through time. And if God and his actions are not in time, can omnipotence, or power of any sort, be meaningfully ascribed to him?

WILLIAM JAMES
"The Will to Believe"

Who Was William James?

William James was a popular essayist, one of the philosophical originators of pragmatism (often considered the first uniquely American philosophy), and one of the founders of academic psychology in America. He was born in 1842 in a New York hotel room. His family lived on a substantial inheritance from William's paternal grandfather (after whom he was named), and his father spent his time in the independent study of theology. Shortly after the birth of William's brother Henry—who was to become a famous writer, author of *The Portrait of a Lady* and *The Bostonians*—the family moved to Europe, living in London, Paris, and Windsor. There, while William was still a young boy, his father had a violent nervous breakdown and found solace in religious mysticism and the "theosophy" of Emanuel Swedenborg.[1] The family sailed back to New

York in 1847, only to return to Europe seven years later in search of a good education for the children: William was educated at a multilingual boarding school near Geneva, the Collège Impérial at Boulogne, and finally the University of Geneva.

As a young man, James was interested in science and painting. Back in Newport, Rhode Island, he embarked on a career as a painter, but quickly switched to the study of chemistry at Harvard in 1861. By then James had already begun his life-long habit of ingesting various, often hallucinogenic, chemicals (such as chloral hydrate, amyl nitrate, or mescaline) out of a scientific interest to see what effect they might have on him. After helping to care for his younger brother Wilky, badly wounded during the Civil War (during and after which the James family made attempts to help the black slaves of the South),

---

1   Swedenborg (1688–1772) was a Swedish scientist who came to believe that, by a special dispensation from God, his mind had been opened to "the other world" so that he could gain knowledge of it and its spiritual

inhabitants, and use this knowledge in a special interpretation of Christian scripture. He was an important influence on the artists William Blake and W.B. Yeats, as well as on the James family.

James entered Harvard Medical School in 1864. He took part in a scientific expedition to Brazil the following year, but was badly seasick on the trip out and suffered temporary blindness from catching a mild form of smallpox in Rio de Janeiro (he suffered from intermittent trouble with his eyes for the rest of his life). Though he decided at that point that he was "cut out for a speculative rather than an active life," he stayed with the expedition as it sailed up the Amazon. Back in Massachusetts, he continued to suffer from ill health and depression, and contemplated suicide.

He spent the period between 1867 and 1868 studying experimental psychology in Germany, and returned to Harvard to take and pass his examination for an MD but then sank into black depression, including bouts of insomnia and nervousness. He resolved never to marry for fear of passing mental illness on to his children. One of the causes of his depression in these years was his inability either to convince himself that modern science had not proved that free will was an illusion, or to resign himself to living in a deterministic, mechanical universe. Famously, in 1870, he apparently decided to shake off this particular worry and simply to decide to believe in free will *despite* all the evidence against it: he wrote in his diary, "my first act of free will shall be to believe in free will." Nevertheless, in 1872 James had a "crisis" which probably resembled that which changed his father's life 28 years earlier: "Suddenly there fell upon me without any warning, just as if it came out of the darkness, a horrible fear of my own existence.... I became a mass of quivering fear. After this the universe was changed for me altogether...."

Probably a psychological lifeline for James at this point was the offer in 1873 to teach compara-tive anatomy and physiology at Harvard (though he hesitated over accepting it, and delayed taking up the appointment for a year due to ill health). By 1877 James was a permanent professor of physiology at Harvard, though he lectured less on physiology than on the relatively new subject of psychology under the auspices of the philosophy department. In 1878 he married Alice Gibbens; "I have found in marriage a calm and repose I never knew before." His first son, Harry, was born the following year.

In 1889 he became the first Alford Professor of Psychology at Harvard University, and the next year he finally completed his first major work, *The Principles of Psychology* (he had signed the book contract in 1878). This book, a modern-day classic, met with instant acclaim. In 1897 he published *The Will to Believe, and Other Essays in Popular Psychology* and the next year, *Human Immortality: Two Supposed Objections to the Doctrine,* then, in 1899, one of his most popular books during his own lifetime *Talks to Teachers on Psychology, and to Students on Some of Life's Ideals.* The 1902 publication of *The Varieties of Religious Experience* met with international praise and sales that substantially boosted James's income.

Throughout his life James's work was dogged by persistent health problems and nervous exhaustion, and in 1903 he tried to resign from Harvard but was persuaded to stay with a reduced teaching load. In 1906 James took a temporary appointment at Stanford University in California, but it was cut short by the great San Francisco earthquake of that year (which James witnessed, and apparently found quite exhilarating). In 1907 he finally retired from Harvard and published *Pragmatism: A New Name for Some Old Ways of Thinking;* this is arguably the most famous single work of American philosophy. That book was followed by *A Pluralistic Universe*, *The Meaning of Truth,* and the posthumous *Some Problems in Philosophy*, all of which try to develop and defend James's overall philosophical framework. James died of a chronic heart condition at his farmhouse in New Hampshire in 1910.

What Was James's Overall Philosophical Project?

James's philosophical work, including "The Will to Believe" and his other essays on religious belief, are rooted in a general metaphysical framework which James came to call "radical empiricism." Radical empiricism has three central elements, each of which has far-reaching philosophical implications.

First, there is James's emphasis on careful attention to what is "directly experienced." He thought philosophers and psychologists had generally failed to look carefully enough at what is actually delivered in experience, and to counteract this he defended what is called "the introspective method" in psychology—essentially, learning to pay close attention to the contents of one's own thought. James argued, as early as *The Principles of Psychology*, that philosophers have tended to read too much into what we experience: for example, he argued (like Hume) that there is no soul or ego or spiritual medium of thought to be seen if we actually look inside ourselves for such a thing. On the other hand, according to James, philosophers (such as Hume) have failed to notice that there is *more* to our experience than is traditionally assumed. We do not simply undergo discrete, repeatable lumps of experience, but experience a continuous stream of thought which includes transitions and relations between the more stable 'substantive' ideas; thus "we ought to say a feeling of *and*, a feeling of *if*, a feeling of *but*, and a feeling of *by*, quite as readily as we say a feeling of *blue* or a feeling of *cold*" (from *Essays in Psychology*).

Second, James rejected the traditional duality of mind and matter. Instead he postulated "a world of pure experience." Ultimately, according to James, the universe is made up not of some kind of 'stuff' but of a huge set of 'pure experiences.' Some of these experiences make up our streams of individual consciousness and, of those, some are taken by us (on the basis of their relations with other experiences) to be 'mental' and some 'physical.'

Third, James felt that he was able, on the basis of this picture of the nature of the universe, to solve the vexing problem of the *meaning of thought* (which philosophers today call "the problem of intentionality"). The problem is this: what is it about your thoughts, your sensations, or your words that makes them *about* some particular object in the external world? What is it, for example, about the word or the thought "cow" that connects it to a certain species of large, smelly mammal? According to James, the answer is relatively simple: your sensation of the cow just is the cow. The succession of pure experiences that makes up the cow, and the sequence of pure experiences that is your stream of consciousness (which is *you*) simply intersect, just as two lines can cross at a point; at that intersection is an experience that is simultaneously both thought and object of thought, mental and non-mental, you and the cow.

Our *idea* of a cow, then, is certainly *about* cows, but that 'aboutness' can now be understood in terms of the prospects for future intersections between, if you like, cow sequences and our personal autobiography. Roughly, for James, the meaning of an idea—including religious and moral ideas like *God* and *free will*—is its "cash-value" in terms of future experience. Importantly, this includes not only predictions about sensations that we might expect lie in store for us, but also the effects such an idea will have on our future behavior; how it will change *us*, and thus affect our future experience. This is the core doctrine of what James called "Pragmatism." "To attain perfect clearness in our thoughts of an object, then, we need only consider what conceivable effects of a practical kind the object may involve—what sensations we are to expect from it, and what reactions we must prepare" (*Pragmatism*).

Finally, once we know how ideas get their meaning, we can ask what it is for an idea to be *true*. For James, the answer is its "workability." Given his radical empiricism and his pragmatism, truth can't possibly consist, for James, in a kind of correspondence or matching between an idea and some sort of external reality—James has rejected that whole way of talking.

For an idea to be called 'true' is not for it to have some special property or value at the moment it occurs but instead it is for it to have particularly *beneficial* effects on our future conduct and our future experiences. An idea might turn out to be true because it is especially valuable for predicting scientific events (such as eclipses, for example), or its truth might lie in the way it is spiritually ennobling to all those who believe in it.

This, then, is a sketch of James's final world-view. This over-arching philosophical structure did not come to James all at once; it was shaped and reshaped, piece by piece, over his lifetime. Its motivation, one of James's key intellectual driving forces, was the tension that he felt between science and religion: between the cold but intelligent detachment and determinism of his 'scientific conscience,' and his attachment to the ideals of free will, morality, and an interested God. "The Will to Believe" was one of James's earlier—and, at the time and ever since, highly popular—attempts to resolve this contradiction.

What Is the Structure of This Reading?

"The Will to Believe," James announces at the outset, is to be "an essay in justification of faith." He starts out by making three distinctions between types of "options" (living or dead, forced or avoidable, momentous or trivial) and suggests that his essay is to be about options that are living, forced, and momentous—what James calls "genuine options."

James begins his discussion of this kind of option—in the second section of the paper—by immediately considering the objection that it is in some way "preposterous" to say that we could or should simply *choose* what to believe. He responds that not only can we and do we believe things on the basis of "our non-intellectual nature," but furthermore that we must and should do so—that willingness to believe is (morally and intellectually) "lawful." He tries to tie this view to the rejection of what he calls "absolutism" in science and the endorsement of "empiricism," and to the quest to "believe truth" rather than merely "avoid error."

In Section VIII James begins to present his actual arguments for the claim that "there are some options between opinions in which [our passional nature] must be regarded both as an inevitable and as a lawful determinant of our choice." He does so partly by arguing that this must be true for what he earlier called *genuine* options, and he gives as examples moral questions, issues to do with personal relationships, and—at greater length—religious faith. One of his central claims in this section is that "a rule of thinking which would absolutely prevent me from acknowledging certain kinds of truth if those truths were really there, would be an irrational rule."

Some Background Information

1. James refers to a number of people in his essay that may no longer be familiar to modern audiences. Here is a run-down of the names James drops, in the order of their appearance:
   - Leslie Stephen (1832–1904): a British writer, editor, and biographer best known as the editor of the *Dictionary of National Biography* and as Virginia Woolf's father.
   - Fridtjof Nansen (1861–1930): a Norwegian explorer, zoologist, and politician who led an Arctic expedition from 1893 to 1896.
   - Blaise Pascal (1623–1662): a French mathematician, physicist and philosopher. James is referring to the book *Pensées*, published (posthumously) in 1670.
   - Arthur Hugh Clough (1819–1861): a British poet. The quote is from a poem sometimes known as "Steadfast."
   - Thomas Henry Huxley (1825–1895): a British biologist and writer, known for championing Darwin's theory of evolution. The quotation is from "The Influence Upon Morality of a Decline in Religious Belief."
   - William Kingdon Clifford (1845–1879): a British mathematician, philosopher, and well-known agnostic who died an early death from tuberculosis. James quotes extensively from his "The Ethics of Belief," published in *Contemporary Review* 29 (1877).
   - Arthur James Balfour (1848–1930): a philosopher who went on to be British Prime Minister from 1902 to 1905 and then Foreign Secretary (1916–1919). James is thinking of his essay "Authority and Reason," published in 1895.

- John Henry Newman (1801–1891): an English theologian who converted to Roman Catholicism in 1845 and became a cardinal in 1879.
- Johann Zöllner (1834–1882): a German astrophysicist who researched psychic phenomena and defended the existence of a "fourth dimension."
- Charles Howard Hinton (1853–1907): an English mathematician who also, independently, postulated a "fourth dimension."
- Thomas Reid (1710–1796): a Scottish philosopher and opponent of the 'skepticism' of David Hume.
- Herbert Spencer (1820–1903): an English philosopher who tried to apply the scientific theory of evolution to philosophy and ethics. He coined the phrase "the survival of the fittest."
- August Wiesmann (1834–1914): a German biologist and one of the founders of modern genetics, who defended the view that hereditary characteristics are transmitted by a germinal plasm (and so ruled out the transmission of acquired characteristics).
- Charles Secrétan (1815–1895): A (rather obscure) late nineteenth-century Swiss philosopher.

2. James's position in "The Will to Believe" is often thought to be a good example of the philosophical position called fideism. This is the thesis that religious belief is based on faith and not on either evidence or reasoning. In other words, the fundamental claims of religion cannot be established by either science or reason but nevertheless (perhaps because we should not place reason ahead of God) they should be believed to be true. Fideism comes in various flavors. Perhaps the mildest version is the view, held by St. Augustine and Pascal, that faith has to come before reason: that is, only faith can persuade us that religious doctrines are true, but once we believe, we can use our intellect to come to better understand them and to see *why* they are true and rational. The most extreme version is typified in the writings of the nineteenth-century Danish philosopher Søren Kierkegaard. Kierkegaard went so far as to say that central tenets of Christianity—e.g., that

God became incarnate in the person of Jesus Christ—are actually self-contradictory, and thus irrational, so belief in them requires a "leap into faith" which cannot in any way be justified.

Some Common Misconceptions

1. James is not anti-science: he does not want to eliminate the scientific attitude in favor of a religious one, but to show that science leaves open the possibility of religious faith and that it can do so without merely ignoring religion or granting it a special sphere insulated from normal rational inquiry.
2. James does not argue that we *must* be religious but only that, even though we are reasonable and scientifically educated people, we still *can* be religious. Religious belief is, for James, a personal choice.

Suggestions for Critical Reflection

1. The American judge Oliver Wendell Holmes, a close friend, once complained that James was inclined "to turn down the lights so as to give miracle a chance," shielding religious issues from the bright light of truth and careful, scientific inquiry. Do you agree with this criticism? How do you think James responded?
2. Do you think James's position in this essay is best understood as saying religious belief is in fact rational, or that religious belief is not rational but nevertheless 'lawful'?
3. James sometimes seems to talk as if we could and should believe things on the basis of our *will*, our decision to do so, and sometimes as if it's a matter of having some beliefs based on *emotion* ("our passional nature") rather than intellect. Do you think there's a conflict between these two ways of talking? If so, which do you think James really meant?
4. W.K. Clifford begins his essay "The Ethics of Belief" with an example of a ship owner who suppresses his own doubts about the seaworthiness of his vessel and "putting his trust in Providence" allows the ship to sail, carrying its

load of immigrants to their death at sea. Clifford argues that, though the ship owner sincerely believes in the soundness of his ship, he has *"no right to believe on such evidence as was before him"* because he did not carry out a proper investigation of the facts. This example is used to support Clifford's central theme: that beliefs must be held responsibly, or ethically, on the basis of careful and conscientious investigation. Although James takes Clifford's essay as a foil to his own position in "The Will to Believe," he never mentions this important example. What do you think of the example? If you think that Clifford makes a good point, how does this affect your view of James's arguments? Is Clifford's example relevant to the case of religious belief, either for the individual or for society as a whole?

5. Some critics of "The Will to Believe" have complained that James seems to be imagining only cases where we have no evidence at all, either for or against a particular possibility, and simply ignoring the much more common case where we are in possession of some evidence and have to weigh the balance of probabilities. Do you agree that James does this, and if so, is it a mistake on his part?

6. Another common criticism of this essay is that the religious belief James defends is highly attenuated: no more than the belief that "perfection is eternal." Do you share this reaction? Is this all that James is defending, in the end? In what way, if so, is this a "momentous" choice?

7. If you have read the Mackie selection "Evil and Omnipotence" you might want to ask yourself how James could respond to Mackie's claim that belief in a Christian/Islamic/Judaic (etc.) God is internally inconsistent and hence that no reasonable person should hold such a belief. Can James and Mackie *both* be right? If not, which of them is (if either)?

Suggestions for Further Reading

The standard edition of William James's works is published (in seventeen volumes) by Harvard University Press. Central works include *The Will to Believe* (1979),

Pragmatism (1975), *The Meaning of Truth* (1975), *Essays in Radical Empiricism* (1976), and *Varieties of Religious Experience* (1985). Biographies of James include the early standard by one of his friends, Ralph Barton Perry, *The Thought and Character of William James* (Little, Brown, 1935); a good more recent one is by Gerald E. Myers, *William James: His Life and Thought* (Yale University Press, 1986).

Other relevant books on James's philosophy include *William James* by Graham Bird (Routledge & Kegan Paul, 1986), *William James and Phenomenology* by James Edie (Indiana University Press, 1987), *William James's Philosophy* by Marcus Peter Ford (University of Massachusetts Press, 1982), *Metaphysics, Experience and Religion in William James's Thought* by David Lamberth (Cambridge University Press, 1999), *James's Will-to-Believe Doctrine: A Heretical View* by James Wernham (University of Toronto Press, 1987), and *The Radical Empiricism of William James* by John Wild (Doubleday, 1989).

There is a *Cambridge Companion to William James* edited by Ruth Anna Putnam (Cambridge University Press, 1997). Three useful articles are: Richard Gale, "William James and the Ethics of Belief," *American Philosophical Quarterly* 17 (1980), Van A. Harvey, "The Ethics of Belief Reconsidered," *Journal of Religion* 59 (1979), and Kauber and Hare, "The Right and Duty to Will to Believe," *Canadian Journal of Philosophy* 4 (1974).

"The Will to Believe"[2]

In the recently published *Life* by Leslie Stephen of his brother, Fitz-James, there is an account of a school to which the latter went when he was a boy. The teacher, a certain Mr. Guest, used to converse with his pupils in this wise: "Gurney, what is the difference between justification and sanctification?—Stephen, prove the

---

2   This essay was an address to the Philosophical Clubs of Yale and Brown Universities, and was first published in the *New World*, June 1896. This reprint is based on the text in *The Will to Believe, and Other Essays in Popular Philosophy* published by Longmans, Green & Co. in 1897.

omnipotence of God!" etc. In the midst of our Harvard freethinking and indifference we are prone to imagine that here at your good old orthodox College conversation continues to be somewhat upon this order; and to show you that we at Harvard have not lost all interest in these vital subjects, I have brought with me to-night something like a sermon on justification by faith to read to you,—I mean an essay in justification *of* faith, a defence of our right to adopt a believing attitude in religious matters, in spite of the fact that our merely logical intellect may not have been coerced. "The Will to Believe," accordingly, is the title of my paper.

I have long defended to my own students the lawfulness of voluntarily adopted faith; but as soon as they have got well imbued with the logical spirit, they have as a rule refused to admit my contention to be lawful philosophically, even though in point of fact they were personally all the time chock-full of some faith or other themselves. I am all the while, however, so profoundly convinced that my own position is correct, that your invitation has seemed to me a good occasion to make my statements more clear. Perhaps your minds will be more open than those with which I have hitherto had to deal. I will be as little technical as I can, though I must begin by setting up some technical distinctions that will help us in the end.

I.

Let us give the name of *hypothesis* to anything that may be proposed to our belief; and just as the electricians speak of live and dead wires, let us speak of any hypothesis as either *live* or *dead*. A live hypothesis is one which appeals as a real possibility to him to whom it is proposed. If I ask you to believe in the Mahdi,[3] the notion makes no electric connection with your nature,—it refuses to scintillate with any credibility at all. As an hypothesis it is completely dead. To an Arab, however (even if he be not one of the Mahdi's followers), the hypothesis is among the mind's possibilities: it is alive. This shows that deadness and liveness in an hypothesis are not intrinsic properties, but relations to the individual thinker. They are

measured by his willingness to act. The maximum of liveness in an hypothesis, means willingness to act irrevocably. Practically, that means belief; but there is some believing tendency wherever there is willingness to act at all.

Next, let us call the decision between two hypotheses an *option*. Options may be of several kinds. They may be—1, *living* or *dead*; 2, *forced* or *avoidable*; 3, *momentous* or *trivial*; and for our purposes we may call an option a *genuine* option when it is of the forced, living, and momentous kind.

1. A living option is one in which both hypotheses are live ones. If I say to you: "Be a theosophist[4] or be a Mohammedan,"[5] it is probably a dead option, because for you neither hypothesis is likely to be alive. But if I say: "Be an agnostic or be a Christian," it is otherwise: trained as you are, each hypothesis makes some appeal, however small, to your belief.

2. Next, if I say to you: "Choose between going out with your umbrella or without it," I do not offer you a genuine option, for it is not forced. You can easily avoid it by not going out at all. Similarly, if I say, "Either love me or hate me," "Either call my theory true or call it false," your option is avoidable. You may remain indifferent to me, neither loving nor hating, and you may decline to offer any judgment as to my theory. But if I say, "Either accept this truth or go without it," I put on you a forced option, for there is no standing place outside of the alternative. Every dilemma based on a complete logical disjunction, with no possibility of not choosing, is an option of this forced kind.

3. Finally, if I were Dr. Nansen and proposed to you to join my North Pole expedition, your option would be momentous; for this would probably be your only similar opportunity, and your choice now would either exclude you from the North Pole sort of immortality alto-

---

3   In Islam, a messianic leader who, it is believed, will appear shortly before the end of the world to establish a reign of righteousness.

4   A member of a religious sect, the Theosophical Society, founded in New York in 1875, which incorporates aspects of Buddhism and Brahmanism.

5   A Muslim.

gether or put at least the chance of it into your hands. He who refuses to embrace a unique opportunity loses the prize as surely as if he tried and failed. *Per contra*,[6] the option is trivial when the opportunity is not unique, when the stake is insignificant, or when the decision is reversible if it later prove unwise. Such trivial options abound in the scientific life. A chemist finds an hypothesis live enough to spend a year in its verification: he believes in it to that extent. But if his experiments prove inconclusive either way, he is quit for his loss of time,[7] no vital harm being done.

It will facilitate our discussion if we keep all these distinctions well in mind.

II.

The next matter to consider is the actual psychology of human opinion. When we look at certain facts, it seems as if our passional and volitional nature lay at the root of all our convictions. When we look at others, it seems as if they could do nothing when the intellect had once said its say. Let us take the latter facts up first.

Does it not seem preposterous on the very face of it to talk of our opinions being modifiable at will? Can our will either help or hinder our intellect in its perceptions of truth? Can we, by just willing it, believe that Abraham Lincoln's existence is a myth, and that the portraits of him in McClure's Magazine[8] are all of some one else? Can we, by any effort of our will, or by any strength of wish that it were true, believe ourselves well and about when we are roaring with rheumatism in bed, or feel certain that the sum of the two one-dollar bills in our pocket must be a hundred dollars? We can say any of these things, but we are absolutely impotent to believe them; and of just such things is the whole fabric of the truths that we do believe in made up,—matters of fact, immediate or

remote, as Hume said,[9] and relations between ideas, which are either there or not there for us if we see them so, and which if not there cannot be put there by any action of our own.

In Pascal's *Thoughts* there is a celebrated passage known in literature as Pascal's wager. In it he tries to force us into Christianity by reasoning as if our concern with truth resembled our concern with the stakes in a game of chance. Translated freely his words are these: You must either believe or not believe that God is—which will you do? Your human reason cannot say. A game is going on between you and the nature of things which at the day of judgment will bring out either heads or tails. Weigh what your gains and your losses would be if you should stake all you have on heads, or God's existence: if you win in such case, you gain eternal beatitude;[10] if you lose, you lose nothing at all. If there were an infinity of chances, and only one for God in this wager, still you ought to stake your all on God; for though you surely risk a finite loss by this procedure, any finite loss is reasonable, even a certain one is reasonable, if there is but the possibility of infinite gain. Go, then, and take holy water, and have masses said; belief will come and stupefy your scruples,—*Cela vous fera croire et vous abêtira.*[11] Why should you not? At bottom, what have you to lose?

You probably feel that when religious faith expresses itself thus, in the language of the gaming table,[12] it is put to its last trumps. Surely Pascal's own personal belief in masses and holy water had far other springs; and this celebrated page of his is but an argument for others, a last desperate snatch at a weapon against the hardness of the unbelieving heart. We feel that a faith in masses and holy water adopted wilfully after such a mechanical calculation—would lack the inner soul of faith's reality; and if we were ourselves in the place of the Deity, we should probably take particular pleasure in cutting off believers of this pattern from their infinite reward. It is evident that unless there be some pre-existing tendency to

---

6   "On the other hand."

7   That is, free to stop with no penalty except for the loss of his time.

8   An influential American muckraking periodical, founded in 1893.

9   See the Hume selections in this chapter and in Chapter 4.

10   Blessedness or happiness.

11   "That will make you believe and will stupefy you."

12   Near to death, in desperate straits.

believe in masses and holy water, the option offered to the will by Pascal is not a living option. Certainly no Turk ever took to masses and holy water on its account; and even to us Protestants these means of salvation seem such foregone impossibilities that Pascal's logic, invoked for them specifically, leaves us unmoved. As well might the Mahdi write to us, saying, "I am the Expected One whom God has created in his effulgence. You shall be infinitely happy if you confess me; otherwise you shall be cut off from the light of the sun. Weigh, then, your infinite gain if I am genuine against your finite sacrifice if I am not!" His logic would be that of Pascal; but he would vainly use it on us, for the hypothesis he offers us is dead. No tendency to act on it exists in us to any degree.

The talk of believing by our volition seems, then, from one point of view, simply silly. From another point of view it is worse than silly, it is vile. When one turns to the magnificent edifice of the physical sciences, and sees how it was reared; what thousands of disinterested moral lives of men lie buried in its mere foundations; what patience and postponement, what choking down of preference, what submission to the icy laws of outer fact are wrought into its very stones and mortar; how absolutely impersonal it stands in its vast augustness,—then how besotted and contemptible seems every little sentimentalist who comes blowing his voluntary smoke-wreaths, and pretending to decide things from out of his private dream! Can we wonder if those bred in the rugged and manly school of science should feel like spewing such subjectivism out of their mouths? The whole system of loyalties which grow up in the schools of science go dead against its toleration; so that it is only natural that those who have caught the scientific fever should pass over to the opposite extreme, and write sometimes as if the incorruptibly truthful intellect ought positively to prefer bitterness and unacceptableness to the heart in its cup.

> It fortifies my soul to know
> That, though I perish, Truth is so —

sings Clough, while Huxley exclaims: "My only consolation lies in the reflection that, however bad our posterity may become, so far as they hold by the plain rule of not pretending to believe what they have no reason to believe, because it may be to their advantage so to pretend [the word 'pretend' is surely here redundant], they will not have reached the lowest depth of immorality." And that delicious *enfant terrible*[13] Clifford writes: "Belief is desecrated when given to unproved and unquestioned statements for the solace and private pleasure of the believer.... Whoso would deserve well of his fellows in this matter will guard the purity of his belief with a very fanaticism of jealous care, lest at any time it should rest on an unworthy object, and catch a stain which can never be wiped away.... If [a] belief has been accepted on insufficient evidence [even though the belief be true, as Clifford on the same page explains] the pleasure is a stolen one.... It is sinful because it is stolen in defiance of our duty to mankind. That duty is to guard ourselves from such beliefs as from a pestilence which may shortly master our own body and then spread to the rest of the town.... It is wrong always, everywhere, and for every one, to believe anything upon insufficient evidence."

III.

All this strikes one as healthy, even when expressed, as by Clifford, with somewhat too much of robustious pathos in the voice. Free-will and simple wishing do seem, in the matter of our credences, to be only fifth wheels to the coach. Yet if any one should thereupon assume that intellectual insight is what remains after wish and will and sentimental preference have taken wing, or that pure reason is what then settles our opinions, he would fly quite as directly in the teeth of the facts.

It is only our already dead hypotheses that our willing nature is unable to bring to life again. But what has made them dead for us is for the most part a previous action of our willing nature of an antagonistic kind. When I say 'willing nature,' I do not mean only such deliberate volitions as may have set up habits of belief that we cannot now escape from,—I mean all such factors of belief as fear and hope, prejudice and passion, imitation and partisanship, the circumpressure of our caste and set. As a matter of fact we find ourselves believing, we hardly know how or why. Mr. Balfour gives

---

13 'Bad boy'—a person whose behavior or ideas shock or embarrass those with more conventional attitudes.

the name of 'authority' to all those influences, born of the intellectual climate, that make hypotheses possible or impossible for us, alive or dead. Here in this room, we all of us believe in molecules and the conservation of energy, in democracy and necessary progress, in Protestant Christianity and the duty of fighting for 'the doctrine of the immortal Monroe,'[14] all for no reasons worthy of the name. We see into these matters with no more inner clearness, and probably with much less, than any disbeliever in them might possess. His unconventionality would probably have some grounds to show for its conclusions; but for us, not insight, but the *prestige* of the opinions, is what makes the spark shoot from them and light up our sleeping magazines[15] of faith. Our reason is quite satisfied, in nine hundred and ninety-nine cases out of every thousand of us, if it can find a few arguments that will do to recite in case our credulity is criticized by someone else. Our faith is faith in someone else's faith, and in the greatest matters this is most the case. Our belief in truth itself, for instance, that there is a truth, and that our minds and it are made for each other,—what is it but a passionate affirmation of desire, in which our social system backs us up? We want to have a truth; we want to believe that our experiments and studies and discussions must put us in a continually better and better position towards it; and on this line we agree to fight out our thinking lives. But if a pyrrhonistic sceptic[16] asks us *how we know* all this, can our logic find a reply? No! certainly it cannot. It is just one volition against another,—we willing to

go in for life upon a trust or assumption which he, for his part, does not care to make.[17]

As a rule we disbelieve all facts and theories for which we have no use. Clifford's cosmic emotions find no use for Christian feelings. Huxley belabors the bishops because there is no use for sacerdotalism[18] in his scheme of life. Newman, on the contrary, goes over to Romanism, and finds all sorts of reasons good for staying there, because a priestly system is for him an organic need and delight. Why do so few 'scientists' even look at the evidence for telepathy, so called? Because they think, as a leading biologist, now dead, once said to me, that even if such a thing were true, scientists ought to band together to keep it suppressed and concealed. It would undo the uniformity of Nature and all sorts of other things without which scientists cannot carry on their pursuits. But if this very man had been shown something which as a scientist he might *do* with telepathy, he might not only have examined the evidence, but even have found it good enough. This very law which the logicians would impose upon us—if I may give the name of logicians to those who would rule out our willing nature here—is based on nothing but their own natural wish to exclude all elements for which they, in their professional quality of logicians, can find no use.

Evidently, then, our non-intellectual nature does influence our convictions. There are passional tendencies and volitions which run before and others which come after belief, and it is only the latter that are too late for the fair; and they are not too late when the previous passional work has been already in their own direction. Pascal's argument, instead of being powerless, then seems a regular clincher, and is the last stroke needed to make our faith in masses and holy water complete. The state of things is evidently far from simple; and pure insight and logic, whatever they might do ideally, are not the only things that really do produce our creeds.

---

14   This is the "Monroe Doctrine," set out by American President James Monroe in 1823, which states that while the US would not interfere with existing European colonies in the Western hemisphere, it would regard additional attempts by European powers to establish new colonies or otherwise interfere in the Americas as acts of aggression. (James himself disliked what he thought of as US threat tactics, which had been recently displayed in a dispute with the British over Venezuela.)

15   A storehouse of explosive ammunition.

16   A radical sceptic, one who is determined to withhold assent from almost all beliefs.

17   [Author's note] Compare the admirable page 310 in S.H. Hodgson's *Time and Space*, London, 1865.

18   The institution of the priesthood.

IV.

Our next duty, having recognized this mixed-up state of affairs, is to ask whether it be simply reprehensible and pathological, or whether, on the contrary, we must treat it as a normal element in making up our minds. The thesis I defend is, briefly stated, this: *Our passional nature not only lawfully may, but must, decide an option between propositions, whenever it is a genuine option that cannot by its nature be decided on intellectual grounds; for to say, under such circumstances, "Do not decide, but leave the question open," is itself a passional decision,—just like deciding yes or no,—and is attended with the same risk of losing the truth.* The thesis thus abstractly expressed will, I trust, soon become quite clear. But I must first indulge in a bit more of preliminary work.

V.

It will be observed that for the purposes of this discussion we are on 'dogmatic' ground,—ground, I mean, which leaves systematic philosophical scepticism altogether out of account. The postulate that there is truth, and that it is the destiny of our minds to attain it, we are deliberately resolving to make, though the sceptic will not make it. We part company with him, therefore, absolutely, at this point. But the faith that truth exists, and that our minds can find it, may be held in two ways. We may talk of the *empiricist* way and of the *absolutist* way of believing in truth. The absolutists in this matter say that we not only can attain to knowing truth, but we can *know* when we have attained to knowing it; while the empiricists think that although we may attain it, we cannot infallibly know when. To *know* is one thing, and to know for certain *that* we know is another. One may hold to the first being possible without the second; hence the empiricists and the absolutists, although neither of them is a sceptic in the usual philosophic sense of the term, show very different degrees of dogmatism in their lives.

If we look at the history of opinions, we see that the empiricist tendency has largely prevailed in science, while in philosophy the absolutist tendency has had everything its own way. The characteristic sort of happiness, indeed, which philosophies yield has

mainly consisted in the conviction felt by each successive school or system that by it bottom-certitude had been attained. "Other philosophies are collections of opinions, mostly false; *my* philosophy gives standing-ground forever,"—who does not recognize in this the key-note of every system worthy of the name? A system, to be a system at all, must come as a *closed* system, reversible in this or that detail, perchance, but in its essential features never!

Scholastic orthodoxy,[19] to which one must always go when one wishes to find perfectly clear statement, has beautifully elaborated this absolutist conviction in a doctrine which it calls that of 'objective evidence.' If, for example, I am unable to doubt that I now exist before you, that two is less than three, or that if all men are mortal then I am mortal too, it is because these things illumine my intellect irresistibly. The final ground of this objective evidence possessed by certain propositions is the *adæquatio intellectus nostri cum rê*.[20] The certitude it brings involves an *apititudinem ad extorquendum certum assensum*[21] on the part of the truth envisaged, and on the side of the subject a *quietem in cognitione*,[22] when once the object is mentally received, that leaves no possibility of doubt behind; and in the whole transaction nothing operates but the *entitas ipsa*[23] of the object and the *entitas ipsa* of the mind. We slouchy modern thinkers dislike to talk in Latin,—indeed, we dislike to talk in set terms at all; but at bottom our own state of mind is very much like this whenever we uncritically abandon ourselves: You believe in objective evidence, and I do. Of some things we feel that we are certain: we know, and we know that we do know. There is something that gives a click inside of us, a bell that strikes twelve, when the hands of our mental clock have swept the dial and meet over

---

19 The dominant philosophy of the Middle Ages, combining remnants of ancient Greek philosophy (especially Aristotle) with Christian theology.

20 "Perfect correspondence of our understanding with the thing."

21 "The aptitude or tendency to force a certain agreement."

22 "Repose in knowledge," i.e., passive acceptance of knowledge.

23 "Being itself," real being.

the meridian hour.[24] The greatest empiricists among us are only empiricists on reflection: when left to their instincts, they dogmatize like infallible popes. When the Cliffords tell us how sinful it is to be Christians on such 'insufficient evidence,' insufficiency is really the last thing they have in mind. For them the evidence is absolutely sufficient, only it makes the other way. They believe so completely in an anti-Christian order of the universe that there is no living option: Christianity is a dead hypothesis from the start.

VI.

But now, since we are all such absolutists by instinct, what in our quality of students of philosophy ought we to do about the fact? Shall we espouse and endorse it? Or shall we treat it as a weakness of our nature from which we must free ourselves, if we can?

I sincerely believe that the latter course is the only one we can follow as reflective men. Objective evidence and certitude are doubtless very fine ideals to play with, but where on this moonlit and dream-visited planet are they found? I am, therefore, myself a complete empiricist so far as my theory of human knowledge goes. I live, to be sure, by the practical faith that we must go on experiencing and thinking over our experience, for only thus can our opinions grow more true; but to hold any one of them—I absolutely do not care which—as if it never could be reinterpretable or corrigible,[25] I believe to be a tremendously mistaken attitude, and I think that the whole history of philosophy will bear me out. There is but one indefectibly certain truth, and that is the truth that pyrrhonistic scepticism itself leaves standing,—the truth that the present phenomenon of consciousness exists. That, however, is the bare starting-point of knowledge, the mere admission of a stuff to be philosophized about. The various philosophies are but so many attempts at expressing what this stuff really is. And if we repair to our libraries what disagreement do we discover! Where is a certainly true answer found? Apart from abstract propositions of comparison (such as two and two are the same as four), propositions

which tell us nothing by themselves about concrete reality, we find no proposition ever regarded by any one as evidently certain that has not either been called a falsehood, or at least had its truth sincerely questioned by some one else. The transcending of the axioms of geometry, not in play but in earnest, by certain of our contemporaries (as Zöllner and Charles H. Hinton), and the rejection of the whole Aristotelian logic by the Hegelians, are striking instances in point.

No concrete test of what is really true has ever been agreed upon. Some make the criterion external to the moment of perception, putting it either in revelation, the *consensus gentium*,[26] the instincts of the heart, or the systematized experience of the race. Others make the perceptive moment its own test,—Descartes, for instance, with his clear and distinct ideas guaranteed by the veracity of God; Reid with his 'common-sense'; and Kant with his forms of synthetic judgment *a priori*.[27] The inconceivability of the opposite; the capacity to be verified by sense; the possession of complete organic unity or self-relation, realized when a thing is its own other,—are standards which, in turn, have been used. The much lauded objective evidence is never triumphantly there; it is a mere aspiration or *Grenzbegriff*,[28] marking the infinitely remote ideal of our thinking life. To claim that certain truths now possess it, is simply to say that when you think them true and they *are* true, then their evidence is objective, otherwise it is not. But practically one's conviction that the evidence one goes by is of the real objective brand, is only one more subjective opinion added to the lot. For what a contradictory array of opinions have objective evidence and absolute certitude been claimed! The world is rational through and through,—its existence is an ultimate brute fact; there is a personal God,—a personal God is inconceivable; there is an extra-mental physical world immediately known,—the mind can only know its own ideas; a moral imperative exists,—obligation is only the resultant of desires; a perma-

---

24 Noon—i.e., the hour when the sun is at its meridian, its highest point in the sky.

25 Correctable.

26 "Public consensus."

27 See Chapter 3 for relevant selections from Descartes and Kant.

28 From Kant's *Critique of Pure Reason*, this literally means a concept at the edge or limit of our understanding; it is often translated "limiting concept."

nent spiritual principle is in every one,—there are only shifting states of mind; there is an endless chain of causes,—there is an absolute first cause; an eternal necessity,—a freedom; a purpose,—no purpose; a primal One,—a primal Many; a universal continuity,—an essential discontinuity in things; an infinity,—no infinity. There is this,—there is that; there is indeed nothing which some one has not thought absolutely true, while his neighbor deemed it absolutely false; and not an absolutist among them seems ever to have considered that the trouble may all the time be essential, and that the intellect, even with truth directly in its grasp, may have no infallible signal for knowing whether it be truth or no. When, indeed, one remembers that the most striking practical application to life of the doctrine of objective certitude has been the conscientious labors of the Holy Office of the Inquisition,[29] one feels less tempted than ever to lend the doctrine a respectful ear.

But please observe, now, that when as empiricists we give up the doctrine of objective certitude, we do not thereby give up the quest or hope of truth itself. We still pin our faith on its existence, and still believe that we gain an ever better position towards it by systematically continuing to roll up experiences and think. Our great difference from the scholastic lies in the way we face. The strength of his system lies in the principles, the origin, the *terminus a quo*[30] of his thought; for us the strength is in the outcome, the upshot, the *terminus ad quem*.[31] Not where it comes from but what it leads to is to decide. It matters not to an empiricist from what quarter an hypothesis may come to him: he may have acquired it by fair means or by foul; passion may have whispered or accident suggested it; but if the total drift of thinking continues to confirm it, that is what he means by its being true.

VII.

One more point, small but important, and our preliminaries are done. There are two ways of looking at our duty in the matter of opinion,—ways entirely different, and yet ways about whose difference the theory of knowledge seems hitherto to have shown very little concern. *We must know the truth*; and *we must avoid error*,—these are our first and great commandments as would-be knowers; but they are not two ways of stating an identical commandment, they are two separable laws. Although it may indeed happen that when we believe the truth *A*, we escape as an incidental consequence from believing the falsehood *B*, it hardly ever happens that by merely disbelieving *B* we necessarily believe *A*. We may in escaping *B* fall into believing other falsehoods, *C* or *D*, just as bad as *B*; or we may escape *B* by not believing anything at all not even *A*.

Believe truth! Shun error—these, we see, are two materially different laws; and by choosing between them we may end by coloring differently our whole intellectual life. We may regard the chase for truth as paramount, and the avoidance of error as secondary; or we may, on the other hand, treat the avoidance of error as more imperative, and let truth take its chance. Clifford, in the instructive passage which I have quoted, exhorts us to the latter course. Believe nothing, he tells us, keep your mind in suspense forever, rather than by closing it on insufficient evidence incur the awful risk of believing lies. You, on the other hand, may think that the risk of being in error is a very small matter when compared with the blessings of real knowledge, and be ready to be duped many times in your investigation rather than postpone indefinitely the chance of guessing true. I myself find it impossible to go with Clifford. We must remember that these feelings of our duty about either truth or error are in any case only expressions of our passional life. Biologically considered, our minds are as ready to grind out falsehood as veracity, and he who says, "Better go without belief forever than believe a lie!" merely shows his own preponderant private horror of becoming a dupe. He may be critical of many of his desires and fears, but this fear he slavishly obeys. He cannot imagine any one questioning its binding force. For my own part, I have also a horror of being duped; but I can believe that worse things than being duped may happen to a man in this world: so Clifford's exhortation has to my ears a thoroughly fantastic sound. It is like a general informing his soldiers that it is better to keep out of

---

29 A tribunal formerly held in the Roman Catholic Church and directed at the forceful suppression of heresy; its best known variant is the notorious Spanish Inquisition of the late fifteenth century.

30 "The point from which it comes."

31 "The point to which it goes."

battle forever than to risk a single wound. Not so are victories either over enemies or over nature gained. Our errors are surely not such awfully solemn things. In a world where we are so certain to incur them in spite of all our caution, a certain lightness of heart seems healthier than this excessive nervousness on their behalf. At any rate, it seems the fittest thing for the empiricist philosopher.

VIII.

And now, after all this introduction, let us go straight at our question. I have said, and now repeat it, that not only as a matter of fact do we find our passional nature influencing us in our opinions, but that there are some options between opinions in which this influence must be regarded both as an inevitable and as a lawful determinant of our choice.

I fear here that some of you my hearers will begin to scent danger, and lend an inhospitable ear. Two first steps of passion you have indeed had to admit as necessary,—we must think so as to avoid dupery, and we must think so as to gain truth; but the surest path to those ideal consummations, you will probably consider, is from now onwards to take no further passional step.

Well, of course, I agree as far as the facts will allow. Wherever the option between losing truth and gaining it is not momentous, we can throw the chance of *gaining truth* away, and at any rate save ourselves from any chance of *believing falsehood*, by not making up our minds at all till objective evidence has come. In scientific questions, this is almost always the case; and even in human affairs in general, the need of acting is seldom so urgent that a false belief to act on is better than no belief at all. Law courts, indeed, have to decide on the best evidence attainable for the moment, because a judge's duty is to make law as well as to ascertain it, and (as a learned judge once said to me) few cases are worth spending much time over: the great thing is to have them decided on *any* acceptable principle, and got out of the way. But in our dealings with objective nature we obviously are recorders, not makers, of the truth; and decisions for the mere sake of deciding promptly and getting on to the next business would be wholly out of place. Throughout the breadth of physical nature facts are

what they are quite independently of us, and seldom is there any such hurry about them that the risks of being duped by believing a premature theory need be faced. The questions here are always trivial options, the hypotheses are hardly living (at any rate not living for us spectators), the choice between believing truth or falsehood is seldom forced. The attitude of sceptical balance is therefore the absolutely wise one if we would escape mistakes. What difference, indeed, does it make to most of us whether we have or have not a theory of the Röntgen rays,[32] whether we believe or not in mind-stuff, or have a conviction about the causality of conscious states? It makes no difference. Such options are not forced on us. On every account it is better not to make them, but still keep weighing reasons *pro et contra*[33] with an indifferent hand.

I speak, of course, here of the purely judging mind. For purposes of discovery such indifference is to be less highly recommended, and science would be far less advanced than she is if the passionate desires of individuals to get their own faiths confirmed had been kept out of the game. See for example the sagacity which Spencer and Weismann now display. On the other hand, if you want an absolute duffer in an investigation, you must, after all, take the man who has no interest whatever in its results: he is the warranted incapable, the positive fool. The most useful investigator, because the most sensitive observer, is always he whose eager interest in one side of the question is balanced by an equally keen nervousness lest he become deceived.[34] Science has organized this nervousness into a regular *technique*, her so-called method of verification; and she has fallen so deeply in love with the method that one may even say she has ceased to care for truth by itself at all. It is only truth as technically verified that interests her. The truth of truths might come in merely affirmative form, and she would decline to touch it. Such truth as that, she might repeat with Clifford, would be stolen in defiance of

---

32   Named for Wilhelm Röntgen, the German physicist who discovered them, these are today called X-rays.

33   "For and against."

34   [Author's note] Compare Wilfrid Ward's Essay, "The Wish to Believe," in his *Witnesses to the Unseen*, Macmillan & Co., 1893.

her duty to mankind. Human passions, however, are stronger than technical rules. "Le coeur a ses raisons," as Pascal says, "que la raison ne connaît pas;"[35] and however indifferent to all but the bare rules of the game the umpire, the abstract intellect, may be, the concrete players who furnish him the materials to judge of are usually, each one of them, in love with some pet 'live hypothesis' of his own. Let us agree, however, that wherever there is no forced option, the dispassionately judicial intellect with no pet hypothesis, saving us, as it does, from dupery at any rate, ought to be our ideal.

The question next arises: Are there not somewhere forced options in our speculative questions, and can we (as men who may be interested at least as much in positively gaining truth as in merely escaping dupery) always wait with impunity till the coercive evidence shall have arrived? It seems *a priori* improbable that the truth should be so nicely adjusted to our needs and powers as that. In the great boarding-house of nature, the cakes and the butter and the syrup seldom come out so even and leave the plates so clean. Indeed, we should view them with scientific suspicion if they did.

IX.

Moral questions immediately present themselves as questions whose solution cannot wait for sensible proof. A moral question is a question not of what sensibly exists, but of what is good, or would be good if it did exist. Science can tell us what exists; but to compare the *worths*, both of what exists and of what does not exist, we must consult not science, but what Pascal calls our heart. Science herself consults her heart when she lays it down that the infinite ascertainment of fact and correction of false belief are the supreme goods for man. Challenge the statement, and science can only repeat it oracularly,[36] or else prove it by showing that such ascertainment and correction bring man all sorts of other goods which man's heart in turn declares. The question of having moral beliefs at all or not having them is decided by our will. Are our

moral preferences true or false, or are they only odd biological phenomena, making things good or bad for *us*, but in themselves indifferent? How can your pure intellect decide? If your heart does not *want* a world of moral reality, your head will assuredly never make you believe in one. Mephistophelian[37] scepticism, indeed, will satisfy the head's play-instincts much better than any rigorous idealism can. Some men (even at the student age) are so naturally cool-hearted that the moralistic hypothesis never has for them any pungent life, and in their supercilious presence the hot young moralist always feels strangely ill at ease. The appearance of knowingness is on their side, of *naïveté*, and gullibility on his. Yet, in the inarticulate heart of him, he clings to it that he is not a dupe, and that there is a realm in which (as Emerson says) all their wit and intellectual superiority is no better than the cunning of a fox.[38] Moral scepticism can no more be refuted or proved by logic than intellectual scepticism can. When we stick to it that there *is* truth (be it of either kind), we do so with our whole nature, and resolve to stand or fall by the results. The sceptic with his whole nature adopts the doubting attitude; but which of us is the wiser, Omniscience only knows.

Turn now from these wide questions of good to a certain class of questions of fact, questions concerning personal relations, states of mind between one man and another. *Do you like me or not?*—for example. Whether you do or not depends, in countless instances, on whether I meet you half-way, am willing to assume that you must like me, and show you trust and expectation. The previous faith on my part in your liking's existence is in such cases what makes your liking come. But if I stand aloof, and refuse to budge an inch until I have objective evidence, until you shall have done something apt, as the absolutists say, *ad extorquendum assensum meum*,[39] ten to one your liking never comes. How many women's hearts

---

35   "The heart has its reasons which reason knows nothing of."

36   In the manner of an oracle: solemnly and enigmatically, but without giving reasons.

37   Mephistopheles is the devil to whom, according to a sixteenth-century German legend, Faust sold his soul: something is "Mephistophelian," therefore, if it is fiendish and tricky.

38   A reference to the poet Ralph Waldo Emerson's essay "The Sovereignty of Ethics" (1884).

39   "To force my unqualified assent."

are vanquished by the mere sanguine insistence of some man that they *must* love him! he will not consent to the hypothesis that they cannot. The desire for a certain kind of truth here brings about that special truth's existence; and so it is in innumerable cases of other sorts. Who gains promotions, boons, appointments, but the man in whose life they are seen to play the part of live hypotheses, who discounts them, sacrifices other things for their sake before they have come, and takes risks for them in advance? His faith acts on the powers above him as a claim, and creates its own verification.

A social organism of any sort whatever, large or small, is what it is because each member proceeds to his own duty with a trust that the other members will simultaneously do theirs. Wherever a desired result is achieved by the co-operation of many independent persons, its existence as a fact is a pure consequence of the precursive faith in one another of those immediately concerned. A government, an army, a commercial system, a ship, a college, an athletic team, all exist on this condition, without which not only is nothing achieved, but nothing is even attempted. A whole train of passengers (individually brave enough) will be looted by a few highwaymen, simply because the latter can count on one another, while each passenger fears that if he makes a movement of resistance, he will be shot before any one else backs him up. If we believed that the whole car-full would rise at once with us, we should each severally rise, and train-robbing would never even be attempted. There are, then, cases where a fact cannot come at all unless a preliminary faith exists in its coming. *And where faith in a fact can help create the fact*, that would be an insane logic which should say that faith running ahead of scientific evidence is the 'lowest kind of immorality' into which a thinking being can fall. Yet such is the logic by which our scientific absolutists pretend to regulate our lives!

X.

In truths dependent on our personal action, then, faith based on desire is certainly a lawful and possibly an indispensable thing.

But now, it will be said, these are all childish human cases, and have nothing to do with great cosmical matters, like the question of religious faith. Let us then pass on to that. Religions differ so much in their accidents[40] that in discussing the religious question we must make it very generic and broad. What then do we now mean by the religious hypothesis? Science says things are; morality says some things are better than other things; and religion says essentially two things.

First, she says that the best things are the more eternal things, the overlapping things, the things in the universe that throw the last stone, so to speak, and say the final word. "Perfection is eternal,"—this phrase of Charles Secrétan seems a good way of putting this first affirmation of religion, an affirmation which obviously cannot yet be verified scientifically at all.

The second affirmation of religion is that we are better off even now if we believe her first affirmation to be true.

Now, let us consider what the logical elements of this situation are *in case the religious hypothesis in both its branches be really true*. (Of course, we must admit that possibility at the outset. If we are to discuss the question at all, it must involve a living option. If for any of you religion be a hypothesis that cannot, by any living possibility be true, then you need go no farther. I speak to the 'saving remnant' alone.) So proceeding, we see, first, that religion offers itself as a *momentous* option. We are supposed to gain, even now, by our belief, and to lose by our non-belief, a certain vital good. Secondly, religion is a *forced* option, so far as that good goes. We cannot escape the issue by remaining sceptical and waiting for more light, because, although we do avoid error in that way *if religion be untrue*, we lose the good, *if it be true*, just as certainly as if we positively chose to disbelieve. It is as if a man should hesitate indefinitely to ask a certain woman to marry him because he was not perfectly sure that she would prove an angel after he brought her home. Would he not cut himself off from that particular angel-possibility as decisively as if he went and married some one else? Scepticism, then, is not avoidance of option; it is option of a certain particular kind of risk. *Better risk loss of truth than chance of*

---

40   Non-essential properties or attributes.

error,—that is your faith-vetoer's exact position. He is actively playing his stake as much as the believer is; he is backing the field against the religious hypothesis, just as the believer is backing the religious hypothesis against the field. To preach scepticism to us as a duty until 'sufficient evidence' for religion be found, is tantamount therefore to telling us, when in presence of the religious hypothesis, that to yield to our fear of its being error is wiser and better than to yield to our hope that it may be true. It is not intellect against all passions, then; it is only intellect with one passion laying down its law. And by what, forsooth, is the supreme wisdom of this passion warranted? Dupery for dupery, what proof is there that dupery through hope is so much worse than dupery through fear? I, for one, can see no proof; and I simply refuse obedience to the scientist's command to imitate his kind of option, in a case where my own stake is important enough to give me the right to choose my own form of risk. If religion be true and the evidence for it be still insufficient, I do not wish, by putting your extinguisher upon my nature (which feels to me as if it had after all some business in this matter), to forfeit my sole chance in life of getting upon the winning side,—that chance depending, of course, on my willingness to run the risk of acting as if my passional need of taking the world religiously might be prophetic and right.

All this is on the supposition that it really may be prophetic and right, and that, even to us who are discussing the matter, religion is a live hypothesis which may be true. Now, to most of us religion comes in a still further way that makes a veto on our active faith even more illogical. The more perfect and more eternal aspect of the universe is represented in our religions as having personal form. The universe is no longer a mere *It* to us, but a *Thou*, if we are religious; and any relation that may be possible from person to person might be possible here. For instance, although in one sense we are passive portions of the universe, in another we show a curious autonomy, as if we were small active centres on our own account. We feel, too, as if the appeal of religion to us were made to our own active good-will, as if evidence might be forever withheld from us unless we met the hypothesis half-way. To take a trivial illustration: just as a man who in a company of gentlemen made no advances, asked a warrant for every concession, and believed no one's word without proof, would cut himself off by such churlishness from all the social rewards that a more trusting spirit would earn—so here, one who should shut himself up in snarling logicality and try to make the gods extort his recognition willy-nilly, or not get it at all, might cut himself off forever from his only opportunity of making the gods' acquaintance. This feeling, forced on us we know not whence, that by obstinately believing that there are gods (although not to do so would be so easy both for our logic and our life) we are doing the universe the deepest service we can, seems part of the living essence of the religious hypothesis. If the hypothesis *were* true in all its parts, including this one, then pure intellectualism, with its veto on our making willing advances, would be an absurdity; and some participation of our sympathetic nature would be logically required. I, therefore, for one, cannot see my way to accepting the agnostic rules for truth-seeking, or wilfully agree to keep my willing nature out of the game. I cannot do so for this plain reason, that *a rule of thinking which would absolutely prevent me from acknowledging certain kinds of truth if those kinds of truth were really there, would be an irrational rule.* That for me is the long and short of the formal logic of the situation, no matter what the kinds of truth might materially be.

I confess I do not see how this logic can be escaped. But sad experience makes me fear that some of you may still shrink from radically saying with me, *in abstracto*,[41] that we have the right to believe at our own risk any hypothesis that is live enough to tempt our will. I suspect, however, that if this is so, it is because you have got away from the abstract logical point of view altogether, and are thinking (perhaps without realizing it) of some particular religious hypothesis which for you is dead. The freedom to 'believe what we will' you apply to the case of some patent superstition; and the faith you think of is the faith defined by the schoolboy when he said, "Faith is when you believe something that you know ain't true." I can only repeat that this is misapprehension. *In concreto*,[42] the freedom to believe can only cover

---

41   "In the abstract."

42   "In concrete (or actual) cases."

living options which the intellect of the individual cannot by itself resolve; and living options never seem absurdities to him who has them to consider. When I look at the religious question as it really puts itself to concrete men, and when I think of all the possibilities which both practically and theoretically it involves, then this command that we shall put a stopper on our heart, instincts, and courage, and *wait*—acting of course meanwhile more or less as if religion were *not* true[43]—till doomsday, or till such time as our intellect and senses working together may have raked in evidence enough,—this command, I say, seems to me the queerest idol ever manufactured in the philosophic cave. Were we scholastic absolutists, there might be more excuse. If we had an infallible intellect with its objective certitudes, we might feel ourselves disloyal to such a perfect organ of knowledge in not trusting to it exclusively, in not waiting for its releasing word. But if we are empiricists, if we believe that no bell in us tolls to let us know for certain when truth is in our grasp, then it seems a piece of idle fantasticality to preach so solemnly our duty of waiting for the bell. Indeed we *may* wait if we will,—I hope you do not think that I am denying that,—but if we do so, we do so at our peril as much as if we believed. In either case we *act*, taking our life in our hands. No one of us ought to issue vetoes to the other, nor should we bandy words of abuse. We ought, on the contrary, delicately and profoundly to respect one another's mental freedom: then only shall we bring about the intellectual republic; then only shall we have that spirit of inner tolerance without which all our outer tolerance is soulless, and which is empiricism's glory; then only shall we live and let live, in speculative as well as in practical things.

I began by a reference to Fitz-James Stephen; let me end by a quotation from him. "What do you think of yourself? What do you think of the world? ... These are questions with which all must deal as it seems good to them. They are riddles of the Sphinx, and in some way or other we must deal with them.... In all important transactions of life we have to take a leap in the dark.... If we decide to leave the riddles unanswered, that is a choice; if we waver in our answer, that, too, is a choice: but whatever choice we make, we make it at our peril. If a man chooses to turn his back altogether on God and the future, no one can prevent him; no one can show beyond reasonable doubt that he is mistaken. If a man thinks otherwise and acts as he thinks, I do not see that any one can prove that he is mistaken. Each must act as he thinks best; and if he is wrong, so much the worse for him. We stand on a mountain pass in the midst of whirling snow and blinding mist, through which we get glimpses now and then of paths which may be deceptive. If we stand still we shall be frozen to death. If we take the wrong road we shall be dashed to pieces. We do not certainly know whether there is any right one. What must we do? 'Be strong and of a good courage.' Act for the best, hope for the best, and take what comes.... If death ends all, we cannot meet death better."[44]

---

43   [Author's note] Since belief is measured by action, he who forbids us to believe religion to be true, necessarily also forbids us to act as we should if we did believe it to be true. The whole defence of religious faith hinges upon action. If the action required or inspired by the religious hypothesis is in no way different from that dictated by the naturalistic hypothesis, then religious faith is a pure superfluity, better pruned away, and controversy about its legitimacy is a piece of idle trifling, unworthy of serious minds. I myself believe, of course, that the religious hypothesis gives to the world an expression which specifically determines our reactions, and makes them in a large part unlike what they might be on a purely naturalistic scheme of belief.

---

44   [Author's note] *Liberty, Equality, Fraternity*, p. 353, 2nd edition. London, 1874.

ALVIN PLANTINGA
"Is Belief in God Properly Basic?"

Who Is Alvin Plantinga?

Alvin Plantinga is the John A. O'Brien Professor of Philosophy at the University of Notre Dame and among the leading American philosophers of religion alive today, as well as being a major figure in contemporary epistemology (theory of knowledge) and metaphysics (specifically the metaphysics of possibility and necessity).

Plantinga was born in 1932 in Ann Arbor, Michigan. His father, who was also an academic, was an immigrant from the Netherlands, and Plantinga was raised in the Dutch Reformed religious tradition, which follows a theology based on the teachings of John Calvin. Plantinga took his undergraduate degree at Calvin College (in Grand Rapids, Michigan), where his father had a position teaching psychology. Alvin was offered a scholarship to Harvard, and attended classes there for one semester, but during spring recess he returned home to visit his parents and sat in on some classes at Calvin by a philosophy professor called William Harry Jellema. This was a turning point for the young Plantinga. While at Harvard he had been troubled by what he called his first encounter with "serious non-Christian thought"; by contrast, he was powerfully struck by Jellema's articulation of the view "that much of the intellectual opposition to Christianity and theism was really a sort of intellectual imperialism with little real basis.... I found Jellema deeply impressive," Plantinga writes in his 'Spiritual Autobiography,' "so impressive that I decided then and there to leave Harvard, return to Calvin, and study philosophy with him. That

was as important a decision, and as good a decision, as I've ever made."[1]

Plantinga later studied as a graduate student at the University of Michigan and completed his PhD at Yale in 1958. He taught there and at Wayne State University (in Detroit, and at the time one of the more active philosophy departments in America) before moving back to Calvin College as a professor in 1963, to replace the retiring Jellema. He took up his position at Notre Dame in 1982.

He has written more than a dozen books on God, metaphysics, and epistemology, and scores of scholarly articles.

What Is the Structure of This Reading?

In this article, Plantinga argues that "the believer is entirely within his intellectual rights in believing [in the existence of God] ... even if he doesn't know of any good theistic argument (deductive or inductive), even if he doesn't believe that there is any such argument, and even if in fact no such argument exists." That is, belief in God does not need to be justified by an argument from *other beliefs*; nevertheless, Plantinga argues, it is a justified, or rational, belief.

Plantinga compares this position with the opposing view, which he calls evidentialism. According to evidentialism, beliefs are rationally justified if they are either properly inferred from other

---

1   "A Christian Life Partly Lived" in *Philosophers Who Believe*, ed. Kelly Clark (Downer's Grove: InterVarsity Press, 1993).

justified beliefs, or are 'basic' beliefs that are self-evidently true without the need for further justification. Since the existence of God is not self-evident, it would follow that some argument is required to establish his existence. Plantinga denies this: according to him, belief in God is "properly basic" *even though* it is not self-evident—that is, he argues that the evidentialists have too narrow an account of what it is to be basic.

Plantinga argues that the 'classical foundationalist' version of what it is to be basic is untenable. Then he considers, and rejects, two possible objections to a broader account of basic belief: first, that beliefs that are held without evidence are thereby groundless or arbitrary; and second, that if belief in God is basic then any old belief could be considered basic too. He argues, against the second objection, that a proper account of basic belief must start from a set of examples of beliefs that are clearly, and pre-theoretically, either basic or non-basic, and that belief in God is a legitimate example of a pre-theoretically basic belief.

Suggestions for Critical Reflection

1. Plantinga asserts that "I believe that 2 + 1 = 3, for example, and don't believe it on the basis of other propositions." Why does Plantinga say this? Are there no more basic beliefs that together justify 2 + 1 = 3? (Are there no more basic *propositions*, whether or not Plantinga actually bases his belief on them? Is this a different question?)
2. When, if ever, is it reasonable to believe something for which there is insufficient evidence?
3. Plantinga very quickly, in this article, rejects the view that belief in God is not properly basic because it is not a belief that is self-evident or incorrigible. Could belief in God be properly considered self-evident? If not, might that be a reason for thinking that it's not a basic belief? Why do you think that Plantinga rejects this line of thought?
4. According to Plantinga, there are "many conditions and circumstances that call forth belief in God." Is he right about this? Are these conditions what Plantinga calls "justifying conditions" for beliefs relevant to the existence of

God? How exactly might this work—how does it compare to the examples of perception and memory that he describes earlier in the essay?
5. Plantinga holds that belief in God is properly basic, while belief in the Great Pumpkin is not only not basic but ungrounded and false. "God has implanted in us a natural tendency to see his hand in the world around us; the same cannot be said for the Great Pumpkin, there being no Great Pumpkin and no natural tendency to accept beliefs about the Great Pumpkin." Is there any problematic circularity in his argument?
6. Is there, in your considered view, sufficient evidence for belief in God? If there is not, what, if any, difference should this make to religious believers?

Suggestions for Further Reading

Two good sources for more of Plantinga's views of the justification of religious belief are *Faith and Rationality* (University of Notre Dame Press, 1983), edited by Alvin Plantinga and Nicholas Wolterstorff, which includes an essay by Plantinga called "Reason and Belief in God," and his *Warranted Christian Belief* (Oxford University Press, 2000). He is also the author of a quite well-known essay called "Advice to Christian Philosophers," *Faith and Philosophy* 1 (1984), pp. 253–271. Two collections of essays on Plantinga's philosophy of religion are *Alvin Plantinga*, ed. James Tomberlin and Peter van Inwagen (D. Reidel, 1985), and *Rational Faith*, ed. Linda Zagzebski (University of Notre Dame Press, 1993).

"Is Belief in God Properly Basic?"[2]

Many philosophers have urged the *evidentialist* objection to theistic belief; they have argued that belief in God is irrational or unreasonable or not rationally acceptable or intellectually irresponsible or noetically[3]

---

2   *Noûs*, Vol. 15, No. 1, 1981 A.P.A. Western Division Meetings (Mar., 1981), pp. 41–51. Reproduced with permission of Wiley-Blackwell Inc.
3   'Noetic' means relating to or based on reason (from the classical Greek word *noûs*, mind).

substandard, because, as they say, there is insufficient evidence for it.[4] Many other philosophers and theologians—in particular, those in the great tradition of natural theology[5]—have claimed that belief in God is intellectually acceptable, but only because the fact is there is sufficient evidence for it. These two groups unite in holding that theistic belief is rationally acceptable only if there is sufficient evidence for it. More exactly, they hold that a person is rational or reasonable in accepting theistic belief only if she has sufficient evidence for it—only if, that is, she knows or rationally believes some *other* propositions which support the one in question, and believes the latter on the basis of the former. In [4] I argued that the evidentialist objection is rooted in *classical foundationalism*,[6] an enormously popular picture or total way of looking at faith, knowledge, justified belief, rationality and allied topics. This picture has been widely accepted ever since the days of Plato and Aristotle; its near relatives, perhaps, remain the dominant ways of thinking about these topics. We may think of the classical foundationalist as beginning with the observation that some of one's beliefs may be *based upon* others; it may be that there are a pair of propositions A and B such that I believe *A on the basis of B*. Although this relation isn't easy to characterize in a revealing and non-trivial fashion, it is nonetheless familiar. I believe that the word 'umbrageous' is spelled u-m-b-r-a-g-e-o-u-s: this belief is based on another belief of mine: the belief that that's how the dictionary says it's spelled. I believe that 72 x 71 =

5112. This belief is based upon several other beliefs I hold: that 1 x 72 = 72; 7 x 2 = 14; 7 x 7 = 49; 49 + 1 = 50; and others.[7] Some of my beliefs, however, I accept but don't accept on the basis of any other beliefs. Call these beliefs *basic*. I believe that 2 + 1 = 3, for example, and don't believe it on the basis of other propositions. I also believe that I am seated at my desk, and that there is a mild pain in my right knee. These too are basic to me; I don't believe them on the basis of any other propositions. According to the classical foundationalist, some propositions are *properly* or *rightly* basic for a person and some are not. Those that are not, are rationally accepted only on the basis of *evidence*, where the evidence must trace back, ultimately, to what is properly basic. The existence of God, furthermore, is not among the propositions that are properly basic; hence a person is rational in accepting theistic belief only if he has evidence for it.

Now many Reformed thinkers and theologians[8] have rejected *natural theology* (thought of as the attempt to provide proofs or arguments for the existence of God). They have held not merely that the proffered arguments are unsuccessful, but that the whole enterprise is in some way radically misguided. In [5], I argue that the reformed rejection of natural theology is best construed as an inchoate and unfocused rejection of classical foundationalism. What these Reformed thinkers really mean to hold, I think, is that belief in God need not be based on argument or evidence from other propositions at all. They mean to hold that the

---

4   [Author's note] See, for example [1], pp. 400 ff, [2], pp. 345 ff, [3], p. 22, [6], pp. 3 ff. and [7], pp. 87 ff. In [4] I consider and reject the evidentialist objection to theistic belief.

5   That is, theology that restricts itself to using the same investigative methods and standards of evidence as are accepted in the rest of philosophy or science.

6   This is the view that, for some given system of belief, there is a set of basic (non-inferential, self-evidently true) propositions from which every other true proposition in the system can be derived. Non-basic beliefs are justified by their derivation from foundational beliefs, and any non-basic beliefs that are not so derivable are not justified.

7   Plantinga is here breaking down the steps by which one would calculate 72 x 71 using the method of long multiplication with a pencil and paper:

$$
\begin{array}{r}
7\ 2 \\
\times\ \ 7\ 1 \\
\hline
7\ 2 \\
1\ \ 4 \\
4\ \ 9 \\
\hline
5\ \ 1\ \ 1\ \ 2 \\
\end{array}
$$

8   [Author's note] A Reformed thinker or theologian is one whose intellectual sympathies lie with the Protestant tradition going back to John Calvin (not someone who was formerly a theologian and has since seen the light).

believer is entirely within his intellectual rights in believing as he does even if he doesn't know of any good theistic argument (deductive or inductive), even if he doesn't believe that there is any such argument, and even if in fact no such argument exists. They hold that it is perfectly rational to accept belief in God without accepting it on the basis of any other beliefs or propositions at all. In a word, they hold that *belief in God is properly basic*. In this paper I shall try to develop and defend this position.

But first we must achieve a deeper understanding of the evidentialist objection. It is important to see that this contention is a normative contention. The evidentialist objector holds that one who accepts theistic belief is in some way irrational or noetically substandard. Here 'rational' and 'irrational' are to be taken as normative or evaluative terms; according to the objector, the theist fails to measure up to a standard he ought to conform to. There is a right way and a wrong way with respect to belief as with respect to actions; we have duties, responsibilities, obligations with respect to the former just as with respect to the latter. So Professor Blanshard:[9]

> ... everywhere and always belief has an ethical aspect. There is such a thing as a general ethics of the intellect. The main principle of that ethic I hold to be the same inside and outside religion. This principle is simple and sweeping: Equate your assent to the evidence. [1] p. 401

This "ethics of the intellect" can be construed variously; many fascinating issues—issues we must here forebear to enter—arise when we try to state more exactly the various options the evidentialist may mean to adopt. Initially it looks as if he holds that there is a duty or obligation of some sort not to accept without evidence such propositions as that God exists—a duty flouted by the theist who has no evidence. If he has no evidence, then it is his duty to cease believing. But there is an oft remarked difficulty: one's beliefs, for the most part, are not directly under one's control. Most of those who believe in God could not divest themselves of that belief just by trying to do so, just as they could

not in that way rid themselves of the belief that the world has existed for a very long time. So perhaps the relevant obligation is not that of divesting myself of theistic belief if I have no evidence (that is beyond my power), but to try to cultivate the sorts of intellectual habits that will tend (we hope) to issue in my accepting as basic only propositions that are properly basic.

Perhaps this obligation is to be thought of *teleologically*:[10] it is a moral obligation arising out of a connection between certain intrinsic goods and evils and the way in which our beliefs are formed and held. (This seems to be W.K. Clifford's way of construing the matter.[11]) Perhaps it is to be thought of *aretetically*: there are valuable noetic or intellectual states (whether intrinsically or extrinsically valuable); there are also corresponding intellectual virtues, habits of acting so as to promote and enhance those valuable states. Among one's obligations, then, is the duty to try to foster and cultivate these virtues in oneself or others. Or perhaps it is to be thought of *deontologically*: this obligation attaches to us just by virtue of our having the sort of noetic equipment human beings do in fact display; it does not arise out of a connection with valuable states of affairs. Such an obligation, furthermore, could be a special sort of moral obligation; on the other hand, perhaps it is a *sui generis*[12] non-moral obligation.

Still further, perhaps the evidentialist need not speak of duty or obligation here at all. Consider someone who believes that Venus is smaller than Mercury, not because he has evidence of any sort, but because he finds it amusing to hold a belief no one else does—

---

9   Brand Blanshard (1892–1987), American rationalist philosopher.

10   Plantinga is drawing a three-way distinction here that is a standard way of understanding the main classes of ethical theory, and applying it to epistemology. An obligation is teleological (or consequentialist) if it is the obligation to produce good results; it is aretetic (from Greek *aretē*) if it is a matter of displaying a certain kind of virtue or excellence; it is deontological if it is a rule for behavior that holds independently of results.

11   William Kingdon Clifford (1845–1879) was an English mathematician and philosopher; his paper "The Ethics of Belief" (1879) was a target of William James's "The Will to Believe."

12   An idea that cannot be included in, or covered by, a broader concept—the only example of its kind.

or consider someone who holds this belief on the basis of some outrageously bad argument. Perhaps there isn't any obligation he has failed to meet. Nevertheless his intellectual condition is deficient in some way; or perhaps alternatively there is a commonly achieved excellence he fails to display. And the evidentialist objection to theistic belief, then, might be understood, as the claim, not that the theist without evidence has failed to meet an obligation, but that he suffers from a certain sort of intellectual deficiency (so that the proper attitude toward him would be sympathy rather than censure).

These are some of the ways, then, in which the evidentialist objection could be developed; and of course there are still other possibilities. For ease of exposition, let us take the claim deontologically; what I shall say will apply *mutatis mutandis*[13] if we take it one of the other ways. The evidentialist objection, therefore, presupposes some view as to what sorts of propositions are correctly, or rightly, or justifiably taken as basic; it presupposes a view as to what is *properly* basic. And the minimally relevant claim for the evidentialist objector is that belief in God is *not* properly basic. Typically this objection has been rooted in some form of *classical foundationalism*, according to which a proposition *p* is properly basic for a person *S* if and only if *p* is either self-evident or incorrigible[14] for *S* (modern foundationalism) or either self-evident or 'evident to the senses' for *S* (ancient and medieval foundationalism). In [4] I argued that both forms of foundationalism are self referentially incoherent and must therefore be rejected.

Insofar as the evidentialist objection is rooted in classical foundationalism, it is poorly rooted indeed: and so far as I know, no one has developed and articulated any other reason for supposing that belief in God is not properly basic. Of course it doesn't follow that it is properly basic; perhaps the class of properly basic propositions is broader than classical

foundationalists think, but still not broad enough to admit belief in God. But why think so? What might be the objections to the Reformed view that belief in God is properly basic?

I've heard it argued that if I have no evidence for the existence of God, then if I accept that proposition, my belief will be groundless, or gratuitous, or arbitrary. I think this is an error; let me explain.

Suppose we consider perceptual beliefs, memory beliefs, and beliefs which ascribe mental states to other persons: such beliefs as

(1)   I see a tree,
(2)   I had breakfast this morning,
and
(3)   That person is angry.

Although beliefs of this sort are typically and properly taken as basic, it would be a mistake to describe them as *groundless*. Upon having experience of a certain sort, I believe that I am perceiving a tree. In the typical case I do not hold this belief on the basis of other beliefs; it is nonetheless not groundless. My having that characteristic sort of experience—to use Professor Chisholm's[15] language, my being appeared treely to—plays a crucial role in the formation and justification of that belief. We might say this experience, together, perhaps, with other circumstances, is what *justifies* me in holding it; this is the *ground* of my justification, and, by extension, the ground of the belief itself.

If I see someone displaying typical pain behavior, I take it that he or she is in pain. Again, I don't take the displayed behavior as *evidence* for that belief; I don't infer that belief from others I hold; I don't accept it on the basis of other beliefs. Still, my perceiving the pain behavior plays a unique role in the formation and justification of that belief; as in the previous case, it forms the ground of my justification for the belief in question. The same holds for memory beliefs. I seem to remember having breakfast this morning; that is, I have an inclination to believe the proposition that I had breakfast, along with a certain past-tinged experience that is familiar to all but hard to describe. Perhaps we

13   After changing what needs to be changed (in the arguments).

14   Incorrigible means, in most philosophical contexts, guaranteed to be correct (as opposed to unmanageable or depraved, which can be part of the everyday meaning of the word).

15   Roderick Chisholm (1916–1999) was an American philosopher; his fairly influential 'adverbial theory' of mental states was presented in *Perceiving* (Routledge & Kegan Paul, 1957).

should say that I am appeared to pastly; but perhaps this insufficiently distinguishes the experience in question from that accompanying beliefs about the past not grounded in my own memory. The phenomenology of memory is a rich and unexplored realm; here I have no time to explore it. In this case as in the others, however, there is a justifying circumstance present, a condition that forms the ground of my justification for accepting the memory belief in question.

In each of these cases, a belief is taken as basic, and in each case properly taken as basic. In each case there is some circumstance or condition that confers justification; there is a circumstance that serves as the *ground* of justification. So in each case there will be some true proposition of the sort

    (4)   In condition *C*, *S* is justified in taking *p* as basic.

Of course *C* will vary with *p*. For a perceptual judgment such as

    (5)   I see a rose colored wall before me,

C will include my being appeared to in a certain fashion. No doubt *C* will include more. If I'm appeared to in the familiar fashion but know that I'm wearing rose colored glasses, or that I am suffering from a disease that causes me to be thus appeared to, no matter what the color of the nearby objects, then I'm not justified in taking (5) as basic. Similarly for memory. Suppose I know that my memory is unreliable; it often plays me tricks. In particular, when I seem to remember having breakfast, then, more often than not, I *haven't* had breakfast. Under these conditions I am not justified in taking it as basic that I had breakfast, even though I seem to remember that I did.

So being appropriately appeared to, in the perceptual case, is not sufficient for justification; some further condition—a condition hard to state in detail—is clearly necessary. The central point, here, however, is that a belief is properly basic only in certain conditions; these conditions are, we might say, the ground of its justification and, by extension, the ground of the belief itself. In this sense, basic beliefs are not, or are not necessarily, *groundless* beliefs.

Now similar things may be said about belief in God. When the Reformers claim that this belief is properly basic, they do not mean to say, of course, that there are no justifying circumstances for it, or

that it is in that sense groundless or gratuitious. Quite the contrary. Calvin[16] holds that God "reveals and daily discloses himself to the whole workmanship of the universe," and the divine art "reveals itself in the innumerable and yet distinct and well ordered variety of the heavenly host." God has so created us that we have a tendency or disposition to see his hand in the world about us. More precisely, there is in us a disposition to believe propositions of the sort *this flower was created by God* or *this vast and intricate universe was created by God* when we contemplate the flower or behold the starry heavens or think about the vast reaches of the universe.

Calvin recognizes, at least implicitly, that other sorts of conditions may trigger this disposition. Upon reading the Bible, one may be impressed with a deep sense that God is speaking to him. Upon having done what I know is cheap, or wrong, or wicked I may feel guilty in God's sight and form the belief *God disapproves of what I've done*. Upon confession and repentance, I may feel forgiven, forming the belief God forgives me for what I've done. A person in grave danger may turn to God, asking for his protection and help; and of course he or she then forms the belief that God is indeed able to hear and help if he sees fit. When life is sweet and satisfying, a spontaneous sense of gratitude may well up within the soul; someone in this condition may thank and praise the Lord for his goodness, and will of course form the accompanying belief that indeed the Lord is to be thanked and praised.

There are therefore many conditions and circumstances that call forth belief in God: guilt, gratitude, danger, a sense of God's presence, a sense that he speaks, perception of various parts of the universe. A complete job would explore the phenomenology of all these conditions and of more besides. This is a large and important topic; but here I can only point to the existence of these conditions.

---

16   John Calvin (1509–1564) was a French theologian who formulated a system of reformed Christian theology, centered in Geneva in the mid-sixteenth century and spreading quickly to Scotland, the Netherlands, and parts of Germany, that became known as Calvinism or the Reformed tradition. Calvin's main written work is *Institutes of the Christian Religion* (1536).

Of course none of the beliefs I mentioned a moment ago is the simple belief that God exists. What we have instead are such beliefs as

> (6)   God is speaking to me,
>
> (7)   God has created all this,
>
> (8)   God disapproves of what I have done,
>
> (9)   God forgives me,

and

> (10)   God is to be thanked and praised.

These propositions are properly basic in the right circumstances. But it is quite consistent with this to suppose that the proposition *there is such a person as God* is neither properly basic nor taken as basic by those who believe in God. Perhaps what they take as basic are such propositions as (6)–(10), believing in the existence of God on the basis of propositions such as those. From this point of view, it isn't exactly right to say that it is belief in God that is properly basic; more exactly, what are properly basic are such propositions as (6)–(10), each of which self-evidently entails that God exists. It isn't the relatively high level and general proposition *God exists* that is properly basic, but instead propositions detailing some of his attributes or actions.

Suppose we return to the analogy between belief in God and belief in the existence of perceptual objects, other persons, and the past. Here too it is relatively specific and concrete propositions rather than their more general and abstract colleagues that are properly basic. Perhaps such items as

> (11)   There are trees,
>
> (12)   There are other persons, and
>
> (13)   The world has existed for more than 5 minutes,

are not in fact properly basic; it is instead such propositions as

> (14)   I see a tree,
>
> (15)   that person is pleased, and
>
> (16)   I had breakfast more than an hour ago,

that deserve that accolade. Of course propositions of the latter sort immediately and self-evidently entail propositions of the former sort; and perhaps there is thus no harm in speaking of the former as properly basic, even though so to speak is to speak a bit loosely.

The same must be said about belief in God. We may say, speaking loosely, that belief in God is prop-

erly basic; strictly speaking, however, it is probably not that proposition but such propositions as (6)–(10) that enjoy that status. But the main point, here, is that belief in God or (6)–(10), are properly basic; to say so, however, is not to deny that there are justifying conditions for these beliefs, or conditions that confer justification on one who accepts them as basic. They are therefore not groundless or gratuitous.

A second objection I've often heard: if belief in God is properly basic, why can't *just any* belief be properly basic? Couldn't we say the same for any bizarre aberration we can think of? What about voodoo or astrology? What about the belief that the Great Pumpkin returns every Halloween? Could I properly take *that* as basic? And if I can't, why can I properly take belief in God as basic? Suppose I believe that if I flap my arms with sufficient vigor, I can take off and fly about the room; could I defend myself against the charge of irrationality by claiming this belief is basic? If we say that belief in God is properly basic, won't we be committed to holding that just anything, or nearly anything, can properly be taken as basic, thus throwing wide the gates to irrationalism and superstition?

Certainly not. What might lead one to think the Reformed epistemologist is in this kind of trouble? The fact that he rejects the criteria for proper basicality purveyed by classical foundationalism? But why should *that* be thought to commit him to such tolerance of irrationality? Consider an analogy. In the palmy days of positivism, the positivists went about confidently wielding their verifiability criterion and declaring meaningless much that was obviously meaningful. Now suppose someone rejected a formulation of that criterion—the one to be found in the second edition of A.J. Ayer's *Language, Truth and Logic*, for example.[17] Would that mean she was committed to holding that

---

17   In one of Ayer's formulations, the principle of verification is: "a statement is held to be literally meaningful if and only if it is either analytic or empirically verifiable" (*Language, Truth and Logic*, second edition [Penguin Books, 1946], p. 176). To a first approximation, a statement is verifiable, according to Ayer, if "some possible sense-experience would be relevant to the determination of its truth or falsehood" (*ibid.*, p. 179).

(17) Twas brillig; and the slithy toves did gyre and gymble in the wabe

contrary to appearances, makes good sense? Of course not. But then the same goes for the Reformed epistemologist; the fact that he rejects the Classical Foundationalist's criterion of proper basicality does not mean that he is committed to supposing just anything is properly basic.

But what then is the problem? Is it that the Reformed epistemologist not only rejects those criteria for proper basicality, but seems in no hurry to produce what he takes to be a better substitute? If he has no such criterion, how can he fairly reject belief in the Great Pumpkin as properly basic?

This objection betrays an important misconception. How do we rightly arrive at or develop criteria for meaningfulness, or justified belief, or proper basicality? Where do they come from? Must one have such a criterion before one can sensibly make any judgments—positive or negative—about proper basicality? Surely not. Suppose I don't know of a satisfactory substitute for the criteria proposed by classical foundationalism; I am nevertheless entirely within my rights in holding that certain propositions are not properly basic in certain conditions. Some propositions seem self-evident when in fact they are not; that is the lesson of some of the Russell paradoxes.[18] Nevertheless it would be irrational to take as basic the denial of a proposition that seems self-evident to

you. Similarly, suppose it seems to you that you see a tree; you would then be irrational in taking as basic the proposition that you don't see a tree, or that there aren't any trees. In the same way, even if I don't know of some illuminating criterion of meaning, I can quite properly declare (17) meaningless.

And this raises an important question—one Roderick Chisholm has taught us to ask. What is the status of criteria for knowledge, or proper basicality, or justified belief? Typically, these are universal statements. The modern foundationalist's criterion for proper basicality, for example, is doubly universal:

(18) For any proposition A and person S, A is properly basic for S if and only if A is incorrigible for S or self-evident to S.

But how could one know a thing like that? What are its credentials? Clearly enough, (18) isn't self-evident or just obviously true. But if it isn't, how does one arrive at it? What sorts of arguments would be appropriate? Of course a foundationalist might find (18) so appealing, he simply takes it to be true, neither offering argument for it, nor accepting it on the basis of other things he believes. If he does so, however, his noetic structure will be self-referentially incoherent.[19] (18) itself is neither self-evident nor incorrigible; hence in accepting (18) as basic, the modern foundationalist violates the condition of proper basicality he himself lays down in accepting it. On the other hand, perhaps the foundationalist will try to produce some argument for it from premises that are self-evident or incorrigible: it is exceedingly hard to see, however, what such an argument might be like. And until he has produced such arguments, what shall the rest of us do—we who do not find (18) at all obvious or compelling? How could he use (18) to show us that belief in God, for example, is not properly basic? Why should we believe (18), or pay it any attention?

The fact is, I think, that neither (18) nor any other revealing necessary and sufficient condition for proper basicality follows from clearly self-evident premisses by clearly acceptable arguments. And hence the proper way to arrive at such a criterion is, broadly

---

18   In a small town there is only one barber; this is the man who shaves all and only those men who do not shave themselves. Who shaves the barber? This is a paradox because, if the barber does not shave himself, then by definition he does (the barber shaves everyone who does not shave themselves), yet if the barber does shave himself then, by definition, he does not (the barber shaves only those men who do not shave themselves). What this reveals is that the initial description of the small town's shaving arrangements, while it may have seemed perfectly straightforward, actually contains a hidden self-contradiction: there could be no such barber. British philosopher Bertrand Russell (1872–1970) used an example of this type in 1901 to show that mathematical set theory, as it was then understood, contained a contradiction.

19   I.e., (roughly) what he takes to be rational will contradict itself: 'believe only basic or justified propositions'; *and* 'believe (18), which is neither basic nor justified.'

speaking, *inductive*. We must assemble examples of beliefs and conditions such that the former are obviously properly basic in the latter, and examples of beliefs and conditions such that the former are obviously *not* properly basic in the latter. We must then frame hypotheses as to the necessary and sufficient conditions of proper basicality and test these hypotheses by reference to those examples. Under the right conditions, for example, it is clearly rational to believe that you see a human person before you: a being who has thoughts and feelings, who knows and believes things, who makes decisions and acts. It is clear, furthermore, that you are under no obligation to reason to this belief from others you hold; under those conditions that belief is properly basic for you. But then (18) must be mistaken; the belief in question, under those circumstances, is properly basic, though neither self-evident nor incorrigible for you. Similarly, you may seem to remember that you had breakfast this morning, and perhaps you know of no reason to suppose your memory is playing you tricks. If so, you are entirely justified in taking that belief as basic. Of course it isn't properly basic on the criteria offered by classical foundationalists; but that fact counts not against you but against those criteria.

Accordingly, criteria for proper basicality must be reached from below rather than above; they should not be presented as *ex Cathedra*,[20] but argued to and tested by a relevant set of examples. But there is no reason to assume, in advance, that everyone will agree on the examples. The Christian will of course suppose that belief in God is entirely proper and rational; if he doesn't accept this belief on the basis of other propositions, he will conclude that it is basic for him and quite properly so. Followers of Bertrand Russell and Madelyn Murray O'Hare [sic][21] may disagree,

but how is that relevant? Must my criteria, or those of the Christian community, conform to their examples? Surely not. The Christian community is responsible to *its* set of examples, not to theirs.

Accordingly, the Reformed epistemologist can properly hold that belief in the Great Pumpkin is not properly basic, even though he holds that belief in God is properly basic and even if he has no full fledged criterion of proper basicality. Of course he is committed to supposing that there is a relevant *difference* between belief in God and belief in the Great Pumpkin, if he holds that the former but not the latter is properly basic. But this should prove no great embarrassment; there are plenty of candidates. These candidates are to be found in the neighborhood of the conditions I mentioned in the last section that justify and ground belief in God. Thus, for example, the Reformed epistemologist may concur with Calvin in holding that God has implanted in us a natural tendency to see his hand in the world around us; the same cannot be said for the Great Pumpkin, there being no Great Pumpkin and no natural tendency to accept beliefs about the Great Pumpkin.

By way of conclusion then: being self-evident, or incorrigible, or evident to the senses is not a necessary condition of proper basicality. Furthermore, one who holds that belief in God is properly basic is not thereby committed to the idea that belief in God is groundless or gratuitous or without justifying circumstances. And even if he lacks a general criterion of proper basicality, he is not obliged to suppose that just any or nearly any belief—belief in the Great Pumpkin, for example—is properly basic. Like everyone should, he begins with examples; and he may take belief in the Great Pumpkin as a paradigm of irrational basic belief.

References

[1] Blanshard, Brand, *Reason and Belief* (London: Allen & Unwin, 1974).

[2] Clifford, W.K., "The Ethics of Belief" in *Lectures and Essays* (London: Macmillan, 1879).

---

20 A pronouncement that is to be considered infallible or authoritative in virtue of the position of the one who utters it. (*Ex cathedra* is Latin for 'from the chair,' and the phrase is often used to characterize the teachings of the Roman Catholic pope, who occupies the 'chair of Peter.')

21 Madelyn Murray O'Hair (1919–1995) was a prominent American atheist, the founder and long-term president of the organization American Atheists; she

is best known for launching one of the lawsuits that led to the Supreme Court decision banning prayer from American public schools in 1963.

[3] Flew, A.G.N., *The Presumption of Atheism* (London: Pemberton Publishing Co., 1976).

[4] Plantinga, A., "Is Belief in God Rational?" in *Rationality and Religious Belief*, ed. C. Delaney (Notre Dame: University of Notre Dame Press, 1979).

[5] ——, "The Reformed Objection to Natural Theology," *Proceedings of the American Catholic Philosophical Association*, 1980.

[6] Russell, Bertrand, "Why I am not a Christian," in *Why I am Not a Christian* (New York: Simon & Schuster, 1957).

[7] Scrivin, Michael, *Primary Philosophy* (New York: McGraw-Hill, 1966).

CHAPTER 3

Epistemology—Is the External World the Way It Appears to Be?

INTRODUCTION TO THE QUESTION

'Epistemology' is the theory of knowledge (the word comes from the Greek *epistēmē*, meaning knowledge). Epistemology can be thought of as arranged around three fundamental questions:

i) *What is knowledge?* For example, what is the difference between believing something that happens to be true and actually *knowing* it to be true? How much justification or proof do we need (if any) before we can be said to know something? Or does knowledge have more to do with, say, the *reliability* of our beliefs than our arguments for them? What is the difference between the conclusions of good science and those of, say, astrology? Or between astrology and religion?

ii) *What can we know?* What are the scope and limits of our knowledge? Can we ever really *know* about the real, underlying nature of the universe? Can we aspire to religious knowledge (e.g., of the true nature of God), or to ethical knowledge (as opposed to mere ethical belief or opinion), or to reliable knowledge of the historical past or the future? Can I ever know what you are thinking, or even *that* you are thinking? Do I even really know what *I* am thinking: e.g., might I have beliefs and desires that I am unaware of, perhaps because they are repressed or simply non-conscious?

iii) *How do we know that we know?* That is, how can we *justify* our claims to know things? What counts as 'enough' justification for a belief? Where does our knowledge—if we have any at all—come from in the first place? Do we acquire knowledge only through sense-experience, or can we also come to know important things through the power of our own naked reason? Do we have some beliefs which are especially 'basic'—which can be so reliably known that they can

form a foundation for all our other beliefs? Or, by contrast, do all our pieces of knowledge fit together like the answers in a giant crossword puzzle, with each belief potentially up for grabs if the rest of the puzzle changes?

The epistemological question that is the focus of this chapter is sometimes called 'the problem of the external world.' In its starkest form, it is simply this: are *any* of our beliefs about the world outside our own heads justified? Can we be sure that any of them at all are *true*? For example, I currently believe that there is a laptop computer in front of me, and a soft-drink can on the table to my left, and a window to my right out of which I can see trees and grass and other houses. Furthermore, I not only believe that these objects exist but I also believe that they have a certain nature: that the pop can is colored red; that the trees outside are further away from me in space than the window I am looking through; that the houses are three-dimensional objects with solid walls, and that they continue to exist even when I close my eyes or turn away; that my computer will continue to behave in a (relatively!) predictable way in accordance with the laws of physics and of computing. But are any of these beliefs of mine justified: do any of them cross the threshold into being *knowledge*, as opposed to mere conjecture? And if some of them are known and not others, *which* are the ones I really know? Which are the beliefs to which a rational person should be committed, and which are the ones a rational person should jettison?

It may seem that these kinds of questions should be fairly straightforward to answer. *Of course* I know that my pop can exists and is really red; it should be pretty easy just to think for a while and give my compelling reasons for having this belief—the reasons which make this belief much more likely to be true than, say, the belief that the can is a figment of my imagination, or is really colorless. However, it turns out, the problem of the external world is a very challenging problem indeed, and one which has been an important philosophical issue since at least the seventeenth century.

The first six readings in this chapter explore different aspects of the problem of the external world. First, we might ask, does the external world exist *at all*—is there any such thing as a world outside my own head, or might reality be just a dream? Descartes is the classic source for the formulation of this problem, which he raises and then tries to answer. However, in 'solving' this problem, Descartes comes to the conclusion that only some of the things we commonsensically believe about the real nature of the external world are true or justifiable. The Locke reading can be thought of as extending this insight and making it more precise through his discussion of the distinction between 'primary qualities' (which resemble our ideas of them) and 'secondary qualities' (which do not). Locke also raises a somewhat different question: what can we know about the sort of 'stuff' that the external world is made of—if it is 'matter,' then what can we say about the kind of *substance* which is matter? Berkeley seizes upon this problem and uses it as a reason to abandon the whole notion of matter: though he does not deny that an 'external' world exists, nor that most of what we normally believe about it is true, Berkeley does deny that our materialist *theory* of the external world is true: he holds that the 'external' world is really a collection of ideas in the mind of God.

Kant, faced with what by this time seemed the intractable problem of proving that mind-independent material objects exist and resemble our ideas of them, attempted to make a radical break with the philosophical assumptions which he thought had generated the puzzle in the first place. Instead of assuming that our mental representations of the world are passive pictures of reality (which, like a portrait, could either be a good likeness or misleadingly inaccurate), he argued that our minds actually *interact* with data

from the external world to *create* 'empirical reality.' For example, he claims, we cannot be mistaken in believing that external objects are three-dimensional, persist through time, and interact causally with each other, since all these features of reality are essential features of empirical experience: it is impossible, according to Kant, that anyone could experience an external reality which was not arranged in this way.

Russell and Moore represent twentieth-century approaches to the problem of the external world. Russell suggests that our belief in the existence of a material external world is justified since it is the simplest hypothesis which could explain the behavior of our 'sense-data.' However, he points out that science tells us that the real nature of this external world is radically different than the way it appears to us. Moore, by contrast, defends a more 'common sense' approach to the problem of the external world, and with great care tries to show that there are many perfectly good proofs available to show that things exist external to our minds: for example, one can solve the problem of the external world by showing that at least two hands exist, and you can do this, Moore thinks, by simply waving your hands in front of your face.

The final two readings in this section introduce two key epistemological innovations of the twentieth century. Gettier's article "Is Justified True Belief Knowledge?" presents a deep problem for the basic philosophical intuition—which in some form goes all the way back to Plato—that any belief that is both true and properly justified counts as an instance of knowledge. Meanwhile, Lorraine Code challenges another generally historically-unquestioned assumption: that the ideal knower should be as objective as possible, such that any item of knowledge should be equally justifiable no matter what standpoint one occupies. Instead, Code argues, knowers are *situated*, and what they (can) know reflects their particular perspectives (as, for example, a woman rather than a man).

There are several good introductory epistemology textbooks currently available if you want more background information. For example: Robert Audi, *Epistemology* (Routledge, 2010); Ralph Baergen, *Contemporary Epistemology* (Harcourt Brace, 1995); Jonathan Dancy, *Introduction to Contemporary Epistemology* (Blackwell, 1985); Everitt and Fisher, *Modern*

Epistemology (McGraw-Hill, 1995); Richard Feldman, *Epistemology* (Prentice Hall, 2002); Keith Lehrer, *Theory of Knowledge* (Westview, 1990); Adam Morton, *A Guide Through the Theory of Knowledge* (Blackwell, 2002); Pollock and Cruz, *Contemporary Theories of Knowledge* (Rowman & Littlefield, 1999); Matthias Steup, *An Introduction to Contemporary Epistemology* (Prentice Hall, 1996); Steup and Sosa (eds.), *Contemporary Debates in* *Epistemology* (Blackwell, 2005); and Michael Williams, *Problems of Knowledge* (Oxford University Press, 2001). There are also a couple of useful reference works on epistemology: Dancy, Sosa, and Steup (eds.), *A Companion to Epistemology* (Blackwell, 2010); Paul K. Moser, *The Oxford Handbook of Epistemology* (Oxford University Press, 2005); and Greco and Sosa (eds.), *The Blackwell Guide to Epistemology* (Blackwell, 1999).

RENÉ DESCARTES
Meditations on First Philosophy

Who Was René Descartes?

René Descartes was born in 1596 in a small town nestled below the vineyards of the Loire in western France; at that time the town was called La Haye, but was later renamed Descartes in his honor. His early life was probably unhappy: he suffered from ill health, his mother had died a year after he was born, and he didn't get on well with his father. (When René sent his father a copy of his first published book, his father's only reported reaction was that he was displeased to have a son "idiotic enough to have himself bound in vellum."[1]) At the age of ten he went to the newly-founded college of La Flèche to be educated by the Jesuits. Descartes later called this college "one of the best schools in Europe," and it was there that he learned the medieval "scholastic" science and philosophy that he was later to decisively reject. Descartes took a law degree at Poitiers and then, at 22, joined first the Dutch army of Prince Maurice of Nassau and then the forces of Maximilian of Bavaria. For the next decade he traveled Europe "resolving to seek no knowledge other than that which could be found either in myself or in the great book of the world."

During this period he developed an intense interest in mathematics, which stayed with him for the rest of his life. In fact, Descartes was one of the most important figures in the development of algebra, which is the branch of mathematics that allows abstract relations to be described without using specific numbers, and which is therefore capable of unifying arithmetic and geometry:

> I came to see that the exclusive concern of mathematics is with questions of order or method, and that it is irrelevant whether the measure in question involves numbers, shapes, stars, sounds, or any other object whatsoever. This made me realize that there must be a general science which explains all the points that can be raised concerning order and measure irrespective of subject matter. (from *Rules for the Direction of our Native Intelligence*)

This insight led Descartes directly to one of the most significant intellectual innovations of the modern age: the conception of science as the exploration of abstract mathematical descriptions of the world.

It was also during this time—in 1619—that Descartes had the experience said to have inspired him to take up the life of a philosopher, and which, perhaps, eventually resulted in the form of the *Meditations*. Stranded by bad weather near Ulm on the river

---

1   Vellum is the parchment made from animal skin which was used to make books.

Danube, Descartes spent the day in a *poêle* or "stove-heated room" engaged in intense philosophical speculations. When he fell asleep that night he had three vivid dreams which he later described as giving him his mission in life. In the first dream Descartes felt himself attacked by phantoms and then a great wind; he was then greeted by a friend who gave him a message about a gift. On awaking after this first dream, Descartes felt a sharp pain which made him fear that the dream was the work of some deceitful evil demon. Descartes eventually fell back asleep and immediately had the second dream: a loud thunderclap, which woke him in terror believing that the room was filled with fiery sparks. The third and last dream was a pleasant one, in which he found an encyclopedia on a table next to a poetry anthology, open to a poem which begins with the line "Which road in life shall I follow?" A man then appeared and said *Est et non*—"it is and is not." While still dreaming, Descartes apparently began to speculate about the meaning of his dreams, and decided, among other things, that the gift of which his friend spoke in the first dream was the gift of solitude, the dictionary represented systematic knowledge, and "*Est et non*" spoke of the distinction between truth and falsity as revealed by the correct scientific method. Descartes concluded that he had a divine mission to found a new philosophical system to underpin all human knowledge.

In 1628 Descartes settled in Holland (at the time the most intellectually vibrant nation in Europe), where he lived for most of his remaining life. His family was wealthy enough that Descartes, who cultivated very modest tastes, was free of the necessity to earn a living and could devote his time to scientific experimentation and writing. By 1633 he had prepared a

book on cosmology and physics, called *Le Monde* (The World), in which he accepted Galileo's revolutionary claim that the Earth orbits the sun (rather than the other way around), but when he heard that Galileo had been condemned by the Inquisition of the Catholic Church, Descartes withdrew the work from publication. In 1637 he published (in French) a sample of his scientific work, the *Optics*, *Meteorology*, and *Geometry*, together with an introduction called *Discourse on the Method of Rightly Conducting One's Reason and Reaching the Truth in the Sciences*. Criticisms of this methodology led Descartes to compose his philosophical masterpiece, *Meditations on First Philosophy*, first published in Latin in 1641. A few years later he produced a summary of his scientific and philosophical views, the *Principles of Philosophy*, which he hoped would become a standard university textbook, replacing the medieval texts used at the time. His last work, published in 1649, was *The Passions of the Soul*, which attempted to extend his scientific methodology to ethics and psychology.

Descartes never married, but in 1635 he had a daughter, Francine, with a serving woman called Hélène Jans. He made arrangements to care for and educate the girl but she died of scarlet fever at the age of five, which was a devastating personal shock for Descartes.

In 1649 Descartes accepted an invitation to visit Stockholm and give philosophical instruction to Queen Kristina of Sweden. He was required to give tutorials at the royal palace at five o'clock in the morning, and it is said that the strain of this sudden break in his habits (he was accustomed to lying late in bed in the morning) caused him to catch pneumonia; he died in February, 1650. His dying words are said to have been, "*ça mon âme; il faut partir*"—so, my soul, it's time to part. His body was returned to France but, apparently, his head was secretly kept in Sweden; in the 1820s a skull bearing the faded inscription "René Descartes" was discovered in Stockholm and is now on display in the Museum of Natural History in Paris.

What Was Descartes' Overall Philosophical Project?

Descartes lived at a time when the accumulated beliefs of centuries—assumptions based on religious doctrine, straightforward observation, and common sense—were being gradually but remorselessly stripped away by exciting new discoveries. (The most striking example of this was the evidence mounting against the centuries-old belief that an unmoving Earth is the center of the universe, orbited by the moon, sun, stars, and all the other planets.) In this intellectual climate, Descartes became obsessed by the thought that no lasting scientific progress was possible without a systematic method for sifting through our preconceived assumptions and distinguishing between those that are reliable and those that are false. Descartes' central intellectual goal was to develop just such a reliable scientific method, and then to construct a coherent and unified theory of the world and of humankind's place within it. This theory, he hoped, would replace the deeply-flawed medieval system of thought (based on the science of Aristotle and Christian theology) called scholasticism.

A key feature of Descartes' system is that all knowledge should be based on utterly reliable foundations, discovered through the systematic rejection of any assumptions that can possibly be called into doubt. Then, as in mathematics, complex conclusions could be reliably derived from these foundations by long chains of reasoning, where each link in the chain is either a basic empirical observation or a simple and certain inference. The human faculty of *reason* was therefore of the greatest importance to Descartes. Furthermore, Descartes urged that scientific knowledge of the external world should be rooted, not in the deceptive and variable testimony of the senses, but on the concepts of pure mathematics.

That is, Cartesian science tries to reduce all physics to "what the geometers call *quantity*, and take as the object of their demonstrations, i.e., that to which every kind of division shape and motion is applicable" (*Principles of Philosophy*).

These ideas (though they have never been uncritically and uniformly accepted) have come to permeate the modern conception of science, including Descartes' influential metaphor of a unified "tree of knowledge," with metaphysics as the roots, physics as the trunk, and the special sciences (like biology, anthropology, or ethics) as the branches. One much less familiar aspect of Descartes' method for the production of knowledge is the central role played by God in his system. For Descartes, all human knowledge of the world around us essentially relies upon our prior knowledge that a non-deceiving God exists. Science, properly understood, not only does not conflict with religion but actually *depends* on religion, he believed.

Finally, one of the best-known results of Descartes' metaphysical reflections is "Cartesian dualism." This doctrine states that mind and body are two completely different substances—that the mind is a non-physical self in which all the operations of thought take place, and which can be wholly separated from the body after death. Like much of Descartes' work, this theory came to have the status of a more or less standard view for some three hundred years after his death, but at the time it was a radical philosophical innovation, breaking with the traditional Aristotelian conception of mental activity as a kind of *attribute* of the physical body (rather than as something entirely separable from the body).

What Is the Structure of This Reading?

The *Meditations* is not intended to be merely an exposition of philosophical arguments and conclusions, but is supposed to be an exercise in philosophical reflection for the reader—as Bernard Williams has put it, "the 'I' that appears throughout them from the first sentence on does not specifically represent [Descartes]: it represents anyone who will step into the position it marks, the position of the thinker who is prepared to reconsider and recast his or her beliefs, as Descartes supposed we might, from the ground up." Descartes aims to convince us of the truth of his conclusions by making us conduct the arguments ourselves.

In the First Meditation the thinker applies a series of progressively more radical doubts to his or her pre-conceived opinions, which leaves her unsure whether she knows anything at all. But then in the Second Meditation the thinker finds a secure foundational belief in her indubitable awareness of her own exis-tence. The rest of this meditation is a reflection on the thinker's own nature as a "thinking thing." In the Third Meditation the thinker realizes that final certainty can only be achieved through the existence of a non-de-ceiving God, and argues from the idea of God found in her own mind to the conclusion that God must re-ally exist and be the cause of this idea (this is some-times nicknamed the "Trademark Argument," from the notion that our possession of the idea of God is God's "trademark" on his creation). The Fourth Medi-tation urges that the way to avoid error in our judg-ments is to restrict our beliefs to things of which we are clearly and distinctly certain. The Fifth Meditation introduces Cartesian science by discussing the math-ematical nature of matter, and also includes a second proof for God's existence which resembles Anselm's ontological argument (see Chapter 2). Finally, in the Sixth Meditation, the thinker re-establishes the real existence of the external world, argues that mind and body are two distinct substances, and reflects on how mind and body are related.

Some Useful Background Information

1. Descartes makes frequent use of the terms "substance," "essence," and "accident." A sub-stance is, roughly, a bearer of attributes, i.e., a thing that has properties. The essence of a substance is its fundamental intrinsic nature: Descartes held that for every substance there is exactly one property which is its essence. A substance's "accidents"[2] are all the rest of its properties, the ones which are not part of its essence.

Take, for example, a red ball: its redness, the spherical shape, the rubbery feel, and so on are all properties—or accidents—of the ball, and the ball's substance is the "stuff" that under-lies and possesses these properties. According to Descartes, the fundamental nature of this stuff—its essence—is that it is extended in three dimensions, that it fills space.

For Descartes and his contemporaries there is also another important aspect to the idea of substance. Unlike an instance of a property, which cannot exist all by itself (there can't be an occurrence of redness without there being something which is red—some bit of substance which is the bearer of that property), sub-stances are not dependent for their existence on something else. In fact, for Descartes, this is actually the *definition* of a substance: "By 'sub-stance' we can understand nothing other than a thing which exists in such a way as to depend on no other things for its existence" (*Principles of Philosophy*). So, for instance, a tree is not really a substance, since trees do depend for their ex-istence on other things (such as soil, light, past trees, and so on). On the other hand, according to Descartes, matter itself—all matter, taken as a whole—is a substance. Matter cannot be de-stroyed or created (except by God), it can only change its local form, gradually moving from the form of a tree to the form of a rotting tree trunk to the form of soil, for example.

2. Another obscure but important phrase fre-quently used by Descartes in the *Meditations* is the "natural light." Descartes has in mind here what in earlier writings he calls "the light of rea-son"—the pure inner light of the intellect, a fac-ulty given to us by God, which allows us to see the truth of the world much more clearly than we can with the confused and fluctuating testi-mony of the senses.

---

2   Strictly speaking, Descartes thought of accidents as being 'modes' of the one essential property of the substance (rather than being really separate proper-ties): shape, for example, is a mode of being extended in space.

3. Descartes, following the scholastic jargon of the time, calls the representational content of an idea its "objective reality" (he uses this term in his attempted proof of the existence of God in the Third Meditation). Confusingly, according to this terminology, for something to have merely objective reality in this sense is for it to belong to the mental world of ideas, and not the mind-independent external world at all. For example, if I imagine Santa Claus as being fat and jolly, then Descartes would say that fatness is "objectively" present in my idea—an idea of fatness forms part of my idea of Santa Claus. By contrast, the baby beluga at the Vancouver Aquarium is fat, but its fatness is not merely the *idea* of fatness but an actual property. To take another example, the objective reality of a stop sign is what it represents—the content "stop"— but its formal reality is the shaped and colored metal from which it is constructed.

4. Although Descartes' talk of a non-physical "soul" was in accord with contemporary Christian theology, his reasons for holding that the mind is immortal and non-material (largely in Meditations Two and Six) were not primarily religious ones. Descartes does not think of the soul as being especially "spiritual" or as being identical with our "better nature," for example. For Descartes the word "soul" simply means the same as the word "mind," and encompasses the whole range of conscious mental activity, including the sensations of sight, touch, sound, taste, and smell; emotions (such as joy or jealousy); and cognitive activities like believing, planning, desiring, or doubting. For Descartes the mind, or soul, is also to be distinguished from the brain: our brains, since they are extended material things, are part of our body and not our mind.

Some Common Misconceptions

1. Descartes is not a skeptic. Although he is famous for the skeptical arguments put forward in the First Meditation, he uses these only in order to go beyond them. It is a bit misleading, however, to think of Descartes as setting out in the *Meditations* to defeat skepticism: his main interest is probably not in proving the skeptic wrong, but in discovering the first principles upon which a proper science can be built. He uses skepticism, surprisingly, in order to *create* knowledge—to show that a properly constituted science would have nothing to fear from even the most radical doubts of the skeptic. Thus, for example, Descartes does not at any point argue that we should actually believe that the external world does not exist—instead, he suspends his belief in external objects until he has a chance to properly build a foundation for this belief (and by the end of the *Meditations* he is quite certain that the external world exists).

2. The "method of doubt" which Descartes uses in the *Meditations* is not an everyday method—it is not supposed to be an appropriate technique for making day-to-day decisions, or even for doing science or mathematics. Most of the time it would be hugely impractical for us to call into question everything that we might possibly doubt, to question all our presuppositions, before we make a judgment. Instead the method of the *Meditations* is supposed to be a once-in-a-lifetime exercise, by which we discover and justify the basic "first principles" that we rely on in everyday knowledge. In short, we always have to rely on certain assumptions when we make decisions or do science, and this is unavoidable but dangerous; the exercise of the *Meditations* can ensure that the assumptions we rely upon are absolutely secure.

3. Although "I think therefore I am" (or "I am, I exist") is the first step in Descartes' reconstruction of human knowledge in the *Meditations*, it is nevertheless not the first piece of *knowledge* that he recognizes—it does not arise out of a complete knowledge vacuum. Before the thinker can come to know that "I think therefore I am" is true, Descartes elsewhere admits that she must know, for example, what is meant by thinking, and that doubting is a kind of thought, and that in order to think one must first exist.

Therefore, it is best to think of "I think therefore I am," not as the first item of knowledge, but as the first *non-trivial* piece of secure knowledge about the world that a thinker can have. It's a piece of information not just about concepts or logic but actually about the world—but, according to Descartes, it's information we can only get if we *already* (somehow) possess a certain set of concepts.

4. It is sometimes supposed that Descartes thought that all knowledge could be mathematically deduced from the foundational beliefs that remain after he has applied his method of doubt. But this is not quite right. He thought that the proper *concepts and terms,* which science must use to describe the world, were purely mathematical and were deducible through pure rational reflection. But he also recognized that only through empirical investigation can we discover which scientific descriptions, expressed in the proper mathematical terms, are actually *true* of the world. For example, reason tells us (according to Descartes—and this was a radically new idea at the time) that matter can be defined simply in terms of extension in three dimensions, and that the laws which guide the movements of particles can be understood mathematically. However, only experience can tell us how the bits of matter in, for example, the human body are actually arranged.

5. Descartes does not conclude that error is impossible, even for those who adopt the proper intellectual methods of science. He argues only that *radical and systematic* error is impossible for the conscientious thinker. For example, even after completing Descartes' course of meditations we might still occasionally be tricked by perceptual illusions, or think we are awake when in fact we are dreaming; what Descartes thinks he has blocked, however, is the possibility that such errors show that our entire picture of reality might be wrong.

6. Descartes is sometimes portrayed as making the following (bad) argument to establish that mind is distinct from body: I can doubt that my body exists; I cannot doubt that my mind exists; there is therefore at least one property that

my mind has which my body lacks (i.e., being doubtable); and therefore mind and body are not identical. Descartes does seem to make an argument which resembles this (in the Second Meditation), but he later denied that this is really what he meant, and he formulates much stronger—though perhaps still flawed—arguments for dualism in the Sixth Meditation.

How Important and Influential Is This Passage?

Descartes is probably the most widely studied of any of the Western philosophers, and his *Meditations on First Philosophy* is his philosophical masterpiece and most important work. John Cottingham, an expert on Descartes, has written of the *Meditations* that:

> The radical critique of preconceived opinions or prejudices which begins that work seems to symbolize the very essence of philosophical inquiry. And the task of finding secure foundations for human knowledge, a reliable basis for science and ethics, encapsulates, for many, what makes philosophy worth doing.

Descartes' foundational claim in the search for truth—*cogito ergo sum*, "I think therefore I am"—is the most famous dictum in the history of philosophy. Although, as it happens, this actual phrase never appears in the *Meditations*—it is used in other writings by Descartes, including *Discourse on the Method* and the *Principles of Philosophy*—the *Meditations* remains Descartes' most complete account of how this principle, today simply called "the Cogito," is established.

The importance of Descartes' work to the history of thought is profound. He is commonly considered the first great philosopher of the modern era, since his work was central in sweeping away medieval scholasticism based on Aristotelian science and Christian theology and replacing it with the methods and questions that dominated philosophy until the twentieth century. This change from scholastic to modern modes of thought was also crucial to the phenomenal growth of natural science and mathematics beginning in the seventeenth century. In recent years, however, it has been fashionable to blame Descartes for what have been seen as philosophical dead ends, and many of the assumptions which he built into philosophy have been questioned (this is one of the reasons why the philosophy of the second half of the twentieth century has been so exciting).

Suggestions for Critical Reflection

1. Descartes, in the *Meditations,* has traditionally been seen as raising and then trying to deal with the problem of radical skepticism: that is, according to this interpretation, he raises the possibility that (almost) all our beliefs might be radically mistaken and then argues that this is, in fact, impossible. A more recent line of interpretation, though, sees Descartes not as attempting to answer the skeptic, but as trying to replace naïve empirical assumptions about science with a more modern, mathematical view—in particular, that Descartes is trying to show our most fundamental pieces of knowledge about mind, God, and the world come not from sensory experience, but directly from the intellect. Which interpretation do you think is more plausible? Could they both be right? If Descartes does want to refute skepticism, is he successful in doing so? If his goal is to overturn naïve scholastic empiricism, do you think he manages to do that?

2. Descartes' foundational claim "I think therefore I am" is usually called the Cogito, from the Latin *cogito ergo sum.* How does Descartes justify this claim? Does he have, or need, an *argument* for it? Is an argument that justifies this claim even possible?

3. David Hume dryly said, of the *Meditations,* "To have recourse to the veracity of the supreme Being, in order to prove the veracity of our senses, is surely making a very unexpected circuit." What do you think? Does Descartes establish the existence of God?

4. On Descartes' picture, do you think an atheist can have any knowledge? Why or why not?

5. A famous objection to Descartes' conclusions in the *Meditations* (raised for the first time by some of his contemporaries) is today known as the problem of the Cartesian Circle. Descartes says in the Third Meditation, "Whatever I perceive very clearly and distinctly is true." Call this the CDP Principle. It is this principle which he thinks will allow him to reconstruct a body of reliable scientific knowledge on the foundations of the Cogito. However, he immediately admits, the CDP Principle will only work if we cannot ever make mistakes about what we clearly and distinctly perceive; to show this, Descartes tries to prove that God exists and has created human beings such that what we clearly and distinctly see to be evidently true really is true. But how does Descartes prove God exists? Apparently, by arguing that we have a clear and distinct idea of God, and so it must be true that God exists. That is, the objection runs, Descartes relies upon the CDP Principle to prove that the CDP Principle is reliable—and this argument just goes in a big circle and doesn't prove anything. What do you think of this objection?

6. "How do I know that I am not ten thinkers thinking in unison?" (Elizabeth Anscombe, "The First Person"). What, if anything, do you think Descartes has proved about the nature of the self?

7. How adequate are Descartes' arguments for mind-body dualism? If mind and body are two different substances, do you think this might cause other philosophical problems to arise? For example, how might mind and body interact? How could we come to know things about other people's minds? How could we be sure whether animals have minds or not, and if they do what they might be like?

8. Descartes recognized no physical properties but size, shape, and motion. Where do you think Descartes would say colors, tastes, smells, and so on come from?

Suggestions for Further Reading

The *Meditations on First Philosophy* was originally published with an extensive set of objections from contemporary thinkers and replies by Descartes. A standard edition of the *Meditations* including selected objections and replies is translated and edited by John Cottingham and published by Cambridge University Press (1996). Cambridge also published Descartes' collected philosophical writings and letters in three volumes, translated by John Cottingham, Robert Stoothoff, Dugald Murdoch, and Anthony Kenny. (Volume II, which includes the *Meditations* and the complete *Objections and Replies*, was published in 1984; Volume I was published in 1985 and the letters in 1991.)

The secondary literature on Descartes is vast, but here are a few starting points. A good recent biography of Descartes is from Stephen Gaukroger, *Descartes: An Intellectual Biography* (Oxford University Press, 1995). Useful general introductions to Descartes' thought are John Cottingham's *Descartes* (Blackwell, 1986), Anthony Kenny's *Descartes: A Study of His Philosophy* (Random House, 1968), Bernard Williams's *Descartes: The Project of Pure Enquiry* (Penguin, 1978), and Margaret Dauler Wilson's *Descartes* (Routledge, 1978). *The Cambridge Companion to Descartes* edited by John Cottingham (Cambridge University Press, 1992) is helpful, and two good collections of articles on the *Meditations* are A.O. Rorty's *Essays on Descartes's* Meditations (University of California Press, 1986) and Vere Chappell's *Descartes's* Meditations: *Critical Essays* (Rowman and Littlefield, 1997). A few of the more influential (and sometimes controversial) recent books on Descartes are Harry Frankfurt's *Demons, Dreamers, and Madmen* (Bobbs-Merrill, 1970), E.M. Curley's *Descartes Against the Sceptics* (Harvard University Press, 1978), Peter J. Markie's *Descartes's Gambit* (Cornell University Press, 1986), Richard Watson's *The Breakdown of Cartesian Metaphysics* (Humanities Press, 1987), and Daniel Garber's *Descartes's Metaphysical Physics* (University of Chicago Press, 1992).

Meditations on First Philosophy

In which are demonstrated the existence of God and the distinction between the human soul and the body.[3]

Synopsis of the following six Meditations

In the First Meditation reasons are provided which give us possible grounds for doubt about all things, especially material things, so long as we have no foundations for the sciences other than those which we have had up till now. Although the usefulness of such extensive doubt is not apparent at first sight, its greatest benefit lies in freeing us from all our preconceived opinions, and providing the easiest route by which the mind may be led away from the senses. The eventual result of this doubt is to make it impossible for us to have any further doubts about what we subsequently discover to be true.

In the Second Meditation, the mind uses its own freedom and supposes the non-existence of all the things about whose existence it can have even the slightest doubt; and in so doing the mind notices that it is impossible that it should not itself exist during this time. This exercise is also of the greatest benefit, since it enables the mind to distinguish without difficulty what belongs to itself, i.e., to an intellectual nature, from what belongs to the body. But since some people may perhaps expect arguments for the immortality of the soul in this section, I think they should be warned here and now that I have tried not to put down anything which I could not precisely demonstrate. Hence the only order which I could follow was that normally employed by geometers, namely to set out all the premises on which a desired proposition depends, before drawing any conclusions about it. Now the first and most important prerequisite for knowledge of the

---

3   First published in Latin in 1641. This translation is by John Cottingham, from *Meditations on First Philosophy, With Selections from the Objections and Replies*, revised edition, Cambridge: Cambridge University Press 1996, pp. 9–62. Copyright © 1996 Cambridge University Press. Reprinted with the permission of Cambridge University Press.

immortality of the soul is for us to form a concept of the soul which is as clear as possible and is also quite distinct from every concept of body; and that is just what has been done in this section. A further requirement is that we should know that everything that we clearly and distinctly understand is true in a way which corresponds exactly to our understanding of it; but it was not possible to prove this before the Fourth Meditation. In addition we need to have a distinct concept of corporeal[4] nature, and this is developed partly in the Second Meditation itself, and partly in the Fifth and Sixth Meditations. The inference to be drawn from these results is that all the things that we clearly and distinctly conceive of as different substances (as we do in the case of mind and body) are in fact substances which are really distinct one from the other; and this conclusion is drawn in the Sixth Meditation. This conclusion is confirmed in the same Meditation by the fact that we cannot understand a body except as being divisible, while by contrast we cannot understand a mind except as being indivisible. For we cannot conceive of half of a mind, while we can always conceive of half of a body, however small; and this leads us to recognize that the natures of mind and body are not only different, but in some way opposite. But I have not pursued this topic any further in this book, first because these arguments are enough to show that the decay of the body does not imply the destruction of the mind, and are hence enough to give mortals the hope of an after-life, and secondly because the premises which lead to the conclusion that the soul is immortal depend on an account of the whole of physics. This is required for two reasons. First, we need to know that absolutely all substances, or things which must be created by God in order to exist, are by their nature incorruptible and cannot ever cease to exist unless they are reduced to nothingness by God's denying his concurrence[5] to them. Secondly, we need to recognize that body, taken in the general sense, is a substance, so that it too never perishes. But the human body, in so far as it differs from other bodies, is simply made up of a certain configuration of limbs

and other accidents of this sort; whereas the human mind is not made up of any accidents in this way, but is a pure substance. For even if all the accidents of the mind change, so that it has different objects of the understanding and different desires and sensations, it does not on that account become a different mind; whereas a human body loses its identity merely as a result of a change in the shape of some of its parts. And it follows from this that while the body can very easily perish, the mind is immortal by its very nature.

In the Third Meditation I have explained quite fully enough, I think, my principal argument for proving the existence of God. But in order to draw my readers' minds away from the senses as far as possible, I was not willing to use any comparison taken from bodily things. So it may be that many obscurities remain; but I hope they will be completely removed later, in my Replies to the Objections.[6] One such problem, among others, is how the idea of a supremely perfect being, which is in us, possesses so much objective reality that it can come only from a cause which is supremely perfect. In the Replies this is illustrated by the comparison of a very perfect machine, the idea of which is in the mind of some engineer. Just as the objective intricacy belonging to the idea must have some cause, namely the scientific knowledge of the engineer, or of someone else who passed the idea on to him, so the idea of God which is in us must have God himself as its cause.

In the Fourth Meditation it is proved that everything that we clearly and distinctly perceive is true, and I also explain what the nature of falsity consists in. These results need to be known both in order to confirm what has gone before and also to make intelligible what is to come later. (But here it should be noted in passing that I do not deal at all with sin, i.e., the error which is committed in pursuing good and evil, but only with the error that occurs in distinguishing truth from falsehood. And there is no discussion of matters pertaining to faith or the conduct of life, but

---

4   Bodily, physical.

5   The continuous divine action which many Christians think necessary to maintain things in existence.

6   Descartes' *Meditations* were originally published with an extensive set of objections from other philosophers, scientists, and theologians of the time, and Descartes' responses to those objections. These Objections and Replies are not reprinted here.

simply of speculative truths which are known solely by means of the natural light.)

In the Fifth Meditation, besides an account of corporeal nature taken in general, there is a new argument demonstrating the existence of God. Again, several difficulties may arise here, but these are resolved later in the Replies to the Objections. Finally I explain the sense in which it is true that the certainty even of geometrical demonstrations depends on the knowledge of God.

Lastly, in the Sixth Meditation, the intellect is distinguished from the imagination; the criteria for this distinction are explained; the mind is proved to be really distinct from the body, but is shown, notwithstanding, to be so closely joined to it that the mind and the body make up a kind of unit; there is a survey of all the errors which commonly come from the senses, and an explanation of how they may be avoided; and, lastly, there is a presentation of all the arguments which enable the existence of material things to be inferred. The great benefit of these arguments is not, in my view, that they prove what they establish—namely that there really is a world, and that human beings have bodies and so on—since no sane person has ever seriously doubted these things. The point is that in considering these arguments we come to realize that they are not as solid or as transparent as the arguments which lead us to knowledge of our own minds and of God, so that the latter are the most certain and evident of all possible objects of knowledge for the human intellect. Indeed, this is the one thing that I set myself to prove in these Meditations. And for that reason I will not now go over the various other issues in the book which are dealt with as they come up.

First Meditation:
What can be called into doubt

Some years ago I was struck by the large number of falsehoods that I had accepted as true in my childhood, and by the highly doubtful nature of the whole edifice that I had subsequently based on them. I realized that it was necessary, once in the course of my life, to demolish everything completely and start again right from the foundations if I wanted to establish anything at all in the sciences that was stable and likely to last. But the task looked an enormous one, and I began to wait until I should reach a mature enough age to ensure that no subsequent time of life would be more suitable for tackling such inquiries. This led me to put the project off for so long that I would now be to blame if by pondering over it any further I wasted the time still left for carrying it out. So today I have expressly rid my mind of all worries and arranged for myself a clear stretch of free time. I am here quite alone, and at last I will devote myself sincerely and without reservation to the general demolition of my opinions.

But to accomplish this, it will not be necessary for me to show that all my opinions are false, which is something I could perhaps never manage. Reason now leads me to think that I should hold back my assent from opinions which are not completely certain and indubitable just as carefully as I do from those which are patently false. So, for the purpose of rejecting all my opinions, it will be enough if I find in each of them at least some reason for doubt. And to do this I will not need to run through them all individually, which would be an endless task. Once the foundations of a building are undermined, anything built on them collapses of its own accord; so I will go straight for the basic principles on which all my former beliefs rested.

Whatever I have up till now accepted as most true I have acquired either from the senses or through the senses. But from time to time I have found that the senses deceive, and it is prudent never to trust completely those who have deceived us even once.

Yet although the senses occasionally deceive us with respect to objects which are very small or in the distance, there are many other beliefs about which doubt is quite impossible, even though they are derived from the senses—for example, that I am here, sitting by the fire, wearing a winter dressing-gown, holding this piece of paper in my hands, and so on. Again, how could it be denied that these hands or this whole body are mine? Unless perhaps I were to liken myself to madmen, whose brains are so damaged by the persistent vapours of melancholia that they firmly maintain they are kings when they are paupers, or say they are dressed in purple when they are naked, or that their heads are made of earthenware, or that they are pumpkins, or made of glass. But such people are insane, and I would be thought equally mad if I took anything from them as a model for myself.

A brilliant piece of reasoning! As if I were not a man who sleeps at night, and regularly has all the same experiences while asleep as madmen do when awake—indeed sometimes even more improbable ones. How often, asleep at night, am I convinced of just such familiar events—that I am here in my dressing-gown, sitting by the fire—when in fact I am lying undressed in bed! Yet at the moment my eyes are certainly wide awake when I look at this piece of paper; I shake my head and it is not asleep; as I stretch out and feel my hand I do so deliberately, and I know what I am doing. All this would not happen with such distinctness to someone asleep. Indeed! As if I did not remember other occasions when I have been tricked by exactly similar thoughts while asleep! As I think about this more carefully, I see plainly that there are never any sure signs by means of which being awake can be distinguished from being asleep. The result is that I begin to feel dazed, and this very feeling only reinforces the notion that I may be asleep.

Suppose then that I am dreaming, and that these particulars—that my eyes are open, that I am moving my head and stretching out my hands—are not true. Perhaps, indeed, I do not even have such hands or such a body at all. Nonetheless, it must surely be admitted that the visions which come in sleep are like paintings, which must have been fashioned in the likeness of things that are real, and hence that at least these general kinds of things—eyes, head, hands and the body as a whole—are things which are not imaginary but are real and exist. For even when painters try to create sirens and satyrs with the most extraordinary bodies, they cannot give them natures which are new in all respects; they simply jumble up the limbs of different animals. Or if perhaps they manage to think up something so new that nothing remotely similar has ever been seen before—something which is therefore completely fictitious and unreal—at least the colours used in the composition must be real. By similar reasoning, although these general kinds of things—eyes, head, hands and so on—could be imaginary, it must at least be admitted that certain other even simpler and more universal things are real. These are as it were

the real colours from which we form all the images of things, whether true or false, that occur in our thought.

This class appears to include corporeal nature in general, and its extension; the shape of extended things; the quantity, or size and number of these things; the place in which they may exist, the time through which they may endure, and so on.

So a reasonable conclusion from this might be that physics, astronomy, medicine, and all other disciplines which depend on the study of composite things, are doubtful; while arithmetic, geometry and other subjects of this kind, which deal only with the simplest and most general things, regardless of whether they really exist in nature or not, contain something certain and indubitable. For whether I am awake or asleep, two and three added together are five, and a square has no more than four sides. It seems impossible that such transparent truths should incur any suspicion of being false.

And yet firmly rooted in my mind is the long-standing opinion that there is an omnipotent God who made me the kind of creature that I am. How do I know that he has not brought it about that there is no earth, no sky, no extended thing, no shape, no size, no place, while at the same time ensuring that all these things appear to me to exist just as they do now? What is more, just as I consider that others sometimes go astray in cases where they think they have the most perfect knowledge, how do I know that God has not brought it about that I too go wrong every time I add two and three or count the sides of a square, or in some even simpler matter, if that is imaginable? But perhaps God would not have allowed me to be deceived in this way, since he is said to be supremely good. But if it were inconsistent with his goodness to have created me such that I am deceived all the time, it would seem equally foreign to his goodness to allow me to be deceived even occasionally; yet this last assertion cannot be made.

Perhaps there may be some who would prefer to deny the existence of so powerful a God rather than believe that everything else is uncertain. Let us not argue with them, but grant them that everything said about God is a fiction. According to their supposition, then, I have arrived at my present state by fate or chance or a continuous chain of events, or by some other means; yet since deception and error seem to be imperfections, the less powerful they make my original cause, the more likely it is that I am so imperfect as to be deceived all the time. I have no answer to these arguments, but am finally compelled to admit that there is not one of my former beliefs about which a doubt may not properly be raised; and this is not a flippant or ill-considered conclusion, but is based on powerful and well thought-out reasons. So in future I must withhold my assent from these former beliefs just as carefully as I would from obvious falsehoods, if I want to discover any certainty.

But it is not enough merely to have noticed this; I must make an effort to remember it. My habitual opinions keep coming back, and, despite my wishes, they capture my belief, which is as it were bound over to them as a result of long occupation and the law of custom. I shall never get out of the habit of confidently assenting to these opinions, so long as I suppose them to be what in fact they are, namely highly probable opinions—opinions which, despite the fact that they are in a sense doubtful, as has just been shown, it is still much more reasonable to believe than to deny. In view of this, I think it will be a good plan to turn my will in completely the opposite direction and deceive myself, by pretending for a time that these former opinions are utterly false and imaginary. I shall do this until the weight of preconceived opinion is counter-balanced and the distorting influence of habit no longer prevents my judgement from perceiving things correctly. In the meantime, I know that no danger or error will result from my plan, and that I cannot possibly go too far in my distrustful attitude. This is because the task now in hand does not involve action but merely the acquisition of knowledge.

I will suppose therefore that not God, who is supremely good and the source of truth, but rather some malicious demon of the utmost power and cunning has employed all his energies in order to deceive me. I shall think that the sky, the air, the earth, colours, shapes, sounds and all external things are merely the delusions of dreams which he has devised to ensnare my judgement. I shall consider myself as not having hands or eyes, or flesh, or blood or senses, but as falsely believing that I have all these things. I shall

stubbornly and firmly persist in this meditation; and, even if it is not in my power to know any truth, I shall at least do what is in my power, that is, resolutely guard against assenting to any falsehoods, so that the deceiver, however powerful and cunning he may be, will be unable to impose on me in the slightest degree. But this is an arduous undertaking, and a kind of laziness brings me back to normal life. I am like a prisoner who is enjoying an imaginary freedom while asleep; as he begins to suspect that he is asleep, he dreads being woken up, and goes along with the pleasant illusion as long as he can. In the same way, I happily slide back into my old opinions and dread being shaken out of them, for fear that my peaceful sleep may be followed by hard labour when I wake, and that I shall have to toil not in the light, but amid the inextricable darkness of the problems I have now raised.

Second Meditation: The nature of the human mind, and how it is better known than the body

So serious are the doubts into which I have been thrown as a result of yesterday's meditation that I can neither put them out of my mind nor see any way of resolving them. It feels as if I have fallen unexpectedly into a deep whirlpool which tumbles me around so that I can neither stand on the bottom nor swim up to the top. Nevertheless I will make an effort and once more attempt the same path which I started on yesterday. Anything which admits of the slightest doubt I will set aside just as if I had found it to be wholly false; and I will proceed in this way until I recognize something certain, or, if nothing else, until I at least recognize for certain that there is no certainty. Archimedes[7] used to demand just one firm and immovable point in order to shift the entire earth; so I too can hope for great things if I manage to find just one thing, however slight, that is certain and unshakeable.

I will suppose then, that everything I see is spurious. I will believe that my memory tells me lies, and that none of the things that it reports ever happened. I have no senses. Body, shape, extension, movement

---

7   A Greek mathematician, engineer, and physicist who died in 212 BCE.

and place are chimeras. So what remains true? Perhaps just the one fact that nothing is certain.

Yet apart from everything I have just listed, how do I know that there is not something else which does not allow even the slightest occasion for doubt? Is there not a God, or whatever I may call him, who puts into me the thoughts I am now having? But why do I think this, since I myself may perhaps be the author of these thoughts? In that case am not I, at least, something? But I have just said that I have no senses and no body. This is the sticking point: what follows from this? Am I not so bound up with a body and with senses that I cannot exist without them? But I have convinced myself that there is absolutely nothing in the world, no sky, no earth, no minds, no bodies. Does it now follow that I too do not exist? No: if I convinced myself of something then I certainly existed. But there is a deceiver of supreme power and cunning who is deliberately and constantly deceiving me. In that case I too undoubtedly exist, if he is deceiving me; and let him deceive me as much as he can, he will never bring it about that I am nothing so long as I think that I am something. So after considering everything very thoroughly, I must finally conclude that this proposition, *I am, I exist*, is necessarily true whenever it is put forward by me or conceived in my mind.

But I do not yet have a sufficient understanding of what this 'I' is, that now necessarily exists. So I must be on my guard against carelessly taking something else to be this 'I', and so making a mistake in the very item of knowledge that I maintain is the most certain and evident of all. I will therefore go back and meditate on what I originally believed myself to be, before I embarked on this present train of thought. I will then subtract anything capable of being weakened, even minimally, by the arguments now introduced, so that what is left at the end may be exactly and only what is certain and unshakeable.

What then did I formerly think I was? A man. But what is a man? Shall I say 'a rational animal'? No; for then I should have to inquire what an animal is, what rationality is, and in this way one question would lead me down the slope to other harder ones, and I do not now have the time to waste on subtleties of this kind. Instead I propose to concentrate on what came into my thoughts spontaneously and quite naturally whenever I used to consider what I was. Well, the first thought to come to mind was that I had a face, hands, arms and the whole mechanical structure of limbs which can be seen in a corpse, and which I called the body. The next thought was that I was nourished, that I moved about, and that I engaged in sense-perception and thinking; and these actions I attributed to the soul. But as to the nature of this soul, either I did not think about this or else I imagined it to be something tenuous, like a wind or fire or ether, which permeated my more solid parts. As to the body, however, I had no doubts about it, but thought I knew its nature distinctly. If I had tried to describe the mental conception I had of it, I would have expressed it as follows: by a body I understand whatever has a determinable shape and a definable location and can occupy a space in such a way as to exclude any other body; it can be perceived by touch, sight, hearing, taste or smell, and can be moved in various ways, not by itself but by whatever else comes into contact with it. For, according to my judgement, the power of self-movement, like the power of sensation or of thought, was quite foreign to the nature of a body; indeed, it was a source of wonder to me that certain bodies were found to contain faculties of this kind.

But what shall I now say that I am, when I am supposing that there is some supremely powerful and, if it is permissible to say so, malicious deceiver, who is deliberately trying to trick me in every way he can? Can I now assert that I possess even the most insignificant of all the attributes which I have just said belong to the nature of a body? I scrutinize them, think about them, go over them again, but nothing suggests itself; it is tiresome and pointless to go through the list once more. But what about the attributes I assigned to the soul? Nutrition or movement? Since now I do not have a body, these are mere fabrications. Sense-perception? This surely does not occur without a body, and besides, when asleep I have appeared to perceive through the senses many things which I afterwards realized I did not perceive through the senses at all. Thinking? At last I have discovered it—thought; this alone is inseparable from me. I am, I exist—that is certain. But for how long? For as long as I am thinking. For it could be that were I totally to cease from thinking, I should totally cease to exist. At present I am not admitting anything except what is necessarily true. I am, then, in the strict sense only a thing that thinks; that is, I am a mind, or intelligence, or intellect, or reason—words whose meaning I have been ignorant of until now. But for all that I am a thing which is real and which truly exists. But what kind of a thing? As I have just said—a thinking thing.

What else am I? I will use my imagination. I am not that structure of limbs which is called a human body. I am not even some thin vapour which permeates the limbs—a wind, fire, air, breath, or whatever I depict in my imagination; for these are things which I have supposed to be nothing. Let this supposition stand; for all that I am still something. And yet may it not perhaps be the case that these very things which I am supposing to be nothing, because they are unknown to me, are in reality identical with the 'I' of which I am aware? I do not know, and for the moment I shall not argue the point, since I can make judgements only about things which are known to me. I know that I exist; the question is, what is this 'I' that I know? If the 'I' is understood strictly as we have been taking it, then it is quite certain that knowledge of it does not depend on things of whose existence I am as yet unaware; so it cannot depend on any of the things which I invent in my imagination. And this very word 'invent' shows me my mistake. It would indeed be a case of fictitious invention if I used my imagination to establish that I was something or other; for imagining is simply contemplating the shape or image of a corporeal thing. Yet now I know for certain both that I exist and at the same time that all such images and, in general, everything relating to the nature of body, could be mere dreams <and chimeras>. Once this point has been grasped, to say 'I will use my imagination to get to know more distinctly what I am' would seem to be as silly as saying 'I am now awake, and see some truth; but since my vision is not yet clear enough, I will deliberately fall asleep so that my dreams may provide a truer and clearer representation.' I thus realize that none of the things that the imagination enables me to grasp is at all relevant to this knowledge of myself which I possess, and that the mind must therefore be most carefully diverted from such things if it is to perceive its own nature as distinctly as possible.

But what then am I? A thing that thinks. What is that? A thing that doubts, understands, affirms, denies, is willing, is unwilling, and also imagines and has sensory perceptions.

This is a considerable list, if everything on it belongs to me. But does it? Is it not one and the same 'I' who is now doubting almost everything, who nonetheless understands some things, who affirms that this one thing is true, denies everything else, desires to know more, is unwilling to be deceived, imagines many things even involuntarily, and is aware of many things which apparently come from the senses? Are not all these things just as true as the fact that I exist, even if I am asleep all the time, and even if he who created me is doing all he can to deceive me? Which of all these activities is distinct from my thinking? Which of them can be said to be separate from myself? The fact that it is I who am doubting and understanding and willing is so evident that I see no way of making it any clearer. But it is also the case that the 'I' who imagines is the same 'I'. For even if, as I have supposed, none of the objects of imagination are real, the power of imagination is something which really exists and is part of my thinking. Lastly, it is also the same 'I' who has sensory perceptions, or is aware of bodily things as it were through the senses. For example, I am now seeing light, hearing a noise, feeling heat. But I am asleep, so all this is false. Yet I certainly *seem* to see, to hear, and to be warmed. This cannot be false; what is called 'having a sensory perception' is strictly just this, and in this restricted sense of the term it is simply thinking.

From all this I am beginning to have a rather better understanding of what I am. But it still appears—and I cannot stop thinking this—that the corporeal things of which images are formed in my thought, and which the senses investigate, are known with much more distinctness than this puzzling 'I' which cannot be pictured in the imagination. And yet it is surely surprising that I should have a more distinct grasp of things which I realize are doubtful, unknown and foreign to me, than I have of that which is true and known—my own self. But I see what it is: my mind enjoys wandering off and will not yet submit to being restrained within the bounds of truth. Very well then; just this once let us give it a completely free rein, so that after a while, when it is time to tighten the reins, it may more readily submit to being curbed.

Let us consider the things which people commonly think they understand most distinctly of all; that is, the bodies which we touch and see. I do not mean bodies in general—for general perceptions are apt to be somewhat more confused—but one particular body. Let us take, for example, this piece of wax. It has just been taken from the honeycomb; it has not yet quite lost the taste of the honey; it retains some of the scent of the flowers from which it was gathered; its colour, shape and size are plain to see; it is hard, cold and can be handled without difficulty; if you rap it with your knuckle it makes a sound. In short, it has everything which appears necessary to enable a body to be known as distinctly as possible. But even as I speak, I put the wax by the fire, and look: the residual taste is eliminated, the smell goes away, the colour changes, the shape is lost, the size increases; it becomes liquid and hot; you can hardly touch it, and if you strike it, it no longer makes a sound. But does the same wax remain? It must be admitted that it does; no one denies it, no one thinks otherwise. So what was it in the wax that I understood with such distinctness? Evidently none of the features which I arrived at by means of the senses; for whatever came under taste, smell, sight, touch or hearing has now altered—yet the wax remains.

Perhaps the answer lies in the thought which now comes to my mind; namely, the wax was not after all the sweetness of the honey, or the fragrance of the flowers, or the whiteness, or the shape, or the sound, but was rather a body which presented itself to me in these various forms a little while ago, but which now exhibits different ones. But what exactly is it that I am now imagining? Let us concentrate, take away everything which does not belong to the wax, and see what is left: merely something extended, flexible and changeable. But what is meant here by 'flexible' and 'changeable'? Is it what I picture in my imagination: that this piece of wax is capable of changing from a round shape to a square shape, or from a square shape to a triangular shape? Not at all; for I can grasp that the wax is capable of countless changes of this kind, yet I am unable to run through this immeasurable number of changes in my imagination, from which

it follows that it is not the faculty of imagination that gives me my grasp of the wax as flexible and changeable. And what is meant by 'extended'? Is the extension of the wax also unknown? For it increases if the wax melts, increases again if it boils, and is greater still if the heat is increased. I would not be making a correct judgement about the nature of wax unless I believed it capable of being extended in many more different ways than I will ever encompass in my imagination. I must therefore admit that the nature of this piece of wax is in no way revealed by my imagination, but is perceived by the mind alone. (I am speaking of this particular piece of wax; the point is even clearer with regard to wax in general.) But what is this wax which is perceived by the mind alone? It is of course the same wax which I see, which I touch, which I picture in my imagination, in short the same wax which I thought it to be from the start. And yet, and here is the point, the perception I have of it is a case not of vision or touch or imagination—nor has it ever been, despite previous appearances—but of purely mental scrutiny; and this can be imperfect and confused, as it was before, or clear and distinct as it is now, depending on how carefully I concentrate on what the wax consists in.

But as I reach this conclusion I am amazed at how <weak and> prone to error my mind is. For although I am thinking about these matters within myself, silently and without speaking, nonetheless the actual words bring me up short, and I am almost tricked by ordinary ways of talking. We say that we see the wax itself, if it is there before us, not that we judge it to be there from its colour or shape; and this might lead me to conclude without more ado that knowledge of the wax comes from what the eye sees, and not from the scrutiny of the mind alone. But then if I look out of the window and see men crossing the square, as I just happen to have done, I normally say that I see the men themselves, just as I say that I see the wax. Yet do I see any more than hats and coats which could conceal automatons? I *judge* that they are men. And so something which I thought I was seeing with my eyes is in fact grasped solely by the faculty of judgement which is in my mind.

However, one who wants to achieve knowledge above the ordinary level should feel ashamed at having taken ordinary ways of talking as a basis for doubt. So let us proceed, and consider on which occasion my perception of the nature of the wax was more perfect and evident. Was it when I first looked at it, and believed I knew it by my external senses, or at least by what they call the 'common' sense[8]—that is, the power of imagination? Or is my knowledge more perfect now, after a more careful investigation of the nature of the wax and of the means by which it is known? Any doubt on this issue would clearly be foolish; for what distinctness was there in my earlier perception? Was there anything in it which an animal could not possess? But when I distinguish the wax from its outward forms—take the clothes off, as it were, and consider it naked—then although my judgement may still contain errors, at least my perception now requires a human mind.

But what am I to say about this mind, or about myself? (So far, remember, I am not admitting that there is anything else in me except a mind.) What, I ask, is this 'I' which seems to perceive the wax so distinctly? Surely my awareness of my own self is not merely much truer and more certain than my awareness of the wax, but also much more distinct and evident. For if I judge that the wax exists from the fact that I see it, clearly this same fact entails much more evidently that I myself also exist. It is possible that what I see is not really the wax; it is possible that I do not even have eyes with which to see anything. But when I see, or think I see (I am not here distinguishing the two), it is simply not possible that I who am now thinking am not something. By the same token, if I judge that the wax exists from the fact that I touch it, the same result follows, namely that I exist. If I judge that it exists from the fact that I imagine it, or for any other reason, exactly the same thing follows. And the result that I have grasped in the case of the wax may be applied to everything else located outside me. Moreover, if my perception of the wax seemed more distinct after it was established not just by sight or touch but by many other considerations, it must be admitted that I now know myself even more distinctly. This is because

every consideration whatsoever which contributes to my perception of the wax, or of any other body, cannot but establish even more effectively the nature of my own mind. But besides this, there is so much else in the mind itself which can serve to make my knowledge of it more distinct, that it scarcely seems worth going through the contributions made by considering bodily things.

I see that without any effort I have now finally got back to where I wanted. I now know that even bodies are not strictly perceived by the senses or the faculty of imagination but by the intellect alone, and that this perception derives not from their being touched or seen but from their being understood; and in view of this I know plainly that I can achieve an easier and more evident perception of my own mind than of anything else. But since the habit of holding on to old opinions cannot be set aside so quickly, I should like to stop here and meditate for some time on this new knowledge I have gained, so as to fix it more deeply in my memory.

Third Meditation: The existence of God

I will now shut my eyes, stop my ears, and withdraw all my senses. I will eliminate from my thoughts all images of bodily things, or rather, since this is hardly possible, I will regard all such images as vacuous, false and worthless. I will converse with myself and scrutinize myself more deeply; and in this way I will attempt to achieve, little by little, a more intimate knowledge of myself. I am a thing that thinks: that is, a thing that doubts, affirms, denies, understands a few things, is ignorant of many things, is willing, is unwilling, and also which imagines and has sensory perceptions; for as I have noted before, even though the objects of my sensory experience and imagination may have no existence outside me, nonetheless the modes of thinking which I refer to as cases of sensory perception and imagination, in so far as they are simply modes of thinking, do exist within me—of that I am certain.

In this brief list I have gone through everything I truly know, or at least everything I have so far discovered that I know. Now I will cast around more carefully to see whether there may be other things within me which I have not yet noticed. I am certain that I

---

8 This is the supposed faculty which integrates the data from the five specialized senses into a single experience. The notion goes back to Aristotle.

am a thinking thing. Do I not therefore also know what is required for my being certain about anything? In this first item of knowledge there is simply a clear and distinct perception of what I am asserting; this would not be enough to make me certain of the truth of the matter if it could ever turn out that something which I perceived with such clarity and distinctness was false. So I now seem to be able to lay it down as a general rule that whatever I perceive very clearly and distinctly is true.

Yet I previously accepted as wholly certain and evident many things which I afterwards realized were doubtful. What were these? The earth, sky, stars, and everything else that I apprehended with the senses. But what was it about them that I perceived clearly? Just that the ideas, or thoughts, of such things appeared before my mind. Yet even now I am not denying that these ideas occur within me. But there was something else which I used to assert, and which through habitual belief I thought I perceived clearly, although I did not in fact do so. This was that there were things outside me which were the sources of my ideas and which resembled them in all respects. Here was my mistake; or at any rate, if my judgement was true, it was not thanks to the strength of my perception.

But what about when I was considering something very simple and straightforward in arithmetic or geometry, for example that two and three added together make five, and so on? Did I not see at least these things clearly enough to affirm their truth? Indeed, the only reason for my later judgement that they were open to doubt was that it occurred to me that perhaps some God could have given me a nature such that I was deceived even in matters which seemed most evident. But whenever my preconceived belief in the supreme power of God comes to mind, I cannot but admit that it would be easy for him, if he so desired, to bring it about that I go wrong even in those matters which I think I see utterly clearly with my mind's eye. Yet when I turn to the things themselves which I think I perceive very clearly, I am so convinced by them that I spontaneously declare: let whoever can do so deceive me, he will never bring it about that I am nothing, so long as I continue to think I am something; or make it true at some future time that I have never

existed, since it is now true that I exist; or bring it about that two and three added together are more or less than five, or anything of this kind in which I see a manifest contradiction. And since I have no cause to think that there is a deceiving God, and I do not yet even know for sure whether there is a God at all, any reason for doubt which depends simply on this supposition is a very slight and, so to speak, metaphysical one. But in order to remove even this slight reason for doubt, as soon as the opportunity arises I must examine whether there is a God, and, if there is, whether he can be a deceiver. For if I do not know this, it seems that I can never be quite certain about anything else.

First, however, considerations of order appear to dictate that I now classify my thoughts into definite kinds, and ask which of them can properly be said to be the bearers of truth and falsity. Some of my thoughts are as it were the images of things, and it is only in these cases that the term 'idea' is strictly appropriate—for example, when I think of a man, or a chimera,[9] or the sky, or an angel, or God. Other thoughts have various additional forms: thus when I will, or am afraid, or affirm, or deny, there is always a particular thing which I take as the object of my thought, but my thought includes something more than the likeness of that thing. Some thoughts in this category are called volitions or emotions, while others are called judgements.

Now as far as ideas are concerned, provided they are considered solely in themselves and I do not refer them to anything else, they cannot strictly speaking be false; for whether it is a goat or a chimera that I am imagining, it is just as true that I imagine the former as the latter. As for the will and the emotions, here too one need not worry about falsity; for even if the things which I may desire are wicked or even non-existent, that does not make it any less true that I desire them. Thus the only remaining thoughts where I must be on my guard against making a mistake are judgements. And the chief and most common mistake which is to

---

9 In Greek mythology, a female fire-breathing monster with a lion's head, a goat's body, and a serpent's tail; more generally, an absurd or horrible idea or wild fancy.

be found here consists in my judging that the ideas which are in me resemble, or conform to, things located outside me. Of course, if I considered just the ideas themselves simply as modes of my thought, without referring them to anything else, they could scarcely give me any material for error.

Among my ideas, some appear to be innate,[10] some to be adventitious,[11] and others to have been invented by me. My understanding of what a thing is, what truth is, and what thought is, seems to derive simply from my own nature. But my hearing a noise, as I do now, or seeing the sun, or feeling the fire, comes from things which are located outside me, or so I have hitherto judged. Lastly, sirens, hippogriffs and the like are my own invention. But perhaps all my ideas may be thought of as adventitious, or they may all be innate, or all made up; for as yet I have not clearly perceived their true origin.

But the chief question at this point concerns the ideas which I take to be derived from things existing outside me: what is my reason for thinking that they resemble these things? Nature has apparently taught me to think this. But in addition I know by experience that these ideas do not depend on my will, and hence that they do not depend simply on me. Frequently I notice them even when I do not want to: now, for example, I feel the heat whether I want to or not, and this is why I think that this sensation or idea of heat comes to me from something other than myself, namely the heat of the fire by which I am sitting. And the most obvious judgement for me to make is that the thing in question transmits to me its own likeness rather than something else.

I will now see if these arguments are strong enough. When I say 'Nature taught me to think this,' all I mean is that a spontaneous impulse leads me to believe it, not that its truth has been revealed to me by some natural light. There is a big difference here. Whatever is revealed to me by the natural light—for example that from the fact that I am doubting it follows that I exist, and so on—cannot in any way be open to doubt. This is because there cannot be another faculty both as trustworthy as the natural light and also

capable of showing me that such things are not true. But as for my natural impulses, I have often judged in the past that they were pushing me in the wrong direction when it was a question of choosing the good, and I do not see why I should place any greater confidence in them in other matters.

Then again, although these ideas do not depend on my will, it does not follow that they must come from things located outside me. Just as the impulses which I was speaking of a moment ago seem opposed to my will even though they are within me, so there may be some other faculty not yet fully known to me, which produces these ideas without any assistance from external things; this is, after all, just how I have always thought ideas are produced in me when I am dreaming.

And finally, even if these ideas did come from things other than myself, it would not follow that they must resemble those things. Indeed, I think I have often discovered a great disparity <between an object and its idea> in many cases. For example, there are two different ideas of the sun which I find within me. One of them, which is acquired as it were from the senses and which is a prime example of an idea which I reckon to come from an external source, makes the sun appear very small. The other idea is based on astronomical reasoning, that is, it is derived from certain notions which are innate in me (or else it is constructed by me in some other way), and this idea shows the sun to be several times larger than the earth. Obviously both these ideas cannot resemble the sun which exists outside me; and reason persuades me that the idea which seems to have emanated most directly from the sun itself has in fact no resemblance to it at all.

All these considerations are enough to establish that it is not reliable judgement but merely some blind impulse that has made me believe up till now that there exist things distinct from myself which transmit to me ideas or images of themselves through the sense organs or in some other way.

But it now occurs to me that there is another way of investigating whether some of the things of which I possess ideas exist outside me. In so far as the ideas are <considered> simply <as> modes of thought, there is no recognizable inequality among them: they all

---

10 Inborn—an idea that is already inside me.

11 Coming from outside.

appear to come from within me in the same fashion. But in so far as different ideas <are considered as images which> represent different things, it is clear that they differ widely. Undoubtedly, the ideas which represent substances to me amount to something more and, so to speak, contain within themselves more objective reality than the ideas which merely represent modes or accidents.[12] Again, the idea that gives me my understanding of a supreme God, eternal, infinite, <immutable,> omniscient, omnipotent and the creator of all things that exist apart from him, certainly has in it more objective reality than the ideas that represent finite substances.

Now it is manifest by the natural light that there must be at least as much <reality> in the efficient and total cause as in the effect of that cause. For where, I ask, could the effect get its reality from, if not from the cause? And how could the cause give it to the effect unless it possessed it? It follows from this both that something cannot arise from nothing, and also that what is more perfect—that is, contains in itself more reality—cannot arise from what is less perfect. And this is transparently true not only in the case of effects which possess <what the philosophers call> actual or formal reality, but also in the case of ideas, where one is considering only <what they call> objective reality. A stone, for example, which previously did not exist, cannot begin to exist unless it is produced by something which contains, either formally or eminently everything to be found in the stone;[13] similarly, heat cannot be produced in an object which was not previously hot, except by something of at least the same order <degree or kind> of perfection as heat, and so on. But it is also true that the *idea* of heat, or of a stone, cannot exist in me unless it is put there by some cause which contains at least as much reality as I conceive to be in the heat or in the stone. For although this cause

does not transfer any of its actual or formal reality to my idea, it should not on that account be supposed that it must be less real. The nature of an idea is such that of itself it requires no formal reality except what it derives from my thought, of which it is a mode. But in order for a given idea to contain such and such objective reality, it must surely derive it from some cause which contains at least as much formal reality as there is objective reality in the idea. For if we suppose that an idea contains something which was not in its cause, it must have got this from nothing; yet the mode of being by which a thing exists objectively <or representatively> in the intellect by way of an idea, imperfect though it may be, is certainly not nothing, and so it cannot come from nothing.

And although the reality which I am considering in my ideas is merely objective reality, I must not on that account suppose that the same reality need not exist formally in the causes of my ideas, but that it is enough for it to be present in them objectively. For just as the objective mode of being belongs to ideas by their very nature, so the formal mode of being belongs to the causes of ideas—or at least the first and most important ones—by *their* very nature. And although one idea may perhaps originate from another, there cannot be an infinite regress here; eventually one must reach a primary idea, the cause of which will be like an archetype which contains formally <and in fact> all the reality <or perfection> which is present only objectively <or representatively> in the idea. So it is clear to me, by the natural light, that the ideas in me are like <pictures, or> images which can easily fall short of the perfection of the things from which they are taken, but which cannot contain anything greater or more perfect.

The longer and more carefully I examine all these points, the more clearly and distinctly I recognize their truth. But what is my conclusion to be? If the objective reality of any of my ideas turns out to be so great that I am sure the same reality does not reside in me, either formally or eminently, and hence that I myself cannot be its cause, it will necessarily follow that I am not alone in the world, but that some other thing which is the cause of this idea also exists. But if no such idea is to be found in me, I shall have no argument to convince me of the existence of anything

---

12   See the notes for background information on "substance," "accident," "objective reality," and "formal reality."

13   That is, it has either the same properties as the stone (e.g., a certain hardness) or possesses even more perfect or pronounced versions of those properties (e.g., perfect hardness). An effect is "eminently" in a cause when the cause is more perfect than the effect.

apart from myself. For despite a most careful and comprehensive survey, this is the only argument I have so far been able to find.

Among my ideas, apart from the idea which gives me a representation of myself, which cannot present any difficulty in this context, there are ideas which variously represent God, corporeal and inanimate things, angels, animals and finally other men like myself.

As far as concerns the ideas which represent other men, or animals, or angels, I have no difficulty in understanding that they could be put together from the ideas I have of myself, of corporeal things and of God, even if the world contained no men besides me, no animals and no angels.

As to my ideas of corporeal things, I can see nothing in them which is so great <or excellent> as to make it seem impossible that it originated in myself. For if I scrutinize them thoroughly and examine them one by one, in the way in which I examined the idea of the wax yesterday, I notice that the things which I perceive clearly and distinctly in them are very few in number. The list comprises size, or extension in length, breadth and depth; shape, which is a function of the boundaries of this extension; position, which is a relation between various items possessing shape; and motion, or change in position; to these may be added substance, duration and number. But as for all the rest, including light and colours, sounds, smells, tastes, heat and cold and the other tactile qualities, I think of these only in a very confused and obscure way, to the extent that I do not even know whether they are true or false, that is, whether the ideas I have of them are ideas of real things or of non-things. For although, as I have noted before, falsity in the strict sense, or formal falsity, can occur only in judgements, there is another kind of falsity, material falsity, which occurs in ideas, when they represent non-things as things. For example, the ideas which I have of heat and cold contain so little clarity and distinctness that they do not enable me to tell whether cold is merely the absence of heat or vice versa, or whether both of them are real qualities, or neither is. And since there can be no ideas which are not as it were of things, if it is true that cold is nothing but the absence of heat, the idea which represents it to me as something real and positive deserves to be called false; and the same goes for other ideas of this kind.

Such ideas obviously do not require me to posit a source distinct from myself. For on the one hand, if they are false, that is, represent non-things, I know by the natural light that they arise from nothing—that is, they are in me only because of a deficiency and lack of perfection in my nature. If on the other hand they are true, then since the reality which they represent is so extremely slight that I cannot even distinguish it from a non-thing, I do not see why they cannot originate from myself.

With regard to the clear and distinct elements in my ideas of corporeal things, it appears that I could have borrowed some of these from my idea of myself, namely substance, duration, number and anything else of this kind. For example, I think that a stone is a substance, or is a thing capable of existing independently, and I also think that I am a substance. Admittedly I conceive of myself as a thing that thinks and is not extended, whereas I conceive of the stone as a thing that is extended and does not think, so that the two conceptions differ enormously; but they seem to agree with respect to the classification 'substance'. Again, I perceive that I now exist, and remember that I have existed for some time; moreover, I have various thoughts which I can count; it is in these ways that I acquire the ideas of duration and number which I can then transfer to other things. As for all the other elements which make up the ideas of corporeal things, namely extension, shape, position and movement, these are not formally contained in me, since I am nothing but a thinking thing; but since they are merely modes of a substance, and I am a substance, it seems possible that they are contained in me eminently.

So there remains only the idea of God; and I must consider whether there is anything in the idea which could not have originated in myself. By the word 'God' I understand a substance that is infinite, <eternal, immutable,> independent, supremely intelligent, supremely powerful, and which created both myself and everything else (if anything else there be) that exists. All these attributes are such that, the more carefully I concentrate on them, the less possible it seems that they could have originated from me alone.

So from what has been said it must be concluded that God necessarily exists.

It is true that I have the idea of substance in me in virtue of the fact that I am a substance; but this would not account for my having the idea of an infinite substance, when I am finite, unless this idea proceeded from some substance which really was infinite.

And I must not think that, just as my conceptions of rest and darkness are arrived at by negating movement and light, so my perception of the infinite is arrived at not by means of a true idea but merely by negating the finite. On the contrary, I clearly understand that there is more reality in an infinite substance than in a finite one, and hence that my perception of the infinite, that is God, is in some way prior to my perception of the finite, that is myself. For how could I understand that I doubted or desired—that is, lacked something—and that I was not wholly perfect, unless there were in me some idea of a more perfect being which enabled me to recognize my own defects by comparison?

Nor can it be said that this idea of God is perhaps materially false and so could have come from nothing, which is what I observed just a moment ago in the case of the ideas of heat and cold, and so on. On the contrary, it is utterly clear and distinct, and contains in itself more objective reality than any other idea; hence there is no idea which is in itself truer or less liable to be suspected of falsehood. This idea of a supremely perfect and infinite being is, I say, true in the highest degree; for although perhaps one may imagine that such a being does not exist, it cannot be supposed that the idea of such a being represents something unreal, as I said with regard to the idea of cold. The idea is, moreover, utterly clear and distinct; for whatever I clearly and distinctly perceive as being real and true, and implying any perfection, is wholly contained in it. It does not matter that I do not grasp the infinite, or that there are countless additional attributes of God which I cannot in any way grasp, and perhaps cannot even reach in my thought; for it is in the nature of the infinite not to be grasped by a finite being like myself. It is enough that I understand[14] the infinite, and that

I judge that all the attributes which I clearly perceive and know to imply some perfection—and perhaps countless others of which I am ignorant—are present in God either formally or eminently. This is enough to make the idea that I have of God the truest and most clear and distinct of all my ideas.

But perhaps I am something greater than I myself understand, and all the perfections which I attribute to God are somehow in me potentially, though not yet emerging or actualized. For I am now experiencing a gradual increase in my knowledge, and I see nothing to prevent its increasing more and more to infinity. Further, I see no reason why I should not be able to use this increased knowledge to acquire all the other perfections of God. And finally, if the potentiality for these perfections is already within me, why should not this be enough to generate the idea of such perfections?

But all this is impossible. First, though it is true that there is a gradual increase in my knowledge, and that I have many potentialities which are not yet actual, this is all quite irrelevant to the idea of God, which contains absolutely nothing that is potential; indeed, this gradual increase in knowledge is itself the surest sign of imperfection. What is more, even if my knowledge always increases more and more, I recognize that it will never actually be infinite, since it will never reach the point where it is not capable of a further increase; God, on the other hand, I take to be actually infinite, so that nothing can be added to his perfection. And finally, I perceive that the objective being of an idea cannot be produced merely by potential being, which strictly speaking is nothing, but only by actual or formal being.

If one concentrates carefully, all this is quite evident by the natural light. But when I relax my concentration, and my mental vision is blinded by the images of things perceived by the senses, it is not so easy for me to remember why the idea of a being more perfect than myself must necessarily proceed from some being which is in reality more perfect. I

---

14   According to Descartes, one can know or understand something without fully grasping it: "In the same way we can touch a mountain with our hands but we can-

not put our arms around it.... To grasp something is to embrace it in one's thought; to know something, it is sufficient to touch it with one's thought," he wrote in one of his letters.

should therefore like to go further and inquire whether I myself, who have this idea, could exist if no such being existed.

From whom, in that case, would I derive my existence? From myself presumably, or from my parents, or from some other beings less perfect than God; for nothing more perfect than God, or even as perfect, can be thought of or imagined.

Yet if I derived my existence from myself, then I should neither doubt nor want, nor lack anything at all; for I should have given myself all the perfections of which I have any idea, and thus I should myself be God. I must not suppose that the items I lack would be more difficult to acquire than those I now have. On the contrary, it is clear that, since I am a thinking thing or substance, it would have been far more difficult for me to emerge out of nothing than merely to acquire knowledge of the many things of which I am ignorant—such knowledge being merely an accident of that substance. And if I had derived my existence from myself, which is a greater achievement, I should certainly not have denied myself the knowledge in question, which is something much easier to acquire, or indeed any of the attributes which I perceive to be contained in the idea of God; for none of them seem any harder to achieve. And if any of them were harder to achieve, they would certainly appear so to me, if I had indeed got all my other attributes from myself, since I should experience a limitation of my power in this respect.

I do not escape the force of these arguments by supposing that I have always existed as I do now, as if it followed from this that there was no need to look for any author of my existence. For a lifespan can be divided into countless parts, each completely independent of the others, so that it does not follow from the fact that I existed a little while ago that I must exist now, unless there is some cause which as it were creates me afresh at this moment—that is, which preserves me. For it is quite clear to anyone who attentively considers the nature of time that the same power and action are needed to preserve anything at each individual moment of its duration as would be required to create that thing anew if it were not yet in existence. Hence the distinction between preservation and creation is only a con-

ceptual one, and this is one of the things that are evident by the natural light.

I must therefore now ask myself whether I possess some power enabling me to bring it about that I who now exist will still exist a little while from now. For since I am nothing but a thinking thing—or at least since I am now concerned only and precisely with that part of me which is a thinking thing—if there were such a power in me, I should undoubtedly be aware of it. But I experience no such power, and this very fact makes me recognize most clearly that I depend on some being distinct from myself.

But perhaps this being is not God, and perhaps I was produced either by my parents or by other causes less perfect than God. No; for as I have said before, it is quite clear that there must be at least as much in the cause as in the effect. And therefore whatever kind of cause is eventually proposed, since I am a thinking thing and have within me some idea of God, it must be admitted that what caused me is itself a thinking thing and possesses the idea of all the perfections which I attribute to God. In respect of this cause one may again inquire whether it derives its existence from itself or from another cause. If from itself, then it is clear from what has been said that it is itself God, since if it has the power of existing through its own might, then undoubtedly it also has the power of actually possessing all the perfections of which it has an idea—that is, all the perfections which I conceive to be in God. If, on the other hand, it derives its existence from another cause, then the same question may be repeated concerning this further cause, namely whether it derives its existence from itself or from another cause, until eventually the ultimate cause is reached, and this will be God.

It is clear enough that an infinite regress is impossible here, especially since I am dealing not just with the cause that produced me in the past, but also and most importantly with the cause that preserves me at the present moment.

Nor can it be supposed that several partial causes contributed to my creation, or that I received the idea of one of the perfections which I attribute to God from one cause and the idea of another from another—the supposition here being that all the perfections are to be found somewhere in the universe but not joined together in a single being, God. On the contrary, the unity, the simplicity, or the inseparability of all the attributes of God is one of the most important of the perfections which I understand him to have. And surely the idea of the unity of all his perfections could not have been placed in me by any cause which did not also provide me with the ideas of the other perfections; for no cause could have made me understand the interconnection and inseparability of the perfections without at the same time making me recognize what they were.

Lastly, as regards my parents, even if everything I have ever believed about them is true, it is certainly not they who preserve me; and in so far as I am a thinking thing, they did not even make me; they merely placed certain dispositions in the matter which I have always regarded as containing me, or rather my mind, for that is all I now take myself to be. So there can be no difficulty regarding my parents in this context. Altogether then, it must be concluded that the mere fact that I exist and have within me an idea of a most perfect being, that is, God, provides a very clear proof that God indeed exists.

It only remains for me to examine how I received this idea from God. For I did not acquire it from the senses; it has never come to me unexpectedly, as usually happens with the ideas of things that are perceivable by the senses, when these things present themselves to the external sense organs—or seem to do so. And it was not invented by me either; for I am plainly unable either to take away anything from it or to add anything to it. The only remaining alternative is that it is innate in me, just as the idea of myself is innate in me.

And indeed it is no surprise that God, in creating me, should have placed this idea in me to be, as it were, the mark of the craftsman stamped on his work—not that the mark need be anything distinct from the work itself. But the mere fact that God created me is a very strong basis for believing that I am somehow made in his image and likeness, and that I perceive that likeness, which includes the idea of God, by the same faculty which enables me to perceive myself. That is, when I turn my mind's eye upon myself, I understand that I am a thing which is incomplete and dependent on another and which aspires without limit

to ever greater and better things; but I also understand at the same time that he on whom I depend has within him all those greater things, not just indefinitely and potentially but actually and infinitely, and hence that he is God. The whole force of the argument lies in this: I recognize that it would be impossible for me to exist with the kind of nature I have—that is, having within me the idea of God—were it not the case that God really existed. By 'God' I mean the very being the idea of whom is within me, that is, the possessor of all the perfections which I cannot grasp, but can somehow reach in my thought, who is subject to no defects whatsoever. It is clear enough from this that he cannot be a deceiver, since it is manifest by the natural light that all fraud and deception depend on some defect.

But before examining this point more carefully and investigating other truths which may be derived from it, I should like to pause here and spend some time in the contemplation of God; to reflect on his attributes, and to gaze with wonder and adoration on the beauty of this immense light, so far as the eye of my darkened intellect can bear it. For just as we believe through faith that the supreme happiness of the next life consists solely in the contemplation of the divine majesty, so experience tells us that this same contemplation, albeit much less perfect, enables us to know the greatest joy of which we are capable in this life.

Fourth Meditation: Truth and falsity

During these past few days I have accustomed myself to leading my mind away from the senses; and I have taken careful note of the fact that there is very little about corporeal things that is truly perceived, whereas much more is known about the human mind, and still more about God. The result is that I now have no difficulty in turning my mind away from imaginable things and towards things which are objects of the intellect alone and are totally separate from matter. And indeed the idea I have of the human mind, in so far as it is a thinking thing, which is not extended in length, breadth or height and has no other bodily characteristics, is much more distinct than the idea of any corporeal thing. And when I consider the fact that I have doubts, or that I am a thing that is incomplete and dependent, then there arises in me a clear and distinct idea of a being who is independent and complete, that is, an idea of God. And from the mere fact that there is such an idea within me, or that I who possess this idea exist, I clearly infer that God also exists, and that every single moment of my entire existence depends on him. So clear is this conclusion that I am confident that the human intellect cannot know anything that is more evident or more certain. And now, from this contemplation of the true God, in whom all the treasures of wisdom and the sciences lie hidden, I think I can see a way forward to the knowledge of other things.

To begin with, I recognize that it is impossible that God should ever deceive me. For in every case of trickery or deception some imperfection is to be found; and although the ability to deceive appears to be an indication of cleverness or power, the will to deceive is undoubtedly evidence of malice or weakness, and so cannot apply to God.

Next, I know by experience that there is in me a faculty of judgement which, like everything else which is in me, I certainly received from God. And since God does not wish to deceive me, he surely did not give me the kind of faculty which would ever enable me to go wrong while using it correctly.

There would be no further doubt on this issue were it not that what I have just said appears to imply that I am incapable of ever going wrong. For if everything that is in me comes from God, and he did not endow me with a faculty for making mistakes, it appears that I can never go wrong. And certainly, so long as I think only of God, and turn my whole attention to him, I can find no cause of error or falsity. But when I turn back to myself, I know by experience that I am prone to countless errors. On looking for the cause of these errors, I find that I possess not only a real and positive idea of God, or a being who is supremely perfect, but also what may be described as a negative idea of nothingness, or of that which is farthest removed from all perfection. I realize that I am, as it were, something intermediate between God and nothingness, or between supreme being and non-being: my nature is such that in so far as I was created by the supreme being, there is nothing in me to enable me to go wrong or lead me astray; but in so far as I participate in nothingness or non-being, that is, in so far as I am not myself the

supreme being and am lacking in countless respects, it is no wonder that I make mistakes. I understand, then, that error as such is not something real which depends on God, but merely a defect. Hence my going wrong does not require me to have a faculty specially bestowed on me by God; it simply happens as a result of the fact that the faculty of true judgement which I have from God is in my case not infinite.

But this is still not entirely satisfactory. For error is not a pure negation, but rather a privation or lack of some knowledge which somehow should be in me. And when I concentrate on the nature of God, it seems impossible that he should have placed in me a faculty which is not perfect of its kind, or which lacks some perfection which it ought to have. The more skilled the craftsman the more perfect the work produced by him; if this is so, how can anything produced by the supreme creator of all things not be complete and perfect in all respects? There is, moreover, no doubt that God could have given me a nature such that I was never mistaken; again, there is no doubt that he always wills what is best. Is it then better that I should make mistakes than that I should not do so?

As I reflect on these matters more attentively, it occurs to me first of all that it is no cause for surprise if I do not understand the reasons for some of God's actions; and there is no call to doubt his existence if I happen to find that there are other instances where I do not grasp why or how certain things were made by him. For since I now know that my own nature is very weak and limited, whereas the nature of God is immense, incomprehensible and infinite, I also know without more ado that he is capable of countless things whose causes are beyond my knowledge. And for this reason alone I consider the customary search for final causes[15] to be totally useless in physics; there is considerable rashness in thinking myself capable of investigating the <impenetrable> purposes of God.

It also occurs to me that whenever we are inquiring whether the works of God are perfect, we

---

15   The final cause of something is (roughly) the purpose or reason for that thing's existence: e.g., the final cause of a statue might be an original idea in the sculptor's head which prompted her to make that particular statue. This terminology goes back to Aristotle.

ought to look at the whole universe, not just at one created thing on its own. For what would perhaps rightly appear very imperfect if it existed on its own is quite perfect when its function as a part of the universe is considered. It is true that, since my decision to doubt everything, it is so far only myself and God whose existence I have been able to know with certainty; but after considering the immense power of God, I cannot deny that many other things have been made by him, or at least could have been made, and hence that I may have a place in the universal scheme of things.

Next, when I look more closely at myself and inquire into the nature of my errors (for these are the only evidence of some imperfection in me), I notice that they depend on two concurrent causes, namely on the faculty of knowledge which is in me, and on the faculty of choice or freedom of the will; that is, they depend on both the intellect and the will simultaneously. Now all that the intellect does is to enable me to perceive the ideas which are subjects for possible judgements; and when regarded strictly in this light, it turns out to contain no error in the proper sense of that term. For although countless things may exist without there being any corresponding ideas in me, it should not, strictly speaking, be said that I am deprived of these ideas, but merely that I lack them, in a negative sense. This is because I cannot produce any reason to prove that God ought to have given me a greater faculty of knowledge than he did; and no matter how skilled I understand a craftsman to be, this does not make me think he ought to have put into every one of his works all the perfections which he is able to put into some of them. Besides, I cannot complain that the will or freedom of choice which I received from God is not sufficiently extensive or perfect, since I know by experience that it is not restricted in any way. Indeed, I think it is very noteworthy that there is nothing else in me which is so perfect and so great that the possibility of a further increase in its perfection or greatness is beyond my understanding. If, for example, I consider the faculty of understanding, I immediately recognize that in my case it is extremely slight and very finite, and I at once form the idea of an understanding which is much greater—indeed supremely great and infinite; and from the very fact that

I can form an idea of it, I perceive that it belongs to the nature of God. Similarly, if I examine the faculties of memory or imagination, or any others, I discover that in my case each one of these faculties is weak and limited, while in the case of God it is immeasurable. It is only the will, or freedom of choice, which I experience within me to be so great that the idea of any greater faculty is beyond my grasp; so much so that it is above all in virtue of the will that I understand myself to bear in some way the image and likeness of God. For although God's will is incomparably greater than mine, both in virtue of the knowledge and power that accompany it and make it more firm and efficacious, and also in virtue of its object, in that it ranges over a greater number of items, nevertheless it does not seem any greater than mine when considered as will in the essential and strict sense. This is because the will simply consists in our ability to do or not do something (that is, to affirm or deny, to pursue or avoid); or rather, it consists simply in the fact that when the intellect puts something forward for affirmation or denial or for pursuit or avoidance, our inclinations are such that we do not feel we are determined by any external force. For in order to be free, there is no need for me to be capable of going in each of two directions; on the contrary, the more I incline in one direction—either because I clearly understand that reasons of truth and goodness point that way, or because of a divinely produced disposition of my inmost thoughts—the freer is my choice. Neither divine grace nor natural knowledge ever diminishes freedom; on the contrary, they increase and strengthen it. But the indifference I feel when there is no reason pushing me in one direction rather than another is the lowest grade of freedom; it is evidence not of any perfection of freedom, but rather of a defect in knowledge or a kind of negation. For if I always saw clearly what was true and good, I should never have to deliberate about the right judgement or choice; in that case, although I should be wholly free, it would be impossible for me ever to be in a state of indifference.

From these considerations I perceive that the power of willing which I received from God is not, when considered in itself, the cause of my mistakes; for it is both extremely ample and also perfect of its kind. Nor is my power of understanding to blame; for since my understanding comes from God, everything that I understand I undoubtedly understand correctly, and any error here is impossible. So what then is the source of my mistakes? It must be simply this: the scope of the will is wider than that of the intellect; but instead of restricting it within the same limits, I extend its use to matters which I do not understand. Since the will is indifferent in such cases, it easily turns aside from what is true and good, and this is the source of my error and sin.

For example, during these past few days I have been asking whether anything in the world exists, and I have realized that from the very fact of my raising this question it follows quite evidently that I exist. I could not but judge that something which I understood so clearly was true; but this was not because I was compelled so to judge by any external force, but because a great light in the intellect was followed by a great inclination in the will, and thus the spontaneity and freedom of my belief was all the greater in proportion to my lack of indifference. But now, besides the knowledge that I exist, in so far as I am a thinking thing, an idea of corporeal nature comes into my mind; and I happen to be in doubt as to whether the thinking nature which is in me, or rather which I am, is distinct from this corporeal nature or identical with it. I am making the further supposition that my intellect has not yet come upon any persuasive reason in favour of one alternative rather than the other. This obviously implies that I am indifferent as to whether I should assert or deny either alternative, or indeed refrain from making any judgement on the matter.

What is more, this indifference does not merely apply to cases where the intellect is wholly ignorant, but extends in general to every case where the intellect does not have sufficiently clear knowledge at the time when the will deliberates. For although probable conjectures may pull me in one direction, the mere knowledge that they are simply conjectures, and not certain and indubitable reasons, is itself quite enough to push my assent the other way. My experience in the last few days confirms this: the mere fact that I found that all my previous beliefs were in some sense open to doubt was enough to turn my absolutely confident belief in their truth into the supposition that they were wholly false.

If, however, I simply refrain from making a judgement in cases where I do not perceive the truth with sufficient clarity and distinctness, then it is clear that I am behaving correctly and avoiding error. But if in such cases I either affirm or deny, then I am not using my free will correctly. If I go for the alternative which is false, then obviously I shall be in error; if I take the other side, then it is by pure chance that I arrive at the truth, and I shall still be at fault since it is clear by the natural light that the perception of the intellect should always precede the determination of the will. In this incorrect use of free will may be found the privation[16] which constitutes the essence of error. The privation, I say, lies in the operation of the will in so far as it proceeds from me, but not in the faculty of will which I received from God, nor even in its operation, in so far as it depends on him.

And I have no cause for complaint on the grounds that the power of understanding or the natural light which God gave me is no greater than it is; for it is in the nature of a finite intellect to lack understanding of many things, and it is in the nature of a created intellect to be finite. Indeed, I have reason to give thanks to him who has never owed me anything for the great bounty that he has shown me, rather than thinking myself deprived or robbed of any gifts he did not bestow.

Nor do I have any cause for complaint on the grounds that God gave me a will which extends more widely than my intellect. For since the will consists simply of one thing which is, as it were, indivisible, it seems that its nature rules out the possibility of anything being taken away from it. And surely, the more widely my will extends, then the greater thanks I owe to him who gave it to me.

Finally, I must not complain that the forming of those acts of will or judgements in which I go wrong happens with God's concurrence. For in so far as these acts depend on God, they are wholly true and good; and my ability to perform them means that there is in a sense more perfection in me than would be the case if I lacked this ability. As for the privation involved—which is all that the essential definition of

---

16   Privation is the state of being deprived of something, or something's being absent.

falsity and wrong consists in—this does not in any way require the concurrence of God, since it is not a thing; indeed, when it is referred to God as its cause, it should be called not a privation but simply a negation. For it is surely no imperfection in God that he has given me the freedom to assent or not to assent in those cases where he did not endow my intellect with a clear and distinct perception; but it is undoubtedly an imperfection in me to misuse that freedom and make judgements about matters which I do not fully understand. I can see, however, that God could easily have brought it about that without losing my freedom, and despite the limitations in my knowledge, I should nonetheless never make a mistake. He could, for example, have endowed my intellect with a clear and distinct perception of everything about which I was ever likely to deliberate; or he could simply have impressed it unforgettably on my memory that I should never make a judgement about anything which I did not clearly and distinctly understand. Had God made me this way, then I can easily understand that, considered as a totality, I would have been more perfect than I am now. But I cannot therefore deny that there may in some way be more perfection in the universe as a whole because some of its parts are not immune from error, while others are immune, than there would be if all the parts were exactly alike. And I have no right to complain that the role God wished me to undertake in the world is not the principal one or the most perfect of all.

What is more, even if I have no power to avoid error in the first way just mentioned, which requires a clear perception of everything I have to deliberate on, I can avoid error in the second way, which depends merely on my remembering to withhold judgement on any occasion when the truth of the matter is not clear. Admittedly, I am aware of a certain weakness in me, in that I am unable to keep my attention fixed on one and the same item of knowledge at all times; but by attentive and repeated meditation I am nevertheless able to make myself remember it as often as the need arises, and thus get into the habit of avoiding error.

It is here that man's greatest and most important perfection is to be found, and I therefore think that today's meditation, involving an investigation into the cause of error and falsity, has been very profit-

able. The cause of error must surely be the one I have explained; for if, whenever I have to make a judgement, I restrain my will so that it extends to what the intellect clearly and distinctly reveals, and no further, then it is quite impossible for me to go wrong. This is because every clear and distinct perception is undoubtedly something, and hence cannot come from nothing, but must necessarily have God for its author. Its author, I say, is God, who is supremely perfect, and who cannot be a deceiver on pain of contradiction; hence the perception is undoubtedly true. So today I have learned not only what precautions to take to avoid ever going wrong, but also what to do to arrive at the truth. For I shall unquestionably reach the truth, if only I give sufficient attention to all the things which I perfectly understand, and separate these from all the other cases where my apprehension is more confused and obscure. And this is just what I shall take good care to do from now on.

Fifth Meditation: The essence of material things, and the existence of God considered a second time

There are many matters which remain to be investigated concerning the attributes of God and the nature of myself, or my mind; and perhaps I shall take these up at another time. But now that I have seen what to do and what to avoid in order to reach the truth, the most pressing task seems to be to try to escape from the doubts into which I fell a few days ago, and see whether any certainty can be achieved regarding material objects.

But before I inquire whether any such things exist outside me, I must consider the ideas of these things, in so far as they exist in my thought, and see which of them are distinct, and which confused.

Quantity, for example, or 'continuous' quantity as the philosophers commonly call it, is something I distinctly imagine. That is, I distinctly imagine the extension of the quantity (or rather of the thing which is quantified) in length, breadth and depth. I also enumerate various parts of the thing, and to these parts I assign various sizes, shapes, positions and local motions; and to the motions I assign various durations.

Not only are all these things very well known and transparent to me when regarded in this general way, but in addition there are countless particular features regarding shape, number, motion and so on, which I perceive when I give them my attention. And the truth of these matters is so open and so much in harmony with my nature, that on first discovering them it seems that I am not so much learning something new as remembering what I knew before; or it seems like noticing for the first time things which were long present within me although I had never turned my mental gaze on them before.

But I think the most important consideration at this point is that I find within me countless ideas of things which even though they may not exist anywhere outside me still cannot be called nothing; for although in a sense they can be thought of at will, they are not my invention but have their own true and immutable[17] natures. When, for example, I imagine a triangle, even if perhaps no such figure exists, or has ever existed, anywhere outside my thought, there is still a determinate nature, or essence, or form of the triangle which is immutable and eternal, and not invented by me or dependent on my mind. This is clear from the fact that various properties can be demonstrated of the triangle, for example that its three angles equal two right angles, that its greatest side subtends its greatest angle, and the like; and since these properties are ones which I now clearly recognize whether I want to or not, even if I never thought of them at all when I previously imagined the triangle, it follows that they cannot have been invented by me.

It would be beside the point for me to say that since I have from time to time seen bodies of triangular shape, the idea of the triangle may have come to me from external things by means of the sense organs. For I can think up countless other shapes which there can be no suspicion of my ever having encountered through the senses, and yet I can demonstrate various properties of these shapes, just as I can with the triangle. All these properties are certainly true, since I am clearly aware of them, and therefore they are something, and not merely nothing; for it is obvious that whatever is true is something; and I have already amply demonstrated that everything of which I am clearly aware is true. And even if I had

not demonstrated this, the nature of my mind is such that I cannot but assent to these things, at least so long as I clearly perceive them. I also remember that even before, when I was completely preoccupied with the objects of the senses, I always held that the most certain truths of all were the kind which I recognized clearly in connection with shapes, or numbers or other items relating to arithmetic or geometry, or in general to pure and abstract mathematics.

But if the mere fact that I can produce from my thought the idea of something entails that everything which I clearly and distinctly perceive to belong to that thing really does belong to it, is not this a possible basis for another argument to prove the existence of God? Certainly, the idea of God, or a supremely perfect being, is one which I find within me just as surely as the idea of any shape or number. And my understanding that it belongs to his nature that he always exists is no less clear and distinct than is the case when I prove of any shape or number that some property belongs to its nature. Hence, even if it turned out that not everything on which I have meditated in these past days is true, I ought still to regard the existence of God as having at least the same level of certainty as I have hitherto attributed to the truths of mathematics.

At first sight, however, this is not transparently clear, but has some appearance of being a sophism.[18] Since I have been accustomed to distinguish between existence and essence in everything else, I find it easy to persuade myself that existence can also be separated from the essence of God, and hence that God can be thought of as not existing. But when I concentrate more carefully, it is quite evident that existence can no more be separated from the essence of God than the fact that its three angles equal two right angles can be separated from the essence of a triangle, or than the idea of a mountain can be separated from the idea of a valley. Hence it is just as much of a contradiction to think of God (that is, a supremely perfect being) lacking existence (that is, lacking a perfection), as it is to think of a mountain without a valley.

---

17   Unchangeable.

18   A clever-sounding argument based on unsound reasoning.

However, even granted that I cannot think of God except as existing, just as I cannot think of a mountain without a valley, it certainly does not follow from the fact that I think of a mountain with a valley that there is any mountain in the world; and similarly, it does not seem to follow from the fact that I think of God as existing that he does exist. For my thought does not impose any necessity on things; and just as I may imagine a winged horse even though no horse has wings, so I may be able to attach existence to God even though no God exists.

But there is a sophism concealed here. From the fact that I cannot think of a mountain without a valley, it does not follow that a mountain and valley exist anywhere, but simply that a mountain and a valley, whether they exist or not, are mutually inseparable. But from the fact that I cannot think of God except as existing, it follows that existence is inseparable from God, and hence that he really exists. It is not that my thought makes it so, or imposes any necessity on any thing; on the contrary, it is the necessity of the thing itself, namely the existence of God, which determines my thinking in this respect. For I am not free to think of God without existence (that is, a supremely perfect being without a supreme perfection) as I am free to imagine a horse with or without wings.

And it must not be objected at this point that while it is indeed necessary for me to suppose God exists, once I have made the supposition that he has all perfections (since existence is one of the perfections), nevertheless the original supposition was not necessary. Similarly, the objection would run, it is not necessary for me to think that all quadrilaterals can be inscribed in a circle; but given this supposition, it will be necessary for me to admit that a rhombus can be inscribed in a circle—which is patently false. Now admittedly, it is not necessary that I ever light upon any thought of God; but whenever I do choose to think of the first and supreme being, and bring forth the idea of God from the treasure house of my mind as it were, it is necessary that I attribute all perfections to him, even if I do not at that time enumerate them or attend to them individually. And this necessity plainly guarantees that, when I later realize that existence is a perfection, I am correct in inferring that the first and supreme

being exists. In the same way, it is not necessary for me ever to imagine a triangle; but whenever I do wish to consider a rectilinear figure having just three angles, it is necessary that I attribute to it the properties which license the inference that its three angles equal no more than two right angles, even if I do not notice this at the time. By contrast, when I examine what figures can be inscribed in a circle, it is in no way necessary for me to think that this class includes all quadrilaterals. Indeed, I cannot even imagine this, so long as I am willing to admit only what I clearly and distinctly understand. So there is a great difference between this kind of false supposition and the true ideas which are innate in me, of which the first and most important is the idea of God. There are many ways in which I understand that this idea is not something fictitious which is dependent on my thought, but is an image of a true and immutable nature. First of all, there is the fact that, apart from God, there is nothing else of which I am capable of thinking such that existence belongs to its essence. Second, I cannot understand how there could be two or more Gods of this kind; and after supposing that one God exists, I plainly see that it is necessary that he has existed from eternity and will abide for eternity. And finally, I perceive many other attributes of God, none of which I can remove or alter.

But whatever method of proof I use, I am always brought back to the fact that it is only what I clearly and distinctly perceive that completely convinces me. Some of the things I clearly and distinctly perceive are obvious to everyone, while others are discovered only by those who look more closely and investigate more carefully; but once they have been discovered, the latter are judged to be just as certain as the former. In the case of a right-angled triangle, for example, the fact that the square on the hypotenuse is equal to the square on the other two sides is not so readily apparent as the fact that the hypotenuse subtends the largest angle; but once one has seen it, one believes it just as strongly. But as regards God, if I were not overwhelmed by preconceived opinions, and if the images of things perceived by the senses did not besiege my thought on every side, I would certainly acknowledge him sooner and more easily than anything else. For what is more self-evident than the fact that the supreme being exists, or that God, to whose essence alone existence belongs, exists?

Although it needed close attention for me to perceive this, I am now just as certain of it as I am of everything else which appears most certain. And what is more, I see that the certainty of all other things depends on this, so that without it nothing can ever be perfectly known.

Admittedly my nature is such that so long as I perceive something very clearly and distinctly I cannot but believe it to be true. But my nature is also such that I cannot fix my mental vision continually on the same thing, so as to keep perceiving it clearly; and often the memory of a previously made judgement may come back, when I am no longer attending to the arguments which led me to make it. And so other arguments can now occur to me which might easily undermine my opinion, if I were unaware of God: and I should thus never have true and certain knowledge about anything, but only shifting and changeable opinions. For example, when I consider the nature of a triangle, it appears most evident to me, steeped as I am in the principles of geometry, that its three angles are equal to two right angles; and so long as I attend to the proof, I cannot but believe this to be true. But as soon as I turn my mind's eye away from the proof, then in spite of still remembering that I perceived it very clearly, I can easily fall into doubt about its truth, if I am unaware of God. For I can convince myself that I have a natural disposition to go wrong from time to time in matters which I think I perceive as evidently as can be. This will seem even more likely when I remember that there have been frequent cases where I have regarded things as true and certain, but have later been led by other arguments to judge them to be false.

Now, however, I have perceived that God exists, and at the same time I have understood that everything else depends on him, and that he is no deceiver; and I have drawn the conclusion that everything which I clearly and distinctly perceive is of necessity true. Accordingly, even if I am no longer attending to the arguments which led me to judge that this is true, as long as I remember that I clearly and distinctly perceived it, there are no counter-arguments which can be adduced to make me doubt it, but on the contrary I have true and certain knowledge of it. And I have knowledge not just of this matter, but of all matters which I remember ever having demonstrated, in geometry and so on. For what objections can now be raised? That the way I am made makes me prone to frequent error? But I now know that I am incapable of error in those cases where my understanding is transparently clear. Or can it be objected that I have in the past regarded as true and certain many things which I afterwards recognized to be false? But none of these were things which I clearly and distinctly perceived: I was ignorant of this rule for establishing the truth, and believed these things for other reasons which I later discovered to be less reliable. So what is left to say? Can one raise the objection I put to myself a while ago, that I may be dreaming, or that everything which I am now thinking has as little truth as what comes to the mind of one who is asleep? Yet even this does not change anything. For even though I might be dreaming, if there is anything which is evident to my intellect, then it is wholly true.

Thus I see plainly that the certainty and truth of all knowledge depends uniquely on my awareness of the true God, to such an extent that I was incapable of perfect knowledge about anything else until I became aware of him. And now it is possible for me to achieve full and certain knowledge of countless matters, both concerning God himself and other things whose nature is intellectual, and also concerning the whole of that corporeal nature which is the subject-matter of pure mathematics.

Sixth Meditation: The existence of material things, and the real distinction between mind and body

It remains for me to examine whether material things exist. And at least I now know they are capable of existing, in so far as they are the subject-matter of pure mathematics, since I perceive them clearly and distinctly. For there is no doubt that God is capable of creating everything that I am capable of perceiving in this manner; and I have never judged that something could not be made by him except on the grounds that there would be a contradiction in my perceiving it distinctly. The conclusion that material things exist is also suggested by the faculty of imagination, which I am aware of using when I turn my mind to material things. For when I give more attentive consideration to what imagination is, it seems to be nothing else but an application of the cognitive faculty to a body which is intimately present to it, and which therefore exists.

To make this clear, I will first examine the difference between imagination and pure understanding. When I imagine a triangle, for example, I do not merely understand that it is a figure bounded by three lines, but at the same time I also see the three lines with my mind's eye as if they were present before me; and this is what I call imagining. But if I want to think of a chiliagon, although I understand that it is a figure consisting of a thousand sides just as well as I understand the triangle to be a three-sided figure, I do not in the same way imagine the thousand sides or see them as if they were present before me. It is true that since I am in the habit of imagining something whenever I think of a corporeal thing, I may construct in my mind a confused representation of some figure; but it is clear that this is not a chiliagon. For it differs in no way from the representation I should form if I were thinking of a myriagon, or any figure with very many sides. Moreover, such a representation is useless for recognizing the properties which distinguish a chiliagon from other polygons. But suppose I am dealing with a pentagon: I can of course understand the figure of a pentagon, just as I can the figure of a chiliagon, without the help of the imagination; but I can also imagine a pentagon, by applying my mind's eye to its five sides and the area contained within them. And in doing this I notice quite clearly that imagination requires a peculiar effort of mind which is not required for understanding; this additional effort of mind clearly shows the difference between imagination and pure understanding.

Besides this, I consider that this power of imagining which is in me, differing as it does from the power of understanding, is not a necessary constituent of my own essence, that is, of the essence of my mind. For if I lacked it, I should undoubtedly remain the same individual as I now am; from which it seems to follow that it depends on something distinct from myself. And I can easily understand that, if there does exist some body to which the mind is so joined that it can apply itself to contemplate it, as it were, whenever it pleases, then it may possibly be this very body that enables me to imagine corporeal things. So the difference between this mode of thinking and pure understanding may simply be this: when the mind understands, it in some way turns towards itself and inspects one of the ideas which are within it; but when it imagines, it turns towards the body and looks at something in the body which conforms to an idea understood by the mind or perceived by the senses. I can, as I say, easily understand that this is how imagination comes about, if the body exists; and since there is no other equally suitable way of explaining imagination that comes to mind, I can make a probable conjecture that the body exists. But this is only a probability; and despite a careful and comprehensive investigation, I do not yet see how the distinct idea of corporeal nature which I find in my imagination can provide any basis for a necessary inference that some body exists.

But besides that corporeal nature which is the subject-matter of pure mathematics, there is much else that I habitually imagine, such as colours, sounds, tastes, pain and so on—though not so distinctly. Now I perceive these things much better by means of the senses, which is how, with the assistance of memory, they appear to have reached the imagination. So in order to deal with them more fully, I must pay equal attention to the senses, and see whether the things which are perceived by means of that mode of thinking which I call 'sensory perception' provide me with any sure argument for the existence of corporeal things.

To begin with, I will go back over all the things which I previously took to be perceived by the senses, and reckoned to be true; and I will go over my reasons for thinking this. Next, I will set out my reasons for subsequently calling these things into doubt. And finally I will consider what I should now believe about them.

First of all then, I perceived by my senses that I had a head, hands, feet and other limbs making up the body which I regarded as part of myself, or perhaps even as my whole self. I also perceived by my senses that this body was situated among many other bodies which could affect it in various favourable or unfavourable ways; and I gauged the favourable effects by a sensation of pleasure, and the unfavourable ones by a sensation of pain. In addition to pain and pleasure, I also had sensations within me of hunger, thirst, and other such appetites, and also of physical propensities towards cheerfulness, sadness, anger and similar emotions. And outside me, besides the extension, shapes and movements of bodies, I also had sensations of their hardness and heat, and of the other tactile qualities. In addition, I had sensations of light, colours, smells, tastes and sounds, the variety of which enabled me to distinguish the sky, the earth, the seas, and all other bodies, one from another. Considering the ideas of all these qualities which presented themselves to my thought, although the ideas were, strictly speaking, the only immediate objects of my sensory awareness, it was not unreasonable for me to think that the items which I was perceiving through the senses were things quite distinct from my thought, namely bodies which produced the ideas. For my experience was that these ideas came to me quite without my consent, so that I could not have sensory awareness of any object, even if I wanted to, unless it was present to my sense organs; and I could not avoid having sensory awareness of it when it was present. And since the ideas perceived by the senses were much more lively and vivid and even, in their own way, more distinct than any of those which I deliberately formed through meditating or which I found impressed on my memory, it seemed impossible that they should have come from within me; so the only alternative was that they came from other things. Since the sole source of my knowledge of these things was the ideas themselves, the supposition that the things resembled the ideas was bound to occur to me. In addition, I remembered that the use of my senses had come first, while the use of my reason came only later; and I saw that the ideas which I formed myself were less vivid than those which I perceived with the senses and were, for the most part, made up of elements of sensory ideas. In this way I easily convinced myself that I had nothing at all in the intellect which I had not previously had in sensation. As for the body which by some special right I called 'mine', my belief that this body, more than any other, belonged to me had some justification. For I could never be separated from it, as I could from other bodies; and I felt all my appetites and emotions in, and on account of, this body; and finally, I was aware of pain and pleasurable ticklings in parts of this body, but not in other bodies external to it. But why should that curious sensation of pain give rise to a particular distress of mind; or why should a certain kind of delight follow on a tickling sensation? Again, why should that curious tugging in the stomach which I call hunger tell me that I should eat, or a dryness of the throat tell me to drink, and so on? I was not able to give any explanation of all this, except that nature taught me so. For there is absolutely no connection (at least that I can understand) between the tugging sensation and the decision to take food, or between the sensation of something causing pain and the mental apprehension of distress that arises from that sensation. These and other judgements that I made concerning sensory objects, I was apparently taught to make by nature; for I had already made up my mind that this was how things were, before working out any arguments to prove it.

Later on, however, I had many experiences which gradually undermined all the faith I had had in the senses. Sometimes towers which had looked round from a distance appeared square from close up; and enormous statues standing on their pediments[19] did not seem large when observed from the ground. In these and countless other such cases, I found that the judgements of the external senses were mistaken. And this applied not just to the external senses but to the internal senses as well. For what can be more internal than pain? And yet I had heard that those who had had a leg or an arm amputated sometimes still seemed to feel pain intermittently in the missing part of the body. So even in my own case it was apparently not quite certain that a particular limb was hurting, even if I felt pain in it. To these reasons for doubting, I recently added two very general ones. The first was that every sensory experience I have ever thought I was having while awake I can also think of myself as sometimes having while asleep; and since I do not

---

19   In classical architecture, a pediment is a wide, triangular, gable-like area forming the front of a building with a two-pitched roof: pediments would often be situated above a door or portico, and might be decorated with statues.

believe that what I seem to perceive in sleep comes from things located outside me, I did not see why I should be any more inclined to believe this of what I think I perceive while awake. The second reason for doubt was that since I did not know the author of my being (or at least was pretending not to), I saw nothing to rule out the possibility that my natural constitution made me prone to error even in matters which seemed to me most true. As for the reasons for my previous confident belief in the truth of the things perceived by the senses, I had no trouble in refuting them. For since I apparently had natural impulses towards many things which reason told me to avoid, I reckoned that a great deal of confidence should not be placed in what I was taught by nature. And despite the fact that the perceptions of the senses were not dependent on my will, I did not think that I should on that account infer that they proceeded from things distinct from myself, since I might perhaps have a faculty not yet known to me which produced them.

But now, when I am beginning to achieve a better knowledge of myself and the author of my being, although I do not think I should heedlessly accept everything I seem to have acquired from the senses, neither do I think that everything should be called into doubt.

First, I know that everything which I clearly and distinctly understand is capable of being created by God so as to correspond exactly with my understanding of it. Hence the fact that I can clearly and distinctly understand one thing apart from another is enough to make me certain that the two things are distinct, since they are capable of being separated, at least by God. The question of what kind of power is required to bring about such a separation does not affect the judgement that the two things are distinct. Thus, simply by knowing that I exist and seeing at the same time that absolutely nothing else belongs to my nature or essence except that I am a thinking thing, I can infer correctly that my essence consists solely in the fact that I am a thinking thing. It is true that I may have (or, to anticipate, that I certainly have) a body that is very closely joined to me. But nevertheless, on the one hand I have a clear and distinct idea of myself, in so far as I am simply a thinking, non-extended thing; and on the other hand I have a distinct idea of body,

in so far as this is simply an extended, non-thinking thing. And accordingly, it is certain that I am really distinct from my body, and can exist without it.

Besides this, I find in myself faculties for certain special modes of thinking, namely imagination and sensory perception. Now I can clearly and distinctly understand myself as a whole without these faculties; but I cannot, conversely, understand these faculties without me, that is, without an intellectual substance to inhere in. This is because there is an intellectual act included in their essential definition; and hence I perceive that the distinction between them and myself corresponds to the distinction between the modes of a thing and the thing itself. Of course I also recognize that there are other faculties (like those of changing position, of taking on various shapes, and so on) which, like sensory perception and imagination, cannot be understood apart from some substance for them to inhere in, and hence cannot exist without it. But it is clear that these other faculties, if they exist, must be in a corporeal or extended substance and not an intellectual one; for the clear and distinct conception of them includes extension, but does not include any intellectual act whatsoever. Now there is in me a passive faculty of sensory perception, that is, a faculty for receiving and recognizing the ideas of sensible objects; but I could not make use of it unless there was also an active faculty, either in me or in something else, which produced or brought about these ideas. But this faculty cannot be in me, since clearly it presupposes no intellectual act on my part, and the ideas in question are produced without my cooperation and often even against my will. So the only alternative is that it is in another substance distinct from me—a substance which contains either formally or eminently all the reality which exists objectively in the ideas produced by this faculty (as I have just noted). This substance is either a body, that is, a corporeal nature, in which case it will contain formally <and in fact> everything which is to be found objectively <or representatively> in the ideas; or else it is God, or some creature more noble than a body, in which case it will contain eminently whatever is to be found in the ideas. But since God is not a deceiver, it is quite clear that he does not transmit the ideas to me either directly from himself, or indirectly, via some creature which contains the objective reality of the ideas not formally but only eminently. For God has given me no faculty at all for recognizing any such source for these ideas; on the contrary, he has given me a great propensity to believe that they are produced by corporeal things. So I do not see how God could be understood to be anything but a deceiver if the ideas were transmitted from a source other than corporeal things. It follows that corporeal things exist. They may not all exist in a way that exactly corresponds with my sensory grasp of them, for in many cases the grasp of the senses is very obscure and confused. But at least they possess all the properties which I clearly and distinctly understand, that is, all those which, viewed in general terms, are comprised within the subject-matter of pure mathematics.

What of the other aspects of corporeal things which are either particular (for example that the sun is of such and such a size or shape), or less clearly understood, such as light or sound or pain, and so on? Despite the high degree of doubt and uncertainty involved here, the very fact that God is not a deceiver, and the consequent impossibility of there being any falsity in my opinions which cannot be corrected by some other faculty supplied by God, offers me a sure hope that I can attain the truth even in these matters. Indeed, there is no doubt that everything that I am taught by nature contains some truth. For if nature is considered in its general aspect, then I understand by the term nothing other than God himself, or the ordered system of created things established by God. And by my own nature in particular I understand nothing other than the totality of things bestowed on me by God.

There is nothing that my own nature teaches me more vividly than that I have a body, and that when I feel pain there is something wrong with the body, and that when I am hungry or thirsty the body needs food and drink, and so on. So I should not doubt that there is some truth in this.

Nature also teaches me, by these sensations of pain, hunger, thirst and so on, that I am not merely present in my body as a sailor is present in a ship, but that I am very closely joined and, as it were, intermingled with it, so that I and the body form a unit. If this were not so, I, who am nothing but a thinking thing, would not feel pain when the body was hurt, but would perceive the damage purely by the intellect, just as a sailor perceives by sight if anything in his ship is broken. Similarly, when the body needed food or drink, I should have an explicit understanding of the fact, instead of having confused sensations of hunger and thirst. For these sensations of hunger, thirst, pain and so on are nothing but confused modes of thinking which arise from the union and, as it were, intermingling of the mind with the body.

I am also taught by nature that various other bodies exist in the vicinity of my body, and that some of these are to be sought out and others avoided. And from the fact that I perceive by my senses a great variety of colours, sounds, smells and tastes, as well as differences in heat, hardness and the like, I am correct in inferring that the bodies which are the source of these various sensory perceptions possess differences corresponding to them, though perhaps not resembling them. Also, the fact that some of the perceptions are agreeable to me while others are disagreeable makes it quite certain that my body, or rather my whole self, in so far as I am a combination of body and mind, can be affected by the various beneficial or harmful bodies which surround it.

There are, however, many other things which I may appear to have been taught by nature, but which in reality I acquired not from nature but from a habit of making ill-considered judgements; and it is therefore quite possible that these are false. Cases in point are the belief that any space in which nothing is occurring to stimulate my senses must be empty; or that the heat in a body is something exactly resembling the idea of heat which is in me; or that when a body is white or green, the selfsame whiteness or greenness which I perceive through my senses is present in the body; or that in a body which is bitter or sweet there is the selfsame taste which I experience, and so on; or, finally, that stars and towers and other distant bodies have the same size and shape which they present to my senses, and other examples of this kind. But to make sure that my perceptions in this matter are sufficiently distinct, I must more accurately define exactly what I mean when I say that I am taught something by nature. In this context I am taking nature to be something more limited than the totality of things bestowed on me by God. For this includes many things that belong to the mind alone—for example my perception that what is done cannot be undone, and all other things that are known by the natural light; but at this stage I am not speaking of these matters. It also includes much that relates to the body alone, like the tendency to move in a downward direction, and so on; but I am not speaking of these matters either. My sole concern here is with what God has bestowed on me as a combination of mind and body. My nature, then, in this limited sense, does indeed teach me to avoid what induces a feeling of pain and to seek out what induces feelings of pleasure, and so on. But it does not appear to teach us to draw any conclusions from these sensory perceptions about things located outside us without waiting until the intellect has examined the matter. For knowledge of the truth about such things seems to belong to the mind alone, not to the combination of mind and body. Hence, although a star has no greater effect on my eye than the flame of a small light, that does not mean that there is any real or positive inclination in me to believe that the star is no bigger than the light; I have simply made this judgement from childhood onwards without any rational basis. Similarly, although I feel heat when I go near a fire and feel pain when I go too near, there is no convincing argument for supposing that there is something in the fire which resembles the heat, any more than for supposing that there is something which resembles the pain. There is simply reason to suppose that there is something in the fire, whatever it may eventually turn out to be, which produces in us the feelings of heat or pain. And likewise, even though there is nothing in any given space that stimulates the senses, it does not follow that there is no body there. In these cases and many others I see that I have been in the habit of misusing the order of nature. For the proper purpose of the sensory perceptions given me by nature is simply to inform the mind of what is beneficial or harmful for the composite of which the mind is a part; and to this extent they are sufficiently clear and distinct. But I misuse them by treating them as reliable touchstones for immediate judgements about the essential nature of the bodies located outside us; yet this is an area where they provide only very obscure information.

I have already looked in sufficient detail at how, notwithstanding the goodness of God, it may happen that my judgements are false. But a further problem now comes to mind regarding those very things which nature presents to me as objects which I should seek out or avoid, and also regarding the internal sensations, where I seem to have detected errors—e.g., when someone is tricked by the pleasant taste of some food into eating the poison concealed inside it. Yet in this case, what the man's nature urges him to go for is simply what is responsible for the pleasant taste, and not the poison, which his nature knows nothing about. The only inference that can be drawn from this is that his nature is not omniscient. And this is not surprising, since man is a limited thing, and so it is only fitting that his perfection should be limited.

And yet it is not unusual for us to go wrong even in cases where nature does urge us towards something. Those who are ill, for example, may desire food or drink that will shortly afterwards turn out to be bad for them. Perhaps it may be said that they go wrong because their nature is disordered, but this does not remove the difficulty. A sick man is no less one of God's creatures than a healthy one, and it seems no less a contradiction to suppose that he has received from God a nature which deceives him. Yet a clock constructed with wheels and weights observes all the laws of its nature just as closely when it is badly made and tells the wrong time as when it completely fulfils the wishes of the clockmaker. In the same way, I might consider the body of a man as a kind of machine equipped with and made up of bones, nerves, muscles, veins, blood and skin in such a way that, even if there were no mind in it, it would still perform all the same movements as it now does in those cases where movement is not under the control of the will or, consequently, of the mind. I can easily see that if such a body suffers from dropsy,[20] for example, and is affected by the dryness of the throat which normally produces in the mind the sensation of thirst, the resulting condition of the nerves and other parts will dispose the body to take a drink, with the result that the disease will be aggravated. Yet this is just as natural as the body's being stimulated by a similar

---

20 An illness characterized by an abnormal accumulation of watery fluid in certain tissues and cavities of the body.

dryness of the throat to take a drink when there is no such illness and the drink is beneficial. Admittedly, when I consider the purpose of the clock, I may say that it is departing from its nature when it does not tell the right time; and similarly when I consider the mechanism of the human body, I may think that, in relation to the movements which normally occur in it, it too is deviating from its nature if the throat is dry at a time when drinking is not beneficial to its continued health. But I am well aware that 'nature' as I have just used it has a very different significance from 'nature' in the other sense. As I have just used it, 'nature' is simply a label which depends on my thought; it is quite extraneous to the things to which it is applied, and depends simply on my comparison between the idea of a sick man and a badly-made clock, and the idea of a healthy man and a well-made clock. But by 'nature' in the other sense I understand something which is really to be found in the things themselves; in this sense, therefore, the term contains something of the truth.

When we say, then, with respect to the body suffering from dropsy, that it has a disordered nature because it has a dry throat and yet does not need drink, the term 'nature' is here used merely as an extraneous label. However, with respect to the composite, that is, the mind united with this body, what is involved is not a mere label, but a true error of nature, namely that it is thirsty at a time when drink is going to cause it harm. It thus remains to inquire how it is that the goodness of God does not prevent nature, in this sense, from deceiving us.

The first observation I make at this point is that there is a great difference between the mind and the body, inasmuch as the body is by its very nature always divisible, while the mind is utterly indivisible. For when I consider the mind, or myself in so far as I am merely a thinking thing, I am unable to distinguish any parts within myself; I understand myself to be something quite single and complete. Although the whole mind seems to be united to the whole body, I recognize that if a foot or arm or any other part of the body is cut off, nothing has thereby been taken away from the mind. As for the faculties of willing, of understanding, of sensory perception and so on, these cannot be termed parts of the mind, since it is one

and the same mind that wills, and understands and has sensory perceptions. By contrast, there is no corporeal or extended thing that I can think of which in my thought I cannot easily divide into parts; and this very fact makes me understand that it is divisible. This one argument would be enough to show me that the mind is completely different from the body, even if I did not already know as much from other considerations.

My next observation is that the mind is not immediately affected by all parts of the body, but only by the brain, or perhaps just by one small part of the brain, namely the part which is said to contain the 'common' sense. Every time this part of the brain is in a given state, it presents the same signals to the mind, even though the other parts of the body may be in a different condition at the time. This is established by countless observations, which there is no need to review here.

I observe, in addition, that the nature of the body is such that whenever any part of it is moved by another part which is some distance away, it can always be moved in the same fashion by any of the parts which lie in between, even if the more distant part does nothing. For example, in a cord ABCD, if one end D is pulled so that the other end A moves, the exact same movement could have been brought about if one of the intermediate points B or C had been pulled, and D had not moved at all. In similar fashion, when I feel a pain in my foot, physiology tells me that this happens by means of nerves distributed throughout the foot, and that these nerves are like cords which go from the foot right up to the brain. When the nerves are pulled in the foot, they in turn pull on inner parts of the brain to which they are attached, and produce a certain motion in them; and nature has laid it down that this motion should produce in the mind a sensation of pain, as occurring in the foot. But since these nerves, in passing from the foot to the brain, must pass through the calf, the thigh, the lumbar region, the back and the neck, it can happen that, even if it is not the part in the foot but one of the intermediate parts which is being pulled, the same motion will occur in the brain as occurs when the foot is hurt, and so it will necessarily come about that the mind feels the same sensation of pain. And we must suppose the same thing happens with regard to any other sensation.

My final observation is that any given movement occurring in the part of the brain that immediately affects the mind produces just one corresponding sensation; and hence the best system that could be devised is that it should produce the one sensation which, of all possible sensations, is most especially and most frequently conducive to the preservation of the healthy man. And experience shows that the sensations which nature has given us are all of this kind; and so there is absolutely nothing to be found in them that does not bear witness to the power and goodness of God. For example, when the nerves in the foot are set in motion in a violent and unusual manner, this motion, by way of the spinal cord, reaches the inner parts of the brain, and there gives the mind its signal for having a certain sensation, namely the sensation of a pain as occurring in the foot. This stimulates the mind to do its best to get rid of the cause of the pain, which it takes to be harmful to the foot. It is true that God could have made the nature of man such that this particular motion in the brain indicated something else to the mind; it might, for example, have made the mind aware of the actual motion occurring in the brain, or in the foot, or in any of the intermediate regions; or it might have indicated something else entirely. But there is nothing else which would have been so conducive to the continued well-being of the body. In the same way, when we need drink, there arises a certain dryness in the throat; this sets in motion the nerves of the throat, which in turn move the inner parts of the brain. This motion produces in the mind a sensation of thirst, because the most useful thing for us to know about the whole business is that we need drink in order to stay healthy. And so it is in the other cases.

It is quite clear from all this that, notwithstanding the immense goodness of God, the nature of man as a combination of mind and body is such that it is bound to mislead him from time to time. For there may be some occurrence, not in the foot but in one of the other areas through which the nerves travel in their route from the foot to the brain, or even in the brain itself; and if this cause produces the same motion which is generally produced by injury to the foot, then pain will be felt as if it were in the foot. This deception of the senses is natural, because a given motion in the brain must always produce the same sensation in the mind; and the origin of the motion in question is much more often going to be something which is hurting the foot, rather than something existing elsewhere. So it is reasonable that this motion should always indicate to the mind a pain in the foot rather than in any other part of the body. Again, dryness of the throat may sometimes arise not, as it normally does, from the fact that a drink is necessary to the health of the body, but from some quite opposite cause, as happens in the case of the man with dropsy. Yet it is much better that it should mislead on this occasion than that it should always mislead when the body is in good health. And the same goes for the other cases.

This consideration is the greatest help to me, not only for noticing all the errors to which my nature is liable, but also for enabling me to correct or avoid them without difficulty. For I know that in matters regarding the well-being of the body, all my senses report the truth much more frequently than not. Also, I can almost always make use of more than one sense to investigate the same thing; and in addition, I can use both my memory, which connects present experiences with preceding ones, and my intellect, which has by now examined all the causes of error. Accordingly, I should not have any further fears about the falsity of what my senses tell me every day; on the contrary, the exaggerated doubts of the last few days should be dismissed as laughable. This applies especially to the principal reason for doubt, namely my inability to distinguish between being asleep and being awake. For I now notice that there is a vast difference between the two, in that dreams are never linked by memory with all the other actions of life as waking experiences are. If, while I am awake, anyone were suddenly to appear to me and then disappear immediately, as happens in sleep, so that I could not see where he had come from or where he had gone to, it would not be unreasonable for me to judge that he was a ghost, or a vision created in my brain, rather than a real man. But when I distinctly see where things come from and where and when they come to me, and when I can connect my perceptions of them with the whole of the rest of my life without a break, then I am quite certain that when I encounter these things I am not asleep but awake. And I ought not to have even the slightest doubt of their reality if, after calling upon all the senses as well as my memory and my intellect in order to check them, I receive no conflicting reports from any of these sources. For from the fact that God is not a deceiver it follows that in cases like these I am completely free from error. But since the pressure of things to be done does not always allow us to stop and make such a meticulous check, it must be admitted that in this human life we are often liable to make mistakes about particular things, and we must acknowledge the weakness of our nature.

JOHN LOCKE

An Essay Concerning Human Understanding

Who Was John Locke?

John Locke was born in the Somerset countryside, near the town of Bristol, in 1632. His parents were small landowners—minor gentry—who subjected the young Locke to a strict Protestant upbringing. Thanks to the influence of one of his father's friends Locke was able to gain a place at Westminster School, at the time the best school in England, where he studied Greek, Latin, and Hebrew. He went on to Christ Church College, Oxford, and graduated with a BA in 1656. Shortly afterwards he was made a senior student of his college—a kind of teaching position—which he was to remain until 1684, when the king of England, Charles II, personally (and illegally) demanded his expulsion.

During the 1650s and early '60s Locke lectured on Greek and rhetoric at Oxford but he was idle and unhappy, and became increasingly bored by the traditional philosophy of his day. He developed an interest in medicine and physical science (in 1675 he tried and failed to gain the degree of Doctor of Medicine), and in 1665 Locke left the confines of the academic world, and began to make his way into the world of politics and science. In the winter of 1665–66 he was ambassador to the German state of Brandenburg, where his first-hand observation of religious toleration between Calvinists, Lutherans, Catholics, and Anabaptists made a big impression on him.

A chance encounter in 1666 was the decisive turning-point in Locke's life: he met a nobleman called Lord Ashley, then the Chancellor of the Exchequer, and soon went to live at Ashley's London house as his confidant and medical advisor. In 1668, Locke was responsible for a life-saving surgical operation on Ashley, implanting a small silver spigot to drain off fluid from a cyst on his liver; the lord never forgot his gratitude (and wore the small tap in his side for the rest of his life). Under Ashley's patronage, Locke had both the leisure to spend several years working on his *Essay Concerning Human Understanding*, and a sequence of lucrative and interesting government positions, including one as part of a group drafting the constitution of the new colony of Carolina in the Americas.

Ashley's support was also essential in giving Locke—an introverted and hyper-sensitive soul, who suffered for most of his life from bad asthma and general poor health—the confidence to do original philosophy. Locke never married, was a life-long celibate, shied away from drinking parties and a hectic social life, but enjoyed the attentions of lady admirers, and throughout his life he had many loyal friends and got on especially well with some of his friends' children.

Locke spent the years from 1675 until 1679 traveling in France (where he expected to die of tuberculosis, but survived—Locke spent a large portion of his life confidently expecting an early death), and when he returned to England it was to a very unsettled political situation. The heir to the British throne, Charles II's younger brother James, was a Catholic, and his succession was feared by many politicians, including Ashley—who was, by this time, the Earl of Shaftesbury—and his political party, the Whigs. Their greatest worry was that the return of a Catholic monarchy would mean the return of religious oppression to England, as was happening in parts of Europe. Charles, however, stood by his brother and in 1681 Shaftesbury was sent to prison in the Tower of London, charged with high treason. Shaftesbury was acquitted by a grand jury, but he fled to Holland and died a few months later (spending his last few hours, the story goes, discussing a draft of Locke's *Essay* with his friends). Locke, in danger as a known associate of Shaftesbury's, followed his example in 1683 and secretly moved to the Netherlands, where he had to spend a year underground evading arrest by the Dutch government's agents on King Charles's behalf. While in Holland he rewrote material for the *Essay*, molding it towards its final state, and published an abridgement of the book in a French scholarly periodical which immediately attracted international attention.

In 1689 the political tumult in England had subsided enough for Locke to return—James's brief reign (as James II) had been toppled by the Protestant William of Orange and his queen Mary—and he moved as a permanent house-guest to an estate called Oates about twenty five miles from London. He returned to political life (though he refused the post of ambassador to Brandenburg, on grounds of ill health), and played a significant role in loosening restrictions on publishers and authors.

It was in this year, when Locke was 57, that the results of his thirty years of thinking and writing were suddenly published in a flood. First, published anonymously, came the *Letter on Toleration*, then *Two Treatises on Government*. In the *Two Treatises*—which was influential in the liberal movements of the next century that culminated in the French and American revolutions—Locke argued that the authority of monarchs is limited by individuals' rights and the public good. Finally, *An Essay Concerning Human Understanding* was published under his own name, to almost instant acclaim: the publication of this book catapulted Locke overnight to what we would now think of as international superstardom.

These three were his most important works, but Locke—by now one of the most famous men in England—continued to write and publish until his death fifteen years later. He wrote, for example, works on the proper control of the currency for the English government; *Some Thoughts Concerning Education* (which, apparently, was historically important in shaping the toilet-training practices of the English educated classes); a work on the proper care and cultivation of fruit trees; and a careful commentary on the *Epistles* of St. Paul. He died quietly, reading in his study, in October 1704.

What Was Locke's Overall Philosophical Project?

Locke is the leading proponent of a school of philosophy now often called "British empiricism." Some of the central platforms of this doctrine are as follows: First, human beings are born like a blank, white sheet of paper—a *tabula rasa*—without any innate knowledge but with certain natural powers, and we use these powers to adapt ourselves to the social and physical environment into which we are born. Two especially important natural powers are the capacity for conscious sense experience and for feeling pleasure and pain, and it is from the interaction of these capacities with the environment that we acquire all of our ideas, knowledge, and habits of mind. All meaningful language must be connected to the ideas that we thus acquire, and the abuse of language to talk about things of which we have no idea is a serious source of intellectual errors—errors that can have harmful consequences for social and moral life, as well as the growth of the sciences. British empiricism—whose other main exponents were Thomas Hobbes (1588–1679), George Berkeley (1685–1753), and David Hume (1711–1776)—was generally opposed to religious fervor and sectarian strife, and cautious about the human capacity for attaining absolute knowledge about things that go beyond immediate experience.

An Essay Concerning Human Understanding is Locke's attempt to present a systematic and detailed empiricist account of the human mind and human knowledge. It also includes an account of the nature of language, and touches on philosophical issues to do with logic, religion, metaphysics, and ethics. Locke was also consciously interested in defending a certain modern way of thinking against the habits of the past: instead of relatively uncritical and conservative acceptance of Greek and Roman history, literature and philosophy, and of Christian theology, Locke defended independent thought, secular values, and the power of modern ideas and social change to produce useful results.

Locke was optimistic about the power and accuracy of his own theory of human understanding—and thus about the powers of human beings to come to know the world—but he nevertheless thought it was a *limited* power. There are some things human beings just cannot ever come to know with certainty, Locke thought, and we should be humble in our attempts to describe reality. Thus, there are some domains in which, according to Locke, our human capacities are sufficient to produce certain knowledge: mathematics, morality, the existence of God, and the existence of things in the world corresponding to our 'simple ideas' (i.e., roughly, the things we perceive). However, there are other areas where the best we can do is to make skillful guesses: these more difficult questions

have to do with the underlying nature and workings of nature—that is, with scientific theory—and with the details of religious doctrine. God has given us the capacity to effectively get by in the world by making these careful guesses, according to Locke, but he has not given us the capacity to ever know for sure whether our guesses are correct or not. (This is one reason why Locke believed we should be tolerant of other people's religious beliefs.)

What Is the Structure of This Reading?

An Essay Concerning Human Understanding is split into four Books, each of which is further divided into chapters, which in turn are divided into sections. The first Book is primarily an attack on the notion, which Locke found especially in Descartes, that human beings are born with certain "innate ideas"—concepts and knowledge which are not the product of experience but which are, perhaps, implanted in us by God. Book II develops Locke's alternative empiricist theory of ideas: here he describes the different sorts of ideas human beings have (such as our ideas of external objects, space, time, number, cause and effect, and so on), and tries to show how these ideas all derive ultimately from reflection on our own sense-experience. In Book III Locke describes the workings of language, and in particular defends the thesis that all meaningful language derives that meaning from its connections to our ideas. Finally, Book IV is where Locke considers the question of human knowledge and asks how much justification there is for our beliefs about God and nature, concluding that, although limited, the scope of our knowledge is more than enough for practical purposes.

The first two selections collected here come from Book II (and so are about ideas), and the third from Book IV (and so is about knowledge). The first selection asks how much our ideas resemble those things in the world that cause them and, among other things, describes and defends an important distinction between "primary" and "secondary" qualities. The second extract deals with the topic of "substance," the 'stuff' of the material world. The third approaches head-on the issue of the extent and limits of our knowledge of the external world.

Some Useful Background Information

1. Locke writes in a very straightforward and clear style—he deliberately set out to write informally, for a general educated readership—but his language is the English of the seventeenth century and some readers might find this a little distracting. Here is a short glossary of the words which might be either unfamiliar or used in an unfamiliar way.

   Admit of: accept

   Apprehension: understanding, perception

   Bare/barely: mere/merely

   Corpuscles: small particles

   Denominate: apply a name to something

   Doth: does

   Evidences: shows

   Experiment: experience

   Extravagant: odd, peculiar

   Fain: gladly, happily

   Figure: shape

   Hath: has

   Impulse: causal impact

   Manna: the sweet dried juice of the Mediterranean ash tree and other plants, which can be used as a mild laxative (also, a substance miraculously supplied as food to the Israelites in the wilderness, according to the Bible)

   Peculiar: particular, specific

   Sensible/insensible: able to be sensed/invisible to the senses

   Superficies: outside surfaces

   V.g.: for example

   Viz.: in other words, that is

   Without: outside (us)

2. Locke's notion of an *idea* is central to his philosophy—which is even sometimes called "the way of ideas"—and he uses the word in his own special and carefully worked out way. For Locke, ideas are not activities of the mind but instead are the *contents* of the mind—they are the things we think about, the objects of our thought. (In fact, for Locke, thought consists entirely in the succession of ideas through consciousness.) Thus, for example, the things we believe, know, remember, or imagine are what Locke would call ideas.

As the term suggests, Locke probably assumes ideas are mental entities—they are things that exist in our minds rather than in the external world. Certainly, there are no ideas floating around that are not part of someone's consciousness; every idea is necessarily the object of some act of thinking. Furthermore, ideas are the *only* things we directly think about—our thought and our mental experience, for Locke, is internally rather than externally directed: it is an experience of our ideas and the operations of our mind, not directly of the world. When Locke uses the word "perception," for example, he often means the mind's perception (awareness) of its own ideas, not, as we would usually mean, perception of objects outside our own minds.

However, this is not to say that we don't think about or perceive the external world; Locke commonsensically thought that we saw trees, tasted oranges, heard the speech of other human beings, and so on. But it does mean that all our thought and perception is mediated by ideas, which intervene between us and external reality. The ideas we have before our minds are the "immediate objects of perception," and the things those ideas represent are the "indirect objects of perception." Yet it is important to remember that, for Locke, ideas *do* naturally and evidently represent things beyond themselves (although not necessarily the whole, or even the most important aspects, of the nature of those things)—Locke does not believe for a moment that we are locked inside our own heads.

Locke distinguishes between lots of different types of ideas, but one especially important contrast is between simple and complex ideas. A simple idea is "nothing but one uniform appearance, or conception in the mind, and is not distinguishable into different ideas," whereas complex ideas are compounded out of more than one simple idea. For example, redness is a simple idea, while the idea of a London double-decker bus is a complex idea. For Locke, all simple ideas are acquired from experience, either through sense perception or through the perception of our own thoughts (often called "introspection"): we are not free to simply invent or ignore such ideas, as they are physically caused by the things they represent. However, we are free to construct complex ideas out of this raw material as we like, and we can do so in various ways: we can add simple ideas together into a single idea (e.g., the idea of a horse), or we can compare two ideas and perceive the relation that holds between them (e.g., the idea of being taller than), or we can generalize about simple ideas to form abstract ideas (e.g., the idea of time or infinity).

3. Locke held the modern (at the time) "corpuscular" theory of matter, which was developed by Pierre Gassendi (1592–1655) and Robert Boyle (1627–1691) and which, though a "mechanical philosophy," contradicted some important elements of Descartes' physical theory. As a corpuscularian, Locke thought that the physical world was made up of tiny indestructible particles, invisible to the human eye, moving around in empty space, and having only the following properties: solidity, extension in three dimensions, shape (or "figure"), motion or rest, number, location ("situation"), volume ("bulk"), and texture. All the phenomena of the material world are built out of or caused by these particles and their properties and powers. Thus, collections of particles big enough to be visible have certain properties (which Locke called "qualities"), e.g., the shape and size of a gold nugget, its color, malleability, luster, chemical inertness, and so on. Our perception of the world—that is to say, our experience of these qualities—is brought about by invisible streams of tiny particles emanating from the objects in our environment and striking our sense-receptors (our eyes, ears, skin, and so on). Locke and his contemporaries thought this stimulation of our senses causes complex reactions in our "animal spirits," and this is what gives rise to our ideas. Animal spirits were supposed to be a fine fluid (itself made up of tiny particles) flowing through our nervous system and carrying signals from one place to another—ultimately to our brain.

Some Common Misconceptions

1. In reading Locke, it is important not to confuse ideas with qualities. Ideas are mental entities; they constitute our *experience* of the world. Qualities are non-mental attributes of chunks of matter in the world; they are the things ideas are *about*. Thus, in Locke's view, our idea of color should not be confused with the property of color itself. The distinction between primary and secondary qualities, then, is mainly a distinction between types of physical property (though it does have implications for the taxonomy of our ideas).

2. The secondary qualities do not only include colors, tastes, smells, sounds, and feels; they also include properties like solubility, brittleness, flammability, being nutritious, being a painkiller, and so on.

3. It is sometimes thought Locke argued that secondary qualities do not really exist, and that color, smell, taste, and so on are only ideas in our mind. But this is not so. Locke does think that material objects in the world really have secondary qualities, but he argues that we have misunderstood the *nature* of these qualities in a particular way.

4. In thinking about the nature of the secondary qualities it is helpful to consider the nature of their connection with our ideas of them. In this context, two concepts are useful but are sometimes confused with each other. The first notion is that of *perceiver-relativity*: this is the idea that how something *seems* depends on who is perceiving it. To say that "beauty is in the eye of the beholder" is to make a claim about perceiver-relativity; more interestingly, being poisonous is an example of a perceiver-relative property, since substances that are poisonous to one kind of perceiver might not be poisonous to others (e.g., chemicals called avermectins are lethal to many invertebrates but harmless to mammals). The second, different, notion is of *perceiver-dependence*: this is the idea that the very existence of something depends upon be-

ing perceived or thought about. An example of this would be a conscious visual image—there can be no such thing as a conscious image that is not in anybody's consciousness, and so mental images must be mind-dependent.

5. In the third selection below, when Locke is writing about substance, his main topic is the *idea* of substance, not substance itself. That is, he does not ask (directly) whether substance really exists; instead, his question is, do we have an idea of substance? And whatever his conclusions about the idea of substance, Locke denied being skeptical about the actual existence of substance.

How Important and Influential Is This Passage?

"The *Essay* has long been recognized as one of the great works of English literature of the seventeenth century, and one of the epoch-making works in the history of philosophy. It has been one of the most repeatedly reprinted, widely disseminated and read, and profoundly influential books of the past three centuries." So writes Peter Nidditch, an expert on Locke's philosophy. Locke's *Essay* is often credited with being the most thorough and plausible formulation and defense of empiricism ever written, and it has exercised a huge influence on, especially, English-speaking philosophers right up until the present day (though with a period in the philosophical wilderness during the 1800s). In the eighteenth century Locke was widely considered as important for philosophy, and what we would today call psychology, as Newton was for physics.

Although the distinction between primary and secondary qualities was certainly not invented by Locke, his account of it was very influential and was taken as the standard line in subsequent discussions of this important idea. Furthermore, the problem Locke raised about the coherence of our idea of material substance has been an important metaphysical problem since he formulated it, and was an important motivator for Berkeley's idealism (which we consider in the next section).

Suggestions for Critical Reflection

1. It is relatively easy to see roughly how Locke's distinction between primary and secondary qualities is supposed to go, but harder to see what Locke's *argument* for this distinction is. Do you think Locke backs up his claims with arguments? If so, how strong do you think they are? In the end, how plausible is the primary/secondary quality distinction?

2. Similarly, while it is relatively easy to see roughly how Locke's distinction between primary and secondary qualities is supposed to go, it is harder to see *precisely* how the distinction works. For example, what might Locke mean by saying that our ideas of primary qualities resemble their causes while our ideas of secondary qualities do not? Does this really make any sense? If it doesn't, then what other criterion should we use to help us make the distinction?

3. There has recently been some controversy about Locke's position on substance. The traditional view is that Locke defended substance, but was wrong to do so since his own arguments had effectively shown that we could have no such idea. The notion of substance in question here is that of a "bare particular" or "substratum"—that which underlies properties, as opposed to any of the properties themselves. A more recent interpretation holds that Locke did indeed defend some notion of substance, but one which is more defensible. This is the idea of substance as the "real essence" of something: roughly, for Locke, something's real essence is supposed to be the (unknown) set of properties that forms the causal basis for the observable properties of that thing (just as the atomic structure of gold is responsible for its color, softness, shininess, and so on). Which of these two conceptions of substance do you find the more plausible? (Can you see why philosophers have typically found the notion of a substratum difficult to make sense of?) Which of these notions of substance do you think fits better with what Locke actually says? Do you perhaps prefer a third interpretation?

4. What do you make of Locke's response to skepticism about the existence of the external world? Does it convince you? Do you find plausible the way Locke carefully divides up different types of knowledge about the external world and gives different answers for them?

5. What kind of entity might a Lockean idea be? What, if anything, is it made of? How determinate must it be? For example, if I clearly perceive the idea of a speckled hen, must we say that I perceive (have the idea of) a particular number of speckles, say 12,372? If not, does that mean the idea does not *have* a determinate number of speckles (even though it's a perfectly clear idea and not blurry at all)? What kind of object could *that* be? Some recent commentators, such as John Yolton, have tried to defend Locke from these kinds of puzzles by suggesting that Locke never meant ideas to be mental *things* at all: what, then, could they be instead?

6. How could an idea, in Locke's sense, really be *caused* by material objects in the external world? What could the last few steps of this causal chain be like?

7. If ideas are the objects of our thought—the things we "perceive" in thought—then what is it that does the perceiving, do you think? Can we distinguish it from the succession of ideas?

Suggestions for Further Reading

The standard edition of Locke's *An Essay Concerning Human Understanding* is edited by Peter H. Nidditch and was published by Oxford University Press in 1975. Several abridgements are also available, such as one by John Yolton in the Everyman Classics series. The standard biography of Locke is Maurice Cranston's *John Locke: A Biography* (Oxford University Press, 1985), though it is now a little out of date. Two good recent collections of essays about Locke are *Locke* (Oxford University Press, 1998) and *A Cambridge Companion to Locke* (Cambridge University Press, 1994), both edited by Vere Chappell. Finally, here are a few useful books on Locke: Michael Ayers, *Locke: Epistemology and Ontology* (Routledge, 1991); Nicholas Jolley, *Locke: His Philosophical Thought* (Oxford University Press, 1999); J.L. Mackie, *Problems from Locke*, (Oxford University Press, 1976); and John Yolton, *Locke: An Introduction* (Blackwell, 1985).

from *An Essay Concerning Human Understanding*[1]

Book II, Chapter VIII: Some Farther Considerations Concerning Our Simple Ideas.

§1. Concerning the simple ideas of Sensation, it is to be considered, that whatsoever is so constituted in nature as to be able, by affecting our senses, to cause any perception in the mind, doth thereby produce in the understanding a simple idea, which, whatever be the external cause of it, when it comes to be taken notice of by our discerning faculty, it is by the mind looked on and considered there to be a real positive idea in the understanding, as much as any other whatsoever; though, perhaps, the cause of it be but a privation[2] of the subject.

§2. Thus the ideas of heat and cold, light and darkness, white and black, motion and rest, are equally clear and positive ideas in the mind, though, perhaps, some of the causes which produce them are barely privations in subjects, from whence our senses derive those ideas. These the understanding, in its view of them, considers all as distinct positive ideas, without taking notice of the causes that produce them; which is an inquiry not belonging to the idea, as it is in the understanding, but to the nature of the things existing without us. These are two very different things, and carefully to be distinguished; it being one thing to perceive and know the idea of white or black, and quite another to examine what kind of particles they must be, and how ranged in the superficies, to make any object appear white or black.

---

1   Locke's *An Essay Concerning Human Understanding* was first published in 1690. The excerpts given here are from the sixth edition of 1710, reprinted from Locke's ten-volume *Collected Works* (first published in 1714 and reprinted with corrections in 1823).

2   A privation is a loss or absence of something.

§3. A painter or dyer, who never inquired into their causes, hath the ideas of white and black, and other colours, as clearly, perfectly, and distinctly in his understanding, and perhaps more distinctly, than the philosopher, who hath busied himself in considering their natures, and thinks he knows how far either of them is in its cause positive or privative; and the idea of black is no less positive in his mind than that of white, however the cause of that colour in the external object may be only a privation.

§4. If it were the design of my present undertaking to inquire into the natural causes and manner of perception, I should offer this as a reason why a privative cause might, in some cases at least, produce a positive idea, viz. that all sensation being produced in us only by different degrees and modes of motion in our animal spirits, variously agitated by external objects, the abatement of any former motion must as necessarily produce a new sensation as the variation or increase of it; and so introduce a new idea, which depends only on a different motion of the animal spirits in that organ.

§5. But whether this be so or not I will not here determine, but appeal to every one's own experience, whether the shadow of a man, though it consists of nothing but the absence of light (and the more the absence of light is, the more discernible is the shadow) does not, when a man looks on it, cause as clear and positive idea in his mind as a man himself, though covered over with clear sunshine? And the picture of a shadow is a positive thing. Indeed, we have negative names, which stand not directly for positive ideas, but for their absence, such as insipid, silence, nihil, &c. which words denote positive ideas; *v.g.* taste, sound, being, with a signification of their absence.

§6. And thus one may truly be said to see darkness. For supposing a hole perfectly dark, from whence no light is reflected, it is certain one may see the figure of it, or it may be painted; or whether the ink I write with makes any other idea, is a question. The privative causes I have here assigned of positive ideas are according to the common opinion; but, in truth, it will be hard to determine whether there be really any ideas from a privative cause, till it be determined, whether rest be any more a privation than motion.

§7. To discover the nature of our ideas the better, and to discourse of them intelligibly, it will be convenient to distinguish them as they are ideas or perceptions in our minds; and as they are modifications of matter in the bodies that cause such perceptions in us: that so we may not think (as perhaps usually is done) that they are exactly the images and resemblances of something inherent in the subject; most of those of sensation being in the mind no more the likeness of something existing without us, than the names that stand for them are the likeness of our ideas, which yet upon hearing they are apt to excite in us.

§8. Whatsoever the mind perceives in itself, or is the immediate object of perception, thought, or understanding, that I call idea; and the power to produce any idea in our mind, I call quality of the subject wherein that power is. Thus a snow-ball having the power to produce in us the ideas of white, cold, and round, the powers to produce those ideas in us, as they are in the snow-ball, I call qualities; and as they are sensations or perceptions in our understandings, I call them ideas; which ideas, if I speak of sometimes as in the things themselves, I would be understood to mean those qualities in the objects which produce them in us.

§9. Qualities thus considered in bodies are, first, such as are utterly inseparable from the body, in what state soever it be; such as in all the alterations and changes it suffers, all the force can be used upon it, it constantly keeps; and such as sense constantly finds in every particle of matter which has bulk enough to be perceived; and the mind finds inseparable from every particle of matter, though less than to make itself singly be perceived by our senses: *v.g.* take a grain of wheat, divide it into two parts; each part has still solidity, extension, figure, and mobility; divide it again, and it retains still the same qualities, and so divide it on, till the parts become insensible, they must retain still each of them all those qualities. For division (which is all that a mill, or pestle, or any other body, does upon another, in reducing it to insensible parts) can never take away either solidity, extension, figure, or mobility from any body, but only makes two or more distinct separate masses of matter, of that which was but one before; all which distinct masses, reckoned as so many distinct bodies, after division make a certain number. These I call original or primary qualities of body, which I think we may observe to produce simple ideas in us, viz. solidity, extension, figure, motion or rest, and number.

§10. Secondly, such qualities which in truth are nothing in the objects themselves, but powers to produce various sensations in us by their primary qualities, i.e., by the bulk, figure, texture, and motion of their insensible parts, as colours, sounds, tastes, &c. these I call secondary qualities. To these might be added a third sort, which are allowed to be barely powers; though they are as much real qualities in the subject as those which I, to comply with the common way of speaking, call qualities, but for distinction, secondary qualities. For the power in fire to produce a new colour, or consistency, in wax or clay, by its primary qualities, is as much a quality in fire, as the power it has to produce in me a new idea or sensation of warmth or burning, which I felt not before, by the same primary qualities, viz. the bulk, texture, and motion of its insensible parts.

§11. The next thing to be considered is, how bodies produce ideas in us; and that is manifestly by impulse, the only way which we can conceive bodies to operate in.

§12. If then external objects be not united to our minds, when they produce ideas therein, and yet we perceive these original qualities in such of them as singly fall under our senses, it is evident that some motion must be thence continued by our nerves, or animal spirits, by some parts of our bodies, to the brains or the seat of sensation, there to produce in our minds the particular ideas we have of them. And since the extension, figure, number, and motion of bodies, of an observable bigness, may be perceived at a distance by the sight, it is evident some singly imperceptible bodies must come from them to the eyes, and thereby convey to the brain some motion, which produces these ideas which we have of them in us.

§13. After the same manner, that the ideas of these original qualities are produced in us, we may conceive that the ideas of secondary qualities are also produced, viz. by the operation of insensible particles on our senses. For it being manifest that there are bodies, and good store of bodies, each whereof are so small that we cannot, by any of our senses, discover either their bulk, figure, or motion, as is evident in the particles of the air and water, and others extremely smaller than those; perhaps as much smaller than the particles of air and water as the particles of air and water are smaller than peas or hail-stones: let us suppose at present, that the different motions and figures, bulk and number of such particles, affecting the several organs of our senses, produce in us those different sensations, which we have from the colours and smells of bodies; v.g. that a violet, by the impulse of such insensible particles of matter of peculiar figures and bulks, and in different degrees and modifications of their motions, causes the ideas of the blue colour and sweet scent of that flower to be produced in our minds, it being no more impossible to conceive that God should annex such ideas to such motions, with which they have no similitude, than that he should annex the idea of pain to the motion of a piece of steel dividing our flesh, with which that idea hath no resemblance.

§14. What I have said concerning colours and smells may be understood also of tastes and sounds, and other the like sensible qualities; which, whatever reality we by mistake attribute to them, are in truth nothing in the objects themselves, but powers to produce various sensations in us, and depend on those primary qualities, viz. bulk, figure, texture, and motion of parts as I have said.

§15. From whence I think it easy to draw this observation, that the ideas of primary qualities of bodies are resemblances of them, and their patterns do really exist in the bodies themselves, but the ideas produced in us by these secondary qualities have no resemblance of them at all. There is nothing like our ideas, existing in the bodies themselves. They are, in the bodies we denominate from them, only a power to produce those sensations in us; and what is sweet, blue, or warm in idea, is but the certain bulk, figure, and motion of the insensible parts, in the bodies themselves, which we call so.

§16. Flame is denominated hot and light; snow white and cold; and manna white and sweet, from the ideas they produce in us: which qualities are commonly thought to be the same in those bodies that those ideas are in us, the one the perfect resemblance of the other, as they are in a mirror; and it would by most men be judged very extravagant if one should say otherwise. And yet he that will consider that the same fire, that at one distance produces in us the sensation of warmth, does at a nearer approach produce in us the far different sensation of pain, ought to bethink himself what reason he has to say, that his idea of warmth, which was produced in him by the fire, is actually in the fire; and his idea of pain, which the same fire produced in him the same way, is not in the fire. Why are whiteness and coldness in snow, and pain not, when it produces the one and the other idea in us, and can do neither but by the bulk, figure, number, and motion of its solid parts?

§17. The particular bulk, number, figure, and motion of the parts of fire, or snow, are really in them, whether any one's senses perceive them or no; and therefore they may be called real qualities, because they really exist in those bodies: but light, heat, whiteness, or coldness, are no more really in them than sickness or pain is in manna. Take away the sensation of them; let not the eyes see light or colours, nor the ears hear sounds; let the palate not taste, nor the nose smell; and all colours, tastes, odours, and sounds, as they are such particular ideas, vanish and cease, and are reduced to their causes, i.e., bulk, figure, and motion of parts.

§18. A piece of manna of a sensible bulk is able to produce in us the idea of a round or square figure, and, by being removed from one place to another, the idea of motion. This idea of motion represents it as it really is in manna moving: a circle or square are the same, whether in idea or existence, in the mind or in the manna; and this, both motion and figure, are really in the manna, whether we take notice of them or no: this every body is ready to agree to. Besides, manna, by the bulk, figure, texture, and motion of its parts, has a power to produce the sensations of sickness, and sometimes of acute pains or gripings in us. That these ideas of sickness and pain are not in the manna, but effects of its operations on us, and are nowhere when we feel them not: this also every one readily agrees to. And yet men are hardly to be brought to think, that sweetness and whiteness are not really in manna; which are but the effects of the operations of manna, by the motion, size, and figure of its particles on the eyes and palate; as the pain and sickness caused by manna are confessedly nothing but the effects of its

operations on the stomach and guts, by the size, motion, and figure of its insensible parts, (for by nothing else can a body operate, as has been proved); as if it could not operate on the eyes and palate, and thereby produce in the mind particular distinct ideas, which in itself it has not, as well as we allow it can operate on the guts and stomach, and thereby produce distinct ideas, which in itself it has not. These ideas being all effects of the operations of manna, on several parts of our bodies, by the size, figure, number, and motion of its parts; why those produced by the eyes and palate should rather be thought to be really in the manna than those produced by the stomach and guts; or why the pain and sickness, ideas that are the effect of manna, should be thought to be nowhere when they are not felt: and yet the sweetness and whiteness, effects of the same manna on other parts of the body, by ways equally as unknown, should be thought to exist in the manna, when they are not seen or tasted, would need some reason to explain.

§19. Let us consider the red and white colours in porphyry:[3] hinder light from striking on it, and its colours vanish, it no longer produces any such ideas in us; upon the return of light it produces these appearances on us again. Can any one think any real alterations are made in the porphyry by the presence or absence of light; and that those ideas of whiteness and redness are really in porphyry in the light, when it is plain it has no colour in the dark? It has, indeed, such a configuration of particles, both night and day, as are apt, by the rays of light rebounding from some parts of that hard stone, to produce in us the idea of redness, and from others the idea of whiteness; but whiteness or redness are not in it at any time, but such a texture that hath the power to produce such a sensation in us.

§20. Pound an almond, and the clear white colour will be altered into a dirty one, and the sweet taste into an oily one. What real alteration can the beating of the pestle make in any body, but an alteration of the texture of it?

§21. Ideas being thus distinguished and understood, we may be able to give an account how the same water, at the same time, may produce the idea of

---

3   A hard red rock filled with large red or white crystals.

cold by one hand and of heat by the other; whereas it is impossible that the same water, if those ideas were really in it, should at the same time be both hot and cold: for if we imagine warmth, as it is in our hands, to be nothing but a certain sort and degree of motion in the minute particles of our nerves or animal spirits, we may understand how it is possible that the same water may, at the same time, produce the sensations of heat in one hand, and cold in the other; which yet figure never does, that never producing the idea of a square by one hand, which has produced the idea of a globe by another. But if the sensation of heat and cold be nothing but the increase or diminution of the motion of the minute parts of our bodies, caused by the corpuscles of any other body, it is easy to be understood, that if that motion be greater in one hand than in the other; if a body be applied to the two hands, which has in its minute particles a greater motion, than in those of one of the hands, and a less than in those of the other; it will increase the motion of the one hand and lessen it in the other, and so cause the different sensations of heat and cold that depend thereon.

§22. I have in what just goes before been engaged in physical inquiries a little further than perhaps I intended. But it being necessary to make the nature of sensation a little understood, and to make the difference between the qualities in bodies, and the ideas produced by them in the mind, to be distinctly conceived, without which it were impossible to discourse intelligibly of them, I hope I shall be pardoned this little excursion into natural philosophy, it being necessary in our present inquiry to distinguish the primary and real qualities of bodies, which are always in them (viz. solidity, extension, figure, number, and motion, or rest; and are sometimes perceived by us, viz. when the bodies they are in are big enough singly to be discerned), from those secondary and imputed qualities, which are but the powers of several combinations of those primary ones, when they operate, without being distinctly discerned; whereby we may also come to know what ideas are, and what are not, resemblances of something really existing in the bodies we denominate from them.

§23. The qualities, then, that are in bodies, rightly considered, are of three sorts. First, The bulk, figure, number, situation, and motion, or rest of their solid parts; those are in them, whether we perceive them or no; and when they are of that size that we can discover them, we have by these an idea of the thing, as it is in itself, as is plain in artificial things. These I call primary qualities.

Secondly, The power that is in any body, by reason of its insensible primary qualities, to operate after a peculiar manner on any of our senses, and thereby produce in us the different ideas of several colours, sounds, smells, tastes, &c. These are usually called sensible qualities.

Thirdly, The power that is in any body, by reason of the particular constitution of its primary qualities, to make such a change in the bulk, figure, texture, and motion of another body, as to make it operate on our senses, differently from what it did before. Thus the sun has a power to make wax white, and fire to make lead fluid. These are usually called powers.

The first of these, as has been said, I think may be properly called real, original, or primary qualities; because they are in the things themselves, whether they are perceived or no; and upon their different modifications it is that the secondary qualities depend.

The other two are only powers to act differently upon other things, which powers result from the different modifications of those primary qualities.

§24. But, though the two latter sorts of qualities are powers barely, and nothing but powers, relating to several other bodies, and resulting from the different modifications of the original qualities, yet they are generally otherwise thought of: for the second sort, viz. the powers to produce several ideas in us by our senses, are looked upon as real qualities in the things thus affecting us; but the third sort are called and esteemed barely powers, *v.g.* the idea of heat, or light, which we receive by our eyes or touch from the sun, are commonly thought real qualities, existing in the sun, and something more than mere powers in it. But when we consider the sun in reference to wax, which it melts or blanches, we look on the whiteness and softness produced in the wax, not as qualities in the sun, but effects produced by powers in it: whereas, if rightly considered, these qualities of light and warmth, which are perceptions in me when I am warmed or enlightened by the sun, are no otherwise in the sun, than the changes made in the wax, when it is blanched or melted, are in the sun. They are all of them equally powers in the sun, depending on its primary qualities; whereby it is able, in the one case, so to alter the bulk, figure, texture, or motion of some of the insensible parts of my eyes or hands, as thereby to produce in me the idea of light or heat; and in the other, it is able so to alter the bulk, figure, texture, or motion of the insensible parts of the wax, as to make them fit to produce in me the distinct ideas of white and fluid.

§25. The reason why the one are ordinarily taken for real qualities, and the other only for bare powers, seems to be, because the ideas we have of distinct colours, sounds, &c., containing nothing at all in them of bulk, figure, or motion, we are not apt to think them the effects of these primary qualities, which appear not, to our senses, to operate in their production, and with which they have not any apparent congruity or conceivable connection. Hence it is that we are so forward to imagine, that those ideas are the resemblances of something really existing in the objects themselves: since sensation discovers nothing of bulk, figure, or motion of parts in their production; nor can reason show how bodies, by their bulk, figure, and motion, should produce in the mind the ideas of blue or yellow, &c. But, in the other case, in the operations of bodies changing the qualities one of another, we plainly discover, that the quality produced hath commonly no resemblance with anything in the thing producing it; wherefore we look on it as a bare effect of power. For, through receiving the idea of heat or light from the sun, we are apt to think it is a perception and resemblance of such a quality in the sun; yet when we see wax, or a fair face, receive change of colour from the sun, we cannot imagine that to be the reception or resemblance of anything in the sun, because we find not those different colours in the sun itself. For our senses being able to observe a likeness or unlikeness of sensible qualities in two different external objects, we forwardly enough conclude the production of any sensible quality in any subject to be an effect of bare power, and not the communication of any quality, which was really in the efficient, when we find no such sensible quality in the thing that produced it. But our senses not being able to discover any unlikeness between the idea produced in us, and the quality of the object producing it, we are apt to imagine, that our ideas are resemblances of something in the objects, and not the effects of certain powers placed in the modification of their primary qualities, with which primary qualities the ideas produced in us have no resemblance.

§26. To conclude, beside those before-mentioned primary qualities in bodies, viz. bulk, figure, extension, number, and motion of their solid parts; all the rest whereby we take notice of bodies, and distinguish them one from another, are nothing else but several powers in them, depending on those primary qualities; whereby they are fitted, either by immediately operating on our bodies to produce several different ideas in us; or else, by operating on other bodies, so to change their primary qualities, as to render them capable of producing ideas in us different from what before they did. The former of these, I think, may be called secondary qualities, immediately perceivable: the latter, secondary qualities, mediately perceivable.

Book II, Chapter XXIII: Of Our Complex Ideas of Substances [§§1–6].

§1. The mind being, as I have declared, furnished with a great number of the simple ideas, conveyed in by the senses, as they are found in exterior things, or by reflection on its own operations, takes notice also, that a certain number of these simple ideas go constantly together; which being presumed to belong to one thing, and words being suited to common apprehensions, and made use of for quick dispatch, are called, so united in one subject, by one name; which, by inadvertency, we are apt afterward to talk of and consider as one simple idea, which indeed is a complication of many ideas together; because, as I have said, not imagining how these simple ideas can subsist by themselves, we accustom ourselves to suppose some substratum wherein they do subsist, and from which they do result; which therefore we call substance.

§2. So that if any one will examine himself concerning his notion of pure substance in general, he will find he has no other idea of it at all, but only a supposition of he knows not what support of such qualities, which are capable of producing simple ideas in us; which qualities are commonly called accidents. If any one should be asked, what is the subject wherein colour or weight inheres, he would have nothing to say, but the solid extended parts: and if he were demanded, what is it that solidity and extension adhere in, he would not be in a much better case than the Indian[4] before mentioned who, saying that the world was supported by a great elephant, was asked what the elephant rested on; to which his answer was a great tortoise. But being again pressed to know what gave support to the broad-backed tortoise, replied, something, he knew not what. And thus here, as in all other cases where we use words without having clear and distinct ideas, we talk like children; who, being questioned what such a thing is, which they know not, readily give this satisfactory answer, that it is something: which in truth signifies no more, when so used, either by children or men, but that they know not what; and that the thing they pretend to know, and talk of, is what they have no distinct idea of at all, and so are perfectly ignorant of it, and in the dark. The idea then we have, to which we give the general name substance, being nothing but the supposed, but unknown support of those qualities we find existing, which we imagine cannot subsist, "*sine re substante,*" without something to support them, we call that support *substantia*; which, according to the true import of the word, is, in plain English, standing under or upholding.

§3. An obscure and relative idea of substance in general being thus made, we come to have the ideas of particular sorts of substances, by collecting such combinations of simple ideas as are, by experience and observation of men's senses taken notice of to exist together, and are therefore supposed to flow from the particular internal constitution, or unknown essence of that substance. Thus we come to have the ideas of a man, horse, gold, water, &c. of which substances, whether any one has any other clear idea, farther than of certain simple ideas co-existent together, I appeal to every one's own experience. It is the ordinary qualities observable in iron, or a diamond, put together, that make the true complex idea of those substances, which a smith or a jeweller commonly knows better than a philosopher; who, whatever substantial forms he may talk of, has no other idea of those substances, than what is framed by a collection of those simple ideas which are to be found in them: only we must take notice, that our complex ideas of substances, besides all those simple ideas they are made up of, have always the confused idea of something to which they belong, and in which they subsist. And therefore when we speak of any sort of substance, we say it is a thing having such or such qualities; as body is a thing that is extended, figured, and capable of motion; spirit, a thing capable of thinking; and so hardness, friability,[5] and power to draw iron, we say, are qualities to be found in a loadstone.[6] These, and the like fashions of speaking, intimate, that the substance is supposed always something besides the extension, figure, solidity, motion, thinking, or other observable ideas, though we know not what it is.

§4. Hence, when we talk or think of any particular sort of corporeal substances, as horse, stone, &c., though the idea we have of either of them be but the complication or collection of those several simple ideas of sensible qualities, which we used to find united in the thing called horse or stone; yet, because we cannot conceive how they should subsist alone, nor one in another, we suppose them existing in and supported by some common subject; which support we denote by the name substance, though it be certain we have no clear or distinct idea of that thing we suppose a support.

§5. The same thing happens concerning the operations of the mind, viz. thinking, reasoning, fearing, &c., which we concluding not to subsist of themselves, nor apprehending how they can belong to body, or be produced by it, we are apt to think these the actions of some other substance, which we call spirit: whereby yet it is evident, that having no other idea or notion of matter, but something wherein those many sensible qualities which affect our senses do subsist; by supposing a substance wherein thinking, knowing, doubting, and a power of moving, &c. do subsist, we have as clear a notion of the substance of spirit, as we have of body; the one being supposed

----

4   A person from the subcontinent of India (rather than a native of North America).

5   Brittleness, crumbliness.

6   A piece of magnetite (iron oxide) that has magnetic properties.

to be (without knowing what it is) the substratum to those simple ideas we have from without; and the other supposed (with a like ignorance of what it is) to be the substratum to those operations we experiment in ourselves within. It is plain then, that the idea of corporeal substance in matter is as remote from our conceptions and apprehensions, as that of spiritual substance, or spirit: and therefore, from our not having any notion of the substance of spirit, we can no more conclude its non-existence, than we can for the same reason deny the existence of body; it being as rational to affirm there is no body, because we have no clear and distinct idea of the substance of matter, as to say there is no spirit, because we have no clear and distinct idea of the substance of a spirit.

§6. Whatever therefore be the secret, abstract nature of substance in general, all the ideas we have of particular distinct sorts of substances are nothing but several combinations of simple ideas co-existing in such, though unknown, cause of their union, as make the whole subsist of itself. It is by such combinations of simple ideas, and nothing else, that we represent particular sorts of substances to ourselves; such are the ideas we have of their several species in our minds; and such only do we, by their specific names, signify to others, *v.g.* man, horse, sun, water, iron: upon hearing which words, every one who understands the language, frames in his mind a combination of those several simple ideas, which he has usually observed, or fancied to exist together under that denomination; all which he supposes to rest in, and be as it were, adherent to that unknown common subject, which inheres not in anything else. Though, in the mean time it be manifest, and every one upon inquiry into his own thoughts will find, that he has no other idea of any substance, *v.g.* let it be gold, horse, iron, man, vitriol,[7] bread, but what he has barely of those sensible qualities, which he supposes to inhere, with a supposition of such a substratum, as gives, as it were, a support to those qualities or simple ideas, which he has observed to exist united together. Thus the idea of the sun, what is it but an aggregate of those several simple ideas, bright, hot, roundish, having a constant regular motion, at a certain distance from us, and perhaps some

other? As he who thinks and discourses of the sun has been more or less accurate in observing those sensible qualities, ideas, or properties, which are in that thing which he calls the sun.

Book IV, Chapter XI: Of Our Knowledge of the Existence of Other Things.

§1. The knowledge of our own being we have by intuition. The existence of a God, reason clearly makes known to us, as has been shown.[8]

The knowledge of the existence of any other thing we can have only by sensation: for there being no necessary connection of real existence with any idea a man hath in his memory, nor of any other existence but that of God, with the existence of any particular man; no particular man can know the existence of any other being, but only when, by actual operating upon him, it makes itself perceived by him. For, the having the idea of anything in our mind no more proves the existence of that thing, than the picture of a man evidences his being in the world, or the visions of a dream make thereby a true history.

§2. It is therefore the actual receiving of ideas from without, that gives us notice of the existence of other things, and makes us know that something doth exist at that time without us, which causes that idea in us, though perhaps we neither know nor consider how it does it: for it takes not from the certainty of our senses, and the ideas we receive by them, that we know not the manner wherein they are produced: *v.g.* whilst I write this, I have, by the paper affecting my eyes, that idea produced in my mind, which, whatever object causes, I call white; by which I know that that quality or accident (i.e., whose appearance before my eyes always causes that idea) doth really exist, and hath a being without me. And of this, the greatest assurance I can possibly have, and to which my faculties can attain, is the testimony of my eyes, which are the proper and sole judges of this thing, whose testimony I have reason to rely on as so certain, that I can no

---

7 Sulphuric acid.

8 These two claims were argued for in his previous two chapters (IX and X). Intuition, for Locke, is roughly direct knowledge—something we can directly see to be true—and is to be contrasted with the indirect knowledge we get from sensation, memory, or reason.

more doubt, whilst I write this, that I see white and black, and that something really exists, that causes that sensation in me, than that I write or move my hand; which is a certainty as great as human nature is capable of, concerning the existence of anything but a man's self alone, and of God.

§3. The notice we have by our senses of the existing of things without us, though it be not altogether so certain as our intuitive knowledge, or the deductions of our reason, employed about the clear abstract ideas of our own minds; yet it is an assurance that deserves the name of knowledge. If we persuade ourselves that our faculties act and inform us right, concerning the existence of those objects that affect them, it cannot pass for an ill-grounded confidence: for I think nobody can, in earnest, be so sceptical as to be uncertain of the existence of those things which he sees and feels. At least, he that can doubt so far (whatever he may have with his own thoughts) will never have any controversy with me; since he can never be sure I say anything contrary to his own opinion. As to myself, I think God has given me assurance enough of the existence of things without me; since by their different application I can produce in myself both pleasure and pain, which is one great concernment of my present state. This is certain, the confidence that our faculties do not herein deceive us, is the greatest assurance we are capable of concerning the existence of material beings. For we cannot act anything, but by our faculties; nor talk of knowledge itself, but by the helps of those faculties, which are fitted to apprehend even what knowledge is. But besides the assurance we have from our senses themselves, that they do not err in the information they give us, of the existence of things without us, when they are affected by them, we are further confirmed in this assurance by other concurrent reasons.

§4. First, it is plain those perceptions are produced in us by exterior causes affecting our senses; because those that want the organs of any sense never can have the ideas belonging to that sense produced in their minds. This is too evident to be doubted: and therefore we cannot but be assured that they come in by the organs of that sense, and no other way. The organs themselves, it is plain, do not produce them; for then the eyes of a man in the dark would produce colours, and his nose smell roses in the winter: but we see nobody gets the relish of a pine-apple till he goes to the Indies, where it is, and tastes it.

§5. Secondly, because sometimes I find that I cannot avoid the having those ideas produced in my mind. For though when my eyes are shut, or windows fast, I can at pleasure recall to my mind the ideas of light, or the sun, which former sensations had lodged in my memory; so I can at pleasure lay by that idea, and take into my view that of the smell of a rose, or taste of sugar. But, if I turn my eyes at noon towards the sun, I cannot avoid the ideas, which the light, or sun, then produces in me. So that there is a manifest difference between the ideas laid up in my memory (over which, if they were there only, I should have constantly the same power to dispose of them, and lay them by at pleasure) and those which force themselves upon me, and I cannot avoid having. And therefore it must needs be some exterior cause, and the brisk acting of some objects without me, whose efficacy I cannot resist, that produces those ideas in my mind, whether I will or no. Besides, there is nobody who doth not perceive the difference in himself between contemplating the sun, as he hath the idea of it in his memory, and actually looking upon it; of which two his perception is so distinct, that few of his ideas are more distinguishable one from another. And therefore he hath certain knowledge, that they are not both memory, or the actions of his mind, and fancies only within him; but that actual seeing hath a cause without.

§6. Thirdly, add to this, that many of those ideas are produced in us with pain, which afterwards we remember without the least offence. Thus, the pain of heat or cold, when the idea of it is revived in our minds, gives us no disturbance; which, when felt, was very troublesome, and is again, when actually repeated; which is occasioned by the disorder the external object causes in our bodies when applied to it. And we remember the pains of hunger, thirst, or the head-ache, without any pain at all; which would either never disturb us, or else constantly do it, as often as we thought of it, were there nothing more but ideas floating in our minds, and appearances entertaining our fancies, without the real existence of things affecting us from abroad. The same may be said of pleasure, accompanying several actual sensations: and though mathematical demonstration depends not upon sense, yet the examining them by diagrams gives great credit to the evidence of our sight, and seems to give it a certainty approaching to that of demonstration itself. For it would be very strange that a man should allow it for an undeniable truth, that two angles of a figure, which he measures by lines and angles of a diagram, should be bigger one than the other; and yet doubt of the existence of those lines and angles, which by looking on he makes use of to measure that by.

§7. Fourthly, our senses in many cases bear witness to the truth of each other's report, concerning the existence of sensible things without us. He that sees a fire may, if he doubt whether it be anything more than a bare fancy, feel it too; and be convinced, by putting his hand in it: which certainly could never be put into such exquisite pain by a bare idea or phantom, unless that the pain be a fancy too; which yet he cannot, when the burn is well, by raising the idea of it, bring upon himself again.

Thus I see, whilst I write this, I can change the appearance of the paper: and by designing the letters, tell beforehand what new idea it shall exhibit the very next moment, by barely drawing my pen over it: which will neither appear (let me fancy as much as I will) if my hands stand still; or though I move my pen, if my eyes be shut: nor, when those characters are once made on the paper, can I choose afterwards but see them as they are; that is, have the ideas of such letters as I have made. Whence it is manifest, that they are not barely the sport and play of my own imagination, when I find that the characters, that were made at the pleasure of my own thought, do not obey them; nor yet cease to be, whenever I shall fancy it; but continue to affect my senses constantly and regularly, according to the figures I made them. To which if we will add, that the sight of those shall, from another man, draw such sounds as I beforehand design they shall stand for; there will be little reason left to doubt that those words I write do really exist without me, when they cause a long series of regular sounds to affect my ears, which could not be the effect of my imagination, nor could my memory retain them in that order.

§8. But yet, if after all this any one will be so sceptical as to distrust his senses, and to affirm that all we see and hear, feel and taste, think and do, dur-

ing our whole being, is but the series and deluding appearances of a long dream, whereof there is no reality; and therefore will question the existence of all things, or our knowledge of any thing; I must desire him to consider, that, if all be a dream, then he doth but dream that he makes the question; and so it is not much matter that a waking man should answer him. But yet, if he pleases, he may dream that I make him this answer, that the certainty of things existing *in rerum natura*,[9] when we have the testimony of our senses for it, is not only as great as our frame can attain to, but as our condition needs. For, our faculties being suited not to the full extent of being, nor to a perfect, clear, comprehensive knowledge of things free from all doubt and scruple; but to the preservation of us, in whom they are, and accommodated to the use of life; they serve to our purpose well enough, if they will but give us certain notice of those things which are convenient or inconvenient to us. For he that sees a candle burning, and hath experimented the force of its flame, by putting his finger in it, will little doubt that this is something existing without him, which does him harm, and puts him to great pain: which is assurance enough, when no man requires greater certainty to govern his actions by than what is as certain as his actions themselves. And if our dreamer pleases to try whether the glowing heat of a glass furnace be barely a wandering imagination in a drowsy man's fancy; by putting his hand into it he may perhaps be wakened into a certainty greater than he could wish, that it is something more than bare imagination. So that this evidence is as great as we can desire, being as certain to us as our pleasure or pain, i.e., happiness or misery; beyond which we have no concernment, either of knowing or being. Such an assurance of the existence of things without us is sufficient to direct us in the attaining the good, and avoiding the evil, which is caused by them; which is the important concernment we have of being made acquainted with them.

§9. In fine, then, when our senses do actually convey into our understandings any idea, we cannot but be satisfied that there doth something at that time really exist without us, which doth affect our senses,

---

9   "In the nature of things," or sometimes, more specifically "in physical reality."

and by them give notice of itself to our apprehensive faculties, and actually produce that idea which we then perceive: and we cannot so far distrust their testimony, as to doubt that such collections of simple ideas as we have observed by our senses to be united together, do really exist together. But this knowledge extends as far as the present testimony of our senses, employed about particular objects that do then affect them, and no further. For if I saw such a collection of simple ideas, as is wont to be called man, existing together one minute since, and am now alone, I cannot be certain that the same man exists now, since there is no necessary connection of his existence a minute since with his existence now: by a thousand ways he may cease to be, since I had the testimony of my senses for his existence. And if I cannot be certain that the man I saw last to-day is now in being, I can less be certain that he is so who hath been longer removed from my senses, and I have not seen since yesterday, or since the last year: and much less can I be certain of the existence of men that I never saw. And, therefore, though it be highly probable that millions of men do now exist, yet, whilst I am alone writing this, I have not that certainty of it which we strictly call knowledge; though the great likelihood of it puts me past doubt, and it be reasonable for me to do several things upon the confidence that there are men (and men also of my acquaintance, with whom I have to do) now in the world: but this is but probability, not knowledge.

§10. Whereby yet we may observe how foolish and vain a thing it is for a man of a narrow knowledge, who having reason given him to judge of the different evidence and probability of things, and to be swayed accordingly,—how vain, I say, it is to expect demonstration and certainty in things not capable of it, and refuse assent to very rational propositions, and act contrary to very plain and clear truths, because they cannot be made out so evident, as to surmount every the least (I will not say reason but) pretence of doubting. He that, in the ordinary affairs of life would admit of nothing but direct plain demonstration, would be sure of nothing in this world, but of perishing quickly. The wholesomeness of his meat or drink would not give him reason to venture on it: and I would fain know, what it is he could do upon such grounds as are capable of no doubt, no objection.

§11. As when our senses are actually employed about any object, we do know that it does exist; so by our memory we may be assured, that heretofore things that affected our senses have existed. And thus we have knowledge of the past existence of several things whereof, our senses having informed us, our memories still retain the ideas; and of this we are past all doubt, so long as we remember well. But this knowledge also reaches no further than our senses have formerly assured us. Thus, seeing water at this instant, it is an unquestionable truth to me that water doth exist: and remembering that I saw it yesterday, it will also be always true, and as long as my memory retains it, always an undoubted proposition to me, that water did exist the 10th of July, 1688, as it will also be equally true that a certain number of very fine colours did exist, which at the same time I saw upon a bubble of that water: but, being now quite out of sight both of the water and bubbles too, it is no more certainly known to me that the water doth now exist, than that the bubbles or colours therein do so; it being no more necessary that water should exist to-day, because it existed yesterday, than that the colours or bubbles exist to-day, because they existed yesterday; though it be exceedingly much more probable, because water hath been observed to continue long in existence but bubbles and the colours on them, quickly cease to be.

§12. What ideas we have of spirits,[10] and how we come by them, I have already shown. But though we have those ideas in our minds, and know we have them there, the having the ideas of spirits does not make us know that any such things do exist without us, or that there are any finite spirits, or any other spiritual beings but the eternal God. We have ground from revelation, and several other reasons, to believe with assurance that there are such creatures: but our senses not being able to discover them, we want the means of knowing their particular existences. For we can no more know, that there are finite spirits really existing, by the idea we have of such beings in our minds, than by the ideas any one has of fairies, or centaurs, he can come to know that things answering those ideas do really exist.

---

10   Spiritual beings such as angels.

And therefore concerning the existence of finite spirits, as well as several other things, we must content ourselves with the evidence of faith; but universal certain propositions concerning this matter are beyond our reach. For however true it may be, *v.g.* that all the intelligent spirits that God ever created do still exist; yet it can never make a part of our certain knowledge. These and the like propositions we may assent to as highly probable, but are not, I fear, in this state capable of knowing. We are not then to put others upon demonstrating, nor ourselves upon search of universal certainty, in all those matters, wherein we are not capable of any other knowledge, but what our senses give us in this or that particular.

§13. By which it appears that there are two sorts of propositions: 1. There is one sort of propositions concerning the existence of any thing answerable to such an idea: as having the idea of an elephant, phoenix, motion, or an angel, in my mind, the first and natural inquiry is, Whether such a thing does anywhere exist? And this knowledge is only of particulars. No existence of anything without us, but only of God, can certainly be known farther than our senses inform us. 2. There is another sort of propositions, wherein is expressed the agreement or disagreement of our abstract ideas, and their dependence on one another. Such propositions may be universal and certain. So having the idea of God and myself, of fear and obedience, I cannot but be sure that God is to be feared and obeyed by me: and this proposition will be certain, concerning man in general, if I have made an abstract idea of such a species, whereof I am one particular. But yet this proposition, how certain soever, that men ought to fear and obey God proves not to me the existence of men in the world, but will be true of all such creatures, whenever they do exist: which certainty of such general propositions depends on the agreement or disagreement to be discovered in those abstract ideas.

§14. In the former case, our knowledge is the consequence of the existence of things producing ideas in our minds by our senses: in the latter, knowledge is the consequence of the ideas (be they what they will) that are in our minds, producing there general certain propositions. Many of these are called *aeternae veritates*,[11] and all of them indeed are so; not from being written all or any of them in the minds of all men; or that they were any of them propositions in any one's mind till he, having got the abstract ideas, joined or separated them by affirmation or negation. But wheresoever we can suppose such a creature as man is, endowed with such faculties, and thereby furnished with such ideas as we have, we must conclude, he must needs, when he applies his thoughts to the consideration of his ideas, know the truth of certain propositions that will arise from the agreement or disagreement which he will perceive in his own ideas. Such propositions are therefore called eternal truths, not because they are eternal propositions actually formed, and antecedent to the understanding, that at any time makes them; nor because they are imprinted on the mind from any patterns, that are anywhere out of the mind, and existed before: but because being once made about abstract ideas, so as to be true, they will, whenever they can be supposed to be made again at any time past or to come, by a mind having those ideas, always actually be true. For names being supposed to stand perpetually for the same ideas, and the same ideas having immutably the same habitudes one to another; propositions concerning any abstract ideas that are once true, must needs be eternal verities.

---

11 "Eternal verities"—things that are eternally true.

GEORGE BERKELEY
Three Dialogues Between Hylas and Philonous

Who Was George Berkeley?

George Berkeley was born in 1685 near Kilkenny, an attractive medieval town in the southern part of Ireland which, in the 1640s, had briefly been the center of Irish resistance to the British. He was the son of a gentleman farmer and went to one of Ireland's leading schools, Kilkenny College, at the age of 11. At the early age of 15 Berkeley entered Trinity College, Dublin (the pre-eminent Irish university), and in 1707 became a Fellow of the College. Two years later he published *An Essay Towards a New Theory of Vision*, an influential scientific work which remained the standard theory of vision until the mid-nineteenth century, but which Berkeley intended, from the outset, to solve a problem for his developing "immaterialist" theories.[1] In fact, Berkeley probably arrived at his main philosophical views in his early twenties, and never wavered from them thereafter.

In 1710 Berkeley was ordained a priest in the protestant Church of Ireland and, in the same year, published *A Treatise Concerning the Principles of Human Knowledge,* in which he put forward his theory, today called "subjective idealism." In a nutshell, he claimed matter does not exist. The book met with a cool reception, and Berkeley felt he was merely dismissed as an eccentric: indeed, a London doctor theorized that Berkeley must be insane, and a bishop publicly expressed pity for Berkeley's need to seek notoriety. Gamely, therefore, he set out to re-present his ideas in a more acceptable form; *Three Dialogues Between Hylas and Philonous*, published in London in 1713, was the result. This book was much more successful, and though it persuaded few to agree with his conclusions it made him something of a literary celebrity in London social circles.

Berkeley, who had moved to London in 1713, spent much of the next decade traveling in France and Italy, first as chaplain to the Earl of Peterborough and then as tutor to the son of a bishop. There is a story (probably untrue) that a fit of apoplexy brought on by arguing with Berkeley caused the death of the important Cartesian philosopher Nicolas Malebranche in 1715.

In 1721 Berkeley published *De Motu* ("On Motion"), attacking Newton's philosophy of space on the basis of Berkeley's own philosophical system (despite his great admiration for Newton's work in general). In the same year he published *An Essay Towards Preventing the Ruin of Great Britain,* which diagnosed Britain's economic problems (the result of a huge stock market crash in 1720, known as the collapse of the South

---

1   The problem that Berkeley needed to solve was the apparent fact that we seem to just 'see' things as being three-dimensional solids located outside of ourselves; he solved it by arguing that vision itself merely provides us with information about a sequence of color patches in our visual field, and we have to learn to make *inferences* about spatial location on the basis of this data and its correlation with the sensations of touch. In other words, he argued that we don't just 'see' that there is a material world located outside of our heads.

Sea Bubble) as being caused by a general decline in religion, morality, and sense of duty to the public good. Berkeley himself, however, attained economic security just two years later when he was made Dean of Derry, a church position which carried with it a very sizeable income.

In 1724 Berkeley enthusiastically embarked on a project for establishing a college in Bermuda to provide Christian education to both colonial and indigenous North Americans. He raised £6,000 in private donations, managed to convince five Fellows of Trinity to give up their secure academic positions in Dublin and commit themselves to becoming teachers in Bermuda, and with his new wife Anne Forster he set sail for the New World in 1728. He settled in Newport, Rhode Island, and bought a farm to provide extra income for his college. Unfortunately, the £20,000 in funding promised by the British government for the college never materialized and in 1731 Berkeley was forced to abandon the project and return to London, hoping instead for advancement in the church. In 1734 he was duly made Bishop of Cloyne (near Cork, in Ireland), and moved there immediately. He devoted most of his energies for the rest of his life to looking after the spiritual and practical interests of the people of the see of Cloyne. His last publication was the strange *Siris: A Chain of Philosophical Reflections and Inquiries*, in which, among other things, he expounded the medicinal benefits of tar-water (a concoction, served cold, made by boiling pine resin in water). Berkeley died suddenly in Oxford in 1753 whilst visiting his second son, George, who was at university there. He was buried a week later (since, out of fear of being buried alive, he had left instructions that he was not to be buried until his body showed signs of decay) in the nave of Christ Church cathedral.

What Was Berkeley's Overall Philosophical Project?

Berkeley is best known as the inventor of the philosophical theory today called "subjective idealism" (and which he called "immaterialism"). This is the theory that the physical world exists only in the experiences that minds have of it—in other words, that the world consists of nothing more than a set of mental experiences. As it is often put, for Berkeley *esse est percipi*: "to exist is to be perceived."[2]

Berkeley's main philosophical project was to attack the prevailing mechanical philosophy, a general world-outlook given early form by the work of Descartes (1596–1650), embodied in the science of Robert Boyle (1627–1691) and Isaac Newton (1642–1727), and provided with its most influential philosophical defender in Locke (1632–1704). What Berkeley saw in the mechanical philosophy was a complete split between mind and matter as two radically different types of thing, combined with the comfortable assumption that our minds can nevertheless interact with and come to know a great deal about the world of matter. He argued throughout his life that these two claims are mutually inconsistent: that to adopt a mechanical view of the external world inevitably commits us to radical skepticism. Furthermore, the new mechanical philosophy, Berkeley felt, tempts us towards materialism (i.e., the denial of the existence of immaterial spirits) and atheism (since Newton's deterministic physics seems to leave little role in the universe for an active God).

Berkeley's way out of what he saw as a deep conceptual confusion was to deny the reality of any non-mental stuff called "matter." That is, Berkeley tries to save us from skepticism by showing that reality is entirely mental, and pointing out that we have extremely close acquaintance with—and so highly reliable knowledge of—our own ideas and their relations with each other. (For most subsequent philosophers, however, this cure has seemed worse than the disease.)

What Is the Structure of This Reading?

Set in a garden, this reading is a dialogue between Hylas and Philonous. Hylas, whose name is derived from *hyle*, the Greek word for matter, defends the mechanistic, scientific account of the material world as existing independently of the mind. Philonous, whose name means "lover of mind," speaks for Berkeley, and defends idealism.

---

2   Actually, the full version of the maxim is *esse est percipi vel percipere*: "to exist is either to be perceived or to perceive."

The *Three Dialogues* have the following scheme. In the First Dialogue, Berkeley lays out most of his arguments for the non-existence of matter. Then, in the Second Dialogue, he tries to show that his conclusions are neither skeptical nor atheistic, and that they in fact refute skepticism and give God a crucial role in the running of the universe. He goes on to argue that the existence of matter is not only unsupported by argument but actually inconceivable. In the Third Dialogue, Berkeley has Philonous defend subjective idealism against a sequence of over twenty objections from Hylas, and especially against the objection that Berkeley's theory is shocking, strange, skeptical, and generally just as indefensible as materialism has turned out to be.

The First Dialogue, the selection reprinted here, pursues several rather complex lines of argument but can be seen as falling into three parts. After an initial exchange on the dangers of skepticism, Philonous argues against the externality of secondary qualities (see the reading from Locke, above, for the classic account of the primary-secondary qualities distinction). Berkeley presents at least three distinct arguments for this conclusion, which today are often called the argument from illusion, the causal argument, and (what Howard Robinson has called) the "assimilation argument." This last works by trying to show that all sensory states essentially contain an irreducibly subjective component, like pain or pleasure.

In the second part of the argument of the First Dialogue, Philonous argues against the externality of the primary qualities. He starts by using similar arguments to those just applied to the secondary qualities, but then comes a fairly long digression in which Hylas raises two interesting suggestions. First, Hylas tries to defend the mind-independence of reality by distinguishing between the *act* of perception and its *object* (i.e., the thing it is a perception of), and arguing that only the first of these is subjective. After Philonous responds to this argument, Hylas then tries appealing to the notion of a material "substratum" or "substance" underlying the qualities we perceive, and Philonous argues that such a notion is meaningless. Finally, Hylas returns to the question of the mind-independence of the primary qualities and tries to defend a view sometimes called the "representative theory of perception" (which can be found in Locke). This theory treats our ideas or sensations not as

being mind-independent themselves but as *representing* or *resembling* mind-independent qualities in the world. Philonous argues that, if this were the case, we could never know anything about the material causes of our ideas.

In the third and final stage of Berkeley's argument, Philonous continues his critique of the representative theory of perception by making two new points. First, he claims in a small section sometimes called his "Master Argument" (since he says he will let everything rest on this argument alone), it is incoherent even to assert that we can conceive of something existing unconceived. It follows that it is incoherent to talk about objects that are not themselves perceived but that cause our perceptions. Second, Berkeley argues that nothing but an idea can be anything like an idea (this is often called Berkeley's "Likeness Principle"). That is, he criticizes the coherence of the view that some of our ideas resemble their material causes.

Some Useful Background Information

1. Berkeley's use of the term "idea," which is crucial to his philosophical system, is taken from Locke; see the background information notes on Locke for an explanation of this usage.

2. Berkeley's metaphysical system contains the following elements. First, Berkeley claims that the only things that exist are minds, and he restricts the list of minds or "spirits" to something like the usual suspects: humans, animals, angels and so on, and God. So humans and animals do exist, but they have no bodies or brains: they are "pure spirit." These minds are each populated by mental entities which Berkeley calls, following Locke, ideas; so now we have two kinds of thing in the universe (and only two): selves and their ideas.[3]

---

3   Another way of putting this is to say there is just one sort of *substance*—mind—and its *modes* or attributes, which include the ideas. This opposes the dualism of Descartes and Locke, where we have *two* substances, mind and matter. (See the background information section on Descartes for more information about the notion of a substance and its modes.)

In humans, these ideas are related to each other in the ways that are familiar from experience: for example, the visual image of a rose is often shortly followed by the sensation of a certain scent, and the sound of horses on the street outside gives rise to the idea of a carriage passing by. Some of our ideas are within our control, such as when we are using our imagination to invent new mythical animals, but others are not, such as when we feel the pain of frostbite. Those ideas not controlled by us are placed in our minds directly by God: it is God, according to Berkeley, who is constantly bringing about our sensory experiences of sight, taste, touch, etc. In other words, instead of causing our experience by the complicated route of creating a mind-independent world which then causes our sensations, God simply produces sensations directly in our minds. These ideas constitute "the real world"—which we can perfectly well call "the physical world" if we want to—and so there is no barrier between us and physical reality: skepticism and atheism are no longer a temptation.

3. Although Berkeley admitted that his theory makes reality mind-dependent (that is, nothing at all can exist without some mind to perceive or contain it, unless it is itself a mind), he denied that our reality—the physical world—was dependent on our *individual* minds. The difference between reality and illusion and hallucination, for Berkeley, is precisely that hallucinations are experienced privately by only one mind, whereas real objects are publicly available to a range of observers. Reality is mind-dependent, but it is dependent on God's mind, not ours.

Some clear terminology might be helpful here. Berkeley defends the existence of "physical reality," but denies that it has "absolute existence." He calls the sort of physical object supposedly capable of absolute existence a "material" thing or "matter"—hence, he denies that matter exists. The kind of "real existence" for physical objects that he does endorse is one where those objects are independent of their perceivers (us), but are not capable of existing

independently of any mind at all. That is, they are ideas in the mind of God.

This problem, of the continued existence of sensible objects even when we are not looking at them, and Berkeley's solution to it, has been summed up in two well-known limericks:

> There was a young man who said "God
> Must think it exceedingly odd
> If he finds that this tree
> Continues to be
> When there's no one about in the Quad."

(A Quad, short for quadrangle, is the courtyard of an Oxford college.) The reply runs as follows:

> Dear Sir:
> Your astonishment's odd;
> I am always about in the Quad.
> And that's why the tree
> Will continue to be,
> Since observed by
> Yours faithfully,
> GOD.

4. There is one important aspect of his metaphysical system about which Berkeley seems to be careful to sit on the fence (or unable to give a definite answer). He holds that "sensible things"—that is, things we perceive or sense—are independent of our minds since they can continue to exist even when we cease to perceive them; this is because they continue to be ideas in the mind of God. This raises the following question, which Berkeley never really answers clearly: in perceiving a sensible thing, is what I perceive an idea in my mind which is a *copy* of an 'archetypal' idea in the mind of God, or (alternatively) do I perceive the very idea in *God's* mind?[4]

---

4   Think of it this way. When I dream about clocks, those clocks are ideas in my mind only; if you also dream of clocks, even if your dream clocks are just like mine, your clock images are in your mind and not in mine. Now consider my sensory image of a tree, and ask: is my tree-image actually, somehow, an idea in *another* mind (God's), or is it just a *copy* of a tree-image in

Some Common Misconceptions

1. Berkeley was emphatic that he did not deny the *reality* of the physical world. He believed in the existence of rocks and trees, other people and animals, cities, and paintings just as fervently as everyone else; we can trip over them, look at them, talk to them, live in them, buy and sell them, and so on, just as we always thought we could. In fact, rightly or wrongly, Berkeley would have said he had a much clearer and more commonsensical view of the real existence of trees and stars than philosophers like Locke and Descartes. (When the contemporary essayist Samuel Johnson kicked a pebble and declared, of Berkeley, "I refute him thus," Johnson was simply missing Berkeley's point.) What Berkeley was denying, then, is not the existence of trees but a particular account of the *nature* of so-called physical objects and their existence. One can put it this way: Berkeley denies that 'trees,' as defined by the philosophers, exist; but he does not want to deny that trees, as understood by pre-theoretical common sense, exist and are independent of our minds.

2. Berkeley was not a skeptic, an (intentional) enemy of common sense, nor a purveyor of paradoxes. His main concern was to defend the solidity and truth of the very reality we see, hear, taste, and touch, against a picture that treats this reality as a flimsy and deceptive veil behind which operates a mysterious, mechanical machinery of which we can never have direct knowledge.

3. Berkeley was not anti-science. Berkeley, like Locke, was an empiricist, and believed that all knowledge comes ultimately from experience. He had an intense and genuine admiration for Newton and his scientific achievements, and he believed his immaterialism was not only compatible with most of the data and laws of empirical science, but improved it by removing unnecessary metaphysical baggage.

God's mind? This is analogous to asking: is my dream-clock actually part of your dream, or is it instead a copy of the one in your dream?

How Important and Influential Is This Passage?

Berkeley's subjective idealism won very few converts during his lifetime, and has continued to be a very unpopular philosophical position since then: Berkeley is the only major philosopher to ever seriously adopt it.[5] Ironically, far from saving religion and common sense from the depredations of atheism and skepticism, Berkeley's philosophy is usually seen as an important stepping stone on the way to David Hume's skeptical atheism. The philosophical value of this selection from Berkeley's *Three Dialogues*, then, is not so much the plausibility of Berkeley's conclusions as his brilliant challenge to the apparent consistency of our common-sense assumptions about the external world and its relation with our mind: it is not enough, Berkeley shows, to just vaguely hope that our notions of substance, perception, causation, representation, knowledge, mind, and so on will all fit together satisfactorily, but instead we must give careful thought to what we believe and be prepared to adjust our assumptions, possibly in some quite radical ways.

Suggestions for Critical Reflection

1. Do you think Berkeley proves that "colors, sounds, tastes, in a word all those termed *secondary qualities*, have certainly no existence without the mind"? What exactly would it be to show such a thing? Would, for example, Locke accept this claim about secondary qualities?

2. What do you make of Berkeley's Likeness Principle, that only an idea can be like another idea? Does it seem plausible? If so how, if at all, does it help to show that there can be no such thing as matter?

3. Berkeley denies that matter exists, but he holds that minds do exist, and minds are not themselves ideas (they are conscious spiritual

---

5   Though, to be fair, some philosophical theories that have had periods of popularity owe quite a lot to Berkeley's influence, such as the British neo-Hegelian theories of the late nineteenth century and the scientific phenomenalism of the early twentieth century.

agents which perceive ideas). Is Berkeley being consistent here? Do his arguments against matter work just as well against spirit? In thinking about this question, you should be aware that Berkeley himself considers it in the Third Dialogue so you might want to go and find out what he has to say there.

4. Berkeley wants us to accept that the physical world really exists, independently of us, since it consists of ideas in the mind of God. How satisfactory do you find this notion? What could the relationship be between our sensations of the external world and God's ideas? Is it any clearer than the relation between our sensations and material objects would be?

5. Berkeley recognized the existence of only two sorts of things: minds and ideas. Ideas, for Berkeley, are entirely passive, and the only active agencies in the world are minds. It follows that there can be no causation, as we would normally understand it. One idea cannot cause another, they can only be somehow connected together by a mind. In other words, (an idea of) fire cannot bring about (an idea of) heat, which in turn cannot cause (an idea of) the expansion of metal: all that can happen is that some mind decides the first idea is followed by the second, the second by the third, and so on. Given all this, could we possibly continue to do science if we accepted Berkeley's metaphysics? If so, what might this new science look like?

6. Locke and Berkeley can be seen as presenting two opposed philosophical world-views: which of them is right? If you think that neither is, then what third position is available? Would it help to abandon some of the presuppositions shared by Locke and Berkeley, such as their notion of an *idea*?

Suggestions for Further Reading

The standard edition of Berkeley's works continues to be *Works of George Berkeley, Bishop of Cloyne*, edited by Luce and Jessop and published in nine volumes between 1948 and 1957 by Nelson & Sons. A good student edition of the *Three Dialogues* was published

by Oxford University Press in 1998, with lots of useful supplementary material from Jonathan Dancy. In the same year Oxford published a similar edition of Berkeley's *The Principles of Human Knowledge*. Any serious student of Berkeley's *Three Dialogues* should begin by reading his *Principles*.

The standard biography of Berkeley is by A.A. Luce, *The Life of George Berkeley, Bishop of Cloyne* (Nelson, 1949). There are various useful books about Berkeley's philosophy, including the short *Berkeley*, by J.O. Urmson (Oxford University Press, 1982), the somewhat longer *Berkeley*, by G.J. Warnock (Pelican, 1953), and the even more substantial *Berkeley: An Introduction*, by Jonathan Dancy (Blackwell, 1987). Also available are *Berkeley: The Central Arguments*, by A.C. Grayling (Duckworth, 1986), *Berkeley*, by George Pitcher (Routledge & Kegan Paul, 1977), and *Berkeley: An Interpretation*, by Kenneth Winkler (Oxford University Press, 1989). A collection of essays can be found in *Essays on Berkeley*, ed. Foster and Robinson (Oxford University Press, 1985), and in *Locke and Berkeley*, ed. Martin and Armstrong (Doubleday, 1968). Finally, Jonathan Bennett's *Locke, Berkeley, Hume: Central Themes* (Oxford, 1971) is well worth consulting.

Three Dialogues Between Hylas and Philonous[6]

First Dialogue

Three dialogues between Hylas and Philonous, the design of which is plainly to demonstrate the reality and perfection of human knowledge, the incorporeal nature of the soul, and the immediate providence of a deity: in opposition to sceptics and atheists; also to open a method for rendering the sciences more easy, useful, and compendious.

---

6   Berkeley's *Three Dialogues* was first published in 1713, reissued in 1725, and then revised for a third edition in 1734. The text reprinted here is from the third edition (with mostly modernized spelling, punctuation, and capitalization).

The First Dialogue

PHILONOUS. Good morrow, Hylas: I did not expect to find you abroad so early.

HYLAS. It is indeed something unusual; but my thoughts were so taken up with a subject I was discoursing of last night, that finding I could not sleep, I resolved to rise and take a turn in the garden.

PHILONOUS. It happened well, to let you see what innocent and agreeable pleasures you lose every morning. Can there be a pleasanter time of the day, or a more delightful season of the year? That purple sky, those wild but sweet notes of birds, the fragrant bloom upon the trees and flowers, the gentle influence of the rising sun, these and a thousand nameless beauties of nature inspire the soul with secret transports; its faculties too being at this time fresh and lively, are fit for those meditations, which the solitude of a garden and tranquillity of the morning naturally dispose us to. But I am afraid I interrupt your thoughts: for you seemed very intent on something.

HYLAS. It is true, I was, and shall be obliged to you if you will permit me to go on in the same vein; not that I would by any means deprive myself of your company, for my thoughts always flow more easily in conversation with a friend, than when I am alone: but my request is, that you would suffer me to impart my reflexions to you.

PHILONOUS. With all my heart, it is what I should have requested myself if you had not prevented me.

HYLAS. I was considering the odd fate of those men who have in all ages, through an affectation of being distinguished from the vulgar,[7] or some unaccountable turn of thought, pretended either to believe nothing at all, or to believe the most extravagant things in the world. This however might be borne, if their paradoxes and scepticism did not draw after them some consequences of general disadvantage to mankind. But the mischief lieth here; that when men of less leisure see them who are supposed to have spent their whole time in the pursuits of knowledge professing an entire ignorance of all things, or advancing such notions as are repugnant to plain and commonly received principles, they will be tempted to entertain suspicions concerning

the most important truths, which they had hitherto held sacred and unquestionable.

PHILONOUS. I entirely agree with you, as to the ill tendency of the affected doubts of some philosophers, and fantastical conceits of others. I am even so far gone of late in this way of thinking, that I have quitted several of the sublime notions I had got in their schools for vulgar opinions. And I give it you on my word, since this revolt from metaphysical notions to the plain dictates of nature and common sense, I find my understanding strangely enlightened, so that I can now easily comprehend a great many things which before were all mystery and riddle.

HYLAS. I am glad to find there was nothing in the accounts I heard of you.

PHILONOUS. Pray, what were those?

HYLAS. You were represented, in last night's conversation, as one who maintained the most extravagant opinion that ever entered into the mind of man, to wit, that there is no such thing as *material substance* in the world.

PHILONOUS. That there is no such thing as what *philosophers call material substance*, I am seriously persuaded: but if I were made to see anything absurd or sceptical in this, I should then have the same reason to renounce this that I imagine I have now to reject the contrary opinion.

HYLAS. What! Can anything be more fantastical, more repugnant to common sense, or a more manifest piece of scepticism, than to believe there is no such thing as *matter*?

PHILONOUS. Softly, good Hylas. What if it should prove that you, who hold there is, are by virtue of that opinion a greater sceptic, and maintain more paradoxes and repugnances to common sense, than I who believe no such thing?

HYLAS. You may as soon persuade me the part is greater than the whole, as that, in order to avoid absurdity and scepticism, I should ever be obliged to give up my opinion in this point.

PHILONOUS. Well then, are you content to admit that opinion for true, which upon examination shall appear most agreeable to common sense, and remote from scepticism?

HYLAS. With all my heart. Since you are for raising disputes about the plainest things in nature, I am content for once to hear what you have to say.

---

7 The common people and their beliefs.

PHILONOUS. Pray, Hylas, what do you mean by a *sceptic*?

HYLAS. I mean what all men mean—one that doubts of everything.

PHILONOUS. He then who entertains no doubts concerning some particular point, with regard to that point cannot be thought a sceptic.

HYLAS. I agree with you.

PHILONOUS. Whether doth doubting consist in embracing the affirmative or negative side of a question?

HYLAS. In neither; for whoever understands English cannot but know that *doubting* signifies a suspense between both.

PHILONOUS. He then that denies any point, can no more be said to doubt of it, than he who affirmeth it with the same degree of assurance.

HYLAS. True.

PHILONOUS. And, consequently, for such his denial is no more to be esteemed a sceptic than the other.

HYLAS. I acknowledge it.

PHILONOUS. How cometh it to pass then, Hylas, that you pronounce me *a sceptic*, because I deny what you affirm, to wit, the existence of matter? Since, for aught you can tell, I am as peremptory[8] in my denial, as you in your affirmation.

HYLAS. Hold, Philonous, I have been a little out in my definition; but every false step a man makes in discourse is not to be insisted on. I said indeed that a *sceptic* was one who doubted of everything; but I should have added, or who denies the reality and truth of things.

PHILONOUS. What things? Do you mean the principles and theorems of sciences? But these you know are universal intellectual notions, and consequently independent of matter. The denial therefore of this doth not imply the denying them.

HYLAS. I grant it. But are there no other things? What think you of distrusting the senses, of denying the real existence of sensible things, or pretending to know nothing of them. Is not this sufficient to denominate a man a *sceptic*?

PHILONOUS. Shall we therefore examine which of us it is that denies the reality of sensible things, or pro-

fesses the greatest ignorance of them; since, if I take you rightly, he is to be esteemed the greatest *sceptic*?

HYLAS. That is what I desire.

PHILONOUS. What mean you by sensible things?

HYLAS. Those things which are perceived by the senses. Can you imagine that I mean anything else?

PHILONOUS. Pardon me, Hylas, if I am desirous clearly to apprehend your notions, since this may much shorten our inquiry. Suffer me then to ask you this farther question. Are those things only perceived by the senses which are perceived immediately? Or, may those things properly be said to be *sensible* which are perceived mediately, or not without the intervention of others?

HYLAS. I do not sufficiently understand you.

PHILONOUS. In reading a book, what I immediately perceive are the letters; but mediately, or by means of these, are suggested to my mind the notions of God, virtue, truth, &c. Now, that the letters are truly sensible things, or perceived by sense, there is no doubt: but I would know whether you take the things suggested by them to be so too.

HYLAS. No, certainly: it were absurd to think *God* or *virtue* sensible things; though they may be signified and suggested to the mind by sensible marks, with which they have an arbitrary connexion.

PHILONOUS. It seems then, that by *sensible things* you mean those only which can be perceived *immediately* by sense?

HYLAS. Right.

PHILONOUS. Doth it not follow from this, that though I see one part of the sky red, and another blue, and that my reason doth thence evidently conclude there must be some cause of that diversity of colours, yet that cause cannot be said to be a sensible thing, or perceived by the sense of seeing?

HYLAS. It doth.

PHILONOUS. In like manner, though I hear variety of sounds, yet I cannot be said to hear the causes of those sounds?

HYLAS. You cannot.

PHILONOUS. And when by my touch I perceive a thing to be hot and heavy, I cannot say, with any truth or propriety, that I feel the cause of its heat or weight?

HYLAS. To prevent any more questions of this kind, I tell you once for all, that by *sensible things* I mean

---

8   Decisive, final, confident.

those only which are perceived by sense; and that in truth the senses perceive nothing which they do not perceive *immediately*: for they make no inferences. The deducing therefore of causes or occasions from effects and appearances, which alone are perceived by sense, entirely relates to reason.

PHILONOUS. This point then is agreed between us— That *sensible things are those only which are immediately perceived by sense.* You will farther inform me, whether we immediately perceive by sight anything beside light, and colours, and figures;[9] or by hearing, anything but sounds; by the palate, anything beside tastes; by the smell, beside odours; or by the touch, more than tangible qualities.

HYLAS. We do not.

PHILONOUS. It seems, therefore, that if you take away all sensible qualities, there remains nothing sensible?

HYLAS. I grant it.

PHILONOUS. Sensible things therefore are nothing else but so many sensible qualities, or combinations of sensible qualities?

HYLAS. Nothing else.

PHILONOUS. *Heat* then is a sensible thing?

HYLAS. Certainly.

PHILONOUS. Doth the *reality* of sensible things consist in being perceived? or, is it something distinct from their being perceived, and that bears no relation to the mind?

HYLAS. To *exist* is one thing, and to be *perceived* is another.

PHILONOUS. I speak with regard to sensible things only. And of these I ask, whether by their real existence you mean a subsistence exterior to the mind, and distinct from their being perceived?

HYLAS. I mean a real absolute being, distinct from, and without any relation to, their being perceived.

PHILONOUS. Heat therefore, if it be allowed a real being, must exist without the mind?

HYLAS. It must.

PHILONOUS. Tell me, Hylas, is this real existence equally compatible to all degrees of heat, which we perceive; or is there any reason why we should attribute it to some, and deny it to others? And if there be, pray let me know that reason.

_____
9   Shapes.

HYLAS. Whatever degree of heat we perceive by sense, we may be sure the same exists in the object that occasions it.

PHILONOUS. What! the greatest as well as the least?

HYLAS. I tell you, the reason is plainly the same in respect of both. They are both perceived by sense; nay, the greater degree of heat is more sensibly perceived; and consequently, if there is any difference, we are more certain of its real existence than we can be of the reality of a lesser degree.

PHILONOUS. But is not the most vehement and intense degree of heat a very great pain?

HYLAS. No one can deny it.

PHILONOUS. And is any unperceiving thing capable of pain or pleasure?

HYLAS. No, certainly.

PHILONOUS. Is your material substance a senseless being, or a being endowed with sense and perception?

HYLAS. It is senseless without doubt.

PHILONOUS. It cannot therefore be the subject of pain?

HYLAS. By no means.

PHILONOUS. Nor consequently of the greatest heat perceived by sense, since you acknowledge this to be no small pain?

HYLAS. I grant it.

PHILONOUS. What shall we say then of your external object; is it a material substance, or no?

HYLAS. It is a material substance with the sensible qualities inhering in it.

PHILONOUS. How then can a great heat exist in it, since you own it cannot in a material substance? I desire you would clear this point.

HYLAS. Hold, Philonous, I fear I was out in yielding intense heat to be a pain. It should seem rather, that pain is something distinct from heat, and the consequence or effect of it.

PHILONOUS. Upon putting your hand near the fire, do you perceive one simple uniform sensation, or two distinct sensations?

HYLAS. But one simple sensation.

PHILONOUS. Is not the heat immediately perceived?

HYLAS. It is.

PHILONOUS. And the pain?

HYLAS. True.

PHILONOUS. Seeing therefore they are both immediately perceived at the same time, and the fire affects you only with one simple or uncompounded idea, it follows that this same simple idea is both the intense heat immediately perceived, and the pain; and, consequently, that the intense heat immediately perceived is nothing distinct from a particular sort of pain.

HYLAS. It seems so.

PHILONOUS. Again, try in your thoughts, Hylas, if you can conceive a vehement sensation to be without pain or pleasure.

HYLAS. I cannot.

PHILONOUS. Or can you frame to yourself an idea of sensible pain or pleasure in general, abstracted from every particular idea of heat, cold, tastes, smells? &c.

HYLAS. I do not find that I can.

PHILONOUS. Doth it not therefore follow, that sensible pain is nothing distinct from those sensations or ideas, in an intense degree?

HYLAS. It is undeniable; and, to speak the truth, I begin to suspect a very great heat cannot exist but in a mind perceiving it.

PHILONOUS. What! are you then in that sceptical state of suspense, between affirming and denying?

HYLAS. I think I may be positive in the point. A very violent and painful heat cannot exist without the mind.

PHILONOUS. It hath not therefore according to you, any *real* being?

HYLAS. I own it.

PHILONOUS. Is it therefore certain, that there is no body in nature really hot?

HYLAS. I have not denied there is any real heat in bodies. I only say, there is no such thing as an intense real heat.

PHILONOUS. But, did you not say before that all degrees of heat were equally real; or, if there was any difference, that the greater were more undoubtedly real than the lesser?

HYLAS. True: but it was because I did not then consider the ground there is for distinguishing between them, which I now plainly see. And it is this: because intense heat is nothing else but a particular kind of painful sensation; and pain cannot exist but in a perceiving being; it follows that no intense heat can really exist in an unperceiving corporeal substance. But this is no reason why we should deny heat in an inferior degree to exist in such a substance.

PHILONOUS. But how shall we be able to discern those degrees of heat which exist only in the mind from those which exist without it?

HYLAS. That is no difficult matter. You know the least pain cannot exist unperceived; whatever, therefore, degree of heat is a pain exists only in the mind. But, as for all other degrees of heat, nothing obliges us to think the same of them.

PHILONOUS. I think you granted before that no unperceiving being was capable of pleasure, any more than of pain.

HYLAS. I did.

PHILONOUS. And is not warmth, or a more gentle degree of heat than what causes uneasiness, a pleasure?

HYLAS. What then?

PHILONOUS. Consequently, it cannot exist without[10] the mind in an unperceiving substance, or body.

HYLAS. So it seems.

PHILONOUS. Since, therefore, as well those degrees of heat that are not painful, as those that are, can exist only in a thinking substance; may we not conclude that external bodies are absolutely incapable of any degree of heat whatsoever?

HYLAS. On second thoughts, I do not think it so evident that warmth is a pleasure as that a great degree of heat is a pain.

PHILONOUS. I do not pretend that warmth is as great a pleasure as heat is a pain. But, if you grant it to be even a small pleasure, it serves to make good my conclusion.

HYLAS. I could rather call it an *indolence*. It seems to be nothing more than a privation of both pain and pleasure. And that such a quality or state as this may agree to an unthinking substance, I hope you will not deny.

PHILONOUS. If you are resolved to maintain that warmth, or a gentle degree of heat, is no pleasure, I know not how to convince you otherwise than by appealing to your own sense. But what think you of cold?

HYLAS. The same that I do of heat. An intense degree of cold is a pain; for to feel a very great cold, is to perceive a great uneasiness: it cannot therefore exist

---

10   "Without," here and elsewhere in this selection, means "outside" (rather than "not having").

without the mind; but a lesser degree of cold may, as well as a lesser degree of heat.

PHILONOUS. Those bodies, therefore, upon whose application to our own, we perceive a moderate degree of heat, must be concluded to have a moderate degree of heat or warmth in them; and those, upon whose application we feel a like degree of cold, must be thought to have cold in them.

HYLAS. They must.

PHILONOUS. Can any doctrine be true that necessarily leads a man into an absurdity?

HYLAS. Without doubt it cannot.

PHILONOUS. Is it not an absurdity to think that the same thing should be at the same time both cold and warm?

HYLAS. It is.

PHILONOUS. Suppose now one of your hands hot, and the other cold, and that they are both at once put into the same vessel of water, in an intermediate state; will not the water seem cold to one hand, and warm to the other?

HYLAS. It will.

PHILONOUS. Ought we not therefore, by your principles, to conclude it is really both cold and warm at the same time, that is, according to your own concession, to believe an absurdity?

HYLAS. I confess it seems so.

PHILONOUS. Consequently, the principles themselves are false, since you have granted that no true principle leads to an absurdity.

HYLAS. But, after all, can anything be more absurd than to say, *there is no heat in the fire*?

PHILONOUS. To make the point still clearer; tell me whether, in two cases exactly alike, we ought not to make the same judgment?

HYLAS. We ought.

PHILONOUS. When a pin pricks your finger, doth it not rend and divide the fibres of your flesh?

HYLAS. It doth.

PHILONOUS. And when a coal burns your finger, doth it any more?

HYLAS. It doth not.

PHILONOUS. Since, therefore, you neither judge the sensation itself occasioned by the pin, nor anything like it to be in the pin; you should not, conformably to what you have now granted, judge the sensation occasioned by the fire, or anything like it, to be in the fire.

HYLAS. Well, since it must be so, I am content to yield this point, and acknowledge that heat and cold are only sensations existing in our minds. But there still remain qualities enough to secure the reality of external things.

PHILONOUS. But what will you say, Hylas, if it shall appear that the case is the same with regard to all other sensible qualities, and that they can no more be supposed to exist without the mind, than heat and cold?

HYLAS. Then indeed you will have done something to the purpose; but that is what I despair of seeing proved.

PHILONOUS. Let us examine them in order. What think you of *tastes*, do they exist without the mind, or no?

HYLAS. Can any man in his senses doubt whether sugar is sweet, or wormwood[11] bitter?

PHILONOUS. Inform me, Hylas. Is a sweet taste a particular kind of pleasure or pleasant sensation, or is it not?

HYLAS. It is.

PHILONOUS. And is not bitterness some kind of uneasiness or pain?

HYLAS. I grant it.

PHILONOUS. If therefore sugar and wormwood are unthinking corporeal substances existing without the mind, how can sweetness and bitterness, that is, pleasure and pain, agree to them?

HYLAS. Hold, Philonous, I now see what it was deluded me all this time. You asked whether heat and cold, sweetness and bitterness, were not particular sorts of pleasure and pain; to which I answered simply, that they were. Whereas I should have thus distinguished: those qualities, as perceived by us, are pleasures or pains, but not as existing in the external objects. We must not therefore conclude absolutely, that there is no heat in the fire, or sweetness in the sugar, but only that heat or sweetness, as perceived by us, are not in the fire or sugar. What say you to this?

PHILONOUS. I say it is nothing to the purpose. Our discourse proceeded altogether concerning sensible things, which you defined to be, *the things we immediately perceive by our senses*. Whatever other qualities, therefore, you speak of as distinct from these, I know nothing of them, neither do they at all belong

---

11   A bitter extract of aromatic herbs and shrubs, used for making absinthe and flavoring certain wines.

to the point in dispute. You may, indeed, pretend to have discovered certain qualities which you do not perceive, and assert those insensible qualities exist in fire and sugar. But what use can be made of this to your present purpose, I am at a loss to conceive. Tell me then once more, do you acknowledge that heat and cold, sweetness and bitterness (meaning those qualities which are perceived by the senses), do not exist without the mind?

HYLAS. I see it is to no purpose to hold out, so I give up the cause as to those mentioned qualities. Though I profess it sounds oddly, to say that sugar is not sweet.

PHILONOUS. But, for your farther satisfaction, take this along with you: that which at other times seems sweet, shall, to a distempered palate, appear bitter. And, nothing can be plainer than that divers persons perceive different tastes in the same food; since that which one man delights in, another abhors. And how could this be, if the taste was something really inherent in the food?

HYLAS. I acknowledge I know not how.

PHILONOUS. In the next place, *odours* are to be considered. And, with regard to these, I would fain know whether what hath been said of tastes doth not exactly agree to them? Are they not so many pleasing or displeasing sensations?

HYLAS. They are.

PHILONOUS. Can you then conceive it possible that they should exist in an unperceiving thing?

HYLAS. I cannot.

PHILONOUS. Or, can you imagine that filth and ordure[12] affect those brute animals that feed on them out of choice, with the same smells which we perceive in them?

HYLAS. By no means.

PHILONOUS. May we not therefore conclude of smells, as of the other forementioned qualities, that they cannot exist in any but a perceiving substance or mind?

HYLAS. I think so.

PHILONOUS. Then as to *sounds*, what must we think of them: are they accidents[13] really inherent in external bodies, or not?

HYLAS. That they inhere not in the sonorous bodies is plain from hence: because a bell struck in the exhausted receiver of an air-pump[14] sends forth no sound. The air, therefore, must be thought the subject of sound.

PHILONOUS. What reason is there for that, Hylas?

HYLAS. Because, when any motion is raised in the air, we perceive a sound greater or lesser, according to the air's motion; but without some motion in the air, we never hear any sound at all.

PHILONOUS. And granting that we never hear a sound but when some motion is produced in the air, yet I do not see how you can infer from thence, that the sound itself is in the air.

HYLAS. It is this very motion in the external air that produces in the mind the sensation of *sound*. For, striking on the drum of the ear, it causeth a vibration, which by the auditory nerves being communicated to the brain, the soul is thereupon affected with the sensation called *sound*.

PHILONOUS. What! is sound then a sensation?

HYLAS. I tell you, as perceived by us, it is a particular sensation in the mind.

PHILONOUS. And can any sensation exist without the mind?

HYLAS. No, certainly.

PHILONOUS. How then can sound, being a sensation, exist in the air, if by the *air* you mean a senseless substance existing without the mind?

HYLAS. You must distinguish, Philonous, between sound as it is perceived by us, and as it is in itself; or (which is the same thing) between the sound we immediately perceive, and that which exists without us. The former, indeed, is a particular kind of sensation, but the latter is merely a vibrative or undulatory motion of the air.

PHILONOUS. I thought I had already obviated that distinction, by the answer I gave when you were applying it in a like case before. But, to say no more of that, are you sure then that sound is really nothing but motion?

HYLAS. I am.

PHILONOUS. Whatever therefore agrees to real sound, may with truth be attributed to motion?

HYLAS. It may.

---

12 Excrement, dung.

13 (Non-essential) properties.

14 A near-vacuum. This experiment was first performed by Otto von Guericke in the 1650s.

PHILONOUS. It is then good sense to speak of *motion* as of a thing that is *loud*, *sweet*, *acute*, or *grave*.[15]

HYLAS. I see you are resolved not to understand me. Is it not evident those accidents or modes belong only to sensible sound, or sound in the common acceptation of the word, but not to *sound* in the real and philosophic sense; which, as I just now told you, is nothing but a certain motion of the air?

PHILONOUS. It seems then there are two sorts of sound—the one vulgar, or that which is heard, the other philosophical and real?

HYLAS. Even so.

PHILONOUS. And the latter consists in motion?

HYLAS. I told you so before.

PHILONOUS. Tell me, Hylas, to which of the senses, think you, the idea of motion belongs? to the hearing?

HYLAS. No, certainly; but to the sight and touch.

PHILONOUS. It should follow then, that, according to you, real sounds may possibly be *seen* or *felt*, but never *heard*.

HYLAS. Look you, Philonous, you may, if you please, make a jest of my opinion, but that will not alter the truth of things. I own, indeed, the inferences you draw me into sound something oddly; but common language, you know, is framed by, and for the use of the vulgar: we must not therefore wonder if expressions adapted to exact philosophic notions seem uncouth and out of the way.

PHILONOUS. Is it come to that? I assure you, I imagine myself to have gained no small point, since you make so light of departing from common phrases and opinions; it being a main part of our inquiry, to examine whose notions are widest of the common road, and most repugnant to the general sense of the world. But, can you think it no more than a philosophical paradox, to say that *real sounds are never heard*, and that the idea of them is obtained by some other sense? And is there nothing in this contrary to nature and the truth of things?

HYLAS. To deal ingenuously,[16] I do not like it. And, after the concessions already made, I had as well grant that sounds too have no real being without the mind.

PHILONOUS. And I hope you will make no difficulty to acknowledge the same of *colours*.

HYLAS. Pardon me: the case of colours is very different. Can anything be plainer than that we see them on the objects?

PHILONOUS. The objects you speak of are, I suppose, corporeal substances existing without the mind?

HYLAS. They are.

PHILONOUS. And have true and real colours inhering in them?

HYLAS. Each visible object hath that colour which we see in it.

PHILONOUS. How! is there anything visible but what we perceive by sight?

HYLAS. There is not.

PHILONOUS. And, do we perceive anything by sense which we do not perceive immediately?

HYLAS. How often must I be obliged to repeat the same thing? I tell you, we do not.

PHILONOUS. Have patience, good Hylas; and tell me once more, whether there is anything immediately perceived by the senses, except sensible qualities. I know you asserted there was not; but I would now be informed, whether you still persist in the same opinion.

HYLAS. I do.

PHILONOUS. Pray, is your corporeal substance either a sensible quality, or made up of sensible qualities?

HYLAS. What a question that is! who ever thought it was?

PHILONOUS. My reason for asking was, because in saying, *each visible object hath that colour which we see in it*, you make visible objects to be corporeal substances; which implies either that corporeal substances are sensible qualities, or else that there is something besides sensible qualities perceived by sight: but, as this point was formerly agreed between us, and is still maintained by you, it is a clear consequence, that your *corporeal substance* is nothing distinct from *sensible qualities*.

HYLAS. You may draw as many absurd consequences as you please, and endeavour to perplex the plainest things; but you shall never persuade me out of my senses. I clearly understand my own meaning.

PHILONOUS. I wish you would make me understand it too. But, since you are unwilling to have your notion

---

15   "Acute" means high-pitched or shrill, and "grave" low-pitched.

16   Openly, honestly.

of corporeal substance examined, I shall urge that point no farther. Only be pleased to let me know, whether the same colours which we see exist in external bodies, or some other.

HYLAS. The very same.

PHILONOUS. What! are then the beautiful red and purple we see on yonder clouds really in them? Or do you imagine they have in themselves any other form than that of a dark mist or vapour?

HYLAS. I must own, Philonous, those colours are not really in the clouds as they seem to be at this distance. They are only apparent colours.

PHILONOUS. *Apparent* call you them? How shall we distinguish these apparent colours from real?

HYLAS. Very easily. Those are to be thought apparent which, appearing only at a distance, vanish upon a nearer approach.

PHILONOUS. And those, I suppose, are to be thought real which are discovered by the most near and exact survey.

HYLAS. Right.

PHILONOUS. Is the nearest and exactest survey made by the help of a microscope, or by the naked eye?

HYLAS. By a microscope, doubtless.

PHILONOUS. But a microscope often discovers colours in an object different from those perceived by the unassisted sight. And, in case we had microscopes magnifying to any assigned degree, it is certain that no object whatsoever, viewed through them, would appear in the same colour which it exhibits to the naked eye.

HYLAS. And what will you conclude from all this? You cannot argue that there are really and naturally no colours on objects: because by artificial managements they may be altered, or made to vanish.

PHILONOUS. I think it may evidently be concluded from your own concessions, that all the colours we see with our naked eyes are only apparent as those on the clouds, since they vanish upon a more close and accurate inspection which is afforded us by a microscope. Then as to what you say by way of prevention: I ask you whether the real and natural state of an object is better discovered by a very sharp and piercing sight, or by one which is less sharp?

HYLAS. By the former without doubt.

PHILONOUS. Is it not plain from *dioptrics*[17] that microscopes make the sight more penetrating, and represent objects as they would appear to the eye in case it were naturally endowed with a most exquisite sharpness?

HYLAS. It is.

PHILONOUS. Consequently the microscopical representation is to be thought that which best sets forth the real nature of the thing, or what it is in itself. The colours, therefore, by it perceived are more genuine and real than those perceived otherwise.

HYLAS. I confess there is something in what you say.

PHILONOUS. Besides, it is not only possible but manifest, that there actually are animals whose eyes are by nature framed to perceive those things which by reason of their minuteness escape our sight. What think you of those inconceivably small animals perceived by glasses?[18] Must we suppose they are all stark blind? Or, in case they see, can it be imagined their sight hath not the same use in preserving their bodies from injuries, which appears in that of all other animals? And if it hath, is it not evident they must see particles less than their own bodies; which will present them with a far different view in each object from that which strikes our senses? Even our own eyes do not always represent objects to us after the same manner. In the jaundice[19] every one knows that all things seem yellow. Is it not therefore highly probable those animals in whose eyes we discern a very different texture from that of ours, and whose bodies abound with different humours,[20] do not see the same colours in every object that we do? From all which, should it not seem to follow that all colours are equally apparent, and that none of those which we perceive are really inherent in any outward object?

HYLAS. It should.

PHILONOUS. The point will be past all doubt, if you consider that, in case colours were real properties or affections inherent in external bodies, they could admit of no alteration without some change wrought in the very bodies themselves: but, is it not evident from what hath

17 The part of optics dealing with the study of refraction.
18 By magnifying lenses (e.g., in a microscope).
19 A yellowing of the skin and the eyes, often caused by liver disease.
20 Bodily fluids.

been said that, upon the use of microscopes, upon a change happening in the humours of the eye, or a variation of distance, without any manner of real alteration in the thing itself, the colours of any object are either changed, or totally disappear? Nay, all other circumstances remaining the same, change but the situation of some objects, and they shall present different colours to the eye. The same thing happens upon viewing an object in various degrees of light. And what is more known than that the same bodies appear differently coloured by candle-light from what they do in the open day? Add to these the experiment of a prism which, separating the heterogeneous rays of light, alters the colour of any object, and will cause the whitest to appear of a deep blue or red to the naked eye. And now tell me whether you are still of opinion that every body hath its true real colour inhering in it; and, if you think it hath, I would fain know farther from you, what certain distance and position of the object, what peculiar texture and formation of the eye, what degree or kind of light is necessary for ascertaining that true colour, and distinguishing it from apparent ones.

HYLAS. I own myself entirely satisfied, that they are all equally apparent, and that there is no such thing as colour really inhering in external bodies, but that it is altogether in the light. And what confirms me in this opinion is, that in proportion to the light colours are still more or less vivid; and if there be no light, then are there no colours perceived. Besides, allowing there are colours on external objects, yet, how is it possible for us to perceive them? For no external body affects the mind, unless it acts first on our organs of sense. But the only action of bodies is motion; and motion cannot be communicated otherwise than by impulse. A distant object therefore cannot act on the eye; nor consequently make itself or its properties perceivable to the soul. Whence it plainly follows that it is immediately some contiguous[21] substance, which, operating on the eye, occasions a perception of colours: and such is light.

PHILONOUS. How! is light then a substance?

HYLAS. I tell you, Philonous, external light is nothing but a thin fluid substance, whose minute particles being agitated with a brisk motion, and in various man-

ners reflected from the different surfaces of outward objects to the eyes, communicate different motions to the optic nerves; which, being propagated to the brain, cause therein various impressions; and these are attended with the sensations of red, blue, yellow, &c.

PHILONOUS. It seems then the light doth no more than shake the optic nerves.

HYLAS. Nothing else.

PHILONOUS. And consequent to each particular motion of the nerves, the mind is affected with a sensation, which is some particular colour.

HYLAS. Right.

PHILONOUS. And these sensations have no existence without the mind.

HYLAS. They have not.

PHILONOUS. How then do you affirm that colours are in the light; since by *light* you understand a corporeal substance external to the mind?

HYLAS. Light and colours, as immediately perceived by us, I grant cannot exist without the mind. But in themselves they are only the motions and configurations of certain insensible particles of matter.

PHILONOUS. Colours then, in the vulgar sense, or taken for the immediate objects of sight, cannot agree to any but a perceiving substance.

HYLAS. That is what I say.

PHILONOUS. Well then, since you give up the point as to those sensible qualities which are alone thought colours by all mankind beside, you may hold what you please with regard to those invisible ones of the philosophers. It is not my business to dispute about *them*; only I would advise you to bethink yourself, whether, considering the inquiry we are upon, it be prudent for you to affirm—*the red and blue which we see are not real colours, but certain unknown motions and figures which no man ever did or can see are truly so*. Are not these shocking notions, and are not they subject to as many ridiculous inferences, as those you were obliged to renounce before in the case of sounds?

HYLAS. I frankly own, Philonous, that it is in vain to stand out any longer. Colours, sounds, tastes, in a word all those termed *secondary qualities*, have certainly no existence without the mind. But by this acknowledgment I must not be supposed to derogate the reality of matter, or external objects; seeing it is no more than several philosophers maintain, who

---

21　Immediately next to, touching.

nevertheless are the farthest imaginable from denying matter. For the clearer understanding of this, you must know sensible qualities are by philosophers divided into *primary* and *secondary*. The former are extension, figure, solidity, gravity, motion, and rest; and these they hold exist really in bodies. The latter are those above enumerated; or, briefly, *all sensible qualities beside the primary*; which they assert are only so many sensations or ideas existing nowhere but in the mind. But all this, I doubt not, you are apprised of. For my part, I have been a long time sensible there was such an opinion current among philosophers, but was never thoroughly convinced of its truth until now.

PHILONOUS. You are still then of opinion that *extension* and *figures* are inherent in external unthinking substances?

HYLAS. I am.

PHILONOUS. But what if the same arguments which are brought against secondary qualities will hold good against these also?

HYLAS. Why then I shall be obliged to think, they too exist only in the mind.

PHILONOUS. Is it your opinion the very figure and extension which you perceive by sense exist in the outward object or material substance?

HYLAS. It is.

PHILONOUS. Have all other animals as good grounds to think the same of the figure and extension which they see and feel?

HYLAS. Without doubt, if they have any thought at all.

PHILONOUS. Answer me, Hylas. Think you the senses were bestowed upon all animals for their preservation and well-being in life? or were they given to men alone for this end?

HYLAS. I make no question but they have the same use in all other animals.

PHILONOUS. If so, is it not necessary they should be enabled by them to perceive their own limbs, and those bodies which are capable of harming them?

HYLAS. Certainly.

PHILONOUS. A mite[22] therefore must be supposed to see his own foot, and things equal or even less than it, as bodies of some considerable dimension; though at the same time they appear to you scarce discernible, or at best as so many visible points?

HYLAS. I cannot deny it.

PHILONOUS. And to creatures less than the mite they will seem yet larger?

HYLAS. They will.

PHILONOUS. Insomuch that what you can hardly discern will to another extremely minute animal appear as some huge mountain?

HYLAS. All this I grant.

PHILONOUS. Can one and the same thing be at the same time in itself of different dimensions?

HYLAS. That were absurd to imagine.

PHILONOUS. But, from what you have laid down it follows that both the extension by you perceived, and that perceived by the mite itself, as likewise all those perceived by lesser animals, are each of them the true extension of the mite's foot; that is to say, by your own principles you are led into an absurdity.

HYLAS. There seems to be some difficulty in the point.

PHILONOUS. Again, have you not acknowledged that no real inherent property of any object can be changed without some change in the thing itself?

HYLAS. I have.

PHILONOUS. But, as we approach to or recede from an object, the visible extension varies, being at one distance ten or a hundred times greater than another. Doth it not therefore follow from hence likewise that it is not really inherent in the object?

HYLAS. I own I am at a loss what to think.

PHILONOUS. Your judgement will soon be determined, if you will venture to think as freely concerning this quality as you have done concerning the rest. Was it not admitted as a good argument, that neither heat nor cold was in the water, because it seemed warm to one hand and cold to the other?

HYLAS. It was.

PHILONOUS. Is it not the very same reasoning to conclude, there is no extension or figure in an object, because to one eye it shall seem little, smooth, and round, when at the same time it appears to the other, great, uneven, and regular?

HYLAS. The very same. But does this latter fact ever happen?

---

22 Any of a large number of species of tiny arachnids, often parasites, some of which are so small that they cannot be seen by the naked eye.

PHILONOUS. You may at any time make the experiment, by looking with one eye bare, and with the other through a microscope.

HYLAS. I know not how to maintain it; and yet I am loath to give up *extension*, I see so many odd consequences following upon such a concession.

PHILONOUS. Odd, say you? After the concessions already made, I hope you will stick at nothing for its oddness. But, on the other hand, should it not seem very odd, if the general reasoning which includes all other sensible qualities did not also include extension? If it be allowed that no idea, nor anything like an idea, can exist in an unperceiving substance, then surely it follows that no figure, or mode of extension, which we can either perceive, or imagine, or have any idea of, can be really inherent in matter; not to mention the peculiar difficulty there must be in conceiving a material substance, prior to and distinct from extension, to be the *substratum* of extension. Be the sensible quality what it will—figure, or sound, or colour, it seems alike impossible it should subsist in that which doth not perceive it.

HYLAS. I give up the point for the present, reserving still a right to retract my opinion, in case I shall hereafter discover any false step in my progress to it.

PHILONOUS. That is a right you cannot be denied. Figures and extension being despatched, we proceed next to *motion*. Can a real motion in any external body be at the same time very swift and very slow?

HYLAS. It cannot.

PHILONOUS. Is not the motion of a body swift in a reciprocal proportion to the time it takes up in describing[23] any given space? Thus a body that describes a mile in an hour moves three times faster than it would in case it described only a mile in three hours.

HYLAS. I agree with you.

PHILONOUS. And is not time measured by the succession of ideas in our minds?

HYLAS. It is.

PHILONOUS. And is it not possible ideas should succeed one another twice as fast in your mind as they do in mine, or in that of some spirit of another kind?

HYLAS. I own it.

---

23   Crossing.

PHILONOUS. Consequently the same body may to another seem to perform its motion over any space in half the time that it doth to you. And the same reasoning will hold as to any other proportion: that is to say, according to your principles (since the motions perceived are both really in the object) it is possible one and the same body shall be really moved the same way at once, both very swift and very slow. How is this consistent either with common sense, or with what you just now granted?

HYLAS. I have nothing to say to it.

PHILONOUS. Then as for *solidity*; either you do not mean any sensible quality by that word, and so it is beside our inquiry: or if you do, it must be either hardness or resistance. But both the one and the other are plainly relative to our senses: it being evident that what seems hard to one animal may appear soft to another, who hath greater force and firmness of limbs. Nor is it less plain that the resistance I feel is not in the body.

HYLAS. I own the very *sensation* of resistance, which is all you immediately perceive, is not in the body; but the *cause* of that sensation is.

PHILONOUS. But the causes of our sensations are not things immediately perceived, and therefore are not sensible. This point I thought had been already determined.

HYLAS. I own it was; but you will pardon me if I seem a little embarrassed: I know not how to quit my old notions.

PHILONOUS. To help you out, do but consider that if *extension* be once acknowledged to have no existence without the mind, the same must necessarily be granted of motion, solidity, and gravity; since they all evidently suppose extension. It is therefore superfluous to inquire particularly concerning each of them. In denying extension, you have denied them all to have any real existence.

HYLAS. I wonder, Philonous, if what you say be true, why those philosophers who deny the secondary qualities any real existence should yet attribute it to the primary. If there is no difference between them, how can this be accounted for?

PHILONOUS. It is not my business to account for every opinion of the philosophers. But, among other reasons which may be assigned for this, it seems probable that pleasure and pain being rather annexed to the former than the latter may be one. Heat and cold, tastes and smells, have something more vividly pleasing or disagreeable than the ideas of extension, figure, and motion affect us with. And, it being too visibly absurd to hold that pain or pleasure can be in an unperceiving substance, men are more easily weaned from believing the external existence of the secondary than the primary qualities. You will be satisfied there is something in this, if you recollect the difference you made between an intense and more moderate degree of heat; allowing the one a real existence, while you denied it to the other. But, after all, there is no rational ground for that distinction; for, surely an indifferent sensation is as truly *a sensation* as one more pleasing or painful; and consequently should not any more than they be supposed to exist in an unthinking subject.

HYLAS. It is just come into my head, Philonous, that I have somewhere heard of a distinction between absolute and sensible extension. Now, though it be acknowledged that *great* and *small*, consisting merely in the relation which other extended beings have to the parts of our own bodies, do not really inhere in the substances themselves; yet nothing obliges us to hold the same with regard to *absolute extension*, which is something abstracted from *great* and *small*, from this or that particular magnitude or figure. So likewise as to motion; *swift* and *slow* are altogether relative to the succession of ideas in our own minds. But, it doth not follow, because those modifications of motion exist not without the mind, that therefore absolute motion abstracted from them doth not.

PHILONOUS. Pray what is it that distinguishes one motion, or one part of extension, from another? Is it not something sensible, as some degree of swiftness or slowness, some certain magnitude or figure peculiar to each?

HYLAS. I think so.

PHILONOUS. These qualities, therefore, stripped of all sensible properties, are without all specific and numerical differences, as the schools call them.

HYLAS. They are.

PHILONOUS. That is to say, they are extension in general, and motion in general.

HYLAS. Let it be so.

PHILONOUS. But it is a universally received maxim that *everything which exists is particular*. How then can motion in general, or extension in general, exist in any corporeal substance?

HYLAS. It will take time to solve your difficulty.

PHILONOUS. But I think the point may be speedily decided. Without doubt you can tell whether you are able to frame this or that idea. Now I am content to put our dispute on this issue. If you can frame in your thoughts a distinct *abstract idea* of motion or extension, divested of all those sensible modes, as swift and slow, great and small, round and square, and the like, which are acknowledged to exist only in the mind, I will then yield the point you contend for. But if you cannot, it will be unreasonable on your side to insist any longer upon what you have no notion of.

HYLAS. To confess ingenuously, I cannot.

PHILONOUS. Can you even separate the ideas of extension and motion from the ideas of all those qualities which they who make the distinction term *secondary*?

HYLAS. What! is it not an easy matter to consider extension and motion by themselves, abstracted from all other sensible qualities? Pray how do the mathematicians treat of them?

PHILONOUS. I acknowledge, Hylas, it is not difficult to form general propositions and reasonings about those qualities, without mentioning any other; and, in this sense, to consider or treat of them abstractedly. But, how doth it follow that, because I can pronounce the word *motion* by itself, I can form the idea of it in my mind exclusive of body? or, because theorems may be made of extension and figures, without any mention of *great* or *small*, or any other sensible mode or quality, that therefore it is possible such an abstract idea of extension, without any particular size or figure, or sensible quality, should be distinctly formed, and apprehended by the mind? Mathematicians treat of quantity, without regarding what other sensible qualities it is attended with, as being altogether indifferent to their demonstrations. But, when laying aside the words, they contemplate the bare ideas, I believe you will find, they are not the pure abstracted ideas of extension.

HYLAS. But what say you to *pure intellect*? May not abstracted ideas be framed by that faculty?

PHILONOUS. Since I cannot frame abstract ideas at all, it is plain I cannot frame them by the help of pure *intellect*, whatsoever faculty you understand by those words. Besides, not to inquire into the nature of pure intellect and its spiritual objects, as *virtue, reason, God*, or the like, thus much seems manifest—that sensible things are only to be perceived by sense, or represented by the imagination. Figures, therefore, and extension, being originally perceived by sense, do not belong to pure intellect: but, for your farther satisfaction, try if you can frame the idea of any figure, abstracted from all particularities of size, or even from other sensible qualities.

HYLAS. Let me think a little—I do not find that I can.

PHILONOUS. And can you think it possible that should really exist in nature which implies a repugnancy in its conception?

HYLAS. By no means.

PHILONOUS. Since therefore it is impossible even for the mind to disunite the ideas of extension and motion from all other sensible qualities, doth it not follow, that where the one exist there necessarily the other exist likewise?

HYLAS. It should seem so.

PHILONOUS. Consequently, the very same arguments which you admitted as conclusive against the secondary qualities are, without any farther application of force, against the primary too. Besides, if you will trust your senses, is it not plain all sensible qualities coexist, or to them, appear as being in the same place? Do they ever represent a motion, or figure, as being divested of all other visible and tangible qualities?

HYLAS. You need say no more on this head. I am free to own, if there be no secret error or oversight in our proceedings hitherto, that all sensible qualities are alike to be denied existence without the mind. But, my fear is that I have been too liberal in my former concessions, or overlooked some fallacy or other. In short, I did not take time to think.

PHILONOUS. For that matter, Hylas, you may take what time you please in reviewing the progress of our inquiry. You are at liberty to recover any slips you might have made, or offer whatever you have omitted which makes for your first opinion.

HYLAS. One great oversight I take to be this—that I did not sufficiently distinguish the *object* from the *sensation*. Now, though this latter may not exist without the mind, yet it will not thence follow that the former cannot.

PHILONOUS. What object do you mean? the object of the senses?

HYLAS. The same.

PHILONOUS. It is then immediately perceived?

HYLAS. Right.

PHILONOUS. Make me to understand the difference between what is immediately perceived and a sensation.

HYLAS. The sensation I take to be an act of the mind perceiving; besides which, there is something perceived; and this I call the *object*. For example, there is red and yellow on that tulip. But then the act of perceiving those colours is in me only, and not in the tulip.

PHILONOUS. What tulip do you speak of? Is it that which you see?

HYLAS. The same.

PHILONOUS. And what do you see beside colour, figure, and extension?

HYLAS. Nothing.

PHILONOUS. What you would say then is that the red and yellow are coexistent with the extension; is it not?

HYLAS. That is not all; I would say they have a real existence without the mind, in some unthinking substance.

PHILONOUS. That the colours are really in the tulip which I see is manifest. Neither can it be denied that this tulip may exist independent of your mind or mine; but, that any immediate object of the senses—that is, any idea, or combination of ideas—should exist in an unthinking substance, or exterior to *all* minds, is in itself an evident contradiction. Nor can I imagine how this follows from what you said just now, to wit, that the red and yellow were on the tulip *you saw*, since you do not pretend to *see* that unthinking substance.

HYLAS. You have an artful way, Philonous, of diverting our inquiry from the subject.

PHILONOUS. I see you have no mind to be pressed that way. To return then to your distinction between *sensation* and *object*; if I take you right, you distinguish in every perception two things, the one an action of the mind, the other not.

HYLAS. True.

PHILONOUS. And this action cannot exist in, or belong to, any unthinking thing; but whatever beside is implied in a perception may?

HYLAS. That is my meaning.

PHILONOUS. So that if there was a perception without any act of the mind, it were possible such a perception should exist in an unthinking substance?

HYLAS. I grant it. But it is impossible there should be such a perception.

PHILONOUS. When is the mind said to be active?

HYLAS. When it produces, puts an end to, or changes, anything.

PHILONOUS. Can the mind produce, discontinue, or change anything, but by an act of the will?

HYLAS. It cannot.

PHILONOUS. The mind therefore is to be accounted *active* in its perceptions so far forth as *volition* is included in them?

HYLAS. It is.

PHILONOUS. In plucking this flower I am active, because I do it by the motion of my hand, which was consequent upon my volition; so likewise in applying it to my nose. But is either of these smelling?

HYLAS. No.

PHILONOUS. I act too in drawing the air through my nose; because my breathing so rather than otherwise is the effect of my volition. But neither can this be called *smelling*: for, if it were, I should smell every time I breathed in that manner?

HYLAS. True.

PHILONOUS. Smelling then is somewhat consequent to all this?

HYLAS. It is.

PHILONOUS. But I do not find my will concerned any farther. Whatever more there is—as that I perceive such a particular smell, or any smell at all—this is independent of my will, and therein I am altogether passive. Do you find it otherwise with you, Hylas?

HYLAS. No, the very same.

PHILONOUS. Then, as to seeing, is it not in your power to open your eyes, or keep them shut; to turn them this or that way?

HYLAS. Without doubt.

PHILONOUS. But, doth it in like manner depend on *your* will that in looking on this flower you perceive *white* rather than any other colour? Or, directing your open eyes towards yonder part of the heaven, can you avoid seeing the sun? Or is light or darkness the effect of your volition?

HYLAS. No, certainly.

PHILONOUS. You are then in these respects altogether passive?

HYLAS. I am.

PHILONOUS. Tell me now, whether *seeing* consists in perceiving light and colours, or in opening and turning the eyes?

HYLAS. Without doubt, in the former.

PHILONOUS. Since therefore you are in the very perception of light and colours altogether passive, what is become of that action you were speaking of as an ingredient in every sensation? And, doth it not follow from your own concessions, that the perception of light and colours, including no action in it, may exist in an unperceiving substance? And is not this a plain contradiction?

HYLAS. I know not what to think of it.

PHILONOUS. Besides, since you distinguish the *active* and *passive* in every perception, you must do it in that of pain. But how is it possible that pain, be it as little active as you please, should exist in an unperceiving substance? In short, do but consider the point, and then confess ingenuously, whether light and colours, tastes, sounds, &c. are not all equally passions or sensations in the soul. You may indeed call them *external objects*, and give them in words what subsistence you please. But, examine your own thoughts, and then tell me whether it be not as I say?

HYLAS. I acknowledge, Philonous, that, upon a fair observation of what passes in my mind, I can discover nothing else but that I am a thinking being, affected with variety of sensations; neither is it possible to conceive how a sensation should exist in an unperceiving substance. But then, on the other hand, when I look on sensible things in a different view, considering them as so many modes and qualities, I find it necessary to suppose a *material substratum*, without which they cannot be conceived to exist.

PHILONOUS. *Material substratum* call you it? Pray, by which of your senses came you acquainted with that being?

HYLAS. It is not itself sensible; its modes and qualities only being perceived by the senses.

PHILONOUS. I presume then it was by reflexion and reason you obtained the idea of it?

HYLAS. I do not pretend to any proper positive *idea* of it. However, I conclude it exists, because qualities cannot be conceived to exist without a support.

PHILONOUS. It seems then you have only a relative *notion* of it, or that you conceive it not otherwise than by conceiving the relation it bears to sensible qualities?

HYLAS. Right.

PHILONOUS. Be pleased therefore to let me know wherein that relation consists.

HYLAS. Is it not sufficiently expressed in the term *substratum*, or *substance*?

PHILONOUS. If so, the word *substratum* should import that it is spread under the sensible qualities or accidents?

HYLAS. True.

PHILONOUS. And consequently under extension?

HYLAS. I own it.

PHILONOUS. It is therefore somewhat in its own nature entirely distinct from extension?

HYLAS. I tell you, extension is only a mode, and matter is something that supports modes.[24] And is it not evident the thing supported is different from the thing supporting?

PHILONOUS. So that something distinct from, and exclusive of, extension is supposed to be the *substratum* of extension?

HYLAS. Just so.

PHILONOUS. Answer me, Hylas. Can a thing be spread without extension? or is not the idea of extension necessarily included in *spreading*?

HYLAS. It is.

PHILONOUS. Whatsoever therefore you suppose spread under anything must have in itself an extension distinct from the extension of that thing under which it is spread?

HYLAS. It must.

PHILONOUS. Consequently, every corporeal substance, being the *substratum* of extension, must have in itself another extension, by which it is qualified to be a *substratum*: and so on to infinity. And I ask whether this be not absurd in itself, and

repugnant to what you granted just now, to wit, that the *substratum* was something distinct from and exclusive of extension?

HYLAS. Aye but, Philonous, you take me wrong. I do not mean that matter is *spread* in a gross literal sense under extension. The word *substratum* is used only to express in general the same thing with *substance*.

PHILONOUS. Well then, let us examine the relation implied in the term *substance*. Is it not that it stands under accidents?

HYLAS. The very same.

PHILONOUS. But, that one thing may stand under or support another, must it not be extended?

HYLAS. It must.

PHILONOUS. Is not therefore this supposition liable to the same absurdity with the former?

HYLAS. You still take things in a strict literal sense. That is not fair, Philonous.

PHILONOUS. I am not for imposing any sense on your words: you are at liberty to explain them as you please. Only, I beseech you, make me understand something by them. You tell me matter supports or stands under accidents. How! is it as your legs support your body?

HYLAS. No; that is the literal sense.

PHILONOUS. Pray let me know any sense, literal or not literal, that you understand it in.—How long must I wait for an answer, Hylas?

HYLAS. I declare I know not what to say. I once thought I understood well enough what was meant by matter's supporting accidents. But now, the more I think on it the less can I comprehend it: in short I find that I know nothing of it.

PHILONOUS. It seems then you have no idea at all, neither relative nor positive, of matter; you know neither what it is in itself, nor what relation it bears to accidents?

HYLAS. I acknowledge it.

PHILONOUS. And yet you asserted that you could not conceive how qualities or accidents should really exist, without conceiving at the same time a material support of them?

HYLAS. I did.

PHILONOUS. That is to say, when you conceive the real existence of qualities, you do withal conceive something which you cannot conceive?

---

24   For Berkeley (as opposed to Locke) a mode is simply a quality, a kind of property.

HYLAS. It was wrong, I own. But still I fear there is some fallacy or other. Pray what think you of this? It is just come into my head that the ground of all our mistake lies in your treating of each quality by itself. Now, I grant that each quality cannot singly subsist without the mind. Colour cannot without extension, neither can figure without some other sensible quality. But, as the several qualities united or blended together form entire sensible things, nothing hinders why such things may not be supposed to exist without the mind.

PHILONOUS. Either, Hylas, you are jesting, or have a very bad memory. Though indeed we went through all the qualities by name one after another, yet my arguments or rather your concessions, nowhere tended to prove that the secondary qualities did not subsist each alone by itself; but, that they were not *at all* without the mind. Indeed, in treating of figure and motion we concluded they could not exist without the mind, because it was impossible even in thought to separate them from all secondary qualities, so as to conceive them existing by themselves. But then this was not the only argument made use of upon that occasion. But (to pass by all that hath been hitherto said, and reckon it for nothing, if you will have it so) I am content to put the whole upon this issue. If you can conceive it possible for any mixture or combination of qualities, or any sensible object whatever, to exist without the mind, then I will grant it actually to be so.

HYLAS. If it comes to that the point will soon be decided. What more easy than to conceive a tree or house existing by itself, independent of, and unperceived by, any mind whatsoever? I do at this present time conceive them existing after that manner.

PHILONOUS. How say you, Hylas; can you see a thing which is at the same time unseen?

HYLAS. No, that were a contradiction.

PHILONOUS. Is it not as great a contradiction to talk of *conceiving* a thing which is *unconceived*?

HYLAS. It is.

PHILONOUS. The, tree or house therefore which you think of is conceived by you?

HYLAS. How should it be otherwise?

PHILONOUS. And what is conceived is surely in the mind?

HYLAS. Without question, that which is conceived is in the mind.

PHILONOUS. How then came you to say, you conceived a house or tree existing independent and out of all minds whatsoever?

HYLAS. That was I own an oversight; but stay, let me consider what led me into it.—It is a pleasant[25] mistake enough. As I was thinking of a tree in a solitary place, where no one was present to see it, methought that was to conceive a tree as existing unperceived or unthought of; not considering that I myself conceived it all the while. But now I plainly see that all I can do is to frame ideas in my own mind. I may indeed conceive in my own thoughts the idea of a tree, or a house, or a mountain, but that is all. And this is far from proving that I can conceive them *existing out of the minds of all spirits*.

PHILONOUS. You acknowledge then that you cannot possibly conceive how any one corporeal sensible thing should exist otherwise than in the mind?

HYLAS. I do.

PHILONOUS. And yet you will earnestly contend for the truth of that which you cannot so much as conceive?

HYLAS. I profess I know not what to think; but still there are some scruples remain with me. Is it not certain I see things at a distance? Do we not perceive the stars and moon, for example, to be a great way off? Is not this, I say, manifest to the senses?

PHILONOUS. Do you not in a dream too perceive those or the like objects?

HYLAS. I do.

PHILONOUS. And have they not then the same appearance of being distant?

HYLAS. They have.

PHILONOUS. But you do not thence conclude the apparitions in a dream to be without the mind?

HYLAS. By no means.

PHILONOUS. You ought not therefore to conclude that sensible objects are without the mind, from their appearance, or manner wherein they are perceived.

HYLAS. I acknowledge it. But doth not my sense deceive me in those cases?

PHILONOUS. By no means. The idea or thing which you immediately perceive, neither sense nor reason informs you that it actually exists without the mind. By sense you only know that you are affected with

---

25 Amusing.

such certain sensations of light and colours, &c. And these you will not say are without the mind.

HYLAS. True: but, beside all that, do you not think the sight suggests something of *outness* or *distance*?

PHILONOUS. Upon approaching a distant object, do the visible size and figure change perpetually, or do they appear the same at all distances?

HYLAS. They are in a continual change.

PHILONOUS. Sight therefore doth not suggest, or any way inform you, that the visible object you immediately perceive exists at a distance, or will be perceived when you advance farther onward; there being a continued series of visible objects succeeding each other during the whole time of your approach.

HYLAS. It doth not; but still I know, upon seeing an object, what object I shall perceive after having passed over a certain distance: no matter whether it be exactly the same or no: there is still something of distance suggested in the case.

PHILONOUS. Good Hylas, do but reflect a little on the point, and then tell me whether there be any more in it than this: from the ideas you actually perceive by sight, you have by experience learned to collect what other ideas you will (according to the standing order of nature) be affected with, after such a certain succession of time and motion.

HYLAS. Upon the whole, I take it to be nothing else.

PHILONOUS. Now, is it not plain that if we suppose a man born blind was on a sudden made to see, he could at first have no experience of what may be suggested by sight?

HYLAS. It is.

PHILONOUS. He would not then, according to you, have any notion of distance annexed to the things he saw; but would take them for a new set of sensations, existing only in his mind?

HYLAS. It is undeniable.

PHILONOUS. But, to make it still more plain: is not *distance* a line turned endwise to the eye?

HYLAS. It is.

PHILONOUS. And can a line so situated be perceived by sight?

HYLAS. It cannot.

PHILONOUS. Doth it not therefore follow that distance is not properly and immediately perceived by sight?

HYLAS. It should seem so.

PHILONOUS. Again, is it your opinion that colours are at a distance?

HYLAS. It must be acknowledged they are only in the mind.

PHILONOUS. But do not colours appear to the eye as co-existing in the same place with extension and figures?

HYLAS. They do.

PHILONOUS. How can you then conclude from sight that figures exist without, when you acknowledge colours do not; the sensible appearance being the very same with regard to both?

HYLAS. I know not what to answer.

PHILONOUS. But, allowing that distance was truly and immediately perceived by the mind, yet it would not thence follow it existed out of the mind. For, whatever is immediately perceived is an idea: and can any idea exist out of the mind?

HYLAS. To suppose that were absurd: but, inform me, Philonous, can we perceive or know nothing beside our ideas?

PHILONOUS. As for the rational deducing of causes from effects, that is beside our inquiry. And, by the senses you can best tell whether you perceive anything which is not immediately perceived. And I ask you, whether the things immediately perceived are other than your own sensations or ideas? You have indeed more than once, in the course of this conversation, declared yourself on those points; but you seem, by this last question, to have departed from what you then thought.

HYLAS. To speak the truth, Philonous, I think there are two kinds of objects:—the one perceived immediately, which are likewise called *ideas*; the other are real things or external objects, perceived by the mediation of ideas, which are their images and representations. Now, I own ideas do not exist without the mind; but the latter sort of objects do. I am sorry I did not think of this distinction sooner; it would probably have cut short your discourse.

PHILONOUS. Are those external objects perceived by sense or by some other faculty?

HYLAS. They are perceived by sense.

PHILONOUS. How! is there any thing perceived by sense which is not immediately perceived?

HYLAS. Yes, Philonous, in some sort there is. For example, when I look on a picture or statue of Julius

Caesar, I may be said after a manner to perceive him (though not immediately) by my senses.

PHILONOUS. It seems then you will have our ideas, which alone are immediately perceived, to be pictures of external things: and that these also are perceived by sense, inasmuch as they have a conformity or resemblance to our ideas?

HYLAS. That is my meaning.

PHILONOUS. And, in the same way that Julius Caesar, in himself invisible, is nevertheless perceived by sight; real things, in themselves imperceptible, are perceived by sense.

HYLAS. In the very same.

PHILONOUS. Tell me, Hylas, when you behold the picture of Julius Caesar, do you see with your eyes any more than some colours and figures, with a certain symmetry and composition of the whole?

HYLAS. Nothing else.

PHILONOUS. And would not a man who had never known anything of Julius Caesar see as much?

HYLAS. He would.

PHILONOUS. Consequently he hath his sight, and the use of it, in as perfect a degree as you?

HYLAS. I agree with you.

PHILONOUS. Whence comes it then that your thoughts are directed to the Roman emperor, and his are not? This cannot proceed from the sensations or ideas of sense by you then perceived; since you acknowledge you have no advantage over him in that respect. It should seem therefore to proceed from reason and memory: should it not?

HYLAS. It should.

PHILONOUS. Consequently, it will not follow from that instance that anything is perceived by sense which is not immediately perceived. Though I grant we may, in one acceptation,[26] be said to perceive sensible things mediately by sense: that is, when, from a frequently perceived connexion, the immediate perception of ideas by one sense *suggests* to the mind others, perhaps belonging to another sense, which are wont to be connected with them. For instance, when I hear a coach drive along the streets, immediately I perceive only the sound; but, from the experience I have had that such a sound is connected with a coach, I am said to hear the coach. It is nevertheless evident that, in truth and strictness, nothing can be *heard* but *sound*; and the coach is not then properly perceived by sense, but suggested from experience. So likewise when we are said to see a red-hot bar of iron; the solidity and heat of the iron are not the objects of sight, but suggested to the imagination by the colour and figure which are properly perceived by that sense. In short, those things alone are actually and strictly perceived by any sense, which would have been perceived in case that same sense had then been first conferred on us. As for other things, it is plain they are only suggested to the mind by experience, grounded on former perceptions. But, to return to your comparison of Caesar's picture, it is plain, if you keep to that, you must hold the real things, or archetypes of our ideas, are not perceived by sense, but by some internal faculty of the soul, as reason or memory. I would therefore fain know what arguments you can draw from reason for the existence of what you call *real things* or *material objects*. Or, whether you remember to have seen them formerly as they are in themselves; or, if you have heard or read of any one that did.

HYLAS. I see, Philonous, you are disposed to raillery; but that will never convince me.

PHILONOUS. My aim is only to learn from you the way to come at the knowledge of *material beings*. Whatever we perceive is perceived immediately or mediately: by sense, or by reason and reflexion. But, as you have excluded sense, pray shew me what reason you have to believe their existence; or what *medium* you can possibly make use of to prove it, either to mine or your own understanding.

HYLAS. To deal ingenuously, Philonous, now I consider the point, I do not find I can give you any good reason for it. But, thus much seems pretty plain, that it is at least possible such things may really exist. And, as long as there is no absurdity in supposing them, I am resolved to believe as I did, till you bring good reasons to the contrary.

PHILONOUS. What! Is it come to this, that you only *believe* the existence of material objects, and that your belief is founded barely on the possibility of its being true? Then you will have me bring reasons against it: though another would think it reasonable the proof should lie on him who holds the affirmative. And,

---

26   In one way of using the word.

after all, this very point which you are now resolved to maintain, without any reason, is in effect what you have more than once during this discourse seen good reason to give up. But, to pass over all this; if I understand you rightly, you say our ideas do not exist without the mind, but that they are copies, images, or representations, of certain originals that do?

HYLAS. You take me right.

PHILONOUS. They are then like external things?

HYLAS. They are.

PHILONOUS. Have those things a stable and permanent nature, independent of our senses; or are they in a perpetual change, upon our producing any motions in our bodies—suspending, exerting, or altering, our faculties or organs of sense?

HYLAS. Real things, it is plain, have a fixed and real nature, which remains the same notwithstanding any change in our senses, or in the posture and motion of our bodies; which indeed may affect the ideas in our minds, but it were absurd to think they had the same effect on things existing without the mind.

PHILONOUS. How then is it possible that things perpetually fleeting and variable as our ideas should be copies or images of anything fixed and constant? Or, in other words, since all sensible qualities, as size, figure, colour, &c., that is, our ideas, are continually changing, upon every alteration in the distance, medium, or instruments of sensation; how can any determinate material objects be properly represented or painted forth by several distinct things, each of which is so different from and unlike the rest? Or, if you say it resembles some one only of our ideas, how shall we be able to distinguish the true copy from all the false ones?

HYLAS. I profess, Philonous, I am at a loss. I know not what to say to this.

PHILONOUS. But neither is this all. Which are material objects in themselves—perceptible or imperceptible?

HYLAS. Properly and immediately nothing can be perceived but ideas. All material things, therefore, are in themselves insensible, and to be perceived only by our ideas.

PHILONOUS. Ideas then are sensible, and their archetypes or originals insensible?

HYLAS. Right.

PHILONOUS. But how can that which is sensible be like that which is insensible? Can a real thing, in itself *in-visible*, be like a *colour*; or a real thing, which is not *audible*, be like a *sound*? In a word, can anything be like a sensation or idea, but another sensation or idea?

HYLAS. I must own, I think not.

PHILONOUS. Is it possible there should be any doubt on the point? Do you not perfectly know your own ideas?

HYLAS. I know them perfectly; since what I do not perceive or know can be no part of my idea.

PHILONOUS. Consider, therefore, and examine them, and then tell me if there be anything in them which can exist without the mind: or if you can conceive anything like them existing without the mind.

HYLAS. Upon inquiry, I find it is impossible for me to conceive or understand how anything but an idea can be like an idea. And it is most evident that *no idea can exist without the mind*.

PHILONOUS. You are therefore, by your principles, forced to deny the *reality* of sensible things; since you made it to consist in an absolute existence exterior to the mind. That is to say, you are a downright sceptic. So I have gained my point, which was to shew your principles led to scepticism.

HYLAS. For the present I am, if not entirely convinced, at least silenced.

PHILONOUS. I would fain know what more you would require in order to a perfect conviction. Have you not had the liberty of explaining yourself all manner of ways? Were any little slips in discourse laid hold and insisted on? Or were you not allowed to retract or reinforce anything you had offered, as best served your purpose? Hath not everything you could say been heard and examined with all the fairness imaginable? In a word have you not in every point been convinced out of your own mouth? And, if you can at present discover any flaw in any of your former concessions, or think of any remaining subterfuge, any new distinction, colour, or comment whatsoever, why do you not produce it?

HYLAS. A little patience, Philonous. I am at present so amazed to see myself ensnared, and as it were imprisoned in the labyrinths you have drawn me into, that on the sudden it cannot be expected I should find my way out. You must give me time to look about me and recollect myself.

PHILONOUS. Hark; is not this the college bell?

HYLAS. It rings for prayers.

PHILONOUS. We will go in then, if you please, and meet here again tomorrow morning. In the meantime, you may employ your thoughts on this morning's discourse, and try if you can find any fallacy in it, or invent any new means to extricate yourself.

HYLAS. Agreed.

IMMANUEL KANT
Critique of Pure Reason

Who Was Immanuel Kant?

Immanuel Kant—by common consent the most important philosopher of the past 300 years, and arguably the most important of the past 2,300—was born in 1724 on the coast of the Baltic Sea, in Königsberg, a regionally important harbor city in East Prussia.[1] Kant spent his whole life living in this town, and never ventured outside its region. His family were devout members of an evangelical Protestant sect (rather like the Quakers or early Methodists) called the Pietists, and Pietism's strong emphasis on moral responsibility, hard work, and distrust of religious dogma had a deep effect on Kant's character. Kant's father was a craftsman (making harnesses and saddles for horses) and his family was fairly poor; Kant's mother, whom he loved deeply, died when he was 13.

Kant's life is notorious for its outward uneventfulness. He was educated at a strict Lutheran school in Königsberg, and after graduating from the University of Königsberg in 1746 (where he supported himself by some tutoring but also by his skill at billiards and card games) he served as a private tutor to various local families until he became a lecturer at the university in 1755. However his position—that of *Privatdozent*—carried no salary, and Kant was expected to support himself by the income from his lecturing; financial need caused Kant to lecture for thirty or more hours a week on a huge range of subjects (including mathematics, physics, geography, anthropology, ethics, and law). During this period Kant published several scientific works and his reputation as a scholar grew; he turned down opportunities for professorships in other towns (Erlangen and Jena), having his heart set on a professorship in Königsberg. Finally, at the age of 46, Kant became professor of logic and metaphysics at the University of Königsberg, a position he held until his retirement twenty-six years later in 1796. After a tragic period of senility he died in 1804, and was buried with pomp and circumstance in the "professors' vault" at the Königsberg cathedral.[2]

Kant's days were structured by a rigorous and unvarying routine—indeed, it is often said that the housewives of Königsberg were able to set their clocks by the regularity of his afternoon walk. He never married (though twice he nearly did), had very few close friends, and lived by all accounts an austere and outwardly unemotional life. He was something of a hypochondriac, hated noise, and disliked all music

---

1   Prussia is a historical region which included what is today northern Germany, Poland, and the western fringes of Russia. It became a kingdom in 1701, and then a dominant part of the newly unified Germany in 1871. Greatly reduced after World War I, the state of Prussia was formally abolished after World War II, and Königsberg—renamed Kaliningrad during the Soviet era, after one of Stalin's henchmen—now sits on the western rump of Russia (between Poland and Lithuania).

2   His body no longer remains there: in 1950 his sarcophagus was broken open by unknown vandals and his corpse was stolen and never recovered.

except for military marches. Nevertheless, anecdotes by those who knew him give the impression of a warm, impressive, rather noble human being, capable of great kindness and dignity and sparkling conversation. He did not shun society, and in fact his regular daily routine included an extended lunchtime gathering at which he and his guests—drawn from the cosmopolitan stratum of Königsberg society—would discuss politics, science, philosophy, and poetry.

Kant's philosophical life is often divided into three phases: his "pre-Critical" period, his "silent" period, and his "Critical" period. His pre-Critical period began in 1747 when he published his first work (*Thoughts on the True Estimation of Living Forces*) and ended in 1770 when he wrote his Inaugural Dissertation—*Concerning the Form and Principles of the Sensible and Intelligible World*—and became a professor. Between 1770 and 1780, Kant published almost nothing. In 1781, however, at the age of 57, Kant made his first major contribution to philosophy with his monumental *Critique of Pure Reason* (written, Kant said, over the course of a few months "as if in flight"). He spent the next twenty years in unrelenting intellectual labor, trying to develop and answer the new problems laid out in this masterwork. First, in order to clarify and simplify the system of the *Critique* for the educated public, Kant published the much shorter *Prolegomena to Any Future Metaphysics* in 1783. In 1785 came Kant's *Foundations of the Metaphysics of Morals* (which is excerpted in Chapter 7 of this anthology), and in 1788 he published what is now known as his "second Critique": the *Critique of Practical Reason*. His third and final Critique, the *Critique of Judgement*, was published in 1790—an amazing body of work produced in less than ten years.

By the time he died, Kant had already become known as a great philosopher, with a permanent place in history. Over his grave was inscribed a quote from the *Critique of Practical Reason*, which sums up the impulse for his philosophy: "Two things fill the

mind with ever new and increasing admiration and reverence, the more often and more steadily one reflects on them: the starry heavens above me and the moral law within me."

What Was Kant's Overall Philosophical Project?

Kant began his philosophical career as a follower of rationalism. Rationalism was an important seventeenth- and eighteenth-century intellectual movement begun by Descartes and developed by Leibniz and his follower Christian Wolff, which held that all knowledge was capable of being part of a single, complete "science": that is, all knowledge can be slotted into a total, unified system of *a priori*, and certainly true, claims capable of encompassing everything that exists in the world, whether we have experience of it or not. In other words, for the German rationalists of Kant's day, metaphysical philosophy—which then included theoretical science—was thought of as being very similar to pure mathematics. Rationalism was also, in Kantian terminology, "dogmatic" as opposed to "critical": that is, it sought to construct systems of knowledge without first attempting a careful examination of the scope and limits of possible knowledge. (This is why Kant's rationalist period is usually called his pre-Critical phase.)

In 1781, after ten years of hard thought, Kant rejected this rationalistic view of philosophy: he came to the view that metaphysics, as traditionally understood, is so far from being a rational science that it is not even a body of knowledge at all. Three major stimuli provoked Kant into being "awakened from his dogmatic slumber," as he put it. First, in about 1769, Kant came to the conclusion that he had discovered several "antinomies"—sets of contradictory propositions *each* of which can apparently be *rationally proven* to be true of reality (if we assume that our intellectual concepts apply to reality at all) and yet which can't both be true. For example, Kant argued that rational arguments are available to prove both that reality is finite but also that it is infinite, and that it is composed of indivisible atoms yet also infinitely divisible. Since both halves of these two pairs can't possibly be true at the same time, Kant argued that this casts serious doubt on the power of pure reason to draw metaphysical conclusions.

Second, Kant was worried about the conflict between free will and natural causality (this is a theme that appears throughout Kant's Critical works). He was convinced that genuine morality must be based on *freely* choosing—or "willing"— to do what is right. To be worthy of moral praise, in Kant's view, one must choose to do *X* rather than *Y*, not because some law of nature causes you to do so, but because your rational self is convinced that it is the right thing to do.[3] Yet he also thought that the rational understanding of reality sought by the metaphysicians could only be founded on universally extending the laws we find in the scientific study of nature—and this includes universal causal determination, the principle that nothing (including choosing *X* over *Y*) happens without a cause. This, for Kant, produces an antinomy: some actions are free (i.e., *not* bound by the laws of nature) and yet everything that happens *is* determined by a law of nature.

Kant resolved this paradox by arguing that the scientific view of reality (including that pursued by the rationalists) must in principle be *incomplete*. Roughly, he held that although we can only rationally understand reality by thinking of it as causally deterministic and governed by scientific laws, our intellectual reason can never encompass *all* of reality. According to Kant, there must be a level of ultimate reality which is beyond the scope of pure reason, and which allows for the free activity of what Kant calls "practical reason" (which therefore holds open the possibility of genuine morality).

The third alarm bell to rouse Kant from his pre-Critical dogmatism was his reading of the Scottish philosopher David Hume (see Chapter 2). Hume was not a rationalist but instead represented the culmination of the other main seventeenth- and

eighteenth-century stream of philosophical thought, usually called empiricism. Instead of thinking of knowledge as a unified, systematic, *a priori* whole, as the rationalists did, empiricists like Locke and Hume saw knowledge as being a piecemeal accumulation of claims derived primarily, not from pure logic, but from *sensation*—from our experience of the world. Science, for Hume, is thus not *a priori* but *a posteriori*: for example, we cannot just *deduce* from first principles that heavy objects tend to fall to the ground, as the rationalists supposed we could; we can only learn this by observing it to happen in our experience. The trouble was that Hume appeared to Kant (and to many others) to have shown that experience is simply *inadequate* for establishing the kind of metaphysical principles that philosophers have traditionally defended: no amount of sense-experience could ever either prove or disprove that God exists, that substance is imperishable, that we have an immortal soul, or even that there exist mind-independent "physical" objects which interact with each other according to causal laws of nature. Not just what we now think of as "philosophy" but theoretical science itself seemed to be called into question by Hume's "skeptical" philosophy. Since Kant was quite sure that mathematics and the natural sciences were genuine bodies of knowledge, he needed to show how such knowledge was possible despite Hume's skepticism: that is, as well as combating the excessive claims of rationalism, he needed to show how empiricism went wrong in the other direction.

Prior to Kant, seventeenth- and eighteenth-century philosophers divided knowledge into exactly two camps: "truths of reason" (or "relations of ideas") on the one hand, and "truths of fact" (or "matters of fact") on the other. Rationalism was characterized by the doctrine that all final, complete knowledge was a truth of reason: that is, it was made up entirely of claims that could be proven *a priori* as being necessarily true, as a matter of logic, since it would be self-contradictory for them to be false. Empiricists, on the other hand, believed that all genuinely *informative* claims were truths of fact: if we wanted to find out about the world itself, rather than merely the logical relations between our own concepts, we had to rely upon the (*a posteriori*) data of sensory experience.

---

3   For more on Kant's ethical views, see his *Foundations of the Metaphysics of Morals* in Chapter 7.

Kant, however, reshaped this distinction in a new framework which, he argued, cast a vital new light upon the nature of metaphysics. Instead of merely drawing a distinction between truths of reason and truths of fact, Kant replaced this with *two* separate distinctions: that between "*a priori*" and "*a posteriori*" propositions, and that between "analytic" and "synthetic" judgments. On this more complex scheme, the rationalists' truths of reason turn out to be "analytic *a priori*" knowledge, while empirical truths of fact are "synthetic *a posteriori*" propositions. But, Kant pointed out, this leaves open the possibility that there is at least a *third* type of knowledge: synthetic *a priori* judgments. These are judgments which we know *a priori* and thus do not need to learn from experience, but which nevertheless go beyond merely "analytic" claims about our own concepts. Kant's central claim in the *Critique of Pure Reason* is that he is the first philosopher in history to understand that the traditional claims of metaphysics—questions about God, the soul, free will, the underlying nature of space, time and matter—consist entirely of synthetic *a priori* propositions. (He also argues that pure mathematics is synthetic *a priori* as well.)

Kant's question therefore becomes: How is synthetic *a priori* knowledge possible? After all, the source of this knowledge can be neither experience (since it is *a priori*) nor the logical relations of ideas (since it is synthetic), so where could this kind of knowledge possibly come from? Once we have discovered the conditions of synthetic *a priori* knowledge, we can ask what its limits are: in particular, we can ask whether the traditional claims of speculative metaphysics meet those conditions, and thus whether they can be known to be true.

In bald (and massively simplified) summary, Kant's answer to these questions in the *Critique of Pure Reason* is the following. Synthetic *a priori* knowledge is possible insofar as it is knowledge of the *conditions of our experience of the world* (or indeed, of any *possible* experience). For example, for Kant, our judgments about the fundamental nature of space and time are not claims about our experiences themselves, nor are they the results of logic: instead, the forms of space and time are the conditions under which we are capable of having experience *at all*—we *can* only undergo sensations (either perceived or imaginary) that are arranged in space, and spread out in time; anything else is just impossible for us. So we can know *a priori*, but not analytically, that space and time must have a certain nature, since they are the forms of (the very possibility of) our experience.

Kant, famously, described this insight as constituting a kind of "Copernican revolution" in philosophy: just as Copernicus set cosmology on a totally new path by suggesting (in 1543) that the Earth orbits the Sun and not the other way around, so Kant wanted to breathe new life into philosophy by suggesting that, rather than assuming that "all our knowledge must conform to objects," we might instead "suppose that objects must conform to our knowledge." That is, rather than merely passively representing mind-independent objects in a "real" world, Kant held that the mind actively *constitutes* its objects—by *imposing* the categories of time, space, and causation onto our sensory experience, the subject actually *creates* the only kind of reality to which it has access. (This is why Kant's philosophy is often called "transcendental idealism." However, Kant is not a full-out idealist in the way that, say, Berkeley is. He does not claim that the *existence* of objects is mind-dependent—only God's mind is capable of this kind of creation, according to Kant. Instead, the *a priori properties* of objects are what we constitute, by the structures of our cognition.)

When we turn to speculative metaphysics, however, we try to go beyond experience and its conditions—we attempt to move beyond what Kant called the "phenomena" of experience, and to make judgments about the nature of a reality that lies behind our sensory experience, what Kant called the "noumenal" realm. And here pure reason reaches its limits. If we ask about the nature of "things in themselves," independently of our experience of them, or if we try to show whether a supra-sensible God really exists, then our faculty of reason is powerless to demonstrate that these synthetic *a priori* judgments are either true or false—these metaphysical questions are neither empirical, nor logical, nor about the basic categories of our experience, so there is simply no way to answer them. The questions are meaningful ones (human beings crave answers to them) but they are beyond the scope of our faculty of reason. In short, we can have knowledge only of things that can be objects of possible experience, and cannot know anything that transcends the phenomenal realm.

This result, according to Kant, finally lets philosophy cease its constant oscillation between dogmatism and skepticism. It sets out the area in which human cognition is capable of attaining lasting truth (theoretical science—the metaphysics of experience—and mathematics), and that in which reason leads to self-contradiction and illusion (speculative metaphysics). Importantly, for Kant, this Copernican revolution provides *morality* with all the metaphysical support it needs, by clearing an area for free will.

What Is the Structure of This Reading?

Kant begins by conceding to the empiricists that, as a matter of psychological fact, we acquire a lot of knowledge through our experience of the world. But, he claims, this does not by itself show that all our knowledge is really *empirical*, and in Section I he draws a distinction between "pure" and "empirical" knowledge in order to make this issue clearer. In the next section he lays out two criteria for distinguishing between pure and empirical knowledge and uses these criteria to argue that we do in fact have a quantity of important pure *a priori* knowledge. However, in Section III, Kant claims that a lot of what we think can be known *a priori* is actually mere fabrication: what is needed, therefore, is a way of accurately *telling the difference* between reliable and unreliable *a priori* judgments. The first step in doing this, according to Kant, is to draw a distinction between analytic and synthetic judgments. He proceeds to do this in Section IV. He then argues, in Section V, that all our interesting *a priori* knowledge—mathematics, the principles of natural science, metaphysics—is synthetic. The "general problem of pure reason," therefore (Section VI) is to develop an account of how synthetic *a priori* judgments are possible, which will in turn tell us when they are reliable and when they are not. According to Kant, we must replace dogmatic philosophy with *critical* and *transcendental* philosophy: i.e., we must undertake a critique of pure reason, as Kant explains in Section VII.

Some Useful Background Information

1. *A priori* is Latin for "what is earlier" and *a posteriori* means "what comes after." These terms were used as early as the fourteenth century to mark a distinction (which dates back to Aristotle) between two different directions of *reasoning*: in this usage, now out of date, an *a priori* argument reasons from a ground to its consequence, while to argue *a posteriori* is to argue backwards from a consequence to its ground. For example, Descartes' "Trademark" argument for the existence of God in the Third Meditation is *a posteriori* in this archaic sense since it starts from his idea of God and moves to the 'only' possible cause of that idea, which is God himself. By contrast, St. Anselm of Canterbury's ontological argument is *a priori* in the medieval sense since, while it also begins with the idea of God, it does not argue 'backwards' to the cause of the idea but 'forwards' to the idea's (alleged) logical consequence, which is the necessary existence of God.

The *modern* usage of *a priori* and *a posteriori*, however, was formulated in the late seventeenth and eighteenth century, primarily by Leibniz and Kant, and has now wholly replaced the older meanings. The selection from Kant reprinted here includes the classic statement of the distinction (though the new usage first appeared much earlier—see, for example, section eight of Leibniz's *Discourse on Metaphysics*, published in 1686). One thing to notice is that the distinction is no longer one between two different directions of reasoning but instead distinguishes primarily between two different types of *knowledge*: the standard example of *a priori* knowledge is the truths of mathematics, and of *a posteriori* knowledge, the results of the natural sciences. This distinction between kinds of knowledge then motivates a similar distinction between two kinds of proposition, two kinds of concept, and two kinds of justification.

Kant himself prefers to use the words "pure" and "empirical" for *a priori* and *a posteriori* knowledge themselves, and usually reserves the terms "*a priori*" and "*a posteriori*" to describe the sources of this knowledge—the way in which it is acquired.

2. At the end of the Introduction to the *Critique*, Kant says that there are "two stems of human knowledge": sensibility and understanding. This is an important assumption of Kant's, and is reflected throughout the reading given here (in, for example, Kant's distinction between intuitions and concepts). Furthermore, it structures the way in which Kant proceeds with his critique of pure reason after the introduction: he deals first with what he calls the Transcendental Aesthetic,[4] which has to do with the faculty of sensibility, and secondly with the Transcendental Analytic, which applies to the faculty of understanding. The faculty of sensibility, according to Kant, is our capacity to passively receive objects into our mental world; this is achieved primarily through sensation, but these sensations are possible only if the objects are *intuited*: that is, roughly, represented as concretely existing in space and time. The faculty of understanding, on the other hand, is our capacity to actively produce knowledge through the application of *concepts*. When concepts are compared with each other, we produce logical knowledge; when concepts (such as space, time, and causation) are combined with intuitions we get empirical knowledge. (However, when concepts that arise out of our knowledge of the empirical world are applied to a realm beyond experience we do not get *any* kind of knowledge, according to Kant: he calls these metaphysical concepts *ideas*, the three most important of which are God, freedom, and immortality.)

A Common Misconception

Some people, on reading Kant for the first time, are thrown off by the word "transcendental." For Kant,

transcendental knowledge is knowledge about the necessary conditions for the possibility of experience (for example, "every event has a cause" is a transcendental claim, according to Kant). Thus, transcendental knowledge is *not*, as would be easy to assume, knowledge of *things which are transcendent* (i.e., of things which lie beyond the empirical world, such as God and other spirits). Therefore Kant's "transcendental philosophy" has nothing to do with, say, Transcendental Meditation.

How Important and Influential Is This Passage?

Within just a few years of the publication of the *Critique of Pure Reason*, Kant was recognized by many of his intellectual contemporaries as one of the great philosophers of all time. The first *Critique* is a candidate for being the single most important philosophical book ever written, and can be thought of as decisively changing the path of Western philosophy. In particular, it did away with the assumption that knowledge is a fixed and stable thing which can be more or less passively received into the mind through either experience or reason, and replaced it with a picture that sees human beings as active *participants* in the construction of our representations of the world. That is, the mind is not a passive receptacle of data but is instead an active *filter* and *creator* of our reality. The implications of this view are still being explored by professional philosophers, such as Hilary Putnam and Richard Rorty, today.

The distinction between analytic and synthetic propositions which Kant formulates in the selection reprinted here, as well as being foundational to his new philosophical system, has also had a great impact on philosophy. From the end of the eighteenth century until the 1950s it was generally accepted as marking a fundamental and important difference between kinds of knowledge. Today, however, the distinction has been thrown into question by philosophers who doubt that we can really make good sense of one concept "containing" or being "synonymous" with another.

---

4   When Kant uses the word "aesthetic"—as in "the transcendental aesthetic"—he means generally "having to do with sense-perception" rather than merely "beautiful."

Suggestions for Critical Reflection

1. Kant's two distinctions—between *a priori* and *a posteriori* propositions, and between analytic and synthetic propositions—allow him to distinguish between *four* different types of knowledge. However, he only entertains the possibility of *three* of those classes of proposition: the analytic *a priori*, synthetic *a priori*, and synthetic *a posteriori*. What is it about the notion of *analytic a posteriori* knowledge which causes Kant to dismiss it as incoherent? Is Kant right about this?

2. There is another distinction between types of propositions which Kant was clearly aware of, and which is often listed along with the *a priori/a posteriori* and analytic/synthetic contrasts: this is the distinction between propositions which are *necessarily* true, and those which are only *contingently* true. (A proposition is necessarily true if it is true no matter what—if no change you could possibly make to the world would make it false. A proposition is contingent if it is possibly, but not necessarily, true.) How, if at all, might this necessary/contingent distinction complicate Kant's classification of knowledge? For example, could some synthetic *a posteriori* propositions be necessary and others be contingent?

3. How adequate is Kant's criterion for the distinction between analytic and synthetic propositions? If you try out this distinction on a number of examples, do you find you can easily tell which are analytic and which synthetic? (How about, for example, "nothing is red all over and green all over at the same time," "water is H₂O," "all tigers are mammals," "2 is less than 3," "contradictions are impossible," or "every event has a cause"?)

4. Kant argues that mathematical knowledge is synthetic rather than analytic. Do you think he is right, or do you think it is more plausible to say that mathematics deals entirely with the *analytic* relations between our mathematical *concepts*? If Kant is wrong about mathematics being synthetic, how much harm do you think

this causes to his overall philosophical framework—for example, would he then be in danger of turning into just a German Hume?

5. Kant claims that some of the principles of natural science are synthetic *a priori*: that is, they are not learned from experience but are in some sense *prior* to experience. (As he hints at the beginning of the reading, Kant's view is that although all our knowledge *begins* with experience it does not all *arise* out of experience.) How plausible do you find this claim? How radical is it—what implications might it have for the way we think of the relationship between our minds and external reality?

6. Do you share Kant's skepticism about speculative metaphysics? If so, do you agree with his reasons for rejecting it? If not, where does Kant go wrong?

7. Are there really any such things as synthetic *a priori* propositions, or are all *a priori* propositions really analytic and all synthetic propositions really *a posteriori*?

Suggestions for Further Reading

Three translations into English of the *Critique of Pure Reason* are currently available: the old standard by Norman Kemp Smith (Macmillan, 1933), the relatively student-friendly version by Werner Pluhar (Hackett, 1997), and the new scholarly edition by Paul Guyer and Allen Wood (Cambridge University Press, 1998). The *Critique of Pure Reason* is notoriously difficult to read, partly because of its philosophical difficulty but also because of its relatively unattractive prose style and complex structure (the German poet Heinrich Heine accused it of having a "colorless, dry, packing-paper style" with a "stiff, abstract form"). Kant himself was aware of this problem, and his *Prolegomena to Any Future Metaphysics* was intended to be a shorter and more lively summary of the main themes of the *Critique*. Cambridge University Press published a good edition translated by Gary Hatfield in 1997; a well-used older translation is by Lewis White Beck, originally published in 1950 by Bobbs-Merrill.

Kant's Life and Thought, by Ernst Cassirer (translated by James Haden and published by Yale University Press in 1981) is a well-respected intellectual biography of Kant, while perhaps the best single, short introduction to the *Critique* itself is Sebastian Gardner's *Kant and the Critique of Pure Reason* (Routledge, 1999). A.C. Ewing's *Short Commentary on Kant's Critique of Pure Reason* (University of Chicago Press, 1938) is an older but still well-respected brief introduction to this work. Two detailed running commentaries on the *Critique* are by Norman Kemp Smith, *A Commentary to Kant's "Critique of Pure Reason"* (revised and enlarged second edition from Humanities Press, 1992) and H.J. Paton, *A Commentary on the First Half of the "Kritik der reinen Vernunft"* (Allen & Unwin, 1936).

Recent critical commentaries on the *Critique* can be divided into two camps depending, roughly, on whether their authors see Kant as primarily an epistemologist, analyzing the limits of our experience, or primarily a metaphysician, showing how the objects that we experience are *constituted* by the knower; that is, it depends on how seriously the authors take Kant's transcendental idealism. Prominent members of the former group are Peter Strawson, with his *The Bounds of Sense* (Methuen, 1966), and Paul Guyer in *Kant and the Claims of Knowledge* (Cambridge University Press, 1987). The idealists have been particularly active and influential in the past few years, and recent important books on Kant and his first Critique from this side include: Henry Allison, *Kant's Transcendental Idealism* (Yale University Press, 1983); Karl Ameriks, *Kant's Theory of Mind* (Oxford University Press, 1982); Robert Pippin, *Kant's Theory of Form* (Yale University Press, 1982); and Ralph Walker, *Kant* (Routledge, 1978).

A seminal modern article which attacks the viability of the distinction between analytic and synthetic propositions is W.V. Quine's "Two Dogmas of Empiricism," which can be found in *From a Logical Point of View* (Harvard University Press, 1953); H.P. Grice and P.F. Strawson replied to Quine in "In Defense of a Dogma," *Philosophical Review* 65 (1956).

There is an old but still useful anthology of essays about Kant's philosophy called *Kant: A Collection of Critical Essays*, edited by Robert Paul Wolff (Doubleday, 1967). Finally, Paul Guyer has edited a collection of articles on Kant designed to summarize the high points of his philosophy: *The Cambridge Companion to Kant* (Cambridge University Press, 1992).

Critique of Pure Reason

Introduction[5]

I. The Distinction between Pure and Empirical Knowledge

There can be no doubt that all our knowledge begins with experience. For how should our faculty[6] of knowledge be awakened into action did not objects affecting our senses partly of themselves produce representations, partly arouse the activity of our understanding to compare these representations, and, by combining or separating them, work up the raw material of the sensible impressions[7] into that knowledge of objects which is entitled experience? In the order of time, therefore, we have no knowledge antecedent to experience, and with experience all our knowledge begins.

But though all our knowledge begins with experience, it does not follow that it all arises out of experience. For it may well be that even our empirical knowledge is made up of what we receive through impressions and of what our own faculty of knowledge (sensible impressions serving merely as the occasion) supplies from itself. If our faculty of knowledge makes any such addition, it may be that we are not in a position to distinguish it from the raw material,

---

5   Kant's *Critique of Pure Reason*, as first published in German in 1781, is usually called the "A" edition. A significantly different second edition, the "B" edition, was published in 1787. The translation used here, of the Introduction to the "B" edition, was made in 1929 by Norman Kemp Smith (Basingstoke, Hants: Palgrave. Copyright © 1929; revised edition 1933). Reproduced with permission of Palgrave Macmillan.

6   A "faculty," in this sense, is an inherent mental power or capacity, such as the faculty of speech or the faculty of memory.

7   A "sensible impression" is an effect produced on the mind which is received by the faculty of sensory perception. Sensible impressions are, roughly, the data we receive from the world (such as, perhaps, colors, sounds, pains, and so on) out of which our conscious perceptual experience (say the experience of being bitten by a squirrel) is constructed.

until with long practice of attention we have become skilled in separating it.

This, then, is a question which at least calls for closer examination, and does not allow of any off-hand answer:—whether there is any knowledge that is thus independent of experience and even of all impressions of the senses. Such knowledge is entitled *a priori*, and distinguished from the *empirical*, which has its sources *a posteriori*, that is, in experience.

The expression '*a priori*' does not, however, indicate with sufficient precision the full meaning of our question. For it has been customary to say, even of much knowledge that is derived from empirical sources, that we have it or are capable of having it *a priori*, meaning thereby that we do not derive it immediately from experience, but from a universal rule—a rule which is itself, however, borrowed by us from experience. Thus we would say of a man who undermined the foundations of his house, that he might have known *a priori* that it would fall, that is, that he need not have waited for the experience of its actual falling. But still he could not know this completely *a priori*. For he had first to learn through experience that bodies are heavy, and therefore fall when their supports are withdrawn.

In what follows, therefore, we shall understand by *a priori* knowledge, not knowledge independent of this or that experience, but knowledge absolutely independent of all experience. Opposed to it is empirical knowledge, which is knowledge possible only *a posteriori*, that is, through experience. *A priori* modes of knowledge are entitled pure when there is no admixture of anything empirical. Thus, for instance, the proposition, 'every alteration has its cause', while an *a priori* proposition, is not a pure proposition, because alteration is a concept which can be derived only from experience.

II. We Are in Possession of Certain Modes of *a priori* Knowledge, and Even the Common Understanding Is Never Without Them

What we here require is a criterion by which to distinguish with certainty between pure and empirical knowledge. Experience teaches us that a thing is so and so, but not that it cannot be otherwise. First, then, if we have a proposition which in being thought is

thought as *necessary*, it is an *a priori* judgment; and if, besides, it is not derived from any proposition except one which also has the validity of a necessary judgment, it is an absolutely *a priori* judgment. Secondly, experience never confers on its judgments true or strict but only assumed and comparative *universality*, through induction.[8] We can properly only say, therefore, that so far as we have hitherto observed, there is no exception to this or that rule. If, then, a judgment is thought with strict universality, that is, in such manner that no exception is allowed as possible, it is not derived from experience, but is valid absolutely *a priori*. Empirical universality is only an arbitrary extension of a validity holding in most cases to one which holds in all, for instance, in the proposition, 'all bodies are heavy'. When, on the other hand, strict universality is essential to a judgment, this indicates a special source of knowledge, namely, a faculty of *a priori* knowledge. Necessity and strict universality are thus sure criteria of *a priori* knowledge, and are inseparable from one another. But since in the employment of these criteria the contingency of judgments is sometimes more easily shown than their empirical limitation, or, as sometimes also happens, their unlimited universality can be more convincingly proved than their necessity, it is advisable to use the two criteria separately, each by itself being infallible.

Now it is easy to show that there actually are in human knowledge judgments which are necessary and in the strictest sense universal, and which are therefore pure *a priori* judgments. If an example from the sciences be desired, we have only to look to any of the propositions of mathematics; if we seek an example from the understanding in its quite ordinary employment, the proposition, 'every alteration must have a cause', will serve our purpose. In the latter case, indeed, the very concept of a cause so manifestly contains the concept of a necessity of connection with an effect and of the strict universality of the rule, that

---

8   Induction is the inference of a general law from particular instances. For example, if you see that one chickadee is chirpy, and you see that the next chickadee is chirpy, and so on, eventually you might conclude that all chickadees are chirpy. See Chapter 4 for more discussion of induction.

the concept would be altogether lost if we attempted to derive it, as Hume has done,[9] from a repeated association of that which happens with that which precedes, and from a custom of connecting representations, a custom originating in this repeated association, and constituting therefore a merely subjective necessity. Even without appealing to such examples, it is possible to show that pure *a priori* principles are indispensable for the possibility of experience, and so to prove their existence *a priori*. For whence could experience derive its certainty, if all the rules, according to which it proceeds, were always themselves empirical, and therefore contingent? Such rules could hardly be regarded as first principles. At present, however, we may be content to have established the fact that our faculty of knowledge does have a pure employment, and to have shown what are the criteria of such an employment.

Such *a priori* origin is manifest in certain concepts, no less than in judgments. If we remove from our empirical concept of a body, one by one, every feature in it which is [merely] empirical, the colour, the hardness or softness, the weight, even the impenetrability, there still remains the space which the body (now entirely vanished) occupied, and this cannot be removed. Again, if we remove from our empirical concept of any object, corporeal or incorporeal, all properties which experience has taught us, we yet cannot take away that property through which the object is thought as substance or as inhering in a substance (although this concept of substance is more determinate than that of an object in general). Owing, therefore, to the necessity with which this concept of substance forces itself upon us, we have no option save to admit that it has its seat in our faculty of *a priori* knowledge.

---

9   Kant is referring to Hume's *An Enquiry Concerning Human Understanding*, which was published in 1748 and translated into German by 1755. (Hume's earlier book, the *Treatise of Human Nature*, was not translated into German until 1791, and Kant probably had no first-hand acquaintance with most of it.) See the Hume reading in Chapter 4 for more information on this philosopher and his views, and especially for some of his views on causation.

III. Philosophy Stands in Need of a Science Which Shall Determine the Possibility, the Principles, and the Extent of All *a priori* Knowledge

But what is still more extraordinary than all the preceding is this, that certain modes of knowledge leave the field of all possible experiences and have the appearance of extending the scope of our judgments beyond all limits of experience, and this by means of concepts to which no corresponding object can ever be given in experience.

It is precisely by means of the latter modes of knowledge, in a realm beyond the world of the senses, where experience can yield neither guidance nor correction, that our reason carries on those enquiries which owing to their importance we consider to be far more excellent, and in their purpose far more lofty, than all that the understanding can learn in the field of appearances. Indeed we prefer to run every risk of error rather than desist from such urgent enquiries, on the ground of their dubious character, or from disdain and indifference. These unavoidable problems set by pure reason itself are *God, freedom*, and *immortality*. The science which, with all its preparations, is in its final intention directed solely to their solution is metaphysics; and its procedure is at first dogmatic, that is, it confidently sets itself to this task without any previous examination of the capacity or incapacity of reason for so great an undertaking.

Now it does indeed seem natural that, as soon as we have left the ground of experience, we should, through careful enquiries, assure ourselves as to the foundations of any building that we propose to erect, not making use of any knowledge that we possess without first determining whence it has come, and not trusting to principles without knowing their origin. It is natural, that is to say, that the question should first be considered, how the understanding can arrive at all this knowledge *a priori*, and what extent, validity, and worth it may have. Nothing, indeed, could be more natural, if by the term 'natural' we signify what fittingly and reasonably ought to happen. But if we mean by 'natural' what ordinarily happens, then on the contrary nothing is more natural and more intelligible than the fact that this enquiry has been so long neglected.

For one part of this knowledge, the mathematical, has long been of established reliability, and so gives rise to a favourable presumption as regards the other part,[10] which may yet be of quite different nature. Besides, once we are outside the circle of experience, we can be sure of not being *contradicted* by experience. The charm of extending our knowledge is so great that nothing short of encountering a direct contradiction can suffice to arrest us in our course; and this can be avoided, if we are careful in our fabrications—which none the less will still remain fabrications. Mathematics gives us a shining example of how far, independently of experience, we can progress in *a priori* knowledge. It does, indeed, occupy itself with objects and with knowledge solely in so far as they allow of being exhibited in intuition.[11] But this circumstance is easily overlooked, since the intuition, in being thought, can itself be given *a priori*, and is therefore hardly to be distinguished from a bare and pure concept. Misled by such a proof of the power of reason, the demand for the extension of knowledge recognises no limits. The light dove, cleaving the air in her free flight, and feeling its resistance, might imagine that its flight would be still easier in empty space. It was thus that Plato left the world of the senses, as setting too narrow limits to the understanding, and ventured out beyond it on the wings of the ideas, in the empty space of the pure understanding. He did not observe that with all his efforts he made no advance—meeting no resistance that might, as it were, serve as a support upon which he could take a stand, to which he could apply his powers, and so set his understanding in motion. It is, indeed, the common fate of human reason to complete its spec-

ulative structures as speedily as may be, and only afterwards to enquire whether the foundations are reliable. All sorts of excuses will then be appealed to, in order to reassure us of their solidity, or rather indeed to enable us to dispense altogether with so late and so dangerous an enquiry. But what keeps us, during the actual building, free from all apprehension and suspicion, and flatters us with a seeming thoroughness, is this other circumstance, namely, that a great, perhaps the greatest, part of the business of our reason consists in analysis of the concepts which we already have of objects. This analysis supplies us with a considerable body of knowledge, which, while nothing but explanation or elucidation of what has already been thought in our concepts, though in a confused manner, is yet prized as being, at least as regards its form, new insight. But so far as the matter or content is concerned, there has been no extension of our previously possessed concepts, but only an analysis of them. Since this procedure yields real knowledge *a priori*, which progresses in an assured and useful fashion, reason is so far misled as surreptitiously to introduce, without itself being aware of so doing, assertions of an entirely different order, in which it attaches to given concepts others completely foreign to them, and moreover attaches them *a priori*. And yet it is not known how reason can be in position to do this. Such a question is never so much as thought of. I shall therefore at once proceed to deal with the difference between these two kinds of knowledge.

IV. The Distinction between Analytic and Synthetic Judgments

In all judgments in which the relation of a subject to the predicate[12] is thought (I take into consideration affirmative judgments only, the subsequent application to negative judgments being easily made), this

---

10   Metaphysics.

11   By "intuition" (*Anschauung*) Kant means the direct perception of an object. An intuition is a mental representation that is *particular* and *concrete*, rather like an image. The main contrast, for Kant, is with *concepts*, which he thinks of as abstract and general representations. For example, the concept of redness is an idea that can apply to many things at once (lots of different things can be red all at the same time); by contrast, an intuition of redness is a sensory impression of some particular instance of red—it is an apprehension of *this* redness.

---

12   A predicate is a describing-phrase, and the subject of a sentence is the thing being described. An affirmative judgment says that some predicate is true of (or "satisfied by") a subject, while a negative judgment says that a subject does not satisfy that predicate. For example, "this nectarine is ripe" is an affirmative judgment (where the nectarine is the subject and '___ is ripe' is the predicate); "this nectarine is not juicy" is a negative judgment.

relation is possible in two different ways. Either the predicate B belongs to the subject A, as something which is (covertly) contained in this concept A; or outside the concept A, although it does indeed stand in connection with it. In the one case I entitle the judgment analytic, in the other synthetic. Analytic judgments (affirmative) are therefore those in which the connection of the predicate with the subject is thought through identity;[13] those in which this connection is thought without identity should be entitled synthetic. The former, as adding nothing through the predicate to the concept of the subject, but merely breaking it up into those constituent concepts that have all along been thought in it, although confusedly, can also be entitled explicative. The latter, on the other hand, add to the concept of the subject a predicate which has not been in any wise thought in it, and which no analysis could possibly extract from it; and they may therefore be entitled ampliative. If I say, for instance, 'All bodies are extended', this is an analytic judgment. For I do not require to go beyond the concept which I connect with 'body' in order to find extension as bound up with it. To meet with this predicate, I have merely to analyse the concept, that is, to become conscious to myself of the manifold which I always think in that concept. The judgment is therefore analytic. But when I say, 'All bodies are heavy', the predicate is something quite different from anything that I think in the mere concept of body in general; and the addition of such a predicate therefore yields a synthetic judgment.

Judgments of experience, as such, are one and all synthetic. For it would be absurd to found an analytic judgment on experience. Since, in framing the judgment, I must not go outside my concept, there is no need to appeal to the testimony of experience in its support. That a body is extended is a proposition that holds *a priori* and is not empirical. For, before appealing to experience, I have already in the concept of body all the conditions required for my judgment. I have only to extract from it, in accordance with the principle of contradiction,[14] the required predicate, and in so doing can at the same time become conscious of the necessity of the judgment—and that is what experience could never have taught me. On the other hand, though I do not include in the concept of a body in general the predicate 'weight', none the less this concept indicates an object of experience through one of its parts, and I can add to that part other parts of this same experience, as in this way belonging together with the concept. From the start I can apprehend the concept of body analytically through the characters of extension, impenetrability, figure, etc., all of which are thought in the concept. Now, however, looking back on the experience from which I have derived this concept of body, and finding weight to be invariably connected with the above characters, I attach it as a predicate to the concept; and in doing so I attach it synthetically, and am therefore extending my knowledge. The possibility of the synthesis of the predicate 'weight' with the concept of 'body' thus rests upon experience. While the one concept is not contained in the other, they yet belong to one another, though only contingently, as parts of a whole, namely, of an experience which is itself a synthetic combination of intuitions.

But in *a priori* synthetic judgments this help is entirely lacking. [I do not here have the advantage of looking around in the field of experience.] Upon what, then, am I to rely, when I seek to go beyond the concept A, and to know that another concept B is connected with it? Through what is the synthesis made possible? Let us take the proposition, 'Everything which happens has its cause'. In the concept

13 By "identity" here Kant means self-identity: for example, to say that rapper Eminem *is identical with* Slim Shady (or that Garth Brooks is identical with Chris Gaines, or even that Cicero is identical with Tully) is to say that they are not two different people but are one and the same person being named in different ways. Another example, more relevant to Kant's concerns in this passage, is that being a vixen *is identical with* being a female fox: these are just two different ways of describing one and the same property.

14 The principle of contradiction states that a proposition and its negation cannot both be true. For example it can't *both* be true that it is now Sunday *and* true that it is not now Sunday; if it is true that the spiny anteater lays eggs then it is not true that it is false that the spiny anteater lays eggs. As Aristotle once pithily put it, "nothing can both be and not be at the same time in the same respect."

of 'something which happens', I do indeed think an existence which is preceded by a time, etc., and from this concept analytic judgments may be obtained. But the concept of a 'cause' lies entirely outside the other concept, and signifies something different from 'that which happens', and is not therefore in any way contained in this latter representation. How come I then to predicate of that which happens something quite different, and to apprehend that the concept of cause, though not contained in it, yet belongs, and indeed necessarily belongs to it? What is here the unknown = X which gives support to the understanding when it believes that it can discover outside the concept A a predicate B foreign to this concept, which it yet at the same time considers to be connected with it? It cannot be experience, because the suggested principle has connected the second representation with the first, not only with greater universality, but also with the character of necessity, and therefore completely *a priori* and on the basis of mere concepts. Upon such synthetic, that is, ampliative principles, all our *a priori* speculative knowledge must ultimately rest; analytic judgments are very important, and indeed necessary, but only for obtaining that clearness in the concepts which is requisite for such a sure and wide synthesis as will lead to a genuinely new addition to all previous knowledge.

V. In All Theoretical Sciences of Reason Synthetic *a priori* Judgments Are Contained as Principles

1. *All mathematical judgments, without exception, are synthetic*. This fact, though incontestably certain and in its consequences very important, has hitherto escaped the notice of those who are engaged in the analysis of human reason, and is, indeed, directly opposed to all their conjectures. For as it was found that all mathematical inferences proceed in accordance with the principle of contradiction[15] (which the nature of all apodeictic[16] certainty requires), it was supposed

that the fundamental propositions of the science can themselves be known to be true through that principle. This is an erroneous view. For though a synthetic proposition can indeed be discerned in accordance with the principle of contradiction, this can only be if another synthetic proposition is presupposed, and if it can then be apprehended as following from this other proposition; it can never be so discerned in and by itself. First of all, it has to be noted that mathematical propositions, strictly so called, are always judgments *a priori*, not empirical; because they carry with them necessity, which cannot be derived from experience. If this be demurred to, I am willing to limit my statement to *pure* mathematics, the very concept of which implies that it does not contain empirical, but only pure *a priori* knowledge.

We might, indeed, at first suppose that the proposition 7 + 5 = 12 is a merely analytic proposition, and follows by the principle of contradiction from the concept of a sum of 7 and 5. But if we look more closely we find that the concept of the sum of 7 and 5 contains nothing save the union of the two numbers into one, and in this no thought is being taken as to what that single number may be which combines both. The concept of 12 is by no means already thought in merely thinking this union of 7 and 5; and I may analyse my concept of such a possible sum as long as I please, still I shall never find the 12 in it. We have to go outside these concepts, and call in the aid of the intuition which corresponds to one of them, our five fingers, for instance, or, as Segner does in his *Arithmetic*,[17] five points, adding to the concept of 7, unit by unit, the five given in intuition. For starting with the number 7, and for the concept of 5 calling in the aid of the fingers of my hand as intuition, I now add one by one to the number 7 the units which I previously took together to form the number 5, and with the aid of that figure [the hand] see the number 12

---

15   By showing that they must be true, since if they were false this would lead to a contradiction.

16   For Kant, an apodeictic proposition states what *must* be the case, i.e., what is necessary. (By contrast, in Kant's

terminology, an "assertoric" proposition says what *is* the case—i.e., what is actual—and a "problematic" proposition asserts what *can* be the case, i.e., what is possible.)

17   The book Kant refers to is *Anfangsgründe der Arithmetik*, translated from the original Latin, the second edition of which was published in 1773.

come into being. That 5 should be added to 7, I have indeed already thought in the concept of a sum = 7 + 5, but not that this sum is equivalent to the number 12. Arithmetical propositions are therefore always synthetic. This is still more evident if we take larger numbers. For it is then obvious that, however we might turn and twist our concepts, we could never, by the mere analysis of them, and without the aid of intuition, discover what [the number is that] is the sum.

Just as little is any fundamental proposition of pure geometry analytic. That the straight line between two points is the shortest, is a synthetic proposition. For my concept of *straight* contains nothing of quantity, but only of quality. The concept of the shortest is wholly an addition, and cannot be derived, through any process of analysis, from the concept of the straight line. Intuition, therefore, must here be called in; only by its aid is the synthesis possible. What here causes us commonly to believe that the predicate of such apodeictic judgments is already contained in our concept, and that the judgment is therefore analytic, is merely the ambiguous character of the terms used. We are required to join in thought a certain predicate to a given concept, and this necessity is inherent in the concepts themselves. But the question is not what we *ought* to join in thought to the given concept, but what we *actually* think in it, even if only obscurely; and it is then manifest that, while the predicate is indeed attached necessarily to the concept, it is so in virtue of an intuition which must be added to the concept, not as thought in the concept itself.

Some few fundamental propositions, presupposed by the geometrician, are, indeed, really analytic, and rest on the principle of contradiction. But, as identical propositions,[18] they serve only as links in the chain of method and not as principles; for instance, $a = a$; the whole is equal to itself; or $(a + b) > a$, that is, the whole is greater than its part. And even these propositions, though they are valid according to pure concepts, are only admitted in mathematics because they can be exhibited in intuition.

2. *Natural science (physics) contains* a priori *synthetic judgments as principles*. I need cite only two such judgments: that in all changes of the mate-

rial world the quantity of matter remains unchanged; and that in all communication of motion, action and reaction must always be equal. Both propositions, it is evident, are not only necessary, and therefore in their origin *a priori*, but also synthetic. For in the concept of matter I do not think its permanence, but only its presence in the space which it occupies. I go outside and beyond the concept of matter, joining to it *a priori* in thought something which I have not thought *in* it. The proposition is not, therefore, analytic, but synthetic, and yet is thought *a priori*; and so likewise are the other propositions of the pure part of natural science.

3. *Metaphysics*, even if we look upon it as having hitherto failed in all its endeavours, is yet, owing to the nature of human reason, a quite indispensable science, and *ought to contain* a priori *synthetic knowledge*. For its business is not merely to analyse concepts which we make for ourselves *a priori* of things, and thereby to clarify them analytically, but to extend our *a priori* knowledge. And for this purpose we must employ principles which add to the given concept something that was not contained in it, and through *a priori* synthetic judgments venture out so far that experience is quite unable to follow us, as, for instance, in the proposition, that the world must have a first beginning, and such like. Thus metaphysics consists, at least *in intention*, entirely of *a priori* synthetic propositions.

VI. The General Problem of Pure Reason

Much is already gained if we can bring a number of investigations under the formula of a single problem. For we not only lighten our own task, by defining it accurately, but make it easier for others, who would test our results, to judge whether or not we have succeeded in what we set out to do. Now the proper problem of pure reason is contained in the question: How are *a priori* synthetic judgments possible?

That metaphysics has hitherto remained in so vacillating a state of uncertainty and contradiction, is entirely due to the fact that this problem, and perhaps even the distinction between analytic and synthetic judgments, has never previously been considered. Upon the solution of this problem, or upon a sufficient proof that the possibility which it desires to have

---

18 As assertions of identities (or non-identities).

explained does in fact not exist at all, depends the success or failure of metaphysics. Among philosophers, David Hume came nearest to envisaging this problem, but still was very far from conceiving it with sufficient definiteness and universality. He occupied himself exclusively with the synthetic proposition regarding the connection of an effect with its cause (*principium causalitatis*[19]), and he believed himself to have shown that such an *a priori* proposition is entirely impossible. If we accept his conclusions, then all that we call metaphysics is a mere delusion whereby we fancy ourselves to have rational insight into what, in actual fact, is borrowed solely from experience, and under the influence of custom has taken the illusory semblance of necessity. If he had envisaged our problem in all its universality, he would never have been guilty of this statement, so destructive of all pure philosophy. For he would then have recognised that, according to his own argument, pure mathematics, as certainly containing *a priori* synthetic propositions, would also not be possible; and from such an assertion his good sense would have saved him.

In the solution of the above problem, we are at the same time deciding as to the possibility of the employment of pure reason in establishing and developing all those sciences which contain a theoretical *a priori* knowledge of objects, and have therefore to answer the questions:

How is pure mathematics possible?

How is pure science of nature possible?

Since these sciences actually exist, it is quite proper to ask *how* they are possible; for that they must be possible is proved by the fact that they exist.[20] But the

poor progress which has hitherto been made in metaphysics, and the fact that no system yet propounded can, in view of the essential purpose of metaphysics, be said really to exist, leaves everyone sufficient ground for doubting as to its possibility.

Yet, in a certain sense, this *kind of knowledge* is to be looked upon as given; that is to say, metaphysics actually exists, if not as a science, yet still as natural disposition (*metaphysica naturalis*[21]). For human reason, without being moved merely by the idle desire for extent and variety of knowledge, proceeds impetuously, driven on by an inward need, to questions such as cannot be answered by any empirical employment of reason, or by principles thence derived. Thus in all men, as soon as their reason has become ripe for speculation, there has always existed and will always continue to exist some kind of metaphysics. And so we have the question:

How is metaphysics, as natural disposition, possible?

that is, how from the nature of universal human reason do those questions arise which pure reason propounds to itself, and which it is impelled by its own need to answer as best it can?

But since all attempts which have hitherto been made to answer these natural questions—for instance, whether the world has a beginning or is from eternity—have always met with unavoidable contradictions, we cannot rest satisfied with the mere natural disposition to metaphysics, that is, with the pure faculty of reason itself, from which, indeed, some sort of metaphysics (be it what it may) always arises. It must be possible for reason to attain to certainty whether we know or do not know the objects of metaphysics, that is, to come to a decision either in regard to the objects of its enquiries or in regard to the capacity or incapacity of reason to pass any judgment upon them, so that we may either with confidence extend our pure reason or set to it sure and determinate limits. This last question, which arises out of the previous general problem, may, rightly stated, take the form:

How is metaphysics, as science, possible?

Thus the critique of reason, in the end, necessarily leads to scientific knowledge; while its dogmatic em-

19   "The origin of causation."

20   [Author's note] Many may still have doubts as regards pure natural science. We have only, however, to consider the various propositions that are to be found at the beginning of (empirical) physics, properly so called, those, for instance, relating to the permanence in the quantity of matter, to inertia, to the equality of action and reaction, etc., in order to be soon convinced that they constitute a *physica pura*, or *rationalis*, which well deserves, as an independent science, to be separately dealt with in its whole extent, be that narrow or wide.

21   "Natural metaphysics."

ployment, on the other hand, lands us in dogmatic assertions to which other assertions, equally specious,[22] can always be opposed—that is, in *scepticism*.

This science cannot be of any very formidable prolixity,[23] since it has to deal not with the objects of reason, the variety of which is inexhaustible, but only with itself and the problems which arise entirely from within itself, and which are imposed upon it by its own nature, not by the nature of things which are distinct from it. When once reason has learnt completely to understand its own power in respect of objects which can be presented to it in experience, it should easily be able to determine, with completeness and certainty, the extent and the limits of its attempted employment beyond the bounds of all experience.

We may, then, and indeed we must, regard as abortive all attempts, hitherto made, to establish a metaphysic *dogmatically*. For the analytic part in any such attempted system, namely, the mere analysis of the concepts that inhere in our reason *a priori*, is by no means the aim of, but only a preparation for, metaphysics proper, that is, the extension of its *a priori* synthetic knowledge. For such a purpose, the analysis of concepts is useless, since it merely shows what is contained in these concepts, not how we arrive at them *a priori*. A solution of this latter problem is required, that we may be able to determine the valid employment of such concepts in regard to the objects of all knowledge in general. Nor is much self-denial needed to give up these claims, seeing that the undeniable, and in the dogmatic procedure of reason also unavoidable, contradictions of reason with itself have long since undermined the authority of every metaphysical system yet propounded. Greater firmness will be required if we are not to be deterred by inward difficulties and outward opposition from endeavouring, through application of a method entirely different from any hitherto employed, at last to bring to a prosperous and fruitful growth a science indispensable to human reason—a science whose every branch may be cut away but whose root cannot be destroyed.

---

22   Superficially plausible, but actually false.
23   Tedious length.

VII. The Idea and Division of a Special Science, under the Title "Critique of Pure Reason"

In view of all these considerations, we arrive at the idea of a special science which can be entitled the Critique of Pure Reason. For reason is the faculty which supplies the principles of *a priori* knowledge. Pure reason is, therefore, that which contains the principles whereby we know anything absolutely *a priori*. An organon[24] of pure reason would be the sum-total of those principles according to which all modes of pure *a priori* knowledge can be acquired and actually brought into being. The exhaustive application of such an organon would give rise to a system of pure reason. But as this would be asking rather much, and as it is still doubtful whether, and in what cases, any extension of our knowledge be here possible, we can regard a science of the mere examination of pure reason, of its sources and limits, as the *propaedeutic*[25] to the system of pure reason. As such, it should be called a critique, not a doctrine, of pure reason. Its utility, in speculation, ought properly to be only negative, not to extend, but only to clarify our reason, and keep it free from errors—which is already a very great gain. I entitle *transcendental* all knowledge which is occupied not so much with objects as with the mode of our knowledge of objects in so far as this mode of knowledge is to be possible *a priori*. A system of such concepts might be entitled transcendental philosophy. But that is still, at this stage, too large an undertaking. For since such a science must contain, with completeness, both kinds of *a priori* knowledge, the analytic no less than the synthetic, it is, so far as our present purpose is concerned, much too comprehensive. We have to carry the analysis so far only as is indispensably necessary in order to comprehend, in their whole extent, the principles of *a priori* synthesis, with which alone we are called upon to deal. It is upon this enquiry, which should be entitled not a doctrine,

---

24   An instrument of thought, especially a system of logic or a method for reasoning. (Aristotle's logical writings were historically grouped together as the *Organon*, and Francis Bacon's influential 1620 book on the scientific method was called the *Novum* (new) *Organon*.)
25   Preliminary or introductory instruction (from the Greek, meaning "to teach beforehand").

but only a transcendental critique, that we are now engaged. Its purpose is not to extend knowledge, but only to correct it, and to supply a touchstone of the value, or lack of value, of all *a priori* knowledge. Such a critique is therefore a preparation, so far as may be possible, for an organon; and should this turn out not to be possible, then at least for a canon,[26] according to which, in due course, the complete system of the philosophy of pure reason—be it in extension or merely in limitation of its knowledge—may be carried into execution, analytically as well as synthetically. That such a system is possible, and indeed that it may not be of such great extent as to cut us off from the hope of entirely completing it, may already be gathered from the fact that what here constitutes our subject-matter is not the nature of things, which is inexhaustible, but the understanding which passes judgment upon the nature of things; and this understanding, again, only in respect of its *a priori* knowledge. These *a priori* possessions of the understanding, since they have not to be sought for without, cannot remain hidden from us, and in all probability are sufficiently small in extent to allow of our apprehending them in their completeness, of judging as to their value or lack of value, and so of rightly appraising them. Still less may the reader here expect a critique of books and systems of pure reason; we are concerned only with the critique of the faculty of pure reason itself. Only in so far as we build upon this foundation do we have a reliable touchstone for estimating the philosophical value of old and new works in this field. Otherwise the unqualified historian or critic is passing judgments upon the groundless assertions of others by means of his own, which are equally groundless.

Transcendental philosophy is only the idea of a science, for which the critique of pure reason has to lay down the complete architectonic[27] plan. That is to say, it has to guarantee, as following from principles, the completeness and certainty of the structure in all its parts. It is the system of all principles of pure reason. And if this critique is not itself to be entitled a transcendental philosophy, it is solely because, to

---

26 A general principle or criterion.

27 Having to do with the scientific systematization of knowledge.

be a complete system, it would also have to contain an exhaustive analysis of the whole of *a priori* human knowledge. Our critique must, indeed, supply a complete enumeration of all the fundamental concepts that go to constitute such pure knowledge. But it is not required to give an exhaustive analysis of these concepts, nor a complete review of those that can be derived from them. Such a demand would be unreasonable, partly because this analysis would not be appropriate to our main purpose, inasmuch as there is no such uncertainty in regard to analysis as we encounter in the case of synthesis, for the sake of which alone our whole critique is undertaken; and partly because it would be inconsistent with the unity of our plan to assume responsibility for the completeness of such an analysis and derivation, when in view of our purpose we can be excused from doing so. The analysis of these *a priori* concepts, which later we shall have to enumerate, and the derivation of other concepts from them, can easily, however, be made complete when once they have been established as exhausting the principles of synthesis, and if in this essential respect nothing be lacking in them.

The critique of pure reason therefore will contain all that is essential in transcendental philosophy. While it is the complete idea of transcendental philosophy, it is not equivalent to that latter science; for it carries the analysis only so far as is requisite for the complete examination of knowledge which is *a priori* and synthetic.

What has chiefly to be kept in view in the division of such a science, is that no concepts be allowed to enter which contain in themselves anything empirical, or, in other words, that it consist in knowledge wholly *a priori*. Accordingly, although the highest principles and fundamental concepts of morality are *a priori* knowledge, they have no place in transcendental philosophy, because, although they do not lay at the foundation of their precepts the concepts of pleasure and pain, of the desires and inclinations, etc., all of which are of empirical origin, yet in the construction of a system of pure morality these empirical concepts must necessarily be brought into the concept of duty, as representing either a hindrance, which we have to overcome, or an allurement, which must not be made into a motive. Transcendental philosophy is therefore a philosophy of pure and merely speculative reason. All that is practical, so far as it contains motives, relates to feelings, and these belong to the empirical sources of knowledge.

If we are to make a systematic division of the science which we are engaged in presenting, it must have first a *doctrine of the elements*,[28] and secondly, a *doctrine of the method of pure reason*. Each of these chief divisions will have its subdivisions, but the grounds of these we are not yet in a position to explain. By way of introduction or anticipation we need only say that

there are two stems of human knowledge, namely, *sensibility*[29] and *understanding*, which perhaps spring from a common, but to us unknown, root. Through the former, objects are given to us; through the latter, they are thought. Now in so far as sensibility may be found to contain *a priori* representations constituting the condition under which objects are given to us, it will belong to transcendental philosophy. And since the conditions under which alone the objects of human knowledge are given must precede those under which they are thought, the transcendental doctrine of sensibility will constitute the first part of the science of the elements.

---

28   The "elements" are the constituents of cognition, which for Kant are intuitions and concepts.

29   The power of sensation.

BERTRAND RUSSELL
The Problems of Philosophy

I heard the beat of centaur's hoofs over the hard turf
As his dry and passionate talk devoured the afternoon.
"He is a charming man"—"But after all what did he
*   mean?"—*
"His pointed ears.... He must be unbalanced,"—
"There was something he said that I might have
*   challenged."*

(from a poem by T.S. Eliot about Bertrand Russell called "Mr. Apollinax")

Who Was Bertrand Russell?

Bertrand Arthur William, 3rd Earl Russell was, with G.E. Moore, the founder of modern analytic philosophy in Britain, and one of the most important logicians of the twentieth century. He had a long and checkered career as an academic, a pacifist, a political activist and social reformer, an educational theorist, and a moral "free-thinker."

Born in 1872, Russell was orphaned at the age of 4 and brought up by his aristocratic grandmother, who

educated him at home with the help of tutors. Russell's interest in philosophical problems began early. His older brother introduced him at the age of 11 to Euclidian geometry (which shows how a large swathe of mathematics can be derived from a few apparently self-evident assumptions, or "axioms"). "This was one of the great events of my life, as dazzling as first love," Russell later wrote; however, when he demanded of his brother to be told how the axioms themselves were justified, he was informed that the axioms must simply be accepted as given. This Russell found a deeply unsatisfying answer.

In 1890 Russell went to study mathematics at Trinity College, Cambridge, but three years later he switched to philosophy. After a rather unhappy and lonely childhood, Russell wrote that "Cambridge opened up for me a new world of infinite delight." In 1895 he was elected to a six-year Fellowship at Trinity on the basis of a dissertation on the foundations of geometry. The intellectual turning-point in Russell's life occurred five years later, at the International Congress of Philosophy in Paris, where Russell met the Italian logician and mathematician Giuseppe Peano, who appeared to have done for arithmetic what Euclid had done for geometry: that is, shown how it could be derived from a small number of axioms. Russell set out to master Peano's notation and results and to use them for the general project of setting mathematics on solid foundations:

> The time was one of intellectual intoxication. My sensations resembled those one has after climbing a mountain in a mist, when, on reaching the summit, the mist suddenly clears, and the country becomes visible for forty miles in every direction.... Suddenly, in the space of a few weeks, I discovered what appeared to be definitive answers to the problems which had baffled me for years. (Russell's *Autobiography*)

This period of intellectual joy for Russell was quickly followed by one of emotional unhappiness as he "suddenly" realized he no longer loved his first wife Alys Pearsall Smith, whom he had married in 1894, and also began to see the cracks emerging in his meta-mathematical theory, showing that his answers might be less definitive than he had hoped.

In 1907 he stood unsuccessfully for Parliament as the candidate for the National Union of Women's Suffrage Societies, and in 1910 he tried to be adopted as the Liberal candidate for a London borough. He was rejected, however, because of his public atheism; Russell later called this rejection a lucky escape since it enabled him to accept a Lectureship at Trinity College, Cambridge, which he was offered that year. Between 1910 and 1916 he was a university lecturer at

Cambridge, but was dismissed because of his pacifist opposition to World War I. In 1918 he was imprisoned for six months for having written that the US Army used intimidation tactics with strikers.

In 1921 Russell married again—to Dora Black—and had his first child. Since he had already given away most of his inherited money and lost his job at Cambridge, he now needed to find some way of making an income. As a result, most of his writings from this point until the mid-1930s were intended for a popular audience, and he went on several well-paid lecture tours of America. Many of his writings were considered scandalous for their liberal attitude towards sex and marriage—the best known of them are *Marriage and Morals* (1929) and *The Conquest of Happiness* (1930)—but they made him a lot of money. On the other hand, the progressive Beacon Hill School he founded with his wife in 1927, which aimed to provide a less authoritarian education than was then generally available, suffered large losses.

In 1936, after another divorce, Russell married his third wife, Patricia ('Peter') Spence, and two years later went to the United States to take up one-year appointments at the University of Chicago and then the University of California at Los Angeles. In 1939 he was offered a professorship at the College of the City of New York; however, there was a public outcry against the appointment on the grounds that Russell's lifestyle was immoral and his writings "lecherous, libidinous, lustful, venerous, erotomaniac, aphrodisiac, irreverent, narrow-minded, untruthful, and bereft of moral fibre." A lawsuit by some outraged taxpayers against the Municipality of New York led to Russell's appointment being revoked. This caused Russell financial problems but he was rescued by a lecturing job at the Barnes Foundation; it was here that he began his monumental book *A History of Western Philosophy*, which was published in 1945 and won him the 1950 Nobel prize for literature.

In 1944 Russell returned to Trinity College, Cambridge, as a Fellow, and in 1952, after the break-up of his third marriage, wed Edith Finch. In 1958 he became president of the Campaign for Nuclear Disarmament and wrote two books on the dangers of nuclear war: *Common Sense and Nuclear Warfare* (1959) and *Has Man a Future?* (1961). He was jailed for a week in 1961, even though he was then 89 years old, for inciting civil disobedience. He was instrumental in founding the Pugwash Conference,[1] at which distinguished scientists from around the world meet to discuss international issues, and in 1963 he became president of the British wing of the Who Killed Kennedy Committee. In 1964 he founded the Bertrand Russell Peace Foundation and in 1967 he set up an International War Crimes Tribunal which, together with his book *War Crimes in Vietnam*, condemned the foreign policy of the United States. Russell died in 1970 at the age of 97.

What Was Russell's Overall Philosophical Project?

Russell's earliest work, and probably his most lasting contribution to philosophy, was in mathematical logic. His project—which today might seem almost unnecessary but which was an extremely important contribution to mathematical thought at the beginning of the twentieth century—was to place all of pure mathematics on a sound footing by showing that it is reducible to a demonstrably sound logical system. This program was called 'logicism,' and its culmination for Russell was the massive *Principia Mathematica*, co-written with Alfred North Whitehead and published between 1910 and 1913. In the process, Russell created essentially the standard formulation of modern classical logic. (The project ran into dif-

ficulties, however, with the discovery of several very deep paradoxes which threaten any sufficiently powerful logical system which makes use of the notion of a class or set;[2] Russell's solution—called the "theory of types"—is generally considered a rather problematic treatment of these paradoxes.) The best introduction to Russell's logicism is his *Introduction to Mathematical Philosophy*, written while he was in prison in 1918.

Lying behind this early work, as well as many of his other philosophical writings, was the dictum that "all sound philosophy should begin with an analysis of propositions": that is, Russell thought, good philosophy starts by examining a particular feature or type of language—such as mathematics—and looking for its underlying logic. This kind of analysis can be seen at work in two of Russell's most seminal papers, "On Denoting" (1905) and "Knowledge by Acquaintance and Knowledge by Description" (1910). The ultimate aim of this philosophical project is to construct an ideal logically correct language to solve or dissolve many, if not all, of our philosophical problems. Such a system, Russell thought, would reveal how mathematical and scientific reality is a "logical construction" of basic data, such as numbers and sense-data.

This philosophical project gave rise to Russell's second important contribution to philosophy: a theory called "logical atomism."[3] This is a metaphysical

---

1   It is named after the village in Nova Scotia where the first meeting was held in 1957. Pugwash conferences still continue, and the organization received the Nobel peace prize in 1995.

2   The most fundamental of these paradoxes is usually called "Russell's paradox," and goes as follows. Some sets are members of themselves and others are not. For example, the set of chimpanzees is not itself a chimp, but the set of sets is itself a set. Now, consider the following (apparently perfectly legitimate) set: the set of all sets that are not members of themselves. Call this set R. The problematic question is: is R a member of itself or not? It can't be true that R *is* a member of itself, since all the members of R are not members of themselves. On the other hand, it can't be true that R is *not* a member of itself, because then it would be a member of itself. Yet it must surely be one or the other. This is a paradox which seems to arise directly out of the notion of a set itself, and it has big implications for logic and mathematics.

3   Ludwig Wittgenstein's book *Tractatus Logico-Philosophicus* (1922) is the other main source for this theory.

doctrine which is simultaneously about the nature of language, knowledge, and the world. Its central claim is that reality is ultimately composed of atomic facts and that these facts are connected together by certain fundamental relations (such as 'and,' 'or,' or 'if … then …') which can be pictured in formal logic. Language, according to this theory, represents the world by sharing its logical structure: that is, *language* (just like reality) is ultimately composed of 'atomic' units which are joined together by logical rules into more complex compounds (i.e., into phrases and sentences). The business of philosophy, according to logical atomism, is to purify our language until it properly reflects the structure of reality, and this goal is achieved through logical analysis. For example, we want the atomic units of our perfect logical language to include the *names* of the atomic individuals and their basic properties, and the grammatical rules for the construction of compound sentences should be the same as the logical relations by which reality is constructed. Finally, human knowledge of the world, according to logical atomism, turns out to have two different components: our acquaintance with the basic elements of reality (which Russell for a long time thought of as sense-data), and our understanding of how these elements can be and are combined (which Russell labeled "knowledge by description").

Three of Russell's works that describe and develop his logical atomism are *Our Knowledge of the External World* (1914), the lectures "The Philosophy of Logical Atomism" (1918), and *The Analysis of Matter* (1927).

After 1938 Russell switched the main focus of his philosophical research to epistemology, the study of the nature of human knowledge. He began by searching for a method that would guarantee the certainty of our beliefs (for example, our scientific beliefs), but he was forced gradually to the conclusion that "all human knowledge is uncertain, inexact, and partial. To this doctrine we have not found any limitation whatever." Part of the reason for Russell's increasing lack of confidence in scientific knowledge was his growing appreciation of "the problem of induction" (see Chapter 4). His work in epistemology can be found in *An Inquiry into Meaning and Truth* (1940) and his last significant philosophical work, *Human Knowledge: Its Scope and Limits* (1948).

Russell's short book *The Problems of Philosophy* (1912), from which our reading is taken, has become one of the most popular introductions to philosophy ever written. In its day it was also important for drawing attention to the previously underrated work of the British empiricists, especially Berkeley and Hume. The book was written while Russell was still developing his logical atomism: in his later work (for a time) he abandoned the notion that matter is *inferred* from our knowledge of sense-data and replaced it with the idea that matter is simply a *logical construction* of actual and possible sense-data. That is, he moved from the theory that matter is the best explanation for what causes our experiences of the world, to the theory that statements about 'matter' are just shorthand statements about past and future experiences themselves.

What Is the Structure of This Reading?

Russell's *Problems of Philosophy* contains fifteen chapters, and the first three are reprinted here. Russell begins his introduction to philosophy by treating it as the search for *certainty*—for knowledge that no "reasonable man" could doubt. In the first chapter he argues that most everyday knowledge about the world we live in fails sadly to live up to this standard and, as the title of the first chapter suggests, he uses simple examples from daily life to draw a distinction between appearance and reality. Russell then distinguishes between two different sorts of questions about the nature of reality: (1) Is there a real table at all? (2) If so, what sort of object can it be? Chapter 2 addresses the first of these questions (and Russell argues that physical tables do exist); Chapter 3 is about the second (where Russell argues that matter cannot resemble our sense-data).

Suggestions for Critical Reflection

1. Do you think philosophy is best thought of as the search for certainty? Does Russell think of it in that way? Judging from the reading, for example, does he require *certainty* in his philosophical arguments?

2. Do you agree that Russell's appearance/reality distinction is a serious blow to our common-sense beliefs about the world? Why, or why not?

3. Do you agree with Russell that "the supposition that the whole of life is a dream ... [is] a less simple hypothesis, viewed as a means of accounting for the facts of our own life, than the common-sense hypothesis that there really are objects independent of us"?

4. How adequate do you find Russell's proof that physical tables exist? What does he mean by "physical" (e.g., does he mean something like "made of sub-atomic particles"?) in this context?

5. What kind of knowledge do you think Russell would be willing to grant us of the real nature of matter? That is, as well as knowing what matter is *not*, how much might we be able to find out (on Russell's picture) about what matter *is*?

Suggestions for Further Reading

After reading the rest of *The Problems of Philosophy* (Oxford University Press, 1912), the best places to start with Russell's philosophy are his *Introduction to Mathematical Philosophy* (George Allen & Unwin, 1919) and the collection of essays edited by R.C. Marsh called *Logic and Knowledge* (George Allen & Unwin, 1956). The latter includes his "The Philosophy of Logical Atomism." Every student of philosophy should at some point read Russell's *A History of Western Philosophy* (George Allen & Unwin, 1945). Probably still the best book about Russell's life is his *Autobiography*, published in three volumes between 1967 and 1969 by George Allen & Unwin. Apart from that, the standard biography continues to be Ronald William Clark's *The Life of Bertrand Russell* (Cape, 1972).

Two useful books about Russell's philosophy are *Bertrand Russell*, by John Slater (Thoemmes Press, 1994) and *Russell*, by R.M. Sainsbury (Routledge & Kegan Paul, 1979). Perhaps the most comprehensive book on Russell's thought is by Ronald Jager, *The Development of Bertrand Russell's Philosophy* (Allen & Unwin, 1972). Essays about Russell's philosophy are collected in David Pears (ed.), *Bertrand Russell: A Collection of Critical Essays* (Anchor Books, 1972).

The Problems of Philosophy

Chapters 1–3[4]

Chapter 1: Appearance and Reality

Is there any knowledge in the world which is so certain that no reasonable man could doubt it? This question, which at first sight might not seem difficult, is really one of the most difficult that can be asked. When we have realized the obstacles in the way of a straightforward and confident answer, we shall be well launched on the study of philosophy—for philosophy is merely the attempt to answer such ultimate questions, not carelessly and dogmatically, as we do in ordinary life and even in the sciences, but critically, after exploring all that makes such questions puzzling, and after realizing all the vagueness and confusion that underlie our ordinary ideas.

In daily life, we assume as certain many things which, on a closer scrutiny, are found to be so full of apparent contradictions that only a great amount of thought enables us to know what it is that we really may believe. In the search for certainty, it is natural to begin with our present experiences, and in some sense, no doubt, knowledge is to be derived from them. But any statement as to what it is that our immediate experiences make us know is very likely to be wrong. It seems to me that I am now sitting in a chair, at a table of a certain shape, on which I see sheets of paper with writing or print. By turning my head I see out of the window buildings and clouds and the sun. I believe that the sun is about ninety-three million miles from the earth; that it is a hot globe many times bigger than the earth; that, owing to the earth's rotation, it rises every morning, and will continue to do so for an indefinite time in the future. I believe that, if any other normal person comes into my room, he will see the same chairs and tables and books and papers as I see, and that the table which I see is the same as the table which I feel pressing against my arm. All this seems to

---

4 *The Problems of Philosophy* was first published in 1912 in the Home University Library series by Williams and Norgate. From Chapters 1–3 of *The Problems of Philosophy*. © Bertrand Russell, 1967. By permission of Oxford University Press.

be so evident as to be hardly worth stating, except in answer to a man who doubts whether I know anything. Yet all this may be reasonably doubted, and all of it requires much careful discussion before we can be sure that we have stated it in a form that is wholly true.

To make our difficulties plain, let us concentrate attention on the table. To the eye it is oblong, brown and shiny, to the touch it is smooth and cool and hard; when I tap it, it gives out a wooden sound. Any one else who sees and feels and hears the table will agree with this description, so that it might seem as if no difficulty would arise; but as soon as we try to be more precise our troubles begin. Although I believe that the table is 'really' of the same colour all over, the parts that reflect the light look much brighter than the other parts, and some parts look white because of reflected light. I know that, if I move, the parts that reflect the light will be different, so that the apparent distribution of colours on the table will change. It follows that if several people are looking at the table at the same moment, no two of them will see exactly the same distribution of colours, because no two can see it from exactly the same point of view, and any change in the point of view makes some change in the way the light is reflected.

For most practical purposes these differences are unimportant, but to the painter they are all-important: the painter has to unlearn the habit of thinking that things seem to have the colour which common sense says they 'really' have, and to learn the habit of seeing things as they appear. Here we have already the beginning of one of the distinctions that cause most trouble in philosophy—the distinction between 'appearance' and 'reality', between what things seem to be and what they are. The painter wants to know what things seem to be, the practical man and the philosopher want to know what they are; but the philosopher's wish to know this is stronger than the practical man's, and is more troubled by knowledge as to the difficulties of answering the question.

To return to the table. It is evident from what we have found, that there is no colour which pre-eminently appears to be *the* colour of the table, or even of any one particular part of the table—it appears to be of different colours from different points of view, and there is no reason for regarding some of these as more really its colour than others. And we know that even from a given point of view the colour will seem different by artificial light, or to a colour-blind man, or to a man wearing blue spectacles, while in the dark there will be no colour at all, though to touch and hearing the table will be unchanged. This colour is not something which is inherent in the table, but something depending upon the table and the spectator and the way the light falls on the table. When, in ordinary life, we speak of *the* colour of the table, we only mean the sort of colour which it will seem to have to a normal spectator from an ordinary point of view under usual conditions of light. But the other colours which appear under other conditions have just as good a right to be considered real; and therefore, to avoid favouritism, we are compelled to deny that, in itself, the table has any one particular colour.

The same thing applies to the texture. With the naked eye one can see the grain, but otherwise the table looks smooth and even. If we looked at it through a microscope, we should see roughnesses and hills and valleys, and all sorts of differences that are imperceptible to the naked eye. Which of these is the 'real' table? We are naturally tempted to say that what we see through the microscope is more real, but that in turn would be changed by a still more powerful microscope. If, then, we cannot trust what we see with the naked eye, why should we trust what we see through a microscope? Thus, again, the confidence in our senses with which we began deserts us.

The *shape* of the table is no better. We are all in the habit of judging as to the 'real' shapes of things, and we do this so unreflectingly that we come to think we actually see the real shapes. But, in fact, as we all have to learn if we try to draw, a given thing looks different in shape from every different point of view. If our table is 'really' rectangular, it will look, from almost all points of view, as if it had two acute angles and two obtuse angles. If opposite sides are parallel, they will look as if they converged to a point away from the spectator; if they are of equal length, they will look as if the nearer side were longer. All these things are not commonly noticed in looking at a table, because experience has taught us to construct the 'real' shape from the apparent shape, and the 'real' shape is what interests us as practical men. But the 'real' shape is not what we see; it is something inferred from what we see. And what we see is constantly changing in shape as we move about the room; so that here again the senses seem not to give us the truth about the table itself, but only about the appearance of the table.

Similar difficulties arise when we consider the sense of touch. It is true that the table always gives us a sensation of hardness, and we feel that it resists pressure. But the sensation we obtain depends upon how hard we press the table and also upon what part of the body we press with; thus the various sensations due to various pressures or various parts of the body cannot be supposed to reveal *directly* any definite property of the table, but at most to be *signs* of some property which perhaps *causes* all the sensations, but is not actually apparent in any of them. And the same applies still more obviously to the sounds which can be elicited by rapping the table.

Thus it becomes evident that the real table, if there is one, is not the same as what we immediately experience by sight or touch or hearing. The real table, if there is one, is not *immediately* known to us at all, but must be an inference from what is immediately known. Hence, two very difficult questions at once arise; namely, (1) Is there a real table at all? (2) If so, what sort of object can it be?

It will help us in considering these questions to have a few simple terms of which the meaning is definite and clear. Let us give the name of 'sense-data' to the things that are immediately known in sensation: such things as colours, sounds, smells, hardnesses, roughnesses, and so on. We shall give the name 'sensation' to the experience of being immediately aware of these things. Thus, whenever we see a colour, we have a sensation *of* the colour, but the colour itself is a sense-datum, not a sensation. The colour is that *of* which we are immediately aware, and the awareness itself is the sensation. It is plain that if we are to know anything about the table, it must be by means of the sense-data—brown colour, oblong shape, smoothness, etc.—which we associate with the table; but, for the reasons which have been given, we cannot say that the table is the sense-data, or even that the sense-data are directly properties of the table. Thus a problem arises as to the relation of the sense-data to the real table, supposing there is such a thing.

The real table, if it exists, we will call a 'physical object'. Thus we have to consider the relation of sense-data to physical objects. The collection of all physical objects is called 'matter'. Thus our two questions may be re-stated as follows: (1) Is there any such thing as matter? (2) If so, what is its nature?

The philosopher who first brought prominently forward the reasons for regarding the immediate objects of our senses as not existing independently of us was Bishop Berkeley (1685–1753). His *Three Dialogues between Hylas and Philonous, in Opposition to Sceptics and Atheists*,[5] undertake to prove that there is no such thing as matter at all, and that the world consists of nothing but minds and their ideas. Hylas has hitherto believed in matter, but he is no match for Philonous, who mercilessly drives him into contradictions and paradoxes, and makes his own denial of matter seem, in the end, as if it were almost common sense. The arguments employed are of very different value: some are important and sound, others are confused or quibbling. But Berkeley retains the merit of having shown that the existence of matter is capable of being denied without absurdity, and that if there are any things that exist independently of us they cannot be the immediate objects of our sensations.

There are two different questions involved when we ask whether matter exists, and it is important to keep them clear. We commonly mean by 'matter' something which is opposed to 'mind', something which we think of as occupying space and as radically incapable of any sort of thought or consciousness. It is chiefly in this sense that Berkeley denies matter; that is to say, he does not deny that the sense-data which we commonly take as signs of the existence of the table are really signs of the existence of *something* independent of us, but he does deny that this something is non-mental, that it is neither mind nor ideas entertained by some mind. He admits that there must be something which continues to exist when we go out of the room or shut our eyes, and that what we call seeing the table does really give us reason for believing in something which persists even when we are not seeing it. But he thinks that this something cannot be radically

---

5   See the Berkeley selection in this chapter.

different in nature from what we see, and cannot be independent of seeing altogether, though it must be independent of *our* seeing. He is thus led to regard the 'real' table as an idea in the mind of God. Such an idea has the required permanence and independence of ourselves, without being—as matter would otherwise be—something quite unknowable, in the sense that we can only infer it, and can never be directly and immediately aware of it.

Other philosophers since Berkeley have also held that, although the table does not depend for its existence upon being seen by me, it does depend upon being seen (or otherwise apprehended in sensation) by *some* mind—not necessarily the mind of God, but more often the whole collective mind of the universe. This they hold, as Berkeley does, chiefly because they think there can be nothing real—or at any rate nothing known to be real—except minds and their thoughts and feelings. We might state the argument by which they support their view in some such way as this: 'Whatever can be thought of is an idea in the mind of the person thinking of it; therefore nothing can be thought of except ideas in minds; therefore anything else is inconceivable, and what is inconceivable cannot exist.'

Such an argument, in my opinion, is fallacious; and of course those who advance it do not put it so shortly or so crudely. But whether valid or not, the argument has been very widely advanced in one form or another; and very many philosophers, perhaps a majority, have held that there is nothing real except minds and their ideas. Such philosophers are called 'idealists'. When they come to explaining matter, they either say, like Berkeley, that matter is really nothing but a collection of ideas, or they say, like Leibniz (1646–1716), that what appears as matter is really a collection of more or less rudimentary minds.

But these philosophers, though they deny matter as opposed to mind, nevertheless, in another sense, admit matter. It will be remembered that we asked two questions; namely, (1) Is there a real table at all? (2) If so, what sort of object can it be? Now both Berkeley and Leibniz admit that there is a real table, but Berkeley says it is certain ideas in the mind of God, and Leibniz says it is a colony of souls. Thus both of them answer our first question in the affirmative, and only diverge from the views of ordinary mortals in their answer to our second question. In fact, almost all philosophers seem to be agreed that there is a real table: they almost all agree that, however much our sense-data—colour, shape, smoothness, etc.—may depend upon us, yet their occurrence is a sign of something existing independently of us, something differing, perhaps, completely from our sense-data whenever we are in a suitable relation to the real table.

Now obviously this point in which the philosophers are agreed—the view that there *is* a real table, whatever its nature may be—is vitally important, and it will be worth while to consider what reasons there are for accepting this view before we go on to the further question as to the nature of the real table. Our next chapter, therefore, will be concerned with the reasons for supposing that there is a real table at all.

Before we go farther it will be well to consider for a moment what it is that we have discovered so far. It has appeared that, if we take any common object of the sort that is supposed to be known by the senses, what the senses *immediately*[6] tell us is not the truth about the object as it is apart from us, but only the truth about certain sense-data which, so far as we can see, depend upon the relations between us and the object. Thus what we directly see and feel is merely 'appearance', which we believe to be a sign of some 'reality' behind. But if the reality is not what appears, have we any means of knowing whether there is any reality at all? And if so, have we any means of finding out what it is like?

Such questions are bewildering, and it is difficult to know that even the strangest hypotheses may not be true. Thus our familiar table, which has roused but the slightest thoughts in us hitherto, has become a problem full of surprising possibilities. The one thing we know about it is that it is not what it seems. Beyond this modest result, so far, we have the most complete liberty of conjecture. Leibniz tells us it is a community of souls: Berkeley tells us it is an idea in the mind of God; sober science, scarcely less wonderful, tells us it is a vast collection of electric charges in violent motion.

---

6   Without an intermediary (as opposed to "straight away").

Among these surprising possibilities, doubt suggests that perhaps there is no table at all. Philosophy, if it cannot *answer* so many questions as we could wish, has at least the power of *asking* questions which increase the interest of the world, and show the strangeness and wonder lying just below the surface even in the commonest things of daily life.

Chapter 2: The Existence of Matter

In this chapter we have to ask ourselves whether, in any sense at all, there is such a thing as matter. Is there a table which has a certain intrinsic nature, and continues to exist when I am not looking, or is the table merely a product of my imagination, a dream-table in a very prolonged dream? This question is of the greatest importance. For if we cannot be sure of the independent existence of objects, we cannot be sure of the independent existence of other people's bodies, and therefore still less of other people's minds, since we have no grounds for believing in their minds except such as are derived from observing their bodies. Thus if we cannot be sure of the independent existence of objects, we shall be left alone in a desert—it may be that the whole outer world is nothing but a dream, and that we alone exist. This is an uncomfortable possibility; but although it cannot be strictly *proved* to be false, there is not the slightest reason to suppose that it is true. In this chapter we have to see why this is the case.

Before we embark upon doubtful matters, let us try to find some more or less fixed point from which to start. Although we are doubting the physical existence of the table, we are not doubting the existence of the sense-data which made us think there was a table; we are not doubting that, while we look, a certain colour and shape appear to us, and while we press, a certain sensation of hardness is experienced by us. All this, which is psychological, we are not calling in question. In fact, whatever else may be doubtful, some at least of our immediate experiences seem absolutely certain.

Descartes (1596–1650), the founder of modern philosophy, invented a method which may still be used with profit—the method of systematic doubt. He determined that he would believe nothing which he did not see quite clearly and distinctly to be true. Whatever he could bring himself to doubt, he would

doubt, until he saw reason for not doubting it. By applying this method he gradually became convinced that the only existence of which he could be *quite* certain was his own. He imagined a deceitful demon, who presented unreal things to his senses in a perpetual phantasmagoria; it might be very improbable that such a demon existed, but still it was possible, and therefore doubt concerning things perceived by the senses was possible.

But doubt concerning his own existence was not possible, for if he did not exist, no demon could deceive him. If he doubted, he must exist; if he had any experiences whatever, he must exist. Thus his own existence was an absolute certainty to him. 'I think, therefore I am,' he said (*Cogito, ergo sum*); and on the basis of this certainty he set to work to build up again the world of knowledge which his doubt had laid in ruins. By inventing the method of doubt, and by showing that subjective things are the most certain, Descartes performed a great service to philosophy, and one which makes him still useful to all students of the subject.

But some care is needed in using Descartes' argument. '*I* think, therefore *I* am' says rather more than is strictly certain. It might seem as though we were quite sure of being the same person to-day as we were yesterday, and this is no doubt true in some sense. But the real Self is as hard to arrive at as the real table, and does not seem to have that absolute, convincing certainty that belongs to particular experiences. When I look at my table and see a certain brown colour, what is quite certain at once is not '*I* am seeing a brown colour', but rather, 'a brown colour is being seen'. This of course involves something (or somebody) which (or who) sees the brown colour; but it does not of itself involve that more or less permanent person whom we call 'I'. So far as immediate certainty goes, it might be that the something which sees the brown colour is quite momentary, and not the same as the something which has some different experience the next moment.

Thus it is our particular thoughts and feelings that have primitive certainty. And this applies to dreams and hallucinations as well as to normal perceptions: when we dream or see a ghost, we certainly do have the sensations we think we have, but for various reasons it is held that no physical object corresponds to these sensations. Thus the certainty of our knowledge of our own experiences does not have to be limited in any way to allow for exceptional cases. Here, therefore, we have, for what it is worth, a solid basis from which to begin our pursuit of knowledge.

The problem we have to consider is this: Granted that we are certain of our own sense-data, have we any reason for regarding them as signs of the existence of something else, which we can call the physical object? When we have enumerated all the sense-data which we should naturally regard as connected with the table have we said all there is to say about the table, or is there still something else—something not a sense-datum, something which persists when we go out of the room? Common sense unhesitatingly answers that there is. What can be bought and sold and pushed about and have a cloth laid on it, and so on, cannot be a *mere* collection of sense-data. If the cloth completely hides the table, we shall derive no sense-data from the table, and therefore, if the table were merely sense-data, it would have ceased to exist, and the cloth would be suspended in empty air, resting, by a miracle, in the place where the table formerly was. This seems plainly absurd; but whoever wishes to become a philosopher must learn not to be frightened by absurdities.

One great reason why it is felt that we must secure a physical object in addition to the sense-data, is that we want the same object for different people. When ten people are sitting round a dinner-table, it seems preposterous to maintain that they are not seeing the same tablecloth, the same knives and forks and spoons and glasses. But the sense-data are private to each separate person; what is immediately present to the sight of one is not immediately present to the sight of another: they all see things from slightly different points of view, and therefore see them slightly differently. Thus, if there are to be public neutral objects, which can be in some sense known to many different people, there must be something over and above the private and particular sense-data which appear to various people. What reason, then, have we for believing that there are such public neutral objects?

The first answer that naturally occurs to one is that, although different people may see the table slightly differently, still they all see more or less similar things when they look at the table, and the variations in what they see follow the laws of perspective and reflection of light, so that it is easy to arrive at a permanent object underlying all the different people's sense-data. I bought my table from the former occupant of my room; I could not buy *his* sense-data, which died when he went away, but I could and did buy the confident expectation of more or less similar sense-data. Thus it is the fact that different people have similar sense-data, and that one person in a given place at different times has similar sense-data, which makes us suppose that over and above the sense-data there is a permanent public object which underlies or causes the sense-data of various people at various times.

Now in so far as the above considerations depend upon supposing that there are other people besides ourselves, they beg the very question at issue.[7] Other people are represented to me by certain sense-data, such as the sight of them or the sound of their voices, and if I had no reason to believe that there were physical objects independent of my sense-data, I should have no reason to believe that other people exist except as part of my dream. Thus, when we are trying to show that there must be objects independent of our own sense-data, we cannot appeal to the testimony of other people, since this testimony itself consists of sense-data, and does not reveal other people's experiences unless our own sense-data are signs of things existing independently of us. We must therefore, if possible, find, in our own purely private experiences, characteristics which show, or tend to show, that there are in the world things other than ourselves and our private experiences.

In one sense it must be admitted that we can never *prove* the existence of things other than ourselves and our experiences. No logical absurdity results from the hypothesis that the world consists of myself and my thoughts and feelings and sensations, and that everything else is mere fancy. In dreams a very complicated world may seem to be present, and yet on waking we find it was a delusion; that is to say, we find that the sense-data in the dream do not appear to have corresponded with such physical objects as we should natu-

---

7   Presuppose the truth of the very thing they are trying to prove.

rally infer from our sense-data. (It is true that, when the physical world is assumed, it is possible to find physical causes for the sense-data in dreams: a door banging, for instance, may cause us to dream of a naval engagement. But although, in this case, there is a physical *cause* for the sense-data, there is not a physical object *corresponding* to the sense-data in the way in which an actual naval battle would correspond.) There is no logical impossibility in the supposition that the whole of life is a dream, in which we ourselves create all the objects that come before us. But although this is not logically impossible, there is no reason whatever to suppose that it is true; and it is, in fact, a less simple hypothesis, viewed as a means of accounting for the facts of our own life, than the common-sense hypothesis that there really are objects independent of us, whose action on us causes our sensations.

The way in which simplicity comes in from supposing that there really are physical objects is easily seen. If the cat appears at one moment in one part of the room, and at another in another part, it is natural to suppose that it has moved from the one to the other, passing over a series of intermediate positions. But if it is merely a set of sense-data, it cannot have ever been in any place where I did not see it; thus we shall have to suppose that it did not exist at all while I was not looking, but suddenly sprang into being in a new place. If the cat exists whether I see it or not, we can understand from our own experience how it gets hungry between one meal and the next; but if it does not exist when I am not seeing it, it seems odd that appetite should grow during non-existence as fast as during existence. And if the cat consists only of sense-data, it cannot be *hungry*, since no hunger but my own can be a sense-datum to me. Thus the behaviour of the sense-data which represent the cat to me, though it seems quite natural when regarded as an expression of hunger, becomes utterly inexplicable when regarded as mere movements and changes of patches of colour, which are as incapable of hunger as a triangle is of playing football.

But the difficulty in the case of the cat is nothing compared to the difficulty in the case of human beings. When human beings speak—that is, when we hear certain noises which we associate with ideas, and simultaneously see certain motions of lips and expressions of face—it is very difficult to suppose that what we hear is not the expression of a thought, as we know it would be if we emitted the same sounds. Of course similar things happen in dreams, where we are mistaken as to the existence of other people. But dreams are more or less suggested by what we call waking life, and are capable of being more or less accounted for on scientific principles if we assume that there really is a physical world. Thus every principle of simplicity urges us to adopt the natural view, that there really are objects other than ourselves and our sense-data which have an existence not dependent upon our perceiving them.

Of course it is not by argument that we originally come by our belief in an independent external world. We find this belief ready in ourselves as soon as we begin to reflect: it is what may be called an *instinctive* belief. We should never have been led to question this belief but for the fact that, at any rate in the case of sight, it seems as if the sense-datum itself were instinctively believed to be the independent object, whereas argument shows that the object cannot be identical with the sense-datum. This discovery, however—which is not at all paradoxical in the case of taste and smell and sound, and only slightly so in the case of touch—leaves undiminished our instinctive belief that there *are* objects *corresponding* to our sense-data. Since this belief does not lead to any difficulties, but on the contrary tends to simplify and systematize our account of our experiences, there seems no good reason for rejecting it. We may therefore admit—though with a slight doubt derived from dreams—that the external world does really exist, and is not wholly dependent for its existence upon our continuing to perceive it.

The argument which has led us to this conclusion is doubtless less strong than we could wish, but it is typical of many philosophical arguments, and it is therefore worth while to consider briefly its general character and validity. All knowledge, we find, must be built up upon our instinctive beliefs, and if these are rejected, nothing is left. But among our instinctive beliefs some are much stronger than others, while many have, by habit and association, become entangled with other beliefs, not really instinctive, but falsely supposed to be part of what is believed instinctively.

Philosophy should show us the hierarchy of our instinctive beliefs, beginning with those we hold most strongly, and presenting each as much isolated and as free from irrelevant additions as possible. It should take care to show that, in the form in which they are finally set forth, our instinctive beliefs do not clash, but form a harmonious system. There can never be any reason for rejecting one instinctive belief except that it clashes with others; thus, if they are found to harmonize, the whole system becomes worthy of acceptance.

It is of course *possible* that all or any of our beliefs may be mistaken, and therefore all ought to be held with at least some slight element of doubt. But we cannot have *reason* to reject a belief except on the ground of some other belief. Hence, by organizing our instinctive beliefs and their consequences, by considering which among them is most possible, if necessary, to modify or abandon, we can arrive, on the basis of accepting as our sole data what we instinctively believe, at an orderly systematic organization of our knowledge, in which, though the *possibility* of error remains, its likelihood is diminished by the interrelation of the parts and by the critical scrutiny which has preceded acquiescence.

This function, at least, philosophy can perform. Most philosophers, rightly or wrongly, believe that philosophy can do much more than this—that it can give us knowledge, not otherwise attainable, concerning the universe as a whole, and concerning the nature of ultimate reality. Whether this be the case or not, the more modest function we have spoken of can certainly be performed by philosophy, and certainly suffices, for those who have once begun to doubt the adequacy of common sense, to justify the arduous and difficult labours that philosophical problems involve.

Chapter 3: The Nature of Matter

In the preceding chapter we agreed, though without being able to find demonstrative reasons, that it is rational to believe that our sense-data—for example, those which we regard as associated with my table—are really signs of the existence of something independent of us and our perceptions. That is to say, over and above the sensations of colour, hardness, noise, and so on, which make up the appearance of the table to me, I assume that there is something else, *of* which these things are appearances. The colour ceases to exist if I shut my eyes, the sensation of hardness ceases to exist if I remove my arm from contact with the table, the sound ceases to exist if I cease to rap the table with my knuckles. But I do not believe that when all these things cease the table ceases. On the contrary, I believe that it is because the table exists continuously that all these sense-data will reappear when I open my eyes, replace my arm, and begin again to rap with my knuckles. The question we have to consider in this chapter is: What is the nature of this real table, which persists independently of my perception of it?

To this question physical science gives an answer, somewhat incomplete it is true, and in part still very hypothetical, but yet deserving of respect so far as it goes. Physical science, more or less unconsciously, has drifted into the view that all natural phenomena ought to be reduced to motions. Light and heat and sound are all due to wave-motions, which travel from the body emitting them to the person who sees light or feels heat or hears sound. That which has the wave-motion is either aether[8] or 'gross matter', but in either case is what the philosopher would call matter. The only properties which science assigns to it are position in space, and the power of motion according to the laws of motion. Science does not deny that it *may* have other properties; but if so, such other properties are not useful to the man of science, and in no way assist him in explaining the phenomena.

It is sometimes said that 'light *is* a form of wave-motion', but this is misleading, for the light which we immediately see, which we know directly by means of

---

8   This is the invisible, all-pervasive substance assumed by classical physics to fill up all the 'empty' space in the universe and to be the medium through which light waves are propagated (just as water is the medium for watery waves). The hypothesis was rendered obsolete by Einstein's theory of special relativity in 1905. (In a foreword to the German edition of 1926, Russell admitted that when *The Problems of Philosophy* was written in 1911 he had not yet sufficiently understood the importance of Einstein's theories. Later Russell became a well-known popularizer of relativity theory, for example, in his *ABC of Relativity* [1925].)

our senses, is *not* a form of wave-motion, but something quite different—something which we all know if we are not blind, though we cannot describe it so as to convey our knowledge to a man who is blind. A wave-motion, on the contrary, could quite well be described to a blind man, since he can acquire a knowledge of space by the sense of touch; and he can experience a wave-motion by a sea voyage almost as well as we can. But this, which a blind man can understand, is not what we mean by *light*: we mean by *light* just that which a blind man can never understand, and which we can never describe to him.

Now this something, which all of us who are not blind know, is not, according to science, really to be found in the outer world: it is something caused by the action of certain waves upon the eyes and nerves and brain of the person who sees the light. When it is said that light *is* waves, what is really meant is that waves are the physical cause of our sensations of light. But light itself, the thing which seeing people experience and blind people do not, is not supposed by science to form any part of the world that is independent of us and our senses. And very similar remarks would apply to other kinds of sensations.

It is not only colours and sounds and so on that are absent from the scientific world of matter, but also *space* as we get it through sight or touch. It is essential to science that its matter should be in *a* space, but the space in which it is cannot be exactly the space we see or feel. To begin with, space as we see it is not the same as space as we get it by the sense of touch; it is only by experience in infancy that we learn how to touch things we see, or how to get a sight of things which we feel touching us. But the space of science is neutral as between touch and sight; thus it cannot be either the space of touch or the space of sight.

Again, different people see the same object as of different shapes, according to their point of view. A circular coin, for example, though we should always *judge* it to be circular, will *look* oval unless we are straight in front of it. When we judge that it *is* circular, we are judging that it has a real shape which is not its apparent shape, but belongs to it intrinsically apart from its appearance. But this real shape, which is what concerns science, must be in a real space, not the same as anybody's apparent space. The real space is public,

the *apparent* space is private to the percipient. In different people's *private* spaces the same object seems to have different shapes; thus the real space, in which it has its real shape, must be different from the private spaces. The space of science, therefore, though *connected* with the spaces we see and feel, is not identical with them, and the manner of its connexion requires investigation.

We agreed provisionally that physical objects cannot be quite like our sense-data, but may be regarded as *causing* our sensations. These physical objects are in the space of science, which we may call 'physical' space. It is important to notice that, if our sensations are to be caused by physical objects, there must be a physical space containing these objects and our sense-organs and nerves and brain. We get a sensation of touch from an object when we are in contact with it; that is to say, when some part of our body occupies a place in physical space quite close to the space occupied by the object. We see an object (roughly speaking) when no opaque body is between the object and our eyes in physical space. Similarly, we only hear or smell or taste an object when we are sufficiently near to it, or when it touches the tongue, or has some suitable position in physical space relatively to our body. We cannot begin to state what different sensations we shall derive from a given object under different circumstances unless we regard the object and our body as both in one physical space, for it is mainly the relative positions of the object and our body that determine what sensations we shall derive from the object.

Now our sense-data are situated in our private spaces, either the space of sight or the space of touch or such vaguer spaces as other senses may give us. If, as science and common sense assume, there is one public all-embracing physical space in which physical objects are, the relative positions of physical objects in physical space must more or less correspond to the relative positions of sense-data in our private spaces. There is no difficulty in supposing this to be the case. If we see on a road one house nearer to us than another, our other senses will bear out the view that it is nearer; for example, it will be reached sooner if we walk along the road. Other people will agree that the house which looks nearer to us is nearer; the ordnance map[9] will take the same view; and thus everything points to a spatial relation between the houses corresponding to the relation between the sense-data which we see when we look at the houses. Thus we may assume that there is a physical space in which physical objects have spatial relations corresponding to those which the corresponding sense-data have in our private spaces. It is this physical space which is dealt with in geometry and assumed in physics and astronomy.

Assuming that there is physical space, and that it does thus correspond to private spaces, what can we know about it? We can know *only* what is required in order to secure the correspondence. That is to say, we can know nothing of what it is like in itself, but we can know the sort of arrangement of physical objects which results from their spatial relations. We can know, for example, that the earth and moon and sun are in one straight line during an eclipse, though we cannot know what a physical straight line is in itself, as we know the look of a straight line in our visual space. Thus we come to know much more about the *relations* of distances in physical space than about the distances themselves; we may know that one distance is greater than another, or that it is along the same straight line as the other, but we cannot have that immediate acquaintance with physical distances that we have with distances in our private spaces, or with colours or sounds or other sense-data. We can know all those things about physical space which a man born blind might know through other people about the space of sight; but the kind of things which a man born blind could never know about the space of sight we also cannot know about physical space. We can know the properties of the relations required to preserve the correspondence with sense-data, but we cannot know the nature of the terms between which the relations hold.

With regard to time, our *feeling* of duration or of the lapse of time is notoriously an unsafe guide as to the time that has elapsed by the clock. Times when we are bored or suffering pain pass slowly, times when we are agreeably occupied pass quickly, and times when we are sleeping pass almost as if they did not exist. Thus, in so far as time is constituted by duration, there is the same necessity for distinguishing a public and a private time as there was in the case of space. But in so far as time consists in an *order* of before and after, there is no need to make such a distinction; the time-order which events seem to have is, so far as we can see, the same as the time-order which they do have. At any rate no reason can be given for supposing that the two orders are not the same. The same is usually true of space: if a regiment of men are marching along a road, the *shape* of the regiment will look different from different points of view, but the men will appear arranged in the same *order* from all points of view. Hence we regard the *order* as true also in physical space, whereas the shape is only supposed to correspond to the physical space so far as is required for the preservation of the order.

In saying that the time-order which events *seem to have* is the same as the time-order which they *really have*, it is necessary to guard against a possible misunderstanding. It must not be supposed that the various states of different physical objects have the same time-order as the sense-data which constitute the perceptions of those objects. Considered as physical objects, the thunder and lightning are simultaneous; that is to say, the lightning is simultaneous with the disturbance of the air in the place where the disturbance begins, namely, where the lightning is. But the sense-datum which we call hearing the thunder does not take place until the disturbance of the air has travelled as far as to where we are. Similarly, it takes about eight minutes for the sun's light to reach us; thus, when we see the sun we are seeing the sun of eight minutes ago. So far as our sense-data afford evidence as to the physical sun they afford evidence as to the physical sun of eight minutes ago; if the physical sun had ceased to exist within the last eight minutes, that would make no difference to the sense-data which we call 'seeing the sun'. This affords a fresh illustration of the necessity of distinguishing between sense-data and physical objects.

What we have found as regards space is much the same as what we find in relation to the correspondence of the sense-data with their physical

---

9   A reference to the standard large-scale maps of Britain made by the Ordnance Survey (originally maps made for the military during the Napoleonic wars).

counterparts. If one object looks blue and another red, we may reasonably presume that there is some corresponding difference between the physical objects; if two objects both look blue, we may presume a corresponding similarity. But we cannot hope to be acquainted directly with the quality in the physical object which makes it look blue or red. Science tells us that this quality is a certain sort of wave-motion, and this sounds familiar, because we think of wave-motions in the space we see. But the wave-motions must really be in physical space, with which we have no direct acquaintance; thus the real wave-motions have not that familiarity which we might have supposed them to have. And what holds for colours is closely similar to what holds for other sense-data. Thus we find that, although the *relations* of physical objects have all sorts of knowable properties, derived from their correspondence with the relations of sense-data, the physical objects themselves remain unknown in their intrinsic nature, so far at least as can be discovered by means of the senses. The question remains whether there is any other method of discovering the intrinsic nature of physical objects.

The most natural, though not ultimately the most defensible, hypothesis to adopt in the first instance, at any rate as regards visual sense-data, would be that, though physical objects cannot, for the reasons we have been considering, be *exactly* like sense-data, yet they may be more or less like. According to this view, physical objects will, for example, really have colours, and we might, by good luck, see an object as of the colour it really is. The colour which an object seems to have at any given moment will in general be very similar, though not quite the same, from many different points of view; we might thus suppose the 'real' colour to be a sort of medium colour, intermediate between the various shades which appear from the different points of view.

Such a theory is perhaps not capable of being definitely refuted, but it can be shown to be groundless. To begin with, it is plain that the colour we see depends only upon the nature of the light-waves that strike the eye, and is therefore modified by the medium intervening between us and the object, as well as by the manner in which light is reflected from the object in the direction of the eye. The intervening air alters colours unless it is perfectly clear, and any strong reflection will alter them completely. Thus the colour we see is a result of the ray as it reaches the eye, and not simply a property of the object from which the ray comes. Hence, also, provided certain waves reach the eye, we shall see a certain colour, whether the object from which the waves start has any colour or not. Thus it is quite gratuitous to suppose that physical objects have colours, and therefore there is no justification for making such a supposition. Exactly similar arguments will apply to other sense-data.

It remains to ask whether there are any general philosophical arguments enabling us to say that, if matter is real, it *must* be of such and such a nature. As explained above, very many philosophers, perhaps most, have held that whatever is real must be in some sense mental, or at any rate that whatever we can know anything about must be in some sense mental. Such philosophers are called 'idealists'. Idealists tell us that what appears as matter is really something mental; namely, either (as Leibniz held) more or less rudimentary minds, or (as Berkeley contended) ideas in the minds which, as we should commonly say, 'perceive' the matter. Thus idealists deny the existence of matter as something intrinsically different from mind, though they do not deny that our sense-data are signs of something which exists independently of our private sensations. In the following chapter we shall consider briefly the reasons—in my opinion fallacious—which idealists advance in favour of their theory.

G.E. MOORE
"Proof of an External World"

Who Was G.E. Moore?

George Edward Moore was a leading figure in the generation of philosophers—including Bertrand Russell and the young Ludwig Wittgenstein—which set British philosophy on a new path at the start of the twentieth century by founding the important stream of thought called "analytic philosophy" (which, in somewhat altered form, is still dominant today in the English-speaking philosophical world).

Born to middle-class, devoutly religious parents in a London suburb in 1873, Moore studied Greek and Latin (but, by his own admission, no science at all) at Dulwich College, and then went up to Trinity College, Cambridge, to study classics. Bertrand Russell, who was a student there at the same time, persuaded Moore to switch to the study of philosophy, and after his undergraduate education (on his second attempt) Moore won a six-year prize fellowship at Trinity. It paid £200 a year, plus board and lodging in college, from 1898 until 1904.

During these early years of his philosophical career Moore had two notable triumphs. First, he published papers (in particular "The Refutation of Idealism," in 1903) which, it turned out, signaled the death knell of the then-dominant form of philosophy in Britain—a philosophy called "absolute idealism" which, roughly, held that the universe is constituted, not of matter, but of the thought of an absolute spirit. Second, he wrote a book on ethics called *Principia Ethica* (also published in 1903) which influentially declared that all previous ethical theories were guilty of a major fallacy, the "naturalistic fallacy" of trying to define moral values in non-ethical terms. By contrast, Moore said, goodness is an intrinsic, unanalyzable quality known to us by intuition. This book, as well as having a major influence on professional philosophers, became the manifesto for a group of artists and writers known as the Bloomsbury Group, which included Virginia and Leonard Woolf, E.M. Forster, John Maynard Keynes, Lytton Strachey, and Clive Bell.

In his later work, Moore became known for his defense of common sense: he believed that whenever a philosophical doctrine contradicts common sense, it was more likely that the philosophical argument had gone awry than that common sense had done so. He disagreed with those philosophers (such as Russell and Wittgenstein) who held that our ordinary language concealed philosophical errors that needed to be eliminated in an artificial, perfect, logical language. Similarly, he did not think that our everyday beliefs were false and in need of replacement by more rigorous philosophical or scientific claims. What, then, is the role of philosophy according to Moore? It is to *analyze* our everyday beliefs and find out what, exactly, they are telling us. What, for example, Moore asks, do we really *mean* when we say, "I think that table over there exists outside of my mind"?

Moore left Cambridge in 1904, lived in Edinburgh and London for a while, but then returned to Cambridge as a university lecturer in 1911. He spent the rest of his life there, except for a lengthy visit to the United States shortly after his retirement in 1939. In 1916 he married one of his students (a "Miss D.M. Ely," who for some reason always called him either "Moore" or "Bill"), and had two sons, one of whom became a poet and the other a musician. Moore quickly became one of the most well-respected philosophers in Britain and, partly under his influence, Cambridge was the most important center for philosophy in the world during these years. Though he had a rather retiring personality, Moore's acute intelligence and his intense concern to lay out problems with total precision and thereby get matters exactly right seems to have exerted a powerful and uplifting influence on those around him. A British philosopher from the generation after Moore's, Gilbert Ryle, said of him:

> For some of us there still lives the Moore whose voice is never quite resuscitated by his printed words. This is the Moore whom we met at Cambridge and at the annual Joint Session of the Mind Association and the Aristotelian Society. Moore was a dynamo of courage. He gave us courage not by making concessions, but by making no concessions to our youth or to our shyness. He treated us as corrigible and therefore as responsible thinkers. He would explode at our mistakes and muddles with just that genial ferocity with which he would explode at the mistakes and muddles of philosophical highups, and with just the genial ferocity with which he would explode at mistakes and muddles of his own. He would listen with minute attention to what we said, and then, without a trace of discourtesy or courtesy, treat our remarks simply on their merits, usually, of course, and justly inveighing against their inadequacy, irrelevance or confusedness, but sometimes, without a trace of politeness or patronage, crediting them with whatever positive utility he thought that they possessed. If, as sometimes happened, he found in someone's interposition the exposure of a confusion or a fallacy of his own, he would announce that this was so, confess to his own unbelievable muddle-headedness or slackness of reasoning, and then with full acknowledgment, adopt and work with the clarification.

What Is the Structure of This Reading?

Moore begins by introducing the problem he will be discussing: the problem of the existence of the external world. He does not proceed immediately to try to answer it, however, but begins by trying to clarify exactly what the question is asking (and thus what would count as a correct answer). He starts with the phrase "things outside of us" and sets out to refine it into a more exact expression, ending up with "things which are to be met with in space." Then he tries to make clearer what precisely this means, contrasting it with "things which are presented in space" in order to do so: this involves showing, first, that some things presented in space are not to be met with in space, and second that some things to be met with in space are not presented in space. Moore now claims (though he admits he has not succeeded in making the notion *absolutely* clear) he has said enough to show that, if only he can prove there exist some things which are to be met with in space (such as tables, stars, and sheets of paper), it would trivially follow that "there are things to be met with in space" is true.

Moore now faces another problem: even if he can prove that there are things to be met with in space, why should we admit that these objects are *external to our minds*? That is, how can Moore prove that tables, even though they are importantly different from after-images, are not nevertheless another kind of mental object? Moore's reasoning needs to be followed carefully here, but his central idea is that statements about things external to our minds are logically independent of claims about experience. That is, for example, its being true that a sheet of paper exists does not logically entail the truth of the claim that someone is perceiving that paper, whereas to say that someone is seeing double at a particular time *commits* one to the claim that someone is having an experience of a double image at that time.

Moore points out that this means that "external to our minds" is not synonymous with "to be met with in space," but suggests that if something *is* to be met with in space then it must also be external to our minds. Moore is now at the point in his argument where, he says, if he can just show that two things are to be met with in space this will prove that some external things exist and so definitively answer his original question. *Can* he show that at least two things are to be met with in space? He can, he says, and demonstrates by proving that his two hands exist.

Philosophers, however, will wonder if it can really be so simple? *Did* Moore actually prove that his hands exist outside of his (and our) mind? Moore completes his paper by attempting to defend his argument against possible objections and showing that it satisfies the three "conditions necessary for a rigorous proof."

Some Common Misconceptions

1. Moore is sometimes caricatured as merely gesticulating with his hands in the air and claiming that he has proved the external world exists. Although there is *some* truth to this, you should be able to see that what Moore is doing is much more complicated and careful than mere hand-waving.

2. "Moore," I said, "have you any apples in that basket?" "No," he replied and smiled seraphically as was his wont. I decided to try a different logical tack. "Moore," I said, "do you then have some apples in that basket?" "No," he said once again. Now I was in a logical cleft-stick, so to speak, and had but one way out. "Moore," I said, "do you then have apples in that basket?" "Yes," he replied, and from that day forth we remained the very best of friends.

This piece of comedy—written by Jonathan Miller for the 1960s show *Beyond the Fringe*—illustrates another common but over-hasty perception of Moore's philosophical method. This is the impression that Moore's work consisted in making, for their own sake, a sequence of trivial and unnecessary logical distinctions and clarifications which perhaps sound clever but which are irrelevant to the "big" concerns of philosophy. You should decide for yourself how fruitful Moore's method of analysis is, but it is certainly untrue that Moore was not at least sincerely *attempting* to deal with real, important philosophical questions by, for example,

distinguishing carefully between the logic of the phrases "to be met with in space" and "presented in space."

Suggestions for Critical Reflection

1. Do you think Moore is attempting to refute philosophical skepticism in this paper, or do you think he might be trying to do something slightly different or more focussed? Does his proof of the existence of the external world, if it works, show that skepticism must be false? Do you think Moore even takes the possibility of skepticism *seriously*? (And if not, should he?)

2. Do you think that Moore manages to prove that the things which are "to be met with in space" (such as shrubbery or furniture) *must* be "external to our minds"? And even if he does that, does he also demonstrate that something like Berkeley's idealism is false: that is, does he show that trees and tables must be external to *any* mind at all (even God's)?

3. How, if at all, does Moore *justify* his claim that he knows his hands exist? Is this a good enough justification (at least, good enough for what Moore is trying to do)?

4. Moore's defense of his final proof that objects exist in the external world may depend upon making a distinction between proving something and proving *that one knows* that thing. Do you think this is a viable distinction? Put it this way: could someone know *p* without knowing that they know *p*?

Suggestions for Further Reading

A good entrée into Moore's philosophy is his book *Some Main Problems of Philosophy* (George Allen & Unwin, 1953). Several of his most important papers are collected in *G.E. Moore: Selected Writings*, edited by Thomas Baldwin (Routledge, 1993); Baldwin also wrote what is probably the best book about Moore's philosophy, *G.E. Moore* (Routledge, 1990). Also interesting is E.D. Klemke, *A Defense of Realism: Reflections on the Metaphysics of G.E. Moore* (Humanity Books, 1999). The best collection of essays about Moore, which includes his rather charming autobiography and replies to the essays, is *The Philosophy of G.E. Moore*, edited by P.A. Schilpp (Open Court, 1968).

"Proof of an External World"[1]

In the Preface to the second edition of Kant's *Critique of Pure Reason* some words occur, which, in Professor Kemp Smith's translation, are rendered as follows:[2]

> It still remains a scandal to philosophy … that the existence of things outside of us … must be accepted merely on *faith*, and that, if anyone thinks good to doubt their existence, we are unable to counter his doubts by any satisfactory proof.[3]

It seems clear from these words that Kant thought it a matter of some importance to give a proof of 'the existence of things outside of us' or perhaps rather (for it seems to me possible that the force of the German words is better rendered in this way) of 'the existence of *the* things outside of us'; for had he not thought it important that a proof should be given, he would scarcely have called it a 'scandal' that no proof had been given. And it seems clear also that he thought that the giving of such a proof was a task which fell properly within the province of philosophy; for, if it did not, the fact that no proof had been given could not possibly be a scandal to *philosophy*.

_____

1 This paper was first published in 1939 in the *Proceedings of the British Academy* (Volume 25, pp. 273–300). It is reprinted here by kind permission of Dr. Thomas Baldwin, Literary Executor to G.E. Moore.

2 The introduction to the second (or 'B') edition of the *Critique of Pure Reason* appears as a reading in this chapter. More information about Kant appears in the notes to that selection.

3 [Author's note] B xxxix, note: Kemp Smith, p.34. The German words are 'so bleibt es immer ein Skandal der Philosophie …, das Dasein der Dinge ausser uns …, bloss auf *Glauben* annehmen zu müssen, und wenn es jemand einfällt es zu bezweifeln, ihm keinen genugtuenden Beweis entgegenstellen zu können'.

Now, even if Kant was mistaken in both of these two opinions there seems to me to be no doubt whatever that it is of some importance and also a matter which falls properly within the province of philosophy, to discuss the question what sort of proof, if any, can be given of 'the existence of things outside of us'. And to discuss this question was my object when I began to write the present lecture. But I may say at once that, as you will find, I have only, at most, succeeded in saying a very small part of what ought to be said about it.

The words 'it … remains a scandal to philosophy … that we are unable …' would, taken strictly, imply that, at the moment at which he wrote them, Kant himself was unable to produce a satisfactory proof of the point in question. But I think it is unquestionable that Kant himself did not think that he personally was at the time unable to produce such a proof. On the contrary, in the immediately preceding sentence, he has declared that he has, in the second edition of his *Critique*, to which he is now writing the Preface, given a 'rigorous proof' of this very thing; and has added that he believes this proof of his to be 'the only possible proof'. It is true that in this preceding sentence he does not describe the proof which he has given as a proof of 'the existence of things outside of us' or of 'the existence of the things outside of us', but describes it instead as a proof of 'the objective reality of outer intuition'. But the context leaves no doubt that he is using these two phrases, 'the objective reality of outer intuition' and 'the existence of things (or 'the things') outside of us', in such a way that whatever is a proof of the first is also necessarily a proof of the second. We must, therefore, suppose that when he speaks as if *we* are unable to give a satisfactory proof, he does not mean to say that he himself, as well as others, is *at the moment* unable; but rather that, until he discovered the proof which he has given, both he himself and everybody else *were* unable. Of course, if he is right in thinking that he has given a satisfactory proof, the state of things which he describes came to an end as soon as his proof was published. As soon as that happened, anyone who read it was able to give a satisfactory proof by simply repeating that which Kant had given, and the 'scandal' to philosophy had been removed once for all.

If, therefore, it were certain that the proof of the point in question given by Kant in the second edition is a satisfactory proof, it would be certain that at least one satisfactory proof can be given; and all that would remain of the question which I said I proposed to discuss would be, firstly, the question as to what *sort* of a proof this of Kant's is, and secondly the question whether (contrary to Kant's own opinion) there may not perhaps be other proofs, of the same or of a different sort, which are also satisfactory. But I think it is by no means certain that Kant's proof is satisfactory. I think it is by no means certain that he did succeed in removing once for all the state of affairs which he considered to be a scandal to philosophy. And I think, therefore, that the question whether it is possible to give *any* satisfactory proof of the point in question still deserves discussion.

But what is the point in question? I think it must be owned that the expression 'things outside of us' is rather an odd expression, and an expression the meaning of which is certainly not perfectly clear. It would have sounded less odd if, instead of 'things outside of us' I had said 'external things', and perhaps also the meaning of this expression would have seemed to be clearer; and I think we make the meaning of 'external things' clearer still if we explain that this phrase has been regularly used by philosophers as short for 'things external to *our minds*'. The fact is that there has been a long philosophical tradition, in accordance with which the three expressions 'external things', 'things external to *us*', and 'things external to *our minds*' have been used as equivalent to one another, and have, each of them, been used as if they needed no explanation. The origin of this usage I do not know. It occurs already in Descartes; and since he uses the expressions as if they needed no explanation, they had presumably been used with the same meaning before. Of the three, it seems to me that the expression 'external to *our minds*' is the clearest, since it at least makes clear that what is meant is not 'external to *our bodies*'; whereas both the other expressions might be taken to mean this: and indeed there has been a good deal of confusion, even among philosophers, as to the relation of the two conceptions 'external things' and 'things external to *our bodies*'. But even the expression 'things external to our minds' seems to me to be far from perfectly clear; and if I am to make really clear what I mean by 'proof of the existence of things outside of us', I cannot do it by merely saying that by 'outside of us' I mean 'external to our minds'.

There is a passage (*Kritik der reinen Vernunft*, A373)[4] in which Kant himself says that the expression 'outside of us' 'carries with it an unavoidable ambiguity'. He says that 'sometimes it means something which exists *as a thing in itself* distinct from us, and sometimes something which merely belongs to external *appearance*'; he calls things which are 'outside of us' in the first of these two senses 'objects which might be called external in the transcendental sense', and things which are so in the second '*empirically external* objects'; and he says finally that, in order to remove all uncertainty as to the latter conception, he will distinguish empirically external objects from objects which might be called 'external' in the transcendental sense, 'by calling them outright things which are *to be met with in space*'.

I think that this last phrase of Kant's, 'things which are to be met with in space', does indicate fairly clearly what sort of things it is with regard to which I wish to inquire what sort of proof, if any, can be given that there are any things of that sort. My body, the bodies of other men, the bodies of animals, plants of all sorts, stones, mountains, the sun, the moon, stars, and planets, houses and other buildings, manufactured articles of all sorts—chairs, tables, pieces of paper, etc., are all of them 'things which are to be met with in space'. In short, all things of the sort that philosophers have been used to call 'physical objects', 'material things', or 'bodies' obviously come under this head. But the phrase 'things that are to be met with in space' can be naturally understood as applying also in cases where the names 'physical object', 'material thing', or 'body' can hardly be applied. For instance, shadows are sometimes to be met with in space, although they could hardly be properly called 'physical objects', 'material things', or 'bodies'; and although in one usage of the term 'thing' it would not be proper to call a shadow a 'thing', yet the phrase 'things which are to be met with in space' can be naturally understood as synonymous

---

4   *Critique of Pure Reason*, first ("A") edition, page 373 (of the original German).

with 'whatever can be met with in space', and this is an expression which can quite properly be understood to include shadows. I wish the phrase 'things which are to be met with in space' to be understood in this wide sense; so that if a proof can be found that there ever have been as many as two different shadows it will follow at once that there have been at least two 'things which were to be met with in space', and this proof will be as good a proof of the point in question as would be a proof that there have been at least two 'physical objects' of no matter what sort.

The phrase 'things which are to be met with in space' can, therefore, be naturally understood as having a very wide meaning—a meaning even wider than that of 'physical object' or 'body', wide as is the meaning of these latter expressions. But wide as is its meaning, it is not, in one respect, so wide as that of another phrase which Kant uses as if it were equivalent to this one; and a comparison between the two will, I think, serve to make still clearer what sort of things it is with regard to which I wish to ask what proof, if any, can be given that there are such things.

The other phrase which Kant uses as if it were equivalent to 'things which are to be met with in space' is used by him in the sentence immediately preceding that previously quoted in which he declares that the expression 'things outside of us' 'carries with it an unavoidable ambiguity' (A373). In this preceding sentence he says that an 'empirical object' 'is called *external*, if it is presented (*vorgestellt*) in space'. He treats, therefore, the phrase 'presented in space' as if it were equivalent to 'to be met with in space'. But it is easy to find examples of 'things', of which it can hardly be denied that they are 'presented in space', but of which it could, quite naturally, be emphatically denied that they are 'to be met with in space'. Consider, for instance, the following description of one set of circumstances under which what some psychologists have called a 'negative after-image' and others a 'negative after-sensation' can be obtained. 'If, after looking steadfastly at a white patch on a black ground, the eye be turned to a white ground, a grey patch is seen for some little time' (Foster's *Text-book of Physiology*, IV, iii, 3, p.1266; quoted in Stout's *Manual of Psychology*, 3rd edition, p. 280). Upon reading these words recently, I took the trouble to cut

out of a piece of white paper a four-pointed star, to place it on a black ground, to 'look steadfastly' at it, and then to turn my eyes to a white sheet of paper: and I did find that I saw a grey patch for some little time—I not only saw a grey patch, but I saw it on the white ground, and also this grey patch was of roughly the same shape as the white four-pointed star at which I had 'looked steadfastly' just before—it also was a four-pointed star. I repeated this simple experiment successfully several times. Now each of those grey four-pointed stars, one of which I saw in each experiment, was what is called an 'after-image' or 'after-sensation'; and can anybody deny that each of these after-images can be quite properly said to have been 'presented in space'? I saw each of them on a real white background, and, if so, each of them was 'presented' on a real white background. But though they were 'presented in space' everybody, I think, would feel that it was gravely misleading to say that they were 'to be met with in space'. The white star at which I 'looked steadfastly', the black ground on which I saw it, and the white ground on which I saw the after-images, were, of course, 'to be met with in space': they were, in fact, 'physical objects' or surfaces of physical objects. But one important difference between them, on the one hand, and the grey after-images, on the other, can be quite naturally expressed by saying that the latter were *not* 'to be met with in space'. And one reason why this is so is, I think, plain. To say that so and so was at a given time 'to be met with in space' naturally suggests that there are conditions such that *any one* who fulfilled them might, conceivably, have 'perceived' the 'thing' in question—might have seen it, if it was a visible object, have felt it, if it was a tangible one, have heard it, if it was a sound, have smelt it, if it was a smell. When I say that the white four-pointed paper star, at which I looked steadfastly, was a 'physical object' and was 'to be met with in space', I am implying that *anyone*, who had been in the room at the time, and who had normal eyesight and a normal sense of touch, might have seen and felt it. But, in the case of those grey after-images which I saw, it is not conceivable that anyone besides myself should have seen any one of them. It is, of course, quite conceivable that other people, if they had been in the room with me at the time, and had carried out the same experiment which I carried out, would have seen grey after-images *very like* one of those which I saw: there is no absurdity in supposing even that they might have seen after-images *exactly* like one of those which I saw. But there is an absurdity in supposing that any one of the after-images which I saw could also have been seen by anyone else: in supposing that two different people can ever see the very same after-image. One reason, then, why we should say that none of those grey after-images which I saw was 'to be met with in space', although each of them was certainly 'presented in space' to me, is simply that none of them could conceivably have been seen by anyone else. It is natural so to understand the phrase 'to be met with in space', that to say of anything which a man perceived that it was to be met with in space is to say that it might have been perceived by *others* as well as by the man in question.

Negative after-images of the kind described are, therefore, one example of 'things' which, though they must be allowed to be 'presented in space', are nevertheless *not* 'to be met with in space', and are *not* 'external to our minds' in the sense with which we shall be concerned. And two other important examples may be given.

The first is this. It is well known that people sometimes see things double, an occurrence which has also been described by psychologists by saying that they have a 'double image', or two 'images', of some object at which they are looking. In such cases it would certainly be quite natural to say that each of the two 'images' is 'presented in space': they are seen, one in one place, and the other in another, in just the same sense in which each of those grey after-images which I saw was seen at a particular place on the white background at which I was looking. But it would be utterly unnatural to say that, when I have a double image, each of the two images is 'to be met with in space'. On the contrary it is quite certain that *both* of them are not 'to be met with in space'. If both were, it would follow that somebody else might see the *very same* two images which I see; and, though there is no absurdity in supposing that another person might see a pair of images exactly similar to a pair which I see, there is an absurdity in supposing that anyone else might see the *same identical pair*. In every case, then,

in which anyone sees anything double, we have an example of at least one 'thing' which, though 'presented in space' is certainly not 'to be met with in space'.

And the second important example is this. Bodily pains can, in general, be quite properly said to be 'presented in space'. When I have a toothache, I feel it *in* a particular region of my jaw or *in* a particular tooth; when I make a cut on my finger smart by putting iodine on it, I feel the pain in a particular place in my finger; and a man whose leg has been amputated may feel a pain *in* a place where his foot might have been if he had not lost it. It is certainly perfectly natural to understand the phrase 'presented in space' in such a way that if, in the sense illustrated, a pain is felt *in* a particular place, that pain is 'presented in space'. And yet of pains it would be quite unnatural to say that they are 'to be met with in space', for the same reason as in the case of after-images or double images. It is quite conceivable that another person should feel a pain exactly like one which I feel, but there is an absurdity in supposing that he could feel *numerically the same*[5] pain which I feel. And pains are in fact a typical example of the sort of 'things' of which philosophers say that they are *not* 'external' to our minds, but 'within' them. Of any pain which I feel they would say that it is necessarily *not* external to my mind but *in* it.

And finally it is, I think, worth while to mention one other class of 'things', which are certainly not 'external' objects and certainly not 'to be met with in space', in the sense with which I am concerned, but which yet some philosophers would be inclined to say are 'presented in space', though they are not 'presented in space' in quite the same sense in which pains, double images, and negative after-images of the sort I described are so. If you look at an electric light and then close your eyes, it sometimes happens that you see, for some little time, against the dark background which you usually see when your eyes are shut, a bright patch similar in shape to the light at which you have just been looking. Such a bright patch, if you see one, is another example of what some psychologists have called 'after-images' and others 'after-sensations'; but, unlike the negative

---

5   One and the same, self-identical with.

after-images of which I spoke before, it is seen when your eyes are shut. Of such an after-image, seen with closed eyes, some philosophers might be inclined to say that this image too was 'presented in space', although it is certainly not 'to be met with in space'. They would be inclined to say that it is 'presented in space', because it certainly is presented as at some little distance from the person who is seeing it: and how can a thing be presented as at some little distance from me, without being 'presented in space'? Yet there is an important difference between such after-images, seen with closed eyes, and after-images of the sort I previously described—a difference which might lead other philosophers to deny that these after-images, seen with closed eyes, are 'presented in space' at all. It is a difference which can be expressed by saying that when your eyes are shut, you are not seeing any part of *physical* space at all—of the space which is referred to when we talk of 'things which are to be met with in *space*'. An after-image seen with closed eyes certainly is presented in *a* space, but it may be questioned whether it is proper to say that it is presented in *space*.

It is clear, then, I think, that by no means everything which can naturally be said to be 'presented in space' can also be naturally said to be 'a thing which is to be met with in space'. Some of the 'things', which are presented in space, are very emphatically *not* to be met with in space: or, to use another phrase, which may be used to convey the same notion, they are emphatically *not* 'physical realities' at all. The conception 'presented in space' is therefore, in one respect, much wider than the conception 'to be met with in space': many 'things' fall under the first conception which do not fall under the second—many after-images, one at least of the pair of 'images' seen whenever anyone sees double, and most bodily pains, are 'presented in space', though none of them are to be met with in space. From the fact that a 'thing' is presented in space, it by no means follows that it is to be met with in space. But just as the first conception is, in one respect, wider than the second, so, in another, the second is wider than the first. For there are many 'things' to be met with in space, of which it is not true that they are presented in space. From the fact that a 'thing' is to be met with in space, it by

no means follows that it is presented in space. I have taken 'to be met with in space' to imply, as I think it naturally may, that a 'thing' *might be* perceived; but from the fact that a thing *might be* perceived, it does not follow that it is perceived; and if it is not actually perceived, then it will not be presented in space. It is characteristic of the sorts of 'things', including shadows, which I have described as 'to be met with in space', that there is no absurdity in supposing with regard to any one of them which is, at a given time, perceived, both (1) that it might have existed at that very time, without being perceived; (2) that it might have existed at another time, without being perceived at that other time; and (3) that during the whole period of its existence, it need not have been perceived at any time at all. There is, therefore, no absurdity in supposing that many things, which were at one time to be met with in space, never were 'presented' at any time at all, and that many things which *are* to be met with in space now, are not now 'presented' and also never were and never will be. To use a Kantian phrase, the conception of 'things which are to be met with in space', embraces not only objects of actual experience, but also objects *of possible* experience; and from the fact that a thing is or was an object of *possible* experience, it by no means follows that it either was or is or will be 'presented' at all.

I hope that what I have now said may have served to make clear enough what sorts of 'things' I was originally referring to as 'things outside us' or 'things external to our minds'. I said that I thought that Kant's phrase 'things that are to be met with in space' indicated fairly clearly the sorts of 'things' in question; and I have tried to make the range clearer still, by pointing out that this phrase only serves the purpose, if (*a*) you understand it in a sense, in which many 'things', e.g., after-images, double images, bodily pains, which might be said to be 'presented in space', are nevertheless *not* to be reckoned as 'things that are to be met with in space', and (*b*) you realise clearly that there is no contradiction in supposing that there have been and are 'to be met with in space' things which never have been, are not now, and never will be perceived, nor in supposing that among those of them which have at some time been perceived many existed at times at which they were not being perceived. I think it will now be clear to everyone that, since I do not reckon as 'external things' after-images, double images, and bodily pains, I also should not reckon as 'external things', any of the 'images' which we often 'see with the mind's eye' when we are awake, nor any of those which we see when we are asleep and dreaming; and also that I was so using the expression 'external' that from the fact that a man was at a given time having a visual hallucination, it will follow that he was seeing at that time something which was *not* 'external' to his mind, and from the fact that he was at a given time having an auditory hallucination, it will follow that he was at the time hearing a sound which was *not* 'external' to his mind. But I certainly have not made my use of these phrases, 'external to our minds' and 'to be met with in space', so clear that in the case of every kind of 'thing' which might be suggested, you would be able to tell at once whether I should or should not reckon it as 'external to our minds' and 'to be met with in space'. For instance, I have said nothing which makes it quite clear whether a reflection which I see in a looking-glass is or is not to be regarded as 'a thing that is to be met with in space' and 'external to our minds', nor have I said anything which makes it quite clear whether the sky is or is not to be so regarded. In the case of the sky, everyone, I think, would feel that it was quite inappropriate to talk of it as 'a thing that is to be met with in space'; and most people, I think, would feel a strong reluctance to affirm, without qualification, that reflections which people see in looking-glasses are 'to be met with in space'. And yet neither the sky nor reflections seen in mirrors are in the same position as bodily pains or after-images in the respect which I have emphasised as a reason for saying of these latter that they are *not* to be met with in space—namely that there is an absurdity in supposing that *the very same* pain which I feel could be felt by someone else or that *the very same* after-image which I see could be seen by someone else. In the case of reflections in mirrors we should quite naturally, in certain circumstances, use language which implies that another person may see the same reflection which we see. We might quite naturally say to a friend: 'Do you see that reddish reflection in the water there? I can't make out what it's a reflection of', just as we might say, pointing to

a distant hill-side: 'Do you see that white speck on the hill over there? I can't make out what it is'. And in the case of the sky, it is quite obviously *not* absurd to say that other people see it as well as I.

It must, therefore, be admitted that I have not made my use of the phrase 'things to be met with in space', nor therefore that of 'external to our minds', which the former was used to explain, so clear that in the case of every kind of 'thing' which may be mentioned, there will be no doubt whatever as to whether things of that kind are or are not 'to be met with in space' or 'external to our minds'. But this lack of a clear-cut definition of the expression 'things that are to be met with in space', does not, so far as I can see, matter for my present purpose. For my present purpose it is, I think, sufficient if I make clear, in the case of many kinds of things, that I am so using the phrase 'things that are to be met with in space', that, in the case of each of these kinds, from the proposition that there are things of that kind it *follows* that there are things to be met with in space. And I have, in fact, given a list (though by no means an exhaustive one) of kinds of things which are related to my use of the expression 'things that are to be met with in space' in this way. I mentioned among others the bodies of men and of animals, plants, stars, houses, chairs, and shadows; and I want now to emphasise that I am so using 'things to be met with in space' that, in the case of each of these kinds of 'things', from the proposition that there are 'things' of that kind it *follows* that there are things to be met with in space: e.g., from the proposition that there are plants or that plants exist it *follows* that there are things to be met with in space, from the proposition that shadows exist, it *follows* that there are things to be met with in space, and so on, in the case of all the kinds of 'things' which I mentioned in my first list. That this should be clear is sufficient for my purpose, because, if it is clear, then it will also be clear that, as I implied before, if you have proved that two plants exist, or that a plant and a dog exist, or that a dog and a shadow exist, etc., etc., you will *ipso facto*[6] have proved that there are things to be met with in space: you will not require *also* to give a separate proof that

_____

6   "By that very fact," "by the fact itself."

from the proposition that there are plants it *does* follow that there are things to be met with in space.

Now with regard to the expression 'things that are to be met with in space' I think it will readily be believed that I may be using it in a sense such that no proof is required that from 'plants exist' there follows 'there are things to be met with in space'; but with regard to the phrase 'things external to our minds' I think the case is different. People may be inclined to say: 'I can see quite clearly that from the proposition "At least two dogs exist at the present moment" there *follows* the proposition "At least two things are to be met with in space at the present moment", so that if you can prove that there are two dogs in existence at the present moment you will *ipso facto* have proved that two things at least are to be met with in space at the present moment. I can see that you do not also require a separate proof that from "Two dogs exist" "Two things are to be met with in space" *does* follow; it is quite obvious that there couldn't be a dog which wasn't to be met with in space. But it is not by any means so clear to me that if you can prove that there are two dogs or two shadows, you will *ipso facto* have proved that there are two things *external to our minds*. Isn't it possible that a dog, though it certainly must be "to be met with in space", might *not* be an external object—an object external to our minds? Isn't a separate proof required that anything that is to be met with in space must be external to our minds? Of course, if you are using "external" as a mere synonym for "to be met with in space", no proof will be required that dogs are external objects: in that case, if you can prove that two dogs exist, you will *ipso facto* have proved that there are some external things. But I find it difficult to believe that you, or anybody else, do really use "external" as a mere synonym for "to be met with in space"; and if you don't, isn't some proof required that whatever is to be met with in space must be external to our minds?

Now Kant, as we saw, asserts that the phrases 'outside of us' or 'external' are in fact used in two very different senses; and with regard to one of these two senses, that which he calls the 'transcendental' sense, and which he tries to explain by saying that it is a sense in which 'external' means 'existing *as a thing in itself* distinct from us', it is notorious that he himself held that things which are to be met with in space are *not* 'external' in that sense.[7] There is, therefore, according to him, *a* sense of 'external', a sense in which the word has been commonly used by philosophers—such that, if 'external' be used in that sense, then from the proposition 'Two dogs exist' it will *not* follow that there are some external things. What this supposed sense is I do not think that Kant himself ever succeeded in explaining clearly; nor do I know of any reason for supposing that philosophers ever have used 'external' in a sense, such that in *that* sense things that are to be met with in space are *not* external. But how about the other sense, in which, according to Kant, the word 'external' has been commonly used—that which he calls 'empirically external'? How is this conception related to the conception 'to be met with in space'? It may be noticed that, in the passages which I quoted (A373), Kant himself does not tell us at all clearly what he takes to be the proper answer to this question. He only makes the rather odd statement that, in order to remove all uncertainty as to the conception 'empirically external', he will distinguish objects to which it applies from those which might be called 'external' in the transcendental sense, by 'calling them outright things which are *to be met with in space*'. These odd words certainly suggest, as one possible interpretation of them, that in Kant's opinion the conception 'empirically external' is *identical* with the conception 'to be met with in space'—that he does think that 'external', when used in this second sense, is a mere synonym for 'to be met with in space'. But, if this is his meaning, I do find it very difficult to believe that he is right. Have philosophers, in fact, ever used 'external' as a mere synonym for 'to be met with in space'? Does he himself do so?

---

7 Basically, this is because, for Kant, the things we "meet with in space" are always *appearances* of things, rather than "things in themselves" (the hidden nature behind those appearances). That is, we never meet with "things in themselves" in space, so if *those* things are what we mean by "the things external to us" then none of the things which we *do* meet with in space could be external. See the notes on the Kant selection in this chapter for more information.

I do not think they have, nor that he does himself; and, in order to explain how they have used it, and how the two conceptions 'external to our minds' and 'to be met with in space' are related to one another, I think it is important expressly to call attention to a fact which hitherto I have only referred to incidentally: namely the fact that those who talk of certain things as 'external to' our minds, do, in general, as we should naturally expect, talk of other 'things', with which they wish to contrast the first, as 'in' our minds. It has, of course, been often pointed out that when 'in' is thus used, followed by 'my mind', 'your mind', 'his mind', etc., 'in' is being used metaphorically. And there are some metaphorical uses of 'in', followed by such expressions, which occur in common speech, and which we all understand quite well. For instance, we all understand such expressions as 'I had you in mind, when I made that arrangement' or 'I had you in mind, when I said that there are some people who can't bear to touch a spider'. In these cases 'I was thinking of you' can be used to mean the same as 'I had you in mind'. But it is quite certain that this particular metaphorical use of 'in' is not the one in which philosophers are using it when they contrast what is 'in' my mind with what is 'external' to it. On the contrary, in their use of 'external', you will be external to my mind even at a moment when I have you in mind. If we want to discover what this peculiar metaphorical use of '*in* my mind' is, which is such that nothing, which is, in the sense we are now concerned with, 'external' to my mind, can ever be 'in' it, we need, I think, to consider instances of the sort of 'things' which they would say are 'in' my mind in this special sense. I have already mentioned three such instances, which are, I think, sufficient for my present purpose: any bodily pain which I feel, any after-image which I see with my eyes shut, and any image which I 'see' when I am asleep and dreaming, are typical examples of the sort of 'thing' of which philosophers have spoken as '*in* my mind'. And there is no doubt, I think, that when they have spoken of such things as my body, a sheet of paper, a star—in short 'physical objects' generally—as 'external', they have meant to emphasize some important difference which they feel to exist between such things as these and such 'things' as a pain, an after-image seen with closed eyes, and a dream-image. But *what* difference? What difference do they feel to exist between a bodily pain which I feel or an after-image which I see with closed eyes, on the one hand, and my body itself, on the other—what difference which leads them to say that whereas the bodily pain and the after-image are 'in' my mind, my body itself is *not* 'in' my mind—not even when I am feeling it and seeing it or thinking of it? I have already said that one difference which there is between the two, is that my body is to be met with in space, whereas the bodily pain and the after-image are not. But I think it would be quite wrong to say that this is *the* difference which has led philosophers to speak of the two latter as 'in' my mind, and of my body as *not* 'in' my mind.

The question what the difference is which has led them to speak in this way, is not, I think, at all an easy question to answer; but I am going to try to give, in brief outline, what I *think* is a right answer.

It should, I think, be noted, first of all, that the use of the word 'mind', which is being adopted when it is said that any bodily pains which I feel are 'in my mind', is one which is not quite in accordance with any usage common in ordinary speech, although we are very familiar with it in philosophy. Nobody, I think, would say that bodily pains which I feel are 'in my mind', unless he was also prepared to say that it is *with* my mind that I feel bodily pains; and to say this latter is, I think, not quite in accordance with common non-philosophic usage. It is natural enough to say that it is with my mind that I remember, and think, and imagine, and feel *mental* pains—e.g., disappointment, but not, I think, quite so natural to say that it is with my mind that I feel *bodily* pains, e.g., a severe headache; and perhaps even less natural to say that it is with my mind that I see and hear and smell and taste. There is, however, a well-established philosophical usage according to which seeing, hearing, smelling, tasting, and having a bodily pain are just as much *mental* occurrences or processes as are remembering, or thinking, or imagining. This usage was, I think, adopted by philosophers, because they saw a real resemblance between such statements as 'I saw a cat', 'I heard a clap of thunder', 'I smelt a strong smell of onions', 'My finger smarted horribly', on the one hand, and such statements as 'I remembered having seen him', 'I was thinking out a plan of action', 'I pictured the scene to myself', 'I felt bitterly disappointed', on the other—a resemblance which puts all these statements in one class together, as contrasted with other statements in which 'I' or 'my' is used, such as, e.g., 'I was less than four feet high', 'I was lying on my back', 'My hair was very long'. What is the resemblance in question? It is a resemblance which might be expressed by saying that all the first eight statements are the sort of statements which furnish data for psychology, while the three latter are not. It is also a resemblance which may be expressed, in a way now common among philosophers, by saying that in the case of all the first eight statements, if we make the statement more specific by adding a date, we get a statement such that, if it is true, then it *follows* that I was 'having an experience' at the date in question, whereas this does not hold for the three last statements. For instance, if it is true that I saw a cat between 12 noon and 5 minutes past, today, it *follows* that I was 'having some experience' between 12 noon and 5 minutes past, today; whereas from the proposition that I was less than four feet high in December 1877, it does not *follow* that I had any experiences in December 1877. But this philosophic use of 'having an experience' is one which itself needs explanation, since it is not identical with any use of the expression that is established in common speech. An explanation, however, which is, I think, adequate for the purpose, can be given by saying that a philosopher, who was following this usage, would say that I was at a given time 'having an experience' if and only if either (1) I was conscious at the time or (2) I was dreaming at the time or (3) something else was true of me at the time, which resembled what is true of me when I am conscious and when I am dreaming, in a certain very obvious respect in which what is true of me when I am dreaming resembles what is true of me when I am conscious, and in which what would be true of me, if at any time, for instance, I had a vision, would resemble both. This explanation is, of course, in some degree vague; but I think it is clear enough for our purpose. It amounts to saying that, in this philosophic usage of 'having an experience', it would be said of me that I was, at a given time, having *no* experience, if I was at the time neither conscious nor dreaming nor having a

vision nor *anything else of the sort*; and, of course, this is vague in so far as it has not been specified what else would be *of the sort*: this is left to be gathered from the instances given. But I think this is sufficient: often at night when I am asleep, I am neither conscious nor dreaming nor having a vision nor *anything else of the sort*—that is to say, I am having no experiences. If this explanation of this philosophic usage of 'having an experience' is clear enough, then I think that what has been meant by saying that any pain which I feel or any after-image which I see with my eyes closed is '*in* my mind', can be explained by saying that what is meant is neither more nor less than that there would be a contradiction in supposing *that very same pain* or *that very same after-image* to have existed at a time at which I was having no experience; or, in other words, that from the proposition, with regard to any time, that *that* pain or *that* after-image existed at that time, it *follows* that I was having some experience at the time in question. And if so, then we can say that the felt difference between bodily pains which I feel and after-images which I see, on the one hand, and my body on the other, which has led philosophers to say that any such pain or after-image is '*in* my mind', whereas my body *never* is but is always 'outside of' or 'external to' my mind, is just this, that whereas there is a contradiction in supposing a pain which I feel or an after-image which I see to exist at a time when I am having no experience, there is no contradiction in supposing my body to exist at a time when I am having no experience; and we can even say, I think, that just this and nothing more is what they have meant by these puzzling and misleading phrases 'in my mind' and 'external to my mind'.

But now, if to say of anything, e.g., my body, that it is external to my mind, means merely that from a proposition to the effect that it existed at a specified time, there in no case follows the further proposition that I was having an experience at the time in question, then to say of anything that it is external to *our* minds, will mean similarly that from a proposition to the effect that it existed at a specified time, it in no case follows that any of us were having experiences at the time in question. And if by *our* minds be meant, as is, I think, usually meant, the minds of human beings living on the earth, then it will follow that any pains which animals may feel, any after-images they may see, any experiences they may have, though not external to *their* minds, yet are external to *ours*. And this at once makes plain how different is the conception 'external to our minds' from the conception 'to be met with in space'; for, of course, pains which animals feel or after-images which they see are no more to be met with in space than are pains which *we* feel or after-images which *we* see. From the proposition that there are external objects—objects that are not in any of *our* minds, it does *not* follow that there are things to be met with in space; and hence 'external to our minds' is not a mere synonym for 'to be met with in space': that is to say, 'external to our minds' and 'to be met with in space' are two different conceptions. And the true relation between these conceptions seems to me to be this. We have already seen that there are ever so many kinds of 'things', such that, in the case of each of these kinds, from the proposition that there is at least one thing of that kind there *follows* the proposition that there is at least one thing to be met with in space: e.g., this follows from 'There is at least one star', from 'There is at least one human body', from 'There is at least one shadow', etc. And I think we can say that of every kind of thing of which this is true, it is also true that from the proposition that there is at least one 'thing' of that kind there *follows* the proposition that there is at least one thing external to our minds: e.g., from 'There is at least one star' there follows not only 'There is at least one thing to be met with in space' but also 'There is at least one external thing', and similarly in all other cases. My reason for saying this is as follows. Consider any kind of thing, such that anything of that kind, if there is anything of it, must be 'to be met with in space': e.g., consider the kind 'soap-bubble'. If I say of anything which I am perceiving, 'That is a soap-bubble', I am, it seems to me, certainly implying that there would be no contradiction in asserting that it existed before I perceived it and that it will continue to exist, even if I cease to perceive it. This seems to me to be part of what is meant by saying that it is a real soap-bubble, as distinguished, for instance, from an hallucination of a soap-bubble. Of course, it by no means follows, that if it really is a soap-bubble, it did in fact exist before I perceived it or will continue to exist after I

cease to perceive it: soap-bubbles are an example of a kind of 'physical object' and 'thing to be met with in space', in the case of which it is notorious that particular specimens of the kind often do exist only so long as they are perceived by a particular person. But a thing which I perceive would not be a soap-bubble unless its existence at any given time were logically *independent* of my perception of it at that time; unless that is to say, from the proposition, with regard to a particular time, that it existed at that time, it *never* follows that I perceived it at that time. But, if it is true that it would not be a soap-bubble, unless it *could* have existed at any given time without being perceived by me at that time, it is certainly also true that it would not be a soap-bubble, unless it *could* have existed at any given time, without its being true that I was having any experience of any kind at the time in question: it would not be a soap-bubble, unless, whatever time you take, from the proposition that it existed at that time it does *not* follow that I was having any experience at that time. That is to say, from the proposition with regard to anything which I am perceiving that it is a soap-bubble, there *follows* the proposition that it is external to *my* mind. But if, when I say that anything which I perceive is a soap-bubble, I am implying that it is external to *my* mind, I am, I think, certainly also implying that it is also external to all other minds: I am implying that it is not a thing of a sort such that things of that sort can only exist at a time when somebody is having an experience. I think, therefore, that from any proposition of the form 'There's a soap-bubble!' there does really *follow* the proposition 'There's an external object!' 'There's an object external to all our minds!' And, if this is true of the kind 'soap-bubble', it is certainly also true of any other kind (including the kind 'unicorn') which is such that, if there are any things of that kind, it follows that there are *some* things to be met with in space.

I think, therefore, that in the case of all kinds of 'things', which are such that if there is a pair of things, both of which are of one of these kinds, or a pair of things one of which is of one of them and one of them of another, then it will follow at once that there are some things to be met with in space, it is true also that if I can prove that there are a pair of things, one of which is of one of these kinds and another of another, or a pair both of which are of one of them, then I shall have proved *ipso facto* that there are at least two 'things outside of us'. That is to say, if I can prove that there exist now both a sheet of paper and a human hand, I shall have proved that there are now 'things outside of us'; if I can prove that there exist now both a shoe and sock, I shall have proved that there are now 'things outside of us', etc.; and similarly I shall have proved it, if I can prove that there exist now two sheets of paper, or two human hands, or two shoes, or two socks, etc. Obviously, then, there are thousands of different things such that, if, at any time, I can prove any one of them, I shall have proved the existence of things outside of us. Cannot I prove any of these things?

It seems to me that, so far from its being true, as Kant declares to be his opinion, that there is only one possible proof of the existence of things outside of us, namely the one which he has given, I can now give a large number of different proofs, each of which is a perfectly rigorous proof; and that at many other times I have been in a position to give many others. I can prove now, for instance, that two human hands exist. How? By holding up my two hands, and saying, as I make a certain gesture with the right hand, 'Here is one hand', and adding, as I make a certain gesture with the left, 'and here is another'. And if, by doing this, I have proved *ipso facto* the existence of external things, you will all see that I can also do it now in numbers of other ways: there is no need to multiply examples.

But did I prove just now that two human hands were then in existence? I do want to insist that I did; that the proof which I gave was a perfectly rigorous one; and that it is perhaps impossible to give a better or more rigorous proof of anything whatever. Of course, it would not have been a proof unless three conditions were satisfied; namely (1) unless the premiss which I adduced as proof of the conclusion was different from the conclusion I adduced it to prove; (2) unless the premiss which I adduced was something which I *knew* to be the case, and not merely something which I believed but which was by no means certain, or something which, though in fact true, I did not know to be so; and (3) unless the conclusion did really follow from the premiss. But all these three

conditions were in fact satisfied by my proof. (1) The premiss which I adduced in proof was quite certainly different from the conclusion, for the conclusion was merely 'Two human hands exist at this moment'; but the premiss was something far more specific than this—something which I expressed by showing you my hands, making certain gestures, and saying the words 'Here is one hand, and here is another'. It is quite obvious that the two were different, because it is quite obvious that the conclusion might have been true, even if the premiss had been false. In asserting the premiss I was asserting much more than I was asserting in asserting the conclusion. (2) I certainly did at the moment *know* that which I expressed by the combination of certain gestures with saying the words 'There is one hand and here is another'. I *knew* that there was one hand in the place indicated by combining a certain gesture with my first utterance of 'here' and that there was another in the different place indicated by combining a certain gesture with my second utterance of 'here'. How absurd it would be to suggest that I did not know it, but only believed it, and that perhaps it was not the case! You might as well suggest that I do not know that I am now standing up and talking—that perhaps after all I'm not, and that it's not quite certain that I am! And finally (3) it is quite certain that the conclusion did follow from the premiss. This is as certain as it is that if there is one hand here and another here *now*, then it follows that there are two hands in existence *now*.

My proof, then, of the existence of things outside of us did satisfy three of the conditions necessary for a rigorous proof. Are there any other conditions necessary for a rigorous proof, such that perhaps it did not satisfy one of them? Perhaps there may be; I do not know; but I do want to emphasise that, so far as I can see, we all of us do constantly take proofs of this sort as absolutely conclusive proofs of certain conclusions—as finally settling certain questions, as to which we were previously in doubt. Suppose, for instance, it were a question whether there were as many as three misprints on a certain page in a certain book. A says there are, B is inclined to doubt it. How could A prove that he is right? Surely he *could* prove it by taking the book, turning to the page, and pointing to three separate places on it, saying 'There's one misprint here, another here, and another here': surely that is a method by which it *might* be proved! Of course, A would not have proved, by doing this, that there were at least three misprints on the page in question, unless it was certain that there was a misprint in each of the places to which he pointed. But to say that he *might* prove it in this way, is to say that it *might* be certain that there was. And if such a thing as that could ever be certain, then assuredly it was certain just now that there was one hand in one of the two places I indicated and another in the other.

I did, then, just now, give a proof that there were *then* external objects; and obviously, if I did, I could *then* have given many other proofs of the same sort that there were external objects *then*, and could now give many proofs of the same sort that there are external objects *now*.

But, if what I am asked to do is to prove that external objects have existed in *the past*, then I can give many different proofs of this also, but proofs which are in important respects of a different *sort* from those just given. And I want to emphasise that, when Kant says it is a scandal not to be able to give a proof of the existence of external objects, a proof of their existence in the past would certainly *help* to remove the scandal of which he is speaking. He says that, if it occurs to anyone to question their existence, we ought to be able to confront him with a satisfactory proof. But by a person who questions their existence, he certainly means not merely a person who questions whether any exist at the moment of speaking, but a person who questions whether any have *ever* existed; and a proof that some have existed in the past would certainly therefore be relevant to *part* of what such a person is questioning. How then can I prove that there have been external objects in the past? Here is one proof. I can say: 'I held up two hands above this desk not very long ago; therefore two hands existed not very long ago; therefore at least two external objects have existed at some time in the past, QED'.[8] This is a perfectly good proof, provided I *know* what is asserted in the premiss. But I do know that I held up two hands above this desk not very long ago. As a

matter of fact, in this case you all know it too. There's no doubt whatever that I did. Therefore I have given a perfectly conclusive proof that external objects have existed in the past; and you will all see at once that, if this is a conclusive proof, I could have given many others of the same sort, and could now give many others. But it is also quite obvious that this sort of proof differs in important respects from the sort of proof I gave just now that there were two hands existing *then*.

I have, then, given two conclusive proofs of the existence of external objects. The first was a proof that two human hands existed at the time when I gave the proof; the second was a proof that two human hands had existed at a time previous to that at which I gave the proof. These proofs were of a different sort in important respects. And I pointed out that I could have given, then, many other conclusive proofs of both sorts. It is also obvious that I could give many others of both sorts now. So that, if these are the sort of proof that is wanted, nothing is easier than to prove the existence of external objects.

But now I am perfectly well aware that, in spite of all that I have said, many philosophers will still feel that I have not given any satisfactory proof of the point in question. And I want briefly, in conclusion, to say something as to why this dissatisfaction with my proofs should be felt.

One reason why, is, I think, this. Some people understand 'proof of an external world' as including a proof of things which I haven't attempted to prove and haven't proved. It is not quite easy to say *what* it is that they want proved—*what* it is that is such that unless they got a proof of it, they would not say that they had a proof of the existence of external things; but I can make an approach to explaining what they want by saying that if I had proved the propositions which I used as *premisses* in my two proofs, then they would perhaps admit that I had proved the existence of external things, but, in the absence of such a proof (which, of course, I have neither given nor attempted to give), they will say that I have not given what they mean by a proof of the existence of external things. In other words, they want a proof of what I assert *now* when I hold up my hands and say 'Here's one hand and here's another'; and, in the other case, they want a proof of what I assert *now* when I say 'I

---

8   *Quod erat demonstrandum*—Latin for "which was to be demonstrated."

did hold up two hands above this desk just now'. Of course, what they really want is not merely a proof of these two propositions, but something like a general statement as to how *any* propositions of this sort may be proved. This, of course, I haven't given; and I do not believe it can be given: if this is what is meant by proof of the existence of external things, I do not believe that any proof of the existence of external things is possible. Of course, in some cases what might be called a proof of propositions which seem like these can be got. If one of you suspected that one of my hands was artificial he might be said to get a proof of my proposition 'Here's one hand, and here's another', by coming up and examining the suspected hand close up, perhaps touching and pressing it, and so establishing that it really was a human hand. But I do not believe that any proof is possible in nearly all cases. How am I to prove now that 'Here's one hand, and here's another'? I do not believe I can do it. In order to do it, I should need to prove for one thing, as Descartes pointed out, that I am not now dreaming. But how can I prove that I am not? I have, no doubt, conclusive reasons for asserting that I am not now dreaming; I have conclusive evidence that I am awake: but that is a very different thing from being able to prove it. I could not tell you what all my evidence is; and I should require to do this at least, in order to give you a proof.

But another reason why some people would feel dissatisfied with my proofs is, I think, not merely that they want a proof of something which I haven't proved, but that they think that, if I cannot give such extra proofs, then the proofs that I have given are not conclusive proofs at all. And this, I think, is a definite mistake. They would say: 'If you cannot prove your premiss that here is one hand and here is another, then you do not know it. But you yourself have admitted that, if you did not know it, then your proof was not conclusive. Therefore your proof was not, as you say it was, a conclusive proof'. This view that, if I cannot prove such things as these, I do not know them, is, I think, the view that Kant was expressing in the sentence which I quoted at the beginning of this lecture, when he implies that so long as we have no proof of the existence of external things, their existence must be accepted merely on *faith*. He means to say, I think, that if I cannot prove that there is a hand here, I must accept it merely as a matter of faith—I cannot know it. Such a view, though it has been very common among philosophers, can, I think, be shown to be wrong—though shown only by the use of premisses which are not known to be true, unless we do know of the existence of external things. I can know things, which I cannot prove; and among things which I certainly did know, even if (as I think) I could not prove them, were the premisses of my two proofs. I should say, therefore, that those, if any, who are dissatisfied with these proofs merely on the ground that I did not know their premisses, have no good reason for their dissatisfaction.

EDMUND L. GETTIER
"Is Justified True Belief Knowledge?"

Who Is Edmund Gettier?

Edmund Gettier's career has been one of the most unusual in contemporary academic philosophy. His first teaching job was at Wayne State University, in Detroit, Michigan. During the early sixties, the chair of his department suggested that, as tenure consideration approached, some publication might help. The result was "Is Justified True Belief Knowledge?" This article took up all of three pages of a 1963 issue of *Analysis*, but it's the best-known article ever published in epistemology. All Gettier did there was to present two examples, but these two showed that the most basic assumption of epistemology since Plato was wrong. David Lewis cited Gettier (and Gödel) as maybe the only philosophers ever who conclusively refuted a philosophical theory.[1]

Opinions differ on the extent of the remainder of Gettier's publication dossier. One of his friends thinks there's a second article in print; the other believes there are two others.[2] The Philosopher's Index lists only two others, both translations; the title listed for one of these, clearly translated into Hungarian and back, is "If Knowledge Is a Justified True Belief?"[3]

But Gettier has not been relaxing since his career began in the late 1950s. His friends agree that, coupled with his "massive indifference to the usual trappings of an academic career," Gettier has shown an "abiding, deep commitment to philosophy."[4] Colleagues and students have enjoyed decades of energetic, creative philosophical interchange. In 1967 Gettier moved to the University of Massachusetts, Amherst, where he is now Professor Emeritus.

What Was Gettier's Overall Philosophical Project?

Gettier attacks a widely-accepted analysis of the concept of *knowledge*. The analysis of knowledge Gettier attacks is the claim that the necessary and sufficient conditions for S knows that P are that (a) P is true; (b) S believes P; (c) S has justification for this belief.

What Is the Structure of This Reading?

Gettier begins with two assumptions. The first is that one can have justification for believing something that's false.

1   *Philosophical Papers*, Vol I (London: Oxford University Press, 1983), p. x.
2   The first opinion from Robert C. Sleigh, Jr., "Knowing Edmund Gettier," *Philosophical Analysis: A Defense by Example*, ed. by David F. Austin (Dordrecht: Kluwer, 1987), p. xiv; the second from Austin's Preface to that book, p. xii.
3   *Magyar Filozofiai Szemle*, no. 1–2, pp. 231–233 (1995).
4   Sleigh, p. xiii.

A tiny bit of background in logic is necessary for understanding the second. Logicians say that a statement P is *entailed* by another statement Q when it's logically impossible for P to be false given the truth of Q. So, for example, *The picnic is off* is entailed by *It's raining; and if it's raining, the picnic is off.*

Gettier's second assumption is that whenever P is entailed by Q, and a person believes Q, and is justified in this belief, and deduces P from Q, and accepts P on this basis, then that person is justified in believing P. Suppose, for example, you believe, with good justification, that it's raining and if it's raining, the picnic is off. And so you deduce from this, and accordingly believe, that the picnic is off. According to Gettier's second assumption, you're justified in believing that the picnic is off.

The second assumption seems quite reasonable. After all, the fact that one's belief that Q is justified means that you'd count Q as likely to be true; and the fact that Q entails P means that P is likely to be true also; so you'd also be justified in believing P.

Applying these reasonable assumptions to Smith's belief in each of Gettier's two examples, we'd conclude that Smith is justified in his belief in both cases. Since both beliefs are true, they should count as knowledge, under the traditional analysis of knowledge as justified true belief; but in neither case would we agree that Smith's true beliefs are knowledge.

There has been an enormous amount of discussion in print concerning what to do about Gettier's examples (and other similar sorts of examples, known as Gettier-type cases). Some philosophers have tried to propose an account of justification that would account better for our judgments about the beliefs of Smith (and the believers in other Gettier-type cases). Others have argued that what's needed is that an additional condition (beside justified true belief) should be added for the correct analysis of knowledge.

Some Useful Background Information

1. In Gettier's time, but less frequently nowadays, philosophers took it that their job (or one of them) was to provide analyses of concepts; an analysis, in this sense, provides the conditions for the concept's application, and it was generally thought that the ideal analysis of any concept would provide a list of *necessary* and *sufficient* application conditions.

   The *necessary conditions* for application of a concept are those such that if something doesn't meet those conditions, the concept doesn't apply to it. Thus, for example, one of the necessary conditions for being someone's brother is being male. You can't be anyone's brother unless you're male. The sufficient conditions are those such that if something does meet these conditions, the concept does apply to it. Thus, being someone's male sibling is sufficient for the application of the concept *brother*. In this case, being someone's male sibling is also necessary. So it's necessary and sufficient; and the successful analysis of the concept *brother* is given by providing this list of conditions which are each necessary and together sufficient: (a) male; (b) somebody's sibling.

2. It's clear, and hardly needs argument, that believing P is necessary for knowing P. If you don't believe it, you wouldn't be said to know it. And the truth of P is another obvious necessary condition; your beliefs that are in fact false aren't knowledge, even though you think they are. The third necessary condition—that P be justified—needs a bit more explanation. This is added to distinguish between genuine knowledge and just a lucky guess. If S believes some true P merely because of a hunch, S's belief has no firm grounding, no justification, so it doesn't merit being called knowledge. When Fred wins the lottery, and says he *knew* he'd win, what he says is false. He may have been firmly convinced he'd win, but he had no justification for this, so he didn't know it. (Note that one may sometimes have justification for a false belief, when a large preponderance of evidence points toward it. But then it's not knowledge either.)

3. The places in Plato's writing Gettier mentions in a footnote, where Plato appears to suggest that knowledge is justified true belief, are these:

From Plato, *Theaetetus*

SOCRATES: But, my friend, if true opinion and knowledge were the same thing in law courts, the best of judges could never have true opinion without knowledge; in fact, however, it appears that the two are different.

THEAETETUS: Oh yes, I remember now, Socrates, having heard someone make the distinction, but I had forgotten it. He said that knowledge was true opinion accompanied by reason, but that unreasoning true opinion was outside of the sphere of knowledge; and matters of which there is not a rational explanation are unknowable—yes, that is what he called them—and those of which there is are knowable.

From Plato, *Meno*

SOCRATES: Well, and a person who had a right opinion as to which was the way, but had never been there and did not really know, might give right guidance, might he not?

MENO: Certainly.

SOCRATES: And so long, I presume, as he has right opinion about that which the other man really knows, he will be just as good a guide—if he thinks the truth instead of knowing it—as the man who has the knowledge.

MENO: Just as good.

SOCRATES: Hence true opinion is as good a guide to rightness of action as knowledge; and this is a point we omitted just now in our consideration of the nature of virtue, when we stated that knowledge is the only guide of right action; whereas we find there is also true opinion.

MENO: So it seems.

SOCRATES: Then right opinion is just as useful as knowledge.

MENO: With this difference, Socrates, that he who has knowledge will always hit on the right way, whereas he who has right opinion will sometimes do so, but sometimes not.

SOCRATES: How do you mean? Will not he who always has right opinion be always right, so long as he opines rightly?

MENO: It appears to me that he must; and therefore I wonder, Socrates, this being the case, that knowledge should ever be more prized than right opinion, and why they should be two distinct and separate things.

SOCRATES: Well, do you know why it is that you wonder, or shall I tell you?

MENO: Please tell me.

SOCRATES: It is because you have not observed with attention the images of Daedalus.[5] But perhaps there are none in your country.

MENO: What is the point of your remark?

SOCRATES: That if they are not fastened up they play truant and run away; but, if fastened, they stay where they are.

MENO: Well, what of that?

SOCRATES: To possess one of his works which is let loose does not count for much in value; it will not stay with you any more than a runaway slave: but when fastened up it is worth a great deal, for his productions are very fine things. And to what am I referring in all this? To true opinion. For these, so long as they stay with us, are a fine possession, and effect all that is good; but they do not care to stay for long, and run away out of the human soul, and thus are of no great value until one makes them fast with causal reasoning. And this process, friend Meno, is recollection,[6] as in our previous talk we have agreed. But when once they are fastened, in the first place they turn into knowledge, and in the second, are abiding. And this is why knowledge is more prized than right opinion: the one transcends the other by its trammels.

MENO: Upon my word, Socrates, it seems to be very much as you say.

[Both translations by Jowett.]

---

5   Socrates refers here to the legend that the first sculptor, Daedalus, put mechanisms inside his works that made them move.

6   Socrates argues earlier in this dialogue that real knowledge comes from recollection of the general Forms of things encountered before birth.

Suggestions for Critical Reflection

1. Sometimes you say, "I just know that …" when what you're saying is merely that you feel certain. But most philosophers would say that feeling certain that P is not a sufficient condition for knowing that P. Do you agree? Why / why not? Perhaps a more likely claim is that feeling certain that P is a necessary condition for knowing that P. Do you agree? Why / why not?

2. One suggestion to deal with Gettier-type cases is to add an additional necessary condition to the traditional analysis: that S's belief not be the result of S's inference from a false belief. But consider this example: S believes that there are sheep in the field, and this is true; but what S in fact has seen is really a large furry dog. So S doesn't know there are sheep there. It's sometimes thought that there's no inference from a false belief in this case—why might this be, and do you agree? If so, why might this show the inadequacy of the current proposal?

3. Another suggestion is that S's belief has to have been arrived at by a generally reliable method. But consider this example: S's watch has kept perfect time for years, so looking at her watch is a generally reliable way of finding out what time it is. Today, S looks at her watch at exactly 1 pm, and the watch shows 1:00. S believes correctly that it's 1 pm. But the watch stopped the previous night at 1 am. So S doesn't know that it's 1 pm. This is sometimes taken to show the inadequacy of this proposal—does it?

4. Here's a third troublesome Gettier-type case. S knows a barn when she sees one. But today, unbeknownst to her, she's traveling in an area where they're making a movie, and have built a large number of barn-facades that look just like real barns from the road. By fortunate coincidence, S sees, however, what is the only real barn in the area, and believes (correctly) that there's a real barn there. Does S know that there's a (real) barn there? Is this true belief justified, given that S is an excellent barn-detector?

Suggestions for Further Reading

These articles survey the problem and its main responses: "An Introduction to the Analysis of Knowledge" by Jack Crumley, in *Introduction to Epistemology* by Jack Crumley (Broadview Press, 2009); "Gettier problem" by Paul K. Moser, in *A Companion to Epistemology* (Blackwell, 1992); "Conditions and Analyses of Knowing" by Robert Shope, in *The Oxford Handbook of Epistemology*, Paul K. Moser, ed. (Oxford University Press, 2002); "Knowledge" by Jonathan Dancy, Chapter 2 of *An Introduction to Contemporary Epistemology* by Jonathan Dancy (Blackwell, 1985); "Gettier Problems" by Stephen Hetherington and "Epistemology" by David A. Truncellito, Part 2d, both online in the *Internet Encyclopedia of Philosophy*; "Epistemology" by Matthias Steup, Part 1.2, online in the *Stanford Encyclopedia of Philosophy*.

These articles argue for important positions responding to Gettier. "Knowledge: Undefeated Justified True Belief" by Keith Lehrer and Thomas D. Paxson, Jr., *Journal of Philosophy*, 66, pp. 225–237. Reprinted in *Epistemology: Contemporary Readings*, Michael Huemer, ed. (Routledge, 2002), and in *Readings in Contemporary Epistemology*, Sven Bernecker and Fred Dretske, eds. (Oxford University Press, 2000), and in *Justification and Knowledge*, G. Pappas and M. Swain, eds. (Cornell University Press, 1978). "A Causal Theory of Knowing" by Alvin I. Goldman, *Journal of Philosophy* 64, pp. 355–372. Reprinted in *Justification and Knowledge*, G. Pappas and M. Swain, eds. (Cornell University Press, 1978). "Epistemic Defeasibility" by Marshal Swain, *American Philosophical Quarterly*, 11, pp. 15–25. Reprinted in *Justification and Knowledge*, G. Pappas and M. Swain, eds. (Cornell University Press, 1978). "Knowledge and Grounds: A Comment on Mr. Gettier's Paper" by Michael Clark, *Analysis* 24 (2) (December, 1963), pp. 46–48. Reprinted in *Epistemology: Contemporary Readings*, Michael Huemer, ed. (Routledge, 2002). "An Alleged Defect in Gettier Counter-Examples" by Richard Feldman, *Australasian Journal of Philosophy* 52 (1), pp. 68–69. Reprinted in *Knowledge: Readings in Contemporary Epistemology*, Sven Bernecker and Fred Dretske, eds. (Oxford University Press, 2000). "Conclusive Reasons" by Fred Dretske, *Australasian Journal of Philosophy* 49, pp. 1–22. Reprinted in *Justification and Knowledge*, G. Pappas and M. Swain, eds. (Cornell University Press, 1978).

"Is Justified True Belief Knowledge?"[7]

Various attempts have been made in recent years to state necessary and sufficient conditions for someone's knowing a given proposition. The attempts have often been such that they can be stated in a form similar to the following:[8]

(a) S knows that P   *IFF*[9]
  (i)   P is true,
  (ii) S believes that P, and
  (iii) S is justified in believing that P.

For example, Chisholm has held that the following gives the necessary and sufficient conditions for knowledge:[10]

(b) S knows that P   *IFF*
  (i)   S accepts P,
  (ii) S has adequate evidence for P, and
  (iii) P is true.

Ayer has stated the necessary and sufficient conditions for knowledge as follows:[11]

(c) S knows that P   *IFF*
  (i)   P is true,
  (ii) S is sure that P is true, and
  (iii) S has the right to be sure that P is true.

I shall argue that (a) is false in that the conditions stated therein do not constitute a *sufficient* condition for the truth of the proposition that S knows that P. The same argument will show that (b) and (c) fail if 'has adequate evidence for' or 'has the right to be sure that' is substituted for 'is justified in believing that' throughout.

I shall begin by noting two points. First, in that sense of 'justified' in which S's being justified in believing P is a necessary condition of S's knowing that P, it is possible for a person to be justified in believing a proposition that is in fact false. Secondly, for any proposition P, if S is justified in believing P, and P entails Q, and S deduces Q from P and accepts Q as a result of this deduction, then S is justified in believing Q. Keeping these two points in mind, I shall now present two cases in which the conditions stated in (a) are true for some proposition, though it is at the same time false that the person in question knows that proposition.

Case I

Suppose that Smith and Jones have applied for a certain job. And suppose that Smith has strong evidence for the following conjunctive proposition:[12]

(d) Jones is the man who will get the job, and Jones has ten coins in his pocket.

Smith's evidence for (d) might be that the president of the company assured him that Jones would in the end be selected, and that he, Smith, had counted the coins in Jones's pocket ten minutes ago. Proposition (d) entails:

(e) The man who will get the job has ten coins in his pocket.

Let us suppose that Smith sees the entailment from (d) to (e), and accepts (e) on the grounds of (d), for

---

7   "Is Justified True Belief Knowledge?" *Analysis* 23, June 1963, pp. 121–123. By permission of Oxford University Press.

8   [Author's footnote] Plato seems to be considering some such definition at *Theaetetus* 201, and perhaps accepting one at *Meno* 98. [See "Some Useful Background Information" in Introduction to this reading.]

9   'IFF' is an abbreviation for 'If and only if.' 'X if and only if Y' means if X then Y, and if Y then X.

10 [Author's footnote] Roderick M. Chisholm, *Perceiving: a Philosophical Study*, Cornell University Press (Ithaca, New York, 1957), p. 16.

11 [Author's footnote] A.J. Ayer, *The Problem of Knowledge*, Macmillan (London, 1956), p. 34.

12 A conjunctive proposition is a statement composed of two propositions connected by 'and.' 'It's raining and it's Tuesday' is an example. A conjunctive proposition is true when both of its components are true; otherwise, it's false.

which he has strong evidence. In this case, Smith is clearly justified in believing that (e) is true.

But imagine, further, that unknown to Smith, he himself, not Jones, will get the job. And, also, unknown to Smith, he himself has ten coins in his pocket. Proposition (e) is then true, though proposition (d), from which Smith inferred (e), is false. In our example, then, all of the following are true: (*i*) (e) is true, (*ii*) Smith believes that (e) is true, and (*iii*) Smith is justified in believing that (e) is true. But it is equally clear that Smith does not *know* that (e) is true; for (e) is true in virtue of the number of coins in Smith's pocket, while Smith does not know how many coins are in Smith's pocket, and bases his belief in (e) on a count of the coins in Jones's pocket, whom he falsely believes to be the man who will get the job.

Case II

Let us suppose that Smith has strong evidence for the following proposition:

(f)   Jones owns a Ford.

Smith's evidence might be that Jones has at all times in the past within Smith's memory owned a car, and always a Ford, and that Jones has just offered Smith a ride while driving a Ford. Let us imagine, now, that Smith has another friend, Brown, of whose whereabouts he is totally ignorant. Smith selects three place-names quite at random, and constructs the following three propositions:

(g)   Either Jones owns a Ford, or Brown is in Boston;

(h)   Either Jones owns a Ford, or Brown is in Barcelona;

(i)   Either Jones owns a Ford, or Brown is in Brest-Litovsk.

Each of these propositions is entailed by (f).[13] Imagine that Smith realizes the entailment of each of these propositions he has constructed by (f), and proceeds to accept (g), (h), and (i) on the basis of (f). Smith has correctly inferred (g), (h), and (i) from a proposition for which he has strong evidence. Smith is therefore completely justified in believing each of these three propositions. Smith, of course, has no idea where Brown is.

But imagine now that two further conditions hold. First, Jones does *not* own a Ford, but is at present driving a rented car. And secondly, by the sheerest coincidence, and entirely unknown to Smith, the place mentioned in proposition (h) happens really to be the place where Brown is. If these two conditions hold then Smith does *not* know that (h) is true, even though (*i*) (h) *is* true, (*ii*) Smith does believe that (h) is true, and (*iii*) Smith is justified in believing that (h) is true.

These two examples show that definition (a) does not state a *sufficient* condition for someone's knowing a given proposition. The same cases, with appropriate changes, will suffice to show that neither definition (b) nor definition (c) do so either.

---

13   Note that a statement 'P' entails 'P or Q,' where 'Q' is any proposition at all. That's because a disjunctive proposition—one composed by connecting two component propositions with 'or'—is true when (at least) one of its components is true. So assuming that P is true, then it follows that P or anything-at-all must also be true.

LORRAINE CODE

"Is the Sex of the Knower Epistemologically Significant?"

Who Is Lorraine Code?

Lorraine Code (1937–) is Distinguished Research Professor of Philosophy at York University, Toronto, Canada. She received her undergraduate degree from Queen's University and her PhD from the University of Guelph, both in Ontario. Her main areas of interest are epistemology, ethics, feminist philosophy, and the politics of knowledge. She was named the Distinguished Woman Philosopher for 2009 by the US Society for Women in Philosophy.

How Important and Influential Is This Passage?

An idea which has moved from the fringes to the mainstream of philosophical ethics and social/political theory in the past few decades is *feminism*. The notion that women have, throughout history, been systematically subordinated and disparaged by male-dominated society—and that this immoral situation must be changed not only through the reform of social structures but also by adjustments to some of our most basic philosophical concepts and assumptions—was once controversial but is now widely accepted by the philosophical community. Thus, there are today a range of feminist projects to critique traditional ways of doing philosophy, and the present article illustrates one of these.

Feminist epistemology examines the assumptions which lie at the basis of traditional epistemology—such as that the ideal knower is perfectly rational and objective, or that the paradigm model for knowledge-acquisition is the scientific method—and subjects them to critical assessment from a feminist point of view. The central concept of feminist epistemology is that of a *situated knower*—and thus of situated knowledge: knowledge that reflects the particular perspectives of the subject—and a central feminist argument is that gender is a particularly important way of being situated. Code lays out these ideas in a clear and careful way.

Suggestions for Critical Reflection

1. Code contrasts the traditional idea that knowledge claims should be assessed "on their own merits" with the claim that "the circumstances of knowledge acquisition" are relevant to their evaluation. Which of these two stances do you think is the most plausible—or epistemically responsible—on the face of it? After reading Code's article carefully, does she change your views?

2. Exactly *how* do "the circumstances of knowledge acquisition," and especially who the knower is, affect the evaluation of knowledge claims, on Code's view? For example, can some factual claim be true or justified if it is asserted by one knower but not if it is asserted by another? (Does Code in fact think that the circumstances of the knower are relevant to the *justification* of knowledge claims at all?) Are all types of knowledge claims equally relative to their knower, or are there differences between kinds of knowledge (e.g., between ethical knowledge and geographical knowledge)?

3. What is the significance of Code's claim that most pieces of knowledge are not 'all or nothing' but are a matter of *degree*?

4. Do you agree with Code—if this is indeed her view—that "there is no universal, unchanging framework or scheme for rational adjudication among competing knowledge claims"? How

radical do you think this claim is? Is the kind of relativism that Code adopts, as she claims, an 'enabling' rather than a problematic position?

5. Code suggests that the nature and circumstances of the knower have not been ignored or treated neutrally in traditional epistemology. Rather, traditional epistemology—such as that of Descartes—has been shaped by tacit, often concealed, and sexist assumptions about the nature of the knower. What do you make of this claim? What is its significance for Code's project?

6. Why does Code reject essentialism about female nature? Is she pragmatically or theoretically right to do so? What is the significance of this stance for her version of feminist epistemology?

Suggestions for Further Reading

Among Lorraine Code's books are *What Can She Know? Feminist Theory and the Construction of Knowledge* (Cornell University Press, 1991), *Rhetorical Spaces: Essays on (Gendered) Locations* (Routledge, 1995), and *Ecological Thinking: The Politics of Epistemic Location* (Oxford University Press, 2006); she has also edited several collections, including the *Encyclopedia of Feminist Theories* (Routledge, 2000) and, with Sandra Burt, *Changing Methods: Feminists Transforming Practice* (Broadview Press, 1995). Some other central readings in feminist epistemology are: Linda Alcoff and Elizabeth Potter, eds., *Feminist Epistemologies* (Routledge, 1993); Louise Antony and Charlotte Witt, eds., *A Mind of One's Own: Feminist Essays on Reason and Objectivity* (Westview Press, 1993); Ann Garry and Marilyn Pearsall, eds., *Women, Knowledge and Reality* (2nd

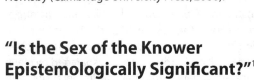

edition, Routledge, 1996); Carol Gilligan, *In a Different Voice* (Harvard University Press, 1982); Sandra Harding, *Whose Science? Whose Knowledge?* (Cornell University Press, 1991); Evelyn Fox Keller, *Reflections on Gender and Science* (Yale University Press, 1985); Kathleen Lennon and Margaret Whitford, eds., *Knowing the Difference: Feminist Perspectives in Epistemology* (Routledge, 1994); Helen Longino, *Science As Social Knowledge* (Princeton University Press, 1990); Genevieve Lloyd, *The Man of Reason: 'Male' and 'Female' in Western Philosophy* (2nd edition, University of Minnesota Press, 1993); and Alessandra Tanesini, *An Introduction to Feminist Epistemologies* (Blackwell, 1999). There is also *The Cambridge Companion to Feminism in Philosophy*, edited by Miranda Fricker and Jennifer Hornsby (Cambridge University Press, 2000).

"Is the Sex of the Knower Epistemologically Significant?"[1]

The Question

A question that focuses on the knower, as the title of this chapter does, claims that there are good reasons for asking who that knower is.[2] Uncontroversial as

---

1 This is Chapter One of Lorraine Code's *What Can She Know? Feminist Theory and the Construction of Knowledge* (Ithaca: Cornell University Press, 1991), pp. 1–26. Copyright © 1991 by Cornell University. Used by permission of the publisher, Cornell University Press.

2 [Author's note] This question is the title of my paper published in *Metaphilosophy* 12 (July–October 1981): pp. 267–276. In this early essay I endorse an essentialism with respect to masculinity and femininity, and

such a suggestion would be in ordinary conversations about knowledge, academic philosophers commonly treat 'the knower' as a featureless abstraction. Sometimes, indeed, she or he is merely a place holder in the proposition 'S knows that p'. Epistemological analyses of the proposition tend to focus on the 'knowing that', to determine conditions under which a knowledge claim can legitimately be made. Once discerned, it is believed, such conditions will hold across all possible utterances of the proposition. Indeed, throughout the history of modern philosophy the central 'problem of knowledge' has been to determine necessary and sufficient conditions for the possibility and justification of knowledge claims. Philosophers have sought ways of establishing a relation of correspondence between knowledge and 'reality' and/or ways of establishing the coherence of particular knowledge claims within systems of already-established truths. They have proposed methodologies for arriving at truth, and criteria for determining the validity of claims to the effect that 'S knows that p'. Such endeavors are guided by the putatively self-evident principle that truth once discerned, knowledge once established, claim their status as truth and knowledge by virtue of a grounding in or coherence within a permanent, objective, ahistorical, and circumstantially neutral framework or set of standards.

The question 'Who is S?' is regarded neither as legitimate nor as relevant in these endeavors. As inquirers into the nature and conditions of human knowledge, epistemologists commonly work from the assumption that they need concern themselves only with knowledge claims that meet certain standards of *purity*. Questions about the circumstances of knowledge acquisition serve merely to clutter and confuse the issue with contingencies and other impurities. The question 'Who is S?' is undoubtedly such a question. If it matters who S is, then it must follow that something peculiar to S's character or nature could bear on the validity of the knowledge she or he claims: that S's *identity* might count among the conditions that make that knowledge claim possible. For many

philosophers, such a suggestion would undermine the cherished assumption that knowledge can—and should—be evaluated on its own merits. More seriously still, a proposal that it matters who the knower is looks suspiciously like a move in the direction of epistemological relativism. For many philosophers, an endorsement of relativism signals the end of knowledge and of epistemology.

Broadly described, epistemological relativists hold that knowledge, truth, or even 'reality' can be understood only in relation to particular sets of cultural or social circumstances, to a theoretical framework, a specifiable range of perspectives, a conceptual scheme, or a form of life. Conditions of justification, criteria of truth and falsity, and standards of rationality are likewise relative: there is no universal, unchanging framework or scheme for rational adjudication among competing knowledge claims.

Critics of relativism often argue that relativism entails incommensurability: that a relativist cannot evaluate knowledge claims comparatively. This argument is based on the contention that epistemological relativism entails conceptual relativism: that it contextualizes language just as it contextualizes knowledge, so that there remains no 'common' or neutral linguistic framework for discussion, agreement, *or* disagreement. Other critics maintain that the very concept 'knowledge' is rendered meaningless by relativism: that the only honest—and logical—move a relativist can make is once and for all to declare her or his skepticism. Where there are no universal standards, the argument goes, there can be no knowledge worthy of the name. Opponents often contend that relativism is simply incoherent because of its inescapable self-referentiality. Relativism, they argue, is subject to the same constraints as every other claim to knowledge and truth. Any claim for the truth of relativism must itself be relative to the circumstances of the claimant; hence relativism itself has no claim to objective or universal truth. In short, relativism is often perceived as a denial of the very possibility of epistemology.[3]

---

convey the impression that 'positive thinking' can bring an end to gender imbalances. I would no longer make these claims.

3   [Author's note] I consider some of these objections to relativism at greater length in "The Importance of Historicism for a Theory of Knowledge," *International Philosophical Quarterly* 22 (June 1982): pp. 157–174.

Now posing the question 'Who is S?'—that is, 'Who is the knowing subject?'—does indeed count as a move in the direction of relativism, and my intention in posing it is to suggest that the answer has epistemological import. But I shall invoke certain caveats[4] to demonstrate that such a move is not the epistemological disaster that many theorists of knowledge believe it to be.

It is true that, on its starkest construal, relativism may threaten to slide into subjectivism, into a position for which knowledge claims are indistinguishable from expressions of personal opinion, taste, or bias. But relativism need not be construed so starkly, nor do its *limitations* warrant exclusive emphasis. There are advantages to endorsing a measure of epistemological relativism that make of it an enabling rather than a constraining position. By no means the least of these advantages is the fact that relativism is one of the more obvious means of avoiding reductive explanations, in terms of drastically simplified paradigms of knowledge, monolithic explanatory modes, or privileged, decontextualized positions. For a relativist, who contends that there can be many valid ways of knowing any phenomenon, there is the possibility of taking several constructions, many perspectives into account. Hence relativism keeps open a range of interpretive possibilities. At the same time, because of the epistemic choices it affirms, it creates stringent accountability requirements of which knowers have to be cognizant. Thus it introduces a moral-political component into the heart of epistemological enquiry.[5]

There probably is no absolute authority, no practice of all practices or scheme of all schemes. Yet it does not follow that conceptual schemes, practices, and paradigms are radically idiosyncratic or purely subjective. Schemes, practices, and paradigms evolve out of communal projects of inquiry. To sustain viability and authority, they must demonstrate their adequacy in enabling people to negotiate the everyday world and to cope with the decisions, problems, and puzzles

they encounter daily. From the claim that no single scheme has absolute explanatory power, it does not follow that all schemes are equally valid. Knowledge is qualitatively variable: some knowledge is *better* than other knowledge. Relativists are in a good position to take such qualitative variations into account and to analyze their implications.

Even if these points are granted, though, it would be a mistake to believe that posing the 'Who is S?' question indicates that the circumstances of the knower are *all* that counts in knowledge evaluation. The point is, rather, that understanding the circumstances of the knower makes possible a more *discerning* evaluation. The claim that certain of those circumstances are epistemologically significant—the sex of the knower, in this instance—by no means implies that they are definitive, capable of bearing the entire burden of justification and evaluation. This point requires special emphasis. Claiming epistemological significance for the sex of the knower might seem tantamount to a dismissal, to a contention that S made such a claim only because of his or her sex. Dismissals of this sort, both of women's knowledge *and* of their claims to be knowers in any sense of the word, are only too common throughout the history of western thought. But claiming that the circumstances of the knower are not epistemologically definitive is quite different from claiming that they are of no epistemological consequence. The position I take in this book is that the sex of the knower is one of a cluster of *subjective* factors (i.e., factors that pertain to the circumstances of cognitive agents) constitutive of received conceptions of knowledge and of what it means to be a knower. I maintain that subjectivity and the specificities of cognitive agency can and must be accorded central epistemological significance, yet that so doing does not commit an inquirer to outright subjectivism. Specificities count, and they require a place in epistemological evaluation, but they cannot tell the whole story.

Knowers and the Known

The only thing that is clear about S from the standard proposition 'S knows that p' is that S is a (would-be) knower. Although the question 'Who is S?' rarely arises, certain assumptions about S as knower perme-

---

4   A caveat is a warning or a reservation.

5   [Author's note] I discuss some of these accountability requirements, and the normative realism from which they derive, in my *Epistemic Responsibility* (Hanover, NH: University Press of New England, 1987).

ate epistemological inquiry. Of special importance for my argument is the assumption that knowers are self-sufficient and solitary individuals, at least in their knowledge-seeking activities. This belief derives from a long and venerable heritage, with its roots in Descartes's quest for a basis of perfect certainty on which to establish his knowledge. The central aim of Descartes's endeavors is captured in this claim: "I shall have the right to conceive high hopes if I am happy enough to discover one thing only which is certain and indubitable."[6] That "one thing," Descartes believed, would stand as the fixed, pivotal, Archimedean point on which all the rest of his knowledge would turn. Because of its systematic relation to that point, his knowledge would be certain and indubitable.

Most significant for this discussion is Descartes's conviction that his quest will be conducted in a private, introspective examination of the contents of his own mind. It is true that, in the last section of the *Discourse on the Method*, Descartes acknowledges the benefit "others may receive from the communication of [his] reflection," and he states his belief that combining "the lives and labours of many"[7] is essential to progress in scientific knowledge. It is also true that this individualistically described act of knowing exercises the aspect of the soul that is common to and alike in all knowers: namely, the faculty of reason. Yet his claim that knowledge seeking is an introspective activity of an individual mind accords no relevance either to a knower's embodiment or to his (or her) intersubjective relations. For each knower, the Cartesian route to knowledge is through private, abstract thought, through the efforts of reason unaided either by the senses or by consultation with other knowers. It is this individualistic, self-reliant, private aspect of Descartes's philosophy that has been influential in shaping subsequent epistemological ideals.

---

6 [Author's note] René Descartes, *Meditations*, in *The Philosophical Works of Descartes*, trans. Elizabeth S. Haldane and G.R.T. Ross (Cambridge: Cambridge University Press, 1969), 1:149.

7 [Author's note] René Descartes, *Discourse on the Method of Rightly Conducting the Reason and Seeking for Truth in the Sciences*, in ibid., pp. 124, 120.

Reason is conceived as autonomous in the Cartesian project in two ways, then. Not only is the quest for certain knowledge an independent one, undertaken separately by each rational being, but it is a journey of reason alone, unassisted by the senses. For Descartes believed that sensory experiences had the effect of distracting reason from its proper course.

The custom of formulating knowledge claims in the 'S knows that p' formula is not itself of Cartesian origin. The point of claiming Cartesian inspiration for an assumption implicit in the formulation is that the knower who is commonly presumed to be the subject of that proposition is modeled, in significant respects, on the Cartesian pure inquirer. For epistemological purposes, all knowers are believed to be alike with respect both to their cognitive capacities and to their methods of achieving knowledge. In the empiricist tradition this assumption is apparent in the belief that simple, basic observational data can provide the foundation of knowledge just because perception is invariant from observer to observer, in standard observation conditions. In fact, a common way of filling the places in the 'S knows that p' proposition is with substitutions such as "Peter knows that the door is open" or "John knows that the book is red." It does not matter who John or Peter is.

Such knowledge claims carry implicit beliefs not only about would-be knowers but also about the knowledge that is amenable to philosophical analysis. Although (Cartesian) rationalists and empiricists differ with respect to what kinds of claim count as foundational, they endorse similar assumptions about the relation of foundational claims to the rest of a body of knowledge. With 'S knows that p' propositions, the belief is that such propositions stand as paradigms for knowledge in general. Epistemologists assume that knowledge is analyzable into propositional 'simples' whose truth can be demonstrated by establishing relations of correspondence to reality, or coherence within a system of known truths. These relatively simple knowledge claims (i.e., John knows that the book is red) could indeed be made by most 'normal' people who know the language and are familiar with the objects named. Knowers would seem to be quite self-sufficient in acquiring such knowledge. Moreover, no one would claim to know "a little" that the book is red or to be in the process of acquiring knowledge about the openness of the door. Nor would anyone be likely to maintain that S knows better than W does that the door is open or that the book is red. Granting such examples paradigmatic status creates the mistaken assumption that all knowledge worthy of the name will be like this.

In some recent epistemological discussion, emphasis has shifted away from simple perceptual claims toward processes of evaluating the 'warranted assertability' of more complex knowledge claims. In such contexts it does make sense to analyze the degree or extent of the knowledge claimed. Yet claims of the simple, perceptual sort are still most commonly cited as exemplary. They are assumed to have an all-or-nothing character; hence they seem not to admit of qualitative assessment. Granting them exemplary status implies that, for knowledge in general, it is appropriate to ask about neither the circumstances of the knowing process nor who the knower is. There would be no point to the suggestion that her or his identity might bear on the *quality* of the knowledge under discussion.

Proposing that the sex of the knower is significant casts doubt both on the autonomy of reason and on the (residual) exemplary status of simple observational knowledge claims. The suggestion that reason might function differently according to whose it is and in what circumstances its capacities are exercised implies that the manner of its functioning is dependent, in some way, on those circumstances, not independent from them. Simple perceptual examples are rendered contestable for their tendency to give a misleading impression of how knowledge is constructed and established and to suppress diversities in knowledge acquisition that derive from the varied circumstances—for example, the sex—of different knowers.

Just what am I asking, then, with this question about the epistemological *significance* of the sex of the knower? First, I do not expect that the question will elicit the answer that the sex of the knower is pertinent among conditions for the existence of knowledge, in the sense that taking it into account will make it possible to avoid skepticism. Again, it is unlikely that information about the sex of the knower could count among criteria of evidence or means of

justifying knowledge claims. Nor is it prima facie obvious that the sex of the knower will have a legitimate bearing on the qualitative judgments that could be made about certain claims to know. Comparative judgments of the following kind are not what I expect to elicit: that if the knower is female, her knowledge is likely to be better grounded; if the knower is male, his knowledge will likely be more coherent.

In proposing that the sex of the knower is epistemologically significant, I am claiming that the scope of epistemological inquiry has been too narrowly defined. My point is not to denigrate projects of establishing the best foundations possible or of developing workable criteria of coherence. I am proposing that even if it is not possible (or not *yet* possible) to establish an unassailable foundationalist or coherentist position, there are numerous questions to be asked about knowledge whose answers matter to people who are concerned to know well. Among them are questions that bear not just on criteria of evidence, justification, and warrantability, but on the 'nature' of cognitive agents: questions about their character; their material, historical, cultural circumstances; their interests in the inquiry at issue. These are questions about how credibility is established, about connections between knowledge and power, about the place of knowledge in ethical and aesthetic judgments, and about political agendas and the responsibilities of knowers. I am claiming that all of these questions are epistemologically significant.

The Sex of the Knower

What, then, of the sex of the knower? In the rest of this chapter—and this book—I examine some attempts to give content to the claim that the sex of the knower *is* epistemologically significant.[8] Many of these en-

---

8   [Author's note] In this chapter I discuss the sex of the knower in a way that may seem to conflate biological sex differences with their cultural elaborations and manifestations as gender differences. I retain the older term—albeit inconsistently—for two reasons. The first, personally historical, reason connects this text with my first thoughts on these matters, published in my *Metaphilosophy* paper (see note [2], above). The second, philosophically historical, reason reflects the

deavors have been less than satisfactory. Nonetheless, I argue that the claim itself is accurate.

Although it has rarely been spelled out prior to the development of feminist critiques, it has long been tacitly assumed that S is male. Nor could S be just any man, the apparently infinite substitutability of the 'S' term notwithstanding. The S who could count as a model, paradigmatic knower has most commonly—if always tacitly—been an adult (but not old), white, reasonably affluent (latterly middle-class) educated man of status, property, and publicly acceptable accomplishments. In theory of knowledge he has been allowed to stand for all men.[9] This assumption does not merely derive from habit or coincidence, but is a manifestation of engrained philosophical convictions. Not only has it been taken for granted that knowers properly so-called are male, but when male philosophers have paused to note this fact, as some indeed have done, they have argued that things are as they should be. Reason may be alike in all men, but it would be a mistake to believe that 'man', in this respect, 'embraces woman'. Women have been judged incapable, for many reasons, of achieving knowledge worthy of the name. It is no exaggeration to say that anyone who wanted to *count* as a knower has commonly had to be male.

In the *Politics*, Aristotle observes: "The freeman rules over the slave after another manner from that in which the male rules over the female, or the man over the child; although the parts of the soul are present in all of them, they are present in different degrees. For the slave has no deliberative faculty at all; the woman has, but it is without authority, and the child has, but it is immature."[10] Aristotle's assumption that a woman will naturally be ruled by a man connects directly with his contention that a woman's deliberative faculty is "without authority." Even if a woman could, in her sequestered, domestic position, acquire deliberative skills, she would remain reliant on her husband for her sources of knowledge and information. She must be ruled by a man because, in the social structure of the *polis*, she enjoys neither the autonomy nor the freedom to put into visible practice the results of the deliberations she may engage in, in private. If she can claim no authority for her rational, deliberative endeavors, then her chances of gaining recognition as a knowledgeable citizen are seriously limited, whatever she may do.[11]

Aristotle is just one of a long line of western thinkers to declare the limitations of women's cognitive capacities.[12] Rousseau maintains that young men and women should be educated quite differently

---

relatively recent appearance of 'gender' as a theoretical term of art. In the history of 'the epistemological project', which I discuss in these early chapters, 'sex' would have been the term used, had these questions been raised.

9   [Author's note] To cite just one example: in *The Theory of Epistemic Rationality* (Cambridge: Harvard University Press, 1987), Richard Foley appeals repeatedly to the epistemic judgments of people who are "like the rest of us" (p. 108). He contrasts their beliefs with beliefs that seem "crazy or bizarre or outlandish ... beliefs to most of the rest of us" (p. 114), and argues that an account of rational belief is plausible only if it can be presented from "some nonweird perspective" (p. 140). Foley contends that "an individual has to be at least minimally like us in order for charges of irrationality even to make sense" (p. 240). Nowhere does he address the question of who 'we' are. (I take this point up again in Chapter 7 [of *What Can She Know?*].)

10 [Author's note] Aristotle, *Politics*, trans. Benjamin Jowett, in *The Basic Works of Aristotle*, ed. Richard McKeon (New York: Random House, 1941), 1260b.

11 [Author's note] I discuss the implications of this lack of authority more fully in Chapters 9 and 6. See Elizabeth V. Spelman, *Inessential Woman: Problems of Exclusion in Feminist Thought* (Boston: Beacon, 1988), for an interesting discussion of some more complex exclusions effected by Aristotle's analysis.

12 [Author's note] It would be inaccurate, however, to argue that this line is unbroken. Londa Schiebinger demonstrates that in the history of science—and, by implication, the history of the achievement of epistemic authority—there were many periods when women's intellectual achievements were not only recognized but respected. The "long line" I refer to is the dominant, historically most visible one. Schiebinger, *The Mind Has No Sex? Women in the Origins of Modern Science* (Cambridge: Harvard University Press, 1989).

because of women's inferiority in reason and their propensity to be dragged down by their sensual natures. For Kierkegaard, women are merely aesthetic beings: men alone can attain the (higher) ethical and religious levels of existence. And for Nietzsche, the Apollonian (intellectual) domain is the male preserve, whereas women are Dionysian (sensuous) creatures. Nineteenth-century philosopher and linguist Wilhelm von Humboldt, who writes at length about women's knowledge, sums up the central features of this line of thought as follows: "A sense of truth exists in [women] quite literally as a sense: ... their nature also contains a lack or a failing of analytic capacity which draws a strict line of demarcation between ego and world; therefore, they will not come as close to the ultimate investigation of truth as man."[13] The implication is that women's knowledge, if ever the products of their projects deserve that label, is inherently and inevitably *subjective*—in the most idiosyncratic sense—by contrast with the best of men's knowledge.

Objectivity, quite precisely construed, is commonly regarded as a defining feature of knowledge per se.[14] So if women's knowledge is declared to be *naturally* subjective, then a clear answer emerges to my question. The answer is that if the would-be knower is female, then her sex is indeed epistemologically significant, for it disqualifies her as a knower in the fullest sense of that term. Such disqualifications will operate differently for women of different classes, races, ages, and allegiances, but in every circumstance they will operate asymmetrically for women and for men. Just what is to be made of these points—how their epistemological significance is to be construed—is the subject of this book.

The presuppositions I have just cited claim more than the rather simple fact that many kinds of knowledge and skill have, historically, been inaccessible to women on a purely practical level. It is true, historically speaking, that even women who were the racial

and social 'equals' of standard male knowers were only rarely able to become learned. The thinkers I have cited (and others like them) claim to find a rationale for this state of affairs through appeals to dubious 'facts' about women's natural incapacity for rational thought. Yet deeper questions still need to be asked: Is there knowledge that is, quite simply, inaccessible to members of the female, or the male, sex? Are there kinds of knowledge that only men, or only women, can acquire? Is the sex of the knower crucially determining in this respect, across all other specificities? The answers to these questions should not address only the *practical* possibilities that have existed for members of either sex. Such practical possibilities are the constructs of complex social arrangements that are themselves constructed out of historically specific choices, and are, as such, open to challenge and change.

Knowledge, as it achieves credence and authoritative status at any point in the history of the male-dominated mainstream, is commonly held to be a product of the individual efforts of human knowers. References to Pythagoras's theorem, Copernicus's revolution, and Newtonian and Einsteinian physics signal an epistemic community's attribution of pathbreaking contributions to certain of its individual members. The implication is that *that* person, single-handedly, has effected a leap of progress in a particular field of inquiry. In less publicly spectacular ways, other cognitive agents are represented as contributors to the growth and stability of public knowledge.

Now any contention that such contributions are the results of independent endeavor is highly contestable. As I argue elsewhere,[15] a complex of historical and other sociocultural factors produces the conditions that make 'individual' achievement possible, and 'individuals' themselves are socially constituted.[16] The claim that individual *men* are the creators of the authoritative (often Kuhn[17]-paradigm-establishing)

---

13 [Author's note] *Humanist without Portfolio: An Anthology of the Writings of Wilhelm von Humboldt*, trans. with intro. by Marianne Cowan (Detroit: Wayne State University Press, 1963), p. 349.

14 [Author's note] I analyze this precise construal of objectivity in Chapter 2.

15 [Author's note] See chap. 7, "Epistemic Community," of my *Epistemic Responsibility*.

16 [Author's note] I discuss the implications of these points for analyses of subjectivity in Chapter 3.

17 Philosopher of science Thomas Kuhn, who is most associated with the notion that paradigms—roughly,

landmarks of western intellectual life is particularly interesting for the fact that the contributions—both practical and substantive—of their lovers, wives, children, servants, neighbors, friends, and colleagues rarely figure in analyses of their work.[18]

The historical attribution of such achievements to specific cognitive agents does, nonetheless, accord a significance to individual efforts which raises questions pertinent to my project. It poses the problem, in another guise, of whether aspects of human specificity could, in fact, constitute conditions for the existence of knowledge or determine the kinds of knowledge that a knower can achieve. It would seem that such incidental physical attributes as height, weight, or hair color would not count among factors that would determine a person's capacities to know (though the arguments that skin color *does* count are too familiar). It is not necessary to consider how much Archimedes weighed when he made his famous discovery,[19] nor is there any doubt that a thinner or a fatter person could have reached the same conclusion. But in cultures in which sex differences figure prominently in virtually every mode of human interaction,[20] being female or male is far more fundamental to the construction of subjectivity than are such attributes as size or hair

color. So the question is whether femaleness or maleness are the kinds of subjective factor (i.e., factors about the circumstances of a knowing subject) that are constitutive of the form and content of knowledge. Attempts to answer this question are complicated by the fact that sex/gender does not function uniformly and universally, even in western societies. Its implications vary across class, race, age, ability, and numerous other interwoven specificities. A separated analysis of sex/gender, then, always risks abstraction and is limited in its scope by the abstracting process. Further, the question seems to imply that sex and gender are themselves constants, thus obscuring the processes of *their* sociocultural construction. Hence the formulation of adequately nuanced answers is problematic and necessarily partial.

Even if it should emerge that gender-related factors play a crucial role in the construction of knowledge, then, the inquiry into the epistemological significance of the sex of the knower would not be complete. The task would remain of considering whether a distinction between 'natural' and socialized capacity can retain any validity. The equally pressing question as to how the hitherto devalued products of *women's* cognitive projects can gain acknowledgment as 'knowledge' would need to be addressed so as to uproot entrenched prejudices about knowledge, epistemology, and women. 'The epistemological project' will look quite different once its tacit underpinnings are revealed.

Reclaiming 'the Feminine'

Whether this project could or should emerge in a *feminist epistemology* is quite another question. Investigations that start from the conviction that the sex of the knower is epistemologically significant will surely question received conceptions of the nature of knowledge and challenge the hegemony[21] of mainstream epistemologies. Some feminist theorists have maintained that there are distinctively female—or feminine—ways of knowing: neglected ways, from which the label 'knowledge', traditionally, is withheld. Many claim that a recognition of these 'ways of knowing' should prompt the development of new, rival, or even separate epistemologies. Others have adopted Mary

---

sets of key experimental concepts and results—govern scientific research.

18 [Author's note] I owe this point—and the list—to Polly Young-Eisendrath, "The Female Person and How We Talk about Her," in Mary M. Gergen, ed., *Feminist Thought and the Structure of Knowledge* (New York: New York University Press, 1988).

19 The principle, which Archimedes is said to have discovered in his bath, that the apparent loss of weight of a body when immersed in a liquid is equal to the weight of the liquid displaced.

20 [Author's note] Marilyn Frye points out: "Sex-identification intrudes into every moment of our lives and discourse, no matter what the supposedly primary focus or topic of the moment is. Elaborate, systematic, ubiquitous and redundant marking of a distinction between two sexes of humans and most animals is customary and obligatory. One *never* can ignore it." Frye, *The Politics of Reality: Essays in Feminist Theory* (Trumansburg, NY: Crossing Press, 1983), p. 19.

---

21 Domination, especially political or social domination.

O'Brien's brilliant characterization of mainstream epistemology as "malestream,"[22] claiming that one of the principal manifestations of its hegemony is its suppression of female—or 'feminine'—knowledge. In this section I sketch some classic and more recent arguments in favor of feminine 'ways of knowing' and offer a preliminary analysis of their strengths and shortcomings.

Claims that there are specifically female or feminine ways of knowing often find support in the contention that women's significantly different experiences (different, that is, from men's experiences) lead them to know 'the world' differently (i.e., from the ways men do). A putatively different female consciousness, in turn, generates different theories of knowledge, politics, metaphysics, morality, and aesthetics. Features of women's experiences commonly cited are a concern with the concrete, everyday world; a connection with objects of experience rather than an objective distance from them; a marked affective tone; a respect for the environment; and a readiness to listen perceptively and responsibly to a variety of 'voices' in the environment, both animate and inanimate, manifested in a tolerance of diversity.

Many of these features are continuous with the attributes with which the dominant discourse of affluent western societies characterizes a good mother. Indeed, one of the best-known advocates of a caring, maternal approach both to knowledge and to a morality based on that knowledge is Sara Ruddick, in her now-classic article "Maternal Thinking." Maternal thinking, Ruddick believes, grows out of the *practice* of caring for and establishing an intimate connection with another being—a growing child. That practice is marked by a "unity of reflection, judgment and emotion ... [which is] ... no more relative to its particular reality (the growing child) than the thinking that arises from scientific, religious, or other practice"[23]

is relevant to scientific or religious matters alone. Just as scientific or religious thought can structure a knower's characteristic approach to experiences and knowledge in general, Ruddick believes that attitudes and skills developed in the attentive and painstaking practices of caring for infants and small children are generalizable across cognitive domains.

Ruddick's celebration of values traditionally associated with mothering and femininity is not the first such in the history of feminist thought. Among nineteenth-century American feminists, both Margaret Fuller and Matilda Gage praised women's intuition as a peculiarly insightful capacity. Fuller, for example, believed that women have an intuitive perception that enables them to "seize and delineate with unerring discrimination" the connections and links among the various life forms that surround them.[24] In this respect, she maintains, women are superior to men. And Gage believed that women have unique intellectual capacities, manifested especially in an intuitive faculty that does not "need a long process of ratiocination" for its operations.[25] Both Fuller and Gage, albeit in quite different contexts, advocate legitimizing this suppressed and undervalued faculty whose deliverances, they believe, are attuned to and hence better able to reveal the secrets of nature and (for Gage) of spirituality, than masculine ratiocinative practices.[26]

This nineteenth-century belief in the powers of female intuition is echoed in the work of two of the best-known twentieth-century radical feminists, Shulamith Firestone and Mary Daly. For Firestone, there are two sharply contrasting modes or styles of response to experience: an "aesthetic response," which she links to femaleness and characterizes as "subjective, intuitive, introverted, wishful, dreamy or fantastic, concerned with the subconscious (the id), emotional, even tem-

---

22 [Author's note] See Mary O'Brien, *The Politics of Reproduction* (London: Routledge & Kegan Paul, 1980).

23 [Author's note] Sara Ruddick, "Maternal Thinking," *Feminist Studies* 6 (1980): p. 348. I develop a critical analysis of Ruddick's position in Chapter 3. It should be noted that in Ruddick's 1989 book, *Maternal Thinking: Toward a Politics of Peace* (Boston: Beacon,

1989), she addresses some of the issues I raise about the essentialism of this earlier article.

24 [Author's note] Margaret Fuller, *Woman in the Nineteenth Century* (1845; New York: Norton, 1971), p. 103.

25 [Author's note] Matilda Jocelyn Gage, *Women, Church, and State* (1893; Watertown, Mass.: Persephone, 1980), p. 238.

26 Practices having to do with reasoning.

peramental (hysterical)"; and a technological response, which she describes as masculine: "objective, logical, extroverted, realistic, concerned with the conscious mind (the ego), rational, mechanical, pragmatic and down-to-earth, stable."[27] Firestone's claim is not that the aesthetic (= the feminine) should dominate, but that there should be a fusion between the two modes. To overcome patriarchal domination, she believes, it is vital for the aesthetic principle to manifest itself in all cultural and cognitive activity and for technology to cease operating to exclude affectivity.

Daly's concern with spirituality and with the celebration of witchcraft places her closer to Gage than to Fuller. Daly invokes the metaphor of spinning to describe the creation of knowledge and to connect the process with women's traditional creative activities. She claims that "Gyn/Ecology Spins around, past, and through the established fields, opening the coffers/coffins in which 'knowledge' has been stored, re-stored, re-covered ... [where] its meaning will be hidden from the Grave Keepers of tradition." These "Grave Keepers" are the arbiters of knowledge in patriarchal culture: the men who determine the legitimacy of knowledge claims. In consequence of their forced adherence to masculine epistemic norms, Daly contends, "women are encouraged, that is, dis-couraged, to adapt to a maintenance level of cognition and behavior by all the myth-masters and enforcers." Gyn/Ecology is a process of breaking the "spell of patriarchal myth"—by which Daly means all 'received' knowledge in patriarchal cultures— "bounding into freedom"; weaving "the tapestries of [one's] own creation."[28] Once freed from patriarchal myth, women will acquire the knowledge they need to validate their pleasures and powers as marks of their own authority and to unmask patriarchy. Daly's is a vision of female empowerment.

Some theorists maintain that research into the lateralization of brain function reveals 'natural' female-male cognitive differences. The findings of this research are frequently interpreted to indicate that in men, "left-brain" functions predominate, whereas "right-brain" functioning is better developed in women. Evidence that women have better verbal skills and fine motor coordination, whereas men are more adept at spatial skills, mathematics, and abstract thinking, is cited as proof of the existence of female and male cognitive differences. Depending on the political orientation of the inquirer, such findings are read either as confirmations of male supremacy and female inferiority or as indications of a need to revalue 'the feminine'. Among the celebratory interpretations are Gina Covina's claim that women, whom she describes as more "rightbrained" than men, deal with experience "in a diffuse non-sequential way, assimilating many different phenomena simultaneously, finding connections between separate bits of information." By contrast, men, whom she labels "leftbrained," engage typically in thinking that is "focused narrowly enough to squeeze out human or emotional considerations ... [and to enable] ... men to kill (people, animals, plants, natural processes) with free consciousnesses."[29] For Covina, there are 'natural' female-male differences. They are marked not just descriptively but evaluatively.

If brain-lateralization studies, or theories like Daly's and Firestone's, can be read as demonstrations of women's and men's necessarily different cognitive capacities, then my title question requires an affirmative answer. But it is not clear that such conclusions follow unequivocally. Consider the fact that allegedly sex-specific differences are not observable in examinations of the structure of the brain itself, and that in small children "both hemispheres appear to be equally proficient."[30] At most, then, it would seem,

27 [Author's note] Shulamith Firestone, *The Dialectic of Sex: The Case for Feminine Revolution* (New York: Bantam, 1971), p. 175.

28 [Author's note] Mary Daly, *Gyn/Ecology: The Meta-ethics of Radical Feminism* (Boston: Beacon, 1978), pp. xiii, 53, 57, 320.

29 [Author's note] Gina Covina, "Rosy Rightbrain's Exorcism/Invocation," in G. Covina and Laurel Galana, eds., *The Lesbian Reader* (Oakland, Calif.: Amazon, 1975), p. 96.

30 [Author's note] See Gordon Rattray Taylor, *The Natural History of the Mind* (London: Granada, 1979), p. 127. In an earlier article Taylor points out that "if the eyelids of an animal are sewn up at birth, and freed at maturity, it cannot see and will never learn to do so. The brain has failed to develop the necessary connections at

the brain may come to control certain processes in sexually differentiated ways. Evidence suggests that the brain *develops* its powers through training and practice.[31] Brains of creatures presented with a wide variety of tasks and stimuli develop strikingly greater performance capacities than brains of creatures kept in impoverished environments. As Ruth Bleier points out, "the biology of the brain itself is shaped by the individual's environment and experiences."[32]

Bleier notes the difficulty of assessing the implications of lateralization research. She observes that there are just as many studies that find no sex differences as there are studies that do, and that variability within each sex is greater than variability between them.[33] Janet Sayers suggests that it is as plausible to argue that sex differences in the results of tests to measure spatial ability are the results of sex-specific strategies that subjects adopt to deal with the tests themselves as it is to attribute them to differences in brain organization. She points out that there is no conclusive demonstration that differences in brain organization actually "*cause* sex differences in spatial

ability."[34] It is not easy to see, then, how these studies can plausibly support arguments about general differences in male and female cognitive abilities or about women's incapacity to enter such specific domains as engineering and architecture, where spatial abilities figure largely.

These are just some of the considerations that recommend caution in interpreting brain-lateralization studies. Differences in female and male brain functioning are just as plausibly attributable to sociocultural factors such as the sex-stereotyping of children's activities or to differing parental attitudes to children of different sexes, even from earliest infancy. It would be a mistake to rely on the research in developing a position about the epistemological significance of the sex of the knower, especially as its results are often elaborated and interpreted to serve political ends.[35]

Now Fuller, Gage, Ruddick, Firestone, Daly, and Covina evidently believe—albeit variously—in the effectiveness of *evaluative reversals* of alleged differences as a fundamental revolutionary move. Philosophers should acknowledge the superiority of feminine ideals in knowledge acquisition as much as in social life and institutions, and masculine ways of thought should give way, more generally, to feminine ways. These recommendations apply to theoretical content and to methodology, to rules for the conduct of inquiry, and to principles of justification and legitimation.

The general thesis that inspires these recommendations is that women have an edge in the development and exercise of just those attributes that merit celebration as feminine: in care, sensitivity, responsiveness and responsibility, intuition and trust. There is no

---

the period when it was able to do so." Taylor, "A New View of the Brain," *Encounter* 36, 2 (1971): 30.

31 [Author's note] In this connection Oliver Sacks recounts an illuminating story of a fifty-nine-year-old, congenitally blind woman with cerebral palsy, whose manual sensory capacities, he determined, were intact and quite normal. But when he met her, she had no use of her hands, referring to them as "useless lumps of dough." It became apparent that her hands were functionless because she had never used them: "being 'protected', 'looked after', 'babied' since birth [had] prevented her from the normal exploratory use of the hands which all infants learn in the first months of life." This woman first learned to use her hands in her sixtieth year. Oliver Sacks, "Hands," in *The Man Who Mistook His Wife for a Hat and Other Clinical Tales* (New York: Summit, 1985), p. 57.

32 [Author's note] Ruth Bleier, "Lab Coat: Robe of Innocence or Klansman's Sheet?" in Teresa de Lauretis, ed., *Feminist Studies / Critical Studies* (Bloomington: Indiana University Press, 1986), p. 65.

33 [Author's note] Ibid., pp. 58–59.

34 [Author's note] Janet Sayers, *Biological Politics* (London: Tavistock, 1982), p. 103.

35 [Author's note] Sayers notes: "So germane do ... findings about sex differences in brain organization appear to the current political debate about the justice of continuing sexual inequalities in professional life that they are now regularly singled out for coverage in newspaper reports of scientific meetings." Ibid., p. 101. See Lynda Birke's elaboration of this point in her *Women, Feminism, and Biology* (Brighton: Harvester, 1986), p. 29.

doubt that these traits are commonly represented as constitutive of femininity. Nor is there much doubt that a society that valued them might be a better society than one that denigrates and discourages them. But these very traits are as problematic, both theoretically and practically, as they are attractive. It is not easy to separate their appeal from the fact that women—at least women of prosperous classes and privileged races—have been encouraged to cultivate them throughout so long a history of oppression and exploitation that they have become marks of acquiescence in powerlessness. Hence there is a persistent tension in feminist thought between a laudable wish to celebrate 'feminine' values as tools for the creation of a better social order and a fear of endorsing those same values as instruments of women's continued oppression.

My recurring critique, throughout this book, of theoretical appeals to an *essential* femininity is one I engage in from a position sensitive to the pull of both sides in this tension. By 'essentialism' I mean a belief in an essence, an inherent, natural, eternal female nature that manifests itself in such characteristics as gentleness, goodness, nurturance, and sensitivity. These are some of women's more positive attributes. Women are also represented, in essentialist thought, as naturally less intelligent, more dependent, less objective, more irrational, less competent, more scatterbrained than men: indeed, essential femaleness is commonly defined against a masculine standard of putatively *human* essence.

Essentialist attributions work both normatively and descriptively. Not only do they purport to describe how women essentially *are*, they are commonly enlisted in the perpetuation of women's (usually inferior) social status. Yet essentialist claims are highly contestable. Their diverse manifestations across class, race, and ethnicity attest to their having a sociocultural rather than a 'natural' source. Their deployment as instruments for keeping women in their place means that caution is always required in appealing to them— even though they often appear to designate women's *strengths*. Claims about masculine essence need also to be treated with caution, though it is worth noting that they are less commonly used to oppress men. Essential masculine aggressiveness, sexual needs, and

ego-enhancing requirements are often added, rather, to reasons why women should remain subservient. Perhaps there are some essential female or male characteristics, but claims that there are always need to be evaluated and analyzed. The burden of proof falls on theorists who appeal to essences, rather than on those who resist them.

As I have noted, some of the thinkers I have cited advocate an evaluative reversal, in a tacit acceptance of stereotypical, essentialist conceptions of masculinity and femininity. To understand the import of the tension in feminist thought, these stereotypes need careful analysis. The issues of power and theoretical hegemony that are inextricably implicated in their maintenance need likewise to be analyzed. As an initial step toward embarking on this task I offer, in the remainder of this section, a critical analysis of three landmark articles that engage with mainstream epistemology with the intention of revealing grounds for feminist opposition to its traditional structures.

(i) In her early piece, "Methodocracy, Misogyny and Bad Faith: Sexism in the Philosophic Establishment," Sheila Ruth characterizes mainstream philosophy in its content, methodology, and practice as male, masculine, and masculinist. Noting, correctly, that most philosophers—even more in the late 1970s than in the 1990s—are men, Ruth maintains that the content of their philosophy reflects masculine interests and that their standard methodologies reflect imperialist masculine values, values whose normative status derives from their association with maleness. Ruth writes that "philosophical sexism, metasexism ... is epistemological, permeating philosophy to its roots—the structure of its methods and the logic of its criticism." She argues that "what should not be is the raising of ... male [intellectual] constructs to the status of universals—the identification of male constructs with allowable constructs so that women cannot 'legitimately' think, perceive, select, argue, etc. from their unique stance."[36] For Ruth, the sex of the knower *is* epistemologically significant at a fundamental level, with all-pervasive implications.

---

36   [Author's note] Sheila Ruth, "Methodocracy, Misogyny, and Bad Faith: Sexism in the Philosophic Establishment," *Metaphilosophy* 10, 1 (1979): pp. 50, 56.

This essay attests to the surprise and anger occasioned by early 'second wave' feminist realizations that theories that had posed, for centuries, as universal, neutral, and impartial were, in fact, deeply invested in furthering the self-interest of a small segment of the human population. Such realizations brought with them a profound shock, which often resulted in an insistence on affirming contrary, feminine interests and values. These early contributions often appear flawed from the present stage of feminist theoretical development, and I shall draw attention to some of those flaws as reasons why I would not, today, wholeheartedly endorse Ruth's claims.[37] They are worthy of rearticulation, though, for this article is one of the classics of feminist philosophy which created space for the development of subsequent critiques.

There is much that is right about Ruth's contentions, but two interconnected problems make it impossible to agree completely with her: the assumptions that "male constructs" exercise a unified, univocal hegemony and that women occupy a single "unique stance." I have argued in the first section of this chapter that epistemological relativism is a strong position because it creates the possibility of raising questions about the *identity* of knowers. It opens the way for analyses of the historical, racial, social, and cultural specificity of knowers and of knowledge. Now its value would be minimal were it possible to demonstrate that cognitive activity and knowledge have been conceived in exactly the same way by all knowers since the dawn of philosophy. Precisely because it allows the interplay of common threads *and* of specific variations, relativism has a significant explanatory capacity. This capacity is tacitly denied in an account such as Ruth's, based, as it apparently is, on implicit claims about essential, eternal conceptions of femininity and masculinity, mirrored in constant interpretations of knowing and knowledge. In the face of historical, ethnographic, political and class-based evidence to the contrary, the onus would fall on Ruth, should she still wish to defend these claims, to demonstrate the constancy of the concepts.

Their assumed rigidity presents a still more serious problem. The content Ruth gives to masculinity and femininity plays directly into their essentialist, stereotypical construal in late-twentieth-century western societies. Yet there is no better reason to believe that feminine and masculine characteristics are constant across a complex society at any one time than there is to believe in their historical or cross-cultural constancy. Norms of masculinity and femininity vary across race, class, age, and ethnicity (to name only a few of the axes) within any society at any time. An acceptance of the stereotypes results in a rigidity of thinking that limits possibilities of developing nuanced analyses. In this article it creates for Ruth the troubling necessity of defining her project both *against* and *with reference to* a taken-for-granted masculine norm. No single such norm is discernible in western thought, yet when Ruth's positive recommendations in favor of different philosophical styles are sketched out by contrast with that assumed norm, their explanatory power is diminished. Ruth is right to assert that women have had "no part in defining the content of philosophical speculation, but they have had even less influence over the categories of concern and the modes of articulation."[38] The predominance of feminine and masculine stereotypes in her argument points to an unhappy implication of such early arguments for evaluative reversal: namely, that had women had such influence, their contribution would have been as monolithic as the 'masculine' one.

The broadest of Ruth's claims remains her strongest: philosophy has oppressed women in ways that feminists are still learning to understand. My point is that analyses of this oppression need to be wary lest they replicate the very structures they deplore. Much depends, in the development of feminist projects, on how women's oppression is analyzed. It is important to prevent the reactive aspects of critical response from

---

37 [Author's note] My *Metaphilosophy* article is another pertinent example. Allan Soble criticizes the essentialism of my argument in "Feminist Epistemology and Women Scientists," *Metaphilosophy* 14 (1983): pp. 291–307.

38 [Author's note] Ruth, "Methodocracy, Misogyny, and Bad Faith," p. 54. In my thinking about Ruth's article I am indebted to Jean Grimshaw's discussion in her *Philosophy and Feminist Thinking* (Minneapolis: University of Minnesota Press, 1986), pp. 53–55, 81–82.

overwhelming its creative possibilities. Ruth's analysis leans rather too heavily toward the reactive mode.

(ii) In another early, landmark article, "The Social Function of the Empiricist Conception of Mind," Sandra Harding confronts stereotypes of femininity from a different direction. Her thesis is that "the empiricist model of mind supports social hierarchy by implicitly sanctioning 'underclass' stereotypes." Emphasizing the passivity of knowers in Humean[39] empiricism, Harding contends, first, that classical empiricism can allow no place for creativity, for historical self-consciousness, or for the adoption of a critical stance. Second, she discerns a striking similarity between 'the Humean mind' and stereotypical conceptions of women's minds: "formless, passive, and peculiarly receptive to direction from outside."[40] Her intention is to show that an espousal of empiricist theory, combined with an uncritical acceptance of feminine stereotypes, legitimates manipulative and controlling treatment of women in the social world. There are striking echoes, as Harding herself notes, with the Aristotelian view of woman's lack of rational authority: a lack that, for Aristotle, likewise justifies women's inferior social position.

Present-day empiricists would no doubt contend that Harding's equation of empiricism with a 'passive' epistemology and theory of mind has little validity, given the varieties of contemporary empiricism in its transformations under the influence of philosophers such as Quine.[41] Yet even if Harding has drawn only a caricature of 'the Humean mind', her account has a heuristic value in highlighting certain tendencies of orthodox, classical empiricism. Empiricism, and its latter-day positivist offspring, could indeed serve,

either as a philosophy of mind or as a theory of knowledge, to legitimate under the guise of objectivity and impartial neutrality just the kinds of social practice feminists are concerned to eradicate. The impartiality of empiricist analysis, the interchangeability of its subjects of study, work to provide rationalizations for treating people as 'cases' or 'types', rather than as active, creative cognitive agents.[42] Such rationalizations are common in positivistic social science.

More intriguing is a 'double standard' Harding discerns in classical empiricist thought. The *explicit* picture of the Humean inquirer, she maintains, is of a person who is primarily passive, receptive, and hence manipulable. Yet the very existence of Hume's own philosophy counts as evidence that he himself escapes that characterization. His intellectual activity is marked by "a critical attitude, firm purposes and a willingness to struggle to achieve them, elaborate principles of inquiry and hypotheses to be investigated, clarity of vision, precision, and facility at rational argument."[43] This description of the *implicit* Humean inquirer, Harding notes, feeds into standard gender stereotypes, in which men come across as "effective historical agents" while women are incapable of historical agency.

Harding accuses the promulgators of the classical empiricist conception of mind of false consciousness. Their own theoretical activity exempts *their* minds from the very model for which they claim universal validity: the contention that no one is a self-directed agent, everyone is a blank tablet, cannot apply to the authors themselves. Hence the empiricists presuppose a we/they structure in which 'they' indeed are as the theory describes them, but 'we', by virtue of our theoretical creativity, escape the description. In consequence, "the empiricist model of mind ... functions as a self-fulfilling *prescription* beneficial to those already in power: treat people as if they are passive and need direction from others, and they will become or remain able to be manipulated and controlled."[44] Harding

39 Relating to David Hume: see the notes to the selection from Hume in Chapter 2.

40 [Author's note] Sandra Harding, "The Social Function of the Empiricist Conception of Mind," *Metaphilosophy* 10 (January 1979): pp. 39, 42.

41 [Author's note] See especially Lynn Hankinson Nelson, *Who Knows: From Quine to a Feminist Empiricism* (Philadelphia: Temple University Press, 1990). Because Nelson's book was published after my manuscript was completed, I have not discussed it in this book.

42 [Author's note] I discuss this consequence of empiricist thinking more fully in Chapter 2.

43 [Author's note] Harding, "Social Function of the Empiricist Conception of Mind," pp. 43, 44.

44 [Author's note] Ibid., p. 46.

maintains that the implicit distinction between active empiricist theorist and passive ordinary inquirer maps onto the stereotypical active male/passive female distinction and acts to legitimate the social and political consequences of that stereotype in androcentered[45] power structures.

Now it is not easy to show that Harding is right either to find an implicit 'double standard' in Humean thought or to suggest that demarcations of the two 'kinds' of knower are appropriately drawn along sexual lines. Hume himself may have meant merely to distinguish a philosopher at his most sophisticated from an ordinary 'vulgar' thinker. His elitism may have been intellect- or class-related, rather than sex-related. If Harding is right, however, the Humean 'double standard' would suggest that the sex of the knower is epistemologically significant, in that it designates men alone as capable of active, creative, critical knowing—and of constructing epistemological theories. By contrast, women are capable only of receiving and shuffling information. Even if she is mistaken in her Humean attributions, then, the parallels Harding draws between the intellectual elitism that empiricism can create and sexual elitism find ample confirmation in the social world. The common relegation of women to low-status forms of employment, which differ from high-status employment partly in the kinds of knowledge, expertise, and cognitive authority they require, is just one confirming practice.[46]

What ensures Harding's paper a place in the history of feminist critiques of philosophy is less the detail of its Hume interpretation than its articulation of the political implications of metaphysical theses. In the face of challenges such as these, which have been more subtly posed both in Harding's later work and elsewhere as feminist thought has increased in sophistication, the neutrality of such theses can never be taken for granted. Should it be declared, the onus is on its declarers to demonstrate the validity of their claims. So despite the flaws in Harding's analysis, her article supports my contention that the

sex of the knower is epistemologically significant. If metaphysical theories are marked by the maleness of their creators, then theories of knowledge informed by them cannot escape the marking. Whether the case can be made that both theoretical levels are thus marked, without playing into sexual stereotypes, is a difficult question, but the evidence points compellingly toward the conclusion that the sex of a philosopher informs his theory-building.

(iii) The influence of stereotypically sex-specific traits on conceptions of the proper way to do philosophy is instructively detailed in Janice Moulton's analysis of "The Adversary Method," as she perceptively names it. Moulton shows that a subtle conceptual "conflation of aggression and competence"[47] has produced a paradigm for philosophical inquiry that is modeled on adversarial confrontation between opponents. This conflation depends, above all, on an association of aggression with such positive qualities as energy, power, and ambition: qualities that count as prerequisites for success in the white, middle-class, male professional world. Moulton questions the validity of this association in its conferral of normative status on styles of behavior stereotypically described as male. Yet what is most seriously wrong with the paradigm, she argues, is not so much its maleness as its constitutive role in the production of truncated philosophical problems, inquiries, and solutions.

The adversarial method is most effective, Moulton claims, in structuring isolated disagreements about specific theses and arguments. Hence it depends for its success on the artificial isolation of such claims and arguments from the contexts that occasion their articulation. Adversarial argument aims to show that an opponent is wrong, often by attacking conclusions implicit in, or potentially consequent on, his basic or alleged premises.[48] Under the adversarial paradigm,

---

45   Male-centered.

46   [Author's note] An example of the hierarchy of cognitive relations created by such assumptions is the theme of Chapter 6.

47   [Author's note] Janice Moulton, "A Paradigm of Philosophy: The Adversary Method," in Sandra Harding and Merrill B. Hintikka, eds., *Discovering Reality* (Dordrecht: Reidel, 1983), p. 151.

48   [Author's note] I am agreeing with Moulton's association of the paradigm with maleness in using the masculine pronoun to refer to its practitioners—even though many women have learned to play the game well.

the point is to confront the most extreme opposing position, with the object of showing that one's own position is defensible even against such stark opposition. Exploration, explanation, and understanding are lesser goals. The irony, Moulton claims, is that the adversarial paradigm produces bad reasoning, because it leads philosophers to adopt the mode of reasoning best suited to defeat an opponent—she uses "counterexample reasoning" to illustrate her point[49]—as the paradigmatic model for reasoning as such. Diverse modes of reasoning which might be more appropriate to different circumstances, tend to be occluded, as does the possibility that a single problem might be amenable to more than one approach.

Moulton's analysis lends support to the contention that the sex of the knower is significant at the 'metaepistemological' level where the legitimacy of epistemological problems is established. The connection between aggressive cognitive styles and stereotypes of masculine behavior is now a commonplace of feminist thought. Moulton's demonstration that such behavior constitutes the dominant mode—the paradigm—in philosophy, which has so long claimed to stand outside 'the commonplace', is compelling. She shows that mainstream philosophy bears the marks of its androcentric derivation out of a stereotypically constructed masculinity, whatever the limitations of that construction are.

Like all paradigms, the adversarial method has a specific location in intellectual history. While it demarcates the kinds of puzzle a philosopher can legitimately consider, a recognition of its historical specificity shows that this is not how philosophy has always been done nor how it must, of necessity, be done. In according the method (interim) paradigm status, Moulton points to the historical contingency of its current hegemony. The fact that many feminist philosophers report a sense of dissonance between the supposed gender neutrality of the method and their own feminine gender[50] puts the paradigm under

serious strains. Such strains create the space and the possibilities for developing alternative methodological approaches. Whether the sex of the knower will be methodologically and/or epistemologically significant in such approaches must, for now, remain an open question.

Knowledge, Methodology, and Power

The adversarial method is but one manifestation of a complex interweaving of power and knowledge which sustains the hegemony of mainstream epistemology. Like the empiricist theory of the mind, it presents a public demeanor of neutral inquiry, engaged in the disinterested pursuit of truth. Despite its evident interest in triumphing over opponents, it would be unreasonable to condemn this disinterest as merely a pose. There is no reason to believe that practitioners whose work is informed by these methodological assumptions have ruthlessly or tyrannically adopted a theoretical stance for the express purpose of engaging in projects that thwart the intellectual pursuits of women or of other marginalized philosophers. Could such a purpose be discerned, the task of revealing the epistemological significance of the sex of the knower would be easy. Critics could simply offer such practitioners a clear demonstration of the errors of their ways and hope that, with a presumption of goodwill on their part, they would abandon the path of error for that of truth and fairness.

Taking these practitioners at their word, acknowledging the sincerity of their convictions about their neutral, objective, impartial engagement in the pursuit of truth, reveals the intricacy of this task. Certain sets of problems, by virtue of their complexity or their intrinsic appeal, often become so engrossing for researchers that they override and occlude other contenders for attention. Reasons for this suppression are often subtle and not always specifically articulable. Nor is it clear that the exclusionary process is wholly conscious. A network of sociopolitical relationships and intellectual assumptions creates an invisible system of acceptance and rejection, discourse and

49   [Author's note] Moulton, "Paradigm of Philosophy," p. 159.

50   [Author's note] See, for example, Genevieve Lloyd's observation that "the exercise of writing feminist philosophy came out of [her] experience of dissonance

between the supposed gender neutrality of philosophy and [her] gender." Lloyd, "Feminist Philosophy and the Idea of the Feminine" (manuscript, 1986), p. 22.

silence, ascendency and subjugation within and around disciplines. Implicit cultural presuppositions work with the personal idiosyncracies of intellectual authorities to keep certain issues from placing high on research agendas. Critics have to learn how to notice their absence.

In "The Discourse on Language," Michel Foucault makes the astute observation that "within its own limits, every discipline recognizes true and false propositions, but it repulses a whole teratology[51] of learning."[52] The observation captures some of the subtleties involved in attempting to understand the often imperceptible workings of hegemonic, usually masculine power in mainstream philosophy. A discipline defines itself both by what it excludes (repulses) and by what it includes. But the self-definition process removes what is excluded (repulsed) from view so that it is not straightforwardly available for assessment, criticism, and analysis. Even in accepting mainstream avowals of neutral objectivity, critics have to learn to see what is repulsed by the disciplinarily imposed limits on methodology and areas of inquiry. The task is not easy. It is much easier to seek the flaws in existing structures and practices and to work at eradicating them than it is to learn to perceive what is not there to be perceived.

Feminist philosophy simply did not exist until philosophers learned to perceive the near-total absence of women in philosophical writings from the very beginning of western philosophy, to stop assuming that 'man' could be read as a generic term. Explicit denigrations of women, which became the focus of philosophical writing in the early years of the contemporary women's movement, were more readily perceptible. The authors of derogatory views about women in classical texts clearly needed power to be able to utter their pronouncements with impunity: a power they claimed from a 'received' discourse that represented women's nature in such a way that women undoubtedly merited the negative judgments that Aristotle or Nietzsche made about them. Women are now in a position to recognize and refuse these overt manifestations of contempt.

The covert manifestations are more intransigent. Philosophers, when they have addressed the issue at all, have tended to group philosophy with science as the most gender-neutral of disciplines. But feminist critiques reveal that this alleged neutrality masks a bias in favor of institutionalizing stereotypical masculine values into the fabric of the discipline—its methods, norms, and contents. In so doing, it suppresses values, styles, problems, and concerns stereotypically associated with femininity. Thus, whether by chance or by design, it creates a hegemonic philosophical practice in which the sex of the knower is, indeed, epistemologically significant.

---

51 [Author's note] A 'teratology' is a collection of tales about marvellous and improbable creatures (such as sea monsters, or people with heads in their chests); Foucault's idea is that disciplines restrict themselves to what is familiar, and rule out or ignore the possibility of things that would be—from the perspective of the discipline—considered strange or unlikely.

52 [Author's note] Michel Foucault, "The Discourse on Language," in *The Archaeology of Knowledge*, trans. Alan Sheridan (New York: Pantheon, 1972), p. 223.

CHAPTER 4

Philosophy of Science—When, if Ever, Are Scientific Inferences Justified?

INTRODUCTION TO THE QUESTION

The philosophy of science can be thought of as being made up of two broad, intersecting streams: the epistemology of science and the metaphysics of science. The epistemology of science concerns itself with the justification, rationality, and objectivity of scientific knowledge and the so-called 'scientific method,' while the metaphysics of science examines philosophical puzzles about the reality uncovered by the various sciences. Furthermore, each of these two types of investigation can be directed at science in general or at one of the particular sciences: there are thus sub-disciplines within the philosophy of science such as 'philosophy of physics,' 'philosophy of mathematics,' 'philosophy of biology,' and 'philosophy of the social sciences.'

Many of the threads of the epistemological strand of philosophy of science can be unraveled from the following question: *What, if anything, is 'the scientific method,' and how rational is it?* Once one attempts to answer this question, a flurry of subsidiary questions arise: What is the methodological difference (if any) between science and other, non-scientific, areas of human endeavor (such as philosophy, history or astrology)? Do all the 'real' sciences share a common methodology? If not, can we discover a single, underlying 'unified science' which is in principle capable of encompassing all the special sciences? How *rational* are the methods of science: how much reason do they give us to accept their conclusions? How *objective* are the methods of science: how much is science influenced by its social context and the personalities of individual scientists? Are the theories produced by science ever in fact true descriptions of reality, and is

that what science should aspire to anyway? What exactly *is* a theory, anyway (for example, is it a set of logical equations, or a kind of model, or a more informal bundle of assumptions and claims)? How adequately does science explain the natural phenomena we want explained, and what counts as a scientific explanation? And so on: these, and other similar questions, are investigated by philosophers of science.

Metaphysical questions about science can be thought of as centered on the following issue: *Are the principles and entities postulated by science actually real?* For example, many scientific theories postulate unobservable entities in order to explain the observed data. Most subatomic particles such as quarks, for instance, have never in any sense been *seen* by a scientist: rather, they are assumed to exist because their existence is the best explanation for a certain set of experimental data. In such situations, are we entitled to infer that such unobservable entities actually do exist, or should we instead treat them as instrumental fictions which are useful in generating observable predictions but which aren't literally real? (After all, plenty of unobserved entities which we now realize do not actually exist have been postulated by science in the past, such as the mythical substance of 'phlogiston' which was invoked to explain many chemical properties, or the massless 'ether' which was thought to fill the gaps between objects and serve as the medium for the transmission of light. Why should our current theories be any luckier in the hypothetical entities they invent?)

One fundamental 'unobservable' principle of science, which has historically been of great interest to philosophers of science, is the principle of *causality*. The sense in which causality is unobservable was pointed out by the philosopher David Hume in the eighteenth century: although we certainly can and do observe that events of type *A* are always followed by events of type *B* (for example, that all objects propelled with force *x* will always accelerate at rate *y*), this necessarily falls short of being able to observe *causation* itself. All we actually see is what Hume called the 'constant conjunction' of *A* things with *B* things, but we do not see the causal law which lies behind and is the reason for this conjunction: that is, we do not *see* laws of nature, but we *infer* them from regularities which we detect in nature. So it is legitimate to ask questions like the following: *Are* there really causal laws lying behind the constant conjunctions we observe—are laws of nature real? If causal laws do exist, how can we reliably tell when we've identified one—how can we tell the difference between a genuine law and a merely accidental constant conjunction? And, if causal laws exist, what is their nature—for example, are they always deterministic, or can they be probabilistic (as quantum mechanics might be taken to suggest)?

The readings in this chapter focus primarily on the epistemological aspects of the philosophy of science: what is the method of science, and how rationally justifiable is it? It is natural to begin with something like the following account of science: scientists first accumulate facts about the world by conducting careful experiments, and then use these observations to support—or 'verify'—one scientific theory rather than another. For example, one might think, by the careful observation of various chemical reactions, scientists are able to formulate and prove true general laws about the underlying chemistry. Furthermore, it is common to suppose that it is this 'experimental' method which is unique to science and the source of its special epistemological power. The first two selections collected here introduce a fundamental problem for this view of scientific method, *the problem of induction*. Induction is, roughly, the process by which we infer general truths from particular observations (for example, inferring that all copper turns green in the rain by noticing that many old copper roofs are now green). The scientific method just described rests

heavily on inductive inferences to move from a finite set of experimental observations to claims about laws of nature. But the question is: is induction rational? Are inductive inferences from the particular to the general justified? David Hume argues compellingly that inductive inferences are *not* rationally justified; and if he is right, then it follows that the scientific method—at least as we have so far understood it—is not rational. In the following reading, Nelson Goodman argues that Hume's problem can be solved … but then promptly introduces what he considers a different and even more difficult version of the problem, which he calls the 'new riddle of induction.'

The next four readings—the authors of all of which are to some degree reacting to the problem of induction—introduce three different accounts of the scientific method, in an effort to improve on the simplistic 'experimental' model described above. Carl Hempel presents a mature version of the influential 'logical positivist' or 'verificationist' account of science; Karl Popper rejects verificationism and argues instead for a 'falsificationist' view of science; and C.S. Peirce describes a view of science which is usually thought of as 'pragmatic.' The other reading in this group, by Wesley Salmon, is critical of all of these attempts to solve the problem of induction, but makes a renewed case for the importance of finding some solution.

The seventh selection in this chapter, from Thomas Kuhn, introduces an important turn in late-twentieth-century philosophy away from the attempt to understand science as a rational enterprise and in favor of seeing it as a sociological phenomenon embedded in a particular historical context. Kuhn has thus been seen as launching an attack on the rationality of science. Finally the article from Helen Longino asks "Can there be a feminist science?" and if so, how different would it look from historical, supposedly 'value-free,' science?

The philosophy of science was a very active area of philosophy for a large part of the twentieth century, and there are many good books which will take you beyond the readings included in this chapter. Among them are: Brody and Grandy, eds., *Readings in the Philosophy of Science* (Prentice Hall, 1989); Alan Chalmers, *What is This Thing Called Science?* (Hackett, 1999); Curd and Cover, eds., *Philosophy of Science: The*

Central Issues (W.W. Norton, 1998); James Franklin, *What Science Knows: And How It Knows It* (Encounter Books, 2009); Donald Gillies, *Philosophy of Science in the Twentieth Century* (Blackwell, 1993); Peter Godfrey-Smith, *Theory and Reality: An Introduction to the Philosophy of Science* (University of Chicago Press, 2003); Ian Hacking, *Representing and Intervening* (Cambridge University Press, 1983); Philip Kitcher, *The Advancement of Science* (Oxford University Press, 1993); Robert Klee, *Introduction to the Philosophy of Science: Cutting Nature at Its Seams* (Oxford University Press, 1996); James Ladyman, *Understanding Philosophy of Science* (Routledge, 2001); W.H. Newton-Smith, *The Rationality of Science* (Routledge, 1981); David Papineau, ed., *The Philosophy of Science* (Oxford University Press, 1996); Alexander Rosenberg, *The Philosophy of Science* (Routledge, 2011); Merrilee Salmon et al., *Introduction to the Philosophy of Science* (Hackett, 1999); and Bas van Fraassen, *The Scientific Image* (Oxford University Press, 1982). Useful references are *A Companion to the Philosophy of Science*, edited by W.H. Newton-Smith (Blackwell, 2001), and Psillos and Curd (eds.), *The Routledge Companion to Philosophy of Science* (Routledge, 2010).

DAVID HUME

An Enquiry Concerning Human Understanding

There is a peculiarly painful chamber inhabited solely by philosophers who have refuted Hume. These philosophers, though in Hell, have not learned wisdom. They continue to be governed by their animal propensity towards induction. But every time that they make an induction, the next instance falsifies it. This, however, happens only during the first hundred years of their damnation. After that, they learn to expect that an induction will be falsified, and therefore it is not falsified until another century of logical torment has altered their expectation. Throughout all eternity surprise continues, but each time at a higher logical level.

(Bertrand Russell)

Who Was David Hume?

David Hume has been called the most important philosopher ever to have written in English. He was born to a strict Calvinist family in Edinburgh, Scotland's capital, in 1711, and spent his youth there and in Ninewells, his family's small land-holding near the border with England. Little is known of Hume's early childhood. His father, Joseph, died when he was two, and he was educated by his mother Katherine—who

never remarried—from an early age. He was a precociously intelligent and well-read child. As his mother put it, in her Scottish dialect: "Our Davie's a fine good-natured crater, but uncommon wake-minded." By the age of 16 he had begun composing his first philosophical master-work, *A Treatise of Human Nature*, on which he was to work, more or less continuously, for the next ten years.

Hume spent the years between 1723 and 1726 (i.e., between the ages of 12 and 15) studying a wide range of subjects at the University of Edinburgh but, like many students of that era, did not take a degree. His father and grandfather had both been lawyers, and his family expected him also to go into law, but, Hume later wrote, he found the law "nauseous" and discovered in himself "an unsurmountable aversion to every thing but the pursuits of philosophy and general learning."

Hume continued to read and write and, as a result of his feverish intellectual activity—motivated by his belief that he had made a major philosophical discovery—he suffered a nervous breakdown in 1734. He was forced to put philosophy aside for several months (during which time he attempted life as a businessman at

Bristol, in the employ of a Portsmouth merchant, but found that it didn't suit him) and then left Britain for France. There, in the following three years, living frugally in the countryside in Anjou (and using up all his savings), he completed most of his book.

Hume's *A Treatise of Human Nature* was published anonymously when he was 27. Hume later wrote, it "fell *dead-born from the press*, without reaching such distinction as even to excite a murmur among the zealots." Hume's career as an intellectual and man of letters seemed to have ended before it had begun, and Hume blamed not the substance of his work but its style. "I was carry'd away by the Heat of Youth & Invention to publish too precipitately. So vast an Undertaking, plan'd before I was one and twenty, & compos'd before twenty-five, must necessarily be very defective. I have repented my Haste a hundred, & a hundred times." Hume returned to Scotland to live with his mother, and began to re-cast the material of the *Treatise* into two new books, which have become philosophical classics in their own right: *An Enquiry Concerning Human Understanding* (1748), and *An Enquiry Concerning the Principles of Morals* (1751). However both these books—though more successful than the *Treatise*—were slow to become influential during Hume's own lifetime.

Needing money, Hume got his first real job at the age of 34 and spent a well-paid year as tutor to a mad nobleman (the Marquess of Annandale). In 1746 Hume accepted a position as secretary to General St. Clair's military expedition to Canada (which never reached Canada and ended, oddly enough, with a brief attack on the French coast), and for two years after that was part of a secret diplomatic and military embassy by St. Clair to the courts of Vienna and Turin. During this period Hume was twice refused academic appointments at Scottish universities—first Edinburgh, then Glasgow—because of his reputation as a religious skeptic. Shortly

afterwards, between 1755 and 1757, unsuccessful attempts were made in Edinburgh to have Hume excommunicated from the Church of Scotland.

In 1752 Hume was offered the Keepership of the Advocates' Library at Edinburgh and there, poorly paid but surrounded by books, he wrote the colossal six-volume *History of England*, which (though unpopular at first) eventually became his first major literary success. At this time he also published a controversial *Natural History of Religion*.

In 1763 Hume was made secretary of the English embassy at Paris, where he found himself very much in fashion and seems to have enjoyed the experience. There he fell in love with, but failed to win the hand of, the Comtesse de Boufflers, the mistress of a prominent French noble. (Some unkindly suggest this might have been partly because at the time, when Hume was in his fifties, he had come to resemble "a fat well-fed Bernardine monk.") In 1767, back in Scotland and now a fairly wealthy man, Hume was appointed an Under-Secretary of State, a senior position in the British civil service.

By the time Hume died in 1776, of cancer of the bowel, he had become respected as one of Europe's leading men of letters and a principal architect of the Enlightenment. His death gave him the reputation of something of a secular saint, as he faced his incurable condition with cheerfulness and resignation and refused to abandon his religious skepticism. In a short autobiography, written just before he died, Hume described his own character.

> I was ... a man of mild dispositions, of command of temper, of an open, social, and cheerful humour, capable of attachment, but little susceptible of enmity, and of great moderation in all my passions. Even my love of literary fame, my rul-

ing passion, never soured my temper, notwith-standing my frequent disappointments. My company was not unacceptable to the young and careless, as well as to the studious and literary; and as I took a particular pleasure in the company of modest women, I had no reason to be displeased with the reception I met from them.… I cannot say there is no vanity in making this funeral oration of myself, but I hope it is not a misplaced one; and this is a matter of fact which is easily cleared and ascertained.

What Was Hume's Overall Philosophical Project?

Hume can be called the first 'post-skeptical' modern philosopher. He was wholly convinced (by, among others, the writings of his predecessors Descartes, Locke, and Berkeley, who appear elsewhere in this volume) that no knowledge that goes beyond the mere data of our own minds has anything like secure and reliable foundations: that is, he believed, we have no certain knowledge of the inner workings of the physical world and its laws, or of God, or of absolute moral 'truth,' or even of our own 'real selves.' All we have secure knowledge of is our own mental states and their relations: our sensory impressions, our ideas, our emotions, and so on.

Despite all this, Hume's philosophical project was a positive one: he wanted to develop a new, constructive science of human nature that would provide a defensible foundation for all the sciences, including ethics, physics, and politics. Where Hume's predecessors tried in vain to argue against philosophical skepticism, Hume assumed that a certain kind of skepticism was actually true and tried to go beyond it, to say something positive about how we are to get on with our lives (including our lives as scientists and philosophers).

Much of Hume's philosophical writing, therefore, begins by showing the unstoppable power of skepticism in some domain—such as skepticism about causation or objective ethical truths—and then goes on to show how we can still talk sensibly about causation or ethics after all. The selection from *An Enquiry Concerning Human Understanding* which appears below follows this pattern.

One of the central aspects of both Hume's skeptical and his constructive philosophy is his strictly empirical methodology—a development of what was called in Hume's day 'the experimental method.' His science of human nature is based firmly on the experimental methods of the natural sciences, which emphasize the data of experience and observation, sometimes combined with mathematical or logical reasoning. Any other method of investigation—such as an appeal to 'innate intuition,' for example—is illegitimate. As Hume put it:

> If we take in our hand any volume; of divinity or school metaphysics, for instance; let us ask, *Does it contain any abstract reasoning concerning quantity or number?* No. *Does it contain any experimental reasoning concerning matter of fact and existence?* No. Commit it then to the flames: for it can contain nothing but sophistry and illusion. [This is the final paragraph of his *An Enquiry Concerning Human Understanding*.]

This assumption that all human knowledge is either a "matter of fact" or a matter of "relations of ideas"—the product of experience or of reason—is often known as 'Hume's Fork.'

What Is the Structure of This Reading?

An Enquiry Concerning Human Understanding first appeared (in 1748) under the title *Philosophical Essays Concerning Human Understanding*, and it does indeed consist of twelve somewhat loosely related philosophical essays. The underlying theme which ties the essays together is the primacy of experience and causal inference in establishing our ideas, especially such philosophically important ideas as necessity and probability, free will, and God.

Hume's argument in this reading has two parts. In the first part he argues there can be no rational justification for our expectations about those parts of the physical world we have not yet observed; in the second he presents his "skeptical solution of these doubts." First, in Section IV Part I, he introduces a distinction between relations of ideas and matters of fact. He then argues that all empirical claims which go beyond "the present testimony of our senses, or the records of our memory" are based on reasonings "founded on the relation of cause and effect." How do we come to discover relations of cause and effect? Not, Hume argues, from "reasonings *a priori*" but from experience. In Part II, Hume addresses the question: "What is the foundation of all conclusions from experience?" and, for the remainder of this part, "contents himself" with a negative answer. He argues that conclusions from experience are not "founded on reasoning, or on any process of the understanding." Part of his argument here has the following structure: Hume tries to show that all experimental arguments rely upon the assumption that nature is generally uniform—the assumption that observed regularities in nature (like the whiteness of swans or day following night) will persist from the present into the future. He then argues—very ingeniously and persuasively—that this assumption is impossible to rationally justify. His conclusion is that inductive inferences are never rationally justifiable.

Hume's constructive project, presented in Section V, has the following pattern. He begins by describing the benefits of a generally skeptical frame of mind. Then he goes on to discuss the principle that *does* cause us to leap to inductive conclusions, since we have no rational reason to do so—this psychological principle, he suggests, is "custom or habit." In Part II, Hume gives us more detail about what he thinks is really going on when we come to have beliefs about the future: he argues that *belief* is a kind of involuntary feeling, "added" to our imagination of some event. That is, we can freely *imagine* almost any future event we like, but we usually cannot make ourselves *believe* that it will happen. This "extra" feeling of belief in a future event, Hume argues, can only be generated automatically in our minds by a certain sequence of past experiences.

Some Useful Background Information

1. Hume, like John Locke (see Chapter 3), began his philosophy with a 'theory of ideas': it is useful to be aware of a few of the basics of this theory when reading this selection. For Hume, the smallest elements of thought are what he called *basic perceptions*. These can usefully be

thought of as analogous to atoms, since these basic perceptions are, in Hume's view, bound together in various ways into larger units—*complex perceptions*—according to certain fundamental psychological laws; Hume called these laws "the principle of the association of ideas." Hume thought of this system as being the counterpart of Newtonian physics: on this view, physics is the science of matter, and Humean philosophy is the science of human nature or mind. Hume himself considered this general picture, and the use he made of it, to be his greatest contribution to human thought. It is especially notable that *rationality* plays relatively little part in Hume's naturalistic picture of human nature: instead, our ideas are connected together by deterministic laws based, for example, on their similarity or their history of "constant conjunction" (that is, a history of having always appeared together in the past). Finally, for Hume, these "laws of association" may defy further explanation: we might need to treat them as basic laws—brute regularities—just as the law of gravity was for Newton.

2. Unlike Locke, Hume divides his "perceptions" into two distinct sorts: *impressions* and *ideas*. Impressions are "all our sensations, passions and emotions, as they make their first appearance in the soul," and come in two flavors: *impressions of sensation* and *impressions of reflection*. Impressions of sensation, according to Hume, appear in the mind "from unknown causes," and the reasons for their occurrence are best studied by "anatomists and natural philosophers," rather than by those, like Hume himself, interested in studying human nature. Examples of such sensations might be the visual image of a cat on the mat, or the taste of a grape-flavored Popsicle. Impressions of reflection (such as disgust, pride, or desire) arise, usually, from our perception of and reaction to our own ideas. Finally, our *ideas* are, according to Hume, "the faint images" of impressions: that is, they are copies of earlier impressions (and so, causally dependent on them: you cannot possibly have an idea of something which you haven't previously experienced). Ideas, for Hume, have been

described as "the mental tokens by which we reason," and would include, for example, our concepts of colors and shapes, of types of objects, of mathematical relationships, of historical individuals, of moral values, and so on.

3. Hume's arguments in this passage rely on two important distinctions, which it is helpful to have clear in your mind as you read. The first is the distinction which is often called 'Hume's fork' between *relations of ideas* and *matters of fact*. Relations of ideas are propositions whose truth or falsity can be discovered merely by thinking about the concepts involved, and which if true are necessarily true. For example, "a triangle has three sides" must be true since *by definition* triangles have three sides—it's just part of the concept 'triangle' that it be three-sided. In modern jargon, relations of ideas are 'analytic *a priori*' propositions. The simplest kind of relation of ideas Hume calls "intuitively certain": these propositions are just self-evidently true to anyone who understands them, such as "1 is smaller than 2."[1] Other propositions, which are also relations of ideas, may be more complex and need to be shown by some kind of 'demonstrative argument' (the proposition that 2^{16} is 65,536, for example, might not be immediately obvious, but it can be proven by a sequence of small and obvious steps).

Matters of fact, by contrast, are 'synthetic *a posteriori*' propositions—that is, only observation and experience can tell us whether they are true or false (and thus they cannot be *necessarily* true, but are only contingently true). An example might be, "sticking your finger inside a hot toaster really hurts." One of Hume's key claims is that propositions about relations of ideas never assert the existence of any non-abstract entities (such as physical objects), while claims about matters of fact often do.

4. The second important distinction used in this reading is one between *demonstrative arguments* and *experimental arguments*. Demonstrative arguments, for Hume, are deductively valid arguments where all the premises are relations of ideas. We can know that the conclusion of a demonstrative argument is true (indeed, necessarily true) without knowing anything about the actual world—this is why Hume often calls them "reasonings *a priori*." Experimental arguments are arguments of any other kind: that is, they are either arguments which have matters of fact among their premises, or arguments which are not deductive, or (most commonly) both.

5. Finally, a word about "induction." Although Hume does not actually use the word in this reading, Section IV Part II of the *Enquiry* is usually thought of as presenting, for the first time, "the problem of induction." Induction is the modern term for the process of arriving at justified beliefs about the future on the basis of experience of the past; to put the same idea in another way, induction is the method for finding out what as-yet unobserved things are like on the basis of a sample of things we have observed. For example, we might notice that every swan we have ever seen has been white, and conclude that, very probably, the next swan we see will also be white. Furthermore, we might think, we've seen enough swans to justify concluding that probably *every* swan is white. Thus we use our experience of observing swans to draw inductive conclusions about unseen swans—generalizations about other swans in the world (such as Australian swans), and predictions about future swans as yet unhatched. This method of reasoning is extremely common. It is what (apparently) supports much of our everyday behavior, such as getting up at a certain time in the morning to go to work or school, using a kettle to make tea, relying on the morning weather forecast to help us decide what to wear, expecting the bus to come at a certain time and place, and so on. All of these

---

1   If you have already read Descartes and Locke you might notice that Hume's notion of 'intuition' is significantly different from that used by his philosophical predecessors. For example, Descartes' "I think therefore I am" would not count as 'intuitively certain' for Hume.

activities and beliefs are based on assuming that past experience is reliable evidence for expectations about the future. Science, too, is largely based on induction—physicists have only observed a tiny, infinitesimal fraction of all the electrons in the universe, for example, yet they assume that all electrons everywhere have the same charge.

We speak of "the problem of induction," because Hume has apparently shown us that we have no rational justification for induction. This would be an extremely radical conclusion if in fact it is so!

Some Common Misconceptions

1. Hume's philosophical concerns were not primarily negative or destructive: although he frequently attacks the role of reason in science and human affairs, and points out the limitations of our own experiential knowledge, he does not do so in order to leave us in a skeptical dead end. Instead, these attacks are part of his attempt to place the science of human nature upon a more reliable footing, by actually examining how we come to have the beliefs that we do.

2. Although there are differences of interpretation on this matter, it seems likely that Hume was not merely pointing out that inductive conclusions cannot be known *with certainty* to be true—that induction cannot be 100% rationally justified. For that would simply be to say that induction is not deduction, which is trivial. (It is today part of the *definition* of an inductive, as opposed to deductive, argument that its conclusion may possibly be false even if all its premises are true, and this seems to correspond reasonably well with Hume's own distinction between experimental and demonstrative methods of reasoning.) Instead, Hume is making the much more radical claim that the conclusions of inductive arguments *have no rational support at all*: they are not "founded on reasoning, or on any process of the understanding." Inductive arguments, if Hume is right, completely fail to justify their conclusions—their

premises, if true, do not make their conclusions *any* more likely to be true. (Analogously, the argument "roses are red, violets are blue, therefore Brad Pitt will become President of America" is not rationally compelling since the truth of the premises—the respective colors of roses and violets—does nothing to make it more likely to be true that this particular actor will have successful political ambitions. Chapter 1 contains more information on inductive and deductive arguments.)

3. On the other hand, Hume is not arguing that induction does not actually *work*—he's not arguing that human beings are systematically *wrong* in their predictions about the future. On the contrary, he thinks that human beings are usually very successful in coming to have true beliefs about the future (that the sun will rise tomorrow, or that the next chunk of copper we mine from the earth will conduct electricity). And although it's admittedly a bit tricky to hold both that this is the case and that induction is not at all justified, it's not flat out inconsistent: it's perfectly coherent to say that some of our beliefs are true but unjustified.

How Important and Influential Is This Passage?

An influential British philosopher named C.D. Broad once called inductive reasoning "the glory of Science ... [and] ... the scandal of Philosophy." The scandal Broad had in mind was the failure of philosophers over the previous two hundred years (he was writing in 1952) to find a convincing answer to Hume's skeptical arguments ... and this despite the wholesale (and apparently successful) reliance of the natural sciences on inductive arguments. If induction is not rationally justified, recall, then neither are most of the claims of physics, biology, chemistry, economics, and so on. Thus Hume, in effect, discovered and incisively formulated a serious new philosophical problem—the problem of induction. (H.H. Price once called Hume's discovery of this problem "one of the most important advances in the whole history of thought.") This problem has very far-reaching consequences indeed, but it is so difficult a puzzle to solve that many philosophers feel Hume has not yet been satisfactorily answered. Hume's problem of induction is still a live problem today; various answers have been proposed but no single solution has yet found widespread acceptance.

Hume's own "skeptical solution" has been much less influential than his skeptical problem: even if Hume's account in Part V is successful (which many contemporary philosophers and psychologists doubt), it will still only be a *psychological* explanation for why we believe the things we do about the future, whereas what we seem to need to defend science— and most of our everyday beliefs—is a *rational justification* for induction.

Suggestions for Critical Reflection

1. *Are* "all the objects of human reason or enquiry" divisible into exactly two piles: relations of ideas and matters of fact? What about, for example, the claim that a wall can't be simultaneously red all over and green all over: which of the two categories does this fall into? How about the statement that water is identical with H_2O?
2. Does Hume think we are being unreasonable or irrational if we continue to act as if inductive inferences are justified? Given what Hume has argued, what do you think?
3. What exactly would it mean to claim that the future resembles the past or that nature is "uniform"? Is nature uniform in *every* respect? (For example, is the sky always blue?) So what *kind* of uniformity do you think we need to look for?
4. Does the past reliability *of induction* provide evidence that future instances of induction will also be reliable? For example, on several hundred occasions in the past I inferred on the basis of previous experience that the Big Mac I was about to eat would not be poisonous, and each time I was right; do these several hundred instances of correct induction provide any evidence that induction is *generally* reliable? Why, or why not?
5. What's the difference (if any) between the psychological claim that people believe certain things about the future only out of habit, rather

than because they have gone through some process of reasoning, and the claim that there is no rational justification available for our beliefs about the future? Which claim is Hume making?
6. Is it possible to formulate a skeptical problem about *deduction* that is similar to Hume's problem about induction?
7. What is the difference between believing something and merely imagining that it is true? Does Hume think that when we believe some future event will occur, as opposed to merely imagining it will occur, there is some *extra* idea present in our mind—a sort of idea of belief itself, added to the idea of the future event? Are Hume's views on the nature of belief plausible?

Suggestions for Further Reading

The following two sections of the *Enquiry* re-cast portions of Part III, Book I of the *Treatise*, so that is a good place to begin your extra reading. A critical edition of Hume's philosophical writings is currently being prepared by Oxford University Press, but in the meantime the standard editions are: *A Treatise of Human Nature* (Oxford University Press, 1978) and *Enquiries Concerning Human Understanding and Concerning the Principles of Morals* (Oxford University Press, 1975), both edited by L.A. Selby-Bigge and P.H. Nidditch.

Many good books have been written about Hume's philosophy: a handful of the best and most relevant are *Hume's Epistemology and Metaphysics* by Georges Dicker (Routledge, 1998), *Hume's Philosophy of Belief* by Antony Flew (Routledge & Kegan Paul, 1961), *Hume's Skepticism* by Robert J. Fogelin (Routledge & Kegan Paul, 1985), *David Hume* by Terence Penelhum (Purdue University Press, 1992), *Probability and Hume's Inductive Scepticism* by David Stove (Oxford University Press, 1973), and *Hume* by Barry Stroud (Routledge, 1977). Tom Beauchamp and Alexander Rosenberg defend the view that Hume is not in fact a skeptic about induction in *Hume and the Problem of Causation* (Oxford University Press, 1981).

The Cambridge Companion to Hume, edited by David Fate Norton (Cambridge University Press, 1993), is a helpful collection of specially written essays on different aspects of Hume's philosophy, which also includes Hume's short autobiography. An old, but still good, collection of critical essays on Hume is V.C. Chappell's *Hume: A Collection of Critical Essays* (Doubleday, 1966).

Some influential attempts to solve Hume's riddle of induction—apart from those encompassed by the next few readings in this text—include: P.F. Strawson in the final chapter of his book *An Introduction to Logical Theory* (Methuen, 1952); Max Black, "Inductive Support of Inductive Rules," in *Problems of Analysis* (Cornell University Press, 1954); and James Van Cleve, "Reliability, Justification, and the Problem of Induction," in *Midwest Studies in Philosophy* IX (1984). A good review article criticizing many of these attempted solutions (and tentatively suggesting another) is Wesley C. Salmon's "Unfinished Business: The Problem of Induction," *Philosophical Studies* 33 (1978) (reprinted below).

from *An Enquiry Concerning Human Understanding*[2]

Section IV: Sceptical Doubts Concerning the Operations of the Understanding.

PART I.

All the objects of human reason or enquiry may naturally be divided into two kinds, to wit,[3] *relations of ideas*, and *matters of fact*. Of the first kind are the sciences of geometry, algebra, and arithmetic; and in short, every affirmation which is either intuitively or demonstratively certain. *That the square of the hypotenuse*[4] *is equal to the square of the two sides*, is a proposition which expresses a relation between these figures. *That three times five is equal to the half*

of *thirty*, expresses a relation between these numbers. Propositions of this kind are discoverable by the mere operation of thought, without dependence on what is anywhere existent in the universe. Though there never were a circle or triangle in nature, the truths demonstrated by Euclid would for ever retain their certainty and evidence.

Matters of fact, which are the second objects of human reason, are not ascertained in the same manner; nor is our evidence of their truth, however great, of a like nature with the foregoing. The contrary of every matter of fact is still possible; because it can never imply a contradiction, and is conceived by the mind with the same facility and distinctness, as if ever so conformable to reality. *That the sun will not rise to-morrow* is no less intelligible a proposition, and implies no more contradiction than the affirmation, *that it will rise*. We should in vain, therefore, attempt to demonstrate its falsehood. Were it demonstratively false, it would imply a contradiction, and could never be distinctly conceived by the mind.

It may, therefore, be a subject worthy of curiosity, to enquire what is the nature of that evidence which assures us of any real existence and matter of fact, beyond the present testimony of our senses, or the records of our memory. This part of philosophy, it is observable, has been little cultivated, either by the ancients or moderns; and therefore our doubts and errors, in the prosecution of so important an enquiry, may be the more excusable; while we march through such difficult paths without any guide or direction. They may even prove useful, by exciting curiosity, and destroying that implicit faith and security, which is the bane of all reasoning and free enquiry. The discovery of defects in the common philosophy, if any such there be, will not, I presume, be a discouragement, but rather an incitement, as is usual, to attempt something more full and satisfactory than has yet been proposed to the public.

All reasonings concerning matter of fact seem to be founded on the relation of *cause and effect*. By means of that relation alone we can go beyond the evidence of our memory and senses. If you were to ask a man, why he believes any matter of fact, which is absent; for instance, that his friend is in the country, or in France; he would give you a reason; and this

---

2   Hume's *An Enquiry Concerning Human Understanding* was first published in 1748. This selection is taken from the 1777 "new edition," generally considered the final version authorized by Hume. Most of the spelling, capitalization, and punctuation have been modernized.

3   "To wit" is a phrase meaning "that is to say" or "namely."

4   The hypotenuse is the side opposite the right angle of a right-angled triangle.

reason would be some other fact; as a letter received from him, or the knowledge of his former resolutions and promises. A man finding a watch or any other machine in a desert island, would conclude that there had once been men in that island. All our reasonings concerning fact are of the same nature. And here it is constantly supposed that there is a connection between the present fact and that which is inferred from it. Were there nothing to bind them together, the inference would be entirely precarious. The hearing of an articulate voice and rational discourse in the dark assures us of the presence of some person: Why? Because these are the effects of the human make and fabric, and closely connected with it. If we anatomize[5] all the other reasonings of this nature, we shall find that they are founded on the relation of cause and effect, and that this relation is either near or remote, direct or collateral. Heat and light are collateral effects of fire, and the one effect may justly be inferred from the other.

If we would satisfy ourselves, therefore, concerning the nature of that evidence, which assures us of matters of fact, we must enquire how we arrive at the knowledge of cause and effect.

I shall venture to affirm, as a general proposition, which admits of no exception, that the knowledge of this relation is not, in any instance, attained by reasonings *a priori*;[6] but arises entirely from experience, when we find that any particular objects are constantly conjoined with each other. Let an object be presented to a man of ever so strong natural reason and abilities; if that object be entirely new to him, he will not be able, by the most accurate examination of its sensible[7] qualities, to discover any of its causes or effects. Adam,[8] though his rational faculties be supposed, at the very first, entirely perfect, could not have inferred from the fluidity and transparency of water that it would suffocate him, or from the light and warmth of fire that it would consume him. No object ever discovers,[9] by the qualities which appear to the senses, either the causes which produced it, or the effects which will arise from it; nor can our reason, unassisted by experience, ever draw any inference concerning real existence and matter of fact.

This proposition, *that causes and effects are discoverable, not by reason but by experience*, will readily be admitted with regard to such objects as we remember to have once been altogether unknown to us; since we must be conscious of the utter inability, which we then lay under, of foretelling what would arise from them. Present two smooth pieces of marble to a man who has no tincture of natural philosophy;[10] he will never discover that they will adhere together in such a manner as to require great force to separate them in a direct line, while they make so small a resistance to a lateral pressure. Such events, as bear little analogy to the common course of nature, are also readily confessed to be known only by experience; nor does any man imagine that the explosion of gunpowder, or the attraction of a loadstone,[11] could ever be discovered by arguments *a priori*. In like manner, when an effect is supposed to depend upon an intricate machinery or secret structure of parts, we make no difficulty in attributing all our knowledge of it to experience. Who will assert that he can give the ultimate reason, why milk or bread is proper nourishment for a man, not for a lion or a tiger?

But the same truth may not appear, at first sight, to have the same evidence with regard to events, which have become familiar to us from our first appearance in the world, which bear a close analogy to the whole course of nature, and which are supposed to depend on the simple qualities of objects, without any secret structure of parts. We are apt to imagine that we could discover these effects by the mere operation of our reason, without experience. We fancy, that were we brought on a sudden into this world, we could at first have inferred that one billiard-ball would com-

---

5   Closely examine.

6   Prior to experience; purely deductively.

7   "Sensible" means, here and elsewhere, able to be perceived or sensed.

8   According to the Old Testament, the first human being.

9   Here (and sometimes elsewhere) "discovers" means reveals or discloses (rather than finds out).

10   That is: no trace of knowledge of physical science.

11   A magnet (made from naturally occurring magnetic iron oxide).

municate motion to another upon impulse;[12] and that we needed not to have waited for the event, in order to pronounce with certainty concerning it. Such is the influence of custom,[13] that, where it is strongest, it not only covers our natural ignorance, but even conceals itself, and seems not to take place, merely because it is found in the highest degree.

But to convince us that all the laws of nature, and all the operations of bodies without exception, are known only by experience, the following reflections may, perhaps, suffice. Were any object presented to us, and were we required to pronounce concerning the effect, which will result from it, without consulting past observation; after what manner, I beseech you, must the mind proceed in this operation? It must invent or imagine some event, which it ascribes to the object as its effect; and it is plain that this invention must be entirely arbitrary. The mind can never possibly find the effect in the supposed cause, by the most accurate scrutiny and examination. For the effect is totally different from the cause, and consequently can never be discovered in it. Motion in the second billiard-ball is a quite distinct event from motion in the first; nor is there any thing in the one to suggest the smallest hint of the other. A stone or piece of metal raised into the air, and left without any support, immediately falls: but to consider the matter *a priori*, is there any thing we discover in this situation which can beget the idea of a downward, rather than an upward, or any other motion, in the stone or metal?

And as the first imagination or invention of a particular effect, in all natural operations, is arbitrary, where we consult not experience; so must we also esteem the supposed tie or connection between the cause and effect, which binds them together, and renders it impossible that any other effect could result from the operation of that cause. When I see, for instance, a billiard-ball moving in a straight line towards another; even suppose motion in the second ball should by accident be suggested to me, as the result of their contact or impulse; may I not conceive, that a hundred different events might as well follow from that cause? May not both these balls remain at absolute rest? May

not the first ball return in a straight line, or leap off from the second in any line or direction? All these suppositions are consistent and conceivable. Why then should we give the preference to one, which is no more consistent or conceivable than the rest? All our reasonings *a priori* will never be able to show us any foundation for this preference.

In a word, then, every effect is a distinct event from its cause. It could not, therefore, be discovered in the cause, and the first invention or conception of it, *a priori*, must be entirely arbitrary. And even after it is suggested, the conjunction of it with the cause must appear equally arbitrary; since there are always many other effects, which, to reason, must seem fully as consistent and natural. In vain, therefore, should we pretend to determine any single event, or infer any cause or effect, without the assistance of observation and experience.

Hence we may discover the reason why no philosopher,[14] who is rational and modest, has ever pretended to assign the ultimate cause of any natural operation, or to show distinctly the action of that power, which produces any single effect in the universe. It is confessed, that the utmost effort of human reason is to reduce the principles, productive of natural phenomena, to a greater simplicity, and to resolve the many particular effects into a few general causes, by means of reasonings from analogy, experience, and observation. But as to the causes of these general causes, we should in vain attempt their discovery; nor shall we ever be able to satisfy ourselves, by any particular explication of them. These ultimate springs and principles are totally shut up from human curiosity and enquiry. Elasticity, gravity, cohesion of parts, communication of motion by impulse; these are probably the ultimate causes and principles which we shall ever discover in nature; and we may esteem ourselves sufficiently happy, if, by accurate enquiry and reasoning, we can trace up the particular phenomena to, or near to, these general principles. The most perfect philosophy of the natural kind only staves off our ignorance a little longer: as perhaps the most perfect philosophy of the moral or metaphysical kind

---

12   Impact, collision.

13   Habit, repeated similar experience.

14   The word "philosopher" at this time included natural scientists.

serves only to discover larger portions of it. Thus the observation of human blindness and weakness is the result of all philosophy, and meets us at every turn, in spite of our endeavours to elude or avoid it.

Nor is geometry, when taken into the assistance of natural philosophy, ever able to remedy this defect, or lead us into the knowledge of ultimate causes, by all that accuracy of reasoning for which it is so justly celebrated. Every part of mixed mathematics[15] proceeds upon the supposition that certain laws are established by nature in her operations; and abstract reasonings are employed, either to assist experience in the discovery of these laws, or to determine their influence in particular instances, where it depends upon any precise degree of distance and quantity. Thus, it is a law of motion, discovered by experience, that the moment[16] or force of any body in motion is in the compound ratio or proportion of its solid contents[17] and its velocity; and consequently, that a small force may remove the greatest obstacle or raise the greatest weight, if, by any contrivance or machinery, we can increase the velocity of that force, so as to make it an overmatch for its antagonist.[18] Geometry assists us in the application of this law, by giving us the just dimensions of all the parts and figures which can enter into any species of machine; but still the discovery of the law itself is owing merely to experience, and all the abstract reasonings in the world could never lead us one step towards the knowledge of it. When we reason *a priori*, and consider merely any object or cause, as it appears to the mind, independent of all observation,

it never could suggest to us the notion of any distinct object, such as its effect; much less, show us the inseparable and inviolable connection between them. A man must be very sagacious[19] who could discover by reasoning that crystal is the effect of heat, and ice of cold, without being previously acquainted with the operation of these qualities.

PART II.

But we have not yet attained any tolerable satisfaction with regard to the question first proposed. Each solution still gives rise to a new question as difficult as the foregoing, and leads us on to farther enquiries. When it is asked, *What is the nature of all our reasonings concerning matter of fact?* the proper answer seems to be, that they are founded on the relation of cause and effect. When again it is asked, *What is the foundation of all our reasonings and conclusions concerning that relation?* it may be replied in one word, Experience. But if we still carry on our sifting humour,[20] and ask, *What is the foundation of all conclusions from experience?* this implies a new question, which may be of more difficult solution and explication. Philosophers, that give themselves airs of superior wisdom and sufficiency,[21] have a hard task when they encounter persons of inquisitive dispositions, who push them from every corner to which they retreat, and who are sure at last to bring them to some dangerous dilemma. The best expedient to prevent this confusion, is to be modest in our pretensions; and even to discover the difficulty ourselves before it is objected to us. By this means, we may make a kind of merit of our very ignorance.

I shall content myself, in this section, with an easy task, and shall pretend[22] only to give a negative answer to the question here proposed. I say then, that, even after we have experience of the operations of cause and effect, our conclusions from that experience are *not* founded on reasoning, or any process of the

---

15 Mathematical physics (mathematics applied to the physical world).
16 Momentum.
17 Mass.
18 Here is what Hume means by this example (which comes from Newtonian physics). Imagine two bodies A and B: suppose that A has a mass of 2 and a velocity of 4 and that B has a mass of 6 and a velocity of 1. Thus the ratios of their respective masses will be 2:6 and their respective velocities 4:1. Then, A will have a higher momentum or force than B (despite only having one third the mass), since the "compound ratio" of its momentum to that of B will be 2x4 to 6x1, which is 8:6.

19 Mentally penetrating, insightful (Hume is being ironic).
20 Searching frame of mind.
21 Here "sufficiency" means ability.
22 Aim, venture.

understanding. This answer we must endeavour both to explain and to defend.

It must certainly be allowed, that nature has kept us at a great distance from all her secrets, and has afforded us only the knowledge of a few superficial qualities of objects; while she conceals from us those powers and principles on which the influence of those objects entirely depends. Our senses inform us of the colour, weight, and consistence[23] of bread; but neither sense nor reason can ever inform us of those qualities which fit it for the nourishment and support of a human body. Sight or feeling conveys an idea of the actual motion of bodies; but as to that wonderful force or power, which would carry on a moving body for ever in a continued change of place, and which bodies never lose but by communicating it to others; of this we cannot form the most distant conception. But notwithstanding this ignorance of natural powers[24] and principles, we always presume, when we see like[25] sensible qualities, that they have like secret powers, and expect that effects, similar to those which we have experienced, will follow from them. If a body of like colour and consistence with that bread, which we have formerly eat,[26] be presented to us, we make no scruple of repeating the experiment,[27] and foresee, with certainty, like nourishment and support. Now this is a process of the mind or thought, of which I would willingly know the foundation. It is allowed on all hands that there is no known connection between the sensible qualities and the secret powers; and consequently, that the mind is not led to form such a conclusion concerning their constant and regular conjunction, by any thing which it knows of their nature. As to past *experience*, it can be allowed to give *direct* and *certain* information of those precise objects only, and that precise period of time, which fell under its cognizance: But why this experience should be extended to future times, and to other objects, which for aught we know, may be only in appearance similar; this is the main question on which I would insist. The bread, which I formerly eat, nourished me; that is, a body of such sensible qualities was, at that time, endued with[28] such secret powers: but does it follow, that other bread must also nourish me at another time, and that like sensible qualities must always be attended with like secret powers? The consequence seems nowise necessary. At least, it must be acknowledged that there is here a consequence drawn by the mind; that there is a certain step taken; a process of thought, and an inference, which wants to be explained. These two propositions are far from being the same, *I have found that such an object has always been attended with such an effect*, and *I foresee, that other objects, which are, in appearance, similar, will be attended with similar effects*. I shall allow, if you please, that the one proposition may justly be inferred from the other: I know, in fact, that it always is inferred. But if you insist that the inference is made by a chain of reasoning, I desire you to produce that reasoning. The connection between these propositions is not intuitive. There is required a medium,[29] which may enable the mind to draw such an inference, if indeed it be drawn by reasoning and argument. What that medium is, I must confess, passes my comprehension; and it is incumbent on those to produce it, who assert that it really exists, and is the origin of all our conclusions concerning matter of fact.

This negative argument must certainly, in process of time, become altogether convincing, if many penetrating and able philosophers shall turn their enquiries this way and no one be ever able to discover any connecting proposition or intermediate step, which supports the understanding in this conclusion. But as the question is yet new, every reader may not trust so far to his own penetration, as to conclude, because an argument escapes his enquiry, that therefore it does not really exist. For this reason it may be requisite to venture upon a more difficult task; and enumerating all the branches of human knowledge, endeavour to show that none of them can afford such an argument.

23 Consistency, texture.

24 [Author's note] The word, Power, is here used in a loose and popular sense. The more accurate explication of it would give additional evidence to this argument. See Sect. 7 [not reprinted here].

25 Similar.

26 Eaten.

27 Experience.

28 Endowed with, possessed of.

29 A ground of inference; a further premise.

All reasonings may be divided into two kinds, namely, demonstrative reasoning, or that concerning relations of ideas, and moral[30] reasoning, or that concerning matter of fact and existence. That there are no demonstrative arguments in the case seems evident; since it implies no contradiction that the course of nature may change, and that an object, seemingly like those which we have experienced, may be attended with different or contrary effects. May I not clearly and distinctly conceive that a body, falling from the clouds, and which, in all other respects, resembles snow, has yet the taste of salt or feeling of fire? Is there any more intelligible proposition than to affirm, that all the trees will flourish in December and January, and decay in May and June? Now whatever is intelligible, and can be distinctly conceived, implies no contradiction, and can never be proved false by any demonstrative argument or abstract reasoning *a priori*.

If we be, therefore, engaged[31] by arguments to put trust in past experience, and make it the standard of our future judgement, these arguments must be probable only, or such as regard matter of fact and real existence according to the division above mentioned. But that there is no argument of this kind, must appear, if our explication of that species of reasoning be admitted as solid and satisfactory. We have said that all arguments concerning existence are founded on the relation of cause and effect; that our knowledge of that relation is derived entirely from experience; and that all our experimental conclusions proceed upon the supposition that the future will be conformable to the past. To endeavour, therefore, the proof of this last supposition by probable arguments, or arguments regarding existence, must be evidently going in a circle, and taking that for granted, which is the very point in question.

In reality, all arguments from experience are founded on the similarity which we discover among natural objects, and by which we are induced to expect effects similar to those which we have found to follow from such objects. And though none but a fool or madman will ever pretend to dispute the authority of experience, or to reject that great guide of human life, it may surely be allowed a philosopher to have so much curiosity at least as to examine the principle of human nature, which gives this mighty authority to experience, and makes us draw advantage from that similarity which nature has placed among different objects. From causes which, appear *similar*, we expect similar effects. This is the sum of all our experimental conclusions. Now it seems evident that, if this conclusion were formed by reason, it would be as perfect at first, and upon one instance, as after ever so long a course of experience. But the case is far otherwise. Nothing so like as eggs; yet no one, on account of this appearing similarity, expects the same taste and relish in all of them. It is only after a long course of uniform experiments in any kind, that we attain a firm reliance and security with regard to a particular event. Now where is that process of reasoning which, from one instance, draws a conclusion, so different from that which it infers from a hundred instances that are nowise different from that single one? This question I propose as much for the sake of information, as with an intention of raising difficulties. I cannot find, I cannot imagine any such reasoning. But I keep my mind still open to instruction, if any one will vouchsafe to bestow it on me.

Should it be said that, from a number of uniform experiments, we *infer* a connection between the sensible qualities and the secret powers; this, I must confess, seems the same difficulty, couched in different terms. The question still recurs, on what process of argument this *inference* is founded? Where is the medium, the interposing ideas, which join propositions so very wide of each other? It is confessed that the colour, consistence, and other sensible qualities of bread appear not, of themselves, to have any connection with the secret powers of nourishment and support. For otherwise we could infer these secret powers from the first appearance of these sensible qualities, without the aid of experience; contrary to the sentiment[32] of all philosophers, and contrary to plain

---

30 Here "moral" means inductive or having at best only a probable conclusion. (Often, however, Hume uses the phrase "moral philosophy" in a somewhat different way, to mean the study of the nature of human beings, contrasted with "natural philosophy," the study of nature.)

31 Induced, persuaded.

32 Opinion.

matter of fact. Here, then, is our natural state of ignorance with regard to the powers and influence of all objects. How is this remedied by experience? It only shows us a number of uniform effects, resulting from certain objects, and teaches us that those particular objects, at that particular time, were endowed with such powers and forces. When a new object, endowed with similar sensible qualities, is produced, we expect similar powers and forces, and look for a like effect. From a body of like colour and consistence with bread we expect like nourishment and support. But this surely is a step or progress of the mind, which wants to be explained. When a man says, *I have found, in all past instances, such sensible qualities conjoined with such secret powers*: and when he says, *similar sensible qualities will always be conjoined with similar secret powers*, he is not guilty of a tautology, nor are these propositions in any respect the same. You say that the one proposition is an inference from the other. But you must confess that the inference is not intuitive; neither is it demonstrative: Of what nature is it, then? To say it is experimental, is begging the question. For all inferences from experience suppose, as their foundation, that the future will resemble the past, and that similar powers will be conjoined with similar sensible qualities. If there be any suspicion that the course of nature may change, and that the past may be no rule for the future, all experience becomes useless, and can give rise to no inference or conclusion. It is impossible, therefore, that any arguments from experience can prove this resemblance of the past to the future; since all these arguments are founded on the supposition of that resemblance. Let the course of things be allowed hitherto ever so regular; that alone, without some new argument or inference, proves not that, for the future, it will continue so. In vain do you pretend to have learned the nature of bodies from your past experience. Their secret nature, and consequently all their effects and influence, may change, without any change in their sensible qualities. This happens sometimes, and with regard to some objects: why may it not happen always, and with regard to all objects? What logic, what process or argument secures you against this supposition? My practice, you say, refutes my doubts. But you mistake the purport of my question. As an agent, I am quite satisfied in the point; but

as a philosopher, who has some share of curiosity, I will not say scepticism, I want to learn the foundation of this inference. No reading, no enquiry has yet been able to remove my difficulty, or give me satisfaction in a matter of such importance. Can I do better than propose the difficulty to the public, even though, perhaps, I have small hopes of obtaining a solution? We shall at least, by this means, be sensible of our ignorance, if we do not augment our knowledge.

I must confess that a man is guilty of unpardonable arrogance who concludes, because an argument has escaped his own investigation, that therefore it does not really exist. I must also confess that, though all the learned, for several ages, should have employed themselves in fruitless search upon any subject, it may still, perhaps, be rash to conclude positively that the subject must, therefore, pass all human comprehension. Even though we examine all the sources of our knowledge, and conclude them unfit for such a subject, there may still remain a suspicion, that the enumeration is not complete, or the examination not accurate. But with regard to the present subject, there are some considerations which seem to remove all this accusation of arrogance or suspicion of mistake.

It is certain that the most ignorant and stupid peasants—nay infants, nay even brute beasts—improve by experience, and learn the qualities of natural objects, by observing the effects which result from them. When a child has felt the sensation of pain from touching the flame of a candle, he will be careful not to put his hand near any candle; but will expect a similar effect from a cause which is similar in its sensible qualities and appearance. If you assert, therefore, that the understanding of the child is led into this conclusion by any process of argument or ratiocination, I may justly require you to produce that argument; nor have you any pretence to refuse so equitable a demand. You cannot say that the argument is abstruse, and may possibly escape your enquiry; since you confess that it is obvious to the capacity of a mere infant. If you hesitate, therefore, a moment, or if, after reflection, you produce any intricate or profound argument, you, in a manner, give up the question, and confess that it is not reasoning which engages us to suppose the past resembling the future, and to expect similar effects from causes which are, to appearance, similar. This is the proposition which I intended to enforce in the present section. If I be right, I pretend not to have made any mighty discovery. And if I be wrong, I must acknowledge myself to be indeed a very backward scholar; since I cannot now discover an argument which, it seems, was perfectly familiar to me long before I was out of my cradle.

Section V: Sceptical Solution of these Doubts.

PART I.

The passion for philosophy, like that for religion, seems liable to this inconvenience, that, though it aims at the correction of our manners, and extirpation of our vices, it may only serve, by imprudent management, to foster a predominant inclination, and push the mind, with more determined resolution, towards that side which already *draws* too much,[33] by the bias and propensity of the natural temper. It is certain that, while we aspire to the magnanimous firmness of the philosophic sage, and endeavour to confine our pleasures altogether within our own minds, we may, at last, render our philosophy like that of Epictetus, and other *Stoics*,[34] only a more refined system of selfishness, and reason ourselves out of all virtue as well as social enjoyment. While we study with attention the vanity of human life, and turn all our thoughts towards the empty and transitory nature of riches and honours, we are, perhaps, all the while flattering our natural indolence, which, hating the bustle of the world, and drudgery of business, seeks a pretence of reason to give itself a full and uncontrolled indulgence. There is, however, one species of philosophy which seems little liable to this inconvenience, and that because it strikes in with no disorderly passion of the human

mind, nor can mingle itself with any natural affection or propensity; and that is the Academic or Sceptical philosophy.[35] The academics always talk of doubt and suspense of judgement, of danger in hasty determinations, of confining to very narrow bounds the enquiries of the understanding, and of renouncing all speculations which lie not within the limits of common life and practice. Nothing, therefore, can be more contrary than such a philosophy to the supine indolence of the mind, its rash arrogance, its lofty pretensions, and its superstitious credulity. Every passion is mortified by it, except the love of truth; and that passion never is, nor can be, carried to too high a degree. It is surprising, therefore, that this philosophy, which, in almost every instance, must be harmless and innocent, should be the subject of so much groundless reproach and obloquy. But, perhaps, the very circumstance which renders it so innocent is what chiefly exposes it to the public hatred and resentment. By flattering no irregular passion, it gains few partisans: by opposing so many vices and follies, it raises to itself abundance of enemies, who stigmatize it as libertine, profane, and irreligious.

Nor need we fear that this philosophy, while it endeavours to limit our enquiries to common life, should ever undermine the reasonings of common life, and carry its doubts so far as to destroy all action, as well as speculation. Nature will always maintain her rights, and prevail in the end over any abstract reasoning whatsoever. Though we should conclude, for instance, as in the foregoing section, that, in all reasonings from experience, there is a step taken by the mind which is not supported by any argument or process of the understanding; there is no danger that these reasonings, on which almost all knowledge depends, will ever be affected by such a discovery. If the mind be not engaged by argument to make this step, it must be induced by some other principle of equal weight and

---

33 Pulls too much—i.e., toward the side we already favor.

34 Epictetus (c. 55–135 CE) was a leading Stoic of the Roman era. Stoicism was a philosophical movement that flourished between roughly 300 BCE and 200 CE, and its main doctrine was that the guiding principle of nature is Reason (*logos*) and the highest virtue is to live in harmony with this rational order.

35 Hume means a kind of moderate scepticism, associated with Plato and the school he founded in Athens around 380 BCE, the Academy. This is to be contrasted with the extreme scepticism sometimes called Pyrrhonism, which seeks to suspend judgment on any question having conflicting evidence—which is to say, on nearly all questions.

authority; and that principle will preserve its influence as long as human nature remains the same. What that principle is may well be worth the pains of enquiry.

Suppose a person, though endowed with the strongest faculties of reason and reflection, to be brought on a sudden into this world; he would, indeed, immediately observe a continual succession of objects, and one event following another; but he would not be able to discover anything farther. He would not, at first, by any reasoning, be able to reach the idea of cause and effect; since the particular powers, by which all natural operations are performed, never appear to the senses; nor is it reasonable to conclude, merely because one event, in one instance, precedes another, that therefore the one is the cause, the other the effect. Their conjunction may be arbitrary and casual. There may be no reason to infer the existence of one from the appearance of the other. And in a word, such a person, without more experience, could never employ his conjecture or reasoning concerning any matter of fact, or be assured of any thing beyond what was immediately present to his memory and senses.

Suppose, again, that he has acquired more experience, and has lived so long in the world as to have observed familiar objects or events to be constantly conjoined together; what is the consequence of this experience? He immediately infers the existence of one object from the appearance of the other. Yet he has not, by all his experience, acquired any idea or knowledge of the secret power by which the one object produces the other; nor is it by any process of reasoning, he is engaged to draw this inference. But still he finds himself determined to draw it: And though he should be convinced that his understanding has no part in the operation, he would nevertheless continue in the same course of thinking. There is some other principle which determines him to form such a conclusion.

This principle is custom or habit. For wherever the repetition of any particular act or operation produces a propensity to renew the same act or operation, without being impelled by any reasoning or process of the understanding, we always say, that this propensity is the effect of *custom*. By employing that word, we pretend not to have given the ultimate reason of such a propensity. We only point out a principle of

human nature, which is universally acknowledged, and which is well known by its effects. Perhaps we can push our enquiries no farther, or pretend to give the cause of this cause; but must rest contented with it as the ultimate principle, which we can assign, of all our conclusions from experience. It is sufficient satisfaction, that we can go so far, without repining at the narrowness of our faculties because they will carry us no farther. And it is certain we here advance a very intelligible proposition at least, if not a true one, when we assert that, after the constant conjunction of two objects—heat and flame, for instance, weight and solidity—we are determined[36] by custom alone to expect the one from the appearance of the other. This hypothesis seems even the only one which explains the difficulty, why we draw, from a thousand instances, an inference which we are not able to draw from one instance, that is, in no respect, different from them. Reason is incapable of any such variation. The conclusions which it draws from considering one circle are the same which it would form upon surveying all the circles in the universe. But no man, having seen only one body move after being impelled by another, could infer that every other body will move after a like impulse. All inferences from experience, therefore, are effects of custom, not of reasoning.[37]

---

36 Caused.

37 [Author's note] Nothing is more usual than for writers, even, on *moral*, *political*, or *physical* subjects to distinguish between *reason* and *experience*, and to suppose, that these species of argumentation are entirely different from each other. The former are taken for the mere result of our intellectual faculties, which, by considering *a priori* the nature of things, and examining the effects, that must follow from their operation, establish particular principles of science and philosophy. The latter are supposed to be derived entirely from sense and observation, by which we learn what has actually resulted from the operation of particular objects, and are thence able to infer, what will, for the future, result from them. Thus, for instance, the limitations and restraints of civil government, and a legal constitution, may be defended, either from *reason*, which reflecting on the great frailty and corruption of human nature, teaches, that no man can safely be

Custom, then, is the great guide of human life. It is

trusted with unlimited authority; or from *experience* and history, which inform us of the enormous abuses, that ambition, in every age and country, has been found to make so imprudent a confidence.

The same distinction between reason and experience is maintained in all our deliberations concerning the conduct of life; while the experienced statesman, general, physician, or merchant is trusted and followed; and the unpractised novice, with whatever natural talents endowed, neglected and despised. Though it be allowed, that reason may form very plausible conjectures with regard to the consequences of such a particular conduct in such particular circumstances; it is still supposed imperfect, without the assistance of experience, which is alone able to give stability and certainty to the maxims, derived from study and reflection.

But notwithstanding that this distinction be thus universally received, both in the active and speculative scenes of life, I shall not scruple to pronounce, that it is, at bottom, erroneous, at least, superficial.

If we examine those arguments, which, in any of the sciences above mentioned, are supposed to be mere effects of reasoning and reflection, they will be found to terminate, at last, in some general principle or, conclusion, for which we can assign no reason but observation and experience. The only difference between them and those maxims, which are vulgarly esteemed the result of pure experience, is, that the former cannot be established without some process of thought, and some reflection on what we have observed, in order to distinguish its circumstances, and trace its consequences: Whereas in the latter, the experienced event is exactly and fully familiar to that which we infer as the result of any particular situation. The history of a Tiberius or a Nero makes us dread a like tyranny, were our monarchs freed from the restraints of laws and senates: but the observation of any fraud or cruelty in private life is sufficient, with the aid of a little thought, to give us the same apprehension; while it serves as an instance of the general corruption of human nature, and shows us the danger which we must incur by reposing an entire confidence in mankind. In both cases, it is experience which is ultimately the foundation of our inference and conclusion.

that principle alone which renders our experience useful to us, and makes us expect, for the future, a similar train of events with those which have appeared in the past. Without the influence of custom, we should be entirely ignorant of every matter of fact beyond what is immediately present to the memory and senses. We should never know how to adjust means to ends, or to employ our natural powers in the production of any effect. There would be an end at once of all action, as well as of the chief part of speculation.

But here it may be proper to remark, that though our conclusions from experience carry us beyond our memory and senses, and assure us of matters of fact which happened in the most distant places and most remote ages, yet some fact must always be present to the senses or memory, from which we may first proceed in drawing these conclusions. A man, who should find in a desert country the remains of pompous[38] buildings, would conclude that the country had, in ancient times, been cultivated by civilized inhabitants; but did nothing of this nature occur to him, he could never form such an inference. We learn the events of former ages from history; but then we must

There is no man so young and inexperienced, as not to have formed, from observation, many general and just maxims concerning human affairs and the conduct of life; but it must be confessed, that, when a man comes to put these in practice, he will be extremely liable to error, till time and farther experience both enlarge these maxims, and teach him their proper use and application. In every situation or incident, there are many particular and seemingly minute circumstances, which the man of greatest talent is, at first, apt to overlook, though on them the justness of his conclusions, and consequently the prudence of his conduct, entirely depend. Not to mention, that, to a young beginner, the general observations and maxims occur not always on the proper occasions, nor can be immediately applied with due calmness and distinction. The truth is, an unexperienced reasoner could be no reasoner at all, were he absolutely unexperienced; and when we assign that character to any one, we mean it only in a comparative sense, and suppose him possessed of experience, in a smaller and more imperfect degree.

38 Splendid, full of pomp.

peruse the volumes in which this instruction is contained, and thence carry up our inferences from one testimony to another, till we arrive at the eyewitnesses and spectators of these distant events. In a word, if we proceed not upon some fact, present to the memory or senses, our reasonings would be merely hypothetical; and however the particular links might be connected with each other, the whole chain of inferences would have nothing to support it, nor could we ever, by its means, arrive at the knowledge of any real existence. If I ask why you believe any particular matter of fact, which you relate, you must tell me some reason; and this reason will be some other fact, connected with it. But as you cannot proceed after this manner, *in infinitum*,[39] you must at last terminate in some fact, which is present to your memory or senses; or must allow that your belief is entirely without foundation.

What, then, is the conclusion of the whole matter? A simple one; though, it must be confessed, pretty remote from the common theories of philosophy. All belief of matter of fact or real existence is derived merely from some object, present to the memory or senses, and a customary conjunction between that and some other object. Or in other words; having found, in many instances, that any two kinds of objects—flame and heat, snow and cold—have always been conjoined together; if flame or snow be presented anew to the senses, the mind is carried by custom to expect heat or cold, and to *believe* that such a quality does exist, and will discover itself upon a nearer approach. This belief is the necessary result of placing the mind in such circumstances. It is an operation of the soul, when we are so situated, as unavoidable as to feel the passion of love, when we receive benefits; or hatred, when we meet with injuries. All these operations are a species of natural instincts, which no reasoning or process of the thought and understanding is able either to produce or to prevent.

At this point, it would be very allowable for us to stop our philosophical researches. In most questions we can never make a single step farther; and in all questions we must terminate here at last, after our most restless and curious enquiries. But still our curiosity will be pardonable, perhaps commendable, if

it carry us on to still farther researches, and make us examine more accurately the nature of this *belief*, and of the *customary conjunction*, whence it is derived. By this means we may meet with some explications and analogies that will give satisfaction; at least to such as love the abstract sciences, and can be entertained with speculations, which, however accurate, may still retain a degree of doubt and uncertainty. As to readers of a different taste; the remaining part of this section is not calculated for them, and the following enquiries may well be understood, though it be neglected.

PART II.

Nothing is more free than the imagination of man; and though it cannot exceed that original stock of ideas furnished by the internal and external senses, it has unlimited power of mixing, compounding, separating, and dividing these ideas, in all the varieties of fiction and vision. It can feign[40] a train of events, with all the appearance of reality, ascribe to them a particular time and place, conceive them as existent, and paint them out to itself with every circumstance, that belongs to any historical fact, which it believes with the greatest certainty. Wherein, therefore, consists the difference between such a *fiction* and *belief*? It lies not merely in any peculiar idea, which is annexed to such a conception as commands our assent, and which is wanting[41] to every known fiction. For as the mind has authority over all its ideas, it could voluntarily annex this particular idea to any fiction, and consequently be able to believe whatever it pleases; contrary to what we find by daily experience. We can, in our conception, join the head of a man to the body of a horse; but it is not in our power to believe that such an animal has ever really existed.

It follows, therefore, that the difference between *fiction* and *belief* lies in some sentiment or feeling, which is annexed to the latter, not to the former, and which depends not on the will, nor can be commanded at pleasure. It must be excited by nature, like all other sentiments; and must arise from the particular situation, in which the mind is placed at any particular juncture. Whenever any object is presented to the

---

39 For ever, to infinity.

40 Simulate, imagine.
41 Lacking.

memory or senses, it immediately, by the force of custom, carries the imagination to conceive that object, which is usually conjoined to it; and this conception is attended with a feeling or sentiment, different from the loose reveries of the fancy. In this consists the whole nature of belief. For as there is no matter of fact which we believe so firmly that we cannot conceive the contrary, there would be no difference between the conception assented to and that which is rejected, were it not for some sentiment which distinguishes the one from the other. If I see a billiard-ball moving toward another, on a smooth table, I can easily conceive it to stop upon contact. This conception implies no contradiction; but still it feels very differently from that conception by which I represent to myself the impulse and the communication of motion from one ball to another.

Were we to attempt a *definition* of this sentiment, we should, perhaps, find it a very difficult, if not an impossible task; in the same manner as if we should endeavour to define the feeling of cold or passion of anger, to a creature who never had any experience of these sentiments. Belief is the true and proper name of this feeling; and no one is ever at a loss to know the meaning of that term; because every man is every moment conscious of the sentiment represented by it. It may not, however, be improper to attempt a *description* of this sentiment; in hopes we may, by that means, arrive at some analogies, which may afford a more perfect explication of it. I say, then, that belief is nothing but a more vivid, lively, forcible, firm, steady conception of an object, than what the imagination alone is ever able to attain. This variety of terms, which may seem so unphilosophical, is intended only to express that act of the mind, which renders realities, or what is taken for such, more present to us than fictions, causes them to weigh more in the thought, and gives them a superior influence on the passions and imagination. Provided we agree about the thing, it is needless to dispute about the terms. The imagination has the command over all its ideas, and can join and mix and vary them, in all the ways possible. It may conceive fictitious objects with all the circumstances of place and time. It may set them, in a manner, before our eyes, in their true colours, just as they might have existed. But as it is impossible that this faculty of imagination can ever, of itself, reach belief, it is evident that belief consists not in the peculiar nature or order of ideas, but in the *manner* of their conception, and in their *feeling* to the mind. I confess, that it is impossible perfectly to explain this feeling or manner of conception. We may make use of words which express something near it. But its true and proper name, as we observed before, is *belief*; which is a term that every one sufficiently understands in common life. And in philosophy, we can go no farther than assert, that *belief* is something felt by the mind, which distinguishes the ideas of the judgement from the fictions of the imagination. It gives them more weight and influence; makes them appear of greater importance; enforces them in the mind; and renders them the governing principle of our actions. I hear at present, for instance, a person's voice, with whom I am acquainted; and the sound comes as from the next room. This impression of my senses immediately conveys my thought to the person, together with all the surrounding objects. I paint them out to myself as existing at present, with the same qualities and relations, of which I formerly knew them possessed. These ideas take faster hold of my mind than ideas of an enchanted castle. They are very different to the feeling, and have a much greater influence of every kind, either to give pleasure or pain, joy or sorrow.

Let us, then, take in the whole compass of this doctrine, and allow, that the sentiment of belief is nothing but a conception more intense and steady than what attends the mere fictions of the imagination, and that this *manner* of conception arises from a customary conjunction of the object with something present to the memory or senses: I believe that it will not be difficult, upon these suppositions, to find other operations of the mind analogous to it, and to trace up these phenomena to principles still more general.

We have already observed that nature has established connections among particular ideas, and that no sooner one idea occurs to our thoughts than it introduces its correlative,[42] and carries our attention towards it, by a gentle and insensible movement. These principles of connection or association we have reduced to three, namely, *resemblance, contiguity*

---

42   The thing normally related or connected to it.

and *causation*; which are the only bonds that unite our thoughts together, and beget that regular train of reflection or discourse, which, in a greater or less degree, takes place among all mankind. Now here arises a question, on which the solution of the present difficulty will depend. Does it happen, in all these relations, that, when one of the objects is presented to the senses or memory, the mind is not only carried to the conception of the correlative, but reaches a steadier and stronger conception of it than what otherwise it would have been able to attain? This seems to be the case with that belief which arises from the relation of cause and effect. And if the case be the same with the other relations or principles of associations, this may be established as a general law, which takes place in all the operations of the mind.

We may, therefore, observe, as the first experiment to our present purpose, that, upon the appearance of the picture of an absent friend, our idea of him is evidently enlivened by the *resemblance*, and that every passion, which that idea occasions, whether of joy or sorrow, acquires new force and vigour. In producing this effect, there concur both a relation and a present impression. Where the picture bears him no resemblance, at least was not intended for[43] him, it never so much as conveys our thought to him: and where it is absent, as well as the person, though the mind may pass from the thought of the one to that of the other, it feels its idea to be rather weakened than enlivened by that transition. We take a pleasure in viewing the picture of a friend, when it is set before us; but when it is removed, rather choose to consider him directly than by reflection in an image, which is equally distant and obscure.

The ceremonies of the Roman Catholic religion may be considered as instances of the same nature. The devotees of that superstition usually plead in excuse for the mummeries,[44] with which they are upbraided, that they feel the good effect of those external motions, and postures, and actions, in enlivening their devotion and quickening their fervour, which otherwise would decay, if directed entirely to distant and immaterial objects. We shadow out the objects of our faith, say they, in sensible types and images, and render them more present to us by the immediate presence of these types, than it is possible for us to do merely by an intellectual view and contemplation. Sensible objects have always a greater influence on the fancy than any other; and this influence they readily convey to those ideas to which they are related, and which they resemble. I shall only infer from these practices, and this reasoning, that the effect of resemblance in enlivening the ideas is very common; and as in every case a resemblance and a present impression must concur, we are abundantly supplied with experiments to prove the reality of the foregoing principle.

We may add force to these experiments by others of a different kind, in considering the effects of *contiguity* as well as of *resemblance*. It is certain that distance diminishes the force of every idea, and that, upon our approach to any object; though it does not discover itself to our senses; it operates upon the mind with an influence, which imitates an immediate impression. The thinking on any object readily transports the mind to what is contiguous; but it is only the actual presence of an object, that transports it with a superior vivacity. When I am a few miles from home, whatever relates to it touches me more nearly than when I am two hundred leagues[45] distant; though even at that distance the reflecting on any thing in the neighbourhood of my friends or family naturally produces an idea of them. But as in this latter case, both the objects of the mind are ideas; notwithstanding there is an easy transition between them; that transition alone is not able to give a superior vivacity to any of the ideas, for want of some immediate impression.[46]

---

43   Supposed to be.
44   Silly rituals.
45   A league is roughly three miles (4.8 km).
46   [Author's note] '*Naturane nobis, inquit, datum dicam, an errore quodam, ut, cum ea loca videamus, in quibus memoria dignos viros acceperimus multim esse versatos, magis moveamur, quam siquando eorum ipsorum aut facta audiamus aut scriptum aliquod legamus? Velut ego nunc moveor. Venit enim mihi Plato in mentem, quem accepimus primum hic disputare solitum; cuius etiam illi hortuli propinqui non memoriam solum mihi afferunt, sed ipsum videntur in conspectu meo hic ponere. Hic Speusippus, hic Xenocrates, hic eius auditor Polemo; cuius ipsa illa sessio fuit, quam*

No one can doubt but causation has the same influence as the other two relations of resemblance and contiguity. Superstitious people are fond of the reliques of saints and holy men, for the same reason, that they seek after types or images, in order to enliven their devotion, and give them a more intimate and strong conception of those exemplary lives, which they desire to imitate. Now it is evident, that one of the best reliques, which a devotee could procure, would be the handywork of a saint; and if his clothes and furniture are ever to be considered in this light, it is because they were once at his disposal, and were moved and affected by him; in which respect they are to be considered as imperfect effects, and as connected with him by a shorter chain of consequences than any of those, by which we learn the reality of his existence.

Suppose, that the son of a friend, who had been long dead or absent, were presented to us; it is evident, that this object would instantly revive its correlative

---

videmus. Equidem etiam curiam nostram, Hostiliam dico, non hanc novam, quae mihi minor esse videtur postquam est maior, solebam intuens, Scipionem, Catonem, Laelium, nostrum vero in primis avum cogitare. Tanta vis admonitionis est in locis; ut non sine causa ex his memopriae deducta sit disciplina.'—Cicero de Finibus. Lib. v. ["Should I say," he asked, "that it is natural or just an error that makes us more greatly moved when we see places where, as we have been told, famous men spent a lot of time, than we are if, at some time or another, we hear about the things which they have done, or read something written by them? I, for example, feel moved at present. For Plato comes to my mind who, we know, was the first to hold regular discussions here: that garden nearby not only brings him to memory but seems to make me see him. Here is Speusippus, here is Xenocrates, and here also is his pupil Polemo: it is the place where he used to sit that we see before us. Similarly, when I looked at our senate house (I mean the one Hostilius built and not the new building which seems to me lesser since it has been enlarged) I used to think of Scipio, Cato, and Lælius, and above all of my grandfather. Places can remind us of so much; it is not without good reason that the formal training of memory is based on them." Cicero, *On the Chief Good and Evil*, from Book V]

idea, and recall to our thoughts all past intimacies and familiarities, in more lively colours than they would otherwise have appeared to us. This is another phenomenon, which seems to prove the principle above mentioned.

We may observe, that, in these phenomena, the belief of the correlative object is always presupposed; without which the relation could have no effect. The influence of the picture supposes, that we *believe* our friend to have once existed. Contiguity to home can never excite our ideas of home, unless we *believe* that it really exists. Now I assert, that this belief, where it reaches beyond the memory or senses, is of a similar nature, and arises from similar causes, with the transition of thought and vivacity of conception here explained. When I throw a piece of dry wood into a fire, my mind is immediately carried to conceive, that it augments, not extinguishes the flame. This transition of thought from the cause to the effect proceeds not from reason. It derives its origin altogether from custom and experience. And as it first begins from an object, present to the senses, it renders the idea or conception of flame more strong and lively than any loose, floating reverie of the imagination. That idea arises immediately. The thought moves instantly towards it, and conveys to it all that force of conception, which is derived from the impression present to the senses. When a sword is levelled at my breast, does not the idea of wound and pain strike me more strongly, than when a glass of wine is presented to me, even though by accident this idea should occur after the appearance of the latter object? But what is there in this whole matter to cause such a strong conception, except only a present object and a customary transition of the idea of another object, which we have been accustomed to conjoin with the former? This is the whole operation of the mind, in all our conclusions concerning matter of fact and existence; and it is a satisfaction to find some analogies, by which it may be explained. The transition from a present object does in all cases give strength and solidity to the related idea.

Here, then, is a kind of pre-established harmony between the course of nature and the succession of our ideas; and though the powers and forces, by which the former is governed, be wholly unknown to us; yet our thoughts and conceptions have still, we find, gone on in the same train with the other works of nature. Custom is that principle, by which this correspondence has been effected; so necessary to the subsistence of our species, and the regulation of our conduct, in every circumstance and occurrence of human life. Had not the presence of an object, instantly excited the idea of those objects, commonly conjoined with it, all our knowledge must have been limited to the narrow sphere of our memory and senses; and we should never have been able to adjust means to ends, or employ our natural powers, either to the producing of good, or avoiding of evil. Those, who delight in the discovery and contemplation of *final causes*,[47] have here ample subject to employ their wonder and admiration.

I shall add, for a further confirmation of the foregoing theory, that, as this operation of the mind, by which we infer like effects from like causes, and *vice*

versa, is so essential to the subsistence of all human creatures, it is not probable, that it could be trusted to the fallacious deductions of our reason, which is slow in its operations; appears not, in any degree, during the first years of infancy; and at best is, in every age and period of human life, extremely liable to error and mistake. It is more conformable to the ordinary wisdom of nature to secure so necessary an act of the mind, by some instinct or mechanical tendency, which may be infallible in its operations, may discover itself at the first appearance of life and thought, and may be independent of all the laboured deductions of the understanding. As nature has taught us the use of our limbs, without giving us the knowledge of the muscles and nerves, by which they are actuated; so has she implanted in us an instinct, which carries forward the thought in a correspondent course to that which she has established among external objects; though we are ignorant of those powers and forces, on which this regular course and succession of objects totally depends.

47   In this context, the purpose for the nature and arrangement of things in the universe.

NELSON GOODMAN
Fact, Fiction, and Forecast

Who Was Nelson Goodman?

Nelson Goodman—who has been called "one of the two or three greatest analytic philosophers of the post-World War II period"—was born in Somerville, Massachusetts in 1906. He graduated in 1928 from Harvard University with a bachelor of science degree and became a successful art dealer and gallery owner in Boston. Still keeping up his art business, he wrote a PhD thesis (according to his colleague Hilary Putnam, "a masterpiece") which he completed in 1941 at Harvard. After serving in the US Army during World War II, Goodman took up a succession of academic positions at Tufts College, the University of Pennsylvania, and

Brandeis University; in 1968 he was appointed Professor of Philosophy at Harvard, where he stayed for the rest of his career.

Goodman published many articles and several books during his lifetime, including *The Structure of Appearance* (1951), *Fact, Fiction, and Forecast* (1954), *Languages of Art* (1968), and *Ways of Worldmaking* (1978). Hilary Putnam has called *Fact, Fiction, and Forecast* "one of the few books that every serious student of philosophy in our time *has* to have read." At the center of Goodman's philosophy is the view that there are no absolute truths or foundations or certainties: according to Goodman there are no propositions, even in logic or mathematics, which are always and everywhere true, and there is no mind-independent, objective world which provides us with a set of 'facts' to which our beliefs should correspond. Instead, in Goodman's view, by creating and using systems of symbols such as mathematics, language, and art we *construct* worlds for ourselves—we *create* facts and standards by choosing to think and talk in one way rather than another.

Goodman's basic argument for this "irrealist" view runs as follows. First, the 'identity conditions' for objects (such as stars) and types (such as purple things) depend entirely upon our system of classification: that is, to ask whether or not something counts as a star is to do no more and no less than to ask whether we would apply the name "star" to it, and *this* fact is not so much a fact about astral bodies as it is a fact about our linguistic categories. For example, we can change a black hole from a non-star into a star (or vice versa) simply by adjusting our usage of the word "star." If this doctrine— a fairly extreme version of a philosophical theory called "nominalism"—is correct, it follows that in adopting a particular system of symbols, such as a language or a scientific theory, *we are determining what things exist*. By choosing how to use words, we are deciding which things are stars and which are not, or even whether anything counts as a star at all (and the same goes for every other possible type of thing). Furthermore, two irreducibly different category schemes must then be about two entirely different sets of things. Two incompatible symbol systems are not to be thought of as two different descriptions of the same thing (the world), one of which might be correct and the other incorrect: instead, they are simply two different collections of things, and hence two different worlds. To put it another way, there are no facts outside of symbol-systems: everything is either true or false only

relative to a particular way of categorizing. There are many worlds if any, and worlds are made rather than found.

None of this, according to Goodman, means that we can do or believe just what we like: to say that there are many possible, equally 'factual' worlds, is not to say that *we* don't live in any world in particular. Propositions are still true or false (within a certain set of community standards) and actions right or wrong (given a set of community practices). It's just that, Goodman says, all we have are practices and community standards, and our practices can only be called right or wrong depending on how they fit with our standards, while our standards are right or wrong according to how they square with our practices. Our choices of scientific theory, or philosophical outlook, or artistic practice are important because they are our 'ways of worldmaking.'

Throughout his life, Goodman was interested not only in science and philosophy but also—and perhaps even more so—in art and arts education. In 1947 he married Katharine Sturgess, a talented painter whom he met when she brought her watercolors to his Boston gallery. He founded and directed the Dance Center of the Harvard Summer School, and was also a founder of Project Zero, an interdisciplinary center for the study of thinking and of aesthetic education at the Harvard Graduate School of Education. Goodman was also passionately devoted to animal welfare, and was especially generous in funding efforts to protect animals from the effects of war or natural disaster (for example, he paid for animal rescue efforts in Kuwait during the first Gulf War, in Bosnia, at Montserrat following a volcanic eruption, and after serious forest fires in Borneo).

Goodman died in Massachusetts in 1998. In the foreword of *Ways of Worldmaking*, Goodman sums up his philosophical approach in the following words:

Few familiar philosophical labels fit comfortably a book that is at odds with rationalism and empiricism alike, with materialism and idealism and dualism, with essentialism and existentialism, with mechanism and vitalism, with mysticism and scientism, and with most other ardent doctrines.… Nevertheless I think of this book as belonging in that mainstream of modern philosophy that began when Kant exchanged the structure of the world for the structure of the mind, continued when C.I. Lewis exchanged the structure of the mind for the structure of concepts, and that now proceeds to exchange the structure of concepts for the structure of the several symbol systems of the sciences, philosophy, the arts, perception, and everyday discourse. The movement is from unique truth and a world fixed and found to a diversity of right and even conflicting versions or worlds in the making.

What Is the Structure of This Reading?

Goodman's book *Fact, Fiction, and Forecast* has two parts. The first part "Predicament—1946" describes Goodman's failed, early attempts to provide a theory of potentiality—of how we can describe and know about what physical objects *will* do or *would* do, even though they are not doing it now. (For example, to say that a glass vase is fragile is to say, roughly, that if it were struck with sufficient force it would shatter.) The second part of the book, "Project—1953," consists of three lectures Goodman gave at the University of London, in which he attempted to make a fresh approach to the solution of his earlier difficulties. In the first lecture Goodman describes the pressing need to develop a theory of potentiality in order to solve a cluster of important philosophical problems (such as, for example, the nature of possibility), and suggests that such a theory would be tantamount to a solution for the problem of induction.

In the second lecture—which is the selection reprinted here—Goodman argues, first, that the traditional problem of induction (raised by Hume in the previous reading) has been widely misunderstood, and when properly understood is perfectly soluble

by an adequate formulation of the rules of inductive inference. Developing such a theory is what Goodman calls, in section 3, "the constructive task of confirmation theory." Goodman describes some of the advances in confirmation theory, but then argues that a deeper philosophical problem remains: this is his "new riddle of induction," which involves the difficulty in distinguishing between general statements which are "lawlike" and those which are merely accidental. Goodman considers several apparently easy ways of dealing with this problem, and argues that none of them work: the new riddle of induction, it turns out, is a very hard philosophical nut to crack.

In the third and final lecture (which is not included here) Goodman lays out his own preliminary attempt to solve the new riddle of induction. His solution is essentially a pragmatic one: he argues that "green" is to be preferred to "grue" as a classification of the inductive evidence for no reason except that the concept of greenness is "entrenched" in our existing habits of thought, and fits more comfortably within the system of classification and explanation that we happen to have used successfully in the past.

Some Common Misconceptions

1. It's not a good objection to Goodman's argument just to point out that "grue" is a made-up word. I could invent a word for my favorite color—such as "Andrewhue"—and use this instead of "green," but this would not make greenness any less genuine (or "projectible") a property. Furthermore, sometimes science discovers previously unknown properties—such as the "charm" or "color" of certain quarks—and has to invent new names for them, but again, this does not all by itself cast any aspersions on the lawlikeness of these properties.

2. It's not a good objection to Goodman's argument just to say that grue is a complicated—often called a 'gruesome' or a 'bent'—predicate. After all, many perfectly respectable predicates are 'bent' in just this way: for example, *being solid and less than 0°C, or liquid and more than 0°C but less than 100°C, or gaseous and more than 100°C.*

3. It's not a good objection to Goodman's argument just to claim that grue is not an 'observable property,' in the same way as greenness or magnetism are. One could build a perfectly good "grue detector" by making a machine which gave a positive result exactly when it was scanning something green before time *t* (by the machine's internal clock) or blue after *t*, and one could then use this grue detector, just like a spectrometer or magnetometer, to observe grue things even without knowing what time it is.

4. It's not a good objection to Goodman's argument just to say that projectible predicates are those that remain after extensive testing—a kind of "survival of the fittest." Even though the claim that an emerald is grue might be ruled out if it continues to be green after time *t*, the real point is that there will *always* be an infinite number of *other* 'bent predicates' which remain to be ruled out (for example, grue': green before time *t* + *n* and blue after).

Suggestions for Critical Reflection

1. Are emeralds really grue? If they were grue, would this mean that they are not green?

2. Hilary Putnam has said, "Goodman totally recasts the problem of induction. For him the problem is not to guarantee that induction will succeed in the future ... but to characterize what induction *is* in a way that is neither too permissive nor too vague." Do you agree with Putnam's assessment? Do you think that Goodman has shown that the "old" problem of induction—the one raised by Hume—has been solved, or at least can be left behind?

3. Another way of understanding Goodman's conclusion is the following: Goodman showed that the strength of inductive inferences is independent of either their syntax (their logical form) or their semantics (the meanings of the words involved). There must therefore be some *third* way to distinguish between good and bad inductive arguments, and 'the new riddle of induction' is to find that third way. What do you

think of this interpretation of Goodman? If it is right, then what has Goodman shown about the difference between deductive and inductive logic?

4. Is there an objective fact of the matter about which predicates are 'projectible' and which are not? Do you think Goodman thinks there is? If projectibility is not objective, where does this leave science? If projectibility is objective, how do you think we could find out about it?

5. How serious is the new riddle of induction? Can you outline a plausible solution to the problem that Goodman has not already rejected? Was Goodman right to reject so quickly the attempted solutions that he considers? If the new riddle of induction cannot be solved, where does that leave us? For example, what implications would this have for science?

Suggestions for Further Reading

In addition to the rest of *Fact, Fiction, and Forecast* (Harvard University Press,1983), Goodman explores the problem of induction in several essays in his *Problems and Projects* (Hackett, 1972). The interested reader can pursue the rest of Goodman's philosophy in his books *The Structure of Appearance* (Reidel, 1977), *Languages of Art: An Approach to a Theory of Symbols* (Hackett, 1976), *Ways of Worldmaking* (Hackett, 1978) and *Of Mind and Other Matters* (Harvard University Press, 1984).

There is a collection of essays specifically about Goodman's new riddle of induction edited by Douglas Stalker and called *Grue! The New Riddle of Induction* (Open Court, 1994), and there have been two special issues of *The Journal of Philosophy* on the new riddle of induction: Volume 63, Issue 11 (1966) and Volume 64, Issue 9 (1967). Goodman's friend and collaborator Catherine Elgin has written about his philosophy in *With Reference to Reference* (Hackett, 1983) and edited a collection of essays on his new riddle *Philosophy of Nelson Goodman* (vol. 2, Garland Publishing, 1997). Peter McCormick's *Starmaking: Realism, Anti-Realism, and Irrealism* (MIT Press, 1996)—a three-way debate between Goodman, Hilary Putnam and Israel Scheffler—contains much of interest about irrealism.

Fact, Fiction, and Forecast
"The New Riddle of Induction"[1]

1. The Old Problem of Induction

At the close of the preceding lecture, I said that today I should examine how matters stand with respect to the problem of induction. In a word, I think they stand ill. But the real difficulties that confront us today are not the traditional ones. What is commonly thought of as the Problem of Induction has been solved, or dissolved; and we face new problems that are not as yet very widely understood. To approach them, I shall have to run as quickly as possible over some very familiar ground.

The problem of the validity of judgments about future or unknown cases arises, as Hume pointed out, because such judgments are neither reports of experience nor logical consequences of it. Predictions, of course, pertain to what has not yet been observed. And they cannot be logically inferred from what has been observed; for what *has* happened imposes no logical restrictions on what *will* happen. Although Hume's dictum that there are no necessary connections of matters of fact has been challenged at times, it has withstood all attacks. Indeed, I should be inclined not merely to agree that there are no necessary connections of matters of fact, but to ask whether there are any necessary connections at all[2]—but that is another story.

---

1   *Fact, Fiction, and Forecast* was originally published in 1954, and was based largely on three lectures Goodman gave at the University of London in 1953. This selection is reprinted from the fourth edition (Harvard University Press, 1983). Reprinted by permission of the publisher from "The New Riddle of Induction" in *Fact, Fiction, and Forecast* by Nelson Goodman, pp. 59–83, Cambridge, Mass.: Harvard University Press, Copyright © 1979, 1983 by Nelson Goodman.

2   [Author's note] Although this remark is merely an aside, perhaps I should explain for the sake of some unusually sheltered reader that the notion of a necessary connection of ideas, or of an absolutely analytic statement, is no longer sacrosanct. Some, like Quine and White, have forthrightly attacked the notion; others,

Hume's answer to the question how predictions are related to past experience is refreshingly non-cosmic. When an event of one kind frequently follows upon an event of another kind in experience, a habit is formed that leads the mind, when confronted with a new event of the first kind, to pass to the idea of an event of the second kind. The idea of necessary connection arises from the felt impulse of the mind in making this transition.

Now if we strip this account of all extraneous features, the central point is that to the question "Why one prediction rather than another?", Hume answers that the elect prediction is one that accords with a past regularity, because this regularity has established a habit. Thus among alternative statements about a future moment, one statement is distinguished by its consonance with habit and thus with regularities observed in the past. Prediction according to any other alternative is errant.

How satisfactory is this answer? The heaviest criticism has taken the righteous position that Hume's account at best pertains only to the source of predictions, not their legitimacy; that he sets forth the circumstances under which we make given predictions—and in this sense explains why we make them—but leaves untouched the question of our license for making them. To trace origins, runs the old complaint, is not to establish validity: the real question is not why a prediction is in fact made but how it can be justified. Since this seems to point to the awkward conclusion that the greatest of modern philosophers completely missed the point of his own problem, the idea has developed that he did not really take his solution very seriously, but regarded the main problem as unsolved and perhaps as insoluble. Thus we come to speak of 'Hume's problem' as though he propounded it as a question without answer.

All this seems to me quite wrong. I think Hume grasped the central question and considered his answer to be passably effective. And I think his answer is reasonable and relevant, even if it is not entirely satisfactory. I shall explain presently. At the moment, I merely want to record a protest against the prevalent notion that the problem of justifying induction,

---

like myself, have simply discarded it; and still others have begun to feel acutely uncomfortable about it.

when it is so sharply dissociated from the problem of describing how induction takes place, can fairly be called Hume's problem.

I suppose that the problem of justifying induction has called forth as much fruitless discussion as has any halfway respectable problem of modern philosophy. The typical writer begins by insisting that some way of justifying predictions must be found; proceeds to argue that for this purpose we need some resounding universal law of the Uniformity of Nature, and then inquires how this universal principle itself can be justified. At this point, if he is tired, he concludes that the principle must be accepted as an indispensable assumption; or if he is energetic and ingenious, he goes on to devise some subtle justification for it. Such an invention, however, seldom satisfies anyone else; and the easier course of accepting an unsubstantiated and even dubious assumption much more sweeping than any actual predictions we make seems an odd and expensive way of justifying them.

2. Dissolution of the Old Problem

Understandably, then, more critical thinkers have suspected that there might be something awry with the problem we are trying to solve. Come to think of it, what precisely would constitute the justification we seek? If the problem is to explain how we know that certain predictions will turn out to be correct, the sufficient answer is that we don't know any such thing. If the problem is to *find* some way of distinguishing antecedently between true and false predictions, we are asking for prevision rather than for philosophical explanation. Nor does it help matters much to say that we are merely trying to show that or why certain predictions are *probable*. Often it is said that while we cannot tell in advance whether a prediction concerning a given throw of a die is true, we can decide whether the prediction is a probable one. But if this means determining how the prediction is related to actual frequency distributions of future throws of the die, surely there is no way of knowing or proving this in advance. On the other hand, if the judgment that the prediction is probable has nothing to do with subsequent occurrences, then the question remains in what sense a probable prediction is any better justified than an improbable one.

Now obviously the genuine problem cannot be one of attaining unattainable knowledge or of accounting for knowledge that we do not in fact have. A better understanding of our problem can be gained by looking for a moment at what is involved in justifying noninductive inferences. How do we justify a *de*duction? Plainly, by showing that it conforms to the general rules of deductive inference. An argument that so conforms is justified or valid, even if its conclusion happens to be false. An argument that violates a rule is fallacious even if its conclusion happens to be true. To justify a deductive conclusion therefore requires no knowledge of the facts it pertains to. Moreover, when a deductive argument has been shown to conform to the rules of logical inference, we usually consider it justified without going on to ask what justifies the rules. Analogously, the basic task in justifying an inductive inference is to show that it conforms to the general rules of *in*duction. Once we have recognized this, we have gone a long way towards clarifying our problem.

Yet, of course, the rules themselves must eventually be justified. The validity of a deduction depends not upon conformity to any purely arbitrary rules we may contrive, but upon conformity to valid rules. When we speak of *the* rules of inference we mean the valid rules—or better, *some* valid rules, since there may be alternative sets of equally valid rules. But how is the validity of rules to be determined? Here again we encounter philosophers who insist that these rules follow from some self-evident axiom, and others who try to show that the rules are grounded in the very nature of the human mind. I think the answer lies much nearer the surface. Principles of deductive inference are justified by their conformity with accepted deductive practice. Their validity depends upon accordance with the particular deductive inferences we actually make and sanction. If a rule yields inacceptable inferences, we drop it as invalid. Justification of general rules thus derives from judgments rejecting or accepting particular deductive inferences.

This looks flagrantly circular. I have said that deductive inferences are justified by their conformity to valid general rules, and that general rules are justified by their conformity to valid inferences. But this circle is a virtuous one. The point is that rules and particular inferences alike are justified by being brought into agreement with each other. *A rule is amended if it yields an inference we are unwilling to accept; an inference is rejected if it violates a rule we are unwilling to amend.* The process of justification is the delicate one of making mutual adjustments between rules and accepted inferences; and in the agreement achieved lies the only justification needed for either.

All this applies equally well to induction. An inductive inference, too, is justified by conformity to general rules, and a general rule by conformity to accepted inductive inferences. Predictions are justified if they conform to valid canons of induction; and the canons are valid if they accurately codify accepted inductive practice.

A result of such analysis is that we can stop plaguing ourselves with certain spurious questions about induction. We no longer demand an explanation for guarantees that we do not have, or seek keys to knowledge that we cannot obtain. It dawns upon us that the traditional smug insistence upon a hard-and-fast line between justifying induction and describing ordinary inductive practice distorts the problem. And we owe belated apologies to Hume. For in dealing with the question how normally accepted inductive judgments are made, he was in fact dealing with the question of inductive validity.[3] The validity of a prediction consisted for him in its arising from habit, and thus in its exemplifying some past regularity. His answer was incomplete and perhaps not entirely correct; but it was not beside the point. The problem of induction is not a problem of demonstration but a problem of defining the difference between valid and invalid predictions.

This clears the air but leaves a lot to be done. As principles of *deductive* inference, we have the familiar and highly developed laws of logic; but there are available no such precisely stated and well-recognized principles of inductive inference. Mill's canons[4] hardly rank with Aristotle's rules of the syllogism, let alone with *Principia Mathematica*.[5] Elaborate and valuable treatises on probability usually leave certain fundamental questions untouched. Only in very recent years has there been any explicit and systematic work upon what I call the constructive task of confirmation theory.

3. The Constructive Task of Confirmation Theory

The task of formulating rules that define the difference between valid and invalid inductive inferences is much like the task of defining any term with an established usage. If we set out to define the term "tree", we try to compose out of already understood words an expression that will apply to the familiar objects that standard usage calls trees, and that will not apply to objects that standard usage refuses to call trees. A proposal that plainly violates either condition is rejected; while a definition that meets these tests may be adopted and used to decide cases

---

3 [Author's note] A hasty reader might suppose that my insistence here upon identifying the problem of justification with a problem of description is out of keeping with my parenthetical insistence in the preceding lecture that the goal of philosophy is something quite different from the mere description of ordinary or scientific procedure. Let me repeat that the point urged there was that the organization of the explanatory account need not reflect the manner or order in which predicates are adopted in practice. It surely must describe practice, however, in the sense that the extensions of predicates as explicated must conform in certain ways to the extensions of the same predicates as applied in practice. Hume's account is a description in just this sense. For it is an attempt to set forth the circumstances under which those inductive judgments are made that are normally accepted as valid; and to do that is to state necessary and sufficient conditions for, and thus to define, valid induction. What I am

maintaining above is that the problem of justifying induction is not something over and above the problem of describing or defining valid induction.

4 Goodman is referring to John Stuart Mill's *System of Logic*, first published in 1843, which tried to lay down general methods for deriving scientific claims from experience.

5 Aristotle developed the foundations of deductive logic—the theory of syllogisms—in the fourth century BCE, and Bertrand Russell and Alfred North Whitehead encapsulated modern logic in their massive *Principia Mathematica*, published in three volumes between 1910 and 1913.

that are not already settled by actual usage. Thus the interplay we observed between rules of induction and particular inductive inferences is simply an instance of this characteristic dual adjustment between definition and usage, whereby the usage informs the definition, which in turn guides extension of the usage.

Of course this adjustment is a more complex matter than I have indicated. Sometimes, in the interest of convenience or theoretical utility, we deliberately permit a definition to run counter to clear mandates of common usage. We accept a definition of "fish" that excludes whales. Similarly we may decide to deny the term "valid induction" to some inductive inferences that are commonly considered valid, or apply the term to others not usually so considered. A definition may modify as well as extend ordinary usage.[6]

Some pioneer work on the problem of defining confirmation or valid induction has been done by Professor Hempel.[7] Let me remind you briefly of a few of his results. Just as deductive logic is concerned primarily with a relation between statements—namely the consequence relation—that is independent of their truth or falsity, so inductive logic as Hempel conceives it is concerned primarily with a comparable relation of confirmation between statements. Thus the problem is to define the relation that obtains between any statement S_1 and another S_2 if and only if S_1 may properly be said to confirm S_2 in any degree.

With the question so stated, the first step seems obvious. Does not induction proceed in just the opposite direction from deduction? Surely some of the evidence-statements that inductively support a general hypothesis are consequences of it. Since the consequence relation is already well defined by deductive

logic, will we not be on firm ground in saying that confirmation embraces the converse relation? The laws of deduction in reverse will then be among the laws of induction.

Let's see where this leads us. We naturally assume further that whatever confirms a given statement confirms also whatever follows from that statement.[8] But if we combine this assumption with our proposed principle, we get the embarrassing result that every statement confirms every other. Surprising as it may be that such innocent beginnings lead to such an intolerable conclusion, the proof is very easy. Start with any statement S_1. It is a consequence of, and so by our present criterion confirms, the conjunction of S_1 and any statement whatsoever—call it S_2. But the confirmed conjunction,[9] $S_1 \cdot S_2$, of course has S_2 as a consequence. Thus every statement confirms all statements.

The fault lies in careless formulation of our first proposal. While some statements that confirm a general hypothesis are consequences of it, not all its consequences confirm it. This may not be immediately evident; for indeed we do in some sense furnish support for a statement when we establish one of its

---

6   [Author's note] For a fuller discussion of definition in general see Chapter I of *The Structure of Appearance* [by Nelson Goodman (Kluwer, 1977)].

7   [Author's note] The basic article is 'A Purely Syntactical Definition of Confirmation', *Journal of Symbolic Logic*, vol. 8 (1943), pp. 122–43. A much less technical account is given in 'Studies in the Logic of Confirmation', *Mind*, n.s., vol. 54 (1945), pp. 1–26 and 97–121. Later work by Hempel and others on defining degree of confirmation does not concern us here.

8   [Author's note] I am not here asserting that this is an indispensable requirement upon a definition of confirmation. Since our commonsense assumptions taken in combination quickly lead us to absurd conclusions, some of these assumptions have to be dropped; and different theorists may make different decisions about which to drop and which to preserve. Hempel gives up the converse consequence condition, while Carnap (*Logical Foundations of Probability*, Chicago and London, 1950, pp. 474–76) drops both the consequence condition and the converse consequence condition. Such differences of detail between different treatments of confirmation do not affect the central points I am making in this lecture.

9   A conjunction is an 'and' statement: "A and B." It is a simple law of logic that if "A and B" is true, then "A" must be as well, and so must "B." For example, if "Sharks are fish and whales are mammals" is true, then it follows that the following two sentences must also be true: "Sharks are fish" and "Whales are mammals."

consequences. We settle one of the questions about it. Consider the heterogeneous conjunction:

> 8497 is a prime number and the other side of the moon is flat and Elizabeth the First was crowned on a Tuesday.

To show that any one of the three component statements is true is to support the conjunction by reducing the net undetermined claim. But support[10] of this kind is not confirmation; for establishment of one component endows the whole statement with no credibility that is transmitted to other component statements. Confirmation of a hypothesis occurs only when an instance imparts to the hypothesis some credibility that is conveyed to other instances. Appraisal of hypotheses, indeed, is incidental to prediction, to the judgment of new cases on the basis of old ones.

Our formula thus needs tightening. This is readily accomplished, as Hempel points out, if we observe that a hypothesis is genuinely confirmed only by a statement that is an instance of it in the special sense of entailing not the hypothesis itself but its relativization or restriction to the class of entities mentioned by that statement. The relativization of a general hypothesis to a class results from restricting the range of its universal and existential quantifiers to the members of that class.[11] Less technically, what the hypothesis says of all things the evidence statement says of one thing (or of one pair or other *n*-ad[12] of things). This obviously covers the confirmation of the conductivity of all copper by the conductivity of a given piece; and it excludes confirmation of our heterogeneous conjunction by any of its components. And, when taken together with the principle that what confirms a statement confirms all its consequences, this criterion does not yield the untoward conclusion that every statement confirms every other.

New difficulties promptly appear from other directions, however. One is the infamous paradox of the ravens. The statement that a given object, say this piece of paper, is neither black nor a raven confirms the hypothesis that all non-black things are non-ravens. But this hypothesis is logically equivalent to the hypothesis that all ravens are black. Hence we arrive at the unexpected conclusion that the statement that a given object is neither black nor a raven confirms the hypothesis that all ravens are black. The prospect of being able to investigate ornithological theories without going out in the rain is so attractive that we know there must be a catch in it. The trouble this time, however, lies not in faulty definition, but in tacit and illicit reference to evidence not stated in our example. Taken by itself, the statement that the given object is neither black nor a raven confirms the hypothesis that everything that is not a raven is not black as well as the hypothesis that everything that is not black is not a raven. We tend to ignore the former hypothesis because we know it to be false from abundant other evidence—from all the familiar things that are not ravens but are black. But we are required to assume that no such evidence is available. Under this circumstance, even a much stronger hypothesis is also obviously confirmed: that nothing is either black or a raven. In the light of this confirmation of the hypothesis that there are no ravens, it is no longer surprising that under the artificial restrictions of the example,

---

10   [Author's note] Any hypothesis is 'supported' by its own positive instances; but support—or better, direct factual support—is only one factor in confirmation. This factor has been separately studied by John G. Kemeny and Paul Oppenheim in 'Degree of Factual Support', *Philosophy of Science*, vol. 19 (1952), pp. 307–24. As will appear presently, my concern in these lectures is primarily with certain other important factors in confirmation, some of them quite generally neglected.

11   For example, a general hypothesis might be that all plants of the genus *Helleborus* are poisonous to humans; one relativization of this hypothesis would be the claim that this sprig of Christmas Rose which I have in my hand is poisonous to humans. (In this case, we have moved from a claim about *all* the members of the genus *Helleborus* to a claim about

one member of that genus: that is we have restricted the range of the universal quantifier word "all" in the original hypothesis.)

12   For example, a triad (three things), tetrad (four things), etc.

the hypothesis that all ravens are black is also confirmed. And the prospects for indoor ornithology vanish when we notice that under these same conditions, the contrary hypothesis that no ravens are black is equally well confirmed.[13]

On the other hand, our definition does err in not forcing us to take into account all the stated evidence. The unhappy results are readily illustrated. If two compatible evidence statements confirm two hypotheses, then naturally the conjunction of the evidence statements should confirm the conjunction of the hypotheses.[14] Suppose our evidence consists of the statements E_1 saying that a given thing b is black, and E_2 saying that a second thing c is not black. By our present definition, E_1 confirms the hypothesis that everything is black, and E_2 the hypothesis that everything is non-black. The conjunction of these perfectly compatible evidence statements will then confirm the self-contradictory hypothesis that everything is both black and non-black. Simple as this anomaly is, it requires drastic modification of our definition. What given evidence confirms is not what we arrive at by generalizing from separate items of it, but—roughly speaking—what we arrive at by generalizing from the total stated evidence. The central idea for an improved definition is that, within certain limitations, what is asserted to be true for the narrow universe of the evidence statements is confirmed for the whole universe of discourse.[15] Thus if our evidence is E_1

and E_2, neither the hypothesis that all things are black nor the hypothesis that all things are non-black is confirmed; for neither is true for the evidence-universe consisting of b and c. Of course, much more careful formulation is needed, since some statements that are true of the evidence-universe—such as that there is only one black thing—are obviously not confirmed for the whole universe. These matters are taken care of by the studied formal definition that Hempel develops on this basis; but we cannot and need not go into further detail here.

No one supposes that the task of confirmation-theory has been completed. But the few steps I have reviewed—chosen partly for their bearing on what is to follow—show how things move along once the problem of definition displaces the problem of justification. Important and long-unnoticed questions are brought to light and answered; and we are encouraged to expect that the many remaining questions will in time yield to similar treatment.

But our satisfaction is shortlived. New and serious trouble begins to appear.

4. The New Riddle of Induction

Confirmation of a hypothesis by an instance depends rather heavily upon features of the hypothesis other than its syntactical form. That a given piece of copper conducts electricity increases the credibility of statements asserting that other pieces of copper conduct electricity, and thus confirms the hypothesis that all copper conducts electricity. But the fact that a given man now in this room is a third son does not increase the credibility of statements asserting that other men now in this room are third sons, and so does not confirm the hypothesis that all men now in this room are third sons. Yet in both cases our hypothesis is a generalization of the evidence statement. The difference is that in the former case the hypothesis is a *lawlike* statement; while in the latter case, the hypothesis is a merely contingent or accidental generality. Only a statement that is *lawlike*—regardless

---

13 [Author's note] An able and thorough exposition of this paragraph is given by Israel Scheffler in his *Anatomy of Inquiry*, New York, 1963, pp. 286–91.

14 [Author's note] The status of the conjunction condition is much like that of the consequence condition—see Note 5 [8 in this text]. Although Carnap drops the conjunction condition also (p. 394), he adopts for different reasons the requirement we find needed above: that the total available evidence must always be taken into account (pp. 211–13).

15 The "universe of discourse" is the collection of things under discussion, whose existence is presupposed by the participants in the discussion. For example, if I say "everyone got ridiculously drunk" then the universe of discourse for our conversation is probably not the whole human race—since not *everybody* in the world

got drunk—but, perhaps, the attendees at a particular New Year's Eve party. In science, the universe of discourse is typically the entire physical universe (but not, for example, angels and immaterial souls).

of its truth or falsity or its scientific importance—is capable of receiving confirmation from an instance of it; accidental statements are not. Plainly, then, we must look for a way of distinguishing lawlike from accidental statements.

So long as what seems to be needed is merely a way of excluding a few odd and unwanted cases that are inadvertently admitted by our definition of confirmation, the problem may not seem very hard or very pressing. We fully expect that minor defects will be found in our definition and that the necessary refinements will have to be worked out patiently one after another. But some further examples will show that our present difficulty is of a much graver kind.

Suppose that all emeralds examined before a certain time t are green.[16] At time t, then, our observations support the hypothesis that all emeralds are green; and this is in accord with our definition of confirmation. Our evidence statements assert that emerald a is green, that emerald b is green, and so on; and each confirms the general hypothesis that all emeralds are green. So far, so good.

Now let me introduce another predicate less familiar than "green". It is the predicate "grue" and it applies to all things examined before t just in case they are green but to other things just in case they are blue. Then at time t we have, for each evidence statement asserting that a given emerald is green, a parallel evidence statement asserting that that emerald is grue. And the statements that emerald a is grue, that emerald b is grue, and so on, will each confirm the general hypothesis that all emeralds are grue. Thus according to our definition, the prediction that all emeralds subsequently examined will be green and the prediction that all will be grue are alike confirmed by evidence statements describing the same observations. But if an emerald subsequently examined is grue, it is blue and hence not green. Thus although we are well aware which of the two incompatible predictions is genuinely confirmed, they are equally well confirmed

according to our present definition. Moreover, it is clear that if we simply choose an appropriate predicate, then on the basis of these same observations we shall have equal confirmation, by our definition, for any prediction whatever about other emeralds—or indeed about anything else.[17] As in our earlier example, only the predictions subsumed under lawlike hypotheses are genuinely confirmed; but we have no criterion as yet for determining lawlikeness. And now we see that without some such criterion, our definition not merely includes a few unwanted cases, but is so completely ineffectual that it virtually excludes nothing. We are left once again with the intolerable result that anything confirms anything. This difficulty cannot be set aside as an annoying detail to be taken care of in due course. It has to be met before our definition will work at all.

Nevertheless, the difficulty is often slighted because on the surface there seem to be easy ways of dealing with it. Sometimes, for example, the problem is thought to be much like the paradox of the ravens. We are here again, it is pointed out, making tacit and illegitimate use of information outside the stated evidence: the information, for example, that different samples of one material are usually alike in conductivity, and, the information that different men in a lecture audience are usually not alike in the number of their older brothers. But while it is true that such information is being smuggled in, this does not by itself settle the matter as it settles the matter of the ravens. There the point was that when the smuggled information is forthrightly declared, its effect upon the confirmation of the hypothesis in question is immediately and properly registered by

---

16   [Author's note] Although the example used is different, the argument to follow is substantially the same as that set forth in my note 'A Query on Confirmation', *Journal of Philosophy*, vol. xliii (1946), pp. 383–85.

17   [Author's note] For instance, we shall have equal confirmation, by our present definition, for the prediction that roses subsequently examined will be blue. Let "emerose" apply just to emeralds examined before time t, and to roses examined later. Then all emeroses so far examined are grue, and this confirms the hypothesis that all emeroses are grue and hence the prediction that roses subsequently examined will be blue. The problem raised by such antecedents has been little noticed, but is no easier to meet than that raised by similarly perverse consequents.

the definition we are using. On the other hand, if to our initial evidence we add statements concerning the conductivity of pieces of other materials or concerning the number of older brothers of members of other lecture audiences, this will not in the least affect the confirmation, according to our definition, of the hypothesis concerning copper or of that concerning this lecture audience. Since our definition is insensitive to the bearing upon hypotheses of evidence so related to them, even when the evidence is fully declared, the difficulty about accidental hypotheses cannot be explained away on the ground that such evidence is being surreptitiously taken into account.

A more promising suggestion is to explain the matter in terms of the effect of this other evidence not directly upon the hypothesis in question but *in*directly through other hypotheses that *are* confirmed, according to our definition, by such evidence. Our information about other materials does by our definition confirm such hypotheses as that all pieces of iron conduct electricity, that no pieces of rubber do, and so on; and these hypotheses, the explanation runs, impart to the hypothesis that all pieces of copper conduct electricity (and also to the hypothesis that none do) the character of lawlikeness—that is, amenability to confirmation by direct positive instances when found. On the other hand, our information about other lecture audiences *dis*confirms many hypotheses to the effect that all the men in one audience are third sons, or that none are; and this strips any character of lawlikeness from the hypothesis that all (or the hypothesis that none) of the men in *this* audience are third sons. But clearly if this course is to be followed, the circumstances under which hypotheses are thus related to one another will have to be precisely articulated.

The problem, then, is to define the relevant way in which such hypotheses must be alike. Evidence for the hypothesis that all iron conducts electricity enhances the lawlikeness of the hypothesis that all zirconium conducts electricity, but does not similarly affect the hypothesis that all the objects on my desk conduct electricity. Wherein lies the difference? The first two hypotheses fall under the broader hypothesis—call it "*H*"—that every class of things of the same material

is uniform in conductivity; the first and third fall only under some such hypothesis as—call it "*K*"—that every class of things that are either all of the same material or all on a desk is uniform in conductivity. Clearly the important difference here is that evidence for a statement affirming that one of the classes covered by *H* has the property in question increases the credibility of any statement affirming that another such class has this property; while nothing of the sort holds true with respect to *K*. But this is only to say that *H* is lawlike and *K* is not. We are faced anew with the very problem we are trying to solve: the problem of distinguishing between lawlike and accidental hypotheses.

The most popular way of attacking the problem takes its cue from the fact that accidental hypotheses seem typically to involve some spatial or temporal restriction, or reference to some particular individual. They seem to concern the people in some particular room, or the objects on some particular person's desk; while lawlike hypotheses characteristically concern all ravens or all pieces of copper whatsoever. Complete generality is thus very often supposed to be a sufficient condition of lawlikeness; but to define this complete generality is by no means easy. Merely to require that the hypothesis contain no term naming, describing, or indicating a particular thing or location will obviously not be enough. The troublesome hypothesis that all emeralds are grue contains no such term; and where such a term does occur, as in hypotheses about men in *this room*, it can be suppressed in favor of some predicate (short or long, new or old) that contains no such term but applies only to exactly the same things. One might think, then, of excluding not only hypotheses that actually contain terms for specific individuals but also all hypotheses that are equivalent to others that do contain such terms. But, as we have just seen, to exclude only hypotheses of which *all* equivalents contain such terms is to exclude nothing. On the other hand, to exclude all hypotheses that have *some* equivalent containing such a term is to exclude everything; for even the hypothesis

All grass is green

has as an equivalent

All grass in London or elsewhere is green.

The next step, therefore, has been to consider ruling out predicates of certain kinds. A syntactically universal hypothesis is lawlike, the proposal runs, if its predicates are 'purely qualitative' or 'non-positional'.[18] This will obviously accomplish nothing if a purely qualitative predicate is then conceived either as one that is equivalent to some expression free of terms for specific individuals, or as one that is equivalent to no expression that contains such a term; for this only raises again the difficulties just pointed out. The claim appears to be rather that at least in the case of a simple enough predicate we can readily determine by direct inspection of its meaning whether or not it is purely qualitative. But even aside from obscurities in the notion of 'the meaning' of a predicate, this claim seems to me wrong. I simply do not know how to tell whether a predicate is qualitative or positional, except perhaps by completely begging the question at issue and asking whether the predicate is 'well-behaved'—that is, whether simple syntactically universal hypotheses applying it are lawlike.

This statement will not go unprotested. "Consider", it will be argued, "the predicates 'blue' and 'green' and the predicate 'grue' introduced earlier, and also the predicate 'bleen' that applies to emeralds examined before time t just in case they are blue and to other emeralds just in case they are green. Surely it is clear", the argument runs, "that the first two are purely qualitative and the second two are not; for the meaning of each of the latter two plainly involves reference to a specific temporal position." To this I reply that indeed I do recognize the first two as well-behaved predicates admissible in lawlike hypotheses, and the second two as ill-behaved predicates. But the argument that the former but not the latter are purely

qualitative seems to me quite unsound. True enough, if we start with "blue" and "green", then "grue" and "bleen" will be explained in terms of "blue" and "green" and a temporal term. But equally truly, if we start with "grue" and "bleen", then "blue" and "green" will be explained in terms of "grue" and "bleen" and a temporal term; "green", for example, applies to emeralds examined before time t just in case they are grue, and to other emeralds just in case they are bleen. Thus qualitativeness is an entirely relative matter and does not by itself establish any dichotomy of predicates. This relativity seems to be completely overlooked by those who contend that the qualitative character of a predicate is a criterion for its good behavior.

Of course, one may ask why we need worry about such unfamiliar predicates as "grue" or about accidental hypotheses in general, since we are unlikely to use them in making predictions. If our definition works for such hypotheses as are normally employed, isn't that all we need? In a sense, yes; but only in the sense that we need no definition, no theory of induction, and no philosophy of knowledge at all. We get along well enough without them in daily life and in scientific research. But if we seek a theory at all, we cannot excuse gross anomalies resulting from a proposed theory by pleading that we can avoid them in practice. The odd cases we have been considering are clinically pure cases that, though seldom encountered in practice, nevertheless display to best advantage the symptoms of a widespread and destructive malady.

We have so far neither any answer nor any promising clue to an answer to the question what distinguishes lawlike or confirmable hypotheses from accidental or non-confirmable ones; and what may at first have seemed a minor technical difficulty has taken on the stature of a major obstacle to the development of a satisfactory theory of confirmation. It is this problem that I call the new riddle of induction.

5. The Pervasive Problem of Projection

At the beginning of this lecture, I expressed the opinion that the problem of induction is still unsolved, but that the difficulties that face us today are not the old ones; and I have tried to outline the changes that have taken place. The problem of justifying induction has been displaced by the problem of defining

---

18 [Author's note] Carnap took this course in his paper 'On the Application of Inductive Logic', *Philosophy and Phenomenological Research*, vol. 8 (1947), pp. 133–47, which is in part a reply to my 'A Query on Confirmation', cited in Note 9 [16 in this text]. The discussion was continued in my note 'On Infirmities of Confirmation Theory', *Philosophy and Phenomenological Research*, vol. 8 (1947), pp. 149–51; and in Carnap's 'Reply to Nelson Goodman', same journal, same volume, pp. 461–62.

confirmation, and our work upon this has left us with the residual problem of distinguishing between confirmable and non-confirmable hypotheses. One might say roughly that the first question was "Why does a positive instance of a hypothesis give any grounds for predicting further instances?"; that the newer question was "What is a positive instance of a hypothesis?"; and that the crucial remaining question is "What hypotheses are confirmed by their positive instances?"

The vast amount of effort expended on the problem of induction in modern times has thus altered our afflictions but hardly relieved them. The original difficulty about induction arose from the recognition that anything may follow upon anything. Then, in attempting to define confirmation in terms of the converse of the consequence relation, we found ourselves with the distressingly similar difficulty that our definition would make any statement confirm any other. And now, after modifying our definition drastically, we still get the old devastating result that any statement will confirm any statement. Until we find a way of exercising some control over the hypotheses to be admitted, our definition makes no distinction whatsoever between valid and invalid inductive inferences.

The real inadequacy of Hume's account lay not in his descriptive approach but in the imprecision of his description. Regularities in experience, according to him, give rise to habits of expectation; and thus it is predictions conforming to past regularities that are normal or valid. But Hume overlooks the fact that some regularities do and some do not establish such habits; that predictions based on some regularities are valid while predictions based on other regularities are not. Every word you have heard me say has occurred prior to the final sentence of this lecture; but that does not, I hope, create any expectation that every word you will hear me say will be prior to that sentence. Again, consider our case of emeralds. All those examined before time t are green; and this leads us to expect, and confirms the prediction, that the next one will be green. But also, all those examined are grue; and this does not lead us to expect, and does not confirm the prediction, that the next one will be grue. Regularity in greenness confirms the prediction of further cases; regularity in grueness does not. To say that valid predictions are those based on past regularities, without being able to say *which* regularities, is thus quite pointless. Regularities are where you find them, and you can find them anywhere. As we have seen, Hume's failure to recognize and deal with this problem has been shared even by his most recent successors.

As a result, what we have in current confirmation theory is a definition that is adequate for certain cases that so far can be described only as those for which it is adequate. The theory works where it works. A hypothesis is confirmed by statements related to it in the prescribed way provided it is so confirmed. This is a good deal like having a theory that tells us that the area of a plane figure is one-half the base times the altitude, without telling us for what figures this holds. We must somehow find a way of distinguishing lawlike hypotheses, to which our definition of confirmation applies, from accidental hypotheses, to which it does not.

Today I have been speaking solely of the problem of induction, but what has been said applies equally to the more general problem of projection. As pointed out earlier, the problem of prediction from past to future cases is but a narrower version of the problem of projecting from any set of cases to others. We saw that a whole cluster of troublesome problems concerning dispositions and possibility can be reduced to this problem of projection. That is why the new riddle of induction, which is more broadly the problem of distinguishing between projectible and non-projectible hypotheses, is as important as it is exasperating.

Our failures teach us, I think, that lawlike or projectible hypotheses cannot be distinguished on any merely syntactical grounds or even on the ground that these hypotheses are somehow purely general in meaning. Our only hope lies in re-examining the problem once more and looking for some new approach. This will be my course in the final lecture.

CARL HEMPEL
"Scientific Inquiry: Invention and Test"

Who Was Carl Hempel?

Carl Gustav ('Peter') Hempel—probably, with Popper and Kuhn, one of the three most influential philosophers of science of the twentieth century—was born in 1905 in Orianenberg, near Berlin, Germany. After attending high school in Berlin, at eighteen he went to study mathematics and logic at the University of Göttingen with the famous mathematician David Hilbert. Although Hempel quickly fell in love with mathematical logic, he left Göttingen within the year to study at the University of Heidelberg, and then in 1924 moved back to Berlin where he studied physics with Hans Reichenbach and Max Planck, and logic with John von Neumann (all destined to become towering figures in their fields). Reichenbach introduced him to the members of a group of intellectuals called the Berlin Circle, and in 1929 Hempel took part in the historic first congress on scientific philosophy in Prague, organized by the founders of an important twentieth-century philosophical movement called 'logical positivism.' At that conference Hempel met the philosopher of science Rudolf Carnap, and was so impressed by him that he moved to Carnap's home town of Vienna, Austria; there, he attended classes by the logical positivists Carnap, Moritz Schlick, and Friedrich Waismann and took part in meetings of the 'Vienna Circle.'

The Vienna and Berlin Circles of the 1920s and early 1930s were fairly informal, diverse, collaborative groups of "scientifically interested philosophers and philosophically interested scientists," as Hempel once put it. The members of these groups, especially the Vienna Circle, thought of themselves as decisively breaking with the past and founding a new, more effective kind of philosophical enterprise—a 'modern scientific philosophy' built on the new techniques of logical analysis and modeled on the successful empirical methods of the exact sciences. The past history of philosophy, the new 'logical empiricists' or 'logical positivists' declared, was one of fruitless strife; by contrast, in Hempel's words, "the Vienna Circle held that the purported problems of metaphysics constitute no genuine problems at all and that in an inquiry making use of an appropriately precise conceptual and linguistic apparatus, metaphysical questions could not even be formulated. They were pseudoproblems, devoid of any clear meaning."

In 1934—just a week before Adolf Hitler anointed himself *Führer* of the German Third Reich—Hempel completed his PhD from the University of Berlin, with a dissertation on probability theory. In the previous year, shortly after Hitler was elected Chancellor of Germany, Hempel's supervisor Hans Reichenbach had been summarily dismissed from his Berlin chair because his father had been Jewish; Hempel himself was of pure 'Aryan' stock, but his wife Eva Ahrends had partly 'Jewish blood' and Hempel was frequently accused of the offense of "philosemitism," sympathy with the Jews. As a consequence, in 1934, Hempel fled Germany to Belgium, where he and Eva were supported by his friend and colleague Paul Oppenheim.

In 1937, because of Carnap's influence, Hempel was invited to become a Rockefeller research associate in philosophy at the University of Chicago, and Hempel officially emigrated to the United States in 1939. Between 1939 and 1948 Hempel taught at City College and Queens College in New York; during these years, Hempel's wife Eva died shortly after giving birth to a son, and Hempel married his second wife, Diane Perlow. In 1948 he moved to Yale University, and in 1955 he was made Stuart Professor of Philosophy at Princeton, a post he held until his mandatory 'retirement' at age 68 in 1973. Even after his retirement, Hempel continued to lecture at Princeton and then, as a visiting professor, at Jerusalem, Berkeley, Carleton College, and Pittsburgh; in 1977 (at the age of 72) he was made University Professor of Philosophy at the University of Pittsburgh, a post he held until 1985. Hempel died at Princeton, New Jersey, in 1997.

In a tribute to him after his death, the well-known Princeton logician Richard Jeffrey wrote of Hempel:

> There was no arrogance in him; he got no thrill of pleasure from proving people wrong. His criticisms were always courteous, never triumphant. This quality was deeply rooted in his character. He was made so as to welcome opportunities for kindness, generosity, courtesy; and he gave his whole mind to such projects spontaneously, for pleasure, so that effort disappeared into zest. [His wife] Diane was another such player. (Once, in a restaurant, someone remarked on their politeness to each other, and she said, "Ah, but you should see us when we are alone together. [Pause] Then we are *really* polite.") And play it was, too. He was notably playful and incapable of stuffiness.

Hempel is commonly credited with a leading role in developing the account of scientific explanation and prediction which came to be labeled the 'Received View' by its critics in the last few decades of the twentieth century. (A more technical name for a central plank of this view is the *deductive-nomological* [D-N] or *covering law* model of scientific explanation.) According to this theory, the scientific explanation of a fact consists in the logical *deduction* of a statement that describes the fact (often called the 'explanan-

dum'), from premises (the 'explanans') which include true scientific laws and statements of initial conditions. For example, a simple scientific explanation for why this piece of copper conducts electricity is that my bit of copper is 'covered' by a general law which says that *all* copper conducts electricity under certain circumstances. In this case, the sentence (1) "This copper conducts electricity" is a *logical consequence* of the statements (2) "All copper conducts electricity under conditions C (e.g., the copper is pure, the metal is within a certain temperature range, etc.)" and (3) "Conditions C presently hold for this bit of copper"; according to Hempel, this logical relationship is why (2) and (3) count as *explaining* (1).

Furthermore, according to Hempel, scientific *prediction* turns out to be just the flip-side of explanation. One can start from an observation, and show that a certain theory *explains* that observation because the observation is deducible from the theory; or one can start with a theory, and show that the theory *predicts* some set of observations because they are logical consequences of the theory being true. Either way, in Hempel's view, the essential logical relationship between statements of laws and statements of observations is the same.

When it comes to the issue of *confirming* which scientific laws are true and which are not (i.e., which can feature in good explanations), one of the things Hempel is best known for is formulating, in 1945, 'Hempel's paradox' (also known as the paradox of the ravens, or the paradox of confirmation). This puzzle calls into question the intuitive assumption that a general law is confirmed only by instances of that law—for example, the idea that the claim that "All ravens are black" is supported by observations of black ravens but not at all by the sighting of a blue jay. Here is the paradox. Suppose I see a white running shoe; this is an instance of the general claim that all non-black things are non-ravens (since a white shoe is neither black nor a raven). Therefore, it appears that my shoe sighting is some evidence for the claim that all non-black things are non-ravens. But "all non-black things are non-ravens" is logically equivalent to "all ravens are black." Thus it turns out that—if our intuitive understanding of induction is correct—observations of white shoes (and blue jays, etc.) do in fact partially confirm the hypothesis that all ravens are black. But this seems absurd—it seems ridiculous to think that we could find out about birds by examining footwear; hence the paradox.

Various attempts have been made to deal with this puzzle. Hempel himself proposed that we resolve the paradox by accepting its apparently absurd conclusion: he held that *all* observations are relevant to any hypothesis, though some of them (such as sightings of white shoes) confirm it only much more weakly than others (sightings of black ravens).

What Is the Structure of This Reading?

In this reading Hempel argues that the traditional, or 'narrow inductivist,' view is incorrect, and argues that it should be replaced in our understanding of science by what he calls the 'method of hypothesis.'

Questions for Further Thought

1. "What particular sorts of data it is reasonable to collect is not determined by the problem under study, but by a tentative answer to it that the investigator entertains in the form of a conjecture or hypothesis." Do you agree? What implications would this have for the working practice of scientists?

2. According to Hempel, there can be no possible mechanical rules for generating inductive generalizations from sets of data; that is, as it is sometimes put, there is no 'logic of discovery.' What are Hempel's reasons for claiming this, and are they persuasive? Even if there are no mechanical methods for scientific discovery, might there nevertheless be some useful non-mechanical methods—and if so, what might these look like?

3. Hempel suggests that, although induction is not a useful method for generating hypotheses, it is important for assessing how well supported a theory is by the evidence. How vulnerable does this make Hempel to the kind of skepticism about induction argued for by David Hume (see the Hume reading in this chapter)?

Suggestions for Further Reading

Philosophy of Natural Science (Prentice-Hall, 1966), from which this selection is taken, is still in print and, though a short book, is considered a useful encapsulation of Hempel's philosophy of science and of the 'received view' in general; it is well worth reading. Several of Hempel's most important and influential papers are contained in *Aspects of Scientific Explanation, and Other Essays in the Philosophy of Science* (Free Press, 1965) and in the more recent anthology *The Philosophy of Carl G. Hempel: Studies in Science, Explanation, and Rationality*, edited by James Fetzer (Oxford University Press, 2000). *Selected Philosophical Essays*, edited by Richard Jeffrey (Cambridge University Press, 2000), fills this out with papers from Hempel's earlier and later philosophical phases.

Science, Explanation, and Rationality: The Philosophy of Carl G. Hempel, edited by James Fetzer (Oxford University Press, 2000), is a collection of essays about Hempel's work. Three good works of philosophy of science which address Hempel's work on explanation and confirmation are Wesley C. Salmon's *Four Decades of Scientific Explanation* (University of Minnesota Press, 1990), Israel Scheffler's *The Anatomy of Inquiry* (Hackett, 1982), and Frederick Suppe's *The Structure of Scientific Theories* (University of Illinois Press, 1979).

from "Scientific Inquiry: Invention and Test"[1]

The Role of Induction in Scientific Inquiry

We have considered some scientific investigations in which a problem was tackled by proposing tentative answers in the form of hypotheses that were then tested by deriving from them suitable test implications and checking these by observation or experiment.

But how are suitable hypotheses arrived at in the first place? It is sometimes held that they are inferred from antecedently collected data by means of a procedure called *inductive inference*, as contradistinguished

---

1 From *Philosophy of Natural Science*, 1st Edition, © 1967; pp. 10–15. Reprinted by permission of Pearson Education, Inc., Upper Saddle River, NJ.

from deductive inference, from which it differs in important respects.

In a deductively valid argument, the conclusion is related to the premises in such a way that if the premisses are true then the conclusion cannot fail to be true as well. This requirement is satisfied, for example, by any argument of the following general form:

> If p, then q.
> It is not the case that q.
> It is not the case that p.

Brief reflection shows that no matter what particular statements may stand at the places marked by the letters 'p' and 'q', the conclusion will certainly be true if the premisses are. In fact, our schema represents the argument form called *modus tollens*....

Another type of deductively valid inference is illustrated by this example:

> Any sodium salt, when put into the flame of a Bunsen burner,[2] turns the flame yellow.
> This piece of rock salt is a sodium salt.
> This piece of rock salt, when put into the flame of a Bunsen burner, will turn the flame yellow.

Arguments of the latter kind are often said to lead from the general (here, the premiss about all sodium salts) to the particular (a conclusion about the particular piece of rock salt). Inductive inferences, by contrast, are sometimes described as leading from premises about particular cases to a conclusion that has the character of a general law or principle. For example, from premises to the effect that each of the particular samples of various sodium salts that have so far been subjected to the Bunsen flame test did turn the flame yellow, inductive inference supposedly leads to the general conclusion that all sodium salts, when put into the flame of a Bunsen burner, turn the flame yellow. But in this case, the truth of the premisses obviously does *not* guarantee the truth of the conclusion; for even if it is the case that all samples

of sodium salts examined so far did turn the Bunsen flame yellow, it remains quite possible that new kinds of sodium salt might yet be found that do not conform to this generalization. Indeed, even some kinds of sodium salt that have already been tested with positive result might conceivably fail to satisfy the generalization under special physical conditions (such as very strong magnetic fields or the like) in which they have not yet been examined. For this reason, the premises of an inductive inference are often said to imply the conclusion only with more or less high probability, whereas the premises of a deductive inference imply the conclusion with certainty.

The idea that in scientific inquiry, inductive inference from antecedently collected data leads to appropriate general principles is clearly embodied in the following account of how a scientist would ideally proceed:

> If we try to imagine how a mind of superhuman power and reach, but normal so far as the logical processes of its thought are concerned, ... would use the scientific method, the process would be as follows: First, all facts would be observed and recorded, *without selection* or *a priori* guess as to their relative importance. Secondly, the observed and recorded facts would be analyzed, compared, and classified, *without hypothesis or postulates* other than those necessarily involved in the logic of thought. Third, from this analysis of the facts generalizations would be inductively drawn as to the relations, classificatory or causal, between them. Fourth, further research would be deductive as well as inductive, employing inferences from previously established generalizations.[3]

This passage distinguishes four stages in an ideal scientific inquiry: (1) observation and recording of all facts, (2) analysis and classification of these facts,

---

2   A common piece of laboratory equipment that produces an adjustable gas flame.

3   [Author's note] A.B. Wolfe, "Functional Economics," in *The Trend of Economics*, ed. R.G. Tugwell (New York: Alfred A. Knopf, Inc., 1924), p. 450 (italics are quoted).

(3) inductive derivation of generalizations from them, and (4) further testing of the generalizations. The first two of these stages are specifically assumed not to make use of any guesses or hypotheses as to how the observed facts might be interconnected; this restriction seems to have been imposed in the belief that such preconceived ideas would introduce a bias and would jeopardize the scientific objectivity of the investigation.

But the view expressed in the quoted passage—I will call it *the narrow inductivist conception of scientific inquiry*—is untenable, for several reasons....

First, our scientific investigation as here envisaged could never get off the ground. Even its first phase could never be carried out, for a collection of *all* the facts would have to await the end of the world, so to speak; and even all the facts *up to now* cannot be collected, since there are an infinite number and variety of them. Are we to examine, for example, all the grains of sand in all the deserts and on all the beaches, and are we to record their shapes, their weights, their chemical composition, their distances from each other, their constantly changing temperature, and their equally changing distance from the center of the moon? Are we to record the floating thoughts that cross our minds in the tedious process? The shapes of the clouds overhead, the changing color of the sky? The construction and the trade name of our writing equipment? Our own life histories and those of our fellow investigators? All these, and untold other things, are, after all, among "all the facts up to now".

Perhaps, then, all that should be required in the first phase is that all the *relevant* facts be collected. But relevant to what? Though the author does not mention this, let us suppose that the inquiry is concerned with a specified *problem*. Should we not then begin by collecting all the facts—or better, all available data— relevant to that problem? This notion still makes no clear sense. Semmelweis sought to solve one specific problem, yet he collected quite different kinds of data at different stages of his inquiry.[4] And rightly so; for

what particular sorts of data it is reasonable to collect is not determined by the problem under study, but by a tentative answer to it that the investigator entertains in the form of a conjecture or hypothesis. Given the conjecture that mortality from childbed fever was increased by the terrifying appearance of the priest and his attendant with the death bell, it was relevant to collect data on the consequences of having the priest change his routine; but it would have been totally irrelevant to check what would happen if doctors and students disinfected their hands before examining their patients. With respect to Semmelweis' eventual contamination hypothesis, data of the latter kind were clearly relevant, and those of the former kind totally irrelevant.

Empirical "facts" or findings, therefore, can be qualified as logically relevant or irrelevant only in reference to a given hypothesis, but not in reference to a given problem.

Suppose now that a hypothesis *H* has been advanced as a tentative answer to a research problem: what kinds of data would be relevant to *H*? Our earlier examples suggest an answer: A finding is relevant to *H* if either its occurrence or its nonoccurrence can be inferred from *H*. Take Torricelli's hypothesis, for example.[5] As we saw, Pascal[6] inferred from it that the mercury column in a barometer should grow shorter if the barometer were carried up a mountain. Therefore, any finding to the effect that this did indeed happen in a particular case is relevant to the hypotheses; but so would be the finding that the length of the mercury column had remained unchanged or that it had decreased

---

4   Hempel is referring here to a case study he described earlier: that of the Viennese doctor Ignaz Semmelweis who in the mid-nineteenth century discovered that incidences of childbed fever—a major cause of death

in young mothers at that time—could be drastically reduced by disinfecting the hands of the attending doctors.

5   This is also a reference to an earlier case study. Evangelista Torricelli (1608–1647) hypothesized that the earth is surrounded by a sea of air which exerts pressure on the surface below because of its weight; thus, the higher that one is off the ground the less downward pressure the atmosphere would exert (because the less air there is above one pushing down).

6   Blaise Pascal (1623–1662) was a French mathematician and physicist.

and then increased during the ascent, for such findings would refute Pascal's test implication and would thus disconfirm Torricelli's hypothesis. Data of the former kind may be called positively, or favorably, relevant to the hypothesis; those of the latter kind negatively, or unfavorably, relevant.

In sum, the maxim that data should be gathered without guidance by antecedent hypotheses about the connections among the facts under study is self-defeating, and it is certainly not followed in scientific inquiry. On the contrary, tentative hypotheses are needed to give direction to a scientific investigation. Such hypotheses determine, among other things, what data should be collected at a given point in a scientific investigation.

...

The second stage envisaged in our quoted passage is open to similar criticism. A set of empirical "facts" can be analyzed and classified in many different ways, most of which will be unilluminating for the purposes of a given inquiry. Semmelweis could have classified the women in the maternity wards according to criteria such as age, place of residence, marital status, dietary habits, and so forth; but information on these would have provided no clue to a patient's prospects of becoming a victim of childbed fever. What Semmelweis sought were criteria that would be significantly connected with those prospects; and for this purpose, as he eventually found, it was illuminating to single out those women who were attended by medical personnel with contaminated hands; for it was with this characteristic, or with the corresponding class of patients, that high mortality from childbed fever was associated.

Thus, if a particular way of analyzing and classifying empirical findings is to lead to an explanation of the phenomena concerned, then it must be based on hypotheses about how those phenomena are connected; without such hypotheses, analysis and classification are blind.

Our critical reflections on the first two stages of inquiry as envisaged in the quoted passage also undercut the notion that hypotheses are introduced only in the third stage, by inductive inference from antecedently collected data. But some further remarks on the subject should be added here.

Induction is sometimes conceived as a method that leads, by means of mechanically applicable rules, from observed facts to corresponding general principles. In this case, the rules of inductive inference would provide effective canons of scientific discovery; induction would be a mechanical procedure analogous to the familiar routine for the multiplication of integers, which leads, in a finite number of predetermined and mechanically performable steps, to the corresponding product. Actually, however, no such general and mechanical induction procedure is available at present; otherwise, the much studied problem of the causation of cancer, for example, would hardly have remained unsolved to this day. Nor can the discovery of such a procedure ever be expected. For—to mention one reason—scientific hypotheses and theories are usually couched in terms that do not occur at all in the description of the empirical findings on which they rest, and which they serve to explain. For example, theories about the atomic and subatomic structure of matter contain terms such as 'atom', 'electron', 'proton', 'neutron', 'psi-function', etc.; yet they are based on laboratory findings about the spectra of various gases, tracks in cloud and bubble chambers, quantitative aspects of chemical reactions, and so forth—all of which can be described without the use of those "theoretical terms". Induction rules of the kind here envisaged would therefore have to provide a mechanical routine for constructing, on the basis of the given data, a hypothesis or theory stated in terms of some quite novel concepts, which are nowhere used in the description of the data themselves. Surely, no general mechanical rule of procedure can be expected to achieve this. Could there be a general rule, for example, which, when applied to the data available to Galileo concerning the limited effectiveness of suction pumps, would, by a mechanical routine, produce a hypothesis based on the concept of a sea of air?

To be sure, mechanical procedures for inductively "inferring" a hypothesis on the basis of given data may be specifiable for situations of special, and relatively simple, kinds. For example, if the length of a copper rod has been measured at several different temperatures, the resulting pairs of associated values for temperature and length may be represented by points in a plane coordinate system, and a curve may be drawn through them in accordance with some particular rule of curve fitting. The curve then graphically represents a general quantitative hypothesis that expresses the length of the rod as a specific function of its temperature. But note that this hypothesis contains no novel terms; it is expressible in terms of the concepts of temperature and length, which are used also in describing the data. Moreover, the choice of "associated" values of temperature and length as data already presupposes a guiding hypothesis; namely, that with each value of the temperature, exactly one value of the length of the copper rod is associated, so that its length is indeed a function of its temperature alone. The mechanical curve-fitting routine then serves only to select a particular function as the appropriate one. This point is important; for suppose that instead of a copper rod, we examine a body of nitrogen gas enclosed in a cylindrical container with a movable piston as a lid, and that we measure its volume at several different temperatures. If we were to use this procedure in an effort to obtain from our data a *general* hypothesis representing the volume of the gas as a function of its temperature, we would fail, because the volume of a gas is a function both of its temperature and of the pressure exerted upon it, so that at the same temperature, the given gas may assume different volumes.

Thus, even in these simple cases, the mechanical procedures for the construction of a hypothesis do only part of the job, for they presuppose an antecedent, less specific hypothesis (i.e., that a certain physical variable is a function of one single other variable), which is not obtainable by the same procedure.

There are, then, no generally applicable "rules of induction", by which hypotheses or theories can be mechanically derived or inferred from empirical data. The transition from data to theory requires creative imagination. Scientific hypotheses and theories are not *derived* from observed facts, but *invented* in order to account for them. They constitute guesses at the connections that might obtain between the phenomena under study, at uniformities and patterns that might underlie their occurrence. "Happy guesses"[7] of this kind require great ingenuity, especially if they involve a radical departure from current modes of scientific thinking, as did, for example, the theory of relativity and quantum theory. The inventive effort required in scientific research will benefit from a thorough familiarity with current knowledge in the field. A complete novice will hardly make an important scientific discovery, for the ideas that may occur to him are likely to duplicate what has been tried before or to run afoul of well-established facts or theories of which he is not aware.

7   [Author's note] This characterization was given already by William Whewell in his work *The Philosophy of the Inductive Sciences*, 2nd ed. (London: John W. Parker, 1847); II, 41. Whewell also speaks of "invention" as "part of induction" (p. 46). In the same vein, K. Popper refers to scientific hypotheses and theories as "conjectures"; see, for example, the essay "Science: Conjectures and Refutations" in his book, *Conjectures and Refutations* (New York and London: Basic Books, 1962). Indeed, A.B. Wolfe, whose narrowly inductivist conception of ideal scientific procedure was quoted earlier, stresses that "the limited human mind" has to use "a greatly modified procedure", requiring scientific imagination and the selection of data on the basis of some "working hypothesis" (p. 450 of the essay cited [above]).

KARL POPPER
"Science: Conjectures and Refutations"

Who Was Karl Popper?

Though Popper's reputation has perhaps waned somewhat since its peak in the 1970s, he is still generally considered one among a small handful of the greatest philosophers of science of the twentieth century. In his day he found a fervent following among prominent scientists such as Peter Medawar (a Nobel Prize winner for medicine, who in 1972 called him "incomparably the greatest philosopher of science that has ever been"), neuroscientist John Eccles (another Nobel laureate, who urged his fellow scientists "to read and meditate upon Popper's writings on the philosophy of science and to adopt them as the basis of one's scientific life"), and mathematician and astronomer Hermann Bondi

(who once stated, "There is no more to science than its method, and there is no more to its method that Popper has said").

Karl Raimund Popper was born in 1902 in Vienna, Austria, to Jewish parents who had converted to Protestantism. His parents were intellectual (his father's library is said to have contained 15,000 volumes) and financially comfortable until rampant inflation in Austria after World War I reduced his family to near-poverty. In his early and middle teens Popper was a Marxist, and then—after witnessing the appalling bloodshed of a brief Communist coup in neighboring Hungary—he became an enthusiastic and active Social Democrat. Vienna after the First World War was a city bubbling over with revolutionary new movements and ideas, and, for Popper, it was a thrilling time and place to be young. As well as studying science and philosophy, Popper was involved with left-wing politics, social work with children, and also the Society for Private Concerts founded by the revolutionary atonal composer Arnold Schönberg (throughout his life, Popper had a great love of music).

During and after his education (he received his PhD in 1928), Popper worked as a schoolteacher in mathematics and physics, and occasionally as a cabinet-maker, but continued to pursue his interest in philosophy. However his ideas were then, as for most of his career, out of tune with contemporary philosophical fashions: Otto Neurath, a member of the "Vienna Circle" of philosophers active during the 1920s and 1930s, nicknamed him "the Official Opposition" for his arguments against the then-dominant philosophy of logical positivism. In 1934 Popper published his first book, *Logik der Forschung*—a heavily edited version of a book originally twice as long—which attacked the main ideas of the logical positivists. This book was later translated into English and published as *The Logic of Scientific Discovery* (1959).

In the 1930s, the Communists and other left wing parties in Austria, Germany, and Italy failed to effectively oppose the rise to power of fascism (believing it to be the last gasp of capitalism before the inevitable Communist revolution, and so offering only a half-hearted resistance) and Popper—accurately foretelling the annexation of Austria by Nazi Germany and the onset of a second European war—fled with his wife to New Zealand. There, from 1937 until 1945, he taught philosophy at the University of Canterbury, at Christchurch. He spent this period teaching himself Greek so he could study the Greek philosophers, and writing *The Open Society and its Enemies* (published in 1943) which, through a critique of the political theories of Plato and Marx, defends the idea of liberty and democracy against that of totalitarianism. Popper considered this to be his contribution to the war against fascism.

According to Popper, no political ideology (either on the political right or the left) can justify large-scale social engineering—it is simply impossible to formulate a demonstrably true, predictive theory of society, and so we should never act as if we alone have the key to the truth about human nature. The proper function of social institutions in an "open society"—one in which any regime can be ousted without violence—is not large-scale utopian planning but, according to Popper, piecemeal reform with the object of minimizing, as much as possible, avoidable suffering. This way, the effectiveness of each small piece of legislation can be publicly assessed, and the society can move forward collectively after learning from its mistakes.

In 1946 Popper moved to England, where he was to live until his death in 1994. Despite his growing reputation (he was knighted in 1965), Popper was never offered a position at either Oxford or Cambridge[1] and he spent the rest of his career as a professor at the London School of Economics, still out of sync with the philosophical tendencies of the day which, during those years in England, were predominantly towards "linguistic" philosophy. Popper was impatient with endless discussion about the meanings of words, and denied that exact precision of terminology was either possible or desirable in science. Popper argued that a

language is an instrument and what matters is what you *do* with that instrument; philosophers who devote their lives exclusively to the analysis of language are, as Bryan Magee has put it, like carpenters who devote all their time to sharpening their tools, but never use them except on each other. Popper wrote in the preface to *The Logic of Scientific Discovery*:

> Language analysts believe that there are no genuine philosophical problems, or that the problems of philosophy, if any, are problems of linguistic usage, or of the meaning of words. I, however, believe that there is at least one problem in which all thinking men are interested. It is the problem of cosmology: *the problem of understanding the world—including ourselves, and our knowledge, as part of the world.* All science is cosmology, I believe, and for me the interest of philosophy, no less than of science, lies solely in the contributions which it has made to it.

Popper's main contribution to the philosophy of science is his proposal of a solution to the 'problem of induction,' which involves the rejection of the previously orthodox view of the scientific method and its replacement with another. The essay reprinted here, "Science: Conjectures and Refutations," is an excellent (and in itself quite influential) summary of these arguments.

What Is the Structure of This Reading?

This article is Popper's own summary of his most important work in the philosophy of science. He begins by laying out the problem which he first became interested in: the problem of the *demarcation* between science and pseudo-science (i.e., of finding a criterion for what makes something a properly scientific theory). By comparing Einstein's relativity theory (an example of science) with the psychoanalytic theories of Freud and Adler (examples of pseudo-science), Popper argues that the proper mark of a scientific theory is its *falsifiability*. In section II Popper goes on to criticize the *ad hoc* modifications of Marxism by Marx's followers that rendered the theory unfalsifiable. However, Popper then takes pains to point out that he does not consider pseudo-scientific theories—or "myths" as he calls them—to be either useless or meaningless. In

---

1   This may have been partly to do with his combative personality. Despite advocating risky conjectures and public refutations, by all accounts Popper was a touchy character, quick to express scorn for those who doubted his ideas. On one famous occasion, at the Moral Sciences Club in Cambridge, he almost came to blows with Ludwig Wittgenstein and—legend has it—had to be restrained by Bertrand Russell (upon which, Wittgenstein stormed out of the room).

section III he contrasts his falsificationism (which is a theory of demarcation and not of meaning) with the logical positivist's "verificationist" account of *meaning*, which did famously entail that all non-science is literally meaningless.

In section IV Popper begins his discussion of the problem of induction. After laying out Hume's description of the problem (see the Hume reading in this chapter), he critiques Hume's psychologistic solution to the problem and uses this critique to motivate his own alternative account: the method of trial and error, or *conjectures and refutations*. In section V Popper suggests that this method of "trial and error" is ultimately rooted in the evolution of the human mind, and he contrasts his views with Kant's doctrine of the *synthetic a priori* (see the Kant reading in Chapter 3). Like Kant, Popper introduces a distinction between *dogmatic* and *critical* thinking, and in section VII he suggests that the scientific, critical attitude has evolved through human history from a pre-scientific dogmatism.

In section VIII Popper turns his attention to the "logic of science," and argues that it is simply a mistake to think that the scientific method is inductive: in fact, Popper asserts, real science proceeds by the method of conjecture and refutation, and scientists have in the past just misdescribed or misunderstood their own practices when they spoke of induction. Popper lays out his final solution to the problem of induction in section IX, and in the last section of the paper he responds to various reformulations of the problem. Particularly important here is his distinction between the claim that science is a *reasonable practice* for human beings to engage in, and the claim that our belief that science will eventually succeed in getting to the truth is a *rational* one: Popper supports the first claim, but unconditionally denies the second one.

Some Useful Background Information

1. Popper sought to replace the traditional inductivist view of science with a quite different account that denies induction plays any role in science at all. In order to see what Popper is reacting against, it is helpful to briefly review the traditional understanding of the scientific method. On this view (sometimes called the "Baconian" view, after Francis Bacon (1561–1626), the first philosopher to systematically lay out rules for good science) the scientist begins by making observations—by carrying out carefully controlled experiments at some outpost on the frontier between our knowledge and our ignorance. The results of these experiments are systematically recorded and shared with other workers in the field. As the body of data grows, certain regularities appear. Individual scientists formulate hypotheses which, if true, would explain all the known facts and reveal an underlying structure explaining the regularities in the data. They then attempt to confirm their hypotheses by performing experiments which will produce supporting evidence. Eventually, after enough experiments are done, some hypothesis is verified and is added to the body of confirmed scientific theory. Science moves on to the next point on the frontier.

    This process, known as the method of induction, was standardly thought to be what marked off scientific investigation from other kinds of intellectual pursuit: science, it might be said, is based on experimental *facts* (rather than, say, on claims rooted in tradition, authority, prejudice, habit, emotion, or whatever). It is this picture of science that Popper attempts to overturn, and replace with his own account of what scientists are actually up to.

2. Popper does not think that good scientific theories are good because they are true. As he once put it, "We cannot identify science with truth, for we think that both Newton's and Einstein's theories belong to science, but they cannot both be true, and they may well both be false." A formative experience for Popper as a young philosopher was the replacement of Newtonian physics—previously the crown jewel of modern science—by Einstein's theories in the early decades of the twentieth century. Newtonian physics was, in 1900, the most successful, well-confirmed, and important scientific theory ever developed, and for more than two hundred years its laws had been unfailingly corroborated by literally billions of scientific ob-

servations and, furthermore, by underpinning the most impressive advances in technology in human history. Yet, despite the huge quantity of inductive evidence apparently confirming the truth of Newtonian physics, it turned out to be false. If this quantity of evidence could not verify a theory, Popper thought, then nothing could. Nothing in science is secure; every scientific theory is open to rejection or revision; all scientific 'knowledge' is probably false, though it aspires eventually to the truth. One of Popper's favorite quotations was from the early Greek philosopher Xenophanes (who lived at about 400 BCE):

The gods did not reveal, from the beginning,
All things to us, but in the course of time
Through seeking we may learn and know
    things better.
But as for certain truth, no man has known it,
Nor shall he know it, neither of the gods
Nor yet of all the things of which I speak.
For even if by chance he were to utter
The final truth, he would himself not know it:
For all is but a woven web of guesses.

3. Popper's approach to knowledge is self-consciously biological in orientation. Human beings, according to Popper, are problem-solving animals, and there is continuity between simple examples of learning by trial and error in the lower animals and the method of conjecture and refutation in human science. The human search for knowledge is ultimately rooted, for Popper, in facts about our evolutionary history.

Some Common Misconceptions

1. Though Popper claims to have "solved the problem of induction," he did not do so by showing that induction *works*. Instead, he 'solves' the problem by issuing a complete ban on induction. The conclusions of science are never positively justified: they are never established as certainly true, or even as probable. In other words, Popper's "corroboration" is not the same

thing as confirmation. Conjectures are not inferences and refutations are not inductive; the failure to refute a hypothesis is *not* evidence in its favor, according to Popper.

2. Unlike the logical positivists, Popper does not dismiss pseudo-science as valueless or meaningless. Falsifiability is not, for him, a demarcation between sense and nonsense, but only between science and non-science. (For the logical positivists, verifiability was a demarcation of both kinds.) Thus, for Popper, although the methods of science have a privileged place in the rational human pursuit of the truth, domains other than science (such as art and religion) can still have substantial value, and can even prove to be valuable starting points—though never finishing posts—in the quest for knowledge.

Suggestions for Critical Reflection

1. Popper claimed to have solved the problem of induction. Did he? If not, did he at least solve the problem of showing how the methods of science could be rational despite Hume's arguments against the rationality of induction?

2. Popper stresses the importance of ruling out *ad hoc* modifications to theories. How helpful is this advice? How easy is to tell when an adjustment to a theory is *ad hoc*, as opposed to when it is a legitimate improvement to a theory under the impact of new data? If it is not so easy, what implications (if any) does this have for Popper's account of science?

3. How plausible is Popper's suggestion that working scientists in fact adopt the method of conjecture and refutation (even though they may not realize they are doing so)? For example, do scientists deliberately pursue highly improbable claims (rather than less contentful, but more probable, hypotheses)? Do they then set out to falsify, rather than to verify, these theories? Do they abandon their theories when faced with single pieces of counter-evidence, rather than modifying their theories to accommodate this new data? If scientists do *not* in fact use the methods Popper prescribes, how much of a problem is this for Popper's philosophy of science?

4. The attempted refutation of our conjectures, according to Popper, can never positively justify those conjectures, or justify us in thinking that they are probably true. On the other hand, according to Popper, the refutation of a conjecture is a step that takes us closer to the truth. Are these two claims compatible?

5. Popper says we ought to act on—provisionally, to believe—those theories that have survived extensive testing. How is this to be distinguished from induction?

6. Popper issues a ban on induction as an irrational method of doing science; but is his own method any more rational? That is, does it give us rational reasons for preferring one theory over another? Does it give us any reason to think scientific theories are getting better and better (i.e., closer to the truth)? Can Popper consistently assert that there is growth in scientific knowledge and that science is a rational activity?

Suggestions for Further Reading

Popper published many books during his lifetime, and since his death a score more have been published based on the papers he left behind. The following six books are among his most important, and together give a fairly complete overview of his thought: *The Logic of Scientific Discovery* (Routledge, 1992), *Conjectures and Refutations: The Growth of Scientific Knowledge* (Routledge 1989), *The Open Society and its Enemies* (Volumes I and II, Princeton University Press, 1972/1976), *Objective Knowledge: An Evolutionary Approach* (Oxford University Press, 1972) and, co-written with John Eccles, *The Self and Its Brain* (Routledge, 1993). A two volume collection of critical essays about Popper's work, with replies from Popper, was published in 1974 by Open Court, edited by Paul A. Schilpp and called *The Philosophy of Karl Popper*. That collection also contains an extended autobiographical essay by Popper, an amended version of which was published under separate cover as *Unended Quest* (Open Court, 1982).

Bryan Magee's *Popper* (Fontana Press, 1973) is short, clear, and stimulating, if sometimes rather

breathless in its adoration of Popper's work. A later, somewhat longer, introduction by Magee is his *Philosophy and the Real World: An Introduction to Karl Popper* (Open Court, 1985). Two other reliable summaries of Popper's philosophical work are Anthony O'Hear, *Popper* (Routledge & Kegan Paul, 1980) and Geoff Stokes, *Popper: Philosophy, Politics and Scientific Method* (Polity Press, 1999). Roberta Corvi's *An Introduction to the Thought of Karl Popper* (Routledge, 1996) was approved by Popper just before his death and constitutes a scholarly account of Popper's final philosophical system; however, it is written rather less accessibly than many of Popper's own writings. Finally, there is a fairly recent collection of essays about Popper's work written by prominent philosophers, edited by Anthony O'Hear: *Karl Popper: Philosophy and Problems* (Cambridge University Press, 1996).

"Science: Conjectures and Refutations"[2]

> Mr. Turnbull had predicted evil consequences, ... and was now doing the best in his power to bring about the verification of his own prophecies.
>
> (Anthony Trollope)[3]

I.

When I received the list of participants in this course and realized that I had been asked to speak to philosophical colleagues I thought, after some hesitation and consultation, that you would probably prefer me

---

2   This was originally a lecture given at Peterhouse College, Cambridge, in 1953. It was first published under the title "Philosophy of Science: A Personal Report" in 1957 in *British Philosophy in Mid-Century*, edited by C.A. Mace. The copy reprinted here is taken, with permission, from Chapter 1 of *Conjectures and Refutations: The Growth of Scientific Knowledge*, fifth revised edition, London: Routledge, 1989. Copyright © University of Klagenfurt/Karl Popper Library.

3   *Phineas Finn*, Chapter XXV.

to speak about those problems which interest me most, and about those developments with which I am most intimately acquainted. I therefore decided to do what I have never done before: to give you a report on my own work in the philosophy of science, since the autumn of 1919 when I first began to grapple with the problem, "*When should a theory be ranked as scientific?*" or "*Is there a criterion for the scientific character or status of a theory?*"

The problem which troubled me at the time was neither, 'When is a theory true?' nor, 'When is a theory acceptable?' My problem was different. I *wished to distinguish between science and pseudo-science*; knowing very well that science often errs, and that pseudo-science may happen to stumble on the truth.

I knew, of course, the most widely accepted answer to my problem: that science is distinguished from pseudo-science—or from 'metaphysics'—by its *empirical method*, which is essentially *inductive*, proceeding from observation or experiment. But this did not satisfy me. On the contrary, I often formulated my problem as one of distinguishing between a genuinely empirical method and a non-empirical or even a pseudo-empirical method—that is to say, a method which, although it appeals to observation and experiment, nevertheless does not come up to scientific standards. The latter method may be exemplified by astrology, with its stupendous mass of empirical evidence based on observation—on horoscopes and on biographies.

But as it was not the example of astrology which led me to my problem I should perhaps briefly describe the atmosphere in which my problem arose and the examples by which it was stimulated. After the collapse of the Austrian Empire[4] there had been a revolution in Austria: the air was full of revolutionary slogans and ideas, and new and often wild theories. Among the theories which interested me Einstein's theory of relativity was no doubt by far the most important. Three others were Marx's theory of history, Freud's psycho-analysis, and Alfred Adler's so-called 'individual psychology'.

There was a lot of popular nonsense talked about these theories, and especially about relativity (as still happens even today), but I was fortunate in those who introduced me to the study of this theory. We all—the small circle of students to which I belonged—were thrilled with the result of Eddington's eclipse observations[5] which in 1919 brought the first important confirmation of Einstein's theory of gravitation. It was a great experience for us, and one which had a lasting influence on my intellectual development.

The three other theories I have mentioned were also widely discussed among students at that time. I myself happened to come into personal contact with Alfred Adler, and even to co-operate with him in his social work among the children and young people in the working-class districts of Vienna where he had established social guidance clinics.

It was during the summer of 1919 that I began to feel more and more dissatisfied with these three theories—the Marxist theory of history, psychoanalysis, and individual psychology; and I began to feel dubious about their claims to scientific status. My problem perhaps first took the simple form, 'What is wrong with Marxism, psycho-analysis, and individual psychology? Why are they so different from physical theories, from Newton's theory, and especially from the theory of relativity?'

To make this contrast clear I should explain that few of us at the time would have said that we believed in the *truth* of Einstein's theory of gravitation. This shows that it was not my doubting the *truth* of those other three theories which bothered me, but something else. Yet neither was it that I merely felt mathematical physics to be more *exact* than the sociological or psychological type of theory. Thus what worried me was neither the problem of truth, at that stage at least, nor the problem of exactness or measurability. It was rather that I felt that these other three theories, though posing as sciences, had in fact more in common with

---

4   In 1918, with Austria-Hungary's defeat in the First World War.

5   Sir Arthur Stanley Eddington (1882–1944), during an expedition to Africa, observed the positions of stars visible around the sun during an eclipse, compared them to the positions of those same stars seen at night (when, of course, the sun is not in the same region of the sky), and deduced from the shift in their positions that the light from those stars must be bent by its passage through the sun's gravitational field.

primitive myths than with science; that they resembled astrology rather than astronomy.

I found that those of my friends who were admirers of Marx, Freud, and Adler, were impressed by a number of points common to these theories, and especially by their apparent *explanatory power*. These theories appeared to be able to explain practically everything that happened within the fields to which they referred. The study of any of them seemed to have the effect of an intellectual conversion or revelation, opening your eyes to a new truth hidden from those not yet initiated. Once your eyes were thus opened you saw confirming instances everywhere: the world was full of *verifications* of the theory. Whatever happened always confirmed it. Thus its truth appeared manifest; and unbelievers were clearly people who did not want to see the manifest truth; who refused to see it, either because it was against their class interest, or because of their repressions which were still 'un-analysed' and crying out for treatment.

The most characteristic element in this situation seemed to me the incessant stream of confirmations, of observations which 'verified' the theories in question; and this point was constantly emphasized by their adherents. A Marxist could not open a newspaper without finding on every page confirming evidence for his interpretation of history; not only in the news, but also in its presentation—which revealed the class bias of the paper—and especially of course in what the paper did *not* say. The Freudian analysts emphasized that their theories were constantly verified by their 'clinical observations'. As for Adler, I was much impressed by a personal experience. Once, in 1919, I reported to him a case which to me did not seem particularly Adlerian, but which he found no difficulty in analysing in terms of his theory of inferiority feelings, although he had not even seen the child. Slightly shocked, I asked him how he could be so sure. 'Because of my thousandfold experience', he replied; whereupon I could not help saying: 'And with this new case, I suppose, your experience has become thousand-and-one-fold.'

What I had in mind was that his previous observations may not have been much sounder than this new one; that each in its turn had been interpreted in the light of 'previous experience', and at the same time counted as additional confirmation. What, I asked myself, did it confirm? No more than that a case could be interpreted in the light of the theory. But this meant very little, I reflected, since every conceivable case could be interpreted in the light of Adler's theory, or equally of Freud's. I may illustrate this by two very different examples of human behaviour: that of a man who pushes a child into the water with the intention of drowning it; and that of a man who sacrifices his life in an attempt to save the child. Each of these two cases can be explained with equal ease in Freudian and in Adlerian terms. According to Freud the first man suffered from repression (say, of some component of his Oedipus complex[6]), while the second man had achieved sublimation. According to Adler the first man suffered from feelings of inferiority (producing perhaps the need to prove to himself that he dared to commit some crime), and so did the second man (whose need was to prove to himself that he dared to rescue the child). I could not think of any human behaviour which could not be interpreted in terms of either theory. It was precisely this fact—that they always fitted, that they were always confirmed—which in the eyes of their admirers constituted the strongest argument in favour of these theories. It began to dawn on me that this apparent strength was in fact their weakness.

With Einstein's theory the situation was strikingly different. Take one typical instance—Einstein's prediction, just then confirmed by the findings of Eddington's expedition. Einstein's gravitational theory had led to the result that light must be attracted by heavy bodies (such as the sun), precisely as material bodies were attracted. As a consequence it could be calculated that light from a distant fixed star whose apparent position was close to the sun would reach the earth from such a direction that the star would seem to be slightly shifted away from the sun; or, in other words, that stars close to the sun would look as if they had moved a little away from the sun, and from one another. This is a thing which cannot normally be observed since such stars are rendered invisible in daytime by the sun's overwhelming brightness; but during an eclipse it is possible to take photographs

---

6   According to Freud, the Oedipus complex consists in subconscious sexual desire in a child (especially a boy) for the parent of the opposite sex, usually combined with repressed hostility towards the parent of the same sex.

of them. If the same constellation is photographed at night one can measure the distances on the two photographs, and check the predicted effect.

Now the impressive thing about this case is the *risk* involved in a prediction of this kind. If observation shows that the predicted effect is definitely absent, then the theory is simply refuted. The theory is *incompatible with certain possible results of observation*—in fact with results which everybody before Einstein would have expected.[7] This is quite different from the situation I have previously described, when it turned out that the theories in question were compatible with the most divergent human behaviour, so that it was practically impossible to describe any human behaviour that might not be claimed to be a verification of these theories.

These considerations led me in the winter of 1919–20 to conclusions which I may now reformulate as follows.

(1) It is easy to obtain confirmations, or verifications, for nearly every theory—if we look for confirmations.

(2) Confirmations should count only if they are the result of *risky predictions*; that is to say, if, unenlightened by the theory in question, we should have expected an event which was incompatible with the theory—an event which would have refuted the theory.

(3) Every 'good' scientific theory is a prohibition: it forbids certain things to happen. The more a theory forbids, the better it is.

(4) A theory which is not refutable by any conceivable event is non-scientific. Irrefutability is not a virtue of a theory (as people often think) but a vice.

(5) Every genuine *test* of a theory is an attempt to falsify it, or to refute it. Testability is falsifiability; but there are degrees of testability: some theories are more testable, more exposed to refutation, than others; they take, as it were, greater risks.

(6) Confirming evidence should not count *except when it is the result of a genuine test of the theory*; and this means that it can be presented as a serious

but unsuccessful attempt to falsify the theory. (I now speak in such cases of 'corroborating evidence'.)

(7) Some genuinely testable theories, when found to be false, are still upheld by their admirers—for example by introducing *ad hoc*[8] some auxiliary assumption, or by re-interpreting the theory *ad hoc* in such a way that it escapes refutation. Such a procedure is always possible, but it rescues the theory from refutation only at the price of destroying, or at least lowering, its scientific status. (I later described such a rescuing operation as a '*conventionalist twist*' or a '*conventionalist stratagem*'.)

One can sum up all this by saying that *the criterion of the scientific status of a theory is its falsifiability, or refutability, or testability.*

II.

I may perhaps exemplify this with the help of the various theories so far mentioned. Einstein's theory of gravitation clearly satisfied the criterion of falsifiability. Even if our measuring instruments at the time did not allow us to pronounce on the results of the tests with complete assurance, there was clearly a possibility of refuting the theory.

Astrology did not pass the test. Astrologers were greatly impressed, and misled, by what they believed to be confirming evidence—so much so that they were quite unimpressed by any unfavourable evidence. Moreover, by making their interpretations and prophecies sufficiently vague they were able to explain away anything that might have been a refutation of the theory had the theory and the prophecies been more precise. In order to escape falsification they destroyed the testability of their theory. It is a typical soothsayer's trick to predict things so vaguely that the predictions can hardly fail: that they become irrefutable.

The Marxist theory of history, in spite of the serious efforts of some of its founders and followers, ultimately adopted this soothsaying practice. In some of its earlier formulations (for example in Marx's analysis of the character of the 'coming social revolution') their predictions were testable, and in fact

---

7   [Author's note] This is a slight oversimplification, for about half of the Einstein effect may be derived from the classical theory, provided we assume a ballistic theory of light.

8   *Ad hoc* means "for the particular situation or case at hand and for no other" (from the Latin "to this").

falsified.[9] Yet instead of accepting the refutations the followers of Marx re-interpreted both the theory and the evidence in order to make them agree. In this way they rescued the theory from refutation; but they did so at the price of adopting a device which made it irrefutable. They thus gave a 'conventionalist twist' to the theory; and by this stratagem they destroyed its much advertised claim to scientific status.

The two psycho-analytic theories were in a different class. They were simply non-testable, irrefutable. There was no conceivable human behaviour which could contradict them. This does not mean that Freud and Adler were not seeing certain things correctly: I personally do not doubt that much of what they say is of considerable importance, and may well play its part one day in a psychological science which is testable. But it does mean that those 'clinical observations' which analysts naïvely believe confirm their theory cannot do this any more than the daily confirmations which astrologers find in their practice.[10] And as for

Freud's epic of the Ego, the Super-ego, and the Id, no substantially stronger claim to scientific status can be made for it than for Homer's collected stories from Olympus.[11] These theories describe some facts, but in the manner of myths. They contain most interesting psychological suggestions, but not in a testable form.

At the same time I realized that such myths may be developed, and become testable; that historically speaking all—or very nearly all—scientific theories originate from myths, and that a myth may contain important anticipations of scientific theories. Examples are Empedocles' theory of evolution by trial and error, or Parmenides' myth of the unchanging block universe[12] in which nothing ever happens and which,

---

9   [Author's note] See, for example, my *Open Society and Its Enemies*, ch. 15, section iii, and notes 13–14.

10   [Author's note] 'Clinical observations', like all other observations, are *interpretations in the light of theories* (see below, sections iv ff.); and for this reason alone they are apt to seem to support those theories in the light of which they were interpreted. But real support can be obtained only from observations undertaken as tests (by 'attempted refutations'); and for this purpose *criteria of refutation* have to be laid down beforehand: it must be agreed which observable situations, if actually observed, mean that the theory is refuted. But what kind of clinical responses would refute to the satisfaction of the analyst not merely a particular analytic diagnosis but psycho-analysis itself? And have such criteria ever been discussed or agreed upon by analysts? Is there not, on the contrary, a whole family of analytic concepts, such as 'ambivalence' (I do not suggest that there is no such thing as ambivalence), which would make it difficult, if not impossible, to agree upon such criteria? Moreover, how much headway has been made in investigating the question of the extent to which the (conscious or unconscious) expectations and theories held by the analyst influence the 'clinical responses' of the patient? (To say

nothing about the conscious attempts to influence the patient by proposing interpretations to him, etc.) Years ago I introduced the term '*Oedipus effect*' to describe the influence of a theory or expectation or prediction *upon the event which it predicts* or describes: it will be remembered that the causal chain leading to Oedipus' parricide was started by the oracle's prediction of this event. This is a characteristic and recurrent theme of such myths, but one which seems to have failed to attract the interest of the analysts, perhaps not accidentally. (The problem of confirmatory dreams suggested by the analyst is discussed by Freud, for example in *Gesammelte Schriften*, III, 1925, where he says on p. 314: 'If anybody asserts that most of the dreams which can be utilized in an analysis ... owe their origin to [the analyst's] suggestion, then no objection can be made from the point of view of analytic theory. Yet there is nothing in this fact', he surprisingly adds, 'which would detract from the reliability of our results.')

11   In Freudian theory, the *ego* is the part of the human psyche which is conscious and most directly in control of our thought and behavior, the *id* is the unconscious reservoir of primitive impulses and instincts, and the *superego* is the mostly unconscious part of our psyche which has internalized our community's moral standards and acts as a restraint on the ego. Olympus is the mythical home of many of the gods of classical Greek mythology, and Homer was a Greek epic poet whose verses often deal with the activities of the gods.

12   Empedocles of Acragas (c. 493–c. 433 BCE), a native of Sicily, was a philosopher, poet, politician, scientist

if we add another dimension,[13] becomes Einstein's block universe (in which, too, nothing ever happens, since everything is, four-dimensionally speaking, determined and laid down from the beginning). I thus felt that if a theory is found to be non-scientific, or 'metaphysical' (as we might say), it is not thereby found to be unimportant, or insignificant, or 'meaningless', or 'nonsensical'.[14] But it cannot claim to be backed by empirical evidence in the scientific sense—although it may easily be, in some genetic[15] sense, the 'result of observation'.

(There were a great many other theories of this pre-scientific or pseudo-scientific character, some of them, unfortunately, as influential as the Marxist interpretation of history; for example, the racialist interpretation of history—another of those impressive

and all-explanatory theories which act upon weak minds like revelations.)

Thus the problem which I tried to solve by proposing the criterion of falsifiability was neither a problem of meaningfulness or significance, nor a problem of truth or acceptability. It was the problem of drawing a line (as well as this can be done) between the statements, or systems of statements, of the empirical sciences, and all other statements—whether they are of a religious or of a metaphysical character, or simply pseudo-scientific. Years later—it must have been in 1928 or 1929—I called this first problem of mine the '*problem of demarcation*'. The criterion of falsifiability is a solution to this problem of demarcation, for it says that statements or systems of statements, in order to be ranked as scientific, must be capable of conflicting with possible, or conceivable, observations.

III.

Today I know, of course, that this *criterion of demarcation*—the criterion of testability, or falsifiability, or refutability—is far from obvious; for even now its significance is seldom realized. At that time, in 1920, it seemed to me almost trivial, although it solved for me an intellectual problem which had worried me deeply, and one which also had obvious practical consequences (for example, political ones). But I did not yet realize its full implications, or its philosophical significance. When I explained it to a fellow student of the Mathematics Department (now a distinguished mathematician in Great Britain), he suggested that I should publish it. At the time I thought this absurd; for I was convinced that my problem, since it was so important for me, must have agitated many scientists and philosophers who would surely have reached my rather obvious solution. That this was not the case I learnt from Wittgenstein's work, and from its reception; and so I published my results thirteen years later in the form of a criticism of Wittgenstein's *criterion of meaningfulness*.

Wittgenstein, as you all know, tried to show in the *Tractatus*[16] (see for example his propositions

---

and—in his own eyes—a miracle worker and a god. He believed in the immortality of the soul and is said to have committed suicide by flinging himself into the volcano Mount Etna. Parmenides of Elea, who was born about twenty years before Empedocles, was perhaps the most important Greek philosopher before Socrates. In his poem "On Nature" he wrote that a goddess had instructed him that, since nature cannot both be and not be, it must necessarily be, and he concluded from this that reality must be perfect, unchanging, motionless, and eternal.

13 The dimension of time.

14 [Author's note] The case of astrology, nowadays a typical pseudo-science, may illustrate this point. It was attacked, by Aristotelians and other rationalists, down to Newton's day, for the wrong reason—for its now accepted assertion that the planets had an 'influence' upon terrestrial ('sublunar') events. In fact Newton's theory of gravity, and especially the lunar theory of the tides, was historically speaking an offspring of astrological lore. Newton, it seems, was most reluctant to adopt a theory which came from the same stable as for example the theory that 'influenza' epidemics are due to an astral 'influence'. And Galileo, no doubt for the same reason, actually rejected the lunar theory of the tides; and his misgivings about Kepler may easily be explained by his misgivings about astrology.

15 Here "genetic" means "having to do with the origins or cause of something."

16 Ludwig Wittgenstein (1889–1951) was one of the twentieth century's most charismatic and influential philosophers. Popper is referring to the *Tractatus*

6.53; 6.54; and 5) that all so-called philosophical or metaphysical propositions were actually non-propositions or pseudo-propositions: that they were senseless or meaningless. All genuine (or meaningful) propositions were truth functions[17] of the elementary or atomic propositions which described 'atomic facts'—i.e., facts which can in principle be ascertained by observation. In other words, meaningful propositions were fully reducible to elementary or atomic propositions which were simple statements describing possible states of affairs, and which could in principle be established or rejected by observation. If we call a statement an 'observation statement' not only if it states an actual observation but also if it states anything that *may* be observed, we shall have to say (according to the *Tractatus*, 5 and 4.52) that every genuine proposition must be a truth-function of, and therefore deducible from, observation statements. All other apparent propositions will be meaningless pseudo-propositions; in fact they will be nothing but nonsensical gibberish.

This idea was used by Wittgenstein for a characterization of science, as opposed to philosophy: We read (for example in 4.11, where natural science is taken to stand in opposition to philosophy): 'The totality of true propositions is the total natural science (or the totality of the natural sciences).' This means that the propositions which belong to science are those deducible from *true* observation statements; they are those propositions which can be *verified* by true observation statements. Could we know all true observation statements, we should also know all that may be asserted by natural science.

This amounts to a crude verifiability criterion of demarcation. To make it slightly less crude, it could be amended thus: 'The statements which may possibly fall within the province of science are those which may possibly be verified by observation statements; and these statements, again, coincide with the class of *all* genuine or meaningful statements.' For this approach, then, *verifiability, meaningfulness, and scientific character all coincide.*

I personally was never interested in the so-called problem of meaning; on the contrary, it appeared to me a verbal problem, a typical pseudo-problem. I was interested only in the problem of demarcation, i.e., in finding a criterion of the scientific character of theories. It was just this interest which made me see at once that Wittgenstein's verifiability criterion of meaning was intended to play the part of a criterion of demarcation as well; and which made me see that, as such, it was totally inadequate, even if all misgivings about the dubious concept of meaning were set aside. For Wittgenstein's criterion of demarcation—to use my own terminology in this context—is verifiability, or deducibility from observation statements. But this criterion is too narrow (*and* too wide): it excludes from science practically everything that is, in fact, characteristic of it (while failing in effect to exclude astrology). No scientific theory can ever be deduced from observation statements, or be described as a truth-function of observation statements.

All this I pointed out on various occasions to Wittgensteinians and members of the Vienna Circle.[18] In 1931–32 I summarized my ideas in a largish book

---

Logico-Philosophicus, published in 1921 and the only book Wittgenstein completed during his lifetime.

17 A 'truth function' is a function from the truth values of input sentences to the truth value of an output sentence. (The two possible 'truth values' are, normally, either True or False.) Thus, a compound sentence is 'truth functional' if its truth value is entirely determined by the truth values of its component sentences: for example, the sentence "*A* and *B*" is true just in case *A* and *B* both have the value 'True,' and is false otherwise. (On the other hand, many other sentences are not, at least on the face of it, truth functional in this way: for example, "*A* because of *B*" does not have its truth value determined entirely by the truth values of *A* and *B*.)

18 The Vienna Circle was a group of like-minded philosophers and scientists who met for Saturday morning seminars in Vienna from 1923 until the late 1930s. Strongly influenced by Wittgenstein's *Tractatus*, they held that the task of philosophy was not the production of new knowledge but the clarification of the basic concepts of science and ordinary language, and one of their most important goals was the unification of science under a single logical language. They spread their ideas through a series of congresses and in a journal, started in 1930, called *Erkenntnis*.

(read by several members of the Circle but never published; although part of it was incorporated in my *Logic of Scientific Discovery*); and in 1933 I published a letter to the Editor of *Erkenntnis* in which I tried to compress into two pages my ideas on the problems of demarcation and induction.[19] In this letter and elsewhere I described the problem of meaning as a pseudo-problem, in contrast to the problem of demarcation. But my contribution was classified by members of the Circle as a proposal to replace the verifiability criterion of *meaning* by a falsifiability criterion of *meaning*—which effectively made nonsense of my views.[20] My protests that I was trying to solve, not their pseudo-problem of meaning, but the problem of demarcation, were of no avail.

My attacks upon verification had some effect, however. They soon led to complete confusion in the camp of the verificationist philosophers of sense and nonsense. The original proposal of verifiability as the criterion of meaning was at least clear, simple, and forceful. The modifications and shifts which were now introduced were the very opposite.[21] This, I should say, is now seen even by the participants. But since I am usually quoted as one of them I wish to repeat that although I created this confusion I never participated in it. Neither falsifiability nor testability were proposed by me as criteria of meaning; and although I may plead guilty to having introduced both terms into the discussion, it was not I who introduced them into the theory of meaning.

Criticism of my alleged views was widespread and highly successful. I have yet to meet a criticism of my views.[22] Meanwhile, testability is being widely accepted as a criterion of demarcation.

---

19 [Author's note] My *Logic of Scientific Discovery* (1959, 1960, 1961), here usually referred to as *L.Sc.D.*, is the translation of *Logik der Forschung* (1934), with a number of additional notes and appendices, including (on pp. 312–14) the letter to the Editor of *Erkenntnis* mentioned here in the text which was first published in *Erkenntnis*, 3, 1933, pp. 426 f. Concerning my never published book mentioned here in the text, see R. Carnap's paper 'Ueber Protokollsätze' (On Protocol-Sentences), *Erkenntnis*, 3, 1932, pp. 215–28 where he gives an outline of my theory on pp. 223–28, and accepts it. He calls my theory 'procedure B', and says (p. 224, top): 'Starting from a point of view different from Neurath's' (who developed what Carnap calls on p. 223 'procedure A'), 'Popper developed procedure B as part of his system.' And after describing in detail my theory of tests, Carnap sums up his views as follows (p. 228): 'After weighing the various arguments here discussed, it appears to me that the second language form with procedure B—that is in the form here described—is the most adequate among the forms of scientific language at present advocated … in the … theory of knowledge.' This paper of Carnap's contained the first published report of my theory of critical testing. (See also my critical remarks in *L.Sc.D.*, note 1 to section 29, p. 104, where the date '1933' should read '1932'; and ch. 11, below, text to note 39.)

20 [Author's note] Wittgenstein's example of a nonsensical pseudo-proposition is: 'Socrates is identical'. Obviously, 'Socrates is not identical' must also be nonsense. Thus the negation of any nonsense will be nonsense, and that of a meaningful statement will be meaningful. *But the negation of a testable (or falsifiable) statement need not be testable*, as was pointed out, first in my *L.Sc.D.*, (e.g., pp. 38 f.) and later by my critics. The confusion caused by taking testability as a criterion of *meaning* rather than of *demarcation* can easily be imagined.

21 [Author's note] The most recent example of the way in which the history of this problem is misunderstood is A.R. White's 'Note on Meaning and Verification', *Mind*, 63, 1954, pp. 66 ff. J.L. Evans's article, *Mind*, 62, 1953, pp. I ff., which Mr. White criticizes, is excellent in my opinion, and unusually perceptive. Understandably enough, neither of the authors can quite reconstruct the story. (Some hints may be found in my *Open Society*, notes 46, 51 and 52 to ch. 11; and a fuller analysis in ch. 11 of the present volume.)

22 [Author's note] In *L.Sc.D.* I discussed, and replied to, some likely objections which afterwards were indeed raised, without reference to my replies. One of them is the contention that the falsification of a natural law is just as impossible as its verification. The answer is that this objection mixes two entirely different levels of analysis (like the objection that mathematical demonstrations are impossible since checking, no matter

IV.

I have discussed the problem of demarcation in some detail because I believe that its solution is the key to most of the fundamental problems of the philosophy of science. I am going to give you later a list of some of these other problems, but only one of them—the *problem of induction*—can be discussed here at any length.

I had become interested in the problem of induction in 1923. Although this problem is very closely connected with the problem of demarcation, I did not fully appreciate the connection for about five years.

I approached the problem of induction through Hume. Hume, I felt, was perfectly right in pointing out that induction cannot be logically justified. He held that there can be no valid logical[23] arguments allow-

ing us to establish '*that those instances, of which we have had no experience, resemble those, of which we have had experience*'. Consequently '*even after the observation of the frequent or constant conjunction of objects, we have no reason to draw any inference concerning any object beyond those of which we have had experience*'. For 'shou'd it be said that we have experience'[24]—experience teaching us that objects constantly conjoined with certain other objects continue to be so conjoined—then, Hume says, 'I wou'd renew my question, *why from this experience we form any conclusion beyond those past instances, of which we have had experience*'. This 'renew'd question' indicates that an attempt to justify the practice of induction by an appeal to experience must lead to an *infinite regress*. As a result we can say that theories can never be inferred from observation statements, or rationally justified by them.

I found Hume's refutation of inductive inference clear and conclusive. But I felt completely dissatisfied with his psychological explanation of induction in terms of custom or habit.

It has often been noticed that this explanation of Hume's is philosophically not very satisfactory. Hume, however, without doubt intended it as a *psychological* rather than a philosophical theory; for it tries to give a causal explanation of a psychological fact—*the fact that we believe in laws*, in statements asserting regularities or constantly conjoined kinds of events. Hume explains this fact by asserting that it is due to (i.e., constantly conjoined with) custom or habit. But even this reformulation of Hume's theory is unacceptable; for what I have just called a 'psychological fact' may itself be described as a custom or habit—our custom or our habit of believing in laws or regularities. It is neither surprising nor enlightening to hear that such a custom or habit can be explained as due to custom or habit, or conjoined with a custom or habit (even though a different one). Only when we

---

how often repeated, can never make it quite certain that we have not overlooked a mistake). On the first level, there is a logical asymmetry: one singular statement—say about the perihelion of Mercury—can formally falsify Kepler's laws; but these cannot be formally verified by any number of singular statements. The attempt to minimize this asymmetry can only lead to confusion. On another level, we may hesitate to accept any statement, even the simplest observation statement; and we may point out that every statement involves *interpretation in the light of theories*, and that it is therefore uncertain. This does not affect the fundamental asymmetry, but it is important: most dissectors of the heart before Harvey observed the wrong things—those, which they expected to see. There can never be anything like a completely safe observation, free from the dangers of misinterpretation. (This is one of the reasons why the theory of induction does not work.) The 'empirical basis' consists largely of a mixture of *theories* of lower degree of universality (of 'reproducible effects'). But the fact remains that, relative to whatever basis the investigator may accept (at his peril), he can test his theory only by trying to refute it.

23   [Author's note] Hume does not say 'logical' but 'demonstrative', a terminology which, I think, is a little misleading. The following two quotations are from the *Treatise of Human Nature*, Book I, Part III, sections vi and xii. (The italics are all Hume's.)

24   [Author's note] This and the next quotation are from *loc. cit.*, section vi. See also Hume's *Enquiry Concerning Human Understanding*, section IV, Part II, and his *Abstract*, edited 1938 by J.M. Keynes and P. Sraffa, p. 15, and quoted in *L.Sc.D.*, new appendix *vii, text to note 6.

remember that the words 'custom' and 'habit' are used by Hume, as they are in ordinary language, not merely to *describe* regular behaviour, but rather to *theorize about its origin* (ascribed to frequent repetition), can we reformulate his psychological theory in a more satisfactory way. Hume's theory becomes then the thesis that, like other habits, *our habit of believing in laws is the product of frequent repetition*—of the repeated observation that things of a certain kind are constantly conjoined with things of another kind.

This genetic-psychological theory is, as indicated, incorporated in ordinary language, and it is therefore hardly as revolutionary as Hume thought. It is no doubt an extremely popular psychological theory—part of 'common sense', one might say. But in spite of my love of both common sense and Hume, I felt convinced that this psychological theory was mistaken; and that it was in fact refutable on purely logical grounds.

Hume's psychology, which is the popular psychology, was mistaken, I felt, about at least three different things: (*a*) the typical result of repetition; (*b*) the genesis of habits; and especially (*c*) the character of those experiences or modes of behaviour which may be described as 'believing in a law' or 'expecting a law-like succession of events'.

(*a*) The typical result of repetition—say, of repeating a difficult passage on the piano—is that movements which at first needed attention are in the end executed without attention. We might say that the process becomes radically abbreviated, and ceases to be conscious: it becomes automatized, 'physiological'. Such a development, far from creating a conscious expectation of law-like succession, or a belief in a law, may on the contrary begin with a conscious belief and destroy it by making it superfluous. In learning to ride a bicycle we may start with the belief that we can avoid falling if we steer in the direction in which we threaten to fall, and this belief may be useful for guiding our movements. After sufficient practice we may forget the rule; in any case, we do not need it any longer. On the other hand, even if it is true that repetition may create unconscious expectations, these become conscious only if something goes wrong (we may not have heard the clock tick, but we may hear that it has stopped).

(*b*) Habits or customs do not, as a rule, *originate* in repetition. Even the habit of walking, or of speaking, or of feeding at certain hours, *begins* before repetition can play any part whatever. We may say, if we like, that they deserve to be called 'habits' or 'customs' only after repetition has played its typical part described under (*a*); but we must not say that the practices in question *originated* as the result of many repetitions.

(*c*) Belief in a law is not quite the same thing as behaviour which betrays an expectation of a law-like succession of events; but these two are sufficiently closely connected to be treated together. They may, perhaps, in exceptional cases, result from a mere repetition of sense impressions (as in the case of the stopping clock). I was prepared to concede this, but I contended that normally, and in most cases of any interest, they cannot be so explained. As Hume admits, even a single striking observation may be sufficient to create a belief or an expectation—a fact which he tries to explain as due to an inductive habit, formed as the result of a vast number of long repetitive sequences which had been experienced at an earlier period of life.[25] But this, I contended, was merely his attempt to explain away unfavourable facts which threatened his theory; an unsuccessful attempt, since these unfavourable facts could be observed in very young animals and babies—as early, indeed, as we like. 'A lighted cigarette was held near the noses of the young puppies', reports F. Bäge. 'They sniffed at it once, turned tail, and nothing would induce them to come back to the source of the smell and to sniff again. A few days later, they reacted to the mere sight of a cigarette or even of a rolled piece of white paper, by bounding away, and sneezing.'[26] If we try to explain cases like this by postulating a vast number of long repetitive sequences at a still earlier age we are not only romancing, but forgetting that in the clever puppies' short lives there must be room not only for repetition but also for a great deal of novelty, and consequently of non-repetition.

---

25 [Author's note] *Treatise*, section xiii; section xv, rule 4.
26 [Author's note] F. Bäge, 'Zur Entwicklung, etc.', *Zeitschrift f. Hundeforschung*, 1933; cp. D. Katz, *Animals and Men*, ch. VI, footnote.

But it is not only that certain empirical facts do not support Hume; there are decisive arguments of a *purely logical* nature against his psychological theory.

The central idea of Hume's psychological theory is that of *repetition, based upon similarity* (or 'resemblance'). This idea is used in a very uncritical way. We are led to think of the water-drop that hollows the stone: of sequences of unquestionably like events slowly forcing themselves upon us, as does the tick of the clock. But we ought to realize that in a psychological theory such as Hume's, only repetition-for-us, based upon similarity-for-us, can be allowed to have any effect upon us. We must respond to situations as if they were equivalent; *take* them as similar; *interpret* them as repetitions. In this way they become for us *functionally equal*. The clever puppies, we may assume, showed by their response, their way of acting or of reacting, that they recognized or interpreted the second situation as a repetition of the first: that they expected its main element, the objectionable smell, to be present. The situation was a repetition-for-them because they responded to it by *anticipating* its similarity to the previous one.

This apparently psychological criticism has a purely logical basis which may be summed up in the following simple argument. (It happens to be the one from which I originally started my criticism.) The kind of repetition envisaged by Hume can never be perfect; the cases he has in mind cannot be cases of perfect sameness; they can only be cases of similarity. Thus *they are repetitions only from a certain point of view*. (What has the effect upon me of a repetition may not have this effect upon a spider.) But this means that, for logical reasons, there must always be a point of view—such as a system of expectations, anticipations, assumptions, or interests—*before* there can be any repetition; which point of view, consequently, cannot be merely the result of repetition. (See now also appendix *x, (1), to my *L.Sc.D.*)

We must thus replace, for the purposes of a psychological theory of the origin of our beliefs, the naïve idea of events which *are* similar by the idea of events to which we react by *interpreting* them as being similar. But if this is so (and I can see no escape from it) then Hume's psychological theory of induction leads to an infinite regress, precisely analogous to that other infinite regress which was discovered by Hume himself, and used by him to explode the logical theory of induction. For what do we wish to explain? In the example of the puppies we wish to explain behaviour which may be described as *recognizing or interpreting* a situation as a repetition of another. Clearly, we cannot hope to explain this by an appeal to earlier repetitions, once we realize that the earlier repetitions must also have been repetitions-for-them, so that precisely the same problem arises again: that of *recognizing or interpreting* a situation as a repetition of another.

To put it more concisely, similarity-for-us is the product of a response involving interpretations (which may be inadequate) and anticipations or expectations (which may never be fulfilled). It is therefore impossible to explain anticipations, or expectations, as resulting from many repetitions, as suggested by Hume. For even the first repetition-for-us must be based upon similarity-for-us, and therefore upon expectations—precisely the kind of thing we wished to explain. (Expectations must come first, *before* repetitions.)

We see that there is an infinite regress involved in Hume's psychological theory.

Hume, I felt, had never accepted the full force of his own logical analysis. Having refuted the logical idea of induction he was faced with the following problem: how do we actually obtain our knowledge, as a matter of psychological fact, if induction is a procedure which is logically invalid and rationally unjustifiable? There are two possible answers: (1) We obtain our knowledge by a non-inductive procedure. This answer would have allowed Hume to retain a form of rationalism. (2) We obtain our knowledge by repetition and induction, and therefore by a logically invalid and rationally unjustifiable procedure, so that all apparent knowledge is merely a kind of belief—belief based on habit. This answer would imply that even scientific knowledge is irrational, so that rationalism is absurd, and must be given up. (I shall not discuss here the age-old attempts, now again fashionable, to get out of the difficulty by asserting that though induction is of course logically invalid if we mean by 'logic' the same as 'deductive logic', it is not irrational by its own standards, and as inductive logic admits; as may be seen from the fact that every reasonable man applies it *as a matter of fact*. As against this, it was Hume's great achievement to break this uncritical identification of the question of fact—*quid facti?*[27]—and the question of justification or validity—*quid juris?*[28] [See below, point (13) of the appendix to the present chapter (not reprinted here).])

It seems that Hume never seriously considered the first alternative. Having cast out the logical theory of induction by repetition he struck a bargain with common sense, meekly allowing the re-entry of induction by repetition, in the guise of a psychological fact. I proposed to turn the tables upon this theory of Hume's. Instead of explaining our propensity to expect regularities as the result of repetition, I proposed to explain repetition-for-us as the result of our propensity to expect regularities and to search for them.

Thus I was led by purely logical considerations to replace the psychological theory of induction by the following view. Without waiting, passively, for repetitions to impress or impose regularities upon us, we actively try to impose regularities upon the world. We try to discover similarities in it, and to interpret it in terms of laws invented by us. Without waiting for premises we jump to conclusions. These may have to be discarded later, should observation show that they are wrong.

This was a theory of trial and error—of *conjectures and refutations*. It made it possible to understand why our attempts to force interpretations upon the world were logically prior to the observation of similarities. Since there were logical reasons behind this procedure, I thought that it would apply in the field of science also; that scientific theories were not the digest of observations, but that they were inventions—conjectures boldly put forward for trial, to be eliminated if they clashed with observations; with observations which were rarely accidental but as a rule undertaken with the definite intention of testing a theory by obtaining, if possible, a decisive refutation.

V.

The belief that science proceeds from observation to theory is still so widely and so firmly held that my denial of it is often met with incredulity. I have even been suspected of being insincere—of denying what nobody in his senses can doubt.

But in fact the belief that we can start with pure observations alone, without anything in the nature of a theory, is absurd; as may be illustrated by the story of the man who dedicated his life to natural science, wrote down everything he could observe, and bequeathed his priceless collection of observations to the Royal Society to be used as inductive evidence. This story should show us that though beetles may profitably be collected, observations may not.

Twenty-five years ago I tried to bring home the same point to a group of physics students in Vienna by beginning a lecture with the following instructions: 'Take pencil and paper; carefully observe, and write down what you have observed!' They asked, of course, *what* I wanted them to observe. Clearly the instruction, 'Observe!' is absurd.[29] (It is not even idiomatic, unless the object of the transitive verb can be taken as understood.) Observation is always selective. It needs a chosen object, a definite task, an interest, a point of view, a problem. And its description presupposes a descriptive language, with property words; it presupposes similarity and classification, which in their turn presuppose interests, points of view, and problems. 'A hungry animal', writes Katz,[30] 'divides the environment into edible and inedible things. An animal in flight sees roads to escape and hiding places.... Generally speaking, objects change ... according to the needs of the animal.' We may add that objects can be classified, and can become similar or dissimilar, *only* in this way—by being related to needs and interests. This rule applies not only to animals but also to scientists: For the animal a point of view is provided by its needs, the task of the moment, and its expectations; for the scientist by his theoretical interests, the special problem under investigation, his conjectures and anticipations, and the theories which he accepts as a kind of background: his frame of reference, his 'horizon of expectations'.

The problem 'Which comes first, the hypothesis (*H*) or the observation (*O*)?' is soluble; as is the problem, 'Which comes first, the hen (*H*) or the egg (*O*)?'.

---

27 What is done?

28 What ought to be done?

29 [Author's note] See section 30 of *L.Sc.D.*

30 [Author's note] Katz, *loc. cit.*

The reply to the latter is, 'An earlier kind of egg'; to the former, 'An earlier kind of hypothesis'. It is quite true that any particular hypothesis we choose will have been preceded by observations—the observations, for example, which it is designed to explain. But these observations, in their turn, presupposed the adoption of a frame of reference: a frame of expectations: a frame of theories. If they were significant, if they created a need for explanation and thus gave rise to the invention of a hypothesis, it was because they could not be explained within the old theoretical framework, the old horizon of expectations. There is no danger here of an infinite regress. Going back to more and more primitive theories and myths we shall in the end find unconscious, *inborn* expectations.

The theory of inborn *ideas* is absurd, I think; but every organism has inborn *reactions* or *responses*; and among them, responses adapted to impending events. These responses we may describe as 'expectations' without implying that these 'expectations' are conscious. The new-born baby 'expects', in this sense, to be fed (and, one could even argue, to be protected and loved). In view of the close relation between expectation and knowledge we may even speak in quite a reasonable sense of 'inborn knowledge'. This 'knowledge', however, is not *valid a priori*;[31] an inborn expectation, no matter how strong and specific, may be mistaken. (The newborn child may be abandoned, and starve.)

Thus we are born with expectations; with 'knowledge' which, although not *valid a priori*, is *psychologically or genetically a priori*, i.e., prior to all observational experience. One of the most important of these expectations is the expectation of finding a regularity. It is connected with an inborn propensity to look out for regularities, or with a *need* to *find* regularities, as we may see from the pleasure of the child who satisfies this need.

This 'instinctive' expectation of finding regularities, which is psychologically *a priori*, corresponds very closely to the 'law of causality' which Kant believed to be part of our mental outfit and to be *a*

priori valid. One might thus be inclined to say that Kant failed to distinguish between psychologically *a priori* ways of thinking or responding and *a priori* valid beliefs. But I do not think that his mistake was quite as crude as that. For the expectation of finding regularities is not only psychologically *a priori*, but also logically *a priori*: it is logically prior to all observational experience, for it is prior to any recognition of similarities, as we have seen; and all observation involves the recognition of similarities (or dissimilarities). But in spite of being logically *a priori* in this sense the expectation is not valid *a priori*. For it may fail: we can easily construct an environment (it would be a lethal one) which, compared with our ordinary environment, is so chaotic that we completely fail to find regularities. (All natural laws could remain valid: environments of this kind have been used in the animal experiments mentioned in the next section.)

Thus Kant's reply to Hume came near to being right; for the distinction between an *a priori* valid expectation and one which is both genetically *and* logically prior to observation, but not *a priori* valid, is really somewhat subtle. But Kant proved too much. In trying to show how knowledge is possible, he proposed a theory which had the unavoidable consequence that our quest for knowledge must necessarily succeed, which is clearly mistaken. When Kant said, 'Our intellect does not draw its laws from nature but imposes its laws upon nature', he was right. But in thinking that these laws are necessarily true, or that we necessarily succeed in imposing them upon nature, he was wrong.[32] Nature very often resists quite success-

---

31 It is not something that can be known with certainty, even independently of any experience of the world, to be true.

32 [Author's note] Kant believed that Newton's dynamics was *a priori* valid. (See his *Metaphysical Foundations of Natural Science*, published between the first and the second editions of the *Critique of Pure Reason*.) But if, as he thought, we can explain the validity of Newton's theory by the fact that our intellect imposes its laws upon nature, it follows, I think, that our intellect must succeed in this; which makes it hard to understand why *a priori* knowledge such as Newton's should be so hard to come by. A somewhat fuller statement of this criticism can be found in ch. 2, especially section x, and chs. 7 and 8 of the present volume [*Conjectures and Refutations*].

fully, forcing us to discard our laws as refuted; but if we live we may try again.

To sum up this logical criticism of Hume's psychology of induction we may consider the idea of building an induction machine. Placed in a simplified 'world' (for example, one of sequences of coloured counters) such a machine may through repetition 'learn', or even 'formulate', laws of succession which hold in its 'world'. If such a machine can be constructed (and I have no doubt that it can) then, it might be argued, my theory must be wrong; for if a machine is capable of performing inductions on the basis of repetition, there can be no logical reasons preventing us from doing the same.

The argument sounds convincing, but it is mistaken. In constructing an induction machine we, the architects of the machine, must decide *a priori* what constitutes its 'world'; what things are to be taken as similar or equal; and what *kind* of 'laws' we wish the machine to be able to 'discover' in its 'world'. In other words we must build into the machine a framework determining what is relevant or interesting in its world: the machine will have its 'inborn' selection principles. The problems of similarity will have been solved for it by its makers who thus have interpreted the 'world' for the machine.

VI.

Our propensity to look out for regularities, and to impose laws upon nature, leads to the psychological phenomenon of *dogmatic thinking* or, more generally, dogmatic behaviour: we expect regularities everywhere and attempt to find them even where there are none; events which do not yield to these attempts we are inclined to treat as a kind of 'background noise'; and we stick to our expectations even when they are inadequate and we ought to accept defeat. This dogmatism is to some extent necessary. It is demanded by a situation which can only be dealt with by forcing our conjectures upon the world. Moreover, this dogmatism allows us to approach a good theory in stages, by way of approximations: if we accept defeat too easily, we may prevent ourselves from finding that we were very nearly right.

It is clear that this *dogmatic attitude*, which makes us stick to our first impressions, is indicative of a strong belief; while a *critical attitude*, which is ready to modify its tenets, which admits doubt and demands tests, is indicative of a weaker belief. Now according to Hume's theory, and to the popular theory, the strength of a belief should be a product of repetition; thus it should always grow with experience, and always be greater in less primitive persons. But dogmatic thinking, an uncontrolled wish to impose regularities, a manifest pleasure in rites and in repetition as such, are characteristic of primitives and children; and increasing experience and maturity sometimes create an attitude of caution and criticism rather than of dogmatism.

I may perhaps mention here a point of agreement with psycho-analysis. Psycho-analysts assert that neurotics and others interpret the world in accordance with a personal set pattern which is not easily given up, and which can often be traced back to early childhood. A pattern or scheme which was adopted very early in life is maintained throughout, and every new experience is interpreted in terms of it; verifying it, as it were, and contributing to its rigidity. This is a description of what I have called the dogmatic attitude, as distinct from the critical attitude, which shares with the dogmatic attitude the quick adoption of a schema of expectations—a myth, perhaps, or a conjecture or hypothesis—but which is ready to modify it, to correct it, and even to give it up. I am inclined to suggest that most neuroses may be due to a partially arrested development of the critical attitude; to an arrested rather than a natural dogmatism; to resistance to demands for the modification and adjustment of certain schematic interpretations and responses. This resistance in its turn may perhaps be explained, in some cases, as due to an injury or shock, resulting in fear and in an increased need for assurance or certainty, analogous to the way in which an injury to a limb makes us afraid to move it, so that it becomes stiff. (It might even be argued that the case of the limb is not merely analogous to the dogmatic response, but an instance of it.) The explanation of any concrete case will have to take into account the weight of the difficulties involved in making the necessary adjustments—difficulties which may be considerable, especially in a complex and changing world: we know from experiments on animals that varying degrees of neurotic behaviour may be produced at will by correspondingly varying difficulties.

I found many other links between the psychology of knowledge and psychological fields which are often considered remote from it—for example the psychology of art and music; in fact, my ideas about induction originated in a conjecture about the evolution of Western polyphony.[33] But you will be spared this story.

VII.

My logical criticism of Hume's psychological theory, and the considerations connected with it (most of which I elaborated in 1926–27, in a thesis entitled 'On Habit and Belief in Laws'[34]) may seem a little removed from the field of the philosophy of science. But the distinction between dogmatic and critical thinking, or the dogmatic and the critical attitude, brings us right back to our central problem. For the dogmatic attitude is clearly related to the tendency to *verify* our laws and schemata by seeking to apply them and to confirm them, even to the point of neglecting refutations, whereas the critical attitude is one of readiness to change them—to test them; to refute them; to *falsify* them, if possible. This suggests that we may identify the critical attitude with the scientific attitude, and the dogmatic attitude with the one which we have described as pseudo-scientific.

It further suggests that genetically speaking the pseudo-scientific attitude is more primitive than, and prior to, the scientific attitude: that it is a pre-scientific attitude. And this primitivity or priority also has its logical aspect. For the critical attitude is not so much opposed to the dogmatic attitude as super-imposed upon it: criticism must be directed against existing and influential beliefs in need of critical revision—in other words, dogmatic beliefs. A critical attitude needs for its raw material, as it were, theories or beliefs which are held more or less dogmatically.

Thus science must begin with myths, and with the criticism of myths; neither with the collection of observations, nor with the invention of experiments, but with the critical discussion of myths, and of magical techniques and practices. The scientific tradition is distinguished from the pre-scientific tradition in having two layers. Like the latter, it passes on its theories; but it also passes on a critical attitude towards them. The theories are passed on, not as dogmas, but rather with the challenge to discuss them and improve upon them. This tradition is Hellenic:[35] it may be traced back to Thales,[36] founder of the first *school* (I do not mean 'of the first *philosophical* school', but simply 'of the first school') which was not mainly concerned with the preservation of a dogma.[37]

The critical attitude, the tradition of free discussion of theories with the aim of discovering their weak spots so that they may be improved upon, is the attitude of reasonableness, of rationality. It makes far-reaching use of both verbal argument and observation—of observation in the interest of argument, however. The Greeks' discovery of the critical method gave rise at first to the mistaken hope that it would lead to the solution of all the great old problems; that it would establish certainty; that it would help to *prove* our theories, to *justify* them. But this hope was a residue of the dogmatic way of thinking; in fact nothing can be justified or proved (outside of mathematics and logic). The demand for rational proofs in science indicates a failure to keep distinct the broad realm of rationality and the narrow realm of rational certainty: it is an untenable, an unreasonable demand.

Nevertheless, the role of logical argument, of deductive logical reasoning, remains all-important for the critical approach; not because it allows us to prove our theories, or to infer them from observation

---

33 Music with two or more independent melodic parts sounded together.

34 [Author's note] A thesis submitted under the title '*Gewohnheit and Gesetzerlebnis*' to the Institute of Education of the City of Vienna in 1927. (Unpublished.)

35 Ancient Greek (from *Hellen*, a Greek).

36 Often described as the first philosopher of the Western tradition, Thales of Miletus flourished around 585 BCE. He is thought to be the first Western thinker in recorded history to attempt to give naturalistic, rather than religious, explanations for natural phenomena (such as magnetism).

37 [Author's note] Further comments on these developments may be found in chs. 4 and 5, below.

statements, but because only by purely deductive reasoning is it possible for us to discover what our theories imply, and thus to criticize them effectively. Criticism, I said, is an attempt to find the weak spots in a theory, and these, as a rule, can be found only in the more remote logical consequences which can be derived from it. It is here that purely logical reasoning plays an important part in science.

Hume was right in stressing that our theories cannot be validly inferred from what we can know to be true—neither from observations nor from anything else. He concluded from this that our belief in them was irrational. If 'belief' means here our inability to doubt our natural laws, and the constancy of natural regularities, then Hume is again right: this kind of dogmatic belief has, one might say, a physiological rather than a rational basis. If, however, the term 'belief' is taken to cover our critical acceptance of scientific theories—a *tentative* acceptance combined with an eagerness to revise the theory if we succeed in designing a test which it cannot pass—then Hume was wrong. In such an acceptance of theories there is nothing irrational. There is not even anything irrational in relying for practical purposes upon well-tested theories, for no more rational course of action is open to us.

Assume that we have deliberately made it our task to live in this unknown world of ours; to adjust ourselves to it as well as we can; to take advantage of the opportunities we can find in it; and to explain it, if possible (we need not assume that it is), and as far as possible, with the help of laws and explanatory theories. *If we have made this our task, then there is no more rational procedure than the method of trial and error—of conjecture and refutation*: of boldly proposing theories; of trying our best to show that these are erroneous; and of accepting them tentatively if our critical efforts are unsuccessful.

From the point of view here developed all laws, all theories, remain essentially tentative, or conjectural, or hypothetical, even when we feel unable to doubt them any longer. Before a theory has been refuted we can never know in what way it may have to be modified. That the sun will always rise and set within twenty-four hours is still proverbial as a law 'established by induction beyond reasonable

doubt'. It is odd that this example is still in use, though it may have served well enough in the days of Aristotle and Pytheas of Massalia[38]—the great traveller who for centuries was called a liar because of his tales of Thule, the land of the frozen sea and the *midnight sun*.

The method of trial and error is not, of course, simply identical with the scientific or critical approach—with the method of conjecture and refutation. The method of trial and error is applied not only by Einstein but, in a more dogmatic fashion, by the amoeba also. The difference lies not so much in the trials as in a critical and constructive attitude towards errors; errors which the scientist consciously and cautiously tries to uncover in order to refute his theories with searching arguments, including appeals to the most severe experimental tests which his theories and his ingenuity permit him to design.

The critical attitude might be described as the result of a conscious attempt to make our theories, our conjectures, suffer in our stead in the struggle for the survival of the fittest. It gives us a chance to survive the elimination of an inadequate hypothesis—when a more dogmatic attitude would eliminate it by eliminating us. (There is a touching story of an Indian community which disappeared because of its belief in the holiness of life, including that of tigers.) We thus obtain the fittest theory within our reach by the elimination of those which are less fit. (By 'fitness' I do not mean merely 'usefulness' but truth; see chapters 3 and 10, below.) I do not think that this procedure is irrational or in need of any further rational justification.

VIII.

Let us now turn from our logical criticism of the *psychology of experience* to our real problem—the problem of the *logic of science*. Although some of the things I have said may help us here, in so far as they may have eliminated certain psychological prejudices

---

38 Aristotle lived from 384 to 322 BCE, and Pytheas flourished around 310 BCE. Pytheas described Thule as being six days sail north of Britain, and the ancients thought of it as being at the northernmost tip of the world; the land he visited was most probably Norway.

that favour induction, my treatment of the *logical problem of induction* is completely independent of this criticism, and of all psychological considerations. Provided you do not dogmatically believe in the alleged psychological fact that we make inductions, you may now forget my whole story with the exception of two logical points: my logical remarks on testability or falsifiability as the criterion of demarcation; and Hume's logical criticism of induction.

From what I have said it is obvious that there was a close link between the two problems which interested me at that time: demarcation, and induction or scientific method. It was easy to see that the method of science is criticism, i.e., attempted falsifications. Yet it took me a few years to notice that the two problems—of demarcation and of induction—were in a sense one.

Why, I asked, do so many scientists believe in induction? I found they did so because they believed natural science to be characterized by the inductive method—by a method starting from, and relying upon, long sequences of observations and experiments. They believed that the difference between genuine science and metaphysical or pseudo-scientific speculation depended solely upon whether or not the inductive method was employed. They believed (to put it in my own terminology) that only the inductive method could provide a satisfactory *criterion of demarcation*.

I recently came across an interesting formulation of this belief in a remarkable philosophical book by a great physicist—Max Born's *Natural Philosophy of Cause and Chance*.[39] He writes: 'Induction allows us to generalize a number of observations into a general rule: that night follows day and day follows night … But while everyday life has no definite criterion for the validity of an induction, … science has worked out a code, or rule of craft, for its application.' Born nowhere reveals the contents of this inductive code (which, as his wording shows, contains a 'definite criterion for the validity of an induction'); but he stresses that 'there is no logical argument' for its acceptance: 'it is a question of faith'; and he is therefore 'willing to

call induction a metaphysical principle'. But why does he believe that such a code of valid inductive rules must exist? This becomes clear when he speaks of the 'vast communities of people ignorant of, or rejecting, the rule of science, among them the members of anti-vaccination societies and believers in astrology. It is useless to argue with them; I cannot compel them to accept the same criteria of valid induction in which I believe: the code of scientific rules.' This makes it quite clear that *'valid induction' was here meant to serve as a criterion of demarcation between science and pseudo-science.*

But it is obvious that this rule or craft of 'valid induction' is not even metaphysical: it simply does not exist. No rule can ever guarantee that a generalization inferred from true observations, however often repeated, is true. (Born himself does not believe in the truth of Newtonian physics, in spite of its success, although he believes that it is based on induction.) And the success of science is not based upon rules of induction, but depends upon luck, ingenuity, and the purely deductive rules of critical argument.

I may summarize some of my conclusions as follows:

(1) Induction, i.e., inference based on many observations, is a myth. It is neither a psychological fact, nor a fact of ordinary life, nor one of scientific procedure.

(2) The actual procedure of science is to operate with conjectures: to jump to conclusions—often after one single observation (as noticed for example by Hume and Born).

(3) Repeated observations and experiments function in science as *tests* of our conjectures or hypotheses, i.e., as attempted refutations.

(4) The mistaken belief in induction is fortified by the need for a criterion of demarcation which, it is traditionally but wrongly believed, only the inductive method can provide.

(5) The conception of such an inductive method, like the criterion of verifiability, implies a faulty demarcation.

(6) None of this is altered in the least if we say that induction makes theories only probable rather than certain. (See especially chapter 10, below.)

---

39 [Author's note] Max Born, *Natural Philosophy of Cause and Chance*, Oxford, 1949, p. 7.

IX.

If, as I have suggested, the problem of induction is only an instance or facet of the problem of demarcation, then the solution to the problem of demarcation must provide us with a solution to the problem of induction. This is indeed the case, I believe, although it is perhaps not immediately obvious.

For a brief formulation of the problem of induction we can turn again to Born, who writes: '…no observation or experiment, however extended, can give more than a finite number of repetitions'; therefore, 'the statement of a law—B depends on A—always transcends experience. Yet this kind of statement is made everywhere and all the time, and sometimes from scanty material.'[40]

In other words, the logical problem of induction arises from (*a*) Hume's discovery (so well expressed by Born) that it is impossible to justify a law by observation or experiment, since it 'transcends experience'; (*b*) the fact that science proposes and uses laws 'everywhere and all the time'. (Like Hume, Born is struck by the 'scanty material', i.e., the few observed instances upon which the law may be based.) To this we have to add (*c*) *the principle of empiricism* which asserts that in science, only observation and experiment may decide upon the *acceptance or rejection* of scientific statements, including laws and theories.

These three principles, (*a*), (*b*), and (*c*), appear at first sight to clash; and this apparent clash constitutes the *logical problem of induction*.

Faced with this clash, Born gives up (*c*), the principle of empiricism (as Kant and many others, including Bertrand Russell, have done before him), in favour of what he calls a 'metaphysical principle'; a metaphysical principle which he does not even attempt to formulate; which he vaguely describes as a 'code or rule of craft'; and of which I have never seen any formulation which even looked promising and was not clearly untenable.

But in fact the principles (*a*) to (*c*) do not clash. We can see this the moment we realize that the acceptance by science of a law or of a theory is *tentative only*; which is to say that all laws and theories are conjec-

tures, or tentative *hypotheses* (a position which I have sometimes called 'hypotheticism'); and that we may reject a law or theory on the basis of new evidence, without necessarily discarding the old evidence which originally led us to accept it.[41]

The principle of empiricism (*c*) can be fully preserved, since the fate of a theory, its acceptance or rejection, is decided by observation and experiment—by the result of tests. So long as a theory stands up to the severest tests we can design, it is accepted; if it does not, it is rejected. But it is never inferred, in any sense, from the empirical evidence. There is neither a psychological nor a logical induction. *Only the falsity of the theory can be inferred from empirical evidence, and this inference is a purely deductive one.*

Hume showed that it is not possible to infer a theory from observation statements; but this does not affect the possibility of refuting a theory by observation statements. The full appreciation of this possibility makes the relation between theories and observations perfectly clear.

This solves the problem of the alleged clash between the principles (*a*), (*b*), and (*c*), and with it Hume's problem of induction.

X.

Thus the problem of induction is solved. But nothing seems less wanted than a simple solution to an age-old philosophical problem. Wittgenstein and his school hold that genuine philosophical problems do not exist;[42] from which it clearly follows that they cannot be solved. Others among my contemporaries do believe that there are philosophical problems, and respect them; but they seem to respect them too much; they seem to believe that they are insoluble, if not taboo; and they are shocked and horrified by the claim that there is a simple, neat, and lucid, solution

---

40   [Author's note] *Natural Philosophy of Cause and Chance*, p. 6.

41   [Author's note] I do not doubt that Born and many others would agree that theories are accepted only tentatively. But the widespread belief in induction shows that the far-reaching implications of this view are rarely seen.

42   [Author's note] Wittgenstein still held this belief in 1946; see note 8 to ch. 2, below.

to any of them. If there is a solution it must be deep, they feel, or at least complicated.

However this may be, I am still waiting for a simple, neat and lucid criticism of the solution which I published first in 1933 in my letter to the Editor of *Erkenntnis*,[43] and later in *The Logic of Scientific Discovery*.

Of course, one can invent new problems of induction, different from the one I have formulated and solved. (Its formulation was half its solution.) But I have yet to see any reformulation of the problem whose solution cannot be easily obtained from my old solution. I am now going to discuss some of these re-formulations.

One question which may be asked is this: how do we really jump from an observation statement to a theory?

Although this question appears to be psychological rather than philosophical, one can say something positive about it without invoking psychology. One can say first that the jump is not from an observation statement, but from a problem-situation, and that the theory must allow us *to explain* the observations which created the problem (that is, *to deduce* them from the theory strengthened by other accepted theories and by other observation statements, the so-called initial conditions). This leaves, of course, an immense number of possible theories, good and bad; and it thus appears that our question has not been answered.

But this makes it fairly clear that when we asked our question we had more in mind than, 'How do we jump from an observation statement to a theory?' The question we had in mind was, it now appears, 'How do we jump from an observation statement to a *good* theory?' But to this the answer is: by jumping first to *any* theory and then testing it, to find whether it is good or not; i.e., by repeatedly applying the critical method, eliminating many bad theories, and inventing many new ones. Not everybody is able to do this; but there is no other way.

Other questions have sometimes been asked. The original problem of induction, it was said, is the problem of *justifying* induction, i.e., of justifying inductive inference. If you answer this problem by

saying that what is called an 'inductive inference' is always invalid and therefore clearly not justifiable, the following new problem must arise: how do you justify your method of trial and error? Reply: the method of trial and error is a *method of eliminating false theories* by observation statements; and the justification for this is the purely logical relationship of deducibility which allows us to assert the falsity of universal statements if we accept the truth of singular ones.

Another question sometimes asked is this: why is it reasonable to prefer non-falsified statements to falsified ones? To this question some involved answers have been produced, for example pragmatic answers. But from a pragmatic point of view the question does not arise, since false theories often serve well enough: most formulae used in engineering or navigation are known to be false, although they may be excellent approximations and easy to handle; and they are used with confidence by people who know them to be false.

The only correct answer is the straightforward one: because we search for truth (even though we can never be sure we have found it), and because the falsified theories are known or believed to be false, while the non-falsified theories may still be true. Besides, we do not prefer *every* non-falsified theory—only one which, in the light of criticism, appears to be better than its competitors: which solves our problems, which is well tested, and of which we think, or rather conjecture or hope (considering other provisionally accepted theories), that it will stand up to further tests.

It has also been said that the problem of induction is, 'Why is it *reasonable* to believe that the future will be like the past?', and that a satisfactory answer to this question should make it plain that such a belief is, in fact, reasonable. My reply is that it is reasonable to believe that the future will be very different from the past in many vitally important respects. Admittedly it is perfectly reasonable to act on the assumption that it will, in many respects, be like the past, and that well-tested laws will continue to hold (since we can have no better assumption to act upon); but it is also reasonable to believe that such a course of action will lead us at times into severe trouble, since some of the laws upon which we now heavily rely may easily prove unreliable. (Remember the midnight sun!) One might even say that to judge from past experience,

---

43   [Author's note] See note 5 [19 in this text] above.

and from our general scientific knowledge, the future will *not* be like the past, in perhaps most of the ways which those have in mind who say that it will. Water will sometimes not quench thirst, and air will choke those who breathe it. An apparent way out is to say that the future will be like the past *in the sense that the laws of nature will not change*, but this is begging the question. We speak of a 'law of nature' only if we think that we have before us a regularity which does not change; and if we find that it changes then we shall not continue to call it a 'law of nature'. Of course our search for natural laws indicates that we hope to find them, and that we believe that there are natural laws; but our belief in any particular natural law cannot have a safer basis than our unsuccessful critical attempts to refute it.

I think that those who put the problem of induction in terms of the *reasonableness* of our beliefs are perfectly right if they are dissatisfied with a Humean, or post-Humean, sceptical despair of reason. We must indeed reject the view that a belief in science is as irrational as a belief in primitive magical practices—that both are a matter of accepting a 'total ideology', a convention or a tradition based on faith. But we must be cautious if we formulate our problem, with Hume, as one of the reasonableness of our *beliefs*. We should split this problem into three—our old problem of demarcation, or of how to *distinguish* between science and primitive magic; the problem of the rationality of the scientific or critical *procedure*, and of the role of observation within it; and lastly the problem of the rationality of our *acceptance* of theories for scientific and for practical purposes. To all these three problems solutions have been offered here.

One should also be careful not to confuse the problem of the reasonableness of the scientific procedure and the (tentative) acceptance of the results of this procedure—i.e., the scientific theories—with the problem of the rationality or otherwise *of the belief that this procedure will succeed*. In practice, in practical scientific research, this belief is no doubt unavoidable and reasonable, there being no better alternative. But the belief is certainly unjustifiable in a theoretical sense, as I have argued (in section V). Moreover, if we could show, on general logical grounds, that the

scientific quest is likely to succeed, one could not understand why anything like success has been so rare in the long history of human endeavours to know more about our world.

Yet another way of putting the problem of induction is in terms of probability. Let *t* be the theory and *e* the evidence: we can ask for $P(t,e)$, that is to say, the probability of *t*, given *e*. The problem of induction, it is often believed, can then be put thus: construct a calculus of probability which allows us to work out for any theory *t* what its probability is, relative to any given empirical evidence *e*; and show that $P(t,e)$ increases with the accumulation of supporting evidence, and reaches high values—at any rate values greater than ½.

In *The Logic of Scientific Discovery* I explained why I think that this approach to the problem is fundamentally mistaken.[44] To make this clear, I introduced there the distinction between *probability* and *degree of corroboration or confirmation*. (The term 'confirmation' has lately been so much used and misused that I have decided to surrender it to the verificationists and to use for my own purposes 'corroboration' only. The term 'probability' is best used in some of the many senses which satisfy the well-known calculus of probability, axiomatized, for example, by Keynes, Jeffreys,[45] and myself; but nothing of course depends on the choice of words, as long as we do not *assume*, uncritically, that degree of corroboration must also be

---

44 [Author's note] *L.Sc.D.* (see note 5 [19 in this text] above), ch. X, especially sections 80 to 83, also section 34 ff. See also my note 'A Set of Independent Axioms for Probability', *Mind*, N.S. 47, 1938, p. 275. (This note has since been reprinted, with corrections, in the new appendix *ii of *L.Sc.D.* See also the next note but one to the present chapter.)

45 John Maynard Keynes (1883–1946) is known primarily as an economist, but he also produced an influential *Treatise on Probability* in 1921. Harold Jeffreys (1891–1989) was a professor of astronomy at Cambridge (and originated the theory that the core of the earth is liquid). His *The Theory of Probability* (1939) was the first attempt to develop a theory of scientific inference based on the ideas of Bayesian statistics.

a probability—that is to say, that it must satisfy the calculus of probability.)[46]

I explained in my book why we are interested in theories with a *high degree of corroboration*. And I explained why it is a mistake to conclude from this that we are interested in *highly probable* theories. I pointed out that the probability of a statement (or set of statements) is always the greater the less the statement says: it is inverse to the content or the deductive power of the statement, and thus to its explanatory power. Accordingly every interesting and powerful statement must have a low probability; and *vice versa*: a statement with a high probability will be scientifically uninteresting, because it says little and has no explanatory power. Although we seek theories with a high degree of corroboration, *as scientists we do not seek highly probable theories but explanations; that is to say, powerful and improbable theories.* The opposite view—that science aims at high probability—is a characteristic development of verificationism: if you find that you cannot verify a theory, or make it certain by induction, you may turn to probability as a kind of '*Ersatz*'[47] for certainty, in the hope that induction may yield at least that much.

I have discussed the two problems of demarcation and induction at some length. Yet since I set out to give you in this lecture a kind of report on the work I have done in this field I shall have to add, in the form of an *Appendix*,[48] a few words about some other problems on which I have been working, between 1934 and 1953. I was led to most of these problems by trying to think out the consequences of the solutions to the two problems of demarcation and induction. But time does not allow me to continue my narrative, and to tell you how my new problems arose out of my old ones. Since I cannot even start a discussion of these further problems now, I shall have to confine myself to giving you a bare list of them, with a few explanatory words here and there. But even a bare list may be useful, I think. It may serve to give an idea of the fertility of the approach. It may help to illustrate what our problems look like; and it may show how many there are, and so convince you that there is no need whatever to worry over the question whether philosophical problems exist, or what philosophy is really about. So this list contains, by implication, an apology for my unwillingness to break with the old tradition of trying to solve problems with the help of rational argument, and thus for my unwillingness to participate wholeheartedly in the developments, trends, and drifts, of contemporary philosophy.

---

46 [Author's note] A definition, in terms of probabilities, of $C(t,e)$, i.e., of the degree of corroboration (of a theory t relative to the evidence e) satisfying the demands indicated in my *L.Sc.D.*, sections 82 to 83, is the following:

$$C(t,e) = E(t,e) (1 + P(t)P(t,e)),$$

where $E(t,e) = (P(e,t) - P(e))/(P(e,t) + P(e))$ is a (non-additive) measure of the explanatory power of t with respect to e. Note that $C(t,e)$ is not a probability: it may have values between -1 (refutation of t by e) and $C(t,t) \leq +1$. Statements t which are lawlike and thus non-verifiable cannot even reach $C(t,e) = C(t,t)$ upon empirical evidence e. $C(t,t)$ is the *degree of corroborability* of t, and is equal to the *degree of testability* of t, or to the *content* of t. Because of the demands implied in point (6) at the end of section I above, I do not think, however, that it is possible to give a complete formalization of the idea of corroboration (or, as I previously used to say, of confirmation).

(Added 1955 to the first proofs of this paper:)

See also my note 'Degree of Confirmation', *British Journal for the Philosophy of Science*, 5, 1954, pp. 143 fl. (See also 5, pp. 334.) I have since simplified this definition as follows (*B.J.P.S.*, 1955, 5, p. 359):

$$C(t,e) = (P(e,t) - P(e))/(P(e,t) - P(e,t) + P(e))$$

For a further improvement, see *B.J.P.S.* 6, 1955, p. 56.

---

47 Inferior substitute (from German "replacement").

48 This Appendix is not reprinted here; it can be found in Popper's book *Conjectures and Refutations* (pages 59 to 65).

WESLEY SALMON

"Unfinished Business: The Problem of Induction"

Who Was Wesley Salmon?

Wesley C. Salmon (1925–2001) was an influential philosopher of science, known especially for his work on the attempt to find a sound basis for scientific explanation. He rejected Carl Hempel's then-dominant deductive-nomological view of scientific explanation (see the Hempel reading in this section for more on the D-N model). Instead, Salmon developed and defended an alternative, causal-mechanical, model of explanation where events are to be explained by the way in which they fit into real, underlying causal processes. In order to provide a proper foundation for this account Salmon also devoted a lot of attention to the nature of causation, and formulated a view of causal processes as those which continuously transmit structure or information from one location, or time, to another. One significant difference between Salmon's causal-mechanical model of explanation and Hempel-style covering-law explanation is that Salmon's model is able to treat unlikely or one-off events as nevertheless explicable.

He authored four books on explanation and causation: *The Foundations of Scientific Inference* (University of Pittsburgh Press, 1967), *Scientific Explanation and the Causal Structure of the World* (Princeton University Press, 1984), *Four Decades of Scientific Explanation* (University of Pittsburgh Press, 1990), and *Causality and Explanation* (Oxford University Press, 1998).

Salmon studied for his PhD at the University of California, Los Angeles, where he worked with the eminent philosopher of science Hans Reichenbach. He taught at Brown University, then for a decade (1963–1973) at Indiana University, Bloomington, where he was one of the founding members of the History and Philosophy of Science program. After a stint at the University of Arizona he moved to the University of Pittsburgh in 1981. He spent the rest of his career at Pittsburgh, during a period in which the department of the history and philosophy of science at Pittsburgh consolidated its status as the top HPS program in the US. From 1983 until his retirement in 1999 he held the post of university professor of philosophy, which Hempel had filled before him.

He died with tragic suddenness in a car crash. "His death was brought about by a causal chain that began with a minor two-car incident and eventuated in an outcome that no one could have predicted would have occurred. Ironically, it was a tragic event of a kind that he himself had frequently discussed in his philosophical work: an improbable occurrence, but not therefore an explicable event!"[1]

What Is the Structure of This Reading?

Salmon begins by reminding us of Hume's formulation of the problem of induction, and asserting that we should take seriously the quest for a satisfactory solution to this problem. He rejects Hume's own solu-

---

1   James H. Fetzer, "In Memoriam: Wesley C. Salmon (1925–2001)," *Synthese* 132 (2002), 1–3, p. 1.

tion, and also canvasses four popular responses each of which, according to Salmon, fails. Indeed, he says, "Hume had already considered and answered each of them." He then goes on to deal in more detail with a succession of more 'serious' responses to the problem of induction. The first sees it as a pseudo-problem, and attempts to dissolve it by marshaling our existing intuitions about when predictions are confirmed (Nowell-Smith, Goodman, Carnap), or by taking a 'Wittgensteinian' or 'ordinary language philosophy' approach (Strawson, Barker, Pollock). Salmon rejects this family of responses to the problem of induction, and also argues fiercely against the second kind of response he considers: Popper's 'method of conjectures and refutations.'

Salmon shows more sympathy for what he calls the 'pragmatic approach' to induction (Feigl, Reichenbach, and himself) but notes the as-yet unsolved problem of justifying the condition that a proper inference rule must be 'symmetrical.' He concludes by asking whether the methods or practices of statistics will be any help in solving the problem of induction—and arguing that they will not—but then making a renewed plea for the importance of finding an answer to Hume's quandary.

Suggestions for Critical Reflection

1. "I must confess, I am not as sanguine as Hume about nature's dependability in keeping us appropriately on course as we plan for the future and make our practical decisions." What does Salmon mean by this? Is he right?

2. Salmon rather cheekily rejects the view that "the fallacy of affirming the consequent—known more politely as the 'hypothetico-deductive method'—is the legitimate method of science." The hypothetico-deductive method is described in a note to this reading, and alluded to elsewhere in this chapter. Why does Salmon call it "the fallacy of affirming the consequent"? Is he right that Goodman makes this mistake? How does Popper seek to avoid it? Does this approach amount to merely aiming to "codify and systematize our feelings about what is or is not legitimate," as Salmon seems to suggest?

3. Salmon argues that, although the principles of induction may not be the kinds of principles that can be *validated*, it is nevertheless reasonable to expect that they should be *vindicated*. What distinction is Salmon making here? What would it be to vindicate induction? Is Hume's problem of induction the problem of vindicating induction?

4. Can the ordinary language approach to induction distinguish in a principled way between induction and other, less rational, principles of inference?

5. How does Salmon argue that, if we adopt Popper's method of conjectures and refutations, "the content of scientific knowledge cannot extend beyond the content of our observation reports"? He suggests that this means that science is no more rational a guide to the future than any other practice (such as astrology): why does he say this? How might Popper reply to Salmon's attack?

6. What do you think Salmon means by the "condition of symmetry" that must be met by any justified basic rule of inference? How difficult a problem do you think it is to justify such a condition? Is this just the problem of induction all over again?

7. "It is manifestly untenable to deny that there is any such thing as rationally grounded prediction," says Salmon. Is it? Is it equally untenable to insist that science is a more rational ground for prediction than, say, reading tea leaves but that we don't know *why* it is (and can't even prove *that* it is)? Is this where the problem of induction leaves us?

Suggestions for Further Reading

Three other articles by Salmon on induction, one earlier and two later than the one reprinted here, are "On Vindicating Induction," *Philosophy of Science* 30 (1963), 252–261; "Rational Prediction," *The British Journal for the Philosophy of Science* 32 (1981), 115–125; and "Hans Reichenbach's Vindication of Induction," *Erkenntnis* 35 (1991), 99–122. Some discussions of Salmon's view of induction are: Brian Skyrms, "On Failing to Vindicate Induction," *Philosophy of Science* 32 (1965), 253–268; Ian Hacking, "Salmon's Vindication of Induction," *The Journal of Philosophy* 62 (1965), 260–266; and Samir Okasha, "What Did Hume Really Show About Induction?", *Philosophical Quarterly* 51 (2001), 307–327.

"Unfinished Business: The Problem of Induction"[2]

Hume's *Enquiry concerning Human Understanding* is widely recognized as a work admirably suited to stimulate genuine epistemological interest and perplexity on the part of beginning students.[3] Composed by a philosophical stylist of consummate skill, it presents, in simple and comprehensible terms, a problem of enormous intellectual and practical import—the problem of the justification of induction. Like most good philosophical problems, this one has proved amazingly refractory against some of the best efforts of first-rate philosophers, past and present. To be sure, many contemporary philosophers believe they possess a definitive answer to this puzzle, but expert opinion differs markedly regarding the nature of the correct answer. Under these circumstances, it seems extraordinary that no mention whatever was made of this problem at the Hume bicentennial conference.[4] Such a lacuna should not, I feel, go unnoticed.

In view of the popularity of the *Enquiry* as an introductory reading, let me continue to pursue the issue from a pedagogic standpoint. How do we go about presenting this material to young minds? We try to challenge them to think about the question of what basis we have for making any inference from the observed to the unobserved. We try to make them grapple with a logical problem: How do we know what's going to happen in the future—in the next few years, the next few hours, the next few minutes? They think they know (partially at least) what's going to happen, and so do we, but how? Not by direct observation, for we do not have the gift of precognition. If we know at all, we know by some sort of inference. And once that is clear, we have them in Hume's grasp. "... [A]s a philosopher, who has some share of curiosity", he said, "I want to learn the foundation of this inference."

As we follow out Hume's analysis for our students, we reveal his inability to find any rational foundation for such inferences. "If there be any suspicion that the course of nature may change, and that the past may be no rule for the future, all experience becomes useless, and can give rise to NO INFERENCE OR CONCLUSION." "... [I]t is not REASONING which engages us to suppose the past resembling the future, and to expect similar effects from causes which are, to appearance, similar." "I am ready to reject ALL BELIEF AND REASONING and look upon *no opinion* as MORE PROBABLE OR LIKELY than another."[5]

Nature, of course, compels us—or exercises friendly persuasion at least—to expect the future to be like the past in significant respects. But psychological expectation is not the same thing as logical inference. Logic—reason—has nothing whatever to do with it. That's what David Hume said, we tell our introductory classes; if Hume is right, any belief about unobserved matters of fact is just as *reasonable* as any other. Not as vivid, or compelling, or natural perhaps—but just as *reasonable* or *probable* or *likely*.

Forgive me for rehearsing this familiar story. My purpose is to ask what response we are to offer. I realize that—if the past be any guide to the future—no vast numbers of students are going to be 'turned on'

---

2   *Philosophical Studies*, Vol. 33, No. 1 (Jan 1978), pp. 1–19. With kind permission from Springer Science+ Business Media.

3   [Author's note] This point was brought home forcefully to me when, recently, trying to free my mind of all philosophical preconceptions, I reread Sections IV–VII of the *Enquiry*. As a result of this effort, I wrote a dialogue, 'An Encounter with David Hume' (published in Joel Feinberg (ed.), *Reason and Responsibility*, 3rd ed., Dickenson Publ. Co., 1975) in which I try to show how this work can speak effectively to contemporary students.

4   The bicentennial of Hume's death was 1976; an international memorial conference was held at the University of Edinburgh in August of that year.

5   [Author's note] The foregoing famous quotations are from the *Enquiry*, Part IV, and the *Treatise*, conclusion of Book I. I have added emphasis.

to any such abstract intellectual problem. But what about the small minority who read the assignment, pay attention to the lecture, and try to understand what is going on? What shall we say to them? Was Hume right? Shall we admit that reason has nothing to do with predicting the future? *I do not think we are quite ready for that concession—at least I fervently hope not.* We believe that there are rational methods of prediction, and that there are irrational ones. Moreover, I must confess, I am not as sanguine as Hume about nature's dependability in keeping us appropriately on course as we plan for the future and make our practical decisions. When I observe human behavior—including my own—I'm not encouraged.

Having been presented with a problem, our students would like to be told 'the answer.' It is, of course, contrary to all accepted principles of philosophic pedagogy to satisfy that desire without further ado, so we tell them that the solution (as if we had one to give them) cannot really be appreciated without going through the salient arguments. We therefore consider various alternative approaches; several immediately suggest themselves either for historical reasons or because of their strong psychological appeal.

(1) Many of the brightest students, when asked why they have confidence in the inductive method, will answer, "because it works." This formula has such compelling psychological appeal that it is easy to overlook the temporal ambiguity of the verb 'works.' What the argument amounts to, as Hume so masterfully explained, is the inference that induction *will work* because it *has worked.* This inference is itself inductive, and thus begs the question. Philosophers have, nevertheless, attempted to show how induction could be supported inductively. It has sometimes been suggested that circles can be 'virtuous' rather than 'vicious,' or that an argument can be circular without committing the fallacy of *petitio principii.*[6] But after all of the philosophical squirming—whether they are circular, the type of circularity, and whether it is bad for an argument to be circular—it remains

possible to 'justify' the counter-inductive method[7] by precisely the same type of argument as was used to justify induction.[8] Whatever 'justifies' everything justifies nothing.

(2) Kant's appeal to the synthetic a priori must be mentioned, and not just for reasons of historical completeness. Hume had severely challenged the status of the principle of uniformity of nature. Awakened from his dogmatic slumbers, Kant argued that this principle (in the form of a principle of universal causation) is secured as a synthetic a priori truth of pure reason.[9] Kant had no doubts about the existence of synthetic a priori truths; he was merely formulating in rather clear and precise terms what philosophers had maintained about the status of geometry for more than two millennia. The subsequent discovery of non-Euclidean geometries,[10] and the searching philosophical investigations of their applicability to the physical world, have thoroughly undercut any such view of the nature of geometry. With that (and other) developments, the basis for the synthetic a priori became tenuous indeed. Nevertheless, the last ditch resort to the synthetic a priori in order to get around the problem of induction is not a thing of the remote past. Two of the greatest scientific philosophers of the twentieth century have taken that refuge—how else can we regard Carnap's

---

6   *Petitio principii* (Latin for 'the taking for granted of the principle or starting point') is the fallacy of begging the question.

7   The counter-inductive method is a method of 'justifying' beliefs that is contrary to induction: for example, the so-called 'gambler's fallacy'—the mistake of believing that if the same thing has happened repeatedly (e.g., a coin landing heads) this makes it more likely that something different will happen soon (e.g., the coin will land tails).

8   [Author's note] My critical discussion of this approach can be found in *The Foundations of Scientific Inference* (University of Pittsburgh Press, Pittsburgh, 1967), pp. 12–17.

9   A synthetic a priori judgment is one which is, of course, both synthetic—i.e., not merely a logical truth (or falsehood)—and a priori, i.e., known prior to, or independently of, sense-experience.

10   Non-Euclidean geometries describe a space that is 'curved' so that lines on a two-dimensional plane that would be parallel in Euclidian geometry will either meet or 'curve away' from each other.

a priori measure functions in confirmation theory[11] or Russell's postulates of scientific inference?[12] Although Russell's theory of non-demonstrative inference does not enjoy a great deal of popularity at present, Carnap's inductive logic does stand as the most highly developed and clearly articulated system we have seen to date.

(3) The tradition of British Empiricism—of which Hume was both the ablest champion and the most devastating challenger—lived on into the nineteenth century with John Stuart Mill. Mill was no friend of global synthetic a priori principles, or a priori principles of any sort. His idea was to assume just as much uniformity of nature (causality) as you need for the job at hand—no more. He seems to have adopted a sort of postulational approach. Russell later provided a critique of postulational method which was both brief and apt: "The method of 'postulating' what we want has many advantages; they are the same as the advantages of theft over honest toil."[13] Mill, in anticipation, seems to have felt that many petty larcenies are more excusable than one big heist. Like all others who have resorted to postulates, Mill never really came to grips with Hume's problem.

(4) It has sometimes been maintained that Hume's critique of induction should be no cause for distress to any but those philosophers engaged in a 'quest for certainty.' Hume showed conclusively, they claim, that the inductive method is not infallible. That is a fact of life we must simply learn to live with.[14] This response, however, seriously fails to appreciate the import of Hume's conclusions and the arguments he adduces in their support. He argues, not that induction may upon occasion yield a false conclusion, but rather, that for all we can know, *it may never again yield a true one*. It is not that inductive conclusions fall short of certainty; rather, we have no reason to place *any confidence whatever in any inductive conclusion*. The ancient philosophers were fully aware that neither perception nor a posteriori reasoning yields absolute certainty. Hume did far more than merely to remind us of that banality.

These four approaches come readily to mind; no doubt there are others that could be placed in the same category. They all have one thing in common. Hume had already considered and answered each of them. If we had read carefully and understood, we could have saved ourselves the trouble of going through them. We should be telling our students, at this point, that Hume's arguments stand up remarkably well against all traditional efforts to refute or circumvent them.

The foregoing attempts to deal with the problem of induction are admittedly not among those which enjoy the greatest current popularity. Let us therefore consider the more serious contenders. Many twentieth century philosophers have tried to dismiss the difficulty as a pseudo-problem; this seems to qualify as the most popular way to get around Hume's embarrassing problem.

The basic idea is that Hume did not formulate a real problem, but became enmeshed in a series of conceptual confusions. Once we straighten out those confusions—which may involve considerable subtlety—the problem will vanish. Here are some of the allegations:

- He confused induction with deduction.
- He tried, unsuccessfully of course, to transform induction into deduction.
- He inappropriately applied deductive standards to induction.
- He failed to recognize that induction has its own standards and criteria—that it is an autonomous type of logic, distinct from deduction.

---

11   Rudolf Carnap (1891–1970) was a German-born American philosopher of science and logician. A priori measure functions are, roughly, functions that assign prior probabilities to states described by scientific theories.

12   [Author's note] See *The Foundations of Scientific Inference*, pp. 27–48, 68–79. Russell's introduction of his postulates in *Human Knowledge, Its Scope and Limits* is strikingly similar to a Kantian 'transcendental deduction.'

13   [Author's note] Bertrand Russell, *Introduction to Mathematical Philosophy* (George Allen and Unwin, London, 1919), p. 71.

14   [Author's note] Such an answer has been suggested by Jerrold Katz, *The Problem of Induction and Its Solution* (University of Chicago Press, Chicago, 1962), p. 115.

The whole attempt to find a justification for induction was, according to this charge, a search for something that would be appropriate only in a deductive context.

There is no doubt that we should make every effort to avoid confusing induction with deduction. But will avoidance of such confusion make Hume's problem of induction vanish? The key notion in this approach is *autonomy*; let us see what it amounts to. The general idea seems to be that there are certain forms of argument which are not valid, but which we are not prepared to give up. When we find that our favorite argument turns out to be fallacious, but we want to cling to it, one way to save it is to call it 'inductive.' Recall Morris R. Cohen's famous quip to the effect that a logic text is a book divided into two parts; in the first part (on deduction) the fallacies are explained, while in the second part (on induction) they are committed.

Similar ploys have been adopted in other areas of philosophy. In a famous passage in the *Treatise*, Hume remarked pointedly upon the logical gap in arguments which purport to derive ought-statements from is-statements. Some moral philosophers who hanker after such inferences have sought ways of circumventing this difficulty. One device, suggested by Patrick Nowell-Smith, is the concept of 'contextual implication': "... a statement *p* contextually implies a statement *q* if anyone who knew the normal conventions of the language would be entitled to infer *q* from *p in the context in which they occur*."[15] Contextual implication, Nowell-Smith notes, does not share with standard logical implication (deductive entailment) the severe drawback of being bound by rigid rules. This very feature of contextual implication suits it for use in the 'anything-goes-if-you-want-it-badly-enough' approach to logic.

Unbridled use of contextual implication may, of course, give rise to some disquieting results. For example, in some places at the present time it seems that the statement, 'the victim of the homicide was homosexual,' contextually implies the statement, 'the homicide was not a serious crime.' But what's wrong

with that kind of logic? If moral philosophers want to derive ought-statements from is-statements, why should they deny themselves? If politicians fancy syllogisms with undistributed middle terms,[16] why should they be subject to logical censure? If a particular sort of argument appeals to you—according to this way of thinking—the fact that it is unjustified should present no obstacle.

I am *not* saying that valid deductive arguments are the only admissible types. Valid deduction has a valuable property. The arguments in this category are truth-preserving; from true premises you cannot validly deduce a false conclusion. But other types of arguments are needed as well; that is precisely the reason we have a problem of justification of induction. I *am* saying that the characteristic of *being an invalid argument we prize* does not constitute a sufficient ground for considering an argument rationally admissible. Better grounds must be found.

Lest there be some feeling that, with the discussion of contextual implication, the is-ought fallacy, and undistributed middle, I have strayed too far from the main issue—induction—let me return forthwith. What reason is there to refuse to grant that the fallacy of affirming the consequent[17]—known more politely as the 'hypothetico-deductive method'[18]—is the legitimate method of science? We

---

16 This is a (fallacious) argument of the following form:
    1. A's are B's
    2. C's are B's
    3. Therefore C's are A's.
For example: beetles are insects; bees are insects; therefore bees are beetles.

17 This is a (deductively invalid) argument of the following form:
    1. If P then Q
    2. Q
    3. Therefore P.
For example: if all swans are white then the next swan I see will be white; the next swan I see is white; so all swans are white. (In this case, the first premise must be true; the second premise was—as it were—repeatedly true for Europeans before the discovery of Australia; but the conclusion is in fact false.)

18 The hypothetico-deductive method is a proposed ac-

15 [Author's note] Patrick Nowell-Smith, *Ethics* (Penguin, 1954), p. 80.

all know, of course, that it is not deductively valid, and no one is claiming otherwise. We can, nevertheless, signify our psychological attachment to this type of argument by calling it 'inductive' and saying that it 'confirms' conclusions rather than entailing them. Am I misrepresenting this attitude of logical tolerence? I do not think so, for I find it stated candidly by some of the most significant modern contributors to the philosophy of induction. Consider a famous statement by Nelson Goodman:

> ... rules and particular inferences alike are justified by being brought into agreement with each other. *A rule is amended if it yields an inference we are unwilling to accept; an inference is rejected if it violates a rule we are unwilling to amend.* The process of justification is the delicate one of making mutual adjustments between rules and accepted inferences; and in the agreement achieved lies the only justification needed for either.
>
> All this applies equally well to induction. An inductive inference, too, is justified by conformity to general rules, and a general rule by conformity to accepted inductive inferences. Predictions are justified if they conform to valid canons of induction; and the canons of induction are valid if they accurately codify accepted inductive practice.[19]

Thus, did Goodman dispatch Hume's problem—'the old riddle of induction.'

Rudolf Carnap used somewhat different terms, but espoused essentially the same view; "The reasons [for accepting any axiom of inductive logic] are based upon our intuitive judgments concerning inductive validity, i.e., concerning inductive rationality of practical decisions (e.g., about bets)."[20]

Two of the most influential philosophers to deal with the problem thus agree that there is nothing more that can be done in inductive logic than to codify and systematize our feelings about what is or is not legitimate. To show that the results of these efforts have any rational justification seems to be regarded as beyond the realm of possibility. Hume's problem is, according to them, utterly recalcitrant. They are extremely reluctant to come right out and say so, but as far as I can see, that's what it boils down to.

In an oft-quoted remark, C.D. Broad[21] said that induction is the glory of science and the scandal of philosophy.[22] If, as Carnap and Goodman seem to admit, the problem is so intractable, why aren't contemporary philosophers more scandalized? How can Carnap, Goodman, and countless others accept the situation with such equanimity? For the answer to this query, let us turn to P.F. Strawson,[23] who seems to have become the most prominent spokesman for a 'Wittgensteinian' approach."[24]

The 'ordinary language dissolution' of the problem of induction rests primarily upon the claim that the principles of induction are ultimate principles; they are not amenable to justification because there are no other principles which are more fundamental that

---

count of the proper methodology of science (dating back at least to the early nineteenth century, when William Whewell introduced the term). On this view, scientific investigation proceeds by formulating empirical hypotheses to explain the observed data, and then performing experiments to test these hypotheses. If an experiment gives a result that is consistent with what we would expect if the hypothesis were true, then the hypothesis is (partially) confirmed; if the experiment gives a result that is inconsistent with the hypothesis, then the hypothesis is falsified (or must be modified).

19 [Author's note] Nelson Goodman, *Fact, Fiction, and Forecast*, 2nd ed. (Bobbs-Merrill, 1965), p. 64.

20 [Author's note] P.A. Schilpp (ed.), *The Philosophy of Rudolf Carnap* (Open Court, 1963), p. 978.

21 Charlie Dunbar Broad (1887–1971) was a prominent philosopher of science and epistemologist who held the Knightbridge Professorship of Moral Philosophy at Cambridge University.

22 [Author's note] *The Philosophy of Francis Bacon*, Cambridge, 1926.

23 Sir Peter Frederick Strawson (1919–2006) was the Waynflete Professor of Metaphysical Philosophy at the University of Oxford, and an influential analytic metaphysician.

24 [Author's note] P.F. Strawson, *Introduction to Logical Theory* (Methuen & Co., 1952), Chap. 9.

could be invoked for the purpose of carrying out a justification of induction. The above-mentioned *autonomy* of inductive logic is a result of the *ultimacy* of its principles. To ask whether induction is justified is to ask whether it is reasonable to employ inductive canons. The demand for such a justification must, so the argument goes, be confused or misplaced, because the canons of induction are themselves constitutive of what it *means* to characterize something as reasonable.

This seductive approach has not gone unchallenged. Employing Herbert Feigl's[25] important distinction between two types of justification—validation and vindication—I pointed out that a straightforward significance could be attached to the request for a justification of induction. While *validation* cannot be carried out without appeal to principles more fundamental than those whose justification is at issue, *vindication* is not subject to any such limitation. To vindicate a rule or principle is to show that its adoption will serve some specified end; this type of justification does not require an appeal to more fundamental inductive principles. Strawson's argument correctly shows that the demand for a justification of the basic canons of induction does take us beyond the limits of possible validation. His argument does *not*, however, show that such a demand takes us beyond the limits of possible *justification*, for vindication is a form of justification, and that type of justification is not touched by the appeal to ultimacy. Strawson suggests that the request for a justification of induction is like asking whether it is reasonable to be reasonable; this, he suggests, is a pointless question. I argued that such a question is not vacuous at all if we recognize two senses of 'reasonable' corresponding to Feigl's two senses of 'justification.'[26]

In a reply of somewhat less than a single page— totally ignoring the crucial distinction between validation and vindication—Strawson dismissed the objections with the remark, "If it is said that there is a problem of induction, and that Hume posed it, it must be added that he solved it."[27] One gets a distinct impression of Strawson's impatience with those who insist on dragging out the old philosophical chestnut.

Hume had, of course, maintained that induction is a matter of 'custom and habit.' This is what Strawson sees as Hume's solution to the problem. It might be reformulated in somewhat more modern terminology by saying that inductive behavior is a matter of psychological conditioning. Knowing what we do of Pavlov's dogs we would rephrase once again: "Verily I say unto you that induction is but a certain watering at the mouth!"[28]

What we know about conditioning, and about various other biological and physiological processes, is known scientifically—inductively. It is not at all clear to me how the proponent of this Strawsonian line would argue against those who, on flagrantly unscientific and non-inductive grounds, simply reject that very scientific claim—namely that inductive behavior, in contrast to various other approaches to finding out about unobserved matters of fact, is enforced upon us by nature. As nearly as I can understand the ordinary language approach, one simply resorts to namecalling. The non-inductionist is smeared with such epithets as 'unscientific' and 'irrational.' On the other hand, "If you use inductive procedures you can call yourself 'reasonable'—*and isn't that nice!*"[29] This, it still seems to me, captures the kernel of the 'ordinary language dissolution' of the problem of induction.

Being reasonable, according to ordinary language theorists, involves fashioning one's beliefs in terms of the evidence—and inductive evidence is normally at least part of the evidence. Once more, we are told, the adoption of inductive procedures determines the

25 Herbert Feigl (1902–1988) was an Austrian-born philosopher of science who spent much of his career in the United States.

26 [Author's note] I offered these arguments in 'Should We Attempt to Justify Induction?,' *Philosophical Studies* 8 (1957), 38–42.

27 [Author's note] P.F. Strawson, 'On Justifying Induction,' *Philosophical Studies* 9 (1958), 20–21.

28 [Author's note] This is a paraphrase of a famous remark allegedly made by A.N. Whitehead in response to a lecture by Bertrand Russell (with much reference to Pavlov's experiments) on ethics: "Verily, I say unto you that the good is but a certain watering at the mouth."

29 [Author's note] Salmon, 'Should We Attempt to Justify Induction?,' p. 42.

very meaning of the concept of evidence, and hence, what it is to be reasonable. This argument, I believe, is vulnerable to the objection that there are many conceivable rules of inference in terms of which one might fashion one's beliefs. To be concrete, one could cite (1) induction by enumeration, (2) an a priori rule, and (3) a counter-inductive rule.[30] Depending upon which rule is adopted, a radically different concept of evidence emerges. A fact which constitutes positive evidence *for* a given hypothesis on the basis of rule (1) is *irrelevant* to that hypothesis on the basis of rule (2), while precisely the same fact is evidence *against* the very same hypothesis on rule (3). If the standard inductive rule, rather than one of the infinitely many pathological alternatives, is constitutive of rationality, it seems to me that we ought to be able to say on what grounds its superiority rests.

In response to these considerations, Stephen Barker rose to the defense of the dissolutionists. He made no secret of his feeling of fatigue:

> Wittgenstein, Strawson, and others have held that the traditional problem of induction is a pseudo-problem, resulting from conceptual confusion; a puzzle to be dissolved, not a problem to be solved in its own terms. Professor Salmon disagrees and tries to rescue the grand old problem from dissolution; or perhaps I ought rather to say that he tries to resurrect that grand old corpse of a problem which many of us had hoped would now be allowed to molder in peace.[31]

Well, I do apologize for being so tiresome, but I fail to see that Hume's problem of justification of induction is a pseudo-problem. Barker elaborates his claim:

Salmon would like us radically to question the practice of induction which shapes our whole form of life, but words fail. We cannot express such a question. We reach one of those points at which, as Wittgenstein says, one feels like uttering an inarticulate cry.[32]

I find Barker's remark incomprehensible. The claim that the problem of induction cannot be formulated seems manifestly false. Hume had formulated it (whether he had also solved it or not). Russell had formulated it. Reichenbach[33] had formulated it. I had just formulated it in the very paper on which Barker was commenting. None of us, as far as I was aware, had been reduced to inarticulate cries. Still, this response by Barker is the most serious and coherent effort to answer these objections of which I am aware.

In spite of damaging attacks—at least they strike me as utterly devastating—and in the absence of any serious defense against them, the 'ordinary language dissolution' continues to be regarded by many as *the definitive answer* to the problem of the justification of induction. As recently as 1974, in a book whose title declares that it is devoted to *Justification and Knowledge*, John Pollock begins his chapter on induction with these remarks:

> The traditional problem of induction was that of justifying induction ... it is almost obvious that nothing could possibly count as a justification. We cannot justify induction inductively, and, as Strawson remarked, to attempt to give a deductive justification of induction is to attempt to turn induction into deduction, which it is not. This, of course, is just what has always made the traditional problem of induction so puzzling. But the lesson to be learned from all this is that the attempt to justify induction is wrongheaded and must be forsaken. This is because the principles of induction are instrumental in our making justified judgments

---

30 [Author's note] I stated these rules in 'The Concept of Inductive Evidence,' *American Philosophical Quarterly* 2 (1965), 1–6, where I also presented the ensuing argument. The same argument was spelled out more fully and precisely in 'The Justification of Inductive Rules of Inference,' in I. Lakatos (ed.), *The Problem of Inductive Logic* (North-Holland, 1968), pp. 29–33.

31 [Author's note] Stephen F. Barker, 'Discussion: Is There a Problem of Induction?,' *American Philosophical Quarterly* 2 (1965), 7.

32 [Author's note] *Ibid.*, p. 9.

33 Hans Reichenbach (1891–1953) was a German philosopher of science who immigrated to America in 1938. He taught at UCLA, and was Salmon's doctoral advisor.

about the world, and as such are involved in the justification conditions of our concepts. Insofar as the principles of induction are involved in the justification conditions of our concepts, they are partially constitutive of the meanings of these concepts. It is simply part of the meaning of these concepts that one can inductively generalize in connection with them. To *justify* induction would be to somehow derive the justification conditions of these concepts from something deeper, but there is nothing deeper. It is in principle impossible to justify induction, and there is no reason why things should be otherwise. The traditional problem of induction is best regarded as a pseudo-problem.[34]

This is Pollock's *total* comment on Hume's problem of induction; the remainder of the chapter is devoted to Goodman's 'new riddle of induction.'

Appalled at the continued popularity of this attempt to evade an unwanted philosophical problem, I once remarked (of P.F. Strawson and A.J. Ayer), "They seem to argue, by a kind of logic that frankly escapes me, that induction needs no defense because it is indefensible."[35] The logic still escapes me, but I now believe I may have a clue to the willingness of so many philosophers to adopt the dissolutionist approach even in the face of the most damaging arguments (which go largely unacknowledged). The fundamental principle distilled from their approach is one which must be admitted, even by those who do not quite comprehend its derivation, to exhibit great philosophic ingenuity. Once formulated, it can easily be applied again: *The ordinary language 'dissolution' of the problem of induction needs no defense precisely because it is indefensible.*

The straightforward candor of Karl Popper's treatment of Hume's problem of induction makes a refreshing contrast to the ordinary language approach. In the opening paragraph of his 1972 book, *Objective Knowledge*, Popper says,

I think that I have solved a major philosophical problem: the problem of induction. (I must have reached the solution in 1927 or thereabouts.) This solution has been extremely fruitful, and it has enabled me to solve a good number of other philosophical problems.[36]

The solution, very simply, is that Hume proved induction to be an untenable mode of inference, and it must therefore be abandoned. It is not the business of science to attempt to establish hypotheses as true or as probable. The hypothetico-deductive form of *confirmation* is illegitimate and has no place in science. Hypotheses can, however, be refuted by the deductively valid *modus tollens*,[37] and this is the most that science can aspire to. Popper's approach has been characterized as 'deductivism' and as 'the method of conjectures and refutations.'

This way of dealing with Hume's problem of induction would seem to give rise to an immediate difficulty. Deduction, as Popper is fully aware, is non-ampliative—that is, the conclusion of a valid deduction has no content which was not already present in the premises. If we grant the plausible assumption that all of our observations are confined to happenings in the past and present, then it follows immediately that observation *plus* deduction can yield no information whatever about the future. Indeed, the total information content of science cannot exceed the content of our observations themselves.

According to Popper's characterization, the method of science is to put forth generalizations as conjectures, and to attempt to falsify them. Let us see how this works. I could use fancier examples of scientific hypotheses, but the principle would be precisely the same. Suppose, on the one hand, that we entertain the

---

34 [Author's note] John Pollock, *Justification and Knowledge* (Princeton University Press, 1974) p. 204.

35 [Author's note] Salmon, 'The Justification of Inductive Rules of Inference,' p. 24.

36 [Author's note] Karl R. Popper, *Objective Knowledge* (Oxford University Press, 1972), p. 1.

37 *Modus tollens* is the name for arguments of the following form:

    1.   If P then Q

    2.   Not-Q

    3.   Therefore Not-P.

For example: if this is an insect then it will have six legs; this does not have six legs; so it's not an insect.

generalization, 'All ravens are black,' and we find that it is impervious to all efforts at falsification. The entire information thereby conveyed is that we have not observed a non-black raven. This says less than a simple report of our observations of birds. Suppose, on the other hand, that we advance the generalization. 'All swans are white,' and find that it is falsified. In this case, the total information conveyed is that we have observed a non-white swan. Again, more would have conveyed by a report of our observations of birds.[38]

According to Popper, bold conjectures and powerful theories are the pride of modern science, but according to the principles of his clearly articulated methodology, the content of scientific knowledge cannot extend beyond the content of our observation reports. Popper has sometimes chided the 'inductivists' for holding the view that science consists merely of observation reports and simple empirical generalizations upon them. He protests that science is not that poverty-stricken—a view with which inductivists heartily agree. But on his theory, the content of scientific knowledge does not even include the generalizations. It is ironic that in recent years Popper and his associates have placed great emphasis upon 'the problem of the growth of knowledge.' According to his own principles, scientific knowledge grows at a rate not exceeding the rate of accumulation of observations. In fairness, I should add, the observations we make are significantly influenced by the hypotheses we are entertaining. But that doesn't change the fact that there is no ampliative form of scientific argument, and consequently, science provides no information whatever about the future. In answer to Hume's question, 'How are we to make reasonable inference from the observed to the unobserved,' Popper's clear and unequivocal answer is, 'No way!'

It may be objected that I am distorting Popper's views by a failure to mention his concept of *corroboration*. Among hypotheses which have not been falsified, some—by reason of greater simplicity, more severe testing, or larger content—receive a higher corroboration rating than others. Popper clearly stresses that 'corroboration' is no synonym for 'confirmation.' If, however, degree of corroboration were some sort of index to the reliance we should place upon a hypothesis for predicting the future, or to the confidence we should have in the truth of the hypothesis, then Popper's deductivism would be polluted with *some* ampliative mode of inference. In that case, Popper would turn out to be an inductivist after all. But Popper adamantly denies that corroboration has any predictive import whatever; the degree of corroboration is an indication of the performance of the generalization *with respect to past occurrences alone.* Popper's deductivism remains pure; science has no predictive import.[39]

When we recover our composure after this shocking news, we may naturally feel impelled to ask on what basis we would make the kind of predictions upon which all of our practical decisions must be grounded. Popper reassures us that for such purposes "a *pragmatic belief in the results of science* is not irrational, because there is nothing more 'rational' than the method of critical discussion [conjectures and refutations], which is the method of science."[40] But recalling what Popper has explicitly stated about the predictive content of science, we must hasten to add that nothing could be *less* 'rational' either. When all methods are on an equal footing with respect to predictive content, Popper seems to draw the astonishing conclusion that belief in the results of none of them is 'irrational.' Predictions based upon the results of science are not irrational, but predictions based upon astrology would likewise not be irrational, since neither science nor astrology has any credentials at all when it comes to predictive value. Popper goes on to say that "it would be irrational to accept any of its [science's] results as certain," but we have recognized from the outset the truism that science is not infallible. Having offered that (unneeded) word of caution (which seems to suggest that those who do not agree with him are

---

38 [Author's note] I have discussed Popper's approach in *The Foundations of Scientific Inference*, pp. 21–27, and again in 'The Justification of Inductive Rules of Inference,' pp. 25–29.

39 [Author's note] See J.W.N. Watkins, 'Non-inductive corroboration,' in I. Lakatos (ed.), *The Problem of Inductive Logic* (North-Holland, 1968), pp. 61–66, and Popper, *Objective Knowledge*, pp. 18–19.

40 [Author's note] Popper, *Objective Knowledge*, p. 27.

committed to an infallibility doctrine), he adds, "there is nothing 'better' [than science] when it comes to practical action: there is no alternative method which might be said to be more rational."[41]

If all methods of making inferences to the future are equally and totally incapable of being justified, then none is any *more* rational than any other, and none is any *less* rational than any other. All are on a par. The correct conclusion to draw, I should think, is that *all* methods, including the scientific method, are irrational bases for prediction. Thus, when the atomic scientists were contemplating the assembly of the first atomic pile in Chicago, it would, according to Popper's principles, have been just as rational to consult a crystal-gazing seer as to consult a scientist for a prediction as to whether a self-sustaining chain reaction would occur, and whether it would engulf the entire city of Chicago and possibly the whole earth in an uncontrolled nuclear blast.

Either science has predictive import or it does not. If it has none, it provides no rational basis for prediction. If it has predictive import, it must incorporate some form of ampliative inference. You can't have it both ways, it has to be one or the other. It is incredible to maintain that the *solution* to the problem of induction lies in the claim that science has no predictive content. *That* sounds a good deal more like a *statement* of the problem.

My own sympathies have lain with an approach by way of a pragmatic vindication of induction, along lines suggested by Herbert Feigl and Hans Reichenbach. Enormous difficulties, however, are encountered along this path. Reichenbach constructed a well-known pragmatic argument based upon the convergence properties of his 'rule of induction.' As he realized, the same argument provided the same sort of justification for an infinite class of 'asymptotic rules'[42] which share the same convergence properties.

On what basis, then, is the 'rule of induction'—the straight rule—to be singled out as the uniquely acceptable member of the class? With a patent misapplication of his principle of descriptive simplicity, Reichenbach claimed to have provided a suitable rationale for the choice. But this answer would not do.

For some time I sought other, more satisfactory, principles on which to narrow down the class of candidates for basic inductive rules. Without boring you with tedious details, let me merely mention two suggestions: (1) a set of *normalizing conditions* and (2) a *criterion of linguistic invariance*. These did seem quite potent in disqualifying large classes of unacceptable asymptotic rules. Moreover, in countering the objection that even Reichenbach's rule of induction would fall victim to the criterion of linguistic invariance, I also offered a proposal for the resolution of Goodman's famous 'grue-bleen paradox'—his 'new riddle of induction'—which still seems fundamentally satisfactory. All of this was enormously pleasing; indeed, in a fit of over-optimism, I thought I had succeeded in providing satisfactory grounds for uniquely justifying the one rule.[43] This happy state of mind was shattered when I. Richard Savage and Ian Hacking independently constructed counter-examples to the general claim.[44]

I do not think either the normalizing conditions or the criterion of linguistic invariance are unsound; the difficulty is that they are not strong enough to do the job I had hoped they would do. Hacking has, however, proved that three principles would be necessary and sufficient to single out Reichenbach's rule of induction: consistency, invariance, and symmetry.[45] If, and only if, it could be shown that a satisfactory basic inductive rule must satisfy these conditions would the desired justification be forthcoming. The question then becomes, what grounds, if any, can be found for imposing just these requirements upon inductive rules.

---

41   [Author's note] *Ibid.*

42   These are rules that are 'asymptotes' with the 'straight rule' of induction by enumeration (i.e., inference to a general rule—"All a's are F"—from a sequence of instances of that rule: Fa_1, Fa_2, Fa_3, and so on). Two rules are asymptotes if their results get closer and closer together, for ever, as the number of instances is multiplied.

43   [Author's note] The details are given in my article 'On Vindicating Induction,' *Philosophy of Science* 30 (1963), 252–261.

44   [Author's note] See I. Lakatos, *The Problem of Inductive Logic*, pp. 50–51 and pp. 86–87.

45   [Author's note] I. Hacking, 'One Problem About Induction,' in I. Lakatos, *The Problem of Inductive Logic*, pp. 57–59.

Skipping over some technical details, I would remark that the consistency requirement is analogous to my normalizing conditions, while my criterion of linguistic invariance can, I think, be legitimately extended to coincide with the invariance condition formulated by Hacking. These two requirements do not seem to me to pose insuperable difficulties. The remaining condition, symmetry, is something else again.[46]

The crucial problem arising out of the symmetry condition can be illustrated by a simple puzzle. Consider the following initial section of a sequence of heads and tails:

H T T H T H T H H H H T H T H H H H T H T H

The relative frequency of heads in this observed sequence is 6/10; on the basis of the rule of induction we might infer—or *posit*, to use Reichenbach's term—that the long run frequency of heads, if the sequence is continued, will be somewhere near that value. If, however, we examine the initial section carefully, we note that each toss corresponding to a prime number—the second, third, fifth, seventh, etc.—is a tail, while every other toss yields heads. If we use the rule of induction on the subsequences, we posit that each prime toss will be a tail and all others will be heads. Since it is known that the limiting frequency of primes among the natural numbers is zero,[47] the induction on the subsequences entails that the limiting frequency of heads in the entire sequence is 1. Unless it can be shown how, and why, one of these inductions must supersede the other,[48] adoption of Reichenbach's rule of induction will lead us into genuine paradox. At present, I do not know how to resolve this paradox—or whether it is, in principle, capable of resolution.

Inasmuch as philosophers have not done an outstanding job of providing answers to Hume's problem of induction, perhaps we might look elsewhere. It would surely make good sense to ask whether statisticians, whose business is to deal with certain kinds of inductive or probabilistic inferences in scientific contexts, can offer any help. The answer, it turns out, is unequivocally negative. There are two major schools of thought regarding foundations of statistics, the bayesian and the orthodox. According to the bayesian school, probabilities are merely subjective degrees of belief; they have no direct bearing upon objective facts in the world. To say that a particular future outcome is highly probable does not mean that it will usually turn out that way in similar circumstances, nor does it mean that we have good reason to believe in any such outcome. The probability, for each individual, is simply the amount of psychological confidence he happens to have—for whatever reason, rational or irrational—in that outcome. The most that statistics can do is to help us avoid a certain type of inconsistency—called *incoherence*—in combinations of beliefs; it cannot tell us whether a given degree of belief is a reasonable basis for predicting the future. L.J. Savage, the most prominent exponent of this viewpoint, explicitly acknowledged that he was a Humean skeptic where prediction is concerned.[49]

Orthodox statisticians regard probabilities as objective entities; if one knows the probabilities that govern certain types of events, one would have a rational basis for prediction and action. The problem, of course, is to establish the values of such objective probabilities. Orthodox statisticians have methods which are used for just such purposes. When these methods are examined carefully, however, it turns out that their application invariably requires synthetic general assumptions about matters of fact. Orthodox statisticians do not, in other words, have methods for making inductive inferences which do not depend upon the results of other,

---

46   A function is symmetrical if it is invariant for any permutations of the constants to which the function is applied. For example, addition is a symmetrical function: $(1 + 7 + 81) = (7 + 81 + 1)$.

47   That is, when you get far enough along the number line—i.e., the natural numbers get big enough—none of them are prime numbers.

48   That is, the basic rule of induction seems to give different results—different predictions about unobserved instances—when applied to subsequences of the series than it does when applied to the series as a whole. The latter application is a symmetrical function—it does not matter in what order the Hs and Ts come in, just how many there are of each—while the former is not.

49   [Author's note] L.J. Savage, 'Implications of Personal Probability for Induction,' *Journal of Philosophy* LXIV (1967), 593–607. In *Foundations of Scientific Inference*, pp. 79–83, I discuss this approach in greater detail.

previous, inductions.[50] Their position is very close, I believe, to that of John Stuart Mill. If we assume some general statistical regularities, we can make inductive inferences. But on what basis are these assumptions—even fairly modest ones—to be justified?

Where can we go from here? Every path we have tried to follow has turned into a blind alley. One feels an almost irresistible tendency to resonate to Hume's own reaction to such frustrations:

> The *intense* view of these manifold contradictions and imperfections in human reason has so wrought upon me, and heated my brain, that I am ready to reject all belief and reasoning, and can look upon no opinion even as more probable or likely than another. Where am I, or what? From what causes do I derive my existence, and to what condition shall I return: Whose favor shall I court, and whose anger must I dread? What beings surround me? and on whom have I any influence, or who have any influence on me? I am confounded with all these questions, and begin to fancy myself in the most deplorable condition imaginable, inviron'd with the deepest darkness, and utterly depriv'd of the use of every member and faculty.
>
> Most fortunately it happens, that since reason is incapable of dispelling these clouds, nature herself suffices to that purpose, and cures me of this philosophical melancholy and delirium, either by relaxing this bent of mind, or by some avocation,[51] and lively impression of my senses, which obliterates all these chimeras.[52] I dine, I play a game of backgammon, I converse, and am merry with my friends; and when after three or four hours' amusement, I wou'd return to these speculations, they appear so cold, and strain'd, and ridiculous, that I cannot find in my heart to enter into them any farther.[53]

Well, perhaps we should just let it rest there. Perhaps these philosophical doubts are empty and sterile. Perhaps, as Robert Ackermann suggests in the Preface of his 1970 introductory text, you have to be crazy to be bothered about such problems:

> I once knew a man who always worried that the roof of any room which he occupied was likely to fall in and injure or kill him. This worry was, in a sense, philosophical; no one could *prove* that the worry was without foundation in fact. But instead of being regarded as a philosopher, this worrier was thought of as a harmless lunatic, known among intimates as 'Crazy Phil.' There is an uncomfortable resemblance between Crazy Phil and many philosophers of science. Like Phil, these philosophers are motivated by private fears.[54]

If this is intended to apply to philosophers who, like Hume, Russell, Reichenbach, and many others, have grappled with the problem of justification of induction, it is a grotesque caricature. Hume was not the victim of neurotic dread.

> Let the course of things be allowed hitherto ever so regular; that alone, without some new argument or inference, proves not that, for the future, it will continue so ... My practice, you say, refutes my doubts. But you mistake the purport of my question. As an agent, I am quite satisfied in the point....[55]

These philosophers were confident that the roof would not fall in, if it was constructed in accord with suitable engineering principles, for they all had full confidence in the laws of physics. Phaedrus, the protagonist of *Zen and the Art of Motorcycle Maintenance*,[56] in

---

50 [Author's note] This matter was surveyed thoroughly by Ben Rogers in 'Foundational Studies in Statistical Inference,' Ph.D. dissertation, Indiana University, 1970.

51 Hobby.

52 Unreal, unpleasant creatures of the imagination.

53 [Author's note] Hume, *Treatise*, Conclusion of Book I.

54 [Author's note] Robert Ackermann, *The Philosophy of Science* (Pegasus, 1970), p. ix.

55 [Author's note] Hume, *Enquiry*, Sec. IV.

56 A 1974 book by Robert M. Pirsig which is a first-person description of a 17-day motorcycle journey across the US, punctuated with philosophical discussions. It has sold more than 4 million copies, making it probably the most widely read work of contemporary philosophy (although Pirsig is not an academic philosopher).

contrast, did end up in an institution on account of his worries about the problem of induction; however he hardly qualifies as a prominent contributor to the philosophical foundations of inductive logic. Concern about the philosophical problem of justification of induction may be pointless; it is not, however, crazy.

But can we really be *that* complacent? Can the problem of induction simply be dismissed as otiose? Much as I'd like to give an affirmative answer, I find I really cannot. Science *is* more reasonable than astrology, superstition, random guessing, divine revelation, and visions in LSD-induced psychedelic states. With scientific techniques we can predict an eclipse. It is reasonable to believe in this prediction. It is not reasonable to accept the prognostication, made by a religious fanatic, that the world will end tomorrow. It is silly to place confidence in forecasts found in fortune cookies in Chinese restaurants.

I am firmly convinced of this—we are all firmly convinced. But how can we show it? With Hume, "I want to know the foundation of this inference."

Without an answer, we open the door to *any mental aberration whatever*—to every form of irrationalism—allowing them all to be just as sound as science. *That simply won't do.* It is unacceptable on philosophical grounds, and it is intolerable on practical grounds. I was not indulging in whimsy when I remarked at the outset that this problem has significant practical ramifications. In a recent case, medical experts agreed that a child with diabetes would die if insulin were not administered. The fundamentalist parents had some sort of divine revelation that the child would not die if medication were halted. No insulin was administered and the child died. In another recent instance, at a commune in Arizona, a 'geomancer'—a person who walks around with hands outstretched sensing the vibrations from the earth—predicted that crops would grow there in arid soil without cultivation or irrigation. The seed was scattered; nothing grew. In this case, the birds and small rodents, at least, benefitted.

It is not intellectually adequate simply to *call* those who practice non-inductive—non-scientific—methods of prediction 'irrational.' It does not solve the

philosophical problem to lock them up, or even to perform lobotomies upon them. Nor is it acceptable to say—as one often hears—that science is, at bottom, a matter of faith; there are many faiths which are all on a par. You just choose the one you like best. It is equally unsatisfactory to give that approach a slight terminological twist and characterize the inductive method as part of 'a form of life'—one among many such 'forms,' I suppose. And it is manifestly untenable to deny that there is any such thing as rationally grounded prediction.

What, then, should we say finally to our students who want to know 'the answer' to Hume's problem of induction? In my opinion we should frankly admit that, as yet, we have no completely satisfactory answer. None of the various attempts—many of them quite ingenious—to solve, resolve, or dissolve the problem is altogether successful. Does that mean that we have been dealing with a pointless question—a pseudoproblem? I do not believe so. The moral seems rather that we have an exceedingly difficult problem on our hands. In his attempts to provide logically adequate foundations of mathematics, Russell turned up a set-theoretical paradox which, he reports, it took him five agonizing years to resolve. We now have every reason to believe that the problems raised by Hume when he said, "I want to learn the foundation of this [inductive] inference," are, if anything, even more difficult. The work of Russell and others on the foundations of mathematics has considerably deepened our understanding of mathematical reasoning. A solution of Hume's problem of induction could plausibly be expected to deepen our understanding of scientific reasoning.

I have been taking an unpopular line—some might even consider it a breach of etiquette on the occasion, when everyone else politely refrained from mentioning this subject. It seems to me, however, that the least we can do on the bicentennial is to acknowledge candidly that part of Hume's legacy is work still to be done. The problem he left us is a tough one, but we have no excuse for pretending that it does not exist. And, I think, we had better not stop trying to solve it.

"The Fixation of Belief"

Who Was C.S. Peirce?

Charles Sanders Peirce was born in 1839 in Cambridge, Massachusetts, the second son of Benjamin and Sarah Peirce. Benjamin Peirce was, at the time, the most respected mathematician in America and a distinguished professor at Harvard College; young Charles was a prodigy in both science and philosophy, and widely viewed as likely to become a more talented mathematician than even his father. Growing up well-connected with America's academic and scientific circles, Charles knew personally most of the leading intellectual figures of his time. However, his undoubted genius, originality, and firm independence of mind—as well as his prickly character—did not make his life an easy one. In an increasingly insular and conservative late nineteenth-century New England, Peirce found his ambitions thwarted at almost every turn, and for the last third of his life he was unable to obtain regular employment. He ended his life living in poverty and relative isolation in rural Pennsylvania.

Peirce was educated at Harvard College (where he got a BA) and the Lawrence Scientific School at Harvard (where he received a BSc in chemistry). In 1861, he joined the US Coast and Geodetic Survey[1] where,

frustrated in his attempts to obtain an academic position, he was to spend the next thirty years of his career. He rose through the ranks of the Survey—partly aided by patronage from his influential father—until he was put in charge of gravity experiments and pendulum research. As part of his duties with the Survey, Peirce took several trips to Europe to attend conferences and compare data with British and European scientists, and he became an internationally respected mathematician and scientist. Between 1869 and 1872 he was also an assistant at the Harvard Observatory, and his first published book, *Photometric Researches*, was the result of his astronomical observations there. In 1879 he was appointed a lecturer in logic at Johns Hopkins University, the first true graduate school in America.

This was the high-point of Peirce's career. In 1876 he had become estranged from his first wife, Harriet Melusina Fay, and in 1883 he divorced her in order to marry Juliette Froissy Pourtalès. In 1884, just as Peirce was confidently expecting to be granted tenure at Johns Hopkins, the university—shocked by Peirce's scandalously "consorting" with a French woman while still legally married to his first wife—declined to renew his lecturing contract. After this, Peirce had no hope of regular academic employment anywhere in America.

Seven years later, in 1891, Peirce was forced to resign from the US Coastal Survey. A new cost-cutting administration in Washington decided to sharply reduce the budget for the Survey's geodetic work, but Peirce refused to submit to the lower standards of accuracy and scientific rigor this imposed and ignored the new regulations. The government then apparently applied behind-the-scenes pressure which meant

---

1   Geodesy is the science of the size and shape of the earth, and a geodetic survey involves the mapping of a large region of the Earth's surface in which adjustments need to be made for the curvature of the planet; the precise measurement of very small variations in gravity at different points on the Earth's surface was an important tool for measuring exactly the planet's shape, and hence for geodetic surveys.

that his major report (on which he had worked for several years) of the results of his gravitational experiments was refused publication—this led to his expulsion from the Survey.

Although Peirce was only 52, and still had a quarter-century of life ahead of him, he was never again able to obtain regular employment. It did not help that Peirce was a notoriously difficult man to get along with, prone to extreme mood swings and sudden onsets of paranoia, combining a very high opinion of his own abilities with a sometimes contemptuous view of others' intelligence. Peirce was reduced to writing huge numbers of book reviews and popular articles to make ends meet, and his life came to be sporadically dominated by a succession of "get rich schemes" that never panned out.

He and Juliette moved to a small farmhouse near Milford, Pennsylvania, and Peirce renamed the house "Arisbe," for the Greek town where some of the earliest philosophers had lived. He embarked on ambitious plans to renovate and expand it, and as he was dealing with the physical architecture of his house Peirce also began thinking about the architecture of his philosophical theories and self-consciously trying to bring his various doctrines together into a single, carefully-assembled structure. He was quite convinced that he was poised to make important and original contributions to human knowledge. However, in the end, both architectural projects remained incomplete: Arisbe never became the rambling manor Peirce hoped it would be, and Peirce felt frustrated in his attempts to summarize his system, describing his writings as "a mere table of contents, so abstract, a very snarl of twine."

Increasingly (and accurately) worried that his public academic career had irreversibly failed and that he would never be able to get his mature philosophical system, and his discoveries in mathematics and logic, into print, Peirce made several book proposals to publishing companies and applied for a number of grants. Most of these were rejected, perhaps partly because of the influence of various enemies he had made during his lifetime. After a long period of ill health, Peirce died at Arisbe in the spring of 1914, a nearly forgotten man, two months before the outbreak of the First World War.

Only twenty years after his death, when the Harvard Philosophy Department published a collection of his papers, did Peirce's philosophical importance come to be glimpsed by the wider world. In recent years—since about the late 1970s—there has been an enormously increased interest in Peirce's work. He is now thought of as important in the development of modern formal logic, as the founder of the science of semiotics, and as one of the main figures in American pragmatism. Indeed for some philosophers, such as Karl Popper, he is "one of the greatest philosophers of all time," and his work inspires intense—sometimes almost uncritical—devotion among many of those who study it today.

What Was Peirce's Overall Philosophical Project?

Peirce wrote voluminously: his extant writings on science, mathematics, philosophy, logic, history, and psychology (not including those lost during his travels to Europe and due to poor storage after his death) would fill over a hundred 500-page volumes. Furthermore, his philosophical beliefs were not static during his lifetime but evolved towards a unified, but complex, diverse, and deeply original, system of doctrines. This makes Peirce's philosophical views difficult to summarize. Some of the most important strands in his mature thought, however, were his pragmatism, his theory of "semiotic," and his metaphysics of objective idealism and evolutionary cosmology.

Pragmatism, in Peirce's view, is a method for resolving conceptual confusions or contradictions by getting clear about the meanings of the claims involved. The central idea is that the meaning of a proposition is not to be found somehow contained *within* it, but consists entirely in a set of *relations* between the claim and its consequences. Perhaps his most famous statement of this view comes in "How to Make Our Ideas Clear," a paper written to be read directly after "The Fixation of Belief":

> Consider what effects, which might conceivably have practical bearings, we conceive the object of our conception to have. Then, our conception of these effects is the whole of our conception of the object.

For example, suppose I want to find out whether a sample of soft, white metal is sodium: I can predict that if it is sodium, then if I drop it into hot water it will explosively catch fire; if I heat it up it will melt at 97.8°C; if I combine it with a wide variety of other substances (such as calcium, fluoride, carbon dioxide, or cyanide) it will react with them and form compounds; and so on. The *complete* set of predications that I could make about the consequences of my actions if the substance were sodium is also, according to Peirce, a complete clarification of the *meaning* of the claim that the sample is sodium.

The method of pragmatism was, for Peirce, inspired by scientific practices, but it is not to be restricted to the laboratory, being a general account of meaning. For example, Peirce argued that the method of pragmatism[2] can be used to clarify, or define, the notions of *truth* and *reality*: "the opinion which is fated to be ultimately agreed to by all who investigate is what we mean by the truth, and the object represented in this opinion is the real."

"Semiotic" was the name that Peirce gave[3] to his theory of information, representation, and communication, a theory which came to have great importance for his system as a whole. For Peirce, the study of *signs* was to replace the theory of knowledge, as traditionally understood. A sign is anything that stands *for* something (its object) *to* something (its interpreter): on Peirce's view, all three parts of this relation (the sign, the object, and the interpreter) are necessary for representation to take place. In particular, nothing can stand for (e.g., be a picture of, be an indication of) something else all by itself; in order to be a sign, it must first be interpreted as such by some observer. Peirce went on to develop an elaborate taxonomy of types of signs, but one three-way distinction is especially important: that between *icons, indices*, and *symbols*. An icon is a sign which resembles its object (such as a photograph or a color swatch); an index is a sign which is naturally correlated with its object (such as clouds indicating rain or returning swallows being a sign of spring); and a symbol is a sign which is conventionally used to refer to objects that it does not physically correspond with or resemble (for example, a "Yield" sign or the English word "cow").

"Objective idealism" was the name that Peirce sometimes gave to his metaphysical beliefs. He was a *monistic realist*, which is to say that he believed that there is a real world whose existence does not depend on our thinking about it, which lies behind and causes our perceptions and about which our beliefs can be true or false, and which is entirely made up of just one kind of stuff. However, Peirce had a rather unusual view of what that 'stuff' is: he held that matter is what he called "effete mind." This is perhaps best explained in terms of Peirce's "evolutionary cosmology." Roughly, this is the view that there are exactly three primary moving forces in the universe: chance, love, and habit. The universe began, according to Peirce, in a state of total chance—pure, random possibility. As it evolved over time, the other two forces (love and habit) emerged out of the chaos, and under their influence the universe became a more ordered place. It began to follow certain laws, though these laws should be thought of, in the first instance, as being primarily *psychological* laws. Over time, in the universe at large as in an individual human being, *habit* has gained more and more of a grip over things' behavior, until much of the universe has become so entrenched in certain regular habits that it has become what we call "matter," blindly obeying (what we call) the laws of physics. One upshot of this is that physical laws should not be thought of as different in kind from psychological laws, and so the habitual aspect of human behavior is just as susceptible to mechanical explanation as is the orbiting of the planets and the erosion of a river bed. On the other hand, love, sympathy, and pure chance are still operative principles in the universe, according to Peirce, so our explanations (of either human beings or the natural world) can never be *purely* mechanical.

Peirce was very much a system-builder, and he intended to fit all of these disparate elements of his philosophy together into an overall unifying structure.

---

2   Peirce re-named his version of the doctrine "pragmaticism" after William James—with due acknowledgements to Peirce—had made the pragmatic theory widely known through lectures and writings; Peirce considered this new label "ugly enough to keep it safe from kidnappers."

3   Though the term was first introduced by John Locke in the seventeenth century.

He believed that all human knowledge can be systematically arrayed within a framework founded on the most basic science, abstract mathematics. Peirce thought of this as the study of the most fundamental and universal *categories*. According to Peirce there are exactly three basic categories, which he called Firstness (that which is as it is in itself, independently of anything else), Secondness (that which is as it is relative to something else), and Thirdness (that which is as it is as mediate between two others).[4] In other words, any language adequate for the description of reality must contain at least three sorts of properties and relations: one-place, two-place, and three-place. In particular, in Peirce's view, Thirdness is ineliminable: the universe cannot be fully captured without a proper understanding of the relation of mediation, and this three-way relation is basic—it cannot be analyzed into any set of two-place relations.

The rest of philosophy then falls into three parts, which Peirce called "phenomenology," "normative science," and "metaphysics." Phenomenology takes phenomena as Firsts, and explores their intrinsic nature. Normative science—which includes both physics and ethics, for example—treats phenomena as Seconds, and examines their relations to various goals such as truth, rightness, or beauty. Thus, normative science asks which physical theories are true or which actions are morally right. Finally, metaphysics treats phenomena as Thirds—as intermediate between us and some underlying reality. The most important examples of Thirds, according to Peirce, are signs.

"The Fixation of Belief" was written fairly early in the development of Peirce's philosophical system, but falls within the domain of "normative science" and is closely connected to his views on pragmatism. It is concerned with how we can best bring our beliefs into line with truth.

What Is the Structure of This Reading?

"The Fixation of Belief" is the first of a sequence of six articles by Peirce published in *Popular Science Monthly*, which together were called "Illustrations of the

Logic of Science." In them, Peirce laid out his view of the nature and importance of the scientific method, which he equates generally with good habits of reasoning. He begins "The Fixation of Belief" by stressing the importance of logic, or good reasoning, to science, and then in section II goes on to sketch his view of the nature of logic. In section III Peirce draws a distinction between doubt and belief, which he uses in section IV to define *inquiry* as the process of replacing doubt with belief. The rest of the article is a consideration of the best and most reliable method of fixing belief in place of doubt: Peirce considers four methods—the method of tenacity, the method of authority, the *a priori* method, and the scientific method—and argues that the scientific method is to be preferred above the others.

Some Useful Background Information

1. Peirce's philosophy was often informed by his wide reading in the history of philosophy, and in "The Fixation of Belief," although he does not mention this explicitly, Peirce can be seen to be reacting against and rejecting Descartes' view of the scientific method. Peirce takes Descartes to recommend the practice of science as a basically solitary pursuit, which begins by calling almost all existing knowledge into doubt and which aspires to prove once and for all the truth of some settled body of scientific knowledge. (See the Descartes reading in Chapter 3 for more information on his views, and to make up your own mind whether Peirce was right about them or not.) By contrast, Peirce thought of science as a collaborative investigation which takes for granted all the propositions of which we have no doubt as the inquiry begins, and seeks only to replace some (more focussed) doubt with belief. Furthermore, in his view, there is no question of jumping suddenly and as individuals to 'the truth': instead, science consists in fallible investigators continually progressing toward the truth by replacing real doubts with settled beliefs, which may in turn be later called into doubt and revised. The real power of the scien-

---

4   Peirce also called these categories "quality," "reaction," and "mediation."

tific method, according to Peirce, is that it is *self-correcting*, rather than infallible.

2. "The Fixation of Belief" introduces Peirce's view of the benefits of the scientific method, but does not go into detail about what exactly he thought that method was. Peirce called it the "inductive method," and he identified three stages of scientific inquiry corresponding to three different patterns of inference: abduction, deduction, and induction. First comes *abduction*, the tentative adoption of an explanatory hypothesis that, if true, would explain the phenomena under investigation. For example, it might occur to a group of scientists that the otherwise mysterious behavior of different materials would be explicable if matter were made up of different types of tiny particles—atoms—which combine with each other in fixed proportions to form compounds. Then *deduction* is the use of logic to derive testable consequences from this tentative theory: for example, it follows from this "atomic theory of matter" that some materials are elements and some are compounds, and that different elements will combine together into compounds only according to particular measurable ratios. Finally *induction* is the testing of these predictions through experimentation—testing to see whether there are indeed identifiable ratios in the combination of elements—and the evaluation of the theory in the light of this experimental data.

A Common Misconception

Peirce is perhaps most commonly thought of as a pragmatist, and indeed "The Fixation of Belief" is the first of a sequence of articles which present a largely pragmatic view of science. This does not mean, as is sometimes assumed, that Peirce placed no value on truth, or the correspondence of our beliefs with reality, and was only concerned about the practical *usefulness* of our beliefs. On the contrary, even at this fairly early stage of his philosophical development Peirce was a realist, and indeed he believed that pragmatism would only be held by someone who was convinced of the

existence of a mind-independent world that would, through the consequences of our actions, check our false beliefs and push us in the direction of truth.

How Important and Influential Is This Passage?

Max Fisch has called Peirce's "Illustrations of the Logic of Science," (of which the article reprinted here is the first of six parts) the nineteenth-century equivalent of Descartes' *Discourse on the Method*. At least in Fisch's view, Peirce definitively captured the essence of the modern scientific method which had replaced the now-outmoded Cartesian understanding of science. In particular, Peirce stresses the importance of collaborative, incremental *experimentation* as part of good scientific reasoning, and places less weight on the power of "pure reason." Peirce also has particular importance for laying the foundations for a *pragmatic* account of science, which elucidates and evaluates scientific claims in terms of their experimental consequences. This idea has been very important in twentieth-century philosophy of science, and is arguably a forerunner of (though not the same doctrine as) the influential theory of "logical positivism," which had as one of its central tenets the claim that the meaning of a statement is its method of verification.

Suggestions for Critical Reflection

1. Why do you think Peirce mocks the medieval assumption that logic consists of nothing more than "syllogistic procedures" (i.e., roughly, deductive logic), suggesting that this component of logic by itself is "very easy"? What do you think is the hard and important part of logic, on Peirce's view? Do you agree? What do you think that Peirce means when he talks of reasoning as something "to be done with one's eyes open, by manipulating real things instead of words and fancies"?

2. Peirce defines the mental states of belief and doubt in terms of their relationships to *action* (a belief is a habit of action, and a doubt is a stimulus to action). Does this seem like a good way to explain them? Does this approach work

for mental states generally? Is there more to be-lieving something than just being disposed to act in certain ways under certain conditions?

3. Peirce defines inquiry as the struggle to elimi-nate doubt and to fix belief; as a consequence, he claims that "the sole object of inquiry is the settlement of opinion." Is this what we normally believe about inquiry, especially scientific in-quiry? Do you think Peirce is right about the goals of science?

4. How persuasive do you find Peirce's discussion of the four different methods of fixing belief? How sincere do you think Peirce is being when he praises the first three methods? What do you think Peirce's attitude was toward religion and its relation with science? Do you agree with him?

5. What exactly are Peirce's *reasons* for prefer-ring the scientific method? How pragmatic are these reasons? How good are they?

6. Why does Peirce think it is an *advantage* of the scientific method that it can sometimes be per-formed badly or incorrectly, while that is not (he claims) true of the other three methods? Is he right that only science can be done badly? Is he right that this is a good sign for science?

Suggestions for Further Reading

The Essential Peirce: Selected Writings (in two volumes edited by Nathan Houser, Christian Kloesel, and mem-bers of the Peirce Edition Project, and published by Indiana University Press in 1992 (Vol. 1) and 1998 (Vol. 2) is a good, representative selection of his writings. The six papers which make up Peirce's "Illustrations of the Logic of Science" appear in the first volume; many of his most important later writings on pragmatism feature in the second. A fairly good account of Peirce's rather tragic and eccentric life is Joseph Brent's *Charles Sanders Peirce: A Life* (Indiana University Press, 1998); also quite interesting is Kenneth Laine Ketner's *His Glassy Essence: An Autobiography of Charles Sand-ers Peirce* (Vanderbilt University Press, 1998).

Four good books about Peirce's philosophy are Max Fisch, *Peirce, Semiotic, and Pragmatism* (Indiana University Press, 1986); Christopher Hookway, *Peirce* (Routledge & Kegan Paul, 1985) and *Truth, Rationality,*

and Pragmatism: Themes from Peirce (Oxford Universi-ty Press, 2000); and Murray Murphey, *The Development of Peirce's Philosophy* (Hackett, 1993).

"The Fixation of Belief"[5]

I.

Few persons care to study logic, because everybody conceives himself to be proficient enough in the art of reasoning already. But I observe that this satisfaction is limited to one's own ratiocination,[6] and does not extend to that of other men.

We come to the full possession of our power of drawing inferences the last of all our faculties, for it is not so much a natural gift as a long and difficult art. The history of its practice would make a grand subject for a book. The mediaeval schoolmen, following the Romans, made logic the earliest of a boy's studies after grammar, as being very easy. So it was, as they understood it. Its fundamental principle, according to them, was, that all knowledge rests on either author-ity or reason; but that whatever is deduced by reason depends ultimately on a premise derived from author-ity. Accordingly, as soon as a boy was perfect in the syllogistic procedure,[7] his intellectual kit of tools was held to be complete.

To Roger Bacon,[8] that remarkable mind who in the middle of the thirteenth century was almost a scientific man, the schoolmen's conception of reason-ing appeared only an obstacle to truth. He saw that experience alone teaches anything—a proposition which to us seems easy to understand, because a dis-

---

5 This article was first printed in *Popular Science Monthly* 12 (November 1877), pp. 1–15. It is the first of six papers, all published in the same magazine, col-lectively titled "Illustrations of the Logic of Science."

6 Methodical or logical reasoning.

7 The rules for argument first laid down by Aristotle in the fourth century BCE.

8 Roger Bacon (c. 1214–1292), an English scientist and philosopher often credited with foreshadowing the empiricist methodology of modern science (and with inventing spectacles). To later ages he had the nickname *Doctor Mirabilis*, or marvelous doctor.

tinct conception of experience has been handed down to us from former generations; which to him also seemed perfectly clear, because its difficulties had not yet unfolded themselves. Of all kinds of experience, the best, he thought, was interior illumination, which teaches many things about Nature which the external senses could never discover, such as the transubstantiation of bread.[9]

Four centuries later, the more celebrated Bacon,[10] in the first book of his *Novum Organum*, gave his clear account of experience as something which must be open to verification and reëxamination. But, superior as Lord Bacon's conception is to earlier notions, a modern reader who is not in awe of his grandiloquence is chiefly struck by the inadequacy of his view of scientific procedure. That we have only to make some crude experiments, to draw up briefs of the results in certain blank forms, to go through these by rule, checking off everything disproved and setting down the alternatives, and that thus in a few years physical science would be finished up—what an idea! "He wrote on science like a Lord Chancellor," indeed.[11]

The early scientists, Copernicus, Tycho Brahe, Kepler, Galileo, and Gilbert,[12] had methods more like those of their modern brethren. Kepler undertook to draw a curve through the places of Mars;[13] and his greatest service to science was in impressing on men's minds that this was the thing to be done if they wished to improve astronomy; that they were not to content themselves with inquiring whether one system of epicycles[14] was better than another, but that they were to sit down to the figures and find out what the curve, in truth, was. He accomplished this by his incomparable energy and courage, blundering along in the most inconceivable way (to us), from one irrational hypothesis to another, until, after trying twenty-two of these, he fell, by the mere exhaustion of his invention, upon the orbit which a mind well furnished with the weapons of modern logic would have tried almost at the outset.

In the same way, every work of science great enough to be well remembered for a few generations affords some exemplification of the defective state of the art of reasoning of the time when it was written; and each chief step in science has been a lesson in logic. It was so when Lavoisier[15] and his contemporaries took up the study of chemistry. The old chemist's maxim had been, "*Lege, lege, lege, labora, ora, et relege.*"[16] Lavoisier's method was not to read and pray, not to dream that some long and complicated

---

9   According to Catholic belief, the changing of the communion wafer into the body of Christ during the sacrament of Eucharist or Mass.

10   Sir Francis Bacon (1561–1626), another English philosopher and scientist, was Lord Chancellor under James I and was arguably the first writer to try to delineate the proper methods of successful science, in the process providing a fairly sophisticated account of the empirical method. The *Novum Organum*, which lays out these methodological principles, was published in 1620.

11   This was a comment on Francis Bacon by William Harvey. Harvey (1578–1657) was the English physician who discovered the circulation of the blood.

12   Nicolaus Copernicus (or Mikoląj Kopernik, 1473–1543) proposed that the planets orbit the sun rather than the earth. Tycho Brahe (1546–1601) made some of the most accurate astronomical observations ever achieved with the naked eye, and Johannes Kepler (1571–1630) used them to formulate three laws governing planetary motion. Galileo Galilei (1564–1642)

formulated the law of the uniform acceleration of falling bodies and was among the first to apply the telescope to astronomy, discovering craters on the moon, sunspots, and Jupiter's satellites. William Gilbert (1544–1603) was an English court physician who discovered how to make magnets and investigated the Earth's magnetic field.

13   [Author's note] Not quite so, but as nearly as can be told in a few words.

14   Epicycles are small circles which move around the circumference of a larger one: epicycles (and epicycles of epicycles) were used in Ptolemaic (i.e., pre-Copernican) astronomy to geometrically describe the movements of the planets.

15   Antoine Lavoisier (1743–1794), often regarded as the father of modern chemistry, discovered oxygen.

16   "Read, read, read, work, pray, and read again" (in Latin). By the "old chemist," Peirce means the alchemists of the Middle Ages.

chemical process would have a certain effect, to put it into practice with dull patience, after its inevitable failure to dream that with some modification it would have another result, and to end by publishing the last dream as a fact: his way was to carry his mind into his laboratory, and to make of his alembics and cucurbits[17] instruments of thought, giving a new conception of reasoning as something which was to be done with one's eyes open, by manipulating real things instead of words and fancies.

The Darwinian controversy is, in large part, a question of logic. Mr. Darwin proposed to apply the statistical method to biology. The same thing had been done in a widely different branch of science, the theory of gases. Though unable to say what the movements of any particular molecule of gas would be on a certain hypothesis regarding the constitution of this class of bodies, Clausius and Maxwell[18] were yet able, by the application of the doctrine of probabilities, to predict that in the long run such and such a proportion of the molecules would, under given circumstances, acquire such and such velocities; that there would take place, every second, such and such a number of collisions, etc.; and from these propositions were able to deduce certain properties of gases, especially in regard to their heat-relations. In like manner, Darwin, while unable to say what the operation of variation and natural selection in any individual case will be, demonstrates that in the long run they will adapt animals to their circumstances. Whether or not existing animal forms are due to such action, or what position the theory ought to take, forms the subject of a discussion in which questions of fact and questions of logic are curiously interlaced.

---

17 A cucurbit is the gourd-shaped flask of an alembic, which was a device used by medieval alchemists for distilling liquids.

18 Rudolf Clausius (1822–1888) developed the concept of entropy and formulated the second law of thermodynamics, as well as carrying out pioneering work on the kinetic theory of gases. James Clerk Maxwell (1831–1879) is best known for unifying the phenomena of electricity and magnetism into a single set of field equations, but he was also important in the development of the kinetic theory of gases.

II.

The object of reasoning is to find out, from the consideration of what we already know, something else which we do not know. Consequently, reasoning is good if it be such as to give a true conclusion from true premises, and not otherwise. Thus, the question of its validity is purely one of fact and not of thinking. A being the premises and B the conclusion, the question is, whether these facts are really so related that if A is B is. If so, the inference is valid; if not, not. It is not in the least the question whether, when the premises are accepted by the mind, we feel an impulse to accept the conclusion also. It is true that we do generally reason correctly by nature. But that is an accident; the true conclusion would remain true if we had no impulse to accept it; and the false one would remain false, though we could not resist the tendency to believe in it.

We are, doubtless, in the main logical animals, but we are not perfectly so. Most of us, for example, are naturally more sanguine[19] and hopeful than logic would justify. We seem to be so constituted that in the absence of any facts to go upon we are happy and self-satisfied; so that the effect of experience is continually to contract our hopes and aspirations. Yet a lifetime of the application of this corrective does not usually eradicate our sanguine disposition. Where hope is unchecked by any experience, it is likely that our optimism is extravagant. Logicality in regard to practical matters is the most useful quality an animal can possess, and might, therefore, result from the action of natural selection; but outside of these it is probably of more advantage to the animal to have his mind filled with pleasing and encouraging visions, independently of their truth; and thus, upon unpractical subjects, natural selection might occasion a fallacious tendency of thought.

That which determines us, from given premises, to draw one inference rather than another, is some habit of mind, whether it be constitutional or acquired. The habit is good or otherwise, according as it produces true conclusions from true premises or not; and an inference is regarded as valid or not, without reference to the truth or falsity of its conclusion specially,

---

19 Optimistic or cheerfully confident.

but according as the habit which determines it is such as to produce true conclusions in general or not. The particular habit of mind which governs this or that inference may be formulated in a proposition whose truth depends on the validity of the inferences which the habit determines; and such a formula is called a *guiding principle* of inference. Suppose, for example, that we observe that a rotating disk of copper quickly comes to rest when placed between the poles of a magnet, and we infer that this will happen with every disk of copper. The guiding principle is, that what is true of one piece of copper is true of another. Such a guiding principle with regard to copper would be much safer than with regard to many other substances—brass, for example.

A book might be written to signalize all the most important of these guiding principles of reasoning. It would probably be, we must confess, of no service to a person whose thought is directed wholly to practical subjects, and whose activity moves along thoroughly-beaten paths. The problems which present themselves to such a mind are matters of routine which he has learned once for all to handle in learning his business. But let a man venture into an unfamiliar field, or where his results are not continually checked by experience, and all history shows that the most masculine intellect will oft-times lose his orientation and waste his efforts in directions which bring him no nearer to his goal, or even carry him entirely astray. He is like a ship in the open sea, with no one on board who understands the rules of navigation. And in such a case some general study of the guiding principles of reasoning would be sure to be found useful.

The subject could hardly be treated, however, without being first limited; since almost any fact may serve as a guiding principle. But it so happens that there exists a division among facts, such that in one class are all those which are absolutely essential as guiding principles, while in the others are all which have any other interest as objects of research. This division is between those which are necessarily taken for granted in asking whether a certain conclusion follows from certain premises, and those which are not implied in that question. A moment's thought will show that a variety of facts are already assumed when the logical question is first asked. It is implied, for instance, that there are such states of mind as doubt and belief—that a passage from one to the other is possible, the object of thought remaining the same, and that this transition is subject to some rules which all minds are alike bound by. As these are facts which we must already know before we can have any clear conception of reasoning at all, it cannot be supposed to be any longer of much interest to inquire into their truth or falsity. On the other hand, it is easy to believe that those rules of reasoning which are deduced from the very idea of the process are the ones which are the most essential; and, indeed, that so long as it conforms to these it will, at least, not lead to false conclusions from true premises. In point of fact, the importance of what may be deduced from the assumptions involved in the logical question turns out to be greater than might be supposed, and this for reasons which it is difficult to exhibit at the outset. The only one which I shall here mention is, that conceptions which are really products of logical reflection, without being readily seen to be so, mingle with our ordinary thoughts, and are frequently the causes of great confusion. This is the case, for example, with the conception of quality. A quality, as such, is never an object of observation. We can see that a thing is blue or green, but the quality of being blue and the quality of being green are not things which we see; they are products of logical reflections. The truth is, that common-sense, or thought as it first emerges above the level of the narrowly practical, is deeply imbued with that bad logical quality to which the epithet *metaphysical* is commonly applied; and nothing can clear it up but a severe course of logic.

III.

We generally know when we wish to ask a question and when we wish to pronounce a judgment, for there is a dissimilarity between the sensation of doubting and that of believing.

But this is not all which distinguishes doubt from belief. There is a practical difference. Our beliefs guide our desires and shape our actions. The Assassins, or followers of the Old Man of the Mountain,[20]

---

20 The Assassins were a militant Muslim religious order founded in Persia in 1090 and, during the time of the

used to rush into death at his least command, because they believed that obedience to him would insure everlasting felicity. Had they doubted this, they would not have acted as they did. So it is with every belief, according to its degree. The feeling of believing is a more or less sure indication of there being established in our nature some habit which will determine our actions. Doubt never has such an effect.

Nor must we overlook a third point of difference. Doubt is an uneasy and dissatisfied state from which we struggle to free ourselves and pass into the state of belief; while the latter is a calm and satisfactory state which we do not wish to avoid, or to change to a belief in anything else.[21] On the contrary, we cling tenaciously, not merely to believing, but to believing just what we do believe.

Thus, both doubt and belief have positive effects upon us, though very different ones. Belief does not make us act at once, but puts us into such a condition that we shall behave in some certain way, when the occasion arises. Doubt has not the least effect of this sort, but stimulates us to action until it is destroyed. This reminds us of the irritation of a nerve and the reflex action produced thereby; while for the analogue of belief, in the nervous system, we must look to what are called nervous associations—for example, to that habit of the nerves in consequence of which the smell of a peach will make the mouth water.

IV.

The irritation of doubt causes a struggle to attain a state of belief. I shall term this struggle *inquiry,* though it must be admitted that this is sometimes not a very apt designation.

The irritation of doubt is the only immediate motive for the struggle to attain belief. It is certainly best for us that our beliefs should be such as may truly guide our actions so as to satisfy our desires; and this reflection will make us reject any belief which does not seem to have been so formed as to insure this result. But it will only do so by creating a doubt in the place of that belief. With the doubt, therefore, the struggle begins, and with the cessation of doubt it ends. Hence, the sole object of inquiry is the settlement of opinion. We may fancy that this is not enough for us, and that we seek, not merely an opinion, but a true opinion. But put this fancy to the test, and it proves groundless; for as soon as a firm belief is reached we are entirely satisfied, whether the belief be true or false. And it is clear that nothing out of the sphere of our knowledge can be our object, for nothing which does not affect the mind can be the motive for mental effort. The most that can be maintained is, that we seek for a belief that we shall *think* to be true. But we think each one of our beliefs to be true, and, indeed, it is mere tautology to say so.

That the settlement of opinion is the sole end of inquiry is a very important proposition. It sweeps away, at once, various vague and erroneous conceptions of proof. A few of these may be noticed here.

1. Some philosophers have imagined that to start an inquiry it was only necessary to utter a question or set it down upon paper, and have even recommended us to begin our studies with questioning everything! But the mere putting of a proposition into the interrogative form does not stimulate the mind to any struggle after belief. There must be a real and living doubt, and without this all discussion is idle.

2. It is a very common idea that a demonstration must rest on some ultimate and absolutely indubitable propositions. These, according to one school, are first principles of a general nature; according to another, are first sensations. But, in point of fact, an inquiry, to have that completely satisfactory result called demonstration, has only to start with propositions perfectly free from all actual doubt. If the premises are not in fact doubted at all, they cannot be more satisfactory than they are.

3. Some people seem to love to argue a point after all the world is fully convinced of it. But no further

---

Crusades, notorious for their widespread acts of terror. Their leader was called Sheik al-Jebal ('Old Man of the Mountain') and he was said to possess the Holy Spirit and to be obeyed with blind obedience. Numbering 50,000 followers at their height, the Assassins—the word comes from the Arabic *haššaš*, hashish-eater—were finally destroyed in 1272.

21   [Author's note] I am not speaking of secondary effects occasionally produced by the interference of other impulses.

advance can be made. When doubt ceases, mental action on the subject comes to an end; and, if it did go on, it would be without a purpose.

V.

If the settlement of opinion is the sole object of inquiry, and if belief is of the nature of a habit, why should we not attain the desired end, by taking any answer to a question which we may fancy, and constantly reiterating it to ourselves, dwelling on all which may conduce to that belief, and learning to turn with contempt and hatred from anything that might disturb it? This simple and direct method is really pursued by many men. I remember once being entreated not to read a certain newspaper lest it might change my opinion upon free-trade. "Lest I might be entrapped by its fallacies and misstatements," was the form of expression. "You are not," my friend said, "a special student of political economy. You might, therefore, easily be deceived by fallacious arguments upon the subject. You might, then, if you read this paper, be led to believe in protection. But you admit that free-trade is the true doctrine; and you do not wish to believe what is not true." I have often known this system to be deliberately adopted. Still oftener, the instinctive dislike of an undecided state of mind, exaggerated into a vague dread of doubt, makes men cling spasmodically to the views they already take. The man feels that, if he only holds to his belief without wavering, it will be entirely satisfactory. Nor can it be denied that a steady and immovable faith yields great peace of mind. It may, indeed, give rise to inconveniences, as if a man should resolutely continue to believe that fire would not burn him, or that he would be eternally damned if he received his *ingesta*[22] otherwise than through a stomach-pump. But then the man who adopts this method will not allow that its inconveniences are greater than its advantages. He will say, "I hold steadfastly to the truth, and the truth is always wholesome." And in many cases it may very well be that the pleasure he derives from his calm faith overbalances any inconveniences resulting from its deceptive character. Thus, if it be true that death is annihilation, then the man who believes that he will

certainly go straight to heaven when he dies, provided he have fulfilled certain simple observances in this life, has a cheap pleasure which will not be followed by the least disappointment. A similar consideration seems to have weight with many persons in religious topics, for we frequently hear it said, "Oh, I could not believe so-and-so, because I should be wretched if I did." When an ostrich buries its head in the sand as danger approaches, it very likely takes the happiest course. It hides the danger, and then calmly says there is no danger; and, if it feels perfectly sure there is none, why should it raise its head to see? A man may go through life, systematically keeping out of view all that might cause a change in his opinions, and if he only succeeds—basing his method, as he does, on two fundamental psychological laws—I do not see what can be said against his doing so. It would be an egotistical impertinence to object that his procedure is irrational, for that only amounts to saying that his method of settling belief is not ours. He does not propose to himself to be rational, and, indeed, will often talk with scorn of man's weak and illusive reason. So let him think as he pleases.

But this method of fixing belief, which may be called the method of tenacity, will be unable to hold its ground in practice. The social impulse is against it. The man who adopts it will find that other men think differently from him, and it will be apt to occur to him, in some saner moment, that their opinions are quite as good as his own, and this will shake his confidence in his belief. This conception, that another man's thought or sentiment may be equivalent to one's own, is a distinctly new step, and a highly important one. It arises from an impulse too strong in man to be suppressed, without danger of destroying the human species. Unless we make ourselves hermits, we shall necessarily influence each other's opinions; so that the problem becomes how to fix belief, not in the individual merely, but in the community.

Let the will of the state act, then, instead of that of the individual. Let an institution be created which shall have for its object to keep correct doctrines before the attention of the people, to reiterate them perpetually, and to teach them to the young; having at the same time power to prevent contrary doctrines

---

22   Food.

from being taught, advocated, or expressed. Let all possible causes of a change of mind be removed from men's apprehensions. Let them be kept ignorant, lest they should learn of some reason to think otherwise than they do. Let their passions be enlisted, so that they may regard private and unusual opinions with hatred and horror. Then, let all men who reject the established belief be terrified into silence. Let the people turn out and tar-and-feather such men, or let inquisitions be made into the manner of thinking of suspected persons, and when they are found guilty of forbidden beliefs, let them be subjected to some signal punishment. When complete agreement could not otherwise be reached, a general massacre of all who have not thought in a certain way has proved a very effective means of settling opinion in a country. If the power to do this be wanting, let a list of opinions be drawn up, to which no man of the least independence of thought can assent, and let the faithful be required to accept all these propositions, in order to segregate them as radically as possible from the influence of the rest of the world.

This method has, from the earliest times, been one of the chief means of upholding correct theological and political doctrines, and of preserving their universal or catholic[23] character. In Rome, especially, it has been practised from the days of Numa Pompilius to those of Pius Nonus.[24] This is the most perfect example in history; but wherever there is a priesthood—and no religion has been without one—this method has been more or less made use of. Wherever there is an aristocracy, or a guild, or any association of a class of men whose interests depend, or are supposed to depend, on certain propositions, there will be inevitably found some traces of this natural product of social feeling. Cruelties always accompany this

system; and when it is consistently carried out, they become atrocities of the most horrible kind in the eyes of any rational man. Nor should this occasion surprise, for the officer of a society does not feel justified in surrendering the interests of that society for the sake of mercy, as he might his own private interests. It is natural, therefore, that sympathy and fellowship should thus produce a most ruthless power.

In judging this method of fixing belief, which may be called the method of authority, we must, in the first place, allow its immeasurable mental and moral superiority to the method of tenacity. Its success is proportionately greater; and, in fact, it has over and over again worked the most majestic results. The mere structures of stone which it has caused to be put together—in Siam,[25] for example, in Egypt, and in Europe—have many of them a sublimity hardly more than rivaled by the greatest works of Nature. And, except the geological epochs, there are no periods of time so vast as those which are measured by some of these organized faiths. If we scrutinize the matter closely, we shall find that there has not been one of their creeds which has remained always the same; yet the change is so slow as to be imperceptible during one person's life, so that individual belief remains sensibly fixed. For the mass of mankind, then, there is perhaps no better method than this. If it is their highest impulse to be intellectual slaves, then slaves they ought to remain.

But no institution can undertake to regulate opinions upon every subject. Only the most important ones can be attended to, and on the rest men's minds must be left to the action of natural causes. This imperfection will be no source of weakness so long as men are in such a state of culture that one opinion does not influence another—that is, so long as they cannot put two and two together. But in the most priest-ridden states some individuals will be found who are raised above that condition. These men possess a wider sort of social feeling; they see that men in other countries and in other ages have held to very different doctrines from those which they themselves have been brought up to believe; and they cannot help seeing that it is the mere accident of their having been taught as they

---

23   Of broad scope, comprehensive, all-embracing (from a Greek word, *katholikos*, meaning "universal").

24   That is, from the earliest days of Rome to the time in which Peirce was writing. Numa Pompilius was, according to legend, the second king of Rome (715–672 BCE) and Pius IX was pope from 1846 until 1878. Pius IX was the pope who first institutionalized the doctrine of papal infallibility (on July 18, 1870), an event which made a deep impression on Peirce.

---

25   Thailand.

have, and of their having been surrounded with the manners and associations they have, that has caused them to believe as they do and not far differently. And their candor cannot resist the reflection that there is no reason to rate their own views at a higher value than those of other nations and other centuries; and this gives rise to doubts in their minds.

They will further perceive that such doubts as these must exist in their minds with reference to every belief which seems to be determined by the caprice either of themselves or of those who originated the popular opinions. The willful adherence to a belief, and the arbitrary forcing of it upon others, must, therefore, both be given up, and a new method of settling opinions must be adopted, which shall not only produce an impulse to believe, but shall also decide what proposition it is which is to be believed. Let the action of natural preferences be unimpeded, then, and under their influence let men, conversing together and regarding matters in different lights, gradually develop beliefs in harmony with natural causes. This method resembles that by which conceptions of art have been brought to maturity. The most perfect example of it is to be found in the history of metaphysical philosophy. Systems of this sort have not usually rested upon any observed facts, at least not in any great degree. They have been chiefly adopted because their fundamental propositions seemed "agreeable to reason." This is an apt expression; it does not mean that which agrees with experience, but that which we find ourselves inclined to believe. Plato, for example, finds it agreeable to reason that the distances of the celestial spheres[26] from one another should be proportional to the different lengths of strings which produce harmonious chords. Many philosophers have been led to their main conclusions by considerations like this; but this is the lowest and least developed form which the method takes, for it is clear that another man might find Kepler's theory, that the celestial spheres are proportional to the inscribed and circumscribed spheres of the different regular solids, more agreeable to *his* reason. But the shock of opinions will soon lead men

to rest on preferences of a far more universal nature. Take, for example, the doctrine that man only acts selfishly—that is, from the consideration that acting in one way will afford him more pleasure than acting in another. This rests on no fact in the world, but it has had a wide acceptance as being the only reasonable theory.

This method is far more intellectual and respectable from the point of view of reason than either of the others which we have noticed. But its failure has been the most manifest. It makes of inquiry something similar to the development of taste; but taste, unfortunately, is always more or less a matter of fashion, and accordingly metaphysicians have never come to any fixed agreement, but the pendulum has swung backward and forward between a more material and a more spiritual philosophy, from the earliest times to the latest. And so from this, which has been called the *a priori* method, we are driven, in Lord Bacon's phrase, to a true induction. We have examined into this *a priori* method as something which promised to deliver our opinions from their accidental and capricious element. But development, while it is a process which eliminates the effect of some casual circumstances, only magnifies that of others. This method, therefore, does not differ in a very essential way from that of authority. The government may not have lifted its finger to influence my convictions; I may have been left outwardly quite free to choose, we will say, between monogamy and polygamy,[27] and, appealing to my conscience only, I may have concluded that the latter practice is in itself licentious.[28] But when I come to see that the chief obstacle to the spread of Christianity among a people of as high culture as the Hindoos has been a conviction of the immorality of our way of treating women, I cannot help seeing that, though governments do not interfere, sentiments in their development will be very greatly determined by accidental causes. Now, there are some people, among whom I must suppose that my reader is to be found, who, when they see that any belief of theirs is deter-

---

26 The positions of the sun, moon, planets, and stars (conceived as a concentric sequence of invisible spherical shells around the earth).

27 Monogamy means having only one spouse (or sexual partner) at a time; polygamy is the practice of having several spouses at once.

28 Lacking moral discipline.

mined by any circumstance extraneous to the facts, will from that moment not merely admit in words that that belief is doubtful, but will experience a real doubt of it, so that it ceases to be a belief.

To satisfy our doubts, therefore, it is necessary that a method should be found by which our beliefs may be caused by nothing human, but by some external permanency—by something upon which our thinking has no effect. Some mystics imagine that they have such a method in a private inspiration from on high. But that is only a form of the method of tenacity, in which the conception of truth as something public is not yet developed. Our external permanency would not be external, in our sense, if it was restricted in its influence to one individual. It must be something which affects, or might affect, every man. And, though these affections are necessarily as various as are individual conditions, yet the method must be such that the ultimate conclusion of every man shall be the same. Such is the method of science. Its fundamental hypothesis, restated in more familiar language, is this: There are real things, whose characters are entirely independent of our opinions about them; those realities affect our senses according to regular laws, and, though our sensations are as different as are our relations to the objects, yet, by taking advantage of the laws of perception, we can ascertain by reasoning how things really are; and any man, if he have sufficient experience and reason enough about it, will be led to the one true conclusion. The new conception here involved is that of reality. It may be asked how I know that there are any realities. If this hypothesis is the sole support of my method of inquiry, my method of inquiry must not be used to support my hypothesis. The reply is this: 1. If investigation cannot be regarded as proving that there are real things, it at least does not lead to a contrary conclusion; but the method and the conception on which it is based remain ever in harmony. No doubts of the method, therefore, necessarily arise from its practice, as is the case with all the others. 2. The feeling which gives rise to any method of fixing belief is a dissatisfaction at two repugnant propositions.[29] But here already is a vague concession

that there is some *one* thing to which a proposition should conform. Nobody, therefore, can really doubt that there are realities, or, if he did, doubt would not be a source of dissatisfaction. The hypothesis, therefore, is one which every mind admits. So that the social impulse does not cause me to doubt it. 3. Everybody uses the scientific method about a great many things, and only ceases to use it when he does not know how to apply it. 4. Experience of the method has not led me to doubt it, but, on the contrary, scientific investigation has had the most wonderful triumphs in the way of settling opinion. These afford the explanation of my not doubting the method or the hypothesis which it supposes; and not having any doubt, nor believing that anybody else whom I could influence has, it would be the merest babble for me to say more about it. If there be anybody with a living doubt upon the subject, let him consider it.

To describe the method of scientific investigation is the object of this series of papers. At present I have only room to notice some points of contrast between it and other methods of fixing belief.

This is the only one of the four methods which presents any distinction of a right and a wrong way. If I adopt the method of tenacity, and shut myself out from all influences, whatever I think necessary to doing this is necessary according to that method. So with the method of authority: the state may try to put down heresy by means which, from a scientific point of view, seem very ill-calculated to accomplish its purposes; but the only test *on that method* is what the state thinks; so that it cannot pursue the method wrongly. So with the *a priori* method. The very essence of it is to think as one is inclined to think. All metaphysicians will be sure to do that, however they may be inclined to judge each other to be perversely wrong. The Hegelian system[30] recognizes every

---

29 Two propositions which repel each other—which seem to be in conflict.

30 The system of philosophy developed by the important German philosopher G.W.F. Hegel (1770–1831). Peirce is thinking here of Hegel's dialectical view of the progress of both reason and history, in which one intellectual current (which Hegel calls a thesis) is faced with another opposing set of ideas, or antithesis, until the contradiction between the two is resolved in a synthesis. This synthesis is then faced with another

natural tendency of thought as logical, although it be certain to be abolished by counter-tendencies. Hegel thinks there is a regular system in the succession of these tendencies, in consequence of which, after drifting one way and the other for a long time, opinion will at last go right. And it is true that metaphysicians do get the right ideas at last; Hegel's system of Nature represents tolerably the science of that day; and one may be sure that whatever scientific investigation has put out of doubt will presently receive *a priori* demonstration on the part of the metaphysicians. But with the scientific method the case is different. I may start with known and observed facts to proceed to the unknown; and yet the rules which I follow in doing so may not be such as investigation would approve. The test of whether I am truly following the method is not an immediate appeal to my feelings and purposes, but, on the contrary, itself involves the application of the method. Hence it is that bad reasoning as well as good reasoning is possible; and this fact is the foundation of the practical side of logic.

It is not to be supposed that the first three methods of settling opinion present no advantage whatever over the scientific method. On the contrary, each has some peculiar convenience of its own. The *a priori* method is distinguished for its comfortable conclusions. It is the nature of the process to adopt whatever belief we are inclined to, and there are certain flatteries to the vanity of man which we all believe by nature, until we are awakened from our pleasing dream by some rough facts. The method of authority will always govern the mass of mankind; and those who wield the various forms of organized force in the state will never be convinced that dangerous reasoning ought not to be suppressed in some way. If liberty of speech is to be untrammeled[31] from the grosser forms of constraint, then uniformity of opinion will be secured by a moral terrorism to which the respectability of society will give its thorough approval. Following the method of authority is the path of peace. Certain non-conformities are permitted; certain others

(considered unsafe) are forbidden. These are different in different countries and in different ages; but, wherever you are, let it be known that you seriously hold a tabooed belief, and you may be perfectly sure of being treated with a cruelty less brutal but more refined than hunting you like a wolf. Thus, the greatest intellectual benefactors of mankind have never dared, and dare not now, to utter the whole of their thought; and thus a shade of *prima facie* doubt[32] is cast upon every proposition which is considered essential to the security of society. Singularly enough, the persecution does not all come from without; but a man torments himself and is oftentimes most distressed at finding himself believing propositions which he has been brought up to regard with aversion. The peaceful and sympathetic man will, therefore, find it hard to resist the temptation to submit his opinions to authority. But most of all I admire the method of tenacity for its strength, simplicity, and directness. Men who pursue it are distinguished for their decision of character, which becomes very easy with such a mental rule. They do not waste time in trying to make up their minds what they want, but, fastening like lightning upon whatever alternative comes first, they hold to it to the end, whatever happens, without an instant's irresolution. This is one of the splendid qualities which generally accompany brilliant, unlasting success. It is impossible not to envy the man who can dismiss reason, although we know how it must turn out at last.

Such are the advantages which the other methods of settling opinion have over scientific investigation. A man should consider well of them; and then he should consider that, after all, he wishes his opinions to coincide with the fact, and that there is no reason why the results of those three first methods should do so. To bring about this effect is the prerogative of the method of science. Upon such considerations he has to make his choice—a choice which is far more than the adoption of any intellectual opinion, which is one of the ruling decisions of his life, to which, when once made, he is bound to adhere. The force of habit will sometimes cause a man to hold on to old beliefs, after he is in a condition to see that they have no sound ba-

---

contradictory set of ideas, which is resolved into a further synthesis, and so on until rational perfection—a state of complete self-consciousness—is reached.

31   Freed from restriction, unhampered.

32   Doubt at first sight; initial doubt, which might or might not be removed by further investigation.

sis. But reflection upon the state of the case will overcome these habits, and he ought to allow reflection its full weight. People sometimes shrink from doing this, having an idea that beliefs are wholesome which they cannot help feeling rest on nothing. But let such persons suppose an analogous though different case from their own. Let them ask themselves what they would say to a reformed Mussulman[33] who should hesitate to give up his old notions in regard to the relations of the sexes; or to a reformed Catholic who should still shrink from reading the Bible. Would they not say that these persons ought to consider the matter fully, and clearly understand the new doctrine, and then ought to embrace it, in its entirety? But, above all, let it be considered that what is more wholesome than any particular belief is integrity of belief, and that to avoid looking into the support of any belief from a fear that it may turn out rotten is quite as immoral as it is disadvantageous. The person who confesses that there is such a thing as truth, which is distinguished from falsehood simply by this, that if acted on it will

carry us to the point we aim at and not astray, and then, though convinced of this, dares not know the truth and seeks to avoid it, is in a sorry state of mind indeed.

Yes, the other methods do have their merits: a clear logical conscience does cost something—just as any virtue, just as all that we cherish, costs us dear. But we should not desire it to be otherwise. The genius[34] of a man's logical method should be loved and reverenced as his bride, whom he has chosen from all the world. He need not contemn[35] the others; on the contrary, he may honor them deeply, and in doing so he only honors her the more. But she is the one that he has chosen, and he knows that he was right in making that choice. And having made it, he will work and fight for her, and will not complain that there are blows to take, hoping that there may be as many and as hard to give, and will strive to be the worthy knight and champion of her from the blaze of whose splendors he draws his inspiration and his courage.

33　Muslim.

34　The prevailing spirit or distinctive character.

35　Despise, show contempt for.

THOMAS KUHN

"Objectivity, Value Judgment, and Theory Choice"

Who Was Thomas Kuhn?

Thomas Kuhn's *The Structure of Scientific Revolutions* (first published in 1962) is the single most influential book in modern philosophy of science ... and indeed, in the opinion of some, is perhaps the most influential book published in the second half of the twentieth century.[1] In it, Kuhn presented a view of science

which seemed radically at variance with what most philosophers of science and scientists had previously supposed. Kuhn argued that most science—what he dubbed "normal science"—takes place against a background of unquestioned theoretical assumptions, which he called a *paradigm*. Typical scientists are

---

1　A report on the "most cited works of the twentieth century" issued by the Arts and Humanities Citation Index lists Lenin as the most cited author but *Structure*, by a fair margin, the most frequently mentioned

book. Kuhn's book is apparently treated with reverence inside the Washington Beltway: Al Gore claimed it as his favorite book, and both Bill Clinton and George Bush Sr. have praised its usefulness. *The Structure of Scientific Revolutions* has sold over a million copies and been translated into some twenty languages.

not, contrary to popular opinion, objective, skeptical, and independent thinkers: rather, according to Kuhn, they are community-minded conservatives who accept what they have been taught by their elders and devote their energies to solving puzzles dictated to them by their theories. Indeed, according to Kuhn, scientists habitually attempt to *ignore* research findings that threaten the existing paradigm. Occasionally, however, the pressures from anomalies—especially inexplicable experimental results—generated within that paradigm become such that a crisis occurs within the scientific community and it is necessary for a *paradigm shift* (a phrase first coined by Kuhn) to take place. These episodes in the history of science are what Kuhn called "revolutions." For example, to caricature Kuhn (who did not hold that paradigm shifts are caused entirely by the actions of single individuals), Galileo's (imagined) experiments—dropping wood and lead balls from the Leaning Tower of Pisa—caused the extinction of the Aristotelian theory that bodies fall at a speed proportional to their weight; Lavoisier's discovery of oxygen signaled the death knell for the older "phlogiston" paradigm of chemistry; Darwin's theory of natural selection overthrew ideas of a world governed by design; and Einstein's theory of relativity completely replaced Newtonian physics. Science, in other words, is "a series of peaceful interludes punctuated by intellectually violent revolutions." The old guard who worked within the previous paradigm then either undergo conversion to the new one, or simply die out and are replaced by younger scientists working in the new paradigm.

The most controversial and stimulating aspect of Kuhn's work has proved to be his claim that there can be no strictly rational reason to choose one new paradigm over another: that is, the adoption of scientific theories, according to Kuhn, is never and can never be a purely rational decision. According to the more extreme of Kuhn's adherents (though not—at least later in his career—Kuhn himself), this means that the logic and philosophy of science is to be replaced by the history and sociology of science: that is, science is best understood not as an ideally rational or logical enterprise, but as a sociological phenomenon. Furthermore, Kuhn has apparently held that successive scientific paradigms are *incommensurable*: scientists before and after a theoretical revolution essentially speak a different language and think in completely different ways, and so—since no one can think within two different paradigms at once—it is not possible for anyone to *compare* the two paradigms and see which is better. If this is the case, it seems to follow that we have no good reason to believe that the history of science is a story of progress or of the cumulative acquisition of scientific knowledge; the scientific revolutions which supplant one paradigm with another do not take us any closer to the truth about the way the world is, they simply replace one set of theoretical puzzles with a new incompatible set. The essay reprinted here, "Objectivity, Value Judgment, and Theory Choice," summarizes some of Kuhn's mature views on these topics.

Thomas Samuel Kuhn was born in Cincinnati, Ohio, in 1922, the son of an industrial engineer. He was educated in New York at a series of progressive, left-leaning schools—where, though bright, Kuhn by his own account felt anxious, isolated, and neurotic (feelings which apparently remained with him to some degree for the rest of his life)—and then in 1940 went to Harvard to take a degree in physics. His undergraduate degree completed in 1943, he joined the US army radar program as a physicist. Kuhn was assigned to work on radar profiles, first in the States and England, but was then sent to Europe in the wake of the Allied invasion—dressed in uniform so he would not be shot as a spy if captured behind enemy lines—to inspect captured German radar installations. He was present (by accident) when the victorious French general Charles de Gaulle entered Paris, and saw the German city of Hamburg after it had been flattened by Allied bombs.

After the war, Kuhn drifted into graduate work and received a PhD in physics from Harvard University in 1949. He remained at Harvard, teaching in the General Education in Science program which was aimed at giving students in the humanities and social sciences a background in natural science. However, in 1955 Kuhn was denied tenure at Harvard—on the grounds that he was insufficiently specialized in any particular academic discipline, either physics or history or philosophy—and he moved to the University of California at Berkeley, where in 1961 he became a full professor of the history of science. In 1964 Kuhn transferred to Princeton and then in 1979, after a divorce, moved again and settled at the Massachusetts Institute of Technology, where he remarried and taught until his retirement in 1991. He died in 1996.

What Is the Structure of This Reading?

Kuhn begins this paper by summarizing passages in *The Structure of Scientific Revolutions* about rational theory choice and progress in science, and claiming that his position on these matters has been seriously misunderstood by many of the book's critics. He then lays out what are sometimes known as his "five ways": five criteria, which are shared by scientists, for rational theory choice. However, he argues these five criteria are insufficient to determine the choice of one theory over another—scientists can only adopt or refuse to adopt a theory on the basis of partly *subjective* criteria. Kuhn then argues that this claim—that there is no single, shared algorithm available for theory choice in science—is a philosophically substantial finding, partly because, on Kuhn's view, there is no distinction to be made between the "contexts of discovery and justification." Furthermore, Kuhn insists, science could not properly function if there were some shared set of criteria that determined what any rational scientist must believe; instead, we should think of the five ways as *values* which influence theory choice rather than

rules which determine it. These five shared values are more or less permanent in the history of science, Kuhn goes on to claim, but they have no rational justification from outside of the practice of science, and furthermore they evolve and change with those practices. Finally, Kuhn addresses the sense in which the idiosyncratic factors that supplement the five ways in theory choice are 'subjective,' and reaffirms and clarifies his claim that paradigms are "incommensurable": that is, roughly, that two scientists who adopt different theories face communication barriers at least as extreme as those faced by two people who speak different languages.

Some Useful Background Information

1. A notion central to Kuhn's critique of the rationality of science is that of *incommensurability*. Two things are 'incommensurable' if they cannot be compared—if one cannot be said to be better, or truer, or more preferable than the other. For example, the number seven and the taste of apples are incommensurable: there is no scale of values on which they can both be compared. In the philosophy of science, two theories (or other linguistic systems) are said to be incommensurable if the claims of one cannot be stated in the language of the other. From this it follows also that there can be no neutral third language in which the claims of both theories can be stated and compared[2]—that is, there can be no neutral standpoint from which we can assess the theories and say that one is better than the other. And from *this*, it seems to be an inescapable conclusion that we cannot give any content to the notion that science is progressing—that scientific theories are be-

---

2 Suppose there were some theoretical language—call it theory *C*—which is capable of stating both the claims of theory *A* and those of theory *B*; then it would follow that *A* and *B* are not incommensurable, since the statements of *A* could be translated into *C* and those *C*-statements in turn could be translated into the language of *B*, and hence the claims of *A* could be stated in the terms of *B* (and vice versa).

coming closer approximations of the truth, for example—since we cannot any longer say that a later theory is better than an earlier one.

There are various reasons why one might think that scientific theories are incommensurable. One of the most influential arguments derives from a certain theory about how theoretical terms get their *meaning*. On this view (roughly), scientific terms like "electron" or "mass" do not, as ordinary words like "cow" and "yellow" may, get their meaning from being attached as labels to observable things in the world. (After all, we cannot *see* electrons, so how can we point to them in order to label them?) Instead, terms applied to theoretical entities get their meaning entirely from their *role in the theory*: for example, the meaning of the word "mass" is, roughly, *whatever it is* that performs the function that mass does in the mathematical equations which make up the theory. If all of this is right, then it seems to follow that *if you change the theory you also change the meanings of all the theoretical terms of that theory*. For example, mass plays a different role in Newton's theory than it does in relativity theory (e.g., mass is independent of velocity in classical mechanics but for Einstein mass increases as velocity does), and hence the word "mass" must mean something different in the two theories—that is, when Einstein talks about "mass" he is using a different language than when Newton talks about it, even though the words they use happen to look and sound the same.

2. Another notion of which Kuhn made influential use and which is often appealed to in arguments for incommensurability is the idea that all observation is "theory-laden." That is, it can be argued—and in fact is generally believed by philosophers of science—that it is impossible for a scientist to make any experimental observations of the world without relying upon certain theoretical assumptions, and furthermore that these observations *are changed* by those assumptions. For example, a scientist who uses equipment—such as a microscope, radio tele-

scope, or fMRI machine—to make observations must rely upon many theoretical claims about the operation of that equipment, and what she believes she is seeing will depend upon how she believes the equipment operates. More fundamentally, it is thought that even unaided observations depend for their content upon the way a scientist categorizes or conceptualizes experience. For example, seventeenth-century chemists reported having *seen* phlogiston (a mythical substance) being emitted by burning objects as flames; a modern day chemist sees much the same phenomenon and observes a violent oxidation reaction. A medieval scientist observing the dawn would have *seen* a moving sun and a static earth; today's observer is aware that she is seeing the rotation of the earth carrying the sun into view. Finally, for many scientists and engineers trained in the Aristotelian science of the Middle Ages, projectiles were apparently *observed* to behave just as they were theoretically expected to—they rose into the air in a straight line until the force of their flight was overcome by the force of their weight, and then fell straight down to the ground; nowadays, *after* Newton has changed our theoretical framework, we observe that projectiles really have a parabolic trajectory.

One of the implications of this—or at least of the most radical versions of this thesis, sometimes called the collapse of the observation-theory distinction—is, once again, a kind of incommensurability. If all observation is infected by theory, the argument goes, then there can be no neutral body of data that can be used to evaluate competing theories. The observations recorded by scientists trained in theory *A* will support that theory because they see what they expect to see; meanwhile the experiments conducted by the partisans of theory *B* will support *their* theory; since all observations are theory-laden, there are no neutral experimental results available with respect to the two theories, and so no data that can legitimately be used to falsify one or confirm the other.

Suggestions for Critical Reflection

1. Kuhn quotes himself, from the *Structure of Scientific Revolutions,* as saying: "What better criterion [for which theory it is rational to adopt] could there be than the decision of the scientific group?" Do you agree with this claim? What better criterion *could* there be? If Kuhn is right about this, could the philosophy of science be replaced by the sociology of science (i.e., by the study of how groups of scientists come to consensus)?

2. What do you think is the philosophical value of studying the history of science? How much does the *actual* behavior of scientists show us about the ideal "scientific method"? In particular, do you think Kuhn establishes that the history of science reveals that there just *is* no completely rational method available to scientists?

3. Kuhn argues that not only do scientists possess no shared set of criteria for theory choice, but that science could not *survive* if there were a rational "scientific method" for confirming or discarding theories. Do you think he is right about this?

4. What do you think Kuhn made of the theories of science represented in this chapter by readings from Hempel and Popper? In what ways do you think his own account differs from theirs?

5. Both Hempel and, especially, Popper make a firm distinction between what Kuhn calls the context of discovery and the context of justification. How successful is Kuhn in arguing that there is no such distinction? What would be the implications if this distinction were collapsed?

6. Many critics have asserted that Kuhn's account of theory choice and paradigm shifts leaves no room for the notion that science *progresses* towards a closer and closer approximation to the *truth* about reality. On the basis of Kuhn's claims in this article, do you think that this is a fair criticism?

7. One unfriendly critic of Kuhn, James Franklin, has said the following: "The basic content of Kuhn's book [*The Structure of Scientific Revolutions*] can be inferred simply by asking: what would the humanities crowd *want* said about science? Once the question is asked, the answer is obvious. Kuhn's thesis is that scientific theories are no better than ones in the humanities.... [S]cience is all theoretical talk and negotiation, which never really establishes anything" (from *The New Criterion*, June 2000). Given what Kuhn says in this article, to what degree do you think that Franklin gets Kuhn right?

Suggestions for Further Reading

The first place to pursue Kuhn's ideas is, of course, his *The Structure of Scientific Revolutions* (University of Chicago Press, 1996). His most important papers are collected in two volumes: *The Essential Tension* (University of Chicago Press, 1977) and *The Road Since Structure: Philosophical Essays, 1970–1993* (University of Chicago Press, 2000), the second of which includes a lengthy autobiographical interview. Kuhn also published two books on case studies from the history of science: *The Copernican Revolution* (Harvard University Press, 1985) and *Black-Body Theory and the Quantum Discontinuity 1894–1912* (University of Chicago Press, 1987).

Currently the most authoritative book on Kuhn's philosophy is probably Paul Hoyningen-Huene's *Reconstructing Scientific Revolutions: Thomas S. Kuhn's Philosophy of Science* (University of Chicago Press, 1993). *Thomas Kuhn* by Alexander Bird (Princeton University Press, 2001) is also helpful. A dense, stimulating, rambling, and quite controversial attack on Kuhn (both his ideas and his person) is Steve Fuller's *Thomas Kuhn: A Philosophical History for Our Times* (University of Chicago Press, 2000). *Criticism and the Growth of Knowledge*, edited by Imre Lakatos and Alan Musgrave (Cambridge University Press, 1970), is an influential collection of articles on *The Structure of Scientific Revolutions*, with a reply from Kuhn, and *World Changes: Thomas Kuhn and the Nature of Science*, edited by Paul Horwich (MIT Press, 1993), is a more recent version along much the same lines. A collection called *Paradigms and Revolutions*, edited by Gary Gutting (University of Notre Dame Press, 1979), seeks to extend Kuhn's ideas to the humanities and social sciences.

"Objectivity, Value Judgment, and Theory Choice"[3]

In the penultimate chapter of a controversial book fifteen years ago, I considered the ways scientists are brought to abandon one time-honored theory or paradigm in favor of another. Such decision problems, I wrote, "cannot be resolved by proof." To discuss their mechanism is, therefore, to talk "about techniques of persuasion, or about argument and counterargument in a situation in which there can be no proof." Under these circumstances, I continued, "lifelong resistance [to a new theory] ... is not a violation of scientific standards.... Though the historian can always find men—Priestley, for instance[4]—who were unreasonable to resist for as long as they did, he will not find a point at which resistance becomes illogical or unscientific." Statements of that sort[5] obviously raise the question of why, in the absence of binding criteria for scientific choice, both the number of solved scientific problems and the precision of individual problem solutions should increase so markedly with the passage of time. Confronting that issue, I sketched in my closing chapter a number of characteristics that scientists share by virtue of the training which licenses their membership in one or another community of specialists. In the absence of criteria able to dictate the choice of each individual, I argued, we do well

to trust the collective judgment of scientists trained in this way. "What better criterion could there be," I asked rhetorically, "than the decision of the scientific group?"[6]

A number of philosophers have greeted remarks like these in a way that continues to surprise me. My views, it is said, make of theory choice "a matter for mob psychology."[7] Kuhn believes, I am told, that "the decision of a scientific group to adopt a new paradigm cannot be based on good reasons of any kind, factual or otherwise."[8] The debates surrounding such choices must, my critics claim, be for me "mere persuasive displays without deliberative substance."[9] Reports of this sort manifest total misunderstanding, and I have occasionally said as much in papers directed primarily to other ends. But those passing protestations have had negligible effect, and the misunderstandings continue to be important. I conclude that it is past time for me to describe, at greater length and with greater precision, what has been on my mind when I have uttered statements like the ones with which I just began. If I have been reluctant to do so in the past, that is largely because I have preferred to devote attention to areas in which my views diverge more sharply from those currently received than they do with respect to theory choice.

What, I ask to begin with, are the characteristics of a good scientific theory? Among a number of quite usual answers I select five, not because they are ex-

---

3   This paper was originally given as the Machette Lecture delivered at Furman University in South Carolina in 1973. It was first published in *The Essential Tension: Selected Studies in Scientific Tradition and Change*, by Thomas Kuhn, Chicago: University of Chicago Press, 1977, pp. 320–339. Copyright © University of Chicago 1977.

4   Joseph Priestley (1733–1804) was an English scientist and theologian who discovered oxygen in 1774, though—in accordance with the terms of the then-current theory—he thought of it as "dephlogisticated air."

5   [Author's note] *The Structure of Scientific Revolutions*, 2d ed. (Chicago, 1970), pp. 148, 151–52, 159. All the passages from which these fragments are taken appeared in the same form in the first edition, published in 1962.

6   [Author's note] Ibid., p. 170.

7   [Author's note] Imre Lakatos, "Falsification and the Methodology of Scientific Research Programmes," in I. Lakatos and A. Musgrave, eds., *Criticism and the Growth of Knowledge* (Cambridge, 1970), pp, 91–195. The quoted phrase, which appears on p. 178, is italicized in the original.

8   [Author's note] Dudley Shapere, "Meaning and Scientific Change," in R.G. Colodny, ed., *Mind and Cosmos: Essays in Contemporary Science and Philosophy*, University of Pittsburgh Series in the Philosophy of Science, vol. 3 (Pittsburgh 1966), pp. 41–85. The quotation will be found on p. 67.

9   [Author's note] Israel Scheffler, *Science and Subjectivity* (Indianapolis, 1967), p. 81.

haustive, but because they are individually important and collectively sufficiently varied to indicate what is at stake. First, a theory should be accurate: within its domain, that is, consequences deducible from a theory should be in demonstrated agreement with the results of existing experiments and observations. Second, a theory should be consistent, not only internally or with itself, but also with other currently accepted theories applicable to related aspects of nature. Third, it should have broad scope: in particular, a theory's consequences should extend far beyond the particular observations, laws, or subtheories it was initially designed to explain. Fourth, and closely related; it should be simple, bringing order to phenomena that in its absence would be individually isolated and, as a set, confused. Fifth—a somewhat less standard item, but one of special importance to actual scientific decisions—a theory should be fruitful of new research findings: it should, that is, disclose new phenomena or unnoted relationships among those already known.[10] These five characteristics—accuracy, consistency, scope, simplicity, and fruitfulness—are all standard criteria for evaluating the adequacy of a theory. If they had not been, I would have devoted far more space to them in my book, for I agree entirely with the traditional view that they play a vital role when scientists must choose between an established theory and an upstart competitor. Together with others of much the same sort, they provide *the* shared basis for theory choice.

Nevertheless, two sorts of difficulties are regularly encountered by the men who must use these criteria in choosing, say, between Ptolemy's astronomical theory and Copernicus's,[11] between the oxygen and phlogiston theories of combustion,[12] or between Newtonian mechanics and the quantum theory.[13] Individually the criteria are imprecise: individuals may legitimately differ about their application to concrete cases. In addition, when deployed together, they repeatedly prove to conflict with one another; accuracy may, for example, dictate the choice of one theory, scope the choice of its competitor. Since these difficulties, especially the first, are also relatively familiar, I shall devote little time to their elaboration. Though my argument does demand that I illustrate them briefly, my views will begin to depart from those long current only after I have done so.

Begin with accuracy, which for present purposes I take to include not only quantitative agreement but qualitative as well. Ultimately it proves the most nearly decisive of all the criteria, partly because it is less equivocal than the others but especially because predictive and explanatory powers, which depend on it, are characteristics that scientists are particularly unwilling to give up. Unfortunately, however, theories cannot always be discriminated in terms of accuracy. Copernicus's system, for example, was not more accurate than Ptolemy's until drastically revised by Kepler[14] more than sixty years after Copernicus's death.

---

10 [Author's note] The last criterion, fruitfulness, deserves more emphasis than it has yet received. A scientist choosing between two theories ordinarily knows that his decision will have a bearing on his subsequent research career. Of course he is especially attracted by a theory that promises the concrete successes for which scientists are ordinarily rewarded.

11 Ptolemy was a second-century CE astronomer from Alexandria, in Egypt, who based his astronomical theory on the belief that all heavenly bodies revolve around a stationary earth. Nicholas Copernicus (1473–1543) was a Polish astronomer who advanced the competing theory that the earth and other planets revolve around the sun.

12 The former theory explains combustion as the violent chemical reaction of a substance with oxygen in the air around it; by contrast, the latter theory (which was current until the eighteenth century) postulated a volatile substance called phlogiston which is contained in all flammable materials and which is released as flame during combustion.

13 According to Newtonian theory, light (and other forms of what we now think of as electromagnetic energy) consisted in the mechanical motions of the particles in an all-enveloping, massless substance called "ether." Quantum theory is the modern scientific account of matter and energy; it is probabilistic rather than mechanical, and abandons the notion of a "medium" through which energy waves propagate.

14 Johannes Kepler (1571–1630), a German astronomer, is often considered the "father of modern astronomy"

If Kepler or someone else had not found other reasons to choose heliocentric astronomy, those improvements in accuracy would never have been made, and Copernicus's work might have been forgotten. More typically, of course, accuracy does permit discriminations, but not the sort that lead regularly to unequivocal choice. The oxygen theory, for example, was universally acknowledged to account for observed weight relations in chemical reactions, something the phlogiston theory had previously scarcely attempted to do. But the phlogiston theory, unlike its rival, could account for the metals' being much more alike than the ores from which they were formed. One theory thus matched experience better in one area, the other in another. To choose between them on the basis of accuracy, a scientist would need to decide the area in which accuracy was more significant. About that matter chemists could and did differ without violating any of the criteria outlined above, or any others yet to be suggested.

However important it may be, therefore, accuracy by itself is seldom or never a sufficient criterion for theory choice. Other criteria must function as well, but they do not eliminate problems. To illustrate I select just two—consistency and simplicity—asking how they functioned in the choice between the heliocentric and geocentric[15] systems. As astronomical theories both Ptolemy's and Copernicus's were internally consistent, but their relation to related theories in other fields was very different. The stationary central earth was an essential ingredient of received physical theory, a tight-knit body of doctrine which explained, among other things, how stones fall, how water pumps function, and why the clouds move slowly across the skies. Heliocentric astronomy, which required the earth's motion, was inconsistent with the existing scientific explanation of these and other terrestrial phenomena. The consistency criterion by itself, therefore, spoke unequivocally for geocentric tradition.

Simplicity, however, favored Copernicus, but only when evaluated in a quite special way. If, on the one hand, the two systems were compared in terms of the actual computational labor required to predict the position of a planet at a particular time, then they proved substantially equivalent. Such computations were what astronomers did, and Copernicus's system offered them no labor-saving techniques; in that sense it was not simpler than Ptolemy's. If, on the other hand, one asked about the amount of mathematical apparatus required to explain, not the detailed quantitative motions of the planets, but merely their gross qualitative features—limited elongation, retrograde motion, and the like—then, as every schoolchild knows, Copernicus required only one circle per planet, Ptolemy two.[16] In that sense the Copernican theory was the simpler, a fact vitally important to the choices made by both Kepler and Galileo and thus essential to the ultimate triumph of Copernicanism. But that sense of simplicity was not the only one available, nor even the one most natural to professional astronomers, men whose task was the actual computation of planetary position.

Because time is short and I have multiplied examples elsewhere, I shall here simply assert that these difficulties in applying standard criteria of choice are typical and that they arise no less forcefully in twentieth-century situations than in the earlier and better-known examples I have just sketched. When scientists must choose between competing theories, two men fully committed to the same list of criteria for choice may nevertheless reach different conclusions. Perhaps they interpret simplicity differently or have different convictions about the range of fields within which the consistency criterion must be met. Or perhaps they agree about these matters but differ about the relative weights to be accorded to these or to other criteria when several are deployed together. With divergences of this sort, no set of choice criteria yet proposed is of any use. One can explain, as the

---

for his formulation of three fundamental laws of planetary motion.

15   "Heliocentric" means centered on the sun; "geocentric" means centered on the earth.

16   In the Ptolemaic system, celestial orbits are described by "epicycles": that is, the orbits of the sun and planets form small circles, the centers of which move around the circumference of a larger circle centered on the earth. For the Copernican system, of course, each planet's orbit is described by a single (elliptical) circle with the sun at its center.

historian characteristically does, why particular men made particular choices at particular times. But for that purpose one must go beyond the list of shared criteria to characteristics of the individuals who make the choice. One must, that is, deal with characteristics which vary from one scientist to another without thereby in the least jeopardizing their adherence to the canons that make science scientific. Though such canons do exist and should be discoverable (doubtless the criteria of choice with which I began are among them), they are not by themselves sufficient to determine the decisions of individual scientists. For that purpose the shared canons must be fleshed out in ways that differ from one individual to another.

Some of the differences I have in mind result from the individual's previous experience as a scientist. In what part of the field was he at work when confronted by the need to choose? How long had he worked there; how successful had he been; and how much of his work depended on concepts and techniques challenged by the new theory? Other factors relevant to choice lie outside the sciences. Kepler's early election of Copernicanism was due in part to his immersion in the Neoplatonic and Hermetic[17] movements of his day; German Romanticism[18] predisposed those it affected toward both recognition and acceptance of

energy conservation; nineteenth-century British social thought had a similar influence on the availability and acceptability of Darwin's concept of the struggle for existence. Still other significant differences are functions of personality. Some scientists place more premium than others on originality and are correspondingly more willing to take risks; some scientists prefer comprehensive, unified theories to precise and detailed problem solutions of apparently narrower scope. Differentiating factors like these are described by my critics as subjective and are contrasted with the shared or objective criteria from which I began. Though I shall later question that use of terms, let me for the moment accept it. My point is, then, that every individual choice between competing theories depends on a mixture of objective and subjective factors, or of shared and individual criteria. Since the latter have not ordinarily figured in the philosophy of science, my emphasis upon them has made my belief in the former hard for my critics to see.

What I have said so far is primarily simply descriptive of what goes on in the sciences at times of theory choice. As description, furthermore, it has not been challenged by my critics, who reject instead my claim that these facts of scientific life have philosophic import. Taking up that issue, I shall begin to isolate some, though I think not vast, differences of opinion. Let me begin by asking how philosophers of science can for so long have neglected the subjective elements which, they freely grant, enter regularly into the actual theory choices made by individual scientists? Why have these elements seemed to them an index only of human weakness, not at all of the nature of scientific knowledge?

One answer to that question is, of course, that few philosophers, if any, have claimed to possess either a complete or an entirely well-articulated list of criteria. For some time, therefore, they could reasonably expect that further research would eliminate residual imperfections and produce an algorithm able to dictate rational, unanimous choice. Pending that achievement, scientists would have no alternative but to supply subjectively what the best current list of objective criteria still lacked. That some of them might still do so even with a perfected list at hand would then be

---

17   Neoplatonism is a school of thought—originating in the third century CE, and influential in medieval and Renaissance philosophy—which fused Plato's philosophy with religious doctrines, and which sees the universe as an emanation from an omnipresent, transcendent, unchanging One. Hermeticism, which was also popular during the Renaissance, involves allegiance to the doctrines found in a collection of occult writings on magical and religious topics which were (wrongly) thought to be the texts of an ancient Egyptian priesthood.

18   Romanticism was a late eighteenth-century movement which reacted against the rationalism of the Enlightenment by embracing spontaneity, imagination, emotion, and inspiration. Among its themes was the belief that reality is ultimately spiritual, and that knowledge of nature cannot be achieved by rational and analytic means but only through a kind of intuitive absorption into the spiritual process of nature.

an index only of the inevitable imperfection of human nature.

That sort of answer may still prove to be correct, but I think no philosopher still expects that it will. The search for algorithmic decision procedures has continued for some time and produced both powerful and illuminating results. But those results all presuppose that individual criteria of choice can be unambiguously stated and also that, if more than one proves relevant, an appropriate weight function is at hand for their joint application. Unfortunately, where the choice at issue is between scientific theories, little progress has been made toward the first of these desiderata[19] and none toward the second. Most philosophers of science would therefore, I think, now regard the sort of algorithm which has traditionally been sought as a not quite attainable ideal. I entirely agree and shall henceforth take that much for granted.

Even an ideal, however, if it is to remain credible, requires some demonstrated relevance to the situations in which it is supposed to apply. Claiming that such demonstration requires no recourse to subjective factors, my critics seem to appeal, implicitly or explicitly, to the well-known distinction between the contexts of discovery and of justification.[20] They concede, that is, that the subjective factors I invoke play a significant role in the discovery or invention of new theories, but they also insist that that inevitably intuitive process lies outside of the bounds of philosophy of science and is irrelevant to the question of scientific objectivity. Objectivity enters science, they continue, through the processes by which theories are tested, justified, or judged. Those processes do not, or at least need not, involve subjective factors at all. They can be governed by a set of (objective) criteria shared by the entire group competent to judge.

I have already argued that that position does not fit observations of scientific life and shall now assume that that much has been conceded. What is now at issue is a different point: whether or not this invocation of the distinction between contexts of discovery and

of justification provides even a plausible and useful idealization. I think it does not and can best make my point by suggesting first a likely source of its apparent cogency. I suspect that my critics have been misled by science pedagogy or what I have elsewhere called textbook science. In science teaching, theories are presented together with exemplary applications, and those applications may be viewed as evidence. But that is not their primary pedagogic function (science students are distressingly willing to receive the word from professors and texts). Doubtless *some* of them were *part* of the evidence at the time actual decisions were being made, but they represent only a fraction of the considerations relevant to the decision process. The context of pedagogy differs almost as much from the context of justification as it does from that of discovery.

Full documentation of that point would require longer argument than is appropriate here, but two aspects of the way in which philosophers ordinarily demonstrate the relevance of choice criteria are worth noting. Like the science textbooks on which they are often modelled, books and articles on the philosophy of science refer again and again to the famous crucial experiments: Foucault's pendulum,[21] which demonstrates the motion of the earth; Cavendish's demonstration of gravitational attraction;[22] or

---

19 Things lacking but needed or desired.

20 [Author's note] The least equivocal example of this position is probably the one developed in Scheffler, *Science and Subjectivity*, chap. 4.

21 This experiment was first performed in 1851 by the French physicist Jean Bernard Léon Foucault (1819–1868) in order to show that the earth spins around its axis. The oscillations of a weight swinging from a very long wire can be observed to slowly rotate (clockwise in the Northern hemisphere and anticlockwise in the Southern); however the pendulum itself must be moving in a straight line, since there is no outside force interrupting its movement; therefore, since the path of the pendulum seems to rotate with respect to the ground and yet we know that the pendulum is not rotating, it must be the *ground* which is spinning.

22 Henry Cavendish (1731–1810) used a sensitive torsion balance to measure the value of the gravitational constant G and this allowed him to estimate the mass of the Earth for the first time. Cavendish's experimental apparatus involved a light, rigid six-foot long rod, suspended from a wire, and having two small metal spheres attached to the ends of the rod. When the rod

Fizeau's measurement of the relative speed of sound in water and air.[23] These experiments are paradigms of good reason for scientific choice; they illustrate the most effective of all the sorts of argument which could be available to a scientist uncertain which of two theories to follow; they are vehicles for the transmission of criteria of choice. But they also have another characteristic in common. By the time they were performed no scientist still needed to be convinced of the validity of the theory their outcome is now used to demonstrate. Those decisions had long since been made on the basis of significantly more equivocal evidence. The exemplary crucial experiments to which philosophers again and again refer would have been historically relevant to theory choice only if they had yielded unexpected results. Their use as illustrations provides needed economy to science pedagogy, but they scarcely illuminate the character of the choices that scientists are called upon to make.

Standard philosophical illustrations of scientific choice have another troublesome characteristic. The only arguments discussed are, as I have previously indicated, the ones favorable to the theory that, in fact, ultimately triumphed. Oxygen, we read, could explain weight relations, phlogiston could not; but nothing is said about the phlogiston theory's power or about the oxygen theory's limitations. Compari-

sons of Ptolemy's theory with Copernicus's proceed in the same way. Perhaps these examples should not be given since they contrast a developed theory with one still in its infancy. But philosophers regularly use them nonetheless. If the only result of their doing so were to simplify the decision situation, one could not object. Even historians do not claim to deal with the full factual complexity of the situations they describe. But these simplifications emasculate by making choice totally unproblematic. They eliminate, that is, one essential element of the decision situation that scientists must resolve if their field is to move ahead. In those situations there are always at least some good reasons for each possible choice. Considerations relevant to the context of discovery are then relevant to justification as well; scientists who share the concerns and sensibilities of the individual who discovers a new theory are ipso facto[24] likely to appear disproportionately frequently among that theory's first supporters. That is why it has been difficult to construct algorithms for theory choice, and also why such difficulties have seemed so thoroughly worth resolving. Choices that present problems are the ones philosophers of science need to understand. Philosophically interesting decision procedures must function where, in their absence, the decision might still be in doubt.

That much I have said before, if only briefly. Recently, however, I have recognized another, subtler source for the apparent plausibility of my critics' position. To present it, I shall briefly describe a hypothetical dialogue with one of them. Both of us agree that each scientist chooses between competing theories by deploying some Bayesian algorithm[25] which permits him to compute a value for $p(T,E)$,

---

is twisted, the torsion of the wire exerts a force which is proportional to the angle of rotation of the rod, and Cavendish carefully calibrated his instrument to determine the relationship between the angle of rotation and the amount of torsional force. He then brought two large lead spheres near the smaller spheres attached to the rod: since all masses attract, the large spheres exerted a gravitational force upon the smaller spheres and twisted the rod a measurable amount. Once the torsional force balanced the gravitational force, the rod and spheres came to rest and Cavendish was able to determine the gravitational force of attraction between the masses.

23   Armand-Hippolyte Fizeau (1819–1896) is best known for experimentally determining the speed of light, and showing that different media (such as still water, moving water, and air) can affect the speed of propagation of light and sound.

24   *Ipso facto* means "by that very fact."

25   Thomas Bayes (1702–1761) was an English clergyman who developed an influential theorem for calculating the probability of a hypothesis given a certain body of evidence. According to this theorem, in its simplest form, the probability of the hypothesis is the product of a) its prior probability (i.e., its probability before the evidence) and b) the probability of the evidence being as it is given the hypothesis, divided by the prior probability of that evidence. That is, $p(T,E) = p(T) \times (p(E,T)/p(E))$.

i.e., for the probability of a theory T on the evidence E available both to him and to the other members of his group at a particular period of time. "Evidence," furthermore, we both interpret broadly to include such considerations as simplicity and fruitfulness. My critic asserts, however, that there is only one such value of p, that corresponding to objective choice, and he believes that all rational members of the group must arrive at it. I assert, on the other hand, for reasons previously given, that the factors he calls objective are insufficient to determine in full any algorithm at all. For the sake of the discussion I have conceded that each individual has an algorithm and that all their algorithms have much in common. Nevertheless, I continue to hold that the algorithms of individuals are all ultimately different by virtue of the subjective considerations with which each must complete the objective criteria before any computations can be done. If my hypothetical critic is liberal, he may now grant that these subjective differences do play a role in determining the hypothetical algorithm on which each individual relies during the early stages of the competition between rival theories. But he is also likely to claim that, as evidence increases with the passage of time, the algorithms of different individuals converge to the algorithm of objective choice with which his presentation began. For him the increasing unanimity of individual choices is evidence for their increasing objectivity and thus for the elimination of subjective elements from the decision process.

So much for the dialogue, which I have, of course, contrived to disclose the non sequitur[26] underlying an apparently plausible position. What converges as the evidence changes over time need only be the values of p that individuals compute from their individual algorithms. Conceivably those algorithms themselves also become more alike with time, but the ultimate unanimity of theory choice provides no evidence whatsoever that they do so. If subjective factors are required to account for the decisions that initially divide the profession, they may still be present later when the profession agrees. Though I shall not here argue the point, consideration of the occasions on which a scientific community divides suggests that they actually do so.

My argument has so far been directed to two points. It first provided evidence that the choices scientists make between competing theories depend not only on shared criteria—those my critics call objective—but also on idiosyncratic factors dependent on individual biography and personality. The latter are, in my critics' vocabulary, subjective, and the second part of my argument has attempted to bar some likely ways of denying their philosophic import. Let me now shift to a more positive approach, returning briefly to the list of shared criteria—accuracy, simplicity, and the like—with which I began. The considerable effectiveness of such criteria does not, I now wish to suggest, depend on their being sufficiently articulated to dictate the choice of each individual who subscribes to them. Indeed, if they were articulated to that extent, a behavior mechanism fundamental to scientific advance would cease to function. What the tradition sees as eliminable imperfections in its rules of choice I take to be in part responses to the essential nature of science.

As so often, I begin with the obvious. Criteria that influence decisions without specifying what those decisions must be are familiar in many aspects of human life. Ordinarily, however, they are called not criteria or rules, but maxims, norms, or values. Consider maxims first. The individual who invokes them when choice is urgent usually finds them frustratingly vague and often also in conflict one with another. Contrast "He who hesitates is lost" with "Look before you leap," or compare "Many hands make light work" with "Too many cooks spoil the broth." Individually maxims dictate different choices, collectively none at all. Yet no one suggests that supplying children with contradictory tags like these is irrelevant to their education. Opposing maxims alter the nature of the decision to be made, highlight the essential issues it presents, and point to those remaining aspects of the decision for which each individual must take responsibility himself. Once invoked, maxims like these alter the nature of the decision process and can thus change its outcome.

Values and norms provide even clearer examples of effective guidance in the presence of conflict and

---

26   A *non sequitur* is something that does not follow, e.g., a conclusion that does not logically follow from the premises.

equivocation. Improving the quality of life is a value, and a car in every garage once followed from it as a norm. But quality of life has other aspects, and the old norm has become problematic. Or again, freedom of speech is a value, but so is preservation of life and property. In application, the two often conflict, so that judicial soul-searching, which still continues, has been required to prohibit such behavior as inciting to riot or shouting fire in a crowded theater. Difficulties like these are an appropriate source for frustration, but they rarely result in charges that values have no function or in calls for their abandonment. That response is barred to most of us by an acute consciousness that there are societies with other values and that these value differences result in other ways of life, other decisions about what may and what may not be done.

I am suggesting, of course, that the criteria of choice with which I began function not as rules, which determine choice, but as values, which influence it. Two men deeply committed to the same values may nevertheless, in particular situations, make different choices as, in fact, they do. But that difference in outcome ought not to suggest that the values scientists share are less than critically important either to their decisions or to the development of the enterprise in which they participate. Values like accuracy, consistency, and scope may prove ambiguous in application, both individually and collectively; they may, that is, be an insufficient basis for a *shared* algorithm of choice. But they do specify a great deal: what each scientist must consider in reaching a decision, what he may and may not consider relevant, and what he can legitimately be required to report as the basis for the choice he has made. Change the list, for example by adding social utility as a criterion, and some particular choices will be different, more like those one expects from an engineer. Subtract accuracy of fit to nature from the list, and the enterprise that results may not resemble science at all, but perhaps philosophy instead. Different creative disciplines are characterized, among other things, by different sets of shared values. If philosophy and engineering lie too close to the sciences, think of literature or the plastic arts. Milton's failure to set *Paradise Lost* in a Copernican universe does not indicate that he agreed with Ptolemy but that he had things other than science to do.

Recognizing that criteria of choice can function as values when incomplete as rules has, I think, a number of striking advantages. First, as I have already argued at length, it accounts in detail for aspects of scientific behavior which the tradition has seen as anomalous or even irrational. More important, it allows the standard criteria to function fully in the earliest stages of theory choice, the period when they are most needed but when, on the traditional view, they function badly or not at all. Copernicus was responding to them during the years required to convert heliocentric astronomy from a global conceptual scheme to mathematical machinery for predicting planetary position. Such predictions were what astronomers valued; in their absence, Copernicus would scarcely have been heard, something which had happened to the idea of a moving earth before. That his own version convinced very few is less important than his acknowledgment of the basis on which judgments would have to be reached if heliocentricism were to survive. Though idiosyncrasy must be invoked to explain why Kepler and Galileo were early converts to Copernicus's system, the gaps filled by their efforts to perfect it were specified by shared values alone.

That point has a corollary which may be more important still. Most newly suggested theories do not survive. Usually the difficulties that evoked them are accounted for by more traditional means. Even when this does not occur, much work, both theoretical and experimental, is ordinarily required before the new theory can display sufficient accuracy and scope to generate widespread conviction. In short, before the group accepts it, a new theory has been tested over time by the research of a number of men, some working within it, others within its traditional rival. Such a mode of development, however, *requires* a decision process which permits rational men to disagree, and such disagreement would be barred by the shared algorithm which philosophers have generally sought. If it were at hand, all conforming scientists would make the same decision at the same time. With standards for acceptance set too low, they would move from one attractive global viewpoint to another, never giving traditional theory an opportunity to supply equivalent attractions. With standards set higher, no one satisfying the criterion of rationality would be inclined to try out the new theory, to articulate it in ways which showed its fruitfulness or displayed its accuracy and scope. I doubt that science would survive the change. What from one viewpoint may seem the looseness and imperfection of choice criteria conceived as rules may, when the same criteria are seen as values, appear an indispensable means of spreading the risk which the introduction or support of novelty always entails.

Even those who have followed me this far will want to know how a value-based enterprise of the sort I have described can develop as a science does, repeatedly producing powerful new techniques for prediction and control. To that question, unfortunately, I have no answer at all, but that is only another way of saying that I make no claim to have solved the problem of induction. If science did progress by virtue of some shared and binding algorithm of choice, I would be equally at a loss to explain its success. The lacuna[27] is one I feel acutely, but its presence does not differentiate my position from the tradition.

It is, after all, no accident that my list of the values guiding scientific choice is, as nearly as makes any difference, identical with the tradition's list of rules dictating choice. Given any concrete situation to which the philosopher's rules could be applied, my values would function like his rules, producing the same choice. Any justification of induction, any explanation of why the rules worked, would apply equally to my values. Now consider a situation in which choice by shared rules proves impossible, not because the rules are wrong but because they are, as rules, intrinsically incomplete. Individuals must then still choose and be guided by the rules (now values) when they do so. For that purpose, however, each must first flesh out the rules, and each will do so in a somewhat different way even though the decision dictated by the variously completed rules may prove unanimous. If I now assume, in addition, that the group is large enough so that individual differences distribute on some normal curve, then any argument that justifies the philosopher's choice by rule should be immediately adaptable to my choice by value. A group too small, or a distribution excessively skewed by external historical pressures, would, of course, pre-

vent the argument's transfer.[28] But those are just the circumstances under which scientific progress is itself problematic. The transfer is not then to be expected.

I shall be glad if these references to a normal distribution of individual differences and to the problem of induction make my position appear very close to more traditional views. With respect to theory choice, I have never thought my departures large and have been correspondingly startled by such charges as "mob psychology," quoted at the start. It is worth noting, however, that the positions are not quite identical, and for that purpose an analogy may be helpful. Many properties of liquids and gases can be accounted for on the kinetic theory[29] by supposing that all molecules

---

27   Hole or gap.

28   [Author's note] If the group is small, it is more likely that random fluctuations will result in its members' sharing an atypical set of values and therefore making choices different from those that would be made by a larger and more representative group. External environment—intellectual, ideological, or economic—must systematically affect the value system of much larger groups, and the consequences can include difficulties in introducing the scientific enterprise to societies with inimical values or perhaps even the end of that enterprise within societies where it had once flourished. In this area, however, great caution is required. Changes in the environment where science is practiced can also have fruitful effects on research. Historians often resort, for example, to differences between national environments to explain why particular innovations were initiated and at first disproportionately pursued in particular countries, e.g., Darwinism in Britain, energy conservation in Germany. At present we know substantially nothing about the minimum requisites of the social milieux within which a sciencelike enterprise might flourish.

29   The kinetic theory is a theory of the thermodynamic behavior of matter, especially the relationships among pressure, volume, and temperature in gases. Among its central notions are that temperature depends on the kinetic energy of the rapidly moving particles of a substance, that energy and momentum are conserved in all collisions between particles, and that the average behavior of the particles in a substance can be deduced by statistical analysis.

travel at the same speed. Among such properties are the regularities known as Boyle's and Charles's law.[30] Other characteristics, most obviously evaporation, cannot be explained in so simple a way. To deal with them one must assume that molecular speeds differ, that they are distributed at random, governed by the laws of chance. What I have been suggesting here is that theory choice, too, can be explained only in part by a theory which attributes the same properties to all the scientists who must do the choosing. Essential aspects of the process generally known as verification will be understood only by recourse to the features with respect to which men may differ while still remaining scientists. The tradition takes it for granted that such features are vital to the process of discovery, which it at once and for that reason rules out of philosophical bounds. That they may have significant functions also in the philosophically central problem of justifying theory choice is what philosophers of science have to date categorically denied.

What remains to be said can be grouped in a somewhat miscellaneous epilogue. For the sake of clarity and to avoid writing a book, I have throughout this paper utilized some traditional concepts and locutions about the viability of which I have elsewhere expressed serious doubts. For those who know the work in which I have done so, I close by indicating three aspects of what I have said which would better represent my views if cast in other terms, simultaneously indicating the main directions in which such recasting should proceed. The areas I have in mind are: value invariance, subjectivity, and partial communication. If my views of scientific development are novel—a matter about which there is legitimate room for doubt—it is in areas such as these, rather than theory choice, that my main departures from tradition should be sought.

30   Boyle's law, formulated by Robert Boyle in 1662, is the principle that, at a constant temperature, the volume of a confined ideal gas varies inversely with its pressure. Charles's law, discovered by French scientist J.A.C. Charles in 1787, states that the volume of a fixed mass of gas held at a constant pressure varies directly with the absolute temperature.

Throughout this paper I have implicitly assumed that, whatever their initial source, the criteria or values deployed in theory choice are fixed once and for all, unaffected by their participation in transitions from one theory to another. Roughly speaking, but only very roughly, I take that to be the case. If the list of relevant values is kept short (I have mentioned five, not all independent) and if their specification is left vague, then such values as accuracy, scope, and fruitfulness are permanent attributes of science. But little knowledge of history is required to suggest that both the application of these values and, more obviously, the relative weights attached to them have varied markedly with time and also with the field of application. Furthermore, many of these variations in value have been associated with particular changes in scientific theory. Though the experience of scientists provides no philosophical justification for the values they deploy (such justification would solve the problem of induction), those values are in part learned from that experience, and they evolve with it.

The whole subject needs more study (historians have usually taken scientific values, though not scientific methods, for granted), but a few remarks will illustrate the sort of variations I have in mind. Accuracy, as a value, has with time increasingly denoted quantitative or numerical agreement, sometimes at the expense of qualitative. Before early modern times, however, accuracy in that sense was a criterion only for astronomy, the science of the celestial region. Elsewhere it was neither expected nor sought. During the seventeenth century, however, the criterion of numerical agreement was extended to mechanics, during the late eighteenth and early nineteenth centuries to chemistry and such other subjects as electricity and heat, and in this century to many parts of biology. Or think of utility, an item of value not on my initial list. It too has figured significantly in scientific development, but far more strongly and steadily for chemists than for, say, mathematicians and physicists. Or consider scope. It is still an important scientific value, but important scientific advances have repeatedly been achieved at its expense, and the weight attributed to it at times of choice has diminished correspondingly.

What may seem particularly troublesome about changes like these is, of course, that they ordinarily occur in the aftermath of a theory change. One of the objections to Lavoisier's new chemistry[31] was the roadblocks with which it confronted the achievement of what had previously been one of chemistry's traditional goals: the explanation of qualities, such as color and texture, as well as of their changes. With the acceptance of Lavoisier's theory such explanations ceased for some time to be a value for chemists; the ability to explain qualitative variation was no longer a criterion relevant to the evaluation of chemical theory. Clearly, if such value changes had occurred as rapidly or been as complete as the theory changes to which they related, then theory choice would be value choice, and neither could provide justification for the other. But, historically, value change is ordinarily a belated and largely unconscious concomitant of theory choice, and the former's magnitude is regularly smaller than the latter's. For the functions I have here ascribed to values, such relative stability provides a sufficient basis. The existence of a feedback loop through which theory change affects the values which led to that change does not make the decision process circular in any damaging sense.

About a second respect in which my resort to tradition may be misleading, I must be far more tentative. It demands the skills of an ordinary language philosopher, which I do not possess. Still no very acute ear for language is required to generate discomfort with the ways in which the terms "objectivity" and, more especially, "subjectivity" have functioned in this paper. Let me briefly suggest the respects in which I believe language has gone astray. "Subjective" is a term with

---

31 Antoine Laurent Lavoisier (1743–1794) isolated the major components of air and water, disproved the phlogiston theory by determining the role of oxygen in combustion, and organized the classification of chemical compounds upon which the modern system is based. He formulated the concept of an element as being a simple substance that cannot be broken down by any known method of chemical analysis, and he showed that although matter changes state during a chemical reaction its mass remains the same, thus leading him to propose the law of conservation of matter. Lavoisier was executed during the Reign of Terror after the French Revolution.

several established uses: in one of these it is opposed to "objective," in another to "judgmental." When my critics describe the idiosyncratic features to which I appeal as subjective, they resort, erroneously I think, to the second of these senses. When they complain that I deprive science of objectivity, they conflate that second sense of subjective with the first.

A standard application of the term "subjective" is to matters of taste, and my critics appear to suppose that that is what I have made of theory choice. But they are missing a distinction standard since Kant when they do so. Like sensation reports, which are also subjective in the sense now at issue, matters of taste are undiscussable. Suppose that, leaving a movie theater with a friend after seeing a western, I exclaim: "How I liked that terrible potboiler!" My friend, if he disliked the film, may tell me I have low tastes, a matter about which, in these circumstances, I would readily agree. But, short of saying that I lied, he cannot disagree with my report that I liked the film or try to persuade me that what I said about my reaction was wrong. What is discussable in my remark is not my characterization of my internal state, my exemplification of taste, but rather my *judgment* that the film was a potboiler. Should my friend disagree on that point, we may argue most of the night, each comparing the film with good or great ones we have seen, each revealing, implicitly or explicitly, something about how he *judges* cinematic merit, about his aesthetic. Though one of us may, before retiring, have persuaded the other, he need not have done so to demonstrate that our difference is one of judgment, not taste.

Evaluations or choices of theory have, I think, exactly this character. Not that scientists never say merely, I like such and such a theory, or I do not. After 1926 Einstein said little more than that about his opposition to the quantum theory. But scientists may always be asked to explain their choices, to exhibit the bases for their judgments. Such judgments are eminently discussable, and the man who refuses to discuss his own cannot expect to be taken seriously. Though there are, very occasionally, leaders of scientific taste, their existence tends to prove the rule. Einstein was one of the few, and his increasing isolation from the scientific community in later life shows how very limited a role taste alone can play in theory choice. Bohr,[32] unlike Einstein, did discuss the bases for his judgment, and he carried the day. If my critics introduce the term "subjective" in a sense that opposes it to judgmental—thus suggesting that I make theory choice undiscussable, a matter of taste—they have seriously mistaken my position.

Turn now to the sense in which "subjectivity" is opposed to "objectivity," and note first that it raises issues quite separate from those just discussed. Whether my taste is low or refined, my report that I liked the film is objective unless I have lied. To my judgment that the film was a potboiler, however, the objective-subjective distinction does not apply at all, at least not obviously and directly. When my critics say I deprive theory choice of objectivity, they must, therefore, have recourse to some very different sense of subjective, presumably the one in which bias and personal likes or dislikes function instead of, or in the face of, the actual facts. But that sense of subjective does not fit the process I have been describing any better than the first. Where factors dependent on individual biography or personality must be introduced to make values applicable, no standards of factuality or actuality are being set aside. Conceivably my discussion of theory choice indicates some limitations of objectivity, but not by isolating elements properly called subjective. Nor am I even quite content with the notion that what I have been displaying are limitations. Objectivity ought to be analyzable in terms of criteria like accuracy and consistency. If these criteria do not supply all the guidance that we have customarily expected of them, then it may be the meaning rather than the limits of objectivity that my argument shows.

Turn, in conclusion, to a third respect, or set of respects, in which this paper needs to be recast. I have assumed throughout that the discussions surrounding theory choice are unproblematic, that the facts appealed to in such discussions are independent of theory, and that the discussions' outcome is appropriately called a choice. Elsewhere I have challenged all three of these assumptions, arguing that communication between proponents of different theories is inevitably partial, that what each takes to be facts depends in part on the theory he espouses, and that an individual's transfer of allegiance from theory to theory is often better described as conversion than as choice. Though all these theses are problematic as well as controversial, my commitment to them is undiminished. I shall not now defend them, but must at least attempt to indicate how what I have said here can be adjusted to conform with these more central aspects of my view of scientific development.

For that purpose I resort to an analogy I have developed in other places. Proponents of different theories are, I have claimed, like native speakers of different languages. Communication between them goes on by translation, and it raises all translation's familiar difficulties. That analogy is, of course, incomplete, for the vocabulary of the two theories may be identical, and most words function in the same ways in both. But some words in the basic as well as in the theoretical vocabularies of the two theories—words like "star" and "planet," "mixture" and "compound," or "force" and "matter"—do function differently. Those differences are unexpected and will be discovered and localized, if at all, only be repeated experience of communication breakdown. Without pursuing the matter further, I simply assert the existence of significant limits to what the proponents of different theories can communicate to one another. The same limits make it difficult or, more likely, impossible for an individual to hold both theories in mind together and compare them point by point with each other and with nature. That sort of comparison is, however, the process on which the appropriateness of any word like "choice" depends.

Nevertheless, despite the incompleteness of their communication, proponents of different theories can exhibit to each other, not always easily, the concrete technical results achievable by those who practice within each theory. Little or no translation is required to apply at least some value criteria to those results. (Accuracy and fruitfulness are most immediately applicable, perhaps followed by scope. Consistency

---

32 Niels Bohr, a Danish physicist, made basic contributions to the theory of atomic structure between 1913 and 1915 and received a Nobel prize in 1922 for this work. His model of the atom made essential use of quantum theory: he suggested that electrons in an atom move in orbits, and that when an electron moves to another orbit it gives off or absorbs a quantum of radiation.

and simplicity are far more problematic.) However incomprehensible the new theory may be to the proponents of tradition, the exhibit of impressive concrete results will persuade at least a few of them that they must discover how such results are achieved. For that purpose they must learn to translate, perhaps by treating already published papers as a Rosetta stone[33] or,

33 The Rosetta stone is a black basalt tablet discovered in 1799 by French troops near Rosetta, a northern Egyptian town in the Nile River delta. It can be seen in the British Museum in London and bears an inscription written in three different scripts—Greek, Egyptian hieroglyphic, and Egyptian demotic. This inscription provided the key to the code of (the hitherto baffling) Egyptian hieroglyphics.

often more effective, by visiting the innovator, talking with him, watching him and his students at work. Those exposures may not result in the adoption of the theory; some advocates of the tradition may return home and attempt to adjust the old theory to produce equivalent results. But others, if the new theory is to survive, will find that at some point in the language-learning process they have ceased to translate and begun instead to speak the language like a native. No process quite like choice has occurred, but they are practicing the new theory nonetheless. Furthermore, the factors that have led them to risk the conversion they have undergone are just the ones this paper has underscored in discussing a somewhat different process, one which, following philosophical tradition, it has labelled theory choice.

HELEN LONGINO

"Can There Be a Feminist Science?"

Who Is Helen Longino?

Helen E. Longino (born 1944) has been perhaps the most influential philosopher to apply contemporary feminist approaches to epistemology and philosophy of science. As an undergraduate, she majored in literary studies, moving to logic and philosophy of science for her graduate work at Johns Hopkins University. During the 1960s and 70s, she was active in anti-war and feminist political action movements. As a faculty member at Mills College, Rice University, and University of Minnesota, she was strongly influential in establishing women's studies courses and programs. At present, she teaches in the philosophy department at Stanford University.

Some Useful Background Information

Longino's target for feminist criticism is the long-held and (for a long time) universal view that the most important feature of good science is its *objectivity*—which was taken to mean that scientific practice, when working right, should be utterly uninfluenced by any values of the scientist, or of his culture or society—any values, that is, other than the internal scientific values of care in observation, honesty, thoroughness, and so on. The idea here was that nature itself—the external facts—should determine what's taken to be true by scientists.

Nobody thinks that real science always works this way: there are numerous high-profile examples brought to light of outright fraud, or unconscious bias, the result of what the scientist himself or the source of his funding, or the dominant culture, hopes to find. But the traditional view counts these as bad science. A very moderate feminist critique of science has, for decades, pointed out how male bias is among the factors that can make for bad science in this sense. Feminists point to scientific studies like these: a study of the causes of heart-attack which studied only males as subjects, blithely considering their conclusions to be applicable to all humans; a study of societal dynamics which looked only at traditional male activities and roles; a study of cognitive abilities that rated subjects on the basis of typically male abilities, concluding with the intellectual inferiority of women.

But this is not Longino's critique.

What Is the Structure of This Reading?

Longino begins by mentioning various sorts of feminist approaches to science that her article will not take. Her subject will instead be a feminist critique of the idea that science should be impersonal, objective, and value-free; feminists, she argues, offer an alternative that makes for better science.

After a number of preliminaries, she reveals her central argument: that confirmation in science often essentially involves background assumptions, and that these assumptions are sometimes not merely established by simple observation or common sense, but are rather tied in with "contextual values"—not mere internal rules of science, but personal, social, or cultural values.

Common Misconceptions

1. Longino does not argue that there are typically feminine characteristics that should be represented more in scientific investigations. She does not reject this view wholesale; she merely argues that this is not what she will talk about.
2. Neither does Longino argue here for a position that some readers, seeing that this is a feminist treatment of scientific practice, might expect: that the current male science gets things all wrong, and that a replacement female science would do better. She mentions that her aim is not to replace one "absolutism" by another.

Suggestions for Critical Reflection

1. Explain in your own words exactly what the difference between "contextual" and "constitutive" values in science is. Do you think that a real distinction can be made here? Do you think that

it's a good idea to try to allow input from the latter, but not from the former?
2. Longino argues that the input of "constitutive values" is sometimes inevitable. But she concludes from this that inquiry with this sort of input is "perfectly respectable." Do you think that follows?
3. Try to imagine a story about *scientifically respectable* theory-testing that includes a significant input of "contextual values." If you have studied science, you may know a bit of the real history of the field that illustrates this. What are the "contextual values" that play a part here?
4. Now try to imagine (or come up with a real example) of such testing where the input of "contextual values" made the scientific procedure unacceptable, invalid. Do you think there's a difference between instances of acceptable and unacceptable value-input science?
5. Explain how Longino uses her example of the study of the influence of sex hormones. What is the "background assumption" she thinks was at work in this study? Why does Longino think that this is connected to particular personal, cultural, or societal values? Is she right? What would have made for a better study? Do you think that a "value-free" inquiry here would have been an improvement? or that it would have been even possible?
6. A central, simple, definition of feminism sees it as a movement to counter discrimination and injustice toward women. What else might be involved in feminism as an intellectual commitment? Can you see why Longino's view of science is properly conceived of as feminist? Explain why you think it is or isn't.
7. Longino does not advocate replacement of scientifically harmful "androcentric" values by supposedly scientifically superior feminist ones. What, exactly, does she advocate?

Suggestions for Further Reading

A good place to start reading more by Longino is online: "The Social Dimensions of Scientific Knowledge," *The Stanford Encyclopedia of Philosophy (Fall 2008 Edition)*, Edward N. Zalta (ed.) <http://plato.stanford.

edu/archives/fall2008/entries/scientific-knowledge-social/>. Other articles by her are "Feminist Epistemology" *Blackwell Guide to Epistemology*, John Greco and Ernest Sosa, eds. (Blackwell, 1999), pp. 327-353; and "Cognitive and Non-Cognitive Values in Science: Rethinking the Dichotomy" *Feminism, Science, and the Philosophy of Science,* Lynn Hankinson Nelson and Jack Nelson, eds. (Kluwer, 1996), 39-58. Her books: *Science as Social Knowledge: Values and Objectivity in Scientific Inquiry* (Princeton University Press, 1990) and *The Fate of Knowledge* (Princeton University Press, 2002). She discusses examples further in Helen Longino and Ruth Doell, "Body, Bias, and Behaviour: A Comparative Analysis of Reasoning in Two Areas of Biological Science" *Signs: Journal of Women in Culture and Society* 9/2 (1983), pp. 206-227.

There has been a great deal written in the past few decades on this subject. A good place to find a variety of important short readings is in any of these anthologies: *Feminist Epistemologies*, Linda Alcoff and Elizabeth Potter, eds. (Routledge, 1993); *A Mind of One's Own: Feminist Essays on Reason and Objectivity*, Louise Antony and Charlotte Witt, eds., (Westview, 1993); *Discovering Reality: Feminist Perspectives in Epistemology, Metaphysics, Methodology and Philosophy of Science*, Sandra Harding and Merrill Hintikka, eds. (Reidel, 1983); *Engendering Rationalities*, Nancy Tuana and Sandra Morgen, eds. (SUNY Press, 2001); and *Feminism and Science*, Nancy Tuana, ed. (Indiana University Press, 1989).

"Can There Be a Feminist Science?"[1]

This paper explores a number of recent proposals regarding "feminist science" and rejects a content-based approach in favor of a process-based approach to characterizing feminist science. Philosophy of science can yield models of scientific reasoning that illuminate the interaction between cultural values and ideology and scientific inquiry. While we can use these models to expose masculine and other forms of bias, we can also use them to defend the introduction of assumptions grounded in feminist political values.

I

The question of this title conceals multiple ambiguities. Not only do the sciences consist of many distinct fields, but the term "science" can be used to refer to a method of inquiry, a historically changing collection of practices, a body of knowledge, a set of claims, a profession, a set of social groups, etc. And as the sciences are many, so are the scholarly disciplines that seek to understand them: philosophy, history, sociology, anthropology, psychology. Any answer from the perspective of some one of these disciplines will, then, of necessity, be partial. In this essay, I shall be asking about the possibility of theoretical natural science that is feminist and I shall ask from the perspective of a philosopher. Before beginning to develop my answer, however, I want to review some of the questions that could be meant, in order to arrive at the formulation I wish to address.

The question could be interpreted as factual, one to be answered by pointing to what feminists in the sciences are doing and saying: "Yes, and this is what it is." Such a response can be perceived as question-begging, however. Even such a friend of feminism as Stephen Gould dismisses the idea of a distinctively feminist or even female contribution to the sciences. In a generally positive review of Ruth Bleier's book, *Science and Gender*, Gould (1984) brushes aside her connection between women's attitudes and values and the interactionist science she calls for. Scientists (male, of course) are already proceeding with wholist[2] and interactionist[3] research programs. Why, he implied, should women or feminists have any particular, distinctive, contributions to make? There is not masculinist and feminist science, just good and

---

2   Wholists reject the assumption, made by positivists, that observation is independent from theory, and claim that confirming or disconfirming observations cannot be specified independently of the theory they are supposed to confirm or disconfirm.

3   This is the view, taken from a theoretical position in sociology, that derives social processes—in this case, the practice of science—from human interaction.

bad science. The question of a feminist science cannot be settled by pointing, but involves a deeper, subtler investigation.

The deeper question can itself have several meanings. One set of meanings is sociological, the other conceptual. The sociological meaning proceeds as follows. We know what sorts of social conditions make misogynist science possible. The work of Margaret Rossiter (1982) on the history of women scientists in the United States and the work of Kathryn Addelson (1983) on the social structure of professional science detail the relations between a particular social structure for science and the kinds of science produced. What sorts of social conditions would make feminist science possible? This is an important question, one I am not equipped directly to investigate, although what I can investigate is, I believe, relevant to it. This is the second, conceptual, interpretation of the question: what sort of sense does it make to talk about a feminist science? Why is the question itself not an oxymoron, linking, as it does, values and ideological commitment with the idea of impersonal, objective, value-free, inquiry? This is the problem I wish to address in this essay.

The hope for a feminist theoretical natural science has concealed an ambiguity between content and practice. In the content sense the idea of a feminist science involves a number of assumptions and calls a number of visions to mind. Some theorists have written as though a feminist science is one of the theories which encode a particular world view, characterized by complexity, interaction and wholism. Such a science is said to be feminist because it is the expression and valorization[4] of a female sensibility or cognitive temperament. Alternatively, it is claimed that women have certain traits (dispositions to attend to particulars, interactive rather than individualist and controlling social attitudes and behaviors) that enable them to understand the true character of natural processes (which are complex and interactive).[5] While propo-

nents of this interactionist view see it as an improvement over most contemporary science, it has also been branded as soft—misdescribed as non-mathematical. Women in the sciences who feel they are being asked to do not better science, but inferior science, have responded angrily to this characterization of feminist science, thinking that it is simply new clothing for the old idea that women can't do science. I think that the interactionist view can be defended against this response, although that requires rescuing it from some of its proponents as well. However, I also think that the characterization of feminist science as the expression of a distinctive female cognitive temperament has other drawbacks. It first conflates feminine with feminist. While it is important to reject the traditional derogation of the virtues assigned to women, it is also important to remember that women are *constructed* to occupy positions of social subordinates. We should not uncritically embrace the feminine.

This characterization of feminist science is also a version of recently propounded notions of a 'women's standpoint' or a 'feminist standpoint' and suffers from the same suspect universalization that these ideas suffer from. If there is one such standpoint, there are many: as Maria Lugones and Elizabeth Spelman spell out in their tellingly entitled article, "Have We Got a Theory for You: Feminist Theory, Cultural Imperialism, and the Demand for 'The Woman's Voice,'" women are too diverse in our experiences to generate a single cognitive framework (Lugones and Spelman 1983). In addition, the sciences are themselves too diverse for me to think that they might be equally transformed by such a framework. To reject this concept of a feminist science, however, is not to disengage science from feminism. I want to suggest that we focus on science as practice rather than content, as process rather than product; hence, not on feminist science, but on doing science as a feminist.

The doing of science involves many practices: how one structures a laboratory (hierarchically or collectively), how one relates to other scientists (competitively or cooperatively), how and whether one engages in political struggles over affirmative action. It extends also to intellectual practices, to the activities of scientific inquiry, such as observation and reasoning. Can there be a feminist scientific inquiry?

---

4   To valorize something is to enhance its value, usually artificially, or to assign a value to it.

5   [Author's note] This seems to be suggested in Bleier (1984), Rose (1983) and in Sandra Harding's (1980) early work.

This possibility is seen to be problematic against the background of certain standard presuppositions about science. The claim that there could be a feminist science in the sense of an intellectual practice is either nonsense because oxymoronic as suggested above or the claim is interpreted to mean that established science (science as done and dominated by men) is wrong about the world. Feminist science in this latter interpretation is presented as correcting the errors of masculine, standard science and as revealing the truth that is hidden by masculine 'bad' science, as taking the sex out of science.

Both of these interpretations involve the rejection of one approach as incorrect and the embracing of the other as the way to a truer understanding of the natural world. Both trade one absolutism for another. Each is a side of the same coin, and that coin, I think, is the idea of a value-free science. This is the idea that scientific methodology guarantees the independence of scientific inquiry from values or value-related considerations. A science or a scientific research program informed by values is *ipso facto* "bad science." "Good science" is inquiry protected by methodology from values and ideology. This same idea underlies Gould's response to Bleier, so it bears closer scrutiny. In the pages that follow, I shall examine the idea of value-free science and then apply the results of that examination to the idea of feminist scientific inquiry.

II

I distinguish two kinds of values relevant to the sciences. Constitutive values, internal to the sciences, are the source of the rules determining what constitutes acceptable scientific practice or scientific method. The personal, social and cultural values, those group or individual preferences about what ought to be, I call contextual values, to indicate that they belong to the social and cultural context in which science is done (Longino 1983c). The traditional interpretation of the value-freedom of modern natural science amounts to a claim that its constitutive and contextual features are clearly distinct from and independent of one another, that contextual values play no role in the inner workings of scientific inquiry, in reasoning and observation. I shall argue that this construal of the distinction cannot be maintained.

There are several ways to develop such an argument. One scholar is fond of inviting her audience to visit any science library and peruse the titles on the shelves. Observe how subservient to social and cultural interests are the inquiries represented by the book titles alone! Her listeners would soon abandon their ideas about the value-neutrality of the sciences, she suggests. This exercise may indeed show the influence of external, contextual considerations on what research gets done/supported (i.e., on problem selection). It does not show that such considerations affect reasoning or hypothesis acceptance. The latter would require detailed investigation of particular cases or a general conceptual argument. The conceptual arguments involve developing some version of what is known in philosophy of science as the underdetermination thesis, i.e., the thesis that a theory is always underdetermined by the evidence adduced in its support, with the consequence that different or incompatible theories are supported by or at least compatible with the same body of evidence. I shall sketch a version of the argument that appeals to features of scientific inference.

One of the rocks on which the logical positivist program foundered was the distinction between theoretical and observational language. Theoretical statements contain, as fundamental descriptive terms, terms that do not occur in the description of data. Thus, hypotheses in particle physics contain terms like "electron," "pion," "muon," "electron spin," etc. The evidence for a hypothesis such as "A pion decays sequentially into a muon, then a positron" is obviously not direct observations of pions, muons and positrons, but consists largely in photographs taken in large and complex experimental apparati: accelerators, cloud chambers, bubble chambers. The photographs show all sorts of squiggly lines and spirals. Evidence for the hypotheses of particle physics is presented as statements that describe these photographs. Eventually, of course, particle physicists point to a spot on a photograph and say things like "Here a neutrino hits a neutron." Such an assertion, however, is an interpretive achievement which involves collapsing theoretical and observational moments. A skeptic would have to be supplied a complicated argument linking the elements of the photograph to traces left by particles and these to particles themselves. What counts as theory and what as data in a pragmatic sense change over time, as some ideas and experimental procedures come to be securely embedded in a particular framework and others take their place on the horizons. As the history of physics shows, however, secure embeddedness is no guarantee against overthrow.

Logical positivists and their successors hoped to model scientific inference formally. Evidence for hypotheses, data, were to be represented as logical consequences of hypotheses. When we try to map this logical structure onto the sciences, however, we find that hypotheses are, for the most part, not just generalizations of data statements. The links between data and theory, therefore, cannot be adequately represented as formal or syntactic, but are established by means of assumptions that make or imply substantive claims about the field over which one theorizes. Theories are confirmed via the confirmation of their constituent hypotheses, so the confirmation of hypotheses and theories is relative to the assumptions relied upon in asserting the evidential connection. Conformation of such assumptions, which are often unarticulated, is itself subject to similar relativization. And it is these assumptions that can be the vehicle for the involvement of considerations motivated primarily by contextual values (Longino 1979, 1983a).

The point of this extremely telescoped argument is that one can't give an a priori specification of confirmation that effectively eliminates the role of value-laden assumptions in legitimate scientific inquiry without eliminating auxiliary hypotheses (assumptions) altogether. This is not to say that all scientific reasoning involves value-related assumptions. Sometimes auxiliary assumptions will be supported by mundane inductive reasoning. But sometimes they will not be. In any given case, they may be metaphysical in character; they may be untestable with present investigative techniques; they may be rooted in contextual, value-related considerations. If, however, there is no a priori way to eliminate such assumptions from evidential reasoning generally, and, hence, no way to rule out value-laden assumptions, then there is no formal basis for arguing that an inference mediated by contextual values is thereby bad science.

A comparable point is made by some historians investigating the origins of modern science. James Jacob (1977) and Margaret Jacob (1976) have, in a series of articles and books, argued that the adoption of conceptions of matter by 17th century scientists like Robert Boyle was inextricably intertwined with political considerations. Conceptions of matter provided the foundation on which physical theories were developed and Boyle's science, regardless of his reasons for it, has been fruitful in ways that far exceed his imaginings. If the presence of contextual influences were grounds for disallowing a line of inquiry, then early modern science would not have gotten off the ground.

The conclusion of this line of argument is that constitutive values conceived as epistemological (i.e., truth-seeking) are not adequate to screen out the influence of contextual values in the very structuring of scientific knowledge. Now the ways in which contextual values do, if they do, influence this structuring and interact, if they do, with constitutive values has to be determined separately for different theories and fields of science. But this argument, if it's sound, tells us that this sort of inquiry is perfectly respectable and involves no shady assumptions or unargued intuitively based rejections of positivism. It also opens the possibility that one can make explicit value commitments and still do "good" science. The conceptual argument doesn't show that all science is value-laden (as opposed to metaphysics-laden)—that must be established on a case-by-case basis, using the tools not just of logic and philosophy but of history and sociology as well. It does show that not all science is value-free and, more importantly, that it is not necessarily in the nature of science to be value-free. If we reject that idea we're in a better position to talk about the possibilities of feminist science.

III

In earlier articles (Longino 1981, 1983b; Longino and Doell 1983), I've used similar considerations to argue that scientific objectivity has to be reconceived as a function of the communal structure of scientific inquiry rather than as a property of individual scientists. I've then used these notions about scientific methodology to show that science displaying masculine bias is not *ipso facto* improper or 'bad' science;

that the fabric of science can neither rule out the expression of bias nor legitimate it. So I've argued that both the expression of masculine bias in the sciences and feminist criticism of research exhibiting that bias are—shall we say—business as usual; that scientific inquiry should be expected to display the deep metaphysical and normative[6] commitments of the culture in which it flourishes; and finally that criticism of the deep assumptions that guide scientific reasoning about data is a proper part of science.

The argument I've just offered about the idea of a value-free science is similar in spirit to those earlier arguments. I think it makes it possible to see these questions from a slightly different angle.

There is a tradition of viewing scientific inquiry as somehow inexorable. This involves supposing that the phenomena of the natural world are fixed in determinate relations with each other, that these relations can be known and formulated in a consistent and unified way. This is not the old "unified science" idea of the logical positivists, with its privileging of physics. In its "unexplicated" or "pre-analytic" state, it is simply the idea that there is one consistent, integrated or coherent, true theoretical treatment of all natural phenomena. (The indeterminacy principle of quantum physics is restricted to our understanding of the behavior of certain particles which themselves underlie the fixities of the natural world. Stochastic[7] theories reveal fixities, but fixities among ensembles rather than fixed relations among individual objects or events.) The scientific inquirer's job is to discover those fixed relations. Just as the task of Plato's philosophers was to discover the fixed relations among forms and the task of Galileo's scientists was to discover the laws written in the language of the grand book of nature, geometry, so the scientist's task in this tradition remains the discovery of fixed relations however conceived. These ideas are part of the realist tradition in the philosophy of science.

It's no longer possible, in a century that has seen the splintering of the scientific disciplines, to give such a unified description of the objects of inquiry.

But the belief that the job is to discover fixed relations of some sort, and that the application of observation, experiment and reason leads ineluctably to unifiable, if not unified, knowledge of an independent reality, is still with us. It is evidenced most clearly in two features of scientific rhetoric: the use of the passive voice as in "it is concluded that ..." or "it has been discovered that ..." and the attribution of agency to the data, as in "the data suggest...." Such language has been criticized for the abdication of responsibility it indicates. Even more, the scientific inquirer, and we with her, become passive observers, victims of the truth. The idea of a value-free science is integral to this view of scientific inquiry. And if we reject that idea we can also reject our roles as passive onlookers, helpless to affect the course of knowledge.

Let me develop this point somewhat more concretely and autobiographically. Biologist Ruth Doell and I have been examining studies in three areas of research on the influence of sex hormones on human behavior and cognitive performance: research on the influence of pre-natal, *in utero*, exposure to higher or lower than normal levels of androgens and estrogens on so-called 'gender-role' behavior in children, influence of androgens (pre- and post-natal) on homosexuality in women, and influence of lower than normal (for men) levels of androgen at puberty on spatial abilities (Doell and Longino, forthcoming).

The studies we looked at are vulnerable to criticism of their data and their observation methodologies. They also show clear evidence of androcentric bias[8]—in the assumption that there are just two sexes and two genders (us and them), in the designation of appropriate and inappropriate behaviors for male and female children, in the caricature of lesbianism, in the assumption of male mathematical superiority. We did not find, however, that these assumptions mediated the inferences from data to theory that we found objectionable. These sexist assumptions did affect the way the data were described. What mediated the inferences from the alleged data (i.e., what functioned as auxiliary hypotheses or what provided auxiliary hypotheses) was what we called the linear model— the assumption that there is a direct one-way causal

---

6   Normative means having to do with a value—a prescribed norm.

7   Probabilistic.

8   I.e., a bias in favor of the male point of view.

relationship between pre- or post-natal hormone levels and later behavior or cognitive performance. To put it crudely, fetal gonadal hormones organize the brain at critical periods of development. The organism is thereby disposed to respond in a range of ways to a range of environmental stimuli. The assumption of unidirectional programming is supposedly supported by the finding of such a relationship in other mammals; in particular, by experiments demonstrating the dependence of sexual behaviors—mounting and lordosis[9]—on peri-natal hormone exposure and the finding of effects of sex hormones on the development of rodent brains. To bring it to bear on humans is to ignore, among other things, some important differences between human brains and those of other species. It also implies a willingness to regard humans in a particular way—to see us as produced by factors over which we have no control. Not only are we, as scientists, victims of the truth, but we are the prisoners of our physiology.[10] In the name of extending an explanatory model, human capacities for self-knowledge, self-reflection, self-determination are eliminated from any role in human action (at least in the behaviors studied).

Doell and I have therefore argued for the replacement of that linear model of the role of the brain in behavior by one of much greater complexity that includes physiological, environmental, historical and psychological elements. Such a model allows not only for the interaction of physiological and environmental factors but also for the interaction of these with a continuously self-modifying, self-representational (and self-organizing) central processing system. In contemporary neurobiology, the closest model is that being developed in the group selectionist approach to higher brain function of Gerald Edelman and other researchers (Edelman and Mountcastle 1978). We argue that a model of at least that degree of complexity is necessary to account for the human behaviors studies in the sex hormones and behavior research

and that if gonadal hormones function at all at these levels, they will probably be found at most to facilitate or inhibit neural processing in general. The strategy we take in our argument is to show that the degree of intentionality involved in the behaviors in question is greater than is presupposed by the hormonal influence researchers and to argue that this degree of intentionality implicates the higher brain processes.

To this point Ruth Doell and I agree. I want to go further and describe what we've done from the perspective of the above philosophical discussion of scientific methodology.

Abandoning my polemical mood for a more reflective one, I want to say that, in the end, commitment to one or another model is strongly influenced by values or other contextual features. The models themselves determine the relevance and interpretation of data. The linear or complex models are not in turn independently or conclusively supported by data. I doubt for instance that value-free inquiry will reveal the efficacy or inefficacy of intentional states or of physiological factors like hormone exposure in human action. I think instead that a research program in neuro-science that assumes the linear model and sex-gender dualism will show the influence of hormone exposure on gender-role behavior. And I think that a research program in neuroscience and psychology proceeding on the assumption that humans do possess the capacities for self-consciousness, self-reflection, and self-determination, and which then asks how the structure of the human brain and nervous system enables the expression of these capacities, will reveal the efficacy of intentional states (understood as very complex sorts of brain states).

While this latter assumption does not itself contain normative terms, I think that the decision to adopt it is motivated by value-laden considerations—by the desire to understand ourselves and others as self-determining (at least some of the time), that is, as capable of acting on the basis of concepts or representations of ourselves and the world in which we act. (Such representations are not necessarily correct, they are surely mediated by our cultures; all we wish to claim is that they are efficacious.) I think further that this desire on Ruth Doell's and my part is, in several ways, an aspect of our feminism. Our preference for

---

9   Arching the spine backwards or downwards, which is a sexual response in some mammals (such as cats and mice).

10   [Author's note] For a striking expression of this point of view see Witelson (1985).

a neurobiological model that allows for agency, for the efficacy of intentionality, is partly a validation of our (and everyone's) subjective experience of thought, deliberation, and choice. One of the tenets of feminist research is the valorization of subjective experience, and so our preference in this regard conforms to feminist research patterns. There is, however, a more direct way in which our feminism is expressed in this preference. Feminism is many things to many people, but it is at its core in part about the expansion of human potentiality. When feminists talk of breaking out and do break out of socially prescribed sex-roles, when feminists criticize the institutions of domination, we are thereby insisting on the capacity of humans—male and female—to act on perceptions of self and society and to act to bring about changes in self and society on the basis of those perceptions. (Not overnight and not by a mere act of will. The point is that we act.) And so our criticism of theories of the hormonal influence or determination of so-called gender-role behavior is not just a rejection of the sexist bias in the description of the phenomena—the behavior of the children studied, the sexual lives of lesbians, etc.—but of the limitations on human capacity imposed by the analytic model underlying such research.[11]

While the argument strategy we adopt against the linear model rests on a certain understanding of intention, the values motivating our adoption of that understanding remain hidden in that polemical context. Our political commitments, however, presuppose a certain understanding of human action, so that when faced with a conflict between these commitments and a particular model of brain-behavior relationships we allow the political commitments to guide the choice.

The relevance of my argument about value-free science should be becoming clear. Feminists—in and out of science—often condemn masculine bias in the sciences from the vantage point of commitment to a value-free science. Androcentric bias, once identified, can then be seen as a violation of the rules, as "bad" science. Feminist science, by contrast, can eliminate that bias and produce better, good, more true or gender free science. From that perspective the process I've just described is anathema. But if scientific methods generated by constitutive values cannot guarantee independent from contextual values, then that approach to sexist science won't work. We cannot restrict ourselves simply to the elimination of bias, but must expand our scope to include the detection of limiting and interpretive frameworks and the finding or construction of more appropriate frameworks. We need not, indeed should not, wait for such a framework to emerge from the data. In waiting, if my argument is correct, we run the danger of working unconsciously with assumptions still laden with values from the context we seek to change. Instead of remaining passive with respect to the data and what the data suggest, we can acknowledge our ability to affect the course of knowledge and fashion or favor research programs that are consistent with the values and commitments we express in the rest of our lives. From this perspective, the idea of a value-free science is not just empty, but pernicious.

Accepting the relevance to our practice as scientists of our political commitments does not imply simple and crude impositions of those ideas onto the corner of the natural world under study. If we recognize, however, that knowledge is shaped by the assumptions, values and interests of a culture and that, within limits, one can choose one's culture, then it's clear that as scientists/theorists we have a choice. We can continue to do establishment science, comfortably wrapped in the myths of scientific rhetoric, or we can alter our intellectual allegiances. While remaining committed to an abstract goal of understanding, we can choose to whom, socially and politically, we are accountable in our pursuit of that goal. In particular we can choose between being accountable to the traditional establishment or to our political comrades.

Such accountability does not demand a radical break with the science one has learned and practiced. The development of a "new" science involves a more dialectical evolution and more continuity with established science than the familiar language of scientific revolutions implies.

---

11 [Author's note] Ideological commitments other than feminist ones may lead to the same assumptions and the variety of feminisms means that feminist commitments can lead to different and incompatible assumptions.

In focusing on accountability and choice, this conception of feminist science differs from those that proceed from the assumption of a congruence between certain models of natural processes and women's inherent modes of understanding.[12] I am arguing instead for the deliberate and active choice of an interpretive model and for the legitimacy of basing that choice on political considerations in this case. Obviously model choice is also constrained by (what we know of) reality, that is, by the data. But reality (what we know of it) is, I have already argued, inadequate to uniquely determine model choice. The feminist theorists mentioned above have focused on the relation between the content of a theory and female values or experiences, in particular on the perceived congruence between interactionist, wholist visions of nature and a form of understanding and set of values widely attributed to women. In contrast, I am suggesting that a feminist scientific practice admits political considerations as relevant constraints on reasoning, which, through their influence on reasoning and interpretation, shape content. In this specific case, those considerations in combination with the phenomena support an explanatory model that is highly interactionist, highly complex. This argument is so far, however, neutral on the issue of whether an interactionist and complex account of natural processes will always be the preferred one. If it is preferred, however, this will be because of explicitly political considerations and not because interactionism is the expression of "women's nature."

The integration of a political commitment with scientific work will be expressed differently in different fields. In some, such as the complex of research programs having a bearing on the understanding of human behavior, certain moves, such as the one described above, seem quite obvious. In others it may not be clear how to express an alternate set of values in inquiry, or what values would be appropriate. The first step, however, is to abandon the idea that scrutiny of the data yields a seamless web of knowledge. The second is to think through a particular field and try to understand just what its unstated and fundamental assumptions are and how they influence the course of inquiry. Knowing something of the history of a field is necessary to this process, as is continued conversation with other feminists.

The feminist interventions I imagine will be local (i.e., specific to a particular area of research); they may not be exclusive (i.e., different feminist perspectives may be represented in theorizing); and they will be in some way continuous with existing scientific work. The accretion of such interventions, of science done by feminists as feminists, and by members of other disenfranchised groups, has the potential, nevertheless, ultimately to transform the character of scientific discourse.

Doing science differently requires more than just the will to do so and it would be disingenuous to pretend that our philosophies of science are the only barrier. Scientific inquiry takes place in a social, political and economic context which imposes a variety of institutional obstacles to innovation, let alone to the intellectual working out of oppositional and political commitments. The nature of university career ladders means that one's work must be recognized as meeting certain standards of quality in order that one be able to continue it. If those standards are intimately bound up with values and assumptions one rejects, incomprehension rather than conversion is likely. Success requires that we present our work in a way that satisfies those standards and it is easier to do work that looks just like work known to satisfy them than to strike out in a new direction. Another push to conformity comes from the structure of support for science. Many of the scientific ideas argued to be consistent with a feminist politics have a distinctively non-production orientation.[13] In the example discussed above, thinking of the brain as hormonally programmed makes intervention and control more likely than does thinking of it as a self-organizing complexly interactive system. The doing of science, however, requires financial support

---

12   [Author's note] Cf. note [5], above.

13   [Author's note] This is not to say that interactionist ideas may not be applied in productive contexts, but that, unlike linear causal models, they are several steps away from the manipulation of natural processes immediately suggested by the latter. See Keller (1985), especially Chapter 10.

and those who provide that support are increasingly industry and the military. As might be expected they support research projects likely to meet their needs, projects which promise even greater possibilities for intervention in and manipulation of natural processes. Our sciences are being harnessed to the making of money and the waging of war. The possibility of alternate understandings of the natural world is irrelevant to a culture driven by those interests. To do feminist science we must change the social and political context in which science is done.

So: can there be a feminist science? If this means: is it in principle possible to do science as a feminist?, the answer must be: yes. If this means: can we in practice do science as feminists?, the answer must be: not until we change present conditions.

Notes

I am grateful to the Wellesley Center for Research on Women for the Mellon Scholarship during which I worked on the ideas in this essay. I am also grateful to audiences at UC Berkeley, Northeastern University, Brandeis University and Rice University for their comments and to the anonymous reviewers for *Hypatia* for their suggestions. An earlier version appeared as Wellesley Center for Research on Women Working Paper #63.

References

Addelson, Kathryn Pine. 1983. The man of professional wisdom. In *Discovering reality*, ed. Sandra Harding and Merrill Hintikka. Dordrecht: Reidel.

Bleier, Ruth. 1984. *Science and gender*. Elmsford, NY: Pergamon.

Doell, Ruth, and Helen E. Longino. N.d. *Journal of Homosexuality*. Forthcoming.

Edelman, Gerald, and Vernon Mountcastle. 1978. *The mindful brain*. Cambridge, MA: MIT Press.

Gould, Stephen J. 1984. Review of Ruth Bleier, *Science and gender*. *New York Times Book Review*, VVI, 7 (August 12): 1.

Harding, Sandra. 1980. The norms of inquiry and masculine experience. In *PSA 1980*, Vol. 2, ed. Peter Asquith and Ronald Giere. East Lansing, MI: Philosophy of Science Association.

Jacob, James R. 1977. *Robert Boyle and the English Revolution, A study in social and intellectual change*. New York: Franklin.

Jacob, Margaret C. 1976. *The Newtonians and the English Revolution, 1689-1720*. Ithaca, NY: Cornell University Press.

Keller, Evelyn Fox. 1985. *Reflections on gender and science*. New Haven, CT: Yale University Press.

Longino, Helen. 1979. Evidence and hypothesis. *Philosophy of Science* 46 (1): 35-56.

———. 1981. Scientific objectivity and feminist theorizing. *Liberal Education* 67 (3): 33-41.

———. 1983a. The idea of a value free science. Paper presented to the Pacific Division of the American Philosophical Association, March 25, Berkeley, CA.

———. 1983b. Scientific objectivity and logics of science. *Inquiry* 26 (1): 85-106.

———. 1983c. Beyond "bad science." *Science, Technology and Human Values* 8 (1): 7-17.

Longino, Helen, and Ruth Doell. 1983. Body, bias and behavior. *Signs* 9 (2): 206-227.

Lugones, Maria, and Elizabeth Spelman. 1983. Have we got a theory for you! Feminist theory, cultural imperialism and the demand for "the woman's voice." *Hypatia 1*, published as a special issue of *Women's Studies International Forum* 6 (6): 573-581.

Rose, Hilary. 1983. Hand, brain, and heart: A feminist epistemology for the natural sciences. *Signs* 9 (1): 73-90.

Rossiter, Margaret. 1982. *Women scientists in America: Struggles and strategies to 1940*. Baltimore, MD: Johns Hopkins University Press.

Witelson, Sandra. 1985. An exchange on gender. *New York Review of Books* (October 24).

CHAPTER 5

Philosophy of Mind—What Is the Place of Mind in the Physical World?

INTRODUCTION TO THE QUESTION

The philosophy of mind has three main parts: the philosophy of psychology, philosophical psychology, and the metaphysics of mental phenomena. The philosophy of psychology (which can also be thought of as a branch of the philosophy of science) consists in the critical evaluation of the claims and methodologies of cognitive science. For example, in the first half of the twentieth century philosophers were involved with assessing the claims made by psychoanalytic theory (such as that of Sigmund Freud) and of psychological behaviorism, which controversially held that the only theoretical goals of psychology are the prediction and control of human behavior. More recently, philosophers have played a role in creating and critiquing psychological models which are based on analogies between the human mind and computer programs. For example, philosophers of mind examine the question of whether Artificial Intelligence is really possible (and how we would know if we found it), and whether the kind of information processing which is performed by the brain more resembles a familiar 'computational' type or a variety of more diffuse 'neural net' processing.

Philosophical psychology, by contrast, does not examine the science of psychology but instead engages in analysis of our ordinary, commonsensical concepts of the mental. It deals with such conceptual questions as the difference between deliberate action and mere behavior, the nature of memory and of perception, the notion of rationality, the concept of personal identity, and so on.

Finally, the metaphysics of the mind has to do with coming to understand the inherent nature of mental phenomena. The questions asked in this area are really at the heart of the philosophy of mind, and the four most important of them are the following:

1) What is the relationship between mind and brain? Of course, everyone knows that our minds and brains are closely connected: when certain things happen in our brains (perhaps caused by the ingestion of hallucinogenic chemicals) certain corresponding things happen in our minds. But what is the nature of this connection? Is the mind *nothing but* the physical brain (so that the brain chemicals *just are* the hallucinations, so to speak), or is it something distinct from the brain, either because it is made of some different metaphysical 'stuff' (such as soul-stuff) or because it belongs to a different level or category of being (as a software program belongs to a different metaphysical category than the hard drive on which it is stored).

2) What explains the fact that some of our mental states are directed at the world: how do some of our mental states come to be *meaningful*? The words on this page are meaningful because we use them as signs—when we learn to read, what we are learning is how to connect certain squiggles on the page with meaningful ideas. It is a much harder problem, however, to understand how bits of our mind or brain can become signs, all by themselves, even though there is no one inside the head to 'read' them and give them meaning.

3) What explains the fact that some of our mental states have a certain qualitative *feel*? Put another way, where does *consciousness* come from? For example, the sensation of being tickled, or the smell of cook-

ing onions, both have a distinctive feel to them: there is 'something it is like' for you to be tickled. However, if you think about it, this is a very unusual and quite puzzling fact; after all, for the vast majority of physical objects in the world, if you tickle them they don't feel a thing. So what makes *minds* special and unique in this respect? How do minds come to have a 'light on inside'—to be centers of consciousness and feeling in an unconscious, unfeeling universe? This is manifestly puzzling if you think of the mind as being nothing more than the three-and-a-bit-pound physico-chemical blob inside our skulls, but it turns out to be an extremely difficult problem for any theory of the mind. (In fact, arguably, it is the most difficult and pressing problem in all of philosophy.)

4) How do our mental states interact causally with the physical world? In particular, if our thoughts obey the laws of rationality instead of brute causality, then how can the workings of our mind be part of, or related to, the natural world? When I believe that this pesto sauce contains pine nuts, and I know that I am allergic to pine nuts and that if I eat any I will swell up like a balloon, and I don't want to swell up like a balloon, then it is (apparently) for this *reason* that I refuse to eat the pesto: my behavior is to be explained by the logical, rational connections between my beliefs and desires. The laws of physics, by contrast, are not rational laws. If a bullet ricochets off a lamppost and hits an innocent bystander during a bank robbery, it does not do so because it *ought* to bounce that way (nor does it do a bad thing because it has bounced *irrationally* or illogically)—its path is merely a physical consequence of the way it glanced off the metal of the lamppost. So, the laws of thought are rational and the laws of nature are arational: the problem is, then, how can thought be part of nature (be *both* rational and arational)? And if it is *not* part of nature, then how can it make things happen in the physical world (and vice versa)?

It is worth noting that, today, all of these questions are asked against the background of a default position called *physicalism*. Generally, in the sciences, we assume that the real world is nothing more than the physical world: that all the things which exist are physical (roughly, made of either matter or energy) and obey exclusively physical laws (i.e., those

described by fundamental physics). In most domains—such as chemistry, biology, or geology—this methodological assumption has proved fruitful; however, in psychology the question is much more vexed. In fact, the mind seems to be the last holdout of the non-physical in the natural world. How can the feeling of pain or the taste of honey be made of either matter or energy? How can falling in love or choosing to become a politician be subject to the laws of physics? If the study of the human mind is ever to be integrated within the rest of (scientific) human knowledge, these phenomena will need to be accounted for in a physicalist framework: the big question is, can this be done, and how?

The issue in the philosophy of mind which is focussed on in this chapter is the mind-body problem: what is the relationship between the mind and the brain? Historically, there have been six main mind-body theories, and all six are introduced in the readings in this chapter. The traditional mind-body theory—the dominant story until about the middle of the twentieth century—is called *substance dualism*: on this view, mind and body are two completely different entities made up of two quite different substances, spirit, and matter. The classic source for this view is Descartes' *Meditations*, which appears in Chapter Three; Gilbert Ryle introduces the theory in this chapter, and then subjects it to a fairly devastating critique, calling it the 'dogma of the ghost in the machine.' The next main mind-body theory to appear, dualism's successor, was called *behaviorism*: this theory holds that the mind is neither brain nor spirit, but instead consists in dispositions to behave in certain ways. Ryle is usually thought of as the primary philosophical practitioner and originator of this approach; all the rest of the readings in this chapter contain elements of a critique of behaviorism.

A natural approach to mental phenomena from a 'scientific' point of view is to attempt to reduce them to brain events. This tactic is called *mind-brain identity theory* in the philosophy of mind, and is represented here by the reading from J.J.C. Smart. An important criticism of identity theory can be found in the Putnam piece, which instead puts forward a theory called *functionalism*. The essential idea behind functionalism is that the mind is best thought of as a sort of abstract information-processing device (rather like a computer program), and a mental state is really a kind of complex input-output relation between sensory stimuli and (internal and external) behavior. Functionalism is attacked in the following three readings, especially the one by John Searle.

Paul Churchland presents a different approach to the mind-body problem, called *eliminativism*. On this view, the mind is not identical with anything since, at least in the way it is normally understood, there is no such thing as 'the mind' at all. Finally, in recent years there has been a resurgence of interest in dualism—not the substance dualism of Descartes, however, but a variant called *property dualism*. This theory agrees that there is nothing in our skulls over and above the brain, but asserts that brains have special non-physical properties which are responsible for the existence of meaning and consciousness. Some of the motivations for a view like this are presented by Thomas Nagel in his article "What Is It Like to Be a Bat?", and further arguments in favor of property dualism are advanced in the readings by Frank Jackson and David Chalmers.

The philosophy of mind has been a particularly active field for the past thirty years or so, and there is any number of good books available which will take you further into these fascinating questions. Some of the best are: David Armstrong, *The Mind-Body Problem* (Westview, 1999); David Braddon-Mitchell and Frank Jackson, *Philosophy of Mind and Cognition* (Blackwell, 2006); Keith Campbell, *Body and Mind* (University of Notre Dame Press, 1984); David Chalmers, *The Conscious Mind* (Oxford University Press, 1996); Paul Churchland, *Matter and Consciousness* (MIT Press, 1988); Tim Crane, *The Mechanical Mind* (Routledge, 2003); Daniel Dennett, *Consciousness Explained* (Little, Brown, 1991); Fred Dretske, *Naturalizing the Mind* (MIT Press, 1995); Owen Flanagan, *The Science of the Mind* (MIT Press, 1991); Jerry Fodor, *Psychosemantics* (MIT Press, 1989); Howard Gardner, *The Mind's New Science* (Basic Books, 1985); John Heil, *Philosophy of Mind* (Routledge, 2004); Ted Honderich, *Mind and Brain* (Oxford University Press, 1990); Jaegwon Kim, *Philosophy of Mind* (Westview, 2005); Colin McGinn, *The Character of Mind* (Oxford University Press, 1982); John Searle, *The Rediscovery of the Mind* (MIT Press, 1992); and Peter Smith and O.R. Jones, *The Philosophy of Mind* (Cambridge University Press, 1986). A good reference work on the philosophy of mind is *A Companion to the Philosophy of Mind*, edited by Samuel Guttenplan (Blackwell, 1996); there is also *The Oxford Handbook of Philosophy of Mind*, edited by Brian P. McLaughlin and Ansgar Beckermann (Oxford University Press, 2009), and *A Companion to Cognitive Science*, edited by William Bechtel and George Graham (Blackwell, 1999).

GILBERT RYLE

The Concept of Mind

Who Was Gilbert Ryle?

Gilbert Ryle, who died in 1976, was one of the most influential figures in British philosophy in the 1950s and 1960s—he is often credited with a large part in reviving philosophy in Britain after the Second World War and with making Oxford University, for a period, the world center of philosophical activity. He was Waynflete Professor of Metaphysical Philosophy at Oxford from 1945 to 1968, and editor of the pre-eminent British journal of philosophy at the time, *Mind*, between 1948 and 1971.

Ryle was born in 1900 in the seaside town of Brighton, in the south of England. His father was a doctor who had a strong interest in philosophy and astronomy; he was in fact one of the founders of the Aristotelian Society, perhaps Britain's most important philosophical society for most of the twentieth century. In 1919 Ryle went to Queen's College, Oxford, to study Classics, but the subject that made the most impression on him was logic, which, he later wrote, unlike Classics, "felt to me like a grown-up subject, in which there were still unsolved problems." He also spent a great deal of time rowing, and captained the Queen's College Boat Club. In 1923 he gained a first-class honors degree in "Greats" (classical studies and philosophy) and in 1924 got *another* first-class undergraduate degree in "Modern Greats" (Philosophy, Politics, and Economics). In the same year he became a lecturer at Christ Church College.

Early in his career, in the 1930s, Ryle became preoccupied with the question of what philosophy itself is: what, if anything, is its special method and subject matter? It is not, he felt, merely the scholarly study of old texts, it's not just science without the experiments,[1] nor is it *simply* the examination of the meanings of words. His view, in the end, was that philosophy consists in the analysis of certain kinds of meaning*less* expressions—with showing how certain combinations of ordinary words make no sense, and so resolving the problems created by these special kinds of nonsense. For example, "Florence hates the thought of going to hospital" is a grammatically misleading sentence, Ryle would say, since it appears to have the same form as "Florence hates Henry," which erroneously suggests that "the thought of going to hospital," like "Henry," is an expression which refers to an individual thing. This creates the apparent philosophical puzzle of trying to explain what kind of thing a thought is, and how they can be "of" one thing rather than another … whereas Ryle would have us *dissolve* the problem by refusing to be trapped by surface grammar and insisting that talk of thoughts as "things" in this way is just *nonsense* created by our loose ways of speaking. Two early articles by Ryle which explore his view of the philosophical method are "Systematically Misleading Expressions" (1932) and "Categories" (1938); both can be found in the second volume of his *Collected Papers*.

Ryle's philosophical method should not be seen as entirely negative. It can be thought of as the attempt to map out the "logical geography" of the problems he considers. That is, he tries to expose the mistaken conceptual maps of other philosophers, and replace them with a new chart giving the correct locations of our ordinary concepts. *The Concept of Mind*, Ryle's first and best-known book and a modern classic of philosophy, applies this method to Cartesian dualism. As he once put it, Ryle was looking around for "some notorious and large-size Gordian Knot" upon which to "exhibit a sustained piece of analytical hatchet-work," and he happened to settle upon our set of traditional—and in his view mistaken—assumptions about the nature of mind. His hatchet-work was immensely successful: partly because of the influence of *The Concept of Mind*, it is today almost (but not entirely) impossible to find a professional philosopher of mind who will admit to believing in the traditional dualism of Descartes (which makes mind and body separate substances).

With the coming of the Second World War in 1939, Ryle volunteered for military service and was commissioned in the Welsh Guards, where he was involved in intelligence work. Immediately after the war Ryle was elected to the Waynflete chair of philosophy at Oxford, and when *The Concept of Mind* came out four years later Ryle was immediately established as a leading British philosopher. Representative book reviews by his peers said, "this is probably one of the two or three most important and original works of

---

1   Ryle was quite candid about his general ignorance of science and psychology, but he did not feel this harmed his philosophy.

general philosophy which have been published in English in the last twenty years" and "it stands head and shoulders above its contemporaries."

During the next thirty years in which Ryle taught at Oxford and edited *Mind*, then perhaps the world's leading philosophical journal, he had a substantial impact on the growth and flourishing of the subject of philosophy in the second half of the twentieth century. Many of his students (such as A.J. Ayer, J.J.C. Smart, and Daniel Dennett) went on to become well-known philosophers; he was a constant presence at philosophical conferences all over the world (but especially the main British annual conference, the Joint Session of the Mind and Aristotelian Societies); and his editorship of *Mind* favored a new style of short, focussed, analytical papers, and was deliberately encouraging to younger philosophers and philosophers from outside of Britain. Ryle retired from his Oxford chair in 1968, but remained philosophically active until his death in 1976.

What Is the Structure of This Reading?

"Descartes's Myth" is the first chapter of *The Concept of Mind*, which contains ten chapters in all. The functions of this first chapter are (a) to lay out Ryle's target, Cartesian dualism, in preparation for Ryle's attack; (b) to describe generally the kind of logical error that dualism makes (a "category mistake"); and (c) to speculate about the historical origins of this mistake. The rest of the book consists, more or less, of a sequence of chapters each of which consider different aspects of mental life—such as intelligence, the will, emotion, sensation, imagination, and self-knowledge—and try to expose the absurdities of the traditional Cartesian "logical geography" of these notions. In place of these faulty conceptual maps, Ryle argues for an account of the mind that generally treats mental states simply as dispositions or tendencies to behave certain ways rather than others. Intelligence, for example, according to Ryle should not be seen as something *additional* to behavior (a kind of ghostly mechanism which plans our behavior by judging possible actions according to a set of internally stored rules) but as itself a *kind* of behavior—a disposition to regularly perform task *X* well, in a variety of different contexts.

Some Useful Background Information

Ryle is often described as rejecting traditional dualism and replacing it with a new philosophical theory of the mind called *behaviorism*. Behaviorism, which was founded by the American psychologist John B. Watson in 1913 (and explained at length in his 1925 book *Behaviorism*), was originally intended to be an experimental method for psychology. Watson's view was that psychology ought to be a strictly empirical and 'respectable' science; it therefore should not rely on the solitary introspective examination of one's own private mental states, but instead should restrict its data to objective, repeatable facts about "what an organism does and says." The business of psychology, then, should be the construction of psychological laws describing correlations between stimuli and reactions; psychology is best seen, not as the study of consciousness, but as the explanation and prediction of behavior. This form of behaviorism is usually called *methodological* (or *scientific*) *behaviorism*, and it is important to notice that it need not actually *deny* the existence of internal mental states but just says that the science of behavior can avoid talking about them.[2]

In the hands of the philosophers, behaviorism became not just a psychological method but a *theory* of the nature of mental states. In its purest form, this is the view that statements about mental phenomena can be completely analyzed in terms of (or reduced to, or translated into) statements about behavior and dispositions to behave. To have a mind *just is* to behave in a certain way. For example, to say that Othello is feeling jealous is, according to behaviorism, to say no more and no less than that he is behaving in a way characteristic of jealousy, or that he would behave in that way given suitable provocation. According to this theory, there are no internal "mental states" *in addition to* the patterns of human behavior. It is this kind of behaviorism—often called *logical* (or *analytic*) *behaviorism*—which is usually attributed to Gilbert Ryle

---

2   Although many behaviorists, such as Watson and B.F. Skinner, do in fact seem to have flirted with the notion that the mind can be eliminated—that it is just a kind of fiction designed to explain the complex movements of human bodies.

(even though he himself, somewhat unconvincingly, denied that he was a behaviorist): indeed, *The Concept of Mind* is frequently cited as the central text of logical behaviorism.

Today, few if any philosophers are logical behaviorists. It is generally accepted that no analysis of the behavior corresponding to any particular belief or desire is possible, since what someone is disposed to do depends not only on a single belief but, in a potentially infinite variety of ways, on a whole system of connected beliefs. For example, the belief that a glass is half full of water will be associated with different behaviors depending on what else one believes about water (e.g., believing that it is a lethal acid), what one desires (e.g., whether or not you are thirsty), what one believes about the current perceptual conditions (e.g., thinking you are dreaming), and so on. There just is no single behavioral analysis of what it is to believe the glass is half full, and so that belief can't just *be* a set of behaviors.

Another major sticking point for behaviorism has been the worry that the behaviorist cannot treat mental states as being the *causes* of behavior since, for them, mentality just *is* a particular pattern of behavior. For example, a behaviorist cannot correctly say that someone winces because they feel pain, or is a crackerjack Scrabble player because they have a large vocabulary, since wincing and playing Scrabble well are *part* of what it is to feel pain or have a large vocabulary, rather than *effects* of those things.

Other forms of philosophical behaviorism live on today however in, for example, the following three modern theories:.

1. *Analytical functionalism* is the view that the meanings of mental terms can be analyzed in terms of their role in our commonsense theory of behavior, "folk psychology." This view was held by, for example, David Lewis.
2. *Eliminative behaviorism* is a theory, associated with W.V. Quine, which denies any reality to internal mental states and talks only of overt behavior.
3. A theory developed by Donald Davidson, sometimes called *interpretivism*, holds that an "ideal interpreter" can have as complete and infallible access as is possible to the mental life of another person (because, for Davidson, to have a certain belief *just is* to be the kind of organism an ideal interpreter would attribute that belief to).

A Common Misconception

It is important to realize that the Ryle selection presented here, though itself a seminal piece of philosophy, is only a small part of a larger work. In this chapter, Ryle does not attempt to present all of his arguments against the doctrine of the ghost in the machine, nor does he explicitly describe his alternative behaviorist theory. Much of the power of Ryle's diagnosis comes from its initial plausibility, rather than from a battery of overt arguments. On the other hand, Ryle does make a couple of arguments, and it is also possible to see the seeds of other lines of argument being planted in this reading.

Suggestions for Critical Reflection

1. Ryle's central conceptual tool in his critique of the doctrine of the ghost in the machine is the notion of a *category mistake*. How clear is this notion? Is it precise enough to do the job Ryle wants it to do?
2. Do you think that what Ryle describes as the "official doctrine" is now defunct? Should it be? Does Ryle persuade you that it is absurd?
3. A big part of Ryle's assault on the ghost in the machine is his attack on the "causal hypothesis." How radical would it be if we abandoned this view of the mind as "para-mechanical"? What consequences would this have for our understanding of the mind and human action?
4. On the basis of the evidence available in this reading, how behavioristic do you think Ryle is? How much does what he has to say about what the mind is *not* tell us about what he thinks the mind *is*?
5. Ryle once said, "science talks about the world, while philosophy talks about talk about the world." How much, if at all, does his admitted ignorance of psychology and neuroscience harm Ryle's arguments about the nature of the mind? What does your answer to this question suggest about the nature of philosophy?

Suggestions for Further Reading

I recommend reading the rest of Ryle's *The Concept of Mind* (issued in various editions, including one from the University of Chicago Press and one from Penguin). His second book, *Dilemmas* (Cambridge University Press, 1954), continues to apply Ryle's philosophical method, and most of his papers are collected in two volumes originally published by Hutchinson in 1971. The two best secondary sources on Ryle's work are *Gilbert Ryle: An Introduction to his Philosophy*, by William Lyons (Harvester Press, 1980), and *Ryle: A Collection of Critical Essays*, edited by O.P. Wood and G.W. Pitcher (Doubleday, 1970).

A modern case for Cartesian dualism has been ably put by John Foster in *The Immaterial Self* (Routledge, 1991). The best source for methodological behaviorism is probably B.F. Skinner's book *Science and Human Behavior* (Macmillan, 1953); he also presented his vision of a utopian society run according to proper behaviorist principles in the novel *Walden Two* (Macmillan, 1948). A short yet rigorous presentation of logical behaviorism is Carl Hempel's "The Logical Analysis of Psychology," which can be found in *Readings in Philosophy of Psychology*, Volume 1, edited by Ned Block (Harvard University Press, 1980). P.T. Geach's book *Mental Acts* (Routledge & Kegan Paul, 1957) is sometimes considered to be the decisive refutation of classical logical behaviorism, while methodological behaviorism is effectively savaged in Noam Chomsky's review of Skinner's *Verbal Behavior* in the journal *Language* 35 (1959).

The Concept of Mind

Descartes's Myth[3]

(1) The Official Doctrine

There is a doctrine about the nature and place of minds which is so prevalent among theorists and even among laymen that it deserves to be described as the official theory. Most philosophers, psychologists and religious teachers subscribe, with minor reservations, to its main articles and, although they admit certain theoretical difficulties in it, they tend to assume that these can be overcome without serious modifications being made to the architecture of the theory. It will be argued here that the central principles of the doctrine are unsound and conflict with the whole body of what we know about minds when we are not speculating about them.

The official doctrine, which hails chiefly from Descartes,[4] is something like this. With the doubtful exceptions of idiots[5] and infants in arms every human being has both a body and a mind. Some would prefer to say that every human being is both a body and a mind. His body and his mind are ordinarily harnessed together, but after the death of the body his mind may continue to exist and function.

Human bodies are in space and are subject to the mechanical laws which govern all other bodies in space. Bodily processes and states can be inspected by external observers. So a man's bodily life is as much a public affair as are the lives of animals and reptiles and even as the careers of trees, crystals and planets.

But minds are not in space, nor are their operations subject to mechanical laws. The workings of one mind are not witnessable by other observers; its career is private. Only I can take direct cognisance of the states and processes of my own mind. A person therefore lives through two collateral histories, one consisting of what happens in and to his body, the other consisting of what happens in and to his mind. The first is public, the second private. The events in the first history are events in the physical world, those in the second are events in the mental world.

---

3   This is the first chapter of Ryle's book *The Concept of Mind*, copyright © 1984 London: Routledge and Chicago: The University of Chicago Press. Reproduced by permission of Taylor & Francis Books UK and with permission of the Principal, Fellows, and Scholars of Hertford College in the University of Oxford.

4   See Descartes' *Meditations on First Philosophy*, especially the Second and Sixth Meditations.

5   The term "idiot" here comes from out-of-date clinical terminology where it means someone so mentally deficient as to be permanently incapable of rational conduct; it was often defined as having a "mental age" below three years.

It has been disputed whether a person does or can directly monitor all or only some of the episodes of his own private history; but, according to the official doctrine, of at least some of these episodes he has direct and unchallengeable cognisance. In consciousness, self-consciousness and introspection he is directly and authentically apprised of the present states and operations of his mind. He may have great or small uncertainties about concurrent and adjacent episodes in the physical world, but he can have none about at least part of what is momentarily occupying his mind.

It is customary to express this bifurcation of his two lives and of his two worlds by saying that the things and events which belong to the physical world, including his own body, are external, while the workings of his own mind are internal. This antithesis of outer and inner is of course meant to be construed as a metaphor, since minds, not being in space, could not be described as being spatially inside anything else, or as having things going on spatially inside themselves. But relapses from this good intention are common and theorists are found speculating how stimuli, the physical sources of which are yards or miles outside a person's skin, can generate mental responses inside his skull, or how decisions framed inside his cranium can set going movements of his extremities.

Even when 'inner' and 'outer' are construed as metaphors, the problem how a person's mind and body influence one another is notoriously charged with theoretical difficulties. What the mind wills, the legs, arms and the tongue execute; what affects the ear and the eye has something to do with what the mind perceives; grimaces and smiles betray the mind's moods and bodily castigations[6] lead, it is hoped, to moral improvement. But the actual transactions between the episodes of the private history and those of the public history remain mysterious, since by definition they can belong to neither series. They could not be reported among the happenings described in a person's autobiography of his inner life, but nor could they be reported among those described in someone else's biography of that person's overt career. They can be inspected neither by introspection nor by laboratory experiment. They are theoretical shuttlecocks which are forever being bandied from the physiologist back to the psychologist and from the psychologist back to the physiologist.

Underlying this partly metaphorical representation of the bifurcation of a person's two lives there is a seemingly more profound and philosophical assumption. It is assumed that there are two different kinds of existence or status. What exists or happens may have the status of physical existence, or it may have the status of mental existence. Somewhat as the faces of coins are either heads or tails, or somewhat as living creatures are either male or female, so, it is supposed, some existing is physical existing, other existing is mental existing. It is a necessary feature of what has physical existence that it is in space and time; it is a necessary feature of what has mental existence that is in time but not in space. What has physical existence is composed of matter, or else is a function of matter; what has mental existence consists of consciousness, or else is a function of consciousness.

There is thus a polar opposition between mind and matter, an opposition which is often brought out as follows. Material objects are situated in a common field, known as 'space', and what happens to one body in one part of space is mechanically connected with what happens to other bodies in other parts of space. But mental happenings occur in insulated fields, known as 'minds', and there is, apart maybe from telepathy, no direct causal connexion between what happens in one mind and what happens in another. Only through the medium of the public physical world can the mind of one person make a difference to the mind of another. The mind is its own place and in his inner life each of us lives the life of a ghostly Robinson Crusoe. People can see, hear and jolt one another's bodies, but they are irremediably blind and deaf to the workings of one another's minds and inoperative upon them.

What sort of knowledge can be secured of the workings of a mind? On the one side, according to the official theory, a person has direct knowledge of the best imaginable kind of the workings of his own mind. Mental states and processes are (or are normally) conscious states and processes, and the consciousness which irradiates them can engender no illusions and leaves the door open for no doubts. A person's

---

6   "Castigation" means "severe punishment."

present thinkings, feelings and willings, his perceivings, rememberings and imaginings are intrinsically 'phosphorescent'; their existence and their nature are inevitably betrayed to their owner. The inner life is a stream of consciousness of such a sort that it would be absurd to suggest that the mind whose life is that stream might be unaware of what is passing down it.

True, the evidence adduced recently by Freud[7] seems to show that there exist channels tributary to this stream, which run hidden from their owner. People are actuated[8] by impulses the existence of which they vigorously disavow; some of their thoughts differ from the thoughts which they acknowledge; and some of the actions which they think they will to perform they do not really will. They are thoroughly gulled[9] by some of their own hypocrisies and they successfully ignore facts about their mental lives which on the official theory ought to be patent to them. Holders of the official theory tend, however, to maintain that anyhow in normal circumstances a person must be directly and authentically seized of the present state and workings of his own mind.

Besides being currently supplied with these alleged immediate data of consciousness, a person is also generally supposed to be able to exercise from time to time a special kind of perception, namely inner perception, or introspection. He can take a (non-optical) 'look' at what is passing in his mind. Not only can he view and scrutinize a flower through his sense of sight and listen to and discriminate the notes of a bell through his sense of hearing; he can also reflectively or introspectively watch, without any bodily organ of sense, the current episodes of his inner life. This self-observation is also commonly supposed to be immune from illusion, confusion or doubt. A mind's reports of its own affairs have a certainty superior to the best that is possessed by its reports of matters in the physical world. Sense-perceptions can, but consciousness and introspection cannot, be mistaken or confused.

On the other side, one person has no direct access of any sort to the events of the inner life of another. He cannot do better than make problematic inferences from the observed behaviour of the other person's body to the states of mind which, by analogy from his own conduct, he supposes to be signalized by that behaviour. Direct access to the workings of a mind is the privilege of that mind itself; in default of such privileged access, the workings of one mind are inevitably occult[10] to everyone else. For the supposed arguments from bodily movements similar to their own to mental workings similar to their own would lack any possibility of observational corroboration. Not unnaturally, therefore, an adherent of the official theory finds it difficult to resist this consequence of his premises, that he has no good reason to believe that there do exist minds other than his own. Even if he prefers to believe that to other human bodies there are harnessed minds not unlike his own, he cannot claim to be able to discover their individual characteristics, or the particular things that they undergo and do. Absolute solitude is on this showing the ineluctable destiny of the soul. Only our bodies can meet.

As a necessary corollary of this general scheme there is implicitly prescribed a special way of construing our ordinary concepts of mental powers and operations. The verbs, nouns and adjectives, with which in ordinary life we describe the wits, characters and higher-grade performances of the people with whom we have to do, are required to be construed as signifying special episodes in their secret histories, or else as signifying tendencies for such episodes to occur. When someone is described as knowing, believing or guessing something, as hoping dreading, intending or shirking something, as designing thus or being

---

7　Sigmund Freud (1856–1939) was, of course, an Austrian psychologist and the main founder of psychoanalysis. One of his main ideas was that the motives for human action are far more numerous and complex than is commonly thought, and that our most basic and constant motives—which result from various significant experiences throughout our life, and particularly in early childhood—are unconscious in the sense that it is difficult for us to acknowledge them and so we "repress" them.

8　Caused to act.

9　Tricked or fooled.

10　Ryle does not literally mean "supernatural," but hidden from human view or beyond the normal range of human knowledge. (The word comes from the Latin for "secret" or "covered over.")

amused at that, these verbs are supposed to denote the occurrence of specific modifications in his (to us) occult stream of consciousness. Only his own privileged access to this stream in direct awareness and introspection could provide authentic testimony that these mental-conduct verbs were correctly or incorrectly applied. The onlooker, be he teacher, critic, biographer or friend, can never assure himself that his comments have any vestige of truth. Yet it was just because we do in fact all know how to make such comments, make them with general correctness and correct them when they turn out to be confused or mistaken, that philosophers found it necessary to construct their theories of the nature and place of minds. Finding mental-conduct concepts being regularly and effectively used, they properly sought to fix their logical geography. But the logical geography officially recommended would entail that there could be no regular or effective use of these mental-conduct concepts in our descriptions of, and prescriptions for, other people's minds.

(2) The Absurdity of the Official Doctrine

Such in outline is the official theory. I shall often speak of it, with deliberate abusiveness, as 'the dogma of the Ghost in the Machine'. I hope to prove that it is entirely false, and false not in detail but in principle. It is not merely an assemblage of particular mistakes. It is one big mistake and a mistake of a special kind. It is, namely, a category-mistake. It represents the facts of mental life as if they belonged to one logical type or category (or range of types or categories), when they actually belong to another. The dogma is therefore a philosopher's myth. In attempting to explode the myth I shall probably be taken to be denying well-known facts about the mental life of human beings, and my plea that I aim at doing nothing more than rectify the logic of mental-conduct concepts will probably be disallowed as mere subterfuge.

I must first indicate what is meant by the phrase 'Category-mistake'. This I do in a series of illustrations.

A foreigner visiting Oxford or Cambridge[11] for the first time is shown a number of colleges, librar-

ies, playing fields, museums, scientific departments and administrative offices. He then asks 'But where is the University? I have seen where the members of the Colleges live, where the Registrar works, where the scientists experiment and the rest. But I have not yet seen the University in which reside and work the members of your University.' It has then to be explained to him that the University is not another collateral institution, some ulterior counterpart to the colleges, laboratories and offices which he has seen. The University is just the way in which all that he has already seen is organized. When they are seen and when their coordination is understood, the University has been seen. His mistake lay in his innocent assumption that it was correct to speak of Christ Church, the Bodleian Library, the Ashmolean Museum[12] *and* the University, to speak, that is, as if 'the University' stood for an extra member of the class of which these other units are members. He was mistakenly allocating the University to the same category as that to which the other institutions belong.

The same mistake would be made by a child witnessing the march-past of a division, who, having had pointed out to him such and such battalions, batteries, squadrons, etc., asked when the division was going to appear. He would be supposing that a division was a counterpart to the units already seen, partly similar to them and partly unlike them. He would be shown his mistake by being told that in watching the battalions, batteries and squadrons marching past he had been watching the division matching past. The march past was not a parade of battalions, batteries, squadrons *and* a division; it was a parade of the battalions, batteries and squadrons *of* a division.

---

collections of 30 or 40 independent colleges and their facilities, plus a few general university buildings used by all the colleges, such as the Examination Schools at Oxford. One consequence of this is that neither Oxford nor Cambridge have a campus or even a central "University" building, but are spread out in various buildings across their respective towns.

11 Oxford and Cambridge, unlike most modern universities, are not single, unified institutions but consist of

12 Christ Church College, the Bodleian, and the Ashmolean are all institutions at Oxford.

One more illustration. A foreigner watching his first game of cricket learns what are the functions of the bowlers, the batsmen, the fielders, the umpires and the scorers. He then says 'But there is no one left on the field to contribute the famous element of team-spirit. I see who does the bowling, the batting and the wicket-keeping, but I do not see whose role it is to exercise *esprit de corps*.' Once more, it would have to be explained that he was looking for the wrong type of thing. Team-spirit is not another cricketing-operation supplementary to all of the other special tasks. It is, roughly, the keenness with which each of the special tasks is performed, and performing a task keenly is not performing two tasks. Certainly exhibiting team spirit is not the same thing as bowling or catching, but nor is it a third thing such that we can say that the bowler first bowls *and* then exhibits team-spirit or that a fielder is at a given moment *either* catching *or* displaying *esprit de corps*.

These illustrations of category-mistakes have a common feature which must be noticed. The mistakes were made by people who did not know how to wield the concepts *University*, *division* and *team-spirit*. Their puzzles arose from inability to use certain items in the English vocabulary.

The theoretically interesting category-mistakes are those made by people who are perfectly competent to apply concepts, at least in the situations with which they are familiar, but are still liable in their abstract thinking to allocate those concepts to logical types to which they do not belong. An instance of a mistake of this sort would be the following story. A student of politics has learned the main differences between the British, the French, and the American Constitutions, and has learned also the differences and connexions between the Cabinet, Parliament, the various Ministries, the Judicature and the Church of England. But he still became embarrassed when asked questions about the connexions between the Church of England, the Home Office and the British Constitution. For while the Church and the Home Office are institutions, the British Constitution is not another institution in the same sense of that noun. So inter-institutional relations which can be asserted or denied to hold

between the Church and the Home Office cannot be asserted or denied to hold between either of them and the British Constitution. 'The British Constitution' is not a term of the same logical type as 'the Home Office' and 'the Church of England'. In a partially similar way, John Doe may be a relative, a friend, an enemy or a stranger to Richard Roe; but he cannot be any of these things to the Average Taxpayer. He knows how to talk sense in certain sorts of discussions about the Average Taxpayer, but he is baffled to say why he could not come across him in the street as he can come across Richard Roe.

It is pertinent to our main subject to notice that, so long as the student of politics continues to think of the British Constitution as a counterpart to the other institutions, he will tend to describe it as a mysteriously occult institution, and so long as John Doe continues to think of the Average Taxpayer as a fellow-citizen, he will tend to think of him as an elusive insubstantial man, a ghost who is everywhere yet nowhere.

My destructive purpose is to show that a family of radical category-mistakes is the source of the double-life theory. The representation of a person as a ghost mysteriously ensconced in a machine derives from this argument. Because, as is true, a person's thinking, feeling and purposive doing cannot be described solely in the idioms of physics, chemistry and physiology, therefore they must be described in counterpart idioms. As the human body is a complex organized unit, so the human mind must be another complex organized unit, though one made of a different sort of stuff and with a different sort of structure. Or, again, as the human body, like any other parcel of matter, is a field of causes and effects, so the mind must be another field of causes and effects, though not (Heaven be praised) mechanical causes and effects.

(3) The Origin of the Category-Mistake

One of the chief intellectual origins of what I have yet to prove to be the Cartesian category-mistake seems to be this. When Galileo showed that his methods of scientific discovery were competent to provide a mechanical theory which should cover every occupant of space, Descartes found in himself two conflicting motives. As a man of scientific genius he could not but endorse the claims of mechanics, yet as a religious and moral man he could not accept, as Hobbes accepted, the discouraging rider to those claims, namely that human nature differs only in degree of complexity from clockwork. The mental could not be just a variety of the mechanical.

He and subsequent philosophers naturally but erroneously availed themselves of the following escape-route. Since mental-conduct words are not to be construed as signifying the occurrence of mechanical processes, they must be construed as signifying the occurrence of non-mechanical processes; since mechanical laws explain movements in space as the effects of other movements in space, other laws must explain some of the non-spatial workings of minds as the effects of other non-spatial workings of minds. The difference between the human behaviours which we describe as intelligent and those which we describe as unintelligent must be a difference in their causation; so, while some movements of human tongues and limbs are the effects of mechanical causes, others must be the effects of non-mechanical causes, i.e., some issue from movements of particles of matter, others from workings of the mind.

The differences between the physical and the mental were thus represented as differences inside the common framework of the categories of 'thing', 'stuff', 'attribute', 'state', 'process', 'change', 'cause' and 'effect'. Minds are things, but different sorts of things from bodies; mental processes are causes and effects, but different sorts of causes and effects from bodily movements. And so on. Somewhat as the foreigner expected the University to be an extra edifice, rather like a college but also considerably different, so the repudiators of mechanism represented minds as extra centres of causal processes, rather like machines but also considerably different from them. Their theory was a paramechanical hypothesis.

That this assumption was at the heart of the doctrine is shown by the fact that there was from the beginning felt to be a major theoretical difficulty in explaining how minds can influence and be influenced by bodies. How can a mental process, such as willing, cause spatial movements like the movements of the tongue? How can a physical change in the optic nerve have among its effects a mind's perception of a flash of light? This notorious crux[13] by itself shows the logical mould into which Descartes pressed his theory of the mind. It was the self-same mould into which he and Galileo set their mechanics. Still unwittingly adhering to the grammar of mechanics, he tried to avert disaster by describing minds in what was merely an obverse[14] vocabulary. The workings of minds had to be described by the mere negatives of the specific descriptions given to bodies; they are not in space, they are not motions, they are not modifications of matter, they are not accessible to public observation. Minds are not bits of clockwork, they are just bits of not-clockwork.

As thus represented, minds are not merely ghosts harnessed to machines, they are themselves just spectral machines. Though the human body is an engine, it is not quite an ordinary engine, since some of its workings are governed by another engine inside it—this interior governor-engine being one of a very special sort. It is invisible, inaudible and it has no size or weight. It cannot be taken to bits and the laws it obeys are not those known to ordinary engineers. Nothing is known of how it governs the bodily engine.

A second major crux points the same moral. Since, according to the doctrine, minds belong to the same category as bodies and since bodies are rigidly governed by mechanical laws, it seemed to many theorists to follow that minds must be similarly governed by rigid non-mechanical laws. The physical world is a deterministic system, so the mental world must be a deterministic system. Bodies cannot help the modifications that they undergo, so minds cannot help pursuing the careers fixed for them. *Responsibility*, *choice*, *merit* and *demerit* are therefore inapplicable concepts—unless the compromise solution is adopted of saying that the laws governing mental processes, unlike those governing physical processes, have the

---

13   The crux of a question is its most basic, critical, or deeply puzzling feature. (This term probably comes from the Medieval Latin phrase *crux interpretum*, or "torment of interpreters.")

14   A thing's obverse is its complement or counterpart: e.g., the obverse of black is white, and the obverse of front is back.

congenial attribute of being only rather rigid. The problem of the Freedom of the Will was the problem how to reconcile the hypothesis that minds are to be described in terms drawn from the categories of mechanics with the knowledge that higher-grade human conduct is not of a piece with the behaviour of machines.

It is an historical curiosity that it was not noticed that the entire argument was broken-backed. Theorists correctly assumed that any sane man could already recognize the differences between, say, rational and non-rational utterances or between purposive and automatic behaviour. Else there would have been nothing requiring to be salved from mechanism. Yet the explanation given presupposed that one person could in principle never recognize the difference between the rational and the irrational utterances issuing from other human bodies, since he could never get access to the postulated immaterial causes of some of their utterances. Save for the doubtful exception of himself, he could never tell the difference between a man and a Robot. It would have to be conceded, for example, that, for all that we can tell, the inner lives of persons who are classed as idiots or lunatics are as rational as those of anyone else. Perhaps only their overt behaviour is disappointing; that is to say, perhaps 'idiots' are not really idiotic, or 'lunatics' lunatic. Perhaps, too, some of those who are classed as sane are really idiots. According to the theory, external observers could never know how the overt behaviour of others is correlated with their mental powers and processes and so they could never know or even plausibly conjecture whether their applications of mental-conduct concepts to these other people were correct or incorrect. It would then be hazardous or impossible for a man to claim sanity or logical consistency even for himself, since he would be debarred from comparing his own performances with those of others. In short, our characterizations of persons and their performances as intelligent, prudent and virtuous or as stupid, hypocritical and cowardly could never have been made, so the problem of providing a special causal hypothesis to serve as the basis of such diagnoses would never have arisen. The question, 'How do persons differ from machines?' arose just because everyone already knew how to apply mental-conduct concepts before the new causal hypothesis was introduced. This causal hypothesis could not therefore be the source of the criteria used in those applications. Nor, of course, has the causal hypothesis in any degree improved our handling of those criteria. We still distinguish good from bad arithmetic, politic[15] from impolitic conduct and fertile from infertile imaginations in the ways in which Descartes himself distinguished them before and after he speculated how the applicability of these criteria was compatible with the principle of mechanical causation.

He had mistaken the logic of his problem. Instead of asking by what criteria intelligent behaviour is actually distinguished from non-intelligent behaviour, he asked 'Given that the principle of mechanical causation does not tell us the difference, what other causal principle will tell it us?' He realized that the problem was not one of mechanics and assumed that it must therefore be one of some counterpart to mechanics. Not unnaturally psychology is often cast for just this role.

When two terms belong to the same category, it is proper to construct conjunctive[16] propositions embodying them. Thus a purchaser may say that he bought a left-hand glove and a right-hand glove, but not that he bought a left-hand glove, a right-hand glove and a pair of gloves. 'She came home in a flood of tears and a sedan-chair'[17] is a well known joke based on the absurdity of conjoining terms of different types. It would have been equally ridiculous to construct the disjunction. 'She came home either in a flood of tears or else in a sedan-chair.' Now the dogma of the Ghost in the Machine does just this. It maintains that there exist both bodies and minds; that there occur physical

---

15 Judicious, careful.

16 A conjunction is an 'and' statement (e.g., "It's 2 AM and you're past curfew"); a disjunction is an 'or' sentence (e.g., "Either he's drunk or very nervous.").

17 A sedan chair is an enclosed chair carried on horizontal poles on the shoulders of two or four porters. This form of transport was common in Europe in the seventeenth and eighteenth centuries and can still sometimes be seen in India and parts of the Far East.

processes and mental processes; that there are mechanical causes of corporeal movements and mental causes of corporeal movements. I shall argue that these and other analogous conjunctions are absurd; but, it must be noticed, the argument will not show that either of the illegitimately conjoined propositions is absurd in itself. I am not, for example, denying that there occur mental processes. Doing long division is a mental process and so is making a joke. But I am saying that the phrase 'there occur mental processes' does not mean the same sort of thing as 'there occur physical processes', and, therefore, that it makes no sense to conjoin or disjoin the two.

If my argument is successful, there will follow some interesting consequences. First, the hallowed contrast between Mind and Matter will be dissipated, but dissipated not by either of the equally hallowed absorptions of Mind by Matter or of Matter by Mind, but in quite a different way. For the seeming contrast of the two will be shown to be as illegitimate as would be the contrast of 'she came home in a flood of tears' and 'she came home in a sedan-chair'. The belief that there is a polar opposition between Mind and Matter is the belief that they are terms of the same logical type.

It will also follow that both Idealism and Materialism are answers to an improper question. The 'reduction' of the material world to mental states and processes, as well as the 'reduction' of mental states and processes to physical states and processes, presupposes the legitimacy of the disjunction 'Either there exist minds or there exist bodies (but not both)'. It would be like saying, 'Either she bought a left-hand and right-hand glove or she bought a pair of gloves (but not both)'.

It is perfectly proper to say, in one logical tone of voice, that there exist minds, and to say, in another logical tone of voice, that there exist bodies. But these expressions do not indicate two different species of existence, for 'existence' is not a generic word like 'coloured' or 'sexed'. They indicate two different senses of 'exist', somewhat as 'rising' has different senses in 'the tide is rising', 'hopes are rising', and 'the average age of death is rising'. A man would be thought to be making a poor joke who said that three things are now rising, namely the tide, hopes and

the average age of death. It would be just as good or bad a joke to say that there exist prime numbers and Wednesdays and public opinions and navies; or that there exist both minds and bodies. In the succeeding chapters I try to prove that the official theory does rest on a batch of category-mistakes by showing that logically absurd corollaries follow from it. The exhibition of these absurdities will have the constructive effect of bringing out part of the correct logic of mental-conduct concepts.

(4) Historical Note

It would not be true to say that the official theory derives solely from Descartes' theories, or even from a more widespread anxiety about the implications of seventeenth-century mechanics. Scholastic and Reformation theology[18] had schooled the intellects of the scientists as well as of the laymen, philosophers and clerics of that age. Stoic-Augustinian[19] theories of the will were embedded in the Calvinist[20] doctrines of sin and grace; Platonic and Aristotelian theories of the intellect shaped the orthodox doctrines of the immortality of the soul. Descartes was reformulating already prevalent

---

18 Scholasticism was the educational tradition of the medieval universities and a system of thought which brought together Catholic doctrine with elements of classical Greek philosophy. The Reformation was a sixteenth-century movement to reform the Roman Catholic church which resulted in the establishment of the Protestant churches.

19 Stoicism is an ancient philosophical system (founded by Zeno of Citium in about 300 BCE) which held, among other things, that the virtuous will should be brought into harmony with *logos*—the rational nature of things, or God. It had a great influence on early Christian thinkers, including Saint Augustine (354–430 CE) who defended the view that humans have free control of their will and so are responsible for their own sin.

20 Calvinism is the theology of John Calvin (1509–1564) and his followers. One of its central doctrines is that human actions are predetermined by God and that we are all sinners, but that God has bestowed his grace on some believers, allowing them to be redeemed by faith.

theological doctrines of the soul in the new syntax of Galileo. The theologian's privacy of conscience became the philosopher's privacy of consciousness, and what had been the bogy of Predestination reappeared as the bogy of Determinism.[21]

---

21 Predestination is the view that God has already decided, at the beginning of time, for every soul whether it will be saved or damned. (The theological problem then is: what use are faith or good works, if our fate is already sealed?) Determinism is the thesis that all events or situations are determined or fixed by prior events or states of affairs: for example, the current situation of a physical particle might be said to be wholly determined by all its previous positions and interactions with other particles. (See Chapter 6.)

It would also not be true to say that the two-worlds myth did no theoretical good. Myths often do a lot of theoretical good, while they are still new. One benefit bestowed by the para-mechanical myth was that it partly superannuated the then prevalent para-political myth. Minds and their Faculties had previously been described by analogies with political superiors and political subordinates. The idioms used were those of ruling, obeying, collaborating and rebelling. They survived and still survive in many ethical and some epistemological discussions. As, in physics, the new myth of occult Forces was a scientific improvement on the old myth of Final Causes, so, in anthropological and psychological theory, the new myth of hidden operations, impulses and agencies was an improvement on the old myth of dictations, deferences and disobediences.

J.J.C. SMART

"Sensations and Brain Processes"

Who Is J.J.C. Smart?

John (Jack) Jamieson Carswell Smart was born in 1920 in Cambridge, England, and was educated at the University of Glasgow and then at Oxford where he was heavily influenced by Gilbert Ryle. He emigrated to Australia in 1950, when he was still not quite 30, to take up a chair in Philosophy at the University of Adelaide, where he stayed until 1972. In that year he moved to La Trobe University in Victoria, and four years later, in 1976, to the Australian National University where he has remained, becoming Professor Emeritus in 1985.

The main tenor of Smart's philosophy has always been uncompromisingly physicalist, realist and objectivist. In metaphysics he has defended a view of the universe which eliminates all reference to particular times, places, individuals, or observers (i.e., to points of view) and which describes it as a four-dimensional manifold containing nothing but entities describable using the basic categories of physics. In the philosophy of mind, Smart was converted to behaviorism by Ryle during his Oxford days but was born again as an "identity theorist" at Adelaide, under the influence of the philosopher and psychologist, U.T. Place. Smart's best known book in this area, published in 1963, is *Philosophy and Scientific Realism*.

Smart is also known for his work in ethics, especially for his defense of a version of the moral theory of utilitarianism in a book co-written with Bernard Williams: *Utilitarianism: For and Against*. His most recent work is a book (co-written with John Haldane) called *Atheism and Theism* in which he vigorously defends atheism.

As he once put it: "In philosophical method my view is that plausibility in the light of total science is a proper touchstone of metaphysical truth."

What Is the Structure of This Reading?

Smart begins his article by denying dualism and describing a behaviorist (or "expressive") account of mental phenomena, which he attributes to Wittgenstein but which also owes a lot to Ryle's influence (see the previous reading). But then he expresses reservations about the ability of behaviorism to handle "sensation statements" and proposes that the account he has just given be supplemented by the hypothesis that "sensations are brain processes" and that sensation statements are reports of these processes.

After an important discussion of his views on the *kind* of identity relation between sensation and brain, Smart goes on to consider eight different philosophical objections to his hypothesis. Several of these objections, Smart suggests, miss the point—attacking a kind of identity claim which he is not making. They attack the thesis that sensations are *necessarily* or *analytically* identical with brain processes, whereas Smart is only claiming that they are *contingently* identical—they will just *turn out* to be the same thing.

As Smart recognizes, the third objection is a key problem for him and it is in his response to it that Smart introduces an idea crucial to his defense of identity theory: the notion of a *topic-neutral* report.

Smart concludes the article by discussing the degree to which the identity theory is open to empirical confirmation. He suggests there are *limits* on what can be empirically proven about the relation between mind and body (and so limits on the degree to which the identity theory can be confirmed by science), but he argues there are always these sorts of limits on scientific theorizing—as in the case of Gosse's creationism—and they don't prevent scientists from legitimately taking one theory as more plausible than another.

Some Useful Background Information

1. This article is about a relation of *identity*. When we say two things are "identical" in everyday speech, we often mean that they are exactly similar, in the way that two black 2008 Honda Civics might look and feel exactly the same. But the philosophical sense of "identity"—sometimes called "numerical identity," as opposed to "qualitative identity"—used in this article is more rigorous than this: in this sense, two different things *cannot* be identical, for identity is the relation that everything bears *with itself*. Thus, I am identical with myself, Cicero is identical with Tully, my dog is identical with the runt of a certain litter of poodles from Minnesota, gold is identical to the substance with atomic number 79, and so on. To say that "two things" are identical is precisely to say that they really are only one thing described in different ways.

2. Smart refers frequently to the philosopher Wittgenstein in the first few pages of his article. Ludwig Wittgenstein (1889–1951) was probably one of the twentieth century's most important philosophers. In 1921 he published an extremely influential book called *Tractatus Logico-Philosophicus*, and then, convinced that he had solved every philosophical problem, quit his position at Cambridge to be a schoolteacher and amateur architect. In 1929, however, he returned to philosophy (and to Cambridge) and, reacting against his own earlier position, developed his complex, elusive, and highly influential "later philosophy." This is encapsulated in the book, *Philosophical Investigations*, published after his death, in 1953.

Later in the essay Smart mentions the "beetle in the box" objection to the identity theory. This is an influential example of Wittgenstein's, designed to show that sensation words like "pain" or "after-image" cannot be thought of as the *names* of internal *objects* and instead should be thought of as the *expressions* of these sensations (in roughly the same way as bursting into tears is an expression of sadness and not a name for sadness). The example works like this. Imagine we all had a matchbox and that all of our matchboxes contained something, but suppose that we never showed anyone else the contents of our own personal box. Even if we adopt the convention of calling our box-contents "beetles" this word would still not act like the *name* of some particular object, since the objects themselves are private and could never play a role in explaining what the word means: what I have in my box and you have in yours would turn out to be actually *irrelevant* to what the phrase "beetle-in-a-box" means. And, says Wittgenstein, the same is true of words like "pain" or "after-image": they could no more function as names than could "beetle-in-a-box," and so must have some other linguistic function.

3. Towards the end of the article Smart discusses the relation between his identity theory and another class of theories called "epiphenomenalism." Epiphenomenalism is the doctrine that mentality is not itself physical but is a by-product of the workings of the physical (in a manner analogous, perhaps, to the way that an old steam-engine's whistle is a by-product of its operation, or the hum of a computer is a side-effect of its workings). The central idea is that only physical things can have causal effects on other physical things, and the mental is completely dependent on the physical but causally impotent to affect the physical world (just as, again analogously, the hum of a computer is irrelevant to its information processing—it may be caused by it, but it does not in turn have any effects on it). For example, for the epiphenomenalist, my feeling an itch does not cause me to slap at the mosquito on my arm, but instead the sensation and the slap are both the results of an underlying physiological state.

Some Common Misconceptions

1. Smart does not argue directly that his mind-brain identity thesis is *true* (though he thinks it is extremely plausible), since he believes that this is, on the whole, an empirical question to be decided by scientists rather than philosophers. What he argues instead is that the identity theory is *not necessarily false*: that is, he argues that philosophers cannot show *a priori* that the identity theory must be wrong before scientists even get a chance to check it.

2. Smart does not defend an identity theory for *all* mental states, but just for those which pose the most difficulty for behaviorism, and in particular for sensations: his view is that, though we do have to admit inner mental items, we should admit as few as possible. He did not, for example, think of a *belief* as being identical with a brain process at the time he was writing this essay, but instead as being a kind of behavioral disposition. (He has since changed his views, however, and now recognizes a greater number of inner states.)

3. Smart is defending an identity between *processes* and not between *objects*. When he uses the word "sensation" he usually means the process of having that sensation—the having of an after-image—rather than the after-image itself. He does not think that yellowy-orange *after-images* are bits of the brain, any more than he thinks the wall behind them is.

Suggestions for Critical Reflection

1. Do you think that sensations, like experiences of after-images, are inner entities—are "things" in our minds? If so, what sort of thing might they be? If not, what *are* after-images? Are you sympathetic to Smart's claim that, if sensations of after-images are things at all, they must be *physical* things ("complex arrangements of physical constituents"), or do you think this might be carrying Occam's razor too far?

2. What do you think of Smart's response to the third objection? Do you agree that our reports

of our own sensations are "topic-neutral"? That is, do you think we are really only reporting on the results of our abilities to discriminate between different stimuli, or do we in fact report that our mental states have certain *properties* like color or itchiness or subjective location (properties that our physical brain states seem to lack)? If Smart is wrong about the "topic-neutrality" of introspection, how serious a problem for the identity theory does this become?

3. What does Smart mean by the difference between *an after-image* (he says there is, in a sense, no such thing in the reply to Objection 4) and *the experience of having an image* (which is identical with a brain process, according to Smart)? Does it really just "miss the point" to ask where the color of an experience goes when a surgeon looks at my brain?

4. One of the most influential objections to identity theory has taken the form of an attack on the whole notion of a *contingent* identity. Smart is clear that he intends the identity between sensations and brain processes to be contingent rather than necessary, but an important American philosopher named Saul Kripke has argued very influentially that *all* identities between two names or "natural kind" terms are necessary identities. The reasoning behind this claim is a bit complex, but the central intuition is something like this. Trivially, everything is necessarily identical with itself: I am necessarily me, and it is logically incoherent to say otherwise. So suppose we point to something (the very same thing) twice and say "*that thing* is identical with *that thing*": this must be not only true but *necessarily* true. Now, according to Kripke, to apply a particular type of label to something, such as a name for an individual (like "Jack") or for a kind of thing (like "water"), is, roughly speaking, to use language to point at something—to indicate *that very thing*, whatever it turns out to be. (Note the similarity of this claim to Smart's notion of "topic-neutral" reporting.) So if we use two names to make an identity claim we are basically just pointing twice, hence if we get the identity claim right it must be necessarily

true. For example, to say, "pain is C-fibers firing" is, if true, *necessarily* true (since "pain" is the name of a type of sensation and "C-fibers firing" is the name of a type of brain process).

Now, here's the pay-off: if Kripke is right about all this, it can be argued that, since the identification of sensations with brain processes is *not* in fact necessarily true, it cannot be true at all. After all, it is surely (?) *possible* that something could feel pain even if it had no C-fibers or had been "turned to stone," and so it can't be *necessarily* true that pain is a brain process, but then it can't be true *at all* that pain is a brain process, even contingently.

So what is Smart to say about all of this? For example, could he change his position and defend a necessary identity between sensations and brain processes, or would he then be subject to some of the objections that he considers and rejects in the article?

5. What is the importance of empirical evidence in thinking about the mind-brain problem? Does Smart overstate its importance? For example, suppose we knew precisely, in every detail, how pain was correlated with states of the brain. Would this count as any evidence at all that, say, substance dualism was false and physicalism true? (What would Descartes say about that?)

Suggestions for Further Reading

Relevant books by J.J.C. Smart include *Philosophy and Scientific Realism* (Routledge & Kegan Paul, 1963), *Essays Metaphysical and Moral* (Blackwell, 1987), and *Our Place in the Universe* (Blackwell, 1989). If you are interested in reading more Wittgenstein, the best place to start is with his *Philosophical Investigations* (Blackwell, 1953). Kripke's account of identity can be found in *Naming and Necessity* (Harvard University Press, 1980), but this is a fairly challenging book for the uninitiated.

A well-known book-length development of identity theory (which he calls "central-state materialism") is David Armstrong's *A Materialist Theory of the Mind*, first published in 1968 and re-released in a revised edition by Routledge in 1993. Keith Campbell's *Body and Mind* (University of Notre Dame Press, 1984) is a short but highly-respected introduction to the philosophy of mind which has a good discussion of identity theory. C.V. Borst (ed.), *The Mind/Brain Identity Theory* (Macmillan, 1970) is a handy collection of articles, which includes Jerome Schaffer's follow-up on Objection 3: "Mental Events and the Brain," *Journal of Philosophy* 60 (1963).

"Sensations and Brain Processes"[1]

Suppose that I report that I have at this moment a roundish, blurry-edged after-image which is yellowish towards its edge and is orange towards its centre. What is it that I am reporting?[2] One answer to this question might be that I am not reporting anything, that when I say that it looks to me as though there is a roundish yellow orange patch of light on the wall I am expressing some sort of *temptation*, the temptation to say that there *is* a roundish yellow orange patch on the wall (though I may know that there is not such a patch on the wall). This is perhaps Wittgenstein's view in the *Philosophical Investigations* (see paragraphs 367, 370). Similarly, when I "report" a pain, I am not really reporting anything (or, if you like, I am reporting in a queer sense of "reporting"), but am doing a sophisticated sort of wince. (See paragraph 244: "The verbal expression of pain replaces crying and does not describe it." Nor does it describe anything else?).[3] I prefer most of the time to discuss an after-image[4] rather than a pain, because the word "pain" brings in something which is irrelevant to my purpose: the notion of "distress." I think that "he is in pain" entails "he is in distress," that is, that he is in a certain agitation-condition.[5] Similarly, to say "I am in pain" may be to do more than "replace pain behavior": it may be partly to report something, though this something is quite nonmysterious, being an agitation-condition, and so susceptible of behavioristic analysis. The suggestion I wish if possible to avoid is a different one, namely that "I am in pain" is a genuine report, and that what it reports is an irreducibly psychical something. And similarly the suggestion I wish to resist is also that to say "I have a yellowish orange after-image" is to report something irreducibly psychical.

Why do I wish to resist this suggestion? Mainly because of Occam's razor.[6] It seems to me that science is increasingly giving us a viewpoint whereby organisms

---

1   This article was first published in 1959 in *The Philosophical Review* (Volume 68, Issue 2, April 1959, pages 141–156). Published by Duke University Press.

2   [Author's note] This paper takes its departure from arguments to be found in U.T. Place's "Is Consciousness a Brain Process?" (*British Journal of Psychology*, XLVII, 1956, 44–50). I have had the benefit of discussing Place's thesis in a good many universities in the United States and Australia, and I hope that the present paper answers objections to his thesis which Place has not considered, and presents his thesis in a more nearly unobjectionable form. This paper is meant also to supplement "The 'Mental' and the 'Physical'," by H. Feigl (in *Minnesota Studies in the Philosophy of Science*, II, 370–497), which argues for much the same thesis as Place's.

3   [Author's note] Some philosophers of my acquaintance, who have the advantage over me in having known Wittgenstein, would say that this interpretation of him is too behavioristic. However, it seems to me a very natural interpretation of his printed words, and whether or not it is Wittgenstein's real view it is certainly an interesting and important one. I wish to consider it here as a possible rival both to the "brain-process" thesis and to straight-out old-fashioned dualism.

4   An after-image is a sensation—typically, though not necessarily, a floating patch of color—retained by one of the senses after the original stimulus has stopped. You can often create your own after-image by rubbing your eyeball or by looking into a bright colored light and then looking at a white expanse of wall.

5   [Author's note] See Ryle, *Concept of Mind* (New York, 1949), p. 93.

6   This is the philosophical maxim that one should not "multiply entities beyond necessity": that is, as a general rule, one should adopt the simplest theory which is consistent with the data. It is named after a medieval philosopher called William of Occam who espoused a similar principle.

are able to be seen as physicochemical mechanisms:[7] it seems that even the behavior of man himself will one day be explicable in mechanistic terms. There does seem to be, so far as science is concerned, nothing in the world but increasingly complex arrangements of physical constituents. All except for one place: in consciousness. That is, for a full description of what is going on in a man you would have to mention not only the physical processes in his tissue, glands, nervous system, and so forth, but also his states of consciousness: his visual, auditory, and tactual sensations, his aches and pains. That these should be *correlated* with brain processes does not help, for to say that they are *correlated* is to say that they are something "over and above." You cannot correlate something with itself. You correlate footprints with burglars, but not Bill Sikes the burglar with Bill Sikes the burglar. So sensations, states of consciousness, do seem to be the one sort of thing left outside the physicalist picture, and for various reasons I just cannot believe that this can be so. That everything should be explicable in terms of physics (together of course with descriptions of the ways in which the parts are put together—roughly, biology is to physics as radio-engineering is to electro-magnetism) except the occurrence of sensations seems to me to be frankly unbelievable. Such sensations would be "nomological danglers," to use Feigl's expression.[8] It is not often realized how odd would be the laws whereby these nomological danglers[9] would dangle. It is sometimes asked, "Why can't there be psycho-physical laws which are of a novel sort, just as

the laws of electricity and magnetism were novelties from the standpoint of Newtonian mechanics?" Certainly we are pretty sure in the future to come across new ultimate laws of a novel type, but I expect them to relate simple constituents: for example, whatever ultimate particles are then in vogue. I cannot believe that ultimate laws of nature could relate simple constituents to configurations consisting of perhaps billions of neurons (and goodness knows how many billion billions of ultimate particles) all put together for all the world as though their main purpose in life was to be a negative feedback mechanism of a complicated sort. Such ultimate laws would be like nothing so far known in science. They have a queer "smell" to them. I am just unable to believe in the nomological danglers themselves, or in the laws whereby they would dangle. If any philosophical arguments seemed to compel us to believe in such things, I would suspect a catch in the argument. In any case it is the object of this paper to show that there are no philosophical arguments which compel us to be dualists.

The above is largely a confession of faith, but it explains why I find Wittgenstein's position (as I construe it) so congenial. For on this view there are, in a sense, no sensations. A man is a vast arrangement of physical particles, but there are not, over and above this, sensations or states of consciousness. There are just behavioral facts about this vast mechanism, such as that it expresses a temptation (behavior disposition) to say "there is a yellowish-red patch on the wall" or that it goes through a sophisticated sort of wince, that is, says "I am in pain." Admittedly Wittgenstein says that though the sensation "is not a something," it is nevertheless "not a nothing either" (paragraph 304), but this need only mean that the word "ache" has a use. An ache is a thing, but only in the innocuous sense in which the plain man, in the first paragraph of Frege's *Foundations of Arithmetic*,[10] answers the

---

7   [Author's note] On this point see Paul Oppenheim and Hilary Putnam, "Unity of Science as a Working Hypothesis," in *Minnesota Studies in the Philosophy of Science*, II, 336; also my note "Plausible Reasoning in Philosophy," *Mind*, LXVI (1957), 75–78.

8   [Author's note] Feigl, *op. cit.*, p. 428.

9   "Nomological" means "scientifically lawlike" (such as the regular way in which bodies attract each other with a force inversely proportional to the square of the distance between them). Something is a "nomological dangler" if it "dangles" from a physical process—if it is just somehow attached to that process in a mysterious way which cannot be explained in terms of scientific laws.

---

10   Gottlob Frege (1848–1925) was a German mathematician and the most important innovator in logic since Aristotle. *Foundations of Arithmetic* (1884) is his relatively (!) non-technical presentation of his logical system. The point of this example is that saying the number one is "a thing" really tells you nothing at all about its nature, just that there is such a number.

question "what is the number one?" by "a thing." It should be noted that when I assert that to say "I have a yellowish-orange after-image" is to express a temptation to assert the physical-object statement "there is a yellowish-orange patch on the wall," I mean that saying "I have a yellowish-orange after-image" is (partly) the exercise of the disposition[11] which is the temptation. It is not to *report* that I have the temptation, any more than is "I love you" normally a report that I love someone. Saying "I love you" is just part of the behavior which is the exercise of the disposition of loving someone.

Though, for the reasons given above, I am very receptive to the above "expressive" account of sensation statements, I do not feel that it will quite do the trick. Maybe this is because I have not thought it out sufficiently, but it does seem to me as though, when a person says "I have an after-image," he *is* making a genuine report, and that when he says "I have a pain," he *is* doing more than "replace pain-behavior," and that "this more" is not just to say that he is in distress. I am not so sure, however, that to admit this is to admit that there are nonphysical correlates of brain processes. Why should not sensations just be brain processes of a certain sort? There are, of course, well-known (as well as lesser-known) philosophical objections to the view that reports of sensations are reports of brain-processes, but I shall try to argue that these arguments are by no means as cogent as is commonly thought to be the case.

Let me first try to state more accurately the thesis that sensations are brain processes. It is not the thesis that, for example, "after-image" or "ache" means the same as "brain process of sort X" (where "X" is replaced by a description of a certain sort of brain process). It is that, in so far as "after-image" or "ache"

is a report of a process, it is a report of a process that *happens to be* a brain process. It follows that the thesis does not claim that sensation statements can be *translated* into statements about brain processes.[12] Nor does it claim that the logic of a sensation statement is the same as that of a brain-process statement. All it claims is that in so far as a sensation statement is a report of something, that something is in fact a brain process. Sensations are nothing over and above brain processes. Nations are nothing "over and above" citizens, but this does not prevent the logic of nation statements being very different from the logic of citizen statements, nor does it insure the translatability of nation statements into citizen statements. (I do not, however, wish to assert that the relation of sensation statements to brain-process statements is very like that of nation statements to citizen statements. Nations do not just *happen to be* nothing over and above citizens, for example. I bring in the "nations" example merely to make a negative point: that the fact that the logic of A-statements is different from that of B-statements does not insure that A's are anything over and above B's.)

Remarks on identity. When I say that a sensation is a brain process or that lightning is an electric discharge, I am using "is" in the sense of strict identity. (Just as in the—in this case necessary—proposition "7 is identical with the smallest prime number greater than 5.") When I say that a sensation is a brain process or that lightning is an electric discharge I do not mean just that the sensation is somehow spatially or temporally continuous with the brain process or that the lightning is just spatially or temporally continuous with the discharge. When on the other hand I say that the successful general is the same person as the small boy who stole the apples I mean only that the successful general I see before me is a time slice[13] of

---

11 [Author's note] Wittgenstein did not like the word "disposition." I am using it to put in a nutshell (and perhaps inaccurately) the view which I am attributing to Wittgenstein. I should like to repeat that I do not wish to claim that my interpretation of Wittgenstein is correct. Some of those who knew him do not interpret him in this way. It is merely a view which I find myself extracting from his printed words and which I think is important and worth discussing for its own sake.

12 [Author's note] See Place, *op. cit.*, p. 45, near top, and Feigl, *op. cit.*, p. 390, near top.

13 [Author's note] See J.H. Woodger, *Theory Construction* (Chicago, 1939), p. 38 (International Encyclopedia of Unified Science, Vol. 2, No. 5). I here permit myself to speak loosely. For warnings against possible ways of going wrong with this sort of talk, see my note "Spatialising Time," *Mind*, LXIV (1955), 239–41.

the same four-dimensional object of which the small boy stealing apples is an earlier time slice. However, the four-dimensional object which has the general-I-see-before-me for its late time slice is identical in the strict sense with the four-dimensional object which has the small-boy-stealing-apples for an early time slice. I distinguish these two senses of "is identical with" because I wish to make it clear that the brain-process doctrine asserts identity in the *strict* sense.

I shall now discuss various possible objections to the view that the processes reported in sensation statements are in fact processes in the brain. Most of us have met some of these objections in our first year as philosophy students. All the more reason to take a good look at them. Others of the objections will be more recondite and subtle.

Objection 1. Any illiterate peasant can talk perfectly well about his after-images, or how things look or feel to him, or about his aches and pains, and yet he may know nothing whatever about neurophysiology. A man may, like Aristotle, believe that the brain is an organ for cooling the body without any impairment of his ability to make true statements about his sensations. Hence the things we are talking about when we describe our sensations cannot be processes in the brain.

Reply. You might as well say that a nation of slug-abeds, who never saw the morning star or knew of its existence, or who had never thought of the expression "the Morning Star,"[14] but who used the expression "the Evening Star" perfectly well, could not use this expression to refer to the same entity as we refer to (and describe as) "the Morning Star."[15]

You may object that the Morning Star is in a sense not the very same thing as the Evening Star, but only something spatio-temporally continuous with it. That is, you may say that the Morning Star is not the Evening Star in the strict sense of "identity" that I distinguished earlier. I can perhaps forestall this objection by considering the slug-abeds to be New Zealanders and the early risers to be Englishmen. Then the thing

the New Zealanders describe as "the Morning Star" could be the very same thing (in the strict sense) as the Englishmen describe as "the Evening Star." And yet they could be ignorant of this fact.

There is, however, a more plausible example. Consider lightning.[16] Modern physical science tells us that lightning is a certain kind of electrical discharge due to ionization of clouds of water-vapor in the atmosphere. This, it is now believed, is what the true nature of lightning is. Note that there are not two things: a flash of lightning and an electrical discharge. There is one thing, a flash of lightning, which is described scientifically as an electrical discharge to the earth from a cloud of ionized water-molecules. The case is not at all like that of explaining a footprint by reference to a burglar. We say that what lightning really is, what its true nature as revealed by science is, is an electric discharge. (It is not the true nature of a footprint to be a burglar.)

To forestall irrelevant objections, I should like to make it clear that by "lightning" I mean the publicly observable physical object, lightning, not a visual sense-datum[17] of lightning. I say that the publicly observable physical object lightning is in fact the electric discharge, not just a correlate of it. The sense-datum, or at least the having of the sense-datum, the "look" of lightning, may well in my view be a correlate of the electric discharge. For in my view it is a brain state *caused* by the lightning. But we should no more confuse sensations of lightning with lightning than we confuse sensations of a table with the table.

In short, the reply to Objection 1 is that there can be contingent[18] statements of the form "A is identical with B," and a person may well know that something is an A without knowing that it is a B. An illiterate peasant might well be able to talk about his sensations without

---

14   "The Morning Star" and "The Evening Star" are two names for one and the same astronomical body: the planet Venus as it appears just before sunrise, and the planet Venus as it appears just after sunset.

15   [Author's note] Cf. Feigl, *op. cit.*, p. 439.

16   [Author's note] See Place, *op. cit.*, p. 47; also Feigl, *op. cit.*, p. 438.

17   A sense-datum is, roughly, a unit of subjective sense experience: a visual image, say, or a sudden whiff of perfume. The plural is "sense-data."

18   "Contingent" means neither necessarily true nor necessarily false—something is contingent if its truth or falsity doesn't depend on logic or language but on the way the world happens to have turned out to be.

knowing about his brain processes, just as he can talk about lightning though he knows nothing of electricity.

Objection 2. It is only a contingent fact (if it is a fact) that when we have a certain kind of sensation there is a certain kind of process in our brain. Indeed it is possible, though perhaps in the highest degree unlikely, that our present physiological theories will be as out of date as the ancient theory connecting mental processes with goings on in the heart. It follows that when we report a sensation we are not reporting a brain-process.

Reply. The objection certainly proves that when we say "I have an after-image" we cannot *mean* something of the form "I have such and such a brain-process." But this does not show that what we report (having an after-image) is not *in fact* a brain process. "I see lightning" does not *mean* "I see an electric discharge." Indeed, it is logically possible (though highly unlikely) that the electrical discharge account of lightning might one day be given up. Again, "I see the Evening Star" does not *mean* the same as "I see the Morning Star," and yet "the Evening Star and the Morning Star are one and the same thing" is a contingent proposition. Possibly Objection 2 derives some of its apparent strength from a "Fido"-Fido theory of meaning.[19] If the meaning of an expression were what the expression named, then of course it *would* follow from the fact that "sensation" and "brain-process" have different meanings that they cannot name one and the same thing.

---

19   A "Fido"-Fido theory of meaning holds that the meaning of a word (say, "Fido") is the object which that word refers to (some particular dog, Fido). This is (or can be) a relatively simple account of meaning, and faces very strong competition from theories such as: (1) The meaning of a sentence is the *idea* which the speaker intends to communicate (or which the word is linked to in a particular language-community); (2) The meaning of a sentence is specified by the conditions under which that sentence would count as *true*; (3) The meaning of a sentence is specified by the ways in which it can be correctly *used* within a particular language-community; or (4) The meaning of a sentence is specified by all its logical relations with other sentences; and so on.

Objection 3.[20] Even if Objections 1 and 2 do not prove that sensations are something over and above brain-processes, they do prove that the qualities of sensations are something over and above the qualities of brain-processes. That is, it may be possible to get out of asserting the existence of irreducibly psychic processes, but not out of asserting the existence of irreducibly psychic *properties*. For suppose we identify the Morning Star with the Evening Star. Then there must be some properties which logically imply that of being the Morning Star, and quite distinct properties which entail that of being the Evening Star. Again, there must be some properties (for example, that of being a yellow flash) which are logically distinct from those in the physicalist story.

Indeed, it might be thought that the objection succeeds at one jump. For consider the property of "being a yellow flash." It might seem that this property lies inevitably outside the physicalist framework within which I am trying to work (either by "yellow" being an objective emergent property of physical objects, or else by being a power to produce yellow sense-data, where "yellow," in this second instantiation of the word, refers to a purely phenomenal or introspectible quality). I must therefore digress for a moment and indicate how I deal with secondary qualities.[21] I shall concentrate on color.

First of all, let me introduce the concept of a normal percipient. One person is more a normal percipient than another if he can make color discriminations that the other cannot. For example, if A can pick a lettuce leaf out of a heap of cabbage leaves, whereas B cannot though he can pick a lettuce leaf out of a heap of beetroot leaves, then A is more normal than B. (I am assuming that A and B are not given time to distinguish the leaves by their slight difference in shape, and so forth.) From the concept of "more normal than" it is easy to see how we can introduce the concept of "normal." Of course, Eskimos may make the finest discrim-

---

20   [Author's note] I think this objection was first put to me by Professor Max Black. I think it is the most subtle of any of those I have considered, and the one which I am least confident of having satisfactorily met.

21   Color, smell, sound, taste, etc. (as opposed to the primary qualities: shape, density, motion, etc.).

inations at the blue end of the spectrum, Hottentots at the red end. In this case the concept of a normal percipient is a slightly idealized one, rather like that of "the mean sun" in astronomical chronology. There is no need to go into such subtleties now. I say that "This is red" means something roughly like "A normal percipient would not easily pick this out of a clump of geranium petals though he would pick it out of a clump of lettuce leaves." Of course it does not exactly mean this: a person might know the meaning of "red" without knowing anything about geraniums, or even about normal percipients. But the point is that a person can be trained to say "This is red" of objects which would not easily be picked out of geranium petals by a normal percipient, and so on. (Note that even a color-blind person can reasonably assert that something is red, though of course he needs to use another human being, not just himself, as his "color meter.") This account of secondary qualities explains their unimportance in physics. For obviously the discriminations and lack of discriminations made by a very complex neurophysiological mechanism are hardly likely to correspond to simple and nonarbitrary distinctions in nature.

I therefore elucidate colors as powers, in Locke's sense, to evoke certain sorts of discriminatory responses in human beings. They are also, of course, powers to cause sensations in human beings (an account still nearer Locke's). But these sensations, I am arguing, are identifiable with brain processes.

Now how do I get over the objection that a sensation can be identified with a brain process only if it has some phenomenal property, not possessed by brain processes, whereby one-half of the identification may be, so to speak, pinned down?

My suggestion is as follows. When a person says, "I see a yellowish-orange after-image," he is saying something like this: "*There is something going on which is like what is going on when* I have my eyes open, am awake, and there is an orange illuminated in good light in front of me, that is, when I really see an orange." (And there is no reason why a person should not say the same thing when he is having a veridical sense-datum,[22] so long as we construe "like" in the

last sentence in such a sense that something can be like itself.) Notice that the italicized words, namely "there is something going on which is like what is going on when," are all quasi-logical or topic-neutral words. This explains why the ancient Greek peasant's reports about his sensations can be neutral between dualistic metaphysics or my materialistic metaphysics. It explains how sensations can be brain-processes and yet how those who report them need know nothing about brain-processes. For he reports them only very abstractly as "something going on which is like what is going on when…." Similarly, a person may say "someone is in the room," thus reporting truly that the doctor is in the room, even though he has never heard of doctors. (There are not two people in the room: "someone" *and* the doctor.) This account of sensation statements also explains the singular elusiveness of "raw feels"—why no one seems to be able to pin any properties on them.[23] Raw feels, in my view, are colorless for the very same reason that *something* is colorless. This does not mean that sensations do not have properties, for if they are brain-processes they certainly have properties. It only means that in speaking of them as being like or unlike one another we need not know or mention these properties.

This, then, is how I would reply to Objection 3. The strength of my reply depends on the possibility of our being able to report that one thing is like another without being able to state the respect in which it is like. I am not sure whether this is so or not, and that is why I regard Objection 3 as the strongest with which I have to deal.

Objection 4. The after-image is not in physical space. The brain-process is. So the after-image is not a brain-process.

Reply. This is an *ignoratio elenchi*.[24] I am not arguing that the after-image is a brain-process, but that the experience of having an after-image is a brain-process. It is the *experience* which is reported in the introspective report. Similarly, if it is objected

---

22   An accurate or true sense perception, as opposed to an illusory one like an after-image.

23   [Author's note] See B.A. Farrell, "Experience," *Mind*, LIX (1950), especially 174.

24   Latin for "a misconception of the refutation"—that is, missing the point and arguing against something the other party has not proposed.

that the after-image is yellowy-orange but that a surgeon looking into your brain would see nothing yellowy-orange, my reply is that it is the experience of seeing yellowy-orange that is being described, and this experience is not a yellowy-orange something. So to say that a brain-process cannot be yellowy-orange is not to say that a brain-process cannot in fact be the experience of having a yellowy-orange after-image. There is, in a sense, no such thing as an after-image or a sense-datum, though there is such a thing as the experience of having an image, and this experience is described indirectly in material object language, not in phenomenal language, for there is no such thing.[25] We describe the experience by saying, in effect, that it is like the experience we have when, for example, we really see a yellow-orange patch on the wall. Trees and wallpaper can be green, but not the experience of seeing or imagining a tree or wallpaper. (Or if they are described as green or yellow this can only be in a derived sense.)

Objection 5. It would make sense to say of a molecular movement in the brain that it is swift or slow, straight or circular, but it makes no sense to say this of the experience of seeing something yellow.

Reply. So far we have not given sense to talk of experiences as swift or slow, straight or circular. But I am not claiming that "experience" and "brain-process" mean the same or even that they have the same logic. "Somebody" and "the doctor" do not have the same logic, but this does not lead us to suppose that talking about somebody telephoning is talking about someone over and above, say, the doctor. The ordinary man when he reports an experience is reporting that

something is going on, but he leaves it open as to what sort of thing is going on, whether in a material solid medium, or perhaps in some sort of gaseous medium, or even perhaps in some sort of nonspatial medium (if this makes sense). All that I am saying is that "experience" and "brain-process" may in fact refer to the same thing, and if so we may easily adopt a convention (which is not a change in our present rules for the use of experience words but an addition to them) whereby it would make sense to talk of an experience in terms appropriate to physical processes.

Objection 6. Sensations are private, brain processes are *public*. If I sincerely say, "I see a yellowish-orange after-image" and I am not making a verbal mistake, then I cannot be wrong. But I can be wrong about a brain-process. The scientist looking into my brain might be having an illusion. Moreover, it makes sense to say that two or more people are observing the same brain-process but not that two or more people are reporting the same inner experience.

Reply. This shows that the language of introspective reports has a different logic from the language of material processes. It is obvious that until the brain-process theory is much improved and widely accepted there will be no *criteria* for saying "Smith has an experience of such-and-such a sort" *except* Smith's introspective reports. So we have adopted a rule of language that (normally) what Smith says goes.

Objection 7. I can imagine myself turned to stone and yet having images, aches, pains, and so on.

Reply. I can imagine that the electrical theory of lightning is false, that lightning is some sort of purely optical phenomenon. I can imagine that lightning is not an electrical discharge. I can imagine that the Evening Star is not the Morning Star. But it is. All the objection shows is that "experience" and "brain-process" do not have the same meaning. It does not show that an experience is not in fact a brain process.

This objection is perhaps much the same as one which can be summed up by the slogan: "What can be composed of nothing cannot be composed of anything."[26] The argument goes as follows: on the

---

25   [Author's note] Dr. J.R. Smythies claims that a sense-datum language could be taught independently of the material object language ("A Note on the Fallacy of the 'Phenomenological Fallacy,'" *British Journal of Psychology*, XLVIII, 1957, 141–144.) I am not so sure of this: there must be some public criteria for a person having got a rule wrong before we can teach him the rule. I suppose someone might *accidentally* learn color words by Dr. Smythies' procedure. I am not, of course, denying that we can learn a sense-datum language in the sense that we can learn to report our experience. Nor would Place deny it.

26   [Author's note] I owe this objection to Mr. C.B. Martin. I gather that he no longer wishes to maintain this objection, at any rate in its present form.

brain-process thesis the identity between the brain-process and the experience is a contingent one. So it is logically possible that there should be no brain-process, and no process of any other sort, either (no heart process, no kidney process, no liver process). There would be the experience but no "corresponding" physiological process with which we might be able to identify it empirically.

I suspect that the objector is thinking of the experience as a ghostly entity. So it is composed of something, of nothing, after all. On his view it is composed of ghost stuff, and on mine it is composed of brain stuff. Perhaps the counter-reply will be[27] that the experience is simple and uncompounded, and so it is not composed of anything after all. This seems to be a quibble, for, if it were taken seriously, the remark "What can be composed of nothing cannot be composed of anything" could be recast as an a priori argument against Democritus and atomism and for Descartes and infinite divisibility.[28] And it seems odd that a question of this sort could be settled a priori. We must therefore construe the word "composed" in a very weak sense, which would allow us to say that even an indivisible atom is composed of something (namely, itself). The dualist cannot really say that an experience can be composed of nothing. For he holds that experiences are something over and above material processes, that is, that they are a sort of ghost stuff. (Or perhaps ripples in an underlying ghost stuff.) I say that the dualist's hypothesis is a perfectly intelligible one. But I say that experiences are not to be identified with ghost stuff but with brain stuff. This is another hypothesis, and in my view a very plausible one. The present argument cannot knock it down a priori.

Objection 8. The "beetle in the box" objection (see Wittgenstein, *Philosophical Investigations*, paragraph 293). How could descriptions of experiences, if these are genuine reports, get a foothold in language? For any rule of language must have public criteria for its correct application.

Reply. The change from describing how things are to describing how we feel is just a change from uninhibitedly saying "this is so" to saying "this looks so." That is, when the naive person might be tempted to say, "There is a patch of light on the wall which moves whenever I move my eyes" or "A pin is being stuck into me," we have learned how to resist this temptation and say "It *looks as though* there is a patch of light on the wallpaper" or "It *feels as though* someone were sticking a pin into me." The introspective account tells us about the individual's state of consciousness in the same way as does "I see a patch of light" or "I feel a pin being stuck into me": it differs from the corresponding perception statement in so far as (a) in the perception statement the individual "goes beyond the evidence of his senses" in describing his environment and (b) in the introspective report he withholds descriptive epithets he is inclined to ascribe to the environment, perhaps because he suspects that they may not be appropriate to the actual state of affairs. Psychologically speaking, the change from talking about the environment to talking about one's state of consciousness is simply a matter of inhibiting descriptive reactions not justified by appearances alone, and of disinhibiting descriptive reactions which are normally inhibited because the individual has learned that they are unlikely to provide a reliable guide to the state of the environment in the prevailing circumstances.[29] To say that something looks green to me is to say that my experience is like the experience I get when I see something that really is green. In my reply to Objection 3, I pointed out the extreme openness or generality of statements which report experiences. This explains why there is no lan-

---

27   [Author's note] Martin did not make this reply, but one of his students did.

28   Democritus (c. 460–c. 370 BCE) was a Greek philosopher who developed an atomistic theory of the universe: he held that the world is made up of an infinite number of tiny, indivisible, and imperishable atoms moving around and colliding with each other in an infinite void. Thus Democritus held that there are ultimate constituents of the world which cannot be divided into smaller parts (the Greek word *atomos* means uncuttable), while Descartes believed that matter can be divided into smaller and smaller parts forever—that it is "infinitely divisible."

---

29   [Author's note] I owe this point to Place, in correspondence.

guage of private qualities. (Just as "someone," unlike "the doctor," is a colorless word.)[30]

If it is asked what is the difference between those brain processes which, in my view, are experiences and those brain processes which are not, I can only reply that this is at present unknown. But it does not seem to me altogether fanciful to conjecture that the difference may in part be that between perception and reception (in Dr. D.M. MacKay's terminology) and that the type of brain process which is an experience might be identifiable with MacKay's active "matching response."[31]

I have now considered a number of objections to the brain-process thesis. I wish now to conclude by some remarks on the logical status of the thesis itself. U.T. Place seems to hold that it is a straight-out scientific hypothesis.[32] If so, he is partly right and partly wrong. If the issue is between (say) a brain-process thesis and a heart thesis, or a liver thesis, or a kidney thesis, then the issue is a purely empirical one, and the verdict is overwhelmingly in favor of the brain. The right sorts of things don't go on in the heart, liver, or kidney, nor do these organs possess the right sort of complexity of structure. On the other hand, if the issue is between a brain-or-heart-or-liver-or-kidney thesis (that is, some form of materialism) on the one hand and epiphenomenalism on the other hand, then the issue is not an empirical one. For there is no conceivable experiment which could decide between materialism and epiphenomenalism. This latter issue is not like the average straight-out empirical issue in science, but like the issue between the nineteenth-century English naturalist Philip Gosse[33] and the

orthodox geologists and paleontologists of his day. According to Gosse, the earth was created about 4000 BC exactly as described in *Genesis*, with twisted rock strata, "evidence" of erosion, and so forth, and all sorts of fossils, all in their appropriate strata, just as if the usual evolutionist story had been true. Clearly this theory is in a sense irrefutable: no evidence can possibly tell against it. Let us ignore the theological setting in which Philip Gosse's hypothesis had been placed, thus ruling out objections of a theological kind, such as "what a queer God who would go to such elaborate lengths to deceive us." Let us suppose that it is held that the universe just *began* in 4004 BC with the initial conditions just everywhere as they were in 4004 BC, and in particular that our own planet began with sediment in the rivers, eroded cliffs, fossils in the rocks, and so on. No scientist would ever entertain this as a serious hypothesis, consistent though it is with all possible evidence. The hypothesis offends against the principles of parsimony and simplicity. There would be far too many brute and inexplicable facts. Why are pterodactyl bones just as they are? No explanation in terms of the evolution of pterodactyls from earlier forms of life would any longer be possible. We would have millions of facts about the world as it was in 4004 BC that just have to be *accepted*.

The issue between the brain-process theory and epiphenomenalism seems to be of the above sort. (Assuming that a behavioristic reduction of introspective reports is not possible.) If it be agreed that there are no cogent philosophical arguments which force us into accepting dualism, and if the brain process theory and dualism are equally consistent with the facts, then the principles of parsimony and simplicity seem to me to decide overwhelmingly in favor of the brain-process theory. As I pointed out earlier, dualism involves a large number of irreducible psychophysical laws (whereby the "nomological danglers" dangle) of a queer sort, that just have to be taken on trust, and are just as difficult to swallow as the irreducible facts about the paleontology of the earth with which we are faced on Philip Gosse's theory.

---

30   [Author's note] The "beetle in the box" objection is, *if it is sound*, an objection to any view, and in particular the Cartesian one, that introspective reports are genuine reports. So it is no objection to a weaker thesis that I would be concerned to uphold, namely, that if introspective reports of "experiences" are genuinely reports, then the things they are reports of are in fact brain processes.

31   [Author's note] See his article "Towards an Information-Flow Model of Human Behaviour," *British Journal of Psychology*, XLVII (1956), 30–43.

32   [Author's note] *Op. cit.*

33   [Author's note] See the entertaining account of Gosse's

book *Omphalos* by Martin Gardner in *Fads and Fallacies in the Name of Science* (2nd ed., New York, 1957).

HILARY PUTNAM
"The Nature of Mental States"

Who Is Hilary Putnam?

Hilary W. Putnam is one of the most important American philosophers since World War II and is today a sort of "elder statesman" for North American philosophy. He was born in Chicago in 1926, the son of a well-known author and translator named Samuel Putnam, and his parents lived in France until he was 8, when they moved to Philadelphia. Putnam did his undergraduate degree at the University of Pennsylvania and his PhD, completed in 1951, at the University of California at Los Angeles, where he worked with the eminent philosophers of science Hans Reichenbach and Rudolph Carnap. Putnam taught for a few years at Northwestern University, Princeton, and the Massachusetts Institute of Technology before moving to Harvard University in 1965, where he is now a Professor Emeritus after retiring in 2000. He is married to Ruth Anna Putnam, who is also a well-known philosopher.

In the 1960s, Putnam was known for his fierce criticism of the US role in the Vietnam War (1954–1975). In 1963, at MIT, he organized one of the first faculty-student committees against the war, and at Harvard he led various campus protests and taught courses on Marxism. He became the official faculty advisor to the Students for a Democratic Society—at that time the main anti-Vietnam-War organization at Harvard—and later joined the "Progressive Labor" faction, which endorsed, in Putnam's words, an "idiosyncratic version of Marxism-Leninism." Though he later abandoned Marxism, Putnam has never ceased to believe that

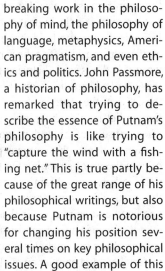

philosophers have a social and political responsibility as well as an academic one.[1]

Putnam began his professional career working in logic and the philosophy of mathematics and science, and since then has done important, often groundbreaking work in the philosophy of mind, the philosophy of language, metaphysics, American pragmatism, and even ethics and politics. John Passmore, a historian of philosophy, has remarked that trying to describe the essence of Putnam's philosophy is like trying to "capture the wind with a fishing net." This is true partly because of the great range of his philosophical writings, but also because Putnam is notorious for changing his position several times on key philosophical issues. A good example of this is the article reprinted here: in "The Nature of Mental States," Putnam founded the theory of mind called functionalism, which is today the most widely held and influential theory of mind. Putnam himself, however, has publicly changed his mind about functionalism and has leveled a battery of arguments against his own theory in his 1988 book *Representation and Reality*.

Putnam's main contributions to philosophy, apart from functionalism, are the following. In the late 1950s and early 1960s Putnam, under the influence

---

1   Biographical details about Hilary Putnam were taken from Lance P. Hickey, "Hilary Putnam," in volume 279, American Philosophers, 1950–2000, of the *Dictionary of Literary Biography* (Thomson Gale, 2003), pp. 226–237.

of a philosopher named W.V. Quine, published a series of devastating articles attacking the then-dominant school of philosophy, headed by his former teachers at UCLA, called logical positivism. (In particular, he attacked positivist doctrines about the "verifiability theory of meaning," the "analytic-synthetic distinction," and the sharp distinction between mathematics and empirical science.)

In the 1970s, together with a philosopher called Saul Kripke, Putnam revolutionized the philosophy of language by developing a new theory of meaning, often called "semantic externalism." The central insight of this theory is that the meanings of words cannot be completely accounted for in terms of what is inside the heads of their users. In other words, we do not give our words meaning simply by *intending* to use them in a particular way, or by somehow "linking" them to a *concept* or a description of what they mean—instead, language gets its meaning from its role in a *community* of speakers and, especially, by its referential connections to the *world*. In Putnam's most famous example, the word "water" gets its meaning not from ideas in the minds of its user, but by the causal connection between our use of the word and the actual stuff—H_2O—we use it about. To illustrate this, Putnam tells a now-famous science fiction story where he imagines a planet called Twin Earth that is molecule-for-molecule identical with ours, except for one difference: on that planet, what we call "water" is not H_2O but is made of some other chemical compound, XYZ. When Oscar on Earth and Twin Oscar on Twin Earth say the words "water is wet," they will be in the same psychological state (since they are molecule-for-molecule identical), but according to Putnam they nevertheless mean *different* things by their utterances: Oscar means that water is wet, whereas Twin Oscar means that twin water is wet. Since nothing about the speakers is different but only their environment, this shows, as Putnam puts it, that "meanings just ain't in the head." Putnam's most influential presentation of these views is in his article "The Meaning of 'Meaning'" (1975).

Finally, Putnam's most radical change of mind, which earned him the nickname "renegade Putnam" in some quarters, was sprung on the philosophical community during his presidential address to the American Philosophical Society in 1976. Up to that time, Putnam had been a leading advocate of "scientific realism": the view that the entities postulated by true scientific theories (such as electrons and black holes) really exist, independently of the theories that describe them. In 1976 he more or less reversed his position, and denied that there is any such thing as theory-independent truth; there is no such thing as an "absolute" perspective from which the "real truth" about reality can be seen. According to Putnam's new "internal realism" (which has close affinities both with Immanuel Kant and with American pragmatism—see the notes to William James in Chapter 2) there is nothing more to truth than what would be rationally accepted after "sufficient" (scientific) inquiry. His books *The Many Faces of Realism* (1986) and *Realism with a Human Face* (1987) pursue this line of thought, but his most famous attack on "metaphysical realism," his so-called brain-in-a-vat argument, appears in *Reason, Truth and History* (1982).

Putnam's approach to philosophy can perhaps be summed up by a quote from the German poet Rainer Maria Rilke that Putnam placed at the front of one of his books:

> Be patient toward all that is unsolved in your heart and try to love the *questions themselves* like locked rooms and like books that are written in a very foreign tongue.… *Live* the questions now. Perhaps you will then gradually, without noticing it, live along some distant day into the answer.

What Is the Structure of This Reading?

Putnam's question in this paper is "Is pain a brain state?" and his answer to that question is that it is not, but for novel and important reasons. He begins by considering the nature of identity questions—that is, of questions which ask whether some thing *A* is identical with (the same thing as) *B*. The point of this section is to argue that the mind-brain identity theory is not an *analytic* claim, and thus is neither analytically true nor analytically false: the claim that pain is a brain state should not be thought of as an analysis of the *concepts* of "pain" and "brain state" (in the same way as "an oculist is an eye doctor" is an analytic claim) but instead as a claim about those *properties* (like the claim that temperature is mean molecular kinetic energy). This means that it cannot be, as many philosophers at the time argued, just a logical mistake to hold that the mind is identical with the brain. So, Putnam is claiming, if identity theory is false it must be false "on empirical and methodological grounds." However, he then argues, it *is* false.

He tries to show that the identity theory is false—that pains are not brain states—by advancing a competing account and showing that it is empirically and methodologically a better theory. Thus, in section II of the paper, he describes his proposal, which has come to be called the theory of *functionalism* (because it identifies mental states with *functions* from inputs to outputs). Then, in section III, he contrasts functionalism with identity theory and argues that it is, empirically, a more adequate theory. Of particular importance in this section is Putnam's argument that the mind-brain identity theory is unlikely to be true. This argument, today called the "multiple realization" thesis, has had an influence out of all proportion with its apparent simplicity. In section IV Putnam contrasts functionalism with behaviorism, and argues that functionalism has all the virtues of behaviorism without its fatal shortcomings. Finally, Putnam closes the article by describing some of the methodological advantages of functionalism as a scientific theory of the mind.

Some Useful Background Information

In his description of functionalism, Putnam relies heavily on the notion of a "Turing Machine." A Turing Machine is an abstract computing device named after the British logician and mathematician who came up with the idea in 1936, Alan Turing. It operates on an indefinitely long tape divided into squares which it "rolls" along, scanning the square which is directly below it. Each square may contain a symbol from a finite alphabet, and when the machine reads a symbol (or detects the absence of a symbol) it is triggered to perform an action: the symbol on the tape can therefore be thought of as the *input* to the machine. In addition to reading these inputs, a Turing Machine

is also capable of occupying any of a finite number of internal states. What action the machine will perform on any particular occasion is determined by these two things: the input, and the machine's current internal state. A Turing Machine can be programmed to perform two types of actions. It can change its internal state. Or it can produce some "output": it can move one square to the left or right, or it can erase what is on the input square, or it can write a symbol on the square.

Here is an example of a program for a Turing Machine (which starts in state S_1) telling it to count to three.

	q_0	q_1
S_1	$q_1 S_1$	LS_2
S_2	$q_1 S_2$	LS_3
S_3	$q_1 S_3$	H

All the possible internal states for our very simple machine are listed on the left and the possible inputs (symbols on the tape) are in the top row. The other cells describe what actions the machine will take for every combination of input and internal state. Suppose the machine starts in internal state S_1. Then, if it looks at the square below it and sees a blank—input q_0—it will produce output q_1 (i.e., write the symbol "1" on the tape) and stay in internal state S_1. On the other hand, if it had seen a 1 already written on the square, it would produce output L (i.e., move one square to the left) and go into internal state S_2. In state S_2, seeing a blank square, it would write 1 and stay in S_2; while detecting a 1 already written would cause it to move to the left without writing anything and to change its internal state to S_3; and so on. Following this program, as long as it is started in state S_1, the Turing Machine will produce a line of exactly three 1s and then halt its operation (output H).

A table of the type written above, which lays out the program for a Turing Machine, is called a Machine Table (or, sometimes, a State Table). It's important for Putnam's paper that the inputs q_0 and q_1 in the Machine Table *need not be* a blank square and a square with "1" written on it, but could be the symbols 0 and 1, or the symbols ↑ and ↓, or a picture of an elephant and a picture of a donkey—any input at all which plays the same role in the system as q_0, counts as q_0. Something similar is true of the internal states S_1, S_2, and S_3. This is what Putnam means when he says that the states and inputs can be specified only "implicitly," i.e., only by describing their role in the program.

Some Common Misconceptions

1. Some people find it initially puzzling to see why functionalism is supposed to be so different from mind-brain identity theory. After all, functionalism is a sort of identity theory—it says that mental states *are identical with* functional states—and functional states are often thought of as just rather abstract physical states. For instance, common examples of functional properties include being a mousetrap and being a computer program. Mousetraps and computers are obviously physical objects, with physical properties, so *why not* talk about, say, a computer-program–hard-drive identity theory and, similarly, mind-brain identities, even if functionalism is true?

    Actually there may well be some philosophical substance to this puzzle (see Jaegwon Kim, "Multiple Realization and the Metaphysics of Reduction," *Philosophy and Phenomenological Research* 52 [1992], if you're interested), but you need to take care not to get involved in a "type-token" confusion: just because each *token* of a property (i.e., each individual instance of the property) is physical, it does not follow that the property is itself physical—that it is a physical *type*. For example, even though it might seem likely that the actual instances, or tokens of some computer program, each happen to be identical with some physical configuration of some hard drive or other, it seems very implausible to say that *every* possible instance of that program *must* be a magnetic trace on a plastic disk, never mind that each installation of the program creates *exactly the same type* of physical pattern on the drive (consider, for example, the fact that the low-level "machine language"

operations of the program might be quite different in the Windows version, the Macintosh version, the UNIX version, and so on). In short, if these kinds of "multiple realizability" considerations are persuasive, functional types are not physical types even though the objects which actually have those functions may all be entirely physical. And the claim that "pains are identical with brain states" is a claim about types rather than tokens: that is, it doesn't just say that some particular pain (say, the pain of my twisted ankle last Tuesday) is identical with some particular brain state (also mine, last Tuesday)—it is the much more ambitious theoretical claim that *all* pains are brain states of a particular sort. (For this reason mind-brain identity theory is often called "type-type physicalism.")

2. When considering the functional description of a human mind, it is tempting to think of the internal states S_i as being the functional specifications of our internal mental states. For example, if you believe that the garden needs watering (i.e., you are in state S_1) then a given input—the sight of rain clouds, say—will produce one sort of output: perhaps a pleased smile. On the other hand if you are in state S_2, hoping to have a barbecue in an hour, then the output might be different. This way of thinking of Turing Machine functionalism is not entirely wrong, but needs one important qualification: at least in the version of functionalism that Putnam describes in his 1967 paper, the state S_1 is *not* a belief and the state S_2 is *not* a desire. Rather, S_1 is the *Total State* of the organism at that particular time; it might in some sense "include" the belief that the garden needs watering, but it isn't itself that belief. For example, a second later you will probably still believe the garden needs watering, but you will no longer be in S_1 (since your *Total State* will be different), but perhaps in state S_3; in fact, plausibly, you will *never* in your lifetime occupy the same internal Total State twice. This means that, as Putnam has put it in another article, "*no psychological state in any customary sense can be a Turing Machine state*" ("Philosophy and Our Mental Life" [1973]).

Suggestions for Critical Reflection

1. Putnam chooses *pain* for his example of a mental state which can be identified with a functional state, and one might gauge his success in this by asking two slightly different questions. First, how successful is he in showing that *the state which is the cause of pain behavior* (and so of our ascriptions of pain to others, and so on) is a functional state, rather than a physical state or a behavioral disposition? Second, how successful is he in showing that *our personal experience of pain* is an experience of a functional state? That is, is it plausible that "what it is like to feel pain" (to use an expression from Thomas Nagel—see his paper in this chapter) can be captured by a functional analysis? If it cannot be, does this matter? Is this a serious problem for functionalism as a theory of the mind?

2. Putnam does not, in this article, talk about cognitive mental states like beliefs and desires. One of the main features of such mental states is that they are *meaningful* (or, in the technical vocabulary, "intentional"); beliefs and perceptions, for example, are standardly understood as *representing* the world as being a certain way, and as such they can be either true or false. Do you think that what makes a mental state *meaningful* could be cashed out in a functionalist way? If so, how do you think this might go? If not, how serious a set-back would this be for functionalism?

3. Putnam gives a functional analysis, spelled out in four conditions, of what it is *for an organism to be in pain*. Is this the same thing as a functional account of what it is for an internal state of the organism to be *a pain state*? If not, how would you functionally specify a pain state— i.e., identify a bit of the brain as having the function of being pain? Can it be done at all using a theory based on the Turing Machine model? If not, is this a problem—does it make the theory less plausible?

4. Does Putnam successfully show that the mind-brain identity theory is almost certainly empirically false?

Suggestions for Further Reading

Putnam's most important papers outlining his functionalism appear in the second volume of his collected papers, *Mind, Language and Reality* (Cambridge University Press, 1975). (This book also contains some of his most important papers on semantic externalism, including "The Meaning of 'Meaning.'") Conversely, Putnam's main attack on functionalism is in *Representation and Reality* (MIT Press, 1988), especially chapter 5: "Why Functionalism Didn't Work." Among the other important books by Putnam are *Reason, Truth and History* (Cambridge University Press, 1981), *Realism and Reason* (Cambridge University Press, 1983), *The Many Faces of Realism* (Open Court, 1987), *Realism With a Human Face* (Harvard University Press, 1990), *Renewing Philosophy* (Harvard University Press, 1992), and *Words and Life* (Harvard University Press, 1994). There is a special issue of the journal *Philosophical Topics* devoted to Putnam's work (Vol. 20, 1992), and a collection of papers edited by Peter Clark and Bob Hale called *Reading Putnam* (Blackwell, 1994).

The literature on functionalism is very large indeed, but it tends to be scattered in the journals and, since the 1970s, fractured among the different species of functionalism which have emerged (machine functionalism or computationalism, teleological functionalism, homuncular functionalism, biosemantics, and so forth). Probably the best starting point is with the papers collected in Part Three of *Readings in Philosophy of Psychology*, Volume One, edited by Ned Block (Harvard University Press, 1980). Especially useful are Block's introduction to the section on functionalism and his classic paper "Troubles with Functionalism." Also, any good introductory text or collection of readings on the philosophy of mind will include a section or more on functionalism (for example Jaegwon Kim's book *Philosophy of Mind* [Westview Press, 1996] and the reader edited by William G. Lycan, *Mind and Cognition*, from Blackwell, second edition, 1999).

"The Nature of Mental States"[2]

The typical concerns of the Philosopher of Mind might be represented by three questions: (1) How do we know that other people have pains? (2) Are pains brain states? (3) What is the analysis of the concept *pain*? I do not wish to discuss questions (1) and (3) in this paper. I shall say something about question (2).[3]

I. Identity Questions

"Is pain a brain state?" (Or, "Is the property of having a pain at time *t* a brain state?")[4] It is impossible to discuss this question sensibly without saying something about the peculiar rules which have grown up in the course of the development of "analytical philosophy"—rules which, far from leading to an end to all conceptual confusions, themselves represent considerable conceptual confusion. These rules—which are, of course, implicit rather than explicit in the practice of most analytical philosophers—are (1) that a statement of the form "being *A* is being *B*" (e.g., "being in pain is being in a certain brain state") can be *correct* only if it follows, in some sense, from the meaning of the terms *A* and *B*; and (2) that a statement

of the form "being A is being B" can be philosophically *informative* only if it is in some sense reductive (e.g., "being in pain is having a certain unpleasant sensation" is not philosophically informative; "being in pain is having a certain behavior disposition" is, if true, philosophically informative). These rules are excellent rules if we still believe that the program of reductive analysis[5] (in the style of the 1930's) can be carried out; if we don't, then they turn analytical philosophy into a mug's game, at least so far as "is" questions are concerned.

In this paper I shall use the term "property" as a blanket term for such things as being in pain, being in a particular brain state, having a particular behavior disposition, and also for magnitudes such as temperature, etc—i.e., for things which can naturally be represented by one-or-more-place predicates or functors.[6] I shall use the term "concept" for things which can be identified with synonymy-classes[7] of

---

2   This paper was written for a 1965 conference at Oberlin College and first published (under the title "Psychological Predicates") in the proceedings of that conference, *Art, Mind, and Religion*, edited by W.H. Capitan and D.D. Merrill (University of Pittsburgh Press, © 1967). It is reprinted by permission of the University of Pittsburgh Press.

3   [Author's note] I have discussed these and related topics in the following papers: "Minds and Machines," in *Dimensions of Mind*, ed. Sidney Hook, New York, 1960, pp. 148–179; "Brains and Behavior," in *Analytical Psychology, second series*, ed. Ronald Butler, Oxford, 1965, pp. 1–20; and "The Mental Life of Some Machines," to appear in a volume edited by Hector Neri Castaneda, Detroit.

4   [Author's note] In this paper I wish to avoid the vexed question of the relation between *pains* and *pain states*. I only remark in passing that one common argument *against* identification of these two—viz., that a pain can be in one's arm but a state (of the organism) cannot be in one's arm—is easily seen to be fallacious.

5   Reductive analysis is the attempt to show that some concept, belief, or theory can be broken down into component parts and that those component elements belong to some more basic category than the thing being analyzed. Examples of the kind of reductive analysis Putnam has in mind here are the attempt to analyze statements about physical objects into sets of reports about sensations (sense-data), and the project of analyzing statements about mental states into sets of statements about actual and possible behavior.

6   A one-place predicate (or "propositional function" or "functor") is simply an incomplete (or "open") sentence which includes a space left open for some referring expression or other. For example, "___ is green" is a one-place predicate, and it can be turned into a (true or false) complete sentence by filling the gap with a name or a description, as in "Polly the Parrot is green," "grass is green," "this cheese is green" or "the Gobi desert is green." "___ is taller than ___" is a two-place predicate, "___ is further south of ___ than ___" is a three-place predicate, and so on.

7   A synonymy-class is a set of all the linguistic expressions which are synonymous with each other. What exactly it is to be "synonymous" turns out to be a philosophically tricky question, but the basic idea is that two bits of language are synonymous if they have

expressions. Thus the concept *temperature* can be identified (I maintain) with the synonymy-class of the word "temperature."[8] (This is like saying that the number 2 can be identified with the class of all pairs. This is quite a different statement from the peculiar statement that 2 *is* the class of all pairs. I do not maintain that concepts *are* synonymy-classes, whatever that might mean, but that they can be identified with synonymy classes, for the purpose of formalization of the relevant discourse.)

The question "What is the concept *temperature*?" is a very "funny" one. One might take it to mean "What is temperature? Please take my question as a conceptual one." In that case an answer might be (pretend for a moment 'heat' and 'temperature' are synonyms) "temperature is heat," or even "the concept of temperature is the same concept as the concept of heat." Or one might take it to mean "What are *concepts*, really? For example, what is 'the concept of temperature'?"

In that case heaven knows what an "answer" would be. (Perhaps it would be the statement that concepts *can be identified with* synonymy-classes.)

Of course, the question "What is the property temperature?" is also "funny." And one way of interpreting it is to take it as a question about the concept of temperature. But this is not the way a physicist would take it.

The effect of saying that the property P_1 can be identical with the property P_2 only if the terms P_1, P_2 are in some suitable sense "synonyms" is, to all intents and purposes, to collapse the two notions of "property" and "concept" into a single notion. The view that concepts (intensions[9]) *are* the same as properties has been explicitly advocated by Carnap[10] (e.g., in *Meaning and Necessity*). This seems an unfortunate view, since "temperature is mean molecular kinetic energy" appears to be a perfectly good example of a true statement of identity of properties, whereas "the concept of temperature is the same concept as the concept of mean molecular kinetic energy" is simply false.

Many philosophers believe that the statement "pain is a brain state" violates some rules or norms of Eng-

---

the same meaning. For example, the following words {rain, rainfall, shower, precipitation, heavy drizzle, light downpour, Scotch mist, *precipitación*, *précipitations*, *Niederschlag*, *pioggia*, …} form (roughly) a synonymy-class.

8   [Author's note] There are some well-known remarks by Alonzo Church on this topic. Those remarks do not bear (as might at first be supposed) on the identification of concepts with synonymy-classes as such, but rather support the view that (in formal semantics) it is necessary to retain Frege's distinction between the normal and the "oblique" use of expressions. That is, even if we say that the concept of temperature *is* the synonymy-class of the word 'temperature,' we must not thereby be led into the error of supposing that 'the concept of temperature' is synonymous with 'the synonymy-class of the word "temperature"'— for then 'the concept of temperature' and 'der Begriff der Temperatur' would not be synonymous, which they are. Rather, we must say that 'the concept of temperature' *refers to* the synonymy-class of the word 'temperature' (on this particular reconstruction); but that class is *identified* not as "the synonymy-class to which such-and-such a word belongs," but in another way (e.g., as the synonymy-class whose members have such-and-such a characteristic use).

9   This is a technical term for, roughly, the meaning of a term or predicate; it is contrasted with a term's *extension*, which is the set of things of which it is true. For example, the intension of the word "marsupial" is, let's suppose, something like what you would discover in a dictionary if you looked the word up. The extension of "marsupial," by contrast, is not any kind of concept or definition but is a large number of non-placental mammals, many but not all of them living in Australasia, including wallabies, wombats, bandicoots, and opossums.

10 Rudolf Carnap (1891–1970), one of the most important analytic philosophers of the first half of the twentieth century, was born in Germany but left Europe in the 1930s to live and work for the rest of his life in America (first at Chicago, then at UCLA). His work is perhaps the most classic example of the "reductive analysis in the style of the 1930s" which Putnam alludes to above, especially his 1928 book *Der logische Aufbau der Welt* ("The Logical Structure of the World"). *Meaning and Necessity*, an important book about formal semantics, was published in 1947.

lish. But the arguments offered are hardly convincing. For example, if the fact that I can know that I am in pain without knowing that I am in brain state *S* shows that pain cannot be brain state *S*, then, by exactly the same argument, the fact that I can know that the stove is hot without knowing that the mean molecular kinetic energy is high (or even that molecules exist) shows that it is *false* that temperature is mean molecular kinetic energy, physics to the contrary. In fact, all that immediately follows from the fact that I can know that I am in pain without knowing that I am in brain state *S* is that the concept of pain is not the same concept as the concept of being in brain state *S*. But either pain, or the state of being in pain, or some pain, or some pain state, might still be brain state *S*. After all, the concept of temperature is not the same concept as the concept of mean molecular kinetic energy. But temperature is mean molecular kinetic energy.

Some philosophers maintain that both 'pain is a brain state' and 'pain states are brain states' are unintelligible. The answer is to explain to these philosophers, as well as we can, given the vagueness of all scientific methodology, what sorts of considerations lead one to make an empirical reduction (i.e., to say such things as "water is H_2O," "light is electromagnetic radiation," "temperature is mean molecular kinetic energy"). If, without giving reasons, he still maintains in the face of such examples that one cannot imagine parallel circumstances for the use of 'pains are brain states' (or, perhaps, 'pain states are brain states') one has grounds to regard him as perverse.

Some philosophers maintain that "P_1 is P_2" is something that can be true, when the 'is' involved is the 'is' of empirical reduction, only when the properties P_1 and P_2 are (a) associated with a spatio-temporal region; and (b) the region is one and the same in both cases. Thus "temperature is mean molecular kinetic energy" is an admissible empirical reduction, since the temperature and the molecular energy are associated with the same space-time region, but "having a pain in my arm is being in a brain state" is not, since the spatial regions involved are different.

This argument does not appear very strong. Surely no one is going to be deterred from saying that mirror images are light reflected from an object and then from the surface of a mirror by the fact that an image can be "located" three feet *behind* the mirror! (Moreover, one can always find *some* common property of the reductions one is willing to allow—e.g., temperature is mean molecular kinetic energy—which is not a property of some one identification one wishes to disallow. This is not very impressive unless one has an argument to show that the very purposes of such identification depend upon the common property in question.)

Again, other philosophers have contended that all the predictions that can be derived from the conjunction of neurophysiological laws with such statements as "pain states are such-and-such brain states" can equally well be derived from the conjunction of the same neurophysiological laws with "being in pain is correlated with such-and-such brain states," and hence (sic)![11] there can be no methodological grounds for saying that pains (or pain states) *are* brain states, as opposed to saying that they are *correlated* (invariantly) with brain states. This argument, too, would show that light is only correlated with electromagnetic radiation. The mistake is in ignoring the fact that, although the theories in question may indeed lead to the same predictions, they open and exclude different *questions*. "Light is invariantly correlated with electromagnetic radiation" would leave open the questions "What is the light then, if it isn't the same as the electromagnetic radiation?" and "What makes the light accompany the electromagnetic radiation?"—questions which are excluded by saying that the light *is* the electromagnetic radiation. Similarly, the purpose of saying that pains are brain states is precisely to exclude from empirical meaningfulness the questions "What is the pain, then, if it isn't the same as the brain state?" and "What makes the pain accompany the brain state?" If there are grounds to suggest that these questions represent, so to speak, the wrong way to look at the matter, then those grounds are grounds for a theoretical identification of pains with brain states.

---

11 *Sic* is the Latin word meaning "so," or "thus," and is used like this after a quotation or paraphrase to mean something like "they really did say this—I'm not making this up, but quoting them exactly!"

If all arguments to the contrary are unconvincing, shall we then conclude that it is meaningful (and perhaps true) to say either that pains are brain states or that pain states are brain states?

(1) It is perfectly meaningful (violates no "rule of English," involves no "extension of usage") to say "pains are brain states."

(2) It is not meaningful (involves a "changing of meaning" or "an extension of usage," etc.) to say "pains are brain states."

My own position is not expressed by either (1) or (2). It seems to me that the notions "change of meaning" and "extension of usage" are simply so ill-defined that one cannot in fact say *either* (1) or (2). I see no reason to believe that either the linguist, or the man-on-the-street, or the philosopher possesses today a notion of "change of meaning" applicable to such cases as the one we have been discussing. The *job* for which the notion of change of meaning was developed in the history of the language was just a *much* cruder job than this one.

But, if we don't assert either (1) or (2)—in other words, if we regard the "change of meaning" issue as a pseudo-issue in this case—then how are we to discuss the question with which we started? "Is pain a brain state?"

The answer is to allow statements of the form "pain is *A*," where 'pain' and '*A*' are in no sense synonyms, and to see whether any such statement can be found which might be acceptable on empirical and methodological grounds. This is what we shall now proceed to do.

II. Is Pain a Brain State?

We shall discuss "Is pain a brain state?," then. And we have agreed to waive the "change of meaning" issue.

Since I am discussing not what the concept of pain comes to, but what pain is, in a sense of 'is' which requires empirical theory-construction (or, at least, empirical speculation), I shall not apologize for advancing an empirical hypothesis. Indeed, my strategy will be to argue that pain is *not* a brain state, not on *a priori* grounds, but on the grounds that another hypothesis is more plausible. The detailed development and verification of my hypothesis would be just as Utopian a task as the detailed development and veri-

fication of the brain state hypothesis. But the putting-forward, not of detailed and scientifically "finished" hypotheses, but of schemata for hypotheses, has long been a function of philosophy. I shall, in short, argue that pain is not a brain state, in the sense of a physical-chemical state of the brain (or even the whole nervous system), but another *kind* of state entirely. I propose the hypothesis that pain, or the state of being in pain, is a functional state of a whole organism.

To explain this it is necessary to introduce some technical notions. In previous papers I have explained the notion of a Turing Machine and discussed the use of this notion as a model for an organism. The notion of a Probabilistic Automaton is defined similarly to a Turing Machine, except that the transitions between "states" are allowed to be with various probabilities rather than being "deterministic." (Of course, a Turing Machine is simply a special kind of Probabilistic Automaton, one with transition probabilities 0, 1.) I shall assume the notion of a Probabilistic Automaton has been generalized to allow for "sensory inputs" and "motor outputs"—that is, the Machine Table specifies, for every possible combination of a "state" and a complete set of "sensory inputs," an "instruction" which determines the probability of the next "state," and also the probabilities of the "motor outputs." (This replaces the idea of the Machine as printing on a tape.) I shall also assume that the physical realization of the sense organs responsible for the various inputs, and of the motor organs, is specified, but that the "states" and the "inputs" themselves are, as usual, specified only "implicitly"—i.e., by the set of transition probabilities given by the Machine Table.

Since an empirically given system can simultaneously be a "physical realization" of many different Probabilistic Automata, I introduce the notion of a *Description* of a system. A Description of S where S is a system, is any true statement to the effect that S possesses distinct states $S_1, S_2, ..., S_n$ which are related to one another and to the motor outputs and sensory inputs by the transition probabilities given in such-and-such a Machine Table. The Machine Table mentioned in the Description will then be called the Functional Organization of S relative to that Description, and the S_i such that S is in state S_i at a given time will be called the Total State of S (at that time) relative to that Description. It should be noted that knowing the Total State of a system relative to a Description involves knowing a good deal about how the system is likely to "behave," given various combinations of sensory inputs, but does not involve knowing the physical realization of the S_i as, e.g., physical-chemical states of the brain. The S_i, to repeat, are specified only *implicitly* by the Description—i.e., specified *only* by the set of transition probabilities given in the Machine Table.

The hypothesis that "being in pain is a functional state of the organism" may now be spelled out more exactly as follows:

(1)   All organisms capable of feeling pain are Probabilistic Automata.

(2)   Every organism capable of feeling pain possesses at least one Description of a certain kind (i.e., being capable of feeling pain is possessing an appropriate kind of Functional Organization).

(3)   No organism capable of feeling pain possesses a decomposition into parts which separately possess Descriptions of the kind referred to in (2).

(4)   For every Description of the kind referred to in (2), there exists a subset of the sensory inputs such that an organism with that Description is in pain when and only when some of its sensory inputs are in that subset.

This hypothesis is admittedly vague, though surely no vaguer than the brain-state hypothesis in its present form. For example, one would like to know more about the kind of Functional Organization that an organism must have to be capable of feeling pain, and more about the marks that distinguish the subset of the sensory inputs referred to in (4). With respect to the first question, one can probably say that the Functional Organization must include something that resembles a "preference function," or at least a preference partial ordering, and something that resembles an "inductive logic" (i.e., the Machine must be able to "learn from experience"). (The meaning of these conditions, for Automata models, is discussed in my paper "The Mental Life of Some Machines.") In addition, it seems natural to require that the Machine possess "pain sensors," i.e., sensory organs which normally signal damage to the Machine's body, or

dangerous temperatures, pressures, etc., which transmit a special subset of the inputs, the subset referred to in (4). Finally, and with respect to the second question, we would want to require at least that the inputs in the distinguished subset have a high disvalue on the Machine's preference function or ordering (further conditions are discussed in "The Mental Life of Some Machines"). The purpose of condition (3) is to rule out such "organisms" (if they can count as such) as swarms of bees as single pain-feelers. The condition (1) is, obviously, redundant, and is only introduced for expository reasons. (It is, in fact, empty, since everything is a Probabilistic Automaton under *some* Description.)

I contend, in passing, that this hypothesis, in spite of its admitted vagueness, is far *less* vague than the "physical-chemical state" hypothesis is today, and far more susceptible to investigation of both a mathematical and an empirical kind. Indeed, to investigate this hypothesis is just to attempt to produce "mechanical" models of organisms—and isn't this, in a sense, just what psychology is about? The difficult step, of course, will be to pass from models of *specific* organisms to a *normal form* for the psychological description of organisms—for this is what is required to make (2) and (4) precise. But this too seems to be an inevitable part of the program of psychology.

I shall now compare the hypothesis just advanced with (a) the hypothesis that pain is a brain state, and (b) the hypothesis that pain is a behavior disposition.

III. Functional State Versus Brain State

It may, perhaps, be asked if I am not somewhat unfair in taking the brain-state theorist to be talking about *physico-chemical* states of the brain. But (a) these are the only sorts of states ever mentioned by brain-state theorists. (b) The brain-state theorist usually mentions (with a certain pride, slightly reminiscent of the Village Atheist) the incompatibility of his hypothesis with all forms of dualism and mentalism.[12] This is

---

12   Mentalism is the view that the causation of human behavior cannot be satisfactorily explained in purely non-mental terms but only by appealing to such psychological entities as beliefs, desires, thoughts, hopes, feelings, and so on.

natural if physical-chemical states of the brain are what is at issue. However, functional states of whole systems are something quite different. In particular, the functional-state hypothesis is *not* incompatible with dualism! Although it goes without saying that the hypothesis is "mechanistic" in its inspiration, it is a slightly remarkable fact that a system consisting of a body and a "soul," if such things there be, can perfectly well be a Probabilistic Automaton. (c) One argument advanced by Smart is that the brain-state theory assumes only "physical" properties, and Smart finds "non-physical" properties unintelligible. The Total States and the "inputs" defined above are, of course, neither mental nor physical *per se*, and I cannot imagine a functionalist advancing this argument. (d) If the brain-state theorist does mean (or at least allow) states other than physical-chemical states, then his hypothesis is completely empty, at least until he specifies *what* sort of "states" he *does* mean.

Taking the brain-state hypothesis in this way, then, what reasons are there to prefer the functional-state hypothesis over the brain-state hypothesis? Consider what the brain-state theorist has to do to make good his claims. He has to specify a physical-chemical state such that *any* organism (not just a mammal) is in pain if and only if (a) it possesses a brain of a suitable physical-chemical structure; and (b) its brain is in that physical-chemical state. This means that the physical-chemical state in question must be a possible state of a mammalian brain, a reptilian brain, a mollusc's brain (octopuses are mollusca, and certainly feel pain), etc. At the same time, it must *not* be a possible (physically possible) state of the brain of any physically possible creature that cannot feel pain. Even if such a state can be found, it must be nomologically certain[13] that it will also be a state of the brain of any extra-terrestrial life that may be found that will be capable of feeling pain before we can even entertain the supposition that it may *be* pain.

It is not altogether impossible that such a state will be found. Even though octopus and mammal are examples of parallel (rather than sequential) evolution, for example, virtually identical structures (physically speaking) have evolved in the eye of the octopus and

in the eye of the mammal, notwithstanding the fact that this organ has evolved from different kinds of cells in the two cases. Thus it is at least possible that parallel evolution, all over the universe, might *always* lead to *one and the same* physical "correlate" of pain. But this is certainly an ambitious hypothesis.

Finally, the hypothesis becomes still more ambitious when we realize that the brain state theorist is not just saying that *pain* is a brain state; he is of course, concerned to maintain that *every* psychological state is a brain state. Thus if we can find even one psychological predicate which can clearly be applied to both a mammal and an octopus (say "hungry"), but whose physical-chemical "correlate" is different in the two cases, the brain-state theory has collapsed. It seems to me overwhelmingly probable that we can do this. Granted, in such a case the brain-state theorist can save himself by *ad hoc* assumptions[14] (e.g., defining the dis-

---

13   Physically necessary, required by the laws of physics.

14   An *ad hoc* assumption is one introduced for no other reason than to defeat a particular objection (rather than for reasons found within the theory itself). Since one can defend even the most ridiculous theory by continually inventing new *ad hoc* assumptions to meet every new refutation, *ad hoc* assumptions are generally thought to be worthless in science. (For example, imagine a scientific law which says that balls of a particular mass will roll down slopes of a particular incline at some particular velocity. Now, suppose that empirical tests show that these types of balls on those types of slope actually travel downhill at a slower velocity. The theory could be defended in various ways, some *ad hoc* and some not. A non-*ad hoc* response would be to point out that the sloping surfaces used in the experiments had surfaces which exerted friction on the rolling balls, and once this is factored in the theory always gives the right answer. Examples of *ad hoc* responses, by contrast, would be to assume that the theory is true but, in the case of these particular experiments, the observers were sleepy and measured badly, or that little invisible demons got in the way of the balls and slowed them down, and so on. It's not that these assumptions wouldn't preserve the theory against refutation; it's that we have no independent reason to believe the assumptions true *except* that they would prevent the theory from being refuted.)

junction of two states to be a single "physical-chemical state"), but this does not have to be taken seriously.

Turning now to the considerations *for* the functional-state theory, let us begin with the fact that we identify organisms as in pain, or hungry, or angry, or in heat, etc., on the basis of their *behavior*. But it is a truism that similarities in the behavior of two systems are at least a reason to suspect similarities in the functional organization of the two systems, and a much *weaker* reason to suspect similarities in the actual physical details. Moreover, we expect the various psychological states—at least the basic ones, such as hunger, thirst, aggression, etc.—to have more or less similar "transition probabilities" (within wide and ill-defined limits, to be sure) with each other and with behavior in the case of different species, because this is an artifact of the way in which we identify these states. Thus, we would not count an animal as *thirsty* if its "unsatiated" behavior did not seem to be directed toward drinking and was not followed by "satiation for liquid." Thus any animal that we count as capable of these various states will at least *seem* to have a certain rough kind of functional organization. And, as already remarked, if the program of finding psychological laws that are not species-specific—i.e., of finding a normal form for psychological theories of different species—ever succeeds, then it will bring in its wake a delineation of the kind of functional organization that is necessary and sufficient for a given psychological state, as well as a precise definition of the notion "psychological state." In contrast, the brain-state theorist has to hope for the eventual development of neurophysiological laws that are species-independent, which seems much less reasonable than the hope that psychological laws (of a sufficiently general kind) may be species-independent, or, still weaker, that a species-independent *form* can be found in which psychological laws can be written.

IV. Functional State Versus Behavior Disposition

The theory that being in pain is neither a brain state nor a functional state but a behavior disposition has one apparent advantage: it appears to agree with the way in which we verify that organisms are in pain. We do not in practice know anything about the brain state of an animal when we say that it is in pain; and

we possess little if any knowledge of its functional organization, except in a crude intuitive way. In fact, however, this "advantage" is no advantage at all: for, although statements about how we verify that x is A may have a good deal to do with what the concept of being A comes to, they have precious little to do with what the property A *is*. To argue on the ground just mentioned that pain is neither a brain state nor a functional state is like arguing that heat is not mean molecular kinetic energy from the fact that ordinary people do not (they think) ascertain the mean molecular kinetic energy of something when they verify that it is hot or cold. It is not necessary that they should; what is necessary is that the marks that they take as indications of heat should in fact be explained by the mean molecular kinetic energy. And, similarly, it is necessary to our hypothesis that the marks that are taken as behavioral indications of pain should be explained by the fact that the organism is in a functional state of the appropriate kind, but not that speakers should *know* that this is so.

The difficulties with "behavior disposition" accounts are so well known that I shall do little more than recall them here. The difficulty—it appears to be more than "difficulty," in fact—of specifying the required behavior disposition except as "the disposition of X to behave as if X were in *pain*," is the chief one, of course. In contrast, we *can* specify the functional state with which we propose to identify pain, at least roughly, without using the notion of pain. Namely, the functional state we have in mind is the state of receiving sensory inputs which play a certain role in the Functional Organization of the organism. This role is characterized, at least partially, by the fact that the sense organs responsible for the inputs in question are organs whose function is to detect damage to the body, or dangerous extremes of temperature, pressure, etc., and by the fact that the "inputs" themselves, whatever their physical realization, represent a condition that the organism assigns a high disvalue to. As I stressed in "The Mental Life of Some Machines," this does *not* mean that the Machine will always *avoid* being in the condition in question ("pain"); it only means that the condition will be avoided unless not avoiding it is necessary to the attainment of some more highly valued goal. Since the behavior of the Machine (in this case, an organism) will depend not merely on the sensory inputs, but also on the Total State (i.e., on other values, beliefs, etc.), it seems hopeless to make any general statement about how an organism in such a condition *must* behave; but this does not mean that we must abandon hope of characterizing the condition. Indeed, we have just characterized it.[15]

Not only does the behavior-disposition theory seem hopelessly vague; if the "behavior" referred to is peripheral behavior, and the relevant stimuli are peripheral stimuli (e.g., we do not say anything about what the organism will do if its brain is operated upon), then the theory seems clearly false. For example, two animals with all motor nerves cut will have the same actual and potential "behavior" (viz., none to speak of); but if one has cut pain fibers and the other has uncut pain fibers, then one will feel pain and the other won't. Again, if one person has cut pain fibers, and another suppresses all pain responses deliberately due to some strong compulsion, then the actual and potential peripheral behavior may be the same, but one will feel pain and the other won't. (Some philosophers maintain that this last case is conceptually impossible, but the only evidence for this appears to be that *they* can't, or don't want to, conceive of it.)[16] If instead of pain, we take some sensation the "bodily expression" of which is easier to suppress—say, a slight coolness in one's left little finger—the case becomes even clearer.

Finally, even if there *were* some behavior disposition invariantly correlated with pain (species-independently!), and specifiable without using the term 'pain,' it would still be more plausible to identify being in pain with some state whose presence *explains* this behavior disposition—the brain state or functional state—than with the behavior disposition itself. Such considerations of plausibility may be somewhat subjective; but if other things were equal (of course, they aren't) why shouldn't we allow considerations of plausibility to play the deciding role?

V. Methodological Considerations

So far we have considered only what might be called the "empirical" reasons for saying that being in pain is a functional state, rather than a brain state or a behavior disposition; viz., that it seems more likely that the functional state we described is invariantly "correlated" with pain, species-independently, than that there is either a physical-chemical state of the brain (must an organism have a *brain* to feel pain? perhaps some ganglia will do) or a behavior disposition so correlated. If this is correct, then it follows that the identification we proposed is at least a candidate for consideration. What of methodological considerations?

The methodological considerations are roughly similar in all cases of reduction, so no surprises need be expected here. First, identification of psychological states with functional states means that the laws of psychology can be derived from statements of the form "such-and-such organisms have such-and-such Descriptions" together with the identification statements ("being in pain is such-and-such a functional state," etc.). Secondly, the presence of the functional state (i.e., of inputs which play the role we have described in the Functional Organization of the organism) is not merely "correlated with" but actually explains the pain behavior on the part of the organism. Thirdly, the identification serves to exclude questions which (if a naturalistic view is correct) represent an altogether wrong way of looking at the matter, e.g., "What *is* pain if it isn't either the brain state or the functional state?" and "What causes the pain to be always accompanied by this sort of functional state?" In short, the identification is to be tentatively accepted as a theory which leads to both fruitful predictions and to fruitful *questions*, and which serves to discourage fruitless and empirically senseless questions, where by 'empirically senseless' I mean "senseless" not merely from the standpoint of verification, but from the standpoint of what there in fact *is*.

---

15   [Author's note] In "The Mental Life of Some Machines" a further, and somewhat independent, characteristic of pain inputs is discussed in terms of Automata models—namely the spontaneity of the inclination to withdraw the injured part, etc. This raises the question, which is discussed in that paper, of giving a functional analysis of the notion of a spontaneous inclination. Of course, still further characteristics come readily to mind—for example, that feelings of pain are (or seem to be) *located* in the parts of the body.

16   [Author's note] C.f. the discussion of "super-spartans" in "Brains and Behavior."

JOHN R. SEARLE
"Minds, Brains and Programs"

Who Is John R. Searle?

John Rogers Searle was born in Denver, Colorado in 1932, the son of an electrical engineer and a doctor. He began his undergraduate work in 1949 at the University of Wisconsin, but in 1952 he went to Oxford University as a Rhodes Scholar and completed a BA in Politics, Philosophy, and Economics there. In 1959 he received his doctorate at Oxford, influenced especially by P.F. Strawson and the famous philosopher of language J.L. Austin. Between 1957 and 1959 he was a lecturer at Christ Church College, Oxford, but he has spent the rest of his career teaching at the University of California, Berkeley.

Searle's early work was devoted to the elaboration and improvement of Austin's theory of "speech acts," and most of his later work has derived in some way from the philosophical theory he developed at this time. A speech act is an action performed by saying (or writing, etc.) something. For example, one might make a promise or a threat, insult somebody and hurt their feelings, assert that something is true or false, ask a question, and so on. Searle holds that all human linguistic communication consists in the performance of speech acts, which he sees as forms of human behavior governed by particular rules. Nearly all the philosophical problems to do with language and meaning, according to Searle, are to be solved by examining these rules (e.g., the rules of promising or of describing). Much of Searle's work in the philosophy of language is encapsulated in his books *Speech Acts* (1969) and *Expression and Meaning* (1979).

This interest in the theory of meaning led to Searle's subsequent career in the philosophy of mind, where his work has had three themes: first, his development of a theory of "intentionality"; second his attack on computationalism and strong AI; and third his attempt to formulate a "naturalized" theory of consciousness.

In his book *Intentionality* (1983), Searle tries to provide a general theory of intentionality (i.e., 'aboutness' or 'representationality'—see the background information below) using a fairly small number of explanatory concepts. For example, he formulated and applied the notions of the "direction of fit" of a mental state (which can be world-to-mind, mind-to-world, or null) and its "direction of causation" (which can be mind-to-world or world-to-mind). Searle does not, however, think that intentionality can be *reduced* to (or analyzed into) these kinds of notions—his view is that intentionality is an irreducible feature of the world, one that can be described or explained but not eliminated.

Searle's most famous attack on strong AI is the extremely controversial article reprinted here.

His work on consciousness appears mainly in the books *The Rediscovery of Mind* (1992) and *The Mystery of Consciousness* (1997). Searle's theory of consciousness has two main features which, independently, are not that unusual, but which Searle is almost alone in holding at the same time. First, his thesis of "ontological subjectivity" insists that consciousness is an irreducibly first-person, subjective phenomenon which, in principle, cannot be fully explained by a third-person, neurological theory. Nevertheless, he *also* defends "biological naturalism," which holds that consciousness is an entirely natural, biological phenomenon; according to Searle, brain processes "cause" conscious states (in much the same way as the molecular structure of water "causes" it to be liquid at room temperature, or gravity "causes" a thrown baseball to come back down), and therefore, he concludes, conscious states *just are* features of the neurobiological substrate. (As Searle put it once, "I think that this is one of those rare questions in philosophy where you can have your cake and eat it too.") Searle argues that most of contemporary cognitive science and philosophy of mind is inadequate because most mental phenomena cannot be understood without a proper understanding of consciousness, and this in turn, he argues, cannot be attained without paying attention to our subjective, phenomenological *experience* of consciousness.

What Is the Structure of This Reading?

Searle begins by describing his target, what he calls "strong Artificial Intelligence," in essence the claim that a suitably adequate AI computer program would not be merely a *simulation* of intelligent thought—it really would *be* thought, and any machine running such a program would be a thinking creature.[1] Searle denies this and (after describing a particular candidate computer program as a concrete target) he presents his argument against it: what is usually called his "Chinese room" thought experiment. He realizes that this argument will not seem persuasive to many workers in cognitive science, so he tries to forestall objections by answering six he has encountered previously from audiences at Berkeley, MIT, Stanford, and Yale: the systems reply, the robot reply, the brain simulator reply, the combination reply, the other minds reply, and the many mansions reply.

Searle then returns to an underlying question, which he had briefly raised earlier: if the Chinese room does not understand, but a human language-user does, what exactly *explains* this different between them? After some comments on this question, he moves on to "state some of the general philosophical points implicit in the [Chinese room] argument," which he does in question-and-answer form, ending by speculating why many, if not most, cognitive scientists are so attracted to the computational model he attacks.

Some Useful Background Information

1. Searle's "Minds, Brains and Programs" is often described as an attack on the form of functionalism called computationalism. Computationalism is the hypothesis that the mind is, quite literally, a computer program (and the brain is the machine which runs it). According to the classical computationalist picture ("classical" in this case meaning dating back to the 1970s), mental representations such as beliefs are symbol structures encoded in the brain, and mental processes—such as playing chess or planning the perfect date—are the manipulations of these representations in accordance with symbolic algorithms; that is, thinking precisely *is* the performance of "computations," in just the same sense as a laptop performs computations. The difference between a human mind and, say, a database program is purely one of complexity and computational power; it is not, according to this theory, a difference in kind.

2. 'Intentionality' is often used as a technical term in philosophy. Sometimes philosophers use "intentional" in the everyday sense, to mean something which is done on purpose, but frequently they use it to mean instead *something which is about* ("directed at," "represents," "of") *something else.* Thus, for example, a sentence, a thought, an action, a sculpture, or a map can be intentional (or "have intentionality") while a person, a star, or a house usually are not. The term was coined in the Middle Ages, and comes from the Latin verb *intendo*, which means "to point at." It was revived in the late nineteenth century by a German philosopher and psychologist called Franz Brentano, who claimed that intentionality was "the mark of the mental"—that is, he held that all mental states are intentional and no physical states are. Nowadays, however, most philosophers think that while many mental states are intentional (such as a fear of snakes) others are not (such as a vague, undirected feeling of anxiety).

   For Searle, it is important that intentionality comes in two different flavors: intrinsic and derived. Some entities, such as thoughts, are *intrinsically* intentional, according to Searle: they have their 'aboutness,' so to speak, objectively built in to them. On the other hand, the intentionality of many other entities is *derived*: they are not about things or for things all by them-

---

1   Thus, its intelligence would be "artificial" in the sense that it was not created in the normal biological way (as in "artificial insemination") but *not* artificial in the sense of being "not really" intelligent (as in "artificial sugar").

selves, but only when they are *interpreted* that way by an observer. For example, a five dollar bill is a meaningless piece of paper unless it is part of a system of conventional exchange created by thinking beings. The sequence of symbols e-l-e-p-h-a-n-t, and the sound you make by sounding out the word, don't by themselves have any magical, objective connection to the largest land mammal—they are just the signs we *use* in English to refer to elephants (and we could just as easily have chosen to use the symbol-strings "heelpant" or "peltahen" instead). Shaking someone's hand is a physical action which we interpret as a friendly gesture, but which in another society might be treated as a mortal insult. And so on. A key point for Searle is that nothing can have derived intentionality unless something else has intrinsic intentionality: that is, only creatures with *minds* can project meaningfulness into the surrounding universe.

3. Searle's argument in this article depends heavily on the distinction between syntax and semantics. The syntax of a language consists of the rules which govern the grammatical formation of sentences in that language (e.g., the rules which say it's OK in English to utter "The cat is on the mat" but not "Cat the mat is on"). In a *formalized* language, such as the various languages of logic, the syntax also includes what are called "transformation rules": these rules specify how one set of strings of symbols can legitimately be turned into another set of symbol-strings. (For example the formula expressing "if P then Q" can be turned into one expressing "not-P or Q.") These logical rules are usually set up so that if the input sentences are all true, the output sentences will all be true as well. However, it is important to notice that the rules themselves pay no attention to the truth or the meaning of the sentences they deal with—they simply take an input of a particular shape or *form*, and produce an output of another form. This is exactly why logic is called "formal" logic—because it deals with the *shapes* of symbol-strings, not directly with their meaning. As Searle puts it, syntactical rules

operate on "uninterpreted formal symbols": on strings of symbols which could mean almost anything at all, or nothing at all. (For example, "(P & Q)" could mean "The corn is high and your Mamma's good looking," or "Hitler and Stalin were not nice men," or "1 + 1 = 3 and 2^3 is 7," or we might not even *know* what it means if the letters remain uninterpreted.)

So where does the meaning come from? The meaning of the symbols in a language is provided by its semantics (a system for specifying what any grammatical sentence of the language *means* and whether or not it is *true*). In a natural language like English the semantics is extremely complicated to specify; but in most formalized languages the semantics is much simpler, consisting of an *interpretation* of the meaning and/or the truth value of all the most elementary building blocks of the language.

4. Finally, another motto of Searle's which deserves explanation is the slogan "everything is a digital computer." This is, in some circles, quite a controversial claim, though there is a widely accepted assumption somewhat similar to this thesis. The widely accepted claim is called the Church-Turing thesis, dates back to 1936, and says that *any* effective mathematical method can be computed on a "Universal Turing Machine." What that means is that any finite computation (no matter how large or complex) can, in principle, be run on any physical system capable of a few very simple operations. These operations are, basically, just moving between a finite number of different internal states, and perhaps "writing" and "erasing" at least two symbols in a large enough workspace. (See the notes to the Putnam selection in this chapter for more details on Turing Machines.) From this it follows that a large number of physical systems that we would not ordinarily think of as computers are nevertheless capable of running computations—they could be *used* as computers: notorious examples include the infinite roll of toilet paper and pile of small stones alluded to by Searle, or the population of Belgium all linked together by two-way radios and fol-

lowing certain simple instructions, or a hive of trained bees shifting position on cue and using eggs and honey as symbols.

The even more radical, and more controversial, claim which Searle wants to make is that any, even remotely complex, hunk of matter can be described as if it *already* is running a computer program and (according to Searle) since there is nothing more to being a computer than being describable in this way, *everything* already *is* a computer. The basic idea here is that anything (even a rock) can be correctly described as passing through a finite sequence of different internal states (e.g., different states of radioactive decay). Therefore, we can always write a program which will describe the transformation of each state into the next, and which will also interpret some aspects of the physical system, at a particular time, as "outputs"—i.e., we can draw up a Machine Table (see the notes on Putnam) to describe the actual behavior of the system over time. The rock is following the instructions laid down in the Machine Table, the Machine Table is a computer program; this means that the system is literally *running* whatever program the Machine Table describes. Thus, rocks are computers—indeed, everything is a computer. Even more strangely, it has been argued (in the appendix to Hilary Putnam's book *Representation and Reality*, for example) that we could interpret the inner states of our rock in any way we choose in order to construct whatever Machine Table we desire. For example, we could interpret the rock as running a program for speaking fluent Chinese.

Some Common Misconceptions

1. Some people reading this article for the first time think Searle is arguing that no computer program could exactly replicate the linguistic behavior of a fluent speaker of Chinese. However this is not correct: by contrast, Searle is actually willing to *assume* without argument that such a program *could* be written, and it is

just this program which he imagines running in the Chinese room (i.e., from the outside, the Chinese room *does* appear to speak Chinese). Furthermore, Searle thinks that Chinese people could also be correctly described as running a language-speaking program, and so whatever program can be read from the brains of sinophones is one which is capable of producing Chinese-language behavior.

2. Despite framing the target of his attack as "strong AI," Searle doesn't in fact argue that computers do not, or could never, really think. He is making the slightly (but importantly) different case that thought is not essentially *just* computation. In other words, according to Searle, computers might well someday be able to really think—but, if they do think, it will not be *because* they are computers but for some other reason.

Suggestions for Critical Reflection

1. Searle uses the Chinese room thought experiment to argue against strong AI. If he is successful in defeating strong AI, do you think *any* form of functionalism could survive? (And, of course, *is* he successful?) What theories of the mind, if any, (e.g., dualism, behaviorism, identity theory) would be left standing by Searle's argument?

2. What do you think of the various responses to his argument which Searle considers and rejects? Are any of them more plausible than Searle gives them credit for? Can you think of any plausible response which Searle has not already considered?

3. Searle is quite ready to admit that *from the outside* the Chinese room really looks like it speaks Chinese. How far does his argument depend upon his insistence that we take a view "from the inside," a so-called "first-person" perspective? Is this methodological maxim legitimate or is it a mistake?

4. What would it be like to look at the details of a physical system which does understand (such as the human brain) and "see the understand-

ing"? Does the fact that we don't "see" the intentionality in the Chinese room cut any philosophical ice?

5. The cognitive scientist Douglas Hofstadter spoke for many in the cognitive science community when he said that Searle's article is more like a "religious diatribe against AI, masquerading as a serious scientific argument" than a serious objection to functionalism or computationalism. What do you think? Is this response warranted, or is it just an expression of the desire to hang onto strong AI at all costs?

6. What is the importance of the distinction between intrinsic and derived intentionality for this argument? (E.g., can you re-state the argument using this distinction, and if so does it make it any stronger and clearer?) Is this distinction a sensible one?

7. Searle argues that computer programs do not have an intrinsic semantics, but at the time he wrote this article he assumed that they do have an objective syntax. Is this right? Or does the claim that "everything is a digital computer" suggest that computer programs don't have an intrinsic syntax either? If computer syntax is also derived rather than intrinsic, does this make Searle's argument stronger or weaker (or neither)?

Suggestions for Further Reading

The journal *Behavioral and Brain Sciences*, where Searle's article originally appeared, is an innovative journal which publishes, in addition to "target articles," extensive "peer commentaries" (dozens of short pieces, often by well-established experts in the relevant field) which raise criticisms of the article, and then a response by the author. The first place to read more about Searle's Chinese room, therefore, is in *Behavioral and Brain Sciences*, Volume 3, Issue 3 (September 1980). Especially notable are the comments by Fodor and Dennett and Searle's response "Intrinsic Intentionality." *Scientific American* 262 (January 1990) also includes a skirmish over the Chinese room between Searle and Paul and Patricia Churchland.

Searle re-presents his Chinese room argument in various places, including *Minds, Brains, and Science* (Harvard University Press, 1984), *The Rediscovery of the Mind* (MIT Press, 1992), and *The Mystery of Consciousness* (New York Review, 1997). One of Searle's latest books, in which he tries to draw together the various threads of his thought, is *Mind, Language and Society: Philosophy in the Real World* (Basic Books, 1998). There is a collection of essays about Searle called *John Searle and His Critics*, edited by Ernest Lepore and Robert van Gulick (Blackwell, 1991), and a book describing his philosophy, *John Searle*, by Nick Fotion (Princeton University Press, 2000).

"Minds, Brains and Programs"[2]

What psychological and philosophical significance should we attach to recent efforts at computer simulations of human cognitive capacities? In answering this question, I find it useful to distinguish what I will call 'strong' AI from 'weak' or 'cautious' AI (Artificial Intelligence). According to weak AI, the principal value of the computer in the study of the mind is that it gives us a very powerful tool. For example, it enables us to formulate and test hypotheses in a more rigorous and precise fashion. But according to strong AI, the computer is not merely a tool in the study of the mind; rather, the appropriately programmed computer really *is* a mind, in the sense that computers given the right programs can be literally said to understand and have other cognitive states. In strong AI, because the programmed computer has cognitive states, the programs are not mere tools that enable us to test psychological explanations; rather, the programs are themselves the explanations.

I have no objection to the claims of weak AI, at least as far as this article is concerned. My discussion here will be directed at the claims I have defined as those of strong AI, specifically the claim that the appropriately programmed computer literally has cognitive states and that the programs thereby explain human cogni-

---

2   This article was first published in *Behavioral and Brain Sciences*, Volume 3, Issue 3 (September 1980), pp. 417–424.

tion. When I hereafter refer to AI, I have in mind the strong version, as expressed by these two claims.

I will consider the work of Roger Schank and his colleagues at Yale (Schank and Abelson 1977), because I am more familiar with it than I am with any other similar claims, and because it provides a very clear example of the sort of work I wish to examine. But nothing that follows depends upon the details of Schank's programs. The same arguments would apply to Winograd's SHRDLU (Winograd 1973), Weizenbaum's ELIZA (Weizenbaum 1965),[3] and indeed any Turing machine[4] simulation of human mental phenomena.

Very briefly, and leaving out the various details, one can describe Schank's program as follows: the aim of the program is to simulate the human ability to understand stories. It is characteristic of human beings' story-understanding capacity that they can answer questions about the story even though the information that they give was never explicitly stated in the story. Thus, for example, suppose you are given the following story: 'A man went into a restaurant and ordered a hamburger. When the hamburger arrived it was burned to a crisp, and the man stormed out of the restaurant angrily, without paying for the hamburger or leaving a tip.' Now, if you are asked 'Did the man eat the hamburger?' you will presumably answer, 'No, he did not.' Similarly, if you are given the following story: 'A man went into a restaurant and ordered a hamburger; when the hamburger came he was very pleased with it; and as he left the restaurant he gave the waitress a large tip before paying his bill,' and you are asked the question, 'Did the man eat the hamburger?', you will presumably answer, 'Yes, he ate the hamburger.' Now Schank's machines can similarly answer questions about restaurants in this fashion. To do this, they have a 'representation' of the sort of information that human beings have about restaurants, which enables them to answer such questions as those above, given these sorts of stories. When the machine is given the story and then asked the question, the machine will print out answers of the sort that we would expect human beings to give if told similar stories. Partisans of strong AI claim that in this question and answer sequence the machine is not only simulating a human ability but also

1.   that the machine can literally be said to *understand* the story and provide the answers to questions, and

2.   that what the machine and its program do *explain* the human ability to understand the story and answer questions about it.

Both claims seem to me to be totally unsupported by Schank's[5] work, as I will attempt to show in what follows.

One way to test any theory of the mind is to ask oneself what it would be like if my mind actually worked on the principles that the theory says all minds work on. Let us apply this test to the Schank program with the following *Gedankenexperiment*.[6] Suppose

---

3   SHRDLU was a program which manipulated virtual blocks in a simulated space and answered questions about them. ELIZA was a program (versions of it can still be found and played with on the Internet) which appears to carry on a conversation with a human interlocutor: that is, if you ask it questions, it will respond to you (in a manner rather like a psychotherapist) and ask you questions in return. Interestingly, Terry Winograd has now repudiated his earlier research project (typified by SHRDLU) and, like Searle, denies that human intelligence can be understood in terms of the computational manipulation of representations. Joseph Weizenbaum, too, has said publicly and forcefully that he thinks people were over-impressed by ELIZA's human-like performance, and that computers can have no real intelligence since they do not understand the symbols they are using.

4   See the notes to the reading by Hilary Putnam in this chapter for more information on Turing Machines.

5   [Author's note] I am not, of course, saying that Schank himself is committed to these claims.

6   This is German for "thought experiment." A thought experiment is a controlled exercise of the imagination in which a test case is carefully constructed to see if it is coherent, or whether it is compatible with some proposed theory. Thought experiments are used by philosophers, but also by theoretical physicists (Galileo and Einstein, for example, made extensive use of them). The idea is to try to find out what is and is not *possibly* true (an *empirical* experiment tries to find out what is actually true).

that I'm locked in a room and given a large batch of Chinese writing. Suppose furthermore (as is indeed the case) that I know no Chinese, either written or spoken, and that I'm not even confident that I could recognize Chinese writing as Chinese writing distinct from, say, Japanese writing or meaningless squiggles. To me, Chinese writing is just so many meaningless squiggles. Now suppose further that after this first batch of Chinese writing I am given a second batch of Chinese script together with a set of rules for correlating the second batch with the first batch. The rules are in English, and I understand these rules as well as any other native speaker of English. They enable me to correlate one set of formal symbols with another set of formal symbols, and all that 'formal' means here is that I can identify the symbols entirely by their shapes. Now suppose also that I am given a third batch of Chinese symbols together with some instructions, again in English, that enable me to correlate elements of this third batch with the first two batches, and these rules instruct me how to give back certain Chinese symbols with certain sorts of shapes in response to certain sorts of shapes given to me in the third batch. Unknown to me, the people who are giving me all these symbols call the first batch 'a script,' they call the second batch a 'story,' and they call the third batch 'questions.' Furthermore, they call the symbols I give them back in response to the third batch 'answers to the questions,' and the set of rules in English that they gave me, they call 'the program.' Now just to complicate the story a little, imagine that these people also give me stories in English, which I understand, and they then ask me questions in English about these stories, and I give them back answers in English. Suppose also that after a while I get so good at following the instructions for manipulating the Chinese symbols and the programmers get so good at writing the programs that from the external point of view—that is, from the point of view of somebody outside the room in which I am locked—my answers to the questions are absolutely indistinguishable from those of native Chinese speakers. Nobody just looking at my answers can tell that I don't speak a word of Chinese. Let us also suppose that my answers to the English questions are, as they no doubt would be, indistinguishable from those of other native English speakers, for the simple reason

that I am a native English speaker. From the external point of view—from the point of view of somebody reading my 'answers'—the answers to the Chinese questions and the English questions are equally good. But in the Chinese case, unlike the English case, I produce the answers by manipulating uninterpreted formal symbols. As far as the Chinese is concerned, I simply behave like a computer; I perform computational operations on formally specified elements. For the purposes of the Chinese, I am simply an instantiation of the computer program.

Now the claims made by strong AI are that the programmed computer understands the stories and that the program in some sense explains human understanding. But we are now in a position to examine these claims in light of our thought-experiment.

1. As regards the first claim, it seems to me quite obvious in the example that I do not understand a word of the Chinese stories. I have inputs and outputs that are indistinguishable from those of the native Chinese speaker, and I can have any formal program you like, but I still understand nothing. For the same reasons, Schank's computer understands nothing of any stories, whether in Chinese, English or whatever, since in the Chinese case the computer is me, and in cases where the computer is not me, the computer has nothing more than I have in the case where I understand nothing.

2. As regards the second claim, that the program explains human understanding, we can see that the computer and its program do not provide sufficient conditions of understanding since the computer and the program are functioning, and there is no understanding. But does it even provide a necessary condition or a significant contribution to understanding? One of the claims made by the supporters of strong AI is that when I understand a story in English, what I am doing is exactly the same—or perhaps more of the same—as what I was doing in manipulating the Chinese symbols. It is simply more formal symbol-manipulation that distinguishes the case in English, where I do understand, from the case in Chinese, where I don't. I have not demonstrated that this claim is false, but it would certainly appear an incredible claim in the example. Such plausibility as the claim has derives from the

supposition that we can construct a program that will have the same inputs and outputs as native speakers, and in addition we assume that speakers have some level of description where they are also instantiations of a program. On the basis of these two assumptions we assume that even if Schank's program isn't the whole story about understanding, it may be part of the story. Well, I suppose that is an empirical possibility, but not the slightest reason has so far been given to believe that it is true, since what is suggested—though certainly not demonstrated—by the example is that the computer program is simply irrelevant to my understanding of the story. In the Chinese case I have everything that artificial intelligence can put into me by way of a program, and I understand nothing; in the English case I understand everything, and there is so far no reason at all to suppose that my understanding has anything to do with computer programs, that is, with computational operations on purely formally specified elements. As long as the program is defined in terms of computational operations on purely formally defined elements, what the example suggests is that these by themselves have no interesting connection with understanding. They are certainly not sufficient conditions, and not the slightest reason has been given to suppose that they are necessary conditions or even that they make a significant contribution to understanding. Notice that the force of the argument is not simply that different machines can have the same input and output while operating on different formal principles—that is not the point at all. Rather, whatever purely formal principles you put into the computer, they will not be sufficient for understanding, since a human will be able to follow the formal principles without understanding anything. No reason whatever has been offered to suppose that such principles are necessary or even contributory, since no reason has been given to suppose that when I understand English I am operating with any formal program at all.

Well, then, what is it that I have in the case of the English sentences that I do not have in the case of the Chinese sentences? The obvious answer is that I know what the former mean, while I haven't the faintest idea what the latter mean. But in what does this consist and

why couldn't we give it to a machine, whatever it is? I will return to this question later, but first I want to continue with the example.

I have had the occasions to present this example to several workers in artificial intelligence, and, interestingly, they do not seem to agree on what the proper reply to it is. I get a surprising variety of replies, and in what follows I will consider the most common of these (specified along with their geographic origins).

But I first want to block some common misunderstandings about 'understanding': in many of these discussions one finds a lot of fancy footwork about the word 'understanding.' My critics point out that there are many different degrees of understanding; that 'understanding' is not a simple two-place predicate;[7] that there are even different kinds and levels of understanding, and often the law of excluded middle[8] doesn't even apply in a straightforward way to statements of the form 'x understands y'; that in many cases it is a matter for decision and not a simple matter of fact whether x understands y; and so on. To all of these points I want to say: of course, of course. But they have nothing to do with the points at issue. There are clear cases in which 'understanding' literally applies and clear cases in which it does not apply; and these two sorts of cases are all I need for this argument.[9] I understand stories in English; to a lesser degree I can understand stories in French; to a

---

7 A two-place predicate is (roughly) a "describing phrase" which is used to describe two things at once: for example "___ is to the left of ___" or "___ and ___ are sisters" or "___ understands ___."

8 This is the logical principle which, when it applies, says that for any proposition p, either p or not-p: that is, there is nothing 'intermediate' between something being so and something not being so. (Incidentally, this should not be confused with the claim that, for any proposition p, p is either true or false: this principle, called the principle of bivalence, is logically different and has somewhat different implications.)

9 [Author's note] Also, 'understanding' implies both the possession of mental (intentional) states and the truth (validity, success) of these states. For the purposes of this discussion we are concerned only with the possession of the states.

still lesser degree, stories in German; and in Chinese, not at all. My car and my adding machine, on the other hand, understand nothing: they are not in that line of business. We often attribute 'understanding' and other cognitive predicates by metaphor and analogy to cars, adding machines, and other artifacts, but nothing is proved by such attributions. We say, 'The door *knows* when to open because of its photoelectric cell,' 'The adding machine *knows how* (*understands how*, is *able*) to do addition and subtraction but not division,' and 'The thermostat *perceives* changes in the temperature.' The reason we make these attributions is quite interesting, and it has to do with the fact that in artifacts we extend our own intentionality,[10] our tools are extensions of our purposes, and so we find it natural to make metaphorical attributions of intentionality to them; but I take it no philosophical ice is cut by such examples. The sense in which an automatic door 'understands instructions' from its photoelectric cell is not at all the sense in which I understand English. If the sense in which Schank's programmed computers understand stories is supposed to be the metaphorical sense in which the door understands, and not the sense in which I understand English, the issue would not be worth discussing. But Newell and Simon (1963) write that the kind of cognition they claim for computers is exactly the same as for human beings. I like the straightforwardness of this claim, and it is the sort of claim I will be considering. I will argue that in the literal sense the programmed computer understands what the car and the adding machine understand, namely, exactly nothing. The computer understanding is not just (like my understanding of German) partial or incomplete; it is zero.

Now to the replies:

1. The Systems Reply (Berkeley)

'While it is true that the individual person who is locked in the room does not understand the story, the fact is that he is merely part of a whole system, and the system does understand the story. The person has a large ledger in front of him in which are written the rules, he has a lot of scratch paper and pencils for doing calculations, he has "data banks" of sets of Chinese symbols. Now, understanding is not being ascribed to the mere individual; rather it is being ascribed to this whole system of which he is a part.'

My response to the systems theory is quite simple: let the individual internalize all of these elements of the system. He memorizes the rules in the ledger and the data banks of Chinese symbols, and he does all the calculations in his head. The individual then incorporates the entire system. There isn't anything at all to the system that he does not encompass. We can even get rid of the room and suppose he works outdoors. All the same, he understands nothing of the Chinese, and *a fortiori*[11] neither does the system, because there isn't anything in the system that isn't in him. If he doesn't understand, then there is no way the system could understand because the system is just a part of him.

Actually I feel somewhat embarrassed to give even this answer to the systems theory because the theory seems to me so unplausible to start with. The idea is that while a person doesn't understand Chinese, somehow the *conjunction* of that person and bits of paper might understand Chinese. It is not easy for me to imagine how someone who was not in the grip of an ideology would find the idea at all plausible. Still, I think many people who are committed to the ideology of strong AI will in the end be inclined to say something very much like this; so let us pursue it a bit further. According to one version of this view, while the man in the internalized systems example doesn't understand Chinese in the sense that a native Chinese speaker does (because, for example, he doesn't know that the story refers to restaurants and hamburgers, etc.), still 'the man as a formal symbol-manipulation system' *really does understand Chinese*. The subsystem of the man that is the formal symbol-manipulation system for Chinese should not be confused with the subsystem for English.

So there are really two subsystems in the man; one understands English, the other Chinese, and 'it's just

---

10 [Author's note] Intentionality is by definition that feature of certain mental states by which they are directed at or about objects and states of affairs in the world. Thus, beliefs, desires, and intentions are intentional states; undirected forms of anxiety and depression are not. For further discussion see Searle (1979b).

---

11 Even more conclusively.

464 PHILOSOPHY OF MIND

that the two systems have little to do with each other.' But, I want to reply, not only do they have little to do with each other, they are not even remotely alike. The subsystem that understands English (assuming we allow ourselves to talk in this jargon of 'subsystems' for a moment) knows that the stories are about restaurants and eating hamburgers, he knows that he is being asked questions about restaurants and that he is answering questions as best he can by making various inferences from the content of the story, and so on. But the Chinese system knows none of this. Whereas the English system knows that 'hamburgers' refers to hamburgers, the Chinese subsystem knows only that 'squiggle squiggle' is followed by 'squoggle squoggle.' All he knows is that various formal symbols are being introduced at one end and manipulated according to rules written in English, and other symbols are going out at the other end. The whole point of the original example was to argue that such symbol manipulation by itself couldn't be sufficient for understanding Chinese in any literal sense because the man could write 'squoggle squoggle' after 'squiggle squiggle' without understanding anything in Chinese. And it doesn't meet that argument to postulate subsystems within the man, because the subsystems are no better off than the man was in the first place; they still don't have anything even remotely like what the English-speaking man (or subsystem) has. Indeed, in the case as described, the Chinese subsystem is simply a part of the English subsystem, a part that engages in meaningless symbol manipulation according to rules in English.

Let us ask ourselves what is supposed to motivate the systems reply in the first place; that is, what *independent* grounds are there supposed to be for saying that the agent must have a subsystem within him that literally understands stories in Chinese? As far as I can tell the only grounds are that in the example I have the same input and output as native Chinese speakers and a program that goes from one to the other. But the whole point of the examples has been to try to show that that couldn't be sufficient for understanding, in the sense in which I understand stories in English, because a person, and hence the set of systems that go to make up a person, could have the right combination of input, output, and program and still not understand anything in the relevant literal sense in which I under-

stand English. The only motivation for saying there *must* be a subsystem in me that understands Chinese is that I have a program and I pass the Turing-test;[12] I can fool native Chinese speakers. But precisely one of the points at issue is the adequacy of the Turing-test. The example shows that there could be two 'systems,' both of which pass the Turing-test, but only one of which understands; and it is no argument against this point to say that since they both pass the Turing-test they must both understand, since this claim fails to meet the argument that the system in me that understands English has a great deal more than the system that merely processes Chinese. In short, the systems reply simply begs the question by insisting without argument that the system must understand Chinese.

Furthermore, the systems reply would appear to lead to consequences that are independently absurd. If we are to conclude that there must be cognition in me on the grounds that I have a certain sort of input and output and a program in between, then it looks like all sorts of noncognitive subsystems are going to turn out to be cognitive. For example, there is a level of description at which my stomach does information processing, and it instantiates any number of computer-programs, but I take it we do not want to say that it has any understanding (cf. Pylyshyn 1980). But if we accept the systems reply, then it is hard to see how we avoid saying that stomach, heart, liver, and so on, are all understanding subsystems, since there is no principled way to distinguish the motivation for saying the Chinese subsystem understands from saying that the stomach understands. It is, by the way, not an answer to this point to say that the Chinese system has information as input and output and the stomach has food and food products as input and output, since

---

12 The Turing test was proposed by the British mathematician Alan Turing in 1950 as a way of determining whether a computer can think. Basically, a person and a computer—whose respective identities are kept hidden during the test—are both asked a series of questions, and are allowed to say anything they like in answer to those questions in order to persuade their interrogator that they are a human being. If the tester cannot tell the difference between them, then the computer passes the test.

from the point of view of the agent, from my point of view, there is no information in either the food or the Chinese—the Chinese is just so many meaningless squiggles. The information in the Chinese case is solely in the eyes of the programmers and the interpreters, and there is nothing to prevent them from treating the input and output of my digestive organs as information if they so desire.

This last point bears on some independent problems in strong AI, and it is worth digressing for a moment to explain it. If strong AI is to be a branch of psychology, then it must be able to distinguish those systems that are genuinely mental from those that are not. It must be able to distinguish the principles on which the mind works from those on which non-mental systems work; otherwise it will offer us no explanations of what is specifically mental about the mental. And the mental–non-mental distinction cannot be just in the eye of the beholder but it must be intrinsic to the systems; otherwise it would be up to any beholder to treat people as non-mental and, for example, hurricanes as mental if he likes. But quite often in the AI literature the distinction is blurred in ways that would in the long run prove disastrous to the claim that AI is a cognitive enquiry. McCarthy, for example, writes, 'Machines as simple as thermostats can be said to have beliefs, and having beliefs seems to be a characteristic of most machines capable of problem solving performances' (McCarthy 1979). Anyone who thinks strong AI has a chance as a theory of the mind ought to ponder the implications of that remark. We are asked to accept it as a discovery of strong AI that the hunk of metal on the wall that we use to regulate the temperature has beliefs in exactly the same sense that we, our spouses, and our children have beliefs, and furthermore that 'most' of the other machines in the room—telephone, tape recorder, adding machine, electric light switch—also have beliefs in this literal sense. It is not the aim of this article to argue against McCarthy's point, so I will simply assert the following without argument. The study of the mind starts with such facts as that humans have belief, while thermostats, telephones, and adding machines don't. If you get a theory that denies this point you have produced a counter-example to the theory and the theory is false. One gets the impression that

people in AI who write this sort of thing think they can get away with it because they don't really take it seriously, and they don't think anyone else will either. I propose for a moment at least, to take it seriously. Think hard for one minute about what would be necessary to establish that that hunk of metal on the wall over there had real beliefs, beliefs with direction of fit, propositional content, and conditions of satisfaction; beliefs that had the possibility of being strong beliefs or weak beliefs; nervous, anxious, or secure beliefs; dogmatic, rational, or superstitious beliefs; blind faiths or hesitant cognitions; any kind of beliefs. The thermostat is not a candidate. Neither is stomach, liver, adding machine, or telephone. However, since we are taking the idea seriously, notice that its truth would be fatal to strong AI's claim to be a science of the mind. For now the mind is everywhere. What we wanted to know is what distinguishes the mind from thermostats and livers. And if McCarthy were right, strong AI wouldn't have a hope of telling us that.

2. The Robot Reply (Yale)

'Suppose we wrote a different kind of program from Schank's program. Suppose we put a computer inside a robot, and this computer would not just take in formal symbols as input and give out formal symbols as output, but rather would actually operate the robot in such a way that the robot does something very much like perceiving, walking, moving about, hammering nails, eating, drinking—anything you like. The robot would, for example, have a television camera attached to it that enabled it to "see," it would have arms and legs that enabled it to "act," and all of this would be controlled by its computer "brain." Such a robot would, unlike Schank's computer, have genuine understanding and other mental states.'

The first thing to notice about the robot reply is that it tacitly concedes that cognition is not solely a matter of formal symbol-manipulation, since this reply adds a set of causal relations with the outside world (cf. Fodor 1980). But the answer to the robot reply is that the addition of such 'perceptual' and 'motor' capacities adds nothing by way of understanding, in particular, or intentionality, in general, to Schank's original program. To see this, notice that the same thought-experiment applies to the robot case. Suppose that instead of the computer inside the robot, you put me inside the room and, as in the original Chinese case, you give me more Chinese symbols with more instructions in English for matching Chinese symbols to Chinese symbols and feeding back Chinese symbols to the outside. Suppose, unknown to me, some of the Chinese symbols that come to me come from a television camera attached to the robot and other Chinese symbols that I am giving out serve to make the motors inside the robot move the robot's legs or arms. It is important to emphasize that all I am doing is manipulating formal symbols: I know none of these other facts. I am receiving 'information' from the robot's 'perceptual' apparatus, and I am giving out 'instructions' to its motor apparatus without knowing either of these facts. I am the robot's homunculus,[13] but unlike the traditional homunculus, I don't know what's going on. I don't understand anything except the rules for symbol manipulation. Now in this case I want to say that the robot has no intentional states at all; it is simply moving about as a result of its electrical wiring and its program. And furthermore, by instantiating the program I have no intentional states of the relevant type. All I do is follow instructions about manipulating formal symbols.

3. The Brain Simulator Reply (Berkeley and MIT)

'Suppose we design a program that doesn't represent information that we have about the world, such as the information in Schank's scripts, but simulates the actual sequence of neuron firings at the synapses of the brain of a native Chinese speaker when he understands stories in Chinese and gives answers to them. The machine takes in Chinese stories and questions about them as input, it simulates the formal structure of actual Chinese brains in processing these stories, and it gives out Chinese answers as outputs. We can even imagine that the machine operates, not with a single serial program, but with a whole set of programs operating in parallel, in the manner that actual human brains presumably operate when they process natural language. Now surely in such a case we would have to say that the machine understood the stories; and if we refuse to say that, wouldn't we also have to deny that native Chinese speakers understood the stories? At the level of the synapses, what would or could be different about the program of the computer and the program of the Chinese brain?'

Before countering this reply I want to digress to note that it is an odd reply for any partisan of artificial intelligence (or functionalism, etc.) to make: I thought the whole idea of strong AI is that we don't need to know how the brain works to know how the mind works. The basic hypothesis, or so I had supposed, was that there is a level of mental operations consisting of computational processes over formal elements that constitute the essence of the mental and can be realized in all sorts of different brain processes, in the same way that any computer program can be realized in different computer hardwares: on the assumptions of strong AI, the mind is to the brain as the program is to the hardware, and thus we can understand the mind without doing neurophysiology. If we had to know how the brain worked to do AI, we wouldn't bother with AI. However, even getting this close to the operation of the brain is still not sufficient to produce understanding. To see this, imagine that instead of a monolingual man in a room shuffling symbols we have the man operate an elaborate set of water pipes with valves connecting them. When the man receives the Chinese symbols, he looks up in the program, written in English, which valves he has to turn on and off. Each water connection corresponds to a synapse in the Chinese brain, and the whole system is rigged up so that after all the right firings, that is after turning on all the right faucets, the Chinese answers pop out at the output end of the series of pipes.

---

13   Literally "little man." The idea behind the (mythical) homuncular theory is that our actions are to be explained by little men in our head, who perform various mental functions such as seeing, hearing, planning, instructing the limbs to move, and so on. Even if the notion of a "little man" is not taken too literally, this general form of psychological theory is often accused of committing the "homunculus fallacy": explaining visual perception by postulating an internal device which "scans" or "views" mental images displayed on a sort of inner screen, for example, is actually to explain nothing at all, since the inner device "sees" the internal images and this *seeing* is precisely what we wanted to explain in the first place.

Now where is the understanding in this system? It takes Chinese as input, it simulates the formal structure of the synapses of the Chinese brain, and it gives Chinese as output. But the man certainly doesn't understand Chinese, and neither do the water pipes, and if we are tempted to adopt what I think is the absurd view that somehow the *conjunction* of man *and* water pipes understands, remember that in principle the man can internalize the formal structure of the water pipes and do all the 'neuron firings' in his imagination. The problem with the brain simulator is that it is simulating the wrong things about the brain. As long as it simulates only the formal structure of the sequence of neuron firings at the synapses, it won't have simulated what matters about the brain, namely its causal properties, its ability to produce intentional states. And that the formal properties are not sufficient for the causal properties is shown by the water pipe example: we can have all the formal properties carved off from the relevant neurobiological causal properties.

4. The Combination Reply (Berkeley and Stanford)

'While each of the previous three replies might not be completely convincing by itself as a refutation of the Chinese room counter-example, if you take all three together they are collectively much more convincing and even decisive. Imagine a robot with a brain-shaped computer lodged in its cranial cavity, imagine the computer programmed with all the synapses of a human brain, imagine the whole behaviour of the robot is undistinguishable from human behaviour, and now think of the whole thing as a unified system and not just as a computer with inputs and outputs. Surely in such a case we would have to ascribe intentionality to the system.'

I entirely agree that in such a case we would find it rational and indeed irresistible to accept the hypothesis that the robot had intentionality, as long as we knew nothing more about it. Indeed, besides appearance and behaviour, the other elements of the combination are really irrelevant. If we could build a robot whose behaviour was indistinguishable over a large range from human behaviour, we would attribute intentionality to it, pending some reason not to. We wouldn't need to know in advance that its computer brain was a formal analogue of the human brain.

But I really don't see that this is any help to the claims of strong AI; and here's why: According to strong AI, instantiating a formal program with the right input and output is a sufficient condition of, indeed is constitutive of, intentionality. As Newell (1979) puts it, the essence of the mental is the operation of a physical-symbol system. But the attributions of intentionality that we make to the robot in this example have nothing to do with formal programs. They are simply based on the assumption that if the robot looks and behaves sufficiently like us, then we would suppose, until proven otherwise, that it must have mental states like ours that cause and are expressed by its behaviour and it must have an inner mechanism capable of producing such mental states. If we knew independently how to account for its behaviour without such assumptions we would not attribute intentionality to it, especially if we knew it had a formal program. And this is precisely the point of my earlier reply to objection 2.

Suppose we knew that the robot's behaviour was entirely accounted for by the fact that a man inside it was receiving uninterpreted formal symbols from the robot's sensory receptors and sending out uninterpreted formal symbols to its motor mechanisms, and the man was doing this symbol manipulation in accordance with a bunch of rules. Furthermore, suppose the man knows none of these facts about the robot, all he knows is which operations to perform on which meaningless symbols. In such a case we would regard the robot as an ingenious mechanical dummy. The hypothesis that the dummy has a mind would now be unwarranted and unnecessary, for there is now no longer any reason to ascribe intentionality to the robot or to the system of which it is a part (except of course for the man's intentionality in manipulating the symbols). The formal symbol manipulations go on, the input and output are correctly matched, but the only real locus of intentionality is the man, and he doesn't know any of the relevant intentional states; he doesn't, for example, *see* what comes into the robot's eyes, he doesn't *intend* to move the robot's arm, and he doesn't *understand* any of the remarks made to or by the robot. Nor, for the reasons stated earlier, does the system of which man and robot are a part.

To see this point, contrast this case with cases in which we find it completely natural to ascribe intentionality to members of certain other primate species such as apes and monkeys and to domestic animals such as dogs. The reasons we find it natural are, roughly, two: we can't make sense of the animal's behaviour without the ascription of intentionality, and we can see that the beasts are made of similar stuff to ourselves—that is an eye, that a nose, this is its skin, and so on. Given the coherence of the animal's behaviour and the assumption of the same causal stuff underlying it, we assume both that the animal must have mental states underlying its behaviour, and that the mental states must be produced by mechanisms made out of the stuff that is like our stuff. We would certainly make similar assumptions about the robot unless we had some reason not to, but as soon as we knew that the behaviour was the result of a formal program, and that the actual causal properties of the physical substance were irrelevant we would abandon the assumption of intentionality. (See Multiple authors 1978.)

There are two other responses to my example that come up frequently (and so are worth discussing) but really miss the point.

5. The Other Minds Reply (Yale)

'How do you know that other people understand Chinese or anything else? Only by their behaviour. Now the computer can pass the behavioural tests as well as they can (in principle), so if you are going to attribute cognition to other people you must in principle also attribute it to computers.'

This objection really is only worth a short reply. The problem in this discussion is not about how I know that other people have cognitive states, but rather what it is that I am attributing to them when I attribute cognitive states to them. The thrust of the argument is that it couldn't be just computational processes and their output because the computational processes and their output can exist without the cognitive state. It is no answer to this argument to feign anesthesia. In 'cognitive sciences'[14] one presupposes the reality and knowability of the mental in the same way that in physical sciences one has to presuppose the reality and knowability of physical objects.

6. The Many Mansions Reply (Berkeley)

'Your whole argument presupposes that AI is only about analogue and digital computers. But that just happens to be the present state of technology. Whatever these causal processes are that you say are essential for intentionality (assuming you are right), eventually we will be able to build devices that have these causal processes, and that will be artificial intelligence. So your arguments are in no way directed at the ability of artificial intelligence to produce and explain cognition.'

I really have no objection to this reply save to say that it in effect trivializes the project of strong AI by redefining it as whatever artificially produces and explains cognition. The interest of the original claim made on behalf of artificial intelligence is that it was a precise, well-defined thesis: mental processes are computational processes over formally defined elements. I have been concerned to challenge that thesis. If the claim is redefined so that it is no longer that thesis, my objections no longer apply because there is no longer a testable hypothesis for them to apply to.

Let us now return to the question I promised I would try to answer: granted that in my original example I understand the English and I do not understand the Chinese, and granted therefore that the machine doesn't understand either English or Chinese, still there must be something about me that makes it the case that I understand English and a corresponding something lacking in me makes it the case that I fail to understand Chinese. Now why couldn't we give those somethings, whatever they are, to a machine?

I see no reason in principle why we couldn't give a machine the capacity to understand English or Chi-

---

14   Cognitive science is an interdisciplinary research program, dating back to about 1956, which includes psychologists, computer scientists, neuroscientists, philosophers, linguists, and anthropologists. It is de-voted to the study and modeling of intelligent activity in humans and other, natural and artificial, organisms, and was founded on the assumption that thought can fruitfully be seen as a kind of information-processing: that is, the mind is an instrument which takes in data from the environment, processes it, and produces behavior as output.

nese, since in an important sense our bodies with our brains are precisely such machines. But I do see very strong arguments for saying that we could not give such a thing to a machine where the operation of the machine is defined solely in terms of computational processes over formally defined elements; that is, where the operation of the machine is defined as an instantiation of a computer program. It is not because I am the instantiation of a computer program that I am able to understand English and have other forms of intentionality (I am, I suppose, the instantiation of any number of computer programs), but as far as we know it is because I am a certain sort of organism with a certain biological (i.e., chemical and physical) structure, and this structure, under certain conditions, is causally capable of producing perception, action, understanding, learning, and other intentional phenomena. And part of the point of the present argument is that only something that had those causal powers could have that intentionality. Perhaps other physical and chemical processes could produce exactly these effects; perhaps, for example, Martians also have intentionality but their brains are made of different stuff. That is an empirical question, rather like the question whether photosynthesis can be done by something with a chemistry different from that of chlorophyll.

But the main point of the present argument is that no purely formal model will ever be sufficient by itself for intentionality because the formal properties are not by themselves constitutive of intentionality, and they have by themselves no causal power except the power, when instantiated, to produce the next stage of the formalism when the machine is running. And any other causal properties that particular realizations of the formal model have, are irrelevant to the formal model because we can always put the same formal model in a different realization where those causal properties are obviously absent. Even if, by some miracle, Chinese speakers exactly realize Schank's program, we can put the same program in English speakers, water pipes, or computers, none of which understand Chinese, the program notwithstanding.

What matters about brain operations is not the formal shadow cast by the sequence of synapses but rather the actual properties of the sequences. All the arguments for the strong version of artificial intelligence that I have seen insist on drawing an outline around the shadows cast by cognition and then claiming that the shadows are the real thing.

By way of concluding I want to try to state some of the general philosophical points implicit in the argument. For clarity I will try to do it in a question and answer fashion, and I begin with that old chestnut of a question:

'Could a machine think?'

The answer is, obviously, yes. We are precisely such machines.

'Yes, but could an artifact, a man-made machine, think?'

Assuming it is possible to produce artificially a machine with a nervous system, neurons with axons and dendrites, and all the rest of it, sufficiently like ours, again the answer to the question seems to be obviously, yes. If you can exactly duplicate the causes, you could duplicate the effects. And indeed it might be possible to produce consciousness, intentionality, and all the rest of it using some other sorts of chemical principles than those that human beings use. It is, as I said, an empirical question.

'OK, but could a digital computer think?'

If by 'digital computer' we mean anything at all that has a level of description where it can correctly be described as the instantiation of a computer program, then again the answer is, of course, yes, since we are the instantiations of any number of computer programs, and we can think.

'But could something think, understand, and so on *solely* in virtue of being a computer with the right sort of program? Could instantiating a program, the right program of course, by itself be a sufficient condition of understanding?'

This I think is the right question to ask, though it is usually confused with one or more of the earlier questions, and the answer to it is no.

'Why not?'

Because the formal symbol-manipulations by themselves don't have any intentionality; they are quite meaningless; they aren't even *symbol* manipulations, since the symbols don't symbolize anything. In the linguistic jargon, they have only a syntax but no semantics. Such intentionality as computers appear to have is solely in the minds of those who program them and those who use them, those who send in the input and those who interpret the output.

The aim of the Chinese room example was to try to show this by showing that as soon as we put something into the system that really does have intentionality (a man), and we program him with the formal program, you can see that the formal program carries no additional intentionality. It adds nothing, for example, to a man's ability to understand Chinese.

Precisely that feature of AI that seemed so appealing—the distinction between the program and the realization—proves fatal to the claim that simulation could be duplication. The distinction between the program and its realization in the hardware seems to be parallel to the distinction between the level of mental operations and the level of brain operations. And if we could describe the level of mental operations as a formal program, then it seems we could describe what was essential about the mind without doing either introspective psychology or neurophysiology of the brain. But the equation, 'mind is to brain as program is to hardware' breaks down at several points, among them the following three:

First, the distinction between program and realization has the consequence that the same program could have all sorts of crazy realizations that had no form of intentionality. Weizenbaum (1976: ch. 2), for example, shows in detail how to construct a computer using a roll of toilet paper and a pile of small stones. Similarly, the Chinese story-understanding program can be programmed into a sequence of water pipes, a set of wind machines, or a monolingual English speaker, none of which thereby acquires an understanding of Chinese. Stones, toilet paper, wind, and water pipes are the wrong kind of stuff to have intentionality in the first place—only something that has the same causal powers as brains can have intentionality—and though the English speaker has the right kind of stuff for intentionality you can easily see that he doesn't get any extra intentionality by memorizing the program, since memorizing it won't teach him Chinese.

Second, the program is purely formal, but the intentional states are not in that way formal. They are defined in terms of their content, not their form. The belief that it is raining, for example, is not defined as a certain formal shape, but as a certain mental content with conditions of satisfaction, a direction of fit (see Searle 1979a), and the like. Indeed the belief as such hasn't even got a formal shape in this syntactic

sense, since one and the same belief can be given an indefinite number of different syntactic expressions in different linguistic systems.

Third, as I mentioned before, mental states and events are literally a product of the operation of the brain, but the program is not in that way a product of the computer.

'Well if programs are in no way constitutive of mental processes, why have so many people believed the converse? That at least needs some explanation.'

I don't really know the answer to that one. The idea that computer simulations could be the real thing ought to have seemed suspicious in the first place because the computer isn't confined to simulating mental operations, by any means. No one supposes that computer simulations of a five-alarm fire will burn the neighbourhood down or that a computer simulation of a rainstorm will leave us all drenched. Why on earth would anyone suppose that a computer simulation of understanding actually understood anything? It is sometimes said that it would be frightfully hard to get computers to feel pain or fall in love, but love and pain are neither harder nor easier than cognition or anything else. For simulation, all you need is the right input and output and program in the middle that transforms the former into the latter. That is all the computer has for anything it does. To confuse simulation with duplication is the same mistake, whether it is pain, love, cognition, fires, or rainstorms.

Still, there are several reasons why AI must have seemed—and to many people perhaps still does seem—in some way to reproduce and thereby explain mental phenomena, and I believe we will not succeed in removing these illusions until we have fully exposed the reasons that give rise to them.

First, and perhaps most important, is a confusion about the notion of 'information-processing': many people in cognitive science believe that the human brain, with its mind, does something called 'information processing,' and analogously the computer with its program does information-processing; but fires and rainstorms, on the other hand, don't do information-processing at all. Thus, though the computer can simulate the formal features of any process whatever, it stands in a special relation to the mind and brain because when the computer is properly programmed, ideally with the same program as the brain, the information-processing is identical in the two cases, and this information-processing is really the essence of the mental. But the trouble with this argument is that it rests on an ambiguity in the notion of 'information.' In the sense in which people 'process information' when they reflect, say, on problems in arithmetic or when they read and answer questions about stories, the programmed computer does not do 'information-processing.' Rather, what it does is manipulate formal symbols. The fact that the programmer and the interpreter of the computer output use the symbols to stand for objects in the world is totally beyond the scope of the computer. The computer, to repeat, has a syntax but no semantics. Thus, if you type into the computer '2 plus 2 equals?' it will type out '4.' But it has no idea that '4' means 4 or that it means anything at all. And the point is not that it lacks some second-order information about the interpretation of its first-order symbols, but rather that its first-order symbols don't have any interpretations as far as the computer is concerned. All the computer has is more symbols. The introduction of the notion of 'information-processing' therefore produces a dilemma: either we construe the notion of 'information processing' in such a way that it implies intentionality as part of the process or we don't. If the former, then the programmed computer does not do information-processing, it only manipulates formal symbols. If the latter, then, though the computer does information-processing, it is only doing so in the sense in which adding machines, typewriters, stomachs, thermostats, rainstorms, and hurricanes do information-processing; namely, they have a level of description at which we can describe them as taking information in at one end, transforming it, and producing information as output. But in this case it is up to outside observers to interpret the input and output as information in the ordinary sense. And no similarity is established between the computer and the brain in terms of any similarity of information processing.

Second, in much of AI there is a residual behaviourism or operationalism.[15] Since appropriately pro-

grammed computers can have input-output patterns similar to those of human beings, we are tempted to postulate mental states in the computer similar to human mental states. But once we see that it is both conceptually and empirically possible for a system to have human capacities in some realm without having any intentionality at all, we should be able to overcome this impulse. My desk adding machine has calculating capacities, but no intentionality, and in this paper I have tried to show that a system could have input and output capabilities that duplicated those of a native Chinese speaker and still not understand Chinese, regardless of how it was programmed. The Turing test is typical of the tradition in being unashamedly behaviouristic and operationalistic, and I believe that if AI workers totally repudiated behaviourism and operationalism much of the confusion between simulation and duplication would be eliminated.

Third, this residual operationalism is joined to a residual form of dualism; indeed strong AI only makes sense given the dualistic assumption that, where the mind is concerned, the brain doesn't matter. In strong AI (and in functionalism, as well) what matters are programs, and programs are independent of their realization in machines; indeed, as far as AI is concerned, the same program could be realized by an electronic machine, a Cartesian mental substance, or a Hegelian world spirit.[16] The single most surprising

---

15 Operationalism is the view, formulated by the physicist P.W. Bridgman in 1927, that a word or concept should be *defined* by the operation we carry out to find out whether the word or concept applies. For example, on this view, the concept 'having a length of one meter' amounts to saying that something of that length will fit exactly against a standard meter stick (which in turn will fit exactly against the distance traveled by light in a vacuum in 1/299,792,458 of a second). Similarly, for the operationalist, to say that someone is hungry is just to say that they will eat if given the chance, claim to be hungry if asked, and so on.

16 G.W.F. Hegel (1770–1831), an extremely influential German philosopher, held that natural entities embody thoughts—mind is embedded in the very structure of the universe—and the passage of human history is a gradual revealing of the categories embedded in nature. In the process, what Hegel called "absolute spirit" (the spirit of the world, or God) ascends to "freedom" and "self-consciousness."

discovery that I have made in discussing these issues is that many AI workers are quite shocked by my idea that actual human mental phenomena might be dependent on actual physical-chemical properties of actual human brains. But if you think about it a minute you can see that I should not have been surprised; for unless you accept some form of dualism, the strong AI project hasn't got a chance. The project is to reproduce and explain the mental by designing programs, but unless the mind is not only conceptually but empirically independent of the brain you couldn't carry out the project, for the program is completely independent of any realization. Unless you believe that the mind is separable from the brain both conceptually and empirically—dualism in a strong form—you cannot hope to reproduce the mental by writing and running programs since programs must be independent of brains or any other particular forms of instantiation. If mental operations consist in computational operations on formal symbols, then it follows that they have no interesting connection with the brain; the only connection would be that the brain just happens to be one of the indefinitely many types of machines capable of instantiating the program. This form of dualism is not the traditional Cartesian variety that claims there are two sorts of substances, but it is Cartesian in the sense that it insists that what is specifically mental about the mind has no intrinsic connection with the actual properties of the brain. This underlying dualism is masked from us by the fact that AI literature contains frequent fulminations against 'dualism'; what the authors seem to be unaware of is that their position presupposes a strong version of dualism.

'Could a machine think?' My own view is that only a machine could think, and indeed only very special kinds of machines, namely brains and machines that had the same causal powers as brains. And that is the main reason strong AI has had little to tell us about thinking, since it has nothing to tell us about machines. By its own definition, it is about programs, and programs are not machines. Whatever else intentionality is, it is a biological phenomenon, and it is as likely to be as causally dependent on the specific biochemistry of its origins as lactation, photosynthesis, or any other biological phenomena. No one would suppose that we could produce milk and sugar by running a computer simulation of the formal sequences in lactation and photosynthesis, but where the mind is concerned many people are willing to believe in such a miracle because of a deep and abiding dualism: the mind they suppose is a matter of formal processes and is independent of quite specific material causes in the way that milk and sugar are not.

In defence of this dualism the hope is often expressed that the brain is a digital computer (early computers, by the way, were often called 'electronic brains'). But that is no help. Of course the brain is a digital computer. Since everything is a digital computer, brains are too. The point is that the brain's causal capacity to produce intentionality cannot consist in its instantiating a computer program, since for any program you like it is possible for something to instantiate that program and still not have any mental states. Whatever it is that the brain does to produce intentionality, it cannot consist in instantiating a program since no program, by itself, is sufficient for intentionality.[17]

References

Fodor, J. A. (1980). 'Methodological Solipsism Considered as a Research Strategy in Cognitive Psychology.' *Behavioral and Brain Sciences* 3: 63–110.

McCarthy, J. (1979). 'Ascribing Mental Qualities to Machines.' In M. Ringle (ed.), *Philosophical Perspectives in Artificial Intelligence*, pp. 161–95. Atlantic Highlands, NJ: Humanities Press.

[Multiple authors] (1978). 'Cognition and Consciousness in Non-Human Species.' *Behavioral and Brain Sciences* 1 (4): entire issue.

Newell, A. (1979). 'Physical Symbol Systems.' Lecture at the La Jolla Conference on Cognitive Science. Later published in *Cognitive Science* 4 (1980): 135–83.

---

17 [Author's note] I am indebted to a rather large number of people for discussion of these matters, and for their patient attempts to overcome my ignorance of artificial intelligence. I would especially like to thank Ned Bock, Hubert Dreyfus, John Haugeland, Roger Schank, Robert Wilensky, and Terry Winograd.

Newell, A. and Simon, H.A. (1963). 'GPS—A Program that Simulates Human Thought.' In E.A. Feigenbaum and J.A. Feldman (eds.), *Computers and Thought*, pp. 279–96. New York: McGraw-Hill.

Pylyshyn, Z.W. (1980). 'Computation and Cognition: Issues in the Foundation of Cognitive Science.' *Behavioral and Brain Sciences* 3: 111–32.

Schank, R.C. and Abelson, R.P. (1977). *Scripts, Plans, Goals, and Understanding*. Hillsdale, NJ: Erlbaum.

Searle, J.R. (1979a). 'Intentionality and the Use of Language.' In A. Margolit (ed.), *Meaning and Use*. Dordrecht: Reidel.

Searle, J.R. (1979b). 'What Is an Intentional State?, *Mind* 88: 74–92.

Weizenbaum, J. (1965). 'ELIZA—A Computer Program for the Study of Natural Language Communication Between Man and Machine.' *Commun. ACM* 9: 36–45.

Weizenbaum, J. (1976). *Computer Power and Human Reason*. San Francisco: W.H. Freeman.

Winograd, T. (1973). 'A Procedural Model of Language Understanding.' In R.C. Schank and K.M. Colby (eds.), *Computer Models of Thought and Language*, pp.152–86. San Francisco: W.H. Freeman.

PAUL CHURCHLAND
"Eliminative Materialism and the Propositional Attitudes"

Who Is Paul Churchland?

Paul M. Churchland was born in Vancouver in 1942, and took his PhD with Wilfrid Sellars at the University of Pittsburgh in 1969. He spent many years teaching at the University of Manitoba, and then became Professor of Philosophy and a member of the Cognitive Science Faculty at the University of California in San Diego in 1984. He is married to Patricia Smith Churchland, a very well-known philosopher of cognitive science in her own right. She also was born in British Columbia and taught at the University of Manitoba before moving to a professorship at San Diego.

Paul Churchland's philosophical work has three main (tightly connected) themes. The first is his "scientific realism," the second his advocacy of "eliminativism," and the third his interest in "connectionism."

Scientific realism is the view that the theoretical entities postulated by a true scientific theory are real things: that is, science does not just produce clever fictions that enable us to manipulate our environment, but actually *describes* the fundamental nature of reality. If a true scientific theory tells us that everything is made up of fermions and bosons, for example, then that should be our metaphysics. An important consequence of this, for Churchland, is that "issues in the philosophy of mind are not independent of the theoretical and experimental results of the natural sciences." Just as physics can radically change our understanding of a chair or a glass, neuroscience can completely upset our philosophical assumptions about such mental entities as beliefs and pains. And, just as the fact that we seem to be able to *see* that a chair is not a mass of tiny fast-moving particles, does not prevent science from over-ruling this perception, similarly the fact that we think we can just look inside our own heads (introspect) and detect our own beliefs, desires, and pains is no barrier to the march of neuroscientific theory. Churchland, in fact, takes one consequence of his general scientific realism to be the doctrine called "eliminativism": that is, he thinks our commonsense account of the nature of the mind is false and destined to be replaced by a completely different, true scientific account. "Eliminative Materialism and the Propositional Attitudes" is his seminal statement and defence of eliminativism.

In his later efforts to describe what this victorious neuroscience might look like, Churchland has come to endorse a general theoretical framework called "connectionism" (also sometimes called "parallel distributed processing" or "neural network modeling"). This research program uses networks of massively interconnected "neural" units to model cognitive processes. The units, which can be thought of as highly simplified versions of neurons, are simple processors that can take on varying numerical "activation values." Each unit is joined to a huge number of other units (and to inputs and outputs outside the system) by connections that can take on different strengths, and that can either excite or inhibit the activation of the units they are connected to. The system processes information in the following way: a particular input causes a ripple of changes in the network as it is propagated through the connections, making a spatially distributed set of units "fire" one after the other or simultaneously, and leading to changes in the overall pattern of activation values and connection strengths for the network. Once the network "settles" into an equilibrium (i.e., when the processing has stopped), this is considered the output state. Thus, for example, in a simple network (which has actually been created) the input might be (code for) "What is the past tense of the English verb *run*?" and the output state might be (code for) the answer "*ran*."

The importance of this cognitive model for Churchland is twofold. First, it (arguably) replicates, in many ways, the features of human cognition. For example, connectionist networks can learn to recognize patterns in ways which resemble human abilities—they make the same sort of mistakes in learning, say, the past tenses of verbs as children do, and respond to information-overload or unexpected inputs in much more "graceful" ways than would a traditional computer program (which would just crash). Second, connectionist networks (allegedly) do not contain any entities which might map onto the categories of folk psychology. Unlike a traditional computer program, neural networks do not manipulate or store symbols according to logical rules; they seem to operate in a different, more holistic way. No particular part of a neural network 'represents' a symbol or a logical rule; instead, the network *as a whole* represents particular outputs, "remembers" past inputs, and performs processing on new inputs. Thus, for example, there is no part of the network which stores the rules "if the input is *run* then output *ran*" or "if the input is *go* then output *went*," and there are no particular sets of units to always represent *run*, *ran*, *go*, or *went*; that is, the system does not contain those symbols. Instead, the network, as a whole, is built to go from *run* to *ran*, and from *go* to *went*, and so on. A sophisticated descendant of connectionism, therefore, is Churchland's current best guess for the type of neuroscientific model that will eliminate folk psychology.

What Is the Structure of This Reading?

The main thesis of "Eliminative Materialism and the Propositional Attitudes" is that our common-sense conception of the mind—which Churchland calls "folk psychology"—is a false theory. Churchland therefore begins by arguing that folk psychology *is* a theory, so that he can later argue it is a false one. Part of his argument is that the laws of folk psychology have exactly the same form as the laws of physical science; "the only difference lies in the respective domain of abstract entities they exploit—numbers in the case of physics, and propositions in the case of psychology." Churchland then moves on, in the next section, to argue that the theory of folk psychology is almost certainly false.

In section three, Churchland turns to defending eliminativism against its critics, especially from the criticisms of "the most popular and best-founded of the competing positions in the philosophy of mind: functionalism." He diagnoses two themes in the attempt to defend folk psychology against elimination: appeals to its abstract nature, and appeals to its normativity. Then he launches an attack on these two notions, one after the other, in an attempt to reveal functionalism "for the short-sighted and reactionary position it is." In the final section of his paper, Churchland describes three speculative scenarios in which folk psychology is replaced by some radically different model of cognition: his aim here is not to *defend* any of these speculations, but to show that alternatives to the commonsense view are possible (and might even be inspiring).

Some Useful Background Information

1. A central theme of Churchland's paper is the inadequacy of the psychological notion of what are called "propositional attitudes." Propositional attitudes are simply attitudes towards propositions (the phrase was coined by Bertrand Russell in 1940). So what is a proposition? It is the thing expressed by different sentences when they all have the same meaning: for example, "*il pleut*," "*es regnet*," and "it is raining" are different sentences, but they all express the same proposition. Now consider the proposition expressed by the sentence "It will snow tomorrow." One might take various attitudes towards this proposition: one might believe it, not believe it, or believe that it is false; one might hope that it is true, desire that it be true, wish that it were true, fear that it is true, or regret that it is true; one might merely entertain the possibility that it is true or be certain of its truth. All of these states (if they exist) are propositional attitudes.

   Many recent philosophers of mind have argued (or assumed) that all of cognitive psychology can be cashed out in terms of propositional attitudes, and even that all cognitive mental states can be treated as belonging to one of exactly two kinds of propositional attitude: a shade of belief or a variety of desire. (This is often called "belief-desire psychology.") This means that human thought and action are described within a model which is not causal (unlike our model for describing and explaining the rest of the world) but which is instead "intentional" or rational: its laws are the logical laws connecting *propositions*, not the laws of physics. (For example, if you hope that it will snow tomorrow and you believe that doing a special snow dance will cause it to snow, then, all things being equal, it would be reasonable for you to do the dance.) It is this kind of psychological model that Churchland is attacking, not merely as being incomplete but as actually being totally false.

2. This article contains several logical formulae, written in a language called "predicate logic." Each formula is translated into English in the notes, but here is a run-down of Churchland's symbols. The letters in italics, such as *x*, *p*, and *m* are variables of different sorts: for example, *p* and *q* are place-holders for any proposition, *m* is a place-holder for a quantity of mass, and *x* is a neutral variable for any individual—an *x* can be anything (at least, anything within the "domain of discourse"). When a variable appears on its own between two brackets—as in (*x*)—this is called a "universal quantifier" (which is also often written (∀*x*)). This is logical shorthand for a phrase like "For any *x*" or "All *x*"—that is, what follows the (*x*) will be a claim about *all* things of type *x*. For example, the formula "(*p*) (*p* is either true or false)" says that all propositions are either true or false. It would be read out loud as, "For any proposition *p*, *p* is either true or false."

   The symbol ⊃ (called the "horseshoe") is logical code for a version of the English connective "if … then …": for example (P ⊃ Q) means that if P is true then Q must be as well (or, strictly speaking, that either P is false or Q is true). Finally, & means "and," and ~ means "not." For example, one might assert that ~(P & ~P): i.e., it's not true that P is both true and false.

Some Common Misconceptions

1. When Churchland calls folk psychology a "theory" he does not (just) mean it is something that is a mere conjecture or hypothesis rather than something already confirmed. He is using the word "theory" in the scientific sense: to mean a body of systematically organized propositions, intended to explain and predict some particu-

lar set of phenomena (in this case, the human mind). As such, a theory can be well confirmed or less well confirmed by the data it is supposed to explain. For example, the theory of quantum mechanics is extremely well confirmed, whereas the theory of astrology is much less so.

2. Churchland's eliminativism, even though he calls it "eliminative materialism," is purely a negative doctrine and not by itself a positive theory of the mind at all. Thus, as he points out, eliminativism is compatible with any theory of the mind that dispenses with folk psychology, and this could include functionalist theories (albeit a functionalism radically different from that currently conceived) or even, though Churchland does not say so, dualist theories. Churchland's own money is on what he calls "naturalistic" theories—that is, roughly, some physical theory of the complex causal configuration of the brain. His defence of naturalism, however, is an *additional* thesis to eliminativism, his main theme in this paper.

Suggestions for Critical Reflection

1. Do you agree that our commonsense understanding of the mind is a theory? For example, do you think Churchland has shown, for instance, that beliefs and desires are *theoretical entities*, like electrons and genes, rather than things we directly *observe*? To put it another way, is introspection about our own propositional attitudes a kind of *perception* or a kind of *theorizing* (or is there no clear difference between the two)? What exactly *are* Churchland's arguments for the claim that folk psychology is a theory, and what if anything is wrong with them?

2. Supposing that folk psychology is a theory, do you agree with Churchland that it's probably a *false* theory? What are Churchland's three arguments for its falsity, and how convincing are they?

3. Churchland's arguments for the falsity of folk psychology are directed at the propositional attitudes: beliefs, desires, hopes, and so on. Would

his arguments be equally successful against other elements of folk psychology, such as sensations and emotions? How significant do you think it would be if these parts of folk psychology resisted elimination?

4. Do you agree that Churchland has shown that functionalism is a "conservative" and "reactionary" theory? Does he manage to show that functionalist responses to eliminativism merely beg the question against it? Is the analogy between functionalism and alchemy a fair one, do you think?

5. Churchland argues that our commonsense grasp of the nature of *rationality* itself is flawed (because we understand it in terms of relations between the propositional attitudes), and suggests that we might transcend this primitive understanding and gain new insight into "cognitive virtue." This is a very radical claim. Do you find it plausible? How adequate are Churchland's arguments for it? If he is wrong about this, could he still be right about (the rest of) eliminativism?

Suggestions for Further Reading

Churchland's eliminativism was first developed in his 1979 book *Scientific Realism and the Plasticity of Mind* (Cambridge University Press), and is further extended in his "Reduction, Qualia, and the Direct Introspection of Brain States," *Journal of Philosophy* 82 (1985). He has also written an entertaining introduction to the philosophy of mind, with a blatant scientific realist bias, called *Matter and Consciousness* (revised edition, MIT Press, 1988); this book includes a final chapter on "Expanding our Perspective" which resembles the speculations in the final section of "Eliminative Materialism and the Propositional Attitudes." Churchland's connectionism can be seen in the collection of essays *A Neurocomputational Perspective* (MIT Press, 1989). One of his latest books, *The Engine of Reason, The Seat of the Soul* (MIT Press, 1995), considers the implications of his philosophical views for the social and moral dimensions of human life. There is a book of essays about the work of Paul and Patricia Churchland called *The Churchlands and Their Critics*, edited by Robert

McCauley (Blackwell, 1996), and an elementary intro-duction to their work by William Hirstein called *On the Churchlands* (Wadsworth, 2001).

There are a number of important books and arti-cles about the prospects for folk psychology, includ-ing *Saving Belief*, by Lynne Rudder Baker (Princeton University Press, 1987); "The Status of Content," by Paul Boghossian, *Philosophical Review* 99 (1990); *The Intentional Stance*, by Daniel Dennett (MIT Press, 1987); *Psycho-semantics*, by Jerry Fodor (MIT Press, 1987); *The Future of Folk Psychology*, edited by John Greenwood (Cambridge University Press, 1991); "Folk Psychology Is Here to Stay," by Terence Horgan and James Wood-ward, *Philosophical Review* 94 (1985); "In Defense of Intentional Psychology," by Patricia Kitcher, *Journal of Philosophy* 81 (1984); and *From Folk Psychology to Cog-nitive Science*, by Stephen Stich (MIT Press, 1983).

"Eliminative Materialism and the Propositional Attitudes"[1,2]

Eliminative materialism is the thesis that our common-sense conception of psychological phenomena consti-tutes a radically false theory, a theory so fundamentally defective that both the principles and the ontology[3] of that theory will eventually be displaced, rather than smoothly reduced, by completed neuroscience. Our mutual understanding and even our introspection may then be reconstituted within the conceptual framework of completed neuroscience, a theory we may expect to be more powerful by far than the common-sense psychology it displaces, and more substantially inte-grated within physical science generally. My purpose in this paper is to explore these projections, especially as they bear on (1) the principal elements of common-sense psychology: the propositional attitudes (beliefs, desires, etc.), and (2) the conception of rationality in which these elements figure.

This focus represents a change in the fortunes of materialism. Twenty years ago, emotions, qualia,[4] and "raw feels" were held to be the principal stumbling blocks for the materialist program. With these barri-ers dissolving,[5] the locus of opposition has shifted. Now it is the realm of the intentional, the realm of the propositional attitude, that is most commonly held up as being both irreducible to and ineliminable in favor of anything from within a materialist framework. Whether and why this is so, we must examine.

Such an examination will make little sense, how-ever, unless it is first appreciated that the relevant network of common-sense concepts does indeed constitute an empirical theory, with all the functions, virtues, *and perils* entailed by that status. I shall therefore begin with a brief sketch of this view and a summary rehearsal of its rationale. The resistance it encounters still surprises me. After all, common sense has yielded up many theories. Recall the view that space has a preferred direction in which all things fall; that weight is an intrinsic feature of a body; that a force-free moving object will promptly return to rest; that the sphere of the heavens turns daily; and so on.

---

1   This paper was first published in February 1981 in *The Journal of Philosophy* (volume LXXVIII, issue 2). Reprinted by permission of *The Journal of Philosophy* and Paul Churchland.

2   [Author's note] An earlier draft of this paper was pre-sented at the University of Ottawa, and to the *Brain, Mind, and Person* colloquium at SUNY/Oswego. My thanks for the suggestions and criticisms that have informed the present version.

3   A theory's ontology is the set of things which the theory says exists. For example, the ontology of mod-ern physics includes leptons and bosons, while the ontology of alchemy involves *materia prima*, the four elements (earth, air, fire, and water), and the Philoso-pher's Stone.

4   "Qualia" is the technical philosophical term for quali-ties as they are immediately felt or perceived, such as the painfulness of pain, the greenness of a color perception, or the smelliness of a whiff of rotten eggs. ("Qualia" is plural; the singular form is "quale," usu-ally pronounced kwa-lay.)

5   [Author's note] See Paul Feyerabend, "Materialism and the Mind-Body Problem," *Review of Metaphysics*, XVII.1, 65 (September 1963): 49–66; Richard Rorty, "Mind-Body Identity, Privacy, and Categories," *ibid.*, XIX.1, 73 (September 1965): 24–54; and my *Scientific Realism and the Plasticity of Mind* (New York: Cam-bridge, 1979).

These examples are clear, perhaps, but people seem willing to concede a theoretical component within common sense only if (1) the theory and the common sense involved are safely located in antiquity, and (2) the relevant theory is now so clearly false that its speculative nature is inescapable. Theories are indeed easier to discern under these circumstances. But the vision of hindsight is always 20/20. Let us aspire to some foresight for a change.

I. Why Folk Psychology Is a Theory

Seeing our common-sense conceptual framework for mental phenomena as a theory brings a simple and unifying organization to most of the major topics in the philosophy of mind, including the explanation and prediction of behavior, the semantics of mental predicates, action theory,[6] the other-minds problem,[7] the intentionality[8] of mental states, the nature of introspection, and the mind-body problem. Any view that can pull this lot together deserves careful consideration.

Let us begin with the explanation of human (and animal) behavior. The fact is that the average person is able to explain, and even predict, the behavior of other persons with a facility and success that is remarkable. Such explanations and predictions standardly make reference to the desires, beliefs, fears, intentions, perceptions, and so forth, to which the agents are presumed subject. But explanations presuppose laws—rough and ready ones, at least—that connect the explanatory conditions with the behavior explained. The same is true for the making of predictions, and for the justification of subjunctive and counterfactual conditionals[9] concerning behavior. Reassuringly, a rich network of common-sense laws can indeed be reconstructed from this quotidian commerce of explanation and anticipation; its principles are familiar homilies; and their sundry functions are transparent. Each of us understands others, as well as we do, because we share a tacit command of an integrated body of lore concerning the lawlike relations holding among external circumstances, internal states, and overt behavior. Given its nature and functions, this body of lore may quite aptly be called "folk psychology."[10]

---

6   As the name suggests, the philosophical study of human action: for example, what is the difference between action and mere behavior? how does action come about in a human agent? how do we specify exactly what kind of action something is (e.g., was it a finger-movement or an assassination or both)? and so on.

7   This is the problem of finding out whether other creatures have minds, and if so what they are like. For example, how can I be sure that my wife or two-year-old child have minds—how good is my evidence for this assumption?—and how can I tell whether they think and feel like me?

8   Roughly, their meaningfulness—their being *about* something. See the notes to the Searle reading for more information on intentionality.

9   A conditional is an 'if ... then ...' statement, such as "if it rains then I will get wet." A counterfactual conditional is an 'if ... then ...' statement about what *would* have happened if something, which did not in fact occur, had occurred: e.g., "if I had dropped this priceless Tang Dynasty vase it would have shattered into a million expensive pieces." Counterfactual conditionals are crucial for scientific theories: the claim that copper conducts electricity, for example, is not merely the assertion that pieces of copper have always conducted in the past whenever we have actually attached them to a current, but that even bits of copper which we *haven't* tried to electrify are nevertheless conductors. A *subjunctive* conditional is an 'if ... then ...' statement where both gaps are filled by subjunctive sentences—that is, by sentences which do not assert that something is true, but instead express a wish, or a fear, or a hypothetical possibility, or a suggestion, or something of that sort. This means all counterfactual conditionals are also subjunctive, but there are also some subjunctive conditionals that are not counterfactual: for example, "If it would only rain, then I would not need to water the garden" or "If I were to drop this vase of yours it would shatter on the tile floor."

10   [Author's note] We shall examine a handful of these laws presently. For a more comprehensive sampling of the laws of folk psychology, see my *Scientific Realism and Plasticity of Mind, op. cit.*, ch. 4. For a detailed examination of the folk principles that underwrite action explanations in particular, see my "The Logical

This approach entails that the semantics of the terms in our familiar mentalistic vocabulary are to be understood in the same manner as the semantics of theoretical terms generally: the meaning of any theoretical term is fixed or constituted by the network of laws in which it figures. (This position is quite distinct from logical behaviorism.[11] We deny that the relevant laws are analytic, and it is the lawlike connections generally that carry the semantic weight, not just the connections with overt behavior. But this view does account for what little plausibility logical behaviorism did enjoy.)

More importantly, the recognition that folk psychology is a theory provides a simple and decisive solution to an old skeptical problem, the problem of other minds. The problematic conviction that another individual is the subject of certain mental states is not inferred deductively from his behavior, nor is it inferred by inductive analogy from the perilously isolated instance of one's own case. Rather, that conviction is a singular *explanatory hypothesis* of a perfectly straightforward kind. Its function, in conjunction with the background laws of folk psychology, is to provide explanations/predictions/understanding of the individual's continuing behavior, and it is credible to the degree that it is successful in this regard over competing hypotheses. In the main, such hypotheses are successful, and so the belief that others enjoy the internal states comprehended by folk psychology is a reasonable belief.

Knowledge of other minds thus has no essential dependence on knowledge of one's own mind. Applying the principles of our folk psychology to our behavior, a Martian could justly ascribe to us the familiar run of mental states, even though his own psychology were very different from ours. He would not, therefore, be "generalizing from his own case."

As well, introspective judgments about one's own case turn out not to have any special status or integrity anyway. On the present view, an introspective judgment is just an instance of an acquired habit of conceptual response to one's internal states, and the

integrity of any particular response is always contingent on the integrity of the acquired conceptual framework (theory) in which the response is framed. Accordingly, one's *introspective* certainty that one's mind is the seat of beliefs and desires may be as badly misplaced as was the classical man's visual certainty that the star-flecked sphere of the heavens turns daily.

Another conundrum is the intentionality of mental states. The "propositional attitudes," as Russell[12] called them, form the systematic core of folk psychology; and their uniqueness and anomalous[13] logical properties have inspired some to see here a fundamental contrast with anything that mere physical phenomena might conceivably display. The key to this matter lies again in the theoretical nature of folk psychology. The intentionality of mental states here emerges not as a mystery of nature, but as a structural feature of the concepts of folk psychology. Ironically, those same structural features reveal the very close affinity that folk psychology bears to theories in the physical sciences. Let me try to explain.

Consider the large variety of what might be called "numerical attitudes" appearing in the conceptual framework of physical science: '... has a mass$_{kg}$ of n', '... has a velocity of n', '... has a temperature$_K$ of n', and so forth. These expressions are predicate-forming expressions: when one substitutes a singular term[14]

---

12 The philosopher Bertrand Russell.

13 "Anomalous" here means not falling under, not being bound by, the laws of physics. ("Nomic" means having to do with laws of nature, so "a-nomalous" means *not* having to do with natural laws.) The idea here is that laws of logic are quite different in kind from physical laws: if we know that either P is true or Q is true, and we know that P is not true, then it follows that Q must be true, but this has nothing to do with causation or physical necessity. Instead, it seems to have something to do with *meaning*—with what it means to say that "either P or Q is true," for example—which is why Churchland goes on to discuss intentionality.

14 A "singular term" is a piece of language which picks out exactly one thing, such as a proper name or a definite description. Churchland has in mind, of course, the names of numbers (or "numerals"): 1, 2, 3, $2/3$, π, $\sqrt{-1}$, etc.

Character of Action Explanations," *Philosophical Review*, LXXIX, 2 (April 1970): 214–236.

11 See the notes to the Ryle reading, in this chapter.

for a number into the place held by '*n*', a determinate predicate results. More interestingly, the relations between the various "numerical attitudes" that result are precisely the relations between the numbers "contained" in those attitudes. More interesting still, the argument place that takes the singular terms for numbers is open to quantification.[15] All this permits the expression of generalizations concerning the lawlike relations that hold between the various numerical attitudes in nature. Such laws involve quantification over numbers, and they exploit the mathematical relations holding in that domain. Thus, for example,

(1) $(x)(f)(m)[((x$ has a mass of $m)$ & $(x$ suffers a net force of $f)) \supset (x$ accelerates at $f/m)]$[16]

Consider now the large variety of propositional attitudes '… believes that *p*', '… desires that *p*', '… fears that *p*', '… is happy that *p*', etc. These expressions are predicate-forming expressions also. When one substitutes a singular term for a proposition into the place held by '*p*', a determinate predicate results, e.g., '… believes that Tom is tall.' (Sentences do not generally function as singular terms, but it is difficult to escape the idea that when a sentence occurs in the place held by '*p*', it is there functioning as or like a singular term. On this, more below.) More interestingly, the relations between the resulting propositional attitudes are characteristically the relations that hold between the propositions "contained" in them, relations such as entailment, equivalence, and mutual inconsistency. More interesting still, the argument place that takes the singular terms for propositions is open to quantification. All this permits the expression of generalizations concerning the lawlike relations that hold among propositional attitudes. Such laws involve quantification over propositions, and they exploit various relations holding in that domain. Thus, for example,

(2) $(x)(p)[(x$ fears that $p) \supset (x$ desires that $\sim p)]$[17]
(3) $(x)(p)[((x$ hopes that $p)$ & $(x$ discovers that $p))$ $\supset (x$ is pleased that $p)]$[18]
(4) $(x)(p)(q)[((x$ believes that $p)$ & $(x$ believes that (if p then $q))) \supset$ (barring confusion, distraction, etc., x believes that $q)]$[19]
(5) $(x)(p)(q)[((x$ desires that $p)$ & $(x$ believes that (if q then $p))$ & $(x$ is able to bring it about that $q)) \supset$ (barring conflicting desires or preferred strategies, x brings it about that $q)]$[20,21]

---

15   This means that the variable *n* in Churchland's examples (the 'argument place') can be 'quantified over,' i.e., that we can coherently say things like "every *n*" or "at least one *n*." For example, we might say "every *n* is either odd or even" or "there is at least one *n* such that … has a velocity of *n*" (this second phrase is just a fancy way of saying "… has some velocity").

16   If anything of mass *m* undergoes a force *f* then it will accelerate at the rate *f/m*.

17   Anyone who fears that *p* desires that *p* be false (e.g., if you fear that your spouse has just crashed the car then it follows that you hope that they didn't crash the car.)

18   If anyone hopes that *p* is true and discovers that it *is* true, then they will be pleased.

19   If you believe *p* and you believe that (if *p* is true then *q* must also be true) then, barring confusion, distraction, etc., you will believe *q*.

20   If anyone desires that *p* be true, *and* believes that if *q* were to be true *p* would be as well, *and* is able to make *q* true, then, barring conflicting desires or preferred strategies, that person would make *q* true. (For example, if you wanted someone to like you, *and* you believed that if you were to dye your hair red they would like you, *and* you were able to dye your hair red, then (all things being equal) you would break out the hair dye and go to it.)

21   [Author's note] Staying within an objectual interpretation of the quantifiers, perhaps the simplest way to make systematic sense of expressions like [x believes that p] and closed sentences formed therefrom is just to construe whatever occurs in the nested position held by '*p*', '*q*', etc. as there having the function of a singular term. Accordingly, the standard connectives, as they occur between terms in that nested position, must be construed as there functioning as operators that form compound singular terms from other singular terms, and not as sentence operators. The compound singular terms so formed denote the appropriate compound propositions. Substitutional quantification will of course underwrite a different interpretation, and there are other approaches as well. Especially appealing is the prosentential approach of Dorothy Grover, Joseph

Not only is folk psychology a theory, it is so *obviously* a theory that it must be held a major mystery why it has taken until the last half of the twentieth century for philosophers to realize it. The structural features of folk psychology parallel perfectly those of mathematical physics; the only difference lies in the respective domain of abstract entities they exploit—numbers in the case of physics, and propositions in the case of psychology.

Finally, the realization that folk psychology is a theory puts a new light on the mind-body problem. The issue becomes a matter of how the ontology of one theory (folk psychology) is, or is not, going to be related to the ontology of another theory (completed neuroscience); and the major philosophical positions on the mind-body problem emerge as so many different anticipations of what future research will reveal about the intertheoretic status and integrity of folk psychology.

The identity theorist optimistically expects that folk psychology will be smoothly *reduced* by completed neuroscience, and its ontology preserved by dint of transtheoretic identities.[22] The dualist expects that it will prove *ir*reducible to completed neuroscience, by dint of being a nonredundant description of an autonomous, nonphysical domain of natural phenomena. The functionalist also expects that it will prove irreducible, but on the quite different grounds that the internal economy characterized by folk psychology is not, in the last analysis, a law-governed economy of natural states, but an abstract organization of functional states, an organization instantiable in a variety of quite dif-

ferent material substrates.[23] It is therefore irreducible to the principles peculiar to any of them.

Finally, the eliminative materialist is also pessimistic about the prospects for reduction, but his reason is that folk psychology is a radically inadequate account of our internal activities, too confused and too defective to win survival through intertheoretic reduction. On his view it will simply be displaced by a better theory of those activities.

Which of these fates is the real destiny of folk psychology, we shall attempt to divine presently. For now, the point to keep in mind is that we shall be exploring the fate of a theory, a systematic, corrigible, speculative *theory*.

II. Why Folk Psychology Might (Really) Be False

Given that folk psychology is an empirical theory, it is at least an abstract possibility that its principles are radically false and that its ontology is an illusion. With the exception of eliminative materialism, however, none of the major positions takes this possibility seriously. None of them doubts the basic integrity or truth of folk psychology (hereafter, "FP"), and all of them anticipate a future in which its laws and categories are conserved. This conservatism is not without some foundation. After all, FP does enjoy a substantial amount of explanatory and predictive success. And what better grounds than this for confidence in the integrity of its categories?

What better grounds indeed? Even so, the presumption in FP's favor is spurious, born of innocence and tunnel vision. A more searching examination reveals a different picture. First, we must reckon not only with FP's successes, but with its explanatory failures, and with their extent and seriousness. Second, we must consider the long-term history of FP, its growth, fertility, and current promise of future development. And third, we must consider what sorts of theories are *likely* to be true of the etiology[24] of our behavior, given what else we have learned about ourselves in recent history. That is, we must evaluate FP with regard to its coherence and continuity with

---

Camp, and Nuel Belnap, "A Prosentential Theory of Truth," *Philosophical Studies*, XXVII, 2 (February 1975): 73–125. But the resolution of these issues is not vital to the present discussion.

22   That is, the things which folk psychology says exist—such as beliefs, desires, and fears—will turn out to be identifiable with (collections of) things that "completed neuroscience" says exist, such as the properties and states of neurons and brain chemicals. By "completed neuroscience," Churchland means something like the final true scientific theory of the human nervous system.

---

23   See the notes to the article by Hilary Putnam, in this chapter.

24   The cause or origin.

fertile and well-established theories in adjacent and overlapping domains—with evolutionary theory, biology, and neuroscience, for example—because active coherence with the rest of what we presume to know is perhaps the final measure of any hypothesis.

A serious inventory of this sort reveals a very troubled situation, one which would evoke open skepticism in the case of any theory less familiar and dear to us. Let me sketch some relevant detail. When one centers one's attention not on what FP can explain, but on what it cannot explain or fails even to address, one discovers that there is a very great deal. As examples of central and important mental phenomena that remain largely or wholly mysterious within the framework of FP, consider the nature and dynamics of mental illness, the faculty of creative imagination, or the ground of intelligence differences between individuals. Consider our utter ignorance of the nature and psychological functions of sleep, that curious state in which a third of one's life is spent. Reflect on the common ability to catch an outfield fly ball on the run, or hit a moving car with a snowball. Consider the internal construction of a 3-D visual image from subtle differences in the 2-D array of stimulations in our respective retinas. Consider the rich variety of perceptual illusions, visual and otherwise. Or consider the miracle of memory, with its lightning capacity for relevant retrieval. On these and many other mental phenomena, FP sheds negligible light.

One particularly outstanding mystery is the nature of the learning process itself, especially where it involves large-scale conceptual change, and especially as it appears in its pre-linguistic or entirely nonlinguistic form (as in infants and animals), which is by far the most common form in nature. FP is faced with special difficulties here, since its conception of learning as the manipulation and storage of propositional attitudes founders on the fact that how to formulate, manipulate, and store a rich fabric of propositional attitudes is itself something that is learned, and is only one among many acquired cognitive skills. FP would thus appear constitutionally incapable of even addressing this most basic of mysteries.[25]

Failures on such a large scale do not (yet) show that FP is a false theory, but they do move that prospect well into the range of real possibility, and they do show decisively that FP is *at best* a highly superficial theory, a partial and unpenetrating gloss on a deeper and more complex reality. Having reached this opinion, we may be forgiven for exploring the possibility that FP provides a positively misleading sketch of our internal kinematics and dynamics,[26] one whose success is owed more to selective application and forced interpretation on our part than to genuine theoretical insight on FP's part.

A look at the history of FP does little to allay such fears, once raised. The story is one of retreat, infertility, and decadence. The presumed domain of FP used to be much larger than it is now. In primitive cultures, the behavior of most of the elements of nature were understood in intentional terms. The wind could know anger, the moon jealousy, the river generosity, the sea fury, and so forth. These were not metaphors. Sacrifices were made and auguries undertaken to placate or divine the changing passions of the gods. Despite its sterility, this animistic approach to nature has dominated our history, and it is only in the last two or three thousand years that we have restricted FP's literal application to the domain of the higher animals.

Even in this preferred domain, however, both the content and the success of FP have not advanced sensibly in two or three thousand years. The FP of the Greeks is essentially the FP we use today, and we are negligibly better at explaining human behavior in its

---

linguaformal in its elements, structures, and processing right from birth. J.A. Fodor, in *The Language of Thought* (New York: Crowell 1975), has erected a positive theory of thought on the assumption that the innate forms of cognitive activity have precisely the form here denied. For a critique of Fodor's view, see Patricia Churchland, "Fodor on Language Learning," *Synthèse*, XXXVIII, 1 (May 1978): 149–159.

26 Kinematics is the study of the movement of a set of bodies without paying attention to the forces which cause their motion; dynamics (sometimes called kinetics) is the study of how forces affect a system of bodies. Together, the two make up the science of mechanics.

---

25 [Author's note] A possible response here is to insist that the cognitive activity of animals and infants is

terms than was Sophocles.[27] This is a very long period of stagnation and infertility for any theory to display, especially when faced with such an enormous backlog of anomalies and mysteries in its own explanatory domain. Perfect theories, perhaps, have no need to evolve. But FP is profoundly imperfect. Its failure to develop its resources and extend its range of success is therefore darkly curious, and one must query the integrity of its basic categories. To use Imre Lakatos'[28] terms, FP is a stagnant or degenerating research program, and has been for millennia.

Explanatory success to date is of course not the only dimension in which a theory can display virtue or promise. A troubled or stagnant theory may merit patience and solicitude on other grounds; for example, on grounds that it is the only theory or theoretical approach that fits well with other theories about adjacent subject matters, or the only one that promises to reduce to or be explained by some established background theory whose domain encompasses the domain of the theory at issue. In sum, it may rate credence because it holds promise of theoretical integration. How does FP rate in this dimension?

It is just here, perhaps, that FP fares poorest of all. If we approach *Homo sapiens* from the perspective of natural history and the physical sciences, we can tell a coherent story of his constitution, development, and behavioral capacities which encompasses particle physics, atomic and molecular theory, organic chemistry, evolutionary theory, biology, physiology, and materialistic neuroscience. That story, though still radically incomplete, is already extremely powerful, outperforming FP at many points even in its own domain. And it is deliberately and self-consciously coherent with the rest of our developing world picture. In short, the greatest theoretical synthesis in the history of the human race is currently in our hands, and parts of it already provide searching descriptions and explanations of human sensory input, neural activity, and motor control.

But FP is no part of this growing synthesis. Its intentional categories stand magnificently alone, without visible prospect of reduction to that larger corpus. A successful reduction cannot be ruled out, in my view, but FP's explanatory impotence and long stagnation inspire little faith that its categories will find themselves neatly reflected in the framework of neuroscience. On the contrary, one is reminded of how alchemy must have looked as elemental chemistry was taking form, how Aristotelean cosmology[29] must have looked as classical mechanics was being articulated, or how the vitalist conception of life must have looked as organic chemistry marched forward.

In sketching a fair summary of this situation, we must make a special effort to abstract from the fact that FP is a central part of our current *lebenswelt*,[30] and serves as the principal vehicle of our interpersonal commerce. For these facts provide FP with a conceptual inertia that goes far beyond its purely theoretical virtues. Restricting ourselves to this latter dimension, what we must say is that FP suffers explanatory failures on an epic scale, that it has been stagnant for at least twenty-five centuries, and that its categories appear (so far) to be incommensurable with or orthogonal to the categories of the background physical science[31] whose long-term claim to explain

---

27 A Greek playwright—with Euripides and Aeschylus one of the three great dramatists of classical Greece—who died in 406 BCE.

28 Lakatos (1922–1974) was a Hungarian-born philosopher of science who taught at the London School of Economics. One of his main ideas, to which Churchland refers here, is that scientific theories are rejected or adopted on the basis of their history of "progress" or "degeneration" in the raising and solving of puzzles, rather than because experiments show them to be "true" or "false."

29 The theory of the natural world based on the philosophy of Aristotle, influential for much of the Middle Ages, but largely replaced in the seventeenth century by the "mechanical philosophy" of Descartes, Bacon, Newton, and others.

30 "Lived world"—that is, the world as it is lived in and experienced by human beings.

31 "Incommensurable with or orthogonal to" means it cannot be compared to, in this case, physical science, or that it is "at right angles" to it. For example, the taste of apples and a description of the atomic structure of lithium might be said to be "incommensurable" because it doesn't even make sense to compare them: to

human behavior seems undeniable. Any theory that meets this description must be allowed a serious candidate for outright elimination.

We can of course insist on no stronger conclusion at this stage. Nor is it my concern to do so. We are here exploring a possibility, and the facts demand no more, and no less, than it be taken seriously. The distinguishing feature of the eliminative materialist is that he takes it very seriously indeed.

III. Arguments Against Elimination

Thus the basic rationale of eliminative materialism: FP is a theory, and quite probably a false one; let us attempt, therefore to transcend it.

The rationale is clear and simple, but many find it uncompelling. It will be objected that FP is not, strictly speaking, an *empirical* theory; that it is not false, or at least not refutable by empirical considerations; and that it ought not or cannot be transcended in the fashion of a defunct empirical theory. In what follows we shall examine these objections as they flow from the most popular and best-founded of the competing positions in the philosophy of mind: functionalism.[32]

An antipathy toward eliminative materialism arises from two distinct threads running through contemporary functionalism. The first thread concerns the *normative*[33] character of FP, or at least of that central core of FP which treats of the propositional attitudes. FP, some will say, is a characterization of an ideal, or at least praiseworthy mode of internal activity. It outlines not only what it is to have and process beliefs and desires, but also (and inevitably) what it is to be rational in their administration. The ideal laid down by FP may be imperfectly achieved by empirical

humans, but this does not impugn FP as a normative characterization. Nor need such failures seriously impugn FP even as a descriptive characterization, for it remains true that our activities can be both usefully and accurately understood as rational *except for* the occasional lapse due to noise, interference, or other breakdown, which defects empirical research may eventually unravel. Accordingly, though neuroscience may usefully augment it, FP has no pressing need to be displaced, even as a descriptive theory; nor could it be replaced, qua normative characterization,[34] by any descriptive theory of neural mechanisms, since rationality is defined over propositional attitudes like beliefs and desires. FP, therefore, is here to stay.

Daniel Dennett[35] has defended a view along these lines.[36] And the view just outlined gives voice to a theme of the property dualists as well. Karl Popper and Joseph Margolis both cite the normative nature of mental and linguistic activity as a bar to their penetration or elimination by any descriptive/materialist theory.[37] I hope to deflate the appeal of such moves below.

The second thread concerns the *abstract* nature of FP. The central claim of functionalism is that the principles of FP characterize our internal states in a fashion that makes no reference to their intrinsic nature or physical constitution. Rather, they are characterized in terms of the network of causal relations they bear to one another, and to sensory circumstances and overt

---

ask if one is true and the other false, or if one is better than the other. They are simply not part of the same set of concerns or way of talking.

32 See "The Nature of Mental States" by Hilary Putnam in this chapter.

33 "Normative" means having to do with prescriptive norms or standards—with things that *ought* to be the case, rather than descriptions of things which in fact are the case. "You should make your bed," is a normative claim, while "34.7% of Canadian beds go unmade in the mornings," is a non-normative, descriptive claim.

34 "*Qua* such-and-such" means in the capacity or character of such-and-such, or as being such-and-such: for example, Napoleon, *qua* general, was a man of great stature, but *qua* human being he was rather short.

35 See the notes to Dennett's article in Chapter 6 for more information.

36 [Author's note] Most explicitly in "Three Kinds of Intentional Psychology" (forthcoming), but this theme of Dennett's goes all the way back to his "Intentional Systems," this Journal, LXVIII, 4 (Feb. 25, 1971): 87–106; reprinted in his *Brainstorms* (Montgomery, Vt.: Bradford Books, 1978).

37 [Author's note] Popper, *Objective Knowledge* (New York: Oxford, 1972); with J. Eccles, *The Self and Its Brain* (New York: Springer Verlag, 1978). Margolis, *Persons and Minds* (Boston: Reidel, 1978).

behavior. Given its abstract specification, that internal economy may therefore be realized in a nomically heterogeneous[38] variety of physical systems. All of them may differ, even radically, in their physical constitution, and yet at another level, they will all share the same nature. This view, says Fodor,[39] "is compatible with very strong claims about the ineliminability of mental language from behavioral theories."[40] Given the real possibility of multiple instantiations in heterogeneous physical substrates,[41] we cannot eliminate the functional characterization in favor of any theory peculiar to one such substrate. That would preclude our being able to describe the (abstract) organization that any one instantiation shares with all the others. A functional characterization of our internal states is therefore here to stay.

This second theme, like the first, assigns a faintly stipulative character to FP, as if the onus were on the empirical systems to instantiate faithfully the organization that FP specifies, instead of the onus being on FP to describe faithfully the internal activities of a naturally distinct class of empirical systems. This impression is enhanced by the standard examples used to illustrate the claims of functionalism—mousetraps, valve-lifters, arithmetical calculators, computers, robots, and the like. These are artifacts, constructed to fill a preconceived bill. In such cases, a failure of fit between the physical system and the relevant functional characterization impugns only the former, not the latter. The functional characterization is thus removed from empirical criticism in a way that is most unlike the case of an empirical theory. One prominent functionalist—Hilary Putnam—has argued outright that FP is not a corrigible[42] theory at all.[43] Plainly, if FP is construed on these models, as regularly it is, the question of its empirical integrity is unlikely ever to pose itself, let alone receive a critical answer.

Although fair to some functionalisms, the preceding is not entirely fair to Fodor. On his view the aim of psychology is to find the *best* functional characterization of ourselves, and what that is remains an empirical question. As well, his argument for the ineliminability of mental vocabulary from psychology does not pick out current FP in particular as ineliminable. It need claim only that *some* abstract functional characterization must be retained, some articulation or refinement of FP perhaps.

His estimate of eliminative materialism remains low, however. First, it is plain that Fodor thinks there is nothing fundamentally or interestingly wrong with FP. On the contrary, FP's central conception of cognitive activity—as consisting in the manipulation of propositional attitudes—turns up as the central element in Fodor's own theory on the nature of thought (*The Language of Thought*, *op. cit.*). And second, there remains the point that, whatever tidying up FP may or may not require, it cannot be displaced by any naturalistic theory of our physical substrate, since it is the abstract functional features of his internal states that make a person, not the chemistry of his substrate.

All of this is appealing. But almost none of it, I think, is right. Functionalism has too long enjoyed

---

38 That is, systems that follow different physical laws: "nomically" means "governed by, or having to do with, laws of nature," and "heterogeneous" means "diverse in character, dissimilar."

39 Jerry A. Fodor (1935–) is a leading American philosopher of mind currently working at Rutgers University and the City University of New York. He defends the view that folk psychological laws are underpinned by a "Language of Thought," which is a computational system of symbols, realized in the brain, having causal laws that mirror the logical structure of chains of thought. He argues that the brain is a physical system mechanically wired to operate according to intentional, normative, and logical principles.

40 [Author's note] *Psychological Explanation* (New York: Random House, 1968), p. 116.

41 See the article by Hilary Putnam in this chapter. To "instantiate" something is to be an instance of it. For example, the piece of paper on which this page is printed is (or at least was) an instantiation of the color white—it is a particular white thing. A swan, say, or a coffee mug might be other instantiations of whiteness, and so on.

42 "Corrigible" means capable of being corrected or improved.

43 [Author's note] "Robots: Machines or Artificially Created Life?", this Journal, LXI, 21 (Nov. 12, 1964): 668–691, pp. 675, 681 ff.

its reputation as a daring and *avant garde* position. It needs to be revealed for the short-sighted and reactionary position it is.

IV. The Conservative Nature of Functionalism

A valuable perspective on functionalism can be gained from the following story. To begin with, recall the alchemists' theory of inanimate matter. We have here a long and variegated tradition, of course, not a single theory, but our purposes will be served by a gloss.

The alchemists conceived the "inanimate" as entirely continuous with animated matter, in that the sensible and behavioral properties of the various substances are owed to the ensoulment of baser matter by various spirits or essences. These nonmaterial aspects were held to undergo development, just as we find growth and development in the various souls of plants, animals, and humans. The alchemist's peculiar skill lay in knowing how to seed, nourish, and bring to maturity the desired spirits enmattered in the appropriate combinations.

On one orthodoxy, the four fundamental spirits (for "inanimate" matter) were named "mercury," "sulphur," "yellow arsenic," and "sal ammoniac." Each of these spirits was held responsible for a rough but characteristic syndrome of sensible, combinatorial, and causal properties. The spirit mercury, for example, was held responsible for certain features typical of metallic substances—their shininess, liquefiability, and so forth. Sulphur was held responsible for certain residual features typical of metals, and for those displayed by the ores from which running metal could be distilled. Any given metallic substance was a critical orchestration principally of these two spirits. A similar story held for the other two spirits, and among the four of them a certain domain of physical features and transformations was rendered intelligible and controllable.

The degree of control was always limited, of course. Or better, such prediction and control as the alchemists possessed was owed more to the manipulative lore acquired as an apprentice to a master, than to any genuine insight supplied by the theory. The theory followed, more than it dictated, practice. But the theory did supply some rhyme to the practice, and in the absence of a developed alternative it was

sufficiently compelling to sustain a long and stubborn tradition.

The tradition had become faded and fragmented by the time the elemental chemistry of Lavoisier and Dalton[44] arose to replace it for good. But let us suppose that it had hung on a little longer—perhaps because the four-spirit orthodoxy had become a thumb-worn part of everyman's common sense—and let us examine the nature of the conflict between the two theories and some possible avenues of resolution.

No doubt the simplest line of resolution, and the one which historically took place, is outright displacement. The dualistic interpretation of the four essences—as immaterial spirits—will appear both feckless and unnecessary given the power of the corpuscularian taxonomy[45] of atomic chemistry. And a reduction of the old taxonomy to the new will appear impossible, given the extent to which the comparatively toothless old theory cross-classifies things relative to the new. Elimination would thus appear the only alternative—*unless* some cunning and determined defender of the alchemical vision has the wit to suggest the following defense.

Being "ensouled by mercury," or "sulphur," or either of the other two so-called spirits, is actually a *functional* state. The first, for example, is defined by the disposition to reflect light, to liquefy under heat, to unite with other matter in the same state, and so forth. And each of these four states is related to the others, in that the syndrome[46] for each varies as a function of which of the other three states is also instantiated in

----

44 Antoine Lavoisier (1743–1794) identified the gas oxygen, and described how it reacted with various substances during combustion; in doing so he is said to have founded modern chemistry. John Dalton (1766–1844) laid the foundation for modern atomic theory by suggesting that all elements are composed of atoms, that all atoms of the same element are identical, and that these atoms can be combined in various ratios to form compound substances.

45 The classification of material substances based on the nature and configuration of the tiny particles (atoms and their constituents) which make them up.

46 A "syndrome" is a characteristic pattern of symptoms or behavior.

the same substrate. Thus the level of description comprehended by the alchemical vocabulary is abstract: various material substances, suitably "ensouled," can display the features of a metal, for example, or even of gold specifically. For it is the total syndrome of occurrent and causal properties which matters, not the corpuscularian details of the substrate. Alchemy, it is concluded, comprehends a level of organization in reality distinct from and irreducible to the organization found at the level of corpuscularian chemistry.

This view might have had considerable appeal. After all, it spares alchemists the burden of defending immaterial souls that come and go; it frees them from having to meet the very strong demands of a naturalistic reduction; and it spares them the shock and confusion of outright elimination. Alchemical theory emerges as basically all right! Nor need they appear too obviously stubborn or dogmatic in this. Alchemy as it stands, they concede, may need substantial tidying up, and experience must be our guide. But we need not fear its naturalistic displacement, they remind us, since it is the particular orchestration of the syndromes of occurrent and causal properties which makes a piece of matter gold, not the idiosyncratic details of its corpuscularian substrate. A further circumstance would have made this claim even more plausible. For the fact is, the alchemists *did* know how to make gold, in this relevantly weakened sense of 'gold', and they could do so in a variety of ways. Their "gold" was never as perfect, alas, as the "gold" nurtured in nature's womb, but what mortal can expect to match the skills of nature herself?

What this story shows is that it is at least possible for the constellation of moves, claims, and defenses characteristic of functionalism to constitute an outrage against reason and truth, and to do so with a plausibility that is frightening. Alchemy is a terrible theory, well-deserving of its complete elimination, and the defense of it just explored is reactionary, obfuscatory, retrograde, and wrong. But in historical context, that defense might have seemed wholly sensible, even to reasonable people.

The alchemical example is a deliberately transparent case of what might well be called "the functionalist stratagem," and other cases are easy to imagine. A cracking good defense of the phlogiston theory of combustion[47] can also be constructed along these lines. Construe being highly phlogisticated and being dephlogisticated as functional states defined by certain syndromes of causal dispositions; point to the great variety of natural substrates capable of combustion and calxification;[48] claim an irreducible functional integrity for what has proved to lack any natural integrity; and bury the remaining defects under a pledge to contrive improvements. A similar recipe will provide new life for the four humors of medieval medicine, for the vital essence or archeus[49] of pre-modern biology, and so forth.

If its application in these other cases is any guide, the functionalist stratagem is a smokescreen for the preservation of error and confusion. Whence derives our assurance that in contemporary journals the same charade is not being played out on behalf of FP? The parallel with the case of alchemy is in all other respects distressingly complete, right down to the parallel between the search for artificial gold and the search for artificial intelligence!

Let me not be misunderstood on this last point. Both aims are worthy aims: thanks to nuclear physics, artificial (but real) gold is finally within our means, if only in submicroscopic quantities; and artificial (but real) intelligence eventually will be. But just as the careful orchestration of superficial syndromes was the wrong way to produce genuine gold, so may the careful orchestration of superficial syndromes be the wrong way to produce genuine intelligence. Just as with gold, what may be required is that our science

---

47 Phlogiston is a mythical substance, formerly thought to be a volatile constituent of all combustible substances and said to be released as flame during combustion. Since the days of Lavoisier, burning has instead been thought of as (roughly) a chemical reaction between a substance and gaseous oxygen.

48 "Calxification" means turning into a powdery metallic oxide after being burnt.

49 The *archeus*, according to the sixteenth-century Swiss alchemist and doctor Theophrastus Bombast von Hohenheim (better known by his pseudonym "Paracelsus"), is the vital principle—or life force—of the world at large. In human beings, the *archeus* is what Paracelsus called the "astral body."

penetrate to the underlying *natural* kind that gives rise to the total syndrome directly.

In summary, when confronted with the explanatory impotence, stagnant history, and systematic isolation of the intentional idioms of FP, it is not an adequate or responsive defense to insist that those idioms are abstract, functional, and irreducible in character. For one thing, this same defense could have been mounted with comparable plausibility no matter *what* haywire network of internal states our folklore had ascribed to us. And for another, the defense assumes essentially what is at issue: it assumes that it is the intentional idioms of FP, plus or minus a bit, that express the *important* features shared by all cognitive systems. But they may not. Certainly it is wrong to assume that they do, and then argue against the possibility of a materialistic displacement on grounds that it must describe matters at a level that is different from the important level. This just begs the question in favor of the older framework.

Finally, it is very important to point out that eliminative materialism is strictly *consistent* with the claim that the essence of a cognitive system resides in the abstract functional organization of its internal states. The eliminative materialist is not committed to the idea that the correct account of cognition *must* be a naturalistic account, though he may be forgiven for exploring the possibility. What he does hold is that the correct account of cognition, whether functionalistic or naturalistic, will bear about as much resemblance to FP as modern chemistry bears to four-spirit alchemy.

Let us now try to deal with the argument, against eliminative materialism, from the normative dimension of FP. This can be dealt with rather swiftly, I believe.

First, the fact that the regularities ascribed by the intentional core of FP are predicated on certain logical relations among propositions is not by itself grounds for claiming anything essentially normative about FP. To draw a relevant parallel, the fact that the regularities ascribed by the classical gas law are predicated on arithmetical relations between numbers does not imply anything essentially normative about the classical gas law. And logical relations between propositions are as much an objective matter of abstract fact as are arithmetical relations between numbers. In this respect, the law

(4) $(x) (p) (q)[((x \text{ believes that } p) \& (x \text{ believes that } (\text{if } p \text{ then } q))) \supset (\text{barring confusion, distraction, etc., } x \text{ believes that } p)]$[50]

is entirely on a par with the classical gas law

(6) $(x) (P) (V) (\mu)[((x \text{ has a pressure } P) \& (x \text{ has a volume } V) \& (x \text{ has a quantity } \mu)) \supset (\text{barring very high pressure or density, } x \text{ has a temperature of } PV/\mu R)]$[51]

A normative dimension enters only because we happen to *value* most of the patterns ascribed by FP. But we do not value all of them. Consider

(7) $(x) (p)[((x \text{ desires with all his heart that } p) \& (x \text{ learns that } \sim p)) \supset (\text{barring unusual strength of character, } x \text{ is shattered that } \sim p)]$[52]

Moreover, and as with normative convictions generally, fresh insight may motivate major changes in what we value.

Second, the laws of FP ascribe to us only a very minimal and truncated rationality, not an ideal rationality as some have suggested. The rationality characterized by the set of all FP laws falls well short of an ideal rationality. This is not surprising. We have no clear or finished conception of ideal rationality anyway; certainly the ordinary man does not. Accordingly, it is just not plausible to suppose that the explanatory failures from which FP suffers are owed primarily to human failure to live up to the ideal standard it provides. Quite to the contrary, the conception of rationality it provides appears limping and superficial, especially when compared with the dialectical complexity of our scientific history, or with the ratiocinative virtuosity displayed by any child.

---

50 If someone believes *p* and they believe if *p* is true then *q* must also be true, then, barring confusion, distraction, etc., they will believe *q*.

51 If a gas has a pressure *P*, a volume *V*, and a quantity μ then, barring very high pressure or density, its temperature will be: its pressure times its volume, divided by its quantity times the gas constant *R* (which is 8.314 joules per Kelvin).

52 If someone desires with all his heart that something is true and learns that it is not, then, barring unusual strength of character, they will be shattered.

Third, even if our current conception of rationality—and more generally, of cognitive virtue—is largely constituted within the sentential/propositional framework of FP, there is no guarantee that this framework is adequate to the deeper and more accurate account of cognitive virtue which is clearly needed. Even if we concede the categorial integrity of FP, at least as applied to language-using humans, it remains far from clear that the basic parameters of intellectual virtue are to be found at the categorial level comprehended by the propositional attitudes. After all, language use is something that is learned, by a brain already capable of vigorous cognitive activity; language use is acquired as only one among a great variety of learned manipulative skills; and it is mastered by a brain that evolution has shaped for a great many functions, language use being only the very latest and perhaps the least of them. Against the background of these facts, language use appears as an extremely peripheral activity, as a racially idiosyncratic mode of social interaction which is mastered thanks to the versatility and power of a more basic mode of activity. Why accept then, a theory of cognitive activity that models its elements on the elements of human language? And why assume that the fundamental parameters of intellectual virtue are or can be defined over the elements at this superficial level?

A serious advance in our appreciation of cognitive virtue would thus seem to *require* that we go beyond FP, that we transcend the poverty of FP's conception of rationality by transcending its propositional kinematics entirely, by developing a deeper and more general kinematics of cognitive activity, and by distinguishing within this new framework which of the kinematically possible modes of activity are to be valued and encouraged (as more efficient, reliable, productive, or whatever). Eliminative materialism thus does not imply the end of our normative concerns. It implies only that they will have to be reconstituted at a more revealing level of understanding, the level that a matured neuroscience will provide.

What a theoretically informed future might hold in store for us, we shall now turn to explore. Not because we can foresee matters with any special clarity, but because it is important to try to break the grip on our imagination held by the propositional kinematics of FP. As far as the present section is concerned, we may summarize our conclusions as follows. FP is nothing more and nothing less than a culturally entrenched theory of how we and the higher animals work. It has no special features that make it empirically invulnerable, no unique functions that make it irreplaceable, no special status of any kind whatsoever. We shall turn a skeptical ear then, to any special pleading on its behalf.

V. Beyond Folk Psychology

What might the elimination of FP actually involve—not just the comparatively straightforward idioms for sensation, but the entire apparatus of propositional attitudes? That depends heavily on what neuroscience might discover, and on our determination to capitalize on it. Here follow three scenarios in which the operative conception of cognitive activity is progressively divorced from the forms and categories that characterize natural language. If the reader will indulge the lack of actual substance, I shall try to sketch some plausible form.

First suppose that research into the structure and activity of the brain, both fine-grained and global, finally does yield a new kinematics and correlative dynamics for what is now thought of as cognitive activity. The theory is uniform for all terrestrial brains, not just human brains, and it makes suitable conceptual contact with both evolutionary biology and non-equilibrium thermodynamics.[53] It ascribes to us, at any given time, a set or configuration of complex states, which are specified within the theory as figurative "solids" within a four- or five-dimensional phase space. The laws of the theory govern the interaction, motion, and transformation of these "solid" states within that space, and also their relations to whatever sensory and motor transducers[54] the system possesses.

---

53 The science of the flow of energy through systems which are not in equilibrium.

54 A transducer is a device to convert one form of energy into another: for example, a speaker is a transducer that turns electrical energy into sound; similarly, the ear turns sound waves into neural signals.

As with celestial mechanics,[55] the exact specification of the "solids" involved and the exhaustive accounting of all dynamically relevant adjacent "solids" is not practically possible, for many reasons, but here also it turns out that the obvious approximations we fall back on yield excellent explanations/predictions of internal change and external behavior; at least in the short term. Regarding long-term activity, the theory provides powerful and unified accounts of the learning process, the nature of mental illness, and variations in character and intelligence across the animal kingdom as well as across individual humans.

Moreover, it provides a straightforward account of "knowledge," as traditionally conceived. According to the new theory, any declarative sentence to which a speaker would give confident assent is merely a one-dimensional *projection*—through the compound lens of Wernicke's and Broca's areas[56] onto the idiosyncratic surface of the speaker's language—a one-dimensional projection of a four- or five-dimensional "solid" that is an element in his true kinematical state. (Recall the shadows on the wall of Plato's cave.[57]) Being projections of that inner reality, such sentences do carry significant information regarding it and are thus fit to function as elements in a communication system. On the other hand, being subdimensional projections, they reflect but a narrow part of the reality projected. They are therefore *un*fit to represent the deeper reality in all its kinematically, dynamically, and even normatively relevant respects. That is to say, a system of propositional attitudes, such as FP, must inevitably fail to capture what is going on here, though it may reflect just enough superficial structure to sustain an alchemy-like tradition among folk who

lack any better theory. From the perspective of the newer theory, however, it is plain that there simply are no law-governed states of the kind FP postulates. The real laws governing our internal activities are defined over different and much more complex kinematical states and configurations, as are the normative criteria for developmental integrity and intellectual virtue.

A theoretical outcome of the kind just described may fairly be counted as a case of elimination of one theoretical ontology in favor of another, but the success here imagined for systematic neuroscience need not have any sensible effect on common practice. Old ways die hard, and in the absence of some practical necessity, they may not die at all. Even so, it is not inconceivable that some segment of the population, or all of it, should become intimately familiar with the vocabulary required to characterize our kinematical states, learn the laws governing their interactions and behavioral projections, acquire a facility in their first-person ascription, and displace the use of FP altogether, even in the marketplace. The demise of FP's ontology would then be complete.

We may now explore a second and rather more radical possibility. Everyone is familiar with Chomsky's[58] thesis that the human mind or brain contains innately and uniquely the abstract structures for learning and using specifically human natural languages. A competing hypothesis is that our brain does indeed contain innate structures, but that those structures have as their original and still primary function the organization of perceptual experience, the administration of linguistic categories being an acquired and additional function for which evolution has only incidentally suited them.[59] This hypothesis has the

---

55 The study of the movements of the stars, planets, and so on.

56 These are areas of the brain associated with language understanding.

57 This is a reference to Book 7 of Plato's *Republic* in which the ascent to true knowledge is compared to walking out of a cave. At first, all we see are shadows cast on the wall in front of us, and we think that that is reality; then we come to see the objects themselves that cast those shadows; and finally we can leave the cave and enter the blinding light of Truth.

58 Noam Chomsky (1928–), a professor at the Massachusetts Institute of Technology, is perhaps the most famous living linguist and has written extensively on the philosophy of mind (as well as on political and social issues).

59 [Author's note] Richard Gregory defends such a view in "The Grammar of Vision," *Listener*, LXXXIII, 2133 (February 1970): 242–246; reprinted in his *Concepts and Mechanisms of Perception* (London: Duckworth, 1975), pp. 622–629.

advantage of not requiring the evolutionary saltation[60] that Chomsky's view would seem to require, and there are other advantages as well. But these matters need not concern us here. Suppose, for our purposes, that this competing view is true, and consider the following story.

Research into the neural structures that fund the organization and processing of perceptual information reveals that they are capable of administering a great variety of complex tasks, some of them showing a complexity far in excess of that shown by natural language. Natural languages, it turns out, exploit only a very elementary portion of the available machinery, the bulk of which serves far more complex activities beyond the ken of the propositional conceptions of FP. The detailed unraveling of what that machinery is and of the capacities it has makes it plain that a form of language far more sophisticated than "natural" language, though decidedly "alien" in its syntactic and semantic structures, could also be learned and used by our innate systems. Such a novel system of communication, it is quickly realized, could raise the efficiency of information exchange between brains by an order of magnitude, and would enhance epistemic evaluation by a comparable amount, since it would reflect the underlying structure of our cognitive activities in greater detail than does natural language.

Guided by our new understanding of those internal structures, we manage to construct a new system of verbal communication entirely distinct from natural language, with a new and more powerful combinatorial grammar over novel elements forming novel combinations with exotic properties. The compounded strings of this alternative system—call them "übersatzen"[61]—are not evaluated as true or false, nor are the relations between them remotely analogous to the relations of entailment, etc., that hold between sentences. They display a different organization and manifest different virtues.

Once constructed, this "language" proves to be learnable; it has the power projected; and in two generations it has swept the planet. Everyone uses the new system. The syntactic forms and semantic categories of so-called "natural" language disappear entirely. And with them disappear the propositional attitudes of FP, displaced by a more revealing scheme in which (of course) "übersatzenal attitudes" play the leading role. FP again suffers elimination.

This second story, note, illustrates a theme with endless variations. There are possible as many different "folk psychologies" as there are possible differently structured communication systems to serve as models for them.

A third and even stranger possibility can be outlined as follows. We know that there is considerable lateralization[62] of function between the two cerebral hemispheres, and that the two hemispheres make use of the information they get from each other by way of the great cerebral commissure—the corpus callosum—a giant cable of neurons connecting them. Patients whose commissure has been surgically severed display a variety of behavioral deficits that indicate a loss of access by one hemisphere to information it used to get from the other. However, in people with callosal agenesis (a congenital defect in which the connecting cable is simply absent), there is little or no behavioral deficit, suggesting that the two hemispheres have learned to exploit the information carried in other less direct pathways connecting them through the subcortical regions. This suggests that, even in the normal case, a developing hemisphere *learns* to make use of the information the cerebral commissure deposits at its doorstep. What we have then, in the case of a normal human, is two physically distinct cognitive systems (both capable of independent function) responding in a systematic and learned fashion to exchanged information. And what is especially interesting about this case is the sheer, amount of information exchanged. The cable of the commissure consists of $\approx$200 million neurons,[63] and even if we assume that each of these fibres is capable

---

60   "Saltation" is a drastic change in an organism's phenotype (its observable physical and behavioral characteristics) caused by one or only a few mutations of its genotype (its genetic make-up).

61   "Super-sentences" (on the model of Nietzsche's word "*Übermensch*," meaning superman).

---

62   Localization to either the left or right side of the brain.

63   [Author's note] M. S. Gazzaniga and J. E. LeDoux, *The Integrated Mind* (New York: Plenum Press, 1975).

of one of only two possible states each second (a most conservative estimate), we are looking at a channel whose information capacity is $> 2 \times 10^8$ binary bits/second. Compare this to the < 500 bits/second capacity of spoken English.

Now, if two distinct hemispheres can learn to communicate on so impressive a scale, why shouldn't two distinct brains learn to do it also? This would require an artificial "commissure" of some kind, but let us suppose that we can fashion a workable transducer for implantation at some site in the brain that research reveals to be suitable, a transducer to convert a symphony of neural activity into (say) microwaves radiated from an aerial in the forehead, and to perform the reverse function of converting received microwaves back into neural activation. Connecting it up need not be an insuperable problem. We simply trick the normal processes of dendritic arborization[64] into growing their own myriad connections with the active microsurface of the transducer.

Once the channel is opened between two or more people, they can learn (*learn*) to exchange information and coordinate their behavior with the same intimacy and virtuosity displayed by your own cerebral hemispheres. Think what this might do for hockey teams, and ballet companies, and research teams! If the entire population were thus fitted out, spoken language of any kind might well disappear completely, a victim of the "why crawl when you can fly?" principle. Libraries become filled not with books, but with long recordings of exemplary bouts of neural activity. These constitute a growing cultural heritage, an evolving "Third World," to use Karl Popper's terms.[65] But they do not consist of sentences or arguments.

How will such people understand and conceive of other individuals? To this question I can only answer, "In roughly the same fashion that your right hemisphere 'understands' and 'conceives of' your left hemisphere—intimately and efficiently, but not propositionally!"

These speculations, I hope, will evoke the required sense of untapped possibilities, and I shall in any case bring them to a close here. Their function is to make some inroads into the aura of inconceivability that commonly surrounds the idea that we might reject FP. The felt conceptual strain even finds expression in an argument to the effect that the thesis of eliminative materialism is incoherent since it denies the very conditions presupposed by the assumption that it is meaningful. I shall close with a brief discussion of this very popular move.

As I have received it, the reductio[66] proceeds by pointing out that the statement of eliminative materialism is just a meaningless string of marks or noises, unless that string is the expression of a certain *belief*, and a certain *intention* to communicate, and a *knowledge* of the grammar of the language, and so forth. But if the statement of eliminative materialism is true, then there are no such states to express. The statement at issue would then be a meaningless string of marks or noises. It would therefore *not* be true. Therefore it is not true. Q.E.D.

The difficulty with any nonformal reductio is that the conclusion against the initial assumption is always no better than the material[67] assumptions invoked to reach the incoherent conclusion. In this case the additional assumptions involve a certain theory of meaning, one that presupposes the integrity of FP. But formally speaking, one can as well infer, from the incoherent result, that this theory of meaning is what must be rejected. Given the independent critique of FP leveled earlier, this would even seem the preferred option. But in any case, one cannot simply assume that particular theory of meaning without begging the question[68] at issue, namely, the integrity of FP.

64   The tree-like growth of dendrites, which are branched protoplasmic extensions of nerve cells that carry impulses from nearby nerves into the cell body.

65   In this context, of course, Churchland does not mean the unaligned less-developed countries but refers to Karl Popper's idea that there are three spheres (each of which has perfectly objective existence): the physical, the mental, and the realm of human knowledge.

66   Short for *reductio ad absurdum*, which means showing that a position is false because it leads to logical absurdity.

67   Non-formal—not strictly logical.

68   To beg the question is to assume as true the very thing which you are arguing for.

The question-begging nature of this move is most graphically illustrated by the following analogue, which I owe to Patricia Churchland.[69] The issue here, placed in the seventeenth century, is whether there exists such a substance as *vital spirit*. At the time, this substance was held, without significant awareness of real alternatives, to be that which distinguished the animate from the inanimate. Given the monopoly enjoyed by this conception, given the degree to which it was integrated with many of our other conceptions, and given the magnitude of the revisions any serious alternative conception would require, the following refutation of any anti-vitalist claim would be found instantly plausible.

> The anti-vitalist says that there is no such thing as vital spirit. But this claim is self-refuting.

---

69   [Author's note] "Is Determinism Self-Refuting?", *Mind*, forthcoming.

The speaker can expect to be taken seriously only if his claim cannot. For if the claim is true, then the speaker does not have vital spirit and must be *dead*. But if he is dead, then his statement is a meaningless string of noises, devoid of reason and truth.

The question-begging nature of this argument does not, I assume, require elaboration. To those moved by the earlier argument, I commend the parallel for examination.

The thesis of this paper may be summarized as follows. The propositional attitudes of folk psychology do not constitute an unbreachable barrier to the advancing tide of neuroscience. On the contrary, the principled displacement of folk psychology is not only richly possible, it represents one of the most intriguing theoretical displacements we can currently imagine.

THOMAS NAGEL

"What Is It Like to Be a Bat?"

Who Is Thomas Nagel?

Thomas Nagel, an important American philosopher, is currently a Professor of Law and Philosophy at New York University. Born in 1937, Nagel was educated at Cornell (BA), Corpus Christi College, Oxford (BPhil), and Harvard (PhD, completed in 1963). After working at Berkeley and Princeton, he moved to New York University in 1980.

Throughout his career a main theme of Nagel's philosophical writing has been the difficulty of reconciling two fundamentally different points of view: our first-person, subjective, personal point of view, and the impartial, third-person, objective perspective.[1]

---

1   "First-person" and "third-person" are terms taken from grammatical categories: "I am hungry," is a first-

The first-person perspective is typically thought of as being more partial than the third-person—partial both in the sense of being constrained by local horizons, and of being infected with personal concerns and biases. (For example, from *my* point of view it is right and natural to eat with a knife and fork, but this seems natural to me only because of the place and manner of my upbringing: speaking objectively, forks are no more nor less 'natural' than chopsticks or fingers.) As a result, subjective impressions are often thought of as being less reliable or 'true' than objective claims, and the first-person perspective tends

---

person sentence as it's about the speaker; "She/he/it is hungry," is a third-person sentence, as it's about a third party. ("You are hungry," would be an example of a second-person sentence.)

to be treated as something to be avoided in serious knowledge-gathering enterprises such as science or good journalism. Nagel's guiding philosophical question is this: *could* we completely understand the universe from the third-person point of view—that is, is the subjective completely reducible to (or eliminable in favor of) the objective? As he puts it in one of his books, he wants to know "how to combine the perspective of a particular person inside the world with an objective view of that same world, the person and his viewpoint included."

The short version of Nagel's response to this problem is the following:

1. The subjective perspective is ineliminable in various highly important ways, and a refusal to notice this can lead to philosophical errors. "Appearance and perspective are essential parts of what there is." Our objectivity is limited by the fact that we cannot leave our own viewpoints entirely behind.

2. However, objectivity is also to be valued and fostered as a crucial method of coming to understand aspects of the world as it is in itself. It is important that we struggle to transcend our local horizons and try to get a better view of our place in the universe.

Most of Nagel's books trace these themes, in one way or another. *The View From Nowhere*, his best-known book, published in 1986, is explicitly about the relation between the subjective and the objective. His first book, *The Possibility of Altruism*, dealt with the conflict between personal and impersonal reasons for individual action, and one of his later books, *Equality and Partiality*, examines the issue of reconciling individual claims with those of a group. Nagel's latest book, *The Last Word*, defends the objectivity and importance of rationality against a kind of "anything goes" subjectivism which Nagel opposes. "What Is It Like to Be a Bat?" is probably Nagel's most famous and influential article. In it he applies his theme to the philosophy of mind, and contends that all current third-person theories of the mind (such as identity-theory, behaviorism, or functionalism) are radically incomplete since they fail to capture "what it is like to be" conscious, and this subjective character of experience, Nagel suggests, is a central aspect of mentality.

In the preface to his book *Mortal Questions,* Nagel describes his view of philosophy, and it is worth repeating here:

> I believe one should trust problems over solutions, intuition over arguments, and pluralistic discord over systematic harmony. Simplicity and elegance are never reasons to think that a philosophical theory is true: on the contrary, they are usually grounds for thinking it false. Given a knockdown argument for an intuitively unacceptable conclusion, one should assume there is probably something wrong with the argument that one cannot detect—though it is always possible that the source of the intuition has been misidentified.... Often the problem has to be reformulated because an adequate answer to the original formulation fails to make the *sense* of the problem disappear.... Superficiality is as hard to avoid in philosophy as it is anywhere else. It is too easy to reach solutions that fail to do justice to the difficulty of the problems. All one can do is try to maintain a desire for answers, a tolerance for long periods without any, an unwillingness to brush aside unexplained intuitions, and an adherence to reasonable standards of clear expression and cogent argument.

What Is the Structure of This Reading?

Nagel begins by saying that the problem of reducing the mental to the physical—of completely describing and explaining our mental life in physical, non-psychological terms—is uniquely difficult because of the nature of conscious experience, and he goes on to explain this by discussing the relation between subjective and objective facts, using bats as an example. After an aside, where he discusses the relation between facts and conceptual schemes for representing those facts, Nagel proceeds to argue that subjective facts about consciousness make the mind-body problem intractable. One of his central claims is that the reduction of experience to neurophysiology (i.e., the physiology of the brain and nervous system) is importantly different from standard cases of reduction (e.g., the reduction of heat to mean molecular motion). Nagel then discusses what philosophical moral should be drawn from all this—what implications it has, for example, for the claim that mental states are identical with brain states. He closes by suggesting that we pursue a solution to the problem he has raised by trying to develop an "objective phenomenology" of the mental.

Some Useful Background Information

Nagel is reacting against attempts in the 1960s and early 1970s to *reduce* the mental to the physical—that is, to show that, properly understood, mental phenomena are nothing more than physical phenomena. There are two central varieties of reduction, sometimes called "ontological reduction" and "theory reduction." Ontological reduction consists in showing that objects (or properties or events) of the first type are identical with—or "realized by"—objects (properties, events) of the second: for example, it might be that genes are identical with DNA molecules, or that lightning is nothing but a kind of electrical discharge, or that the color purple is just reflected light of a particular wavelength. Theory reduction consists in showing that all the statements of one higher-level theory can be translated into (or otherwise deduced from) statements of another more fundamental theory: for example (roughly speaking), the Mendelian

laws of genetics are entailed by molecular biology, and our commonsense "theory" of temperature can be translated into the kinetic theory of matter.

Nagel's anti-reductive claim is, therefore, that any optimism we might feel, that mental entities such as beliefs and emotions can be shown to be identical with neurological or functional states, or that psychological theories can someday be translated into some non-psychological language, is seriously misguided.

Some Common Misconceptions

1. It is sometimes thought Nagel argues that physicalism is false: that is, that the mental involves something *extra* over and above the physical. (This would make Nagel some kind of dualist.) However, Nagel does not claim this: instead, he argues that *existing* physicalist theories of the mental (behaviorism, identity theory, functionalism) must be wrong, and he suggests that, although physicalism may be true—or even demonstrably true—it will be very hard for us to understand *how* it can be true. That is, he worries about the difficulty of giving any kind of objective theory of the mind.

2. There are various kinds of "subjectivity," and it has sometimes puzzled people exactly which kind Nagel is worrying about (perhaps because Nagel himself does not distinguish between some of them). One variety of non-objectivity that Nagel is clear he is *not* endorsing, however, is a particular kind of privacy of the mental. Some philosophers (such as Descartes) have held that consciousness is radically private in the sense that we have a special kind of access to our own mental states which, in principle, we cannot have to physical states. If this were true, then I could look as hard as I liked at your brain (which is a physical object) and *never* see any of your mental states; it would mean that the only access to consciousness must necessarily be from the first person, and thus that science would be forever excluded from studying and describing it. It is easy to see how this view might be confused with the one Nagel develops in this article, but nevertheless it is

importantly different. For example, Nagel actually *denies* that we could never come to know anything at all about other people's consciousness, and even asserts that we can be corrected by other people when we make mistakes about what we ourselves are feeling (i.e., we are not "incorrigible"). For Nagel, the problem is not some metaphysical difference of access to the mental and physical, but a problem about reconciling subjective and objective categories. Other versions of "subjectivity" which may (or may not) be in play in this article include:

- having a particular point of view or perspective;
- being phenomenal or experiential (i.e., feeling a certain way);
- having a sense of oneself as being a subject—as being a creature that, for example, undergoes sensations, forms intentions to do things, and controls its own actions;
- being infallibly known or present to one's awareness (like the kind of raging toothache which is impossible to ignore and which one couldn't possibly be mistaken about).

Suggestions for Critical Reflection

1. Many commentators suggest (as hinted above) that Nagel collapses together two or three different kinds of subjectivity that would be better kept separate. Do you agree with this criticism? If so, how much of a problem (if any) does this cause for Nagel's arguments?

2. Do you think Nagel makes a good case for the claim that the reduction of, say, pain to some objectively-describable physical state is a very different ball game than the reduction of, for example, heat or liquidity to microphysical properties? If he's right about this, what philosophical implications are there (if any)?

3. Do you agree that there must be some facts—some things which are true—which could never be known by any human being, no matter how smart or well-informed?

4. Given Nagel's arguments, do you think that physicalism could possibly be true? That is,

does Nagel leave open the possibility that everything that exists is, at bottom, physical (e.g., composed out of matter and energy)?

5. What do you think of Nagel's proposal for an "objective phenomenology"? What might such a theory look like? Is it even possible? Does Nagel *really* hold open the possibility of an objective description of the subjective character of experience?

Suggestions for Further Reading

Nagel's main works are *The Possibility of Altruism* (Oxford University Press, 1970), *The View From Nowhere* (Oxford University Press, 1986), *The Last Word* (Oxford, 1997), and the collection of papers *Mortal Questions* (Cambridge University Press, 1979), which includes "What Is It Like to Be a Bat?" "Brain Bisection and the Unity of Consciousness," another of Nagel's influential papers on the philosophy of mind, also appears in this volume. He has also written a popular short introduction to philosophy, *What Does It All Mean?* (Oxford University Press, 1987). Nagel's views on the subjectivity of consciousness are discussed in many works: two useful discussions to start with are found in Daniel Dennett's *Consciousness Explained* (Little, Brown, 1991) and John Searle's *The Rediscovery of Mind* (MIT Press, 1992). Dennett argues Nagel is wrong; Searle says he is right, but that it doesn't matter.

"What Is It Like to Be a Bat?"[2]

Consciousness is what makes the mind-body problem really intractable. Perhaps that is why current discussions of the problem give it little attention or get it obviously wrong. The recent wave of reductionist euphoria has produced several analyses of mental phenomena and mental concepts designed to explain the possibility of some variety of materialism,

---

2   This article was first published in 1974 in *The Philosophical Review* (Volume 83, Issue 4, October 1974, pp. 435–450). Published by Duke University Press.

psychophysical identification, or reduction.[3] But the problems dealt with are those common to this type of reduction and other types, and what makes the mind-body problem unique, and unlike the water-H_2O problem or the Turing machine–IBM machine problem[4] or the lightning–electrical discharge problem or the gene-DNA problem or the oak tree–hydrocarbon problem, is ignored.

Every reductionist has his favorite analogy from modern science. It is most unlikely that any of these unrelated examples of successful reduction will shed

---

3 [Author's note] Examples are J.J.C. Smart, *Philosophy and Scientific Realism* (London, 1963); David K. Lewis, "An Argument for the Identity Theory," *Journal of Philosophy*, LXIII (1966), reprinted with addenda in David M. Rosenthal, *Materialism & the Mind-Body Problem* (Englewood Cliffs, N. J., 1971); Hilary Putnam, "Psychological Predicates" in Capitan and Merrill, *Art, Mind, & Religion* (Pittsburgh, 1967), reprinted in Rosenthal, *op. cit.*, as "The Nature of Mental States"; D.M. Armstrong, *A Materialist Theory of the Mind* (London, 1968); D.C. Dennett, *Content and Consciousness* (London, 1969). I have expressed earlier doubts in "Armstrong on the Mind," *Philosophical Review*, LXXIX (1970), 394–403; "Brain Bisection and the Unity of Consciousness," *Synthèse*, 22 (1971); and a review of Dennett, *Journal of Philosophy*, LXIX (1972). See also Saul Kripke, "Naming and Necessity" in Davidson and Harman, *Semantics of Natural Language* (Dordrecht, 1972), esp. pp. 334–342; and M.T. Thornton, "Ostensive Terms and Materialism," *The Monist*, 56 (1972).

4 By "IBM machine" Nagel simply means a computer. A Turing machine is an idealized computing device (thought up by the British mathematician Alan Turing in 1936) which consists in nothing more than a (potentially infinite) paper tape divided into squares, and a read-write head which moves left or right one square at a time and can write or erase the symbol "1" on the tape. Turing argued that any effective mathematical method or "algorithm"—and thus any computer program whatever, such as say Microsoft Word for the Macintosh—can in principle be run on a Turing machine. See the notes to the Putnam reading in this chapter for more information.

light on the relation of mind to brain. But philosophers share the general human weakness for explanations of what is incomprehensible in terms suited for what is familiar and well understood, though entirely different. This has led to the acceptance of implausible accounts of the mental largely because they would permit familiar kinds of reduction. I shall try to explain why the usual examples do not help us to understand the relation between mind and body—why, indeed, we have at present no conception of what an explanation of the physical nature of a mental phenomenon would be. Without consciousness the mind-body problem would be much less interesting. With consciousness it seems hopeless. The most important and characteristic feature of conscious mental phenomena is very poorly understood. Most reductionist theories do not even try to explain it. And careful examination will show that no currently available concept of reduction is applicable to it. Perhaps a new theoretical form can be devised for the purpose, but such a solution, if it exists, lies in the distant intellectual future.

Conscious experience is a widespread phenomenon. It occurs at many levels of animal life, though we cannot be sure of its presence in the simpler organisms, and it is very difficult to say in general what provides evidence of it. (Some extremists have been prepared to deny it even of mammals other than man.) No doubt it occurs in countless forms totally unimaginable to us, on other planets in other solar systems throughout the universe. But no matter how the form may vary, the fact that an organism has conscious experience *at all* means, basically, that there is something it is like to *be* that organism. There may be further implications about the form of the experience; there may even (though I doubt it) be implications about the behavior of the organism. But fundamentally an organism has conscious mental states if and only if there is something that it is like to *be* that organism—something it is like *for* the organism.

We may call this the subjective character of experience. It is not captured by any of the familiar, recently devised reductive analyses of the mental, for all of them are logically compatible with its absence. It is not analyzable in terms of any explanatory system of functional states, or intentional states,[5] since these could be ascribed to robots or automata that behaved like people though they experienced nothing.[6] It is not analyzable in terms of the causal role of experiences in relation to typical human behavior—for similar reasons.[7] I do not deny that conscious mental states and events cause behavior, nor that they may be given functional characterizations. I deny only that this kind of thing exhausts their analysis. Any reductionist program has to be based on an analysis of what is to be reduced. If the analysis leaves something out, the problem will be falsely posed. It is useless to base the defense of materialism on any analysis of mental phenomena that fails to deal explicitly with their subjective character. For there is no reason to suppose that a reduction which seems plausible when no attempt is made to account for conscious-

ness can be extended to include consciousness. Without some idea, therefore, of what the subjective character of experience is, we cannot know what is required of a physicalist theory.

While an account of the physical basis of mind must explain many things, this appears to be the most difficult. It is impossible to exclude the phenomenological[8] features of experience from a reduction in the same way that one excludes the phenomenal features of an ordinary substance from a physical or chemical reduction of it—namely, by explaining them as effects on the minds of human observers.[9] If physicalism is to be defended, the phenomenological features must themselves be given a physical account. But when we examine their subjective character it seems that such a result is impossible. The reason is that every subjective phenomenon is essentially connected with a single point of view, and it seems inevitable that an objective, physical theory will abandon that point of view.

Let me first try to state the issue somewhat more fully than by referring to the relation between the subjective and the objective, or between the *pour-soi* and the *en-soi*.[10] This is far from easy. Facts about what it is like to be an *X* are very peculiar, so peculiar that some may be inclined to doubt their reality, or the significance of claims about them. To illustrate the connection between subjectivity and a point of view, and to make evident the importance of subjective features, it will help to explore the matter in relation to an example

---

5 A functional state is characterized by its causal role (rather than by, say, what it is made of). *Being a can opener* is a functional property since anything which takes a certain kind of input—closed cans—and produces a certain kind of output—cans neatly opened at one end—is a can opener. (By contrast, *being a piece of gold* is usually considered a physical but not a functional property: it has to do with what the lump is made of, rather than what it does.)

An intentional state is one which has what philosophers call "intentionality," a technical term for 'aboutness' or, roughly, meaningfulness. Thus an intentional state is one which is about something else (such as the state of a register in a computer's CPU, as compared with, say, the position of a randomly chosen pebble on a beach). See the notes to the Searle reading in this chapter for more information on intentionality.

6 [Author's note] Perhaps there could not actually be such robots. Perhaps anything complex enough to behave like a person would have experiences. But that, if true, is a fact which cannot be discovered merely by analyzing the concept of experience.

7 [Author's note] It is not equivalent to that about which we are incorrigible, both because we are not incorrigible about experience and because experience is present in animals lacking language and thought, who have no beliefs at all about their experiences.

8 "Phenomenological" means having to do with phenomenology, and phenomenology is the description of the features of our lived conscious experience (as opposed to the features of what it is experience *of*). So, for example, the phenomenology of our perception of trees does not concern itself with actual trees and their relations to perceivers, but instead examines what it *feels* like to see a tree—what kind of picture we have in our head, if you like.

9 [Author's note] Cf. Richard Rorty, "Mind-Body Identity, Privacy, and Categories," *The Review of Metaphysics*, XIX (1965), esp. 37–38.

10 *Pour-soi* means "for itself" and *en-soi* means "in itself." In this context, the phrase refers to the contrast between consciousness and mere thing-hood.

that brings out clearly the divergence between the two types of conception, subjective and objective.

I assume we all believe that bats have experience. After all, they are mammals, and there is no more doubt that they have experience than that mice or pigeons or whales have experience. I have chosen bats instead of wasps or flounders because if one travels too far down the phylogenetic tree,[11] people gradually shed their faith that there is experience there at all. Bats, although more closely related to us than those other species, nevertheless present a range of activity and a sensory apparatus so different from ours that the problem I want to pose is exceptionally vivid (though it certainly could be raised with other species). Even without the benefit of philosophical reflection, anyone who has spent some time in an enclosed space with an excited bat knows what it is to encounter a fundamentally *alien* form of life.

I have said that the essence of the belief that bats have experience is that there is something that it is like to be a bat. Now we know that most bats (the microchiroptera, to be precise) perceive the external world primarily by sonar, or echolocation, detecting the reflections, from objects within range, of their own rapid, subtly modulated, high-frequency shrieks. Their brains are designed to correlate the outgoing impulses with the subsequent echoes, and the information thus acquired enables bats to make precise discriminations of distance, size, shape, motion, and texture comparable to those we make by vision. But bat sonar, though clearly a form of perception, is not similar in its operation to any sense that we possess, and there is no reason to suppose that it is subjectively like anything we can experience or imagine. This appears to create difficulties for the notion of what it is like to be a bat. We must consider whether any method will permit us to extrapolate to the inner life of the bat from our own case,[12] and if not, what alternative methods there may be for understanding the notion.

---

11 (Roughly) the scale of evolutionary development.

12 [Author's note] By "our own case" I do not mean just "my own case," but rather the mentalistic ideas that we apply unproblematically to ourselves and other human beings.

Our own experience provides the basic material for our imagination, whose range is therefore limited. It will not help to try to imagine that one has webbing on one's arms, which enables one to fly around at dusk and dawn catching insects in one's mouth; that one has very poor vision, and perceives the surrounding world by a system of reflected high-frequency sound signals; and that one spends the day hanging upside down by one's feet in an attic. In so far as I can imagine this (which is not very far), it tells me only what it would be like for *me* to behave as a bat behaves. But that is not the question. I want to know what it is like for a *bat* to be a bat. Yet if I try to imagine this, I am restricted to the resources of my own mind, and those resources are inadequate to the task. I cannot perform it either by imagining additions to my present experience, or by imagining segments gradually subtracted from it, or by imagining some combination of additions, subtractions, and modifications.

To the extent that I could look and behave like a wasp or a bat without changing my fundamental structure, my experiences would not be anything like the experiences of those animals. On the other hand, it is doubtful that any meaning can be attached to the supposition that I should possess the internal neurophysiological constitution of a bat. Even if I could by gradual degrees be transformed into a bat, nothing in my present constitution enables me to imagine what the experiences of such a future stage of myself thus metamorphosed would be like. The best evidence would come from the experiences of bats, if we only knew what they were like.

So if extrapolation from our own case is involved in the idea of what it is like to be a bat, the extrapolation must be incompletable. We cannot form more than a schematic conception of what it is like. For example, we may ascribe general *types* of experience on the basis of the animal's structure and behavior. Thus we describe bat sonar as a form of three-dimensional forward perception; we believe that bats feel some versions of pain, fear, hunger, and lust, and that they have other, more familiar types of perception besides sonar. But we believe that these experiences also have in each case a specific subjective character, which it is beyond our ability to conceive. And if there is conscious life elsewhere in the universe, it is likely that some of it will not be describable even in the most general experiential terms available to us.[13] (The problem is not confined to exotic cases, however, for it exists between one person and another. The subjective character of the experience of a person deaf and blind from birth is not accessible to me, for example, nor presumably is mine to him. This does not prevent us each from believing that the other's experience has such a subjective character.)

If anyone is inclined to deny that we can believe in the existence of facts like this whose exact nature we cannot possibly conceive, he should reflect that in contemplating the bats we are in much the same position that intelligent bats or Martians[14] would occupy if they tried to form a conception of what it was like to be us. The structure of their own minds might make it impossible for them to succeed, but we know they would be wrong to conclude that there is not anything precise that it is like to be us: that only certain general types of mental state could be ascribed to us (perhaps perception and appetite would be concepts common to us both; perhaps not). We know they would be wrong to draw such a skeptical conclusion because we know what it is like to be us. And we know that while it includes an enormous amount of variation and complexity, and while we do not possess the vocabulary to describe it adequately, its subjective character is highly specific, and in some respects describable in terms that can be understood only by creatures like us. The fact that we cannot expect ever to accommodate in our language a detailed description of Martian or bat phenomenology should not lead us to dismiss as meaningless the claim that bats and Martians have experiences fully comparable in richness of detail to our own. It would be fine if someone were to develop concepts and a theory that enabled us to think about those things; but such an understanding may be permanently denied to us by the limits of our nature. And to deny the reality or logical significance of what we can never describe or understand is the crudest form of cognitive dissonance.

This brings us to the edge of a topic that requires much more discussion than I can give it here: namely, the relation between facts on the one hand and conceptual schemes or systems of representation on the other. My realism about the subjective domain in all its forms implies a belief in the existence of facts beyond the reach of human concepts. Certainly it is possible for a human being to believe that there are facts which humans never *will* possess the requisite concepts to represent or comprehend. Indeed, it would be foolish to doubt this, given the finiteness of humanity's expectations. After all, there would have been transfinite numbers even if everyone had been wiped out by the Black Death before Cantor[15] discovered them. But one might also believe that there are facts which *could* not ever be represented or comprehended by human beings, even if the species lasted forever—simply because our structure does not permit us to operate with concepts of the requisite type. This impossibility might even be observed by other beings, but it is not clear that the existence of such beings, or the possibility of their existence, is a precondition of the significance of the hypothesis that there are humanly inaccessible facts. (After all, the nature of beings with access to humanly inaccessible facts is presumably itself a humanly inaccessible fact.) Reflection on what it is like to be a bat seems to lead us, therefore, to the conclusion that there are facts that do not consist in the truth of propositions expressible in a human language. We can be compelled to recognize the existence of such facts without being able to state or comprehend them.

I shall not pursue this subject, however. Its bearing on the topic before us (namely, the mind-body problem) is that it enables us to make a general observation about the subjective character of expe-

---

13   [Author's note] Therefore the analogical form of the English expression "what it is *like*" is misleading. It does not mean "what (in our experience) it *resembles*," but rather "how it is for the subject himself."

14   [Author's note] Any intelligent extraterrestrial beings totally different from us.

15   Georg Cantor (1845–1918) was a German mathematician. His theory of transfinite numbers is a mathematical theory of infinity which introduces a sequence of infinite cardinal numbers (called 'aleph-numbers,' and written $\aleph_0$, $\aleph_1$, $\aleph_2$ ...) of increasing size. That is, intuitively, Cantor formalized the fact that some infinities are bigger than others.

rience. Whatever may be the status of facts about what it is like to be a human being, or a bat, or a Martian, these appear to be facts that embody a particular point of view.

I am not adverting here to the alleged privacy of experience to its possessor. The point of view in question is not one accessible only to a single individual. Rather it is a *type*. It is often possible to take up a point of view other than one's own, so the comprehension of such facts is not limited to one's own case. There is a sense in which phenomenological facts are perfectly objective: one person can know or say of another what the quality of the other's experience is. They are subjective, however, in the sense that even this objective ascription of experience is possible only for someone sufficiently similar to the object of ascription to be able to adopt his point of view—to understand the ascription in the first person as well as in the third, so to speak. The more different from oneself the other experiencer is, the less success one can expect with this enterprise. In our own case we occupy the relevant point of view, but we will have as much difficulty understanding our own experience properly if we approach it from another point of view as we would if we tried to understand the experience of another species without taking up *its* point of view.[16]

This bears directly on the mind-body problem. For if the facts of experience—facts about what it is like *for* the experiencing organism—are accessible only from one point of view, then it is a mystery how the true character of experiences could be revealed in the physical operation of that organism. The latter is a domain of objective facts *par excellence*[17]—the kind that can be observed and understood from many points of view and by individuals with differing perceptual systems. There are no comparable imaginative obstacles to the acquisition of knowledge about bat neurophysiology by human scientists, and intelligent bats or Martians might learn more about the human brain than we ever will.

This is not by itself an argument against reduction. A Martian scientist with no understanding of visual perception could understand the rainbow, or lightning, or clouds as physical phenomena, though he would never be able to understand the human concepts of rainbow, lightning, or cloud, or the place these things occupy in our phenomenal world. The objective nature of the things picked out by these concepts could be apprehended by him because, although the concepts themselves are connected with a particular point of view and a particular visual phenomenology, the things apprehended from that point of view are not: they are observable from the point of view but external to it; hence they can be comprehended from other points of view also, either by the same organisms or by others. Lightning has an objective character that is not exhausted by its visual appearance, and this can be investigated by a Martian without vision. To be precise, it has a *more* objective character than is revealed in its visual appearance. In speaking of the move from subjective to objective characterization, I wish to remain noncommittal about the existence of an end point, the completely objective intrinsic nature of the thing, which one might or might not be able to reach. It may be more accurate to think of objectivity as a direction in which the understanding can travel.

---

16   [Author's note] It may be easier than I suppose to transcend inter-species barriers with the aid of the imagination. For example, blind people are able to detect objects near them by a form of sonar, using vocal clicks or taps of a cane. Perhaps if one knew what that was like, one could by extension imagine roughly what it was like to possess the much more refined sonar of a bat. The distance between oneself and other persons and other species can fall anywhere on a continuum. Even for other persons the understanding of what it is like to be them is only partial, and when one moves to species very different from oneself, a lesser degree of partial understanding may still be available. The imagination is remarkably flexible. My point, however, is not that we cannot *know* what it is like to be a bat. I am not raising that epistemological problem. My point is rather that even to form a *conception* of what it is like to be a bat (and a fortiori to know what it is like

to be a bat) one must take up the bat's point of view. If one can take it up roughly, or partially, then one's conception will also be rough or partial. Or so it seems in our present state of understanding.

17   French for "being the best example of its kind."

And in understanding a phenomenon like lightning, it is legitimate to go as far away as one can from a strictly human viewpoint.[18]

In the case of experience, on the other hand, the connection with a particular point of view seems much closer. It is difficult to understand what could be meant by the *objective* character of an experience, apart from the particular point of view from which its subject apprehends it. After all, what would be left of what it was like to be a bat if one removed the viewpoint of the bat? But if experience does not have, in addition to its subjective character, an objective nature that can be apprehended from many different points of view, then how can it be supposed that a Martian investigating my brain might be observing physical processes which were my mental processes (as he might observe physical processes which were bolts of lightning), only from a different point of view? How, for that matter, could a human physiologist observe them from another point of view?[19]

We appear to be faced with a general difficulty about psychophysical reduction. In other areas the process of reduction is a move in the direction of greater objectivity, toward a more accurate view of the real nature of things. This is accomplished by reducing our dependence on individual or species-specific points of view toward the object of investigation. We describe it not in terms of the impressions it makes on our senses, but in terms of its more general effects and of properties detectable by means other than the human senses. The less it depends on a specifically human viewpoint, the more objective is our description. It is possible to follow this path because although the concepts and ideas we employ in thinking about the external world are initially applied from a point of view that involves our perceptual apparatus, they are used by us to refer to things beyond themselves—toward which we *have* the phenomenal point of view. Therefore we can abandon it in favor of another, and still be thinking about the same things.

Experience itself, however, does not seem to fit the pattern. The idea of moving from appearance to reality seems to make no sense here. What is the analogue in this case to pursuing a more objective understanding of the same phenomena by abandoning the initial subjective viewpoint toward them in favor of another that is more objective but concerns the same thing? Certainly it *appears* unlikely that we will get closer to the real nature of human experience by leaving behind the particularity of our human point of view and striving for a description in terms accessible to beings that could not imagine what it was like to be us. If the subjective character of experience is fully comprehensible only from one point of view, then any shift to greater objectivity—that is, less attachment to a specific viewpoint—does not take us nearer to the real nature of the phenomenon: it takes us farther away from it.

In a sense, the seeds of this objection to the reducibility of experience are already detectable in successful cases of reduction; for in discovering sound to be, in reality, a wave phenomenon in air or other media, we leave behind one viewpoint to take up another, and the auditory, human or animal viewpoint that we leave behind remains unreduced. Members of radically different species may both understand the same physical events in objective terms, and this does not require that they understand the phenomenal forms in which those events appear to the senses of members of the other species. Thus it is a condition of their referring to a common reality that their more particular viewpoints are not part of the common reality that they both apprehend. The reduction can succeed only if the species-specific viewpoint is omitted from what is to be reduced.

But while we are right to leave this point of view aside in seeking a fuller understanding of the external

---

18   [Author's note] The problem I am going to raise can therefore be posed even if the distinction between more subjective and more objective descriptions or viewpoints can itself be made only within a larger human point of view. I do not accept this kind of conceptual relativism, but it need not be refuted to make the point that psychophysical reduction cannot be accommodated by the subjective-to-objective model familiar from other cases.

19   [Author's note] The problem is not just that when I look at the "Mona Lisa," my visual experience has a certain quality, no trace of which is to be found by someone looking into my brain. For even if he did observe there a tiny image of the "Mona Lisa," he would have no reason to identify it with the experience.

world, we cannot ignore it permanently, since it is the essence of the internal world, and not merely a point of view on it. Most of the neobehaviorism of recent philosophical psychology results from the effort to substitute an objective concept of mind for the real thing, in order to have nothing left over which cannot be reduced. If we acknowledge that a physical theory of mind must account for the subjective character of experience, we must admit that no presently available conception gives us a clue how this could be done. The problem is unique. If mental processes are indeed physical processes, then there is something it is like, intrinsically,[20] to undergo certain physical processes.

---

20   [Author's note] The relation would therefore not be a contingent one, like that of a cause and its distinct effect. It would be necessarily true that a certain physical state felt a certain way. Saul Kripke (*op. cit.*) argues that causal behaviorist and related analyses of the mental fail because they construe, e.g., "pain" as a merely contingent name of pains. The subjective character of an experience ("its immediate phenomenological quality" Kripke calls it [p. 340]) is the essential property left out by such analyses, and the one in virtue of which it is, necessarily, the experience it is. My view is closely related to his. Like Kripke, I find the hypothesis that a certain brain state should *necessarily* have a certain subjective character incomprehensible without further explanation. No such explanation emerges from theories which view the mind-brain relation as contingent, but perhaps there are other alternatives, not yet discovered.

A theory that explained how the mind-brain relation was necessary would still leave us with Kripke's problem of explaining why it nevertheless appears contingent. That difficulty seems to me surmountable, in the following way. We may imagine something by representing it to ourselves either perceptually, sympathetically, or symbolically. I shall not try to say how symbolic imagination works, but part of what happens in the other two cases is this. To imagine something perceptually, we put ourselves in a conscious state resembling the state we would be in if we perceived it. To imagine something sympathetically, we put ourselves in a conscious state resembling the thing itself. (This method can be used only to imagine mental events and

What it is for such a thing to be the case remains a mystery.

What moral should be drawn from these reflections, and what should be done next? It would be a mistake to conclude that physicalism must be false. Nothing is proved by the inadequacy of physicalist hypotheses that assume a faulty objective analysis of mind. It would be truer to say that physicalism is a position we cannot understand because we do not at present have any conception of how it might be true. Perhaps it will be thought unreasonable to require such a conception as a condition of understanding. After all, it might be said, the meaning of physicalism is clear enough: mental states are states of the body; mental events are physical events. We do not know *which* physical states and events they are, but that should not prevent us from understanding the hypothesis. What could be clearer than the words "is" and "are"?

But I believe it is precisely this apparent clarity of the word "is" that is deceptive. Usually, when we are told that *X* is *Y* we know *how* it is supposed to be true, but that depends on a conceptual or theoretical background and is not conveyed by the "is" alone.

---

states—our own or another's.) When we try to imagine a mental state occurring without its associated brain state, we first sympathetically imagine the occurrence of the mental state: that is, we put ourselves into a state that resembles it mentally. At the same time, we attempt to perceptually imagine the non-occurrence of the associated physical state, by putting ourselves into another state unconnected with the first: one resembling that which we would be in if we perceived the nonoccurrence of the physical state. Where the imagination of physical features is perceptual and the imagination of mental features is sympathetic, it appears to us that we can imagine any experience occurring without its associated brain state, and vice versa. The relation between them will appear contingent even if it is necessary, because of the independence of the disparate types of imagination.

(Solipsism, incidentally, results if one misinterprets sympathetic imagination as if it worked like perceptual imagination: it then seems impossible to imagine any experience that is not one's own.)

We know how both "X" and "Y" refer, and the kinds of things to which they refer, and we have a rough idea how the two referential paths[21] might converge on a single thing, be it an object, a person, a process, an event, or whatever. But when the two terms of the identification are very disparate it may not be so clear how it could be true. We may not have even a rough idea of how the two referential paths could converge, or what kind of things they might converge on, and a theoretical framework may have to be supplied to enable us to understand this. Without the framework, an air of mysticism surrounds the identification.

This explains the magical flavor of popular presentations of fundamental scientific discoveries, given out as propositions to which one must subscribe without really understanding them. For example, people are now told at an early age that all matter is really energy. But despite the fact that they know what "is" means, most of them never form a conception of what makes this claim true, because they lack the theoretical background.

At the present time the status of physicalism is similar to that which the hypothesis that matter is energy would have had if uttered by a pre-Socratic philosopher.[22] We do not have the beginnings of a conception of how it might be true. In order to understand the hypothesis that a mental event is a physical event, we require more than an understanding of the word "is." The idea of how a mental and a physical term might refer to the same thing is lacking, and the usual analogies with theoretical identification in other fields fail to supply it. They fail because if we construe the reference of mental terms to physical events on the usual model, we either get a reappearance of separate subjective events as the effects through which mental reference to physical events is secured, or else we get a false account of how mental terms refer (for example, a causal behaviorist[23] one).

Strangely enough, we may have evidence for the truth of something we cannot really understand. Suppose a caterpillar is locked in a sterile safe by someone unfamiliar with insect metamorphosis, and weeks later the safe is reopened, revealing a butterfly. If the person knows that the safe has been shut the whole time, he has reason to believe that the butterfly is or was once the caterpillar, without having any idea in what sense this might be so. (One possibility is that the caterpillar contained a tiny winged parasite that devoured it and grew into the butterfly.)

It is conceivable that we are in such a position with regard to physicalism. Donald Davidson has argued that if mental events have physical causes and effects, they must have physical descriptions. He holds that we have reason to believe this even though we do not—and in fact *could* not—have a general psycho-physical theory.[24] His argument applies to intentional mental events, but I think we also have some reason to believe that sensations are physical processes, without being in a position to understand how. Davidson's position is that certain physical events have irreducibly mental properties, and perhaps some view describable in this way is correct. But nothing of which we can now form a conception corresponds to it; nor have we any idea what a theory would be like that enabled us to conceive of it.[25]

Very little work has been done on the basic question (from which mention of the brain can be entirely omitted) whether any sense can be made of experi-

---

21   By "referential paths" Nagel means something like the various ways in which we fix the reference of our words to a certain thing (e.g., by personal acquaintance or by a description in a text book). For example, I have at least two "referential paths" to the stuff picked out by the word *water*: it is the liquid which comes out of the tap in my kitchen, and it is the substance which has the molecular composition H_2O.

22   A philosopher who lived before or around the time of Socrates (a Greek philosopher who died in 399 BCE).

23   Nagel presumably means the idea that our mental states are defined as whatever physically causes certain characteristic patterns of behavior (e.g., the word "pain" refers to the cause of pain behavior).

24   [Author's note] See "Mental Events" in Foster and Swanson, *Experience and Theory* (Amherst, 1970); though I don't understand the argument against psychophysical laws.

25   [Author's note] Similar remarks apply to my paper "Physicalism," *Philosophical Review* LXXIV (1965), 339–356, reprinted with postscript in John O'Connor, *Modern Materialism* (New York, 1969).

ences' having an objective character at all. Does it make sense, in other words, to ask what my experiences are *really* like, as opposed to how they appear to me? We cannot genuinely understand the hypothesis that their nature is captured in a physical description unless we understand the more fundamental idea that they *have* an objective nature (or that objective processes can have a subjective nature).[26]

I should like to close with a speculative proposal. It may be possible to approach the gap between subjective and objective from another direction. Setting aside temporarily the relation between the mind and the brain, we can pursue a more objective understanding of the mental in its own right. At present we are completely unequipped to think about the subjective character of experience without relying on the imagination—without taking up the point of view of the experiential subject. This should be regarded as a challenge to form new concepts and devise a new method—an objective phenomenology not dependent on empathy or the imagination. Though presumably it would not capture everything, its goal would be to describe, at least in part, the subjective character of experiences in a form comprehensible to beings incapable of having those experiences.

We would have to develop such a phenomenology to describe the sonar experiences of bats; but it would also be possible to begin with humans. One might try, for example, to develop concepts that could be used to explain to a person blind from birth what it was like to see. One would reach a blank wall eventually, but it should be possible to devise a method of expressing in objective terms much more than we can at present, and with much greater precision. The loose intermodal[27] analogies—for example, "Red is like the sound of a trumpet"—which crop up in discussions of this subject are of little use. That should be clear to any-

one who has both heard a trumpet and seen red. But structural features of perception might be more accessible to objective description, even though something would be left out. And concepts alternative to those we learn in the first person may enable us to arrive at a kind of understanding even of our own experience which is denied us by the very ease of description and lack of distance that subjective concepts afford.

Apart from its own interest, a phenomenology that is in this sense objective may permit questions about the physical[28] basis of experience to assume a more intelligible form. Aspects of subjective experience that admitted this kind of objective description might be better candidates for objective explanations of a more familiar sort. But whether or not this guess is correct, it seems unlikely that any physical theory of mind can be contemplated until more thought has been given to the general problem of subjective and objective. Otherwise we cannot even pose the mind-body problem without sidestepping it.[29]

---

26 [Author's note] This question also lies at the heart of the problem of other minds, whose close connection with the mind-body problem is often overlooked. If one understood how subjective experience could have an objective nature, one would understand the existence of subjects other than oneself.

27 Crossing between modes of sensation, such as sight and touch.

28 [Author's note] I have not defined the term "physical." Obviously it does not apply just to what can be described by the concepts of contemporary physics, since we expect further developments. Some may think there is nothing to prevent mental phenomena from eventually being recognized as physical in their own right. But whatever else may be said of the physical, it has to be objective. So if our idea of the physical ever expands to include mental phenomena, it will have to assign them an objective character—whether or not this is done by analyzing them in terms of other phenomena already regarded as physical. It seems to me more likely, however, that mental-physical relations will eventually be expressed in a theory whose fundamental terms cannot be placed clearly in either category.

29 [Author's note] I have read versions of this paper to a number of audiences, and am indebted to many people for their comments.

FRANK JACKSON

"Epiphenomenal Qualia" and "What Mary Didn't Know"

Who Is Frank Jackson?

Frank Cameron Jackson was born in Australia in 1943. He studied mathematics and philosophy at the University of Melbourne and received his PhD in philosophy from La Trobe University. His main appointments have been in Australia: at the University of Adelaide, Monash University, and the Australian National University. He has also had numerous visiting appointments, at (among other places) Harvard, Princeton, Oxford, and Cambridge. He is the author of many books and articles; his research covers philosophical logic, cognitive science, epistemology and metaphysics, and meta-ethics, but has concentrated mainly on the philosophy of mind. His example of Mary the brain scientist is extremely well-known and widely discussed; his somewhat less famous yet still influential example is Fred the tomato sorter. Both were introduced in his article "Epiphenomenal Qualia," (1982); his later article "What Mary Didn't Know" (1986) deals with Mary's case in more detail. Both articles are excerpted below. In these articles Jackson, like Chalmers, defends dualism about mind and body on the basis of the impossibility of providing a physical explanation of experience. It should be noted, however, that in articles published in 1995 and later, Jackson recanted his earlier dualism.

What Is the Structure of These Articles?

After some introductory remarks, Jackson introduces the case of Fred, who consistently sorts ripe tomatoes by means of an apparent color-difference nobody else can see. Jackson uses this thought-experiment to show that there would be something about Fred that we don't know and couldn't know, despite all the knowledge one could wish about his discrimination-behavior and physiology: what these new colors are to Fred, as he experiences them. Because there's something left out when the whole physical story is spelled out to us, it follows, argues Jackson, that the physical story leaves something out.

Jackson then introduces his second famous example: Mary, a super brain-scientist, who knows all there is to know about the physical story of how we perceive, process, and recognize colors, but who has never seen color. Jackson suggests that when Mary sees colors for the first time she learns something new, something that all that physical knowledge did not provide her with. Again, the physical information is shown to be incomplete.

Jackson, like Chalmers in the next reading, is willing to grant that the causes for external behavior and internal mental and physical events are all purely physical. Thus, the whole story explaining Fred's discriminations among tomatoes would be given in terms of physical events involving reflected light from the tomatoes, and in Fred's eyes and brain. What Mary knows would, similarly, give us all the information needed to fit into the causal explanation of behavior based on color perception, and of results of such perception. Experience—what's missing from the physical story—then, according to both philosophers, has no causal influence over anything in Fred or Mary or us. Experience, is caused (in this case) by physical neural stimulation, but has no physical effects. For both philosophers, the character of experience is entirely an *epiphenomenon* of the physical situation. (An epiphenomenon in a system is something caused by the system, but without effects. The noise your car makes when it's running, for example, is caused by the physical events in your car, but has no effect on them; it's an epiphenomenon.)

Jackson considers three objections to an epiphenomenal theory of mind: (i) It seems obvious that qualia are causes. (ii) If qualia have no effects, having them is not conducive to fitness; so why did they evolve? And (iii) if qualia have no behavioral effects, how could we have evidence that other minds have them? Jackson responds to each of these objections, and finally reacts to the criticism that qualia "*do* nothing, they *explain* nothing, they serve merely to soothe the intuitions of dualists, and it is left a total mystery how they fit into the world view of science. In short we do not and cannot understand the how and why of them." His retort is that all this may be true, but that it is overly optimistic to think that the human mind can understand everything.

The selection from "What Mary Didn't Know" is entitled "Three Clarifications"; they are in fact three responses to objections to Jackson's Mary argument in the earlier paper. The first interprets Jackson's claim about Mary to be what Mary can't imagine (as, for example, in the Nagel article printed earlier, there appears to be the claim that we can't imagine what it's like to be a bat). But Jackson replies that his point is about limits of knowledge, not of imagination. The second responds to an objection to the Knowledge Argument that antedates Jackson's paper: that the fact that someone knows that X is there, but doesn't know that Y is there, doesn't show that X is not in fact Y. We'll have more to say about this matter below, in the Suggestions for Critical Reflection section. The third points out that Mary's lack of knowledge when in her cell is about others, not about herself.

Some Useful Background Information

Jackson, in our readings, defends epiphenomenalism about the mental, the position that certain mental events—experiences of qualia—are caused by physical (presumably neural) events, but that these mental events have no effects of any kind on physical events in one's nervous system, or in one's behavior. Chalmers, one of whose papers is reprinted below, does not claim to be an epiphenomenalist, but it has seemed clear to commentators on his work that this is a consequence of his position.

Epiphenomenalism about mind has a long philosophical history. It came into its own with the growth of modern science, beginning in the Renaissance; it gradually seemed more and more likely that physical events of every sort had physical causes only. Descartes (the most influential historical substance dualist) ran into a good deal of criticism because he held that mental events could cause physical ones. By the twentieth century, the most common response to this difficulty was to deny dualism: to hold that mental events actually were physical ones, so could be causes (and effects) of other physical events. But epiphenomenalists attempted to maintain dualism while accepting the idea that mental could not cause physical, by denying that mental events could be causes.

A very influential mid-twentieth-century argument against epiphenomenalism about mind (and about dualism in general) was due to Herbert Feigl. If physical events caused mental ones, he argued, there would presumably be scientific laws connecting them; but such laws would be, in his words, "nomological danglers." ("Nomological" means *having to do with scientific laws.*) These are, Feigl argued, at least very suspect, in that they cannot be accounted for, being outside of the scope of, science. They "dangle" from the web of scientific theory and its laws.[1]

---

1   Feigl's essay "The 'Mental' and the 'Physical'" first appeared in Volume II of *Minnesota Studies in the Philosophy of Science: Concepts, Theories, and the Mind-Body Problem*, edited by Herbert Feigl, Michael Scriven, and Grover Maxwell and published

Suggestions for Critical Reflection

1. Anti-epiphenomenalists claim that it's just obvious that our thoughts and feelings have causal influence on our other thoughts and feelings, and on our actions. Does Jackson give an adequate rebuttal to this idea?

2. Consider this objection; is it right?

    If Mary knows everything physical there is to know about colors and color-perception, then she'd know what it's like to experience red things, even though while locked in her cell she'd never done that. To argue that there's something she doesn't know is simply to beg the question.

3. Consider this objection; is it right?

    What Mary gets when she emerges from her room is not new knowledge of some sort of fact. It's new "acquaintance-knowledge"—a new way of experiencing something that may have been (in Mary's case, *would* have been) otherwise experienced earlier.

4. Consider this objection; is it right?

    The difference between Fred and us is that he has color-discrimination abilities which are more finely tuned than ours. It's a difference in know-how, not knowing-that, and this difference in know-how, Jackson agrees, might totally be accounted for by a story about Fred's physical perceptual and neural system.

5. As mentioned above, Jackson now has changed his mind about the knowledge argument. Here's his account of what went wrong with his knowledge argument:

Intensionalism means that no amount of tub-thumping assertion by dualists (including by me in the past) that the *redness* of seeing red cannot be accommodated in the austere physicalist picture carries any weight. That striking feature is a feature of how things are being represented to be, and if, as claimed by the tub thumpers, it is transparently a feature that has no place in the physicalist picture, what follows is that physicalists should deny that anything has that striking feature. And this is no argument against physicalism. Physicalists can allow that people are sometimes in states that represent that things have a non-physical property. Examples are people who believe that there are fairies. What physicalists must deny is that such properties are instantiated.[2]

See if you can explain what he means here in your own terms: what might it be to deny that there is any such thing as "the *redness* of seeing red"? By contrast, how does Jackson try to deal with the intensionality of knowledge in "What Mary Didn't Know"? Who do you think is right, the earlier or the later Jackson?

Suggestions for Further Reading

Excellent detailed surveys of the state of the art regarding epiphenomenalism and the Knowledge Argument are both online in the *Stanford Encyclopedia of Philosophy*: "Epiphenomenalism" by William Robinson, <http://plato.stanford.edu/entries/epiphenomenalism/> and "Qualia—The Knowledge Argument" by Martine Nida-Rümelin <http://plato.stanford.edu/entries/qualia-knowledge/>. The best place to look for articles about Mary is a collection by noted philosophers devoted entirely to the Mary argument: *There's Something about Mary*, Peter Ludlow, Yujin Nagasawa, and Daniel Stoljar (eds.), Cambridge, MA: MIT Press, 2004.

---

by the University of Minnesota Press in 1958. It was republished in 1967 as a book with a new Postscript, a preface to the Postscript, and an additional bibliography; and it appears online at http://www.ditext.com/feigl/mp/mp.html. J.J.C. Smart used the objectionable nature of nomological danglers to argue for his version of the physicalist identity theory in his equally influential paper, "Sensations and Brain Processes," which appears in this chapter.

2   "Mind and Illusion" in *Minds and Persons: Royal Institute of Philosophy Supplement* 53, edited by A. O'Hear (Cambridge: Cambridge University Press, 2003). Online at http://consc.net/neh/papers/jackson.htm.

from "Epiphenomenal Qualia"[3]

It is undeniable that the physical, chemical and biological sciences have provided a great deal of information about the world we live in and about ourselves. I will use the label 'physical information' for this kind of information, and also for information that automatically comes along with it. For example, if a medical scientist tells me enough about the processes that go on in my nervous system, and about how they relate to happenings in the world around me, to what has happened in the past and is likely to happen in the future, to what happens to other similar and dissimilar organisms, and the like, he or she tells me—if I am clever enough to fit it together appropriately—about what is often called the functional role of those states in me (and in organisms in general in similar cases). This information, and its kin, I also label 'physical'.

I do not mean these sketchy remarks to constitute a definition of 'physical information', and of the correlative notions of physical property, process, and so on, but to indicate what I have in mind here. It is well known that there are problems with giving a precise definition of these notions, and so of the thesis of Physicalism that all (correct) information is physical information. But—unlike some—I take the question of definition to cut across the central problems I want to discuss in this paper.

I am what is sometimes known as a "qualia freak".[4] I think that there are certain features of the bodily sensations especially, but also of certain perceptual experiences, which no amount of purely physical information includes. Tell me everything physical there is to tell about what is going on in a living brain, the kind of states, their functional role, their relation to what goes on at other times and in other brains, and so on and so forth, and be I as clever as can be in fitting it all together, you won't have told me about the hurtfulness of pains, the itchiness of itches, the pangs of jealousy, or about the characteristic experience of tasting a lemon, smelling a rose, hearing a loud noise or seeing the sky.

There are many qualia freaks, and some of them say that their rejection of Physicalism is an unargued intuition. I think that they are being unfair to themselves. They have the following argument. Nothing you could tell of a physical sort captures the smell of a rose, for instance. Therefore, Physicalism is false. By our lights this is a perfectly good argument. It is obviously not to the point to question its validity, and the premise is intuitively obviously true both to them and to me.

I must, however, admit that it is weak from a polemical point of view. There are, unfortunately for us, many who do not find the premise intuitively obvious. The task then is to present an argument whose premises are obvious to all, or at least to as many as possible. This I try to do in §I with what I will call "the Knowledge argument". In §II I contrast the Knowledge argument with the Modal argument and in §III with the "What is it like to be" argument. In §IV I tackle the question of the causal role of qualia. The major factor in stopping people from admitting qualia is the belief that they would have to be given a causal role with respect to the physical world and especially the brain; and it is hard to do this without sounding like someone who believes in fairies. I seek in §IV to turn this objection by arguing that the view that qualia are epiphenomenal[5] is a perfectly possible one.

I. The Knowledge Argument for Qualia

People vary considerably in their ability to discriminate colours. Suppose that in an experiment to catalogue this variation Fred is discovered. Fred has better colour vision than anyone else on record; he makes

---

3   From *The Philosophical Quarterly* Volume 32, Number 127, April 1982; pp. 127–130 and pp. 133–136. Reproduced by permission of Wiley-Blackwell Inc.

4   Qualia (pronounced KWAH-lee-a; singular *quale* [KWAH-lay]) are subjective qualities of conscious experience, for example, pains, tastes, the visual experience of colors.

5   An epiphenomenon (plural *epiphenomena*) is something caused by some system of events, but having no effects in that system. An example is the sound made by a running car: it's caused by vibrations at various places in the car, but it has no effect on the car. An epiphenomenalist about mind holds that mental events are epiphenomena—physically caused, but having no mental or physical effect.

every discrimination that anyone has ever made, and moreover he makes one that we cannot even begin to make. Show him a batch of ripe tomatoes and he sorts them into two roughly equal groups and does so with complete consistency. That is, if you blindfold him, shuffle the tomatoes up, and then remove the blindfold and ask him to sort them out again, he sorts them into exactly the same two groups.

We ask Fred how he does it. He explains that all ripe tomatoes do not look the same colour to him, and in fact that this is true of a great many objects that we classify together as red. He sees two colours where we see one, and he has in consequence developed for his own use two words 'red$_1$' and 'red$_2$' to mark the difference. Perhaps he tells us that he has often tried to teach the difference between red$_1$ and red$_2$ to his friends but has got nowhere and has concluded that the rest of the world is red$_1$- red$_2$ colourblind—or perhaps he has had partial success with his children, it doesn't matter. In any case he explains to us that it would be quite wrong to think that because 'red' appears in both 'red$_1$' and 'red$_2$' that the two colours are shades of the one colour. He only uses the common term 'red' to fit more easily into our restricted usage. To him red$_1$ and red$_2$ are as different from each other and all the other colours as yellow is from blue. And his discriminatory behaviour bears this out: he sorts red$_1$ from red$_2$ tomatoes with the greatest of ease in a wide variety of viewing circumstances. Moreover, an investigation of the physiological basis of Fred's exceptional ability reveals that Fred's optical system is able to separate out two groups of wave-lengths in the red spectrum as sharply as we are able to sort out yellow from blue.

I think that we should admit that Fred can see, really see, at least one more colour than we can; red$_1$ is a different colour from red$_2$. We are to Fred as a totally red-green colour-blind person is to us. H.G. Wells' story "The Country of the Blind" is about a sighted person in a totally blind community.[6] This person never manages to convince them that he can see, that he has an extra sense. They ridicule this sense as quite inconceivable, and treat his capacity to avoid falling

into ditches, to win fights and so on as precisely that capacity and nothing more. We would be making their mistake if we refused to allow that Fred can see one more colour than we can.

What kind of experience does Fred have when he sees red$_1$ and red$_2$? What is the new colour or colours like? We would dearly like to know but do not; and it seems that no amount of physical information about Fred's brain and optical system tells us. We find out perhaps that Fred's cones respond differentially to certain light waves in the red section of the spectrum that make no difference to ours (or perhaps he has an extra cone) and that this leads in Fred to a wider range of those brain states responsible for visual discriminatory behaviour. But none of this tells us what we really want to know about his colour experience. There is something about it we don't know. But we know, we may suppose, everything about Fred's body, his behaviour and dispositions to behaviour and about his internal physiology, and everything about his history and relation to others that can be given in physical accounts of persons. We have all the physical information. Therefore, knowing all this is *not* knowing everything about Fred. It follows that Physicalism leaves something out.

To reinforce this conclusion, imagine that as a result of our investigations into the internal workings of Fred we find out how to make everyone's physiology like Fred's in the relevant respects; or perhaps Fred donates his body to science and on his death we are able to transplant his optical system into someone else—again the fine detail doesn't matter. The important point is that such a happening would create enormous interest. People would say, "At last we will know what it is like to see the extra colour, at last we will know how Fred has differed from us in the way he has struggled to tell us about for so long". Then it cannot be that we knew all along all about Fred. But *ex hypothesi* we did know all along everything about Fred that features in the physicalist scheme; hence the physicalist scheme leaves something out.

Put it this way. *After* the operation, we will know *more* about Fred and especially about his colour experiences. But beforehand we had all the physical information we could desire about his body and brain, and indeed everything that has ever featured

---

6   [Author's note] H.G. Wells, *The Country of the Blind and Other Stories* (London, n.d.).

in physicalist accounts of mind and consciousness. Hence there is more to know than all that. Hence Physicalism is incomplete.

Fred and the new colour(s) are of course essentially rhetorical devices. The same point can be made with normal people and familiar colours. Mary is a brilliant scientist who is, for whatever reason, forced to investigate the world from a black and white room *via* a black and white television monitor. She specialises in the neurophysiology of vision and acquires, let us suppose, all the physical information there is to obtain about what goes on when we see ripe tomatoes, or the sky, and use terms like 'red', 'blue', and so on. She discovers, for example, just which wave-length combinations from the sky stimulate the retina, and exactly how this produces *via* the central nervous system the contraction of the vocal chords and expulsion of air from the lungs that results in the uttering of the sentence 'The sky is blue'. (It can hardly be denied that it is in principle possible to obtain all this physical information from black and white television, otherwise the Open University[7] would *of necessity* need to use colour television.)

What will happen when Mary is released from her black and white room or is given a colour television monitor? Will she *learn* anything or not? It seems just obvious that she will learn something about the world and our visual experience of it. But then it is inescapable that her previous knowledge was incomplete. But she had *all* the physical information. *Ergo* there is more to have than that, and Physicalism is false.

Clearly the same style of Knowledge argument could be deployed for taste, hearing, the bodily sensations and generally speaking for the various mental states which are said to have (as it is variously put) raw feels, phenomenal features or qualia. The conclusion in each case is that the qualia are left out of the physicalist story. And the polemical strength of the Knowledge argument is that it is so hard to deny the central claim that one can have all the physical information without having all the information there is to have.

...

___

7   A British university offering distance education, partly through broadcast lectures.

IV. The Bogey of Epiphenomenalism

Is there any really *good* reason for refusing to countenance the idea that qualia are causally impotent with respect to the physical world? I will argue for the answer no, but in doing this I will say nothing about two views associated with the classical epiphenomenalist position. The first is that mental *states* are inefficacious with respect to the physical world. All I will be concerned to defend is that it is possible to hold that certain *properties* of certain mental states, namely those I've called qualia, are such that their possession or absence makes no difference to the physical world. The second is that the mental is *totally* causally inefficacious. For all I will say it may be that you have to hold that the instantiation of *qualia* makes a difference to *other mental states* though not to anything physical. Indeed general considerations to do with how you could come to be aware of the instantiation of qualia suggest such a position.

Three reasons are standardly given for holding that a quale like the hurtfulness of a pain must be causally efficacious in the physical world, and so, for instance, that its instantiation must sometimes make a difference to what happens in the brain. None, I will argue, has any real force....

(i) It is supposed to be just obvious that the hurtfulness of pain is partly responsible for the subject seeking to avoid pain, saying 'It hurts' and so on. But, to reverse Hume, anything can fail to cause anything. No matter how often B follows A, and no matter how initially obvious the causality of the connection seems, the hypothesis that A causes B can be overturned by an over-arching theory which shows the two as distinct effects of a common underlying causal process.

To the untutored the image on the screen of Lee Marvin's fist moving from left to right immediately followed by the image of John Wayne's head moving in the same general direction looks as causal as anything. And of course throughout countless Westerns images similar to the first are followed by images similar to the second. All this counts for precisely nothing when we know the over-arching theory concerning how the relevant images are both effects of an underlying causal process involving the projector and the film. The epiphenomenalist can say exactly the same about the connection between, for example, hurtfulness and behaviour. It is simply a consequence of the fact that certain happenings in the brain cause both.

(ii) The second objection relates to Darwin's Theory of Evolution. According to natural selection the traits that evolve over time are those conducive to physical survival. We may assume that qualia evolved over time—we have them, the earliest forms of life do not—and so we should expect qualia to be conducive to survival. The objection is that they could hardly help us to survive if they do nothing to the physical world.

The appeal of this argument is undeniable, but there is a good reply to it. Polar bears have particularly thick, warm coats. The Theory of Evolution explains this (we suppose) by pointing out that having a thick, warm coat is conducive to survival in the Arctic. But having a thick coat goes along with having a heavy coat, and having a heavy coat is *not* conducive to survival. It slows the animal down.

Does this mean that we have refuted Darwin because we have found an evolved trait—having a heavy coat—which is not conducive to survival? Clearly not. Having a heavy coat is an unavoidable concomitant of having a warm coat (in the context, modern insulation was not available), and the advantages for survival of having a warm coat outweighed the disadvantages of having a heavy one. The point is that all we can extract from Darwin's theory is that we should expect any evolved characteristic to be either conducive to survival *or* a by-product of one that is so conducive. The epiphenomenalist holds that qualia fall into the latter category. They are a by-product of certain brain processes that are highly conducive to survival.

(iii) The third objection is based on a point about how we come to know about other minds. We know about other minds by knowing about other behaviour, at least in part. The nature of the inference is a matter of some controversy, but it is not a matter of controversy that it proceeds from behaviour. That is why we think that stones do not feel and dogs do feel. But, runs the objection, how can a person's behaviour provide any reason for believing he has qualia like mine, or indeed any qualia at all, unless this behaviour can be regarded as the *outcome* of the

qualia. Man Friday's footprint was evidence of Man Friday because footprints are causal outcomes of feet attached to people. And an epiphenomenalist cannot regard behaviour, or indeed anything physical, as an outcome of qualia.

But consider my reading in *The Times* that Spurs[8] won. This provides excellent evidence that *The Telegraph* has also reported that Spurs won, despite the fact that (I trust) *The Telegraph* does not get the results from *The Times*. They each send their own reporters to the game. *The Telegraph*'s report is in no sense an outcome of *The Times*', but the latter provides good evidence for the former nevertheless.

The reasoning involved can be reconstructed thus. I read in *The Times* that Spurs won. This gives me reason to think that Spurs won because I know that Spurs' winning is the most likely candidate to be what caused the report in *The Times*. But I also know that Spurs' winning would have had many effects, including almost certainly a report in *The Telegraph*.

I am arguing from one effect back to its cause and out again to another effect. The fact that neither effect causes the other is irrelevant. Now the epiphenomenalist allows that qualia are effects of what goes on in the brain. Qualia cause nothing physical but are caused by something physical. Hence the epiphenomenalist can argue from the behaviour of others to the qualia of others by arguing from the behaviour of others back to its causes in the brains of others and out again to their qualia.

You may well feel for one reason or another that this is a more dubious chain of reasoning than its model in the case of newspaper reports. You are right. The problem of other minds is a major philosophical problem, the problem of other newspaper reports is not. But there is no special problem of Epiphenomenalism as opposed to, say, Interactionism here.

There is a very understandable response to the three replies I have just made. "All right, there is no knockdown refutation of the existence of epiphenomenal qualia. But the fact remains that they are an excrescence. They *do* nothing, they *explain* nothing, they serve merely to soothe the intuitions of dualists, and it is left a total mystery how they fit into the

---

8   The London soccer team Tottenham Hotspur.

world view of science. In short we do not and cannot understand the how and why of them."

This is perfectly true; but is no objection to qualia, for it rests on an overly optimistic view of the human animal, and its powers. We are the products of Evolution. We understand and sense what we need to understand and sense in order to survive. Epiphenomenal qualia are totally irrelevant to survival. At no stage of our evolution did natural selection favour those who could make sense of how they are caused and the laws governing them, or in fact why they exist at all. And that is why we can't.

It is not sufficiently appreciated that Physicalism is an extremely optimistic view of our powers. If it is true, we have, in very broad outline admittedly, a grasp of our place in the scheme of things. Certain matters of sheer complexity defeat us—there are an awful lot of neurons—but in principle we have it all. But consider the antecedent probability that everything in the Universe be of a kind that is relevant in some way or other to the survival of *homo sapiens*. It is very low surely. But then one must admit that it is very likely that there is a part of the whole scheme of things, maybe a big part, which no amount of evolution will ever bring us near to knowledge about or understanding. For the simple reason that such knowledge and understanding is irrelevant to survival.

Physicalists typically emphasise that we are a part of nature on their view, which is fair enough. But if we are a part of nature, we are as nature has left us after however many years of evolution it is, and each step in that evolutionary progression has been a matter of chance constrained just by the need to preserve or increase survival value. The wonder is that we understand as much as we do, and there is no wonder that there should be matters which fall quite outside our comprehension. Perhaps exactly how epiphenomenal qualia fit into the scheme of things is one such.

This may seem an unduly pessimistic view of our capacity to articulate a truly comprehensive picture of our world and our place in it. But suppose we discovered living on the bottom of the deepest oceans a sort of sea slug which manifested intelligence. Perhaps survival in the conditions required rational powers. Despite their intelligence, these sea slugs have only a very restricted conception of the world by comparison with ours, the explanation for this being the nature of their immediate environment. Nevertheless they have developed sciences which work surprisingly well in these restricted terms. They also have philosophers, called slugists. Some call themselves tough-minded slugists, others confess to being soft-minded slugists.

The tough-minded slugists hold that the restricted terms (or ones pretty like them which may be introduced as their sciences progress) suffice in principle to describe everything without remainder. These tough-minded slugists admit in moments of weakness to a feeling that their theory leaves something out. They resist this feeling and their opponents, the soft-minded slugists, by pointing out—absolutely correctly—that no slugist has ever succeeded in spelling out how this mysterious residue fits into the highly successful view that their sciences have and are developing of how their world works.

Our sea slugs don't exist, but they might. And there might also exist super beings which stand to us as we stand to the sea slugs. We cannot adopt the perspective of these super beings, because we are not them, but the possibility of such a perspective is, I think, an antidote to excessive optimism.

from "What Mary Didn't Know"[9]

...

I. Three Clarifications

The knowledge argument does not rest on the dubious claim that logically you cannot imagine what sensing red is like unless you have sensed red. Powers of imagination are not to the point. The contention about Mary is not that, despite her fantastic grasp of neurophysiology and everything else physical, she *could not imagine* what it is like to sense red; it is that, as a matter of fact, she *would not know*. But if physicalism is true, she would know; and no great powers of imagination would be called for. Imagination is a faculty that those who *lack* knowledge need to fall back on.

---

9   From *The Journal of Philosophy* 83 (May 1986), pp. 291–295 (excerpt).

Secondly, the intensionality of knowledge[10] is not to the point. The argument does not rest on assuming falsely that, if S knows that a is F and if $a = b$, then S knows that b is F. It is concerned with the nature of Mary's total body of knowledge before she is released: is it complete, or do some facts escape it? What is to the point is that S may know that a is F and *know* that $a = b$, yet arguably not know that b is F, by virtue of not being sufficiently logically alert to follow the consequences through. If Mary's lack of knowledge were at all like this, there would be no threat to physicalism in it. But it is very hard to believe that her lack of knowledge could be remedied merely by her explicitly following through enough logical consequences of her vast physical knowledge. Endowing her with great logical acumen and persistence is not in itself enough to fill in the gaps in her knowledge. On being let out, she will not say "I could have worked all this out before by making some more purely logical inferences."

Thirdly, the knowledge Mary lacked which is of particular point for the knowledge argument against physicalism is *knowledge about the experiences of others*, not about her own. When she is let out, she has new experiences, color experiences she has never had before. It is not, therefore, an objection to physicalism that she learns *something* on being let out. Before she was let out, she could not have known facts about her experience of red, for there were no such facts to know. That physicalist and nonphysicalist alike can agree on. After she is let out, things change; and physicalism can happily admit that she learns this; after all, some physical things will change, for instance, her brain states and their functional roles. The trouble for physicalism is that, after Mary sees her first ripe tomato, she will realize how impoverished her conception of the mental life of *others* has been *all along*. She will realize that there was, all the time she was carrying out her laborious investigations into the neurophysiologies of others and into the functional roles of their internal states, something about these people she was quite unaware of. All along their experiences (or many of them, those got from tomatoes, the sky, ...) had a feature conspicuous to them but until now hidden from her (in fact, not in logic). But she knew all the physical facts about them all along; hence, what she did not know until her release is not a physical fact about their experiences. But it is a fact about them. That is the trouble for physicalism....

---

10 To say that knowledge is intensional is to say that one might know something when it is expressed in one way but not know *the same thing* when it is expressed another way. For example, I might know that Snoop Dogg is a rap musician but deny any knowledge of Calvin Cordozar Broadus, Jr. Yet they're the same person.

DAVID CHALMERS
"The Puzzle of Conscious Experience"

Who Is David Chalmers?

David Chalmers was born in Australia in 1966. His undergraduate degree, at the University of Adelaide, concentrated in mathematics and computer science, and he went to the University of Oxford to do graduate work in mathematics, but then, his interest in the philosophy of mind having become dominant, he switched to Indiana University, working in Douglas Hofstadter's Center for Research on Concepts and Cognition there. After his PhD in 1993, he had a two-year post-doctoral fellowship at Washington University in St. Louis, then taught at UC Santa Cruz, and then at the University of Arizona. He moved to the Australia National University in August 2004, and is also part-time at New York University. He looks and dresses like a rock star.

What Is Chalmers's Overall Philosophical Project?

Chalmers may be the best-known of the group of contemporary philosophers of mind known (mostly by their philosophical opponents) as Mysterians: those who claim that the central feature of the mental is conscious experience, and that this feature must forever remain a mystery to physical science (though Chalmers himself, in the article we include here, claims he is not a Mysterian). Famously he distinguished what he called the "easy problem" and the "hard problem" for a science of mind. The former—not really easy, but at least doable—was to give a scientific account of mental functions, such as sensory discriminations. The latter—not merely hard, but rather, he argued impossible—was to give a physical account of the experiences that were the constituents of our conscious minds.

The view that consciousness must elude physical scientific treatment is not a new one. It was a gener-ally held view among philosophers of mind for centuries; usually this was a consequence of their substance dualism: their view that mind and matter were two completely different kinds of stuff. But, with the advance of science, explaining more and more of what had previously seemed inexplicable, Mysterianism gradually became more and more rare. In the twentieth century, however, it had a rebirth in various forms, in the view that although everything in the universe might turn out to be constructed of physical matter obeying physical laws, it would not follow that physical laws could explain mental goings-on. (See the section below, Some Useful Background Information, for brief descriptions of these positions.) Importantly, however, these positions shared the view that, notwithstanding the impossibility of explanation of the mental by physicalist science, mental events might each be identical to physical events, and that the basic tenet of physicalism, that everything that exists is physical, could still be true.

Chalmers, however, has placed himself in a small minority of philosophers of mind by arguing that physicalism is false, and that the properties that constitute conscious experience may be fundamentally non-physical properties.

What Is the Structure of This Reading?

Chalmers begins with a distinction he thinks is fundamental to the philosophy of mind: between the functions carried out by the mental faculties, of gathering information from sensation, directing muscular activity, and so on, on the one hand, and the experiences of conscious life—of our impressions of shapes and colors, our feelings of pain and pleasure, our emotions and thoughts: in sum, our mental life—on the other. He's willing to grant that neuroscience could give a physicalist explanation of all of the former phenomena; his argument is that science can never begin to explain our mental life, to answer questions like: Why do we have *that* experience when we eat strawberries? Why are there any experiences at all? The first job of explanation he calls the "easy problem"—not meaning that it's easy to do, but rather just that science knows how to approach it, and it's scientifically doable; the second he calls the "hard problem"—not meaning that it's simply more difficult, but rather that it's really impossible for physicalist science.

His first section refers to the case of Mary the brain scientist. This is a famous example due to Frank Jackson, and is the subject of the previous reading in this chapter. Chalmers next goes on to consider some work by neuropsychologists and philosophers on the subject of consciousness; his claim is that almost all of this (properly) addresses part of the 'easy' problem, leaving the 'hard' problem untouched.

He then suggests that the right way of approaching the 'hard' problem would be to abandon the idea that only physical entities and properties and events are the ground-floor basis for explanation, and to accept mental items as basic, or "irreducible," as well. Then science can correlate mental types with physical (presumably neurological) types, with the ultimate goal of producing psychophysical laws—laws relating the two basic types of events. This sort of "theory of everything" could solve the 'hard' problem, because it includes the mental as basic, instead of trying to explain it in terms of the physical. He finishes by suggesting that such a theory might centrally involve the concept of information.

Some Useful Background Information

As science made enormous progress during the nineteenth and early twentieth centuries, a growing number of philosophers came to believe that the physical, scientific categories that had been deployed so successfully in explaining events elsewhere would someday have equal success in dealing with the mental; equally, more and more philosophers came to think that a unified view of reality was the correct one: a view that took there to be one sort of physical stuff that everything was made of.

These two ideas, however, were separable. While (probably) most philosophers remained physicalist, believing that everything was ultimately constructed out of the same sort of matter, basically obeying the same sorts of laws, doubts grew during the second half of the twentieth century that physical explanation for mental events would be possible—that is, that there was, for example, a kind of brain event that happened every time anyone thought about dinner, that *constituted* thinking about dinner.

The most common theory denying the explainability of the mental by the physical came from the functionalists, who typically held that mental events were classified functionally—that is, by their typical causes and effects—and instances of a single mental type (e.g., wishing you had a hamburger now) might be realized by any of a possibly infinite number of different physical types of event. We can imagine, for example, that a Martian, whose brain was built on entirely different principles from ours, might also yearn for a hamburger, but this yearning might be identical in his case to a totally different physical brain event than in you. If there could not be a physical type corresponding, in an exceptionless way, to any mental type, then there could not be mental-physical bridge laws, and thus no physical explanation of the mental. (Most functionalists are, however, physicalists—believing that each particular mental event really is a physical event. See the selection by Hilary Putnam in this chapter.)

Other arguments to the same conclusion relied on the basically normative character of mental ascriptions; the idea here is that whenever we assign beliefs and desires to others, we assume their rationality (otherwise their behavior might be correlated with any beliefs and desires whatever). Rationality is essentially an evaluative notion, thus having no place in physical sciences like neurophysiology. Thus mental categories must cut up phenomena differently from physical ones; and again exceptionless "bridge" laws linking the two would be impossible. (Again, philosophers who accept this argument are generally physicalists.)

Chalmers, by contrast, accepts the idea that there are relations between the mental and the physical that can be described in terms of scientific laws. He denies, however, that these can be completely physical laws: they would have to describe correlations between the physical and the irreducibly mental.

Suggestions for Critical Reflection

1. Chalmers (but not in the reading we have) gives an argument for his position based on the premise that it's possible (though not actual) that zombies exist. Zombies (in the sense philosophers of mind speak of them) are organisms physically just like us, inside and out, behaving in the same ways we do; the only difference is that they have no consciousness. See if you can fill in the rest of the argument: what is the conclusion we're supposed to draw from the possibility of zombies? How is that conclusion supposed to follow?

2. Valerie Gray Hardcastle suggests we

   consider the following exchange. A water-mysterian wonders why water has this peculiar property [being wet]. She inquires and you give an explanation of the molecular composition of water and a brief story about the connection between micro-chemical properties and macro-phenomena. Ah, she says … I am convinced that you have properly correlated water with its underlying mo-

lecular composition. I also have no reason to doubt that your story about the macro-effects of chemical properties to be wrong. But I still am not satisfied, for you have left off in your explanation what I find most puzzling. Why *is* water H_2O? Why couldn't it be XYZ? Why couldn't it have some other radically different chemical story behind it? I can imagine a possible world in which water has all the macro-properties that it has now, but is not composed of H_2O … What *can* one say? I think nothing. Water-mysterians are antecedently convinced of the mysteriousness of water and no amount of scientific data is going to change that perspective. Either you already believe that science is going to give you a correct identity statement, or you don't and you think that there is always going to be something left over, the wateriness of water.[1]

What analogy is Hardcastle drawing with Chalmers's position? The suggestion here is that consciousness-mysterianism is just as baseless as water-mysterianism, but that there are no arguments that could convince either mysterian that their positions are wrong. Do you agree?

3. Hardcastle points out that both materialists and dualists accept some facts as "brute facts"—unexplainable features of the universe, just the way it is; but she remarks that "it seems highly unlikely that some relatively chauvinistic *biological* fact should ever be brute." If this is to be a criticism of Chalmers, what's the "relatively chauvinistic biological fact" in his view? (What does "chauvinistic" mean in this context?) See if you can explain why Hardcastle thinks that this view is "highly unlikely."

4. There's something discreditable about being a Mysterian. What do you suppose it is? Why does Chalmers claim he's not a Mysterian? Do you think he sufficiently rebuts the charge of discreditable Mysterianism?

1   "The Why of Consciousness: A Non-issue for Materialists." *Journal of Consciousness Studies*, 3, No.1, 1996, pp. 7–13.

5. What is Chalmers's "principle of organizational invariance"? What are its implications, if it's true? (Is it true?)

6. At the end of the reading Chalmers raises the prospect of 'panpsychism': the view that everything (or at least everything that 'processes information,' including certainly thermostats and All Wheel Drive traction systems, and possibly even natural processes such as convection) is conscious. How palatable is this notion? If we must reject it, what problems might this cause for Chalmers?

Suggestions for Further Reading

The definitive statement of Chalmers's ideas is found in his book, *The Conscious Mind: In Search of a Fundamental Theory* (Oxford: Oxford University Press, 1996). *Explaining Consciousness: The Hard Problem*, edited by Jonathan Shear (MIT Press, 1997), is a collection of articles responding to Chalmers. These articles, and others by and responding to Chalmers, are in various issues of the *Journal of Consciousness Studies*.

"The Puzzle of Conscious Experience"[2]

Conscious experience is at once the most familiar thing in the world and the most mysterious. There is nothing we know about more directly than consciousness, but it is extraordinarily hard to reconcile it with everything else we know. Why does it exist? What does it do? How could it possibly arise from neural processes in the brain? These questions are among the most intriguing in all of science.

From an objective viewpoint, the brain is relatively comprehensible. When you look at this page, there is a whir of processing: photons strike your retina, electrical signals are passed up your optic nerve and between different areas of your brain,

and eventually you might respond with a smile, a perplexed frown or a remark. But there is also a subjective aspect. When you look at the page, you are conscious of it, directly experiencing the images and words as part of your private, mental life. You have vivid impressions of the colors and shapes of the images. At the same time, you may be feeling some emotions and forming some thoughts. Together such experiences make up consciousness: the subjective, inner life of the mind.

For many years, consciousness was shunned by researchers studying the brain and the mind. The prevailing view was that science, which depends on objectivity, could not accommodate something as subjective as consciousness. The behaviorist movement in psychology, dominant earlier in this century, concentrated on external behavior and disallowed any talk of internal mental processes. Later, the rise of cognitive science focused attention on processes inside the head. Still, consciousness remained off-limits, fit only for late-night discussion over drinks.

Over the past several years, however, an increasing number of neuroscientists, psychologists and philosophers have been rejecting the idea that consciousness cannot be studied and are attempting to delve into its secrets. As might be expected of a field so new, there is a tangle of diverse and conflicting theories, often using basic concepts in incompatible ways. To help unsnarl the tangle, philosophical reasoning is vital.

The myriad views within the field range from reductionist theories, according to which consciousness can be explained by the standard methods of neuroscience and psychology, to the position of the so-called mysterians, who say we will never understand consciousness at all. I believe that on close analysis both of these views can be seen to be mistaken and that the truth lies somewhere in the middle.

Against reductionism I will argue that the tools of neuroscience cannot provide a full account of conscious experience, although they have much to offer. Against mysterianism I will hold that consciousness might be explained by a new kind of theory. The full details of such a theory are still out of reach, but careful reasoning and some educated inferences can

---

2   This article was published in *Scientific American* in December 1995. It was reprinted, slightly updated, in 2002 in the Scientific American Special Edition *The Hidden Mind* (Volume 12 Issue 1), pp. 90–100.

reveal something of its general nature. For example, it will probably involve new fundamental laws, and the concept of information may play a central role. These faint glimmerings suggest that a theory of consciousness may have startling consequences for our view of the universe and of ourselves.

The Hard Problem

Researchers use the word "consciousness" in many different ways. To clarify the issues, we first have to separate the problems that are often clustered together under the name. For this purpose, I find it useful to distinguish between the "easy problems" and the "hard problem" of consciousness. The easy problems are by no means trivial—they are actually as challenging as most in psychology and biology—but it is with the hard problem that the central mystery lies.

The easy problems of consciousness include the following: How can a human subject discriminate sensory stimuli and react to them appropriately? How does the brain integrate information from many different sources and use this information to control behavior? How is it that subjects can verbalize their internal states? Although all these questions are associated with consciousness, they all concern the objective mechanisms of the cognitive system. Consequently, we have every reason to expect that continued work in cognitive psychology and neuroscience will answer them.

The hard problem, in contrast, is the question of how physical processes in the brain give rise to subjective experience. This puzzle involves the inner aspect of thought and perception: the way things feel for the subject. When we see, for example, we experience visual sensations, such as that of vivid blue. Or think of the ineffable sound of a distant oboe, the agony of an intense pain, the sparkle of happiness or the meditative quality of a moment lost in thought. All are part of what I call consciousness. It is these phenomena that pose the real mystery of the mind.

To illustrate the distinction, consider a thought experiment devised by the Australian philosopher Frank Jackson. Suppose that Mary, a neuroscientist in the 23rd century, is the world's leading expert on the brain processes responsible for color vision. But Mary has lived her whole life in a black-and-white room and has never seen any other colors. She knows everything there is to know about physical processes in the brain—its biology, structure and function. This understanding enables her to grasp all there is to know about the easy problems: how the brain discriminates stimuli, integrates information and produces verbal reports. From her knowledge of color vision, she knows how color names correspond with wave-lengths on the light spectrum. But there is still something crucial about color vision that Mary does not know: what it is like to experience a color such as red. It follows that there are facts about conscious experience that cannot be deduced from physical facts about the functioning of the brain.

Indeed, nobody knows why these physical processes are accompanied by conscious experience at all. Why is it that when our brains process light of a certain wavelength, we have an experience of deep purple? Why do we have any experience at all? Could not an unconscious automaton have performed the same tasks just as well? These are questions that we would like a theory of consciousness to answer.

Is Neuroscience Enough?

I am not denying that consciousness arises from the brain. We know, for example, that the subjective experience of vision is closely linked to processes in the visual cortex. It is the link itself that perplexes, however. Remarkably, subjective experience seems to emerge from a physical process. But we have no idea how or why this is.

Given the flurry of recent work on consciousness in neuroscience and psychology, one might think this mystery is starting to be cleared up. On closer examination, however, it turns out that almost all the current work addresses only the easy problems of consciousness. The confidence of the reductionist view comes from the progress on the easy problems, but none of this makes any difference where the hard problem is concerned.

Consider the hypothesis put forward by neurobiologists Francis Crick of the Salk Institute for Biological Studies in San Diego and Christof Koch of the California Institute of Technology. They suggest that consciousness may arise from certain oscillations in the cerebral cortex, which become synchronized as neurons fire 40 times per second. Crick and Koch believe the phenomenon might explain how different attributes of a single perceived object (its color and shape, for example), which are processed in different parts of the brain, are merged into a coherent whole. In this theory, two pieces of information become bound together precisely when they are represented by synchronized neural firings.

The hypothesis could conceivably elucidate one of the easy problems about how information is integrated in the brain. But why should synchronized oscillations give rise to a visual experience, no matter how much integration is taking place? This question involves the hard problem, about which the theory has nothing to offer. Indeed, Crick and Koch are agnostic about whether the hard problem can be solved by science at all.

The same kind of critique could be applied to almost all the recent work on consciousness. In his 1991 book *Consciousness Explained*, philosopher Daniel C. Dennett laid out a sophisticated theory of how numerous independent processes in the brain combine to produce a coherent response to a perceived event. The theory might do much to explain how we produce verbal reports on our internal states, but it tells us very little about why there should be a subjective experience behind these reports. Like other reductionist theories, Dennett's is a theory of the easy problems.

The critical common trait among these easy problems is that they all concern how a cognitive or behavioral function is performed. All are ultimately questions about how the brain carries out some task— how it discriminates stimuli, integrates information, produces reports and so on. Once neurobiology specifies appropriate neural mechanisms, showing how the functions are performed, the easy problems are solved.

The hard problem of consciousness, in contrast, goes beyond problems about how functions are performed. Even if every behavioral and cognitive function related to consciousness were explained, there would still remain a further mystery: Why is the performance of these functions accompanied by conscious experience? It is this additional conundrum that makes the hard problem hard.

The Explanatory Gap

Some have suggested that to solve the hard problem, we need to bring in new tools of physical explanation: nonlinear dynamics, say, or new discoveries in neuroscience, or quantum mechanics. But these ideas suffer from exactly the same difficulty. Consider a proposal from Stuart R. Hameroff of the University of Arizona and Roger Penrose of the University of Oxford. They hold that consciousness arises from quantum-physical processes taking place in microtubules, which are protein structures inside neurons. It is possible (if not likely) that such a hypothesis will lead to an explanation of how the brain makes decisions or even how it proves mathematical theorems, as Hameroff and Penrose suggest. But even if it does, the theory is silent about how these processes might give rise to conscious experience. Indeed, the same problem arises with any theory of consciousness based only on physical processing.

The trouble is that physical theories are best suited to explaining why systems have a certain physical structure and how they perform various functions. Most problems in science have this form; to explain life, for example, we need to describe how a physical system can reproduce, adapt and metabolize. But consciousness is a different sort of problem entirely, as it goes beyond the scientific explanation of structure and function.

Of course, neuroscience is not irrelevant to the study of consciousness. For one, it may be able to reveal the nature of the neural correlate of consciousness—the brain processes most directly associated with conscious experience. It may even give a detailed correspondence between specific processes in the brain and related components of experience. But until we know why these processes give rise to conscious experience at all, we will not have crossed what philosopher Joseph Levine has called the explanatory gap between physical processes and consciousness. Making that leap will demand a new kind of theory.

In searching for an alternative, a key observation is that not all entities in science are explained in terms of more basic entities. In physics, for example, space-time, mass and charge (among other things) are regarded as fundamental features of the world, as they are not reducible to anything simpler. Despite this irreducibility, detailed and useful theories relate these entities to one another in terms of fundamental laws. Together these features and laws explain a great variety of complex and subtle phenomena.

A True Theory of Everything

It is widely believed that physics provides a complete catalogue of the universe's fundamental features and laws. As physicist Steven Weinberg puts it in his 1992 book *Dreams of a Final Theory*, the goal of physics is a "theory of everything" from which all there is to know about the universe can be derived. But Weinberg concedes that there is a problem with consciousness. Despite the power of physical theory, the existence of consciousness does not seem to be derivable from physical laws. He defends physics by arguing that it might eventually explain what he calls the objective correlates of consciousness (that is, the neural correlates), but of course to do this is not to explain consciousness itself. If the existence of consciousness cannot be derived from physical laws, a theory of physics is not a true theory of everything. So a final theory must contain an additional fundamental component.

Toward this end, I propose that conscious experience be considered a fundamental feature, irreducible to anything more basic. The idea may seem strange at first, but consistency seems to demand it. In the 19th century it turned out that electromagnetic phenomena could not be explained in terms of previously known principles. As a consequence, scientists introduced electromagnetic charge as a new fundamental entity and studied the associated fundamental laws. Similar reasoning should be applied to consciousness. If existing fundamental theories cannot encompass it, then something new is required.

Where there is a fundamental property, there are fundamental laws. In this case, the laws must relate experience to elements of physical theory. These laws will almost certainly not interfere with those of the physical world; it seems that the latter form a closed system in their own right. Rather the laws will serve as a bridge, specifying how experience depends on underlying physical processes. It is this bridge that will cross the explanatory gap.

Thus, a complete theory will have two components: physical laws, telling us about the behavior of physical systems from the infinitesimal to the cosmological, and what we might call psychophysical laws, telling us how some of those systems are associated with conscious experience. These two components will constitute a true theory of everything.

Supposing for the moment that they exist, how might we uncover such psychophysical laws? The greatest hindrance in this pursuit will be a lack of data. As I have described it, consciousness is subjective, so there is no direct way to monitor it in others. But this difficulty is an obstacle, not a dead end. For a start, each one of us has access to our own experiences, a rich trove that can be used to formulate theories. We can also plausibly rely on indirect information, such as subjects' descriptions of their experiences. Philosophical arguments and thought experiments also have a role to play. Such methods have limitations, but they give us more than enough to get started.

These theories will not be conclusively testable, so they will inevitably be more speculative than those of more conventional scientific disciplines. Nevertheless, there is no reason they should not be strongly constrained to account accurately for our own first-person experiences, as well as the evidence from subjects' reports. If we find a theory that fits the data better than any other theory of equal simplicity, we will have good reason to accept it. Right now we do not have even a single theory that fits the data, so worries about testability are premature.

We might start by looking for high-level bridging laws, connecting physical processes to experience at an everyday level. The basic contour of such a law might be gleaned from the observation that when we are conscious of something, we are generally able to act on it and speak about it—which are objective, physical functions. Conversely, when some information is directly available for action and speech, it is generally conscious. Thus, consciousness correlates well with what we might call "awareness": the process by which information in the brain is made globally available to motor processes such as speech and bodily action.

Objective Awareness

The notion may seem trivial. But as defined here, awareness is objective and physical, whereas consciousness is not. Some refinements to the definition of awareness are needed, in order to extend the concept to animals and infants, which cannot speak. But at least in familiar cases, it is possible to see the rough outlines of a psychophysical law: where there is awareness, there is consciousness, and vice versa.

To take this line of reasoning a step further, consider the structure present in the conscious experience. The experience of a field of vision, for example, is a constantly changing mosaic of colors, shapes and patterns and as such has a detailed geometric structure. The fact that we can describe this structure, reach out in the direction of many of its components and perform other actions that depend on it suggests that the structure corresponds directly to that of the information made available in the brain through the neural processes of objective awareness.

Similarly, our experiences of color have an intrinsic three-dimensional structure that is mirrored in the structure of information processes in the brain's visual cortex. This structure is illustrated in the color wheels and charts used by artists. Colors are arranged in a systematic pattern—red to green on one axis, blue to yellow on another, and black to white on a third. Colors that are close to one another on a color wheel are experienced as similar. It is extremely likely that they also correspond to similar perceptual representations in the brain, as one part of a system of complex three-dimensional coding among neurons that is not yet fully understood. We can recast the underlying concept as a principle of structural coherence: the structure of conscious experience is mirrored by the structure of information in awareness, and vice versa.

Another candidate for a psychophysical law is a principle of organizational invariance. It holds that physical systems with the same abstract organization will give rise to the same kind of conscious experience, no matter what they are made of. For example, if the precise interactions between our neurons could be duplicated with silicon chips, the same conscious experience would arise. The idea is somewhat controversial, but I believe it is strongly supported by thought experiments describing the gradual replacement of neurons by silicon chips. The remarkable implication is that consciousness might someday be achieved in machines.

Theory of Consciousness

The ultimate goal of a theory of consciousness is a simple and elegant set of fundamental laws, analogous to the fundamental laws of physics. The principles described above are unlikely to be fundamental, however. Rather they seem to be high-level psychophysical laws, analogous to macroscopic principles in physics such as those of thermodynamics or kinematics. What might the underlying fundamental laws be? No one really knows, but I don't mind speculating.

I suggest that the primary psychophysical laws may centrally involve the concept of information. The abstract notion of information, as put forward in the 1940s by Claude E. Shannon of the Massachusetts Institute of Technology, is that of a set of separate states with a basic structure of similarities and differences between them. We can think of a 10-bit binary code as an information state, for example. Such information states can be embodied in the physical world. This happens whenever they correspond to physical states (voltages, say) and when differences between them can be transmitted along some pathway, such as a telephone line.

We can also find information embodied in conscious experience. The pattern of color patches in a visual field, for example, can be seen as analogous to that of the pixels covering a display screen. Intriguingly, it turns out that we find the same information states embedded in conscious experience and in underlying physical processes in the brain. The three-dimensional encoding of color spaces, for example, suggests that the information state in a color experience corresponds directly to an information state in the brain. Thus, we might even regard the two states as distinct aspects of a single information state, which is simultaneously embodied in both physical processing and conscious experience.

Aspects of Information

A natural hypothesis ensues. Perhaps information, or at least some information, has two basic aspects: a physical one and an experiential one. This hypothesis has the status of a fundamental principle that might underlie the relation between physical processes and experience. Wherever we find conscious experience, it exists as one aspect of an information state, the other aspect of which is embedded in a physical process in the brain. This proposal needs to be fleshed out to make a satisfying theory. But it fits nicely with the principles mentioned earlier—systems with the same organization will embody the same information, for example—and it could explain numerous features of our conscious experience.

The idea is at least compatible with several others, such as physicist John A. Wheeler's suggestion that information is fundamental to the physics of the universe. The laws of physics might ultimately be cast in informational terms, in which case we would have a satisfying congruence between the constructs in both physical and psychophysical laws. It may even be that a theory of physics and a theory of consciousness could eventually be consolidated into a single grander theory of information.

A potential problem is posed by the ubiquity of information. Even a thermostat embodies some information, for example, but is it conscious? There are at least two possible responses. First, we could constrain the fundamental laws so that only some information has an experiential aspect, perhaps depending on how it is physically processed. Second, we might bite the bullet and allow that all information has an experiential aspect—where there is complex information processing, there is complex experience, and where there is simple information processing, there is simple experience. If this is so, then even a thermostat might have experiences, although they would be much simpler than even a basic color experience, and there would certainly be no accompanying emotions or thoughts. This seems odd at first, but if experience is truly fundamental, we might expect it to be widespread. In any case, the choice between these alternatives should depend on which can be integrated into the most powerful theory.

Of course, such ideas may be all wrong. On the other hand, they might evolve into a more powerful proposal that predicts the precise structure of our conscious experience from physical processes in our brains. If this project succeeds, we will have good reason to accept the theory. If it fails, other avenues will be pursued, and alternative fundamental theories may be developed. In this way, we may one day resolve the greatest mystery of the mind.

CHAPTER 6

Metaphysics—Do We Have Free Will?

INTRODUCTION TO THE QUESTION

Metaphysics is the philosophical study of the most fundamental categories of existence. It deals with questions about reality which lie beyond or behind those capable of being tackled by the methods of empirical science (typically because they address phenomena that are taken as unquestioned *givens* by science).[1] Central topics in metaphysics include, therefore, the nature of space and time, the nature of causation, the real nature of substance (such as matter), and the nature of possibility and necessity. Other metaphysical questions address very basic questions about *existence*. Why is there something rather than nothing? Does the 'external world' exist independently of our minds, or is it in some sense constituted by our perceptions of it?

Is the world fundamentally a collection of *events*, or of *states of affairs*, or what? Do abstract objects (such as numbers, propositions, or moral values) actually in some sense *exist*, over and above the concrete spatio-temporal furniture of the world? Do *properties* exist over and above the individual objects which possess them: is there such a thing as redness, for example, *in addition to* all the particular red things in the world? (This is known by philosophers as 'the problem of universals,' and is harder to answer than it may at first seem: after all, if there is nothing to redness over and above all the red things, then how can we explain what *makes* a red thing red—how can we talk about what all the red things *have in common*?)

Even everyday individual objects such as trees, boats and human beings can generate metaphysical puzzles. In particular, there are deep problems about the *identity* of particular objects: What makes this boat an individual thing (rather than, say, a collection of things)? What makes it the *same* boat as the one that existed yesterday or will exist tomorrow? What properties are *necessary* for something to be the thing it is, and which are merely 'accidental'? And, for people, what is it that gives me my *personal identity*? (E.g., is it my body? my history? my memories? my consciousness?)

Finally, a perennial topic in metaphysics, oddly enough, is whether metaphysics is even possible. After all, metaphysics explicitly tries to go beyond the possible reach of empirical knowledge—it tries to think about phenomena which in principle cannot be addressed by the methods of any conceivable empirical science, phenomena which go beyond (or lie

---

1   The word 'metaphysics' originally comes from the Greek phrase *ta meta ta physika*, meaning 'what comes after physics,' but this etymology is really only an accident of history. When the works of Aristotle were collected together in the first century BCE, his books on 'first philosophy'—the fundamental categories of reality, such as being, substance, causality, and so on—were placed by his editors *after* his books on physics, and so were known as "the books after the books on physics."

One popular sense of 'metaphysics,' which connects it to the study of supernatural, occult, or mystical phenomena (such as ghosts, messages from the afterlife, ley lines, and what-have-you), is strictly *non*-philosophical, insofar as most of these phenomena are questionable on both scientific and philosophical (and commonsensical) grounds.

behind) any possible human experience. It is a serious philosophical question whether such an endeavor is at all fruitful, or whether 'metaphysics' is a sphere where no real knowledge can ever be gained—a realm where we are doomed to endless futile speculation, or even to uttering claims which are, strictly speaking, *meaningless* because they have no connection to any possible human experience.

Six good general introductions to metaphysics, all of which go by the title *Metaphysics*, are those by Bruce Aune (University of Minnesota Press, 1985), D.W. Hamlyn (Cambridge University Press, 1984), Michael J. Loux (Routledge, 2006), John Post (Paragon House, 1991), Richard Taylor (Prentice Hall, 1991), and Peter Van Inwagen (Westview Press, 2008). Of these, Loux is my favorite and Taylor is the shortest. There is also *A Survey of Metaphysics* by E.J. Lowe (Oxford University Press, 2002). Two very good anthologies of contemporary papers in metaphysics are Kim and Sosa (eds.), *Metaphysics: An Anthology* (Blackwell, 1999) and Laurence and Macdonald (eds.), *Contemporary Readings in the Foundations of Metaphysics* (Blackwell, 1998). Kim and Sosa (eds.), *A Companion to Metaphysics* (Blackwell, 2009), is a fine work of reference.

The particular metaphysical topic which is addressed in this chapter is the problem of free will. This problem is generated by the following argument:

(i) All human behavior is determined: that is, the state of the world at a particular time (e.g., the moment of your birth) entirely fixes what the state of the world will be at every moment into the future (e.g., now), and that includes fixing what actions you will ever perform.

(ii) If determinism is true, then human beings are (in at least one important sense) not free to choose their actions—we could not have done otherwise than we did, and so we do not possess genuine free will.

(iii) Therefore human beings do not have free will (and, furthermore, may lack moral responsibility for their actions, lead lives that have no meaning, and so on).

This is a straightforwardly valid argument. The problem, of course, is that both of the premises (i) and (ii) are highly plausible (or at least, can be made to seem so with a certain amount of argumentation), and yet the conclusion is, we hope and believe, *false*: we feel like free agents, able to choose to do one thing rather than another; we believe that people often have moral (and other kinds of) responsibility for their action; we think that people can guide their own destinies in a meaningful way. The philosophical problem, therefore, is to say what if anything is wrong with the argument, and since the argument is valid the only way to criticize it is to call into question the truth of the premises. This means there are exactly three main philosophical positions on the problem of free will:

The first position, usually called *hard determinism* or just *determinism*, is the view that the argument is sound: that is, both of the premises are true and hence freedom (and moral responsibility and so on) is a mere illusion. This stance is represented here by the reading from Paul Rée. The second position, usually called *libertarianism* (or *metaphysical libertarianism*), accepts premise (ii) but argues that the first premise is false—that is, libertarians agree that determinism is incompatible with freedom, but argue that we have free will because *indeterminism* is true. This tactic is represented in this chapter by a reading from C.A. Campbell (a classic statement of libertarianism) .

The third and by far the most popular philosophical approach to free will is known as *soft determinism* or *compatibilism*. Compatibilists typically accept premise (i), determinism, but deny premise (ii): that is, they deny that the truth of determinism implies that we lack at least one important variety of freedom. Instead, they argue in a variety of ways that determinism is compatible with all the types of freedom worth wanting: that we can be *both* free and determined. Two compatibilist accounts are reprinted here, from A.J. Ayer (a classic version of compatibilism) and Daniel Dennett. Finally, there is an influential discussion by Bernard Williams and Thomas Nagel of "moral luck"— the degree to, and complex ways in which, matters of chance and determination interact with the question of moral responsibility.

There are many decent collections of articles on the problem of free will, including Gerald Dworkin (ed.), *Determinism, Free Will, and Moral Responsibility* (Prentice Hall, 1970); John Martin Fischer (ed.), *Moral Responsibility* (Cornell University Press, 1986); Robert

Kane (ed.), *Free Will* (Blackwell, 2009) and *The Oxford Handbook of Free Will* (Oxford University Press, 2005); Timothy O'Connor (ed.), *Agents, Causes, and Events* (Oxford University Press, 1995); and Gary Watson (ed.), *Free Will* (Oxford University Press, 2003). Useful and fairly accessible single-author discussions of the problem of free will include Daniel Dennett, *Elbow Room* (MIT Press, 1985); Ted Honderich, *How Free Are You?* (Oxford University Press, 1993); Robert Kane, *A Contemporary Introduction to Free Will* (Oxford University Press, 2005); Graham McFee, *Free Will* (McGill-Queen's University Press, 2000); Daniel John O'Connor, *Free Will* (Macmillan, 1971); Timothy O'Connor, *Persons and Causes* (Oxford University Press, 2000); and Jennifer Trusted, *Free Will and Responsibility* (Oxford University Press, 1984).

Finally, here are a few recent influential books on free will which are not cited in the Further Reading sections elsewhere in the chapter: Richard Double, *The Non-Reality of Free Will* (Oxford University Press, 1991); John Martin Fischer, *The Metaphysics of Free Will* (Blackwell, 1996); Ted Honderich, *A Theory of Determinism* (two volumes, Oxford University Press, 1988); Murphy and Brown (eds.), *Did My Neurons Make Me Do It?: Philosophical and Neurobiological Perspectives on Moral Responsibility and Free Will* (Oxford University Press, 2009); Derk Pereboom, *Living Without Free Will* (Cambridge University Press, 2001); Galen Strawson, *Freedom and Belief* (Oxford University Press, 1986); Peter Van Inwagen, *An Essay on Free Will* (Oxford University Press, 1983); and Daniel Wegner, *The Illusion of Conscious Will* (MIT Press, 2005).

PAUL RÉE
The Illusion of Free Will

Who Was Paul Rée?

Paul Rée, a German philosopher and psychologist, is best remembered for his association with Friedrich Nietzsche and for his uncompromising moral relativism and atheism. Born in 1849, Rée was the son of a wealthy Prussian landowner. In his early twenties he fought in the Franco-Prussian war of 1870–71, in which Prussian troops advanced into France and decisively defeated the French army at Sedan (a town near the Belgian border). The outcome was the fall of the French Second Empire and the establishment of a new, united German Empire—the first Reich—under its first chancellor, Prince Otto Leopold von Bismarck. On his return from the war, wounded, Rée went to Switzerland to recuperate and, abandoning the law studies he had begun before the war, devoted himself to the study of philosophy and psychology. In 1875 he received a doctorate in philosophy from the University of Halle (a city in central Germany), and also

published a book of psychological aphorisms, *Psychologische Beobachtungen*.

In 1873 Rée had met the famous German philosopher Friedrich Nietzsche in Basel, and after the publication of Rée's *Psychological Observations* Nietzsche wrote him a letter complimenting the work. As a result, the two struck up a close friendship—which Nietzsche's biographer, Walter Kaufmann, has called "among the best things which ever happened to Nietzsche"—that lasted about seven years. However, Rée was ethnically Jewish (though not a religious practitioner), and several of Nietzsche's anti-Semitic friends and Nietzsche's unpleasant sister resented his influence on Nietzsche. In 1882, after Nietzsche bitterly broke off his relationship with the tempestuous and bewitching Lou Salomé, to whom Rée had originally introduced him, Rée's friendship with the famous philosopher came to an end, and they never spoke again. Later, Rée was to dismiss Nietzsche's ethical writings as "a mixture of insanity and nonsense."

In 1877 Rée published *Ursprung der moralischen Empfindungen* (The Origin of the Moral Sentiments). In this book, strongly influenced by Charles Darwin and David Hume, Rée argued that there are no universally true moral principles, and that what is regarded as morally right or wrong, in any given society, is a function of its needs and cultural conditions. *The Illusion of Free Will*, in which Rée advocates abandoning notions of moral responsibility in practical as well as philosophical life, was published in 1885, when Rée was 36. In the same year, he published *Die Entstehung des Gewissens* (The Origin of Conscience) and in the process of writing this book he became concerned about his own lack of knowledge of the natural sciences. The next year Rée enrolled at the University of Munich to study medicine. After obtaining his MD, Rée returned to his family estate in Stibbe, West Prussia. There he practiced medicine, charging no fees, and when his own medical knowledge fell short in particular cases, paid all the hospital expenses for the peasants and laborers who were his patients.

For the last ten years of his life, Rée led an isolated, ascetic existence living at Stibbe with his brother, and spent much of his time working on a major book which would encapsulate all his philosophical reflections. Rée told a friend that when it was finished he would give up philosophy, but that since he could not live without doing philosophy, there would be nothing left for him but to die. This is more or less what happened: in 1900, when his book was almost completed, Rée, a passionate mountain climber, returned to live in Switzerland and fell to his death from the icy ridge of a Swiss mountain in 1901. His book, *Philosophie*, was published posthumously in 1903 and, to this day, has been almost completely ignored. In this work, Rée roundly condemned metaphysics as a system of "fairy tales" and "lies," and argued that religions "are true neither in the literal nor in an allegorical sense—they are untrue in every sense. Religion issues from a marriage of error and fear."

Lou von Salomé, Paul Rée, and Friedrich Nietzsche. In the studio of Jules Bonnet, Luzern 1882.

What Is the Structure of This Reading?

This selection contains most of Chapters 1 and 2 of Paul Rée's 1885 book *Die Illusion der Willensfreiheit* (The Illusion of Free Will). The final (third) chapter of the book, which is not reprinted here, contains a detailed critique of Immanuel Kant's views on free will. Rée begins by defining freedom of the will as the ability to act as "an absolute beginning"—i.e., a thought or action is free, according to Rée, just in the case where it is not the necessary result of prior causes. Rée then goes on to argue that *no* event is uncaused, and thus that there can be no such thing as free will. To show this, he first examines the example of an act of decision in a donkey and then extends similar considerations to human beings. He insists that even actions performed solely from a sense of duty are not genuinely free, and he argues that one must be careful to distinguish between correct and incorrect senses of the claim "I can do what I want." Finally, he diagnoses our mistaken belief in free will as being the result of ignorance of the causes of our own actions. Because we do not see how our actions are caused, we fallaciously assume that they are not caused.

In section 5, which marks the start of Chapter 2 of his book, Rée explores the implications for morality of the truth of determinism. He argues that if all our actions are necessary effects of prior causes, then we cannot be held morally responsible for them: we cannot legitimately be praised or blamed for our actions. The true philosopher, Rée hints, will try to rid herself of the bad habit of assigning moral responsibility. On the other hand, we certainly do *prefer* some actions (and some types of people) over others, and this is legitimate; but our preferences themselves are to be explained as causal effects of our genetic inheritance and social upbringing.

Some Useful Background Information

There is a useful and commonly made philosophical distinction which is helpful for understanding Rée's position on free will: the contrast between necessary and sufficient conditions. *A* is a *necessary* condition for *B* if *B* could not have occurred (or been true) without *A*—that is, if there would be no *B* unless *A*. For example, being connected to a power supply is a necessary condition for a bulb to light up (the bulb could not light unless connected to a source of electricity). On the other hand, *A* is a *sufficient* condition for *B* if the occurrence (or truth) of *A* is *sufficient* for the occurrence (or truth) of *B*—that is, if *B* happens every time *A* does. Being connected in the right way to a properly functioning circuit with an adequate source of power, under normal physical circumstances, with the power switch in the "on" position is, altogether, a sufficient circumstance for a bulb to light.

It follows from this that if *A* is a sufficient condition for *B*, then if *A* occurs *B* must *necessarily* occur as well.[1] (On the other hand, if *A* is merely a necessary condition for *B*, the occurrence of *A* only tells us that *B* may happen, but not that it actually will.)

---

1   This claim is a bit more complicated than it seems, however, because of the various flavors which necessity can come in: for example, the fact that *B* always follows *A* in the actual world perhaps means that *B* is a '*physically* necessary' consequence of *A*, but it need not follow that *B* follows from *A* by *logical* necessity.

Suggestions for Critical Reflection

1. "To say that the will is not free means that it is subject to the law of causality." Is this right? Or could the will somehow be *both* free and subject to causal laws?

2. Rée admits that "man has the ability to free himself from being dominated by his drives." Does this undermine his claim that determinism is incompatible with moral responsibility?

3. Rée suggests that anyone who comes to properly grasp the truth of determinism will immediately abandon any belief in moral responsibility (though perhaps will be unable to shake off the habit of making moral judgments). Is this claim plausible? How strong are his reasons for making it?

4. Here are two claims:
   a) Some event *A* will occur *whenever* its sufficient cause is present.
   b) Some event *A* will occur *only* when its sufficient cause is present.
   Do these two claims say different things (i.e., could one be true when the other one is false)? Does Rée clearly differentiate between the two of them? How might the difference between the two claims cause problems for Rée's argument?

5. "Observation teaches us that for every act of will, some causes were the determining factors." Is this true and, if so, is it sufficient to establish determinism?

6. One of the consequences of Rée's determinism, he suggests, is that people can *only* do what they want to do—that is, according to Rée, it is impossible to deliberately do something that you do not want to do. Does this seem right to you? Does it actually follow from the thesis of determinism?

7. Is it *fair* to prefer some people over others, to seek the company of the former, and to shun the latter, if they are not responsible for their character traits? For example, is it okay to dislike depressed people if it's not their fault they are depressed? Is the question of 'fairness' even appropriate, if human beings have no free will?

Suggestions for Further Reading

The Rée reading and much of the information reprinted here about him comes from the third edition of *A Modern Introduction to Philosophy*, edited by Paul Edwards and Arthur Pap (Free Press, 1973). As far as I am aware, no more of Rée's writings have yet been published in English. One of the best-known "determinists" of the century before Rée was Paul-Henri Thiry, the Baron d'Holbach (1723–1789). His most important book is *The System of Nature* (1770—reissued by Clinamen Press, 2000), in which he defended an unflinching atheistic materialism; however, unlike Rée, d'Holbach took pains to argue that determinism is compatible with altruism and moral virtue. Another precursor was the French mathematician Pierre-Simon de Laplace (1749–1827), famous for formulating the idea that a superhuman intelligence, capable of knowing the entire state of the universe at a given moment, could compute exactly how everything in the universe would evolve, down to the minutest detail, for the rest of time. (Such a being is now usually known as "Laplace's demon.") A rigorous intellectual biography of Laplace, with information about his demon, is Charles Coulston Gillespie's *Pierre Simon Laplace, 1749–1827* (Princeton University Press, 2000).

Two particularly notorious twentieth-century determinist tracts are Clarence Darrow's, *Crime, Its Cause and Treatment* (Crowell, 1922) and B.F. Skinner's, *Beyond Freedom and Dignity* (Knopf, 1971). Probably the best recent book on the scientific basis for determinism is John Earman's *A Primer on Determinism* (Kluwer, 1986), and a useful recent exploration of its philosophical consequences is Roy Weatherford's *The Implications of Determinism* (Routledge, 1991).

The Illusion of Free Will

Chapters 1 and 2[2]

1. Nothing Happens without a Cause

… To say that the will is not free means that it is subject to the law of causality. Every act of will is in fact preceded by a sufficient cause. Without such a cause the act of will cannot occur; and, if the sufficient cause is present, the act of will must occur.

To say that the will is free would mean that it is not subject to the law of causality. In that case every act of will would be an absolute beginning [a first cause] and not a link [in a chain of events]: it would not be the effect of preceding causes.

The reflections that follow may serve to clarify what is meant by saying that the will is not free.… Every object—a stone, an animal, a human being— can pass from its present state to another one. The stone that now lies in front of me may, in the next moment, fly through the air, or it may disintegrate into dust or roll along the ground. If, however, one of these *possible* states is to be *realized*, its sufficient cause must first be present. The stone will fly through the air if it is tossed. It will roll if a force acts upon it. It will disintegrate into dust, given that some object hits and crushes it.

It is helpful to use the terms "potential" and "actual" in this connection. At any moment there are innumerably many potential states. At a given time, however, only *one* can become actual, namely, the one that is triggered by its sufficient cause.

The situation is no different in the case of an animal. The donkey that now stands motionless between two piles of hay may, in the next moment, turn to the left or to the right, or he may jump into the air or put his head between his legs. But here, too, the sufficient

---

2   Paul Rée's *Die Illusion der Willensfreiheit* was first published in Berlin in 1885. This selection was translated by Stefan Bauer-Mengelberg and edited by Paul Edwards and Arthur Pap (who also supplied the section headings) in 1973. It is reprinted here with the kind permission of Dr. Tim Madigan, Literary Executor to Paul Edwards.

cause must first be present if of the *possible* modes of behavior one is to be *realized*.

Let us analyze one of these modes of behavior. We shall assume that the donkey has turned toward the bundle on his right. This turning presupposes that certain muscles were contracted. The cause of this muscular contraction is the excitation of the nerves that lead to them. The cause of this excitation of the nerves is a state of the brain. It was in a state of decision. But how did the brain come to be in that condition? Let us trace the states of the donkey back a little farther.

A few moments before he turned, his brain was not yet so constituted as to yield the sufficient cause for the excitation of the nerves in question and for the contraction of the muscles; for otherwise the movement would have occurred. The donkey had not yet "decided" to turn. If he then moved at some subsequent time, his brain must in the meantime have become so constituted as to bring about the excitation of the nerves and the movement of the muscles. Hence the brain underwent some change. To what causes is this change to be attributed? To the effectiveness of an impression that acts as an external stimulus, or to a sensation that arose internally; for example, the sensation of hunger and the idea of the bundle on the right, by jointly affecting the brain, change the way in which it is constituted so that it now yields the sufficient cause for the excitation of the nerves and the contraction of the muscles. The donkey now "wants" to turn to the right; he now turns to the right.

Hence, just as the position and constitution of the stone, on the one hand and the strength and direction of the force that acts upon it, on the other, necessarily determine the kind and length of its flight, so the movement of the donkey—his turning to the bundle on the right—is no less necessarily the result of the way in which the donkey's brain and the stimulus are constituted at a given moment. That the donkey turned toward this particular bundle was determined by something trivial. If the bundle that the donkey did not choose had been positioned just a bit differently, or if it had smelled different, or if the subjective factor—the donkey's sense of smell or his visual organs—had developed in a somewhat different way, then, so we may assume, the donkey would have turned to the left.

But the cause was not complete there, and that is why the effect could not occur, while with respect to the other side, where the cause was complete, the effect could not fail to appear.

For the donkey, consequently, just as for the stone, there are innumerably many *potential* states at any moment; he may walk or run or jump, or move to the left, to the right, or straight ahead. But only the one whose sufficient cause is present can ever become *actual*.

At the same time, there is a difference between the donkey and the stone in that the donkey moves because he wants to move, while the stone moves because it is moved. We do not deny this difference. There are, after all, a good many other differences between the donkey and the stone. We do not by any means intend to prove that this dissimilarity does not exist. We do not assert that the donkey is a stone, but only that the donkey's every movement and act of will has causes just as the motion of the stone does. The donkey moves because he wants to move. But that he wants to move at a given moment, and in this particular direction, is causally determined.

Could it be that there was no sufficient cause for the donkey's wanting to turn around—that he simply wanted to turn around? His act of will would then be an absolute beginning. An assumption of that kind is contradicted by experience and the universal validity of the law of causality. By experience, since observation teaches us that for every act of will some causes were the determining factors. By the universal validity of the law of causality, since, after all, nothing happens anywhere in the world without a sufficient cause. Why, then, of all things should a donkey's act of will come into being without a cause? Besides, the state of willing, the one that immediately precedes the excitation of the motor nerves, is no different in principle from other states—that of indifference, of lassitude, or of weariness. Would anyone believe that all of these states exist without a cause? And if one does not believe that, why should just the state of willing be thought to occur without a sufficient cause?

It is easy to explain why it seems to us that the motion of the stone is necessary while the donkey's act of will is not. The causes that move the stone are, after all, external and visible. But the causes of the donkey's act of will are internal and invisible; between us and the locus of their effectiveness lies the skull of the donkey. Let us consider this difference somewhat more closely. The stone lies before us as it is constituted. We can also see the force acting upon it, and from these two factors, the constitution of the stone and the force, there results, likewise visible, the rolling of the stone. The case of the donkey is different. The state of his brain is hidden from our view. And, while the bundle of hay is visible, its effectiveness is not. It is an internal process. The bundle does not come into visible contact with the brain but acts at a distance. Hence the subjective and the objective factor—the brain and the impact that the bundle has upon it—are invisible.

Let us suppose that we could depict the donkey's soul in high relief, taking account of and making visible all those states, attitudes, and feelings that characterize it before the donkey turns. Suppose further that we could see how an image detaches itself from the bundle of hay and, describing a visible path through the air, intrudes upon the donkey's brain and how it produces a change there in consequence of which certain nerves and muscles move. Suppose, finally, that we could repeat this experiment arbitrarily often, that, if we returned the donkey's soul into the state preceding his turning and let exactly the same impression act upon it, we should always observe the very same result. Then we would regard the donkey's turning to the right as necessary. We would come to realize that the brain, constituted as it was at that moment, had to react to such an impression in precisely that way.

In the absence of this experiment it seems as though the donkey's act of will were not causally determined. We just do not see its being causally determined and consequently believe that no such determination takes place. The act of will, it is said, is the cause of the turning, but it is not itself determined; it is said to be an absolute beginning.

The opinion that the donkey's act of will is not causally determined is held not only by the outsider; the donkey himself, had he the gift of reflection, would share it. The causes of his act of will would elude him, too, since in part they do not become conscious at all and in part pass through consciousness fleetingly, with the speed of lightning. If, for example, what tipped the scales was that he was closer by a hair's breadth to the bundle on the right, or that it smelled a shade better, how should the donkey notice something so trivial, something that so totally fails to force itself upon his consciousness?

In *one* sense, of course, the donkey is right in thinking "I could have turned to the left." His state at the moment, his position relative to the bundle, or its constitution need merely have been somewhat different, and he really would have turned to the left. The statement "I could have acted otherwise" is, accordingly, true in this sense: turning to the left is one of the movements possible for me (in contrast, for example, to the movement of flying); it lies within the realm of my possibilities.

We arrive at the same result if we take the law of inertia as our point of departure. It reads: every object strives to remain in its present state. Expressed negatively this becomes: without a sufficient cause no object can pass from its present state to another one. The stone will lie forever just as it is lying now; it will not undergo the slightest change if no causes—such as the weather or a force—act upon it to bring about a change. The donkey's brain will remain in the same state unchanged for all eternity if no causes—the feeling of hunger or fatigue, say, or external impressions—bring about a change.

If we reflect upon the entire life of the donkey *sub specie necessitatis*,[3] we arrive at the following result. The donkey came into the world with certain properties of mind and body, his genetic inheritance. Since the day of his birth, impressions—of the companions with whom he frolicked or worked, his feed, the climate—have acted upon these properties. These two factors, his inborn constitution and the way in which it was formed through the impressions of later life, are the cause of all of his sensations, ideas, and moods, and of all of his movements, even the most trivial

---

3 Latin for "under the aspect of necessity"—that is, seen from the standpoint of necessity. (This expression is modeled on philosopher Baruch Spinoza's coinage *sub specie aeternitatis*, "under the aspect of eternity," which Spinoza uses in his *Ethics* (1677) to characterize the highest form of knowledge as that in which the world is seen from the standpoint of timelessness or eternity.)

ones. If, for example, he cocks his left ear and not the right one, that is determined by causes whose historical development could be traced back ad infinitum;[4] and likewise when he stands, vacillating,[5] between the two bundles. And when action, the act of feeding, takes the place of vacillation, that, too, is determined: the idea of the one bundle now acts upon the donkey's mind, when it has become receptive to the idea of that particular sheaf, in such a way as to produce actions.

2. Human Beings and the Law of Causality

Let us now leave the realm of animals and proceed to consider man. Everything is the same here. Man's every feeling is a necessary result. Suppose, for example, that I am stirred by a feeling of pity at this moment. To what causes is it to be attributed? Let us go back as far as possible. An infinite amount of time has elapsed up to this moment. Time was never empty; objects have filled it from all eternity. These objects ... have continually undergone change. All of these changes were governed by the law of causality; not one of them took place without a sufficient cause.

We need not consider what else may have characterized these changes. Only their *formal* aspect, only this *one* point is of concern to us: no change occurred without a cause.

At some time in the course of this development, by virtue of some causes, organic matter was formed, and finally man. Perhaps the organic world developed as Darwin described it. Be that as it may, it was in any case due to causes that I was born on a particular day, with particular properties of body, of spirit, and of heart. Impressions then acted upon this constitution; I had particular governesses, teachers, and playmates. Teaching and example in part had an effect and in part were lost upon me; the former, when my inborn constitution made me receptive to them, when I had an affinity for them. And that is how it has come to be, through the operation of [a chain of] causes, that I am stirred by a feeling of pity at this moment. The course of the world would have had to be somewhat different if my feelings were to be different now.

It is of no consequence for the present investigation whether the inborn capacity for pity, for taking pleasure in another's pain, or for courage remains constant throughout life or whether teaching, example, and activity serve to change it. In any case the pity or pleasure in another's pain, the courage or cowardice, that a certain person feels or exhibits at a given moment is a necessary result, whether these traits are inborn—an inheritance from his ancestors—or were developed in the course of his own life.

Likewise every intention, indeed, every thought that ever passes through the brain, the silliest as well as the most brilliant, the true as well as the false, exists of necessity. In that sense there is no freedom of thought. It is necessary that I sit in this place at this moment, that I hold my pen in my hand in a particular way, and that I write that every thought is necessary; and if the reader should perchance be of the opinion that this is not the case, i.e., if he should believe that thoughts may not be viewed as effects, then he holds this false opinion of necessity also.

Just as sensations and thoughts are necessary, so, too, is action. It is, after all, nothing other than their externalization, their objective embodiment. Action is born of sensations and thoughts. So long as the sensations are not sufficiently strong, action cannot occur, and when the sensations and thoughts are constituted so as to yield the sufficient cause for it, then it must occur; then the appropriate nerves and muscles are set to work. Let us illustrate this by means of an action that is judged differently at different levels of civilization, namely, murder.[6] Munzinger,[7] for example, says that among the Bogos[8] the murderer, the terror

---

4   Without limit, forever.

5   Swaying indecisively between one course of action and another.

6   The German word Rée used here was *Raubmord*, a compound noun denoting a combination of murder and robbery (with overtones of pillage and rape).

7   Werner Munzinger (1832–1875) was a Swiss linguist and explorer. He spent many years traveling in Eritrea, Abyssinia, and the Sudan, three countries in northeast Africa south of Egypt (Abyssinia is now known as Ethiopia).

8   The Bogos were a tribe living in the highlands of northern Abyssinia and southern Eritrea. Munzinger described the customs of the Bogos in his 1859 book *Über die Sitten und das Recht der Bogos*.

of the neighborhood, who never tires of blood and murder, is a man of respect. Whoever has been raised with such views will not be deterred from murder either by external or by internal obstacles. Neither the police nor his conscience forbids him to commit it. On the contrary, it is his habit to praise murder; his parents and his gods stimulate him to commit it, and his companions encourage him by their example. And so it comes to be that, if there is a favorable opportunity, he does the deed. But is this not terribly trivial? After all, everyone knows that an act of murder is due to *motives*! True, but almost no one (except perhaps a philosopher) knows that an act of murder, and indeed every action, has a *cause*. Motives are a part of the cause. But to admit that there are motives for an action is not yet to recognize that it is causally determined, or to see clearly that the action is determined by thoughts and sensations—which in turn are effects—just as the rolling of a ball is determined by a force. But it is this point, and only this one, to which we must pay heed.

Let us now consider the act of murder from the same point of view in the case of civilized peoples. Someone raised at a higher level of civilization has learned from childhood on to disapprove of murder and to regard it as deserving punishment. God, his parents, and his teachers—in short, all who constitute an authority for him—condemn acts of this kind. It is, moreover, inconsistent with his character, which has been formed in an era of peace. Lastly, too, fear of punishment will deter him. Can murder prosper on such soil? Not easily. Fear, pity, the habit of condemning murder—all these are just so many bulwarks that block the path to such an action. Nevertheless need, passion, or various seductive influences will perhaps remove one after another of these bulwarks. Let us consider the cause of an act of murder more closely. First it is necessary to distinguish between two components, the subjective and the objective, in the total cause. The *subjective* part of the cause consists of the state of the murderer at the moment of the deed. To this we must assign all ideas that he had at the time, the conscious as well as the unconscious ones, his sensations, the temperature of his blood, the state of his stomach, of his liver—of each and every one of his bodily organs. The *objective* component consists

of the appearance of the victim, the locality in which the deed took place, and the way it was illuminated. The act of murder was necessarily consummated at that moment because these impressions acted upon a human being constituted in that particular way at the time. "Necessarily" means just that the act of murder is an effect; the state of the murderer and the impressions acting upon it are its cause. If the cause had not been complete, the effect could not have occurred. If, for example, the murderer had felt even a trifle more pity at that moment, if his idea of God or of the consequences that his deed would have here on earth had been somewhat more distinct, or if the moon had been a little brighter, so that more light would have fallen upon the victim's face and his pleading eyes—then, perhaps, the cause of the act of murder would not have become complete, and in consequence the act would not have taken place.

Thus for man, as for animal and stone, there are at any moment innumerably many *potential* states. The murderer might, at the moment when he committed the murder, have climbed a tree instead or stood on his head. If, however, instead of the murder one of these actions were to have become *actual*, then its sufficient cause would have had to be present. He would have climbed a tree if he had had the intention of hiding, or of acting as a lookout, that is to say, if at that moment he had had other ideas and sensations. But this could have been the case only if the events that took place in the world had been somewhat different [stretching back in time] ad infinitum.

3. Determinism and Will-Power

But I can, after all, break through the network of thoughts, sensations, and impressions that surrounds me by resolutely saying "I will not commit murder!" No doubt. We must, however, not lose sight of the fact that a resolute "I will" or "I will not" is also, wherever it appears, a necessary result; it does not by any means exist without a cause. Let us return to our examples. Although the Bogo really has reasons only to commit murder, it is nevertheless possible for a resolute "I will not commit murder" to assert itself. But is it conceivable that this "I will not" should occur without a sufficient cause? Fear, pity, or some other feeling, which in turn is an effect, overcomes him and gives rise to this "I will not" before the cause of the murder has yet become complete. Perhaps Christian missionaries have had an influence upon him; hence the idea of a deity that will visit retribution on him for murder comes before his soul, and that is how the "I will not" comes to be. It is easier to detect the causes of the resolute "I will not commit murder" in someone raised at a higher level of civilization; fear, principles, or the thought of God in most cases produce it in time.

A resolute will can be characteristic of a man. No matter how violently jealousy, greed, or some other passion rages within him, he does not want to succumb to it; he does not succumb to it. The analogue of this constitution is a ball that, no matter how violent a force acts upon it, does not budge from its place. A billiard cue will labor in vain to shake the earth. The earth victoriously resists the cue's thrusts with its mass. Likewise man resists the thrusts of greed and jealousy with the mass of his principles. A man of that kind, accordingly, is free—from being dominated by his drives. Does this contradict determinism? By no means. A man free from passion is still subject to the law of causality. He is necessarily free. It is just that the word "free" has different meanings. It may be correctly predicated of man in every sense except a single one: he is not free from the law of causality. Let us trace the causes of his freedom from the tyranny of the passions.

Let us suppose that his steadfastness of will was not inherited, or, if so, merely as a disposition. Teaching, example, and, above all, the force of circumstances developed it in him. From early childhood on he found himself in situations in which he had to control himself if he did not want to perish. Just as someone standing at the edge of an abyss can banish dizziness by thinking "If I become dizzy, then I will plunge," so thinking "If I yield to my excitation—indeed, if I so much as betray it[9]—I will perish" has led him to control of his drives.

It is often thought that those who deny that the will is free want to deny that man has the ability to free himself from being dominated by his drives. However, one can imagine man's power to resist passions to be

as great as one wants, even infinitely great; that is to say, a man may possibly resist even the most violent passion: his love of God or his principles have still more power over him than the passion. The question whether even the most resolute act of will is an effect is entirely independent of this.

But is being subject to the law of causality not the weak side of the strong? By no means. Is a lion weak if he can tear a tiger apart? Is a hurricane weak if it can uproot trees? And yet the power by means of which the lion dismembers and the storm uproots is an effect, and not an absolute beginning. By having causes, by being an effect, strength is not diminished.

Just as resolute willing is to be considered an effect, so is irresolute willing. A vacillating man is characterized by the fact that he alternately wants something and then doesn't want it. To say that someone contemplating murder is still vacillating means that at one time the desire for possessions, greed, and jealousy predominate—then he wants to commit murder, at another time fear of the consequences, the thought of God, or pity overcomes him, and then he does not want to commit murder. In the decisive moment, when his victim is before him, everything depends upon which feeling has the upper hand. If at that moment passion predominates, then he wants to commit murder; and then he commits murder.

We see that, from whatever point of view we look at willing, it always appears as a necessary result, as a link [in a chain of events], and never as an absolute beginning.

But can we not prove by means of an experiment that willing is an absolute beginning? I lift my arm because I *want* to lift it.... Here my *wanting* to lift my arm is the cause of the lifting, but this wanting, we are told, is not itself causally determined; rather, it is an absolute beginning. I simply want to lift my arm, and that is that. We are deceiving ourselves. This act of will, too, has causes; my intention to demonstrate by means of an experiment that my will is free gives rise to my wanting to lift my arm. But how did this intention come to be? Through a conversation, or through reflecting on the freedom of the will. Thus the thought "I want to demonstrate my freedom" has the effect that I want to lift my arm. There is a gap in

---

9   Reveal it, let it show.

this chain. Granted that my intention to demonstrate that my will is free stands in some relation to my wanting to lift my arm, why do I not demonstrate my freedom by means of some other movement? Why is it *just my arm* that I want to lift? This specific act of will on my part has not yet been causally explained. Does it perhaps not have causes? Is it an uncaused act of will? Let us note first that someone who wishes to demonstrate that his will is free will usually really extend or lift his arm, and in particular his right arm. He neither tears his hair nor wiggles his belly. This can be explained as follows. Of all of the parts of the body that are subject to our voluntary control, there is none that we move more frequently than the right arm. If, now, we wish to demonstrate our freedom by means of some movement, we will automatically make that one to which we are most accustomed.... Thus we first have a conversation about or reflection on the freedom of the will; this leads to the intention of demonstrating our freedom; this intention arises in an organism with certain [physiological] habits [such as that of readily lifting the right arm], and as a result we want to lift (and then lift) the right arm.

I remember once discussing the freedom of the will with a left-handed man. He asserted "My will is free; I can do what I want." In order to demonstrate this he extended his *left* arm.

It is easy to see, now, what the situation is with regard to the assertion "I can do what I want." In one sense it is indeed correct; in another, however, it is wrong. The *correct* sense is to regard willing as a cause and action as an effect. For example, I can kill my rival if I want to kill him. I can walk to the left if I want to walk to the left. The causes are *wanting* to kill and *wanting* to walk; the effects are killing and walking. In some way every action must be preceded by the act of willing it, whether we are aware of it or not. According to this view, in fact, I can do *only* what I want to do, and only if I want to do it. The *wrong* sense is to regard willing *merely* as a cause, and not at the same time as the effect of something else. But, like everything else, it is cause *as well as effect*. An absolutely initial act of will does not exist. Willing stands in the middle: it brings about killing and walking to the left; it is the effect of thoughts and sensations (which in turn are effects).

4. Ignorance of the Causation of Our Actions

Hence our volition (with respect to some action) is always causally determined. But it seems to be free (of causes); it seems to be an absolute beginning. To what is this appearance due?

We do not perceive the causes by which our volition is determined, and that is why we believe that it is not causally determined at all.

How often do we do something while "lost in thought"! We pay no attention to what we are doing, let alone to the causes from which it springs. While we are thinking, we support our head with our hand. While we are conversing, we twist a piece of paper in our hand. If we then reflect on our behavior—stimulated perhaps by a conversation about the freedom of the will—and if we are quite incapable of finding a sufficient cause for it, then we believe that there was no sufficient cause for it at all, that, consequently, we could have proceeded differently at that moment, e.g., supporting our head with the left hand instead of the right....

To adduce yet another example: suppose that there are two eggs on the table. I take one of them. Why not the other one? Perhaps the one I took was a bit closer to me, or some other trivial matter, which would be very difficult to discover and is of the kind that almost never enters our consciousness, tipped the scales. If I now look back but do not see why I took *that* particular egg, then I come to think that I could just as well have taken the other.

Let us replace "I could have taken the other egg" by other statements containing the expression "I could have." For example, I could, when I took the egg, have chopped off my fingers instead, or I could have jumped at my neighbor's throat. Why do we never adduce such statements ... but always those contemplating an action close to the one that we really carried out? Because at the moment when I took the egg, chopping off my fingers and murder were far from my mind. From this point of view the two aspects of our subject matter—the fact that acts of will are necessary and that they appear not to be necessary—can be perceived especially clearly. *In fact* taking the other egg was at that moment just as impossible as chopping off a finger. For, whether a nuance of a sensation or a whole army of sensations and thoughts is lacking in the complete cause obviously does not matter; the effect cannot occur so long as the cause is incomplete. But it *seems* as though it would have been possible to take the other egg at that moment; if something almost happened, we think that it could have happened.

While in the case of unimportant matters we perhaps do not notice the causes of our act of will and therefore think that it has no causes, the situation is quite different—it will be objected—in the case of important matters. We did not, after all, marry one girl rather than another while "lost in thought." We did not close the sale of our house while "lost in thought." Rather, everyone sees that motives determined such decisions. In spite of this, however, we think "I could have acted differently." What is the source of this error?

In the case of unimportant matters we do not notice the cause of our action at all; in the case of important ones we perceive it, but not adequately. We do, to be sure, see the separate parts of the cause, but the special relation in which they stood to one another at the moment of the action eludes us.

Let us first consider another example from the realm of animals. A vixen vacillated whether to sneak into the chicken coop, to hunt for mice, or to return to her young in her den. At last she sneaked into the chicken coop. Why? Because she wanted to. But why did she want to? Because this act of will on her part resulted from the relation in which her hunger, her fear of the watchdog, her maternal instinct, and her other thoughts, sensations, and impressions stood to one another at that time. But a vixen with the gift of reflection would, were she to look back upon her action, say "I could have willed differently." For, although she realizes that hunger influenced her act of will, the *degree* of hunger on the one hand, and of fear and maternal instinct on the other, present at the moment of the action elude her. Having become a different animal since the time of the action, perhaps because of it, she thinks—by way of a kind of optical illusion—that she was that other animal already then. It is the same in the case of man. Suppose, for example, that someone has slain his rival out of jealousy. What does he himself, and what do others, perceive with respect to this action? We see that on the one hand jealousy, the desire for possessions, hatred, and

rage were present in him, and on the other fear of punishment, pity, and the thought of God. We do not, however, see the particular relation in which hatred and pity, and rage and fear of punishment, stood to one another at the moment of the deed. If we could see this, keep it fixed, and recreate it experimentally, then everyone would regard this action as an effect, as a necessary result.

Let us now, with the aid of our imagination, suppose that the sensations and thoughts of the murderer at the moment of the deed were spread out before us, clearly visible as if on a map. From this reflection we shall learn that *in fact* we are lacking such an overview, and that this lack is the reason why we do not ascribe a cause (or "necessity") to the action.

The kaleidoscopically changing sensations, thoughts, and impressions would, in order for their relation to one another to become apparent, have to be returned to the state in which they were at the moment of the deed, and then made rigid, as if they were being nailed to their place. But beyond that, the thoughts and sensations would have to be spatially extended and endowed with a colored surface; a stronger sensation would have to be represented by a bigger lump. A clearer thought would have to wear, say, a bright red color, a less clear one a gray coloration. Jealousy and rage, as well as pity and the thought of God, would have to be plastically exhibited[10] for us in this way. We would, further, have to see how the sight of the victim acts upon these structures of thoughts and sensations, and how there arises from these two factors first the desire to commit murder and then the act of murder itself.

Moreover, we would have to be able to repeat the process, perhaps as follows: we return the murderer to the state of mind that he had some years before the act of murder; we equip his mind with precisely the same thoughts and sensations, and his body with the same constitution. Then we let the very same impressions act upon them; we bring him into contact with the same people, let him read the same books, nourish him with the same food, and, finally, we will place the murdered person, after having called him back to life, before the murderer with the very same

---

10   Modeled in three dimensions.

facial expression, in the same illumination and at the same distance. Then, as soon as the parts of the cause have been completely assembled, we would always see that the very same effect occurs, namely, wanting to commit, and then committing, murder.

Finally, too, we would have to vary the experiment, in the manner of the chemists; we would have to be able now to weaken a sensation, now to strengthen it, and to observe the result that this produces.

If these conditions were fulfilled, if we could experimentally recreate the process and also vary it, if we were to see its components and, above all, their relation to one another with plastic clarity before us—on the one hand, the *degree* of jealousy and of rage present at the moment; on the other, the *degree* of fear of punishment and of pity—then we would acknowledge that wanting to commit murder and committing murder are necessary results. But as it is we merely see that, on the one hand, jealousy and related feelings, and, on the other, pity and the idea of God, were present in the murderer. But, since we do not see the particular relation in which the sensations and thoughts stood to one another at the moment of the deed, we simply think that the *one* side could have produced acts of will and actions as well as the *other*, that the murderer could, at the moment when he wanted to commit and did commit murder, just as well have willed and acted differently, say compassionately.

It is the same if we ourselves are the person who acts. We, too, think "I could have willed differently." Let us illustrate this by yet another example. Yesterday afternoon at 6:03 o'clock I sold my house. Why? Because I wished to do so. But why did I wish to do so? Because my intention to change my place of residence, and other circumstances, caused my act of will. But was I compelled to will? Could I not have postponed the sale or forgone it altogether? It seems so to me, because I do not see the particular relation in which my thoughts, sensations, and impressions stood to one another yesterday afternoon at 6:03 o'clock.

Thus: we do not see the sufficient cause (either not at all, in the case of unimportant matters; or inadequately, in the case of important ones); consequently it does not exist for us; consequently we think that our volition and our actions were not causally determined at all, that we could just as well have willed and acted differently. No one would say "I could have willed differently" if he could see his act of will and its causes displayed plastically before him, in an experiment permitting repetition.

But who are the mistaken "we" of whom we are speaking here? Patently the author does not consider himself to be one of them. Does he, then, set himself, along with a few fellow philosophers, apart from the rest of mankind, regarding them as ignorant of the truth? Well, it really is not the case that mankind has always concerned itself with the problem of the freedom of the will and only a small part arrived at the result that the will is not free; rather, in precivilized ages no one, and in civilized ages almost no one, concerned himself with this problem. But of the few who did address themselves to this question, as the history of philosophy teaches us, almost all recognized that there is no freedom of the will. The others became victims of the illusion described above, without ever coming to grips with the problem in its general form (is the will subject to the law of causality or not?) ….

5. Determinism is Inconsistent with Judgments of Moral Responsibility

We hold ourselves and others responsible without taking into account the problem of the freedom of the will.

Experience shows that, if someone has lied or murdered, he is told that he has acted reprehensibly and deserves punishment. Whether his action is uncaused or whether, like the other processes in nature, it is subject to the law of causality—how would people come to raise such questions in the ordinary course of their lives? Or has anyone ever heard of a case in which people talking about an act of murder, a lie, or an act of self-sacrifice discussed these actions in terms of the freedom of the will? It is the same if we ourselves are the person who acted. We say to ourselves "Oh, if only I had not done this! Oh, if only I had acted differently!" or "I have acted laudably, as one should act." At best a philosopher here or there chances upon the question whether our actions are causally determined or not, certainly not the rest of mankind.

Suppose, however, that someone's attention is directed to the fact that the will is not free. At first it will be very difficult to make this plausible to him. His volition is suspended from threads that are too nearly invisible, and that is why he comes to think that it is not causally determined at all. At last, however—so we shall assume—he does come to recognize that actions are effects, that their causes are thoughts and impressions, that these must likewise be viewed as effects, and so on. How will he then judge these actions? Will he continue to maintain that murder is to be punished by *reprisal* and that benevolent actions are to be considered *meritorious*? By no means. Rather, the first conclusion that he will—validly—draw from his newly acquired insight is that we cannot hold anyone responsible. "*Tout comprendre c'est tout pardonner*";[11] no one can be made to answer for an *effect*.

In order to illustrate this important truth, that whoever considers intentions to be effects will cease to assign merit or blame for them, let us resume discussion of the examples above. From early childhood on the Bogo … has learned to praise murder. The praiseworthiness of such an action already penetrated the consciousness of the child as a secondary meaning of the word "murder," and afterward it was confirmed by every impression: his gods and his fellow men praise murder. In consequence he involuntarily judges acts of murder to be praiseworthy, no matter whether it was he himself or someone else who committed them. Let us assume, now, that a philosopher had succeeded in persuading the Bogos that the act of murder and the intention to practice cruelty are causally determined. Then their judgment would undergo an essential modification.

To conceive of actions and intentions as causally determined, after all, means the following. We go back in the history of the individual, say to his birth, and investigate which of his characteristics are inborn and to what causes they are due.[12] Then, ever guided by the law of causality, we trace the development or transformation of these properties; we see how impressions, teachings, and examples come to him

and, if his inborn constitution has an affinity for them, are taken up and transformed by it, otherwise passing by without leaving a trace. Finally we recognize that the keystone, the necessary result of this course of development, is the desire to commit murder and the act of murder.

A Bogo who looks upon murder and the intention to practice cruelty in this way—that is, as an effect—will say that it is impossible to regard them as meritorious.

But will he now look upon these actions with apathy, devoid of all feeling? By no means. He will still consider them to be pleasant or unpleasant, agreeable or disagreeable.

When the action is directed against himself, he will perceive it as pleasant or as unpleasant; the prospect of being murdered is unpleasant for everyone, whether he considers the action to be causally determined or uncaused.

Similarly our liking or dislike for the character of a human being will persist even if we regard it as the result of causes. To say that I find someone agreeable means that I am drawn to him; I like him. Of a landscape, too, one says that it is agreeable, and, just as this liking cannot be diminished even if we consider the trees, meadows, and hills to be the result of causes, so our liking for the character of a human being is not diminished if we regard it *sub specie necessitatis*. Hence to the Bogo who has come to see that murder is causally determined it is still agreeable or disagreeable. Usually he will consider it to be agreeable. He will say that it warms the cockles of his heart to observe such an action; it accords with his wild temperament, as yet untouched by civilization. Therefore he will, in view of the necessity, suspend only the specifically moral practice of regarding it as meritorious. But his liking may become love, and even esteem and reverence. It will be objected, however, that "I revere a mode of behavior" entails "I consider it meritorious for a person to behave in that way," and similarly for esteem. To be sure, the words "reverence" and "esteem" *frequently* have this meaning, and *to the extent that they do* a determinist would cease using them. But all words that denote human feelings have not only one, but several meanings. They have, if I may express it in that way, a harem of meanings,

---

11   "To understand all is to forgive all" (old French saying).

12   [Author's note] An investigation as detailed as that is, of course, never possible in practice.

and they couple now with this one, now with that one. So, if I "revere" someone, it means also that I esteem him, that he impresses me, and that I wish to be like him…. Reverence and esteem in *this* sense can coexist with determinism.

Hence the Bogo who conceives of the intention to practice cruelty and the act of murder as effects can nevertheless consider them to be agreeable or disagreeable, and in a certain sense he can also have esteem and reverence for them, but he will not regard them as meritorious.

Let us now consider the act of murder at high levels of civilization. Civilization, as it progressed, stigmatized murder and threatened penalties for it on earth and in heaven. This censure already penetrates the consciousness of the child as a secondary meaning of the word "murder" and afterward is confirmed through every impression. All the people whom one knows, all the books that one reads, the state with its institutions, pulpit and stage always use "murder" in a censorious sense. That is how it comes to be that we involuntarily declare an act of murder to be blameworthy, be it that others or that we ourselves, driven by passion, committed it. Whether the action was determined by causes or uncaused—that question is raised neither by the person who acted nor by the uninvolved observers. But *if* it is raised, if someone considers the act of murder *sub specie necessitatis*, then he ceases to regard it as blameworthy. He will then no longer want to see punishment in the proper sense—suffering as retribution—meted out for it, but merely punishment as a safety measure.[13] The feelings of liking and dislike, however, will continue to exist even then. On the whole, someone raised at a high level of civilization will have a feeling of dislike for acts of murder; he will not feel drawn to whoever commits it; he will not like him. For such an act does not accord with his temperament, which was formed as he was engaged in non-violent occupations. In spite of the recognition that the action was necessary, this dislike can at times grow to revulsion, and even to contempt—given that the latter notion is stripped of the specifically moral elements that it contains (the

attribution of blame). It will then mean something like this: I do not want to be like that person.

The situation is the same in the case of benevolent actions and those performed out of a sense of duty; we cease to regard them as meritorious if we consider them to be effects. Let us look more closely at actions performed out of a sense of duty. To say that someone acts out of a sense of duty means that he performs an action, perhaps contrary to his inclinations, because his conscience commands him to do it. But how does conscience come to issue such commandments? As follows: with some actions (and intentions) there is linked for us from early childhood on a categorical "thou shalt do (or have) them"; for example, "you *should* help everyone as much as possible." If someone then makes this habitual judgment into the guiding principle of his behavior, if he helps a person because his conscience commands "thou *shalt* help thy fellow man," then he is acting "out of a sense of duty"…. If we want to consider such an action from the point of view of eternity and necessity, we shall have to proceed as follows: we investigate (1) the constitution of the child who receives the teaching "thou shalt help," (2) the constitution of those who give it to him. The child absorbing this doctrine has some inborn constitution of nerves, of blood, of imagination, and of reason. The commandment "thou shalt help" is impressed upon this substance with some degree of insistence; the deity, heaven, hell, approval of his fellow men and of his own conscience—these ideas are presented to him, depending upon his teachers, as being more or less majestic and inspiring. And the child transforms them with greater or lesser intensity, depending upon his receptivity. The ultimate constitution of a man, the preponderance within him of the sense of duty over his own desires, is in any case a necessary result, a product of his inborn constitution and the impressions received. To someone who contemplates this, such a temperament may, to be sure, still seem agreeable (perhaps because he himself is or would like to be similarly constituted), but no one can regard as *meritorious* behavior that he conceives to be an *effect*.

But what if we ourselves are the person who acted? Then the circumstances are analogous; then, too, liking and dislike remain, while the attribution of merit or blame (the "pangs of conscience") disappears.

---

13   [Author's note] Punishments are causes that prevent the repetition of the action punished.

Our own action, too, can remain agreeable or become disagreeable for us after it has occurred. It is agreeable if the disposition from which we acted persists after the action; it will become disagreeable if we change our frame of mind. Suppose, for example, that we have acted vengefully and are still in the same mood; then the act of revenge is still agreeable, whether we conceive it to be an effect or not. If, however, a feeling of pity takes the place of our desire for revenge, then we come to dislike our action; we cannot stand our earlier self—the less so, the more pronounced our feeling of pity is. The reflection that the action is an effect in no way affects this feeling of dislike, perhaps of disgust, or even of revulsion for ourselves. We say to ourselves that the desire for revenge was, to be sure, necessarily stronger than the ideas and impressions that stood in its way, hence the action took place necessarily, too; but now it happens that pity is necessarily present, and, along with it, regrets that we acted as we did....

6. Can We Abandon Judgments of Moral Responsibility?

But is it really possible to shake off feelings of guilt so easily? Do they disappear, like a spook, when the magic word *effect* is pronounced? Is the situation with respect to this feeling not quite like that with regard to dislike? It was, to be sure, necessary that I took revenge, but now I necessarily feel dislike for my own action, along with guilt. I can no more prevent the onset of the one feeling than of the other. But if the feeling of guilt asserts itself in spite of the recognition that actions are effects, should we not suspect that our holding others responsible, too, will persist in spite of this insight? Did we commit an error somewhere? Is it that responsibility and necessity do not exclude each other? The situation is as follows. The reason why we assign moral praise to some actions and moral censure to others has already been mentioned repeatedly. Censure already penetrates the consciousness of the child as a secondary meaning of the words "murder," "theft," "vengefulness," and "pleasure in another's pain," and praise as a secondary meaning of the words "benevolence" and "mercy." That is why censure seems to him to be a constituent part of murder, and praise, of benevolence. At a later point

in his life, perhaps in his twentieth year, the insight comes to him from somewhere that all actions are effects and therefore cannot earn merit or blame. What can this poor little insight accomplish against the accumulated habits of a lifetime of judging? The habit of mind of assigning blame for actions like murder makes it very difficult to think of them without this judgment. It is all very well for reason to tell us that we may not assign blame for such actions, since they are effects—our habit of judging, which has become a feeling, will see to it that it is done anyway. But—let habit confront habit! Suppose that, whenever someone involuntarily wants to assign blame or merit for an action, he ascends to the point of view of eternity and necessity. He then regards the action as the necessary result of [a chain of events stretching back into] the infinite past. Through that way of looking at things the *instinctive* association between the action and the judgment will be severed, if not the first time, then perhaps by the thousandth. Such a man will shed the habit of assigning blame or merit for any action whatsoever.

In fact, of course, human beings almost never behave like that; this way of looking at things is completely foreign to them. Furthermore, human beings determine their actions by considering whether they will make them happy or unhappy; but shedding the habit of making judgments [of moral responsibility] would hardly increase their happiness....

The situation with respect to a person's character is no different from that with respect to his individual actions. *Customarily* one assigns blame or merit, whether to himself or to others, for a single action: a single act of cheating or of giving offense. But *sometimes* we go back from the action to its source, to a person's character. In reality, of course, character, in its broadest as well as its smallest traits, is just as necessary as an individual action; it is the product of [a chain of events stretching back into] the infinite past, be it that it was inherited in its entirety or that it was formed in part during the individual's lifetime. But with regard to character, too, hardly anyone adopts this point of view. Just as in the case of particular actions, character is regarded neither as free nor as necessary; that is to say, people do not raise the question at all whether the law of causality is applicable also to actions and character. Hence one assigns blame and merit for character as for actions, though they are effects; for one does not see that they are effects. If one sees this, if one regards character *sub specie necessitatis*, then he ceases to assign blame or merit for it. Liking and dislike, on the other hand, nevertheless persist even then: a character closely related to mine will garner my liking, my love, and perhaps even, in the sense mentioned above, my esteem and reverence—whether I conceive of it as an effect or not.

Hence we assign blame or merit for character and actions out of the habit of judging, without concerning ourselves with the question whether they are causally determined or not. We cease to assign blame or merit for character and actions as soon as we recognize that they are causally determined (if we ignore the remnants of our habits).

Let us recapitulate: the character, the intentions, and the actions of every human being are effects, and it is impossible to assign blame or merit for effects.

C.A. CAMPBELL

On Selfhood and Godhood

Who Was C.A. Campbell?

Charles Arthur Campbell (known to his friends as Arthur) was born in Scotland in 1897 and died there in 1974. He served with the Tenth Border Regiment during the First World War but was invalided out in 1917: his injuries put an end to what might have been a successful athletic career and left him plagued with intermittently serious health problems for the rest of his life. After attending university at Glasgow and at Balliol College, Oxford, he lectured in the moral philosophy department of Glasgow University. From 1932 to 1938 he was professor of philosophy at the University of North Wales, Bangor, and then returned to Glasgow where he was appointed to the chair of Logic and Rhetoric, a position which he held until retirement in 1961.

Campbell's main publications were *Scepticism and Construction* (1931), *Moral Intuition and the Principle of Self-Realisation* (1948), *On Selfhood and Godhood* (1957), and *In Defence of Free Will* (1967). *On Selfhood and Godhood* has been called (by the philosopher H.D. Lewis) "one of the most impressive defences of theism ever attempted."

It's fair to say that, for much of his career, Campbell was considered rather old fashioned and out of step with the spirit of the philosophical times. As Campbell writes in the preface to *On Selfhood and Godhood*,

> Readers of this book will not be long in discovering my inability to do obeisance to the twin gods of so much recent British philosophy—linguisticism and empiricism.... Perhaps it was a little naïve of the older generation of contemporary British philosophers to be so taken aback by [the] apparently total absence [of readiness to re-examine their first principles] in logical positivists and later heralds of a new dawn. Perhaps also, however, it was pardonable that philosophers whose reflections upon the premises of latter-day empiricism and of linguisticism left them profoundly sceptical of their validity should have been disquieted, incensed, or infuriated—according to temperament—by the practice that prevailed in most modernist quarters of automatically dismissing as worthless all writings which did not conform to modernist preconceptions (on the assump-

tion, apparently, that their authors could only be philosophic Rip Van Winkles talking in their sleep).… The more tranquil and judicial assessment of gains and losses which is now practicable, and of which there are some instructive examples already in being, must surely be welcomed by all who do not think it priggish to believe that philosophy is neither a word-game, nor a social accomplishment, nor a gladiatorial exhibition, but, quite simply, the rational pursuit of such truth as is attainable by human minds about the general character of the universe in which we find ourselves.

H.D. Lewis described Campbell as "a peculiarly sharp controversialist, [but] he was also totally devoid of rancour or bitterness."

The lecture reprinted here is a classic statement of one important version of the *libertarian* position on free will: that, although most events are causally determined, some human actions—those we do, not from personal inclination, but from moral duty—are not determined by anything except moral law. That is, we are free because, if we choose to, we can do what we *ought* to do as opposed to what we *want* to do.

What Is the Structure of This Reading?

Campbell begins his lecture by stressing the importance of carefully and precisely formulating the problem of free will, before we can see what would count as a solution to it. He defines the kind of freedom at issue: a freedom belonging to "inner acts," of which the self is the sole author, and which are such that the agent, categorically, could have acted otherwise. On the other hand, it is not necessary that these acts be morally good ones; if we are free, then we are free to choose to behave immorally. Having defined the kind of free will he is concerned with, Campbell goes on to discuss (from section 5 onwards) whether such freedom exists in reality. He defends the view that it *is* real, though its area of functioning is limited to moral decisions made in response to situations of moral temptation. He argues by:

a) Claiming we have "phenomenological" evidence for the existence of this kind of free will—that we know from our own experience that we sometimes act out of duty, against our own inclinations;

b) Arguing that if this result conflicts with *theoretical* reasons for doubting free will, it is not necessarily the phenomenological—practical—side that must concede defeat; and

c) Rejecting what he considers the two main theoretical objections to the existence of genuinely free will: the claim that our free will is inconsistent with facts about human predictability; and the claim that the free-will doctrine is unintelligible, since it apparently disconnects 'our' actions from our selves.

Some Useful Background Information

1. Campbell rejected what he calls a "naturalistic" study of the human mind: i.e., he rejected the assumption that the human mind is just one among all the other objects in the natural world, and that it is fully open to study and explanation using the methods of the natural sciences. His main objection to naturalizing the mind is captured by the following quotation (from Lecture III of *On Selfhood and Godhood*):

The naturalistic standpoint, the standpoint proper to, and indeed alone possible for, the study of physical objects, is the standpoint of the external observer. But that standpoint is bound to be inadequate to the study of that which is something not merely for an external observer, but also *for itself*. It will not afford us even a glimpse of this latter aspect of the thing's being; and in the degree that this latter aspect is important to the thing's being, any account which abstracts from it is bound to result in travesty.… Accordingly it seems to me clear that the naturalistic approach to the study of the mind, abstracting wholly from the standpoint of the experiencing subject, which can alone throw light upon what the mind is for itself, is in principle hopelessly incapable of revealing to us mental experience as it really is, and as, in our less doctrinaire moments, we all believe it to be.

2. Although Campbell does not say so explicitly, when he defines the problem of free will in this selection he sets it up as an "incompatibilist" thesis. He argues that the existence of (the right kind of) free will is *incompatible* with the claim that all of our actions are causally determined.

Suggestions for Critical Reflection

1. How accurate is Campbell's characterization of the free-will problem? Are actions genuinely free *only* if they are inner acts for which the agent is solely responsible and which are such that the agent could (categorically) have chosen not to do them?

2. Does Campbell have to admit that most of our choices or actions are *not* free? That is, do we exercise free will, on his account, when we do what we want—when we do things without exerting any "moral effort"? If not, is this a serious blow to his account of free will?

3. How much legitimate evidence for freedom of the will comes from the fact that we *feel* free? After all, don't people sometimes sincerely, but falsely, believe they are acting freely (e.g., when they are under the influence of hypnotism, or suffering from a brain disorder)?

4. Campbell passes lightly over "criticisms based upon the universality of causal law as a supposed postulate of science." Is he right to do so? Campbell tacitly appeals to the probabilistic mathematics of quantum mechanics to suggest that even scientists are uncertain about the universality of causality. Does this help his case? Is there an important difference between quantum randomness and the kind of freedom Campbell wants to defend?

5. "A free will is *ex hypothesi* the sort of thing of which the request for an *explanation* is absurd." Do you agree?

6. Campbell argues that, from the "inner standpoint" it is clear we sometimes do things that go against our own character: roughly, we do things we really do not want to do. But is this really true? Or is the internal conflict we sometimes feel really a conflict between different things we *do* want to do—such as visiting our sick mother in hospital or going skiing—and our inner struggles just a matter of finding out what we want to do *most*?

Suggestions for Further Reading

The two books in which C.A. Campbell paid most attention to the problem of free will are *On Selfhood and Godhood* (George Allen & Unwin, 1957) and *In Defence of Free Will* (George Allen & Unwin, 1967). One of his articles, which is frequently anthologized, is "Is 'Free Will' a Pseudo-Problem?" *Mind* 60 (1951). In this article Campbell criticizes compatibilist accounts of free will. Ideas similar to those expressed by Campbell can be found in the writings of the eighteenth-century Scottish "common sense" philosopher Thomas Reid. See his *Essays on the Active Powers of the Human Mind* (1788, reprinted by MIT Press, 1969).

Articles that defend or are generally sympathetic to Campbell's line include Keith Lehrer's "Can We Know That We Have Free Will by Introspection?" *Journal of Philosophy* 57 (1960); "The Moral and Religious Philosophy of C.A. Campbell" by H.P. Owen, *Religious Studies* 3 (1967); and Betty Powell's "Uncharacteristic Actions," *Mind* 68 (1959). Three articles which attack Campbell's views are Phillip Gosselin "C.A. Campbell's Effort of Will Argument" *Religious Studies* 13 (1977); J.J.C. Smart, "Free-Will, Praise and Blame," *Mind* 70 (1961); and Edward Walter, "Is Libertarianism Logically Coherent?" *Philosophy and Phenomenological Research* 38 (1978). A good discussion of the evidence for freedom from introspection is Douglas Browning's "The Feeling of Freedom," *Review of Metaphysics* 18 (1964).

On Selfhood and Godhood

Lecture IX, "Has the Self Free Will?"[1]

1.

... It is something of a truism that in philosophic enquiry the exact formulation of a problem often takes one a long way on the road to its solution. In the case of the Free Will problem I think there is a rather special need of careful formulation. For there are many sorts of human freedom; and it can easily happen that one wastes a great deal of labour in proving or disproving a freedom which has almost nothing to do with the freedom which is at issue in the traditional problem of Free Will. The abortiveness of so much of the argument for and against Free Will in contemporary philosophical literature seems to me due in the main to insufficient pains being taken over the preliminary definition of the problem. There is, indeed, one outstanding exception, Professor Broad's[2] brilliant inaugural lecture entitled, 'Determinism, Indeterminism, and Libertarianism,'[3] in which forty-three pages are devoted to setting out the problem, as against seven to its solution! I confess that the solution does not seem to myself to follow upon the formulation quite as easily as all that:[4] but Professor Broad's

---

1   This selection is taken from Chapter IX of *On Selfhood and Godhood* (pages 158–179), London: HarperCollins Publishers Ltd. (Originally published by George Allen & Unwin, 1957.) Copyright © C.A. Campbell, 1957. Reprinted by permission of Taylor & Francis Books UK. The book is based on the Gifford Lectures which Campbell gave at the University of St. Andrews, in Scotland, between 1953 and 1955.

2   C.D. Broad was the well-respected professor of moral philosophy at Cambridge from 1933 to 1953. Broad's typical method was a detailed and careful elaboration of all the possible answers to a particular philosophical question, and then a tentative suggestion as to which of them was most plausible.

3   [Author's note] Reprinted in *Ethics and the History of Philosophy, Selected Essays.*

4   [Author's note] I have explained the grounds for my dissent from Broad's final conclusion on pp. 27 ff. of *In Defence of Free Will* (Jackson Son & Co., 1938).

eminent example fortifies me in my decision to give here what may seem at first sight a disproportionate amount of time to the business of determining the essential characteristics of the kind of freedom with which the traditional problem is concerned.

Fortunately we can at least make a beginning with a certain amount of confidence. It is not seriously disputable that the kind of freedom in question is the freedom which is commonly recognised to be in some sense a precondition of moral responsibility. Clearly, it is on account of this integral connection with moral responsibility that such exceptional importance has always been felt to attach to the Free Will problem. But in what precise sense is free will a precondition of moral responsibility, and thus a postulate of the moral life in general? This is an exceedingly troublesome question; but until we have satisfied ourselves about the answer to it, we are not in a position to state, let alone decide, the question whether 'Free Will' in its traditional, ethical, significance is a reality.

Our first business, then, is to ask, exactly what kind of freedom is it which is required for moral responsibility? And as to method of procedure in this inquiry, there seems to me to be no real choice. I know of only one method that carries with it any hope of success; viz.[5] the critical comparison of those acts for which, on due reflection, we deem it proper to attribute moral praise or blame to the agents, with those acts for which, on due reflection, we deem such judgments to be improper. The ultimate touchstone, as I see it, can only be our moral consciousness as it manifests itself in our more critical and considered moral judgments. The 'linguistic' approach by way of the analysis of moral *sentences* seems to me, despite its present popularity, to be an almost infallible method for reaching wrong results in the moral field; but I must reserve what I have to say about this.

2.

The first point to note is that the freedom at issue (as indeed the very name 'Free *Will* Problem' indicates) pertains primarily not to overt acts but to inner acts. The nature of things has decreed that, save in the case of one's self, it is only overt acts which one can direct-

---

5   Namely, that is (from the Latin *videlicet*).

ly observe. But a very little reflection serves to show that in our moral judgments upon others their overt acts are regarded as significant only insofar as they are the expression of inner acts. We do not consider the acts of a robot to be morally responsible acts; nor do we consider the acts of a man to be so save in so far as they are distinguishable from those of a robot by reflecting an inner life of choice. Similarly, from the other side, if we are satisfied (as we may on occasion be, at least in the case of ourselves) that a person has definitely elected to follow a course which he believes to be wrong, but has been prevented by external circumstances from translating his inner choice into an overt act, we still regard him as morally blameworthy. Moral freedom, then, pertains to *inner* acts.

The next point seems at first sight equally obvious and uncontroversial; but, as we shall see, it has awkward implications if we are in real earnest with it (as almost nobody is). It is the simple point that the act must be one of which the person judged can be regarded as the *sole* author. It seems plain enough that if there are any *other* determinants of the act, external to the self, to that extent the act is not an act which the *self* determines, and to that extent not an act for which the self can be held morally responsible. The self is only part-author of the act, and his moral responsibility can logically extend only to those elements within the act (assuming for the moment that these can be isolated) of which he is the *sole* author.

The awkward implications of this apparent truism will be readily appreciated. For, if we are mindful of the influences exerted by heredity and environment, we may well feel some doubt whether there is any act of will at all of which one can truly say that the self is sole author, sole determinant. No man has a voice in determining the raw material of impulses and capacities that constitute his hereditary endowment, and no man has more than a very partial control of the material and social environment in which he is destined to live his life. Yet it would be manifestly absurd to deny that these two factors do constantly and profoundly affect the nature of a man's choices. That this is so we all of us recognise in our moral judgments when we 'make allowances,' as we say, for a bad heredity or a vicious environment, and acknowledge in the victim of them a diminished moral

responsibility for evil courses. Evidently we do *try*, in our moral judgments, however crudely, to praise or blame a man only in respect of that of which we can regard him as *wholly* the author. And evidently we do recognise that, for a man to be the author of an act in the full sense required for moral responsibility, it is not enough merely that he 'wills' or 'chooses' the act: since even the most unfortunate victim of heredity or environment does, as a rule, 'will' what he does. It is significant, however, that the ordinary man, though well enough aware of the influence upon choices of heredity and environment, does not feel obliged thereby to give up his assumption that moral predicates *are* somehow applicable. Plainly he still believes that there is *something* for which a man is morally responsible, something of which we can fairly say that he is the sole author. *What is this something?* To that question commonsense is not ready with an explicit answer—though an answer is, I think, implicit in the line which its moral judgments take. I shall do what I can to give an explicit answer later in this lecture. Meantime it must suffice to observe that, if we are to be true to the deliverances of our moral consciousness, it is very difficult to deny that *sole* authorship is a necessary condition of the morally responsible act.

Thirdly we come to a point over which much recent controversy has raged. We may approach it by raising the following question. Granted an act of which the agent is sole author, does this 'sole authorship' suffice to make the act a morally free act? We may be inclined to think that it does, until we contemplate the possibility that an act of which the agent is sole author might conceivably occur as a necessary expression of the agent's nature; the way in which, e.g., some philosophers have supposed the Divine act of creation to occur. This consideration excites a legitimate doubt; for it is far from easy to see how a person can be regarded as a proper subject for moral praise or blame in respect of an act which he *cannot help* performing—even if it be his own 'nature' which necessitates it. Must we not recognise it as a condition of the morally free act that the agent 'could have acted otherwise' than he in fact did? It is true, indeed, that we sometimes praise or blame a man for an act about which we are prepared to say, in the light of our knowledge of his established character, that he 'could no other.' But I think that a little reflection shows that in such cases we are not praising or blaming the man strictly for what he does *now* (or at any rate we ought not to be), but rather for those past acts of his which have generated the firm habit of mind from which his *present* act follows 'necessarily.' In other words, our praise and blame, so far as justified, are really retrospective, being directed not to the agent *qua*[6] performing *this* act, but to the agent *qua* performing those past acts which have built up his present character, and in respect to which we presume that he *could* have acted otherwise, that there really *were* open possibilities before him. These cases, therefore, seem to me to constitute no valid exception to what I must take to be the rule, viz. that a man can be morally praised or blamed for an act only if he could have acted otherwise.

Now philosophers today are fairly well agreed that it is a postulate[7] of the morally responsible act that the agent 'could have acted otherwise' in *some* sense of that phrase. But sharp differences of opinion have arisen over the way in which the phrase ought to be interpreted. There is a strong disposition to water down its apparent meaning by insisting that it is not (as a postulate of moral responsibility) to be understood as a straightforward categorical proposition, but rather as a disguised hypothetical proposition.[8] All that we really require to be assured of, in order to justify our holding X morally responsible for an act, is, we are told, that X could have acted otherwise *if* he had *chosen* otherwise (Moore, Stevenson[9]); or perhaps that X could have acted otherwise *if* he had had a different character, or *if* he had been placed in different circumstances.

I think it is easy to understand, and even, in a measure, to sympathise with, the motives which induce

___

6   *Qua* means "as being," "in the capacity of."

7   A presupposition or basic principle.

8   A categorical proposition asserts that something is true; a hypothetical proposition says only that something is true *if* something else is. It's the difference between, for example, "Billy is a good boy" and "Billy is a good boy if someone is watching."

9   G.E. Moore (1873–1958) and C.L. Stevenson (1908–1979). Both philosophers are known for their (widely divergent) moral theories.

philosophers to offer these counter-interpretations. It is not just the fact that 'X could have acted otherwise,' as a bald categorical statement, is incompatible with the universal sway of causal law—though this is, to some philosophers, a serious stone of stumbling. The more widespread objection is that it at least looks as though it were incompatible with that causal continuity of an agent's character with his conduct which is implied when we believe (surely with justice) that we can often tell the sort of thing a man will do from our knowledge of the sort of man he is.

We shall have to make our accounts with that particular difficulty later. At this stage I wish merely to show that neither of the hypothetical propositions suggested—and I think the same could be shown for *any* hypothetical alternative—is an acceptable substitute for the categorical proposition 'X could have acted otherwise' as the presupposition of moral responsibility.

Let us look first at the earlier suggestion—'X could have acted otherwise *if* he had chosen otherwise.' Now clearly there are a great many acts with regard to which we are entirely satisfied that the agent is thus situated. We are often perfectly sure that—for this is all it amounts to—if X had chosen otherwise, the circumstances presented no external obstacle to the translation of that choice into action. For example, we often have no doubt at all that X, who in point of fact told a lie, could have told the truth *if* he had so chosen. But does our confidence on this score allay all legitimate doubts about whether X is really blameworthy? Does it entail that X is free in the sense required for moral responsibility? Surely not. The obvious question immediately arises: 'But *could* X have *chosen* otherwise than he did?' It is doubt about the true answer to *that* question which leads most people to doubt the reality of moral responsibility. Yet on this crucial question the hypothetical proposition which is offered as a sufficient statement of the condition justifying the ascription of moral responsibility gives us no information whatsoever.

Indeed this hypothetical substitute for the categorical 'X could have acted otherwise' seems to me to lack all plausibility unless one contrives to forget why it is, after all, that we ever come to feel fundamental doubts about man's moral responsibility. Such doubts are born, surely, when one becomes aware of certain reputable world-views in religion or philosophy, or of certain reputable scientific beliefs, which in their several ways imply that man's actions are necessitated, and thus could not be otherwise than they in fact are. But clearly a doubt so based is not even touched by the recognition that a man could very often act otherwise *if* he so chose. That proposition is entirely compatible with the necessitarian theories which generate our doubt: indeed it is this very compatibility that has recommended it to some philosophers, who are reluctant to give up either moral responsibility or Determinism. The proposition which we *must* be able to affirm if moral praise or blame of X is to be justified is the categorical proposition that X could have acted otherwise because—not if—he could have chosen otherwise; or, since it is essentially the inner side of the act that matters, the proposition simply that X could have chosen otherwise.

For the second of the alternative formulae suggested we cannot spare more than a few moments. But its inability to meet the demands it is required to meet is almost transparent. 'X could have acted otherwise,' as a statement of a precondition of X's moral responsibility, really means (we are told) 'X could have acted otherwise *if* he were differently constituted, or *if* he had been placed in different circumstances.' It seems a sufficient reply to this to point out that the person whose moral responsibility is at issue is X; a specific individual, in a specific set of circumstances. It is totally irrelevant to X's moral responsibility that we should be able to say that some person differently constituted from X, or X in a different set of circumstances, could have done something different from what X did.

3.

Let me, then, briefly sum up the answer at which we have arrived to our question about the kind of freedom required to justify moral responsibility. It is that a man can be said to exercise free will in a morally significant sense only in so far as his chosen act is one of which he is the sole cause or author, and only if—in the straightforward, categorical sense of the phrase—he 'could have chosen otherwise.'

I confess that this answer is in some ways a disconcerting one; disconcerting, because most of us,

however objective we are in the actual conduct of our thinking, would *like* to be able to believe that moral responsibility is real: whereas the freedom required for moral responsibility, on the analysis we have given, is certainly far more difficult to establish than the freedom required on the analyses we found ourselves obliged to reject. If, e.g., moral freedom entails only that I could have acted otherwise *if* I had chosen otherwise, there is no real 'problem' about it at all. I am 'free' in the normal case where there is no external obstacle to prevent my translating the alternative choice into action, and not free in other cases. Still less is there a problem if all that moral freedom entails is that I could have acted otherwise *if* I had been a differently constituted person, or been in different circumstances. Clearly I am *always* free in *this* sense of freedom. But, as I have argued, these so-called 'freedoms' fail to give us the pre-conditions of moral responsibility, and hence leave the freedom of the traditional free-will problem, the freedom that people are really concerned about, precisely where it was.

4.

Another interpretation of freedom which I am bound to reject on the same general ground, i.e., that it is just not the kind of freedom that is relevant to moral responsibility, is the old idealist[10] view which identifies the *free* will with the *rational* will; the rational will in its turn being identified with the will which wills the moral law in whole-hearted, single-minded obedience to it. This view is still worth at least a passing mention, if only because it has recently been resurrected in an interesting work by Professor A.E. Teale.[11] Moreover, I cannot but feel a certain nostalgic tenderness for a view in which I myself was (so to speak) philosophically cradled. The almost apostolic fervour with which my revered nursing-mother, the late Sir Henry Jones, was wont to impart it to his charges, and, hardly less, his ill-concealed scorn for

---

10 By "idealist" here, Campbell means the view that reality is, in some sense, fundamentally mental or spiritual in nature. He is thinking mainly of Immanuel Kant's "transcendental idealism."

11 [Author's note] *Kantian Ethics.*

ignoble natures (like my own) which still hankered after a free will in the old 'vulgar' sense, are vividly recalled for me in Professor Teale's stirring pages.

The true interpretation of free will, according to Professor Teale, the interpretation to which Kant, despite occasional back-slidings, adhered in his better moments, is that 'the will is free in the degree that it is informed and disciplined by the moral principle.'[12]

Now this is a perfectly intelligible sense of the word 'free'—or at any rate it can be made so with a little explanatory comment which Professor Teale well supplies but for which there is here no space. But clearly it is a very different sort of freedom from that which is at issue in the traditional problem of free will. This idealist 'freedom' sponsored by Teale belongs, on his own showing, only to the self in respect of its *good* willing. The freedom with which the traditional problem is concerned, inasmuch as it is the freedom presupposed by moral responsibility, must belong to the self in respect of its *bad*, no less than its *good*, willing. It is, in fact, the freedom to decide between genuinely open alternatives of good and bad willing.

Professor Teale, of course, is not unaware that the freedom he favours differs from freedom as traditionally understood. He recognises the traditional concept under its Kantian title of 'elective' freedom. But he leaves the reader in no kind of doubt about his disbelief in both the reality and the value of this elective freedom to do, or forbear from doing, one's duty.

The question of the reality of elective freedom I shall be dealing with shortly; and it will occupy us to the end of the lecture. At the moment I am concerned only with its value, and with the rival view that all that matters for the moral life is the 'rational' freedom which a man has in the degree that his will is 'informed and disciplined by the moral principle.' I confess that to myself the verdict on the rival view seems plain and inescapable. No amount of verbal ingenuity or argumentative convolutions can obscure the fact that it is in flat contradiction to the implications of moral responsibility. The point at issue is really perfectly straightforward. If, as this idealist theory maintains, my acting in defiance of what I deem to be my duty is not a 'free' act in *any* sense, let alone in

the sense that 'I could have acted otherwise,' then I cannot be morally blameworthy, and that is all there is to it. Nor, for that matter, is the idealist entitled to say that I am morally praiseworthy if I act dutifully; for although that act is a 'free' act in the idealist sense, it is on his own avowal not free in the sense that 'I could have acted otherwise.'

It seems to me idle, therefore, to pretend that if one has to give up freedom in the traditional elective sense one is not giving up anything important. What we are giving up is, quite simply, the reality of the moral life. I recognise that to a certain type of religious nature (as well as, by an odd meeting of extremes, to a certain type of secular nature) that does not appear to matter so very much; but, for myself, I still think it sufficiently important to make it well worthwhile enquiring seriously into the possibility that the elective freedom upon which it rests may be real after all.

5.

That brings me to the second, and more constructive, part of this lecture. From now on I shall be considering whether it is reasonable to believe that man does in fact possess a free will of the kind specified in the first part of the lecture. If so, just how and where within the complex fabric of the volitional[13] life are we to locate it?—for although free will must presumably belong (if anywhere) to the volitional side of human experience, it is pretty clear from the way in which we have been forced to define it that it does not pertain simply to volition as such; not even to all volitions that are commonly dignified with the name of 'choices.' It has been, I think, one of the more serious impediments to profitable discussion of the Free Will problem that Libertarians and Determinists alike have so often failed to appreciate the comparatively narrow area within which the free will that is necessary to 'save' morality is required to operate. It goes without saying that this failure has been gravely prejudicial to the case for Libertarianism. I attach a good deal of importance, therefore, to the problem of locating free will correctly within the volitional orbit.

---

12   [Author's note] *Op. cit.*, p. 261.

13   "Volitional" means concerned with volitions, which are exercises of the will; consciously doing one thing rather than another.

Its solution forestalls and annuls, I believe, some of the more tiresome clichés of Determinist criticism.

We saw earlier that Common Sense's practice of 'making allowances' in its moral judgments for the influence of heredity and environment indicates Common Sense's conviction, both that a just moral judgment must discount determinants of choice over which the agent has no control, and also (since it still accepts moral judgments as legitimate) that *something* of moral relevance survives which can be regarded as genuinely self-originated. We are now to try to discover what this 'something' is. And I think we may still usefully take Common Sense as our guide. Suppose one asks the ordinary intelligent citizen *why* he deems it proper to make allowances for X, whose heredity and/or environment are unfortunate. He will tend to reply, I think, in some such terms as these: that X has more and stronger temptations to deviate from what is right than Y or Z, who are normally circumstanced, so that he must put forth a *stronger moral effort* if he is to achieve the same level of external conduct. The intended implication seems to be that X is just as morally praiseworthy as Y or Z *if* he exerts an equivalent moral effort, even though he may not thereby achieve an equal success in conforming his will to the 'concrete' demands of duty. And this implies, again, Common Sense's belief that *in moral effort* we have something for which a man is responsible *without qualification*, something that is not affected by heredity and environment but depends *solely* upon the self itself.

Now in my opinion Common Sense has here, in principle, hit upon the one and only defensible answer. Here, and here alone, so far as I can see, in the act of deciding whether to put forth or withhold the moral effort required to resist temptation and rise to duty, is to be found an act which is free in the sense required for moral responsibility; an act of which the self is sole author, and of which it is true to say that 'it could be' (or, after the event, 'could have been') 'otherwise.' Such is the thesis which we shall now try to establish.

6.

The species of argument appropriate to the establishment of a thesis of this sort should fall, I think, into two phases. First, there should be a consideration of the evidence of the moral agent's own inner experience. What *is* the act of moral decision, and what does it imply, from the standpoint of the actual participant? Since there is no way of knowing the act of moral decision—or for that matter any other form of activity—except by actual participation in it, the evidence of the subject, or agent, is on an issue of this kind of palmary[14] importance. It can hardly, however, be taken as in itself conclusive. For even if that evidence should be overwhelmingly to the effect that moral decision does have the characteristics required by moral freedom, the question is bound to be raised—and in view of considerations from other quarters pointing in a contrary direction is *rightly* raised—Can we *trust* the evidence of inner experience? That brings us to what will be the second phase of the argument. We shall have to go on to show, if we are to make good our case, that the extraneous[15] considerations so often supposed to be fatal to the belief in moral freedom are in fact innocuous to it.

In the light of what was said in the last lecture[16] about the self's experience of moral decision as a *creative* activity, we may perhaps be absolved from developing the first phase of the argument at any great length. The appeal is throughout to one's own experience in the actual taking of the moral decision in the situation of moral temptation. 'Is it possible,' we must ask, 'for anyone so circumstanced to *dis*believe that he could be deciding otherwise?' The answer is surely not in doubt. When we decide to exert moral effort to resist a temptation, we feel quite certain that we *could* withhold the effort; just as, if we decide to withhold the effort and yield to our desires, we feel quite certain that we *could* exert it—otherwise we should not blame ourselves afterwards for having succumbed. It may be, indeed, that this conviction is mere self-delusion. But that is not at the moment our concern. It is enough at present to establish that the act of deciding to exert or to withhold moral effort, as we know it from the inside in actual moral living, belongs to the category of acts which 'could have been otherwise.'

---

14 Great, outstanding.

15 External, coming from outside.

16 "Self-Activity and Its Modes."

Mutatis mutandis,[17] the same reply is forthcoming if we ask, 'Is it possible for the moral agent in the taking of his decision to *dis*believe that he is the *sole* author of that decision?' Clearly he cannot disbelieve that it is *he* who takes the decision. That, however, is not in itself sufficient to enable him, on reflection, to regard himself as *solely* responsible for the act. For his 'character' as so far formed might conceivably be a factor in determining it, and no one can suppose that the constitution of his 'character' is uninfluenced by circumstances of heredity and environment with which *he* has nothing to do. But as we pointed out in the last lecture, the very essence of the moral decision as it is experienced is that it is a decision whether or not to *combat* our strongest desire, and our strongest desire *is* the expression in the situation of our character as so far formed. Now clearly our character cannot be a factor in determining the decision whether or not to *oppose* our character. I think we are entitled to say, therefore, that the act of moral decision is one in which the self is for itself not merely 'author' but 'sole author.'

7.

We may pass on, then, to the second phase of our constructive argument; and this will demand more elaborate treatment. Even if a moral agent *qua* making a moral decision in the situation of 'temptation' cannot help believing that he has free will in the sense at issue—a moral freedom between real alternatives, between genuinely open possibilities—are there, nevertheless, objections to a freedom of this kind so cogent that we are bound to distrust the evidence of 'inner experience'?

I begin by drawing attention to a simple point whose significance tends, I think, to be underestimated. If the phenomenological analysis we have offered is substantially correct, no one while functioning as a moral agent can help believing that he enjoys free will. Theoretically he may be completely convinced by Determinist arguments, but when actually confronted with a personal situation of conflict between duty and desire he is quite certain that it lies with him

here and now whether or not he will rise to duty. It follows that if Determinists could produce convincing theoretical arguments against a free will of this kind, the awkward predicament would ensue that man has to deny as a theoretical being what he has to assert as a practical being. Now I think the Determinist ought to be a good deal more worried about this than he usually is. He seems to imagine that a strong case on general theoretical grounds is enough to prove that the 'practical' belief in free will, even if inescapable for us as practical beings, is mere illusion. But in fact it proves nothing of the sort. There is no reason whatever why a belief that we find ourselves obliged to hold *qua* practical beings should be required to give way before a belief which we find ourselves obliged to hold *qua* theoretical beings; or, for that matter, *vice versa*. All that the theoretical arguments of Determinism can prove, unless they are reinforced by a refutation of the phenomenological analysis that supports Libertarianism, is that there is a radical conflict between the theoretical and the practical sides of man's nature, an antinomy[18] at the very heart of the self. And this is a state of affairs with which no one can easily rest satisfied. I think therefore that the Determinist ought to concern himself a great deal more than he does with phenomenological analysis, in order to show, if he can, that the assurance of free will is not really an inexpugnable[19] element in man's practical consciousness. There is just as much obligation upon him, convinced though he may be of the soundness of his theoretical arguments, to expose the errors of the Libertarian's phenomenological analysis, as there is upon us, convinced though we may be of the soundness of the Libertarian's phenomenological analysis, to expose the errors of the Determinist's theoretical arguments.

8.

However, we must at once begin the discharge of our own obligation. The rest of this lecture will be devoted to trying to show that the arguments which seem to carry the most weight with Determinists are, to say the least of it, very far from compulsive.

---

17   With appropriate alterations. The Latin means "things having been changed that need to be changed."

18   Contradiction, paradox.

19   Impossible to put aside or overcome.

Fortunately, a good many of the arguments which at an earlier time in the history of philosophy would have been strongly urged against us make almost no appeal to the bulk of philosophers today, and we may here pass them by. That applies to any criticism of 'open possibilities' based on a metaphysical theory about the nature of the universe as a whole. Nobody today *has* a metaphysical theory about the nature of the universe as a whole! It applies also, with almost equal force, to criticisms based upon the universality of causal law as a supposed postulate of science. There have always been, in my opinion, sound philosophic reasons for doubting the validity, as distinct from the convenience, of the causal postulate in its universal form, but at the present time, when scientists themselves are deeply divided about the need for postulating causality even within their own special field, we shall do better to concentrate our attention upon criticisms which are more confidently advanced. I propose to ignore also, on different grounds, the type of criticism of free will that is sometimes advanced from the side of religion, based upon religious postulates of Divine Omnipotence and Omniscience.[20] So far as I can see, a postulate of human freedom is every bit as necessary to meet certain religious demands (e.g., to make sense of the 'conviction of sin'), as postulates of Divine Omniscience and Omnipotence are to meet certain other religious demands. If so, then it can hardly be argued that religious experience as such tells more strongly against than for the position we are defending; and we may be satisfied, in the present context, to leave the matter there. It will be more profitable to discuss certain arguments which contemporary philosophers do think important, and which recur with a somewhat monotonous regularity in the literature of anti-Libertarianism.

These arguments can, I think, be reduced in principle to no more than two: first, the argument from 'predictability'; second, the argument from the alleged meaninglessness of an act supposed to be the self's act and yet not an expression of the self's character. Contemporary criticism of free will seems to me to consist almost exclusively of variations on these two themes. I shall deal with each in turn.

9.

On the first we touched in passing at an earlier stage. Surely it is beyond question (the critic urges) that when we know a person intimately we can foretell with a high degree of accuracy how he will respond to at least a large number of practical situations. One feels safe in predicting that one's dog-loving friend will not use his boot to repel the little mongrel that comes yapping at his heels; or again that one's wife will not pass with incurious eyes (or indeed pass at all) the new hat shop in the city. So to behave would not be (as we say) 'in character.' But, so the criticism runs, you with your doctrine of 'genuinely open possibilities,' of a free will by which the self can diverge from its own character, remove all rational basis from such prediction. You require us to make the absurd supposition that the success of countless predictions of the sort in the past has been mere matter of chance. If you *really* believed in your theory, you would not be surprised if tomorrow your friend with the notorious horror of strong drink should suddenly exhibit a passion for whisky and soda, or if your friend whose taste for reading has hitherto been satisfied with the sporting columns of the newspapers should be discovered on a fine Saturday afternoon poring over the works of Hegel. But of course you *would* be surprised. Social life would be sheer chaos if there were not well-grounded social expectations; and social life is not sheer chaos. Your theory is hopelessly wrecked upon obvious facts.

Now whether or not this criticism holds good against some versions of Libertarian theory I need not here discuss. It is sufficient if I can make it clear that against the version advanced in this lecture, according to which free will is localised in a relatively narrow field of operation, the criticism has no relevance whatsoever.

Let us remind ourselves briefly of the setting within which, on our view, free will functions. There is X, the course which we believe we ought to follow, and Y, the course towards which we feel our desire is strongest. The freedom which we ascribe to the agent is the freedom to put forth or refrain from putting forth the

---

20   Roughly, that God can do anything (omnipotence) and knows everything (omniscience).

moral effort required to resist the pressure of desire and do what he thinks he ought to do.

But then there is surely an immense range of practical situations—covering by far the greater part of life—in which there is no question of a conflict within the self between what he most desires to do and what he thinks he ought to do? Indeed such conflict is a comparatively rare phenomenon for the majority of men. Yet over that whole vast range there is nothing whatever in our version of Libertarianism to prevent our agreeing that character determines conduct. In the absence, real or supposed, of any 'moral' issue, what a man chooses will be simply that course which, after such reflection as seems called for, he deems most likely to bring him what he most strongly desires; and that is the same as to say the course to which his present character inclines him.

Over by far the greater area of human choices, then, our theory offers no more barrier to successful prediction on the basis of character than any other theory. For where there is no clash of strongest desire with duty, the free will we are defending has no business. There is just nothing for it to do.

But what about the situations—rare enough though they may be—in which there is this clash and in which free will does therefore operate? Does our theory entail that there, at any rate, as the critic seems to suppose, 'anything may happen'?

Not by any manner of means. In the first place, and by the very nature of the case, the range of the agent's possible choices is bounded by what he thinks he ought to do on the one hand, and what he most strongly desires on the other. The freedom claimed for him is a freedom of decision to make or withhold the effort required to do what he thinks he ought to do. There is no question of a freedom to act in some 'wild' fashion, out of all relation to his characteristic beliefs and desires. This so-called 'freedom of caprice,' so often charged against the Libertarian, is, to put it bluntly, a sheer figment of the critic's imagination, with no *habitat*[21] in serious Libertarian theory. Even in situations where free will does come into play it is perfectly possible, on a view like ours, given the ap-

propriate knowledge of a man's character, to predict within certain limits how he will respond.

But 'probable' prediction in such situations can, I think, go further than this. It is obvious that where desire and duty are at odds, the felt 'gap' (as it were) between the two may vary enormously in breadth in different cases. The moderate drinker and the chronic tippler may each want another glass, and each deem it his duty to abstain, but the felt gap between desire and duty in the case of the former is trivial beside the great gulf which is felt to separate them in the case of the latter. Hence it will take a far harder moral effort for the tippler than for the moderate drinker to achieve the same external result of abstention. So much is matter of common agreement. And we are entitled, I think, to take it into account in prediction, on the simple principle that the harder the moral effort required to resist desire the less likely it is to occur. Thus in the example taken, most people would predict that the tippler will very probably succumb to his desires, whereas there is a reasonable likelihood that the moderate drinker will make the comparatively slight effort needed to resist them. So long as the prediction does not pretend to more than a measure of probability, there is nothing in our theory which would disallow it.

I claim, therefore, that the view of free will I have been putting forward is consistent with predictability of conduct on the basis of character over a very wide field indeed. And I make the further claim that that field will cover all the situations in life concerning which there is any empirical evidence that successful prediction is possible.

10.

Let us pass on to consider the second main line of criticism. This is, I think, much the more illuminating of the two, if only because it compels the Libertarian to make explicit certain concepts which are indispensable to him, but which, being desperately hard to state clearly, are apt not to be stated at all. The critic's fundamental point might be stated somewhat as follows:

'Free will as you describe it is completely unintelligible. On your own showing no *reason* can be given, because there just *is* no reason, why a man decides to exert rather than to withhold moral effort, or *vice*

---

21   Dwelling place.

versa. But such an act—or more properly, such an 'occurrence'—it is nonsense to speak of as an act of a *self*. If there is nothing in the self's character to which it is, even in principle, in any way traceable, the self has nothing to do with it. Your so-called 'freedom,' therefore, so far from supporting the self's moral responsibility, destroys it as surely as the crudest Determinism could do.'

If we are to discuss this criticism usefully, it is important, I think, to begin by getting clear about two different senses of the word 'intelligible.'

If, in the first place, we mean by an 'intelligible' act one whose occurrence is in principle capable of being inferred, since it follows necessarily from something (though we may not know in fact from what), then it is certainly true that the Libertarian's free will is unintelligible. But that is only saying, is it not, that the Libertarian's 'free' act is not an act which follows necessarily from something! This can hardly rank as a *criticism* of Libertarianism. It is just a description of it. That there can be nothing unintelligible in *this* sense is precisely what the Determinist has got to *prove*.

Yet it is surprising how often the critic of Libertarianism involves himself in this circular mode of argument. Repeatedly it is urged against the Libertarian, with a great air of triumph, that on his view he can't say *why* I now decide to rise to duty, or now decide to follow my strongest desire in defiance of duty. Of course he can't. If he could he wouldn't *be* a Libertarian. To 'account for' a 'free' act is a contradiction in terms. A free will is *ex hypothesi*[22] the sort of thing of which the request for an *explanation* is absurd. The assumption that an explanation must be in principle possible for the act of moral decision deserves to rank as a classic example of the ancient fallacy of 'begging the question.'[23]

But the critic usually has in mind another sense of the word 'unintelligible.' He is apt to take it for granted that an act which is unintelligible in the *above* sense (as the morally free act of the Libertarian undoubtedly is) is unintelligible in the *further* sense that we can attach no meaning to it. And this is an altogether more serious matter. If it could really be shown that the Libertarian's 'free will' were unintelligible in this sense of being meaningless, that, for myself at any rate, would be the end of the affair. Libertarianism would have been conclusively refuted.

But it seems to me manifest that this can *not* be shown. The critic has allowed himself, I submit, to become the victim of a widely accepted but fundamentally vicious[24] assumption. He has assumed that whatever is meaningful must exhibit its meaningfulness to those who view it from the standpoint of external observation. Now if one chooses thus to limit one's self to the rôle of external observer, it is, I think, perfectly true that one can attach no meaning to an act which is the act of something we call a 'self' and yet follows from nothing in that self's character. But then *why should we* so limit ourselves, when what is under consideration is a subjective activity? For the apprehension of subjective acts there is *another* standpoint available, that of *inner experience*, of the practical consciousness in its actual functioning. If our free will should turn out to be something to which we can attach a meaning from *this* standpoint, no more is required. And no more ought to be expected. For I must repeat that only from the inner standpoint of living experience *could* anything of the nature of 'activity' be directly grasped. Observation from without is in the nature of the case impotent to apprehend the active *qua* active. We can from without observe sequences of states. If into these we read activity (as we sometimes do), this can only be on the basis of what we discern in ourselves from the inner standpoint. It follows that if anyone insists upon taking his criterion of the meaningful simply from the standpoint of external observation, he is really deciding in advance of the evidence that the notion of activity, and *a fortiori*[25] the notion of a free will, is 'meaningless.' He looks for the free act through a medium which is in the nature of the case incapable of revealing it, and then, because inevitably he doesn't find it, he declares that it doesn't exist!

But if, as we surely ought in this context, we adopt the inner standpoint, then (I am suggesting) things appear in a totally different light. From the inner

---

22   On this (libertarian) hypothesis, given this assumption.

23   Assuming as true that which needs to be proved.

24   Faulty, defective.

25   Even more so.

standpoint, it seems to me plain, there is no difficulty whatever in attaching meaning to an act which is the self's act and which nevertheless does not follow from the self's character. So much I claim has been established by the phenomenological analysis, in this and the previous lecture, of the act of moral decision in face of moral temptation. It is thrown into particularly clear relief where the moral decision is to make the moral effort required to rise to duty. For the very function of moral effort, as it appears to the agent engaged in the act, is to enable the self to act against the line of least resistance, against the line to which his character as so far formed most strongly inclines him. But if the self is thus conscious here of *combating* his formed character, he surely cannot possibly suppose that the act, although his own act, *issues from* his formed character? I submit, therefore, that the self knows very well indeed—from the inner standpoint—what is meant by an act which is the *self*'s act and which nevertheless does not follow from the self's *character*.

What this implies—and it seems to me to be an implication of cardinal importance for any theory of the self that aims at being more than superficial—is that the nature of the self is for itself something more than just its character as so far formed. The 'nature' of the self and what we commonly call the 'character' of the self are by no means the same thing, and it is utterly vital that they should not be confused. The 'nature' of the self comprehends, but is not without remainder reducible to, its 'character'; it must, if we are to be true to the testimony of our experience of it, be taken as including *also* the authentic creative power of fashioning and refashioning 'character.'

The misguided, and as a rule quite uncritical, belittlement, of the evidence offered by inner experience has, I am convinced, been responsible for more bad argument by the opponents of Free Will than has any other single factor. How often, for example, do we find the Determinist critic saying, in effect, '*Either* the act follows necessarily upon precedent states, *or* it is a mere matter of chance and accordingly of no moral significance.' The disjunction is invalid for it does not exhaust the possible alternatives. It seems to the critic to do so only because he *will* limit himself to the standpoint which is proper, and indeed alone possible, in dealing with the physical world, the standpoint of the external observer. If only he would allow himself to assume the standpoint which is not merely proper for, but necessary to, the apprehension of subjective activity, the inner standpoint of the practical consciousness in its actual functioning, he would find himself obliged to recognise the falsity of his disjunction. Reflection upon the act of moral decision as apprehended from the inner standpoint would force him to recognise a *third* possibility, as remote from chance as from necessity, that, namely, of *creative activity*, in which (as I have ventured to express it) nothing determines the act save the agent's doing of it.

11.

There we must leave the matter. But as this lecture has been, I know, somewhat densely packed, it may be helpful if I conclude by reminding you, in bald summary, of the main things I have been trying to say. Let me set them out in so many successive theses.

1. The freedom which is at issue in the traditional Free Will problem is the freedom which is presupposed in moral responsibility.

2. Critical reflection upon carefully considered attributions of moral responsibility reveals that the only freedom that will do is a freedom which pertains to inner acts of choice, and that these acts must be acts (*a*) of which the self is *sole* author, and (*b*) which the self could have performed otherwise.

3. From phenomenological analysis of the situation of moral temptation we find that the self as engaged in this situation is inescapably convinced that it possesses a freedom of precisely the specified kind, located in the decision to exert or withhold the moral effort needed to rise to duty where the pressure of its desiring nature is felt to urge it in a contrary direction.

Passing to the question of the *reality* of this moral freedom which the moral agent believes himself to possess, we argued:

4. Of the two types of Determinist criticism which seem to have most influence today, that based on the predictability of much human behaviour fails to touch a Libertarianism which confines the area of free will as above indicated. Libertarianism so understood is compatible with all the predictability that the empirical facts warrant. And:

5. The second main type of criticism, which alleges the 'meaninglessness' of an act which is the self's act and which is yet not determined by the self's character, is based on a failure to appreciate that the standpoint of inner experience is not only legitimate but indispensable where what is at issue is the reality and nature of a subjective activity. The creative act of moral decision is inevitably meaningless to the mere external observer; but from the inner standpoint it is as real, and as significant, as anything in human experience.[26]

---

26   [Author's note] An earlier, but not in substance dissimilar, version of my views on the Free Will problem has been criticised at length in Mr. Nowell-Smith's *Ethics*. A detailed reply to these criticisms will be found in Appendix B [of Part One of *On Selfhood and Godhood*].

A.J. AYER

"Freedom and Necessity"

Who was A.J. Ayer?

Sir Alfred Jules Ayer (1910–1989), known to all his friends as Freddie, was born into a wealthy European-origin family in London. He attended the pre-eminent English private school Eton, then went on scholarship to Oxford. He served as an officer in a British espionage and sabotage unit during World War II, then taught at University College London and at Oxford.

When only 24, Ayer wrote *Language, Truth, and Logic,* the book that made his name. In it, he briefly, simply, and persuasively to many, argued for logical positivism, a form of radical empiricism that had been developed largely by the group of philosophers called the Vienna Circle, whose ideas Ayer had picked up while studying with them in Austria. Logical positivism dominated Anglophone philosophy for decades; while objections (especially to Ayer's rather simplified version) came thick and fast, everyone was at least aware of it as a philosophical force to be reckoned with.

While *Language, Truth, and Logic* was by far his best-seller, Ayer wrote a good deal of other important work, especially in epistemology. While his work is not now generally included in lists of all-time philosophical landmarks, he was considered, in terms of influence if not of originality, second only to Bertrand Russell among the English philosophers of his day.

Ayer was extraordinarily well-known by the British public. He wrote and spoke on all sorts of popular issues, all over the media. In those days, TV networks programed witty intellectual chatter, and Ayer was a master at this. He loved his celebrity, and hobnobbed with the famous and influential.

What Is the Structure of This Reading?

The problem Ayer will talk about, clearly set out in the first few paragraphs of his article, is how free action—action for which one is morally responsible—is possible, given the assumption that all human action, like everything else in the world, is determined by causes, and, given the causes, could not have been otherwise.

Ayer points out that the alternative to an action's being determined by causes appears to be that it is totally random; and that would certainly not be the sort of action for which we could count someone as morally responsible. He admits that libertarians often deny that total randomness is the non-determination they argue is a pre-requisite for freedom and responsibility; but he asks, then, what do they argue for? If what they're thinking of as what one is responsible for is action in accord with one's character, then that seems to be wholly compatible with universal causality: one's character itself may well be entirely determined by antecedent causes.

He then reveals his main positive argument: that freedom (thus responsibility) is incompatible with *constraint*, not with causal determination. One is constrained when one's choice over actions is not operative: for example, if one were hypnotized, or if someone held a gun at one's head, or if one had a compelling psychological influence over what one did.

He concludes by attempting to explain and defuse the tendency many philosophers have of counting causal determination as constraining. A constrained action, he argues, is one that you'll do whatever you decide, if anything. But free actions, on his understanding, are those in which your decision is operative: they would not have occurred had you not decided to do them. Your decision, for a determinist, is itself causally determined; but that's not relevant. The fact that the causal chain behind the action includes your decision is what makes it a "free" action, an action for which you're responsible.

Suggestions for Critical Reflection

1. Consider the following case. An ingenious physiologist has hooked up wires to your brain; by pushing buttons, he can cause you to have a variety of "volitions"; these are what Ayer would presumably count as decisions to act, so he would count your resulting actions as free. But it is plausible to claim that in this case you would be entirely unfree—merely the physiologist's puppet. Which position is right? Where does the other position go wrong?

2. You've been called to act as a witness for the prosecution in a criminal trial, and friends of the accused tell you that all of your family will be in great danger if you testify honestly. You decide that all you can do is to lie to the court, and say you can't remember anything. This is ordinarily an immoral act, but is it under the circumstances? Are you constrained to act as you did? (Compare Ayer's example of someone's holding a gun to your head.) If this is genuine constraint, then does that mean you're not morally responsible for lying?

3. Fatalism is the position that something will happen in the future *no matter what*. In the last few paragraphs, Ayer attempts to distinguish determinism from fatalism, and to argue that it is the second, not the first, that is incompatible with responsibility and freedom. Try to explain his argument, in your own terms. Some philosophers think that determinism and fatalism are the same thing. Why do you think they would say this? Who is right?

Suggestions for Further Reading

There are really two independent positions here: *determinism* (the thesis that all events, including human actions and decisions, are determined by antecedent causes) and *compatibilism* (the thesis that freedom and responsibility are compatible with determinism). A classic essay on both, and their connection, is "Of Liberty and Necessity" by David Hume; this is a section of Hume's great work, *An Enquiry Concerning Human Understanding*, available online and in many anthologies and editions. Hume's influence is certainly apparent in Ayer. An excellent and very thorough survey of compatibilist positions and arguments, with a thorough bibliography, is online: McKenna, Michael, "Compatibilism", *The Stanford Encyclopedia of Philosophy (Winter*

2009 Edition), Edward N. Zalta (ed.), <http://plato.stanford.edu/archives/win2009/entries/compatibilism/>. *The Stanford Encyclopedia* does a similarly good job on determinism: Hoefer, Carl, "Causal Determinism", *The Stanford Encyclopedia of Philosophy (Spring 2010 Edition)*, Edward N. Zalta (ed.), <http://plato.stanford.edu/archives/spr2010/entries/determinism-causal/>. A very interesting and accessible work on freedom, modifying the compatibilist view considerably, is Harry Frankfurt's article "Freedom of the Will and the Concept of the Person." This was originally published in *Journal of Philosophy*, LXVII, No. 1 (Jan. 1971), but it's also widely anthologized. Another one is Daniel Dennet's book *Elbow Room: The Varieties of Free Will Worth Wanting* (Bradford, 1984).

"Freedom and Necessity"[1]

When I am said to have done something of my own free will it is implied that I could have acted otherwise; and it is only when it is believed that I could have acted otherwise that I am held to be morally responsible for what I have done. For a man is not thought to be morally responsible for an action that it was not in his power to avoid. But if human behaviour is entirely governed by causal laws, it is not clear how any action that is done could ever have been avoided. It may be said of the agent that he would have acted otherwise if the causes of his action had been different, but they being what they were, it seems to follow that he was bound to act as he did. Now it is commonly assumed both that men are capable of acting freely, in the sense that is required to make them morally responsible, and that human behaviour is entirely governed by causal laws: and it is the apparent conflict between these two assumptions that gives rise to the philosophical problem of the freedom of the will.

Confronted with this problem, many people will be inclined to agree with Dr. Johnson: 'Sir, we *know*

our will is free, and *there's* an end on't.'[2] But, while this does very well for those who accept Dr. Johnson's premiss, it would hardly convince anyone who denied the freedom of the will. Certainly, if we do know that our wills are free, it follows that they are so. But the logical reply to this might be that since our wills are not free, it follows that no one can know that they are: so that if anyone claims, like Dr. Johnson, to know that they are, he must be mistaken. What is evident, indeed, is that people often believe themselves to be acting freely; and it is to this 'feeling' of freedom that some philosophers appeal when they wish, in the supposed interests of morality, to prove that not all human action is causally determined. But if these philosophers are right in their assumption that a man cannot be acting freely if his action is causally determined, then the fact that someone feels free to do, or not to do, a certain action does not prove that he really is so. It may prove that the agent does not himself know what it is that makes him act in one way rather than another: but from the fact that a man is unaware of the causes of his action, it does not follow that no such causes exist.

So much may be allowed to the determinist; but his belief that all human actions are subservient to causal laws still remains to be justified. If, indeed, it is necessary that every event should have a cause, then the rule must apply to human behaviour as much as to anything else. But why should it be supposed that every event must have a cause? The contrary is not unthinkable. Nor is the law of universal causation a necessary presupposition of scientific thought. The scientist may try to discover causal laws, and in many cases he succeeds; but sometimes he has to be content with statistical laws, and sometimes he comes upon events which, in the present state of his knowledge, he is not able to subsume under any law at all. In the case of these events he assumes that if he knew more he would be able to discover some law, whether causal or statistical, which would enable him to account for them. And this assumption cannot be disproved. For

---

1   This paper first appeared in *Polemic* No. 5 in 1946; it is reprinted from Ayer's *Philosophical Essays*, published in New York by St. Martin's Press, 1969. Reproduced with permission of Palgrave Macmillan.

2   Samuel Johnson (1709–84) was a prominent English essayist and the compiler of the first great *Dictionary of the English Language*; he is quoted in James Boswell's *Life of Johnson* (1769: AETAT, 60).

however far he may have carried his investigation, it is always open to him to carry it further; and it is always conceivable that if he carried it further he would discover the connection which had hitherto escaped him. Nevertheless, it is also conceivable that the events with which he is concerned are not systematically connected with any others: so that the reason why he does not discover the sort of laws that he requires is simply that they do not obtain.

Now in the case of human conduct the search for explanations has not in fact been altogether fruitless. Certain scientific laws have been established; and with the help of these laws we do make a number of successful predictions about the ways in which different people will behave. But these predictions do not always cover every detail. We may be able to predict that in certain circumstances a particular man will be angry, without being able to prescribe the precise form that the expression of his anger will take. We may be reasonably sure that he will shout, but not sure how loud his shout will be, or exactly what words he will use. And it is only a small proportion of human actions that we are able to forecast even so precisely as this. But that, it may be said, is because we have not carried our investigations very far. The science of psychology is still in its infancy and, as it is developed, not only will more human actions be explained, but the explanations will go into greater detail. The ideal of complete explanation may never in fact be attained: but it is theoretically attainable. Well, this may be so: and certainly it is impossible to show *a priori* that it is not so: but equally it cannot be shown that it is. This will not, however, discourage the scientist who, in the field of human behaviour, as elsewhere, will continue to formulate theories and test them by the facts. And in this he is justified. For since he has no reason *a priori* to admit that there is a limit to what he can discover, the fact that he also cannot be sure that there is no limit does not make it unreasonable for him to devise theories, nor, having devised them, to try constantly to improve them.

But now suppose it to be claimed that, so far as men's actions are concerned, there is a limit: and that this limit is set by the fact of human freedom. An obvious objection is that in many cases in which a person feels himself to be free to do, or not to do, a certain action, we are even now able to explain, in causal terms, why it is that he acts as he does. But it might be argued that even if men are sometimes mistaken in believing that they act freely, it does not follow that they are always so mistaken. For it is not always the case that when a man believes that he has acted freely we are in fact able to account for his action in causal terms. A determinist would say that we should be able to account for it if we had more knowledge of the circumstances, and had been able to discover the appropriate natural laws. But until those discoveries have been made, this remains only a pious hope. And may it not be true that, in some cases at least, the reason why we can give no causal explanation is that no causal explanation is available; and that this is because the agent's choice was literally free, as he himself felt it to be?

The answer is that this may indeed be true, inasmuch as it is open to anyone to hold that no explanation is possible until some explanation is actually found. But even so it does not give the moralist what he wants. For he is anxious to show that men are capable of acting freely in order to infer that they can be morally responsible for what they do. But if it is a matter of pure chance that a man should act in one way rather than another, he may be free but he can hardly be responsible. And indeed when a man's actions seem to us quite unpredictable, when, as we say, there is no knowing what he will do, we do not look upon him as a moral agent. We look upon him rather as a lunatic.

To this it may be objected that we are not dealing fairly with the moralist. For when he makes it a condition of my being morally responsible that I should act freely, he does not wish to imply that it is purely a matter of chance that I act as I do. What he wishes to imply is that my actions are the result of my own free choice: and it is because they are the result of my own free choice that I am held to be morally responsible for them.

But now we must ask how it is that I come to make my choice. Either it is an accident that I choose to act as I do or it is not. If it is an accident, then it is merely a matter of chance that I did not choose otherwise; and if it is merely a matter of chance that I did not choose otherwise, it is surely irrational to hold me morally responsible for choosing as I did. But if it is not an accident that I choose to do one thing rather than another, then presumably there is some causal explanation of my choice: and in that case we are led back to determinism.

Again, the objection may be raised that we are not doing justice to the moralist's case. His view is not that it is a matter of chance that I choose to act as I do, but rather that my choice depends upon my character. Nevertheless he holds that I can still be free in the sense that he requires; for it is I who am responsible for my character. But in what way am I responsible for my character? Only, surely, in the sense that there is a causal connection between what I do now and what I have done in the past. It is only this that justifies the statement that I have made myself what I am: and even so this is an over-simplification, since it takes no account of the external influences to which I have been subjected. But, ignoring the external influences, let us assume that it is in fact the case that I have made myself what I am. Then it is still legitimate to ask how it is that I have come to make myself one sort of person rather than another. And if it be answered that it is a matter of my strength of will, we can put the same question in another form by asking how it is that my will has the strength that it has and not some other degree of strength. Once more, either it is an accident or it is not. If it is an accident, then by the same argument as before, I am not morally responsible, and if it is not an accident we are led back to determinism.

Furthermore, to say that my actions proceed from my character or, more colloquially, that I act in character, is to say that my behaviour is consistent and to that extent predictable: and since it is, above all, for the actions that I perform in character that I am held to be morally responsible, it looks as if the admission of moral responsibility, so far from being incompatible with determinism, tends rather to presuppose it. But how can this be so if it is a necessary condition of moral responsibility that the person who is held responsible should have acted freely? It seems that if we are to retain this idea of moral responsibility, we must either show that men can be held responsible for actions which they do not do freely, or else find some way of reconciling determinism with the freedom of the will.

It is no doubt with the object of effecting this reconciliation that some philosophers[3] have defined freedom as the consciousness of necessity. And by so doing they are able to say not only that a man can be acting freely when his action is causally determined, but even that his action must be causally determined for it to be possible for him to be acting freely. Nevertheless this definition has the serious disadvantage that it gives to the word 'freedom' a meaning quite different from any that it ordinarily bears. It is indeed obvious that if we are allowed to give the word 'freedom' any meaning that we please, we can find a meaning that will reconcile it with determinism: but this is no more a solution of our present problem than the fact that the word 'horse' could be arbitrarily used to mean what is ordinarily meant by 'sparrow' is a proof that horses have wings. For suppose that I am compelled by another person to do something 'against my will'. In that case, as the word 'freedom' is ordinarily used, I should not be said to be acting freely: and the fact that I am fully aware of the constraint to which I am subjected makes no difference to the matter. I do not become free by becoming conscious that I am not. It may, indeed, be possible to show that my being aware that my action is causally determined is not incompatible with my acting freely: but it by no means follows that it is in this that my freedom consists. Moreover, I suspect that one of the reasons why people are inclined to define freedom as the consciousness of necessity is that they think that if one is conscious of necessity one may somehow be able to master it. But this is a fallacy. It is like someone's saying that he wishes he could see into the future, because if he did he would know what calamities lay in wait for him and so would be able to avoid them. But if he avoids the calamities then they don't lie in the future and it is not true that he foresees them. And similarly if I am able to master necessity, in the sense of escaping the operation of a necessary law, then the law in question is not necessary. And if the law is not necessary, then

---

3   Karl Marx is a prominent example of a philosopher who makes this claim.

neither my freedom nor anything else can consist in my knowing that it is.

Let it be granted, then, that when we speak of reconciling freedom with determinism we are using the word 'freedom' in an ordinary sense. It still remains for us to make this usage clear: and perhaps the best way to make it clear is to show what it is that freedom, in this sense, is contrasted with. Now we began with the assumption that freedom is contrasted with causality: so that a man cannot be said to be acting freely if his action is causally determined. But this assumption has led us into difficulties and I now wish to suggest that it is mistaken. For it is not, I think, causality that freedom is to be contrasted with, but constraint. And while it is true that being constrained to do an action entails being caused to do it, I shall try to show that the converse does not hold. I shall try to show that from the fact that my action is causally determined it does not necessarily follow that I am constrained to do it: and this is equivalent to saying that it does not necessarily follow that I am not free.

If I am constrained, I do not act freely. But in what circumstances can I legitimately be said to be constrained? An obvious instance is the case in which I am compelled by another person to do what he wants. In a case of this sort the compulsion need not be such as to deprive one of the power of choice. It is not required that the other person should have hypnotized me, or that he should make it physically impossible for me to go against his will. It is enough that he should induce me to do what he wants by making it clear to me that, if I do not, he will bring about some situation that I regard as even more undesirable than the consequences of the action that he wishes me to do. Thus, if the man points a pistol at my head I may still choose to disobey him: but this does not prevent its being true that if I do fall in with his wishes he can legitimately be said to have compelled me. And if the circumstances are such that no reasonable person would be expected to choose the other alternative, then the action that I am made to do is not one for which I am held to be morally responsible.

A similar, but still somewhat different, case is that in which another person has obtained an habitual ascendancy over me. Where this is so, there may be no question of my being induced to act as the other person wishes by being confronted with a still more disagreeable alternative: for if I am sufficiently under his influence this special stimulus will not be necessary. Nevertheless I do not act freely, for the reason that I have been deprived of the power of choice. And this means that I have acquired so strong a habit of obedience that I no longer go through any process of deciding whether or not to do what the other person wants. About other matters I may still deliberate; but as regards the fulfilment of this other person's wishes, my own deliberations have ceased to be a causal factor in my behaviour. And it is in this sense that I may be said to be constrained. It is not, however, necessary that such constraint should take the form of subservience to another person. A kleptomaniac is not a free agent, in respect of his stealing, because he does not go through any process of deciding whether or not to steal. Or rather, if he does go through such a process, it is irrelevant to his behaviour. Whatever he resolved to do, he would steal all the same. And it is this that distinguishes him from the ordinary thief.

But now it may be asked whether there is any essential difference between these cases and those in which the agent is commonly thought to be free. No doubt the ordinary thief does go through a process of deciding whether or not to steal, and no doubt it does affect his behaviour. If he resolved to refrain from stealing, he could carry his resolution out. But if it be allowed that his making or not making this resolution is causally determined, then how can he be any more free than the kleptomaniac? It may be true that unlike the kleptomaniac he could refrain from stealing if he chose: but if there is a cause, or set of causes, which necessitate his choosing as he does, how can he be said to have the power of choice? Again, it may be true that no one now compels me to get up and walk across the room: but if my doing so can be causally explained in terms of my history or my environment, or whatever it may be, then how am I any more free than if some other person had compelled me? I do not have the feeling of constraint that I have when a pistol is manifestly pointed at my head; but the chains of causation by which I am bound are no less effective for being invisible.

The answer to this is that the cases I have mentioned as examples of constraint do differ from the others: and they differ just in the ways that I have tried to bring out. If I suffered from a compulsion neurosis, so that I got up and walked across the room, whether I wanted to or not, or if I did so because somebody else compelled me, then I should not be acting freely. But if I do it now, I shall be acting freely, just because these conditions do not obtain; and the fact that my action may nevertheless have a cause is, from this point of view, irrelevant. For it is not when my action has any cause at all, but only when it has a special sort of cause, that it is reckoned not to be free.

But here it may be objected that, even if this distinction corresponds to ordinary usage, it is still very irrational. For why should we distinguish, with regard to a person's freedom, between the operations of one sort of cause and those of another? Do not all causes equally necessitate? And is it not therefore arbitrary to say that a person is free when he is necessitated in one fashion but not when he is necessitated in another?

That all causes equally necessitate is indeed a tautology, if the word 'necessitate' is taken merely as equivalent to 'cause': but if, as the objection requires, it is taken as equivalent to 'constrain' or 'compel', then I do not think that this proposition is true. For all that is needed for one event to be the cause of another is that, in the given circumstances, the event which is said to be the effect would not have occurred if it had not been for the occurrence of the event which is said to be the cause, or *vice versa*, according as causes are interpreted as necessary, or sufficient, conditions: and this fact is usually deducible from some causal law which states that whenever an event of the one kind occurs then, given suitable conditions, an event of the other kind will occur in a certain temporal or spatio-temporal relationship to it. In short, there is an invariable concomitance[4] between the two classes of events; but there is no compulsion, in any but a metaphorical sense. Suppose, for example, that a psycho-analyst is able to account for some aspect of my behaviour by referring it to some lesion[5] that I suffered in my childhood. In that case, it may be said that my childhood experience, together with certain other events, necessitates my behaving as I do. But all that this involves is that it is found to be true in gen-

eral that when people have had certain experiences as children, they subsequently behave in certain specifiable ways; and my case is just another instance of this general law. It is in this way indeed that my behaviour is explained. But from the fact that my behaviour is capable of being explained, in the sense that it can be subsumed under some natural law, it does not follow that I am acting under constraint.

If this is correct, to say that I could have acted otherwise is to say, first, that I should have acted otherwise if I had so chosen; secondly, that my action was voluntary in the sense in which the actions, say, of the kleptomaniac are not; and thirdly, that nobody compelled me to choose as I did: and these three conditions may very well be fulfilled. When they are fulfilled, I may be said to have acted freely. But this is not to say that it was a matter of chance that I acted as I did, or, in other words, that my action could not be explained. And that my actions should be capable of being explained is all that is required by the postulate of determinism.

If more than this seems to be required it is, I think, because the use of the very word 'determinism' is in some degree misleading. For it tends to suggest that one event is somehow in the power of another, whereas the truth is merely that they are factually correlated. And the same applies to the use, in this context, of the word 'necessity' and even of the word 'cause' itself. Moreover, there are various reasons for this. One is the tendency to confuse causal with logical necessitation, and so to infer mistakenly that the effect is contained in the cause. Another is the uncritical use of a concept of force which is derived from primitive experiences of pushing and striking. A third is the survival of an animistic conception of causality, in which all causal relationships are modelled on the example of one person's exercising authority over another. As a result we tend to form an imaginative picture of an unhappy effect trying vainly to escape from the clutches of an overmastering cause. But, I repeat, the fact is simply that when an event of one type occurs, an event of another type occurs also, in a certain temporal or spatio-temporal relation to the first. The rest is only metaphor. And it is because of the metaphor, and not because of the fact, that we come to think that there is an antithesis between causality and freedom.

---

4   Co-occurrence or co-existence.

5   Abnormal or damaged brain tissue; an injury.

Nevertheless, it may be said, if the postulate of determinism is valid, then the future can be explained in terms of the past: and this means that if one knew enough about the past one would be able to predict the future. But in that case what will happen in the future is already decided. And how then can I be said to be free? What is going to happen is going to happen and nothing that I do can prevent it. If the determinist is right, I am the helpless prisoner of fate.

But what is meant by saying that the future course of events is already decided? If the implication is that some person has arranged it, then the proposition is false. But if all that is meant is that it is possible, in principle, to deduce it from a set of particular facts about the past, together with the appropriate general laws, then, even if this is true, it does not in the least entail that I am the helpless prisoner of fate. It does not even entail that my actions make no difference to the future: for they are causes as well as effects; so that if they were different their consequences would be different also. What it does entail is that my behaviour can be predicted: but to say that my behaviour can be predicted is not to say that I am acting under constraint. It is indeed true that I cannot escape my destiny if this is taken to mean no more than that I shall do what I shall do. But this is a tautology, just as it is a tautology that what is going to happen is going to happen. And such tautologies as these prove nothing whatsoever about the freedom of the will.

DANIEL DENNETT

"On Giving Libertarians What They Say They Want"

Who Is Daniel Dennett?

Daniel Clement Dennett, one of the most prominent living philosophers of mind, was born in Boston in 1942, the son of an American historian of the same name, but spent some of his childhood in Beirut, Lebanon. After majoring in philosophy at Harvard, he took his doctorate at Oxford where he was one of Gilbert Ryle's last students. He taught at the University of California at Irvine from 1965 until 1971, and then moved to Tufts University in Massachusetts, where he has taught ever since. He is now University Professor and Austin B. Fletcher Professor of Philosophy, and Director of the Center for Cognitive Studies there.

The center of gravity of Dennett's philosophical interests is the philosophy of mind, and in this area he identifies two main topics, which he calls *content* and *consciousness*. Furthermore, Dennett has argued since early in his career (against the then-prevailing assumption in the philosophy of mind) that the former, content, is a more fundamental phenomenon than the latter—that consciousness is to be explained as a special sort of content, rather than mental content as a special sort of consciousness.

Perhaps the central plank of Dennett's theory of content is that, as he puts it, "brains are syntactic engines that can mimic the competence of semantic engines." By this he means that brains are fundamentally complex, mechanical systems which follow the laws of *physics* and not the principles of rationality or meaning; however, according to Dennett, evolution has 'designed' the human brain so that its mechanical (or "syntactic") processes closely *approximate* those of a system which intelligently manipulates meaningful symbols (semantics). Therefore, meaning is something that brains—and thus human beings—seem to have only *from the outside*. Moreover since this is, in Dennett's view, all there is to having mental content, any system which is complex enough to act *as if* it has beliefs or desires—such as a thermostat, a simple robot, or an ant—really *does* have mental states in just the same way as, though in a more rudimentary form than, a human being.

Dennett's theory of consciousness is equally radical and is called the Multiple Drafts Model. He develops it as a contrast to what he thinks of as the traditional model of consciousness, which he labels (after the influence of René Descartes on modern philosophy) the "Cartesian Theater." According to this traditional picture, consciousness consists in a sort of metaphorical theater where all the data of consciousness 'come together' into a single experience at a particular time, and this experience is 'observed' by a metaphorical self (which then responds to it in some way—by interpreting it, acting on it, storing it in memory, and so on). For example, according to the tradition, all of my sensory experiences of the office in which I am currently working—the sight of my desk and computer, the sound of Fleetwood Mac playing quietly in the background, the sensation of the chair underneath me—are brought together into a single conscious experience, and this conscious experience is made available to me in my 'mind's eye,' on a more or less "real time" basis, so that I can respond to it in whatever way seems appropriate to me.

Dennett rejects nearly all the elements of the Cartesian theater: the idea of a self, a mind's eye, or a central place where all the pieces of a single conscious image come together. Instead, he thinks of consciousness as the multiple, simultaneous processing of various different bits of data, distributed across the brain and even across time. For example, the processing of the visual information about my room as it was at 11:29 PM might be occurring a few moments later than the processing of the aural information about the room at that time, and will certainly take place at a different location in my brain. Furthermore, there is no particular point at which this processing 'stops'

and spills its results into consciousness—my perceptions of the state of my office at 11:29 are subject to constant adjustment and revision as they go on, and there is no particular threshold they cross to become conscious. Thus, according to Dennett, there just *is* no "mental image" in our minds when we are conscious and so, roughly, the traditional "problem of consciousness" is dissolved.

Although his formal education was almost exclusively devoted to philosophy, Dennett has a strong bent for practical issues and problems and for finding out "how things work." He has described himself as "playing catch-up" since graduate school on the scientific areas most closely connected to his research, especially psychology, biology, and computer science. While still a student, he seriously considered a career as a sculptor, and he still throws the occasional pot and makes carved wood sculptures. He and his family own a farm in Maine where Dennett grows apples, blueberries, hay, and timber, and designs and builds equipment for his cider-making hobby. Dennett is also an avid sailor (he has cruised and raced a variety of boats, including ocean-going catamarans and windsurfers), skier, and scuba diver.

What Is the Structure of This Reading?

After some initial remarks—in which he comments that the "free will problem" is really a *cluster* of different questions and not a single unitary issue—Dennett announces that his paper will be an attempt to "diagnose" one of the lingering attractions of the libertarian position; his aim is to show that it is possible for compatibilism to take these libertarian intuitions more seriously and, in effect, give the libertarian a large dollop of "what they say they want."

Dennett begins by considering a paper from David Wiggins (which overturns a "standard," but fallacious, objection to libertarianism), and explains what Wiggins says he wants from a libertarian theory—in essence, a theory combining the *indeterminacy* of human actions with their *intelligibility* as "intentional" acts. Dennett then provides a description of a case which, he says, fits both of these criteria. This is his "answer box" example. However, he admits, libertarians will not be satisfied with this kind of case, as it locates the indeterminacy outside of the agent. Therefore, Dennett next provides a different case which places the "answer box" inside the agent, and puts the indeterminacy at "choice points" which are so trivial that they do not affect the overall psychological predictability and intelligibility of the agent. Still, however, libertarians will not be satisfied, precisely *because* the indeterminacy Dennett has described affects only trivial components of action. Dennett therefore gives his third, and final, example where the indeterminacy is pushed back to the initial stages of the agent's decision-making procedure and yet, he argues, still does not affect the rational intelligibility of ensuing actions.

Dennett goes on to argue that this third type of case—decision-making involving "a non-deterministic generate-and-test procedure"—should satisfy many libertarian demands, and he gives six reasons for its plausibility. However, he points out, this kind of "libertarian" model, though consistent with genuine indeterminism, does not require it: that is, the theory Dennett ultimately develops is not so much a variety of libertarianism as a kind of "reflective compatibilism."

Some Useful Background Information

1. One of the fundamental ideas in Dennett's philosophy is that of the "intentional stance," and it plays a significant role in this article. To take an intentional stance towards a system (such as a person, a government, a computer, or a bat) is to treat it as if it is a rational agent with appropriate beliefs and desires, and then to use this theoretical framework to predict and explain its actions. For example, I might adopt the intentional stance to try to predict the future foreign policy of, say, France: that is, I would treat France as an entity with particular interests (desires) and certain attitudes about itself and the rest of the world (beliefs), and then try to work out what a system with these beliefs and desires would be likely to do under various conditions. The "intentional level" is thus the level of description needed to understand a system in terms of its rational behavior. (The main, contrasting, kinds of "stance," for Dennett, are what he calls the "physical stance," which examines the material make-up of a system, and the "design stance," which investigates the mechanisms necessary to get it to do what it does.)

2. Dennett begins his consideration of a "plausible libertarianism" with an appeal to "Maxwell's Demon." This was a thought-experiment devised by the great physicist James Clerk Maxwell (1831–1879) in an effort to describe a possible "perpetual motion machine"—a mechanism which neither creates nor loses energy, and so could keep on operating for an infinite amount of time (forever) on a fixed supply of energy (or even no energy supply at all). One version of Maxwell's Demon is the everlasting air conditioner. The Demon sits on the doorstep of your room on a hot day, and watches the molecules meandering back and forth over the threshold. Those moving faster than some speed limit he allows only to pass *out* of the room, and those moving slower than this limit he allows only to *enter* the room. He doesn't need to expend physical energy to affect the molecules' motions: he simply closes a shutter at precisely the right moment to make them bounce back the way they came. All the Demon needs is a sharp eye, quick reflexes, and the intelligence to herd molecules. The net effect of the Demon's activities is to slow the average speed of molecules in the room—i.e., to cool down the air temperature. If this thought-experiment worked (a possibility contemporary physicists deny, essentially because the Demon would have to exchange energy with the system in order to 'see' the molecules—for example, he might need a tiny flashlight) then

the Demon would be violating the second law of thermodynamics, sometimes called the law of entropy or "time's arrow," which states that energy spontaneously tends to flow only from being concentrated in one place to becoming diffused and spread out.

A Common Misconception

Dennett refers frequently to the idea that human actions can be seen as "intentional": it is very easy, especially in the context of a discussion of free will, to assume that "intentional" here means deliberate, intended, purposeful. However, it does not. "Intentionality," in the way Dennett is using it here, is a technical term in philosophy, and means, roughly, *aboutness*. That is, something is "intentional" just in case it is directed at, or is about, something else, as a sentence, a road sign or a thought can be about things (e.g., I might think *about* bumbleberry pie). So when Dennett refers to human behavior as "intentional," he means it is guided by meaningful mental states, such as beliefs, desires, or reasons: that is, from the intentional stance, we do the things we do because we *want* to achieve certain goals and *believe* that this is a way to attain them.

Suggestions for Critical Reflection

1. Is the characterization of libertarianism (or "indeterminism") by David Wiggins, which is Dennett's starting point, an attractive and plausible one? Do you think it leaves out anything which is crucial to libertarianism?

2. "Whenever we choose to perform an action of a certain sort, there are no doubt slight variations in timing, style, and skeletal implementation of those actions that are within our power but beneath our concern. For all we know, which variation occurs is *undetermined*." Is this last sentence an empirically plausible claim? For Dennett's purposes, does it matter whether it is plausible or not?

3. In Dennett's first two cases, it seems it is not human *actions* that are macroscopically infected with indeterminism but merely human *behavior*: i.e., it is not the action which is undetermined, but the physical way the action is carried out. Do you think this really gives Wiggins the kind of indeterminacy the libertarian is looking for? If not, then what do you think is the point (if any) of the first two cases?

4. Does Dennett's final model of human decision-making really capture "what Russell was looking for"? For example, according to Dennett, does our intelligence "make improbable things happen" by *indeterministically* deciding which of the various options being considered should be acted on?

5. Dennett draws a distinction between "invention"—which is "the intelligent selection from among randomly generated candidates"—and mere mechanical computation, and he argues we can claim authorship of, and responsibility for, our moral decisions as long as they are our inventions. How viable is this distinction? Is it persuasive, or is Dennett really engaging in his own kind of "prestidigitation"? For example, does Dennett give us any reasons to believe that, using his model of human decision-making, the selection of one action rather than another (from a randomly generated list) is *not* purely mechanical and deterministic?

6. Dennett emphasizes the importance, for free will, of the ability to decide to cease deliberating at a certain point (even though there is more deliberating left to be done) and to act. Does his model of decision-making include any component to make *this* action—of stopping deliberating—non-deterministic? If not, how much less attractive does this make his account for the libertarian?

7. Towards the end of his paper, Dennett suggests that his model shows that libertarians can preserve what they find attractive about "moral authorship" *whether or not* our actions are genuinely undetermined. Do you agree with Dennett? Would it make a real difference to human freedom whether considerations for choice are generated with genuine randomness or merely unpredictably?

8. Dennett declares in this paper that his aim is to give libertarians one of the things they say they want, but he admits that there may be still other components of the attractiveness of libertarianism which he has not dealt with. How satisfied do you think a libertarian should be with Dennett's model of human decision-making? How important are the libertarian intuitions, if any, which are not accommodated by it? Would such libertarian worries (if any) be a reason to *replace* Dennett's model, or just to *add* to it in some way?

Suggestions for Further Reading

Dennett has written one book and several articles on the free-will problem. The book—which is highly accessible and quite influential—is *Elbow Room: The Varieties of Free Will Worth Wanting* (MIT Press, 1984). The articles include "Mechanism and Responsibility," reprinted in Dennett's collection *Brainstorms* (MIT Press, 1978); "I Could Not Have Done Otherwise—So What?" *Journal of Philosophy* 81 (1984); and, with Christopher Taylor, "Who's Afraid of Determinism…?" in *The Free Will Handbook*, edited by Robert Kane (Oxford University Press, 2002).

Dennett's work on intentional systems can be found primarily in two of his books: *Brainstorms* (MIT Press, 1978) and *The Intentional Stance* (MIT Press, 1987). An important later essay in this area is "Real Patterns," *Journal of Philosophy* 88 (1991), which is also reprinted in Dennett's latest book *Brainchildren* (MIT Press, 1998). Dennett has also done very prominent work on consciousness—especially his *Consciousness Explained* (Little, Brown, 1991)—and the theory of evolution—*Darwin's Dangerous Idea* (Simon & Schuster, 1995).

Three books which collect specially-written papers about Dennett's philosophy are *Daniel Dennett*, edited by Andrew Brook and Don Ross (Cambridge University Press, 2001), *Dennett and His Critics*, edited by Bo Dahlbom (Blackwell, 1993), and *Dennett's Philosophy: A Comprehensive Assessment*, edited by Don Ross, Andrew Brook, and David Thompson (MIT Press, 2000).

"On Giving Libertarians What They Say They Want"[1]

Why is the free will problem so persistent? Partly, I suspect, because it is called *the* free will problem. Hilliard, the great card magician,[2] used to fool even his professional colleagues with a trick he called the tuned deck. Twenty times in a row he'd confound the quidnuncs,[3] as he put it, with the same trick, a bit of prestidigitation that resisted all the diagnostic hypotheses of his fellow magicians. The trick, as he eventually revealed, was a masterpiece of subtle misdirection; it consisted entirely of the *name*, "the tuned deck", plus a peculiar but obviously non-functional bit of ritual. It was, you see, *many* tricks, however many different but familiar tricks Hilliard had to perform in order to stay one jump ahead of the solvers. As soon as their experiments and subtle arguments had conclusively eliminated one way of doing the trick, that was the way he would do the trick on future trials. This would have been obvious to his sophisticated onlookers had they not been so intent on finding *the* solution to *the* trick.

The so called free will problem is in fact many not very closely related problems tied together by a name and lots of attendant anxiety. Most people can be brought by reflection to care very much what the truth is on these matters, for each problem poses a threat: to our self-esteem, to our conviction that we are not living deluded lives, to our conviction that we may justifiably trust our grasp of such utterly familiar notions as possibility, opportunity and ability.[4] There

---

1 This article was written in 1976 and first published in a collection of Dennett's papers called *Brainstorms: Philosophical Essays on Mind and Psychology*, pp. 286–299. Copyright © 1981, Massachusetts Institute of Technology, by permission of The MIT Press.

2 John Northern Hilliard (1872–1935), author of the influential book *Greater Magic* (published posthumously in 1938).

3 A busybody (from the Latin "what now?").

4 [Author's note] An incomplete list of the very different questions composing the free will problem: (1) How can a material thing (a mechanism?) be correctly said to reason, to have reasons, to act on reasons? (a ques-

is no very good reason to suppose that an acceptable solution to *one* of the problems will be, or even point to, an acceptable solution to the others, and we may be misled by residual unallayed worries into rejecting or undervaluing partial solutions, in the misguided hope that we might allay all the doubts with one overarching doctrine or theory. But we don't have any good theories. Since the case for determinism is persuasive and since we all want to believe we have free will, *compatibilism* is the strategic favorite, but we must admit that no compatibilism free of problems while full of the traditional flavors of responsibility has yet been devised.

The alternatives to compatibilism are anything but popular. Both the libertarian and the hard determinist believe that free will and determinism are incompatible. The hard determinist says: "So much the worse for free will." The libertarian says: "So much the worse for determinism," at least with regard to human action. Both alternatives have been roundly and routinely dismissed as at best obscure, at worst incoherent. But alas for the compatibilist, neither view will oblige us by fading away. Their persistence, like Hilliard's success, probably has many explanations. I hope to diagnose just one of them.

In a recent paper, David Wiggins has urged us to look with more sympathy at the program of libertari-

___

tion I attempt to answer in Chapter 12 ["Mechanism and Responsibility"]). (2) How can the unique four dimensional non-branching world-worm that comprises all that has happened and will happen admit of a notion of possibilities that are not actualities? What does an *opportunity* look like when the world is viewed *sub specie aeternitatis* [under the aspect of eternity]? (3) How can a person be an author of decisions, and not merely the locus of causal summation for external influences? (4) How can we make sense of the intuition that an agent can only be responsible if he could have done otherwise? (5) How can we intelligibly describe the relevant mental history of the truly culpable agent—the villain or rational cheat with no excuses? As Socrates asked, can a person knowingly commit evil?

anism.[5] Wiggins first points out that a familiar argument often presumed to demolish libertarianism begs the question. The first premise of this argument is that every event is either causally determined or random. Then since the libertarian insists that human actions cannot be both free and determined, the libertarian must be supposing that any and all free actions are random. But one would hardly hold oneself responsible for an action that merely happened at random, so libertarianism, far from securing a necessary condition for responsible action, has unwittingly secured a condition that would defeat responsibility altogether. Wiggins points out that the first premise, that every event is either causally determined or random, is not the innocent logical truth it appears to be. The innocent logical truth is that every event is either causally determined or not causally determined. There may be an established sense of the word "random" that is unproblematically synonymous with "not causally determined", but the word "random" in common parlance has further connotations of pointlessness or arbitrariness, and it is these very connotations that ground our acquiescence in the further premise that one would not hold oneself responsible for one's random actions. It may be the case that whatever is random in the sense of being causally undetermined, is random in the sense connoting utter meaninglessness, but that is just what the libertarian wishes to deny. This standard objection to libertarianism, then, assumes what it must prove; it fails to show that undetermined action would be random action, and hence action for which we could not be held responsible.

But is there in fact any reasonable hope that the libertarian can find some defensible ground between the absurdity of "blind chance" on the one hand and on the other what Wiggins calls the cosmic unfairness of the determinist's view of these matters? Wiggins thinks there is. He draws our attention to a speculation of Russell's: "It might be that without infringing the laws of physics, intelligence could make improbable things happen, as Maxwell's demon would have de-

___

5   [Author's note] D. Wiggins, "Towards a Reasonable Libertarianism" in T. Honderich, ed., *Essays on Freedom of Action* (London: Routledge & Kegan Paul, 1973).

feated the second law of thermo-dynamics by opening the trap door to fast-moving particles and closing it to slow-moving particles."[6] Wiggins sees many problems with the speculation, but he does, nevertheless, draw a glimmer of an idea from it.

> For indeterminism maybe all we really need to imagine or conceive is a world in which (a) there is some macroscopic indeterminacy founded in microscopic indeterminacy, and (b) an appreciable number of the free actions or policies or deliberations of individual agents, although they are not even in principle hypothetico-deductively derivable[7] from antecedent conditions, can be such as to persuade us to fit them into meaningful sequences. We need not trace free actions back to volitions construed as little pushes aimed from outside the physical world. What we must find instead are patterns which are coherent and intelligible in the low level terms of practical deliberation, even though they are not amenable to the kind of generalization or necessity which is the stuff of rigorous theory. (p. 52)

The "low level terms of practical deliberation" are, I take it, the familiar terms of intentional or reason-giving explanation. We typically render actions intelligible by citing their reasons, the beliefs and desires of the agent that render the actions at least marginally reasonable under the circumstances. Wiggins is suggesting then that if we could somehow *make sense* of human actions at the level of intentional explanation, then in spite of the fact that those actions might be physically undetermined, they would not be random. Wiggins invites us to take this possibility seriously, but he has little further to say in elaboration or defense of this. He has said enough, however, to suggest to me a number of ways in which we could give libertarians what they seem to want.

Wiggins asks only that human actions be seen to be *intelligible* in the low-level terms of practical deliberation. Surely if human actions were *predictable* in the low-level terms of practical deliberation, they would be intelligible in those terms. So I propose first to demonstrate that there is a way in which human behavior could be strictly undetermined from the physicist's point of view while at the same time accurately predictable from the intentional level. This demonstration, alas, will be very disappointing, for it relies on a cheap trick and what it establishes can be immediately seen to be quite extraneous to the libertarian's interests. But it is a necessary preamble to what I hope will be a more welcome contribution to the libertarian's cause. So let us get the disappointing preamble behind us.

Here is how a bit of human behavior could be undetermined from the physicist's point of view, but quite clearly predictable by the intentionalist. Suppose we were to build an electronic gadget that I will call an answer box. The answer box is designed to record a person's answers to simple questions. It has two buttons, a Yes button, and a No button, and two foot pedals, a Yes pedal, and a No pedal, all clearly marked. It also has a little display screen divided in half, and on one side it says "use the buttons" and on the other side it says "use the pedals". We design this bit of apparatus so that only one half of this display screen is illuminated at any one time. Once a minute, a radium randomizer[8] determines, in an entirely undetermined

---

6   [Author's note] Bertrand Russell, *Human Knowledge; Its Scope and Limits* (New York: Simon and Schuster, 1948), Chapter 15, "The Physiology of Sensation and Volition", p. 54.

7   The hypothetico-deductive method is a way of testing scientific hypotheses. A prediction is "hypothetico-deductively derivable" from a theory when it is the case that, if the theory is true, the prediction must also be true. For example, if it is true that gold is a non-reactive substance and that this ring is gold, then it follows logically that if I drop this ring into a beaker full of a certain kind of acid it will not be affected. Hence, if the ring does dissolve, this shows either that it was not gold or that some of our theoretical assumptions about gold are false.

8   A mechanism which makes use of the genuine physical (quantum) randomness of the decay of a particle of radium, a highly radioactive element. A radioactive substance decays by spontaneously emitting a particle or gamma ray (i.e., radiation) at random intervals, and a radium randomizer would probably work by detecting whether or not the radium had emitted a particle in a particular direction within a particular time span.

way of course, whether the display screen says "use the buttons" or "use the pedals". I now propose the following experiment. First, we draw up a list of ten very simple questions that have Yes or No answers, questions of the order of difficulty of "Do fish swim?" and "Is Texas bigger than Rhode Island?" We seat a subject at the answer box and announce that a handsome reward will be given to those who correctly follow all the experimental instructions, and a bonus will be given to those who answer all our questions correctly.

Now, can the physicist in principle predict the subject's behavior? Let us suppose the subject is in fact a physically deterministic system, and let us suppose further that the physicist has perfect knowledge of the subject's initial state, all the relevant deterministic laws, and all the interactions within the closed situation of the experimental situation. Still, the unpredictable behavior of the answer box will infect the subject on a macroscopic scale with its own indeterminacy on at least ten occasions during the period the physicist must predict. So the best the physicist can do is issue a multiple disjunctive or multiple conditional prediction. Can the intentionalist do any better? Yes, of course. The intentionalist, having read the instructions given to the subject, and having sized up the subject as a person of roughly normal intelligence and motivation, and having seen that all the odd numbered questions have Yes answers and the even numbered questions have No answers, confidently predicts that the subject will behave as follows: "The subject will give Yes answers to questions *1*, *3*, *5*, *7*, and *9*, and the subject will answer the rest of the questions in the negative". There are no *if's*, *or's* or *maybe's* in those predictions. They are categorical and precise—precise enough for instance to appear in a binding contract or satisfy a court of law.

This is, of course, the cheap trick I warned you about. There is no real difference in the predictive power of the two predictors. The intentionalist for instance is no more in a position to predict whether the subject will move finger or foot than the physicist is, and the physicist may well be able to give predictions that are tantamount to the intentionalist's. The physicist may for instance be able to make this prediction: "When question *6* is presented, if the illuminated

sign on the box reads use the pedals, the subject's right foot will move at velocity k until it depresses the No pedal n inches, and if the illuminated sign says use the buttons, the subject's right index finger will trace a trajectory terminating on the No button." Such a prediction is if anything more detailed than the intentionalist's simple prediction of the negative answer to question *6*, and it might in fact be more reliable and better grounded as well. But so what? What we are normally interested in, what we are normally interested in *predicting*, moreover, is not the skeletal motion of human beings but their actions, and the intentionalist can predict the actions of the subject (at least insofar as most of us would take any interest in them) without the elaborate rigmarole and calculations of the physicist. The possibility of indeterminacy in the environment of the kind introduced here, and hence the possibility of indeterminacy in the subject's reaction to that environment, is something with regard to which the intentionalistic predictive power is quite neutral. Still, we could not expect the libertarian to be interested in this variety of undetermined human behavior, behavior that is undetermined simply because the behavior of the answer box, something entirely external to the agent, is undetermined.

Suppose then we move something like the answer box inside the agent. It is a commonplace of action theory that virtually all human actions can be accomplished or realized in a wide variety of ways. There are, for instance, indefinitely many ways of insulting your neighbor, or even of asserting that snow is white. And we are often not much interested, nor should we be, in exactly which particular physical motion accomplishes the act we intend. So let us suppose that our nervous system is so constructed and designed that whenever in the implementation of an intention, our control system is faced with two or more options with regard to which we are non-partisan, a purely undetermined tie-breaking "choice" is made. There you are at the supermarket, wanting a can of Campbell's Tomato Soup, and faced with an array of several hundred identical cans of Campbell's Tomato Soup, all roughly equidistant from your hands. What to do? Before you even waste time and energy pondering this trivial problem, let us suppose, a perfectly random factor determines which can your hand reaches out for. This is of course simply a variation on the ancient theme of Buridan's ass, that unfortunate beast who, finding himself hungry, thirsty and equidistant between food and water, perished for lack of the divine nudge that in a human being accomplishes a truly free choice.[9] This has never been a promising vision of the free choice of responsible agents, if only because it seems to secure freedom for such a small and trivial class of our choices. What does it avail me if I am free to choose *this* can of soup, but not free to choose between buying and stealing it? But however unpromising the idea is as a centerpiece for an account of free will, we must not underestimate its possible scope of application. Such trivial choice points seldom obtrude in our conscious deliberation, no doubt, but they are quite possibly ubiquitous nonetheless at an unconscious level. Whenever we choose to perform an action of a certain sort, there are no doubt slight variations in timing, style and skeletal implementation of those actions that are within our power but beneath our concern. For all we know, which variation occurs is *undetermined*. That is, the implementation of any one of our intentional actions may encounter undetermined *choice points* in many places in the causal chain. The resulting behavior would not be distinguishable to our everyday eyes, or from the point of view of our everyday interests, from behavior that was rigidly determined. What we are mainly interested in, as I said before, are actions, not motions, and what we are normally interested in predicting are actions.

It is worth noting that not only can we typically predict actions from the intentional stance without paying heed to possibly undetermined variations of implementation of these actions, but we can even put together chains of intentional predictions that are relatively immune to such variation. In the summer of 1974 many people were confidently predicting that Nixon would resign. As the day and hour approached, the prediction grew more certain and more specific as to time and place; Nixon would resign not just in the near future, but in the next hour, and in the White House and in the presence of television cameramen and so forth. Still, it was not plausible to claim to know just how he would resign, whether he would resign with grace, or dignity, or with an attack on his critics, whether he would enunciate clearly or mumble or tremble. These details were not readily predictable, but most of the further dependent predictions we were interested in making did not hinge on these subtle variations. However Nixon resigned, we could predict that Goldwater would publicly approve of it, Cronkite would report that Goldwater had so approved of it, Sevareid would comment on it, Rodino would terminate the proceedings of the Judiciary Committee, and Gerald Ford would be sworn in as Nixon's successor.[10] Of course some predictions we might have made at the time would have hinged crucially on particular details of the precise manner of Nixon's resignation, and if these details happened to be undetermined both by Nixon's intentions and by any other feature of the moment, then some human actions of perhaps great importance would be infected by the indeterminacy of Nixon's manner at the moment just as our exemplary subject's behavior was infected by the indeterminacy

9 Jean Buridan (c. 1295–1358) was a significant French medieval philosopher, scientist, and logician (who is said to have been thrown into the river Seine in a sack for dallying with the Queen of France). The notion of "Buridan's ass" is probably not his example—it appears nowhere in his writings—but one which was used against him by his contemporaries. Buridan held that choice is always a matter of finding the best reason for action, and thus that it is delayed until reason has decided in favor of one action or another; freedom of the will, for Buridan, was simply the ability to defer choice in the absence of any compelling reason.

10 Barry Goldwater was a conservative Republican senator from Arizona (who ran unsuccessfully for President in 1964); after his resignation, he called Richard Nixon "a disaster for the Republicans." Walter Cronkite was an influential broadcast journalist and anchor of the *CBS Evening News*, and Eric Sevareid was a well-known correspondent and commentator on the *Evening News*. Peter Rodino, a Democrat, was chair of the House Judiciary Committee which recommended Nixon be impeached and removed from office. Gerald Ford was Nixon's Vice President (after Spiro Agnew resigned in 1973), and became President after Nixon's resignation over the Watergate scandal in August 1974.

of the answer box. That would not, however, make these actions any the less intelligible to us as actions.

This result is not just what the libertarian is looking for, but it is a useful result nevertheless. It shows that we can indeed install indeterminism in the internal causal chains affecting human behavior *at the macroscopic level* while preserving the intelligibility of practical deliberation that the libertarian requires. We may have good reasons from other quarters for embracing determinism, but we need not fear that macroscopic indeterminism in human behavior would of necessity rob our lives of intelligibility by producing chaos. Thus, philosophers such as Ayer and Hobart,[11] who argue that free will requires determinism, must be wrong. There are *some* ways our world could be macroscopically indeterministic, without that fact remotely threatening the coherence of the intentionalistic conceptual scheme of action description presupposed by claims of moral responsibility.

Still, it seems that all we have done is install indeterminism in a harmless place by installing it in an *irrelevant* place. The libertarian would not be relieved to learn that although his decision to murder his neighbor was quite determined, the style and trajectory of the death blow was not. Clearly, what the libertarian has in mind is indeterminism at some earlier point, prior to the ultimate decision or formation of intention, and unless we can provide that, we will not aid the libertarian's cause. But perhaps we can provide that as well.

Let us return then, to Russell's speculation that intelligence might make improbable things happen. Is there any way that something like this could be accomplished? The idea of intelligence exploiting randomness is not unfamiliar. The poet, Paul Valéry,[12] nicely captures the basic idea:

> It takes two to invent anything. The one makes up combinations; the other one chooses, recognizes what he wishes and what is important to him in the mass of the things which the former has imparted to him. What we call genius is much less the work of the first one than the readiness of the second one to grasp the value of what has been laid before him and to choose it.[13]

Here we have the suggestion of an intelligent *selection* from what may be a partially arbitrary or chaotic or random *production*, and what we need is the outline of a model for such a process in human decision-making.

An interesting feature of most important human decision-making is that it is made under time pressure. Even if there are, on occasion, algorithmic[14] decision procedures giving guaranteed optimal solutions to our problems, and even if these decision procedures are in principle available to us, we may not have time or energy to utilize them. We are rushed, but moreover, we are all more or less lazy, even about terribly critical decisions that will affect our lives—our own lives, to say nothing of the lives of others. We invariably settle for a *heuristic*[15] decision procedure; we *satisfice*;[16,17]

---

11 [Author's note] A.J. Ayer, "Freedom and Necessity", in *Philosophical Essays* (London: MacMillan, 1954); R.B. Hobart, "Free Will as Involving Determination and Inconceivable Without It", *Mind* (1934).

12 Paul-Ambroise Valéry (1871–1945) was a French poet, critic, and essayist. He often explored abstract and philosophical ideas in his verse and prose.

13 [Author's note] Quoted by Jacques Hadamard, in *The Psychology of Invention in the Mathematical Field*, Princeton University Press, 1949, p. 30. I discuss the implications of Valéry's claim in Chapter 5 ["Why the Law of Effect Will Not Go Away"].

14 Finite and mechanical.

15 Something is "heuristic" if—like a template or a shortcut—it helps one to arrive more quickly at a result that would otherwise require a long and tedious process of discovery. For example, today's chess-playing programs do not calculate the permutations of every possible move for several turns ahead (which would take a very large amount of time or processing power), but instead use "heuristic rules" to spot moves that are most likely to be successful and then focus on choosing between them.

16 [Author's note] The term is Herbert Simon's. See his *The Sciences of the Artificial* (1969) for a review of the concept.

17 To satisfice is to choose a solution which is good enough to do the job required, without expending extra effort to look for another solution which might be just a little bit better.

we poke around hoping for inspiration; we do our best to think about the problem in a more or less directed way until we must finally stop mulling, summarize our results as best we can, and act. A realistic model of such decision-making just might have the following feature: When someone is faced with an important decision, something in him generates a variety of more or less relevant considerations bearing on the decision. Some of these considerations, we may suppose, are determined to be generated, but others may be non-deterministically generated. For instance, Jones, who is finishing her dissertation on Aristotle and the practical syllogism,[18] must decide within a week whether to accept the assistant professorship at the University of Chicago, or the assistant professorship at Swarthmore. She considers the difference in salaries, the probable quality of the students, the quality of her colleagues, the teaching load, the location of the schools, and so forth. Let us suppose that considerations A, B, C, D, E, and F occur to her and that those are the only considerations that occur to her, and that on the basis of those, she decides to accept the job at Swarthmore. She does this *knowing* of course that she could devote more time and energy to this deliberation, could cast about for other relevant considerations, could perhaps dismiss some of A–F as being relatively unimportant and so forth, but being no more meticulous, no more obsessive, than the rest of us about such matters, she settles for the considerations that have occurred to her and makes her decision.

Let us suppose though, that after sealing her fate with a phone call, consideration G occurs to her, and she says to herself: "If only G had occurred to me before, I would certainly have chosen the University of Chicago instead, but G didn't occur to me". Now it just might be the case that *exactly* which considerations occur to one in such circumstances is to some degree strictly undetermined. If that were the case,

then even the intentionalist, knowing everything knowable about Jones' settled beliefs and preferences and desires, might nevertheless be unable to predict her decision, except perhaps conditionally. The intentionalist might be able to argue as follows: "If considerations A–F occur to Jones, then she will go to Swarthmore," and this would be a prediction that would be grounded on a rational argument based on considerations A–F according to which Swarthmore was the best place to go. The intentionalist might go on to add, however, that if consideration G also occurs to Jones (which is strictly unpredictable unless we interfere and draw Jones' attention to G), Jones will choose the University of Chicago instead. Notice that although we are supposing the decision is in this way strictly unpredictable except conditionally by the intentionalist, whichever choice Jones makes is retrospectively intelligible. There will be a rationale for the decision in either case; in the former case a rational argument in favor of Swarthmore based on A–F, and in the latter case, a rational argument in favor of Chicago, based on A–G. (There may, of course be yet another rational argument based on A–H, or I, or J, in favor of Swarthmore, or in favor of going on welfare, or in favor of suicide.) Even if *in principle* we couldn't predict which of many rationales could ultimately be correctly cited in justification or retrospective explanation of the choice made by Jones, we could be confident that there would be some sincere, authentic, and not unintelligible rationale to discover.

The model of decision making I am proposing has the following feature: when we are faced with an important decision, a consideration-generator whose output is to some degree undetermined produces a series of considerations, some of which may of course be immediately rejected as irrelevant by the agent (consciously or unconsciously). Those considerations that are selected by the agent as having a more than negligible bearing on the decision then figure in a reasoning process, and if the agent is in the main reasonable, those considerations ultimately serve as predictors and explicators of the agent's final decision. What can be said in favor of such a model, bearing in mind that there are many possible substantive variations on the basic theme?

---

18 A "practical syllogism" is an argument which purports to show that one ought to perform some action or other. For example, one might argue as follows: I want a drink; beer is a drink; so I shall have a beer. It is highly controversial whether such syllogisms really do show the logical form of practical reasoning, or indeed that Aristotle ever thought they did.

First, I think it captures what Russell was looking for. The intelligent selection, rejection and weighting of the considerations that do occur to the subject is a matter of intelligence making the difference. Intelligence makes the difference here because an intelligent selection and assessment procedure determines which microscopic indeterminacies get amplified, as it were, into important macroscopic determiners of ultimate behavior.

Second, I think it installs indeterminism in the right place for the libertarian, if there is a right place at all. The libertarian could not have wanted to place the indeterminism *at the end* of the agent's assessment and deliberation. It would be insane to hope that after all rational deliberation had terminated with an assessment of the best available course of action, indeterminism would then intervene to flip the coin before action. It is a familiar theme in discussions of free will that the important claim that one could have done otherwise under the circumstances is not plausibly construed as the claim that one could have done otherwise given *exactly* the set of convictions and desires that prevailed at the end of rational deliberation. So if there is to be a crucial undetermined nexus, it had better be prior to the final assessment of the considerations on the stage, which is right where we have located it.

Third, I think that the model is recommended by considerations that have little or nothing to do with the free will problem. It may well turn out to be that from the point of view of biological engineering, it is just more efficient and in the end more rational that decision-making should occur in this way. Time rushes on, and people must act, and there may not be time for a person to canvass all his beliefs, conduct all the investigations and experiments that he would see were relevant, assess every preference in his stock before acting, and it may be that the best way to prevent the inertia of Hamlet[19] from overtaking us is for our decision-making processes to be expedited by a process of partially random generation and test. Even in the rare circumstances where we know there is, say, a decision procedure for determining the optimal solution to a decision problem, it is often more reasonable to proceed swiftly and by heuristic methods, and this strategic principle may in fact be incorporated as a design principle at a fairly fundamental level of cognitive-conative[20] organization.

A fourth observation in favor of the model is that it permits moral education to make a difference, without making all of the difference. A familiar argument against the libertarian is that if our moral decisions were not in fact determined by our moral upbringing, or our moral education, there would be no point in providing such an education for the young. The libertarian who adopted our model could answer that a moral education, while not completely determining the generation of considerations and moral decision-making, can nevertheless have a prior selective effect on the sorts of considerations that will occur. A moral education, like mutual discussion and persuasion generally, could adjust the boundaries and probabilities of the generator without rendering it deterministic.

Fifth—and I think this is perhaps the most important thing to be said in favor of this model—it provides some account of our important intuition that we are the authors of our moral decisions. The unreflective compatibilist is apt to view decision-making on the model of a simple balance or scale on which the pros and cons of action are piled. What gets put on the scale is determined by one's nature and one's nurture, and once all the weights are placed, gravity as it were determines which way the scale will tip, and hence determines which way we will act. On such a view, the agent does not seem in any sense to be the author of the decisions, but at best merely the locus at which the environmental and genetic factors bearing on him interact to produce a decision. It all looks terribly mechanical and inevitable, and seems to leave no room for creativity or genius. The model proposed, however, holds out the promise of a distinc-

---

19   Hamlet, the title character of Shakespeare's famous play, is the prince of Denmark who cannot decide whether or not to act on his belief that his father was murdered by his uncle (who then seized the crown and married Hamlet's mother).

20   Cognition is concerned with beliefs about the world and conation is directed toward action in the world.

tion between authorship and mere implication in a causal chain.[21]

Consider in this light the difference between completing a lengthy exercise in long division and constructing a proof in, say, Euclidian geometry. There is a sense in which I can be the author of a particular bit of long division, and can take credit if it turns out to be correct, and can take pride in it as well, but there is a stronger sense in which I can claim authorship of a proof in geometry, even if thousands of school children before me have produced the very same proof. There is a sense in which this is something original that I have created. To take pride in one's *computational accuracy* is one thing, and to take pride in one's *inventiveness* is another, and as Valéry claimed, the essence of invention is the intelligent selection from among randomly generated candidates. I think that the sense in which we wish to claim authorship of our moral decisions, and hence claim responsibility for them, requires that we view them as products of intelligent invention, and not merely the results of an assiduous application of formulae. I don't want to overstate this case; certainly many of the decisions we make are so obvious, so black and white, that no one would dream of claiming any special creativity in having made them and yet would still claim complete responsibility for the decisions thus rendered. But if we viewed all our decision-making on those lines, I think our sense of our dignity as moral agents would be considerably impoverished.

Finally, the model I propose points to the multiplicity of decisions that encircle our moral decisions and suggests that in many cases our ultimate decision as to which way to act is less important phenomenologically as a contributor to our sense of free will than the prior decisions affecting our deliberation process itself: the decision, for instance, not to consider any further, to terminate deliberation; or the decision to ignore certain lines of inquiry.

These prior and subsidiary decisions contribute, I think, to our sense of ourselves as responsible free agents, roughly in the following way: I am faced with an important decision to make, and after a certain amount of deliberation, I say to myself: "That's enough. I've considered this matter enough and now I'm going to act," in the full knowledge that I could have considered further, in the full knowledge that the eventualities may prove that I decided in error, but with the acceptance of responsibility in any case.

I have recounted six recommendations for the suggestion that human decision-making involves a non-deterministic generate-and-test procedure. First, it captures whatever is compelling in Russell's hunch. Second, it installs determinism in the only plausible locus for libertarianism (something we have established by a process of elimination). Third, it makes sense from the point of view of strategies of biological engineering. Fourth, it provides a flexible justification of moral education. Fifth, it accounts at least in part for our sense of authorship of our decisions. Sixth, it acknowledges and explains the importance of decisions internal to the deliberation process. It is embarrassing to note, however, that the very feature of the model that inspired its promulgation is *apparently* either gratuitous or misdescribed or both, and that is the causal indeterminacy of the generator. We have been supposing, for the sake of the libertarian, that the process that generates considerations for our assessment generates them at least in part by a physically or causally undetermined or random process. But here we seem to be trading on yet another imprecision or ambiguity in the word "random". When a system designer or programmer relies on a "random" generation process, it is not a *physically undetermined* process that is required, but simply a *patternless* process. Computers are typically equipped with a random number generator, but the process that generates the sequence is a perfectly deterministic and determinate process. If it is a good random number generator (and designing one is extraordinarily difficult, it turns out) the sequence will be locally and globally patternless. There will be a complete absence of regularities on which to base predictions about unexamined portions of the sequence.

Isn't it the case that the new improved proposed model for human deliberation can do as well with a random-but-deterministic generation process as

---

21 [Author's note] Cf. the suggestive discussion of genius in Kant's *Critique of Judgment*, Sections 46, 47.

with a causally undetermined process? Suppose that to the extent that the considerations that occur to me are unpredictable, they are unpredictable simply because they are fortuitously determined by some arbitrary and irrelevant factors, such as the location of the planets or what I had for breakfast. It appears that this alternative supposition diminishes not one whit the plausibility or utility of the model that I have proposed. Have we in fact given the libertarians what they really want without giving them indeterminism? Perhaps. We have given the libertarians the materials out of which to construct an account of personal authorship of moral decisions, and this is something that the compatibilistic views have never handled well. But something else has emerged as well. Just as the presence or absence of macroscopic indeterminism in the implementation style of intentional actions turned out to be something essentially undetectable from the vantage point of our *Lebenswelt*,[22] a feature with no significant repercussions in the "manifest image", to use Sellars' term,[23] so the rival descriptions of the consideration generator, as random-but-causally-deterministic *versus* random-and-causally-*in*deterministic, will have no clearly testable and contrary

implications at the level of micro-neurophysiology, even if we succeed beyond our most optimistic fantasies in mapping deliberation processes onto neural activity.

That fact does not refute libertarianism, or even discredit the motivation behind it, for what it shows once again is that we need not fear that causal indeterminism would make our lives unintelligible. There may not be compelling grounds from *this* quarter for favoring an indeterministic vision of the springs of our action, but if considerations from other quarters favor indeterminism, we can at least be fairly sanguine about the prospects of incorporating indeterminism into our picture of deliberation, even if we cannot yet see what point such an incorporation would have. Wiggins speaks of the cosmic unfairness of determinism, and I do not think the considerations raised here do much to allay our worries about *that*. Even if one embraces the sort of view I have outlined, the deterministic view of the unbranching and inexorable history of the universe can inspire terror or despair, and perhaps the libertarian is right that there is no way to allay these feelings short of a brute denial of determinism. Perhaps such a denial, and only such a denial, would permit us to make sense of the notion that our actual lives are created by us over time out of possibilities that exist in virtue of our earlier decisions; that we trace a path through a branching maze that both defines who we are, and why, to some extent (if we are fortunate enough to maintain against all vicissitudes the integrity of our deliberational machinery) we are *responsible* for being who we are. That prospect deserves an investigation of its own. All I hope to have shown here is that it is a prospect we can and should take seriously.

---

22   "Life-world." This term comes from the work of the German philosopher Edmund Husserl (1859–1938) and refers to the pre-scientific world in which we live our day-to-day lives, and which has to underpin any adequate science. (For Husserl the mathematical understanding of *shapes*, to pick just one example, has to be understood in terms of the "idealized construction" of those ideas from our everyday experience of shaped objects.)

23   Wilfrid Sellars (1912–1989) distinguished between the "manifest image" of humanity (as beings with beliefs, desires, perception, and intentions) and the "scientific image" of humankind (as a physical organism studied by physicists, biochemists, and neurologists). The trick, according to Sellars, is to reconcile these two images in such a way that we do justice to both viewpoints, but, in particular, to ensure that our understanding of the manifest image does not invoke anything repugnant to the scientific image (such as incompatibilist free will).

BERNARD WILLIAMS AND THOMAS NAGEL
"Moral Luck"

Who Was Bernard Williams?

His obituary in the [London] *Times*, June 14, 2003, called Sir Bernard Williams "the most brilliant and most important British moral philosopher of his time," remarking, however, that his work "effortlessly spanned the entire discipline of philosophy." Williams, born in 1929, turned to philosophy during his Oxford education, and following his military service, taught at Oxford, then at University College London, Bedford College (also part of the University of London), and, from 1967 until 1988, Cambridge. Unhappy with Thatcherite educational policy, he moved to UC Berkeley, but returned in 1990 to Oxford. He was knighted in 1999 and died in 2003.

What Was Williams's Overall Philosophical Project?

Williams is known, in moral philosophy, as a critic of both utilitarianism and Kantianism. His contribution to the book *Utilitarianism, For and Against*, argued that the utilitarian framework was wrong in its basic approach because (among other faults) it ignored individuals' connections to those nearer to them. His criticism of Kantianism, seen in his article here, is that it purifies ethics of all contingent matters such as your circumstances and the consequences of your actions. The emotional aspects of morality, he argued contrary to Kant, must be integrated into a full understanding of ethics.

In a remembrance of Williams published in the *Boston Review* (Oct/Nov 2003), the influential political philosopher Martha Nussbaum wrote that, according to Williams,

> Utilitarianism and Kantianism ... simplified the moral life in ways that he found egregious, failing to understand, or even actively denying, the heterogeneity of values, the sometimes

tragic collisions between one thing we care for and another. They also underestimated the importance of personal attachments and projects in the ethical life and, in a related way, neglected the valuable role emotions play in good choice.

His work on political theory and on personal identity has also been very important.

For information on Thomas Nagel and his overall project, please see the notes on Nagel's "What Is It Like to Be a Bat?" in Chapter 5.

What Is the Structure of These Readings?

I.

Williams begins his article by mentioning the old philosophical tradition which argues for the central value of internal tranquility immune from contingent "luck"—from how the external world happens to turn out. The more modern correlate of this, he points out, is the Kantian tradition which chooses a life of morally correct action as the most important thing, but equally sees this as independent of luck. For Kantians, a morally good action is one that arises from the right intentions, however its effects turn out. It is Williams's intention in this article, to show that this view is false.

If moral considerations were the most important thing—the only intrinsically important thing—then moral regret would be the most basic form of regret; and if morality was "unconditioned"—independent of worldly eventualities—moral regret should not depend on how things turned out. But Williams claims that the most basic kind of regret we have in fact is partly determined by outside events—things beyond our control. Thus his overall point: this sort of unconditioned morality could not be the only thing of basic importance in our lives.

To demonstrate the "conditioned" nature of basic regret, Williams considers the life of 'Gauguin' (loosely based on the French artist of that name), who left his job, family, and country to live in the South Seas and pursue his painting. Whether he can justify this radical choice to himself, in the long run, can be determined only retrospectively, once he knows how it turns out. He will find it justified (or else regret it), in the profound way that one judges the justifiability of one's own most basic decisions, depending on whether he eventually takes himself to realize what he thought were his gifts as a painter.

Williams distinguishes this sort of justification from, on the one hand, Kantian moral justification, which can be done in advance: it depends supposedly only on the good will and its intentions based on moral principle; it has nothing to do with how one's actions turn out. And he also distinguishes it, on the other hand, from utilitarian moral justification, which would consider whether, all in all, the world as a whole was better off as the result of Gauguin's actions and their consequences. This sort of justification considers merely whether it is better or worse that it happened, not whether the person who did it can consider himself a success or a failure.

This particular kind of regret, Williams argues, is appropriate only when failure is "intrinsic to the project itself." Thus, if Gauguin failed in his plans because of an accidental injury, he would not have been unjustified in his earlier decision, and would not regret it in that way. Williams discusses Anna Karenina's disastrous affair, for which she left her family, as a clearer case of intrinsic failure of a project: in Williams's words, "her hopes were not just negated, but refuted, by what happened."

Williams goes on to distinguish this kind of "agent-regret" from other sorts of regret at bad luck in various ways, including the fact that one can express the former by gestures of reparation to those harmed.

His overall point here is that this sort of action is shown to be justified or unjustified by events out of one's control—by good or bad luck—and that the values expressed here are deep and important; Kant's narrower conception of morality is, he indicates, certainly not what he conceives it to be: the only basic value there is.

II.

Nagel begins his response to Williams by accusing him of sidestepping the question: ignoring *moral* luck altogether, he instead describes cases involving values that have nothing to do with morality, though luck may certainly play a part there. He reminds us that the problem raised by moral luck arises because, on the one hand, there is a plausible general principle that people cannot be assessed, be praised or blamed, because of events beyond their control; but on the other, most of our assessments are in fact based on things not in the agents' control.

Nagel distinguishes several ways in which assessments are "disturbingly subject to luck": those involving *constitutive luck* (the kind of person the agent is—his inclinations, capacities, and temperament); involving *one's circumstances* (the kinds of situation one happens to find oneself in); and involving the *causes and effects* of one's actions.

He says that Williams's cases (involving effects) do not show *moral* luck: the agents' regret is not a matter of moral assessment at all. In moral cases, one can make assessment of actions in advance, for oneself or others, but often this will be a hypothetical judgment, depending on outcome. The truck driver who negligently fails to check his brakes is morally more to blame if he kills a child who runs into the road than if he luckily completes his trip without incident—even though whether a child runs into his path or not is not something within his control.

Nagel, in other words, does admit that our ordinary *moral* judgments do take account of events beyond agents' control; this is problematic. It's clearly irrational to hold someone morally responsible for what he has no control over.

One response to this problem is to "pare down each act to the morally essential core," for example, by judging merely the pure will and intentions of the agent, and ignoring consequences. Similarly, one might ignore "constitutive" differences by paring away the antecedent kind of person the agent is, considering only the person's immediate will. But this shrinks the area of genuine agency "down to an extensionless point": when all external factors are removed, it seems nothing is left.

Nagel then leaves us with what he calls a "paradox"—a problem with no solution. Moral judgment must exclude luck, but this leaves us with a mysterious inner self we have no grasp of. The problem is, it seems, the result of an irreconcilable conflict between the inner view we have of ourselves as responsible agents, and the external view that "forces itself on us when we see how everything we do belongs to a world that we have not created."

Some Useful Background Information

1. The famous passage from Kant in which he presents his view that the only morally relevant thing is a good will which is totally independent of effects, appears in his *Foundations of the Metaphysics of Morals*; selections from this are reprinted and discussed in Chapter 7, below. Here is the passage, from Part I:

> The good will is not good because of what it effects or accomplishes or because of its competence to achieve some intended end; it is good only because of its willing (i.e., it is good in itself).... Even if it should happen that, by a particularly unfortunate fate or by the niggardly provision of a step-motherly nature, this will should be wholly lacking in power to accomplish its purpose, and even if the greatest effort should not avail it to achieve anything of its end, and if there remained only the good will—not as a mere wish, but as the summoning of all means in our power—it would sparkle like a jewel all by itself, as something that had its full worth in itself. Usefulness or fruitlessness can neither diminish nor augment this worth.

2. Nagel remarks on the connection between the issue of moral luck and the long-standing debate about free will and moral responsibility. This issue is discussed in depth in the other readings in this chapter, but we'll here briefly indicate how our current topic hooks up with the free-will debate.

Libertarians hold that one can be morally responsible only for actions that are uncaused; and they believe that the will is capable of uncaused action. Thus they would accept the Kantian view that antecedent events have no causal relevance to morally significant acts of the will; so that category of "moral luck" (Nagel's third) would be empty. Determinists, however, believe that the will, like all other natural phenomena, is caused. Some determinists, as a result, reject moral responsibility altogether—and this corresponds to Nagel's point that the realm of morally relevant action seems to dwindle and disappear from the external viewpoint, as causes (and other things beyond one's control) are discovered. Other determinists are compatibilists, holding that the fact that one's decisions and actions have causes does not imply that one is not morally responsible for them. Nagel mentions the corresponding possibility of compatibilism in the moral-luck debate: one might hold, and Williams actually seems to, that moral responsibility is not compromised by the existence of "moral luck"—factors in the action under consideration that are outside one's power.

Suggestions for Critical Reflection

1. What situation does Williams take to be an example that shows that we have "deep and persistent reasons to be grateful" that morality is not universally respected? What's his reasoning here?

2. Why does Williams think that the sort of justification he's thinking about could not be provided in advance?

3. What is, according to Williams, the wrong sort of question utilitarians would ask about the Gauguin case?

4. What is the difference Williams draws between extrinsic and intrinsic luck? Which one does he think "relates to unjustification"? Explain.

5. What is the difference, for Williams, between the cases of Gauguin and Anna Karenina?

6. Explain what Williams means when he says that "real supremacy of the moral would imply its ubiquity.... If it were to be genuinely unconditioned, there would have to be nothing to condition it." What does he think is wrong with the idea that the moral is thus supreme?

7. Why does Nagel deny that Williams's two examples, Gauguin and Anna Karenina, are cases of *moral* luck?

8. What is the "condition of control" Nagel speaks about? He admits that there are numerous highly plausible counterexamples to this condition. Why does he not conclude that this condition is false? Explain his reasoning in the paragraphs following "What rules out this escape...."

9. Nagel's argument (contra Williams) is that one can give a moral evaluation of one's acts in advance—but a *hypothetical* evaluation. Explain his point.

10. Explain what Nagel means when he says that "The area of genuine agency, and therefore of legitimate judgment, seems to shrink under this scrutiny to an extensionless point." Under what scrutiny? Why does this scrutiny "shrink" these areas?

11. Explain what Nagel means when he says that "The problem arises ... because the self ... is threatened with dissolution by the absorption of its acts and impulses into the class of events." Why does the "acknowledgement that we are parts of the world" leave us with "no one to be"?

Suggestions for Further Reading

Williams's major work including this article and others more or less related is *Moral Luck* (Cambridge University Press, 1981). He has also written a postscript to this article, printed in *Moral Luck*, D. Statman, ed. (State University of New York Press, 1993).

For Nagel's major works, see Suggestions for Further Reading in the introduction to his article in Chapter 5 of this book.

An important anthology of articles on the topic is D. Statman (ed.), *Moral Luck* (State University of New York Press, 1993).

Two excellent online surveys of the problem, each including an extensive bibliography, are: A. Latus, 2001, "Moral Luck," *The Internet Encyclopedia of Philosophy*, J. Feiser (ed.) <http://www.iep.utm.edu/moralluc/> and Dana K. Nelkin, "Moral Luck", *The Stanford Encyclopedia of Philosophy (Fall 2008 Edition)*, Edward N. Zalta (ed.), <http://plato.stanford.edu/archives/fall2008/entries/moral-luck/>.

"Moral Luck"[1]

I—B.A.O. Williams

There has been a strain of philosophical thought which has identified the end of life as happiness, happiness as reflective tranquillity, and tranquillity as the product of self-sufficiency—for what is not in the domain of the self is not in its control, and so is subject to luck and the contingent enemies of tranquillity. The most extreme versions of this outlook in the Western tradition are certain doctrines of classical antiquity; though it is a notable fact about them that while the good man, the sage, was immune to the impact of incident luck, it was a matter of what may be called constitutive luck[2] that one was a sage, or capable of becoming one: for the many and vulgar this was not (on the prevailing view) an available course.

The idea that one's whole life can in some such way be rendered immune to luck has perhaps rarely prevailed since (it did not prevail, for instance, in mainstream Christianity), but its place has been taken by the still powerfully influential idea that there is one basic form of value, moral value, which is immune to luck and—in the crucial term of the idea's most rigorous exponent[3]—"unconditioned". Both the disposition to correct moral judgment, and the objects of such judgment, are on this view free from external contingency, for both are, in their related ways, the product of the unconditioned will. Anything which is the product of happy or unhappy contingency is no proper object of moral assessment, and no proper determinant of it either. Just as in the realm of character it is motive, not style, or powers, or endowment, that counts, so in action, it is not changes actually effected in the world, but intention. With these considerations

---

1   From *Proceedings of the Aristotelian Society, Supplementary Volume.* Volume 50, 1976; pp. 115–135 and pp. 137–151. Reprinted by courtesy of the Editor of the Aristotelian Society: © 1976.

2   This concerns what Nagel calls, below, "the kind of person you are, where this is not just a question of what you deliberately do, but of your inclinations, capacities, and temperament."

3   Immanuel Kant (1724–1804).

there is supposed to disappear even that constitutive luck which the ancient sages were happy to benefit from; the capacity for moral agency is supposedly present to any rational agent whatever, to anyone for whom the question can even present itself. The successful moral life, removed from considerations of birth, lucky upbringing, or indeed of the incomprehensible Grace of a non-Pelagian[4] God, is presented as a career open not merely to the talents, but to a talent which all rational beings necessarily possess in the same degree. Such a conception has an ultimate form of justice at its heart, and that is its allure. Kantianism is only superficially repulsive[5]—despite appearances, it offers an inducement, solace to a sense of the world's unfairness.

Any conception of "moral luck", on this view, is radically incoherent, and the fact that the phrase indeed sounds strange may express a fit, not unexpected, between that view and some of our implicit conceptions of morality. But the view is false. Morality itself cannot be rendered immune to luck: most basically, the dispositions of morality, however far back they are placed in the area of intention and motive, are as "conditioned" as anything else. This, the matter of what I have called "constitutive" luck, I shall leave entirely on one side. But there is a further issue. Even if moral value had been radically unconditioned by luck, it would not have been enough merely to exhibit it as one kind of value among others. Little would be affirmed unless moral values possessed some special,

indeed supreme, kind of dignity or importance: the thought that there is a kind of value which is, unlike others, accessible to all rational agents, offers little encouragement if that kind of value is merely a last resort, the doss-house[6] of the spirit. Rather, it must have a claim on one's most fundamental concerns as a rational agent, and in one's recognition of that, one is supposed to grasp, not only morality's immunity to luck, but one's own partial immunity to luck through morality.

It has notoriously not been easy for Kantianism to make clear what the recognition consists in.[7] But one consequence of it, at least, would be something very widely held: that anyone who is genuinely open to moral considerations must regard moral regret for his actions as the most basic form of regret there is, and (connectedly), in so far as he is rational, will not let his most basic regrets be determined by other than what he was fully responsible for, what lay within his voluntary control. In this way, though his life may be subject to luck, at the most basic level of his self-assessment as a rational agent, he will not be.

It is in this area of regret, justification, and the retrospective view of one's own actions, that I shall raise my questions. Some views of regret which I shall

---

4   Pelagianism, an early version of Christianity based on the thought of the (possibly British) monk Pelagius (354–c. 420), taught that humans were completely free to do good or evil, and were completely responsible for their own actions and salvation. The mainstream church had this view declared heretical, believing instead that humans were evil by nature, because of original sin, and could achieve goodness and salvation only through the unearned grace of God.

5   Williams does, however, find Kant's view repulsive (if only superficially) in the sense that it repels rather than attracts, due to its insistence that the only source for morality is abstract duty, and that desires other than to do one's duty are irrelevant, as are considerations of the values of happiness or pleasure.

6   A very cheap boarding-house, or a shelter provided by a municipality or charity—minimal accommodation for those who can get nothing better.

7   [Author's note] The question centres on the rôle of the Categorical Imperative. On the major issue here, I agree with what I take to be the substance of Philippa Foot's position ("Morality as a System of Hypothetical Imperatives", *Phil. Rev.* 1972; and her reply to Frankena, *Philosophy* 1975), but not at all with her way of putting it. In so far as there is a clear distinction between categorical and hypothetical imperatives, and in so far as morality consists of imperatives, it consists of categorical imperatives. The point is that the fact that an imperative is (in this sense) categorical provides no reason at all for obeying it. Nor need Kant think it does: the authority of the Categorical Imperative is supposed (mysteriously enough) to derive not just from its being (in this sense) categorical, but from its being categorical and self-addressed by the agent as a rational being.

question (roughly that the most profound aspects of first-personal[8] regret must attach to voluntary actions) are implied by this conception of morality, but may well not imply it, or indeed any specific view of morality, as opposed to certain conceptions of rationality. In so far as that is so, the discussion will have broader implications for the self's exposure to luck, though the examples centrally in question do essentially involve considerations of morality.

I shall use the notion of "luck" generously, undefinedly, but, I think, comprehensibly. (I hope it will be clear that when I say of something that it is a matter of luck, this is not meant to carry any implication that it is uncaused.) My procedure in general will be to invite reflection about how to think and feel about some rather less usual situations, in the light of an appeal to how we—many people—tend to think and feel about other more usual situations, not in terms of substantive moral opinions or "intuitions" but in terms of the experience of those kinds of situation. There is no suggestion that it is impossible for human beings to lack these feelings and experiences. In the case of the less usual there is only the claim that the thoughts and experiences I consider are possible, coherent, and intelligible, and that there is no ground for condemning them as irrational. In the case of the more usual, there are suggestions, with the outline of a reason for them, that unless we were to be merely confused or unreflective, life without these experiences would involve a much vaster reconstruction of our sentiments and our views of ourselves than may be supposed: supposed, in particular, by those philosophers who discuss these matters as though our experience of our own agency and the sense of our regrets not only could be tidied up to accord with a very simple image of rationality, but already had been.

Let us take first an outline example of the creative artist who turns away from definite and pressing human claims on him in order to live a life in which, as he supposes, he can pursue his art. Without feeling that we are limited by any historical facts, let us call

him *Gauguin*.[9] Gauguin might have been a man who was not at all interested in the claims on him, and simply preferred to live another life, and from that life, and perhaps from that preference, his best paintings came. That sort of case, in which the claims of others simply have no hold on the agent, is not what concerns us now: though it serves to remind us of something related to the present concerns, that while we are sometimes guided by the notion that it would be the best of worlds in which morality were universally respected and all men were of a disposition to affirm it, we have in fact deep and persistent reasons to be grateful that that is not the world we have.

We are interested here in a narrower phenomenon, more intimate to moral thought itself. Let us take, rather, a Gauguin who is concerned about these claims and what is involved in their being neglected (we may suppose this to be grim), and that he nevertheless, in the face of that, opts for the other life. This other life he might perhaps not see very determinately under the category of realising his gifts as a painter: but to make consideration simpler, let us add that he does see it determinately in that light—it is as a life which will enable him really to be a painter that he opts for it. It will then be more clear what will count for him as eventual success in his project: at least some possible outcomes will be clear examples of success (which of course is not meant to be equivalent to recognition), however many others may be unclear.

Whether he will succeed cannot, in the nature of the case, be foreseen; we are not dealing here with the removal of an external obstacle to something which, once that is removed, will fairly predictably go through. Gauguin, in our story, is putting a great deal on a possibility which has not unequivocally declared itself. I want to explore and uphold the claim that it is possible that in such a situation the only thing that will justify his choice will be success itself. If he fails—and we shall come shortly to what, more precisely, failure may be—then he did the wrong thing,

---

8   The "first person" in grammar is the person speaking—"I." So first-personal regret is regret about one's own actions, not about someone else's.

9   Williams's choice of this name for his hypothetical agent is an allusion to the French post-impressionist painter Paul Gauguin (1848–1903), who left his wife and family, and job as a stockbroker, to live among the natives in tropical islands and paint.

not just in the sense in which that platitudinously follows, but in the sense that having done the wrong thing in those circumstances he has no basis for the thought that he was justified in acting as he did; while if he succeeds, he does have a basis for that thought. This notion of justification, which I shall try to make clearer, is not one by which, if he succeeds, he will necessarily be able to justify himself *to others*. The reproaches of others he may never have an answer to, in the sense of having a right that they accept or even listen to what he has to say; but if he fails, he will not even have anything to say.

The justification, if there is to be one, will be essentially retrospective. Gauguin could not do something which is often thought to be essential to rationality and to the notion of justification itself, which is to apply the justifying considerations at the time of the choice and in advance of knowing whether one was right (in the sense of its coming out right). How this can be in general, will form a major part of the discussion. First, however, we should consider a more limited question, whether there could be a moral justification in advance. A moral theorist, recognizing that some value attached to the success of Gauguin's project and hence possibly to his choice, might try to accommodate that choice within a framework of moral rules, by forming a subsidiary rule which could, before the outcome, justify that choice. What could that rule be? It could not be that one is morally justified in deciding to neglect other claims if one is a great creative artist: apart from basic doubts about its moral content, that saving clause begs the question which at the relevant time one is in no position to answer. On the other hand, ".... if one is convinced that one is a great creative artist" will serve to make obstinacy and fatuous self-delusion conditions of justification; while "... if one is reasonably convinced that one is a great creative artist" is, if anything, worse. What is reasonable conviction supposed to be in such a case? Should Gauguin consult professors of art? The absurdity of such riders surely expresses an absurdity in the whole enterprise of trying to find a place for such cases within the rules.

If there cannot be a moral justification which is accessible in advance, then, according to the conception of morality which purges it of luck, there cannot

be a moral justification at all. Whether there could in *any* sense be a moral justification of the Gauguin-type decision is not a question I shall try to resolve here. There are other issues that need discussion first, and I suspect that when they have been discussed, that will turn out to be a question of diminishing interest. But there is one point that needs to be mentioned. One consequence of finding a moral justification (a motive, perhaps for trying to find one) might be thought to be that those who suffer from the decision would then have no justified, or at least correct, ground of reproach. There is no reason to think that we want that result. But there is also no obvious reason to think that it would be a consequence: one needs some very strong assumption about the nature of ethical consistency in order to deliver it.

Utilitarian formulations are not going to contribute any more to understanding these situations than do formulations in terms of rules. They can offer the thought "it is better (worse) that he did it", where the force of that is, approximately, "it is better (worse) that it happened", but this in itself does not help to a characterization of the agent's decision or its possible justification, and Utilitarianism has no special materials of its own to help in that. It has its own well-known problems, too, in spelling out the content of the "better"—on standard doctrine, Gauguin's decision would seem to have been a better thing, the more popular a painter he eventually became. But more interesting than that class of difficulty is the point that the Utilitarian perspective, not uniquely but clearly, will fail to attach importance to something which is actually important for these thoughts, the question of what "failure" may relevantly be. From the perspective of consequences, the goods or benefits for the sake of which Gauguin's choice was made either materialize in some degree, or do not materialize. But it matters considerably to the thoughts we are considering, in what way the project fails to come off, if it fails. If Gauguin sustains some injury on the way to Tahiti which prevents his ever painting again, that certainly means that his decision (supposing it now to be irreversible) was for nothing, and indeed there is nothing in the outcome to set against the other people's loss. But that train of events does not provoke the thought in question, that after all he was wrong and unjustified: he does not, and never will, know whether he was wrong. What would prove him wrong in his project would not just be that it failed, but that he failed.

This distinction shows that while Gauguin's justification is in some ways a matter of luck, it is not equally a matter of all kinds of luck. It matters how intrinsic the cause of failure is to the project itself. The occurrence of an injury is, relative to these undertakings at least, luck of the most external and incident kind. Irreducibly, luck of this kind affects whether he will be justified or not, since if it strikes, he will not be justified. But it is too external for it to unjustify him, something which only his failure as a painter can do: yet still that is, at another level, luck, the luck of being able to be as he hoped he might be. It might be wondered whether that is luck at all, or, if so, whether it may not be luck of that constitutive kind which affects everything and which we have already left on one side. But it is more than that. It is not merely luck that he is such a man, but luck relative to the deliberations that went into his decision, that he turns out to be such a man: he might (epistemically) not have been.[10] That is what sets the problem.

In some cases, though perhaps not in Gauguin's, success in such decisions might be thought not to be a matter of epistemic luck relative to the decision: there might be grounds for saying that the person who was prepared to take the decision, and was in fact right, actually knew that he would succeed, however subjectively uncertain he may have been. But even if this is right for some cases, it does not help with the problems of retrospective justification. For the concept of knowledge here is itself applied restrospectively, and while there is nothing necessarily wrong with that, it does not enable the agent at the time of his decision to make any distinctions he could not already make. As one might say, even if it did turn out in such a case that the agent did know, it was still luck, relative to the considerations available to him at the time and at the level at which he made his decision, that he should turn out to have known.

Some luck, in a decision of Gauguin's kind, is extrinsic to his project, some intrinsic; both are necessary for success, and hence for actual justification, but only the latter relates to unjustification. If we now broaden the range of cases slightly, we shall be able to see more clearly the notion of intrinsic luck. In Gauguin's case the nature of the project is such that two distinctions do, roughly, coincide: the distinction between luck intrinsic to the project, and luck extrinsic to it, and another distinction between what is, and what is not, determined by him and by what he is. The intrinsic luck in Gauguin's case concentrates itself on virtually the one question of whether he is a genuinely gifted painter who can succeed in doing genuinely valuable work. Not all the conditions of the project's coming off lie in him, obviously, since others' actions and refrainings provide many necessary conditions of its coming off—and that is an important locus of extrinsic luck. But the conditions of its coming off which are relevant to unjustification, the locus of intrinsic luck, largely lie in him—which is not to say, of course, that they depend on his will, though some may. This rough coincidence of two distinctions is a feature of this case. But in others, the locus of intrinsic luck (intrinsic, that is to say, to the project) may lie partly outside the agent, and this is an important, and indeed the more typical, case.

Consider an almost equally schematized account of another example, that of Anna Karenina.[11] Anna remains conscious in her life with Vronsky of the cost exacted from others, above all her son. She could have lived with that consciousness, we may suppose, if things had gone better; and relative to her state of understanding when she left Karenin, they could have gone better. As it turns out, the social situation and her own state of mind are such that the relationship with Vronsky has to carry too much weight, and the more obvious that becomes, the more it has to carry; and that I take that to be a truth not only about society

---

10 That is, given what we currently know, he might not have been. A claim is epistemically possible if it may be true, for all we know.

11 She is the central character in the great 1878 novel bearing her name, by the Russian author Leo Tolstoy (1828–1910). The moral and psychological depth of this novel is of course not done justice by this plot summary: Anna abandons a loveless marriage for a doomed affair with the handsome Count Vronsky.

but about her and Vronsky, a truth which, however inevitable Tolstoy ultimately makes it seem, could, relative to her earlier thoughts, have been otherwise. It is, in the present terms, a matter of intrinsic luck, and a failure in the heart of her project. But its locus is not by any means entirely in her, for it also lies in him.

It would have been an intrinsic failure, also, if Vronsky had actually committed suicide. But it would not have been that, but rather an extrinsic misfortune, if Vronsky had been accidentally killed: though her project would have been at an end, it would not have failed as it does fail. This difference illustrates precisely the thoughts we are concerned with. For if Anna had then committed suicide, her thought might essentially have been something like: "there is nothing more for me". But I take it that as things are, her thought in killing herself is not just that, but relates inescapably also to the past and to what she has done. What she did she now finds insupportable, because she could have been justified only by the life she hoped for, and those hopes were not just negated, but refuted, by what happened.

It is these thoughts that I want to explore and to place in a structure which will make their sense plainer. The discussion is not in the first place directed to what we or others might say or think of these agents (though it has implications for that), but on what they can be expected coherently to think about themselves. A notion we shall be bound to use in describing their state of mind is *regret*, and there are certain things that need, first, to be said about this notion.

The constitutive thought of regret in general is something like "how much better if it had been otherwise", and the feeling can in principle apply to anything of which one can form some conception of how it might have been otherwise, together with consciousness of how things would then have been better. In this general sense of regret, what are regretted are states of affairs, and they can be regretted, in principle, by anyone who knows of them. But there is a particularly important species of regret, which I shall call "agent-regret", which a person can feel only towards his own past actions (or, at most, actions in which he regards himself as a participant). In this case, the supposed possible difference is that one might have acted otherwise, and the focus of the regret is

on that possibility, the thought being formed in part by first-personal conceptions of how one might have acted otherwise. "Agent-regret" is not distinguished from regret in general solely or simply in virtue of its subject-matter. There can be cases of regret directed to one's own past actions which are not cases of agent-regret, because the past action is regarded purely externally, as one might regard anyone else's action. Agent-regret requires not merely a first-personal subject-matter, nor yet merely a particular kind of psychological content, but also a particular kind of expression, something which I hope will become a little clearer in what follows.

The sentiment of agent-regret is by no means restricted to *voluntary* agency. It can extend far beyond what one intentionally did to almost anything for which one was causally responsible in virtue of something one intentionally did. Yet even at deeply accidental or non-voluntary levels of agency, sentiments of agent-regret are different from regret in general, such as might be felt by a spectator, and are acknowledged in our practice as being different. The lorry driver[12] who, through no fault of his, runs over a child, will feel differently from any spectator, even a spectator next to him in the cab, except perhaps to the extent that the spectator takes on the thought that he might have prevented it, an agent's thought. Doubtless, and rightly, people will try, in comforting him, to move the driver from this state of feeling, move him indeed from where he is to something more like the place of a spectator; but it is important that this is seen as something that should need to be done, and indeed some doubt would be felt about a driver who too blandly or readily moved to that position. We feel sorry for the driver, but that sentiment co-exists with, indeed presupposes, that there is something special about his relation to this happening, something which cannot merely be eliminated by the consideration that it was not his fault. It may be still more so in cases where agency is fuller than in such an accident, though still involuntary through ignorance.

The differences between agent-regret and any felt by a spectator come out not just in thoughts and im-

---

12   British for truck driver.

ages that enter into the sentiment, but in differences of expression. The lorry driver may act in some way which he hopes will constitute or at least symbolise some kind of recompense or restitution, and this will be an expression of his agent-regret. But the willingness to give compensation, even the recognition that one should give it, does not necessarily express agent-regret, and the preparedness to compensate can present itself at very different levels of significance in these connexions. We may recognize the need to pay compensation for damage we involuntarily cause, and yet this recognition be of an external kind, accompanied only by regret of a general kind, or by no regret at all. The general structure of these situations may merely be that it would be unfair for the sufferer to bear the cost if there is an alternative, and there is an alternative to be found in the agent whose intentional activities produced the damage as a side-effect. This area of compensation can be seen as part of the general regulation of boundary effects between agents' activities.

In such cases, the relevant consciousness of having done the harmful thing is basically that of its having happened as a consequence of one's acts, together with the thought that the cost of its happening can in the circumstances fairly be allocated to one's account. A test of whether that is an agent's state of mind in acknowledging that he should compensate is offered by the question whether from his point of view insurance cover would do at least as well. Imagine the premiums already paid (by someone else, we might add, if that helps to clarify the test): then if knowledge that the victim received insurance payments would settle any unease the agent feels, then it is for him an external case. It is an obvious and welcome consequence of this test that whether an agent can acceptably regard a given case externally is a function not only of his relations to it, but of what sort of case it is—besides the question of whether he should compensate rather than the insurance company, there is the question whether it is the sort of loss that can be compensated at all by insurance. If it is not, an agent conscious that he was unintentionally responsible for it might still feel that he should do something, not necessarily because he could actually compensate where insurance money could not, but because (if he is lucky) his actions might have some reparative significance other than compensation.

In other cases, again, there is no room for any appropriate action at all. Then only the desire to make reparation remains, with the painful consciousness that nothing can be done about it; some other action, perhaps less directed to the victims, may come to express this. What degree of such feeling is appropriate, and what attempts at reparative action or substitutes for it, are questions for particular cases, and that there is room in the area for irrational and self-punitive excess, no one is likely to deny. But equally it would be a kind of insanity never to experience sentiments of this kind towards anyone, and it would be an insane concept of rationality which insisted that a rational person never would. To insist on such a conception of rationality, moreover, would, apart from other kinds of absurdity, suggest a large falsehood: that we might, if we conducted ourselves clear-headedly enough, entirely detach ourselves from the unintentional aspects of our actions, relegating their costs to, so to speak, the insurance fund, and yet still retain our identity and character as agents. One's history as an agent is a web in which anything that is the product of the will is surrounded and held up and partly formed by things that are not, in such a way that reflection can go only in one of two directions: either in the direction of saying that responsible agency is a fairly superficial concept, which has a limited use in harmonizing what happens, or else that it is not a superficial concept, but that it cannot ultimately be purified—if one attaches importance to the sense of what one is in terms of what one has done and what in the world one is responsible for, one must accept much that makes its claim on that sense solely in virtue of its being actual.[13]

---

13   [Author's note] That acceptance is central to tragedy, something which presses the question of how we want to think about these things. When Oedipus says "I did not do it" (Sophocles *OC* 539) he speaks as one whose exile proclaims that he did do it, and to persons who treat him as quite special because he did. Could we have, and do we want, a concept of agency by which what Oedipus said would be simply true, and by which he would be seeing things rightly if for him it

The cases we are concerned with are, of course, cases of voluntary agency, but they share something with the involuntary cases just mentioned, for the "luck" of the agents relates to those elements which are essential to the outcome but lie outside their control, and what we are discussing is in this way a very drastic example of determination by the actual, the determination of the agent's judgment on his decision by what, beyond his will, actually occurs. Besides that, the discussion of agent-regret about the involuntary also helps us to get away from a dichotomy which is often relied on in these matters, expressed in such terms as *regret* and *remorse*, where "regret" is identified in effect as the regret of a spectator, while "remorse" is what we have called "agent-regret", but under the restriction that it applies only to the voluntary. The fact that we have agent-regret about the involuntary, and would not readily recognize a life without it (though we may think we might), shows already that there is something wrong with this dichotomy: such regret is neither mere spectator's regret, nor (by this definition) remorse.

There is a difference between agent-regret as we have so far discussed it, and the agents' feelings in the present cases. As we elicited it from the non-voluntary examples, agent-regret involved a wish on the agent's part that he had not done it: he deeply wishes that he had made that change which, had he known it, was in his power and which would have altered the outcome. But Gauguin or Anna Karenina, as we have represented them, wish they had acted otherwise only if they are unsuccessful. (At least, that wish attends their unsuccess under the simplifying assumption that their subsequent thoughts and feelings are still essentially formed by the projects we have ascribed to them. This is an oversimplification, since evidently they might form new projects in the course of unsuccess itself; though Anna did not. I shall sustain the assumption in what follows.) Whatever feelings these agents had after their decision, but before the declaration of their success or failure, lacked the fully-developed wish to

have acted otherwise—that wish comes only when failure is declared.

Regret necessarily involves a wish that things had been otherwise, for instance that one had not had to act as one did. But it does not necessarily involve the wish, all things taken together, that one had acted otherwise. An example of this, largely independent of the present issues, is offered by the cases of conflict between two courses of action each of which is morally required, where either course of action, even if it is judged to be for the best, leaves regrets—which are, in our present terms, agent-regrets about something voluntarily done.[14] We should not entirely assimilate agent-regret and the wish, all things taken together, to have acted otherwise. We must now look at some connexions of these to each other, and to certain ideas of justification. This will add the last element to our attempt to characterize our cases.

It will be helpful to contrast our cases with more straightforward cases of practical deliberation and the types of retrospective reflexion appropriate to them. We may take first the simplest cases of pure egoistic deliberation, where not only is the agent's attention confined to egoistic projects, but moral critics would agree that it is legitimately so confined. Here, in one sense the agent does not have to justify his deliberative processes, since there is no one he is answerable to; but it is usually supposed that there is some sense in which even such an agent's deliberative processes can be justified or unjustified—the sense, that is, in which his decision can be reasonable or unreasonable relative to his situation, whatever its actual outcome. Considerations bearing on this include at least the consistency of his thoughts, the rational assessment of probabilities, and the optimal ordering of actions in time.[15]

While the language of justification is used in this connexion, it is less clear than is usually assumed what its content is, and, in particular, what the point

---

was straight off as though he had no part in it? (These questions have little to do with how the law should be: punishment and public amends are a different matter.)

14   [Author's note] For some discussion of this see "Ethical Consistency", in *Problems of the Self* (Cambridge 1973), pp. 166–186.

15   [Author's note] A useful outline of such considerations is in D.A.J. Richards, *A Theory of Reasons for Action* (Oxford 1971), ch. 3.

is of an agent's being retrospectively concerned with the rationality of his decision, and not just with its success. How are we to understand the retrospective thought of one who comes to see a mismatch between his deliberations and the outcome? If he deliberates badly, and as a result of this his projects go wrong, it is easy to see *in that case* how his regret at the outcome appropriately attaches itself to his deliberations. But if he deliberates well, and things go wrong; particularly if, as sometimes happens, they would have gone better if he had deliberated worse; what is the consciousness that he was "justified" supposed to do for the disposition of his undoubted regret about how things actually turned out? His thought that he was justified seems to carry with it something like this: while he is sorry that things turned out as they did, and, in a sense corresponding to that, he wishes he had acted otherwise, at the same time he does not wish he had acted otherwise, for he stands by the processes of rational deliberation which led to what he did. Similarly with the converse phenomenon, where having made and too late discovered some mistake of deliberation, the agent is by luck successful, and indeed would have been less successful if he had done anything else. Here his gladness that he acted as he did (his lack of a wish to have acted otherwise) operates at a level at which it is compatible with such feelings as self-reproach or retrospective alarm at having acted as he did.

These observations are truisms, but it remains obscure what their real content is. Little is effected by talk of self-reproach or regret at all, still less of co-existent regret and contentment, unless some expression, at least, of such sentiments can be identified. Certainly it is not to be identified in this case with any disposition to compensate other persons, for none is affected. Connected with that, criticism by other persons would be on a different basis from criticism offered where they had a grievance, as in a case where an agent risks goods of which he is a trustee, through deliberative error or (interestingly) merely through the choice of a high-risk strategy to which he would be perfectly entitled if he were acting solely in his own interests. The trustee is not entitled to gamble with the infants' money even if any profits will certainly go to the infants, and success itself will not remove, or start

to remove, that objection. That sort of criticism is of course not appropriate in the purely egoistic case; and in fact there is no reason to think that criticism by others is more than a consequential consideration in the egoistic case, derived from others' recommendation of the virtues of rational prudence, which need to be explained first.

Granted that there is no issue of compensation to others in the purely egoistic case, the form of expression of regret seems necessarily to be, as Richards has said,[16] the agent's resolutions for his future deliberations. Regrets about his deliberations express themselves as resolves, at least, to think better next time; satisfaction with the deliberation, however disappointing the particular outcome, expresses itself in this, that he finds nothing to be *learned* from the case, and is sure that he will have no better chance of success (at a given level of payoff) next time by changing his procedures. If this is right, then the notions of regret or lack of regret at the past level of deliberative excellence make sense only in the context of a policy or disposition of rational deliberation applied to an on-going class of cases.

This is a modest enough conception—it is important to see how modest it is. It implies a class of cases sufficiently similar for deliberative practices to be translated from one to another of them; it does not imply that these cases are all conjointly the subject of deliberative reasoning. I may make a reasoned choice between alternatives of a certain kind today, and, having seen how it turns out, resolve to deal rather differently with the next choice of that kind; but I need not either engage in or resolve to engage in any deliberative reasoning which weighs the options of more than one such occasion together.[17]

---

16 [Author's note] *Op. cit.* pp. 70–71, and *cf.* ch. 13.

17 [Author's note] The notion of treating cases together, as opposed to treating them separately but in the light of experience, applies not only to deliberation which yields in advance a conjunctive resolution of a number of cases, but also to deliberation which yields hypothetical conclusions to the effect that a later case will receive a certain treatment if an earlier case turns out in a certain way: as in a staking system.

In so far as the outcomes of different such situations affect one another, there is indeed pressure to say that rational deliberation should in principle consider them together. But, further, if one knew enough, any choice would be seen to affect all later ones; so it has seemed to some that the ideal limit of this process is something which is a far more ambitious extension of the modest notion of an ongoing disposition to rational deliberation: this is the model of rational deliberation as directed to a *life-plan*, in Rawls' sense, which treats all times of one's life as of equal concern to one.[18] The theorists of this picture agree that as a matter of fact ignorance and other factors do usually make it rational to discount over remoteness in time,[19] but these are subsequent considerations brought to a model which is that of one's life as a rectangle, so to speak, presented all at once and to be optimally filled in. This model is presented not only as embodying the ideal fulfilment of a rational urge to harmonize all one's projects. It is also supposed to provide a special grounding for the idea that a more fundamental form of regret is directed to deliberative error than to mere mistake. The regret takes the form of self-reproach, and the idea is that we protect ourselves against reproaches from our future self if we act with deliberative rationality: "nothing can protect us from the ambiguities and limitations of our knowledge, or guarantee that we find the best alternative open to us. Acting with deliberative rationality can only ensure that our conduct is above reproach, and that we are responsible to ourselves as one person over time."[20] These strains come together in Rawls' advocacy of "... the guiding principle that a rational individual is always to act so that he need never blame himself no matter how things finally transpire."[21]

Rawls seems to regard this injunction as, in a sense, formal, and as not determining how risky or conservative a strategy the agent should adopt; but it is worth remarking that if any grounding for self-reproach about deliberative error is to be found in the notion of the recriminations of one's later self, the injunction will in fact have to be taken in a more materially cautious sense. For the grounding relies on an analogy with the responsibility to other persons: I am a trustee for my own future. If this has any force at all, it is hard to see why it does not extend to my being required, like any other trustee, to adopt a cautious strategy with the entrusted goods—which are, in this case, almost everything I have.

However that may be, the model that gives rise to the injunction is false. Apart from other difficulties,[22] it implicitly ignores the obvious fact that what one does and the sort of life one leads condition one's later desires and judgments: the standpoint of that retrospective judge who will be my later self will be the product of my earlier choices. So there is no set of preferences both fixed and relevant, relative to which the various fillings of my life-space can be compared; if the fillings are to be evaluated by reference to what I variously, in them, want, the relevant preferences are not fixed, while if they are to be evaluated by what I now (for instance) want, this will give a fixed set of preferences, but one which is not necessarily relevant. The recourse from this within the life-space model is to assume (as Utilitarianism does) that there is some currency of satisfactions, in terms of which it is possible to compare quite neutrally the value of one set of preferences together with their fulfilments, as against a quite different set of preferences together with their fulfilments. But there is no reason to suppose that there is any such currency, nor (still less) that the idea of practical rationality should implicitly presuppose it.

If there is no such currency, then we can only to a limited extent abstract from the projects and preferences we actually have, and cannot in principle gain a standpoint from which the alternative fillings of our life-rectangle could be compared without prejudice. The perspective of deliberative choice on one's life

---

18   [Author's note] John Rawls, *A Theory of Justice* (Oxford, 1972), esp. ch VII; Thomas Nagel, *The Possibility of Altruism* (Oxford, 1970).

19   That is, to treat events or situations further away in time as less important than those closer in time.

20   [Author's note] Rawls, pp. 422–423.

21   [Author's note] p. 422.

22   [Author's note] It ignores also the very basic fact that the size of the rectangle is up to me: I have said something about this in "Persons, Character and Morality", in Amélie Rorty, ed., *The Identity of Persons*, (California UP, forthcoming).

is constitutively *from here*. Correspondingly the perspective of assessment with greater knowledge is necessarily *from there*, and not only can I not guarantee how factually it will then be, but I cannot ultimately guarantee from what standpoint of assessment my major and most fundamental regrets will be.

For many decisions which are part of the agent's ongoing activity (the "normal science",[23] so to speak, of the moral life) we can see why it is that the presence or absence of regrets is more basically conditioned by the retrospective view of the deliberative processes, than by the particular outcomes. Oneself and one's viewpoint are more basically identified with the dispositions of rational deliberation, applicable to an ongoing series of decisions, than they are with the particular projects which succeed or fail on those occasions. But there are certain other decisions, as on the cases we are considering, which are not like this. There is indeed some room for the presence and subsequent assessment of deliberative rationality: the agents in our cases might well not be taken as seriously as they would otherwise if they did not, to the limited extent which the situation permits, take as rational thought as they can about the realities of their situation. But this is not the aspect under which they will primarily look back on it, nor is it as a contribution to a series of deliberative situations that it will have its importance for them; though they will learn from it, it will not be in that way. In these cases, the project in the interests of which the decision is made is one with which the agent is identified in such a way that if it succeeds, his standpoint of assessment will be from a life which then derives an important part of its significance for him from that very fact; while if he fails, it can, necessarily, have no such significance in his life. If he succeeds, it cannot be that while welcoming the outcome he more basically regrets the decision; while if he fails, his standpoint

---

23   This term was brought into philosophical currency by Thomas Kuhn, in his book, *The Structure of Scientific Revolutions*. He uses it to describe the sort of science carried on within stable accepted "paradigms" for basic theory and procedures, without attempt to challenge these underlying assumptions. Scientific revolution challenges and replaces them.

will be of one for whom the ground project of the decision has proved worthless, and this (under the simplifying assumption that other adequate projects are not generated in the process) must leave him with the most basic regrets. So if he fails, his most basic regrets will attach to his decision, and if he succeeds, they cannot. That is the sense in which his decision can be justified, for him, by success.

On this account, it is clear that the type of decisions we are concerned with is not merely very risky ones, or even very risky ones with a substantial outcome. The outcome has to be substantial in a special way—in a way which importantly conditions the agent's sense of what is significant in his life, and hence his standpoint of retrospective assessment. It follows from this that they are, indeed, risky, and in a way which helps to explain the importance for such projects of the difference between extrinsic and intrinsic failure. With an intrinsic failure, the project which generated the decision is revealed as an empty thing, incapable of grounding the agent's life. With extrinsic failure, it is not so revealed, and while he must acknowledge that it has failed, nevertheless it has not been discredited, and may, perhaps in the form of some new aspiration, contribute to making sense of what is left. In his retrospective thought, and its allocation of basic regret, he cannot in the fullest sense identify with his decision, and so does not find himself justified; but he is not totally alienated from it either, cannot just see it as a disastrous error, and so does not find himself unjustified.

This structure of retrospective understanding can occur without the concern introduced by the interests of others, which is central to our cases; but that concern is likely to be present in such decisions, and certainly it contributes importantly to their nature when it is present. The risks taken by our agents are taken in part with others' goods. The risks are taken also with their own, which increases our respect for them. But for themselves, they have a chance of winning, while the others do not; worse off than those served by the gambling trustee, the others' loss is settled from the start. There is no ground, whatever happens, for demanding that they drop their resentment. If they are eventually going to feel better towards him, it will not be through having received an answer to their complaints—nor, far from it, need it be because the agent is successful. They are not recompensed by the agent's success—or only if they are prepared to be.

But what about the rest of us? Here, for the first time, it is worth mentioning a difference between our cases, that if Gauguin's project succeeds, it could yield a good for the world as Anna's success could not. There is no reason why those who suffer from Gauguin's decision should be impressed by this fact, and there are several reasons (one of which we touched on earlier, in the matter of moral justification) why Gauguin should not. Nor should we be overimpressed by the difference, in considering what can be learned from such cases. But eventually the spectator has to consider the fact that he has reason to be glad that Gauguin succeeded, and hence that he tried. At the very least, this may stand as an emblem for cases in which we are glad. Perhaps fewer of us than is pretended care about the existence of Gauguin's paintings, but we are supposed to care, which gives an opportunity for reflection to start out and work towards the cases where we really care, where we salute the project. The fact is that if we believe in any other values at all, then it is likely that at some point we shall have reason to be glad that moral values (taken here in the simple sense of a concern for others' rights and interests) have been treated as one value among others, and not as unquestionably supreme. Real supremacy of the moral would imply its ubiquity. Like Spinoza's substance, if it were to be genuinely unconditioned,[24] there would have to be nothing to condition it.

There is a public dimension of appreciation for such cases: how Gauguin stands with us (taking him emblematically as one whose project is saluted); whether we are, taking it all together, glad that he did it; depends on his success. That question, moreover, whether we are, taking it all together, glad, is the question we should take seriously. The various dichotomies which can be brought in to break up that question—such as moral v. non-moral, or agent v. act, or act v. outcome—often only help to evade the basic and connected questions of what one really wants the world to be like and what human dispositions are involved in its being like that.

These questions for the spectator we will leave; they would arise, as we noticed at the beginning, even if the agent had no concern for others' interests at all. But assuming (as we have throughout) that he has such a concern, then for him success makes a special kind of difference. It runs against the widely held view mentioned before, that moral regret is ultimate, and ultimate regret is immune to luck. If he fails, above all if he intrinsically fails, nothing is left except the cost to others for which (we are supposing) he in any case feels regret. In success, it must be dishonest or confused of him to regard that regret as his most basic feeling about the situation; if it were, he would at the most basic level wish that he had acted otherwise. In failure, that regret can consistently be part of his most basic feelings about what he has done. This is one way—only one of many—in which an agent's moral view of his life can depend on luck.

II—T. Nagel

Williams sidesteps the fascinating question raised in his paper.[25] He does not defend the possibility of moral luck against Kantian doubts, but instead redescribes the case which seems to be his strongest candidate in terms which have nothing to do with moral judgment. Gauguin's talent as a painter may be a matter of luck, but it does not, according to Williams, warrant the retrospective judgment that his desertion of his family is morally acceptable. In fact, it does not warrant any judgment about his prior decision that pretends to objective validity for everyone, or even to timeless validity for him. According to Williams, the effect of the fortunate outcome on Gauguin's attitude to his earlier choice will be merely to make him not regret, at the most basic level, having made it. He will not regret it because it has resulted in a success which

---

24   What is unconditioned is without limits or restrictions from, or influenced or brought about by, anything else. Spinoza argues that since unconditioned substance must be infinite, include all attributes, etc., it (= God) must encompass everything: there *can't be* anything else.

25   [Author's note] "Moral Luck", *Aristotelian Society Supplementary Volume* 1976.

forms the centre of his life. This attitude can hardly be called a judgment at all, let alone a moral judgment. Williams says Gauguin cannot use it to justify himself to others. It does not even imply the truth of an hypothetical judgment made in advance, of the form "If I leave my family and become a great painter, I will be justified by success; if I don't become a great painter, the act will be unforgivable." And if the rest of us are glad that Gauguin left his family, Williams says that this is because we do not always give priority to moral values.

The importance of luck in human life is no surprise, even in respect of those matters about which we feel most deeply glad or regretful. It is the place of luck in ethics that is puzzling. Williams misdescribes his result in the closing paragraph of the paper: he has argued not that an agent's moral view of his life can depend on luck but that ultimate regret is not immune to luck because ultimate regret need not be moral. This is consonant with his tendency, here and in other recent writings,[26] to reject the impersonal claims of morality in favour of more personal desires and projects. Even if Williams has successfully explained away the appearance of moral luck in the case of Gauguin, however, the explanation applies only to a narrow range of phenomena and leaves most of the area untouched. Williams acknowledges that he has dealt with only one type of case, but I do not believe these cases can be treated in isolation from the larger problem.

Why is there a problem? Not because morality seems too basic to be subject to luck. Some very important non-moral assessments of people deal with what is not their fault. We deplore madness or leprosy in ourselves and others, we rejoice in beauty or talent, but these, though very basic, are not moral judgments. If we ask ourselves why, the natural explanation is that these attributes are not the responsibility of their possessors, they are merely good or back luck. Prior to reflection it is intuitively plausible that people cannot be morally assessed for what is not their fault, or

for what is due to factors beyond their control. This proposition uses an unanalysed concept of moral assessment that is presumably logically independent of the idea of control—otherwise the problem could not arise. Such a judgment is different from the evaluation of something as a good or bad thing, or state of affairs. The latter may be present in addition to moral judgment, but when we blame someone for his actions we are not merely saying it is bad that they happened, or bad that he exists: we are judging *him*, saying he is bad, which is different from his being a bad thing. This kind of judgment takes only a certain kind of object. Without being able to explain exactly why, we feel that the appropriateness of moral assessment is easily undermined by the discovery that the act or attribute, no matter how good or bad, is not under the person's control. While other evaluations remain, this one seems to lose its footing.

However, if the condition of control is consistently applied, it threatens to erode most of the moral assessments we find it natural to make. For in various ways, to be discovered, the things for which people are morally judged are not under their control, or are determined to some extent by what is beyond their control. And when the seemingly natural requirement of fault or responsibility is applied in light of these facts, it leaves few pre-reflective moral judgments intact.

Why not conclude, then, that the condition of control is false—that it is an initially plausible hypothesis refuted by clear counter-examples? One could in that case look instead for a more refined condition which picked out the *kinds* of lack of control that really undermine certain moral judgments, without yielding the unacceptable conclusion derived from the broader condition, that most or all ordinary moral judgments are illegitimate.

What rules out this escape is that we are dealing not with a theoretical conjecture but with a philosophical problem. The condition of control does not suggest itself merely as a generalization from certain clear cases. It seems correct in the further cases to which it is extended beyond the original set. When we undermine moral assessment by considering new ways in which control is absent, we are not just discovering what *would* follow given the general hypothesis, but

---

26 [Author's note] "Egoism and Altruism", in *Problems of the Self* (Cambridge, 1973); "Persons, Character, and Morality", in A. Rorty, ed., *The Identities of Persons* (Berkeley, Calif., forthcoming).

are actually being persuaded that in itself the absence of control is relevant in these cases too. The erosion of moral judgment emerges not as the absurd consequence of an over-simple theory, but as a natural consequence of the ordinary idea of moral assessment, when it is applied in view of a more complete and precise account of the facts. It would therefore be a *mistake* to argue from the unacceptability of the conclusions to the need for a different account of the conditions of moral responsibility. The view that moral luck is paradoxical is not a mistake, ethical or logical, but a perception of one of the ways in which the intuitively acceptable conditions of moral judgment threaten to undermine it all.

It resembles the situation in another area of philosophy, the theory of knowledge. There too conditions which seem perfectly natural, and which grow out of the ordinary procedures for challenging and defending claims to knowledge, threaten to undermine all such claims if consistently applied.[27] Most sceptical arguments have this quality: they do not depend on the imposition of arbitrarily stringent standards of knowledge, arrived at by misunderstanding, but appear to grow inevitably from the consistent application of ordinary standards.[28] There is a substantive parallel as well, for epistemological scepticism arises from consideration of the respects in which our beliefs and their relation to reality depend on factors beyond our control. External and internal causes produce our beliefs. We may subject these processes to scrutiny in an effort to avoid error, but our conclusions at this next level also result, in part, from influences which we do not control directly. The same will be true no matter how far we carry the investigation. Our beliefs are always, ultimately, due to factors outside our control, and the impossibility of encompassing those factors without being at the mercy of others leads us to doubt whether we know anything. It looks as though, if any of our beliefs are true, it is pure biological luck rather than knowledge.

Moral luck is like this because while there are various respects in which the natural objects of moral assessment are out of our control or influenced by what is out of our control, we cannot reflect on these facts without losing our grip on the judgments.

There are roughly four ways in which the natural objects of moral assessment are disturbingly subject to luck. One is the phenomenon of constitutive luck mentioned by Williams at the beginning of his paper—the kind of person you are, where this is not just a question of what you deliberately do, but of your inclinations, capacities, and temperament. Another category is luck in one's circumstances—the kind of problems and situations one faces. The other two have to do with the causes and effects of action. Williams' discussion is confined to the last category, but all of them present a common problem. They are all opposed by the idea that one cannot be more culpable or estimable for anything than one is for that fraction of it which is under one's control. It seems irrational to take or dispense credit or blame for matters over which a person has no control, or for their influence on results over which he has partial control. Such things may create the conditions for action, but action can be judged only to the extent that it goes beyond these conditions and does not just result from them.

Let us first consider luck, good and bad, in the way things turn out—the type of case Williams examines. We may note that the category includes a range of examples, from the truck driver who accidentally runs over a child to Gauguin and beyond. The driver, if he is entirely without fault, will feel terrible about his rôle in the event, but will not have to reproach himself. Therefore this example of what Williams calls agent-regret is not yet a case of *moral* bad luck. However, if the driver was guilty of even a minor degree of negligence—failing to have his brakes checked recently, for example—then if that negligence contributes to the death of the child, he will not merely feel terrible. He will blame himself for its death. And what makes this an example of moral luck is that he would have to blame himself only slightly for the negligence itself if no situation arose which

---

27 Nagel is thinking of a family of familiar problems, e.g., how to justify your belief that you really do perceive an external world (and are not dreaming, or hallucinating, or being fed false experience by a computer wired into your brain). See Chapter 3.

28 [Author's note] See Thompson Clarke, "The Legacy of Skepticism", *Journal of Philosophy* LXIX (1972), pp. 754–769.

required him to brake suddenly and violently to avoid hitting a child. Yet the *negligence* is the same in both cases, and the driver has no control over whether a child will run into his path.

The same is true at higher levels of negligence. If someone has had too much to drink and his car swerves on to the sidewalk, he can count himself morally lucky if there are no pedestrians in its path. If there were, he would be to blame for their deaths, and would probably be prosecuted for manslaughter. But if he hurts no one, although his recklessness is exactly the same, he is guilty of a far less serious legal offence and will certainly reproach himself and be reproached by others much less severely. To take another legal example, the penalty for attempted murder is less than that for successful murder—however similar the intentions and motives of the assailant may be in the two cases. His degree of culpability can depend, it would seem, on whether the victim happened to be wearing a bullet-proof vest, or whether a bird flew into the path of the bullet—matters beyond his control.

Finally, there are cases of decision under uncertainty—common in public and in private life. Anna Karenina goes off with Vronsky, Gauguin leaves his family, Chamberlain signs the Munich agreement,[29] the Decembrists persuade the troops under their command to revolt against the Czar,[30] the American colonies declare their independence from Britain, you introduce two people in an attempt at match-making. It is tempting in all such cases to feel that some decision must be possible, in the light of what is known at the time, which will make reproach unsuitable no mat-

ter how things turn out. But, as Williams says, this is not true; when someone acts in such ways he takes his life, or his moral position, into his hands, because how things turn out determines what he has done. It is possible *also* to assess the decision from the point of view of what could be known at the time, but this is not the end of the story. If the Decembrists had succeeded in overthrowing Nicholas I in 1825 and establishing a constitutional regime, they would be heroes. As it is, not only did they fail and pay for it, but they bore some responsibility for the terrible punishments meted out to the troops who had been persuaded to follow them. If the American Revolution had been a bloody failure resulting in greater repression, then Jefferson, Franklin and Washington would still have made a noble attempt, and might not even have regretted it on their way to the scaffold, but they would also have had to blame themselves for what they had helped to bring on their compatriots. (Perhaps peaceful efforts at reform would eventually have succeeded.) If Hitler had not overrun Europe and exterminated millions, but instead had died of a heart attack after occupying the Sudetenland, Chamberlain's action at Munich would still have utterly betrayed the Czechs, but it would not be the great moral disaster that has made his name a household word.[31]

In many cases of difficult choice the outcome cannot be foreseen with certainty. One kind of assessment of the choice is possible in advance, but another kind must await the outcome, because the outcome determines what has been done. The same degree of culpability or estimability in intention, motive, or concern is compatible with a wide range of judgments, positive or negative, depending on what happened beyond the point of decision. The *mens rea*[32] which could have existed in the absence of any consequences does not exhaust the grounds of moral judgment.

---

29 Neville Chamberlain, British Prime Minister, signed an agreement with Hitler in Munich in 1939 yielding the Sudetenland (a portion of Czechoslovakia) to Germany in exchange for Hitler's promise that this would end Germany's expansion. Chamberlain famously announced "peace for our time"; but Hitler's promise was soon broken, and Chamberlain has ever since been blamed for useless appeasement with tragic results.

30 The Decembrists were imperial Russian army officers who led a failed revolt against Nicholas I's assumption of the throne in 1825 (because they were loyal to his older brother, Constantine, who should constitutionally have been the next czar rather than Nicholas).

31 [Author's note] For a fascinating but morally repellent discussion of the topic of justification by history, see Maurice Merleau-Ponty, *Humanism and Terror* (Beacon Press, Boston: 1969).

32 Latin: *guilty mind*. One is usually not considered guilty of a criminal act without this: the understanding of what one's actions would or might involve, thus the intentionality of the action.

I have said that Williams does not defend the view that these are instances of moral luck. The fact that Gauguin will or will not feel basic regret over his decision is a separate matter, and does nothing to explain the influence of actual results on culpability or esteem in those unquestionably ethical cases ranging from negligence through political choice. In such cases one can say *in advance* how the moral verdict will depend on the results. If one negligently leaves the bath running with the baby in it, one will realize, as one bounds up the stairs toward the bathroom, that if the baby has drowned one has done something awful, whereas if it has not one has merely been careless. Someone who launches a violent revolution against an authoritarian regime knows that if he fails he will be responsible for much suffering that is in vain, but if he succeeds he will be justified by the outcome. I don't mean that any action can be retroactively justified by history. Certain things are so bad in themselves, or so risky, that no results can make them all right. Nevertheless, when moral judgment does depend on the outcome, it is objective and timeless and not dependent on a change of standpoint produced by success or failure. The judgment after the fact follows from an hypothetical judgment that can be made beforehand, and it can be made as easily by someone else as by the agent.

From the point of view which makes responsibility dependent on control, all this seems absurd. How is it possible to be more or less culpable depending on whether a child gets into the path of one's car, or a bird into the path of one's bullet? Perhaps it is true that what is done depends on more than the agent's state of mind or intention. The problem then is, why is it not irrational to base moral assessment on what people do, in this broad sense? It amounts to holding them responsible for the contributions of fate as well as for their own—provided they have made some contribution to begin with. If we look at cases of negligence or attempt, the pattern seems to be that overall culpability corresponds to the product of mental or intentional fault and the seriousness of the outcome. Cases of decision under uncertainty are less easily explained in this way, for it seems that the overall judgment can even shift from positive to negative depending on the outcome. But here too it seems rational to subtract the effects of occurrences subsequent to the choice, that were merely possible at the time, and concentrate moral assessment on the actual decision in light of the probabilities. If the object of moral judgment is the *person*, then to hold him accountable for what he has done in the broader sense is akin to strict liability,[33] which may have its legal uses but seems irrational as a moral position.

The result of such a line of thought is to pare down each act to its morally essential core, an inner act of pure will assessed by motive and intention. Adam Smith advocates such a position in *The Theory of Moral Sentiments*, but notes that it runs contrary to our actual judgments.

> But how well soever we may seem to be persuaded of the truth of this equitable maxim, when we consider it after this manner, in abstract, yet when we come to particular cases, the actual consequences which happen to proceed from any action, have a very great effect upon our sentiments concerning its merit or demerit, and almost always either enhance or diminish our sense of both. Scarce, in any one instance, perhaps, will our sentiments be found, after examination, to be entirely regulated by this rule, which we all acknowledge ought entirely to regulate them.[34]

Joel Feinberg points out further that restricting the domain of moral responsibility to the inner world will not immunize it to luck. Factors beyond the agent's control, like a coughing fit, can interfere with his decisions as surely as they can with the path of a bullet from his gun.[35]

---

33   This legal term refers to the responsibility to compensate for the damages inflicted by one's actions, even though the damage was unintentional or unforeseen or unforeseeable, and even though the actions were reasonable and not negligent. This is the kind of responsibility relevant to a civil suit, not a criminal trial.

34   [Author's note] Part II, Section III, Introduction, paragraph 5 [1759].

35   [Author's note] "Problematic Responsibility in Law and Morals", in Joel Feinberg, *Doing and Deserving* (Princeton, 1970).

Nevertheless the tendency to cut down the scope of moral assessment is pervasive, and does not limit itself to the influence of effects. It attempts to isolate the will from the other direction, so to speak, by separating out what Williams calls constitutive luck. Let us consider that next.

Kant was particularly insistent on the moral irrelevance of qualities of temperament and personality that are not under the control of the will. Such qualities as sympathy or coldness might provide the background against which obedience to moral requirements is more or less difficult, but they could not be objects of moral assessment themselves, and might well interfere with confident assessment of its proper object—the determination of the will by the motive of duty. This rules out moral judgment of many of the virtues and vices, which are states of character that influence choice but are certainly not exhausted by dispositions to act deliberately in certain ways. A person may be greedy, envious, cowardly, cold, ungenerous, unkind, vain, or conceited, but *behave* perfectly by a monumental effort of will. To possess these vices is to be unable to help having certain feelings under certain circumstances, and to have strong spontaneous impulses to act badly. Even if one controls the impulses, one still has the vice. An envious person hates the greater success of others. He can be morally condemned as envious even if he congratulates them cordially and does nothing to denigrate or spoil their success. Conceit, likewise, need not be displayed. It is fully present in someone who cannot help dwelling with secret satisfaction on the superiority of his own achievements, talents, beauty, intelligence, or virtue. To some extent such a quality may be the product of earlier choices; to some extent it may be amenable to change by current actions. But it is largely a matter of constitutive bad fortune. Yet people are morally condemned for such qualities, and esteemed for others equally beyond control of the will: they are assessed for what they are *like*.

To Kant this seems incoherent because virtue is enjoined on everyone and therefore must be in principle possible for everyone. It may be easier for some than for others, but it must be possible to achieve it by making the right choices, against whatever temperamental background.[36] One may want to have a generous spirit, or regret not having one, but it makes no sense to condemn oneself or anyone else for a quality which is not within the control of the will. Condemnation implies that you shouldn't be like that, not that it's unfortunate that you are.

Nevertheless, Kant's conclusion remains intuitively unacceptable. We may be persuaded that these moral judgments are irrational, but they reappear involuntarily as soon as the argument is over. This is the pattern throughout the subject.

The third category to consider is luck in one's circumstances, and I shall mention it briefly. The things we are called upon to do, the moral tests we face, are importantly determined by factors beyond our control. It may be true of someone that in a dangerous situation he would behave in a cowardly or heroic fashion, but if the situation never arises, he will never have the chance to distinguish or disgrace himself in this way, and his moral record will be different.[37]

---

36 [Author's note] "... if nature has put little sympathy in the heart of a man, and if he, though an honest man, is by temperament cold and indifferent to the sufferings of others, perhaps because he is provided with special gifts of patience and fortitude and expects or even requires that others should have the same—and such a man would certainly not be the meanest product of nature—would not he find in himself a source from which to give himself a far higher worth than he could have got by having a good-natured temperament?" *Foundations of the Metaphysics of Morals*, Akademie edition p. 398.

37 [Author's note] *Cf.* Thomas Gray, "Elegy Written in a Country Churchyard":
"Some mute inglorious Milton here may rest,
Some Cromwell, guiltless of his country's blood."
An unusual example of circumstantial moral luck is provided by the kind of moral dilemma with which someone can be faced through no fault of his own, but which leaves him with nothing to do which is not wrong. See T. Nagel, "War and Massacre", *Philosophy and Public Affairs* Vol. 1 No. 2 (Winter 1972); and B. Williams, "Ethical Consistency", *PASS* XXXIX (1965), also in *Problems of the Self*.

A conspicuous example of this is political. Ordinary citizens of Nazi Germany had an opportunity to behave heroically by opposing the regime. They also had an opportunity to behave badly, and most of them are culpable for having failed this test. But it is a test to which the citizens of other countries were not subjected, with the result that even if they, or some of them, would have behaved as badly as the Germans in like circumstances, they simply didn't and therefore are not similarly culpable. Here again one is morally at the mercy of fate, and it may seem irrational upon reflection, but our ordinary moral attitudes would be unrecognizable without it. We judge people for what they actually do or fail to do, not just for what they would have done if circumstances had been different.[38]

This form of moral determination by the actual is also paradoxical, but we can begin to see how deep in the concept of responsibility the paradox is embedded. A person can be morally responsible only for what he does; but what he does results from a great deal that he does not do; therefore he is not morally responsible for what he is and is not responsible for. (This is not a contradiction, but it is a paradox.)

It should be obvious that there is a connection between these problems about responsibility and control and an even more familiar problem, that of freedom of the will. That is the last type of moral luck I want to take up, though I can do no more within the scope of this paper than indicate its connection with the other types.

If one cannot be responsible for consequences of one's acts due to factors beyond one's control, or for antecedents of one's acts that are properties of temperament not subject to one's will, or for the circumstances that pose one's moral choices, then how can one be responsible even for the stripped-down acts of the will itself, if *they* are the product of antecedent circumstances outside of the will's control?

The area of genuine agency, and therefore of legitimate moral judgment, seems to shrink under this scrutiny to an extensionless point. Everything seems to result from the combined influence of factors, antecedent and posterior to action, that are not within the agent's control. Since he cannot be responsible for them, he cannot be responsible for their results—thought it may remain possible to take up the aesthetic or other evaluative analogues of the moral attitudes that are thus displaced.

It is also possible, of course, to brazen it out and refuse to accept the results, which indeed seem unacceptable as soon as we stop thinking about the arguments. Admittedly, if certain surrounding circumstances had been different, then no unfortunate consequences would have followed from a wicked intention, and no seriously culpable act would have been performed; but since the circumstances were *not* different, and the agent *in fact* succeeded in perpetrating a particularly cruel murder, *that* is what he did, and that is what he is responsible for. Similarly, we may admit that if certain antecedent circumstances had been different, the agent would never have developed into the sort of person who would do such a thing; but since he *did* develop (as the inevitable result of those antecedent circumstances) into the sort of swine he is, and into the person who committed such a murder, *that* is what he is blameable for. In both cases one is responsible for what one actually does—even if what one actually does depends in important ways on what is not within one's control.

---

38 [Author's note] Circumstantial luck can extend to aspects of the situation other than individual behaviour. For example, during the Vietnam War even US citizens who had opposed their country's actions vigorously from the start often felt compromised by its crimes. Here they were not even responsible; there was probably nothing they could do to stop what was happening, so the feeling of being implicated may seem unintelligible. But it is nearly impossible to view the crimes of one's own country in the same way that one views the crimes of another country, no matter how equal one's lack of power to stop them in the two cases. One is a citizen of one of them, and has a connexion with its actions (even if only through taxes that cannot be withheld)—that one does not have with the other's. This makes it possible to be ashamed of one's country, and to feel a victim of moral bad luck that one was an American in the 'sixties.

This compatibilist account[39] of our moral judgments would leave room for the ordinary conditions of responsibility—the absence of coercion, ignorance, or involuntary movement—as part of the determination of what someone has done—but it is understood not to exclude the influence of a great deal that he has not done.[40] It is essentially what Williams means when he says, above,

> One's history as an agent is a web in which anything that is the product of the will is surrounded and held up and partly formed by things that are not, in such a way that reflection can go only in one of two directions: either in the direction of saying that responsible agency is a fairly superficial concept, which has a limited use in harmonizing what happens, or else that it is not a superficial concept, but that it cannot ultimately be purified—if one attaches importance to the sense of what one is in terms of what one has done and what in the world one is responsible for, one must accept much that makes its claim on that sense solely in virtue of its being actual.

The only thing wrong with this solution is its failure to explain how sceptical problems arise. For they arise not from the imposition of an arbitrary external requirement, but from the nature of moral judgment itself. Something in the ordinary idea of what someone does must explain how it can seem necessary to subtract from it anything that merely happens—even though the ultimate consequence of such subtraction is that nothing remains. And something in the ordinary idea of knowledge must explain why it seems to be undermined by any influences on belief not within the control of the subject—so that knowledge seems impossible without an impossible foundation in autonomous reason. But let us leave epistemology aside and concentrate on action, character, and moral assessment.

The problem arises, I believe, because the self which acts and is the object of moral judgment is threatened with dissolution by the absorption of its acts and impulses into the class of events. Moral judgment of a person is judgment not of what happens to him, but of him. It does not say merely that a certain event or state of affairs is fortunate or unfortunate or even terrible. It is not an evaluation of a state of the world, or of an individual as part of the world. We are not thinking just that it would be better if he were different, or didn't exist, or hadn't done some of the things he has done. We are judging *him*, rather than his existence or characteristics. The effect of concentrating on the influence of what is not under his control is to make this responsible self seem to disappear, swallowed up by the order of mere events.

What, however, do we have in mind that a person must be to be the object of these moral attitudes? While the concept of agency is easily undermined, it is very difficult to give it a positive characterization. That is familiar from the literature on Free Will.

I believe that in a sense the problem has no solution, because something in the idea of agency is incompatible with actions being events, or people being things. But as the external determinants of what someone has done are gradually exposed, in their effect on consequences, character, and choice itself, it becomes gradually clear that actions are events and people things. Eventually nothing remains which can be ascribed to the responsible self, and we are left with nothing but a portion of the larger sequence of events, which can be deplored or celebrated, but not blamed or praised.

Though I cannot define the idea of the active self that is thus undermined, it is possible to say

---

39   Compatibilism is the position that moral responsibility for one's actions is compatible with the fact that those actions are ultimately causally determined by facts outside one's control—provided that those actions are caused by one's decisions (even though those decisions themselves are determined by external causes).

40   [Author's note] The corresponding position in epistemology would be that knowledge consists of true beliefs formed in certain ways, and that it does not require all aspects of the process to be under the knower's control, actually or potentially. Both the correctness of these beliefs and the process by which they are arrived at would therefore be importantly subject to luck. The Nobel Prize is not awarded to people who turn out to be wrong, no matter how brilliant their reasoning.

something about its sources. Williams is right to point out the important difference between agent-regret and regret about misfortunes from which one is detached, but he does not emphasise the corresponding distinction in our attitudes toward others, which comes from the extension to them of external agent-centred evaluations corresponding to the agent-regret that they can feel about themselves. This causes him to miss the truly moral character of such judgments, which can be made not only by the agent himself, though they involve the agent's point of view.

There is a close connexion between our feelings about ourselves and our feelings about others. Guilt and indignation, shame and contempt, pride and admiration are internal and external sides of the same moral attitudes. We are unable to view ourselves simply as portions of the world, and from inside we have a rough idea of the boundary between what is us and what is not, what we do and what happens to us, what is our personality and what is an accidental handicap. We apply the same essentially internal conception of the self to others. About ourselves we feel pride, shame, guilt, remorse—and what Williams calls agent-regret. We do not regard our actions and our characters merely as fortunate or unfortunate episodes—though they may also be that. We cannot *simply* take an external evaluative view of ourselves—of what we most essentially are and what we do. And this remains true even when we have seen that we are not responsible for our own existence, or our nature, or the choices we have to make, or the circumstances that give our acts the consequences they have. Those acts remain ours and we remain ourselves, despite the persuasiveness of the reasons that seem to argue us out of existence.

It is this internal view that we extend to others in moral judgment—when we judge *them* rather than their desirability or utility. We extend to others the refusal to limit ourselves to external evaluation, and we accord to them selves like our own. But in both cases this comes up against the brutal inclusion of humans and everything about them in a world from which they cannot be separated and of which they are nothing but contents. The external view forces itself on us at the same time that we resist it. One way this

occurs is through the gradual erosion of what we do by the subtraction of what happens.[41]

The inclusion of consequences in the conception of what we have done is an acknowledgement that we are parts of the world, but the paradoxical character of moral luck which emerges from this acknowledgement shows that we are unable to operate with such a view, for it leaves us with no one to be. The same thing is revealed in the appearance that determinism obliterates responsibility. Once we see an aspect of what we or someone else does as something that happens, we lose our grip on the idea that it has been done and that we can judge the doer and not just the happening. This explains why the absence of determinism is no more hospitable to the concept of agency than its presence is—a point that has been noticed often. Either way the act is viewed externally, as part of the course of events.

The problem of moral luck cannot be understood without an account of the internal conception of agency and its special connection with the moral attitudes as opposed to other types of value. I do not have such an account. The degree to which the problem has a solution can be determined only by seeing whether in some degree the incompatibility between this conception and the various ways in which we do not control what we do is only apparent. I have nothing to offer on that topic either. But it is not enough to say merely that our basic moral attitudes toward ourselves and others are determined by what is actual; for they are also threatened by the sources of that actuality, and by the external view of action which forces itself on us when we see how everything we do belongs to a world that we have not created.

---

41 [Author's note] See P.F. Strawson's discussion of the conflict between the objective attitude and personal reaction attitudes in "Freedom and Resentment", *Proceedings of the British Academy*, 1962, reprinted in Strawson, ed., *Studies in the Philosophy of Thought and Action* (London, O.U.P., 1968), and in Strawson, *Freedom and Resentment and Other Essays* (London, Methuen, 1974).

CHAPTER 7

Ethics—How Ought We to Live Our Lives?

INTRODUCTION TO THE QUESTION

Ethics, of course, is the philosophical sub-discipline which examines morality;[1] along with metaphysics and epistemology, it is one of the largest and most important areas of philosophy. It can usefully be thought of as divided into three main parts: *normative ethics*, *applied ethics* and *meta-ethics*.

i) Normative ethics is the philosophical study of the standards of right and wrong, or of good and bad. Normative ethical theories do not attempt to merely *describe* how people actually do behave, or report what people *think* is right: they lay out prescriptions (rooted in rationally supported philosophical theory) for how people *really ought* to think and behave. It is common—though by no means universal—to assume that the proper aim of normative ethics should be to develop a systematic and comprehensive moral theory which has as many of the virtues of a scientific theory as possible: it should capture all the phenomena of moral life, place them within a simple and unified theoretical structure, and provide the resources for answering any ethical question whatsoever—i.e.,

an adequate moral theory should always be able to tell you what to do, and it should always give you the correct answer.

One way of classifying different normative moral theories is in terms of their emphasis on 'the Right' or 'the Good.' Some moral theories—such as that of Kant—are primarily theories of *right action*: they are moral codes (usually derived from, and justified by, some fundamental principle or set of principles, such as Kant's Categorical Imperative) that define the duties human beings have to themselves and others. A (morally) good life is then defined simply as a life of duty—a life spent doing the right thing. By contrast, other moral theories—such as Mill's utilitarianism—*begin* by developing a theory of the good: they are accounts of those things that are *good in themselves* (or at least which are essential components of human flourishing). For example, for Mill, what is good is the happiness of sentient creatures. Right actions are then defined derivatively as those (whichever they are) that best contribute to the good.

ii) Applied ethics is the study of how ethical norms or rules ought to be applied in particular cases of unusual difficulty, such as abortion, mercy-killing, the treatment of animals, genetic research, corporate responsibility to the community, 'just' wars, and so on. It encompasses several sub-fields, such as bioethics, business ethics, environmental ethics, legal ethics, and so forth.

iii) Metaethics deals with the philosophical underpinnings of normative ethics: that is, it applies philosophical scrutiny to a part of philosophy itself. The main kinds of metaethical inquiry are the study of

---

1   There are various important philosophical usages which treat 'ethical' and 'moral' as meaning slightly different things. For example, some philosophers (such as Bernard Williams) use the word 'ethics' to denote systems of *rules* for conduct, whilst 'morality' has a more open-ended, less institutionalized content ... while others (such as Jürgen Habermas), interestingly, use the terms in almost exactly the opposite way! I am ignoring such niceties here, however, and simply treat the two words as being interchangeable.

the ethical *concepts* used in normative ethics (such as 'duty,' 'right,' 'good,' 'responsibility'), moral *epistemology* (questions about whether and how moral truths can be known), and moral *ontology* (which is concerned with the nature of 'moral reality'— e.g., whether it is objective or subjective, relative or absolute).

The sequence of readings in this chapter begins in the realm of metaethics, then moves into normative ethics, and finally returns to metaethics; the question which is being pursued throughout is simple, but profound: it is "How should I live my life?" That is, what kind of *person* should I be? What *values* should guide my plans and choices? Which kinds of *behavior* are morally acceptable, and which unacceptable?

The first selection, from Plato, is a metaethical consideration of the notion of moral value itself: what exactly is the connection between moral virtue and 'the good life'? Are moral goodness and well-being *simply the same thing* (perhaps because only the virtuous are really happy, as Plato goes on to argue, or because what is morally good just is happiness, which is Mill's view)? Or do happiness and virtue come apart (as Kant believes): could one be moral but miserable, vicious yet fulfilled?

The next readings introduce three of the historically most important and influential theories of normative ethics. Aristotle lays the foundations for a theory called 'virtue ethics,' which holds that morality cannot be captured by any set of moral rules or principles— instead that what is right or wrong will vary from situation to situation and the trick is to educate people to be wise in their ethical judgments. Kant defends the view that moral actions have to be understood independently of their merely contingent motivations, and thus that certain actions are simply right or wrong *in themselves*. Mill lays out a moral theory, called utilitarianism, which is based on the principle that the moral value of actions must be understood in terms of their effect on human happiness or well-being.

The final three readings can be thought of as critiques of traditional approaches to ethics. Nietzsche, who called himself an 'immoralist,' argues that our modern moral views are merely historically contingent opinion (rather than any kind of insight into 'the truth'), and furthermore that they are heavily infected with what he labels "slave morality." He urges a 'revaluation' of our moral values which will take us "beyond good and evil." Virginia Held presents a feminist critique of traditional moral theory, arguing that the history of ethical thought has been dominated by sexist attitudes towards women and that only a *radical transformation* of moral philosophy will allow us to escape from these distorting preconceptions. Mary Midgley argues that we need to develop a more flexible notion of moral personhood that will allow us to treat non-human animals as morally important in their own right.

Many good introductory books on moral philosophy are available, including: Piers Benn, *Ethics* (McGill-Queen's University Press, 1998); Simon Blackburn, *Being Good: A Short Introduction to Ethics* (Oxford University Press, 2003); Julia Driver, *Ethics: The Fundamentals* (Blackwell, 2006); Fred Feldman, *Introductory Ethics* (Prentice Hall, 1978); William Frankena, *Ethics* (Prentice Hall, 1988); Gilbert Harman, *The Nature of Morality* (Oxford University Press, 1977); Colin McGinn, *Moral Literacy, or How to Do The Right Thing* (Hackett, 1992); Louis Pojman, *Ethics: Discovering Right and Wrong* (Wadsworth, 2005); James Rachels, *The Elements of Moral Philosophy* (McGraw Hill, 2006); Peter Singer, *Practical Ethics* (Cambridge University Press, 1999); and Bernard Williams, *Morality: An Introduction to Ethics* (Cambridge University Press, 1993). Good reference works are Hugh LaFollette (ed.), *The Blackwell Guide to Ethical Theory* (Blackwell, 2000) and Peter Singer (ed.), *A Companion to Ethics* (Blackwell, 1991).

PLATO
Republic

Who Was Plato?

The historical details of Plato's life are shrouded in uncertainty. He is traditionally thought to have been born in about 427 BCE and to have died in 347 BCE. His family, who lived in the Greek city-state of Athens, was aristocratic and wealthy. Legend has it that Plato's father, Ariston, was descended from Codrus, the last king of Athens, and his mother, Perictione, was related to the great Solon, who wrote the first Athenian constitution. While Plato was still a boy, his father died and his mother married Pyrilampes, a friend of the revered Athenian statesman, Pericles, who in the 450s had transformed Athens into one of the greatest cities in the Greek world.

As a young man, Plato probably fought with the Athenian army against Sparta during the Peloponnesian war (431–404 BCE)—which Athens lost—and he may have served again when Athens was involved in the Corinthian war (395–386 BCE).

Given his family connections, Plato looked set for a prominent role in Athenian political life and, as it happens, when he was about 23, a political revolution occurred in Athens which could have catapulted Plato into public affairs. The coup swept the previous democratic rulers—who had just lost the war against Sparta—out of power and into exile, and replaced them with the so-called Thirty Tyrants, several of whom were Plato's friends and relatives. Plato, an idealistic young man, expected this would usher in a new era of justice and good government, but he was soon disillusioned when the new regime was even more violent and corrupt than the old. He withdrew from public life in disgust. The rule of the Thirty lasted only about 90 days before the exiled democrats were restored to power, and Plato—impressed by their relative lenience towards the coup leaders—apparently thought again about entering politics. But then, in 399 BCE, the city rulers arrested Plato's old friend and mentor, Socrates, and accused him of the trumped-up charge of impiety towards the city's gods and of corrupting the youth of Athens. Socrates was convicted by a jury of the townspeople, and—since he declared that he would rather die than give up philosophy, even though he was given a chance to escape—he was executed by being forced to drink poison.

The result was that I, who had at first been full of eagerness for public affairs, when I considered all this and saw how things were shifting about every which way, at last became dizzy. I didn't cease to consider ways of improving this particular situation, however, and, indeed, of reforming the whole constitution. But as far as action was concerned, I kept waiting for favorable moments and finally saw clearly that the constitutions of all actual cities are bad and that their laws are almost beyond redemption without extraordinary resources and luck as well. Hence I was compelled to say in praise of the true philosophy that it enables us to discern what is just for a city or an individual in every case and that the human race will have no respite from evils until those who are really and truly philosophers acquire political power or until, through some divine dispensation, those who rule and have political authority in cities become real philosophers.[1]

After the death of Socrates, it appears that Plato, along with some other philosophical followers of Socrates, fled Athens and went to the city of Megara in east-central Greece to stay with the philosopher Eucleides (a follower of the great Greek philosopher Parmenides of Elea). He may also have visited Egypt, though his travels at this time are shrouded in myth. It appears that Plato started doing philosophy in earnest at about this time, and his earliest writings date from this point. Almost all of Plato's writings are in the form of dialogues between two or more characters and, in most of them, the character leading the discussion is Socrates. Since Plato never wrote himself into any of his dialogues, it is usually—though not uncontroversially—assumed that the views expressed by the character of Socrates more or less correspond with those that Plato is trying to put forward in his dialogues.

Later, when Plato was about 40, he made another trip away from Athens, visiting Italy to talk with the Pythagorean philosophers. Plato was deeply impressed by Pythagorean philosophy—especially their emphasis on mathematics—but he was horrified by the luxury and sensuality of life in Italy, "with men gorging themselves twice a day and never sleeping alone at night."

After Italy, Plato visited Syracuse on the island of Sicily where, during a long stay, he became close friends with Dion, the brother-in-law of the ruling tyrant Dionysius I.[2] Dion became Plato's pupil, and (according to legend) came to prefer the philosophical life of moral goodness to the pleasure, luxury, and power of his surroundings. Exactly what happened next is historically unclear, but there is some reason to believe Plato was captured by a displeased Dionysius, sold into slavery, and subsequently rescued from the slave market when his freedom was purchased by an unidentified benevolent stranger.

On Plato's return to Athens, he bought land in a precinct named for an Athenian hero called Academus, and there, in about 385, he founded the first European university (or at least, the first of which there is any real historical knowledge). Because of its location, this school was called the Academy, and it was to remain in existence for over 900 years, until 529 CE. For most of the rest of his life, Plato stayed at the Academy, directing its studies, and he probably wrote the *Republic* there (in about 380 BCE). Very quickly, the school became a vital center for research in all kinds of subjects, both theoretical and practical. It was probably one of the first cradles for the subjects of metaphysics, epistemology, psychology, ethics, politics, aesthetics, and mathematical science, and members were invited, by various Greek city-states, to help draft new political constitutions.

In 368 Dionysius I of Sicily died and Dion persuaded his successor, Dionysius II, to send for Plato to advise him on how the state should be run. Plato, by now about 60, agreed with some misgivings, possibly hoping to make the younger Dionysius an example of a philosopher-king and to put the doctrines of the *Republic* into practice. However, the experiment was a disastrous failure. Dionysius II—though he gave himself airs as a philosopher—had no inclination to learn philosophy and mathematics in order to become a better ruler. Within four months Dion was banished, and Plato returned to Greece shortly afterwards. However, four years later Dionysius II persuaded Plato to return, pressuring him with testimonials from eminent philosophers describing Dionysius's love for philosophy, and bribing him by offering to reinstate Dion at Syracuse within a year. Once again, the king proved false: he not only kept Dion in exile but confiscated and sold his lands and property. Plato was imprisoned on Sicily for nearly two years until, in 360, he finally

---

1   This is a quotation from the so-called *Seventh Letter*, supposed to have been written by Plato when he was 70 years old. It is not certain that Plato actually wrote this document, but if it was not his, it was probably written by one of his disciples shortly after his death. (This translation is by C.D.C. Reeve.)

2   Indeed, Plato later wrote a poem about Dion and spoke of being driven out of his mind with love for him.

escaped and returned to Athens for good. He died thirteen years later, at the ripe age of 80.[3]

What Was Plato's Overall Philosophical Project?

Plato is probably the single person with the best claim to being the inventor of western philosophy. His thought encompassed nearly all the areas central to philosophy today—metaphysics, epistemology, ethics, political theory, aesthetics, and the philosophy of science and mathematics—and, for the first time in European history, dealt with them in a unified way.[4] Plato thought of philosophy as a special discipline with its own intellectual method, and he was convinced it had foundational importance in human life. Only philosophy, Plato thought, could provide genuine understanding, since only philosophy scrutinized the assumptions that other disciplines left unquestioned. Furthermore, according to Plato, philosophy reveals a realm of comprehensive and unitary hidden truths—indeed, a whole level of reality that the senses cannot detect—which goes far beyond everyday common sense and which, when properly understood, has the power to revolutionize the way we live our lives and organize our societies. Philosophy, and only philosophy, holds the key to genuine human happiness and well-being.

This realm of objects which Plato claimed to have discovered is generally known as that of the Platonic Forms. The Forms—according to Plato—are changeless, eternal objects, which lie outside of both the physical world and the minds of individuals, and which can only be encountered through pure thought rather than through sensation. One of Pla-

to's favorite examples of a Form is the mathematical property of Equality. In a dialogue called the *Phaedo* he argues that Equality itself cannot be identical with two equal sticks, or with any other group of physical objects of equal length, since we could always be mistaken about whether any two observed objects are really equal with one another, but we could not possibly be mistaken about Equality itself and somehow take *it* to be unequal. When two sticks are equal in length, therefore, they "participate in" Equality—it is their relation to Equality which makes them equal rather than unequal—but Equality itself is an abstract object which exists over and above all the instances of equal things. The form of Equality is what one succeeds in understanding when one has a proper conception of what Equality really is in itself: real knowledge, therefore, comes not from observation but from acquaintance with the Forms. Other central examples of Platonic Forms, are Sameness, Number, Motion, Beauty, Justice, Piety, and (the most important Form of all) Goodness.

Plato describes the relation of the ordinary world of perceivable, concrete objects to the realm of the Forms in Book VII of the *Republic,* using the allegory of a cave. Ordinary people, lacking the benefit of a philosophical education, are like prisoners trapped underground in a cave since birth and forced to look only at shadows cast on the wall in front of them by puppets behind their backs, dancing in front of a fire. With the proper philosophical encouragement, they can—if they have the courage to do so—break their bonds and turn around to see that what they believed was reality was really only an illusory puppet show. The philosophers among them can even leave the cave to encounter the true reality—of which even the puppets are only copies—illuminated by the light of the sun which, for Plato, represents the form of the Good. The perceptible world is thus merely an imperfect image of—and sustained by—the quasi-divine, eternal realm of the unchanging and unobservable Forms.

What Is the Structure of This Reading?

The *Republic* is written in the form of a dramatic dialogue. The narrator, Socrates, speaking directly to the reader, describes a conversation in which he took part

---

3   Dion, meanwhile, attempted to recover his position at Syracuse by force—an endeavor Plato, wisely, refused to support—and was later assassinated by a supposed friend, and fellow member of the Academy, called Callippus.

4   In fact the mathematician and philosopher Alfred North Whitehead (1861–1947) famously was moved to say that: "The safest general characterization of the European philosophical tradition is that it consists of a series of footnotes to Plato."

and which is supposed to have happened yesterday at the Athenian port city of Piraeus. The dialogue is traditionally divided into ten parts or "Books," and the first half of Book II is reprinted here. In the first book, Thrasymachus, a boorish character, has asserted that justice, or morality, is simply the rule of the strong over the weak, and that it is, in fact, not in everybody's self-interest to be just—it is only in the best interests of the ruling powers for everyone else to follow the social rules they lay down. Socrates has, characteristically, attempted to show that Thrasymachus' reasons for this claim are muddled and confused, but although Thrasymachus is unable to defend himself against Socrates' attacks he remains convinced of the truth of his position. As Book II opens, two brothers, Glaucon and Adeimantus, take up Thrasymachus's cause ... not because they think he is right, but because they want to challenge Socrates to defeat it properly and to conclusively show that being a just and moral person is valuable *in itself*.

Glaucon begins by introducing a classification of "goods" into three types and asks Socrates to which class justice belongs. Socrates replies it belongs to the highest type of good, but Glaucon points out this conflicts with the popularly held assumption that justice belongs in the lowest class of good. Glaucon then presents three arguments in favor of this common view. First, he describes an account of the "origin and essence of justice" which treats it as only a 'second best' solution to a social problem. Second, he uses the myth of the Ring of Gyges to argue that people are unwillingly just and that, given the chance, anyone would behave immorally. Finally, he describes 'ideal cases' of just and unjust people to show that, if one had the option of living a perfectly just or a totally unjust life, the only rational choice would be the latter. When Glaucon has finished, Adeimantus argues at length that even those who defend justice—parents, poets, and politicians—only defend it on the basis of its beneficial *effects*, and never go so far as to claim it is intrinsically worthwhile to be a morally just person. Glaucon and Adeimantus challenge Socrates to refute all of these arguments.

The reading breaks off just as Socrates is about to respond to this challenge (a response not completed until at least the end of Book IX of the *Republic*). Socra-

tes argues, in effect, that the virtue of justice is such a good thing that it is better to be a just person, even if severe misfortune and loss of reputation occur, than it is to be unjust and to enjoy all possible social rewards; that being a just person always makes you *happier* than being an unjust one, no matter what other circumstances may hold.

In crude outline, Plato's response goes like this. There are three fundamentally different kinds of psychological impulses in human beings: *appetitive desires* (e.g., food, sex, money), *spirited desires* (e.g., fame, power, honor), and *rational desires* (knowledge and truth). Because of this three-fold division of desire, the human soul must also be divided into three parts, and people can be classified according to the dominant part of their soul: that is, people are either money-lovers, honor-lovers, or wisdom-lovers (philosophers). Since these three types of people have very different sorts of desires, they must also have quite different views of what it is to lead a good and morally virtuous life. For one it is a life of hedonistic pleasure, for the second, a life of political power and influence, and for the philosopher, a life spent in the pursuit of knowledge.

However, according to Plato, only one of these views of the good life is *correct*. Only the philosopher, he argues, has access to the genuinely good life. This is so because the true nature of reality—including moral reality—is the realm of the Forms, and only the philosopher has knowledge of this fundamental reality. Since philosophers are the only ones to understand the true nature of virtue, it seems, to Plato, to follow that they are the only ones with the specialized knowledge necessary to live a truly good life.[5] Since capacity for the good life is thus connected with the *kind of person* one is (i.e., a money-lover, an honor-lover, or a philosopher), the Platonic conception of

---

5   There is also a quasi-religious interpretation of Plato which sees him holding that the Forms—rather than anything in the shifting, illusory spatio-temporal world—are the supreme objects of value. Instead of wealth, power, or pleasure, the most perfect object of devotion is the realm of the Forms, and in particular the Form of the Good (which Plato seems to think of as almost a kind of divinity).

virtue can thus be understood as a particular kind of balance in the soul. According to Plato, to be virtuous is to have a soul ruled by its rational part. Morality, properly understood, fulfils one's highest nature—it is a kind of psychic harmony or mental health—and so leads to the deepest and most genuine form of happiness.[6]

Some Useful Background Information

1. All the characters who take part in discussions in the *Republic* were historical figures. Of those mentioned here, Glaucon and Adeimantus were actually Plato's brothers and Thrasymachus was a well-known contemporary teacher of rhetoric, oratory, and "sophist" philosophy (roughly, what we might think of today as a "self-help" guru). The main character of the *Republic,* however, is its narrator Socrates, Plato's primary intellectual influence. Though he left no writings, Socrates' personality and ideas were so powerful that he appears to have had a tremendous impact upon everyone he encountered, inspiring either fervent devotion or intense irritation. Socrates' main philosophical concern was the ethical question of how one's life should best be lived, and his method was to engage in systematic cross-examination (*elenchus*) of those he encountered, challenging them to state and then justify their beliefs about justice and virtue. The effect of this was to demonstrate to them that their uncritically held beliefs about moral virtue are self-contradictory and hence *have* no justification. The state of bewildered awareness of their own ignorance in which Socrates left his unfortunate victims is called *aporia,* and Socrates' technique of remorseless questioning is sometimes known as the "aporetic method."

Though famous for insisting he was wiser than his fellow Athenians only because he alone realized that he knew nothing, Socrates did subscribe to a handful of substantive philosophical positions, two of which he passed on to Plato. First, for Socrates, virtue (*aretē*) is a kind of knowledge. To be a virtuous person is, fundamentally, to *understand* what virtue is, in much the same way as being an expert shoemaker consists in knowing everything there is to know about shoes. Socrates (and Plato after him) held that it was vitally important to find correct definitions—to understand the essence (*eidos*)—of ethical concepts, otherwise we will not know how to live. The second crucial Socratic doctrine is that the real essence of a person is not their body but their soul, and that this soul is immortal. The health of one's own soul is thus of paramount importance, far more significant than the mere slings and arrows of physical life. Indeed, Socrates was convinced that, even while we are living in the physical world, the quality of our souls is a far more important determinant of our happiness than external circumstances like health, wealth, popularity, or power.

2. The topic of the *Republic* is *dikaiosunē,* a Greek word usually translated into English as "justice." Strangely enough, it is a matter of some controversy just what Plato means by *dikaiosunē* (and thus just what, exactly, the *Republic* is about!); clearly, though, the notion covers more than we might normally understand by the word "justice," though probably somewhat less than we would, today, understand by "morality." Plato is not merely interested in the virtue of treating other people fairly and impartially (and, in the *Republic*, he is hardly interested at all in the formulation and administration of civil and criminal law). Rather, Plato is discussing some-

---

6   Plato introduces and explains this account of justice in the human soul by drawing an analogy with the structure of an ideal city-state (which is why the dialogue is called the *Republic*). Briefly, a properly run state would contain three specialized types of citizens: craftspeople, warrior-guardians, and rulers. The rulers would have to have a proper philosophical education, in order to truly know what is best for the state and its citizens, and for this reason they are often called "philosopher kings." The state only functions properly and justly, according to Plato, when these three classes work together in harmony—for example, the craftspeople must be appropriately skilled and must also be properly subservient to the other two classes.

thing like *the right way to live*, where it is understood (as was generally assumed by the ancient Greeks) that human beings are *social* animals, for whom the good life can only exist in a particular sort of political context and all the virtues—such as courage, moderation, generosity, and even piety—have to do, in one way or another, with our relationships with other people. Therefore, by "justice," Plato probably means all the areas of morality that regulate our relationships with other people.

On the other hand, it is important to notice that Plato does *not* think of justice as primarily a way of behaving, as a set of rules for correct action, or as a kind of relationship between people. Justice, for Plato, is an *internal property of individual souls*, and only secondarily of their actions. You have the virtue of justice if your soul has a certain configuration, and then it is this virtue of yours which regulates your treatment of other people; but your treatment of other people is not *itself* justice, it is just the manifestation of your justice. To put it another way, you are not a just person because your actions are just—on the contrary, your actions are just because you are.

3. The description of the "popular view" of justice by Glaucon and Adeimantus is philosophically more complicated than it might at first seem, and the following distinction is a useful one to bear in mind when you are trying to get it straight. This distinction is one between what are often called the "artificial" and the "natural" consequences of justice. The artificial consequences of justice are those "rewards and reputations" which society provides for those who give the appearance of being just. They are artificial rewards because they would not exist if it were not for human social conventions and practices and, more importantly, because they are connected only to the *appearance* of justice rather than justice itself. Thus, someone who appeared just, but was not, would still get all of the artificial rewards of justice. On the other hand, the natural rewards of being just are supposed to follow simply from justice itself, in the way that health, sight, and knowledge have, in themselves, beneficial consequences for their possessors.

Some Common Misconceptions

1. All the protagonists in this section—Glaucon, Adeimantus, and Socrates—*agree* that justice is good in itself. Glaucon and Adeimantus present certain arguments as strongly as they can in order to force Socrates to properly respond to them, but they do not, themselves, endorse the conclusion of those arguments (and they hope Socrates will give them a way to legitimately evade that conclusion).

2. The discussion is about the benefits of justice *for just people themselves*, not for those with whom they interact or for society generally. The topic asks whether *acting justly* is intrinsically worthwhile (rather than whether it is nice to be *treated* justly).

How Important and Influential Is This Passage?

The *Republic* is generally acknowledged to be Plato's greatest work (indeed, one of the very greatest works in all philosophy), and is often thought of as the centerpiece of Plato's philosophy. Though it presents only a partial picture of his developing philosophical views, it is the dialogue where most of Plato's central ideas about ethics, metaphysics, epistemology, politics, psychology, aesthetics, and so on, come together into a single unified theory. This excerpt from the *Republic* is by no means the best-known part of the work, but it is where Plato sets up the philosophical question his book is intended to answer. As with much of Plato's writing, it is the questions he asked which have proved to be of enduring philosophical importance as much as the answers he gave to them. The questions developed here about the relationship between morality and self-interest lie at the very foundation of ethical study, and the myth of the Ring of Gyges, in particular, has been a particularly evocative image through the centuries for exploring these issues.

Suggestions for Critical Reflection

1. How does Glaucon distinguish between the three different kinds of good? Do his examples make sense, and can you think of any examples of goods that do not fit easily into his classification? Into which of the three classes would *you* place justice?

2. Most modern debates about justice or morality tend to assume that there are only two fundamental, mutually exclusive positions one might take. Either something is morally right in itself, *regardless* of its consequences—often called a "deontological" view—or things are morally right or wrong *because* of their consequences (a view called "consequentialism"). For example, one might hold that taking human life is intrinsically morally wrong, no matter what the justification (e.g., because human life is 'sacred'); alternately, one might believe killing is wrong because of its harmful consequences (suffering, death, etc.), or perhaps even that sometimes it can be morally justified to kill human beings if the net consequences of doing so are sufficiently desirable (e.g., if a killing prevents more deaths than it brings about). How does the view of justice Socrates is being asked to defend fit here? Is his position *either* deontological or consequentialist? If not, what is it? How tenable a view is it?

3. How plausible is Glaucon's story of the origin of justice? If he were historically right about it, what would this show us (if anything) about the *moral* value of behaving justly?

4. If you had the Ring of Gyges, how would you behave? Do you agree with the claim that nearly everybody who possessed such a ring would behave immorally? What, if anything, would the answer to this question show about how people *ought* to behave?

5. Do unjust people generally lead more pleasant lives than just people? If so, what, if anything, would this show about the nature of morality?

6. Some commentators have claimed that the speeches of Glaucon and Adeimantus are not, as they purport to be, making the same point, but, in fact, are arguing for two quite *different* conclusions. Glaucon, it is said, emphasizes the need to defend justice *in itself*, without concern for the consequences, while Adeimantus urges that the virtue of justice must be shown to have beneficial *consequences* for those who have it. What do you think about this? Is this characterization of the speeches correct and, if so, does it mean they must be arguing for different conclusions?

7. Socrates agrees with Glaucon and Adeimantus that if justice is to be properly defended, it must be defended in isolation from its artificial or conventional consequences (such as reputation, wealth, and political influence). He also agrees that a good theory of justice must be capable of accommodating such extreme and unrealistic examples as the Ring of Gyges. But is this the right methodology to adopt? Couldn't we say that an essential part of what makes justice valuable is its pragmatic role in regulating social interactions in the kind of political societies in which we find ourselves? For example, perhaps part of the *point* of being just *is* that it entitles us to certain social rewards, or allows us to escape social penalties, and so justice does lose at least some of its value if this connection to social reality breaks down. What do you think?

8. If being just would make a person unhappy, would it then be irrational to be moral? Does Plato think so? Why does Socrates accept the challenge of showing that being just is in one's self-interest? Why not agree that justice is onerous, but is, nevertheless, our moral duty?

Suggestions for Further Reading

Various translations of the *Republic* are available. The one used here is by G.M.A. Grube and C.D.C. Reeve and was published by Hackett in 1992. Another much-used translation is F.M. Cornford's *The Republic of Plato* (Oxford University Press, 1941), and an interesting newer one is *Republic*, translated by Robin Waterfield (Oxford University Press, 1993). The rest of Plato's writings can be found in either *The Collected Dialogues of Plato*, edited by Hamilton and Cairns (Princeton University Press, 1971) or *Plato: Complete Works*, edited by

John Cooper (Hackett, 1997). If you like the fragments of poetry quoted by Plato, you can find more of it in Richard Lattimore's *Greek Lyrics* (University of Chicago Press, 1960). There isn't enough historical detail available about Plato's life for extensive biographies to be possible, but an entertaining historical novel, which includes a fictionalized account of Plato's adventures in Syracuse, is *The Mask of Apollo* by Mary Renault (Pantheon Books, 1966).

Probably the best short introduction to the philosophical context in which Plato was writing is Terence Irwin's superb *Classical Thought* (Oxford University Press, 1989). A fine, brief account of the theories of Plato's predecessors is Edward Hussey's, *The Presocratics* (Hackett, 1972). The British Joint Association of Classical Teachers has produced a reliable, readable (illustrated) book called *The World of Athens: An Introduction to Classical Athenian Culture* (Cambridge University Press, 1984). Finally, K.J. Dover's *Greek Popular Morality in the Time of Plato and Aristotle* (Basil Blackwell, 1974, reprinted by Hackett in 1994) is immensely interesting.

Plato's mentor Socrates wrote nothing, and the best access to his views is in Plato's early dialogues, the *Apology*, *Crito*, *Euthyphro*, *Protagoras*, and *Gorgias*. In fact, Socrates' trial and conviction are the setting for a sequence of Platonic dialogues: in the *Euthyphro* Socrates is on his way to court to be indicted; the *Apology* depicts his trial; in the *Crito* Socrates refuses his friends' pleas to escape from prison; and the *Phaedo* describes Socrates' last conversation and his death. Modern accounts of the trial of Socrates include Brickhouse and Smith, *Socrates on Trial* (Princeton University Press, 1989) and C.D.C. Reeve, *Socrates in the Apology* (Hackett, 1989). A general account of the philosophy of Socrates is Gregory Vlastos, *Socrates: Ironist and Moral Philosopher* (Cambridge University Press, 1991).

The history of modern Plato scholarship dates back to the nineteenth century and, as you might expect, there is a wealth of published description and analysis of his philosophical views. Some of the best (accessible, relatively recent) work is: I.M. Crosbie, *An Examination of Plato's Doctrines* (2 vols., Routledge & Kegan Paul, 1962/1963); J.C.B. Gosling, *Plato* (Routledge & Kegan Paul, 1973); G.M.A. Grube, *Plato's Thought* (Hackett, 1980); W.K.C. Guthrie, *A History of Greek Philosophy*, Vols. 4 and 5 (Cambridge University Press, 1986); Terence Irwin, *Plato's Moral Theory* (Oxford University Press, 1977); Richard Kraut (ed.), *The Cambridge Companion to Plato* (Cambridge University Press, 1992); W.D. Ross, *Plato's Theory of Ideas* (Oxford University Press, 1951); Gregory Vlastos (ed.), *Plato: A Collection of Critical Essays* (2 vols., Doubleday, 1971); Gregory Vlastos, *Platonic Studies* (Princeton University Press, 1981); and Nicholas White, *Plato on Knowledge and Reality* (Hackett, 1976).

There are also a number of works specifically about Plato's *Republic*. The best is by Julia Annas, *An Introduction to Plato's Republic* (Oxford University Press, 1981). Nicholas White, *A Companion to Plato's Republic* (Hackett, 1979), Cross and Woozley, *Plato's Republic: A Philosophical Commentary* (Macmillan, 1964), and C.D.C. Reeve, *Philosopher-Kings* (Princeton University Press, 1988) are also good. The following articles deal with material found in the first half of Book II of the *Republic* and are well worth looking at: C.A. Kirwan, "Glaucon's Challenge," *Phronesis* 10 (1965); J.D. Mabbott, "Is Plato's *Republic* Utilitarian?" *Mind* 46 (1937); H.A. Prichard, "Duty and Interest" in *Moral Obligation and Duty and Interest* (Oxford University Press, 1968); David Sachs, "A Fallacy in Plato's *Republic*," *Philosophical Review* 72 (1963); and Nicholas White, "The Classification of Goods in Plato's *Republic*," *Journal of the History of Philosophy* 22 (1984).

Republic

Book II
(357a–367e)[7]

When I said this, I thought I had done with the discussion, but it turned out to have been only a prelude. Glaucon showed his characteristic courage on this occasion too and refused to accept Thrasymachus'

---

7   The *Republic* was probably written in about 380 BCE. This translation is by G.M.A. Grube, revised by C.D.C. Reeve, and published in 1992 by the Hackett Publishing Company. Reprinted by permission of Hackett Publishing Company, Inc. All rights reserved.

abandonment of the argument. Socrates, he said, do you want to seem to have persuaded us that it is better in every way to be just than unjust, or do you want truly to convince us of this?

I want truly to convince you, I said, if I can.

Well, then, you certainly aren't doing what you want. Tell me, do you think there is a kind of good we welcome, not because we desire what comes from it, but because we welcome it for its own sake—joy, for example, and all the harmless pleasures that have no results beyond the joy of having them?

Certainly, I think there are such things.

And is there a kind of good we like for its own sake and also for the sake of what comes from it—knowing, for example, and seeing and being healthy? We welcome such things, I suppose, on both counts.

Yes.

And do you also see a third kind of good, such as physical training, medical treatment when sick, medicine itself, and the other ways of making money? We'd say that these are onerous[8] but beneficial to us, and we wouldn't choose them for their own sakes, but for the sake of the rewards and other things that come from them.

There is also this third kind. But what of it?

Where do you put justice?

I myself put it among the finest goods, as something to be valued by anyone who is going to be blessed with happiness, both because of itself and because of what comes from it.

That isn't most people's opinion. They'd say that justice belongs to the onerous kind, and is to be practiced for the sake of the rewards and popularity that come from a reputation for justice, but is to be avoided because of itself as something burdensome.

I know that's the general opinion. Thrasymachus faulted justice on these grounds a moment ago and praised injustice, but it seems that I'm a slow learner.

Come, then, and listen to me as well, and see whether you still have that problem, for I think that Thrasymachus gave up before he had to, charmed by you as if he were a snake.[9] But I'm not yet satisfied by the argument on either side. I want to know

what justice and injustice are and what power each itself has when it's by itself in the soul. I want to leave out of account their rewards and what comes from each of them. So, if you agree, I'll renew the argument of Thrasymachus. First, I'll state what kind of thing people consider justice to be and what its origins are. Second, I'll argue that all who practice it do so unwillingly, as something necessary, not as something good. Third, I'll argue that they have good reason to act as they do, for the life of an unjust person is, they say, much better than that of a just one.

It isn't, Socrates, that I believe any of that myself. I'm perplexed, indeed, and my ears are deafened listening to Thrasymachus and countless others. But I've yet to hear anyone defend justice in the way I want, proving that it is better than injustice. I want to hear it praised *by itself*, and I think that I'm most likely to hear this from you. Therefore, I'm going to speak at length in praise of the unjust life, and in doing so I'll show you the way I want to hear you praising justice and denouncing injustice. But see whether you want me to do that or not.

I want that most of all. Indeed, what subject could someone with any understanding enjoy discussing more often?

Excellent. Then let's discuss the first subject I mentioned—what justice is and what its origins are.

They say that to do injustice is naturally good and to suffer injustice bad, but that the badness of suffering it so far exceeds the goodness of doing it that those who have done and suffered injustice and tasted both, but who lack the power to do it and avoid suffering it, decide that it is profitable to come to an agreement with each other neither to do injustice nor to suffer it. As a result, they begin to make laws and covenants, and what the law commands they call lawful and just. This, they say, is the origin and essence of justice. It is intermediate between the best and the worst. The best is to do injustice without paying the penalty; the worst is to suffer it without being able to take revenge. Justice is a mean between these two extremes. People value it not as a good but because they are too weak to do injustice with impunity. Someone who has the power to do this, however, and is a true man wouldn't make an agreement with anyone not to do injustice in

---

8   Burdensome, troublesome.

9   As if he were calmed by the music of a snake-charmer.

order not to suffer it. For him that would be madness. This is the nature of justice, according to the argument, Socrates, and these are its natural origins.

We can see most clearly that those who practice justice do it unwillingly and because they lack the power to do injustice, if in our thoughts we grant to a just and an unjust person the freedom to do whatever they like. We can then follow both of them and see where their desires would lead. And we'll catch the just person red-handed travelling the same road as the unjust. The reason for this is the desire to outdo others and get more and more.[10] This is what anyone's nature naturally pursues as good, but nature is forced by law into the perversion of treating fairness with respect.

The freedom I mentioned would be most easily realized if both people had the power they say the ancestor of Gyges of Lydia[11] possessed. The story goes that he was a shepherd in the service of the ruler of Lydia. There was a violent thunderstorm, and an earthquake broke open the ground and created a chasm at the place where he was tending his sheep. Seeing this, he was filled with amazement and went down into it. And there, in addition to many other wonders of which we're told, he saw a hollow bronze horse. There were windowlike openings in it, and, peeping in, he saw a corpse, which seemed to be of more than human size, wearing nothing but a gold ring on its finger. He took the ring and came out of the chasm. He wore the ring at the usual monthly meeting that reported to the king on the state of the flocks. And as he was sitting among the others, he happened to turn the setting[12] of the ring towards himself to the inside of his hand. When he did this, he became invisible to those sitting near him, and they went on talking as if he had gone. He wondered at this, and, fingering the ring, he turned the setting outwards again and became visible. So he experimented with the ring to test whether it indeed had this power—and it did. If he turned the setting inward, he became invisible; if he turned it outward, he became visible again. When he realized this, he at once arranged to become one of the messengers sent to report to the king. And when he arrived there, he seduced the king's wife, attacked the king with her help, killed him, and took over the kingdom.

Let's suppose, then, that there were two such rings, one worn by a just and the other by an unjust person. Now, no one, it seems, would be so incorruptible that he would stay on the path of justice or stay away from other people's property, when he could take whatever he wanted from the marketplace with impunity, go into people's houses and have sex with anyone he wished, kill or release from prison anyone he wished, and do all the other things that would make him like a god among humans. Rather his actions would be in no way different from those of an unjust person and both would follow the same path. This, some would say, is a great proof that one is never just willingly but only when compelled to be. No one believes justice to be a good when it is kept private, since, wherever either person thinks he can do injustice with impunity, he does it. Indeed, every man believes that injustice is far more profitable to himself than justice. And any exponent of this argument will say he's right, for someone who didn't want to do injustice, given this sort of opportunity, and who didn't touch other people's property would be thought wretched and stupid by everyone aware of the situation, though, of course, they'd praise him in public, deceiving each other for fear of suffering injustice. So much for my second topic.

As for the choice between the lives we're discussing, we'll be able to make a correct judgment about that only if we separate the most just and the most unjust. Otherwise we won't be able to do it. Here's the

---

10   This is the vice of *pleonexia*, the desire to out-compete everybody else and get more than you are entitled to. According to Plato, *pleonexia* is the root cause of injustice, and proper virtue consists in keeping *pleonexia* in check; Thrasymachus, however, has argued that *pleonexia* is not a vice at all, but a reasonable impulse which is only stifled by artificial social conventions.

11   Lydia was an ancient kingdom located in western Asia Minor, where northwestern Turkey lies today. Gyges was king of Lydia from 670 to 652 BCE. Probably the first realm to use coins as money, Lydia was renowned for its immense wealth and reached the height of its power in the seventh century BCE. In 546 BCE its final king, Croesus, was defeated by the Persians and Lydia was absorbed into the Persian Empire.

12   The setting for a jewel.

separation I have in mind. We'll subtract nothing from the injustice of an unjust person and nothing from the justice of a just one, but we'll take each to be complete in his own way of life. First, therefore, we must suppose that an unjust person will act as clever craftsmen do: A first-rate captain or doctor, for example, knows the difference between what his craft can and can't do. He attempts the first but lets the second go by, and if he happens to slip, he can put things right. In the same way, an unjust person's successful attempts at injustice must remain undetected, if he is to be fully unjust. Anyone who is caught should be thought inept, for the extreme of injustice is to be believed to be just without being just. And our completely unjust person must be given complete injustice; nothing may be subtracted from it. We must allow that, while doing the greatest injustice, he has nonetheless provided himself with the greatest reputation for justice. If he happens to make a slip, he must be able to put it right. If any of his unjust activities should be discovered, he must be able to speak persuasively or to use force. And if force is needed, he must have the help of courage and strength and of the substantial wealth and friends with which he has provided himself.

Having hypothesized such a person, let's now in our argument put beside him a just man, who is simple and noble and who, as Aeschylus[13] says, doesn't want to be believed to be good but to be so.[14] We must take away his reputation, for a reputation for justice would bring him honour and rewards, so that it wouldn't be clear whether he is just for the sake of justice itself or for the sake of those honours and rewards. We must strip him of everything except justice and make his situation the opposite of an unjust person's. Though he does no injustice, he must have the greatest reputation

for it, so that his justice may be tested full-strength and not diluted by wrong-doing and what comes from it. Let him stay like that unchanged until he dies—just, but all his life believed to be unjust. In this way, both will reach the extremes, the one of justice and the other of injustice, and we'll be able to judge which of them is happier.

Whew! Glaucon, I said, how vigorously you've scoured each of the men for our competition, just as you would a pair of statues for an art competition.

I do the best I can, he replied. Since the two are as I've described, in any case, it shouldn't be difficult to complete the account of the kind of life that awaits each of them, but it must be done. And if what I say sounds crude, Socrates, remember that it isn't I who speak but those who praise injustice at the expense of justice. They'll say that a just person in such circumstances will be whipped, stretched on a rack, chained, blinded with fire, and, at the end, when he has suffered every kind of evil, he'll be impaled, and will realize then that one shouldn't want to be just but to be believed to be just. Indeed, Aeschylus' words are far more correctly applied to unjust people than to just ones, for the supporters of injustice will say that a really unjust person, having a way of life based on the truth about things and not living in accordance with opinion, doesn't want simply to be believed to be unjust but actually to be so —

Harvesting a deep furrow in his mind,
Where wise counsels propagate.

He rules his city because of his reputation for justice; he marries into any family he wishes; he gives his children in marriage to anyone he wishes; he has contracts and partnerships with anyone he wants; and besides benefiting himself in all these ways, he profits because he has no scruples about doing injustice. In any contest, public or private, he's the winner and outdoes his enemies. And by outdoing them, he becomes wealthy, benefiting his friends and harming his enemies. He makes adequate sacrifices to the gods and sets up magnificent offerings to them. He takes better care of the gods, therefore, (and, indeed, of the human beings he's fond of) than a just person does. Hence it's likely that the gods, in turn, will take better care of him than of a just person. That's what they say,

13 Aeschylus (525–456 BCE) was a great and influential Greek tragic dramatist. He is sometimes said to have created drama itself, through his innovative introduction of multiple actors speaking different parts. His most famous plays are the *Oresteia* trilogy—*Agamemnon, The Libation Bearers,* and *The Eumenides.*

14 This refers to Aeschylus's play *Seven Against Thebes.* It is said of a character that "he did not wish to be believed to be the best but to be it." The next two lines of the passage are quoted by Glaucon below.

Socrates, that gods and humans provide a better life for unjust people than for just ones.

When Glaucon had said this, I had it in mind to respond, but his brother Adeimantus intervened: You surely don't think that the position has been adequately stated?

Why not? I said.

The most important thing to say hasn't been said yet.

Well, then, I replied, a man's brother must stand by him, as the saying goes.[15] If Glaucon has omitted something, you must help him. Yet what he has said is enough to throw me to the canvas[16] and make me unable to come to the aid of justice.

Nonsense, he said. Hear what more I have to say, for we should also fully explore the arguments that are opposed to the ones Glaucon gave, the ones that praise justice and find fault with injustice, so that what I take to be his intention may be clearer.

When fathers speak to their sons, they say that one must be just, as do all the others who have charge of anyone. But they don't praise justice itself, only the high reputations it leads to and the consequences of being thought to be just, such as the public offices, marriages, and other things Glaucon listed. But they elaborate even further on the consequences of reputation. By bringing in the esteem of the gods, they are able to talk about the abundant good things that they themselves and the noble Hesiod and Homer say that the gods give to the pious, for Hesiod says that the gods make the oak trees

Bear acorns at the top and bees in the middle
And make fleecy sheep heavy laden with wool[17]

for the just, and tells of many other good things akin to these. And Homer is similar:

When a good king, in his piety,
Upholds justice, the black earth bears
Wheat and barley for him, and his trees are
* heavy with fruit.*
His sheep bear lambs unfailingly, and the sea
* yields up its fish.*[18]

Musaeus[19] and his son make the gods give the just more headstrong goods than these. In their stories, they lead the just to Hades,[20] seat them on couches, provide them with a symposium[21] of pious people, crown them with wreaths, and make them spend all their time drinking—as if they thought drunkenness was the finest wage of virtue. Others stretch even further the wages that virtue receives from the gods, for they say that someone who is pious and keeps his promises leaves his children's children and a whole race behind him. In these and other similar ways, they praise justice. They bury the impious and unjust in mud in Hades; force them to carry water in a sieve; bring them into bad repute while they're still alive, and all those penalties that Glaucon gave to the just person they give to the unjust. But they have nothing else to say. This, then, is the way people praise justice and find fault with injustice.

Besides this, Socrates, consider another form of argument about justice and injustice employed both by private individuals and by poets. All go on repeating with one voice that justice and moderation are

---

15   In Homer's *Odyssey* (part 16, lines 97–98).

16   To throw me to the floor of a wrestling ring.

17   Hesiod, *Works and Days*, lines 232–234. Hesiod was an early Greek poet—considered the second greatest Greek epic poet after Homer—who lived around 700 BCE. His poem *Works and Days* reflects his experiences as a farmer, giving practical advice on how to live, and also shows Hesiod lamenting the loss of a historic Golden Age which has been replaced, he complains, with a modern era of immorality and suffering.

18   Homer, *Odyssey*, part 19, lines 109 and 111–113.

19   This Musaeus (as opposed to a Greek poet of the same name, who lived some 1000 years later) was a mythical poet and singer connected with the cult of Orphism, a Greek mystery religion of the sixth century BCE. His son, Eumolpus, is said to have founded the Eleusinian mysteries, an annual celebration to honor Demeter, goddess of agriculture and fertility.

20   The site of the Greek afterlife, where the good were rewarded and the wicked punished.

21   A gathering for drinking, music, and intellectual conversation. (Greek—*sumposion*, literally, drinking party.)

fine things, but hard and onerous, while licentious-ness and injustice are sweet and easy to acquire and are shameful only in opinion and law. They add that unjust deeds are for the most part more profitable than just ones, and, whether in public or private, they will-ingly honour vicious people[22] who have wealth and other types of power and declare them to be happy. But they dishonour and disregard the weak and the poor, even though they agree that they are better than the others.

But the most wonderful of all these arguments concerns what they have to say about the gods and virtue. They say that the gods, too, assign misfortune and a bad life to many good people, and the opposite fate to their opposites. Begging priests and prophets frequent the doors of the rich and persuade them that they possess a god-given power founded on sacri-fices and incantations. If the rich person or any of his ancestors has committed an injustice, they can fix it with pleasant rituals. Moreover, if he wishes to injure some enemy, then, at little expense, he'll be able to harm just and unjust alike, for by means of spells and enchantments they can persuade the gods to serve them. And the poets are brought forward as witnesses to all these accounts. Some harp on the ease of vice, as follows:

> *Vice in abundance is easy to get;*
> *The road is smooth and begins beside you,*
> *But the gods have put sweat between us and*
> *virtue,*[23]

and a road that is long, rough, and steep. Others quote Homer to witness that the gods can be influenced by humans, since he said:

> *The gods themselves can be swayed by prayer,*
> *And with sacrifices and soothing promises,*
> *Incense and libations, human beings turn*
> *them from their purpose*
> *When someone has transgressed and sinned.*[24]

And they present a noisy throng of books by Musaeus and Orpheus,[25] offspring as they say of Selene and the Muses,[26] in accordance with which they perform their rituals. And they persuade not only individuals but whole cities that the unjust deeds of the living or the dead can be absolved or purified through sacrifices and pleasant games, whether those who have com-mitted them are still alive, or have died. These initia-tions, as they call them, free people from punishment hereafter, while a terrible fate awaits those who have not performed rituals.

When all such sayings about the attitudes of gods and humans to virtue and vice are so often repeated, Socrates, what effect do you suppose they have on the souls of young people? I mean those who are clever and are able to flit from one of these sayings to another, so to speak, and gather from them an im-pression of what sort of person he should be and of how best to travel the road of life. He would surely ask himself Pindar's[27] question, "Should I by justice or by crooked deceit scale this high wall and live my life guarded and secure?" And he'll answer: "The various sayings suggest that there is no advantage in my being just if I'm not also thought just, while the troubles and penalties of being just are apparent. But they tell me that an unjust person, who has secured for himself a reputation for justice, lives the life of a god. Since, then, 'opinion forcibly overcomes truth'

22   Those having many vices, wicked people.

23   *Works and Days*, lines 287–289.

24   *Iliad*, part 9, lines 497 and 499–501.

25   Orpheus was a legendary poet who lived (if he is a real figure at all) in the sixth or seventh century BCE. According to Greek myth, he was the first living mortal to travel to the underworld, on a quest to retrieve his dead wife Eurydice. Hades, ruler of the underworld, was so moved by the poet's music that he gave back Eurydice, on the condition that Orpheus not look back at her until they reached the world of the living. Or-pheus glanced back a moment too soon, and Eurydice vanished. Heart-broken, he wandered alone in the wilds until a band of Thracian women killed him and threw his severed head in the river, where it continued to call for his lost love, Eurydice.

26   Selene is the Greek goddess of the Moon. The Muses were nine goddesses, daughters of Zeus, who presided over the arts and sciences.

27   Pindar (520–440 BCE) was a Greek lyric poet.

and 'controls happiness,' as the wise men[28] say, I must surely turn entirely to it. I should create a façade of illusory virtue around me to deceive those who come near, but keep behind it the greedy and crafty fox of the wise Archilochus."[29]

"But surely," someone will object, "it isn't easy for vice to remain always hidden." We'll reply that nothing great is easy. And, in any case, if we're to be happy, we must follow the path indicated in these accounts. To remain undiscovered we'll form secret societies and political clubs. And there are teachers of persuasion to make us clever in dealing with assemblies and law courts. Therefore, using persuasion in one place and force in another, we'll outdo others without paying a penalty.

"What about the gods? Surely, we can't hide from them or use violent force against them!" Well, if the gods don't exist or don't concern themselves with human affairs, why should we worry at all about hiding from them? If they do exist and do concern themselves with us, we've learned all we know about them from the laws and the poets who give their genealogies—nowhere else. But these are the very people who tell us that the gods can be persuaded and influenced by sacrifices, gentle prayers, and offerings. Hence, we should believe them on both matters or neither. If we believe them, we should be unjust and offer sacrifices from the fruits of our injustice. If we are just, our only gain is not to be punished by the gods, since we lose the profits of injustice. But if we are unjust, we get the profits of our crimes and transgressions and afterwards persuade the gods by prayer and escape without punishment.

"But in Hades won't we pay the penalty for crimes committed here, either ourselves or our children's children?" "My friend," the young man will say as he does his calculation, "mystery rites have great power and the gods have great power of absolution. The greatest cities tell us this, as do those children of the gods who have become poets and prophets."

Why, then, should we still choose justice over the greatest injustice? Many eminent authorities agree that, if we practice such injustice with a false façade, we'll do well at the hands of gods and humans, living and dying as we've a mind to. So, given all that has been said, Socrates, how is it possible for anyone of any power—whether of mind, wealth, body, or birth—to be willing to honor justice and not laugh aloud when he hears it praised? Indeed, if anyone can show that what we've said is false and has adequate knowledge that justice is best, he'll surely be full not of anger but of forgiveness for the unjust. He knows that, apart from someone of godlike character who is disgusted by injustice or one who has gained knowledge and avoids injustice for that reason, no one is just willingly. Through cowardice or old age or some other weakness, people do indeed object to injustice. But it's obvious that they do so only because they lack the power to do injustice, for the first of them to acquire it is the first to do as much injustice as he can.

And all of this has no other cause than the one that led Glaucon and me to say to you: "Socrates, of all of you who claim to praise justice, from the original heroes of old whose words survive, to the men of the present day, not one has ever blamed injustice or praised justice except by mentioning the reputations, honours, and rewards that are their consequences. No one has ever adequately described what each itself does of its own power by its presence in the soul of the person who possesses it, even if it remains hidden from gods and humans. No one, whether in poetry or in private conversations, has adequately argued that injustice is the worst thing a soul can have in it and that justice is the greatest good. If you had treated the subject in this way and persuaded us from youth, we wouldn't now be guarding against one another's injustices, but each would be his own best guardian, afraid that by doing injustice he'd be living with the worst thing possible."

Thrasymachus or anyone else might say what we've said, Socrates, or maybe even more, in discussing justice and injustice—crudely inverting their powers, in my opinion. And, frankly, it's because I want to hear the opposite from you that I speak with all the force I can muster. So don't merely give us a theoretical argument that justice is stronger than in-

---

28 Simonides of Ceos (c. 556–468 BCE), a Greek poet.
29 Archilochus of Paros (who lived around 650 BCE), yet another Greek poet, and author of the famous fable about a fox and a hedgehog.

justice, but tell us what each itself does, because of its own powers, to someone who possesses it, that makes injustice bad and justice good. Follow Glaucon's advice, and don't take reputations into account, for if you don't deprive justice and injustice of their true reputations and attach false ones to them, we'll say that you are not praising them but their reputations and that you're encouraging us to be unjust in secret. In that case, we'll say that you agree with Thrasymachus that justice is the good of another, the advantage of the stronger, while injustice is one's own advantage and profit, though not the advantage of the weaker.

You agree that justice is one of the greatest goods, the ones that are worth getting for the sake of what comes from them, but much more so for their own sake, such as seeing, hearing, knowing, being healthy, and all other goods that are fruitful by their own nature and not simply because of reputation. Therefore, praise justice as a good of that kind, explaining how—because of its very self—it benefits its possessors and how injustice harms them. Leave wages and reputations for others to praise.

Others would satisfy me if they praised justice and blamed injustice in that way, extolling the wages of one and denigrating those of the other. But you, unless you order me to be satisfied, wouldn't, for you've spent your whole life investigating this and nothing else. Don't, then, give us only a theoretical argument that justice is stronger than injustice, but show what effect each has because of itself on the person who has it—the one for good and the other for bad—whether it remains hidden from gods and human beings or not....

ARISTOTLE

The Nicomachean Ethics

Who Was Aristotle?

Aristotle was born in 384 BCE in Stageira, a small town in the northeast corner of the Chalcidice peninsula in the kingdom of Macedon, many days journey north of the intellectual centers of Greece. His father—Nicomachus, a physician at the Macedonian court—died when Aristotle was young, and he was brought up by his mother's wealthy family. At 17 Aristotle traveled to Athens to study at Europe's most important center of learning, the Academy, set up and presided over by Plato. As a young philosopher, Aristotle showed exceptional promise and made a name for himself as being industrious and clever, a good speaker, argumentative (if rather sarcastic), original, and independent of thought. He was apparently a bit of a dandy—cutting his hair in a fashionably short style, and wearing jeweled rings—and is said to have suffered from poor digestion, to have lisped, and to have had spindly legs.

After Plato's death in about 347 BCE, Aristotle left Athens (possibly pushed out by a surge of anti-Macedonian feeling in the city—though one story suggests he left in a fit of pique after failing to be granted leadership of the Academy, and yet another account has it that Aristotle was unhappy with the Academy's turn towards pure mathematics under Plato's successor Speusippus). He traveled to Atarneus on the coast of Asia Minor (present-day Turkey) where his mother's family had connections and where the pro-Macedonian tyrant, Hermias, was a patron of philosophical studies. There, with three colleagues from the Academy, Aristotle started his own school at the town of Assos. Aristotle married Hermias's niece and adopted daughter, Pythias, and they had a daughter, also called Pythias.

This happy familial situation did not last long, however. In about 345 BCE Hermias was betrayed and executed (in a particularly grisly fashion) by the Persians. Aristotle and his family fled to the nearby island of Lesbos, in the eastern Aegean Sea, where Aristotle founded another school at a town called Mytilene. There, with his student Theophrastus, he engaged in a hugely impressive series of studies in botany, zoology, and marine biology, collecting observations which were still of unrivaled scientific interest some 2000 years later. (Indeed, as late as the nineteenth century, Charles Darwin was able to praise Aristotle's biological researches as a work of genius which every professional biologist should read.)

Aristotle's stay on Lesbos was of short duration. In 343 BCE, invited by Philip II, the ruler of Macedonia, he returned home to tutor the 13-year-old prince Alexander. Little is reliably known about Aristotle's life during this period, though many fanciful stories have been written, enshrouding it in myth. Three years later, on Philip's death, Alexander became king and launched the military career which, in fairly short order, made him conqueror of much of the known world and earned him the epithet Alexander the Great. (One history claims that when Alexander embarked on his conquest of the East—his armies advanced as far as the Indian sub-continent—he took along scientists whose sole job it was to report their discoveries back to Aristotle.)

In 335 BCE, after Alexander's troops had completed their conquest of the Greek city-states, Aristotle moved back to Athens where, once again, he started his own research institute. This university became known as the Lyceum (after the grove, dedicated to Apollo Lyceus, where it was located), and it continued to flourish for 500 years after Aristotle's death.[1] There

he spent the next twelve years teaching, writing, and building up the first great library of the ancient world. Most of his known philosophical writings probably date from this time. After his wife Pythias died, Aristotle became the lover of a woman called Herpyllis. Their son Nicomachus, was named, following the Greek custom, after his grandfather.

This peaceful existence was shattered in 323 BCE by news of Alexander's death in Babylon at the age of 33. Almost instantly, open revolt against the Macedonian conquerors broke out, and Aristotle—because of his connection with Alexander—was suddenly no longer welcome in Athens. One of the citizens brought an indictment of impiety towards him—the same 'crime' for which the Athenians had executed Socrates three-quarters of a century earlier. In order, as one tradition has it, to prevent the Athenians from sinning against philosophy a second time, Aristotle and his family beat a hasty retreat to Chalcis, on the island of Euboea, where his mother's family had estates. There Aristotle soon died, in November 322 BCE, at age 62. In his humane and sensible will, which has been preserved for posterity, Aristotle directed that Pythias's bones should be placed in his grave, in accordance with her wishes. He also freed several of his slaves and made generous and flexible financial provisions for Herpyllis and Nicomachus.

What Was Aristotle's Overall Philosophical Project?

Aristotle's life-work was nothing less than the attempt to collect together and systematically arrange all human knowledge. His consuming ambition was to get

---

1   Because philosophical discussions at the Lyceum were often conducted whilst strolling around a colonnaded walk called a *peripatos*, Aristotle's group became known as "the Peripatetics" (the walkers).

as close as possible to *knowing everything*—about the natural world, the human social world, and even the unchanging and eternal world of the heavens and the gods. However, unlike many other philosophers with similar ambitions before and since, Aristotle probably did not believe that there is some single, unified set of truths—some single *theory*—which provides the key to unlocking all of reality. He was not looking for a deeper, more authentic realm lying behind and explaining the world we live in, but instead was simply trying to find out as much as he could about *our* world, as we experience it. Thus, it is sometimes said, Aristotle's basic theoretical commitment was to *common sense*: he wanted to develop a system that provided a place for both scientific and moral-political truths, but did not depend on mysteriously invisible and inaccessible objects such as Plato's Forms (see the notes to the previous reading).[2] For Aristotle, the ultimate reality is the concrete world with which we are already acquainted—people, animals, plants, minerals—which Aristotle thought of as *substances* and their properties.

Often, Aristotle worked in the following way: after choosing a domain of study (such as rhetoric or metaphysics), he would begin by summarizing and laying out all the serious claims made about it—"what seems to be the case," including all the "reputable opinions." He would also pay attention to the way in which the matters in question were ordinarily spoken of—the assumptions about them built into everyday language. Then, Aristotle would survey the puzzles or problems generated by this material, and would set out to solve those puzzles, preferably without disturbing too many of the received opinions. Typically he would not stop there: new puzzles or objections

would be raised by the solutions, and he would try to clear up those matters, and then the new puzzles generated, and so on, each time, he hoped, getting closer to the final truth.

Since Aristotle did not believe in a single "theory of everything," he divided the branches of knowledge, or "sciences," into three main groups: theoretical sciences (whose aim is to discover truths), practical sciences (governing the performance of actions), and productive sciences (whose goal is the making of objects). The major theoretical sciences, according to Aristotle, are theology (which he thought of as the study of "changeless items"), mathematics, and the natural sciences. The chief practical sciences are ethics and politics. Examples of productive sciences are poetics, rhetoric, medicine, and agriculture. According to Aristotle, these various sciences are quite different: although they add up to a composite picture of reality, they share no single set of theoretical concepts or assumptions, no single methodology, and no single set of standards for scientific rigor. The proper methods of mathematics differ from those of zoology, which differ again from those of ethics.

On the other hand, Aristotle hoped each science, or at least all theoretical sciences, would share the same *structure*: Aristotle was the first philosopher to conceive of science as a body of knowledge arranged according to a particular logical structure, which he modeled on that of geometry. As in geometry, there are two kinds of scientific truth, according to Aristotle: truths which are simply "evident" and need no explanation, and a much larger body of further truths which are justified or explained by being logically derived from the self-evident truths. (Aristotle, more or less single-handedly, *invented* the study of logic—which he called the science of "syllogisms"—partly to be able to describe the proper structure of scientific knowledge.) Unlike the case with geometry, however, Aristotle insisted that the "axioms" of any theoretical science—the self-evident truths upon which it is based—should ideally capture the *essences* of the things being described by that science. In this way, according to Aristotle, the logical structure of science would exactly reflect the structure of the world itself. Just as the properties of things (say, plants) are caused by their essential natures, so will the claims of

---

2   Another, then contemporary, theory which Aristotle opposed, also on the grounds of mystery-mongering, was a theory called "atomism," put forward by philosophers like Leucippus (who flourished between 450 and 420 BCE) and Democritus (c. 460–371 BCE). This theory postulated the existence of huge numbers of invisibly tiny, eternal, unchangeable particles—*atoma*, Greek for "uncuttables"—whose hidden behaviors and interactions were supposed to explain all the observable properties of the visible spatio-temporal world.

the relevant science (e.g., botany) be logically derived from its basic assumptions about the essences of the things in its domain.

So *where*, according to Aristotle, do we get these first principles of the different sciences? The answer, Aristotle believed, was not from the exercise of pure reason but from careful *observation* of the world around us. By looking very hard and carefully at a particular domain (such as botany or ethics) we discern some fundamental truths about the things in that domain, from which everything else about it will follow. Because of this practical emphasis on observation rather than mere thought, Aristotle is described as "the father of modern empiricism." On the other hand, Aristotle never developed anything like an experimental method: his method for testing theories—verifying and falsifying them—consisted more in reasoned analysis than in empirical testing.

What Is the Structure of This Reading?

Judging by Alexandrian-age library catalogues, Aristotle wrote some 150 works in his lifetime—ranging in length from essays to books—covering a huge variety of topics: logic, physics, biology, meteorology, philosophy of science, history of science, metaphysics, psychology (including works on love, friendship, and the emotions), ethics and political theory, political science, rhetoric, poetics (and some original poetry), and political and legal history. Only a fraction of these writings—perhaps less than a fifth—survive: many of Aristotle's works, including all the dialogues he wrote for popular consumption, are now lost.[3] Most of what remains are summaries of lectures delivered at various times during his career, which were deposited in Aristotle's own library at the Lyceum to be consulted by teachers and students. Most of these notes were probably edited and re-edited, both by Aristotle and his successors; the *Nicomachean Ethics*, for example, is so-called because it is thought to have been edited by Aristotle's son Nicomachus after his father's death.[4]

The *Nicomachean Ethics* is traditionally divided into ten books (though the divisions were probably not Aristotle's own). Book I examines the nature of the good for human beings—happiness—and divides it into two categories: intellectual excellence and moral excellence. Books II to IV deal with moral excellence, beginning with a general account of it and going on to discuss several of the moral virtues in detail. Book V looks at the virtue of justice, while Book VI describes some of the forms of intellectual excellence. Book VII deals with moral self-control and the nature of pleasure, and Books VIII and IX are about friendship. Finally, Book X concludes with a discussion of *eudaimonia* or well-being, and of the role that education and society play in bringing about individual happiness.

Excerpted here are the first few pages of Book I, which introduce Aristotle's view of the study of ethics, and then section 7 of Book I, where Aristotle lays out his so-called "function argument" for the view that human happiness consists in a life of excellent activity in accordance with reason. There follows the second half of Book II, where Aristotle defines moral virtue as a disposition to choose the mean—illustrating this with examples of particular moral virtues—and then discusses the practical corollaries of this account of virtue. Finally, part of Book X is included: here, Aristotle discusses further the nature of happiness and argues that the highest form of happiness is to be found in a life of philosophical "contemplation."

Much of Book V of the *Nicomachean Ethics* is also reprinted in Chapter 8.

---

3   This lost *oeuvre* is a particular tragedy because Aristotle's prose style was greatly admired by the ancients—more so than Plato's, for example—and yet (not unnaturally, considering their purpose) the lecture notes, which are the only things of Aristotle's we have left to us, are generally agreed to be rather dryly written: terse and elliptical, full of abrupt transitions, inadequate explanations, and technical jargon.

---

4   Aristotle's other main ethical work—an earlier set of lecture notes, generally thought to be superseded by the more mature *Nicomachean Ethics*—is similarly called the *Eudemian Ethics*, possibly after its ancient editor Eudemus of Rhodes.

Some Useful Background Information

1. Aristotle categorized ethics as a practical, rather than a theoretical, science. The *Nicomachean Ethics* is written "not in order to know what virtue is, but in order to become good." In other words, for Aristotle, the point of ethics is not merely to know what good people are like, but to learn to act as good people do: the *Nicomachean Ethics* is intended to foster what he calls "practical wisdom" (*phronesis*) in those who study it. The science of ethics is continuous, for Aristotle, with two others—biology and politics. It is continuous with biology because ethics is the study of the good life for humankind *as a biological species*. A good life for the member of *any* species (whether a horse or a rubber plant) is a life of continuous flourishing, but what *counts* as flourishing will depend upon the biological nature of that species. Ethics is continuous with politics—the study of human society—because the arena in which human beings live their lives, in which they develop as moral agents and exercise their moral capacities, is necessarily a social one.

2. According to Aristotle, the goal of human life is to achieve *eudaimonia*. *Eudaimonia* is usually—as it is in our selection—translated as "happiness," but this can be misleading. The Greek word does not refer to a psychological state or feeling, such as pleasure, but instead means a certain kind of desirable *activity* or *way of life*—it is the activity of living well. The happy person is, for Aristotle, someone who has lived a genuinely *successful* or fulfilling life.

3. Aristotle's understanding of nature, and in particular of biology, is what is called *teleological*: a thing's *telos* is its goal or purpose and, for Aristotle, all of nature is goal-directed. For example, the nature of some processes (such as digestion) or biological organs (such as the eye) is plausibly determined by their *function*—their goal or *telos*—and not by their physical composition at some particular time. Eyes are things—any things—that have the function of seeing. Aristotle extended this model to the entire natural world, so that, in his view, the essence of fire consists in its goal (of, roughly, rising upwards), the essence of an acorn is its purpose to grow into an oak tree, and the essence of the species *horse* is to flourish and procreate as horses are supposed to do. Since human beings are as much a part of the biological world as anything else, it follows that a proper understanding of human nature—and thus of the good life for human beings—must involve an investigation into the function of the human species.

Some Common Misconceptions

1. When Aristotle refers to the *telos*—the function or goal—of living creatures like plants, animals, and human beings, he is not thinking of these creatures as having a purpose for *something else*. He is not, for example, assuming that there is some great universal plan (perhaps God's plan) and that living creatures have a role to play in fulfilling this plan. Instead, the *telos* of living creatures is *internal* to them: it is, so to speak, built into their biological natures.

2. It is sometimes easy to forget that Aristotle's Doctrine of the Mean urges us to avoid *both* excess and deficiency. Aristotle's account not only instructs us to moderate our anger or curb our drinking, it also warns us against feeling too *little* anger or not drinking *enough* wine.

3. When Aristotle refers to "the mean" of a spectrum of behavior, he does not intend to speak of something like an arithmetical average, and thus does not suggest we should, literally, choose the *mid-point* of that range of behavior. The mean or mid-point of two numbers (as 6 is the mean of 2 and 10) is an example of what Aristotle calls a mean "in terms of the object." Aristotle contrasts this mathematical use with his own usage of "mean," which is a mean "relatively to us." For example, we should eat neither too many, nor too few, cookies; but exactly how many cookies we should eat depends on our personal circumstances (our weight, our lifestyle, how many other people also want cookies, whether we are allergic to ingredients in the

cookies, and so on). Certainly, Aristotle does not want to say that we should eat *exactly half* of all the available cookies. As Jonathan Barnes put it, "it is as though I were to hand a man a pack of cards and urge him to pick the middle one—adding that by 'middle' I meant 'middle relative to the chooser,' and that any card in the pack may be middle in this sense."

4. Aristotle does not think of his ethical theory as a sort of moral rulebook. Unlike most modern moral philosophers, such as Immanuel Kant and J.S. Mill, Aristotle is not trying to find a theory that will, by itself, generate moral principles to tell us how to act. Instead, he is trying to develop an account of moral *character*—a theory of the good person. It is salutary to recall that, although the topic of Aristotle's book is indeed *ēthika*, which is usually translated as "ethics," the Greek word means "matters to do with character." Similarly, when Aristotle writes of *ēthikē aretē*—which is almost invariably translated as "moral virtue"—the literal meaning is "excellence of character," and by "excellence" is meant simply what we would mean if we spoke of an excellent horse or an excellent ax. The modern sense of ethics, as involving *obedience to some sort of moral law,* is substantially more recent than Aristotle, and arose (more or less) with the monotheistic religions of Judaism, Christianity, and Islam.

5. The Doctrine of the Mean does not apply to particular *actions*, but to *virtues*—to states of character. Thus, the idea is not that one always *acts* in a way which is intermediate between two extremes, but that one's actions are guided by a *character trait* which is neither excessive nor insufficient. For example, in certain situations, someone possessing the virtue of generosity might nevertheless refuse to give anything at all to a particular person in a particular circumstance (or, conversely, might give away everything they own); or a person with the virtue of being even-tempered might nevertheless find it appropriate, sometimes, to become very angry (or, in another situation, to meekly suppress any angry feelings whatsoever).

How Important and Influential Is This Passage?

Many professional philosophers consider Aristotle to be the greatest philosopher who ever lived (for example, Oxford philosopher J.L. Ackrill calls him "a philosophical super-genius"); throughout the Middle Ages he was simply "the Philosopher." The system of ethics developed in the *Nicomachean Ethics* has had a profound effect on all subsequent moral philosophy. In every age of philosophy it has been either fervently embraced or fiercely rejected, but never ignored. Several of its central tenets—that morality consists in finding a "golden mean," or that the rational aim of human life is happiness (though not necessarily pleasure)—have become part of our everyday moral consciousness. On the other hand, for much of the post-medieval period, Aristotle's emphasis on the *virtues*, rather than on *types of action*, as the basis of morality was paid relatively little attention. More recently, there has been a surge of interest in so-called "virtue ethics," and Aristotle is generally considered the original source for this 'new' theory. (Modern virtue theories, however, diverge from Aristotle's ethical philosophy in important ways. In particular, they tend to reject or ignore his emphasis on *eudaimonia* as the ultimate moral good.)

Suggestions for Critical Reflection

1. When Aristotle talks of the "precision" of a subject matter, what exactly does he mean? What kind of precision can mathematics have which ethics must always lack? Does this mean there can be no universally true moral principles (but, perhaps, just 'rules of thumb')?

2. Does Aristotle assume there is just one thing which is the goal of every human life? Is he right?

3. Aristotle seems to define the (biological) function of human beings as the thing "which is peculiar to man"—i.e., as something only human beings can do. Is this a plausible way of identifying the human function? Is reason the *only* capacity which human beings have uniquely? Does Aristotle believe that only human beings are rational, or does he say things elsewhere which are inconsistent with this?

4. What if human beings do not *have* a function? How much damage would this do to Aristotle's moral theory?

5. Aristotle concedes that not every *vice* is a matter of degree, but he does seem to hold that every *virtue is* in the middle between two vices. Does this claim seem plausible? What about, for example, the virtue of kindness?

6. Does Aristotle's Doctrine of the Mean actually help us at all in making moral decisions? If not, how much of a problem is this for Aristotle's ethics? Do you think Aristotle *expects* his Doctrine of the Mean to guide our moral behavior? If the Doctrine of the Mean *cannot* tell us what to do, then what (if anything) is its point?

7. Many commentators on Aristotle's ethics have worried about what is sometimes called the "Aristotelian circle." Aristotle can be seen as making the following claims: virtuous action is what the practically wise person would choose; the practically wise are those who can successfully act in such a way as to achieve *eudaimonia*; but *eudaimonia*, for Aristotle, simply consists in wise action (it is "activity of soul exhibiting excellence"). If this is an accurate description of Aristotle's claims, how are we to *recognize* wise or virtuous action without an independent standard by which to judge it, and when Aristotle's inter-connected definitions go around in an endless circle? Do you agree that Aristotle's theory is circular? If so, do you think that makes it simply vacuous?

8. How plausible do you find Aristotle's arguments that the life of a philosopher is the best and happiest possible kind of life for human beings? How consistent is the emphasis in Book X on the activity of *theoria*—on *theoretical* reason—with Aristotle's earlier focus on *practical* wisdom?

9. Is Aristotle too egoistic? Does he pay too much attention to the question of how *individuals* can lead a good life, and not enough on moral issues to do with helping other people? For example, is generosity a virtue just because of its good effects on others, or simply because being generous makes one happy?

Suggestions for Further Reading

The standard English edition of Aristotle's works is *The Complete Works of Aristotle*, edited by Jonathan Barnes (2 vols., Princeton University Press, 1984). The translation of the *Nicomachean Ethics* reprinted here—that by W.D. Ross, revised by J.L. Ackrill and J.O. Urmson (Oxford University Press, 1998)—is the classic English version, but there are several other good ones, including the translations by J.A.K. Thomson, revised by Hugh Tredennick (Penguin, 1976), and Terence Irwin, which includes very extensive notes (Hackett, 1999).

By common consensus, the best short introduction to Aristotle's philosophy is J.L. Ackrill's *Aristotle the Philosopher* (Oxford University Press, 1981). Another good short book (which gives a strong impression of the breadth of Aristotle's interests, though it places very little emphasis on his ethics) is *Aristotle* by Jonathan Barnes (Oxford University Press, 1982). Somewhat longer but very valuable books are: W.D. Ross, *Aristotle* (Routledge, 1995); Jonathan Lear, *Aristotle: The Desire to Understand* (Cambridge University Press, 1988); G.E.R. Lloyd, *Aristotle: The Growth and Structure of his Thought* (Cambridge University Press, 1968); and Terence Irwin, *Aristotle's First Principles* (Oxford University Press, 1990). *The Cambridge Companion to Aristotle*, edited by Jonathan Barnes (Cambridge University Press, 1995), is also very good.

Perhaps the best guide to Aristotle's ethical philosophy is W.F.R. Hardie's *Aristotle's Ethical Theory* (Oxford University Press, 1980). Sarah Broadie's *Ethics with Aristotle* (Oxford University Press, 1995), John M. Cooper's *Reason and Human Good in Aristotle* (Hackett, 1986), Gerard Hughes's *Aristotle's Ethics* (Routledge, 2001), D.S. Hutchinson's *The Virtues of Aristotle* (Routledge & Kegan Paul, 1986), Harold H. Joachim's *Aristotle: The Nicomachean Ethics* (Oxford University Press, 1955), Richard Kraut's *Aristotle on the Human Good* (Princeton University Press, 1990), C.D.C. Reeve's *Practices of Reason: Aristotle's Nicomachean Ethics* (Oxford University Press, 1995), and J.O. Urmson's *Aristotle's Ethics* (Blackwell, 1988) are also good.

There are two particularly useful collections of articles on the *Nicomachean Ethics*: Nancy Sherman (ed.), *Aristotle's Ethics: Critical Essays* (Rowman and Littlefield, 1999), and Amélie O. Rorty (ed.), *Essays on Aristo-*

tle's Ethics (University of California Press, 1981). Three additional interesting articles, not included in these collections, are: J.E. Whiting, "Aristotle's Function Argument: A Defence," *Ancient Philosophy* 8 (1988); Richard Kraut, "Two Conceptions of Happiness," *Philosophical Review* 88 (1979); and Gavin Lawrence, "Aristotle on the Ideal Life," *Philosophical Review* 102 (1993).

Finally, descendents of Aristotle's ethical ideas are discussed in Georg Henrik Von Wright, *The Varieties of Goodness* (Routledge & Kegan Paul, 1963); Peter Geach, *The Virtues* (Cambridge University Press, 1977); Stuart Hampshire, *Two Theories of Morality* (Oxford University Press, 1977); Philippa Foot, *Virtues and Vices* (University of California Press, 1978); James D. Wallace, *Virtues and Vices* (Cornell University Press, 1978); Bernard Williams, *Ethics and the Limits of Philosophy* (Harvard University Press, 1986); Michael Slote, *From Morality to Virtue* (Oxford University Press, 1995); Crisp and Slote (eds.), *Virtue Ethics* (Oxford University Press, 1997); Roger Crisp (ed.), *How Should One Live?* (Oxford University Press, 1998); Christine MacKinnon, *Character, Virtue Theories, and the Vices* (Broadview Press, 1999); and Thomas Hurka, *Virtue, Vice, and Value* (Oxford University Press, 2000).

from *The Nicomachean Ethics*[5]

Book I

1: All human activities aim at some good: some goods subordinate to others.

Every art and every inquiry, and similarly every action and pursuit, is thought to aim at some good; and for this reason the good has rightly been declared to be that at which all things aim.[6] But a certain difference is found among ends;[7] some are activities, others are products apart from the activities that produce them. Where there are ends apart from the actions, it is the nature of the products to be better than the activities. Now, as there are many actions, arts, and sciences, their ends also are many; the end of the medical art is health, that of shipbuilding a vessel, that of strategy victory, that of economics wealth. But where such arts fall under a single capacity—as bridle-making and the other arts concerned with the equipment of horses fall under the art of riding, and this and every military action under strategy, in the same way other arts fall under yet others—in all of these the ends of the master arts are to be preferred to all the subordinate ends; for it is for the sake of the former that the latter are pursued. It makes no difference whether the activities themselves are the ends of the actions, or something else apart from the activities, as in the case of the sciences just mentioned.

2: The science of the good for man is politics.

If, then, there is some end of the things we do, which we desire for its own sake (everything else being desired for the sake of this), and if we do not choose everything for the sake of something else (for at that rate the process would go on to infinity, so that our desire would be empty and vain), clearly this must be the good and the chief good. Will not the knowledge of it, then, have a great influence on life? Shall we not, like archers who have a mark to aim at, be more likely to hit upon what is right? If so, we must try, in outline at least, to determine what it is, and of which of the sciences or capacities it is the object. It would seem to belong to the most authoritative art and that which

---

5   The *Nicomachean Ethics* was probably written, as a series of lecture notes which would have undergone frequent revision, sometime between 334 and 322 BCE. This selection is reprinted from *Aristotle: The Nicomachean Ethics*, translated with an Introduction by David Ross [aka W.D. Ross], revised by J.O. Urmson and J.L. Ackrill (Oxford World's Classics, 1998), by permission of Oxford University Press. The section headings are not Aristotle's own, but are supplied by the translators.

6   This definition is consistent with the views of Plato, but Aristotle is probably thinking mostly of the work of a philosopher, mathematician, and astronomer called Eudoxus of Cnidus. Eudoxus taught at Plato's Academy in Athens from 368 until his death in 355 BCE, and was in charge of the school (during one of Plato's absences in Sicily) when Aristotle arrived there to study at the age of 17.

7   Here, and throughout this reading, "end" means "goal" or "purpose," rather than merely "stopping place."

is most truly the master art. And politics[8] appears to be of this nature; for it is this that ordains which of the sciences should be studied in a state, and which each class of citizens should learn and up to what point they should learn them; and we see even the most highly esteemed of capacities to fall under this, e.g., strategy, economics, rhetoric; now, since politics uses the rest of the sciences, and since, again, it legislates as to what we are to do and what we are to abstain from, the end of this science must include those of the others, so that this end must be the good for man. For even if the end is the same for a single man and for a state, that of the state seems at all events something greater and more complete whether to attain or to preserve; though it is worth while to attain the end merely for one man, it is finer and more godlike to attain it for a nation or for city-states. These, then, are the ends at which our inquiry aims, since it is political science, in one sense of that term.

3: We must not expect more precision than the subject-matter admits of.

Our discussion will be adequate if it has as much clearness as the subject-matter admits of, for precision is not to be sought for alike in all discussions, any more than in all the products of the crafts. Now fine and just actions, which political science investigates, admit of much variety and fluctuation of opinion, so that they may be thought to exist only by convention, and not by nature. And goods also give rise to a similar fluctuation because they bring harm to many people; for before now men have been undone by reason of their wealth, and others by reason of their courage. We must be content, then, in speaking of such subjects and with such premises to indicate the truth roughly and in outline, and in speaking about things which are only for the most part true and with premises of the

same kind to reach conclusions that are no better. In the same spirit, therefore, should each type of statement be received; for it is the mark of an educated man to look for precision in each class of things just so far as the nature of the subject admits; it is evidently equally foolish to accept probable reasoning from a mathematician and to demand from a rhetorician scientific proofs....

7: The good must be something final and self-sufficient. Definition of happiness reached by considering the characteristic function of man.

Let us again return to the good we are seeking, and ask what it can be. It seems different in different actions and arts; it is different in medicine, in strategy, and in the other arts likewise. What then is the good of each? Surely that for whose sake everything else is done. In medicine this is health, in strategy victory, in architecture a house, in any other sphere something else, and in every action and pursuit the end; for it is for the sake of this that all men do whatever else they do. Therefore, if there is an end for all that we do, this will be the good achievable by action, and if there are more than one, these will be the goods achievable by action.

So the argument has by a different course reached the same point; but we must try to state this even more clearly. Since there are evidently more than one end, and we choose some of these (e.g., wealth, flutes,[9] and in general instruments) for the sake of something else, clearly not all ends are final ends; but the chief good is evidently something final. Therefore, if there is only one final end, this will be what we are seeking, and if there are more than one, the most final of these will be what we are seeking. Now we call that which is in itself worthy of pursuit more final than that which is worthy of pursuit for the sake of something else, and that which is never desirable for the sake of something else more final than the things that are desirable both in themselves and for the sake of that other thing, and therefore we call final without qualification that which is always desirable in itself and never for the sake of something else.

---

8   For Aristotle the study of politics (*politikē*) would be broader than our modern political science, and would include all aspects of the study of society. The goal of political science, according to Aristotle, ought to be to achieve happiness (*eudaimonia*) for all the citizens of the state, and this is why he thinks that the investigation into human happiness (ethics) is continuous with politics.

9   Strictly speaking, Aristotle means an *aulos*, an ancient Greek double-reed instrument.

Now such a thing happiness,[10] above all else, is held to be; for this we choose always for itself and never for the sake of something else, but honour, pleasure, reason, and every virtue we choose indeed for themselves (for if nothing resulted from them we should still choose each of them), but we choose them also for the sake of happiness, judging that by means of them we shall be happy. Happiness, on the other hand, no one chooses for the sake of these, nor, in general, for anything other than itself.

From the point of view of self-sufficiency the same result seems to follow; for the final good is thought to be self-sufficient. Now by self-sufficient we do not mean that which is sufficient for a man by himself, for one who lives a solitary life, but also for parents, children, wife, and in general for his friends and fellow citizens, since man is born for citizenship. But some limit must be set to this; for if we extend our requirement to ancestors and descendants and friends' friends we are in for an infinite series. Let us examine this question, however, on another occasion; the self-sufficient we now define as that which when isolated makes life desirable and lacking in nothing; and such we think happiness to be; and further we think it most desirable of all things, without being counted as one good thing among others—if it were so counted it would clearly be made more desirable by the addition of even the least of goods; for that which is added becomes an excess of goods, and of goods the greater is always more desirable. Happiness, then, is something final and self-sufficient, and is the end of action.

Presumably, however, to say that happiness is the chief good seems a platitude, and a clearer account of what it is is still desired. This might perhaps be given, if we could first ascertain the function of man. For just as for a flute-player, a sculptor, or any artist, and, in general, for all things that have a function or activity, the good and the 'well' is thought to reside in the function, so would it seem to be for man, if he has a function. Have the carpenter, then, and the tanner certain functions or activities, and has man none? Is he born without a function?[11] Or as eye, hand,

foot, and in general each of the parts evidently has a function, may one lay it down that man similarly has a function apart from all these? What then can this be? Life seems to belong even to plants, but we are seeking what is peculiar to man. Let us exclude, therefore, the life of nutrition and growth. Next there would be a life of perception, but *it* also seems to be shared even by the horse, the ox, and every animal. There remains, then, an active life of the element that has a rational principle; of this, one part has such a principle in the sense of being obedient to one, the other in the sense of possessing one and exercising thought. And, as 'life of the rational element' also has two meanings, we must state that life in the sense of activity is what we mean; for this seems to be the more proper sense of the term. Now if the function of man is an activity of soul[12] which follows or implies a rational principle, and if we say 'a so-and-so' and 'a good so-and-so' have a function which is the same in kind, e.g., a lyre-player and a good lyre-player, and so without qualification in all cases, eminence in respect of goodness being added to the name of the function (for the function of a lyre-player is to play the lyre, and that of a good lyre-player is to do so well): if this is the case [and we state the function of man to be a certain kind of life, and this to be an activity or actions of the soul implying a rational principle, and the function of a good man to be the good and noble performance of these, and if any action is well performed when it is performed in accordance with the appropriate excellence: if this is the case], human good turns out to be activity of soul exhibiting excellence, and if there are more than one excellence, in accordance with the best and most complete.

But we must add 'in a complete life'. For one swallow does not make a summer, nor does one day; and

---

10   *Eudaimonia* (see the introductory notes to this reading).

11   In the original Greek, this would have been a pun: the word for being "without function" (*argon*) was also

used colloquially to mean a "good for nothing" or a "dropout."

12   By "soul"—*psuchē*—Aristotle means, very roughly, that which makes us alive or animates us. The religious or Cartesian connotations of the word—the notion of the soul as a sort of substantial spiritual self, housed in a temporary material vessel (the body)—only came about much later in history.

so too one day, or a short time, does not make a man blessed and happy.

Let this serve as an outline of the good; for we must presumably first sketch it roughly, and then later fill in the details. But it would seem that any one is capable of carrying on and articulating what has once been well outlined, and that time is a good discoverer or partner in such a work; to which facts the advances of the arts are due; for any one can add what is lacking. And we must also remember what has been said before, and not look for precision in all things alike, but in each class of things such precision as accords with the subject-matter, and so much as is appropriate to the inquiry. For a carpenter and a geometer investigate the right angle in different ways; the former does so in so far as the right angle is useful for his work, while the latter inquires what it is or what sort of thing it is; for he is a spectator of the truth. We must act in the same way, then, in all other matters as well, that our main task may not be subordinated to minor questions. Nor must we demand the cause in all matters alike; it is enough in some cases that the *fact* be well established, as in the case of the first principles; the fact is a primary thing or first principle. Now of first principles we see some by induction,[13] some by perception,[14] some by a certain habituation,[15] and others too in other ways. But each set of principles we must try to investigate in the natural way, and we must take pains to determine them correctly, since they have a great influence on what follows. For the beginning

is thought to be more than half of the whole,[16] and many of the questions we ask are cleared up by it....

Book II

5: The genus of moral virtue: it is a state of character, not a passion, nor a faculty.

Next we must consider what virtue is. Since things that are found in the soul are of three kinds—passions, faculties, states of character—virtue must be one of these. By passions I mean appetite, anger, fear, confidence, envy, joy, friendly feeling, hatred, longing, emulation, pity, and in general the feelings that are accompanied by pleasure or pain; by faculties the things in virtue of which we are said to be capable of feeling these, e.g., of becoming angry or being pained or feeling pity; by states of character the things in virtue of which we stand well or badly with reference to the passions, e.g., with reference to anger we stand badly if we feel it violently or too weakly, and well if we feel it moderately; and similarly with reference to the other passions.

Now neither the virtues nor the vices are *passions*, because we are not called good or bad on the ground of our passions, but are so called on the ground of our virtues and our vices, and because we are neither praised nor blamed for our passions (for the man who feels fear or anger is not praised, nor is the man who simply feels anger blamed, but the man who feels it in a certain way), but for our virtues and our vices we *are* praised or blamed.

Again, we feel anger and fear without choice, but the virtues are modes of choice or involve choice. Further, in respect of the passions we are said to be moved, but in respect of the virtues and the vices we are said not to be moved but to be disposed in a particular way.

For these reasons also they are not *faculties*; for we are neither called good nor bad, nor praised nor blamed, for the simple capacity of feeling the passions; again, we have the faculties by nature, but we are not made good or bad by nature; we have spoken of this before.

---

13   This, for Aristotle, is the process of moving from particular facts, observations, or examples to a general or universal claim (for example, from particular examples of courage and cowardice to a general understanding of the relation between them). The Greek word is *epagōgē*, which literally means "leading on."

14   The word Aristotle uses, *aisthēsis*, can be used to mean sense-perception, but Aristotle probably means something more like "direct intuition" of (moral) facts—just *seeing* that something is right or wrong.

15   This, in Aristotle's view, is how the moral virtues are inculcated: by repeatedly and self-consciously acting in a particular way (e.g., bravely) until that manner of behaving (e.g., bravery) becomes a habit or a character trait.

---

16   This was apparently a Greek proverb.

If, then, the virtues are neither passions nor faculties, all that remains is that they should be *states of character*.

Thus we have stated what virtue is in respect of its genus.

6: The differentia of moral virtue: it is a disposition to choose the mean.

We must, however, not only describe virtue as a state of character, but also say what sort of state it is. We may remark, then, that every virtue or excellence both brings into good condition the thing of which it is the excellence and makes the work of that thing be done well; e.g., the excellence of the eye makes both the eye and its work good; for it is by the excellence of the eye that we see well. Similarly the excellence of the horse makes a horse both good in itself and good at running and at carrying its rider and at awaiting the attack of the enemy. Therefore, if this is true in every case, the virtue of man also will be the state of character which makes a man good and which makes him do his own work well.

How this is to happen we have stated already, but it will be made plain also by the following consideration of the specific nature of virtue. In everything that is continuous and divisible it is possible to take more, less, or an equal amount, and that either in terms of the thing itself or relatively to us; and the equal is an intermediate between excess and defect. By the intermediate in the object I mean that which is equidistant from each of the extremes, which is one and the same for all men; by the intermediate relatively to us that which is neither too much nor too little—and this is not one, nor the same for all. For instance, if ten is many and two is few, six is the intermediate, taken in terms of the object; for it exceeds and is exceeded by an equal amount; this is intermediate according to arithmetical proportion. But the intermediate relatively to us is not to be taken so; if ten pounds are too much for a particular person to eat and two too little, it does not follow that the trainer will order six pounds; for this also is perhaps too much for the person who is to take it, or too little—too little for Milo,[17] too much

for the beginner in athletic exercises. The same is true of running and wrestling. Thus a master of any art avoids excess and defect, but seeks the intermediate and chooses this—the intermediate not in the object but relatively to us.

If it is thus, then, that every art does its work well—by looking to the intermediate and judging its works by this standard (so that we often say of good works of art that it is not possible either to take away or to add anything, implying that excess and defect destroy the goodness of works of art, while the mean preserves it; and good artists, as we say, look to this in their work), and if, further, virtue is more exact and better than any art, as nature also is, then virtue must have the quality of aiming at the intermediate. I mean moral virtue; for it is this that is concerned with passions and actions, and in these there is excess, defect, and the intermediate. For instance, both fear and confidence and appetite and anger and pity and in general pleasure and pain may be felt both too much and too little, and in both cases not well; but to feel them at the right times, with reference to the right objects, towards the right people, with the right motive, and in the right way, is what is both intermediate and best, and this is characteristic of virtue. Similarly with regard to actions also there is excess, defect, and the intermediate. Now virtue is concerned with passions and actions, in which excess is a form of failure, and so is defect, while the intermediate is praised and is a form of success; and being praised and being successful are both characteristics of virtue. Therefore virtue is a kind of mean, since, as we have seen, it aims at what is intermediate.

Again, it is possible to fail in many ways (for evil belongs to the class of the unlimited, as the Pythagoreans[18] conjectured, and good to that of the limited), while to succeed is possible only in one way (for

---

17   Milo of Croton, supposed to have lived in the second half of the sixth century BCE in southern Italy, was a legendary wrestler and athlete, famous for his immense strength.

18   The followers of philosopher and mystic Pythagoras of Samos (c. 570–495 BCE). One of their most influential beliefs was that everything in the universe can be understood in terms of *harmonia* or number, and the notion of a "limit" which Aristotle refers to here is a quasi-mathematical notion.

which reason also one is easy and the other difficult—to miss the mark easy, to hit it difficult); for these reasons also, then, excess and defect are characteristic of vice, and the mean of virtue;

> *For men are good in but one way, but bad in many.*[19]

Virtue, then, is a state of character concerned with choice, lying in a mean, i.e., the mean relative to us, this being determined by a rational principle, and by that principle by which the man of practical wisdom would determine it. Now it is a mean between two vices, that which depends on excess and that which depends on defect; and again it is a mean because the vices respectively fall short of or exceed what is right in both passions and actions, while virtue both finds and chooses that which is intermediate. Hence in respect of what it is, i.e., the definition which states its essence, virtue is a mean, with regard to what is best and right an extreme.

But not every action nor every passion admits of a mean; for some have names that already imply badness, e.g., spite, shamelessness, envy, and in the case of actions adultery, theft, murder; for all of these and suchlike things imply by their names that they are themselves bad, and not the excesses or deficiencies of them. It is not possible, then, ever to be right with regard to them; one must always be wrong. Nor does goodness or badness with regard to such things depend on committing adultery with the right woman, at the right time, and in the right way, but simply to do any of them is to go wrong. It would be equally absurd, then, to expect that in unjust, cowardly, and voluptuous action there should be a mean, an excess, and a deficiency; for at that rate there would be a mean of excess and of deficiency, an excess of excess, and a deficiency of deficiency. But as there is no excess and deficiency of temperance and courage because what is intermediate is in a sense an extreme, so too of the actions we have mentioned there is no mean nor any excess and deficiency, but however they are done they are wrong; for in general there is neither a mean of excess and deficiency, nor excess and deficiency of a mean.

---

19   The source of this quotation is unknown.

7: The above proposition illustrated by reference to particular virtues.

We must, however, not only make this general statement, but also apply it to the individual facts. For among statements about conduct those which are general apply more widely, but those which are particular are more true, since conduct has to do with individual cases, and our statements must harmonize with the facts in these cases. We may take these cases from our table.[20] With regard to feelings of fear and confidence courage is the mean; of the people who exceed, he who exceeds in fearlessness has no name (many of the states have no name), while the man who exceeds in confidence is rash, and he who exceeds in fear and falls short in confidence is a coward. With regard to pleasures and pains—not all of them, and not so much with regard to the pains—the mean is temperance, the excess self-indulgence. Persons deficient with regard to the pleasures are not often found; hence such persons also have received no name. But let us call them 'insensible'.

With regard to giving and taking of money the mean is liberality, the excess and the defect prodigality and meanness. In these actions people exceed and fall short in contrary ways; the prodigal exceeds in spending and falls short in taking, while the mean man exceeds in taking and falls short in spending. (At present we are giving a mere outline or summary, and are satisfied with this; later these states will be more exactly determined.) With regard to money there are also other dispositions—a mean, magnificence (for the magnificent man differs from the liberal man; the former deals with large sums, the latter with small ones), an excess, tastelessness and vulgarity, and a deficiency, niggardliness; these differ from the states opposed to liberality, and the mode of their difference will be stated later.

With regard to honour and dishonour the mean is proper pride, the excess is known as a sort of 'empty vanity', and the deficiency is undue humility; and as we said liberality was related to magnificence, differing from it by dealing with small sums, so there is a state similarly related to proper pride, being concerned

---

20   Aristotle must have used a diagram at this point during his lectures, to illustrate graphically the various virtues and their extremes.

with small honours while that is concerned with great. For it is possible to desire honour as one ought, and more than one ought, and less, and the man who exceeds in his desires is called ambitious, the man who falls short unambitious, while the intermediate person has no name. The dispositions also are nameless, except that that of the ambitious man is called ambition. Hence the people who are at the extremes lay claim to the middle place; and we ourselves sometimes call the intermediate person ambitious and sometimes unambitious, and sometimes praise the ambitious man and sometimes the unambitious. The reason of our doing this will be stated in what follows; but now let us speak of the remaining states according to the method which has been indicated.

With regard to anger also there is an excess, a deficiency, and a mean. Although they can scarcely be said to have names, yet since we call the intermediate person good-tempered let us call the mean good temper; of the persons at the extremes let the one who exceeds be called irascible, and his vice irascibility, and the man who falls short an unirascible sort of person, and the deficiency unirascibility.

There are also three other means, which have a certain likeness to one another, but differ from one another: for they are all concerned with intercourse in words and actions, but differ in that one is concerned with truth in this sphere, the other two with pleasantness; and of this one kind is exhibited in giving amusement, the other in all the circumstances of life. We must therefore speak of these too, that we may the better see that in all things the mean is praise-worthy, and the extremes neither praiseworthy nor right, but worthy of blame. Now most of these states also have no names, but we must try, as in the other cases, to invent names ourselves so that we may be clear and easy to follow. With regard to truth, then, the intermediate is a truthful sort of person and the mean may be called truthfulness, while the pretence which exaggerates is boastfulness and the person characterized by it a boaster, and that which understates is mock modesty and the person characterized by it mock-modest. With regard to pleasantness in the giving of amusement the intermediate person is ready-witted and the disposition ready wit, the excess is buffoonery and the person characterized by it a buffoon, while the man who falls

short is a sort of boor and his state is boorishness. With regard to the remaining kind of pleasantness, that which is exhibited in life in general, the man who is pleasant in the right way is friendly and the mean is friendliness, while the man who exceeds is an obsequious person if he has no end in view, a flatterer if he is aiming at his own advantage, and the man who falls short and is unpleasant in all circumstances is a quarrelsome and surly sort of person.

There are also means in the passions and concerned with the passions; since shame is not a virtue, and yet praise is extended to the modest man. For even in these matters one man is said to be intermediate, and another to exceed, as for instance the bashful man who is ashamed of everything; while he who falls short or is not ashamed of anything at all is shameless, and the intermediate person is modest. Righteous indignation is a mean between envy and spite, and these states are concerned with the pain and pleasure that are felt at the fortunes of our neighbours; the man who is characterized by righteous indignation is pained at undeserved good fortune, the envious man, going beyond him, is pained at all good fortune, and the spiteful man falls so far short of being pained that he even rejoices.[21] But these states there will be an opportunity of describing elsewhere; with regard to justice, since it has not one simple meaning, we shall, after describing the other states, distinguish its two kinds and say how each of them is a mean; and similarly we shall treat also of the rational virtues.

8: The extremes are opposed to each other and to the mean.

There are three kinds of disposition, then, two of them vices, involving excess and deficiency respectively, and one a virtue, viz.[22] the mean, and all are in a sense opposed to all; for the extreme states are contrary both to the intermediate state and to each other, and the intermediate to the extremes; as the equal is greater relatively to the less, less relatively to the greater, so the middle states are excessive relatively to the deficiencies, deficient relatively to the excesses, both in passions and in actions. For the brave man appears

---

21 At the misfortune of others.

22 "In other words."

rash relatively to the coward, and cowardly relatively to the rash man; and similarly the temperate man appears self-indulgent relatively to the insensible man, insensible relatively to the self-indulgent, and the liberal man prodigal relatively to the mean man, mean relatively to the prodigal. Hence also the people at the extremes push the intermediate man each over to the other, and the brave man is called rash by the coward, cowardly by the rash man, and correspondingly in the other cases.

These states being thus opposed to one another, the greatest contrariety is that of the extremes to each other, rather than to the intermediate; for these are further from each other than from the intermediate, as the great is further from the small and the small from the great than both are from the equal. Again, to the intermediate some extremes show a certain likeness, as that of rashness to courage and that of prodigality to liberality; but the extremes show the greatest unlikeness to each other; now contraries are defined as the things that are furthest from each other, so that things that are further apart are more contrary.

To the mean in some cases the deficiency, in some the excess, is more opposed; e.g., it is not rashness, which is an excess, but cowardice, which is a deficiency, that is more opposed to courage, and not insensibility, which is a deficiency, but self-indulgence, which is an excess, that is more opposed to temperance. This happens from two reasons, one being drawn from the thing itself; for because one extreme is nearer and liker to the intermediate, we oppose not this but rather its contrary to the intermediate. E.g., since rashness is thought liker and nearer to courage, and cowardice more unlike, we oppose rather the latter to courage; for things that are further from the intermediate are thought more contrary to it. This, then, is one cause, drawn from the thing itself; another is drawn from ourselves; for the things to which we ourselves more naturally tend seem more contrary to the intermediate. For instance, we ourselves tend more naturally to pleasures, and hence are more easily carried away towards self-indulgence than towards propriety. We describe as contrary to the mean, then, rather the directions in which we more often go to great lengths; and therefore self-indulgence, which is an excess, is the more contrary to temperance.

9: The mean is hard to attain, and is grasped by perception, not by reasoning.

That moral virtue is a mean, then, and in what sense it is so, and that it is a mean between two vices, the one involving excess, the other deficiency, and that it is such because its character is to aim at what is intermediate in passions and in actions, has been sufficiently stated. Hence also it is no easy task to be good. For in everything it is no easy task to find the middle, e.g., to find the middle of a circle is not for every one but for him who knows; so, too, any one can get angry—that is easy—or give or spend money; but to do this to the right person, to the right extent, at the right time, with the right motive, and in the right way, *that* is not for every one, nor is it easy; wherefore goodness is both rare and laudable and noble.

Hence he who aims at the intermediate must first depart from what is the more contrary to it, as Calypso advises—

Hold the ship out beyond that surf and spray.[23]
For of the extremes one is more erroneous, one less so; therefore, since to hit the mean is hard in the extreme, we must as a second best, as people say, take the least of the evils; and this will be done best in the way we describe.

But we must consider the things towards which we ourselves also are easily carried away; for some of us tend to one thing, some to another; and this will be recognizable from the pleasure and the pain we feel. We must drag ourselves away to the contrary extreme; for we shall get into the intermediate state by drawing well away from error, as people do in straightening sticks that are bent.

Now in everything the pleasant or pleasure is most to be guarded against; for we do not judge it impar-

23   A line from Homer's *Odyssey* (part 12, lines 219–220). However, it is actually Circe (an enchantress), not Calypso (the nymph who detained Odysseus and his crew on her island), who gave the advice. The actual quotation is from Odysseus' orders to his steersman when he acts on Circe's suggestion that he take the ship closer to Scylla (a sea monster) than to Charybdis (a great whirlpool). Aristotle's quotations from Homer were apparently made from memory, and are rarely exact.

tially. We ought, then, to feel towards pleasure as the elders of the people felt towards Helen, and in all circumstances repeat their saying;[24] for if we dismiss pleasure thus we are less likely to go astray. It is by doing this, then, (to sum the matter up) that we shall best be able to hit the mean.

But this is no doubt difficult, and especially in individual cases; for it is not easy to determine both how and with whom and on what provocation and how long one should be angry; for we too sometimes praise those who fall short and call them good-tempered, but sometimes we praise those who get angry and call them manly. The man, however, who deviates little from goodness is not blamed, whether he do so in the direction of the more or of the less, but only the man who deviates more widely; for *he* does not fail to be noticed. But up to what point and to what extent a man must deviate before he becomes blameworthy it is not easy to determine by reasoning, any more than anything else that is perceived by the senses; such things depend on particular facts, and the decision rests with perception. So much, then, is plain, that the intermediate state is in all things to be praised, but that we must incline sometimes towards the excess, sometimes towards the deficiency; for so shall we most easily hit the mean and what is right....

Book X

6: Happiness is good activity, not amusement.

Now that we have spoken of the virtues, the forms of friendship, and the varieties of pleasure, what remains is to discuss in outline the nature of happiness, since

24   See Homer's *Iliad*, part 3, lines 156–160 (here translated by Richmond Lattimore):
   Surely there is no blame on Trojans and strong-greaved Achaians
   if for long time they suffer hardship for a woman like this one.
   Terrible is the likeness of her face to immortal goddesses.
   Still, though she be such, let her go away in the ships, lest
   she be left behind, a grief for us and our children.

this is what we state the end of human affairs to be. Our discussion will be the more concise if we first sum up what we have said already. We said, then, that it is not a state; for if it were it might belong to someone who was asleep throughout his life, living the life of a plant, or, again, to someone who was suffering the greatest misfortunes. If these implications are unacceptable, and we must rather class happiness as an activity, as we have said before, and if some activities are necessary, and desirable for the sake of something else, while others are so in themselves, evidently happiness must be placed among those desirable in themselves, not among those desirable for the sake of something else; for happiness does not lack anything, but is self-sufficient. Now those activities are desirable in themselves from which nothing is sought beyond the activity. And of this nature virtuous actions are thought to be; for to do noble and good deeds is a thing desirable for its own sake.

Pleasant amusements also are thought to be of this nature: we choose them not for the sake of other things; for we are injured rather than benefited by them, since we are led to neglect our bodies and our property. But most of the people who are deemed happy take refuge in such pastimes, which is the reason why those who are ready-witted at them are highly esteemed at the courts of tyrants; they make themselves pleasant companions in the tyrants' favourite pursuits, and that is the sort of man they want. Now these things are thought to be of the nature of happiness because people in despotic positions spend their leisure in them, but perhaps such people prove nothing; for virtue and reason, from which good activities flow, do not depend on despotic position; nor, if these people, who have never tasted pure and generous pleasure, take refuge in the bodily pleasures, should these for that reason be thought more desirable; for boys, too, think the things that are valued among themselves are the best. It is to be expected, then, that, as different things seem valuable to boys and to men, so they should to bad men and to good. Now, as we have often maintained, those things are both valuable and pleasant which are such to the good man; and to each man the activity in accordance with his own disposition is most desirable, and, therefore, to the good man that which is in accordance with virtue. Happiness, therefore, does not lie in amusement; it would, indeed, be strange if the end were amusement, and one were to take trouble and suffer hardship all one's life in order to amuse oneself. For, in a word, everything that we choose we choose for the sake of something else—except happiness, which is an end. Now to exert oneself and work for the sake of amusement seems silly and utterly childish. But to amuse oneself in order that one may exert oneself, as Anacharsis[25] puts it, seems right; for amusement is a sort of relaxation, and we need relaxation because we cannot work continuously. Relaxation, then, is not an end; for it is taken for the sake of activity.

The happy life is thought to be virtuous; now a virtuous life requires exertion, and does not consist in amusement. And we say that serious things are better than laughable things and those connected with amusement, and that the activity of the better of any two things—whether it be two elements of our being or two men—is the more serious; but the activity of the better is *ipso facto*[26] superior and more of the nature of happiness. And any chance person—even a slave—can enjoy the bodily pleasures no less than the best man; but no one assigns to a slave a share in happiness—unless he assigns to him also a share in human life. For happiness does not lie in such occupations, but, as we have said before, in virtuous activities.

7: Happiness in the highest sense is the contemplative life.

If happiness is activity in accordance with virtue, it is reasonable that it should be in accordance with the highest virtue; and this will be that of the best thing in us. Whether it be reason or something else that is this element which is thought to be our natural ruler and guide and to take thought of things noble and divine, whether it be itself also divine or only the most divine

element in us, the activity of this in accordance with its proper virtue will be perfect happiness. That this activity is contemplative[27] we have already said.

Now this would seem to be in agreement both with what we said before and with the truth. For, firstly, this activity is the best (since not only is reason the best thing in us, but the objects of reason are the best of knowable objects); and secondly, it is the most continuous, since we can contemplate truth more continuously than we can *do* anything. And we think happiness ought to have pleasure mingled with it, but the activity of philosophic wisdom is admittedly the pleasantest of virtuous activities; at all events the pursuit of it is thought to offer pleasures marvellous for their purity and their enduringness, and it is to be expected that those who know will pass their time more pleasantly than those who inquire. And the self-sufficiency that is spoken of must belong most to the contemplative activity. For while a philosopher, as well as a just man or one possessing any other virtue, needs the necessaries of life, when they are sufficiently equipped with things of that sort the just man needs people towards whom and with whom he shall act justly, and the temperate man, the brave man, and each of the others is in the same case, but the philosopher, even when by himself, can contemplate truth, and the better the wiser he is; he can perhaps do so better if he has fellow-workers, but still he is the most self-sufficient. And this activity alone would seem to be loved for its own sake; for nothing arises from it apart from the contemplating, while from practical activities we gain more or less apart from the action. And happiness is thought to depend on leisure; for we are busy that we may have leisure, and make war that

---

25 Anacharsis was a prince of Scythia (today the southern Ukraine), said to have lived early in the sixth century BCE, whose travels throughout the Greek world gave him a reputation for wisdom. He was known for his aphorisms, which were believed to be particularly profound.

26 "By that very fact."

27 The Greek word *theōria*, translated here as "contemplation," denotes something like the theoretical study of reality for the sake of knowledge alone, and would include, for example, astronomy, biology, mathematics, and anthropology as well as what we call philosophy. Furthermore, it is not so much the *search* for this knowledge that Aristotle is thinking of, but the quasi-aesthetic *appreciation* of it—a tranquil surveying of it in one's mind—once it has been acquired. (*Theōrein* is a Greek verb which originally meant to look at something, to gaze at it steadily.)

we may live in peace. Now the activity of the practical virtues is exhibited in political or military affairs, but the actions concerned with these seem to be unleisurely. Warlike actions are completely so (for no one chooses to be at war, or provokes war, for the sake of being at war; anyone would seem absolutely murderous if he were to make enemies of his friends in order to bring about battle and slaughter); but the action of the statesman is also unleisurely, and aims—beyond the political action itself—at despotic power and honours, or at all events happiness, for him and his fellow citizens—a happiness different from political action, and evidently sought as being different. So if among virtuous actions political and military actions are distinguished by nobility and greatness, and these are unleisurely and aim at an end and are not desirable for their own sake, but the activity of reason, which is contemplative, seems both to be superior in serious worth and to aim at no end beyond itself, and to have its pleasure proper to itself (and this augments the activity), and the self-sufficiency, leisureliness, unweariedness (so far as this is possible for man), and all the other attributes ascribed to the supremely happy man are evidently those connected with this activity, it follows that this will be the complete happiness of man, if it be allowed a complete term of life (for none of the attributes of happiness is *in*complete).

But such a life would be too high for man; for it is not in so far as he is man that he will live so, but in so far as something divine is present in him; and by so much as this is superior to our composite nature[28] is its activity superior to that which is the exercise of the other kind of virtue. If reason is divine, then, in comparison with man, the life according to it is divine in comparison with human life. But we must not follow those who advise us, being men, to think of human things, and, being mortal, of mortal things, but must, so far as we can, make ourselves immortal, and strain every nerve to live in accordance with the best thing in us; for even if it be small in bulk, much more does it in power and worth surpass everything. This would seem, too, to *be* each man himself, since it is the authoritative and better part of him. It would

be strange, then, if he were to choose not the life of his self but that of something else. And what we said before will apply now; that which is proper to each thing is by nature best and most pleasant for each thing; for man, therefore, the life according to reason is best and pleasantest, since reason more than anything else *is* man. This life therefore is also the happiest.

8: Superiority of the contemplative life further considered.

But in a secondary degree the life in accordance with the other kind of virtue is happy; for the activities in accordance with this befit our human estate. Just and brave acts, and other virtuous acts, we do in relation to each other, observing our respective duties with regard to contracts and services and all manner of actions and with regard to passions; and all of these seem to be typically human. Some of them seem even to arise from the body, and virtue of character to be in many ways bound up with the passions. Practical wisdom, too, is linked to virtue of character, and this to practical wisdom, since the principles of practical wisdom are in accordance with the moral virtues and rightness in morals is in accordance with practical wisdom. Being connected with the passions also, the moral virtues must belong to our composite nature; and the virtues of our composite nature are human; so, therefore, are the life and the happiness which correspond to these. The excellence of the reason is a thing apart; we must be content to say this much about it, for to describe it precisely is a task greater than our purpose requires. It would seem, however, also to need external equipment but little, or less than moral virtue does. Grant that both need the necessaries, and do so equally, even if the statesman's work is the more concerned with the body and things of that sort; for there will be little difference there; but in what they need for the exercise of their activities there will be much difference. The liberal man will need money for the doing of his liberal deeds, and the just man too will need it for the returning of services (for wishes are hard to discern, and even people who are not just *pretend* to wish to act justly); and the brave man will need power if he is to accomplish any of the acts that correspond to his virtue, and the temperate man will need opportunity; for how else is either he or any of

---

28   The view that human beings are made up of both soul and body, while the divine is pure intellect.

the others to be recognized? It is debated, too, whether the will or the deed is more essential to virtue, which is assumed to involve both; it is surely clear that its perfection involves both; but for deeds many things are needed, and more, the greater and nobler the deeds are. But the man who is contemplating the truth needs no such thing, at least with a view to the exercise of his activity; indeed they are, one may say, even hindrances, at all events to his contemplation; but in so far as he is a man and lives with a number of people, he chooses to do virtuous acts; he will therefore need such aids to living a human life.

But that perfect happiness is a contemplative activity will appear from the following consideration as well. We assume the gods to be above all other beings blessed and happy; but what sort of actions must we assign to them? Acts of justice? Will not the gods seem absurd if they make contracts and return deposits, and so on? Acts of a brave man, then, confronting dangers and running risks because it is noble to do so? Or liberal acts? To whom will they give? It will be strange if they are really to have money or anything of the kind. And what would their temperate acts be? Is not such praise tasteless, since they have no bad appetites? If we were to run through them all, the circumstances of action would be found trivial and unworthy of gods. Still, every one supposes that they *live* and therefore that they are active; we cannot suppose them to sleep like Endymion.[29] Now if you take away from a living being action, and still more production, what is left but contemplation? Therefore the activity of God, which surpasses all others in blessedness, must be contemplative; and of human activities, therefore, that which is most akin to this must be most of the nature of happiness.

This is indicated, too, by the fact that the other animals have no share in happiness, being completely deprived of such activity. For while the whole life of the gods is blessed, and that of men too in so far as some likeness of such activity belongs to them, none of the other animals is happy, since they in no way

share in contemplation. Happiness extends, then, just so far as contemplation does, and those to whom contemplation more fully belongs are more truly happy, not as a mere concomitant but in virtue of the contemplation; for this is in itself precious. Happiness, therefore, must be some form of contemplation.

But, being a man, one will also need external prosperity; for our nature is not self-sufficient for the purpose of contemplation, but our body also must be healthy and must have food and other attention. Still, we must not think that the man who is to be happy will need many things or great things, merely because he cannot be supremely happy without external goods; for self-sufficiency and action do not involve excess, and we can do noble acts without ruling earth and sea; for even with moderate advantages one can act virtuously (this is manifest enough; for private persons are thought to do worthy acts no less than despots—indeed even more); and it is enough that we should have so much as that; for the life of the man who is active in accordance with virtue will be happy. Solon,[30] too, was perhaps sketching well the happy man when he described him[31] as moderately furnished with externals but as having done (as Solon thought) the noblest acts, and lived temperately; for one can with but moderate possessions do what one ought. Anaxagoras[32] also seems to have supposed the happy man not to be rich nor a despot, when he said that he would not be surprised if the happy man were to seem to most people a strange person; for they judge by externals, since these are all they perceive. The opinions of the wise seem, then, to harmonize with our arguments. But while even such things carry some conviction, the truth in practical matters is discerned from the facts of life; for these are the

---

29 According to Greek myth, Endymion was such a beautiful man that the Moon fell in love with him. She made him immortal, but cast him into an eternal sleep so that she could descend and embrace him every night.

30 Solon (c. 640–558 BCE) was an Athenian lawmaker and poet, considered the founder of Athenian democracy, whose name was a byword for wisdom.

31 As quoted in Book I of Herodotus's *History*.

32 Anaxagoras of Clazomenae (c. 500–428 BCE) was the first philosopher to teach in Athens—though he, like Socrates and Plato, was prosecuted for impiety by the Athenians (in part for believing that the sun is a fiery body larger than Greece and that the light of the moon is reflected light from the sun).

decisive factor. We must therefore survey what we have already said, bringing it to the test of the facts of life, and if it harmonizes with the facts we must accept it, but if it clashes with them we must suppose it to be mere theory. Now he who exercises his reason and cultivates it seems to be both in the best state of mind and most dear to the gods. For if the gods have any care for human affairs, as they are thought to have, it would be reasonable both that they should delight in that which was best and most akin to them (i.e., reason) and that they should reward those who love and honour this most, as caring for the things that are dear to them and acting both rightly and nobly. And that all these attributes belong most of all to the philosopher is manifest. He, therefore, is the dearest to the gods. And he who is that will presumably be also the happiest; so that in this way too the philosopher will more than any other be happy.

IMMANUEL KANT

Foundations of the Metaphysics of Morals

Who Was Immanuel Kant?

Immanuel Kant—by common consent the most important philosopher of the past 300 years, and arguably the most important of the past 2,300—was born in 1724 on the coast of the Baltic Sea, in Königsberg, a regionally important harbor city in East Prussia.[1] Kant spent his whole life living in this town, and never ventured outside its region. His family were devout members of an evangelical Protestant sect (rather like the Quakers or early Methodists) called the Pietists, and Pietism's strong emphasis on moral responsibility, hard work, and distrust of religious dogma had a deep effect on Kant's character. Kant's father was a craftsman (making harnesses and saddles for horses) and his family was fairly poor; Kant's mother, whom he loved deeply, died when he was 13.

Kant's life is notorious for its outward uneventfulness. He was educated at a strict Lutheran school in Königsberg, and after graduating from the University of Königsberg in 1746 (where he supported himself by some tutoring but also by his skill at billiards and card games) he served as a private tutor to various local families until he became a lecturer at the university in 1755. However his position—that of *Privatdozent*—carried no salary, and Kant was expected to support himself by the income from his lecturing; financial need caused Kant to lecture for thirty or more hours a week on a huge range of subjects (including mathematics, physics, geography, anthropology, ethics, and law). During this period Kant published several scientific works and his reputation as a scholar grew; he turned down opportunities for professorships in other towns (Erlangen and Jena), having his heart set on a professorship in Königsberg. Finally, at the age of 46, Kant became professor of logic and metaphysics at the University of Königsberg, a position he held until his retirement twenty-six years later in 1796. After a tragic period of senility he died in

---

1   Prussia is a historical region which included what is today northern Germany, Poland, and the western fringes of Russia. It became a kingdom in 1701, and then a dominant part of the newly unified Germany in 1871. Greatly reduced after World War I, the state of Prussia was formally abolished after World War II, and Königsberg—renamed Kaliningrad during the Soviet era, after one of Stalin's henchmen—now sits on the western rump of Russia (between Poland and Lithuania).

1804, and was buried with pomp and circumstance in the "professors' vault" at the Königsberg cathedral.[2]

Kant's days were structured by a rigorous and unvarying routine—indeed, it is often said that the housewives of Königsberg were able to set their clocks by the regularity of his afternoon walk. He never married (though twice he nearly did), had very few close friends, and lived by all accounts an austere and outwardly unemotional life. He was something of a hypochondriac, hated noise, and disliked all music except for military marches. Nevertheless, anecdotes by those who knew him give the impression of a warm, impressive, rather noble human being, capable of great kindness and dignity and sparkling conversation. He did not shun society, and in fact his regular daily routine included an extended lunchtime gathering at which he and his guests—drawn from the cosmopolitan stratum of Königsberg society—would discuss politics, science, philosophy, and poetry.

Kant's philosophical life is often divided into three phases: his "pre-Critical" period, his "silent" period, and his "Critical" period. His pre-Critical period began in 1747 when he published his first work (*Thoughts on the True Estimation of Living Forces*) and ended in 1770 when he wrote his Inaugural Dissertation—*Concerning the Form and Principles of the Sensible and Intelligible World*—and became a professor. Between 1770 and 1780, Kant published almost nothing. In 1781, however, at the age of 57, Kant made his first major contribution to philosophy with his monumental *Critique of Pure Reason* (written, Kant said, over the course of a few months "as if in flight"). He spent the next twenty years in unrelenting intellectual labor, trying to develop and answer the new problems laid out in this masterwork. First, in order to clarify and simplify the system of the *Critique* for the educated public, Kant published the much shorter *Prolegomena to Any Future Metaphysics* in 1783. In 1785 came Kant's *Foundations of the Metaphysics of Morals*, and in 1788 he published what is now known as his "second Critique": the *Critique of Practical Reason*. His third and final Critique, the *Critique of Judgement*, was published in 1790—an amazing body of work produced in less than ten years.

By the time he died, Kant had already become known as a great philosopher, with a permanent place in history. Over his grave was inscribed a quote from the *Critique of Practical Reason*, which sums up the impulse for his philosophy: "Two things fill the mind with ever new and increasing admiration and reverence, the more often and more steadily one reflects on them: the starry heavens above me and the moral law within me."

What Was Kant's Overall Philosophical Project?

Kant began his philosophical career as a follower of rationalism. Rationalism was an important seventeenth- and eighteenth-century intellectual movement begun by Descartes and developed by Leibniz and his follower Christian Wolff, which held that all knowledge was capable of being part of a single, complete "science": that is, all knowledge can be slotted into a total, unified system of *a priori*, and certainly true, claims capable of encompassing everything that exists in the world, whether we have experience of it or not. In other words, for the German rationalists of Kant's day, metaphysical philosophy—which then

---

2   His body no longer remains there: in 1950 his sarcophagus was broken open by unknown vandals and his corpse was stolen and never recovered.

included theoretical science—was thought of as being very similar to pure mathematics. Rationalism was also, in Kantian terminology, "dogmatic" as opposed to "critical": that is, it sought to construct systems of knowledge without first attempting a careful examination of the scope and limits of possible knowledge. (This is why Kant's rationalist period is usually called his pre-Critical phase.)

In 1781, after ten years of hard thought, Kant rejected this rationalistic view of philosophy: he came to the view that metaphysics, as traditionally understood, is so far from being a rational science that it is not even a body of knowledge at all. Three major stimuli provoked Kant into being "awakened from his dogmatic slumber," as he put it. First, in about 1769, Kant came to the conclusion that he had discovered several "antinomies"—sets of contradictory propositions *each* of which can apparently be *rationally proven* to be true of reality (if we assume that our intellectual concepts apply to reality at all) and yet which can't both be true. For example, Kant argued that rational arguments are available to prove both that reality is finite but also that it is infinite, and that it is composed of indivisible atoms yet also infinitely divisible. Since both halves of these two pairs can't possibly be true at the same time, Kant argued that this casts serious doubt on the power of pure reason to draw metaphysical conclusions.

Second, Kant was worried about the conflict between free will and natural causality (this is a theme that appears throughout Kant's Critical works). He was convinced that genuine morality must be based on *freely* choosing—or "willing"— to do what is right. To be worthy of moral praise, in Kant's view, one must choose to do *X* rather than *Y*, not because some law of nature causes you to do so, but because your rational self is convinced that it is the right thing to do. Yet he also thought that the rational understanding of reality sought by the metaphysicians could only be founded on universally extending the laws we find in the scientific study of nature—and this includes universal causal determination, the principle that nothing (including choosing *X* over *Y*) happens without a cause. This, for Kant, produces an antinomy: some actions are free (i.e., *not* bound by the laws of nature) and yet everything that happens *is* determined by a law of nature.

Kant resolved this paradox by arguing that the scientific view of reality (including that pursued by the rationalists) must in principle be *incomplete*. Roughly, he held that although we can only rationally understand reality by thinking of it as causally deterministic and governed by scientific laws, our intellectual reason can never encompass *all* of reality. According to Kant, there must be a level of ultimate reality which is beyond the scope of pure reason, and which allows for the free activity of what Kant calls "practical reason" (which therefore holds open the possibility of genuine morality).

The third alarm bell to rouse Kant from his pre-Critical dogmatism was his reading of the Scottish philosopher David Hume. Hume was not a rationalist but instead represented the culmination of the other main seventeenth- and eighteenth-century stream of philosophical thought, usually called empiricism. Instead of thinking of knowledge as a unified, systematic, *a priori* whole, as the rationalists did, empiricists like Locke and Hume saw knowledge as being a piecemeal accumulation of claims derived primarily, not from pure logic, but from *sensation*— from our experience of the world. Science, for Hume, is thus not *a priori* but *a posteriori*: for example, we cannot just *deduce* from first principles that heavy objects tend to fall to the ground, as the rationalists supposed we could; we can only learn this by observing it to happen in our experience. The trouble was that Hume appeared to Kant (and to many others) to have shown that experience is simply *inadequate* for establishing the kind of metaphysical principles that philosophers have traditionally defended: no amount of sense-experience could ever either prove or disprove that God exists, that substance is imperishable, that we have an immortal soul, or even that there exist mind-independent "physical" objects which interact with each other according to causal laws of nature. Not just what we now think of as "philosophy" but theoretical science itself seemed to be called into question by Hume's "skeptical" philosophy. Since Kant was quite sure that mathematics and the natural sciences were genuine bodies of knowledge, he needed to show how such knowledge was possible despite Hume's skepticism: that is, as well as combatting the excessive claims of rationalism, he needed to show how empiricism went wrong in the other direction.

Prior to Kant, seventeenth- and eighteenth-century philosophers divided knowledge into exactly two camps: "truths of reason" (or "relations of ideas") on the one hand, and "truths of fact" (or "matters of fact") on the other. Rationalism was characterized by the doctrine that all final, complete knowledge was a truth of reason: that is, it was made up entirely of claims that could be proven *a priori* as being necessarily true, as a matter of logic, since it would be self-contradictory for them to be false. Empiricists, on the other hand, believed that all genuinely *informative* claims were truths of fact: if we wanted to find out about the world itself, rather than merely the logical relations between our own concepts, we had to rely upon the (*a posteriori*) data of sensory experience.

Kant, however, reshaped this distinction in a new framework which, he argued, cast a vital new light upon the nature of metaphysics. Instead of merely drawing a distinction between truths of reason and truths of fact, Kant replaced this with *two* separate distinctions: that between "*a priori*" and "*a posteriori*" propositions, and that between "analytic" and "synthetic" judgments. On this more complex scheme, the rationalists' truths of reason turn out to be "analytic *a priori*" knowledge, while empirical truths of fact are "synthetic *a posteriori*" propositions. But, Kant pointed out, this leaves open the possibility that there is at least a *third* type of knowledge: *synthetic a priori* judgments. These are judgments which we know *a priori* and thus do not need to learn from experience, but which nevertheless go beyond merely "analytic" claims about our own concepts. Kant's central claim in the *Critique of Pure Reason* is that he is the first philosopher in history to understand that the traditional claims of metaphysics—questions about God, the soul, free will, the underlying nature of space, time and matter—consist entirely of synthetic *a priori* propositions. (He also argues that pure mathematics is synthetic *a priori* as well.)

Kant's question therefore becomes: *How* is synthetic *a priori* knowledge possible? After all, the source of this knowledge can be neither experience (since it is *a priori*) nor the logical relations of ideas (since it is synthetic), so where could this kind of knowledge possibly come from? Once we have discovered the conditions of synthetic *a priori* knowledge, we can ask what its limits are: in particular, we can ask whether the traditional claims of speculative metaphysics meet those conditions, and thus whether they can be known to be true.

In bald (and massively simplified) summary, Kant's answer to these questions in the *Critique of Pure Reason* is the following. Synthetic *a priori* knowledge is possible insofar as it is knowledge of the *conditions of our experience of the world* (or indeed, of any *possible* experience). For example, for Kant, our judgments about the fundamental nature of space and time are not claims about our experiences themselves, nor are they the results of logic: instead, the forms of space and time are the conditions under which we are capable of having experience *at all*—we *can* only undergo sensations (either perceived or imaginary) that are arranged in space, and spread out in time; anything else is just impossible for us. So we can know *a priori*, but not analytically, that space and time must have a certain nature, since they are the forms of (the very possibility of) our experience.

Kant, famously, described this insight as constituting a kind of "Copernican revolution" in philosophy: just as Copernicus set cosmology on a totally new path by suggesting (in 1543) that the Earth orbits the Sun and not the other way around, so Kant wanted to breathe new life into philosophy by suggesting that, rather than assuming that "all our knowledge must conform to objects," we might instead "suppose that objects must conform to our knowledge." That is, rather than merely passively representing mind-independent objects in a "real" world, Kant held that the mind actively *constitutes* its objects—by *imposing* the categories of time, space, and causation onto our sensory experience, the subject actually *creates* the only kind of reality to which it has access. (This is why Kant's philosophy is often called "transcendental idealism." However, Kant is not a full-out idealist in the way that, say, George Berkeley is. He does not claim that the *existence* of objects is mind-dependent—only God's mind is capable of this kind of creation, according to Kant. Instead, the *a priori properties* of objects are what we constitute, by the structures of our cognition.)

When we turn to speculative metaphysics, however, we try to go beyond experience and its conditions—we attempt to move beyond what Kant called the "phenomena" of experience, and to make judgments about the nature of a reality that lies behind our sensory experience, what Kant called the "noumenal" realm. And here pure reason reaches its limits. If we ask about the nature of "things in themselves," independently of our experience of them, or if we try to show whether a supra-sensible God really exists, then our faculty of reason is powerless to demonstrate that these synthetic *a priori* judgments are either true or false—these metaphysical questions are neither empirical, nor logical, nor about the basic categories of our experience, so there is simply no way to answer them. The questions are meaningful ones (human beings crave answers to them) but they are beyond the scope of our faculty of reason. In short, we can have knowledge only of things that can be objects of possible experience, and cannot know anything that transcends the phenomenal realm.

This result, according to Kant, finally lets philosophy cease its constant oscillation between dogmatism and skepticism. It sets out the area in which human cognition is capable of attaining lasting truth (theoretical science—the metaphysics of experience—and mathematics), and that in which reason leads to self-contradiction and illusion (speculative metaphysics). Importantly, for Kant, this Copernican revolution provides *morality* with all the metaphysical support it needs, by clearing an area for free will.

What Is the Structure of This Reading?

Kant's *Foundations of the Metaphysics of Morals* was written, not just for professional philosophers, but for the general educated reader. Nevertheless, it can be pretty hard going, especially for those coming to Kant for the first time; the effort, however, is richly rewarded.

The *Foundations* forms a single, continuous argument running the whole length of the book, and each step of that overall argument is supported by sub-arguments. Its aim is to lay the preliminary groundwork for the study of morality. It is not intended to be, all by itself, a *moral theory* (though that is often the way it

has been treated in the past). Kant's goals for the work are ambitious enough: first, to establish that there is such a thing as morality—that there really are laws that should govern our conduct—and, second, to discover and justify "the supreme principle of morality." This "supreme principle," which Kant announces he has uncovered, is now famous as the Categorical Imperative.

Each section of the *Foundations* plays a role in Kant's overall argument. He begins, in the First Section, by simply trying to discover *what we already think morality is*. He is not, at this stage, trying to *justify* these beliefs: he merely wants to analyze our moral "common sense" to bring to light the principle behind it. He argues that the only thing which is "unconditionally" morally good is a good will, and that this insight is embedded in our ordinary moral judgments. (He then backs this argument with another, longer but less plausible, which appeals to "the purpose of nature.") The key to understanding morality, therefore, must be a proper understanding of the good will; if we can understand the principles that people of good will try to act on, Kant thinks, then we can see what the moral law tells us to do. In order to carry out this investigation, Kant announces he will focus on examples that make the moral will especially clear: i.e., on cases where the person performing an action has other motives that would normally lead to *not* doing that thing, but where she does it anyway because she recognizes it as her moral duty. He illustrates this contrast between people doing things "from duty" and doing them for some other reason by giving examples (each of which can be done for the sake of duty or not): a merchant who does not overcharge customers, a person who refrains from committing suicide, a man who performs kind actions to help others, and someone taking care to preserve their own happiness.

Consideration of examples like these shows us, Kant argues, that what gives a particular action moral worth is not the kind of action it is, nor the consequences of that action, nor even the purpose for which the action is performed, but the psychological *maxim* motivating that action. This in turn, Kant claims, shows moral worth is a kind of *respect for moral law* and that, in order to have the form of a law, moral principles must be *universalizable*. This important result is then illustrated and further explained using the example of truth-telling.

Kant concludes the First Section by explaining the need for philosophy to bolster these insights of common sense. The Second Section, therefore, is devoted to developing the fundamental elements of a proper "metaphysics of morals," which, in turn, Kant argues, must ultimately be embedded within a general theory of *practical reason*. Since the theory of practical reason is a theory of what reason tells us we ought to do (whether or not we actually do it), it must be a theory of what Kant calls *imperatives*. Kant therefore embarks on a discussion of the different types of imperative, distinguishing between *hypothetical* imperatives and *categorical* imperatives. Moral imperatives, he argues, must be categorical and not hypothetical.

He then asks: What makes these imperatives "possible," that is, what makes them legitimate requirements of rationality? Why are they *laws* that are binding on rational beings? The answer for hypothetical imperatives, Kant argues, is easy: that hypothetical imperatives are laws of reason is an *analytic* truth. However, in the case of categorical imperatives, the issue is more difficult. That these imperatives are rationally binding can only be, in Kant's terms, a *synthetic a priori* practical principle—something which we can know, independently of experience, to be true, but which is not merely true 'logically' or by virtue of the meanings of the words involved. Thus, showing there really *are* moral laws that are binding on all rational creatures is a difficult problem for Kant—and he postpones it until the Third Section of his book.

First, he turns to a more detailed analysis of the concept of a categorical imperative and, by emphasizing the *unconditional* character of categorical imperatives, arrives at his first major formulation of the moral law: the so-called Formula of Universal Law. Kant then illustrates how this law constrains our duties by ruling out certain maxims as being immoral. He gives four (carefully chosen) examples: someone contemplating suicide, someone considering borrowing money by making a false promise to repay it, someone wasting their talents in a life of self-indulgence and idleness, and someone refusing to help others.

If this helps us see *what* the categorical imperative requires us, morally, to do, the next issue is to discover *why* our wills should be consistent with the categorical imperative: what could motivate us to adopt universalizable maxims? The imperative is categorical and not hypothetical, so we cannot appeal to any contingent or variable motivations: the goal of morality—the *value* of being moral—must be something shared by every possible rational creature, no matter how they are situated. This, Kant argues, means all rational creatures must be ends-in-themselves and the ultimate source of all objective value. The categorical imperative can thus be expressed according to the Formula of Humanity as End in Itself. The reason non-universalizable maxims are immoral is, according to Kant, because they fail to properly respect rational creatures as ends in themselves; Kant illustrates this by re-considering his four examples in light of this latest formulation.

This notion of rational beings as having (and indeed being the source of) objective, intrinsic worth leads Kant to the idea of the *kingdom of ends*: an ideal human community in which people treat each other as ends in themselves. Acting morally, Kant claims, can be thought of as *legislating* moral laws for this ideal community: we guide our own behavior by principles which we realize should be followed by all the free and equal members of the kingdom of ends. This formulation of the categorical imperative is often called the Formula of Autonomy (autonomy comes from the Greek words for self—*autos*—and law—*nomos*—and hence means something like "following one's own laws"). Again, this shows us something new about the categorical imperative: the reason we ought to follow the moral law is not because we are forced to conform to it by something outside ourselves (such as society or God), but because these are laws that rational people lay down *for themselves*.[3] Morality, thus, does

---

3   Moreover, we do not need to be told, by some external authority, what the moral law is. We can each reliably discover *for ourselves* what we ought to do. In fact, for Kant, acting in accordance with a moral law merely because some moral authority has told you to does not make you a good person. That would be to obey a merely hypothetical, and not a categorical, imperative.

not infringe on freedom—on the contrary, it is the fullest expression of freedom, and also of respect for the freedom of others. Furthermore, it is the capacity of rational creatures to be legislators in the kingdom of ends which is the source of what Kant calls their *dignity*.

This brings us to the final stage of Kant's argument: the last problem he faces is that of showing moral law really does exist—that we really are rationally bound by it. He has shown that we *would* be bound by it if we were autonomous, rational beings capable of being legislative citizens in the kingdom of ends; now Kant has to show that human beings really do have an autonomous will, and this is the project of the Third Section (which is not reprinted here). To do this, Kant needs to show that the human will is not subject to the laws of nature, for otherwise we would not be free to legislate the moral law for ourselves. On the other hand, if we are free, then—since our wills must be governed by *some* law or other or they would not be causal—we must be governed by the moral law. Morality and freedom are thus intimately connected, for Kant, and we cannot have one without the other. He then argues that if we are to think of ourselves as *rational,* we must necessarily think of ourselves as free. Thus, to be rational just is to be governed by the moral law.

But how is this freedom possible—how *can* human beings be rational, given that we are surely part of the natural world and hence entangled in the web of the laws of nature? Here Kant appeals to and summarizes parts of his *Critique of Pure Reason*, where he argued that the empirical world of appearance—the world of nature—is not the way things are in themselves, but merely how they appear to us: 'behind' this world of appearance is the deeper reality of things as they are in themselves. Human beings, too, are subject to this duality: as members of the natural world, we are subject to the laws of causality, but our real selves—our *egos*—are "above nature" and so, at least potentially, are autonomous. Kant's overall conclusion in the *Foundations of the Metaphysics of Morals*, then, is not that we can actually know there *is* a moral law, but that a) if there were a moral law it would have to be the way he has described, b) it is at least possible the moral law really does exist, and c) in any case we

are forced to *believe* the moral law exists, simply in virtue of thinking of ourselves as rational beings.

Some Useful Background Information

1. The goal of Kant's *Foundations* is not to tell people how to act or to introduce a new theory of morality. Kant thought that, on the whole, people know perfectly well what they are and are not supposed to do and, indeed, that any moral theory having prescriptions that substantially diverged from "common sense" beliefs about morality was likely to be erroneous. When criticized by his contemporaries for merely providing a new formula for old beliefs, Kant replied, "… who would even want to introduce a new principle of all morality and, as it were, first invent it? Just as if, before him, the world had been ignorant of what duty is, or in thoroughgoing error about it." Instead, Kant aimed to provide a new philosophical *underpinning* for morality: he thought people had misunderstood *why* the prescriptions of morality are the way they are, and that they lacked a reliable *method* for making sure they always did the right thing.

2. In the Preface to the *Foundations of the Metaphysics of Morals* Kant divides philosophy into three parts: logic (the study of thought), physics (the study of the way the world is), and ethics (the study of what we ought to do). Kant thinks of each of these as a domain of *laws*: logic deals with the laws of thought, physics deals with the laws of nature, and ethics deals with what Kant calls the *laws of freedom*—that is, with laws governing the conduct of those beings not subject to the laws of nature. In this way, Kant sets up the study of morality as the study of a particular kind of law (as opposed to, say, of character traits, states of affairs, or types of actions), and he thinks of these laws as being analogous to, but different from, laws of nature.

3. According to Kant, there are in general two routes to knowledge: experience and reason. The study of logic is within the domain of pure reason, but for Kant physics and ethics each have both a "pure" and an empirical part. Par-

ticular physical laws—for example that infection is transmitted by micro-organisms—are empirical, but the general *framework* for these laws—the idea that all events must have a law-like cause—is not itself empirical (after all, we have not *seen* every event and its cause). That ethics must be built upon a non-empirical foundation is even more obvious, according to Kant. Ethics is the study, not of how things actually are, but of how things *ought* to be. Scrutinizing the way human beings actually behave, and describing the things they actually believe, will never be sufficient to tell you what we *ought* to do and think. Moral laws and concepts, therefore, must be established by pure reason alone (though experience will certainly play a role in determining the *concrete content* of moral principles in actual circumstances). This body of non-empirical knowledge, which sets out what Kant calls the "synthetic *a priori*" framework for physics and ethics, is called *metaphysics*; that is why Kant labels the subject of this work the "metaphysics of morals."

4. While all things in nature are bound by laws, rational beings instead govern their behavior by their *conception* of laws. For example, while objects fall because of the law of gravity, rational entities refrain from stepping off high places, not because of this law itself, but because of their *understanding* or conception of the law. A *maxim*, for Kant, is the subjective psychological principle that lies behind volition. It is, roughly, a stable motive that makes people do things in one way rather than another, a tacit 'rule' that guides their behavior. Examples of maxims might be "never kill innocent people," "don't tell lies unless it is clearly to your advantage to do so," "don't eat meat (except on special occasions)," "always give people the correct change," "never sleep with someone before the third date," and "never shoplift, but it's okay to take office supplies from your workplace."

5. Kant makes frequent mention of the *formal* nature of moral law. Something is *formal* if it concerns the form of something and *material* if it concerns what it is made of. The "matter" of a maxim is typically the action intended (such as keeping someone's car keys) plus the goal of that action (such as wanting to keep someone safe or wanting their car). The form of the maxim consists in the way those parts are put together. Consider, for example, the way the moral worth of the following maxims changes as their matter is rearranged: (1) "I will keep your car keys because you have had too much to drink and might hurt yourself or others," (2) "I will keep your car keys because I want the car for myself," (3) "I will keep my car keys because I want the car for myself." Maxims 1 and 2 involve the same action and maxims 2 and 3 have the same goal, yet—because of their different forms—1 and 3 are moral maxims while 2 is not.

Some Common Misconceptions

1. Kant is not an ethical grinch or an unfeeling puritan. He does not claim that we cannot be glad to perform a moral action, that we only act morally when we do something we don't want to do, or that happiness is incompatible with goodness. Kant's examples in the *Foundations* are only supposed to be thought experiments which pull apart, as clearly as possible, actions we *want* to do from actions we *ought* to do, in order to show what makes actions distinctively moral. He does not claim that the mere presence of an inclination to do something detracts from its moral worth: the key idea is just that one's *motive* must be duty and not inclination. (In fact, Kant argues that we have a kind of indirect moral duty to seek our own happiness, and that since generous inclinations are helpful in doing good actions, we should cultivate these feelings in ourselves.)

2. Similarly, Kant does not—as is sometimes claimed—assert that the good will is the *only thing* which is good, that everything else which is good is merely a *means* to the achievement of a good will, or even that a good will is *all* we require for a completely good life. It is perfectly consistent with Kant's views to point out that, say, health or pleasure are valuable for their

own sake. Kant's claim is that the good will is the *highest* good, and that it is the *precondition* of all the other goods (i.e., nothing else is good unless it is combined with a good will). When Kant says health is not "unconditionally" good, what he means is that it is not good at all unless it is combined with a good will—though when it *is* so combined, it really does have value in itself. By contrast, a good will is unconditionally good: it has its goodness in all possible circumstances, independently of its relation to anything else, and this is what makes it the "highest" good.

3. The categorical imperative is (arguably) not intended by Kant to be *itself* a recipe for moral action. It does not, and is not supposed to, tell you what you ought to do. Instead, the categorical imperative acts as a *test* for particular maxims—ruling some in and others out—and it is these *maxims* which provide the content of morality. To put it another way, Kant does not expect us to *deduce* particular moral maxims from the categorical imperative alone; rather, we take the maxims upon which we are *already* disposed to act and scrutinize them to see if they are formally consistent with the moral law.

4. The categorical imperative—say, the Formula of Universal Law—applies to maxims, not to actions or even intentions. Thus, for example, there is no requirement that our *actions* be universalizable: it need not be immoral for me to use my toothbrush or live in my house, even though not *everyone* could do those things. Instead, the *maxims* which guide my actions must be universalizable, and one and the same maxim (e.g., the principle of taking care of one's teeth) can give rise to different actions by different people in different circumstances. Conversely, two actions of exactly the same type (e.g., refusing to give someone a loan) could be of vastly different moral significance since the maxims that lie behind them might be of vastly different moral worth. It is also important to notice that maxims are not the same thing as *intentions*: one can intend to do something (such as make someone happy) for any of several quite different maxims (e.g., because you realize that being nice to people is part of moral duty, or because you want to be remembered in their will), and thus sometimes this intention is moral and sometimes it is not.[4]

5. When Kant claims certain maxims cannot be universalized, he cannot mean by this merely that it would be *immoral* or *bad* if these maxims were universal laws. (This would make his reasoning circular; if he is trying to define immorality in terms of non-universalizable maxims, he can't turn around and define universalizability in terms of immorality. Also, Kant has disavowed the relevance of the *consequences* of an action as part of what makes it moral or immoral, so he cannot now appeal to the consequences of making a maxim universal.) Instead, Kant means it is *literally impossible* to will that certain maxims be universal laws—that it would go against rationality itself to do so, rather like willing that 2+2=5 or wanting my will to be always and everywhere frustrated.

6. Kant did not hold that *all* universalizable maxims are moral; it would be a problem for his account if he had done so, since some obviously trivial and non-moral maxims appear to be consistent with the categorical imperative (e.g., a policy of always wearing socks on Tuesdays). Kant is able to exclude such examples from the sphere of the moral by distinguishing between actions that merely *conform* to a law, and actions performed *because* of a law. It is these latter kind of actions that are genuinely moral, since in these cases I decide what to do *by* working out what I would will that every rational being should do (rather than doing

---

4   One significant consequence of this is that Kant is not coldly saying that all of our actions should be done *because* it is our duty, in the sense that the purpose of our acting is to be dutiful. On the contrary, good people will typically do the things they do because they want to help others, or to cultivate their own talents, or to be good parents, and so on: it is just that the maxims they are following in acting on these intentions are maxims which are consistent with the moral law.

something for *other* reasons—e.g., to keep my feet warm—that also happens to be something that every rational being could do).

7. Kant's philosophy is not, as is often assumed, authoritarian or dictatorial. Although he places great emphasis on a rigid adherence to duty, it is important to realize that, for Kant, this duty is not imposed from the outside: it is not a matter of the laying down of moral laws by the state, society, or even by God. Quite the opposite: for Kant, constraining one's own behavior by the moral law actually *constitutes* genuine freedom or autonomy, which is being guided by rationality and not by mere inclination. Moral duty, for Kant, is *self*-legislated.

How Important and Influential Is This Passage?

Kant's *Foundations of the Metaphysics of Morals* is one of the most important ethical works ever written. Philosopher H.J. Patton called it "one of the small books which are truly great: it has exercised on human thought an influence almost ludicrously disproportionate to its size…. Its main topic—the supreme principle of morality—is of the utmost importance to all who are not indifferent to the struggle of good against evil." Since their introduction in this work, some of Kant's themes—the idea that human beings are ends-in-themselves and so not to be treated as mere means by others; that our own humanity finds its greatest expression through the respect we have for others; that morality is freedom and vice a form of enslavement—have become central parts of contemporary moral culture. Many modern moral philosophers have been heavily influenced by his work, and descendents of his moral theory form one of the main strands in contemporary ethical theory. Kant's ethical theory is very much a 'live' philosophical position today.

Suggestions for Critical Reflection

1. Kant gives four examples in which it is supposed to be impossible to will that your maxim become universal law. Just exactly *how* does Kant think this is impossible? Is there more than one kind of 'impossibility' here? Is Kant *correct* that it is, in some way, impossible to universalize these four maxims? (If you don't think he is, what does this show about his moral theory?)

2. Could Kant's moral theory lead to a potential conflict of duties? For example, the duty to tell the truth seems to conflict, potentially, with the duty to save the lives of innocent people: what, for example, if you are faced with a mad axeman demanding to know where his victim—whom you happen to know is cowering under your kitchen table—is hiding? (Here the key idea is that, in some situations, two universalizable *maxims* must tend toward different and incompatible actions. Mere conflicts of rules for action—e.g., "always return what you have borrowed"—will tend to miss the mark as criticisms of Kant, as the maxims which lie behind them may well allow for exceptions in particular cases.) If duties mandated by the categorical imperative *can* conflict with each other, how much destruction does this wreak on Kant's moral theory?

3. On the other hand, does Kant's moral theory produce any concrete ethical prescriptions at all? The German philosopher G.W.F. Hegel called Kant's Formula of Universal Law an "empty formalism" and said it reduced "the science of morals to the preaching of duty for duty's sake…. No transition is possible to the specification of particular duties nor, if some such particular content for acting comes under consideration, is there any criterion in that principle for deciding whether it is or is not a duty. On the contrary, by this means any wrong or immoral line of conduct may be justified." What do you make of this objection?

4. Kant provides several—up to five—different formulations of the categorical imperative. What is the relationship between them? For example, do some of the formulations yield different sets of duties than the others?

5. Kant denies that "the principles of morality are … to be sought anywhere in knowledge of human nature." Does this seem like a reasonable

position to take? What reasons does he have for this striking claim, and how persuasive are they?

6. At one point Kant argues that the function of reason cannot, primarily, be to produce happiness, since then it would not have been well adapted by nature to its purpose, and it must therefore have some other purpose (to produce a will which is good in itself). What do you think of this argument? How much does it rely upon the assumption that nature has purposes?

7. Kant suggests our ordinary, everyday moral beliefs and practices contain within them the "ultimate principle" of morality (the categorical imperative). Is he successful in showing we *already* tacitly believe the categorical imperative? If not, how much of a problem is this for his later arguments?

8. Do all of our actions rest on maxims? Do you think that Kant thinks they do (and if so, how does that affect your understanding of what he means by "maxim")? If they do not, does this cause serious problems for Kant's moral theory?

9. "There are … many persons so sympathetically constituted that without any motive of vanity or selfishness they find an inner satisfaction in spreading joy and rejoice in the contentment of others which they have made possible. But I say that, however dutiful and however amiable it may be, that kind of action has no true moral worth." What do you think of this claim of Kant's? When properly understood, do you think it is plausible?

10. Does Kant's moral theory require us to be perfectly rational in order to be perfectly moral? If so, is this a reasonable expectation? What place can the irrational elements of human psychology—such as emotions—have in Kant's moral philosophy?

11. How well can Kant's moral theory handle the following question: Now you've shown me what morality is, *why* should I be moral? Why is morality binding on me? For example, when Kant rules out all hypothetical imperatives as grounds for moral behavior, does he thereby rule out all possible *reasons* to be moral?

12. How accurately can we make moral judgments about *other people*, if Kant's theory is correct? How easily could we tell what maxim is guiding their behavior? For that matter, how accurately can we make moral judgments about our *own* behavior? Do we always know our own motives for action? How much, if at all, is any of this a problem for Kant's theory?

13. Even if you disagree with the details in Kant's moral theory, do you think his fundamental claim is sound? Is there a sharp distinction between moral actions and those performed for the sake of self-interest or emotional inclination? Must genuinely moral actions be motivated by a categorical or universally rational duty?

Suggestions for Further Reading

It is important to realize that the *Foundations for the Metaphysics of Morals* is only *part* of Kant's ethical system, and some things which are puzzling or incomplete in the *Foundations* are fleshed out elsewhere. There are three main places to look for the rest of Kant's ethics. In the *Critique of Practical Reason* Kant re-examines the question of whether a categorical imperative is really possible—that is, whether a "purely rational" consideration can provide any kind of incentive for action. In the *Metaphysics of Morals* Kant discusses, in detail, the problems of moral choice in concrete situations, and tries to show how the categorical imperative yields precise and plausible moral prescriptions in everyday life. And in *Religion Within the Limits of Reason Alone* Kant explores important questions about moral choice and responsibility. *The Cambridge Edition of the Works of Immanuel Kant: Practical Philosophy*, translated and edited by Mary J. Gregor (Cambridge University Press, 1996), contains most of his writings on ethics. The Cambridge Edition volume on *Religion and Rational Theology*, translated and edited by Allen Wood and George diGiovanni (Cambridge University Press, 1996), contains *Religion Within the Limits of Reason Alone*.

Mary Gregor's translation of the *Foundations* is also published separately, with an extremely helpful introduction by Christine Korsgaard, as *Kant: Groundwork of the Metaphysics of Morals* (Cambridge University Press, 1997). *Immanuel Kant: Ethical Philosophy* (Hackett, 1994), contains translations by James Ellington of (what is there called) the *Grounding for the Metaphysics of Morals* and the second part of the *Metaphysics of Morals*, along with a clear and useful introductory essay by Warner Wick. Another well-known translation of the *Foundations* is H.J. Paton's *The Moral Law: Kant's Groundwork of the Metaphysic of Morals* (Hutchinson, 1948).

There are many books and articles on Kant's ethical theory, and the *Foundations* in particular. Here are some of the best of recent years: H.B. Acton, *Kant's Moral Philosophy* (Macmillan, 1970); Henry Allison, *Idealism and Freedom: Essays on Kant's Theoretical and Practical Philosophy* (Cambridge University Press, 1996); Bruce Aune, *Kant's Theory of Morals* (Princeton University Press, 1979); Lewis White Beck, *Studies in the Philosophy of Kant* (Bobbs-Merrill, 1965); A.R.C. Duncan, *Practical Reason and Morality: A Study of Immanuel Kant's Foundations for the Metaphysics of Morals* (Thomas Nelson, 1957); Mary J. Gregor, *Laws of Freedom* (Basil Blackwell, 1963); Paul Guyer (ed.), *The Cambridge Companion to Kant* (Cambridge University Press, 1992) and *Kant's Groundwork of the Metaphysics of Morals: Critical Essays* (Rowman & Littlefield, 1998); Barbara Herman, *The Practice of Moral Judgment* (Harvard University Press, 1993); Thomas E. Hill, Jr., *Dignity and Practical Reason in Kant's Moral Theory* (Cornell University Press, 1992); Christine Korsgaard, *Creating the Kingdom of Ends* (Cambridge University Press, 1996); Onora Nell (O'Neill), *Acting on Principle: An Essay on Kantian Ethics* (Columbia University Press, 1975); Onora O'Neill, *Constructions of Reason: Explorations of Kant's Moral Philosophy* (Cambridge University Press, 1989); H.J. Paton, *The Categorical Imperative: A Study in Kant's Moral Philosophy* (University of Chicago Press, 1948); Roger J. Sullivan, *Immanuel Kant's Moral Theory* (Cambridge University Press, 1989) and the shorter *An Introduction to Kant's Ethics* (Cambridge University Press, 1994); Robert Paul Wolff, *The Autonomy of Reason: A Commentary on Kant's Groundwork of the Metaphysics of Morals* (Harper & Row, 1973); Robert Paul Wolff (ed.), *Foundations of the Metaphysics of Morals with Critical Essays* (Bobbs-Merrill, 1969); and Allen Wood, *Kant's Ethical Thought* (Cambridge University Press, 1999).

Kantian ideas have played an important role in recently-published original moral and political philosophy, including Stephen Darwall's *Impartial Reason* (Cornell University Press, 1983), Alan Donagan's *The Theory of Morality* (University of Chicago Press, 1977), Alan Gewirth's *Reason and Morality* (University of Chicago Press, 1978), Thomas Hill, Jr.'s *Autonomy and Self-Respect* (Cambridge University Press, 1991), Christine Korsgaard's *The Sources of Normativity* (Cambridge University Press, 1996), Thomas Nagel's *The Possibility of Altruism* (Princeton University Press, 1978), Onora O'Neill's *Towards Justice and Virtue* (Cambridge University Press, 1996), and, especially, John Rawls's *A Theory of Justice* (Harvard University Press, 1971).

Foundations of the Metaphysics of Morals[5]

First Section

Transition from the Common Rational Moral Cognition to the Philosophical Moral Cognition

Nothing can possibly be conceived in the world, or even out of it, which can be called good without qualification, except a *good will*. Intelligence, wit, judgment, and the other *talents* of the mind, however they may be named, or courage, resolution, perseverance, as qualities of *temperament*, are undoubtedly good and desirable in many respects; but these gifts of nature may also become extremely bad and mischievous if the will which is to make use of them, and which, therefore, constitutes what is called *character*, is not good. It is the same with the *gifts of fortune*. Power, riches, honor, even health, and the general well-being

---

5   Kant's *Grundlegung zur Metaphysik der Sitten* was first published in Riga in 1785. This translation is by Thomas K. Abbott with revisions by Lara Denis, *Groundwork for the Metaphysics of Morals* (Peterborough, ON: Broadview Press, 2005).

and contentment with one's condition which is called *happiness*, inspire pride, and often presumption, if there is not a good will to correct the influence of these on the mind, and with this also to rectify the whole principle of acting, and adapt it to its end. The sight of a being who is not adorned with a single feature of a pure and good will, enjoying unbroken prosperity, can never give pleasure to an impartial spectator. Thus a good will appears to constitute the indispensable condition even of being worthy of happiness.

There are even some qualities which are of service to this good will itself, and may facilitate its action, yet which have no inner unconditional value, but always presuppose a good will, and this qualifies the esteem that we justly have for them, and does not permit us to regard them as absolutely good. Moderation in the affections and passions, self-control, and calm deliberation are not only good in many respects, but even seem to constitute part of the *inner* worth of the person; but they are far from deserving to be called good without qualification, although they have been so unconditionally praised by the ancients. For without the principles of a good will, they may become extremely evil; and the coldness of a villain not only makes him far more dangerous, but also directly makes him more abominable in our eyes than he would have been without it.

A good will is good not because of what it accomplishes or effects, not by its aptness for the attainment of some proposed end, but simply by virtue of the volition—that is, it is good in itself, and considered by itself is to be esteemed much higher than all that can be brought about by it in favor of any inclination, or even the sum total of all inclinations.[6] Even if it should happen that, owing to a step-motherly nature, this will should wholly lack power to accomplish its purpose, if with its greatest efforts it should yet achieve nothing, and there should remain only the good will (not, to be sure, a mere wish, but the summoning of all means in our power), then, like a jewel, it would still shine by its own light, as a thing which has its whole value in itself. Its usefulness or fruitlessness can neither add to nor take away anything from this value. It would be, as it were, only the setting to

enable us to handle it more conveniently in common commerce, or to attract to it the attention of those who are not yet connoisseurs, but not to recommend it to true connoisseurs, or to determine its value.

There is, however, something so strange in this idea of the absolute value of a mere will, in which no account is taken of its utility, that notwithstanding the thorough assent of even common reason to the idea, yet a suspicion must arise that it may perhaps really be the product of mere high-flown fancy, and that we may have misunderstood the purpose of nature in assigning reason as the governor of our will. Therefore we will examine this idea from this point of view.

In the natural constitution of an organized being, that is, a being adapted suitably to the purposes of life, we assume it as a fundamental principle that no organ for any purpose will be found but what is also the fittest and best adapted for that purpose. Now in a being which has reason and a will, if the proper object of nature were its *preservation*, its *welfare*, in a word, its *happiness*, then nature would have hit upon a very bad arrangement in selecting the reason of the creature to carry out this purpose. For all the actions which the creature has to perform with a view to this purpose, and the whole rule of its conduct, would be far more surely prescribed to it by instinct, and that end would have been attained thereby much more certainly than it ever can be by reason. Should reason have been imparted to this favored creature over and above, it must only have served it to contemplate the happy constitution of its nature, to admire it, to congratulate itself on it, and to feel thankful for it to the beneficent cause, but not that it should subject its desires to that weak and delusive guidance, and meddle incompetently with the purpose of nature. In a word, nature would have taken care that reason should not break forth into *practical use*, nor have the presumption, with its weak insight, to think out for itself the plan of happiness and of the means of attaining it. Nature would not only have taken on herself the choice of the ends but also of the means, and with wise foresight would have entrusted both to instinct.

And, in fact, we find that the more a cultivated reason applies itself with deliberate purpose to the enjoyment of life and happiness, so much more does one fall short of true satisfaction. And from this cir-

---

6   One's inclinations are things one wants or likes to do.

cumstance there arises in many, if they are candid enough to confess it, a certain degree of *misology*, that is, hatred of reason, especially in the case of those who are most experienced in the use of it, because after calculating all the advantages they derive—I do not say from the invention of all the arts of common luxury, but even from the sciences (which seem to them to be after all only a luxury of the understanding)—they find that they have, in fact, only brought more trouble on their shoulders rather than gained in happiness; and they end by envying rather than despising the more common run of human beings who keep closer to the guidance of mere instinct, and do not allow their reason much influence on their conduct. And this we must admit, that the judgment of those who would very much lower the lofty eulogies of the advantages which reason gives us in regard to the happiness and satisfaction of life, or who would even reduce them below zero, is by no means morose or ungrateful to the goodness with which the world is governed, but that there lies at the root of these judgments the idea that our existence has a different and far worthier end, to which, and not to happiness, is reason's proper vocation, and which must, therefore, be regarded as the supreme condition to which private ends of human beings must, for the most part, defer.

For as reason is not competent to guide the will with certainty in regard to its objects and the satisfaction of all our needs (which it to some extent even multiplies), this being an end to which an implanted instinct would have led with much greater certainty; and since, nevertheless, reason is imparted to us as a practical faculty, that is, as one which is to have influence on the *will*, therefore admitting that nature generally in the distribution of her capacities has adapted the means to the end, its true vocation must be to produce a *will*, not merely good as a *means* to something else, but *good in itself*, for which reason was absolutely necessary. This will then, though not indeed the sole and complete good, must be the supreme good and the condition of every other, even of the desire of happiness. Under these circumstances, there is nothing inconsistent with the wisdom of nature in the fact that the cultivation of reason, which is requisite for the first and unconditioned purpose, does in many ways interfere, at least in this life,

with the attainment of the second, which is always conditional—namely, happiness. Indeed, it may even reduce it to nothing, without nature thereby failing of her purpose. For reason recognizes the establishment of a good will as its highest practical vocation, and in attaining this purpose is capable only of a satisfaction of its own proper kind, namely, that from the attainment of an end, which in turn is determined by reason only, notwithstanding that this may involve many a disappointment to the ends of inclination.

We have then to develop the concept of a will which deserves to be highly esteemed for itself, and is good without a view to anything further, a concept which exists already in the sound natural understanding, requiring rather to be clarified than to be taught, and which in estimating the value of our actions always takes the first place and constitutes the condition of all the rest. In order to do this, we will take concept of duty, which includes that of a good will, although implying certain subjective limitations and hindrances. These, however, far from concealing it or rendering it unrecognizable, rather bring it out by contrast and make it shine forth so much the brighter.

I omit here all actions which are already recognized as contrary to duty, although they may be useful for this or that purpose, for with these the question whether they are done *from duty* cannot arise at all, since they even conflict with it. I also set aside those actions which really conform to duty, but to which men have *no* immediate *inclination*, performing them because they are impelled thereto by some other inclination. For in this case we can readily distinguish whether the action which agrees with duty is done *from duty* or from a selfish purpose. It is much harder to make this distinction when the action accords with duty, and the subject has besides an *immediate* inclination to it. For example, it is always a matter of duty that a dealer should not overcharge an inexperienced purchaser; and wherever there is much commerce the prudent tradesman does not overcharge, but keeps a fixed price for everyone, so that a child buys from him as well as any other. People are thus *honestly* served; but this is not enough to make us believe that the tradesman has so acted from duty and from principles of honesty; his own advantage required it; it is unwarranted in this case to suppose that he might besides have an immediate inclination in favor of the buyers, so that, as it were, from love he should give no advantage to one over another. Accordingly the action was done neither from duty nor from immediate inclination, but merely with a selfish purpose.

On the other hand, it is a duty to preserve one's life; and, in addition, everyone has also an immediate inclination to do so. But on this account the often anxious care which most people take for it has no intrinsic worth, and their maxim has no moral content. They preserve their life *in conformity with duty*, no doubt, but not *from duty*. On the other hand, if adversity and hopeless sorrow have completely taken away the relish for life, if the unfortunate one, strong in mind, indignant to his fate rather than desponding or dejected, wishes for death, and yet preserves his life without loving it—not from inclination or fear, but from duty—then his maxim has moral content.

To be beneficent when one can is a duty; and besides this, there are many minds so sympathetically constituted that, without any other motive of vanity or self-interest, they find a pleasure in spreading joy around them, and can take delight in the satisfaction of others so far as it is their own work. But I maintain that in such a case an action of this kind, however proper, however amiable it may be, has nevertheless no true moral worth, but is on a level with other inclinations, for example, the inclination to honor, which if it is happily directed to that which is in fact of public utility and accordant with duty, and consequently honorable, deserves praise and encouragement, but not esteem. For the maxim lacks the moral content, namely, that such actions be done *from duty*, not from inclination. Put the case that the mind of that philanthropist was clouded by sorrow of his own, extinguishing all sympathy with the lot of others, and that while he still has the power to benefit others in distress, he is not touched by their trouble because he is absorbed with his own; and now suppose that he tears himself out of this dead insensibility and performs the action without any inclination to it, but simply from duty, then for the first time his action has its genuine moral worth. Further still, if nature has put little sympathy in the heart of this or that man, if he, supposed to be an upright man, is by temperament cold and indifferent to the sufferings of others, perhaps because in respect of his

own he is provided with the special gifts of patience and fortitude, and supposes, or even requires, that others should have the same—and such a man would certainly not be the meanest product of nature—but if nature had not specially framed him for a philanthropist, would he not still find in himself a source from which to give himself a far higher worth than that of a good-natured temperament could be? Unquestionably. It is just in this that the moral worth of the character is brought out which is incomparably the highest of all, namely, that he is beneficent, not from inclination, but from duty.

To secure one's own happiness is a duty, at least indirectly; for discontent with one's condition, under a pressure of many anxieties and amidst unsatisfied needs, might easily become a great *temptation to transgression of duty*. But here again, without looking to duty, all men have already the strongest and most intimate inclination to happiness, because it is just in this idea[7] that all inclinations are combined in one total. But the precept of happiness is often of such a sort that it greatly interferes with some inclinations, and yet a human being cannot form any definite and certain conception of the sum of satisfaction of all of them which is called happiness. It is not then to be wondered at that a single inclination, definite both as to what it promises and as to the time within which it can be gratified, is often able to overcome such a fluctuating idea, and that a gouty[8] patient, for instance, can choose to enjoy what he likes, and to suffer what he may, since, according to his calculation, on this occasion at least, he has not sacrificed the enjoyment of the present mo-

---

7   Kant used the word *Idee,* which means a pure concept of reason corresponding to no sensory "intuition"—roughly, concepts that (though they may be derived from the empirical world) correspond to nothing within the empirical world but only to 'something' outside it. Kant thought that ideas, although they do not 'picture reality' in any way we can understand, can act as *precepts* that guide our thoughts and actions in particular directions.

8   Gout is a chronic illness (caused by elevated levels of uric acid in the blood) traditionally thought to be brought on by eating too much rich food and drinking too much alcohol.

ment to a possibly mistaken expectation of a happiness which is supposed to be found in health. But even in this case, if the general inclination to happiness did not influence his will, and supposing that in his particular case health was not a necessary element in this calculation, there yet remains in this, as in all other cases, this law—namely, that he should promote his happiness not from inclination but from duty, and by this would his conduct first acquire true moral worth.

It is in this manner, undoubtedly, that we are to understand those passages of Scripture also in which we are commanded to love our neighbor, even our enemy. For love, as an inclination, cannot be commanded, but beneficence for duty's sake may, even though we are not impelled to it by any inclination—indeed, are even repelled by a natural and unconquerable aversion. This is *practical*[9] love, and not *pathological*[10]—a love which is seated in the will, and not in the propensities of feeling—in principles of action and not of tender sympathy; and it is this love alone which can be commanded.

The second proposition is: That an action done from duty derives its moral worth, *not from the purpose* which is to be attained by it, but from the maxim by which it is determined, and therefore does not depend on the realization of the object of the action, but merely on the *principle of volition* by which the action has taken place, without regard to any object of desire. It is clear from what precedes that the purposes which we may have in view in our action, or their effects regarded as ends and incentives of the will, cannot give to actions any unconditional or moral worth. In what, then, can their worth lie if it is not to consist in the will in reference to its expected effect? It cannot lie anywhere but in the *principle of the will* without regard to the ends which can be attained by the action. For the will stands between its *a priori* principle, which is formal, and its *a posteriori* incentive, which is material,[11] as between two roads, and as

it must be determined by something, it follows that it must be determined by the formal principle of volition when an action is done from duty, in which case every material principle has been withdrawn from it.

The third proposition, which is a consequence of the two preceding, I would express thus: *Duty is the necessity of acting from respect for the law*. I may have *inclination* for an object as the effect of my proposed action, but *never respect* for it, just because it is an effect and not an activity of will. Similarly, I cannot have respect for inclination, whether my own or another's; I can at most, if my own, approve it; if another's, sometimes even love it, that is, look on it as favorable to my own interest. It is only what is connected with my will as a principle, by no means as an effect—what does not serve my inclination, but outweighs it, or at least in case of choice excludes it from its calculation—in other words, simply the law of itself, which can be an object of respect, and hence a command. Now an action done from duty must wholly exclude the influence of inclination, and with it every object of the will, so that nothing remains which can determine the will except objectively the *law*, and subjectively *pure respect* for this practical law, and consequently the maxim[12] that I should follow this law even to the thwarting of all my inclinations.

Thus the moral worth of an action does not lie in the effect expected from it, nor in any principle of action which needs to borrow its motive from this expected effect. For all these effects—agreeableness of one's condition, and even the promotion of the happiness of others—could have been also brought

---

9   Based on practical reason.

10 Kant means simply motives and actions arising from feeling or bodily impulses. No suggestion of abnormality or disease is intended.

11 *A priori* means "prior to experience": a proposition is *a priori* if it can be known to be true prior to, or

independently of, any specific empirical events. By contrast, something is *a posteriori* if it must be derived from experience. "1 + 1 = 2" is an *a priori* claim whilst "The sky is blue" is *a posteriori*. In order to know the first, one need not have had any particular experience of the external world, but to know that the second is true, you (or some reliable source) must have seen the sky.

12 [Author's note] A maxim is the subjective principle of volition. The objective principle (i.e., that which would serve all rational beings also subjectively as a practical principle if reason had full power over the faculty of desire) is the practical law.

about by other causes, so that for this there would have been no need of the will of a rational being; whereas it is in this alone that the supreme and unconditional good can be found. The pre-eminent good which we call moral can therefore consist in nothing else than *the representation of the law* in itself, *which certainly is only possible in a rational being*, insofar as this representation, and not the expected effect, determines the will. This is a good which is already present in the person who acts accordingly, and we need not wait for it to appear first in the result.[13]

But what sort of law can that be, the conception of which must determine the will, even without pay-

ing any regard to the effect experienced from it, in order that this will may be called good absolutely and without qualification? As I have deprived the will of every impulse which could arise for it from obedience to any particular law, there remains nothing but the universal conformity of its actions to law in general, which alone is to serve the will as a principle, that is, I am never to act otherwise than so *that I could also will that my maxim should become a universal law*. Here, now, it is the simple lawfulness in general, without assuming any particular law applicable to certain actions, that serves the will as its principle, and must so serve it if duty is not to be a vain delusion and a chimerical notion. The common reason of human beings in its practical judgments perfectly coincides with this, and always has in view the principle here suggested.

Let the question be, for example: May I when in distress make a promise with the intention not to keep it? I readily distinguish here between the two significations which the question may have: whether it is prudent or whether it is right to make such a false promise. The former may undoubtedly often be the case. I see clearly indeed that it is not enough to extricate myself from a present difficulty by means of this subterfuge, but it must be well considered whether there may not hereafter spring from this lie much greater inconvenience than that from which I now seek to free myself, and as, with all my supposed *cunning*, the consequences cannot be so easily foreseen but that credit once lost may be much more injurious to me than any mischief which I seek to avoid at present, it should be considered whether it would not be *more prudent* to act herein according to a universal maxim, and to make it a habit to promise nothing except with the intention of keeping it. But it is soon clear to me that such a maxim will still only be based on the fear of consequences. Now it is a wholly different thing to be truthful from duty than to be so from apprehension of injurious consequences. In the first case, the very notion of the action already implies a law for me; in the second case, I must first look about elsewhere to see what results may be combined with it which would affect myself. For to deviate from the principle of duty is beyond all doubt evil; but to be unfaithful to my maxim of prudence may often

---

13 [Author's note] It might be objected that I seek to take refuge in an obscure feeling behind the word "respect," instead of clearly resolving the question with a concept of reason. But though respect is a feeling, it is not one received through any [outer] influence but is self-wrought by a rational concept; thus it differs specifically from all feelings of the former kind which may be referred to inclination or fear. What I recognize directly as a law for myself I recognize with respect, which means merely the consciousness of the submission of my will to a law without the intervention of other influences on my mind. The direct determination of the will by law and the consciousness of this determination is respect; thus respect can be regarded as the effect of the law on the subject and not as the cause of the law. Respect is properly the conception of a worth which thwarts my self-love. Thus it is regarded as an object neither of inclination nor of fear, though it has something analogous to both. The only object of respect is law, and indeed only the law which we impose on ourselves and yet recognize as necessary in itself. As a law we are subject to it without consulting self-love; as imposed on us by ourselves, it is a consequence of our will. In the former respect it is analogous to fear and in the latter to inclination. All respect for a person is only respect for the law (of righteousness, etc.) of which the person provides an example. Because we see the improvement of our talents as a duty, we think of a person of talent as the example of a law, as it were (the law that we should by practice become like him in his talents), and that constitutes our respect. All so-called moral interest consists solely in respect for the law.

be very advantageous to me, although to abide by it is certainly safer. The shortest way, however, and an unerring one, to discover the answer to this question whether a lying promise is consistent with duty, is to ask myself: Would I be content that my maxim (to extricate myself from difficulty by a false promise) should hold as a universal law, for myself as well as for others? And would I be able to say to myself, "Everyone may make a deceitful promise when he finds himself in a difficulty from which he cannot otherwise extricate himself"? Then I presently become aware that, while I can will the lie, I can by no means will that lying become a universal law. For with such a law there would be no promises at all, since it would be in vain to profess my intention in regard to my future actions to those who would not believe this profession, or if they over-hastily did so, would pay me back in my own coin. Hence my maxim, as soon as it should be made a universal law, would necessarily destroy itself.

I do not, therefore, need any far-reaching penetration to discern what I have to do in order that my volition may be morally good. Inexperienced in the course of the world, incapable of being prepared for all its contingencies, I only ask myself: Can you also will that your maxim should be a universal law? If not, then it must be rejected, and that not because of a disadvantage accruing from it to myself or even to others, but because it cannot enter as a principle into a possible universal legislation, and reason extorts from me immediate respect for such legislation. I do not indeed as yet *discern* on what this respect is based (this the philosopher may inquire), but at least I understand this—that it is an estimation of the worth which far outweighs all worth of what is recommended by inclination, and that the necessity of acting from *pure* respect for the practical law is what constitutes duty, to which every other motive must give place because it is the condition of a will that is good *in itself*, and the worth of such a will is above everything.

Thus, then, without quitting the moral cognition of common human reason, we have arrived at its principle. And although, no doubt, common human reason does not conceive it in such an abstract and universal form, yet it really always has it before its eyes and uses it as the standard of judgment. Here it would be easy to show how, with this compass in hand, common human reason is well able to distinguish, in every case that occurs, what is good, what evil, conformably to duty or inconsistent with it, if, without in the least teaching it anything new, we only, like Socrates,[14] direct its attention to the principle it itself employs; and that, therefore, we do not need science and philosophy to know what we should do to be honest and good, yes, even to be wise and virtuous. Indeed we might well have conjectured beforehand that the acquaintance with what every human being is obligated to do, and therefore also to know, would be within the reach of every human being, even the commonest. Here we cannot withhold admiration when we see how great an advantage practical judgment has over the theoretical in the common human understanding. In the latter, if common reason ventures to depart from the laws of experience and from the perceptions of the senses, it falls into mere inconceivabilities and self-contradictions, at least into a chaos of uncertainty, obscurity, and instability. But in the practical sphere it is just when the common understanding excludes all sensible incentives from practical laws that its power of judgment begins to show itself to advantage. It then becomes even subtle, whether it be that it quibbles with its own conscience or with other claims regarding what is to be called right, or whether it desires for its own instruction to determine honestly the worth of its actions; and, in the latter case, it may even have as good a hope of hitting the mark as any philosopher whatever can promise himself. Indeed it is almost more sure of doing so, because the philosopher cannot have any other principle, while he may easily perplex his judgment by a multitude of considerations foreign to the matter, and so turn aside from the right way. Would it not therefore be wiser in moral concerns

---

14 This ancient Athenian is famous for (among other things) a technique of teaching—today called the "Socratic method"—in which the master, instead of imparting knowledge, asks a sequence of questions to prompt the pupil to reflect on their own ideas and to uncover knowledge they already have within themselves. Because of this technique, Socrates compared himself to a midwife helping people give birth to philosophical ideas.

to acquiesce in the judgment of common reason, or at most only to call in philosophy for the purpose of rendering the system of morals more complete and intelligible, and its rules more convenient for use (especially disputation), but not so as to draw off the common understanding from its happy simplicity, or bring it by means of philosophy into a new path of inquiry and instruction?

Innocence is indeed a glorious thing; but, on the other hand, it is very sad that it cannot well maintain itself, and is easily seduced. On this account even wisdom—which otherwise consists more in conduct than in knowledge—still has need of science, not in order to learn from it, but to secure for its precepts admission and permanence. Against all the commands of duty which reason represents to the human being as so deserving of respect, he feels in himself a powerful counterweight in his needs and inclinations, the entire satisfaction of which he sums up under the name of happiness. Now reason issues commands unyieldingly, without promising anything to the inclinations, and, as it were, with disregard and contempt for these claims, which are so impetuous and at the same time so plausible, and which will not allow themselves to be suppressed by any command. Hence there arises a *natural dialectic*,[15] that is, a disposition to argue against these strict laws of duty and to question their validity, or at least their purity and strictness; and if possible, to make them more compatible with our wishes and inclinations, that is to say, to corrupt them at their very source and entirely destroy their worth[16]—a thing which even common practical reason cannot ultimately approve.

Thus is the *common human reason* compelled to go out of its sphere and to take a step into the field of *practical philosophy*, not to satisfy any speculative need (which never occurs to it as long as it is content to be mere sound reason), but rather on practical grounds, in order to attain in it information and clear instruction respecting the source of its principle, and the correct determination of it in opposition to the maxims which are based on wants and inclinations, so that it may escape from the perplexity of opposite claims, and not run the risk of losing all genuine moral principles through the equivocation into which it easily falls. Thus, when practical reason cultivates itself, there insensibly arises in it a dialectic which forces it to seek aid in philosophy, just as happens to it in its theoretical use; and in this case, therefore, as well as in the other, it will find rest nowhere but in a thorough critical examination of our reason.

Second Section

Transition from Popular Moral Philosophy to the Metaphysics of Morals

If we have so far drawn our notion of duty from the common use of our practical reason, it is by no means to be inferred that we have treated it as an empirical concept. On the contrary, if we attend to the experience of human conduct, we meet frequent and, as we ourselves allow, just complaints that one cannot find a single, certain example of the disposition to act from pure duty. Although many things are done *in conformity with* what *duty* prescribes, it is nevertheless always doubtful whether they are done strictly *from duty*, and so have moral worth. Hence there have at all times been philosophers who have altogether denied that this disposition actually exists at all in human actions, and have ascribed everything to a more or less refined self-love. Not that they have on that account questioned the soundness of the conception of morality; on the contrary, they spoke with sincere regret of the frailty and impurity of human nature, which, though noble enough to take as its rule an idea so worthy of respect, is yet too weak to follow it; and employs reason, which ought to give it the law, only for the purpose of providing for the interest of the inclinations, whether singly or at the best in the greatest possible harmony with one another.

In fact, it is absolutely impossible to make out by experience with complete certainty a single case in which the maxim of an action, however right in itself, rested simply on moral grounds and on the representation of duty. Sometimes it happens that with the sharpest self-examination we can find nothing beside the

---

15   In Kant's special usage, a dialectic is the "logic of illusion," a process of fallacious or misleading reasoning.

16   For Kant, "dignity" is a technical term meaning something like *intrinsic worth*.

moral principle of duty which could have been powerful enough to move us to this or that action and to so great a sacrifice; yet we cannot from this infer with certainty that it was not really some secret impulse of self-love, under the false appearance of duty, that was the actual determining cause of the will. We like then to flatter ourselves by falsely taking credit for a more noble motive; whereas in fact we can never, even by the strictest examination, get completely behind the secret incentives, since, when the question is of moral worth, it is not with the actions which we see that we are concerned, but with those inward principles of them which we do not see.

Moreover, we cannot better serve the wishes of those who ridicule all morality as mere chimera of human imagination overstepping itself from vanity, than by conceding to them that concepts of duty must be drawn only from experience (as, from indolence, people are ready to think is the case with all other concepts also); for this is to prepare for them a certain triumph. I am willing to admit out of love for humanity that even most of our actions are in conformity with duty; but if we look closer at them we everywhere come upon the dear self which is always prominent; and it is this they have in view, and not the strict command of duty, which would often require self-denial. Without being an enemy of virtue, a cool observer, one that does not mistake the wish for good, however lively, for its reality, may sometimes doubt whether true virtue is actually found anywhere in the world, and this especially as years increase and the judgment is partly made wiser by experience, and partly also more acute in observation. This being so, nothing can secure us from falling away altogether from our ideas of duty, or maintain in the soul a well-grounded respect for its law, but the clear conviction that although there should never have been actions which really sprang from such pure sources, yet whether this or that takes place is not at all the question; but that reason itself, independent of all experience, ordains what ought to take place, that accordingly actions of which perhaps the world has so far never given an example, the feasibility even of which might be very much doubted by one who founds everything on experience, are nevertheless inflexibly commanded by reason; that, for example, even though there might

never have been a sincere friend, yet not a whit less is pure sincerity in friendship required of everyone, because, prior to all experience, this duty is involved (as duty in general) in the idea of a reason determining the will by *a priori* principles.

When we add further that, unless we deny that the notion of morality has any truth or reference to any possible object, we must admit that its law must be valid, not merely for human beings, but for all *rational beings as such*, not merely under certain contingent conditions or with exceptions, but with *absolute necessity*, then it is clear that no experience could enable us to infer even the possibility of such apodictic[17] laws. For with what right could we bring into unbounded respect as a universal precept for all rational nature that which perhaps holds only under the contingent conditions of humanity? Or how could laws of the determination of *our* will be regarded as laws of the determination of the will of rational beings as such, and for us only as such, if they were merely empirical and did not take their origin wholly *a priori* from pure but practical reason?

Nor could anything be more fatal to morality than that we should wish to derive it from examples. For every example of it that is set before me must first itself be judged by principles of morality, as to whether it is worthy to serve as an original example, that is, as a model; but by no means can it authoritatively furnish the conception of morality. Even the Holy One of the Gospels[18] must first be compared with our ideal of moral perfection before we can recognize Him as such; and so He says of Himself, "Why do you call Me (whom you see) good; none is good (the model of good) but God only (whom you do not see)?"[19] But whence have we the conception of God as the supreme good? Simply from the *idea* of moral perfection, which reason frames *a priori* and connects inseparably with the notion of a free will. Imitation finds no place at all in morality, and examples serve only for encouragement, that is, they put beyond all doubt the feasibility of what the law commands, they make visible that which the practical rule expresses

---

17 Necessarily true, clearly demonstrated or established.
18 Jesus Christ.
19 Matthew 19:17.

more generally, but they can never authorize us to set aside the true original which lies in reason, and to guide ourselves by examples.

If there is no genuine supreme principle of morality but what must rest simply on pure reason, independent on all experience, I think it is not necessary even to ask the question whether it is good to exhibit these concepts in their generality (*in abstracto*[20]) as they are established *a priori* along with the principles belonging to them, if our knowledge is to be distinguished from the *common* and to be called philosophical. In our times indeed this might perhaps be necessary; for if we collected votes, whether pure rational knowledge separated from everything empirical, that is to say, a metaphysics of morals, or whether popular practical philosophy is to be preferred, it is easy to guess which side would predominate.

This descending to popular notions is certainly very commendable if the ascent to the principles of pure reason has first taken place and been satisfactorily accomplished. This implies that we first *ground* the doctrine of morals on metaphysics, and then, when it is firmly established, procure *entry* for it by giving it a popular character. But it is quite absurd to try to be popular in the first inquiry, on which the soundness of the principles depends. It is not only that this procedure can never lay claim to the very rare merit of a true *philosophical popularity*, since there is no art in being intelligible if one renounces all thoroughness of insight; but also it produces a disgusting medley of compiled observations and half-reasoned principles. Shallow minds enjoy this because it can be used for everyday chat, but the sagacious find in it only confusion, and being unsatisfied and unable to help themselves, they turn away their eyes, while philosophers, who see quite well through this delusion, are little listened to when they call people off for a time from this pretended popularity in order that they might be rightfully popular after they have attained a definite insight.

We need only to look at the attempts of moralists in that favorite fashion, and we will find at one time the special constitution of human nature (including, however, the idea of a rational nature generally), at one time perfection, at another time happiness, here moral sense, there fear of God, a little of this and a little of that, in marvelous mixture, without its occurring to them to ask whether the principles of morality are to be sought in the knowledge of human nature at all (which we can have only from experience); and, if this is not so—if these principles are to be found altogether *a priori*, free from everything empirical, in pure rational concepts only, and nowhere else, not even in the smallest degree—then rather to adopt the method of making this a separate inquiry, as pure practical philosophy, or (if one may use a name so decried) as metaphysics[21] of morals, to bring it by itself to completeness, and to require the public, which wishes for popular treatment, to await the outcome of this undertaking.

Such a metaphysics of morals, completely isolated, not mixed with any anthropology, theology, physics, or hyperphysics, or still less with occult qualities (which we might call hypophysical),[22] is not only an indispensable substratum of all sound theoretical knowledge of duties, but is at the same time a desideratum[23] of the highest importance to the actual fulfilment of their precepts. For the pure thought of duty, unmixed with any foreign addition of empirical attractions, and, in a word, the thought of the moral law, exercises on the human heart, by way of reason alone (which first becomes aware with this that it can of itself be practical), an influence so

---

20 "In the abstract."

21 [Author's note] If one wishes, the pure philosophy (metaphysics) of morals can be distinguished from the applied (i.e., applied to human nature), just as pure mathematics and pure logic are distinguished from applied mathematics and applied logic. By this designation one is immediately reminded that moral principles are not founded on the peculiarities of human nature but must stand of themselves *a priori*, and that from such principles practical rules for every rational nature, and accordingly for man, must be derivable.

22 Hyperphysics is that which goes beyond physics. The term is usually used in a similar way as "paranormal" or "supernatural." "Hypophysics" is a coinage meaning that which lies *below* physics.

23 Something very much needed or desired.

much more powerful than all other incentives[24] which may be derived from the field of experience that in the consciousness of its dignity it despises the latter, and can by degrees become their master; whereas a mixed doctrine of morals, compounded partly of incentives drawn from feelings and inclinations, and partly also of conceptions of reason, must make the mind waver between motives which cannot be brought under any principle, which lead to good only by mere accident, and very often also to evil.

From what has been said, it is clear that all moral concepts have their seat and origin completely *a priori* in reason, and that, moreover, in the commonest reason just as truly as in that which is in the highest degree speculative; that they cannot be obtained by abstraction from any empirical, and therefore merely contingent, cognitions; that it is just this purity of their origin that makes them worthy to serve as our supreme practical principle, and that just in proportion as we add anything empirical, we detract from their genuine influence and from the absolute value of actions; that it is not only of the greatest necessity, in a purely speculative point of view, but is also

---

24   [Author's note] I have a letter from the late excellent Sulzer [Johann Georg Sulzer (1720–1790), translator of Hume into German and director of the philosophical division of the Berlin Academy] in which he asks me why the theories of virtue accomplish so little even though they contain so much that is convincing to reason. My answer was delayed in order that I might make it complete. The answer is only that the teachers themselves have not completely clarified their concepts, and when they wish to make up for this by hunting in every quarter for motives to the morally good so as to make their physic right strong, they spoil it. For the commonest observation shows that if we imagine an act of honesty performed with a steadfast soul and sundered from all view to any advantage in this or another world and even under the greatest temptations of need or allurement, it far surpasses and eclipses any similar action which was affected in the least by any foreign incentive; it elevates the soul and arouses the wish to be able to act in this way. Even moderately young children feel this impression, and one should never represent duties to them in any other way.

of the greatest practical importance, to derive these concepts and laws from pure reason, to present them pure and unmixed, and even to determine the compass of this practical or pure rational cognition, that is, to determine the whole faculty of pure practical reason; and, in doing so, we must not make its principles dependent on the particular nature of human reason, though in speculative philosophy this may be permitted, or may even at times be necessary; but since moral laws ought to hold good for every rational being, we must derive them from the universal concept of a rational being. In this way, although for its *application* to human beings morality has need of anthropology, yet, in the first instance, we must treat it in itself (a thing which in such distinct branches of science is easily done); knowing well that, unless we are in possession of this, it would not only be vain to determine the moral element of duty in right actions for purposes of speculative criticism, but it would be impossible to base morals on their genuine principles, even for common practical purposes, especially for moral instruction, so as to produce pure moral dispositions, and to engraft them on people's minds to the promotion of the greatest possible good in the world.

But in order that in this study we may not merely advance by the natural steps from the common moral judgment (in this case very worthy of respect) to the philosophical, as has been already done, but also from a popular philosophy, which goes no further than it can reach by groping with the help of examples, to metaphysics (which does not allow itself to be checked by anything empirical and, as it must measure the whole extent of this kind of rational knowledge, goes as far as ideal conceptions, where even examples fail us), we must follow and clearly describe the practical faculty of reason, from the general rules of its determination to the point where the concept of duty springs from it.

Everything in nature works according to laws. Rational beings alone have the capacity to act *in accordance with the representation* of laws—that is, according to principles, that is, have a *will*. Since the deduction of actions from principles requires *reason*, the will is nothing but practical reason. If reason infallibly determines the will, then the actions of such a being which are recognized as objectively necessary[25] are subjectively necessary also, that is, the will is a capacity to choose *that only* which reason independent of inclination recognizes as practically necessary, that is, as good. But if reason of itself does not sufficiently determine the will, if the latter is subject also to subjective conditions (particular incentives) which do not always coincide with the objective conditions, in a word, if the will does not *in itself* completely accord with reason (which is actually the case with human beings), then the actions which objectively are recognized as necessary are subjectively contingent, and the determination of such a will according to objective laws is *necessitation*, that is to say, the relation of the objective laws to a will that is not thoroughly good is conceived as the determination of the will of a rational being by principles of reason, but which the will from its nature does not necessarily follow.

The conception of an objective principle, in so far as it is obligatory for a will, is called a command (of reason), and the formula of the command is called an **imperative**.

All imperatives are expressed through an *ought*, and thereby indicate the relation of an objective law of reason to a will which from its subjective constitution is not necessarily determined by it (a necessitation). They say that something would be good to do or to forbear, but they say it to a will which does not always do a thing because it is represented to be good to do it. That is *practically good*, however, which determines the will by means of the representations of reason, and consequently not from subjective causes, but objectively, that is, on principles which are valid for every rational being as such. It is distinguished from the agreeable as that which influences the will only by means of feeling from merely subjective causes, valid only for the senses of this or that one, and not as a principle of reason which holds for everyone.[26]

A perfectly good will would therefore be equally subject to objective laws (viz. laws of good), but could not be conceived as *necessitated* thereby to act lawfully, because of itself from its subjective constitution it can only be determined by the conception of good. Therefore no imperatives hold for the Divine will, or in general for a *holy* will; *ought* is here out of place because the volition is already of itself necessarily in unison with the law. Therefore imperatives are only formulae to express the relation of objective laws of all volition to the subjective imperfection of the will of this or that rational being, for example, a human will.

Now all imperatives command either *hypothetically* or *categorically*. The former represent the practical necessity of a possible action as means to something else that is willed (or at least which one might possibly will). The categorical imperative would be that which represented an action as necessary of itself without reference to another end, that is, as objectively necessary.

Since every practical law represents a possible action as good, and on this account, for a subject who is practically determinable by reason, as necessary, all imperatives are formulae determining an action which is necessary according to the principle of a will good in some respects. If now the action is good only as a means *to something else*, then the imperative is

___

25 As determined by the objective principles of rationality.

26 [Author's note] The dependence of the faculty of desire on sensations is called inclination, and inclination always indicates a need. The dependence of a contingently determinable will on principles of reason, however, is called interest. An interest is present only in a dependent will which is not of itself always in accord with reason; in the divine will we cannot conceive of an interest. But even the human will can take an interest in something without thereby acting from interest. The former means the practical interest in the action; the latter, the pathological interest in the object of the action. The former indicates only the dependence of the will on principles of reason in themselves, while the latter indicates dependence on the principles of reason for the purpose of inclination, since reason gives only the practical rule by which the needs of inclination are to be aided. In the former case the action interests me, and in the latter the object of the action (so far as it is pleasant for me) interests me. In the First Section we have seen that, in the case of an action done from duty, no regard must be given to the interest in the object, but merely to the action itself and its principle in reason (i.e., the law).

hypothetical; if it is conceived as good *in itself* and consequently as being necessarily the principle of a will which of itself conforms to reason, then it is *categorical*.

Thus the imperative declares what action possible by me would be good, and presents the practical rule in relation to a will which does not forthwith perform an action simply because it is good, whether because the subject does not always know that it is good, or because, even if it know this, yet its maxims might be opposed to the objective principles of practical reason.

Accordingly the hypothetical imperative only says that the action is good for some purpose, *possible* or *actual*. In the first case, it is a **problematic**, in the second an **assertoric**, practical principle. The categorical imperative which declares an action to be objectively necessary in itself without reference to any purpose, without any other end, is valid as an **apodictic** (practical) principle.

Whatever is possible only by the power of some rational being may also be conceived as a possible purpose of some will; and therefore the principles of action as regards the means necessary to attain some possible purpose are in fact infinitely numerous. All sciences have a practical part consisting of problems expressing that some end is possible for us, and of imperatives directing how it may be attained. These may, therefore, be called in general imperatives of **skill**. Here there is no question whether the end is rational and good, but only what one must do in order to attain it. The precepts for the physician to make his patient thoroughly healthy, and for a poisoner to ensure certain death, are of equal value in this respect, that each serves to effect its purpose perfectly. Since in early youth it cannot be known what ends are likely to occur to us in the course of life, parents seek to have their children taught a *great many things*, and provide for their *skill* in the use of means for all sorts of *discretionary* ends, of none of which can they determine whether it may not perhaps hereafter be an object to their pupil, but which it is at all events *possible* that he might aim at; and this anxiety is so great that they commonly neglect to form and correct their children's judgment of the value of the things which may be chosen as ends.

There is *one* end, however, which may be assumed to be actually such to all rational beings (so far as imperatives apply to them, viz. as dependent beings), and therefore, one purpose which they not merely *may* have, but which we may with certainty assume that they all actually *do have* by a natural necessity, and this is *happiness*. The hypothetical imperative which expresses the practical necessity of an action as means to the advancement of happiness is *assertoric*. We are not to present it as necessary for an uncertain and merely possible purpose, but for a purpose which we may presuppose with certainty and *a priori* in every human being, because it belongs to his being. Now skill in the choice of means to his own greatest well-being may be called *prudence*,[27] in the narrowest sense. And thus the imperative which refers to the choice of means to one's own happiness, that is, the precept of prudence, is still always *hypothetical*; the action is not commanded absolutely, but only as means to another purpose.

Finally, there is an imperative which commands a certain conduct immediately, without having as its condition any other purpose to be attained by it. This imperative is **categorical**. It concerns not the matter of the action, or its intended result, but its form and the principle of which it is itself a result; and what is essentially good in it consists in the mental disposition, let the consequence be what it may. This imperative may be called that of **morality**.

There is a marked distinction also between the volitions on these three sorts of principles in the *dissimilarity* of the necessitation of the will. In order to mark this difference more clearly, I think they would be most suitably named in their order if we said they

---

27 [Author's note] The word "prudence" may be taken in two senses, and it may bear the names of prudence with reference to things of the world and private prudence. The former sense means the skill of a man in having an influence on others so as to use them for his own purposes. The latter is the ability to unite all these purposes to his own lasting advantage. The worth of the first is finally reduced to the latter, and of one who is prudent in the former sense but not in the latter we might better say that he is clever and cunning yet, on the whole, imprudent.

are either *rules* of skill, or *counsels* of prudence, or *commands* (*laws*) of morality. For it is law only that involves the concept of an *unconditional* and objective necessity, which is consequently universally valid; and commands are laws which must be obeyed, that is, must be followed, even in opposition to inclination. *Counsels*, indeed, involve necessity, but one which can only hold under a contingent subjective condition, viz., they depend on whether this or that human being counts this or that as part of his happiness; the categorical imperative, on the contrary, is not limited by any condition, and as being absolutely, although practically, necessary may be quite properly called a command. We might also call the first kind of imperatives *technical* (belonging to art), the second *pragmatic*[28] (belonging to welfare), and the third *moral* (belonging to free conduct as such, that is, to morals).

Now arises the question, how are all these imperatives possible? This question does not seek to know how we can conceive the performance of the action which the imperative ordains, but merely how we can conceive the necessitation of the will which the imperative expresses. No special explanation is needed to show how an imperative of skill is possible. Whoever wills the end wills also (so far as reason has decisive influence on his action) the means in his power which are indispensably necessary to it. This proposition is, as regards the volition, analytic;[29]

for in willing an object as my effect there is already thought the causality of myself as an acting cause, that is to say, the use of the means; and the imperative educes from the concept of a volition of an end the concept of actions necessary to this end. Synthetic propositions must no doubt be employed in defining the means to a proposed end; but they do not concern the principle, the act of the will, but the object and its realization. For example, that in order to bisect a line on an unerring principle I must draw from its extremities two intersecting arcs; this no doubt is taught by mathematics only in synthetic propositions; but if I know that it is only by this process that the intended operation can be performed, then to say that if I fully will the operation, I also will the action required for it, is an analytic proposition; for it is one and the same thing to represent something as an effect which I can produce in a certain way, and to represent myself as acting in this way.

If it were only equally easy to give a definite conception of happiness, the imperatives of prudence would correspond exactly with those of skill, and would likewise be analytic. For in this case as in that, it could be said whoever wills the end wills also (necessarily in accordance with reason) the indispensable means thereto which are in his power. But, unfortunately, the notion of happiness is so indeterminate that although every human being wishes to attain it, yet he never can say definitely and consistently what it is that he really wishes and wills. The reason for this is that all the elements which belong to the concept of happiness are altogether empirical, that is, they must be borrowed from experience, and nevertheless the idea of happiness requires an absolute whole, a maximum of welfare in my present and all future circumstances. Now it is impossible that the most clear-sighted and at the same time most powerful being (supposed finite) should frame for himself a definite conception of what he really wills in this. If he wills riches, how much anxiety, envy, and snares might he not thereby draw upon his shoulders? If he wills knowledge and discernment, perhaps it might prove to be only an eye

---

28   [Author's note] It seems to me that the proper meaning of the word "pragmatic" could be most accurately defined in this way. For sanctions which properly flow not from the law of states as necessary statutes but from provision for the general welfare are called pragmatic. A history is pragmatically composed when it teaches prudence (i.e., instructs the world how it could provide for its interest better than, or at least as well as, has been done in the past).

29   Something is analytically true if it is true in virtue of the meanings involved, particularly in cases where, as Kant put it, the concept of the predicate is "contained in" the concept of the subject (e.g., "All aunts are female" or "This poodle is a dog"). Synthetic propositions, according to Kant, are simply propositions that are not analytic: thus, in synthetic propositions, the

predicate provides *new* information about the subject (e.g., "My aunt is called Dora" or "Poodles come in many colors").

so much sharper to show him so much the more fearfully the evils that are now concealed from him and that cannot be avoided, or to impose more wants on his desires, which already give him concern enough. Would he have long life? Who guarantees to him that it would not be a long misery? Would he at least have health? How often has uneasiness of the body restrained from excesses into which perfect health would have allowed one to fall, and so on? In short, he is unable, on any principle, to determine with certainty what would make him truly happy; because to do so he would need to be omniscient. We cannot therefore act on any definite principles to secure happiness, but only on empirical counsels, for example, of regimen, frugality, courtesy, reserve, etc., which experience teaches do, on the average, most promote well-being. Hence it follows that the imperatives of prudence do not, strictly speaking, command at all, that is, they cannot present actions objectively as practically *necessary*; that they are rather to be regarded as counsels (*consilia*) than precepts (*praecepta*) of reason, that the problem to determine certainly and universally what action would promote the happiness of a rational being is completely insoluble, and consequently no imperative respecting it is possible which would, in the strict sense, command him to do what makes him happy; because happiness is not an ideal of reason but of imagination, resting solely on empirical grounds, and it is vain to expect that these should determine an action by which one could attain the totality of a series of consequences which is really endless. This imperative of prudence would, however, be an analytic proposition if we assume that the means to happiness could be certainly assigned; for it is distinguished from the imperative of skill only by this, that in the latter the end is merely *possible*, in the former it is *given*; as, however, both only ordain the means to that which we suppose to be willed as an end, it follows that the imperative which ordains the willing of the means to him who wills the end is in both cases analytic. Thus there is no difficulty in regard to the possibility of an imperative of this kind either.

On the other hand, the question, how the imperative of *morality* is possible, is undoubtedly one, the only one, demanding a solution, as this is not at all hypothetical, and the objective necessity which it presents cannot rest on any hypothesis, as is the case with the hypothetical imperatives. Only here we must never leave out of consideration that we *cannot* make out *by means of any example*, in other words, empirically, whether there is such an imperative at all; but it is rather to be feared that all those which seem to be categorical may yet be at bottom hypothetical. For instance, when the precept is: "You ought not to promise deceitfully," and it is assumed that the necessity of this is not a mere counsel to avoid some other ill, so that it should mean: "You shall not make a lying promise, lest if it become known you should destroy your credit," but that an action of this kind must be regarded as evil in itself, so that the imperative of the prohibition is categorical; then we cannot show with certainty in any example that the will was determined merely by the law, without any other incentives, although it may appear to be so. For it is always possible that fear of disgrace, perhaps also obscure dread of other dangers, may have a secret influence on the will. Who can prove by experience the non-existence of a cause when all that experience tells us is that we do not perceive it? But in such a case the so-called moral imperative, which as such appears to be categorical and unconditional, would in reality be only a pragmatic precept, drawing our attention to our own interests, and merely teaching us to take these into consideration.

We will therefore have to investigate *a priori* the possibility of a *categorical* imperative, as we have not in this case the advantage of its reality being given in experience, so that [the elucidation of]its possibility should be requisite only for its explanation, not for its establishment. In the meantime it may be discerned beforehand that the categorical imperative alone has the purport of a practical law; and the rest may indeed be called *principles* of the will but not laws, since whatever is only necessary for the attainment of some discretionary purpose may be considered as in itself contingent, and we can at any time be free from the precept if we give up the purpose; on the contrary, the unconditional command leaves the will no liberty to choose the opposite, consequently it alone carries with it that necessity which we require of a law.

Secondly, in the case of this categorical imperative or law of morality, the difficulty (of describing its possibility) is a very profound one. It is an *a priori* synthetic practical proposition;[30] and as there is so much difficulty in discerning the possibility of speculative propositions of this kind, it may readily be supposed that the difficulty will be no less with the practical.

In this problem we will first inquire whether the mere concept of a categorical imperative may not perhaps supply us also with the formula of it, containing the proposition which alone can be a categorical imperative; for even if we know the tenor of such an absolute command, yet how it is possible will require further special and laborious study, which we postpone to the last section.

When I conceive a hypothetical imperative, in general I do not know beforehand what it will contain until I am given the condition. But when I conceive a categorical imperative, I know at once what it contains. For as the imperative contains besides the law only the necessity that the maxims[31] shall conform to this law, while the law contains no conditions restricting it, there remains nothing but the general statement that the maxim of the action should conform to universal law, and it is this conformity alone that the imperative properly represents as necessary.

There is therefore but one categorical imperative, namely, this: *Act only on that maxim whereby you can at the same time will that it become a universal law.*[32]

Now if all imperatives of duty can be deduced from this one imperative as their principle, then, although it should remain undecided whether what is called duty is not merely a vain notion, yet at least we shall be able to show what we understand by it and what this notion means.

Since the universality of the law according to which effects are produced constitutes what is properly called *nature* in the most general sense (as to form)—that is, the existence of things so far as it is determined by general laws—the imperative of duty may be expressed thus: *Act as if the maxim of your action were to become by your will a **universal law of nature**.*[33]

We will now enumerate a few duties, adopting the usual division of them into duties to ourselves and duties to others, and into perfect and imperfect duties.[34]

1. Someone reduced to despair by a series of misfortunes feels wearied of life, but is still so far in possession of his reason that he can ask himself whether it would not be contrary to his duty to himself take his own life. Now he inquires whether the maxim of his action could become a universal law of nature. His maxim is: From self love I adopt it as my principle to shorten my life when its longer duration is likely to bring more ill than satisfaction. It is asked then

---

30 [Author's note] I connect a priori, and hence necessarily, the action with the will without supposing as a condition that there is any inclination [to the action] (though I do so only objectively, i.e., under the Idea of a reason which would have complete power over all subjective motives). This is, therefore, a practical proposition which does not analytically derive the willing of an action from some other volition already presupposed (for we do not have such a perfect will); it rather connects it directly with the concept of the will of a rational being as something which is not contained within it.

31 [Author's note] A maxim is the subjective principle of acting and must be distinguished from the objective principle (i.e., the practical law). The former contains the practical rule which reason determines according to the conditions of the subject (often his ignorance or inclinations) and is thus the principle according to which the subject acts. The law, on the other hand, is the objective principle valid for every rational being, and the principle by which it ought to act, i.e., an imperative.

32 This formulation of the categorical imperative is often called the Formula of Universal Law.

33 This is often called the Formula of the Law of Nature.

34 [Author's note] It must be noted here that I reserve the division of duties for a future *Metaphysics of Morals* and that the division here stands as only an arbitrary one (chosen in order to arrange my examples). For the rest, by a perfect duty I here understand a duty which permits no exception in the interest of inclination; thus I have not merely outer but also inner perfect duties. This runs contrary to the usage adopted in the schools, but I am not disposed to defend it here because it is all one to my purpose whether this is conceded or not.

simply whether this principle founded on self-love can become a universal law of nature. Now we can see at once that a system of nature of which it should be a law to destroy life by means of the very feeling whose vocation it is to impel to the improvement of life would contradict itself, and therefore could not exist as a system of nature; hence that maxim cannot possibly exist as a universal law of nature, and consequently would be wholly inconsistent with the supreme principle of all duty.

2. Another finds himself forced by necessity to borrow money. He knows that he will not be able to repay it, but sees also that nothing will be lent to him unless he promises firmly to repay it within in a determinate time. He wants to make this promise, but he has still so much conscience as to ask himself: Is it not unlawful and inconsistent with duty to get out of a difficulty this way? Suppose, however, that he resolves to do so, then the maxim of his action would be expressed thus: When I think myself in want of money, I will borrow money and promise to repay it, although I know that I never can do so. Now this principle of self-love or of one's own advantage may perhaps be consistent with my whole future welfare; but the question now is, Is it right? I change then the suggestion of self-love into a universal law, and state the question thus: How would it be if my maxim were a universal law? Then I see at once that it could never hold as a universal law of nature, but would necessarily contradict itself. For supposing it to be a universal law that everyone when he thinks himself in a difficulty should be able to promise whatever he pleases, with the purpose of not keeping his promise, the promise itself would become impossible, as well as the end that he might have in view in it, since no one would consider that anything was promised to him, but would ridicule all such statements as vain pretenses.

3. A third finds in himself a talent which with the help of some culture might make him a useful human being in many respects. But he finds himself in comfortable circumstances and prefers to indulge in pleasure rather than to take pain in enlarging and improving his fortunate natural predispositions. He asks, however, whether his maxim of neglect of his natural gifts, besides agreeing with his inclination to indulgence, agrees also with what is called duty. He sees then that a system of nature could indeed subsist with such a universal law, although human beings (like the South Sea islanders[35]) should let their talents rust and resolve to devote their lives merely to idleness, amusement, and propagation of their species—in a word, to enjoyment; but he cannot possibly **will** that this should be a universal law of nature, or be implanted in us as such by a natural instinct. For as a rational being, he necessarily wills that his faculties be developed, since they serve him, and have been given him, for all sorts of purposes.

4. Yet a fourth, who is in prosperity, while he sees that others have to contend with great wretchedness and that he could help them, thinks: What concern is it of mine? Let everyone be as happy as heaven pleases, or as he can make himself; I will take nothing from him nor even envy him, only I do not wish to contribute anything to his welfare or to his assistance in need! Now no doubt, if such a mode of thinking were a universal law, the human race might very well subsist, and doubtless even better than in a state in which everyone talks of sympathy and good-will, or even takes care occasionally to put it into practice, but, on the other side, also cheats when he can, betrays the rights of human beings, or otherwise violates them. But although it is possible that a universal law of nature might exist in accordance with that maxim, it is impossible to **will** that such a principle should have the universal validity of a law of nature. For a will which resolved this would contradict itself, inasmuch as many cases might occur in which one would have need of the love and sympathy of others, and in which, by such a law of nature, sprung from his own will, he would deprive himself of all hope of the aid he desires.

These are a few of the many actual duties, or at least what we regard as such, which obviously fall into two classes on the one principle that we have laid down. We must *be able to will* that a maxim of our action should be a universal law. This is the canon of the moral judgment of the action generally. Some actions are of such a character that their maxim cannot without contradiction be even *conceived* as a universal law of nature, far from it being possible that we should

---

35 The inhabitants of the islands of the southern Pacific, such as Polynesia and Micronesia.

will that it *should* be so. In others, this intrinsic impossibility is not found, but still it is impossible to *will* that their maxim should be raised to the universality of a law of nature, since such a will would contradict itself. It is easily seen that the former violate strict or rigorous (inflexible) duty; the latter only wide (meritorious) duty. Thus it has been completely shown by these examples how all duties depend as regards the nature of the obligation (not the object of the action) on the same principle.

If now we attend to ourselves on occasion of any transgression of duty, we will find that we in fact do not will that our maxim should be a universal law, for that is impossible for us; on the contrary, we will that the opposite should remain a universal law, only we assume the liberty of making an *exception* in our own favor or (just for this time only) in favor of our inclination. Consequently, if we considered all cases from one and the same point of view, namely, that of reason, we should find a contradiction in our own will, namely, that a certain principle should be objectively necessary as a universal law, and yet subjectively should not be universal, but admit of exceptions. As, however, we at one moment regard our action from the point of view of a will wholly conformed to reason, and then again look at the same action from the point of view of a will affected by inclination, there is not really any contradiction, but an opposition (*antagonismus*) of inclination to the precept of reason, whereby the universality (*universalitas*) of the principle is changed into a mere generality (*generalitas*), so that the practical principle of reason shall meet the maxim half way. Now, although this cannot be justified in our own impartial judgment, yet it proves that we do really recognize the validity of the categorical imperative and (with all respect for it) only allow ourselves a few exceptions which we think unimportant and forced upon us.

We have thus established at least this much—that if duty is a conception which is to have any import and real legislative authority for our actions, it can only be expressed in categorical, and not at all in hypothetical, imperatives. We have also, which is of great importance, exhibited clearly and definitely for every practical application the content of the categorical imperative, which must contain the principle of all duty if there is such a thing at all. We have not yet, however, advanced so far as to prove *a priori* that there actually is such an imperative, that there is a practical law which commands absolutely of itself and without any other incentive, and that the following of this law is duty.

With the view of attaining to this it is of extreme importance to remember that we must not allow ourselves to think of deducing the reality of this principle from the *particular attributes of human nature*. For duty is to be a practical, unconditional necessity of action; it must therefore hold for all rational beings (to whom an imperative can apply at all), and *for this reason only* be also a law for all human wills. On the contrary, whatever is deduced from the particular natural characteristics of humanity, from certain feelings and propensities, or even, if possible, from any particular tendency proper to human reason, and which need not necessarily hold for the will of every rational being—this may indeed supply us with a maxim but not with a law; with a subjective principle on which we may have a propensity and inclination to act, but not with an objective principle on which we should be *enjoined* to act, even though all our propensities, inclinations, and natural dispositions were opposed to it. In fact, the sublimity and intrinsic dignity of the command in duty are so much the more evident, the less the subjective impulses favor it and the more they oppose it, without being able in the slightest degree to weaken the obligation of the law or to diminish its validity.

Here then we see philosophy brought to a critical position, since it has to be firmly fixed, notwithstanding that it has nothing to support it in heaven or on earth. Here it must show its purity as absolute director of its own laws, not the herald of those which are whispered to it by an implanted sense or who knows what tutelary nature. Although these may be better than nothing, yet they can never afford principles dictated by reason, which must have their source wholly *a priori* and, at the same time, their commanding authority from this, expecting everything from the supremacy of the law and the due respect for it, nothing from inclination, or else condemning the human being to self-contempt and inward abhorrence.

Thus every empirical element is not only quite incapable of being an aid to the principle of morality, but is even highly prejudicial to the purity of morals; for the proper and inestimable worth of an absolutely good will consists just in this, that the principle of action is free from all influence of contingent grounds, which alone experience can furnish. We cannot too much or too often repeat our warning against this lax and even mean habit of thought which seeks for its principle among empirical motives and laws; for human reason in its weariness is glad to rest on this pillow, and in a dream of sweet illusions (in which, instead of Juno, it embraces a cloud[36]) it substitutes for morality a bastard patched up from limbs of various derivation, which looks like anything one chooses to see in it; only not like virtue to one who has once beheld her in her true form.[37]

The question then is this: Is it a necessary law *for all rational beings* that they should always judge their actions by maxims of which they can themselves will that they should serve as universal laws? If there is such a law, then it must be connected (altogether *a priori*) with the very concept of the will of a rational being as such. But in order to discover this connection we must, however reluctantly, take a step into metaphysics, although into a domain of it which is distinct from speculative philosophy—namely, the metaphysics of morals. In a practical philosophy, where it is not the grounds of what *happens* that we have to ascertain, but the laws of what *ought to happen*, even though it never does, that is, objective practical laws, there it is not necessary to inquire into the grounds why anything pleases or displeases, how the pleasure of mere sensation differs from taste, and whether the latter is distinct from a general satisfaction of reason; on what the feeling of pleasure or pain rests, and how from it desires and inclinations arise, and from these again maxims by the cooperation of reason; for all this belongs to an empirical psychology, which would constitute the second part of the doctrine of nature, if we regard physics as the *philosophy of nature*, so far as it is based *on empirical laws*. But there we are concerned with objective practical laws, and consequently with the relation of the will to itself so far as it is determined by reason alone, in which case whatever has reference to anything empirical is necessarily excluded; since if *reason of itself alone* determines the conduct (and it is the possibility of this that we are now investigating), it must necessarily do so *a priori*.

The will is conceived as a capacity of determining itself to action in accordance with the *representation of certain laws*. And such a capacity can be found only in rational beings. Now that which serves the will as the objective ground of its self-determination is the *end*, and if this is assigned by reason alone, it must hold for all rational beings. On the other hand, that which merely contains the ground of possibility of the action of which the effect is the end, this is called the *means*. The subjective ground of the desire is the *incentive*, the objective ground of the volition is the *motive*; hence the distinction between subjective ends which rest on incentives, and objective ends which depend on motives valid for every rational being. Practical principles are *formal* when they abstract from all subjective ends; they are *material* when they assume these, and therefore particular incentives. The ends which a rational being proposes to himself at pleasure as *effects* of his actions (material ends) are all only relative, for it is only their relation to the particular desires of the subject that gives them their worth, which therefore cannot furnish principles universal and necessary for all rational beings and for every volition, that is to say, practical laws. Hence all these relative ends can give rise only to hypothetical imperatives.

---

36   Juno is the Roman name for the Greek goddess Hera, wife and sister of the god Zeus. The human king Ixion was tricked into making love to a cloud, mistaking it for Juno, and so became the father of the "bastard" race of centaurs, half horse and half human. (Ixion was later punished for his attempted seduction by being pinned for eternity to a burning, revolving wheel in Hades.)

37   [Author's note] To behold virtue in her proper form is nothing else than to exhibit morality stripped of all admixture of sensuous things and of every spurious adornment of reward or self-love. How much she then eclipses everything which appears charming to the senses can easily be seen by everyone with the least effort of his reason, if it be not spoiled for all abstraction.

Supposing, however, that there were something *whose existence* has *in itself* an absolute worth, something which, being *an end in itself*, could be a source of definite laws, then in this and this alone would lie the source of a possible categorical imperative, that is, a practical law.

Now I say: the human being and in general every rational being exists as an end[38] in itself, *not merely as a means* to be arbitrarily used by this or that will, but in all his actions, whether they concern himself or other rational beings, must be always regarded at the same time as an end. All objects of the inclinations have only a conditional worth; for if the inclinations and the needs founded on them did not exist, then their object would be without any value. But the inclinations themselves, being sources of needs, are so far from having an absolute worth for which they should be desired that, on the contrary, it must be the universal wish of every rational being to be wholly free from them. Thus the worth of any object which is *to be acquired* by our action is always conditional. Beings whose existence depends not on our will but on nature's, have nevertheless, if they are nonrational beings, only a relative value as means, and are therefore called *things*; rational beings, on the contrary, are called *persons*, because their very nature restricts all choice (and is an object of respect). These, therefore, are not merely subjective ends whose existence has a worth *for us* as an effect of our action, but *objective ends*, that is, things whose existence is an end in itself—an end, moreover, for which no other can be substituted, to which they should serve *merely* as means, for otherwise nothing whatever would possess *absolute worth*; but if all worth were conditioned and therefore contingent, then there would be no supreme practical principle of reason whatever.

If then there is a supreme practical principle or, with respect to the human will, a categorical imperative, it must be one which, being drawn from the conception of that which is necessarily an end for everyone because it is *an end in itself*, constitutes an *objective* principle of will, and can therefore serve as a universal practical law. The foundation of this principle is: *rational nature exists as an end in itself.*

The human being necessarily conceives of his own existence as being so; so far then this is a *subjective* principle of human actions. But every other rational being regards its existence similarly, just on the same rational principle that holds for me;[39] so that it is at the same time an objective principle from which as a supreme practical law all laws of the will must be capable of being deduced. Accordingly the practical imperative will be as follows: *So act as to treat humanity, whether in your own person or in that of any other, in every case at the same time as an end, never as a means only.*[40] We will now inquire whether this can be practically carried out.

To abide by the previous examples:

First, under the head of necessary duty to oneself: Someone who contemplates suicide should ask himself whether his action can be consistent with the idea of humanity *as an end in itself.* If he destroys himself in order to escape from painful circumstances, he uses a person merely as a *means* to maintain a tolerable condition up to the end of life. But a human being is not a thing, that is to say, something which can be used merely as a means, but must in all his actions be always considered as an end in itself. I cannot, therefore, dispose in any way of a human being in my own person by mutilating, damaging, or killing him. (It belongs to morals proper to define this principle more precisely, so as to avoid all misunderstanding, for example, as to the amputation of the limbs in order to preserve myself; as to exposing my life to danger with a view to preserve it, etc. This question is therefore omitted here.)

Second, as regards necessary duties, or those of strict obligation, towards others: He who is thinking of making a lying promise to others will see at once that he would be using another human being *merely as a means*, without the latter at the same time containing in himself the end. For he whom I propose by such a promise to use for my own purposes cannot possibly assent to my mode of acting toward him,

---

38   A source of value and meaning, a goal or purpose.

39   [Author's note] Here I present this proposition as a postulate, but in the last Section grounds for it will be found.

40   This is often called the Formula of Humanity as End in Itself.

and therefore cannot himself contain the end of this action. This violation of the principle of humanity in other human beings is more obvious if we take in examples of attacks on the freedom and property of others. For then it is clear that he who transgresses the rights of human beings intends to use the person of others merely as means, without considering that as rational beings they ought always to be esteemed also as ends, that is, as beings who must be capable of containing in themselves the end of the very same action.[41]

Third, as regards contingent (meritorious) duties to oneself: It is not enough that the action does not violate humanity in our own person as an end in itself, it must also *harmonize with* it. Now there are in humanity capacities of greater perfection which belong to the end that nature has in view with regard to humanity in ourselves as the subject; to neglect these might perhaps be consistent with the *maintenance* of humanity as an end in itself, but not with the *advancement* of this end.

Fourth, as regards meritorious duties toward others: The natural end which all human beings have is their own happiness. Now humanity might indeed subsist although no one should contribute anything to the happiness of others, provided he did not intentionally withdraw anything from it; but after all, this would only harmonize negatively, not positively, with *humanity as an end in itself*, if everyone does not also endeavor, as far as he can, to forward the ends of others. For the ends of any subject which is an end in itself ought as far as possible to be *my* ends also, if that conception is to have its *full* effect in me.

This principle that humanity and generally every rational nature is *an end in itself* (which is the supreme limiting condition of every human being's freedom of action), is not borrowed from experience, *first*, because it is universal, applying as it does to all rational beings whatever, and experience is not capable of determining anything about them; *second*, because it does not present humanity as an end to human beings (subjectively), that is, as an object which human beings do of themselves actually adopt as an end; but as an objective end which must as a law constitute the supreme limiting condition of all our subjective ends, let them be what they will; it must therefore spring from pure reason. In fact the ground of all practical legislation lies (according to the first principle) *objectively in the rule* and its form of universality which makes it capable of being a law (say, for example, a law of nature); but *subjectively* in the *end*; now by the second principle, the subject of all ends is each rational being inasmuch as it is an end in itself. From this follows the third practical principle of the will, which is the ultimate condition of its harmony with the universal practical reason, viz., the idea of *the will of every rational being as a will giving universal law*.[42]

On this principle all maxims are rejected which are inconsistent with the will being itself universal legislator. Thus the will is not merely subject to the law, but subject to it so that it must be regarded *as itself giving the law*, and on this ground only subject to the law (of which it can regard itself as the author).

In the previous imperatives, namely, that based on the conception of the conformity of actions to general laws, as in a *system of nature*, and that based on the universal *prerogative* of rational beings as *ends* in themselves—these imperatives just because they were conceived as categorical excluded from any share in their authority all admixture of any interest as an incentive; they were, however, only *assumed* to be categorical, because such an assumption was necessary to explain the conception of duty. But we

---

41   [Author's note] Let it not be thought that the banal "what you do not wish to be done to you..." could here serve as guide or principle, for it is only derived from the principle and is restricted by various limitations. It cannot be a universal law, because it contains the ground neither of duties to one's self nor of the benevolent duties to others (for many a man would gladly consent that others should not benefit him, provided only that he might be excused from showing benevolence to them). Nor does it contain the ground of obligatory duties to another, for the criminal would argue on this ground against the judge who sentences him. And so on.

---

42   This is sometimes called the Formula of Autonomy.

could not prove independently that there are practical propositions which command categorically, nor can it be proved in this section; one thing, however, could be done, namely, to indicate in the imperative itself, by some determinate expression, that in the case of volition from duty all interest is renounced, which is the specific criterion of categorical as distinguished from hypothetical imperatives. This is done in the present third formula of the principle, namely, in the idea of the will of every rational being as a *will giving universal law*.

For although a will *which is subject to laws* may be attached to this law by means of an interest, yet a will which is itself a supreme lawgiver, so far as it is such, cannot possibly depend on any interest, since a will so dependent would itself still need another law restricting the interest of its self-love by the condition that it should be valid as universal law.

Thus the *principle* of every human will as *a will which in all its maxims*[43] *gives universal laws*, provided it be otherwise correct, would be very *well suited* to be the categorical imperative in this respect, namely, that just because of the idea of universal legislation it is *not based on any interest*, and therefore it alone among all possible imperatives can be *unconditional*. Or still better, converting the proposition, if there is a categorical imperative (that is, a law for the will of every rational being), it can only command that everything be done from maxims of one's will regarded as a will which could at the same time will that it should itself give universal laws, for in that case only the practical principle and the imperative which it obeys are unconditional, since they cannot be based on any interest.

Looking back now on all previous attempts to discover the principle of morality, we need not wonder why they all failed. It was seen that the human being is bound to laws by duty, but it was not observed that the laws to which he is subject are *only those of his own giving*, though at the same time they are *universal*, and that he is only bound to act in conformity with his own

---

43   [Author's note] I may be excused from citing examples to elucidate this principle, for those that have already illustrated the categorical imperative and its formula can here serve the same purpose.

will—a will, however, which is designed by nature to give universal laws. For when one has conceived the human being only as subject to a law (no matter what), then this law required some interest, either by way of attraction or constraint, since it did not originate as a law from *his own* will, but this will was according to a law obliged by *something else* to act in a certain manner. Now by this necessary consequence all the labor spent in finding a supreme principle of *duty* was irrevocably lost. For one never elicited duty, but only a necessity of acting from a certain interest. Whether this interest was private or otherwise, in any case the imperative had to be conditional, and could not by any means be capable of being a moral command. I will therefore call this the principle of **autonomy** of the will, in contrast with every other which I accordingly count under **heteronomy**.

The concept of every rational being as one which must consider itself as giving in all the maxims of its will universal laws, so as to judge itself and its actions from this point of view—this concept leads to another which depends on it and is very fruitful, namely, that of a *kingdom of ends*.

By a *kingdom* I understand the systematic union of different rational beings through common laws. Now since it is by laws that the universal validity of ends are determined, hence, if we abstract from the personal differences of rational beings, and likewise from all the content of their private ends, we shall be able to conceive all ends combined in a systematic whole (including both rational beings as ends in themselves, and also the special ends which each may propose to himself), that is to say, we can conceive a kingdom of ends, which on the preceding principles is possible.

For all rational beings come under the *law* that each of them must treat itself and all others *never merely as means*, but in every case *at the same time as ends in themselves*. From this results a systematic union of rational beings through common objective laws, that is, a kingdom which may be called a kingdom of ends, since what these laws have in view is just the relation of these beings to one another as ends and means. It is certainly only an ideal.

A rational being belongs as a *member* to the kingdom of ends when, although giving universal laws in it, he is also himself subject to these laws. He belongs to it *as sovereign* when, while giving laws, he is not subject to the will of any other.

A rational being must always regard himself as giving laws either as member or as sovereign in a kingdom of ends which is rendered possible by the freedom of will. He cannot, however, maintain the latter position merely by maxims of his will, but only in case he is a completely independent being without needs and with unrestricted power adequate to his will.

Morality consists then in the reference of all action to the legislation which alone can render a kingdom of ends possible.[44] This legislation must be capable of existing in every rational being, and of emanating from his will, so that the principle of this will is never to act on any maxim which could not without contradiction be also a universal law, and accordingly always so to act that *the will could at the same time regard itself as giving through its maxims universal laws*. If now the maxims of rational beings are not by their own nature coincident with this objective principle, then the necessity of acting on it is called practical necessitation, that is, *duty*. Duty does not apply to the sovereign in the kingdom of ends, but it does apply to every member of it and to all in the same degree.

The practical necessity of acting on this principle, that is, duty, does not rest at all on feelings, impulses, or inclinations, but solely on the relation of rational beings to one another, a relation in which the will of a rational being must always be regarded as *legislative*, since otherwise it could not be regarded as *an end in itself*. Reason then refers every maxim of the will, regarding it as legislative universally, to every other will and also to every action towards oneself; and this not on account of any other practical motive or any future advantage, but from the idea of the *dignity* of a rational being, obeying no law but that which he himself also gives.

In the kingdom of ends everything has either *price* or *dignity*. Whatever has price can be replaced by something else which is *equivalent*; whatever, on the other hand, is above all price, and therefore admits of no equivalent, has a dignity.

Whatever has reference to the general inclinations and wants of humankind has a *market price*; whatever, without presupposing a need, corresponds to a certain taste, that is, to a delight in the mere purposeless play of our faculties, has a *fancy price*; but that which constitutes the condition under which alone anything can be an end in itself, this has not merely relative worth, that is, price, but an inner worth, that is, *dignity*.

Now morality is the condition under which alone a rational being can be an end in himself, since by this alone it is possible that he should be a legislating member in the kingdom of ends. Thus morality, and humanity, insofar as it is capable of morality, is that which alone has dignity. Skill and diligence in labor have a market price; wit, lively imagination, and humor have a fancy price; on the other hand, fidelity to promises, benevolence from principle (not from instinct), have an inner worth. Neither nature nor art contains anything which in default of these it could put in their place, for their worth consists not in the effects which spring from them, not in the use and advantage which they secure, but in the disposition, that is, the maxims of the will which are ready to manifest themselves in such actions, even if they do not have the desired effect. These actions also need no recommendation from any subjective taste or sentiment, that they may be looked upon with immediate favor and delight; they need no immediate propensity or feeling for them; they exhibit the will that performs them as an object of an immediate respect, and nothing but reason is required to *impose* them on the will; not to *flatter* it into them, which, in the case of duties, would be a contradiction. This estimation therefore shows that the worth of such a disposition is dignity, and places it infinitely above all price, with which it cannot for a moment be brought into comparison or competition without as it were violating its sanctity.

What then is it which justifies virtue or the morally good disposition, in making such lofty claims? It is nothing less than the *privilege* it secures to the rational being of participating *in the giving of*

---

44   This is sometimes called the Formula of the Kingdom of Ends.

universal laws, by which it qualifies him to be a member of a possible kingdom of ends, a privilege to which he was already destined by his own nature as being an end in itself, and on that account legislating in the kingdom of ends; free as regards all laws of nature, and obeying only those laws which he himself gives, and by which his maxims can belong to a system of universal law to which at the same time he submits himself. For nothing has any worth except what the law assigns it. Now the legislation itself which assigns the worth of everything must for that very reason possess dignity, that is, an unconditional incomparable worth; and the word *respect*[45] alone supplies a becoming expression for the esteem which a rational being must have for it. *Autonomy* then is the basis of the dignity of human nature and of every rational nature.

The three modes of presenting the principle of morality that have been adduced are at bottom only so many formulae of the very same law, and each unites in itself the other two. There is, however, a difference among them, but it is subjectively rather than objectively practical, intended, namely, to bring an idea of reason nearer to intuition (by means of a certain analogy), and thereby nearer to feeling. All maxims, in fact, have—

1. A *form*, consisting in universality; and in this view the formula of the moral imperative is expressed thus, that the maxims must be so chosen as if they were to serve as universal laws of nature.

2. A *matter*, namely, an end, and here the formula says that the rational being, as it is an end by its own nature and therefore an end in itself, must in every maxim serve as the condition limiting all merely relative and arbitrary ends.

3. A *complete determination* of all maxims by means of that formula, namely, that all maxims ought, by their own legislation, to harmonize with a possible kingdom of ends as with a kingdom of nature.[46] There is a progression here in the order of the categories of *unity* of the form of the will (its universality), *plurality* of the matter (the objects, that is, the ends), and *totality* of the system of these. In forming our moral *judgment* of actions it is better to proceed always on the strict method, and start from the universal formula of the categorical imperative: *Act according to a maxim which can at the same time make itself a universal law.* If, however, we wish to gain an *entrance* for the moral law, it is very useful to bring one and the same action under the three specified conceptions, and thereby as far as possible to bring it nearer to intuition.

---

45 Other translators have preferred the English word "reverence." The German word is *Achtung*, which in this context has religious overtones of awe before the sublimity of the moral law.

---

46 [Author's note] Teleology considers nature as a realm of ends; morals regards a possible realm of ends as a realm of nature. In the former the realm of ends is a theoretical Idea for the explanation of what actually is. In the latter it is a practical Idea for bringing about that which does not exist but which can become actual through our conduct and for making it conform with this Idea.

JOHN STUART MILL
Utilitarianism

Who Was John Stuart Mill?

John Stuart Mill, the most important British philosopher of the nineteenth century, was born in London in 1806, the eldest son of Scottish utilitarian philosopher and political radical James Mill. His childhood was shaped—some might say, misshaped—by his father's fervent belief in the importance of education. James Mill held that every variation in the talents and capacities of individual human beings could be explained by their education and experiences, and thus that a proper educational regime, beginning more or less from birth, could train any child to be an almost superhuman intellect. To prove these theories, James Mill brought up his first son, John Stuart, to be the British radical movement's secret weapon—a prodigious intellect who would be a living demonstration of what could be achieved through properly scientific educational methods, and who would go out into the world to spread the secular gospel of utilitarianism and liberalism.

His father took sole charge of little John Stuart's education from the time when he was a toddler, keeping him isolated from other children (who might be harmful influences) and even from other adults who were not Mill's own philosophical compatriots. John was therefore kept out of schools—which his father believed reinforced ignorant and immoral social attitudes—and educated at home, learning Greek and Latin in the same large study where his father was hard at work on a monumental history of India (and, since no English-Greek dictionary had yet been written, frequently interrupting his father to ask questions about vocabulary). In his autobiography, Mill wrote, "I have no remembrance of the time when I began to learn Greek. I have been told that it was when I was three years old." By the time he was 8—the age at which he began to learn Latin and arithmetic—he had studied much of Greek literature in the original, including all of Herodotus's *Histories* and six dialogues by Plato. At 12 he started on logic and the serious study of philosophy; political economy at 13; and at 20 he was sent to France for a year to become fluent in that language and to study chemistry and mathematics.[1]

Despite these prodigious achievements, Mill's early life seems not to have been a happy one. He had no toys or children's books—not so much, apparently, because his father forbade them as simply because it never occurred to him to provide them—and John Stuart later remarked that he had never learned to play. Until he was 14 he never really mixed with children his own age at all. An early draft of his autobiography contained the following passage, deleted before publication:

---

1   At around this time Mill was offered a place at Cambridge University. His father refused it for him saying he already knew more than Cambridge could ever teach him.

I believe there is less personal affection in England than in any other country of which I know anything, and I give my father's family not as peculiar in this respect but only as a faithful exemplification of the ordinary fact. That rarity in England, a really warm hearted mother, would in the first place have made the children grow up loving and being loved. But my mother with the very best intentions, only knew how to pass her life in drudging for them ... but to make herself loved, looked up to, or even obeyed, required qualities which she unfortunately did not possess. I thus grew up in the absence of love and in the presence of fear: and many and indelible are the effects of this bringing-up, in the stunting of my moral growth.

At the age of 22 Mill suffered a nervous breakdown and was plunged into suicidal despair. The trigger—according to his autobiography—was a sudden realization that living the life for which his father had trained him could not make him happy:

> ... [I]t occurred to me to put the question directly to myself, "Suppose that all your objects in life were realized; that all the changes in institutions and opinions which you are looking forward to, could be completely effected this very instant: would this be a great joy and happiness to you?" And an irrepressible self-consciousness distinctly answered, "No!" At this my heart sank within me: the whole foundation on which my life was constructed fell down. All my happiness was to have been found in the continual pursuit of this end. The end had ceased to charm, and how could there ever again be any interest in the means? I seemed to have nothing left to live for.

Mill's response to this crisis was not to *abandon* utilitarianism and the radical philosophy of his father, but instead to *modify* the theories by which he had been brought up. He came to adopt the view that "those only are happy ... who have their minds fixed on some object other than their own happiness": that is, true happiness—which, as his father had taught him, is the measure of all action—comes not from the

pursuit of one's own happiness in itself, but from living a life filled with concern for the happiness of others and with a love of other things, such as poetry and music, for their own sake. Mill, in fact, claimed his sanity was saved by his discovery of Romantic poetry—especially that of William Wordsworth, Samuel Taylor Coleridge, and Johann Wolfgang von Goethe—and he later placed great emphasis on the proper development of the emotional and sentimental side of one's character, as well as one's intellect.

In 1830, at 24, Mill began a deeply passionate (but non-sexual) love affair with a beautiful, vivacious, but married woman, Harriet Hardy Taylor, the wife of John Taylor, a merchant. Mill's relationship with Harriet Taylor was central to his life, and she had a great influence on his writings. For fifteen years, between 1834 and John Taylor's death in 1849, Harriet and the two Johns lived out a curiously Victorian compromise. Harriet and Mill agreed never to be seen in "society" as a couple—which would cause a scandal—but were allowed by Harriet's husband to go on frequent holidays together. In 1851, two years after her husband's death, Harriet and Mill were finally able to marry, but in 1858, Harriet died of tuberculosis—a disease she probably caught from her new husband, who in turn had probably caught it from his father (James Mill died of TB in 1836).

Mill never held an academic position, but spent 35 years working as an administrator for the British East India Company in London. The East India Company, which had also employed Mill's father, was a private trading company formed in 1600 which, by the end of the eighteenth century, had its own army and political service and was effectively administering the sub-continent of India on behalf of the British Government. Mill started his career in 1823, at 17, as a clerk in the office of the Examiner of India Correspondence; by 1856 he had become Chief Examiner of India Correspondence, as his father had been before him. In 1858 the East India Company was taken over by the British Crown following the Indian Mutiny of 1857, and Mill retired with a substantial pension.

Mill's work for the company left him plenty of time for his writing, and he was also very active in public life. In 1823 he was arrested for distributing birth-control pamphlets, and in 1825 he helped to found the London Debating Society. In 1824 James Mill had founded the *Westminster Review*, a quarterly magazine advocating a radically liberal political and social agenda, and John Stuart Mill—only 18 years old at the time—was a frequent and enthusiastic contributor of articles during its early years. In 1835 John Stuart started his own radical periodical, the *London Review*, which soon became the influential *London and Westminster Review* and ran, under his editorship, until 1840. Between 1865 and 1868 Mill was the Liberal Member of Parliament for Westminster, and in 1866 he secured a law guaranteeing freedom of speech in London's Hyde Park.[2] In 1867 he tried, but failed, to amend the second Reform Bill to introduce proportional representation and the vote for women. In 1866—by now something of a "grand old man" of English society—he was made Rector of the University of St. Andrew's in Scotland. In 1872 he became 'godfather' to the newborn Bertrand Russell.

Mill died suddenly, from a fever, in 1873 at Aix-en-Provence, France. From about 1860 until 1870 he had been at the peak of his powers and influence. The moral philosopher Henry Sidgwick wrote in 1873, "from about 1860–1865 or thereabouts he ruled England in the region of thought as very few men ever did. I do not expect to see anything like it again." A few decades later the former Prime Minister James Arthur Balfour noted that the authority of Mill's thought in English universities had been "comparable to that wielded ... by Hegel in Germany and in the middle ages by Aristotle." By the First World War, however, Mill's reputation as a philosopher had suffered a precipitous decline, and he remained in ill-favor in the English-speaking philosophical world until the early 1970s, when new scholarship and changing philosophical fashions made possible a gradual increase in the appreciation of Mill as a major philosophical figure—the finest flowering of nineteenth-century British philosophy, and a precursor for the "naturalist" philosophers of the second half of the twentieth century.

---

2   This is the location, since that date, of London's famous Speakers' Corner—a place where "soapbox orators" can say whatever they like with legal impunity.

What Was Mill's Overall Philosophical Project?

Mill is important less for the *originality* of his philosophic thought than for its brilliant *synthesis* of several major strands in nineteenth-century (and especially British) thought into a single, compelling, well-developed picture. The main ingredients for his world-view were empiricism, associationism, utilitarianism, and elements of German Romanticism. Together, these elements became what John Skorupski has called Mill's "liberal naturalism."

The bedrock of Mill's philosophy was empiricism: he believed all human knowledge comes ultimately from sense-experience, and his most substantial intellectual project was the attempt to construct a system of empirical knowledge that could underpin not just science but also moral and social affairs. One of his main interests was in showing that empiricism need not lead to skepticism, such as that espoused by the eighteenth-century Scottish philosopher David Hume. Mill's main discussion of the foundation of knowledge and the principles of inference is the massive *System of Logic*, published in six volumes in 1843. In this work he discussed both deductive inference (including mathematics, which Mill argued was—like all human knowledge—reducible to a set of generalizations of relations among sense-experiences) and inductive inference in the natural sciences. He also tried to show how these methods could be applied in politics and the social sciences. Social phenomena, he argued, are just as much the result of causal laws as are natural events, and thus the social sciences—though they will never make us perfectly able to predict human behavior—are capable of putting social policy on an objective footing which goes beyond the mere "intuitions" of conservative common sense.

His prescriptions for scientific practice—today called "Mill's methods"—were highly influential in the development of the philosophy of science in the twentieth century, and his work is still the foundation of modern methodologies for discovering causal laws. The key engine of science, for Mill, is simply *enumerative induction* or generalization from experience. Crudely put, once we have observed a sequence of events which all obey some regularity—ravens which are black, say, or moving magnetic fields being accompanied by an electrical current—we are justified in inferring that all future events of that type will follow the same law.

Mill's work was also a precursor of what is today called "naturalized epistemology." He proposed that all the phenomena of the human mind, including rationality, be treated as the upshot of the operation of psychological laws acting upon the data of experience. This psychological theory is called "associationism"—since it holds that ideas arise from the psychological *associations* between sensations—and was particularly defended by Mill in his *Examination of Sir William Hamilton's Philosophy* (1865).

In his own time, Mill was for many years most widely known for his *Principles of Political Economy* (1848), which tried to show that the science of economics—criticized in his day as a "dismal science" that could only predict disaster and starvation—could be reformulated as a progressive force for social progress. Mill pointed out the mismatch between what economics measures and what human beings really value, and this led him to argue for limiting economic growth for the sake of the environment, controlling populations in order to allow an adequate standard of living for everyone, and for what he considered the economically ideal form of society—a system of worker-owned cooperatives.

Mill's main ethical position, of course, is utilitarianism, which he sets out in the selection reprinted here. As he wrote in his autobiography, of reading Jeremy Bentham's work on utilitarianism (at the age of 15), "it gave unity to my conceptions of things. I now had opinions; a creed, a doctrine, a philosophy; in one among all the best senses of the word, a religion; the inculcation and diffusion of which could be made the principal outward purpose of a life." Mill was also concerned to apply this moral theory to wider questions of social policy. Of all social institutions—including both formal institutions such as laws and churches, and informal ones like social norms—Mill wants to ask: does this institution contribute to human welfare, and does it do so better than any of the alternatives? If the answer was "No," Mill argued, then that institution should (gradually and non-violently) be changed for the better.

Mill's *On Liberty* (1859)—which, during his lifetime, was probably his most notorious writing—is a classic defence of the freedom of thought and discussion, arguing that "the only purpose for which power can be rightfully exercised over any member of a civilized community, against his will, is to prevent harm to others. His own good, either physical or moral, is not a sufficient warrant." This essay—sections of which are reprinted in Chapter 8—was sparked partly by Mill's growing fear of the middle-class conformism (which he saw in America and detected increasing signs of in Britain) which he thought dangerously stifled originality and the critical consideration of ideas. Central to these concerns is Mill's view of human nature as "progressive," and the importance of individuality and autonomy. These themes, with their emphasis on the power and importance of the human spirit, were part of what he took from the European Romantic movement.

One of Mill's last works, *The Subjection of Women* (1869), is a classic statement of liberal feminism. Mill argues that women should have just as much freedom as men, and attacks the conservative view that women and men have different "natures" which suit them for different spheres of life by arguing that no one could possibly know this—since all knowledge comes only from experience—unless women were first allowed to throw off their oppression and, over several generations, to *try* and do all the things that men were allowed to do.

What Is the Structure of This Reading?

Utilitarianism was not written as a scholarly treatise but as a sequence of articles, published in a monthly magazine, and intended for the general educated reader: consequently, although *Utilitarianism* is philosophically weighty and—just below the surface—often quite difficult, its overall structure is pretty straightforward. Mill begins by making some general remarks in the first chapter, attacking moral intuitionism and suggesting, among other things, that the principle of utilitarianism has always had a major tacit influence on moral beliefs. In Chapter 2 he defines utilitarianism, attempts to head off several common misunderstandings of the doctrine, and raises and responds to about ten possible objections to the theory (such as that utilitarianism is a godless morality worthy only of pigs, or alternatively that it sets an impracticably high standard which can never be attained by mere mortal human beings). In the third chapter, Mill considers the question of moral motivation, and discusses how people might come to feel themselves morally bound by the principles of utilitarianism, arguing that utilitarianism is grounded in the natural social feelings of humanity. In Chapter 4 Mill sets out to give a positive "proof" (insofar as that is possible) for the claim that utilitarianism is the correct moral theory: he argues, first, that one's own happiness is desirable to oneself; second that it follows that happiness is simply desirable in itself, no matter whose it is; and third that *only* happiness is intrinsically desirable. It is this third stage in the argument which takes up most of the chapter. The final chapter of *Utilitarianism*, which is not reprinted here, is a long discussion dealing with the relationship between utilitarianism and justice.

Some Useful Background Information

1. Mill frames much of *Utilitarianism* in terms of a debate between two basic positions on the nature of morality: the "intuitive" school versus the "inductive" school. The intuitionists, whom Mill attacks, believed that ethical facts—though as real and as objectively true as any others—are *non-empirical*: that is, moral truths cannot be detected or confirmed using the five senses, but instead are known through the special faculty of "moral intuition." This philosophical position was represented in Mill's time by, among others, Sir William Hamilton (1788–1856) and William Whewell (1794–1866), and Mill's frequent criticism of the notion of "transcendental" moral facts is directed at intuitionists such as these. Mill considered intuitionism to be not only false but also a serious obstacle to social and moral progress. He thought the claim that (educated) human beings can 'just tell' which moral principles are true, without needing or being able to cite *evidence for these beliefs*, tended to act as a disguise for prejudice and social conservatism.

Mill's own moral methodology, by contrast, was what he called "inductive": he believed *all* human knowledge, including ethical knowledge, comes ultimately from sense experience, and thus that moral judgments must be explained and defended by showing their connections to actual human experience.

2. The notion of *happiness* is a very important part of Mill's moral philosophy, so it is useful to be clear about exactly what his theory of happiness was. Because of Mill's empiricist and associationist philosophical upbringing, it was most natural for him to adopt a kind of *hedonistic* view of happiness. In keeping with his emphasis on sense experience as the key to understanding knowledge and the mind, Mill thinks of happiness as a kind of *pleasurable mental state* (*hēdonē* is the classical Greek word for "pleasure"). For Mill, a happy life is, roughly, one filled with as many pleasurable sensations as possible, and as few painful ones.

Mill followed his philosophical predecessors in thinking that pleasurable experiences can be classified according to their duration and their intensity: thus rational people seeking their own happiness will aim to arrange their lives so that, over time, they will have more longer-lasting pleasures than short-lived ones, and more intense pleasures than dilute ones. For example, the initial painfulness of learning the violin, might be more than off-set by the intense and long-lasting pleasure of playing it well.[3] In addition, however, Mill distinguished

---

3   Mill's mentor Jeremy Bentham even proposed what he called a "felicific calculus": a mathematical system for measuring the total net quantity of pleasure to be expected from a given course of action. (Roughly, calculate the balance of pleasure and pain that would accompany a particular outcome of your actions—taking into account their intensity and duration—and then multiply this number by the probability of that outcome actually occurring. This yields what Bentham called the "expected utility" of an action. The rational agent—according to Bentham—acts in a way which has the greatest expected utility.)

between different *qualities* of pleasure. For Mill (unlike, say, Bentham), pleasure is not just one type of mental sensation but comes in "higher" and "lower" varieties. For example, according to Mill, the pleasant feeling that accompanies advanced intellectual or creative activity is a more valuable kind of pleasure—even if it is no more intense or long-lasting—than that which comes from physical satisfactions like eating and sex.

3. One of Mill's philosophical presuppositions which is significant for his moral and social philosophy is *individualism*. Mill assumed that individual persons are the basic unit of political analysis—that social structures are nothing more than constructions out of these individuals and are nothing over and above particular people and the relations between them. It follows that the analysis of social phenomena must be approached through a study of the actions and intentions of individuals, and similarly that social change is only possible through a large number of changes to individual people. What mattered to Mill was not "the general happiness" in some abstract sense, but the happiness of large numbers of individual human beings. Social institutions were seen as merely *instruments* for benefiting all these people. Furthermore, for Mill (influenced, as he was, by European Romanticism), there is a special kind of *value* in individuality: the particular uniqueness of each person is a thing to be treasured in itself.

Some Common Misconceptions

1. For Mill, mere *exemption* from pain is not itself a good. He holds that pleasure is the only good, and pain the only bad, and the overall goodness of states of affairs consists in the *balance* of pleasure over pain. The absence of pain is thus merely morally neutral, unless it is accompanied by the positive presence of pleasure.

2. Mill is not arguing that people already *do* act in order to produce the greatest happiness of the greatest number: he is arguing that we *should*.

He is not merely describing an already prevalent moral psychology, but arguing for a certain set of moral attitudes which he thinks we ought to cultivate in ourselves and in society in general.

3. Utilitarianism is a theory of actions and not motives. It does not require that people *intend* to maximize utility, just that their behavior, in fact, does so. Mill insists the criterion for what makes an action right is that it maximize utility; it does not follow from this that all our actions must have the conscious goal of maximizing utility. In fact, there is a good case to be made that a community where everyone is *trying* to maximize utility all the time would actually be self-defeating and a much less happy society than it would be if people acted from other motivations. If this is right, it would follow that, according to utilitarianism itself, it would be immoral to be always consciously trying to maximize utility. This is not a paradox or a problem for the theory, however; it simply shows there is a difference between the criterion of right action and the best advice one can give moral agents for actually meeting that criterion.

Actions, according to Mill, include within themselves two parts: an *intention* (which is different from a motive—it is not *why* the action is done but *what* the action is intended to achieve), and the action's *effects*. Mill sometimes appeals to differences of intention to distinguish between kinds of actions (as in his Chapter 3 footnote about a tyrant rescuing a drowning man), but, strictly speaking, only the *effects* or consequences of an action can be morally relevant to the utilitarian.

4. One common complaint against utilitarianism is that it makes *every* action, no matter how trivial, a moral issue: pretty much everything we do (e.g., getting a haircut) will have *some* effect on someone's pleasure and pain, and so it appears we have a moral duty to ensure we *always* act in such a way as to maximize the general happiness—and this, to say the least, would seem to put a bit of a strain on everyday life. However, even if this, in fact, is an implica-

tion of Mill's utilitarian theory, he did not intend to commit us to such an onerous regime. Here is a quote from another of Mill's works (*Auguste Comte and Positivism*): "It is not good that persons should be bound, by other people's opinion, to do everything that they would deserve praise for doing. There is a standard of altruism to which all should be required to come up, and a degree beyond which it is not obligatory, but meritorious."

5. Despite the way *Utilitarianism* can strike us today, in the aftermath of the grand and often massively destructive social engineering projects of the twentieth century, Mill was actually a bitter foe of what might be called "social constructivism." He emphatically did *not* see society as merely a machine built to help human beings to live together, a machine which can be broken into bits and reconstructed if it is not working optimally, and one where the rational, technical vision of collective planners should override individual initiative in the public good. On the contrary, Mill was very much an *individualist* and a humanist. He saw society as built from the actions of separate individual human beings and held that it is a kind of historical "consensus" which has created traditions and cultural practices that are continually but gradually evolving over time. Mill's vision for the reform of society, then, was not the imposition of central planning, but instead the gradual construction of a set of cultural norms—including, especially, a progressive educational system—to create human beings with the best possible moral character.

How Important and Influential Is This Passage?

John Stuart Mill did not *invent* utilitarianism (and never pretended to have done so). Indeed, he was brought up by people who already considered themselves utilitarians. Mill's importance to utilitarianism is that he gave it what is arguably its single greatest and most influential formulation, in the essay *Utilitarianism*. It is this work which, ever since it was written,

has been the starting point for both defenders and foes of utilitarianism. Furthermore, utilitarianism is itself a very important and influential moral theory. Along with Marxism, it was arguably the most prevalent moral theory among philosophers, economists, political scientists, and other social theorists for much of the twentieth century (completely eclipsing—or in some cases, like G.E. Moore's moral philosophy, absorbing—the moral "intuitionism" which Mill saw as his theory's main competitor in 1861). Utilitarianism's influence has waned since the 1970s and it has been subjected to several damaging philosophical attacks, but it is still, uncontroversially, one of the three or four main moral theories.

Suggestions for Critical Reflection

1. One of the attractions of utilitarianism, it is often supposed, is that it is 'scientific' or objective in a way that "intuitionism" (or even Kantianism, or virtue theory) is not. The Greatest Happiness Principle apparently provides a quasi-mathematical, bias-free, and theoretically motivated way of working out what we ought to do in literally any moral situation. But is this really so? For example, can the pleasures and pains of sentient creatures really be 'objectively' measured and compared, in order to calculate the net effect of my actions on utility? Even if pleasures and pains are measurable, do you think *all* the consequences of an action can be properly predicted and measured? How serious are these problems for utilitarianism?

2. Does Mill's notion of "higher" or more "noble" pleasure make sense? How could the "nobility" of an experience add to the pleasure of it? Why couldn't an experience be noble but not pleasant? In that case, would Mill have to say that it is still valuable? In other words, is Mill *really* a hedonist?

3. An influential criticism of the hedonistic component of utilitarianism was invented by philosopher Robert Nozick and is called the "experience machine." The experience machine is a fictional device which keeps your body alive in a tank of fluids, for a normal human

life-span, all the while stimulating your brain so that you continuously feel as if you are having the most pleasant and satisfying experiences imaginable. Since—properly designed—this would be an utterly reliable way of maximizing the quality and number of pleasant sensations during your lifetime, it seems that the utilitarian is forced to conclude that it would be our *moral duty* to plug ourselves into one of these machines (especially if they are such reliable and long-lasting devices that nearly *everyone* can be plugged in at the same time). But Nozick argues that this result is clearly unsatisfactory: surely there is more to a valuable life than a mere succession of pleasant experiences, and so utilitarianism must be a faulty moral theory. What do you think about Nozick's argument? What exactly does it suggest is wrong with utilitarianism (or at least Mill's version of the theory)? Could this problem—if it is a problem—be fixed?

4. The third paragraph of the fourth chapter of *Utilitarianism* has been called "the most notorious [passage] in Mill's writings" (Roger Crisp). In it Mill compares desirability with visibility, in an effort to argue that desire is a faculty which reveals what we morally ought to do. The most famous and apparently devastating criticism of this argument came from G.E. Moore in 1903: "The fact is that 'desirable' does not mean 'able to be desired' as 'visible' means 'able to be seen.' The desirable means simply what *ought* to be desired or deserves to be desired." How does Moore's complaint cause problems for Mill's argument? Does Mill really make the mistake Moore is suggesting? If Mill's own arguments fail to show that we *ought* to desire happiness, is there any other way a utilitarian could consistently argue for this claim? Does utilitarianism *need* to provide arguments for it?

5. How well does Mill refute moral egoism? That is, does his argument show that I ought to care about *everyone's* happiness, and not just my own? Does he have an *argument* for the "impartiality" component of utilitarianism? Does he need one?

6. Is Mill right that we *only* desire happiness—is his claim, "to desire anything, except in proportion as the idea of it is pleasant, is a physical and metaphysical impossibility," a plausible one? If he is wrong, how seriously does this undercut his argument for the truth of utilitarianism? For example, what about Mill's own example of virtue: is he right in arguing that we value our own virtue only as a kind or "part" of our happiness?

7. Utilitarianism is a kind of moral theory which is sometimes called "welfarist": for such theories, the only thing of intrinsic value is the welfare of moral agents (according to Mill, sentient beings). One consequence of welfarism is that *nothing else* is of intrinsic value. Thus, for example, the beauty of art and nature, ecological sustainability, scientific knowledge, justice, equality, loyalty, kindness, or self-sacrifice—none of these things have any value in themselves, but are valuable *only* insofar as they increase the welfare of sentient creatures (and are actually *immoral* if they reduce this welfare). Does this seem to be an acceptable consequence of a moral theory?

8. Utilitarianism is often accused of being an extremely demanding moral theory. According to utilitarianism, a certain unit of pleasure or pain should matter *equally* to me whether it belongs to me, to a member of my family, to a stranger half-way across the world, or even to an animal. Utilitarianism requires us to maximize happiness generally, and does not allow us to think of the happiness of ourselves and our friends as being especially important. If you or I were to spend all of our free time, and use almost all of our money, working to help victims of famine and other natural disasters around the world, this might well produce more overall utility than the lives we currently lead. If so, then utilitarianism commits us to a moral *duty* to behave in this way, and we are being flat-out *immoral* in spending time with our families or watching movies. Is this acceptable? If not, what is wrong with it?

9. According to utilitarianism, should we be morally responsible for all the consequences of our

actions, including the unforeseen ones? What would Mill say? Are we just as responsible for *not* doing things that could have prevented great pain? For example, according to utilitarianism, am I equally morally deficient if I fail to give money to charity as I am if I send poisoned food to famine-stricken areas (supposing the outcomes in terms of human death and suffering would be the same)?

10. Act (or "direct") utilitarianism is the view that one should act in any circumstance so as to produce the greatest overall balance of pleasure over pain. (You would have a moral duty to break an important promise to your best friend if it would increase overall utility by even a tiny amount, for example.) Rule (or "indirect") utilitarianism, on the other hand, is the view that one should act in accordance with certain moral rules, rules fixed as those which, over time, can be expected to maximize utility if they are generally followed. (For example, you should never break an important promise, even if you can foresee that keeping it, in a particular case, will cause far more pain than pleasure.) Is Mill an act or rule utilitarian? Which is the better theory? Is *either* version attractive and, if not, can you think of a third option for utilitarianism?

11. According to utilitarianism, *how* should we maximize utility? Should we aim to maximize the *total* utility of the world, the *average* utility, or what? (For example, if we chose to maximize total utility, we might be morally obliged to aim for an extremely large population, even if each member has only a low level of happiness; on the other hand, if we opt for the highest possible average utility we might be committed to keeping the population small and select, perhaps killing, before birth, people who look as though they might drag the average down.) What would Mill say?

12. Mill thought utilitarianism to be the one true fundamental moral theory, and to be consistent with (what is right in) the moral theories of Aristotle and Kant. If you have read the selections by those thinkers in this chapter, you might want to think about whether utilitarianism *is* in fact consistent with the views of Aristotle and Kant. For example, could Kant accept that consequences are what is morally important about our actions?

Suggestions for Further Reading

Mill's writings have been published as *The Collected Works of John Stuart Mill*, under the general editorship of John Robson (33 volumes, University of Toronto Press, 1963–91). A very good edition of Mill's *Utilitarianism* is by Roger Crisp (ed.) in the Oxford Philosophical Texts series (Oxford University Press, 1998); it is also widely available in other editions (such as that published by Penguin Books in 1987). Mill's *Autobiography* is available from Penguin (1990), and a good edition of his *On Liberty*, with interesting supplemental material, was edited by Edward Alexander and published by Broadview Press (1999). Jeremy Bentham's *Introduction to the Principles of Morals and Legislation*, J.H. Burns and H.L.A. Hart (eds.) (Oxford University Press, 1996) is also essential reading for any serious student of Mill's *Utilitarianism*.

Three worthwhile books about Mill's philosophy as a whole are Alan Ryan's *J.S. Mill* (Routledge & Kegan Paul, 1974) and *The Philosophy of John Stuart Mill* (Prometheus Books, 1990), and John Skorupski's *John Stuart Mill* (Routledge, 1989). Roger Crisp has written a *Routledge Philosophical Guidebook to Mill on Utilitarianism* (Routledge, 1997), and there are a number of good books on Mill's moral theory, including: Fred Berger, *Happiness, Justice, and Freedom: The Moral and Political Philosophy of John Stuart Mill* (University of California Press, 1984); Wendy Donner, *The Liberal Self: John Stuart Mill's Moral and Political Philosophy* (Cornell University Press, 1992); David Lyons, *Rights, Welfare, and Mill's Moral Theory* (Oxford University Press, 1994); and Bernard Semmel, *John Stuart Mill and the Pursuit of Virtue* (Yale University Press, 1984).

G.E. Moore's attack on Mill's argument for utilitarianism appears in *Principia Ethica*, Thomas Baldwin (ed.) (Cambridge University Press, 1994, originally published 1903). An early defense of Mill against this attack is James Seth's "The Alleged Fallacies in Mill's 'Utilitarianism,'" *Philosophical Review* 17 (1908); more recently, Necip Fikri Alican has written a book called

Mill's Principle of Utility: A Defense of John Stuart Mill's Notorious Proof (Rodopi, 1994).

Three useful collections of essays about Mill are J.B. Schneewind (ed.), *Mill: A Collection of Critical Essays* (Doubleday, 1968); David Lyons (ed.), *Mill's 'Utilitarianism': Critical Essays* (Rowman and Littlefield, 1997); and John Skorupski (ed.), *The Cambridge Companion to Mill* (Cambridge University Press, 1998). Other useful articles include: J.O. Urmson, "The Interpretation of the Moral Philosophy of J.S. Mill," *Philosophical Quarterly* 3 (1953); Rex Martin, "A Defence of Mill's Qualitative Hedonism," *Philosophy* 47 (1972); R.M. Adams, "Motive Utilitarianism," *Journal of Philosophy* 73 (1976); Henry R. West, "Mill's Qualitative Hedonism," *Philosophy* 51 (1976); Roger Crisp, "Utilitarianism and the Life of Virtue," *Philosophical Quarterly* 42 (1992); and L.W. Sumner, "Welfare, Happiness and Pleasure," *Utilitas* 4 (1992).

Finally, there is a substantial literature on the moral theory of utilitarianism in its own right. Perhaps the best starting point is J.J.C. Smart and Bernard Williams, *Utilitarianism: For and Against* (Cambridge University Press, 1973). James Griffin's "Modern Utilitarianism," *Revue Internationale de Philosophie* 141 (1982) is a very useful review of the modern development of the theory. The following books are also valuable: Richard Brandt, *Morality, Utilitarianism, and Rights* (Cambridge University Press, 1992); David Lyons, *Forms and Limits of Utilitarianism* (Oxford University Press, 1965); Derek Parfit, *Reasons and Persons* (Oxford University Press, 1986); Anthony Quinton, *Utilitarian Ethics* (Open Court, 1989); Geoffrey Scarre, *Utilitarianism* (Routledge, 1996); Samuel Scheffler (ed.), *Consequentialism and Its Critics* (Oxford University Press, 1988); Samuel Scheffler, *The Rejection of Consequentialism* (Oxford University Press, 1994); Amartya Sen and Bernard Williams (eds.), *Utilitarianism and Beyond* (Cambridge University Press, 1982); and William Shaw, *Contemporary Ethics: Taking Account of Utilitarianism* (Blackwell, 1999).

Utilitarianism[4]

Chapter 1: General Remarks

There are few circumstances among those which make up the present condition of human knowledge, more unlike what might have been expected, or more significant of the backward state in which speculation on the most important subjects still lingers, than the little progress which has been made in the decision of the controversy respecting the criterion of right and wrong. From the dawn of philosophy, the question concerning the *summum bonum*,[5] or, what is the same thing, concerning the foundation of morality, has been accounted the main problem in speculative thought, has occupied the most gifted intellects, and divided them into sects and schools, carrying on a vigorous warfare against one another. And after more than two thousand years the same discussions continue, philosophers are still ranged under the same contending banners, and neither thinkers nor mankind at large seem nearer to being unanimous on the subject, than when the youth Socrates[6] listened to the old Protagoras,[7]

---

4   *Utilitarianism* was first published in 1861 as a series of three essays in volume 64 of *Fraser's Magazine*. It was first published as a book in 1863; this text is from the fourth edition, published in 1871 (by Longmans, Green, Reader, and Dyer), the last to be printed in Mill's lifetime.

5   "The highest good": that thing which is an end-in-itself, which gives everything else its value, and the achievement of which is (arguably) the goal of an ethical system. Candidates for the "highest good" might be— indeed, historically have been—pleasure, human flourishing, the rational comprehension of reality, or God.

6   Socrates (469–399 BCE) was a highly influential philosopher from Athens, in Greece, who—particularly through his great impact on Plato—is often thought to be the main originator of the western philosophical tradition. He wrote nothing himself, but appears as a character in nearly all of Plato's dialogues.

7   Protagoras (c. 490–c. 420 BCE) was the greatest of the Sophist philosophers—itinerant teachers of rhetoric and practical philosophy—and is most famous for his doctrine that "Man is the measure of all things," which is usually interpreted as an extreme form of relativism.

and asserted (if Plato's dialogue be grounded on a real conversation[8]) the theory of utilitarianism against the popular morality of the so-called sophist.

It is true that similar confusion and uncertainty, and in some cases similar discordance, exist respecting the first principles of all the sciences, not excepting that which is deemed the most certain of them, mathematics; without much impairing, generally indeed without impairing at all, the trustworthiness of the conclusions of those sciences. An apparent anomaly, the explanation of which is, that the detailed doctrines of a science are not usually deduced from, nor depend for their evidence upon, what are called its first principles. Were it not so, there would be no science more precarious, or whose conclusions were more insufficiently made out, than algebra; which derives none of its certainty from what are commonly taught to learners as its elements, since these, as laid down by some of its most eminent teachers, are as full of fictions as English law, and of mysteries as theology. The truths which are ultimately accepted as the first principles of a science, are really the last results of metaphysical analysis, practised on the elementary notions with which the science is conversant; and their relation to the science is not that of foundations to an edifice, but of roots to a tree, which may perform their office equally well though they be never dug down to and exposed to light. But though in science the particular truths precede the general theory, the contrary might be expected to be the case with a practical art, such as morals or legislation. All action is for the sake of some end, and rules of action, it seems natural to suppose, must take their whole character and colour from the end to which they are subservient. When we engage in a pursuit, a clear and precise conception of what we are pursuing would seem to be the first thing we need, instead of the last we are to look forward to. A test of right and wrong must be the means, one would think, of ascertaining what is right or wrong, and not a consequence of having already ascertained it.

The difficulty is not avoided by having recourse to the popular theory of a natural faculty, a sense or instinct, informing us of right and wrong. For—besides that the existence of such a moral instinct is itself one of the matters in dispute—those believers in it who have any pretensions to philosophy, have been obliged to abandon the idea that it discerns what is right or wrong in the particular case in hand, as our other senses discern the sight or sound actually present. Our moral faculty, according to all those of its interpreters who are entitled to the name of thinkers, supplies us only with the general principles of moral judgments; it is a branch of our reason, not of our sensitive faculty;[9] and must be looked to for the abstract doctrines of morality, not for perception of it in the concrete. The intuitive, no less than what may be termed the inductive, school of ethics, insists on the necessity of general laws. They both agree that the morality of an individual action is not a question of direct perception, but of the application of a law to an individual case. They recognise also, to a great extent, the same moral laws; but differ as to their evidence, and the source from which they derive their authority. According to the one opinion, the principles of morals are evident *a priori*,[10] requiring nothing to command assent, except that the meaning of the terms be understood. According to the other doctrine, right and wrong, as well as truth and falsehood, are questions of observation and experience. But both hold equally that morality must be deduced from principles; and the intuitive school affirm as strongly as the inductive, that there is a science of morals. Yet they seldom attempt to make out a list of the *a priori* principles which are to serve as the premises of the science; still more rarely do they make any effort to

---

8   Mill first read this dialogue—called the *Protagoras*—during the "more advanced" period of his education (after he had reached the age of 12). It is questionable whether Socrates does indeed put forward utilitarianism in that dialogue (and almost certain that he was not himself a utilitarian). Mill, however, was always anxious to portray utilitarianism as a doctrine already widespread in the history of philosophy (and especially in ancient Greek philosophy: in *On Liberty,* for example, he describes Aristotle's ethics as "judicious utilitarianism").

9   Mill means our faculty of sensation.

10   Obviously true, independently of any actual experience. ("*A priori*" means knowable prior to experience.)

reduce those various principles to one first principle, or common ground of obligation. They either assume the ordinary precepts[11] of morals as of *a priori* authority, or they lay down as the common groundwork of those maxims, some generality much less obviously authoritative than the maxims themselves, and which has never succeeded in gaining popular acceptance. Yet to support their pretensions there ought either to be some one fundamental principle or law, at the root of all morality, or if there be several, there should be a determinate order of precedence among them; and the one principle, or the rule for deciding between the various principles when they conflict, ought to be self-evident.

To inquire how far the bad effects of this deficiency have been mitigated in practice, or to what extent the moral beliefs of mankind have been vitiated or made uncertain by the absence of any distinct recognition of an ultimate standard, would imply a complete survey and criticism, of past and present ethical doctrine. It would, however, be easy to show that whatever steadiness or consistency these moral beliefs have attained, has been mainly due to the tacit influence of a standard not recognised. Although the non-existence of an acknowledged first principle has made ethics not so much a guide as a consecration of men's actual sentiments, still, as men's sentiments, both of favour and of aversion, are greatly influenced by what they suppose to be the effects of things upon their happiness, the principle of utility, or as Bentham[12] latterly called it,

the greatest happiness principle, has had a large share in forming the moral doctrines even of those who most scornfully reject its authority. Nor is there any school of thought which refuses to admit that the influence of actions on happiness is a most material and even predominant consideration in many of the details of morals, however unwilling to acknowledge it as the fundamental principle of morality, and the source of moral obligation. I might go much further, and say that to all those *a priori* moralists who deem it necessary to argue at all, utilitarian arguments are indispensable. It is not my present purpose to criticise these thinkers; but I cannot help referring, for illustration, to a systematic treatise by one of the most illustrious of them, the *Metaphysics of Ethics*, by Kant.[13] This remarkable man, whose system of thought will long remain one of the landmarks in the history of philosophical speculation, does, in the treatise in question, lay down a universal first principle as the origin and ground of moral obligation; it is this: "So act, that the rule on which thou actest would admit of being adopted as a law by all rational beings." But when he begins to deduce from this precept any of the actual duties of morality, he fails, almost grotesquely, to show that there would be any contradiction, any logical (not to say physical) impossibility, in the adoption by all rational beings of the most outrageously immoral rules of conduct. All he shows is that the *consequences* of their universal adoption would be such as no one would choose to incur.

On the present occasion, I shall, without further discussion of the other theories, attempt to contribute something towards the understanding and appreciation of the Utilitarian or Happiness theory, and towards such proof as it is susceptible of. It is evident that this cannot be proof in the ordinary and popular meaning of the term. Questions of ultimate ends are not amenable to direct proof. Whatever can be proved to be good, must be so by being shown to be a means to something

---

11   A precept is an instruction or command prescribing a particular course of action (such as, "always tell the truth" or "do not commit adultery").

12   Jeremy Bentham (1748–1832) was an English philosopher of law and ethics who is usually thought of as the founder of utilitarianism, which he intended as a coherent and sensible foundation for the large-scale reform of social and legal policy. His main theoretical work was *An Introduction to the Principles of Morals and Legislation*, published in 1789, and it is in this book that the Greatest Happiness Principle was first clearly formulated and defended. It was while reading a French edition of Bentham's *Principles of Morals* in 1821 that, according to Mill's autobiography, he was permanently "converted" to utilitarianism. (Bentham

is also the founder of University College London, and his embalmed body, topped with a wax death mask, is still preserved there in a glass box which is wheeled out for special occasions.)

13   Mill is actually thinking of Kant's *Foundations of the Metaphysics of Morals* (see the previous reading).

admitted to be good without proof. The medical art is proved to be good by its conducing to health; but how is it possible to prove that health is good? The art of music is good, for the reason, among others, that it produces pleasure; but what proof is it possible to give that pleasure is good? If, then, it is asserted that there is a comprehensive formula, including all things which are in themselves good, and that whatever else is good, is not so as an end, but as a mean, the formula may be accepted or rejected, but is not a subject of what is commonly understood by proof. We are not, however, to infer that its acceptance or rejection must depend on blind impulse, or arbitrary choice. There is a larger meaning of the word proof, in which this question is as amenable to it as any other of the disputed questions of philosophy. The subject is within the cognisance[14] of the rational faculty; and neither does that faculty deal with it solely in the way of intuition. Considerations may be presented capable of determining the intellect either to give or withhold its assent to the doctrine; and this is equivalent to proof.

We shall examine presently of what nature are these considerations; in what manner they apply to the case, and what rational grounds, therefore, can be given for accepting or rejecting the utilitarian formula. But it is a preliminary condition of rational acceptance or rejection, that the formula should be correctly understood. I believe that the very imperfect notion ordinarily formed of its meaning, is the chief obstacle which impedes its reception; and that could it be cleared, even from only the grosser misconceptions, the question would be greatly simplified, and a large proportion of its difficulties removed. Before, therefore, I attempt to enter into the philosophical grounds which can be given for assenting to the utilitarian standard, I shall offer some illustrations of the doctrine itself; with the view of showing more clearly what it is, distinguishing it from what it is not, and disposing of such of the practical objections to it as either originate in, or are closely connected with, mistaken interpretations of its meaning. Having thus prepared the ground, I shall afterwards endeavour to throw such light as I can upon the question, considered as one of philosophical theory.

---

14   Sphere of concern or awareness.

Chapter 2: What Utilitarianism Is.

A passing remark is all that needs be given to the ignorant blunder of supposing that those who stand up for utility as the test of right and wrong, use the term in that restricted and merely colloquial sense in which utility is opposed to pleasure. An apology is due to the philosophical opponents of utilitarianism, for even the momentary appearance of confounding them with any one capable of so absurd a misconception; which is the more extraordinary, inasmuch as the contrary accusation, of referring everything to pleasure, and that too in its grossest form, is another of the common charges against utilitarianism: and, as has been pointedly remarked by an able writer,[15] the same sort of persons, and often the very same persons, denounce the theory "as impracticably dry when the word utility precedes the word pleasure, and as too practicably voluptuous when the word pleasure precedes the word utility." Those who know anything about the matter are aware that every writer, from Epicurus[16] to Bentham, who maintained the theory of utility, meant by it, not something to be contradistinguished from pleasure, but pleasure itself, together with exemption from pain; and instead of opposing the useful to the agreeable or the ornamental, have always declared that the useful means these, among other things. Yet the common herd, including the herd of writers, not only in newspapers and periodicals, but in books of weight and pretension, are perpetually falling into

---

15   The identity of this writer remains mysterious.

16   Epicurus (341–270 BCE) was a Greek philosopher and founder of the loosely-knit school of thought called Epicureanism. A central plank of this doctrine is—as the modern connotations of the word "epicurean" suggest—that the good life is one filled with pleasure. Indeed, for Epicurus, the only rational goal in life is one's own pleasure. However, contrary to the popular association of "Epicureanism" with mere sensual self-indulgence, Epicurus placed much greater emphasis on stable, non-sensory pleasures (say, the pleasures of friendship and psychological contentment), and also stressed the importance of dispensing with unnecessary desires, harmful fears (such as the fear of death), and hollow gratifications.

this shallow mistake. Having caught up the word utilitarian, while knowing nothing whatever about it but its sound, they habitually express by it the rejection, or the neglect, of pleasure in some of its forms; of beauty, of ornament, or of amusement. Nor is the term thus ignorantly misapplied solely in disparagement, but occasionally in compliment; as though it implied superiority to frivolity and the mere pleasures of the moment. And this perverted use is the only one in which the word is popularly known, and the one from which the new generation are acquiring their sole notion of its meaning. Those who introduced the word, but who had for many years discontinued it as a distinctive appellation, may well feel themselves called upon to resume it, if by doing so they can hope to contribute anything towards rescuing it from this utter degradation.[17]

The creed which accepts as the foundation of morals, Utility, or the Greatest Happiness Principle, holds that actions are right in proportion as they tend to promote happiness, wrong as they tend to produce the reverse of happiness. By happiness is intended pleasure, and the absence of pain; by unhappiness, pain, and the privation of pleasure. To give a clear view of the moral standard set up by the theory, much more requires to be said; in particular, what things it includes in the ideas of pain and pleasure; and to what extent this is left an open question. But these supplementary explanations do not affect the theory of life on which this theory of morality is grounded—namely, that pleasure, and freedom from pain, are the only things desirable as ends; and that all desirable things (which are as numerous in the utilitarian as in any other scheme) are desirable either for the pleasure inherent in themselves, or as means to the promotion of pleasure and the prevention of pain.

Now, such a theory of life excites in many minds, and among them in some of the most estimable in feeling and purpose, inveterate dislike. To suppose that life has (as they express it) no higher end than pleasure—no better and nobler object of desire and pursuit—they designate as utterly mean and grovelling; as a doctrine worthy only of swine, to whom the followers of Epicurus were, at a very early period, contemptuously likened;[18] and modern holders of the doctrine are occasionally made the subject of equally polite comparisons by its German, French, and English assailants.

When thus attacked, the Epicureans have always answered, that it is not they, but their accusers, who represent human nature in a degrading light; since the accusation supposes human beings to be capable of no pleasures except those of which swine are capable. If this supposition were true, the charge could not be gainsaid, but would then be no longer an imputation; for if the sources of pleasure were precisely the same to human beings and to swine, the rule of life which is good enough for the one would be good enough for the other. The comparison of the Epicurean life to that of beasts is felt as degrading, precisely because a beast's pleasures do not satisfy a human being's conceptions of happiness. Human beings have faculties more elevated than the animal appetites, and when once made conscious of them, do not regard anything as happiness which does not include their gratification. I do not, indeed, consider the Epicureans to have been by any means faultless in drawing out their scheme of consequences from the utilitarian principle. To do this in any sufficient manner, many Stoic,[19] as well as Christian elements require to be

17 [Author's note] The author of this essay has reason for believing himself to be the first person who brought the word utilitarian into use. He did not invent it, but adopted it from a passing expression in Mr. Galt's *Annals of the Parish*. After using it as a designation for several years, he and others abandoned it from a growing dislike to anything resembling a badge or watchword of sectarian distinction. But as a name for one single opinion, not a set of opinions—to denote the recognition of utility as a standard, not any particular way of applying it—the term supplies a want in the language, and offers, in many cases, a convenient mode of avoiding tiresome circumlocution.

18 For example, in Diogenes Laertius' *Lives of Eminent Philosophers*, written in about 230 CE.

19 Stoicism was, with Epicureanism, one of the two main strands of "Hellenistic" philosophy (roughly, that associated with Greek culture during the 300 years after the death of Alexander the Great in 323 BCE). Its main ethical doctrine was that the wise and virtuous man

included. But there is no known Epicurean theory of life which does not assign to the pleasures of the intellect, of the feelings and imagination, and of the moral sentiments, a much higher value as pleasures than to those of mere sensation. It must be admitted, however, that utilitarian writers in general have placed the superiority of mental over bodily pleasures chiefly in the greater permanency, safety, uncostliness, etc., of the former—that is, in their circumstantial advantages rather than in their intrinsic nature. And on all these points utilitarians have fully proved their case; but they might have taken the other, and, as it may be called, higher ground, with entire consistency. It is quite compatible with the principle of utility to recognise the fact, that some *kinds* of pleasure are more desirable and more valuable than others. It would be absurd that while, in estimating all other things, quality is considered as well as quantity, the estimation of pleasures should be supposed to depend on quantity alone.

If I am asked, what I mean by difference of quality in pleasures, or what makes one pleasure more valuable than another, merely as a pleasure, except its being greater in amount, there is but one possible answer. Of two pleasures, if there be one to which all or almost all who have experience of both give a decided preference, irrespective of any feeling of moral obligation to prefer it, that is the more desirable pleasure. If one of the two is, by those who are competently acquainted with both, placed so far above the other that they prefer it, even though knowing it to be attended with a greater amount of discontent, and would not resign it for any quantity of the other pleasure which their nature is capable of, we are justified in ascribing to the preferred enjoyment a superiority in quality, so far outweighing quantity as to render it, in comparison, of small account.

Now it is an unquestionable fact that those who are equally acquainted with, and equally capable of appreciating and enjoying, both, do give a most marked preference to the manner of existence which employs their higher faculties. Few human creatures would consent to be changed into any of the lower animals, for a promise of the fullest allowance of a beast's pleasures; no intelligent human being would consent to be a fool, no instructed person would be an ignoramus, no person of feeling and conscience would be selfish and base, even though they should be persuaded that the fool, the dunce, or the rascal is better satisfied with his lot than they are with theirs. They would not resign what they possess more than he for the most complete satisfaction of all the desires which they have in common with him. If they ever fancy they would, it is only in cases of unhappiness so extreme, that to escape from it they would exchange their lot for almost any other, however undesirable in their own eyes. A being of higher faculties requires more to make him happy, is capable probably of more acute suffering, and certainly accessible to it at more points, than one of an inferior type; but in spite of these liabilities, he can never really wish to sink into what he feels to be a lower grade of existence. We may give what explanation we please of this unwillingness; we may attribute it to pride, a name which is given indiscriminately to some of the most and to some of the least estimable feelings of which mankind are capable: we may refer it to the love of liberty and personal independence, an appeal to which was with the Stoics one of the most effective means for the inculcation of it; to the love of power, or to the love of excitement, both of which do really enter into and contribute to it: but its most appropriate appellation is a sense of dignity, which all human beings possess in one form or other, and in some, though by no means in exact, proportion to their higher faculties, and which is so essential a part of the happiness of those in whom it is strong, that nothing which conflicts with it could be, otherwise than momentarily, an object of desire to them. Whoever supposes that this preference takes place at a sacrifice of happiness—that the superior being, in anything like equal circumstances, is not happier than the inferior—confounds the two very different ideas, of happiness, and content. It is indisputable that the being whose capacities of enjoyment are low, has the greatest chance of having them fully satisfied; and a highly endowed being will always

accepts, with calm indifference, his place in the impartial, rational, inevitable order of the universe—even if it is his fate to suffer hardship or painful death—but also works dutifully to foster a social order that mirrors the rational order of the cosmos.

feel that any happiness which he can look for, as the world is constituted, is imperfect. But he can learn to bear its imperfections, if they are at all bearable; and they will not make him envy the being who is indeed unconscious of the imperfections, but only because he feels not at all the good which those imperfections qualify. It is better to be a human being dissatisfied than a pig satisfied; better to be Socrates dissatisfied than a fool satisfied. And if the fool, or the pig, are of a different opinion, it is because they only know their own side of the question. The other party to the comparison knows both sides.

It may be objected, that many who are capable of the higher pleasures, occasionally, under the influence of temptation, postpone them to the lower. But this is quite compatible with a full appreciation of the intrinsic superiority of the higher. Men often, from infirmity of character, make their election for[20] the nearer good, though they know it to be the less valuable; and this no less when the choice is between two bodily pleasures, than when it is between bodily and mental. They pursue sensual indulgences to the injury of health, though perfectly aware that health is the greater good.

It may be further objected, that many who begin with youthful enthusiasm for everything noble, as they advance in years sink into indolence and selfishness. But I do not believe that those who undergo this very common change, voluntarily choose the lower description of pleasures in preference to the higher. I believe that before they devote themselves exclusively to the one, they have already become incapable of the other. Capacity for the nobler feelings is in most natures a very tender plant, easily killed, not only by hostile influences, but by mere want of sustenance; and in the majority of young persons it speedily dies away if the occupations to which their position in life has devoted them, and the society into which it has thrown them, are not favourable to keeping that higher capacity in exercise. Men lose their high aspirations as they lose their intellectual tastes, because they have not time or opportunity for indulging them; and they addict themselves to inferior pleasures, not because they deliberately prefer them, but because they are either the only ones to which they have access, or the only ones which they are any longer capable of enjoying. It may be questioned whether any one who has remained equally susceptible to both classes of pleasures, ever knowingly and calmly preferred the lower; though many, in all ages, have broken down in an ineffectual attempt to combine both.

From this verdict of the only competent judges, I apprehend there can be no appeal. On a question which is the best worth having of two pleasures, or which of two modes of existence is the most grateful to the feelings, apart from its moral attributes and from its consequences, the judgment of those who are qualified by knowledge of both, or, if they differ, that of the majority among them, must be admitted as final. And there needs be the less hesitation to accept this judgment respecting the quality of pleasures, since there is no other tribunal to be referred to even on the question of quantity. What means are there of determining which is the acutest of two pains, or the intensest of two pleasurable sensations, except the general suffrage[21] of those who are familiar with both? Neither pains nor pleasures are homogeneous, and pain is always heterogeneous with pleasure. What is there to decide whether a particular pleasure is worth purchasing at the cost of a particular pain, except the feelings and judgment of the experienced? When, therefore, those feelings and judgment declare the pleasures derived from the higher faculties to be preferable *in kind*, apart from the question of intensity, to those of which the animal nature, disjoined from the higher faculties, is susceptible, they are entitled on this subject to the same regard.

I have dwelt on this point, as being a necessary part of a perfectly just conception of Utility or Happiness, considered as the directive rule of human conduct. But it is by no means an indispensable condition to the acceptance of the utilitarian standard; for that standard is not the agent's own greatest happiness, but the greatest amount of happiness altogether; and if it may possibly be doubted whether a noble character is always the happier for its nobleness, there can be no doubt that it makes other people happier, and that

---

20   Choose.

21   A view expressed by voting (or the right to make such a vote).

the world in general is immensely a gainer by it. Utilitarianism, therefore, could only attain its end by the general cultivation of nobleness of character, even if each individual were only benefited by the nobleness of others, and his own, so far as happiness is concerned, were a sheer deduction[22] from the benefit. But the bare enunciation of such an absurdity as this last, renders refutation superfluous.

According to the Greatest Happiness Principle, as above explained, the ultimate end, with reference to and for the sake of which all other things are desirable (whether we are considering our own good or that of other people), is an existence exempt as far as possible from pain, and as rich as possible in enjoyments, both in point of quantity and quality; the test of quality, and the rule for measuring it against quantity, being the preference felt by those who in their opportunities of experience, to which must be added their habits of self-consciousness and self-observation, are best furnished with the means of comparison. This, being, according to the utilitarian opinion, the end of human action, is necessarily also the standard of morality; which may accordingly be defined, the rules and precepts for human conduct, by the observance of which an existence such as has been described might be, to the greatest extent possible, secured to all mankind; and not to them only, but, so far as the nature of things admits, to the whole sentient creation.[23]

Against this doctrine, however, arises another class of objectors, who say that happiness, in any form, cannot be the rational purpose of human life and action; because, in the first place, it is unattainable: and they contemptuously ask, what right hast thou to be happy? a question which Mr. Carlyle[24] clenches by the addition, What right, a short time ago, hadst thou even *to be*? Next, they say, that men can do *without* happiness; that all noble human beings have felt this, and could not have become noble but by learning the lesson of Entsagen,[25] or renunciation; which lesson, thoroughly learnt and submitted to, they affirm to be the beginning and necessary condition of all virtue.

The first of these objections would go to the root of the matter were it well founded; for if no happiness is to be had at all by human beings, the attainment of it cannot be the end of morality, or of any rational conduct. Though, even in that case, something might still be said for the utilitarian theory; since utility includes not solely the pursuit of happiness, but the prevention or mitigation of unhappiness; and if the former aim be chimerical,[26] there will be all the greater scope and more imperative need for the latter, so long at least as mankind think fit to live, and do not take refuge in the simultaneous act of suicide recommended under certain conditions by Novalis.[27] When, however, it is thus positively asserted to be impossible that human life should be happy, the assertion, if not something like a verbal quibble, is at least an exaggeration. If by happiness be meant a continuity of highly pleasurable excitement, it is evident enough that this is impossible. A state of exalted pleasure lasts only moments, or in some cases, and with some intermissions, hours or days, and is the occasional brilliant flash of enjoy-

---

22 Subtraction (as opposed to an inference).
23 To all creatures capable of sensation (and thus of feeling pleasure and pain).
24 Thomas Carlyle (1795–1881) was a popular Scottish writer and (somewhat reactionary) social critic. This quote is from his 1836 book, *Sartor Resartus*. As a young man Mill was heavily influenced by Carlyle's allegiance to German Romanticism, but once Carlyle began to realize that Mill did not see himself as one of his disciples their relationship took a sharp turn for the worse. (The fact that Mill's maid accidentally used the only manuscript copy of Carlyle's *History of the French Revolution* to light a fire when Carlyle was visiting him—forcing Carlyle to rewrite all of Volume I—cannot have helped.) *Utilitarianism* is largely intended as a response to criticisms of Mill's moral theories leveled by Carlyle and others.
25 German for "to renounce or abjure." The idea it is supposed to capture is that moral behavior must be painful or difficult to be genuinely virtuous.
26 Unrealistic, fanciful.
27 Novalis was the pseudonym of an early German poet and philosopher in the "Romantic" movement, Friedrich von Hardenberg (1772–1801). His most famous poem, "Hymns to the Night," was written after the death of his young fiancée from tuberculosis in 1799. Just months after its publication, von Hardenberg also succumbed to the disease.

ment, not its permanent and steady flame. Of this the philosophers who have taught that happiness is the end of life were as fully aware as those who taunt them. The happiness which they meant was not a life of rapture; but moments of such, in an existence made up of few and transitory pains, many and various pleasures, with a decided predominance of the active over the passive, and having as the foundation of the whole, not to expect more from life than it is capable of bestowing. A life thus composed, to those who have been fortunate enough to obtain it, has always appeared worthy of the name of happiness. And such an existence is even now the lot of many, during some considerable portion of their lives. The present wretched education, and wretched social arrangements, are the only real hindrance to its being attainable by almost all.

The objectors perhaps may doubt whether human beings, if taught to consider happiness as the end of life, would be satisfied with such a moderate share of it. But great numbers of mankind have been satisfied with much less. The main constituents of a satisfied life appear to be two, either of which by itself is often found sufficient for the purpose: tranquillity, and excitement. With much tranquillity, many find that they can be content with very little pleasure: with much excitement, many can reconcile themselves to a considerable quantity of pain. There is assuredly no inherent impossibility in enabling even the mass of mankind to unite both; since the two are so far from being incompatible that they are in natural alliance, the prolongation of either being a preparation for, and exciting a wish for, the other. It is only those in whom indolence amounts to a vice, that do not desire excitement after an interval of repose: it is only those in whom the need of excitement is a disease, that feel the tranquillity which follows excitement dull and insipid, instead of pleasurable in direct proportion to the excitement which preceded it. When people who are tolerably fortunate in their outward lot do not find in life sufficient enjoyment to make it valuable to them, the cause generally is, caring for nobody but themselves. To those who have neither public nor private affections, the excitements of life are much curtailed, and in any case dwindle in value as the time approaches when all selfish interests must

be terminated by death: while those who leave after them objects of personal affection, and especially those who have also cultivated a fellow-feeling with the collective interests of mankind, retain as lively an interest in life on the eve of death as in the vigour of youth and health. Next to selfishness, the principal cause which makes life unsatisfactory is want[28] of mental cultivation. A cultivated mind—I do not mean that of a philosopher, but any mind to which the fountains of knowledge have been opened, and which has been taught, in any tolerable degree, to exercise its faculties—finds sources of inexhaustible interest in all that surrounds it; in the objects of nature, the achievements of art, the imaginations of poetry, the incidents of history, the ways of mankind, past and present, and their prospects in the future. It is possible, indeed, to become indifferent to all this, and that too without having exhausted a thousandth part of it; but only when one has had from the beginning no moral or human interest in these things, and has sought in them only the gratification of curiosity.

Now there is absolutely no reason in the nature of things why an amount of mental culture sufficient to give an intelligent interest in these objects of contemplation, should not be the inheritance of every one born in a civilised country. As little is there an inherent necessity that any human being should be a selfish egotist, devoid of every feeling or care but those which centre in his own miserable individuality. Something far superior to this is sufficiently common even now, to give ample earnest of what the human species may be made. Genuine private affections and a sincere interest in the public good, are possible, though in unequal degrees, to every rightly brought up human being. In a world in which there is so much to interest, so much to enjoy, and so much also to correct and improve, every one who has this moderate amount of moral and intellectual requisites is capable of an existence which may be called enviable; and unless such a person, through bad laws, or subjection to the will of others, is denied the liberty to use the sources of happiness within his reach, he will not fail to find this enviable existence, if he escape the positive evils of life, the great sources of physical and mental suffer-

28 Lack.

ing—such as indigence, disease, and the unkindness, worthlessness, or premature loss of objects of affection. The main stress of the problem lies, therefore, in the contest with these calamities, from which it is a rare good fortune entirely to escape; which, as things now are, cannot be obviated, and often cannot be in any material degree mitigated. Yet no one whose opinion deserves a moment's consideration can doubt that most of the great positive evils of the world are in themselves removable, and will, if human affairs continue to improve, be in the end reduced within narrow limits. Poverty, in any sense implying suffering, may be completely extinguished by the wisdom of society, combined with the good sense and providence of individuals. Even that most intractable of enemies, disease, may be indefinitely reduced in dimensions by good physical and moral education, and proper control of noxious influences; while the progress of science holds out a promise for the future of still more direct conquests over this detestable foe. And every advance in that direction relieves us from some, not only of the chances which cut short our own lives, but, what concerns us still more, which deprive us of those in whom our happiness is wrapt up.[29] As for vicissitudes of fortune, and other disappointments connected with worldly circumstances, these are principally the effect either of gross imprudence, of ill-regulated desires, or of bad or imperfect social institutions. All the grand sources, in short, of human suffering are in a great degree, many of them almost entirely, conquerable by human care and effort; and though their removal is grievously slow—though a long succession of generations will perish in the breach before the conquest is completed, and this world becomes all that, if will and knowledge were not wanting, it might easily be made—yet every mind sufficiently intelligent and generous to bear a part, however small and unconspicuous, in the endeavour, will draw a noble enjoyment from the contest itself, which he would not for any bribe in the form of selfish indulgence consent to be without.

And this leads to the true estimation of what is said by the objectors concerning the possibility, and the obligation, of learning to do without happiness. Unquestionably it is possible to do without happiness; it is done involuntarily by nineteen-twentieths of mankind, even in those parts of our present world which are least deep in barbarism; and it often has to be done voluntarily by the hero or the martyr, for the sake of something which he prizes more than his individual happiness. But this something, what is it, unless the happiness of others or some of the requisites of happiness? It is noble to be capable of resigning entirely one's own portion of happiness, or chances of it: but, after all, this self-sacrifice must be for some end; it is not its own end; and if we are told that its end is not happiness, but virtue, which is better than happiness, I ask, would the sacrifice be made if the hero or martyr did not believe that it would earn for others immunity from similar sacrifices? Would it be made if he thought that his renunciation of happiness for himself would produce no fruit for any of his fellow creatures, but to make their lot like his, and place them also in the condition of persons who have renounced happiness? All honour to those who can abnegate for themselves the personal enjoyment of life, when by such renunciation they contribute worthily to increase the amount of happiness in the world; but he who does it, or professes to do it, for any other purpose, is no more deserving of admiration than the ascetic mounted on his pillar.[30] He may be an inspiriting proof of what men *can* do, but assuredly not an example of what they *should*.

Though it is only in a very imperfect state of the world's arrangements that any one can best serve the happiness of others by the absolute sacrifice of his own, yet so long as the world is in that imperfect state, I fully acknowledge that the readiness to make such a sacrifice is the highest virtue which can be found in man. I will add, that in this condition of the world, paradoxical as the assertion may be, the conscious ability to do without happiness gives the best prospect of realising such happiness as is attainable. For nothing except that consciousness can raise a person

---

29 For example, Mill's wife Harriet Taylor, who died of "pulmonary congestion" in 1858.

30 Mill is probably thinking of St. Simeon Stylites (c. 390–459), a Syrian ascetic who spent more than thirty years living at the top of various pillars, the highest of which was twenty meters tall.

above the chances of life, by making him feel that, let fate and fortune do their worst, they have not power to subdue him: which, once felt, frees him from excess of anxiety concerning the evils of life, and enables him, like many a Stoic in the worst times of the Roman Empire,[31] to cultivate in tranquillity the sources of satisfaction accessible to him, without concerning himself about the uncertainty of their duration, any more than about their inevitable end.

Meanwhile, let utilitarians never cease to claim the morality of self-devotion as a possession which belongs by as good a right to them, as either to the Stoic or to the Transcendentalist.[32] The utilitarian morality does recognise in human beings the power of sacrificing their own greatest good for the good of others. It only refuses to admit that the sacrifice is itself a good. A sacrifice which does not increase, or tend to increase, the sum total of happiness, it considers as wasted. The only self-renunciation which it applauds, is devotion to the happiness, or to some of the means of happiness, of others; either of mankind collectively, or of individuals within the limits imposed by the collective interests of mankind.

I must again repeat, what the assailants of utilitarianism seldom have the justice to acknowledge, that the happiness which forms the utilitarian standard of what is right in conduct, is not the agent's own happiness, but that of all concerned. As between his own happiness and that of others, utilitarianism requires him to be as strictly impartial as a disinterested[33] and benevolent spectator. In the golden rule of Jesus of Nazareth, we read the complete spirit of the ethics of utility. To do as you would be done by, and to love your neighbour as yourself, constitute the ideal perfection of utilitarian morality. As the means of making the nearest approach to this ideal, utility would enjoin, first, that laws and social arrangements should place the happiness, or (as speaking practically it may be called) the interest, of every individual, as nearly as possible in harmony with the interest of the whole; and secondly, that education and opinion, which have so vast a power over human character, should so use that power as to establish in the mind of every individual an indissoluble association between his own happiness and the good of the whole; especially between his own happiness and the practice of such modes of conduct, negative and positive, as regard for the universal happiness prescribes; so that not only he may be unable to conceive the possibility of happiness to himself, consistently with conduct opposed to the general good, but also that a direct impulse to promote the general good may be in every individual one of the habitual motives of action, and the sentiments connected therewith may fill a large and prominent place in every human being's sentient existence. If the impugners of the utilitarian morality represented it to their own minds in this, its true character, I know not what recommendation possessed by any other morality they could possibly affirm to be wanting to it; what more beautiful or more exalted developments of human nature any other ethical system can be supposed to foster, or what springs of action, not accessible to the utilitarian, such systems rely on for giving effect to their mandates.

The objectors to utilitarianism cannot always be charged with representing it in a discreditable light. On the contrary, those among them who entertain anything like a just idea of its disinterested character, sometimes find fault with its standard as being too high for humanity. They say it is exacting too much to require that people shall always act from the inducement of promoting the general interests of society. But this is to mistake the very meaning of a standard of morals, and confound the rule of action with the motive of it. It is the business of ethics to tell us what are our duties, or by what test we may know them; but no system of ethics requires that the sole motive of all we do shall be a feeling of duty; on the contrary, ninety-nine hundredths of all our actions are done from other motives, and rightly so done, if the rule of duty does not condemn them. It is the more unjust to utilitarianism that this particular misapprehension should be made a ground of objection to it, inasmuch as utilitarian moralists have gone beyond almost all others in affirming

---

31   Many Stoics were punished or killed for opposition to dictatorial Roman emperors.

32   Those—such as Kant—who think the evidence for moral truths "transcends" human sense experience.

33   Free from bias or self-interest (not *un*interested or bored!).

that the motive has nothing to do with the morality of the action, though much with the worth of the agent. He who saves a fellow creature from drowning does what is morally right, whether his motive be duty, or the hope of being paid for his trouble; he who betrays the friend that trusts him, is guilty of a crime, even if his object be to serve another friend to whom he is under greater obligations.[34]

---

34 [Author's note] An opponent, whose intellectual and moral fairness it is a pleasure to acknowledge (the Rev. J. Llewellyn Davies), has objected to this passage, saying, "Surely the rightness or wrongness of saving a man from drowning does depend very much upon the motive with which it is done. Suppose that a tyrant, when his enemy jumped into the sea to escape from him, saved him from drowning simply in order that he might inflict upon him more exquisite tortures, would it tend to clearness to speak of that action as 'a morally right action'? Or suppose again, according to one of the stock illustrations of ethical inquiries, that a man betrayed a trust received from a friend, because the discharge of it would fatally injure that friend himself or some one belonging to him, would utilitarianism compel one to call the betrayal 'a crime' as much as if it had been done from the meanest motive?"

I submit, that he who saves another from drowning in order to kill him by torture afterwards, does not differ only in motive from him who does the same thing from duty or benevolence; the act itself is different. The rescue of the man is, in the case supposed, only the necessary first step of an act far more atrocious than leaving him to drown would have been. Had Mr. Davies said, "the rightness of wrongness of saving a man from drowning does depend very much"—not upon the motive but—"upon the *intention*," no utilitarian would have differed from him. Mr. Davies, by an oversight too common not to be quite venial, has in this case confounded the very different ideas of Motive and Intention. There is no point at which utilitarian thinkers (and Bentham pre-eminently) have taken more pains to illustrate than this. The morality of the action depends entirely upon the intention—that is, upon what the agent *wills to do*. But the motive, that is, the feeling which makes him will to do so, when it makes no difference to the act, makes none in the morality: though it

But to speak only of actions done from the motive of duty, and in direct obedience to principle: it is a misapprehension of the utilitarian mode of thought, to conceive it as implying that people should fix their minds upon so wide a generality as the world, or society at large. The great majority of good actions are intended not for the benefit of the world, but for that of individuals, of which the good of the world is made up; and the thoughts of the most virtuous man need not on these occasions travel beyond the particular persons concerned, except so far as is necessary to assure himself that in benefiting them he is not violating the rights—that is, the legitimate and authorised expectations—of any one else. The multiplication of happiness is, according to the utilitarian ethics, the object of virtue: the occasions on which any person (except one in a thousand) has it in his power to do this on an extended scale, in other words to be a public benefactor, are but exceptional; and on these occasions alone is he called on to consider public utility; in every other case, private utility, the interest or happiness of some few persons, is all he has to attend to. Those alone the influence of whose actions extends to society in general, need concern themselves habitually about so large an object. In the case of abstinences indeed—of things which people forbear to do from moral considerations, though the consequences in the particular case might be beneficial—it would be unworthy of an intelligent agent not to be consciously aware that the action is of a class which, if practised generally, would be generally injurious, and that this is the ground of the obligation to abstain from it. The amount of regard for the public interest implied in this recognition, is no greater than is demanded by every system of morals, for they all enjoin to abstain from whatever is manifestly pernicious to society.

The same considerations dispose of another reproach against the doctrine of utility, founded on a still grosser misconception of the purpose of a standard of

---

makes a great difference in our moral estimation of the agent, especially if it indicates a good or a bad habitual *disposition*—a bent of character from which useful, or from which hurtful actions are likely to arise.

morality, and of the very meaning of the words right and wrong. It is often affirmed[35] that utilitarianism renders men cold and unsympathising; that it chills their moral feelings towards individuals; that it makes them regard only the dry and hard consideration of the consequences of actions, not taking into their moral estimate the qualities from which those actions emanate. If the assertion means that they do not allow their judgment respecting the rightness or wrongness of an action to be influenced by their opinion of the qualities of the person who does it, this is a complaint not against utilitarianism, but against having any standard of morality at all; for certainly no known ethical standard decides an action to be good or bad because it is done by a good or a bad man, still less because done by an amiable, a brave, or a benevolent man, or the contrary. These considerations are relevant, not to the estimation of actions, but of persons; and there is nothing in the utilitarian theory inconsistent with the fact that there are other things which interest us in persons besides the rightness and wrongness of their actions. The Stoics, indeed, with the paradoxical misuse of language which was part of their system, and by which they strove to raise themselves above all concern about anything but virtue, were fond of saying that he who has that has everything; that he, and only he, is rich, is beautiful, is a king. But no claim of this description is made for the virtuous man by the utilitarian doctrine. Utilitarians are quite aware that there are other desirable possessions and qualities besides virtue, and are perfectly willing to allow to all of them their full worth. They are also aware that a right action does not necessarily indicate a virtuous character, and that actions which are blameable, often proceed from qualities entitled to praise. When this is apparent in any particular case, it modifies their estimation, not certainly of the act, but of the agent. I grant that they are, notwithstanding, of opinion, that in the long run the best proof of a good character is good actions; and resolutely refuse to consider any mental disposition as good, of which the predominant tendency is to produce bad conduct. This makes them

unpopular with many people; but it is an unpopularity which they must share with every one who regards the distinction between right and wrong in a serious light; and the reproach is not one which a conscientious utilitarian need be anxious to repel.

If no more be meant by the objection than that many utilitarians look on the morality of actions, as measured by the utilitarian standard, with too exclusive a regard, and do not lay sufficient stress upon the other beauties of character which go towards making a human being lovable or admirable, this may be admitted. Utilitarians who have cultivated their moral feelings, but not their sympathies nor their artistic perceptions, do fall into this mistake; and so do all other moralists under the same conditions. What can be said in excuse for other moralists is equally available for them, namely, that, if there is to be any error, it is better that it should be on that side. As a matter of fact, we may affirm that among utilitarians as among adherents of other systems, there is every imaginable degree of rigidity and of laxity in the application of their standard: some are even puritanically rigorous, while others are as indulgent as can possibly be desired by sinner or by sentimentalist. But on the whole, a doctrine which brings prominently forward the interest that mankind have in the repression and prevention of conduct which violates the moral law, is likely to be inferior to no other in turning the sanctions of opinion again such violations. It is true, the question, What does violate the moral law? is one on which those who recognise different standards of morality are likely now and then to differ. But difference of opinion on moral questions was not first introduced into the world by utilitarianism, while that doctrine does supply, if not always an easy, at all events a tangible and intelligible mode of deciding such differences.

It may not be superfluous to notice a few more of the common misapprehensions of utilitarian ethics, even those which are so obvious and gross that it might appear impossible for any person of candour and intelligence to fall into them; since persons, even of considerable mental endowments, often give themselves so little trouble to understand the bearings of any opinion against which they entertain a prejudice, and men are in general so little conscious of this

---

35   For example, in Charles Dickens's novel *Hard Times* (1854), especially through the character of Gradgrind.

voluntary ignorance as a defect, that the vulgarest misunderstandings of ethical doctrines are continually met with in the deliberate writings of persons of the greatest pretensions both to high principle and to philosophy. We not uncommonly hear the doctrine of utility inveighed against as a *godless* doctrine. If it be necessary to say anything at all against so mere an assumption, we may say that the question depends upon what idea we have formed of the moral character of the Deity. If it be a true belief that God desires, above all things, the happiness of his creatures, and that this was his purpose in their creation, utility is not only not a godless doctrine, but more profoundly religious than any other. If it be meant that utilitarianism does not recognise the revealed will of God as the supreme law of morals, I answer, that a utilitarian who believes in the perfect goodness and wisdom of God, necessarily believes that whatever God has thought fit to reveal on the subject of morals, must fulfil the requirements of utility in a supreme degree. But others besides utilitarians have been of opinion that the Christian revelation was intended, and is fitted, to inform the hearts and minds of mankind with a spirit which should enable them to find for themselves what is right, and incline them to do it when found, rather than to tell them, except in a very general way, what it is; and that we need a doctrine of ethics, carefully followed out, to *interpret* to us the will God. Whether this opinion is correct or not, it is superfluous here to discuss; since whatever aid religion, either natural or revealed, can afford to ethical investigation, is as open to the utilitarian moralist as to any other. He can use it as the testimony of God to the usefulness or hurtfulness of any given course of action, by as good a right as others can use it for the indication of a transcendental law, having no connection with usefulness or with happiness.

Again, Utility is often summarily stigmatised as an immoral doctrine by giving it the name of Expediency, and taking advantage of the popular use of that term to contrast it with Principle. But the Expedient, in the sense in which it is opposed to the Right, generally means that which is expedient for the particular interest of the agent himself; as when a minister sacrifices the interests of his country to keep himself in place. When it means anything better than this, it means that which is expedient for some immediate object, some temporary purpose, but which violates a rule whose observance is expedient in a much higher degree. The Expedient, in this sense, instead of being the same thing with the useful, is a branch of the hurtful. Thus, it would often be expedient, for the purpose of getting over some momentary embarrassment, or attaining some object immediately useful to ourselves or others, to tell a lie. But inasmuch as the cultivation in ourselves of a sensitive feeling on the subject of veracity, is one of the most useful, and the enfeeblement of that feeling one of the most hurtful, things to which our conduct can be instrumental; and inasmuch as any, even unintentional, deviation from truth, does that much towards weakening the trustworthiness of human assertion, which is not only the principal support of all present social well-being, but the insufficiency of which does more than any one thing that can be named to keep back civilisation, virtue, everything on which human happiness on the largest scale depends; we feel that the violation, for a present advantage, of a rule of such transcendant expediency, is not expedient, and that he who, for the sake of a convenience to himself or to some other individual, does what depends on him to deprive mankind of the good, and inflict upon them the evil, involved in the greater or less reliance which they can place in each other's word, acts the part of one of their worst enemies. Yet that even this rule, sacred as it is, admits of possible exceptions, is acknowledged by all moralists; the chief of which is when the withholding of some fact (as of information from a malefactor, or of bad news from a person dangerously ill) would save an individual (especially an individual other than oneself) from great and unmerited evil, and when the withholding can only be effected by denial. But in order that the exception may not extend itself beyond the need, and may have the least possible effect in weakening reliance on veracity, it ought to be recognised, and, if possible, its limits defined; and if the principle of utility is good for anything, it must be good for weighing these conflicting utilities against one another, and marking out the region within which one or the other preponderates.

Again, defenders of utility often find themselves called upon to reply to such objections as this—that there is not time, previous to action, for calculating and weighing the effects of any line of conduct on the general happiness. This is exactly as if any one were to say that it is impossible to guide our conduct by Christianity, because there is not time, on every occasion on which anything has to be done, to read through the Old and New Testaments. The answer to the objection is, that there has been ample time, namely, the whole past duration of the human species. During all that time, mankind have been learning by experience the tendencies of actions; on which experience all the prudence, as well as all the morality of life, are dependent. People talk as if the commencement of this course of experience had hitherto been put off, and as if, at the moment when some man feels tempted to meddle with the property or life of another, he had to begin considering for the first time whether murder and theft are injurious to human happiness. Even then I do not think that he would find the question very puzzling; but, at all events, the matter is now done to his hand. It is truly a whimsical supposition that, if mankind were agreed in considering utility to be the test of morality, they would remain without any agreement as to what *is* useful, and would take no measures for having their notions on the subject taught to the young, and enforced by law and opinion. There is no difficulty in proving any ethical standard whatever to work ill, if we suppose universal idiocy to be conjoined with it; but on any hypothesis short of that, mankind must by this time have acquired positive beliefs as to the effects of some actions on their happiness; and the beliefs which have thus come down are the rules of morality for the multitude, and for the philosopher until he has succeeded in finding better. That philosophers might easily do this, even now, on many subjects; that the received code of ethics is by no means of divine right; and that mankind have still much to learn as to the effects of actions on the general happiness, I admit, or rather, earnestly maintain. The corollaries from the principle of utility, like the precepts of every practical art, admit of indefinite improvement, and, in a progressive state of the human mind, their improvement is perpetually going on. But to consider the rules of morality as improvable, is one thing; to pass over the intermediate generalisations entirely, and endeavour to test each individual action

directly by the first principle, is another. It is a strange notion that the acknowledgment of a first principle is inconsistent with the admission of secondary ones. To inform a traveller respecting the place of his ultimate destination, is not to forbid the use of landmarks and direction-posts on the way. The proposition that happiness is the end and aim of morality, does not mean that no road ought to be laid down to that goal, or that persons going thither should not be advised to take one direction rather than another. Men really ought to leave off talking a kind of nonsense on this subject, which they would neither talk nor listen to on other matters of practical concernment. Nobody argues that the art of navigation is not founded on astronomy, because sailors cannot wait to calculate the Nautical Almanack.[36] Being rational creatures, they go to sea with it ready calculated; and all rational creatures go out upon the sea of life with their minds made up on the common questions of right and wrong, as well as on many of the far more difficult questions of wise and foolish. And this, as long as foresight is a human quality, it is to be presumed they will continue to do. Whatever we adopt as the fundamental principle of morality, we require subordinate principles to apply it by; the impossibility of doing without them, being common to all systems, can afford no argument against any one in particular; but gravely to argue as if no such secondary principles could be had, and as if mankind had remained till now, and always must remain, without drawing any general conclusions from the experience of human life, is as high a pitch, I think, as absurdity has ever reached in philosophical controversy.

The remainder of the stock arguments against utilitarianism mostly consist in laying to its charge the common infirmities of human nature, and the general difficulties which embarrass conscientious

---

36   An annual government publication that tabulates the astronomical data required for maritime navigation. (For example, the almanac might give the coordinates of the constellation Orion as it would be seen at the horizon on a particular date from various places on the earth's surface: observation of Orion at certain coordinates on that date will therefore tell you where you are.)

persons in shaping their course through life. We are told that a utilitarian will be apt to make his own particular case an exception to moral rules, and, when under temptation, will see a utility in the breach of a rule, greater than he will see in its observance. But is utility the only creed which is able to furnish us with excuses for evil doing, and means of cheating our own conscience? They are afforded in abundance by all doctrines which recognise as a fact in morals the existence of conflicting considerations; which all doctrines do, that have been believed by sane persons. It is not the fault of any creed, but of the complicated nature of human affairs, that rules of conduct cannot be so framed as to require no exceptions, and that hardly any kind of action can safely be laid down as either always obligatory or always condemnable. There is no ethical creed which does not temper the rigidity of its laws, by giving a certain latitude, under the moral responsibility of the agent, for accommodation to peculiarities of circumstances; and under every creed, at the opening thus made, self-deception and dishonest casuistry[37] get in. There exists no moral system under which there do not arise unequivocal cases of conflicting obligation. These are the real difficulties, the knotty points both in the theory of ethics, and in the conscientious guidance of personal conduct. They are overcome practically, with greater or with less success, according to the intellect and virtue of the individual; but it can hardly be pretended that any one will be the less qualified for dealing with them, from possessing an ultimate standard to which conflicting rights and duties can be referred. If utility is the ultimate source of moral obligations, utility may be invoked to decide between them when their demands are incompatible. Though the application of the standard may be difficult, it is better than none at all: while in other systems, the moral laws all claiming independent authority, there is no common umpire entitled to interfere between them; their claims to precedence one over another rest on little better than sophistry,[38] and unless determined, as they generally are, by the unacknowledged influence of considerations of utility, afford a free scope for the action of personal desires and partialities. We must remember that only in these cases of conflict between secondary principles is it requisite that first principles should be appealed to. There is no case of moral obligation in which some secondary principle is not involved; and if only one, there can seldom be any real doubt which one it is, in the mind of any person by whom the principle itself is recognised.

Chapter 3: Of the Ultimate Sanction[39] of the Principle of Utility.

The question is often asked, and properly so, in regard to any supposed moral standard—What is its sanction? what are the motives to obey it? or more specifically, what is the source of its obligation? whence does it derive its binding force? It is a necessary part of moral philosophy to provide the answer to this question; which, though frequently assuming the shape of an objection to the utilitarian morality, as if it had some special applicability to that above others, really arises in regard to all standards. It arises, in fact, whenever a person is called on to *adopt* a standard, or refer morality to any basis on which he has not been accustomed to rest it. For the customary morality, that which education and opinion have consecrated, is the only one which presents itself to the mind with the feeling of being *in itself* obligatory; and when a person is asked to believe that this morality *derives* its obligation from some general principle round which custom has not thrown the same halo, the assertion is to him a paradox; the supposed corollaries seem to have a more binding force than the original theorem; the superstructure seems to stand better without, than with, what is represented as its foundation. He says to

---

37   Specious rationalizing.

38   Plausible but misleading argument.

39   "Sanction" was a technical term in eighteenth- and nineteenth-century philosophy. Sanctions are the *sources* of the pleasures and pains which motivate people to act. For example, Bentham—in his *Introduction to the Principles of Morals and Legislation*—distinguished between four different types of sanction: "physical" sanctions (e.g., hunger or sexual desire), "political" sanctions (e.g., prison), "religious" sanctions (e.g., heaven and hell), and "moral" sanctions (e.g., social disapproval).

himself, I feel that I am bound not to rob or murder, betray or deceive; but why am I bound to promote the general happiness? If my own happiness lies in something else, why may I not give that the preference?

If the view adopted by the utilitarian philosophy of the nature of the moral sense be correct, this difficulty will always present itself, until the influences which form moral character have taken the same hold of the principle which they have taken of some of the consequences—until, by the improvement of education, the feeling of unity with our fellow-creatures shall be (what it cannot be denied that Christ intended it to be) as deeply rooted in our character, and to our own consciousness as completely a part of our nature, as the horror of crime is in an ordinarily well brought up young person. In the meantime, however, the difficulty has no peculiar application to the doctrine of utility, but is inherent in every attempt to analyse morality and reduce it to principles; which, unless the principle is already in men's minds invested with as much sacredness as any of its applications, always seems to divest them of a part of their sanctity.

The principle of utility either has, or there is no reason why it might not have, all the sanctions which belong to any other system of morals. Those sanctions are either external or internal. Of the external sanctions it is not necessary to speak at any length. They are, the hope of favour and the fear of displeasure, from our fellow creatures or from the Ruler of the Universe, along with whatever we may have of sympathy or affection for them, or of love and awe of Him, inclining us to do his will independently of selfish consequences. There is evidently no reason why all these motives for observance should not attach themselves to the utilitarian morality, as completely and as powerfully as to any other. Indeed, those of them which refer to our fellow creatures are sure to do so, in proportion to the amount of general intelligence; for whether there be any other ground of moral obligation than the general happiness or not, men do desire happiness; and however imperfect may be their own practice, they desire and commend all conduct in others towards themselves, by which they think their happiness is promoted. With regard to the religious motive, if men believe, as most profess to do, in the goodness of God, those who think that conduciveness to the general happiness is the essence, or even only the criterion of good, must necessarily believe that it is also that which God approves. The whole force therefore of external reward and punishment, whether physical or moral, and whether proceeding from God or from our fellow men, together with all that the capacities of human nature admit of disinterested devotion to either, become available to enforce the utilitarian morality, in proportion as that morality is recognised; and the more powerfully, the more the appliances of education and general cultivation are bent to the purpose.

So far as to external sanctions. The internal sanction of duty, whatever our standard of duty may be, is one and the same—a feeling in our own mind; a pain, more or less intense, attendant on violation of duty, which in properly cultivated moral natures rises, in the more serious cases, into shrinking from it as an impossibility. This feeling, when disinterested, and connecting itself with the pure idea of duty, and not with some particular form of it, or with any of the merely accessory circumstances, is the essence of Conscience; though in that complex phenomenon as it actually exists, the simple fact is in general all encrusted over with collateral associations, derived from sympathy, from love, and still more from fear; from all the forms of religious feeling; from the recollections of childhood and of all our past life; from self-esteem, desire of the esteem of others, and occasionally even self-abasement. This extreme complication is, I apprehend, the origin of the sort of mystical character which, by a tendency of the human mind of which there are many other examples, is apt to be attributed to the idea of moral obligation, and which leads people to believe that the idea cannot possibly attach itself to any other objects than those which, by a supposed mysterious law, are found in our present experience to excite it. Its binding force, however, consists in the existence of a mass of feeling which must be broken through in order to do what violates our standard of right, and which, if we do nevertheless violate that standard, will probably have to be encountered afterwards in the form of remorse. Whatever theory we have of the nature or origin of conscience, this is what essentially constitutes it.

The ultimate sanction, therefore, of all morality (external motives apart) being a subjective feeling in our own minds, I see nothing embarrassing to those whose standard is utility, in the question, what is the sanction of that particular standard? We may answer, the same as of all other moral standards—the conscientious feelings of mankind. Undoubtedly this sanction has no binding efficacy on those who do not possess the feelings it appeals to; but neither will these persons be more obedient to any other moral principle than to the utilitarian one. On them morality of any kind has no hold but through the external sanctions. Meanwhile the feelings exist, a fact in human nature, the reality of which, and the great power with which they are capable of acting on those in whom they have been duly cultivated, are proved by experience. No reason has ever been shown why they may not be cultivated to as great intensity in connection with the utilitarian, as with any other rule of morals.

There is, I am aware, a disposition to believe that a person who sees in moral obligation a transcendental fact, an objective reality belonging to the province of "Things in themselves," is likely to be more obedient to it than one who believes it to be entirely subjective, having its seat in human consciousness only. But whatever a person's opinion may be on this point of Ontology,[40] the force he is really urged by is his own subjective feeling, and is exactly measured by its strength. No one's belief that duty is an objective reality is stronger than the belief that God is so; yet the belief in God, apart from the expectation of actual reward and punishment, only operates on conduct through, and in proportion to, the subjective religious feeling. The sanction, so far as it is disinterested, is always in the mind itself, and the notion therefore of the transcendental moralists must be, that this sanction will not exist *in* the mind unless it is believed to have its root out of the mind; and that if a person is able to say to himself, This which is restraining me, and which is called my conscience, is only a feeling in my own mind, he may possibly draw the conclusion that when the feeling ceases the obligation ceases, and that if he find the feeling inconvenient, he may disregard it, and endeavour to get rid of it. But is this danger confined to the utilitarian morality? Does the belief that moral obligation has its seat outside the mind make the feeling of it too strong to be got rid of? The fact is so far otherwise, that all moralists admit and lament the ease with which, in the generality of minds, conscience can be silenced or stifled. The question, Need I obey my conscience? is quite as often put to themselves by persons who never heard of the principle of utility, as by its adherents. Those whose conscientious feelings are so weak as to allow of their asking this question, if they answer it affirmatively, will not do so because they believe in the transcendental theory, but because of the external sanctions.

It is not necessary, for the present purpose, to decide whether the feeling of duty is innate[41] or implanted. Assuming it to be innate, it is an open question to what objects it naturally attaches itself, for the philosophic supporters of that theory are now agreed that the intuitive perception is of principles of morality and not of the details. If there be anything innate in the matter, I see no reason why the feeling which is innate should not be that of regard to the pleasures and pains of others. If there is any principle of morals which is intuitively obligatory, I should say it must be that. If so, the intuitive ethics would coincide with the utilitarian, and there would be no further quarrel between them. Even as it is, the intuitive moralists, though they believe that there are other intuitive moral obligations, do already believe this to be one; for they unanimously hold that a large *portion* of morality turns upon the consideration due to the interests of our fellow-creatures. Therefore, if the belief in the transcendental origin of moral obligation gives any additional efficacy to the internal sanction, it appears to me that the utilitarian principle has already the benefit of it.

On the other hand, if, as is my own belief, the moral feelings are not innate, but acquired, they are

---

40 Ontology is the study of what exists or of the nature of 'being' itself (*on* is Greek for "being"). Questions about the reality of numbers, of fictional characters, or of theoretical entities (such as quarks or genes) are ontological questions. The particular ontological question Mill has in mind here, is the existence of transcendent moral laws.

41 Inborn, possessed at birth.

not for that reason the less natural. It is natural to man to speak, to reason, to build cities, to cultivate the ground, though these are acquired faculties. The moral feelings are not indeed a part of our nature, in the sense of being in any perceptible degree present in all of us; but this, unhappily, is a fact admitted by those who believe the most strenuously in their transcendental origin. Like the other acquired capacities above referred to, the moral faculty, if not a part of our nature, is a natural outgrowth from it; capable, like them, in a certain small degree, of springing up spontaneously; and susceptible of being brought by cultivation to a high degree of development. Unhappily it is also susceptible, by a sufficient use of the external sanctions and of the force of early impressions, of being cultivated in almost any direction: so that there is hardly anything so absurd or so mischievous that it may not, by means of these influences, be made to act on the human mind with all the authority of conscience. To doubt that the same potency might be given by the same means to the principle of utility, even if it had no foundation in human nature, would be flying in the face of all experience.

But moral associations which are wholly of artificial creation, when intellectual culture goes on, yield by degrees to the dissolving force of analysis: and if the feeling of duty, when associated with utility, would appear equally arbitrary; if there were no leading department of our nature, no powerful class of sentiments, with which that association would harmonise, which would make us feel it congenial, and incline us not only to foster it in others (for which we have abundant interested motives), but also to cherish it in ourselves; if there were not, in short, a natural basis of sentiment for utilitarian morality, it might well happen that this association also, even after it had been implanted by education, might be analysed away.

But there *is* this basis of powerful natural sentiment; and this it is which, when once the general happiness is recognised as the ethical standard, will constitute the strength of the utilitarian morality. This firm foundation is that of the social feelings of mankind; the desire to be in unity with our fellow creatures, which is already a powerful principle in human nature, and happily one of those which tend to become stronger,

even without express inculcation,[42] from the influences of advancing civilisation. The social state is at once so natural, so necessary, and so habitual to man, that, except in some unusual circumstances or by an effort of voluntary abstraction, he never conceives himself otherwise than as a member of a body; and this association is riveted more and more, as mankind are further removed from the state of savage independence. Any condition, therefore, which is essential to a state of society, becomes more and more an inseparable part of every person's conception of the state of things which he is born into, and which is the destiny of a human being. Now, society between human beings, except in the relation of master and slave, is manifestly impossible on any other footing than that the interests of all are to be consulted. Society between equals can only exist on the understanding that the interests of all are to be regarded equally. And since in all states of civilisation, every person, except an absolute monarch, has equals, every one is obliged to live on these terms with somebody; and in every age some advance is made towards a state in which it will be impossible to live permanently on other terms with anybody. In this way people grow up unable to conceive as possible to them a state of total disregard of other people's interests. They are under a necessity of conceiving themselves as at least abstaining from all the grosser injuries, and (if only for their own protection) living in a state of constant protest against them. They are also familiar with the fact of co-operating with others and proposing to themselves a collective, not an individual interest as the aim (at least for the time being) of their actions. So long as they are co-operating, their ends are identified with those of others; there is at least a temporary feeling that the interests of others are their own interests. Not only does all strengthening of social ties, and all healthy growth of society, give to each individual a stronger personal interest in practically consulting the welfare of others; it also leads him to identify his *feelings* more and more with their good, or at least with an even greater degree of practical consideration for it. He comes, as though instinctively, to be conscious of himself as a being who *of course* pays regard to oth-

---

42 Frequent repetition or instruction, intended to firmly impress something in someone's mind.

ers. The good of others becomes to him a thing naturally and necessarily to be attended to, like any of the physical conditions of our existence. Now, whatever amount of this feeling a person has, he is urged by the strongest motives both of interest and of sympathy to demonstrate it, and to the utmost of his power encourage it in others; and even if he has none of it himself, he is as greatly interested as any one else that others should have it. Consequently the smallest germs of the feeling are laid hold of and nourished by the contagion of sympathy and the influences of education; and a complete web of corroborative association is woven round it, by the powerful agency of the external sanctions. This mode of conceiving ourselves and human life, as civilisation goes on, is felt to be more and more natural. Every step in political improvement renders it more so, by removing the sources of opposition of interest, and levelling those inequalities of legal privilege between individuals or classes, owing to which there are large portions of mankind whose happiness it is still practicable to disregard. In an improving state of the human mind, the influences are constantly on the increase, which tend to generate in each individual a feeling of unity with all the rest; which, if perfect, would make him never think of, or desire, any beneficial condition for himself, in the benefits of which they are not included. If we now suppose this feeling of unity to be taught as a religion, and the whole force of education, of institutions, and of opinion, directed, as it once was in the case of religion, to make every person grow up from infancy surrounded on all sides both by the profession and the practice of it, I think that no one, who can realise this conception, will feel any misgiving about the sufficiency of the ultimate sanction for the Happiness morality. To any ethical student who finds the realisation difficult, I recommend, as a means of facilitating it, the second of M. Comte's two principle works, the *Système de Politique Positive*.[43] I entertain the strongest objections to the system of

43 This 1854 book by French political philosopher and sociologist Auguste Comte (1798–1857) advocated a capitalist dictatorship based on science as the ideal form of society, and urged that theistic conceptions of religion be replaced by a scientific "religion of humanity."

politics and morals set forth in that treatise; but I think it has superabundantly shown the possibility of giving to the service of humanity, even without the aid of belief in a Providence, both the psychical power and the social efficacy of a religion; making it take hold of human life, and colour all thought, feeling, and action, in a manner of which the greatest ascendancy ever exercised by any religion may be but a type and foretaste; and of which the danger is, not that it should be insufficient but that it should be so excessive as to interfere unduly with human freedom and individuality.

Neither is it necessary to the feeling which constitutes the binding force of the utilitarian morality on those who recognise it, to wait for those social influences which would make its obligation felt by mankind at large. In the comparatively early state of human advancement in which we now live, a person cannot indeed feel that entireness of sympathy with all others, which would make any real discordance in the general direction of their conduct in life impossible; but already a person in whom the social feeling is at all developed, cannot bring himself to think of the rest of his fellow creatures as struggling rivals with him for the means of happiness, whom he must desire to see defeated in their object in order that he may succeed in his. The deeply rooted conception which every individual even now has of himself as a social being, tends to make him feel it one of his natural wants that there should be harmony between his feelings and aims and those of his fellow creatures. If differences of opinion and of mental culture make it impossible for him to share many of their actual feelings—perhaps make him denounce and defy those feelings—he still needs to be conscious that his real aim and theirs do not conflict; that he is not opposing himself to what they really wish for, namely their own good, but is, on the contrary, promoting it. This feeling in most individuals is much inferior in strength to their selfish feelings, and is often wanting altogether. But to those who have it, it possesses all the characters of a natural feeling. It does not present itself to their minds as a superstition of education, or a law despotically imposed by the power of society, but as an attribute which it would not be well for them to be without. This conviction is the ultimate sanction of the greatest happiness morality. This it is which makes any mind, of well-developed feelings, work with, and not against, the outward motives to care for others, afforded by what I have called the external sanctions; and when those sanctions are wanting, or act in an opposite direction, constitutes in itself a powerful internal binding force, in proportion to the sensitiveness and thoughtfulness of the character; since few but those whose mind is a moral blank, could bear to lay out their course of life on the plan of paying no regard to others except so far as their own private interest compels.

Chapter 4: Of what Sort of Proof the Principle of Utility is Susceptible.

It has already been remarked, that questions of ultimate ends do not admit of proof, in the ordinary acceptation of the term. To be incapable of proof by reasoning is common to all first principles; to the first premises of our knowledge,[44] as well as to those of our conduct. But the former, being matters of fact, may be the subject of a direct appeal to the faculties which judge of fact—namely, our senses, and our internal consciousness.[45] Can an appeal be made to the same faculties on questions of practical ends? Or by what other faculty is cognisance taken of them?

Questions about ends are, in other words, questions about what things are desirable. The utilitarian doctrine is, that happiness is desirable, and the only thing desirable, as an end; all other things being only desirable as means to that end. What ought to be required of this doctrine—what conditions is it requisite that the doctrine should fulfil—to make good its claim to be believed?

The only proof capable of being given that an object is visible, is that people actually see it. The only proof that a sound is audible, is that people hear it: and so of the other sources of our experience. In like manner, I apprehend, the sole evidence it is possible to produce that anything is desirable, is that people do actually desire it. If the end which the utilitarian doctrine proposes to itself were not, in theory and in practice, acknowledged to be an end, nothing could

ever convince any person that it was so. No reason can be given why the general happiness is desirable, except that each person, so far as he believes it to be attainable, desires his own happiness. This, however, being a fact, we have not only all the proof which the case admits of, but all which it is possible to require, that happiness is a good: that each person's happiness is a good to that person, and the general happiness, therefore, a good to the aggregate of all persons. Happiness has made out its title as *one* of the ends of conduct, and consequently one of the criteria of morality.

But it has not, by this alone, proved itself to be the sole criterion. To do that, it would seem, by the same rule, necessary to show, not only that people desire happiness, but that they never desire anything else. Now it is palpable that they do desire things which, in common language, are decidedly distinguished from happiness. They desire, for example, virtue, and the absence of vice, no less really than pleasure and the absence of pain. The desire of virtue is not as universal, but it is as authentic a fact, as the desire of happiness. And hence the opponents of the utilitarian standard deem that they have a right to infer that there are other ends of human action besides happiness, and that happiness is not the standard of approbation and disapprobation.

But does the utilitarian doctrine deny that people desire virtue, or maintain that virtue is not a thing to be desired? The very reverse. It maintains not only that virtue is to be desired, but that it is to be desired disinterestedly, for itself. Whatever may be the opinion of utilitarian moralists as to the original conditions by which virtue is made virtue; however they may believe (as they do) that actions and dispositions are only virtuous because they promote another end than virtue; yet this being granted, and it having been decided, from considerations of this description, what is virtuous, they not only place virtue at the very head of the things which are good as means to the ultimate end, but they also recognise as a psychological fact the possibility of its being, to the individual, a good in itself, without looking to any end beyond it; and hold, that the mind is not in a right state, not in a state conformable to Utility, not in the state most conducive to the general happiness, unless it does love virtue in this

---

44 Sense experience.

45 Mill means the memory of something previously experienced.

manner—as a thing desirable in itself, even although, in the individual instance, it should not produce those other desirable consequences which it tends to produce, and on account of which it is held to be virtue. This opinion is not, in the smallest degree, a departure from the Happiness principle. The ingredients of happiness are very various, and each of them is desirable in itself, and not merely when considered as swelling an aggregate. The principle of utility does not mean that any given pleasure, as music, for instance, or any given exemption from pain, as for example health, is to be looked upon as means to a collective something termed happiness, and to be desired on that account. They are desired and desirable in and for themselves; besides being means, they are a part of the end. Virtue, according to the utilitarian doctrine, is not naturally and originally part of the end, but it is capable of becoming so; and in those who love it disinterestedly it has become so, and is desired and cherished, not as a means to happiness, but as a part of their happiness.

To illustrate this farther, we may remember that virtue is not the only thing, originally a means, and which if it were not a means to anything else, would be and remain indifferent, but which by association with what it is a means to, comes to be desired for itself, and that too with the utmost intensity. What, for example, shall we say of the love of money? There is nothing originally more desirable about money than about any heap of glittering pebbles. Its worth is solely that of the things which it will buy; the desires for other things than itself, which it is a means of gratifying. Yet the love of money is not only one of the strongest moving forces of human life, but money is, in many cases, desired in and for itself, the desire to possess it is often stronger than the desire to use it, and goes on increasing when all the desires which point to ends beyond it, to be compassed by it, are falling off. It may, then, be said truly, that money is desired not for the sake of an end, but as part of the end. From being a means to happiness, it has come to be itself a principal ingredient of the individual's conception of happiness. The same may be said of the majority of the great objects of human life—power, for example, or fame; except that to each of these there is a certain amount of immediate pleasure annexed, which has at least the semblance of being naturally inherent in them; a

thing which cannot be said of money. Still, however, the strongest natural attraction, both of power and of fame, is the immense aid they give to the attainment of our other wishes; and it is the strong association thus generated between them and all our objects of desire, which gives to the direct desire of them the intensity it often assumes, so as in some characters to surpass in strength all other desires. In these cases the means have become a part of the end, and a more important part of it than any of the things which they are means to. What was once desired as an instrument for the attainment of happiness, has come to be desired for its own sake. In being desired for its own sake it is, however, desired as *part* of happiness. The person is made, or thinks he would be made, happy by its mere possession; and is made unhappy by failure to obtain it. The desire of it is not a different thing from the desire of happiness, any more than the love of music, or the desire of health. They are included in happiness. They are some of the elements of which the desire of happiness is made up. Happiness is not an abstract idea, but a concrete whole; and these are some of its parts. And the utilitarian standard sanctions and approves their being so. Life would be a poor thing, very ill provided with sources of happiness, if there were not this provision of nature, by which things originally indifferent, but conducive to, or otherwise associated with, the satisfaction of our primitive desires, become in themselves sources of pleasure more valuable than the primitive pleasures, both in permanency, in the space of human existence that they are capable of covering, and even in intensity.

Virtue, according to the utilitarian conception, is a good of this description. There was no original desire of it, or motive to it, save its conduciveness to pleasure, and especially to protection from pain. But through the association thus formed, it may be felt a good in itself, and desired as such with as great intensity as any other good; and with this difference between it and the love of money, of power, or of fame, that all of these may, and often do, render the individual noxious to the other members of the society to which he belongs, whereas there is nothing which makes him so much a blessing to them as the cultivation of the disinterested love of virtue. And consequently, the utilitarian standard, while it tolerates and approves those other acquired desires, up to the point beyond which they would be more injurious to the general happiness than promotive of it, enjoins and requires the cultivation of the love of virtue up to the greatest strength possible, as being above all things important to the general happiness.

It results from the preceding considerations, that there is in reality nothing desired except happiness. Whatever is desired otherwise than as a means to some end beyond itself, and ultimately to happiness, is desired as itself a part of happiness, and is not desired for itself until it has become so. Those who desire virtue for its own sake, desire it either because the consciousness of it is a pleasure, or because the consciousness of being without it is a pain, or for both reasons united; as in truth the pleasure and pain seldom exist separately, but almost always together, the same person feeling pleasure in the degree of virtue attained, and pain in not having attained more. If one of these gave him no pleasure, and the other no pain, he would not love or desire virtue, or would desire it only for the other benefits which it might produce to himself or to persons whom he cared for.

We have now, then, an answer to the question, of what sort of proof the principle of utility is susceptible. If the opinion which I have now stated is psychologically true—if human nature is so constituted as to desire nothing which is not either a part of happiness or a means of happiness, we can have no other proof, and we require no other, that these are the only things desirable. If so, happiness is the sole end of human action, and the promotion of it the test by which to judge of all human conduct; from whence it necessarily follows that it must be the criterion of morality, since a part is included in the whole.

And now to decide whether this is really so; whether mankind do desire nothing for itself but that which is a pleasure to them, or of which the absence is a pain; we have evidently arrived at a question of fact and experience, dependent, like all similar questions, upon evidence. It can only be determined by practised self-consciousness and self-observation, assisted by observation of others. I believe that these sources of evidence, impartially consulted, will declare that desiring a thing and finding it pleasant, aversion to it and thinking of it as painful, are phenomena entirely inseparable, or rather two parts of the same phenomenon; in strictness of language, two different modes of naming the same psychological fact: that to think of an object as desirable (unless for the sake of its consequences), and to think of it as pleasant, are one and the same thing; and that to desire anything, except in proportion as the idea of it is pleasant, is a physical and metaphysical[46] impossibility.

So obvious does this appear to me, that I expect it will hardly be disputed: and the objection made will be, not that desire can possibly be directed to anything ultimately except pleasure and exemption from pain, but that the will is a different thing from desire; that a person of confirmed virtue, or any other person whose purposes are fixed, carries out his purposes without any thought of the pleasure he has in contemplating them, or expects to derive from their fulfilment; and persists in acting on them, even though these pleasures are much diminished, by changes in his character or decay of his passive sensibilities, or are outweighed by the pains which the pursuit of the purposes may bring upon him. All this I fully admit, and have stated it elsewhere, as positively and emphatically as any one. Will, the active phenomenon, is a different thing from desire, the state of passive sensibility, and though originally an offshoot from it, may in time take root and detach itself from the parent stock; so much so, that in the case of an habitual purpose, instead of willing the thing because we desire it, we often desire it only because we will it. This, however, is but an instance of that familiar fact, the power of habit, and is nowise confined to the case of virtuous actions. Many indifferent things, which men originally did from a motive of some sort, they continue to do from habit. Sometimes this is done unconsciously, the consciousness coming only after the action: at other times with conscious volition, but volition which has become habitual, and is put in operation by the force of habit, in opposition perhaps

---

46   Mill probably means "psychological." In his view, not only do human beings actually desire things "in proportion as the idea of it is pleasant," but there is no possible human psychology which would be otherwise.

to the deliberate preference, as often happens with those who have contracted habits of vicious or hurtful indulgence. Third and last comes the case in which the habitual act of will in the individual instance is not in contradiction to the general intention prevailing at other times, but in fulfilment of it; as in the case of the person of confirmed virtue, and of all who pursue deliberately and consistently any determinate end. The distinction between will and desire thus understood is an authentic and highly important psychological fact; but the fact consists solely in this—that will, like all other parts of our constitution, is amenable to habit, and that we may will from habit what we no longer desire for itself or desire only because we will it. It is not the less true that will, in the beginning, is entirely produced by desire; including in that term the repelling influence of pain as well as the attractive one of pleasure. Let us take into consideration, no longer the person who has a confirmed will to do right, but him in whom that virtuous will is still feeble, conquerable by temptation, and not to be fully relied on; by what means can it be strengthened? How can the will to be virtuous, where it does not exist in sufficient force, be implanted or awakened? Only by making the person *desire* virtue—by making him think of it in a pleasurable light, or of its absence in a painful one. It is by associating the doing right with pleasure, or the doing wrong with pain, or by eliciting and impressing and bringing home to the person's experience the pleasure naturally involved in the one or the pain in the other, that it is possible to call forth that will to be virtuous, which, when confirmed, acts without any thought of either pleasure or pain. Will is the child of desire, and passes out of the dominion of its parent only to come under that of habit. That which is the result of habit affords no presumption of being intrinsically good; and there would be no reason for wishing that the purpose of virtue should become independent of pleasure and pain, were it not that the influence of the pleasurable and painful associations which prompt to virtue is not sufficiently to be depended on for unerring constancy of action until it has acquired the support of habit. Both in feeling and in conduct, habit is the only thing which imparts certainty; and it is because of the importance to others of being able to rely absolutely on one's feelings and conduct, and to oneself of being able to rely on one's own, that the will to do right ought to be cultivated into this habitual independence. In other words, this state of the will is a means to good, not intrinsically a good; and does not contradict the doctrine that nothing is a good to human beings but in so far as it is either itself pleasurable, or a means of attaining pleasure or averting pain.

But if this doctrine be true, the principle of utility is proved. Whether it is so or not, must now be left to the consideration of the thoughtful reader.

FRIEDRICH NIETZSCHE
Beyond Good and Evil

In the end, what is there for it? There is no other means to bring philosophy again into honor: one must first hang all moralists.

(Friedrich Nietzsche)

Who Was Friedrich Nietzsche?

Friedrich Wilhelm Nietzsche was one of the most original, important, and—belatedly—influential voices of the nineteenth century, and is (arguably) among the greatest of the German-speaking philosophers since Kant. He was born in 1844, on the birthday of King Friedrich Wilhelm IV of Prussia (after whom he was named), in the village of Röcken near Leipzig in the region of Saxony. His father and both grandfathers were Lutheran ministers. Nietzsche's father, Carl Ludwig, died of a head injury before he was five and Nietzsche's younger brother died the next year, and so he and his sister Elisabeth were brought up by their mother, Franziska, and two aunts. As a young boy he struggled with his schoolwork, but persevered, rising at 5 A.M. to begin his school day and then studying extra hours in the evening to keep up with his Greek. He spent much of his free time playing the piano—Nietzsche was a skilled pianist—and, beginning before the age of ten and continuing throughout his life, composed many pieces of music and wrote a great deal of poetry.

In 1858 Nietzsche was admitted to Schulpforta, one of Germany's oldest and most prestigious private boarding schools. The fourteen-year-old Nietzsche found the transition to the school's rigorous, almost monastic, regime hard, but again he persevered and played an energetic role in the school's intellectual, musical, and cultural life. By 1861, however, he was beginning to be plagued by headaches, fevers, eyestrain, and weakness—the first signs of the ill health from which he would suffer for the rest of his life. In 1864 Nietzsche graduated, and although his grades were patchy he had already shown signs of great intellectual promise, especially in the study of languages.

After a brief stint as a theology student at the University of Bonn, Nietzsche enrolled at the university in Leipzig and began work in classical philology—studying the linguistic, interpretative, and historical aspects of Greek and Roman literature. At this time, he discovered the work of philosopher Arthur Schopenhauer (1788–1860), a pessimistic German philosopher who saw the world as an irrational, godless sequence of ceaseless striving and suffering. He also met and became friends with the composer Richard Wagner (1813–1883), a creative genius who revolutionized opera with his concept of "music drama" which fused music, poetry, drama, and legend, culminating with his famous

Ring cycle. Both these men would greatly influence Nietzsche's philosophical thought.

Even before he had completed his studies and at the unprecedentedly young age of 24, Nietzsche was invited to take up a post as professor of classical philology at the University of Basel in Switzerland. Leipzig University hastily gave him a doctorate, not even bothering with the formality of an examination. Nietzsche began work at Basel in 1869, after renouncing his Prussian citizenship, and in 1870 was promoted to the rank of full professor. In that same year, the French parliament declared war on Prussia and Nietzsche volunteered for military service but, because of Switzerland's neutrality, he was allowed only to serve as a medical orderly. He was on the front lines for approximately a week before he fell ill—of diphtheria—and spent most of the rest of the short Franco-Prussian war (Paris surrendered in January 1871) recuperating and continuing his academic work.

His first book, *The Birth of Tragedy out of the Spirit of Music*, appeared in 1872 and was expected to secure his reputation as a brilliant young scholar. Instead, it caused a small tempest of academic controversy, a battle which Nietzsche was deemed by his professional contemporaries to have lost. Rather than publishing a traditional work of classical scholarship, Nietzsche presented a rhapsodic, free-flowing essay which attempted to apply Schopenhauer's philosophical ideas to an interpretation of the origins of Greek tragedy, and which argued that the spirit of Greek tragedy was reborn in the music-dramas of Richard Wagner. Nietzsche hoped this work would establish him as a philosopher (and allow him to transfer to the philosophy department at Basel), but it did not resemble a traditional work of philosophy either. Nietzsche's reputation as a professional scholar was irreparably damaged.

Nietzsche continued to teach philology at Basel—where, for several years after the publication of *The Birth of Tragedy* he was generally shunned by the students—until 1879. In that year he resigned due to ill health: by this time he could hardly see to read and write, and was beset with headaches and other pains. He was given a pension of two-thirds his salary, not quite enough money for Nietzsche to live comfort-

ably, but this freed him to devote all his time to his real love—the writing of philosophy.

Disliking the increasingly nationalist climate of Bismarck's "Second Reich," Nietzsche spent most of the next decade, from 1880 until 1889, in self-imposed exile from Germany, wandering around Europe (France, Italy, Switzerland) staying with various friends. In 1882, in Rome, Nietzsche met the bewitching Lou von Andreas-Salomé, fell madly in love with her, and within two months asked her to marry him; she refused. A month later, in Lucerne, he proposed again, and was again rejected. Nevertheless, Nietzsche, Salomé, and their mutual friend Paul Rée became, for a time, firm companions, traveling together and calling themselves the *Dreieinigkeit* or "trinity" of free spirits. The capricious Salomé, however, was not warmly received by Nietzsche's possessive mother and sister—eventually his mother refused to have Lou in the house. This caused such family bickering that Nietzsche, upset and depressed, broke off his relations with Rée and Salomé and also ceased his correspondence with his mother and sister for a few months. On his (rather bumpy) reconciliation with his sister Elisabeth, she began a campaign to turn Nietzsche decisively against Rée and Salomé, and was quickly successful in making the split between Nietzsche and his former friends irrevocable.

Despite this and various other emotional upsets, Nietzsche produced several substantial philosophical books during the first few years of his "wandering" decade: *Human, All Too Human: A Book for Free Spirits* (1878–1880), *Daybreak: Thoughts on the Prejudices of Morality* (1881), *The Gay Science* (1882), and *Thus Spake Zarathustra* (1883–1885). They sold so few copies, however, that by the time he came to write *Beyond Good and Evil* (1886) he was having great difficulty finding publishers and was rapidly running out of money. The late 1880s were lonely, worried years: his health was very bad, he had little money, he had destroyed his relationships with most of his friends (including Wagner and his circle), and his philosophical work was falling on deaf ears.

In 1887 Nietzsche published *On the Genealogy of Morals* and, at long last, in 1888 began to see the first signs of public recognition—for example, public lectures on his work were held in Copenhagen. However, by this time Nietzsche, never a modest man, was starting to show signs of full-blown megalomania, referring to himself in letters as, for example, "the first spirit of the age" and "a genius of the Truth." Yet in this final year of his sanity he managed to write no fewer than five new books: *The Case of Wagner*, *Twilight of the Idols (or How to Philosophize with a Hammer)*, *The Anti-Christ: Curse on Christianity*, *Ecce Homo*, and *Nietzsche Contra Wagner*. By January of 1889, however, his communications were so bizarre—they are the so-called *Wahnbriefe*, or "mad letters"—that his remaining friends became concerned and called in the director of the Psychiatric Clinic in Basel, Dr. Ludwig Wille.

Nietzsche, by now completely insane, was tracked down in Turin and (with the help of a local dentist named Dr. Bettmann) was brought back to Basel and quickly transferred to a psychiatric clinic in the central German city of Jena. He was only 44. The doctors quickly agreed that the prospects for recovery were slim, even after Nietzsche's condition improved somewhat with confinement and treatment. They reported that he

> speaks more coherently and … the episodes with screaming are more seldom. Different delirious notions appear continually, and auditory hallucinations still occur…. He recognizes his environment only partially, e.g., he calls the chief orderly Prince Bismarck etc. He does not know exactly where he is.

In 1890, Nietzsche was released into the care of his mother and his mental health declined into a kind of permanent apathy and, gradually, paralysis.

Meanwhile, his sister Elisabeth seized control of Nietzsche's literary remains.[1] She created a Nietzsche Archive in Naumburg, near Leipzig, in 1894 and quick-

ly turned out a biography of her brother in which she presented herself as his major influence and closest friend. She even hired a tutor, Rudolf Steiner, to teach her about her brother's philosophy, but after a few months Steiner resigned in disgust, declaring it was impossible to teach her anything about philosophy. After much legal wrangling, editions of many of Nietzsche's previously unpublished works were released, several of his books were translated into English and other languages, and (partly because of his sister's energetic, if self-serving, proselytizing) Nietzsche's intellectual influence began to increase. However, despite her role in publicizing Nietzsche's philosophy, it is now widely agreed that Elisabeth's appalling editing practices caused great harm to Nietzsche's reputation for many years after his death. She had twisted his thoughts to fit her virulent German nationalism and anti-Semitism, and even her own fervent Christianity.

Nietzsche finally died[2] on August 25, 1900, in the German city of Weimar where Elisabeth had relocated the Nietzsche Archive and her helpless brother. For some time before his death, his sister—who was still enthusiastically encouraging a "Nietzsche cult"—had taken to dressing the half-paralyzed Nietzsche in ridiculous "holy" outfits and propping him up on the balcony of his home for adoring groups below to witness, an indignity which Nietzsche would have loathed.

What Was Nietzsche's Overall Philosophical Project?

Nietzsche's philosophical project was essentially a critique of all previous philosophical projects. He held that all philosophers before him, although they may have *believed* that they sought the pure and objective truth, were in fact merely laying out and defending *their own prejudices*—their philosophical theories were really nothing more than a personal statement, "a rarefied and abstract version of their heart's desire." They were often tricked into sincerely believing in

---

1 She and her racist husband Bernhard Förster (whom Nietzsche detested) had been living in Paraguay, South America, where Förster was attempting to establish the pure Aryan colony of "New Germany." However Förster committed suicide in 1889 and, after unsuccessfully trying for a few months to hold the colony together, Elisabeth returned to Germany.

2 Although there is still controversy, most commentators agree that he probably suffered from and succumbed to syphilis.

their own objectivity, through the apparent simplicity and clarity of their statements (such as Descartes'"I think, therefore I am") but this, according to Nietzsche, is a form of deception built into the very nature of language. For example, the claim "I think" is not *at all* clear and simple when one considers it carefully: the concept of thinking is not clear, and even if it could be *made* clear it would (in Nietzsche's view) fail to capture the reality of things. The world itself has no sharp edges and is not divided sharply into thinking and non-thinking things, for example, but instead contains subtle gradations and complexities. In fact, for Nietzsche, there is no stable, enduring, fixed reality lying behind the endless flux of experience; there is only experience and the human attempt to impose an individual perspective upon it.

The result of all this, for Nietzsche, is that the proper business of philosophy has been misunderstood. The point is not to scrutinize our most fundamental concepts, in order to come closer to a 'true description of reality'; the point is to ask what *function* our concepts have—to ask why we have adopted them, whether they are life-enhancing or destructive, whether it is necessary for us to have them at all. The goal is to affirm life, to live it free from superstitious illusions.

In urging this change, Nietzsche (probably[3]) does not simply *give up* on the whole project of acquiring 'knowledge,' but he does radically recast it. His philosophers of the future will realize that there is no such thing as 'objective,' non-perspectival knowledge, since this requires the defunct assumption of a 'real' world underlying our ever-changing experience. Instead they will take a *multi*-perspectival approach to understanding reality; roughly, since *all there is* is a set of different individual perspectives on the world, the

best way to achieve as full a comprehension of reality as possible is simply to strive to adopt *as many perspectives as possible* (through art, metaphor, construction of dramatic personas, and so on). Clearly, this is a task which can never be completed; there can never be a 'final understanding' of the world, and we should not look for such a thing, since there will always be a new perspective around the next corner not previously encountered.

Nietzsche's term for his new breed of philosopher was "free spirits" (*freien Geistes*), and he believed that these free spirits would be superior human beings who would assume a place of authority in a future social and intellectual hierarchy. Nietzsche's free spirits disdain democracy, equality, and social convention; and are "*delivered* from the crowd, the multitude, the majority, where he is allowed to forget the rule of 'humanity,' being the exception to it." Instead of toiling for 'objectivity' and consensus, they will revel in their subjectivity and strive for the *extraordinary*. They will be in touch with their own instinctual life—their "will to power"—and will rise beyond, or "overcome," traditional morality and religion.[4] Traditional ethical systems are merely historical creations, according to Nietzsche, that serve the self-interested purposes of their creators and artificially constrain the horizons of human possibility.

The kind of future morality Nietzsche envisages for his "free spirits" is rather elusive. All his mature life, Nietzsche planned a great work, to be called *The Revaluation of All Values*, which would fill in all of the details, but he never seems to have felt able to get beyond the first step of this project. Furthermore, Nietzsche had a deep distrust of systematization: in his view, the desire to make everything "fit together" and "make sense" is really a desire for death and the end of creativity. As he writes in *Beyond Good and Evil* (section 32):

> The overcoming of morality, or even (in a certain sense) the self-overcoming of morality: let

---

3   It should be pointed out that the interpretation of Nietzsche is a tricky business. His philosophical approach is highly unusual, with no sustained arguments or clear statements of philosophical conclusions, and his writing style is more often polemical or metaphorical than analytic. As a result, even more so than for other philosophers, it is more or less impossible to present a summary of 'Nietzsche's views' with which some commentators will not disagree strongly (and this attempt will be no exception).

---

4   One of Nietzsche's most famous aphorisms occurs in *The Gay Science*, where he proclaims, "God is dead" (Book 3, Section 125). In *Beyond Good and Evil* he calls Christianity "an ongoing suicide of reason."

that be the name for the long, clandestine work that was kept in reserve for the most subtle and honest (and also the most malicious) people of conscience today, living touchstones of the human heart.

Nevertheless, there are things that can be said about Nietzsche's positive view of morality (or, as he might have put it, the value system that lies *beyond* morality). First, Nietzsche approaches morality *naturalistically*. He treats it as a natural phenomenon, observable in certain living things such as human beings, and not as something rooted in a supernatural or metaphysical 'other world.' The emergence of value is to be explained in a roughly Darwinian fashion, as the result of human evolution. The "free spirits" or *Übermensch* (supermen) of our future, with their "revalued" values, will not somehow escape this evolutionary progress, but will be the next stage in the development of the human race.

Second, for Nietzsche, genuine moral worth is not a matter of our conscious intentions or rational choices; it's not a matter of following the right rules. Instead, moral value is somehow built into our unconscious, non-autonomous, non-rational "inner nature"—the *noble spirit*. For Nietzsche, there is a natural hierarchy (*Rangordnung*) among human beings, a natural division between those with "noble" souls and the lesser creatures of the "herd." Only a value-system which recognizes this, he thought, is biologically natural, life-affirming, creative, and vital.

Finally, another famous thesis of Nietzsche's which is morally relevant (though it does not appear in *Beyond Good and Evil*) is the notion of "eternal recurrence": the idea that time is cyclical, repeating itself in an endless loop over and over again. It is not fully clear whether Nietzsche actually *believed* this cosmological claim, but he did use it as a way of expressing what he thought of as a more positive attitude to life than the moral or Christian one. Instead of the value of one's life being judged *at its end*, Nietzsche suggests that we should see our lives as being subject to eternal recurrence, and thus that we should strive to make *each moment* of life one that we would want to repeat over and over again for eternity.

What Is the Structure of This Reading?

Despite its title, *Beyond Good and Evil* is not only—or even primarily—about moral philosophy. It is a general statement of much of Nietzsche's philosophical thought, including reflections on religion, epistemology, art, and politics. Its central theme is that philosophers must strip themselves of their preconceptions and contingently existing values, and become perfectly non-dogmatic; only then can they begin a "philosophy of the future" which will, for the first time in history, approach the truth. One of Nietzsche's central concerns in this work, as in much of his philosophy, is to persuade us to abandon previously accepted 'truths' inherited both from philosophy and religion. He is much less interested in laying out a new moral system with which to replace them.

Beyond Good and Evil is structured as a set of loosely connected aphorisms—tersely phrased statements, each dealing with a single focussed claim. The aphorisms (numbered 1 through 296) are self-standing, and each has its own point to make: but together—like threads in a tapestry or notes in a piece of music—they combine to form an overall picture. Ideally, the book needs to be read as a whole to get its full effect. Nietzsche arranged the aphorisms into nine chapters, eight of which are designed to pursue a particular theme:

1. On the Prejudices of the Philosophers
2. The Free Spirit
3. The Religious Disposition
4. Epigrams and Interludes
5. Towards a Natural History of Morals
6. We Scholars
7. Our Virtues
8. Peoples and Fatherlands
9. What is Noble?

The book concludes with a poem—in the style of a Greek ode—called "From High Mountains."

The three aphorisms reprinted here are from the final chapter, What is Noble? Aphorism 259 urges the "exploitative character" of all living things, 260 describes a distinction, very important for Nietzsche's philosophy, between "master moralities" and "slave moralities," and 261, while primarily a rumination on the nature of vanity, also contains important comments on the *source* of value—juxtaposed with 260 it gives further insight into the nature of "slave morality."

Some Useful Background Information

One of the central concepts in Nietzsche's philosophy is the *will to power*. According to Nietzsche, the will to power is the basic disposition of all life, including human life—it is the principle which provides the ultimate motive force for everything that happens in the natural (or at least the biological) world. Thus, every organic phenomenon—such as plant growth, animal predation, or the establishment of a religion—can be understood, according to Nietzsche, as being brought about by an underlying set of power relationships, where each term of the relation is exerting a "force of will" which strives, with varying success, to expand towards and transform the other terms. For example, a hunting lioness is driven by her will to power to kill antelope, whilst the will to power of her prey impels them to attempt to frustrate her.

Some Common Misconceptions

1. Though Nietzsche makes it amply clear in his text that he admires master morality more than slave morality, there is nevertheless controversy over whether Nietzsche actually *endorsed* master morality. (The textual evidence on this is mixed. For example, in a later book called *The Antichrist* Nietzsche asserts: "When the exceptional human being treats the mediocre more tenderly than himself and his peers, this is not mere courtesy of the heart—it is simply his *duty*.") The revalued values of free spirits might have more in common with master morality than slave morality, but might nevertheless supersede *both* types and be a third form of 'morality' entirely.

2. Nietzsche's "master" and "slave" moralities are ideal types, and cannot be identified in the modern world—where types of morality are jumbled—by simply looking at what contemporary people say and do. Instead, clear paradigms can only be found in the distant historical past: perhaps Homer's *Iliad* as an illustration of master morality, and the *New Testament* to exemplify slave morality.

3. Nietzsche called himself an "immoralist," and was (on the surface at least) centrally concerned with *attacking* morality, but this does not mean Nietzsche encourages people to *behave immorally*—he is certainly not saying that people should do the opposite of what traditional moral systems prescribe. In one of his earlier works, *Daybreak* (1881), he firmly asserts:

   > it goes without saying that I do not deny, presupposing I am no fool, that many actions called immoral ought to be avoided and resisted, or that many called moral ought to be done and encouraged—but *for different reasons than formerly*.

4. Although not a philosophical point, it may be worth mentioning that—although Nietzsche certainly did equate the rise of Judeo-Christianity with the ascendance of "slave morality"—his notorious so-called anti-Semitism, and supposed sympathy for what became ideological themes of the Nazi party, are largely a *myth* created by misunderstandings and deliberate distortions of his work during the fifty years after his death. In fact, Nietzsche had difficulty finding a publisher for *Beyond Good and Evil* because he had split from the publisher of his previous books, Ernst Schmeitzner, in part because Nietzsche *objected* to Schmeitzner's close association with the anti-Semitic movement in Germany and did not want it to seem that he had similar racist sympathies.[5] (On the other hand, it *does* seem that Nietzsche, at least late in his life, was avowedly—and very unpleas-

---

5 In the end, Nietzsche had to pay for printing *Beyond Good and Evil* himself. He needed to sell 300 copies to cover his costs, but after a year only 114 had been purchased (and 66 given away to reviewers). As Nietzsche mournfully put it, "I—may no longer afford the luxury of print."

antly—misogynist, and a fierce opponent of the first wave of tentative female emancipation then moving across Germany.[6])

How Important and Influential Is This Passage?

Beyond Good and Evil is widely considered to be the work which best introduces and encapsulates many of the themes of Nietzsche's mature philosophy. Like the rest of his writings, it had little influence during his sane lifetime, and from 1930 to 1960 Nietzsche (tarred by his supposed association with fascism) was hardly considered worthy of study at all. However, since revisionist scholarship on his work began in earnest in the 1960s, Nietzsche's philosophical reputation has been in the ascendant (especially on the European continent), and *Beyond Good and Evil* has now come to be recognized as one of the most important books of the nineteenth century. As Walter Kaufmann, a leading Nietzsche translator and commentator since 1950, puts it:

> It is possible to say briefly what makes this book great: the prophetic independence of its spirit; the hundreds of doors it opens for the mind, revealing new vistas, problems, and relationships; and what it contributes to our understanding of much of recent thought and literature and history.

The particular sections excerpted here, though merely a small part of the book and not in any way a 'summary' of the whole, are especially interesting for the introduction of Nietzsche's notorious distinction between "master" and "slave" moralities, and for some hints as to the connection of this distinction with his concept of a "will to power."

---

6   On the other, other hand, Nietzsche was one of the minority of University of Basel faculty members who voted in *favor* of allowing women to be admitted to doctoral programs in 1874. Clearly, Nietzsche was a complex character.

Suggestions for Critical Reflection

1. Why could "good manners" never be an adequate basic principle of society? What does Nietzsche mean when he says that this would be to "deny life"? How plausible do you find his reasons for saying so?

2. Nietzsche distinguishes between two possible understandings of the difference between good and bad: "noble" vs. "despicable," and "good" vs. "evil." How important is this difference? Are they both really *moral* distinctions, or is one of them dealing with a different sort of value altogether? If they are different kinds of value, does this hurt Nietzsche's argument or help it?

3. "It is obvious that moral value distinctions everywhere are first attributed to *people* and only later and in a derivative fashion applied to *actions*." Is it? If this claim *is* true, then what does it show about the nature of morality?

4. How *historically* and *psychologically* plausible do you find Nietzsche's description of the difference between the moral outlooks of the powerful and their 'slaves'? If it is plausible as a *description* of moral attitudes, what implications should this have (if any) for the moral views we *ought* to hold? What implications would Nietzsche think it has?

5. "Within a slave mentality a good person must in any event be *harmless*." What do you think of this claim?

6. What do Nietzsche's claims about the nature of vanity reveal about his views on the way we, as individuals, come to *endorse* or *reject* particular values? Are these views plausible?

7. What do you think Nietzsche's view of democracy is? What reasons might he have for his views?

8. What is your judgment of Nietzsche's style: do you think that it is 'philosophical' in the right way? For example, is it a productive way of pursuing the truth (if that is indeed the proper goal of philosophy), or is it in the end (merely?) a sophisticated kind of creative writing?

Suggestions for Further Reading

A readable modern translation of *Beyond Good and Evil*, from which this excerpt is taken, is that by Marion Faber in the Oxford World's Classics series (Oxford University Press, 1998). Two older, well-established translations are those by Walter Kaufmann (Random House, 1966) and R.J. Hollingdale (Penguin, 1973). Nietzsche's famous book *Thus Spake Zarathustra* (published between 1883 and 1885) also lays out the central tenets of his mature philosophy—and thus covers much of the same ground as *Beyond Good and Evil*—but does so in a series of enigmatic parables, in a style intended to parody the Bible. Nietzsche's *On the Genealogy of Morality* (1887) was intended as a "supplement and clarification" of *Beyond Good and Evil*. Meanwhile, *Human, All Too Human* (1878–80), *Daybreak* (1881), and *The Gay Science* (1882) are earlier works in which Nietzsche developed his naturalistic approach to morality. Standard translations of Nietzsche's works are by Walter Kaufmann, but other good ones are available. It is also interesting to consult Arthur Schopenhauer's *The World as Will and Representation* (trans. E.F. Payne, 2 vols., Dover, 1969), a book which had a big influence on Nietzsche's philosophical development. (One can also, incidentally, buy recordings of Nietzsche's musical compositions: for example, *The Music of Friedrich Nietzsche*, Atma Records, 1999.)

There is a vast secondary literature on Nietzsche, but its quality is rather uneven. General accounts of Nietzsche's life and work appear in R.J. Hollingdale's *Nietzsche: The Man and His Philosophy* (Cambridge University Press, 2001), Michael Tanner's *Nietzsche* (Oxford University Press, 1994), and Ronald Hayman's *Nietzsche: A Critical Life* (Oxford University Press, 1980). Nietzsche also published an autobiographical work (published posthumously in 1908) called *Ecce Homo* ("Behold the Man"). Other high-quality, comprehensive works on Nietzsche's philosophy include: Walter Kaufmann, *Nietzsche: Philosopher, Psychologist, Antichrist* (Princeton University Press, 1974); Gilles Deleuze, *Nietzsche and Philosophy* (Cambridge University Press, 1983); Alexander Nehemas, *Nietzsche: Life as Literature* (Harvard University Press, 1985); Richard Schacht, *Nietzsche* (Routledge and Kegan Paul, 1983) and *Making Sense of Nietzsche* (University of Illinois Press, 1994); and David Allison, *Reading the New Nietzsche* (Rowman and Littlefield,

2001). Also helpful are Maudemarie Clark's *Nietzsche on Truth and Philosophy* (Cambridge University Press, 1990), Geoff Waite, *Nietzsche's Corps/e* (Duke University Press, 1996), and Peter Berkowitz, *Nietzsche: The Ethics of an Immoralist* (Harvard University Press, 1995). A *Routledge Philosophy Guidebook to Nietzsche on Morality* by Brian Leiter was published in 2002.

There are also several good collections of articles, including: Richardson and Leiter (eds.), *Nietzsche* (Oxford University Press, 2001); Magnus and Higgins (eds.), *The Cambridge Companion to Nietzsche* (Cambridge University Press, 1996); Peter Sedgwick (ed.), *Nietzsche: A Critical Reader* (Blackwell, 1995); Richard Schacht (ed.), *Nietzsche, Genealogy, Morality* (University of California Press, 1994); Solomon and Higgins (eds.), *Reading Nietzsche* (Oxford University Press, 1990); David Allison (ed.), *The New Nietzsche* (MIT Press, 1985); and Robert Solomon (ed.), *Nietzsche: A Collection of Critical Essays* (University of Notre Dame Press, 1980).

Beyond Good and Evil
§§259–261[7]

259

To refrain from injuring, abusing, or exploiting one another; to equate another person's will with our own: in a certain crude sense this can develop into good manners between individuals, if the preconditions are in place (that is, if the individuals have truly similar strength and standards and if they are united within one single social body). But if we were to try to take this principle further and possibly even make it the *basic principle of society*, it would immediately be revealed for what it is: a will to *deny* life, a principle for dissolution and decline. We must think through

---

7   *Jenseits von Gut und Böse: Vorspiel einer Philosophie der Zukunft* [*Beyond Good and Evil: Prelude to a Philosophy of the Future*] was first published in Leipzig in 1886. This excerpt is reprinted from *Friedrich Nietzsche: Beyond Good and Evil*, a new translation by Marion Faber (Oxford World's Classics, 1998). Copyright © 1998. Reprinted by permission of Oxford University Press.

the reasons for this and resist all sentimental frailty: life itself *in its essence* means appropriating, injuring, overpowering those who are foreign and weaker; oppression, harshness, forcing one's own forms on others, incorporation, and at the very least, at the very mildest, exploitation—but why should we keep using this kind of language, that has from time immemorial been infused with a slanderous intent? Even that social body whose individuals, as we have just assumed above, treat one another as equals (this happens in every healthy aristocracy) must itself, if the body is vital and not moribund, do to other bodies everything that the individuals within it refrain from doing to one another: it will have to be the will to power incarnate, it will want to grow, to reach out around itself, pull towards itself, gain the upper hand—not out of some morality or immorality, but because it is *alive*, and because life simply *is* the will to power. This, however, more than anything else, is what the common European consciousness resists learning; people everywhere are rhapsodizing, even under the guise of science, about future social conditions that will have lost their 'exploitative character'—to my ear that sounds as if they were promising to invent a life form that would refrain from all organic functions. 'Exploitation' is not part of a decadent or imperfect, primitive society: it is part of the *fundamental nature* of living things, as its fundamental organic function; it is a consequence of the true will to power, which is simply the will to life.

Assuming that this is innovative as theory—as reality it is the *original fact* of all history: let us at least be this honest with ourselves!

260

While perusing the many subtler and cruder moral codes that have prevailed or still prevail on earth thus far, I found that certain traits regularly recurred in combination, linked to one another—until finally two basic types were revealed and a fundamental difference leapt out at me. There are *master moralities* and *slave moralities*.[8] I would add at once that in

all higher and more complex cultures, there are also apparent attempts to mediate between the two moralities, and even more often a confusion of the two and a mutual misunderstanding, indeed sometimes even their violent juxtaposition—even in the same person, within one single breast. Moral value distinctions have emerged either from among a masterful kind, pleasantly aware of how it differed from those whom it mastered, or else from among the mastered, those who were to varying degrees slaves or dependants. In the first case, when it is the masters who define the concept 'good', it is the proud, exalted states of soul that are thought to distinguish and define the hierarchy. The noble person keeps away from those beings who express the opposite of these elevated, proud inner states: he despises them. Let us note immediately that in this first kind of morality the opposition 'good' and 'bad' means about the same thing as 'noble' and 'despicable'—the opposition 'good' and '*evil*' has a different origin. The person who is cowardly, or anxious or petty or concerned with narrow utility is despised; likewise the distrustful person with his constrained gaze, the self-disparager, the craven kind of person who endures maltreatment, the importunate flatterer, and above all the liar: all aristocrats hold the fundamental conviction that the common people are liars. 'We truthful ones'—that is what the ancient Greek nobility called themselves. It is obvious that moral value distinctions everywhere are first attributed to *people* and only later and in a derivative fashion applied to *actions*: for that reason moral historians commit a crass error by starting with questions such as: 'Why do we praise an empathetic action?' The noble type of person feels *himself* as determining value—he does not need approval, he judges that 'what is harmful to me is harmful per se,'[9] he knows that he is the one who causes things to be revered in the first place, he *creates values*. Everything that he knows of himself he reveres: this kind of moral code is self-glorifying. In the foreground is a feeling of fullness, of overflowing power, of happiness in great tension, an awareness of a wealth that

---

8   This distinction was first introduced—though not given these now-famous names—in Nietzsche's *Human, All Too Human* (1878), and plays an important role in Es-

say One of his next book, *On the Genealogy of Morals* (1887).

9   *Per se* is Latin for "in itself" or "intrinsically."

would like to bestow and share—the noble person will also help the unfortunate, but not, or not entirely, out of pity, but rather from the urgency created by an excess of power. The noble person reveres the power in himself, and also his power over himself, his ability to speak and to be silent, to enjoy the practice of severity and harshness towards himself and to respect everything that is severe and harsh. 'Wotan[10] placed a harsh heart within my breast,' goes a line in an old Scandinavian saga: that is how it is written from the heart of a proud Viking—and rightly so. For this kind of a person is proud *not* to be made for pity; and so the hero of the saga adds a warning: 'If your heart is not harsh when you are young, it will never become harsh.' The noble and brave people who think like this are the most removed from that other moral code which sees the sign of morality in pity or altruistic behaviour or *désintéressement*;[11] belief in ourselves, pride in ourselves, a fundamental hostility and irony towards 'selflessness'—these are as surely a part of a noble morality as caution and a slight disdain towards empathetic feelings and 'warm hearts'.

It is the powerful who *understand* how to revere, it is their art form, their realm of invention. Great reverence for old age and for origins (all law is based upon this twofold reverence), belief in ancestors and prejudice in their favour and to the disadvantage of the next generation—these are typical in the morality of the powerful; and if, conversely, people of 'modern ideas' believe in progress and 'the future' almost by instinct and show an increasing lack of respect for old age, that alone suffices to reveal the ignoble origin of these 'ideas'. Most of all, however, the master morality is foreign and embarrassing to current taste because of the severity of its fundamental principle: that we have duties only towards our peers, and that we may treat those of lower rank, anything foreign, as we think best or 'as our heart dictates' or in any event

'beyond good and evil'[12]—pity and the like should be thought of in this context. The ability and duty to feel enduring gratitude or vengefulness (both only within a circle of equals), subtlety in the forms of retribution, a refined concept of friendship, a certain need for enemies (as drainage channels for the emotions of envy, combativeness, arrogance—in essence, in order to be a good *friend*): these are the typical signs of a noble morality, which, as we have suggested, is not the morality of 'modern ideas' and is therefore difficult to sympathize with these days, also difficult to dig out and uncover.

It is different with the second type of morality, *slave morality*. Assuming that the raped, the oppressed, the suffering, the shackled, the weary, the insecure engage in moralizing, what will their moral value judgements have in common? They will probably express a pessimistic suspicion about the whole human condition, and they might condemn the human being along with his condition. The slave's eye does not readily apprehend the virtues of the powerful: he is sceptical and distrustful, he is *keenly* distrustful of everything that the powerful revere as 'good'—he would like to convince himself that even their happiness is not genuine. Conversely, those qualities that serve to relieve the sufferers' existence are brought into relief and bathed in light: this is where pity, a kind, helpful hand, a warm heart, patience, diligence, humility, friendliness are revered—for in this context, these qualities are most useful and practically the only means of enduring an oppressive existence. Slave morality is essentially a morality of utility. It is upon this hearth that the famous opposition 'good' and '*evil*' originates—power and dangerousness, a certain fear-inducing, subtle strength that keeps contempt from surfacing, are translated by experience into evil. According to slave morality, then, the 'evil' person evokes fear; according to master morality, it is exactly the 'good' person who evokes fear and wants to evoke it, while the 'bad' person is felt to be despicable. The opposition comes to a head when, in terms of slave morality, a hint of condescension (it may be slight and well intentioned) clings even to

---

10   Also called Odin, Wotan was the supreme god of Scandinavian and German mythology: creator of the world and god of war, wisdom, poetry, magic, and the dead. He was usually depicted as a one-eyed, wise old man, accompanied by two great ravens. Wednesday— "Wotan's day"—is named for him.

11   French—"disinterestedness."

---

12   This phrase, in German, has religious as well as moral overtones. *Jenseits* not only means "beyond" but also refers to the afterlife.

those whom this morality designates as 'good', since within a slave mentality a good person must in any event be *harmless*: he is good-natured, easily deceived, perhaps a bit stupid, a *bonhomme*.[13] Wherever slave morality gains the upper hand, language shows a tendency to make a closer association of the words 'good' and 'stupid'.

A last fundamental difference: the longing for *freedom*, an instinct for the happiness and nuances of feeling free, is as necessarily a part of slave morals and morality as artistic, rapturous reverence and devotion invariably signal an aristocratic mentality and judgement.

From this we can immediately understand why *passionate* love (our European speciality) absolutely must have a noble origin: the Provençal poet-knights are acknowledged to have invented it, those splendid, inventive people of the '*gai saber*'[14] to whom Europe owes so much—virtually its very self.

261

Among the things that a noble person finds most difficult to understand is vanity: he will be tempted to deny its existence, even when a different kind of person thinks that he grasps it with both hands. He has trouble imagining beings who would try to elicit a good opinion about themselves that they themselves do not hold (and thus do not 'deserve', either) and who then themselves nevertheless *believe* this good opinion. To him, that seems in part so tasteless and irreverent towards one's self, and in part so grotesquely irrational that he would prefer to consider vanity an anomaly and in most of the cases when it is mentioned, doubt that it exists. He will say, for example: 'I may be

---

13   French—a simple, good man.
14   "Gay science" or "joyful art" in the dialect of Provence, in south-eastern France. One of Nietzsche's earlier books is called *The Gay Science* (1882). The phrase was coined in the early fourteenth century to refer to the art of the troubadours: lyric poets and musicians— mostly noblemen, and sometimes even kings—who flourished in southern France, northern Italy, and eastern Spain from the end of the eleventh to the close of the thirteenth century. Their songs typically dealt with themes of chivalry and courtly love.

wrong about my worth, but on the other hand require that others recognize the worth that I assign—but that is not vanity (rather it is arrogance, or more often what is called "humility", and also "modesty").' Or he will say: 'There are many reasons to be glad about other people's good opinion of me, perhaps because I revere and love them and am happy about every one of their joys, or else perhaps because their good opinion underscores and strengthens my belief in my own private good opinion, or perhaps because the good opinion of others, even in the cases where I do not share it, is nevertheless useful or promises to be useful to me—but none of that is vanity.' It takes compulsion, particularly with the help of history, for the noble person to realize that in every sort of dependent social class, from time immemorial, a common person *was* only what he was *thought to be*—completely unused to determining values himself, he also attributed to himself no other value than what his masters attributed to him (creating values is truly the *master's privilege*). We may understand it as the result of a tremendous atavism[15] that even now, the ordinary person first *waits* for someone else to have an opinion about him, and then instinctively submits to it—and by no means merely to 'good' opinions, but also to bad or improper ones (just think, for example, how most pious women esteem or under-esteem themselves in accordance with what they have learned from their father confessors, or what pious Christians in general learn from their Church). Now, in fact, in conformity with the slow emergence of a democratic order of things (this in turn caused by mixing the blood of masters and slaves), the originally noble and rare impulse to ascribe one's own value to oneself and to 'think well' of oneself, is more and more encouraged and widespread: but always working against it is an older, broader, and more thoroughly entrenched tendency—and when it comes to 'vanity', this older tendency becomes master of the newer. The vain person takes pleasure in *every* good opinion that he hears about himself (quite irrespective of any prospect of its

---

15   A throwback: a trait which resembles those possessed by remote ancestors, and which has returned after being absent for many generations. (The word comes from *atavus*, which is Latin for one's great-grandfather's grandfather.)

utility, and likewise irrespective of truth or falsehood), just as he suffers at any bad opinion: for he submits himself to both, he *feels* submissive to both, from that old submissive instinct that breaks out in him.

It is the 'slave' in the blood of the vain person, a remnant of the slave's craftiness (and how much of the 'slave' is still left, for example, in women today!) that tries to *seduce* him to good opinions of himself; and it is likewise the slave who straightway kneels down before these opinions, as if he himself were not the one who had called them forth.

So I repeat: vanity is an atavism.

VIRGINIA HELD

"Feminist Transformations of Moral Theory"

Who Is Virginia Held?

Virginia P. Held received her PhD from Columbia University and is now a Distinguished Professor in the philosophy program of the Graduate Center at the City University of New York. She is the author of three books—*Feminist Morality: Transforming Culture, Society and Politics* (University of Chicago Press, 1993), *Rights and Goods: Justifying Social Action* (Free Press, 1984), and *The Public Interest and Individual Interests* (Basic Books, 1972)—and many articles on social and political philosophy, ethics, and feminist philosophy.

What Is the Structure of This Reading?

Held begins her article by arguing that, historically, all ethical theories have been built upon assumptions biased in favor of men and against women. She illustrates this by exploring the implications of the historically important dichotomies of reason vs. emotion and public vs. private, and by discussing the history of our concept of the self or personhood. She then goes on, in the next three sections, to discuss feminist approaches to the transformation of each of these three conceptual areas. In particular, she emphasizes a feminist re-valuing of *emotional responses* in ethics, the importance of *mothering* (which breaks through the public-private distinction), and the notion of the self as being importantly constituted by its *relations* to others.

Suggestions for Critical Reflection

1. Do you agree with Held that there has historically been a characteristically 'male point of view'? Do you think there is today? If so, what does this show about ethics? (Similarly, do you think there is a characteristically *female* point of view, and what would that show?) Do you think it is possible to remove the male bias from ethical philosophy without merely replacing it with a female bias?

2. Held argues that the male bias in the history of ethics requires, for its correction, a *wholesale transformation* of ethical theory: she does not think women should want "simply to be accorded entry as equals into the enterprise of morality as so far developed." How persuasively does Held make this case? If—unlike Held—you think traditional ethical theory might be repaired rather than transformed, how might one go about removing the gender bias that Held detects in, for example, utilitarianism or Kantian ethics?

3. Held writes, "The associations between ... philosophical concepts and gender cannot be merely dropped, and the concepts retained regardless of gender, because gender has been built into them in such a way that without it, they will have to be different concepts." What do you make of this argument? What implications does it have for philosophy today?

4. Held suggests that our very concept of *human* has historically been infected with male-biased assumptions. Does this seem plausible? If so, how important a philosophical discovery is this? In what ways should the existing concept be changed (or with what sort of concept should it be replaced)?

5. Should "a mother's sacrifice for her child" be considered an act of moral super-erogation (something it is good to do but not a moral duty)? Why, or why not? What implications, if any, does this have for ethical theory?

6. Do you think Held's portrayal of the history of philosophy is, on the whole, accurate?

7. Held draws a contrast between an "ethic of care" and an "ethic of justice," and suggests the former is more appropriate to women's experience than the latter. Does this claim seem right to you? If so, in what ways—if any— does that make an ethic of care a *better moral theory* than an ethic of justice? What potential benefits and pitfalls can you see in the notion of an ethic of care?

8. Held argues that women are no more biologically determined than men, and, in particular, that the activity of mothering is no less 'human' than, say, politics or trade. What implications

does this have for our view of human relationships, and for morality?

9. Feminist ethicists often pay particular attention to a domain of people intermediate between the self and 'everyone': i.e., they focus on our moral relationships to "particular others," our friends, family, and other individuals with whom we have personal relationships. How important, and how defensible, is this shift in focus? *Do* we have special moral responsibilities to particular people—which we do not have to others—just because, for example, they are our friends? If so, is feminist ethics the only theory able to accommodate this insight?

10. Held describes a model of the self which treats it as at least partly constituted by its *relationships* with other people. Does Held mean to suggest that only *women* have a "relational self" or that men do as well? If this model is correct, what are its implications for ethics? For example, how does it affect the problem of moral motivation? What would it do to our conception of justice, rights, and duties? How does it change the nature and value of human autonomy?

Suggestions for Further Reading

In addition to the books mentioned above, several of Held's articles are on topics related to issues she discusses in "Feminist Transformations of Moral Theory": for example, "On the Meaning of Trust," *Ethics* 78 (1968); "Can a Random Collection of Individuals Be Morally Responsible?" *Journal of Philosophy* 67 (1970); "Egalitarianism and Relevance," *Ethics* 81 (1971); "Feminism and Moral Theory," in Eva Feder Kittay (ed.), *Women and Moral Theory* (Rowman and

Littlefield, 1987); "Birth and Death," *Ethics* 99 (1989); "The Meshing of Care and Justice," *Hypatia* 10 (1995); "Feminist Reconceptualizations in Ethics," in Janet Kourany (ed.), *Philosophy in a Feminist Voice* (Princeton University Press, 1998); and "Feminist Ethical Theory," in Klaus Brinkmann (ed.), *Proceedings of the Twentieth World Congress of Philosophy, Volume 1: Ethics* (Philosophy Documentation Center, 1999). There is also a book of specially written essays on Held's work called *Norms and Values: Essays on the Work of Virginia Held*, edited by Joram Haber and Mark Halfon (Rowman and Littlefield, 1998).

On feminist ethics generally, the following collections of articles are a useful starting point: *On Feminist Ethics and Politics*, ed. Claudia Card (University of Kansas Press, 1999); *Justice and Care: Essential Readings in Feminist Ethics*, ed. Virginia Held (Westview Press, 1995); *Explorations in Feminist Ethics*, ed. Cole and Coultrap-McQuinn (Indiana University Press, 1992); *Feminist Ethics*, ed. Claudia Card (University of Kansas Press, 1991); and *Science, Morality and Feminist Theory*, ed. Hanen and Nielsen (University of Calgary Press, 1987). Other interesting articles include: Samantha Brennan, "Recent Work in Feminist Ethics," *Ethics* 109 (1999); Cheshire Calhoun, "Justice, Care, Gender Bias," *Journal of Philosophy* 85 (1988); Monique Deveaux, "New Directions in Feminist Ethics," *European Journal of Philosophy* 3 (1995); Christine James, "Feminist Ethics, Mothering, and Caring," *Kinesis* 22 (1995); Kuhse, Singer, and Rickard, "Reconciling Impartial Morality and a Feminist Ethic of Care," *Journal of Value Inquiry* 32 (1998); Alison Jaggar, "Feminist Ethics: Some Issues for the Nineties," *Journal of Social Philosophy* 20 (1989); Alison Jaggar, "Globalizing Feminist Ethics," *Hypatia* 13 (1998); and Margaret Walker, "Moral Understandings: Alternative 'Epistemology' for a Feminist Ethics," *Hypatia* 4 (1989).

Finally, some books: *Care, Autonomy, and Justice: Feminism and the Ethic of Care*, by Grace Clement (Westview Press, 1999); *Caring: Gender-Sensitive Ethics*, by Peta Bowden (Routledge, 1997); *Moral Understanding: A Feminist Study in Ethics*, by Margaret Walker (Routledge, 1997); *Feminine and Feminist Ethics*, by Rosemarie Tong (Wadsworth, 1993); *Justice, Gender and the Family*, by Susan Moller Okin (Basic Books, 1989); *Caring: A Feminine Approach to Ethics and Moral*

Education, by Nel Noddings (University of California Press, 1984); and *In A Different Voice: Psychological Theory and Women's Development*, by Carol Gilligan (Harvard University Press, 1982).

"Feminist Transformations of Moral Theory"[1]

The history of philosophy, including the history of ethics, has been constructed from male points of view, and has been built on assumptions and concepts that are by no means gender-neutral.[2] Feminists characteristically begin with different concerns and give different emphases to the issues we consider than do nonfeminist approaches. And, as Lorraine Code expresses it, "starting points and focal points shape the impact of theoretical discussion."[3] Within philosophy, feminists often start with, and focus on, quite different issues than those found in standard philosophy and ethics, however "standard" is understood. Far from providing mere additional insights which can be incorporated into traditional theory, feminist explorations often require radical transformations of existing fields of inquiry and theory.[4] From a feminist point of view, moral theory along with almost all theory will have to be transformed to take adequate account of the experience of women.

I shall in this paper begin with a brief examination of how various fundamental aspects of the history

---

1   This article was originally published in *Philosophy and Phenomenological Research*, Volume 50 (Supplement Autumn 1990), pp. 321–344. Reproduced with permission of Wiley-Blackwell Inc.

2   [Author's note] See e.g., Cheshire Calhoun, "Justice, Care, Gender Bias," *The Journal of Philosophy* 85 (September, 1988): 451–63.

3   [Author's note] Lorraine Code, "Second Persons," in *Science, Morality and Feminist Theory*, ed. Marsha Hanen and Kai Nielsen (Calgary: University of Calgary Press, 1987), p. 360.

4   [Author's note] See e.g., *Revolutions in Knowledge: Feminism in the Social Sciences*, ed. Sue Rosenberg Zalk and Janice Gordon-Kelter (Boulder: Westview Press, forthcoming).

of ethics have not been gender-neutral. And I shall discuss three issues where feminist rethinking is transforming moral concepts and theories.

The History of Ethics

Consider the ideals embodied in the phrase "the man of reason." As Genevieve Lloyd has told the story, what has been taken to characterize the man of reason may have changed from historical period to historical period, but in each, the character ideal of the man of reason has been constructed in conjunction with a rejection of whatever has been taken to be characteristic of the feminine. "Rationality," Lloyd writes, "has been conceived as transcendence of the 'feminine,' and the 'feminine' itself has been partly constituted by its occurrence within this structure."[5]

This has of course fundamentally affected the history of philosophy and of ethics. The split between reason and emotion is one of the most familiar of philosophical conceptions. And the advocacy of reason "controlling" unruly emotion, of rationality guiding responsible human action against the blindness of passion, has a long and highly influential history, almost as familiar to non-philosophers as to philosophers. We should certainly now be alert to the ways in which reason has been associated with male endeavor, emotion with female weakness, and the ways in which this is of course not an accidental association. As Lloyd writes, "From the beginnings of philosophical thought, femaleness was symbolically associated with what Reason supposedly left behind—the dark powers of the earth goddesses, immersion in unknown forces associated with mysterious female powers. The early Greeks saw women's capacity to conceive as connecting them with the fertility of Nature. As Plato later expressed the thought, women 'imitate the earth.'"[6]

Reason, in asserting its claims and winning its status in human history, was thought to have to conquer the female forces of Unreason. Reason and clarity of thought were early associated with maleness, and as Lloyd notes, "what had to be shed in develop-

ing culturally prized rationality was, from the start, symbolically associated with femaleness."[7] In later Greek philosophical thought, the form/matter distinction was articulated,[8] and with a similar hierarchical and gendered association. Maleness was aligned with active, determinate, and defining form; femaleness with mere passive, indeterminate, and inferior matter. Plato, in the *Timaeus*,[9] compared the defining aspect of form with the father, and indefinite matter with the mother; Aristotle also compared the form/matter distinction with the male/female distinction. To quote Lloyd again, "This comparison … meant that the very nature of knowledge was implicitly associated with the extrusion of what was symbolically associated with the feminine."[10]

The associations, between Reason, form, knowledge, and maleness, have persisted in various guises, and have permeated what has been thought to be moral knowledge as well as what has been thought to be scientific knowledge, and what has been thought to be the practice of morality. The associations between the philosophical concepts and gender cannot be merely dropped, and the concepts retained regardless of gender, because gender has

---

5   [Author's note] Genevieve Lloyd, *The Man of Reason: 'Male' and 'Female' in Western Philosophy* (Minneapolis: University of Minnesota Press, 1984), p. 104.

6   [Author's note] Ibid., p. 2.

7   [Author's note] Ibid., p. 3.

8   For Plato and Aristotle, the matter of something (roughly) is the stuff it is made of, while its form is the organization, shape, or pattern which gives that thing its particular nature. A simple example would be a clay bowl, where the matter—a lump of clay—has been given the form of a bowl by the potter.

9   A dialogue by Plato (427–347 BCE), which describes how a divine (though not omnipotent) craftsman transformed the chaotic materials of the universe into an ordered and harmonious cosmos by consulting the unchanging Forms and using them as his template for the construction of (rather shoddily inadequate and fluctuating) earthly images of those paradigms. See the Plato reading in this chapter for more information on the Forms.

10   [Author's note] Ibid., p. 4. For a feminist view of how reason and emotion in the search for knowledge might be reevaluated, see Alison M. Jaggar, "Love and Knowledge: Emotion in Feminist Epistemology," *Inquiry* 32 (June, 1989): 151–76.

been built into them in such a way that without it, they will have to be different concepts. As feminists repeatedly show, if the concept of "human" were built on what we think about "woman" rather than what we think about "man," it would be a very different concept. Ethics, thus, has not been a search for universal, or truly human guidance, but a gender-biased enterprise.

Other distinctions and associations have supplemented and reinforced the identification of reason with maleness, and of the irrational with the female; on this and other grounds "man" has been associated with the human, "woman" with the natural. Prominent among distinctions reinforcing the latter view has been that between the public and the private, because of the way they have been interpreted. Again, these provide as familiar and entrenched a framework as do reason and emotion, and they have been as influential for non-philosophers as for philosophers. It has been supposed that in the public realm, man transcends his animal nature and creates human history. As citizen, he creates government and law; as warrior, he protects society by his willingness to risk death; and as artist or philosopher, he overcomes his human mortality. Here, in the public realm, morality should guide human decision. In the household, in contrast, it has been supposed that women merely "reproduce" life as natural, biological matter. Within the household, the "natural" needs of man for food and shelter are served, and new instances of the biological creature that man is are brought into being. But what is distinctively human, and what transcends any given level of development to create human progress, are thought to occur elsewhere.

This contrast was made highly explicit in Aristotle's conceptions of polis[11] and household; it has continued to affect the basic assumptions of a remarkably broad swath of thought ever since. In ancient Athens, women were confined to the household; the public sphere was literally a male domain. In more recent history, though women have been permitted to venture into public space, the associations of the public, historically male sphere with the distinctively human, and of the household, historically a female sphere, with the merely natural and repetitive, have persisted. These associations have deeply affected moral theory, which has often supposed the transcendent, public domain to be relevant to the foundations of morality in ways that the natural behavior of women in the household could not be. To take some recent and representative examples, David Heyd, in his discussion of supererogation,[12] dismisses a mother's sacrifice for her child as an example of the supererogatory because it belongs, in his view, to "the sphere of natural relationships and instinctive feelings (which lie outside morality)."[13] J.O. Urmson had earlier taken a similar position. In his discussion of supererogation, Urmson said, "Let us be clear that we are not now considering cases of natural affection, such as the sacrifice made by a mother for her child; such cases may be said with some justice not to fall under the concept of morality...."[14] And in a recent article called "Distrusting Economics," Alan Ryan argues persuasively about the questionableness of economics and other branches of the social sciences built on the assumption that human beings are ra-

---

11 The *polis* is the ancient Greek city-state. See the Aristotle reading in this chapter for more on his interwoven views on politics and society.

12 "Supererogation" means acting in a way which is not strictly required by moral duty but which goes beyond it, as in cases of exceptional generosity or heroism (from Latin—"beyond what is asked"). The key idea is that a supererogatory act is morally good, but to fail to perform it would not be morally bad. Such acts are of interest partly because several major moral theories— such as utilitarianism, Kantianism, and some versions of Protestantism—appear to be unable to recognize the existence of supererogation.

13 [Author's note] David Heyd, *Supererogation: Its Status in Ethical Theory* (New York: Cambridge University Press, 1982), p. 134.

14 [Author's note] J.O. Urmson, "Saints and Heroes," in *Essays in Moral Philosophy*, ed. A.I. Melden (Seattle: University of Washington Press, 1958), p. 202. I am indebted to Marcia Baron for pointing out this and the previous example in her "Kantian Ethics and Supererogation," *The Journal of Philosophy* 84 (May, 1987): 137–62.

tional, self-interested calculators; he discusses various examples of non-self-interested behavior, such as of men in wartime, which show the assumption to be false, but nowhere in the article is there any mention of the activity of mothering, which would seem to be a fertile locus for doubts about the usual picture of rational man.[15] Although Ryan does not provide the kind of explicit reason offered by Heyd and Urmson for omitting the context of mothering from consideration as relevant to his discussion, it is difficult to understand the omission without a comparable assumption being implicit here, as it so often is elsewhere. Without feminist insistence on the relevance for morality of the experience in mothering, this context is largely ignored by moral theorists. And yet, from a gender-neutral point of view, how can this vast and fundamental domain of human experience possibly be imagined to lie "outside morality"?

The result of the public/private distinction, as usually formulated, has been to privilege the points of view of men in the public domains of state and law, and later in the marketplace, and to discount the experience of women. Mothering has been conceptualized as a primarily biological activity, even when performed by humans, and virtually no moral theory in the history of ethics has taken mothering, as experienced by women, seriously as a source of moral insight, until feminists in recent years have begun to.[16] Women have been seen as emotional rather than as rational beings, and thus as incapable of full moral personhood. Women's behavior has been interpreted as either "natural" and driven by instinct, and thus as irrelevant to morality and to the construction of moral principles, or it has been interpreted as, at best, in need

of instruction and supervision by males better able to know what morality requires and better able to live up to its demands.

The Hobbesian[17] conception of reason is very different from the Platonic or Aristotelian conceptions before it, and from the conceptions of Rousseau or Kant or Hegel later; all have in common that they ignore and disparage the experience and reality of women. Consider Hobbes' account of man in the state of nature contracting with other men to establish society. These men hypothetically come into existence fully formed and independent of one another, and decide on entering or staying outside of civil society. As Christine Di Stefano writes, "What we find in Hobbes's account of human nature and political order is a vital concern with the survival of a self conceived in masculine terms…. This masculine dimension of Hobbes's atomistic egoism is powerfully underscored in his state of nature, which is effectively built on the foundation of denied maternity."[18] In *The Citizen*, where Hobbes gave his first systematic exposition of the state of nature, he asks us to "consider men as if but even now sprung out of the earth, and suddenly, like mushrooms, come to full maturity, without all kind of engagement with each other."[19] As Di Stefano says, it is a most incredible and problematic feature of Hobbes's state of nature that the men in it "are not born of, much less nurtured by, women, or anyone else."[20] To abstract from the complex web of human reality an abstract man for rational perusal, Hobbes has, Di Stefano continues, "expunged human reproduction and early nurturance, two of the most basic

---

15 [Author's note] Alan Ryan, "Distrusting Economics," *New York Review of Books* (May 18, 1989): 25–27. For a different treatment, see *Beyond Self-Interest*, ed. Jane Mansbridge (Chicago: University of Chicago Press, 1990).

16 [Author's note] See especially *Mothering: Essays in Feminist Theory*, ed. Joyce Trebilcot (Totowa, New Jersey: Rowman and Allanheld, 1984); and Sara Ruddick, *Maternal Thinking: Toward a Politics of Peace* (Boston: Beacon Press, 1989).

17 That found in the philosophy of Thomas Hobbes (1588–1679). See the notes to the selection from Hobbes in Chapter 8.

18 [Author's note] Christine Di Stefano, "Masculinity as Ideology in Political Theory: Hobbesian Man Considered," *Women's Studies International Forum* (Special Issue: *Hypatia*), Vol. 6, No. 6 (1983): 633–44, p. 637.

19 [Author's note] Thomas Hobbes, *The Citizen: Philosophical Rudiments Concerning Government and Society*, ed. B. Gert (Garden City, New York: Doubleday, 1972 (1651)), p. 205.

20 [Author's note] Di Stefano, op. cit., p. 638.

and typically female-identified features of distinctively human life, from his account of basic human nature. Such a strategy ensures that he can present a thoroughly atomistic subject...."[21] From the point of view of women's experience, such a subject or self is unbelievable and misleading, even as a theoretical construct. The Leviathan,[22] Di Stefano writes, "is effectively comprised of a body politic of orphans who have reared themselves, whose desires are situated within and reflect nothing but independently generated movement.... These essential elements are natural human beings conceived along masculine lines."[23]

Rousseau, and Kant, and Hegel, paid homage to the emotional power, the aesthetic sensibility, and the familial concerns, respectively, of women. But since in their views morality must be based on rational principle, and women were incapable of full rationality, or a degree or kind of rationality comparable to that of men, women were deemed, in the view of these moralists, to be inherently wanting in morality. For Rousseau,[24] women must be trained from childhood to submit to the will of men lest their sexual power lead both men and women to disaster. For Kant,[25] women were thought incapable of achieving full moral personhood, and women lose all charm if they try to behave like men by engaging in rational pursuits. For Hegel,[26] women's moral concern for their

families could be admirable in its proper place, but is a threat to the more universal aims to which men, as members of the state, should aspire.[27]

These images, of the feminine as what must be overcome if knowledge and morality are to be achieved, of female experience as naturally irrelevant to morality, and of women as inherently deficient moral creatures, are built into the history of ethics. Feminists examine these images, and see that they are not the incidental or merely idiosyncratic suppositions of a few philosophers whose views on many topics depart far from the ordinary anyway. Such views are the nearly uniform reflection in philosophical and ethical theory of patriarchal attitudes pervasive throughout human history. Or they are exaggerations even of ordinary male experience, which exaggerations then reinforce rather than temper other patriarchal conceptions and institutions. They distort the actual experience and aspirations of many men as well as of women. Annette Baier recently speculated about why it is that moral philosophy has so seriously overlooked the trust between human beings that in her view is an utterly central aspect of moral life. She noted that "the great moral theorists in our tradition not only are all men, they are mostly men who had minimal adult dealings with (and so were then minimally influenced by) women."[28] They were for the most part "clerics, misogynists, and puritan bachelors," and thus it is not surprising that they focus their philosophical attention

---

21 [Author's note] Ibid.

22 Hobbes's term for the state, in his book *Leviathan* (1651). A leviathan is something monstrously large and powerful—from the name of a sea monster in the Old Testament—and the term was in part supposed to reflect the state's absolute power over its citizens.

23 [Author's note] Ibid., p. 639.

24 Jean-Jacques Rousseau (1712–1778) was a French-speaking philosopher, born in Geneva, whose early-Romantic writings on human nature were highly influential in the eighteenth and nineteenth centuries; perhaps his most famous work is *The Social Contract* (1762).

25 Immanuel Kant (1724–1804); see the selections in this chapter for more on his philosophy.

26 Georg Wilhelm Friedrich Hegel (1770–1831), who had a huge influence on nineteenth-century German

philosophy and who saw history as progressing towards a fully self-conscious and rationally-organized community or state.

27 [Author's note] For examples of relevant passages, see *Philosophy of Woman: Classical to Current Concepts*, ed. Mary Mahowald (Indianapolis: Hackett, 1978); and *Visions of Women*, ed. Linda Bell (Clifton, New Jersey: Humana, 1985). For discussion, see Susan Moller Okin, *Women in Western Political Thought* (Princeton, New Jersey: Princeton University Press, 1979); and Lorenne Clark and Lynda Lange, eds., *The Sexism of Social and Political Theory* (Toronto: University of Toronto Press, 1979).

28 [Author's note] Annette Baier, "Trust and Anti-Trust," *Ethics* 96 (1986): 231–60, pp. 247–48.

"so single-mindedly on cool, distanced relations between more or less free and equal adult strangers...."[29]

As feminists, we deplore the patriarchal attitudes that so much of philosophy and moral theory reflect. But we recognize that the problem is more serious even than changing those attitudes. For moral theory as so far developed is incapable of correcting itself without an almost total transformation. It cannot simply absorb the gender that has been "left behind," even if both genders would want it to. To continue to build morality on rational principles opposed to the emotions and to include women among the rational will leave no one to reflect the promptings of the heart, which promptings can be moral rather than merely instinctive. To simply bring women into the public and male domain of the polis will leave no one to speak for the household. Its values have been hitherto unrecognized, but they are often moral values. Or to continue to seek contractual restraints on the pursuits of self-interest by atomistic individuals, and to have women join men in devotion to these pursuits, will leave no one involved in the nurturance of children and cultivation of social relations, which nurturance and cultivation can be of greatest moral import.

There are very good reasons for women not to want simply to be accorded entry as equals into the enterprise of morality as so far developed. In a recent survey of types of feminist moral theory, Kathryn Morgan notes that "many women who engage in philosophical reflection are acutely aware of the masculine nature of the profession and tradition, and feel their own moral concerns as women silenced or trivialized in virtually all the official settings that define the practice."[30] Women should clearly not agree, as the price of admission to the masculine realm of traditional morality, to abandon our own moral concerns as women.

And so we are groping to shape new moral theory. Understandably, we do not yet have fully worked out feminist moral theories to offer. But we can suggest some directions our project of developing such theories is taking. As Kathryn Morgan points out, there is not likely to be a "star" feminist moral theorist on the order of a Rawls or Nozick:[31] "There will be no individual singled out for two reasons. One reason is that vital moral and theoretical conversations are taking place on a large dialectical scale as the feminist community struggles to develop a feminist ethic. The second reason is that this community of feminist theoreticians is calling into question the very model of the individualized autonomous self presupposed by a star-centered male-dominated tradition.... We experience it as a common labour, a common task."[32]

The dialogues that are enabling feminist approaches to moral theory to develop are proceeding. As Alison Jaggar makes clear in her useful overview of them, there is no unitary view of ethics that can be identified as "feminist ethics." Feminist approaches to ethics share a commitment to "rethinking ethics with a view to correcting whatever forms of male bias it may contain."[33] While those who develop these approaches are "united by a shared project, they diverge widely in their views as to how this project is to be accomplished."[34]

Not all feminists, by any means, agree that there are distinctive feminist virtues or values. Some are especially skeptical of the attempt to give positive value to such traditional "feminine virtues" as a willingness to nurture, or an affinity with caring, or reluctance to seek independence. They see this approach as playing into the hands of those who would confine women to traditional roles.[35] Other feminists are skeptical

---

29   [Author's note] Ibid.

30   [Author's note] Kathryn Pauly Morgan, "Strangers in a Strange Land: Feminists Visit Relativists" in *Perspectives on Relativism*, ed. D. Odegaard and Carole Stewart (Toronto: Agathon Press, 1990).

31   John Rawls, Robert Nozick: see Chapter 8 for information on these contemporary philosophers.

32   [Author's note] Kathryn Morgan, "Women and Moral Madness," in *Science, Morality and Feminist Theory*, ed. Hanen and Nielsen, p. 223.

33   [Author's note] Alison M. Jaggar, "Feminist Ethics: Some Issues for the Nineties," *Journal of Social Philosophy* 20 (Spring/Fall 1989), p. 91.

34   [Author's note] Ibid.

35   [Author's note] One well-argued statement of this position is Barbara Houston, "Rescuing Womanly Virtues: Some Dangers of Moral Reclamation," in *Science, Morality and Feminist Theory*, ed. Hanen and Nielsen.

of all claims about women as such, emphasizing that women are divided by class and race and sexual orientation in ways that make any conclusions drawn from "women's experience" dubious.[36]

Still, it is possible, I think, to discern various important focal points evident in current feminist attempts to transform ethics into a theoretical and practical activity that could be acceptable from a feminist point of view. In the glimpse I have presented of bias in the history of ethics, I focused on what, from a feminist point of view, are three of its most questionable aspects: 1) the split between reason and emotion and the devaluation of emotion; 2) the public/private distinction and the relegation of the private to the natural; and 3) the concept of the self as constructed from a male point of view. In the remainder of this article, I shall consider further how some feminists are exploring these topics. We are showing how their previous treatment has been distorted, and we are trying to reenvision the realities and recommendations with which these aspects of moral theorizing do and should try to deal.

I. Reason and Emotion

In the area of moral theory in the modern era, the priority accorded to reason has taken two major forms. A) On the one hand has been the Kantian, or Kantian-inspired search for very general, abstract, deontological,[37] universal moral principles by which rational beings should be guided. Kant's Categorical Imperative is a foremost example: it suggests that all moral problems can be handled by applying an impartial, pure, rational principle to particular cases. It requires that we try to see what the general features of the problem before us are, and that we apply an abstract principle, or rules derivable from it, to this problem. On this view, this procedure should be adequate for all moral decisions. We should thus be able to act as reason recommends, and resist yielding to emotional inclinations and desires in conflict with our rational wills.

B) On the other hand, the priority accorded to reason in the modern era has taken a Utilitarian form. The Utilitarian approach, reflected in rational choice theory, recognizes that persons have desires and interests, and suggests rules of rational choice for maximizing the satisfaction of these. While some philosophers in this tradition espouse egoism,[38] especially of an intelligent and long-term kind, many do not. They begin, however, with assumptions that what are morally relevant are gains and losses of utility to theoretically isolatable individuals, and that the outcome at which morality should aim is the maximization of the utility of individuals. Rational calculation about such an outcome will, in this view, provide moral recommendations to guide all our choices. As with the Kantian approach, the Utilitarian approach relies on abstract general principles or rules to be applied to particular cases. And it holds that although emotion is, in fact, the source of our desires for certain objectives, the task of morality should be to instruct us on how to pursue those objectives most rationally. Emotional attitudes toward moral issues themselves interfere with rationality and should be disregarded. Among the questions Utilitarians can ask can be questions about which emotions to cultivate, and which desires to try to change, but these questions are to be handled in the terms of rational calculation, not of what our feelings suggest.

Although the conceptions of what the judgments of morality should be based on, and of how reason should guide moral decision, are different in Kantian and in Utilitarian approaches, both share a reliance on a highly abstract, universal principle as the appropriate source of moral guidance, and both share the view that moral problems are to be solved by the application of such an abstract principle to particular cases. Both share an admiration for the rules of reason

---

36 [Author's note] See e.g., Elizabeth V. Spelman, *Inessential Woman: Problems of Exclusion in Feminist Thought* (Boston: Beacon Press, 1988). See also Sarah Lucia Hoagland, *Lesbian Ethics: Toward New Value* (Palo Alto, California: Institute of Lesbian Studies, 1989); and Katie Geneva Cannon, *Black Womanist Ethics* (Atlanta, Georgia: Scholars Press, 1988).

37 Based on the notion of a duty or a right (rather than on the value of some kind of state of affairs or type of character).

38 That one either is, or ought to be, exclusively motivated by self-interest.

to be appealed to in moral contexts, and both denigrate emotional responses to moral issues.

Many feminist philosophers have questioned whether the reliance on abstract rules, rather than the adoption of more context-respectful approaches, can possibly be adequate for dealing with moral problems, especially as women experience them.[39] Though Kantians may hold that complex rules can be elaborated for specific contexts, there is nevertheless an assumption in this approach that the more abstract the reasoning applied to a moral problem, the more satisfactory. And Utilitarians suppose that one highly abstract principle, The Principle of Utility, can be applied to every moral problem no matter what the context.

A genuinely universal or gender-neutral moral theory would be one which would take account of the experience and concerns of women as fully as it would take account of the experience and concerns of men. When we focus on the experience of women, however, we seem to be able to see a set of moral concerns becoming salient that differs from those of traditional or standard moral theory. Women's experience of moral problems seems to lead us to be especially concerned with actual relationships between embodied persons, and with what these relationships seem to require. Women are often inclined to attend to rather than to dismiss the particularities of the context in which a moral problem arises. And we often pay attention to feelings of empathy and caring to suggest what we ought to do rather than relying as fully as possible on abstract rules of reason.

Margaret Walker, for instance, contrasts feminist moral "understanding" with traditional moral "knowledge." She sees the components of the former as involving "attention, contextual and narrative appreciation, and communication in the event of moral deliberation."[40] This alternative moral epistemology holds that "the adequacy of moral understanding decreases as its form approaches generality through abstraction."[41]

The work of psychologists such as Carol Gilligan and others has led to a clarification of what may be thought of as tendencies among women to approach moral issues differently. Rather than interpreting moral problems in terms of what could be handled by applying abstract rules of justice to particular cases, many of the women studied by Gilligan tended to be more concerned with preserving actual human relationships, and with expressing care for those for whom they felt responsible. Their moral reasoning was typically more embedded in a context of particular others than was the reasoning of a comparable group of men.[42] One should not equate tendencies women in fact display with feminist views, since the former may well be the result of the sexist, oppressive conditions in which women's lives have been lived. But many feminists see our own consciously considered experience as lending confirmation to the view that what has come to be called "an ethic of care" needs to be developed. Some think it should supercede "the ethic of justice" of traditional or standard moral theory. Others think it should be integrated with the ethic of justice and rules.

In any case, feminist philosophers are in the process of reevaluating the place of emotion in morality in at least two respects. First, many think morality requires the development of the moral emotions, in contrast to moral theories emphasizing the primacy of reason. As Annette Baier notes, the rationalism typical of traditional moral theory will be challenged when we pay attention to the role of parent. "It might be

---

39   [Author's note] For an approach to social and political as well as moral issues that attempts to be context-respectful, see Virginia Held, *Rights and Goods. Justifying Social Action* (Chicago: University of Chicago Press, 1989).

40   [Author's note] Margaret Urban Walker, "Moral Understandings: Alternative 'Epistemology' for a Feminist Ethics," *Hypatia* 4 (Summer, 1989): 15–28, p. 19.

41   [Author's note] Ibid., p. 20. See also Iris Marion Young, "Impartiality and the Civic Public. Some Implications of Feminist Critiques of Moral and Political Theory," in Seyla Benhabib and Drucilla Cornell, *Feminism as Critique* (Minneapolis: University of Minnesota Press, 1987).

42   [Author's note] See especially Carol Gilligan, *In a Different Voice. Psychological Theory and Women's Development* (Cambridge, Massachusetts: Harvard University Press, 1988); and Eva Feder Kittay and Diana T. Meyers eds., *Women and Moral Theory* (Totowa, New Jersey: Rowman and Allanheld, 1987).

important," she writes, "for father figures to have rational control over their violent urges to beat to death the children whose screams enrage them, but more than control of such nasty passions seems needed in the mother or primary parent, or parent-substitute, by most psychological theories. They need to love their children, not just to control their irritation."[43] So the emphasis in many traditional theories on rational control over the emotions, "rather than on cultivating desirable forms of emotion,"[44] is challenged by feminist approaches to ethics.

Secondly, emotion will be respected rather than dismissed by many feminist moral philosophers in the process of gaining moral understanding. The experience and practice out of which feminist moral theory can be expected to be developed will include embodied feeling as well as thought. In a recent overview of a vast amount of writing, Kathryn Morgan states that "feminist theorists begin ethical theorizing with embodied, gendered subjects who have particular histories, particular communities, particular allegiances, and particular visions of human flourishing. The starting point involves valorizing what has frequently been most mistrusted and despised in the western philosophical tradition...."[45] Among the elements being reevaluated are feminine emotions. The "care" of the alternative feminist approach to morality appreciates rather than rejects emotion. The caring relationships important to feminist morality cannot be understood in terms of abstract rules or moral reasoning. And the "weighing" so often needed between the conflicting claims of some relationships and others cannot be settled by deduction or rational calculation. A feminist ethic will not just acknowledge emotion, as do Utilitarians, as giving us the objectives toward which moral rationality can direct us. It will embrace emotion as providing at least a partial basis for morality itself, and for moral understanding.

Annette Baier stresses the centrality of trust for an adequate morality.[46] Achieving and maintaining trusting, caring relationships is quite different from acting in accord with rational principles, or satisfying the individual desires of either self or other. Caring, empathy, feeling with others, being sensitive to each other's feelings, all may be better guides to what morality requires in actual contexts than may abstract rules of reason, or rational calculation, or at least they may be necessary components of an adequate morality.

The fear that a feminist ethic will be a relativistic "situation ethic" is misplaced. Some feelings can be as widely shared as are rational beliefs, and feminists do not see their views as reducible to "just another attitude."[47] In her discussion of the differences between feminist medical ethics and nonfeminist medical ethics, Susan Sherwin gives an example of how feminists reject the mere case by case approach that has come to predominate in nonfeminist medical ethics. The latter also rejects the excessive reliance on abstract rules characteristic of standard ethics, and in this way resembles feminist ethics. But the very focus on cases in isolation from one another deprives this approach from attending to general features in the institutions and practices of medicine that, among other faults, systematically contribute to the oppression of women.[48] The difference of approach can be seen in the treatment of issues in the new reproductive technologies, where feminists consider how the new technologies may further decrease the control of women over reproduction.

This difference might be thought to be one of substance rather than of method, but Sherwin shows the implications for method also. With respect to reproductive technologies one can see especially clearly the deficiencies of the case by case approach: what needs to be considered is not only choice in the purely individualistic interpretation of the case by case approach, but control at a more general level and how it affects the structure of gender in society. Thus, a

---

43 [Author's note] Annette Baier, "The Need for More Than Justice," in *Science, Morality and Feminist Theory*, ed. Hanen and Nielsen, p. 55.

44 [Author's note] Ibid.

45 [Author's note] Kathryn Pauly Morgan, "Strangers in a Strange Land...," p. 2.

46 [Author's note] Annette Baier, "Trust and Anti-Trust."

47 [Author's note] See especially Kathryn Pauly Morgan, "Strangers in a Strange Land...."

48 [Author's note] Susan Sherwin, "Feminist and Medical Ethics: Two Different Approaches to Contextual Ethics," *Hypatia* 4 (Summer, 1989): 57–72.

feminist perspective does not always counsel attention to specific case vs. appeal to general considerations, as some sort of methodological rule. But the general considerations are often not the purely abstract ones of traditional and standard moral theory, they are the general features and judgments to be made about cases in actual (which means, so far, patriarchal) societies. A feminist evaluation of a moral problem should never omit the political elements involved; and it is likely to recognize that political issues cannot be dealt with adequately in purely abstract terms any more than can moral issues.

The liberal tradition in social and moral philosophy argues that in pluralistic society[49] and even more clearly in a pluralistic world, we cannot agree on our visions of the good life, on what is the best kind of life for humans, but we can hope to agree on the minimal conditions for justice, for coexistence within a framework allowing us to pursue our visions of the good life.[50] Many feminists contend that the commitment to justice needed for agreement *in actual conditions* on even minimal requirements of justice is as likely to demand relational feelings as a rational recognition of abstract principles. Human beings can and do care, and are capable of caring far more than at present, about the sufferings of children quite distant from them, about the prospects for future generations, and about the well-being of the globe. The liberal tradition's mutually disinterested rational individualists would seem unlikely to care enough to take the actions needed to achieve moral decency at a global level, or environmental sanity for decades hence, as they would seem unable to represent caring relationships within the family and among friends. As Annette Baier puts it, "A moral theory, it can plausibly be claimed, cannot regard concern for new and future persons as

an optional charity left for those with a taste for it. If the morality the theory endorses is to sustain itself, it must provide for its own continuers, not just take out a loan on a carefully encouraged maternal instinct or on the enthusiasm of a self-selected group of environmentalists, who make it their business or hobby to be concerned with what we are doing to mother earth."[51]

The possibilities as well as the problems (and we are well aware of some of them) in a feminist reenvisioning of emotion and reason need to be further developed, but we can already see that the views of nonfeminist moral theory are unsatisfactory.

II. The Public and the Private

The second questionable aspect of the history of ethics on which I focused was its conception of the distinction between the public and the private. As with the split between reason and emotion, feminists are showing how gender-bias has distorted previous conceptions of these spheres, and we are trying to offer more appropriate understandings of "private" morality and "public" life.

Part of what feminists have criticized has been the way the distinction has been accompanied by a supposition that what occurs in the household occurs as if on an island beyond politics, whereas the personal is highly affected by the political power beyond, from legislation about abortion to the greater earning power of men, to the interconnected division of labor by gender both within and beyond the household, to the lack of adequate social protection for women against domestic violence.[52] Of course we recognize that the family is not identical to the state, and we need concepts for thinking about the private or personal, and

49 A society which values (or at least tolerates) a range of different, and even mutually incompatible, views among its members of what constitutes a "good life." For example, toleration of different religions and sexual orientations is a form of pluralism.

50 [Author's note] See especially the work of John Rawls and Ronald Dworkin; see also Charles Larmore, *Patterns of Moral Complexity* (Cambridge: Cambridge University Press, 1987).

51 [Author's note] Annette Baier, "The Need for More Than Justice," pp. 53–54.

52 [Author's note] See e.g., Linda Nicholson, *Gender and History. The Limits of Social Theory in the Age of the Family* (New York: Columbia University Press, 1986); and Jean Bethke Elshtain, *Public Man, Private Woman* (Princeton, New Jersey: Princeton University Press, 1981). See also Carole Pateman, *The Sexual Contract* (Stanford, California: Stanford University Press, 1988).

the public or political. But they will have to be very different from the traditional concepts.

Feminists have also criticized deeper assumptions about what is distinctively human and what is "natural" in the public and private aspects of human life, and what is meant by "natural" in connection with women.[53] Consider the associations that have traditionally been built up: the public realm is seen as the distinctively human realm in which man transcends his animal nature, while the private realm of the household is seen as the natural region in which women merely reproduce the species.[54] These associations are extraordinarily pervasive in standard concepts and theories, in art and thought and cultural ideals, and especially in politics.

Dominant patterns of thought have seen women as primarily mothers, and mothering as the performance of a primarily biological function. Then it has been supposed that while engaging in political life is a specifically human activity, women are engaged in an activity which is not specifically human. Women accordingly have been thought to be closer to nature than men,[55] to be enmeshed in a biological function involving processes more like those in which other animals are involved than like the rational discussion of the citizen in the polis, or the glorious battles of noble soldiers, or the trading and rational contracting of "economic man." The total or relative exclusion of women from the domain of public life has then been seen as either inevitable or appropriate.

53 [Author's note] See e.g., Susan Moller Okin, *Women in Western Political Thought*. See also Alison M. Jaggar, *Feminist Politics and Human Nature* (Totowa, New Jersey: Rowman and Allanheld, 1983).

54 [Author's note] So entrenched is this way of thinking that it was even reflected in Simone de Beauvoir's pathbreaking feminist text *The Second Sex*, published in 1949. Here, as elsewhere, feminists have had to transcend our own early searches for our own perspectives.

55 [Author's note] See e.g., Sherry B. Ortner, "Is Female to Male as Nature is to Culture?" in *Woman, Culture, and Society*, ed. Michelle Z. Rosaldo and Louise Lamphere (Stanford: Stanford University Press, 1974).

The view that women are more determined by biology than are men is still extraordinarily prevalent. It is as questionable from a feminist perspective as many other traditional misinterpretations of women's experience. Human mothering is an extremely different activity from the mothering engaged in by other animals. The work and speech of men is recognized as very different from what might be thought of as the "work" and "speech" of other animals. Human mothering is fully as different from animal mothering. Of course all human beings are animal as well as human. But to whatever extent it is appropriate to recognize a difference between "man" and other animals, so would it be appropriate to recognize a comparable difference between "woman" and other animals, and between the activities—including mothering—engaged in by women and the behavior of other animals.

Human mothering shapes language and culture, it forms human social personhood, it develops morality. Animal behavior can be highly impressive and complex, but it does not have built into it any of the consciously chosen aims of morality. In creating human social persons, human mothering is different in kind from merely propagating a species. And human mothering can be fully as creative an activity as those activities traditionally thought of as distinctively human, because to create *new* persons, and new types of *persons*, can surely be as creative as to make new objects, products, or institutions. *Human* mothering is no more "natural" or "primarily biological" than is any other human activity.

Consider nursing an infant, often thought of as the epitome of a biological process with which mothering is associated and women are identified. There is no reason to think of human nursing as any more simply biological than there is to think of, say, a businessmen's lunch this way. Eating is a biological process, but what and how and with whom we eat are thoroughly cultural. Whether and how long and with whom a woman nurses an infant, are also human, cultural matters. If men transcend the natural by conquering new territory and trading with their neighbors and making deals over lunch to do so, women can transcend the natural by choosing not to nurse their children when they could, or choosing to nurse them when their culture tells them not to, or singing songs to their infants as they nurse, or nursing in restaurants to overcome the prejudices against doing so, or thinking human thoughts as they nurse, and so forth. Human culture surrounds and characterizes the activity of nursing as it does the activities of eating, or governing, or writing, or thinking.

We are continually being presented with images of the humanly new and creative as occurring in the public realm of the polis, or the realms of marketplace or of art and science outside the household. The very term 'reproduction' suggests mere repetition, the "natural" bringing into existence of repeated instances of the same human animal. But human reproduction is not repetition.[56] This is not to suggest that bringing up children in the interstices[57] of patriarchal society, in society structured by institutions supporting male dominance, can achieve the potential of transformation latent in the activity of human mothering. But the activity of creating new social persons and new kinds of persons is potentially the most transformative human activity of all. And it suggests that morality should concern itself first of all with this activity, with what its norms and practices ought to be, and with how the institutions and arrangements throughout society and the world ought to be structured to facilitate the right kinds of development of the best kinds of new persons. The flourishing of children ought to be at the very center of moral and social and political and economic and legal thought, rather than, as at present, at the periphery, if attended to at all.

Revised conceptions of public and private have significant implications for our conceptions of human beings and relationships between them. Some feminists suggest that instead of seeing human relationships in terms of the impersonal ones of the "public" sphere, as standard political and moral theory has so often done, we might consider seeing human relationships in terms of those experienced in the sphere of the "private," or of what these relationships could be imagined to be like in post-patriarchal society.[58] The traditional approach is illustrated by those who generalize, to other regions of human life than the economic, assumptions about "economic man" in contractual relations with other men. It sees such impersonal, contractual relations as paradigmatic, even, on some views, for moral theory. Many feminists, in contrast, consider the realm of what has been misconstrued as the "private" as offering guidance to what human beings and their relationships should be like even in regions beyond those of family and friendship. Sara Ruddick looks at the implications of the practice of mothering for the conduct of peace politics.[59] Marilyn Friedman and Lorraine Code consider friendship, especially as women understand it, as a possible model for human relationships.[60] Others see society as non-contractual rather than as contractual.

Clearly, a reconceptualization is needed of the ways in which every human life is entwined with personal and with social components. Feminist theorists are contributing imaginative work to this project.

III. The Concept of Self

Let me turn now to the third aspect of the history of ethics which I discussed and which feminists are re-envisioning: the concept of self. One of the most important emphases in a feminist approach to morality is the recognition that more attention must be paid to the domain between, on the one hand, the self as ego, as self-interested individual, and, on the other hand, the universal, everyone, others in general.[61] Traditionally, ethics has dealt with these poles of individual self and universal all. Usually, it has called for impartiality against the partiality of the egoistic self; sometimes

---

56   [Author's note] For further discussion and an examination of surrounding associations, see Virginia Held, "Birth and Death," in *Ethics* 99 (January 1989): 362–88.

57   Intervening spaces, cracks.

58   [Author's note] See e.g., Virginia Held, "Non-contractual Society: A Feminist View," in *Science, Morality and Feminist Theory*, ed. Hanen and Nielsen.

59   [Author's note] Sara Ruddick, *Maternal Thinking*.

60   [Author's note] See Marilyn Friedman, "Feminism and Modern Friendship: Dislocating the Community," *Ethics* 99 (January 1989): 275–90; and Lorraine Code, "Second Persons."

61   [Author's note] See Virginia Held, "Feminism and Moral Theory," in *Women and Moral Theory*, ed. Kittay and Meyers.

it has defended egoism against claims for a universal perspective. But most standard moral theory has hardly noticed as morally significant the intermediate realm of family relations and relations of friendship, of group ties and neighborhood concerns, especially from the point of view of women. When it has noticed this intermediate realm it has often seen its attachments as threatening to the aspirations of the Man of Reason, or as subversive of "true" morality. In seeing the problems of ethics as problems of reconciling the interests of the self with what would be right or best for "everyone," standard ethics has neglected the moral aspects of the concern and sympathy which people actually feel for particular others, and what moral experience in this intermediate realm suggests for an adequate morality.

The region of "particular others" is a distinct domain, where what can be seen to be artificial and problematic are the very egoistic "self" and the universal "all others" of standard moral theory. In the domain of particular others, the self is already constituted to an important degree by relations with others, and these relations may be much more salient and significant than the interests of any individual self in isolation.[62] The "others" in the picture, however, are not the "all others," or "everyone," of traditional moral theory; they are not what a universal point of view or a view from nowhere could provide.[63] They are, characteristically, actual flesh and blood other human beings for whom we have actual feelings and with whom we have real ties.

From the point of view of much feminist theory, the individualistic assumptions of liberal theory and of most standard moral theory are suspect. Even if we would be freed from the debilitating aspects of dominating male power to "be ourselves" and to pursue our own interests, we would, as persons, still have ties to other persons, and we would at least in part be constituted by such ties. Such ties would be part of what we inherently are. We are, for instance, the daughter or son of given parents, or the mother or father of given children, and we carry with us at least some ties to the racial or ethnic or national group within which we developed into the persons we are.

If we look, for instance, at the realities of the relation between mothering person (who can be female or male) and child, we can see that what we value in the relation cannot be broken down into individual gains and losses for the individual members in the relation. Nor can it be understood in universalistic terms. Self-development apart from the relation may be much less important than the satisfactory development of the relation. What matters may often be the health and growth of and the development of the relation-and-its-members in ways that cannot be understood in the individualistic terms of standard moral theories designed to maximize the satisfaction of self-interest. The universalistic terms of moral theories grounded in what would be right for "all rational beings" or "everyone" cannot handle, either, what has moral value in the relation between mothering person and child.

Feminism is of course not the only locus of criticism of the individualistic and abstractly universalistic features of liberalism and of standard moral theory. Marxists[64] and communitarians[65] also see the self as

62 [Author's note] See Seyla Benhabib, "The Generalized and the Concrete Other. The Kohlberg-Gilligan Controversy and Moral Theory," in *Women and Moral Theory*, ed. Kittay and Meyers. See also Caroline Whitbeck, "Feminist Ontology: A Different Reality," in *Beyond Domination*, ed. Carol Gould (Totowa, New Jersey: Rowman and Allanheld, 1983).

63 [Author's note] See Thomas Nagel, *The View from Nowhere* (New York: Oxford University Press, 1986). For a feminist critique, see Susan Bordo, "Feminism, Postmodernism, and Gender-Skepticism," in *Feminism/Postmodernism*, ed. Linda Nicholson (New York: Routledge, 1989).

64 See Chapter 8 for more on Marx.

65 Communitarian political theories tend to stress the social role of a shared sense of common purpose and tradition and mutual ties of kinship and affection, as opposed to the typically "liberal" conception of society as constructed out of a set of contractual relations between otherwise unattached individuals. In North America, communitarianism is especially associated with a wave of criticism of liberalism in the 1980s, spearheaded by such philosophers as Alasdair MacIntyre, Michael Sandel, Charles Taylor, and Michael Walzer.

constituted by its social relations. But in their usual form, Marxist and communitarian criticisms pay no more attention than liberalism and standard moral theory to the experience of women, to the context of mothering, or to friendship as women experience it.[66] Some recent nonfeminist criticisms, such as offered by Bernard Williams, of the impartiality required by standard moral theory, stress how a person's identity may be formed by personal projects in ways that do not satisfy universal norms, yet ought to be admired. Such views still interpret morality from the point of view of an individual and his project, not a social relationship such as that between mothering person and child. And recent nonfeminist criticisms in terms of traditional communities and their moral practices, as seen for instance in the work of Stuart Hampshire and Alasdair MacIntyre, often take traditional gender roles as given, or provide no basis for a radical critique of them.[67] There is no substitute, then, for feminist exploration of the area between ego and universal, as women experience this area, or for the development of a refocused concept of relational self that could be acceptable from a feminist point of view.

Relationships can be evaluated as trusting or mistrustful, mutually considerate or selfish, harmonious or stressful, and so forth. Where trust and considera-tion are appropriate, which is not always, we can find ways to foster them. But understanding and evaluating relationships, and encouraging them to be what they can be at their best, require us to look at relationships between actual persons, and to see what both standard moral theories and their nonfeminist critics often miss. To be adequate, moral theories must pay attention to the neglected realm of particular others in the actual relationships and actual contexts of women's experi-ence. In doing so, problems of individual self-interest vs. universal rules may recede to a region more like background, out-of-focus insolubility or relative un-importance. The salient problems may then be seen to be how we ought best to guide or to maintain or to reshape the relationships, both close and more distant, that we have, or might have, with actual other human beings. Particular others can be actual children in need in distant continents, or the anticipated children of generations not yet even close to being born. But they are not "all rational beings" or "the greatest number," and the self that is in relationships with particular others and is composed to a significant degree by such relations is not a self whose ego must be pitted against abstract, universal claims. Developing the needed guidance for maintaining and reshaping rela-tionships presents enormous problems, but a first step is to recognize how traditional and nonfeminist moral theory of both an individualistic and communitarian kind falls short in providing it.

The concept of the relational self which is evolv-ing within feminist thought is leading to interesting inquiry in many fields. An example is the work be-ing done at the Stone Center at Wellesley College.[68]

---

66   [Author's note] On Marxist theory, see e.g., *Women and Revolution*, ed. Lydia Sargent (Boston: South End Press, 1981); Alison Jaggar, *Feminist Politics and Human Nature*; and Ann Ferguson, *Blood at the Root. Motherhood, Sexuality and Male Dominance* (London: Pandora, 1989). On communitarian theory, see Marilyn Friedman, "Feminism and Modern Friendship...," and also her paper "The Social Self and the Partial-ity Debates," presented at the Society for Women in Philosophy meeting in New Orleans, April 1990.

67   [Author's note] Bernard Williams, *Moral Luck* (Cam-bridge: Cambridge University Press, 1981); *Public and Private Morality*, ed. Stuart Hampshire (Cambridge: Cambridge University Press, 1978); Alasdair Ma-cIntyre, *After Virtue. A Study in Moral Theory* (Notre Dame, Indiana: University of Notre Dame Press, 1981). For discussion see Susan Moller Okin, *Justice, Gender, and the Family* (New York: Basic Books, 1989).

68   [Author's note] On the Stone Center concept of the self see especially Jean Baker Miller, "The Development of Women's Sense of Self," Wellesley, Massachusetts: Stone Center Working Paper No. 12; Janet Surrey, "The 'Self-in-Relation': A Theory of Women's Develop-ment" (Wellesley, Massachusetts: Stone Center Work-ing Paper No. 13); and Judith Jordan, "The Meaning of Mutuality" (Wellesley, Massachusetts: Stone Center Working Paper No. 23). For a feminist but critical view of this work, see Marcia Westkott, "Female Re-lationality and the Idealized Self," *American Journal of Psychoanalysis* 49 (September, 1989): 239–50.

Psychologists there have posited a self-in-relation theory and are conducting empirical inquiries to try to establish how the female self develops. They are working with a theory that a female relational self develops through a mutually empathetic mother-daughter bond.

The work has been influenced by Jean Baker Miller's re-evaluation of women's psychological qualities as strengths rather than weaknesses. In her book *Toward a New Psychology of Women*, published in 1976, Miller identified women's "great desire for affiliation" as one such strength.[69] Nancy Chodorow's *The Reproduction of Mothering*, published in 1978, has also had a significant influence on the work done at the Stone Center, as it has on much feminist inquiry.[70] Chodorow argued that a female affiliative self is reproduced by a structure of parenting in which mothers are the primary caretakers, and sons and daughters develop differently in relation to a parent of the same sex, or a parent of different sex, as primary caretaker. Daughters develop a sense of self by identifying themselves with the mother; they come to define themselves as connected to or in relation with others. Sons, in contrast, develop a sense of self by differentiating themselves from the mother; they come to define themselves as separate from or unconnected to others. An implication often drawn from Chodorow's work is that parenting should be shared equally by fathers and mothers so that children of either sex can develop with caretakers of both same and different sex.

In 1982, Carol Gilligan, building on both Miller and Chodorow, offered her view of the "different voice" with which girls and women express their understanding of moral problems.[71] Like Miller and Chodorow, Gilligan valued tendencies found especially in women to affiliate with others and to interpret their moral responsibilities in terms of their relation-

ships with others. In all, the valuing of autonomy and individual independence over care and concern for relationships, was seen as an expression of male bias. The Stone Center has tried to elaborate and to study a feminist conception of the relational self. In a series of Working Papers, researchers and clinicians have explored the implications of this conception for various issues in women's psychology (e.g., power, anger, work inhibitions, violence, eating patterns) and for therapy.

The self as conceptualized in these studies is seen as having both a need for recognition and a need to understand the other, and these needs are seen as compatible. They are created in the context of mother-child interaction, and are satisfied in a mutually empathetic relationship. This does not require a loss of self, but a relationship of mutuality in which self and other both express intersubjectivity. Both give and take in a way that not only contributes to the satisfaction of their needs as individuals, but also affirms the "larger relational unit" they compose.[72] Maintaining this larger relational unit then becomes a goal, and maturity is seen not in terms of individual autonomy but in terms of competence in creating and sustaining relations of empathy and mutual intersubjectivity.

The Stone Center psychologists contend that the goal of mutuality is rarely achieved in adult male-female relationships because of the traditional gender system. The gender system leads men to seek autonomy and power over others, and to undervalue the caring and relational connectedness that is expected of women. Women rarely receive the nurturing and empathetic support they provide. Accordingly, these psychologists look to the interaction that occurs in mother-daughter relationships as the best source of insight into the promotion of the healthy, relational self. This research provides an example of exploration into a refocused, feminist conception of the self, and into empirical questions about its development and implications.

In a quite different field, that of legal theory, a refocused concept of self is leading to reexamina-

---

69   [Author's note] Jean Baker Miller, *Toward a New Psychology of Women* (Boston: Beacon Press, 1976).

70   [Author's note] Nancy Chodorow, *The Reproduction of Mothering: Psychoanalysis and the Sociology of Gender* (Berkeley: University of California Press, 1978).

71   [Author's note] Carol Gilligan, *In a Different Voice*.

72   [Author's note] J. V. Jordan, "The Meaning of Mutuality," p. 2.

tions of such concepts as property and autonomy and the role these have played in political theory and in constitutional law. For instance, the legal theorist Jennifer Nedelsky questions the imagery that is dominant in constitutional law and in our conceptions of property: the imagery of a bounded self, a self contained within boundaries and having rights to property within a wall allowing it to exclude others and to exclude government. The boundary metaphor, she argues, obscures and distorts our thinking about human relationships and what is valuable in them. "The boundedness of selves," Nedelsky writes, "may seem to be a self-evident truth, but I think it is a wrong-headed and destructive way of conceiving of the human creatures law and government are created for."[73] In the domain of the self's relation to the state, the central problem, she argues, is not "maintaining a sphere into which the state cannot penetrate, but fostering autonomy when people are already within the sphere of state control or responsibility."[74] What we can from a feminist perspective think of as the male "separative self" seems on an endless quest for security behind such walls of protection as those of property. Property focuses the quest for security "in ways that are paradigmatic of the efforts of separative selves to protect themselves through boundaries...."[75] But of course property is a social construction, not a thing; it requires the involvement of the state to define what it is and to defend it. What will provide what it seeks to offer will not be boundaries and exclusions, but constructive relationships.

In an article on autonomy, Nedelsky examines the deficiencies in the concept of self with which so much of our political and legal thinking about autonomy has been developed. She well recognizes that of course feminists are centrally concerned with freedom and autonomy, with enabling women to live our own lives. But we need a language with which to express these concerns which will also reflect "the equally important feminist precept that any good theorizing will start with people in their social contexts. And the notion of social context must take seriously its constitutive quality; social context cannot simply mean that individuals will, of course, encounter one another."[76] The problem, then, is how to combine the claim of the constitutiveness of social relations with the value of self-determination. Liberalism has been the source of our language of freedom and self-determination, but it lacks the ability to express comprehension of "the reality we know: the centrality of relationships in constituting the self."[77]

In developing a new conception of autonomy that avoids positing self-sufficient and thus highly artificial individuals, Nedelsky points out first that "the capacity to find one's own law can develop only in the context of relations with others (both intimate and more broadly social) that nurture this capacity, and second, that the 'content' of one's own law is comprehensible only with reference to shared social norms, values, and concepts."[78] She sees the traditional liberal view of the self as implying that the most perfectly autonomous man is the most perfectly isolated, and finds this pathological.

Instead of developing autonomy through images of walls around one's property, as does the Western liberal tradition and as does U.S. constitutional law, Nedelsky suggests that "the most promising model, symbol, or metaphor for autonomy is not property, but childrearing. There we have encapsulated the emergence of autonomy through relationship with others.... Interdependence [is] a constant component of autonomy."[79] And she goes on to examine how

73   [Author's note] Jennifer Nedelsky, "Law, Boundaries, and the Bounded Self," *Representations* 30 (Spring, 1990): 162–89, at 167.

74   [Author's note] Ibid., p. 169.

75   [Author's note] Ibid., p. 181.

76   [Author's note] Jennifer Nedelsky, "Reconceiving Autonomy: Sources, Thoughts and Possibilities," *Yale Journal of Law and Feminism* 1 (Spring, 1989): 7–36, p. 9. See also Diana T. Meyers, *Self, Society, and Personal Choice* (New York: Columbia University Press, 1989).

77   [Author's note] Ibid.

78   [Author's note] Ibid, p. 11.

79   [Author's note] Ibid., p. 12. See also Mari J. Matsuda, "Liberal Jurisprudence and Abstracted Visions of Human Nature," *New Mexico Law Review* 16 (Fall, 1986): 613–30.

law and bureaucracies can foster autonomy within relationships between citizen and government. This does not entail extrapolating from intimate relations to largescale ones; rather, the insights gained from experience with the context of childrearing allow us to recognize the relational aspects of autonomy. In work such as Nedelsky's we can see how feminist reconceptualizations of the self can lead to the rethinking of fundamental concepts even in terrains such as law, thought by many to be quite distant from such disturbances.

To argue for a view of the self as relational does not mean that women need to remain enmeshed in the ties by which they are constituted. In recent decades, especially, women have been breaking free of relationships with parents, with the communities in which they grew up, and with men, relationships in which they defined themselves through the traditional and often stifling expectations of others.[80] These quests for self have often involved wrenching instability and painful insecurity. But the quest has been for a new and more satisfactory relational self, not for the self-sufficient individual of liberal theory. Many might share the concerns expressed by Alison Jaggar that disconnecting ourselves from particular others, as ideals of individual autonomy seem to presuppose we should, might make us incapable of morality, rather than capable of it, if, as so many feminists think, "an ineliminable part of morality consists in responding emotionally to particular others."[81]

I have examined three topics on which feminist philosophers and feminists in other fields are thinking anew about where we should start and how we should focus our attention in ethics. Feminist reconceptualizations and recommendations concerning the relation between reason and emotion, the distinction between public and private, and the concept of the self, are providing insights deeply challenging to standard moral theory. The implications of this work are that we need an almost total reconstruction of social and political and economic and legal theory in all their traditional forms as well as a reconstruction of moral theory and practice at more comprehensive, or fundamental, levels.[82]

---

80 [Author's note] See e.g., *Women's Ways of Knowing. The Development of Self, Voice, and Mind*, by Mary Field Belenky, Blyth McVicker Clinchy, Nancy Rule Goldberger, and Jill Mattuck Tarule (New York: Basic Books, 1986).

81 [Author's note] Alison Jaggar, "Feminist Ethics: Some Issues for the Nineties," p. 11.

82 [Author's note] This paper is based in part on my Truax Lectures on "The Prospect of Feminist Morality" at Hamilton College on November 2 and 9, 1989. Early versions were also presented at Colgate University; at Queen's University in Kingston, Ontario; at the University of Kentucky; and at the New School for Social Research. I am grateful to all who made possible these occasions and commented on the paper at these times, and to Alison Jaggar, Laura Purdy, and Sara Ruddick for additional discussion.

MARY MIDGLEY

"Is a Dolphin a Person?"

Who Is Mary Midgley?

Mary Midgley (1919–) is a moral philosopher, re-nowned for her no-nonsense, highly practical ap-proach to fundamental human issues. She writes mainly on religion, science, and ethics. Formerly a pro-fessor of philosophy at the University of Newcastle (now retired), she is one of Britain's most popular and well-known philosophical figures. Fiercely combative, she has been described as possibly "the most fright-ening philosopher in the country: the one before whom it is least pleasant to appear a fool."

Midgley studied Classics at Somerville College, Ox-ford, but never completed a PhD. (In 2005 she pub-lished a newspaper article called "Proud not to be a doctor," in which she argued that a PhD may give you the skills of a lawyer, but it can also obscure the big issues in a mass of detail.) She wrote her first book in her fifties, after raising a family,[1] but has since pro-duced more than a dozen volumes including *Beast and Man* (revised edition, Routledge, 1995); *Animals and Why They Matter* (reprint edition, University of Georgia Press, 1998); *Wickedness* (revised edition, Routledge, 2001); *Evolution as a Religion* (revised edi-tion, Routledge, 2002); *The Ethical Primate* (Routledge, 1994); and *Science and Poetry* (Routledge, 2001). Be-tween 1979 and 1983 Midgley was involved in a high-ly public, very heated exchange of articles after she attacked Richard Dawkins' "selfish gene" thesis.

The article reprinted here, "Is a Dolphin a Person?" is included in her book *Utopias, Dolphins and Comput-ers* (Routledge, 1996). In it, she argues that we need to develop a more flexible notion of moral personhood that will allow us to treat animals as morally impor-tant in their own right.

How Important and Influential Is This Passage?

This article represents the vastly increased attention that has been paid by professional philosophers in recent decades to the possibility that human beings *have moral obligations to the natural environment* and, in particular, to non-human animals. Though certainly not a new idea, the notion that the so-called 'lower' animals might have moral claims upon us, and that our species might have a moral duty to care for and preserve the planet's various ecosystems, is today playing an unprecedentedly significant role in main-stream moral theorizing.

Suggestions for Critical Reflection

1. Can non-humans be persons? Are all humans persons? How do we decide who is a person and what isn't?
2. What, if anything, is *special* about human beings?
3. What makes cruelty immoral? Is there a moral difference between cruelty to people and cruelty to animals?
4. How far should we allow human interests to be overridden by those of non-humans? Should these considerations affect what we eat or wear? How we farm? The economic and cul-tural practices of some cultures (such as those that, for example, hunt seals or whales)? When, if ever, should we sacrifice human comfort, health or even life for non-humans?
5. What is the relationship between law and mo-rality? What should it be?

---

1   As she once put it: "I wrote no books until I was a good 50, and I'm jolly glad because I didn't know what I thought before then."

Suggestions for Further Reading

Midgley has published a memoir, *The Owl of Minerva* (Routledge, 2005). Her article "Proud not to be a doctor," is in *The Guardian*, October 3, 2005. In addition to her books listed above, her articles that address the moral status of animals include "Towards a More Humane View of the Beasts?" in *The Environment in Question: Ethics and Global Issues*, ed. David E. Cooper (Routledge, 1992), and "Beasts Versus the Biosphere?" *Environmental Values* 1 (1992).

A good overview of the question of animals in ethics is provided by Angus Taylor's *Animals and Ethics* (Broadview Press, 2009). Rosalind Hursthouse, *Ethics, Humans and Other Animals* (Routledge, 2000) is another introduction which includes a collection of readings, and there is also Armstrong and Botzler, eds., *The Animal Ethics Reader* (Routledge, 2008). Peter Singer's *Animal Liberation* (Harper Perennial, 2009) is a very famous defense of the view that animals have substantial moral claims on us; see also Tom Regan's "The Case for Animal Rights" in a collection edited by Singer, *In Defence of Animals* (Basil Blackwell, 1985)—see also Regan's book also called *The Case for Animal Rights* (University of California Press, 2004). Robert Nozick responded to Singer in a section of his *Anarchy, State and Utopia* (Basic Books, 1974), pp. 34–42.

Decent introductions to philosophy of the environment include Zimmerman et al. (eds.), *Environmental Philosophy: From Animal Rights to Radical Ecology* (Prentice Hall, 2004) and Andrew Light and Holmes Rolston III (eds.), *Environmental Ethics: An Anthology* (Blackwell, 2002).

"Is a Dolphin a Person?"[2]

The Undoubting Judge

This question came up during the trial of the two people who, in May 1977, set free two bottle-nosed dolphins used for experimental purposes by the University of Hawaii's Institute of Marine Biology. It is an interesting question for a number of reasons, and I want to use most of this discussion in interpreting it, and tracing its connexion with several others which may already be of concern to us. I shall not go into details of the actual case, but shall rely on the very clear and thoughtful account which Gavin Daws gives in his paper, "'Animal Liberation" as Crime'.[3]

Kenneth le Vasseur, the first of the two men to be tried, attempted through his counsel what is called a 'choice of evils' defence. In principle the law allows this in cases where an act, otherwise objectionable, is necessary to avoid a greater evil. For this defence to succeed, the act has to be (as far as the defendant knows) the only way of avoiding an imminent, and more serious, harm or evil to himself or to 'another'.

Le Vasseur, who had been involved in the care of the dolphins, believed that their captivity, with

---

2 This article was first published under the title "Persons and Non-Persons" in *In Defence of Animals*, edited by Peter Singer (Oxford: Basil Blackwell, 1985). Copyright © 1985, pp. 52-62. The version reprinted here appeared as Chapter Nine of *Utopias, Dolphins and Computers* (London: Routledge, 1996). Reprinted with permission of Wiley-Blackwell Inc.

3 [Author's note] Gavin Daws, "'Animal Liberation' as Crime" in Harlan B. Miller and William H. Williams (eds.), *Ethics and Animals* (Totowa, NJ: Humana Press, 1983).

the conditions then prevailing in it, actually endangered their lives. His counsel, in his opening statement for the defence, spoke of the exceptional nature of dolphins as animals; bad and rapidly deteriorating physical conditions at the laboratory; a punishing regimen for the dolphins, involving overwork, reductions in their food rations, the total isolation they endured, deprived of the company of other dolphins, even of contact with humans in the tank, deprived of all toys which they had formerly enjoyed playing with—to the point where Puka, having refused to take part consistently in experimental sessions, developed self-destructive behaviours symptomatic of deep disturbance, and finally became lethargic—'comatose'. Le Vasseur, seeing this, fearing that death would be the outcome, and knowing that there was no law that he could turn to, believed himself authorized, in the interests of the dolphins' well-being, to release them. The release was not a theft in that Le Vasseur did not intend to gain anything for himself. It was intended to highlight conditions in the laboratory. (Daws: 356–67)

But was a dolphin 'another'? The judge thought not. He said that 'another' would have to be another person, and he defined dolphins as property, not as persons, as a matter of law. A dolphin could not be 'another person' under the penal code. The defence tried and failed to get the judge disqualified for prejudice. It then asked leave to go to Federal Court in order to claim that Thirteenth Amendment rights in respect of involuntary servitude might be extended to dolphins. This plea the judge rejected:

Judge Doi said, 'We get to dolphins, we get to orangutans, chimpanzees, dogs, cats. I don't know at what level you say intelligence is insufficient to have that animal or thing, or whatever you want to call it, a human being under the penal code. I'm saying that they're not under the penal code and that's my answer.' (Daws: 365)

At this point—which determined the whole outcome of the trial—something seemed perfectly obvious to the judge about the meaning of the words 'other' and 'person'. What was it? And how obvious is it to everybody else? In the answer just given, he raises the possibility that it might be a matter of intelligence, but he rejects it. That consideration, he says, is not needed. The question is quite a simple one; no tests are called for. The word 'person' just means a human being.

What Are Persons?

I think that this is a very natural view, but not actually a true one, and the complications which we find when we look into the use of this interesting word are instructive. In the first place, there are several well-established and indeed venerable precedents for calling non-human beings 'persons'.

One concerns the persons of the Trinity, and indeed the personhood of God. Another is the case of 'legal persons'—corporate bodies such as cities or colleges, which count as persons for various purposes, such as sueing and being sued. As Blackstone says, these 'corporations or bodies politic ... are formed and created by human laws for the purposes of society and government'; unlike 'natural persons', who can only be created by God.[4] The law, then, can if it chooses create persons; it is not a mere passive recorder of their presence (as indeed Judge Doi implied in making his ruling a matter of law and not of fact). Thirdly, what may look nearer to the dolphins, the word is used by zoologists to describe the individual members of a compound or colonial organism, such as jellyfish or coral, each having (as the dictionary reasonably puts it) 'a more or less independent life'.[5]

There is nothing stretched or paradoxical about these uses, for the word does not in origin mean 'human being' or anything like it. It means a mask, and its basic general sense comes from the drama. The

---

4   Sir William Blackstone's *Commentaries on the Laws of England*, published in four volumes between 1765 and 1767, codified the common law—law based on judicial custom and precedent—which today forms a major part of the law of many countries which were once British territories or colonies.

5   [Author's note] It is also interesting that 'personal identity' is commonly held to belong to continuity of consciousness rather than of bodily form, in stories where the two diverge. Science fiction strongly supports this view, which was first mooted by John Locke, *Essay Concerning Human Understanding*, bk. 2, ch. 27, sect. 15.

'masks' in a play are the characters who appear in it. Thus, to quote the Oxford Dictionary again, after 'a mask', it means 'a character or personage acted, one who plays or performs any part, a character, relation or capacity in which one acts, a being having legal rights, a juridical person'.

The last two meanings throw a sharp light on the difference between this notion and that of being human. Not all human beings need be persons. The word *persona* in Latin does not apply to slaves, though it does apply to the State as a corporate person. Slaves have, so to speak, no speaking part in the drama; they do not figure in it; they are extras.

There are some entertaining similar examples about women. Thus:

> One case, brought before the US Supreme Court in the 1890s, concerned Virginia's exclusion of a woman from the practice of the law, although the pertinent statute was worded in terms of 'persons'. The Court argued that it was indeed up to the State's Supreme Court '*to determine whether the word 'person' as used (in the Statute) is confined to males*, and whether women are admitted to practise law in that Commonwealth'. The issue of whether women must be understood as included by the word 'persons' continued even into the twentieth century ... In a Massachusetts case in 1931 ... women were denied eligibility for jury service, although the statute stated that every 'person qualified to vote' was so eligible. The Massachusetts Supreme Court asserted: 'No intention to include women can be deduced from the omission of the word male.'[6]

Finding the Right Drama

What is going on here? We shall not understand it, I think, unless we grasp how deeply drama is interwoven with our thinking, how intimately its categories shape our ideas. People who talk like this have a clear notion of the drama which they think is going on around them. They know who is supposed to count in

it and who is not. Attempts to introduce fresh characters irritate them. They are inclined to dismiss these attempts sharply as obviously absurd and paradoxical. The question who is and who is not a person seems at this point a quite simple and clear-cut one. Bertie Wooster simply is not a character in *Macbeth* and that is the end of the matter.

It is my main business here to point out that this attitude is too crude. The question is actually a very complex one, much more like 'who is important?' than 'who has got two legs?' If we asked 'who is important?' we would know that we needed to ask further questions, beginning with 'important for what?' Life does not contain just one purpose or one drama, but many interwoven ones. Different characters matter in different ways. Beings figure in some who are absent from others, and we all play different parts in different scripts.

Even in ordinary human life, it is fatal to ignore this. To insist on reducing all relationships to those prescribed by a single drama—such, for instance, as the Social Contract[7]—is disastrous. Intellectuals are prone to such errors, and need to watch out for them. But when we come to harder cases, where the variation is greater—cases such as abortion, euthanasia or the treatment of other species—this sort of mistake is still more paralysing. That is why these cases are so helpful in illuminating the more central ones.

It is clear that, over women, those who limited the use of the concept 'person' felt this difficulty. They did not want to deny altogether that women were persons, since in the dramas of private life women figured prominently. Public life, however, was a different stage, whose rules and conventions excluded them (queens apart) as completely as elephants or angels. The fact that private life often impinges on public

---

6   [Author's note] Susan Möller Okin, *Women in Western Political Thought* (Princeton, NJ, 1979), p. 251.

7   The idea of a *social contract* is typically appealed to in order to justify constraints on people's individual freedom, on the basis that people voluntarily agree (or would agree, or ought to agree) to these restrictions because in the long run they make everybody better off. For example, one might argue, we tacitly agree to submit appropriately to the authority of the police because we are better off living in a society where there is a police force than one where there is not.

was an informal matter and could not affect this ruling. Similarly at Rome, it is clear that slaves actually played a considerable part in life. In Greek and Roman comedy ingenious slaves, both male and female, often figure as central characters, organizing the intrigue and supplying the brains which the hero and heroine themselves unfortunately lack. This, however, was not going to get them legal rights. The boundaries of particular situations and institutions served to compartmentalize thought and to stop people raising questions about the rights and status of those who were for central purposes currently disregarded.

I think it will be helpful here to follow out a little further the accepted lines of usage for the word person. How complete is its link with the human bodily form? What, for instance, about intelligent alien beings? Could we call them persons? If not, then contact with them—which is certainly conceivable—would surely require us to coin a new word to do the quite subtle moral job which is done at present by 'person'. The idea of a person in the almost technical sense required by morality today is the one worked out by Kant.[8] It is the idea of a rational being, capable of choice and therefore endowed with dignity, worthy of respect, having rights; one that must be regarded always as an end in itself, not only as a means to the ends of others.

Because this definition deals solely with rational qualities, it makes no mention of human form or human descent, and the spirit behind it would certainly not license us to exclude intelligent aliens, any more than disembodied spirits. The moral implications of the word 'person' would therefore, on our current Kantian principles, surely still have to attach to whatever word we might coin to include aliens. C.S. Lewis, describing a planet where there are three distinct rational species, has them use the word *hnau* for the condition which they all share, and this term is naturally central to the morality of all of them.[9]

Now if intelligence is really so important to the issue, a certain vertigo descends when we ask 'where do we draw the line?' because intelligence is a matter of degree. Some inhabitants of our own planet, including whales and dolphins, have turned out to be a lot brighter than was once thought. Quite how bright they are is not yet really clear to us. Indeed it may never become so, because of the difference in the kind of brightness appropriate to beings with very different sorts of life. How can we deal with such a situation?

Attending to the Middle Ground

The first thing needed is undoubtedly to get away from the single, simple, black-and-white antithesis with which Kant started, the antithesis between persons and things. Most of Kant's argument is occupied with this, and while it remains so he does not need to make finer distinctions. *Things* (he says) can properly be used as means to human ends in a way in which *people* cannot. Things have no aims of their own; they are not subjects but objects.

Thing-treatment given to people is exploitation and oppression. It is an outrage, because, as Kant exclaims, 'a man is not a thing'. Masters sell slaves; rulers deceive and manipulate their subjects; employers treat their secretaries as part of the wallpaper. By dwelling on the simple, stark contrast involved here, Kant was able to make some splendid moral points which are still vital to us today, about the thoroughgoing respect which is due to every free and rational human being. But the harsh, bright light which he turned on these situations entirely obscured the intermediate cases. A mouse is not a thing either, before we even start to think about a dolphin.

I find it interesting that, just as the American courts could not quite bring themselves to say that women were not persons, so Kant cannot quite get around to saying what his theory certainly implies, that animals are things. He does say that they 'are not self-conscious and are there merely as a means to an end',[10] that end being ours. But he does not

---

8   [Author's note] See Immanuel Kant, *Foundations of the Metaphysics of Morals* (tr. Lewis White Beck, Bobbs-Merrill, 1959), sect. 428–432, p. 46. In the UK a more available translation is that called *The Moral Law* (tr. H.J. Paton, Hutchinson, 1948), pp. 90–92.

9   [Author's note] C.S. Lewis, *Out of the Silent Planet* (London, John Lane, 1938).

10 [Author's note] Immanuel Kant, 'Duties towards Animals and Spirits' in his *Lectures on Ethics* (tr. Louis Infield, Methuen, London, 1930), p. 239.

actually call them things, nor does he write off their interests. In fact he emphatically condemns cruel and mean treatment of them. But, like many other humane people who have got stuck with an inadequate moral theory, he gives ingeniously unconvincing reasons for this. He says—what has gone on being said ever since—that it is only because cruelty to animals may lead on to cruelty to humans, or degrade us, or be a sign of a bad moral character, that we have to avoid it.

This means that if we can show that, for instance, venting our ill-temper on the dog will prevent our doing it on our families, or if we can produce certificates to show that we are in general people of firm moral character, not easily degraded, we can go ahead with a clear conscience. Dog-bashing, properly managed, could count as a legitimate form of therapy, along with gardening, pottery and raffia-work. In no case would the physical materials involved be directly considered, because all equally would be only objects, not subject. And there is nothing degrading about simply hitting an object.

In spite of the appalling cruelty which human beings show towards animals the world over, it does not seem likely that anyone regards them consistently in this light, as objects. Spasms of regard, tenderness, comradeship and even veneration, alternating with unthinking callousness, seem to make up the typical human attitude to them. And towards fellow-human-beings too, a rather similar alternation is often found. So this cannot really be an attitude confined to things. Actually even cruelty itself, when it is deliberate, seems to require that its objects should not be mere physical objects, but should be capable of minding what is done to them, of responding as separate characters in the drama.

More widely, the appeal of hunting, and also of sports such as bullfighting, seems to depend on the sense of outwitting and defeating a conscious quarry or opponent, 'another', able to be one's opposite in the game or drama. The script distinctly requires non-human characters, who can play their parts well or badly. Moby Dick is not an extra. And the degradingness of deliberate cruelty itself surely requires this other-regarding element. 'Another' is not always another human being.

Indirect Justifications

The degradingness of cruelty is of course widely admitted, and le Vasseur's counsel used this admission as the ground of an alternative defence. He drew attention to his client's status as a state employee, which conferred authority on him to act as he did in coming to the defence of 'another', in this case the United States, whose social values were injured by what was being done to the dolphins. This argument was rejected, on the ground that, in the eyes of the law, cruelty to animals is merely a misdemeanour, whereas theft is a felony. Accordingly the choice of evils could not properly be resolved in such a way as to make theft the less serious offence. It is interesting that this argument makes no objection to treating the United States as 'another' or 'another person'—it does not insist that a person simply means a human being—but rests instead on contending that this 'other' finds its values more seriously attacked by theft than by cruelty to dolphins.

This sort of argument is not easy to come to grips with, even in the case of an ordinary individual person, still less in that of a nation. How serious an evil is cruelty? Once it is conceded that the victim's point of view does not count, that the injury is only to the offender or some body of which he is part, we seem to be cut off from the key considerations of the argument and forced to conduct it in a strained manner, from grounds which are not really central. Is cruelty necessarily depraving? On this approach, that seems partly to be a factual question about how easily people are depraved, and partly perhaps an aesthetic one about how far cruel acts are necessarily disgusting and repellent.

These acts seem to be assimilated now to others which are repellent without being clearly immoral, such as eating the bodies of people whom one has not killed, or watching atrocities over which one has no control. The topic becomes a neighbour of pornography rather than of abortion and euthanasia. (In the disputes about permissiveness in the 1960s, an overlap actually developed here at times, as when a London art gallery organized a happening in which some fish were to be electrocuted as part of the show, and efforts to ban this were attacked as censorious manifestations of aesthetic narrow-mindedness.)

Something seems to have gone wrong with the thinking here. The distinctive feature of actions attacked on purely aesthetic grounds should surely be that their effects are confined to those who actually perform them. No other sentient being is harmed by them. That is why they pose problems for libertarians, when bystanders object to them. But cruelty does not pose this kind of problem, since the presence of 'another' who is harmed is essential to it. In our case it is the dolphin, who does seem to be 'another'. Can we avoid thinking of it in this way? Can the central objection to cruelty really be something rather indirect, such as its being in bad taste?

Moral Change and the Law

The law seems to have ruled thus here. And in doing this, the law shows itself to be in a not uncommon difficulty, one that arises when public opinion is changing. Legal standards are not altogether independent of moral standards. They flow from them and crystallize in ways designed to express certain selected moral insights. When those insights change deeply enough, the law changes. But there are often jolts and discrepancies here, because the pace of change is different. New moral perceptions require the crystals to be broken up and reformed, and this process takes time. Changes of this kind have repeatedly altered the rules surrounding the central crux which concerns us here; the stark division of the world into persons and property. Changing attitudes to slavery are a central case, to which we must come back in a minute. But it is worth noticing first that plain factual discoveries too can make a difference.

When our civilization formed the views on the species barrier which it still largely holds, all the most highly-developed non-human animals were simply unknown. Legend apart, it was assumed that whales and dolphins were much like fish. The great apes were not even discovered till the eighteenth century and no real knowledge of their way of living was acquired until within the last few decades. About better-known creatures too, there was a very general ignorance and unthinking dismissal of available evidence; their sociality was not noticed or believed in. The central official intellectual tradition of our culture never expected to be forced to subtilize its crude, extreme,

unshaded dichotomy between man and beast. In spite of the efforts of many concerned thinkers, from Plutarch to Montaigne and from Blake to John Stuart Mill, it did not develop other categories.[11]

If alien beings landed tomorrow, lawyers, philosophers and social scientists would certainly have to do some very quick thinking. (I don't expect the aliens myself, but they are part of the imaginative furniture of our age, and it is legitimate to use them to roust us from our dogmatic slumbers.) Science fiction, though sometimes helpful, has far too often side-tracked the problem by making its aliens just scientists with green antennae—beings whose 'intelligence' is of a kind to be instantly accepted at the Massachusetts Institute of Technology, only of course a little greater. Since neither dolphins nor gorillas write doctoral theses, this would still let us out as far as terrestrial non-human creatures were concerned. 'Persons' and their appropriate rights could still go on being defined in terms of this sort of intelligence, and we could quietly continue to poison the pigeons in the park any time that we felt like it.

The question is, why should this kind of intelligence be so important, and determine the limits of our moral concern? It is often assumed that we can only owe duties to beings capable of speech. Why this should be thought is not altogether clear. At a simple level, Bentham[12] surely got it right: 'The question is not *can they talk*? Nor *can they reason*? But *can they suffer*?'[13] With chimps, gorillas and dolphins, however, there is now a further problem, because people have been trying, apparently with some degree of success, to teach them certain kinds of language.

---

11   Plutarch lived in Greece around 100 CE and Michel de Montaigne was born in France in 1533; both were famous essayists. William Blake, a British Romantic poet, died in 1827 and the philosopher Mill in 1873.

12   Jeremy Bentham, an English philosopher and advocate of legal reform, was an influential formulator of the principle of 'utilitarianism'—the principle that actions are right insofar as they contribute to general happiness, and wrong insofar as they contribute to unhappiness—and was a great influence on John Stuart Mill.

13   [Author's note] Jeremy Bentham, *Introduction to the Principles of Morals and Legislation*, ch. 17.

This project might have taught us a great deal about just what new categories we need in our attempt to classify beings more subtly. But unluckily it has been largely obscured by furious opposition from people who still have just the two categories, and who see the whole proceeding as an illicit attempt to smuggle contraband from one to the other.

This reaction is extremely interesting. What is the threat? Articulate apes and cetaceans[14] are scarcely likely to take over the government. What might happen, however, is that it would become much harder to exclude them from moral consideration. In particular, their use as experimental subjects might begin to look very different. Can the frontier be defended by a resolute and unbreakable refusal to admit that these animals can talk?

The Meaning of Fellowship

It is understandable that people have thought so, but this surely cannot really be the issue. What makes creatures our fellow-beings, entitled to basic consideration, is not intellectual capacity, but emotional fellowship. And if we ask what powers can give a higher claim, bringing some creatures nearer to the degree of consideration which is due to humans, what is most relevant seems to be sensibility, social and emotional complexity of the kind which is expressed by the forming of deep, subtle and lasting relationships. The gift of imitating certain intellectual skills which are important to humans is no doubt an indicator of this, but it cannot be central. We already know that both apes and dolphins have this kind of social and emotional complexity.

If we ask what elements in 'persons' are central in entitling them to moral consideration, we can, I think, get some light on the point by contrasting the claim of these sensitive social creatures with that of a computer of the present generation, programmed in a manner which entitles it, by current controversial usage, to be called 'intelligent' and certainly able to perform calculations impossible to human beings. That computer does not trouble our sleep with any moral claims, and would not do so however much more 'intelligent' it

___

14   Whales, dolphins, and porpoises.

became, unless it eventually seemed to be conscious, sensitive and endowed with emotions.

If it did seem so, we should have the Frankenstein problem in an acute form. (The extraordinary eagerness with which Frankenstein drove his researches to this disastrous point is something which contemporary monster-makers might like to ponder.) But those who at present emphasize the intelligence of computers do not see any reason to want to call them persons, nor to allow for them as members of the moral community. Speech alone, then, would scarcely do this job for the apes. What is at issue is the already glaring fact, which speech would make it finally impossible to deny, that they mind what happens to them—that they are highly sensitive social beings.

These considerations are not, I think, ones confined to cranks or extremists. They seem fairly widespread today, and probably occur at times to all of us, however uncertain we may be what to do about them. If so, and if the law really allows them no possible weight, then we seem to have reached the situation where the law will have to be changed, because it shocks morality. There is an obvious precedent, to which the dolphin-liberators tried to appeal:

> When the dolphins were taken from the tanks, a message was left behind identifying the releasers as the 'Undersea Railroad', a reference to the Underground Railroad, the Abolitionists' slave-freeing network of pre–Civil War days. Along the Underground Railroad in the 1850s, it sometimes happened that juries refused to convict people charged with smuggling slaves to freedom. That was the kind of vindication le Vasseur and Sipman were looking for ... They did not consider themselves to be criminals. In fact they took the view that, if there was a crime, it was the crime of keeping dolphins—intelligent, highly aware creatures with no criminal record of their own—in solitary confinement, in small, concrete tanks, made to do repetitious experiments, for life. (Daws: 362)

If we go back to the alien beings for a moment and consider whether even the most intelligent of them would have the right to keep any visiting human beings, however stupid, in these conditions, even those of us least partial to astronauts may begin to see the point which le Vasseur and Sipman were making. It surely cannot be dismissed merely by entrenching the law round the definition of the word 'person'. We need new thinking, new concepts and new words, not (of course) just about animals but about our whole relation to the non-human world. We are not less capable of providing these than people were in the 1850s, so we should get on with it.

CHAPTER 8

Social/Political Philosophy— What Is Justice?

INTRODUCTION TO THE QUESTION

Social and political philosophy is made up of our attempts to understand and map the basic categories of social life, and to ethically evaluate different forms of social organization. It has three closely interwoven strands: *conceptual analysis* of various important social dimensions, *normative assessment* of the ways society ought to be structured along these dimensions, and *empirical investigation* of issues relevant to the implementation of these social ideals. It includes social philosophy, political philosophy, philosophy of law, and philosophy of the social sciences (such as economics and sociology).

Among the central concepts studied within social and political philosophy are society, culture, human nature, political obligation, power, democracy, toleration, rights, equality, autonomy or freedom, justice, merit, welfare, property, social class, public interest, and social stability. Different analyses of these notions, and different emphases on some ideas (e.g., equality) over others (e.g., autonomy), give rise to differing political philosophies—differing ideological stances as to what the ideal society should look like, and thus different views on how current societies should be modified in order to move them closer to this ideal. Some of the main social-political ideologies (not all of which are mutually exclusive) are:

- *Anarchism,* which denies that any coercive government institutions are ever justified;
- *Libertarianism* (or 'classical liberalism'), which holds that government infringements on individual liberty are always inappropriate, but accepts that a 'minimal' state is consistent with

this; libertarians also hold that failing to help people in need is not an infringement on their liberty, and that the state therefore has no duty to provide this form of support for its citizens;
- *Liberalism* (or 'welfare liberalism'), which is also concerned with promoting individual liberty but holds that a guaranteed social minimum standard of living and enforced equal opportunity are necessary to provide citizens with genuinely substantive autonomy;
- *Communitarianism,* which denies that the rights of individuals are basic and asserts that collectives (states, cultures, communities) have moral claims that are prior to, and sometimes even opposed to, the rights which liberals ascribe to individuals; usually, this is because communitarians hold some version of the thesis that individual identity is constituted by one's social setting, and thus that the liberal notion of an 'isolated individual' who exists independently of society is a mere myth;
- *Fascism,* which is an extreme communitarian view stressing the overriding importance of national culture and giving the state authority to control almost all aspects of social life;
- *Socialism,* which takes neither individual liberty nor community to be a fundamental ideal, but instead emphasizes the value of equality, and justifies coercive social institutions insofar as they promote social equality;
- *Communism,* which advocates a society in which private property is abolished in favor of communal ownership of all goods, in the belief

that it is only in such conditions that human be-ings can truly flourish;

- *Conservatism*, which distrusts naked political power and is skeptical of social planning, and which therefore seeks to channel and constrain government within historically-evolved, time-tested social institutions and relationships; and
- *Feminism*, which advocates social reform (e.g., to the institution of the family) in order to take better account of the fact that women have the same basic social rights as men.

In addition to conceptual and ethical analysis, there are also many substantive empirical questions which have an important bearing on the choice and implementation of social philosophies. For example, once a set of principles of distributive justice have been decided on, it is still a substantial empirical problem to decide which social and economic ar-rangements will best instantiate those principles. A sampling of other important questions: What checks and balances on government power will be most ef-fective without being inefficient? How can the self-in-terest of individuals best be harnessed for the public good? What is the most effective body of legislation for fostering social stability? Can equality of oppor-tunity be preserved without infringing on personal autonomy (e.g., on people's choices about who to hire or rent to)? Which forms of punishment are the most effective deterrent of crime? How much is human na-ture shaped and changed by social circumstances? What is the relationship between free economic mar-kets and democratic political structures? And so on.

The particular social-political issue which is the focus of this chapter is the problem of justice. The readings approach the topic in all three of the inter-connected ways identified above: they deal with the philosophical analysis of the concept of justice, make claims about how society should be organized in order to take proper account of justice, and touch on some of the empirical data relevant to the con-struction of a just society. They also deal with some of the different *aspects* of justice: justice as a prop-erty of a political system, a set of social relationships, of actions, or of individuals; and justice considered as a problem of specifying how social benefits and

burdens should be distributed among the members of that society (*distributive justice*), and the problem of determining the appropriate way to correct injus-tices or compensate for illegitimate inequalities (*rec-tificatory justice*).

Aristotle provides an influential initial analysis of the notion of justice which sets some of the terms for the following debate. The reading from Hobbes pursues similar questions and also introduces an ad-ditional theme: the pressing problem of justifying (and defining the limits of) coercive state power over individuals. Hobbes, famously, answers this question with the device of a 'social contract,' by which ration-ally self-interested individuals agree to leave the 'state of nature' and submit themselves to the authority of the state. Mill is also, in the reading reprinted here, concerned with the question of the justice of gov-ernment intervention in the lives of citizens, and he formulates and defends the classical liberal position which limits government action to the prevention of harm. Three of the following readings then present three of the most important twentieth-century po-litical ideologies on justice, and particularly distribu-tive justice. Marx and Engels argue for the inevitable ascendance of communism; Rawls carefully lays out the most influential contemporary version of welfare liberalism; and Nozick attempts to rebut Rawls with a lively and fast-moving defense of libertarianism. There are also two readings representing another very important social-political movement, feminism: Simone de Beauvoir criticizes the historical domina-tion of society by males, while the more recent writer Susan Moller Okin presents a feminist critique of con-temporary liberal theory.

There are a number of good books which will take you deeper into social and political philosophy. Perhaps the best place to start is with Will Kymlicka's excellent *Contemporary Political Philosophy* (Oxford University Press 2001). Also good are Arthur and Shaw (eds.), *Social and Political Philosophy* (Prentice Hall 1992); Benn and Peters, *The Principles of Political Thought* (Free Press 1965); Carl Cohen, *Communism, Fascism, and Democracy: The Theoretical Foundations* (McGraw-Hill 1997); Iain Hampsher-Monk, *A History of Modern Political Thought, Major Political Thinkers from Hobbes to Marx* (Blackwell 1992); J.R. Lucas, *The*

Principles of Politics (Oxford University Press, 1986); Gerald MacCallum, *Political Philosophy* (Prentice Hall, 1987); George Sher, *Social and Political Philosophy* (Wadsworth, 1999); and Jonathan Wolff, *An Introduction to Political Philosophy* (Oxford University Press, 2006). Goodin and Pettit (eds.), *A Companion to Contemporary Political Philosophy* (Blackwell, 1996) and Robert Simon (ed.), *The Blackwell Guide to Social and Political Philosophy* (Blackwell, 2002) are both well worth consulting.

The modern literature on justice is rich and extensive. Here are some relevant books (focussing mainly on books not already included in the Further Reading sections of the selections in this chapter): Brian Barry, *Theories of Justice*, Volume 1 (University of California Press, 1991); G.A. Cohen, *Self-Ownership, Freedom, and Equality* (Cambridge University Press, 1995); Ronald Dworkin, *Taking Rights Seriously* (Harvard University Press, 1978); Friedrich A. Hayek, *The Constitution of Liberty* (Routledge and Kegan Paul, 1960); David Miller, *Principles of Social Justice* (Harvard University Press, 2001); Stephen Nathanson, *Economic Justice* (Prentice Hall, 1998); D.D. Raphael, *Concepts of Justice* (Oxford University Press, 2001); John Roemer, *Theories of Distributive Justice* (Harvard University Press, 1996); Michael Sandel, *Liberalism and the Limits of Justice* (Cambridge University Press, 1998) and *Justice* (Farrar, Straus and Giroux, 2009); Amartya Sen, *The Idea of Justice* (Harvard University Press, 2009); Arthur and Shaw (eds.), *Justice and Economic Distribution* (Prentice Hall, 1991); and Michael Walzer, *Spheres of Justice* (Basic Books, 1984).

ARISTOTLE

The Nicomachean Ethics

For information on Aristotle's life and his overall philosophical project, please see Chapter 7.

What Is the Structure of This Reading?

The overall structure of the *Nicomachean Ethics* is described in the notes in Chapter 7. Book V, in which Aristotle discusses justice, comes after discussions of various moral virtues, such as courage, temperance, generosity, good temper, and truthfulness. It is fairly clear that Aristotle thinks justice is a particularly important virtue, however, since it is the one to which he devotes by far the most space.

The first five sections of Book V are reprinted here. After distinguishing between the particular virtue of justice and "universal justice," Aristotle goes on, in section two, to divide particular justice into two types: distributive justice and rectificatory justice. In the next three sections, however, he discusses, in turn, *three* varieties of justice—distributive justice in section three, rectificatory justice in section four, and "justice in exchange" in section five. The rest of Book V, which is not included here, deals with the difference between natural and legal justice and emphasizes the role of choice in the virtue of justice (roughly, that people are unjust, according to Aristotle, only if they deliberately *choose* to take unfair advantage of others).

Some Useful Background Information

1. The Greek words for "just" and "unjust" (*dikaios* and *adikos*) are ambiguous in a way which is much less evident in their English counterparts, and Aristotle commences by discussing this ambiguity. The Greek words apply not only to people or actions that we would call just or unjust—i.e., roughly, those that are fair or unfair—but also to moral rightness or wrongness *in general*. Thus

what Aristotle calls "particular justice" is one virtue (albeit a particularly important one) among
others, while "universal justice" corresponds to
moral virtue in general (or at least, "complete virtue … in relation to our neighbor").

2. For Aristotle, justice is not primarily a state of affairs (such as an even distribution of wealth) or
a framework of social rules (such as a fair taxation system). Instead, justice is a *virtue*, just as
courage and truthfulness are virtues—justice is,
at bottom, a sort of *character trait*. Just actions,
then, are (roughly) those performed by just
people; a just society is one which is governed
by just people; and just laws are those which
prescribe moral virtue, and especially the particular virtue of justice.

3. Furthermore, the virtue of justice, for Aristotle,
is defined not merely by one's disposition to
behave in certain ways, but also by one's *motive* for that behavior. That is, unjust people,
according to Aristotle, are motivated by what
he calls *pleonexia,* usually translated as being
"grasping," "greedy," or "overreaching." Literally,
it means desiring to have more than other people or wanting more than one's share. (People
who possess the particular virtue of justice, presumably, are those who are *not* motivated by
pleonexia.)

4. At one point Aristotle refers to "those who have
a share in the constitution," and this is a significant indicator of his view of the political dimension of distributive justice. For Aristotle, and in
ancient Greek thought generally, the free citizens of a political state were like *shareholders*
or *partners* in the state. Public property (such
as the land of a new colony) or public rewards
and honors (such as political office) were to be
divided up among citizens in accordance with
their merit (i.e., their wealth, nobility, or virtue).
The question of just distribution of rewards
was therefore, for Aristotle, fundamentally a
question about how social goods should be divided up among the (free, male, land-owning)
members of the society—that is, of how people
should fairly be rewarded for their contribution
to a common political enterprise.

A Common Misconception

Aristotle's focus is on *acting* justly or unjustly, rather
than on what it is to be *treated* justly or not. Thus, for
example, in his discussion of rectificatory justice, his
main focus is on how the judge or arbiter should act,
and not on the 'injustice' of the state of affairs which the
judge is concerned to redress. To put it another way, for
Aristotle, justice is a virtue, and since being treated fairly
or unfairly manifests neither virtue nor vice, Aristotle's
real interest is in those who *do the treating*.

How Important and Influential Is This Passage?

The huge influence of Aristotle's *Nicomachean Ethics* as a whole has already been discussed in notes
to the Aristotle reading in the previous chapter. Furthermore, many concepts introduced in Book V specifically have also been particularly influential. For
example, the distinction between the just *distribution
and exchange of goods* and justice considered as *the
redressing of wrongs*, has become a standard part of
debates about justice since Aristotle's time. Also, Aristotle's analysis of reciprocal justice is one of the first
discussions of political economy and is often hailed
as an example of his visionary analytic genius. On the
other hand, Aristotle's actual theories of justice—such
as that distributive justice is a matter of geometrical
proportion—are usually considered useful *starting
points* for discussion but are often criticized as being
too unsophisticated to be taken seriously today as
complete accounts of justice.

Suggestions for Critical Reflection

1. Aristotle seems to suggest the law does (or at
least, should) forbid any behavior that conflicts
with the virtues—that a good system of law
prescribes universal justice. Is Aristotle right
about this? For example, should the laws of
the state attempt to ensure that I am exactly as
generous, even-tempered, courageous, friendly,
witty, truthful (and so on) as I ought to be?

2. Do you think people can behave unjustly even
if they are not motivated by greed (*pleonexia*)?

If so, can Aristotle take account of this, or is it a problem for his view of justice? Do you think he is entirely consistent throughout this reading in his view that injustice is always connected to *pleonexia*?

3. How adequate is Aristotle's account of distributive justice? If Aristotle is mainly thinking of the fairness of the distribution of goods *by the state*, can his theory of distributive justice work for other forms of distribution (e.g., by a parent to her children, or an employer to her staff)? Are all fair ways of dividing things up connected to the *worth* or *merit* of those receiving shares, as Aristotle seems to think? If so, should more worthy people get a bigger share of *every* good—more money, more food, more respect, and so on—than their less worthy counterparts?

4. How adequately can Aristotle's account of distributive justice deal with cases of goods that cannot be shared (such as, say, a political office like the Presidency of the United States)? Do cases like this cause problems for his theory?

5. Aristotle points out that people disagree about the sort of merit that is relevant to distributive justice: "democrats identify it with the status of freeman, supporters of oligarchy with wealth (or with noble birth), and supporters of aristocracy with excellence." What does Aristotle have to say about the *proper* kind of merit? Do you think he has a view on this? If more than one kind of merit is relevant, does this cause problems for Aristotle's account of distributive justice?

6. How adequate is Aristotle's account of rectificatory justice? For example, is it always possible to take from the offender what has been stolen and restore it to the victim? (What about, for example, cases of adultery or murder?) Is it even *sufficient* merely to restore the situation to the previous status quo? For example, is it an adequate response to theft merely to require the thief to return exactly what has been stolen (no more and no less)?

7. How adequate is Aristotle's account of justice in exchange? How close to modern economic theory is Aristotle's analysis? (For example, how

does modern economics square with Aristotle's view of justice as a kind of *character trait*?) What do you think Aristotle means by "demand"?

8. What is the relationship between justice in exchange and the other two kinds of justice Aristotle deals with? Why do you think Aristotle announces there are *two* kinds of justice and then, apparently, describes three?

9. Does Aristotle have a theory of *criminal* justice (i.e., of just punishment for crimes)? If so, which of the three types of justice does it belong to? If not, then *why* do you think Aristotle neglects this sphere of justice?

10. How does Aristotle's account of the virtue of "particular justice" fit in with his general account of virtue (as presented in the selection from *Nicomachean Ethics* in Chapter 7)? For example, is the virtue of justice really a mean between two vices?

Suggestions for Further Reading

References to Aristotle's works are given in the Aristotle selection in Chapter 7. As well as reading more from Aristotle's *Nicomachean Ethics* and *Politics*, it is also illuminating to compare Plato's *Republic*, especially the section reprinted in Chapter 7. Many of the books recommended in Chapter 7 are also of value in thinking about Aristotle on justice, particularly W.F.R. Hardie's *Aristotle's Ethical Theory* (Oxford University Press, 1980), Terence Irwin's *Aristotle's First Principles* (Oxford University Press, 1990), and David Bostock's *Aristotle's Ethics* (Oxford University Press, 2000). There is also an old but useful commentary by Henry Jackson, *Peri Dikaiosunēs: The Fifth Book of the Nicomachean Ethics of Aristotle* (Cambridge University Press, 1879). Wolfgang von Leyden's *Aristotle on Equality and Justice* (Macmillan, 1985) is also worth looking at.

A seminal article on Aristotelian justice is Bernard Williams's "Justice as a Virtue," which appears in Amelie O. Rorty (ed.), *Essays on Aristotle's Ethics* (University of California Press, 1981). David O'Connor responded to Williams's critique in "Aristotelian Justice as a Personal Virtue," *Midwest Studies in Philosophy* 13 (1988). Other interesting articles on Book V of the *Nicomachean Ethics* include Renford Bambrough, "Aristotle on Justice, a

Paradigm of Philosophy," in Renford Bambrough (ed.), *New Essays on Plato and Aristotle* (Humanities Press, 1965); M.I. Finley, "Aristotle and Economic Analysis," *Past and Present* 47 (1970); A.R.W. Harrison, "Aristotle's *Nicomachean Ethics*, Book V, and the Law of Athens," *Journal of Hellenic Studies* 77 (1957); Lindsay Judson, "Aristotle on Fair Exchange," *Oxford Studies in Ancient Philosophy* 15 (1997); Hans Kelsen, "Aristotle's Doctrine of Justice," in Walsh and Shapiro (eds.), *Aristotle's Ethics* (1967); Paul Keyser, "A Proposed Diagram in Aristotle, *EN* V 3, 1131a24–b20 for Distributive Justice in Proportion," *Apeiron* 25 (1992); David Keyt, "Aristotle's Theory of Distributive Justice," in Keyt and Miller (eds.), *A Companion to Aristotle's Politics* (Blackwell, 1991); Konrad Marc-Wogau, "Aristotle's Theory of Corrective Justice and Reciprocity," in his *Philosophical Essays* (Lund, Gleerup, 1967); Stanley Rosen, "The Political Context of Aristotle's Theories of Justice," *Phronesis* 20 (1975); and Ernest Weinrib, "Aristotle's Forms of Justice," in Spiro Panagiotou (ed.), *Justice, Law, and Method in Plato and Aristotle* (Academic, 1987).

The Nicomachean Ethics[1]

Book V, Sections 1–5

1: The just as the lawful (universal justice) and the just as the fair and equal (particular justice): the former considered.

With regard to justice and injustice we must consider (1) what kind of actions they are concerned with, (2) what sort of mean justice is, and (3) between what extremes the just act is intermediate. Our investigation shall follow the same course as the preceding discussions.

---

1   The *Nicomachean Ethics* was probably written as a series of lecture notes, which would have undergone frequent revision, some time between 334 and 322 BCE. This selection is reprinted from *Aristotle: The Nicomachean Ethics*, translated with an Introduction by David Ross [W.D. Ross], revised by J.O. Urmson and J.L. Ackrill (Oxford World's Classics, 1998), by permission of Oxford University Press. The section headings are not Aristotle's own, but supplied by the translators.

We see that all men mean by justice that kind of state of character which makes people disposed to do what is just and makes them act justly and wish for what is just; and similarly by injustice that state which makes them act unjustly and wish for what is unjust. Let us too, then, lay this down as a general basis. For the same is not true of the sciences and the faculties[2] as of states of character. A faculty or a science which is one and the same is held to relate to contrary objects,[3] but a state of character which is one of two contraries does *not* produce the contrary results; e.g., as a result of health we do not do what is the opposite of healthy, but only what is healthy; for we say a man walks healthily, when he walks as a healthy man would.

Now often one contrary state is recognized from its contrary, and often states are recognized from the subjects that exhibit them; for (A) if good condition is known, bad condition also becomes known, and (B) good condition is known from the things that are in good condition, and they from it. If good condition is firmness of flesh, it is necessary both that bad condition should be flabbiness of flesh and that the wholesome should be that which causes firmness in flesh. And it follows for the most part that if one contrary is ambiguous the other also will be ambiguous; e.g., if 'just' is so, that 'unjust' will be so too.

Now 'justice' and 'injustice' seem to be ambiguous, but because their different meanings approach near to one another the ambiguity escapes notice and is not obvious as it is, comparatively, when the meanings are far apart, e.g., (for here the difference in outward form is great) as the ambiguity in the use of *kleis* for the collar-bone of an animal and for that with which we lock a door. Let us take as a starting-point, then, the various meanings of 'an unjust man'. Both the lawless man and the grasping and unfair man are thought to be unjust, so that evidently both the law-abiding and the fair man will be just. The just, then, is the lawful and the fair, the unjust the unlawful and the unfair.

---

2   Sciences are structured bodies of knowledge. Faculties are capacities or skills.

3   For example, medicine deals with disease as well as health; an engineer has the skill necessary to either build or destroy a bridge.

Since the unjust man is grasping, he must be concerned with goods—not all goods, but those with which prosperity and adversity have to do, which taken absolutely are always good, but for a particular person are not always good.[4] Now men pray for and pursue these things; but they should not, but should pray that the things that are good absolutely may also be good for them, and should choose the things that *are* good for them. The unjust man does not always choose the greater, but also the less—in the case of things bad absolutely; but because the lesser evil is itself thought to be in a sense good, and graspingness is directed at the good, therefore he is thought to be grasping. And he is unfair; for this contains and is common to both.

Since the lawless man was seen to be unjust and the law-abiding man just, evidently all lawful acts are in a sense just acts; for the acts laid down by the legislative art are lawful, and each of these, we say, is just. Now the laws in their enactments on all subjects aim at the common advantage either of all or of the best or of those who hold power, or something of the sort; so that in one sense we call those acts just that tend to produce and preserve happiness and its components for the political society. And the law bids us do both the acts of a brave man (e.g., not to desert our post nor take to flight nor throw away our arms), and those of a temperate man (e.g., not to commit adultery nor to gratify one's lust), and those of a good-tempered man (e.g., not to strike another nor to speak evil), and similarly with regard to the other virtues and forms of wickedness, commanding some acts and forbidding others; and the rightly-framed law does this rightly, and the hastily conceived one less well.

This form of justice, then, is complete virtue, although not without qualification, but in relation to our neighbour. And therefore justice is often thought to be the greatest of virtues, and 'neither evening nor morning star' is so wonderful;[5] and proverbially 'in justice is every virtue comprehended'.[6] And it is complete virtue in its fullest sense, because it is the actual exercise of complete virtue. It is complete because he who possesses it can exercise his virtue not only in himself but towards his neighbour also; for many men can exercise virtue in their own affairs, but not in their relations to their neighbour. This is why the saying of Bias[7] is thought to be true, that 'rule will show the man'; for a ruler is necessarily in relation to other men and a member of a society. For this same reason justice, alone of the virtues, is thought to be 'another's good', because it is related to our neighbour; for it does what is advantageous to another, either a ruler or a co-partner. Now the worst man is he who exercises his wickedness both towards himself and towards his friends, and the best man is not he who exercises his virtue towards himself but he who exercises it towards another; for this is a difficult task. Justice in this sense, then, is not part of virtue but virtue entire, nor is the contrary injustice a part of vice but vice entire. What the difference is between virtue and justice in this sense is plain from what we have said; they are the same but their essence is not the same; what, as a relation to one's neighbour, is justice is, as a certain kind of state without qualification, virtue.

2: The just as the fair and the equal: divided into distributive and rectificatory justice.

But at all events what we are investigating is the justice which is a *part* of virtue; for there is a justice of this kind, as we maintain. Similarly it is with injustice in the particular sense that we are concerned.

That there is such a thing is indicated by the fact that while the man who exhibits in action the other forms of wickedness acts wrongly indeed, but not graspingly (e.g., the man who throws away his shield through cowardice or speaks harshly through bad temper or

---

4 For example, wealth is something which can always contribute to a good life, but for people with defective characters—i.e., those who do not use money wisely— it can make them less happy.

5 According to some ancient commentaries, this is a quotation from Euripides' lost play *Melanippe* (of which just a fragment remains today).

6 This saying is attributed to the poet Theognis of Megara and to another poet called Phocylides (both of whom lived around the middle of the sixth century BCE).

7 Bias of Priene (who lived in the sixth century BCE) was one of the Seven Sages—a group of seventh- and sixth-century Greek politicians and philosophers renowned in later ages for their practical wisdom.

fails to help a friend with money through meanness), when a man acts graspingly he often exhibits none of these vices—no, nor all together, but certainly wickedness of some kind (for we blame him) and injustice. There is, then, another kind of injustice which is a part of injustice in the wide sense, and a use of the word 'unjust' which answers to a part of what is unjust in the wide sense of 'contrary to the law'. Again if one man commits adultery for the sake of gain and makes money by it, while another does so at the bidding of appetite though he loses money and is penalized for it, the latter would be held to be self-indulgent rather than grasping, but the former is unjust, but not self-indulgent; evidently, therefore, he is unjust by reason of his making gain by his act. Again, all other unjust acts are ascribed invariably to some particular kind of wickedness, e.g., adultery to self-indulgence, the desertion of a comrade in battle to cowardice, physical violence to anger; but if a man makes gain, his action is ascribed to no form of wickedness but injustice. Evidently, therefore, there is apart from injustice in the wide sense another, 'particular', injustice which shares the name and nature of the first, because its definition falls within the same genus; for the significance of both consists in a relation to one's neighbour, but the one is concerned with honour or money or safety—or that which includes all these, if we had a single name for it—and its motive is the pleasure that arises from gain; while the other is concerned with all the objects with which the good man is concerned.

It is clear, then, that there is more than one kind of justice, and that there is one which is distinct from virtue entire; we must try to grasp its genus and differentia.[8]

The unjust has been divided into the unlawful and the unfair, and the just into the lawful and the fair. To the unlawful answers the aforementioned sense of injustice. But since the unfair and the unlawful are not the same, but are different as a part is from its whole (for all that is unfair is unlawful, but not all that is unlawful is unfair), the unjust and injustice in the sense of the unfair are not the same as but different from the former kind, as part from whole; for injustice in this sense is a part of injustice in the wide sense, and similarly justice in the one sense of justice in the other. Therefore we must speak also about particular justice and particular injustice and similarly about the just and the unjust. The justice, then, which answers to the whole of virtue, and the corresponding injustice, one being the exercise of virtue as a whole, and the other that of vice as a whole, towards one's neighbour, we may leave on one side. And how the meanings of 'just' and 'unjust' which answer to these are to be distinguished is evident; for practically the majority of the acts commanded by the law are those which are prescribed from the point of view of virtue taken as a whole; for the law bids us practise every virtue and forbids us to practise any vice. And the things that tend to produce virtue taken as a whole are those of the acts prescribed by the law which have been prescribed with a view to education for the common good. But with regard to the education of the individual as such, which makes him without qualification a good *man*, we must determine later whether this is the function of the political art or of another; for perhaps it is not the same to be a good man and a good citizen of any state taken at random.

Of particular justice and that which is just in the corresponding sense, (A) one kind is that which is manifested in distributions of honour or money or the other things that fall to be divided among those who have a share in the constitution[9] (for in these it is possible for one man to have a share either unequal or equal[10] to that of another), and (B) one is that which plays a rectifying part in transactions between man and man. Of this there are two divisions; of transactions (1) some are voluntary and (2) others involuntary—voluntary such transactions as sale, purchase, loan for consumption, pledging, loan for use, depositing, letting (they are called voluntary because the *origin* of these transactions is voluntary), while of the involuntary (*a*) some are clandestine, such as theft, adultery, poisoning, procuring, enticement of slaves,

---

8   That is, its overall type (genus) and the particular kinds which make up that type (differentia).

9   The political system, public life.

10   The Greek words *anisos* and *isos,* translated here as "unequal" and "equal," have a wider meaning than their English equivalents. In particular, they can also be rendered as "unfair" and "fair."

assassination, false witness, and (*b*) others are violent, such as assault, imprisonment, murder, robbery with violence, mutilation, abuse, insult.

3: Distributive justice, in accordance with geometrical proportion.

(A) We have shown that both the unjust man and the unjust act are unfair or unequal; now it is clear that there is also an intermediate between the two unequals involved in either case. And this is the equal; for in any kind of action in which there's a more and a less there is also what is equal. If, then, the unjust is unequal, the just is equal, as all men suppose it to be, even apart from argument. And since the equal is intermediate, the just will be an intermediate. Now equality implies at least two things. The just, then, must be both intermediate and equal and relative (i.e., for certain persons). And *qua*[11] intermediate it must be between certain things (which are respectively greater and less); *qua* equal, it involves *two* things; *qua* just, it is for certain people. The just, therefore, involves at least four terms; for the persons for whom it is in fact just are two, and the things in which it is manifested, the objects distributed, are two. And the same equality will exist between the persons and between the things concerned; for as the latter—the things concerned—are related, so are the former; if they are not equal, they will not have what is equal, but this is the origin of quarrels and complaints—when either equals have and are awarded unequal shares, or unequals equal shares. Further, this is plain from the fact that awards should be 'according to merit'; for all men agree that what is just in distribution must be according to merit in some sense, though they do not all specify the same sort of merit, but democrats identify it with the status of freeman, supporters of oligarchy with wealth (or with noble birth), and supporters of aristocracy with excellence.

The just, then, is a species of the proportionate (proportion being not a property only of the kind of number which consists of abstract units, but of number in general[12]). For proportion is equality of ratios, and involves four terms at least (that discrete proportion involves four terms is plain, but so does continuous proportion,[13] for it uses one term as two and mentions it twice; e.g., 'as the line A is to the line B, so is the line B to the line C'; the line B, then, has been mentioned twice, so that if the line B be assumed twice, the proportional terms will be four); and the just, too, involves at least four terms, and the ratio between one pair is the same as that between the other pair; for there is a similar distinction between the persons and between the things. As the term A, then, is to B, so will C be to D, and therefore, *alternando*,[14] as A is to C, B will be to D. Therefore also the whole is in the same ratio to the whole;[15] and this coupling the distribution effects, and, if the terms are so combined, effects justly. The conjunction, then, of the term A with C and of B with D is what is just in distribution, and this species of the just is intermediate, and the unjust is what violates the proportion; for the proportional is intermediate, and the just is proportional. (Mathematicians call this kind of proportion geometrical; for it is in geometrical proportion that it follows that the whole is to the whole as either part is to the corresponding part.) This proportion is not

---

11   "*Qua* such-and-such" means "considered as being such-and-such," "in the capacity of such-and-such." For example, Queen Elizabeth II might be thought of *qua* monarch, *qua* mother or *qua* Canadian head of state.

12   The contrast here is, roughly, between numbers considered as mathematical entities and numbers of *things*—between *the number two* and *two apples*, for example.

13   An example of "discrete proportion" would be A : B = C : D. An example of "continuous proportion" would be A : B = B : C. (Note that Aristotle uses the terms "discrete" and "continuous" in a way unrelated to their meanings in modern mathematics.)

14   By alternation, taking them alternately.

15   Suppose that A and B are people, and C and D are goods. The idea Aristotle expresses here is that if the ratios of A to B and C to D are the same, then the ratios of A to C and B to D will be the same, and therefore the ratio of (A + C) to (B + D) will be the same as that of A to B. In other words, the goods will be divided according to the same ratio as the difference in merit between the people.

continuous; for we cannot get a single term standing for a person and a thing.

This, then, is what the just is—the proportional; the unjust is what violates the proportion. Hence one term becomes too great, the other too small, as indeed happens in practice; for the man who acts unjustly has too much, and the man who is unjustly treated too little, of what is good. In the case of evil the reverse is true; for the lesser evil is reckoned a good in comparison with the greater evil, since the lesser evil is rather to be chosen than the greater, and what is worthy of choice is good, and what is worthier of choice a greater good.

This, then, is one species of the just.

4: Rectificatory justice, in accordance with arithmetical proportion.

(B) The remaining one is the rectificatory, which arises in connexion with transactions both voluntary and involuntary. This form of the just has a different specific character from the former. For the justice which distributes common possessions is always in accordance with the kind of proportion mentioned above (for in the case also in which the distribution is made from the common funds of a partnership it will be according to the same ratio which the funds put into the business by the partners bear to one another); and the injustice opposed to this kind of justice is that which violates the proportion. But the justice in transactions between man and man is a sort of equality indeed, and the injustice a sort of inequality; not according to that kind of proportion, however, but according to arithmetical proportion.[16] For it makes no difference whether a good man has defrauded a bad man or a bad man a good one, nor whether it is a good or a bad

man that has committed adultery; the law looks only to the distinctive character of the injury, and treats the parties as equal, if one is in the wrong and the other is being wronged, and if one inflicted injury and the other has received it. Therefore, this kind of injustice being an inequality, the judge tries to equalize it; for in the case also in which one has received and the other has inflicted a wound, or one has slain and the other been slain, the suffering and the action have been unequally distributed; but the judge tries to equalize by means of the penalty, taking away from the gain of the assailant. For the term 'gain' is applied generally to such cases—even if it be not a term appropriate to certain cases, e.g., to the person who inflicts a wound—and 'loss' to the sufferer; at all events when the suffering has been estimated, the one is called loss and the other gain. Therefore the equal is intermediate between the greater and the less, but the gain and the loss are respectively greater and less in contrary ways; more of the good and less of the evil are gain, and the contrary is loss; intermediate between them is, as we saw, the equal, which we say is just; therefore corrective justice will be the intermediate between loss and gain. This is why, when people dispute, they take refuge in the judge; and to go to the judge is to go to justice; for the nature of the judge is to be a sort of animate justice; and they seek the judge as an intermediate, and in some states[17] they call judges mediators, on the assumption that if they get what is intermediate they will get what is just. The just, then, is an intermediate, since the judge is so. Now the judge restores equality; it is as though there were a line divided into unequal parts, and he took away that by which the greater segment exceeds the half, and added it to the smaller segment. And when the whole has been equally divided, then they say they have 'their own'—i.e., when they have got what is equal. The equal is intermediate between the greater and the lesser line according to arithmetical proportion. It is for this reason also that it is called just (*dikaion*), because it is a division into two equal parts (*dikha*), just as if one were to call it *dikaion*; and the judge (*dikastes*) is one who bisects (*dikhastes*).[18] For

---

16   An arithmetical proportion is, actually, not so much what we would call a "proportion" at all, but a series in a particular sort of mathematical progression. In such a series, the first term is larger than the second by the same amount by which the third term is larger than the fourth (and so on); thus, $A - B = C - D$. For example, the series 8, 6, 4, 2 would be an arithmetical proportion, since $8 - 6 = 4 - 2$. Aristotle calls this "a sort of equality" because in an arithmetical proportion the sum of the extremes is equal to the sum of the means, i.e., $A + D = B + C$.

17   Such as Larissa (eastern Greece) or Abydos (on the Dardanelles Strait).

18   This is not the actual etymology of these words (Aris-

when something is subtracted from one of two equals and added to the other, the other is in excess by these two; since if what was taken from the one had not been added to the other, the latter would have been in excess by one only. It therefore exceeds the intermediate by one, and the intermediate exceeds by one that from which something was taken. By this, then, we shall recognize both what we must subtract from that which has more, and what we must add to that which has less; we must add to the latter that by which the intermediate exceeds it, and subtract from the greatest that by which it exceeds the intermediate. Let the lines AA', BB', CC' be equal to one another; from the line AA' let the segment AE have been subtracted, and to the line CC' let the segment CD[19] have been added, so that the whole line DCC' exceeds the line EA' by the segment CD and the segment CF;[20] therefore it exceeds the line BB' by the segment CD.

These names, both loss and gain, have come from voluntary exchange; for to have more than one's own is called gaining, and to have less than one's original share is called losing, e.g., in buying and selling and in all other matters in which the law has left people free to make their own terms; but when they get neither more nor less but just what belongs to themselves, they say that they have their own and that they neither lose nor gain.

Therefore the just is intermediate between a sort of gain and a sort of loss, viz. those which are involuntary; it consists in having an equal amount before and after the transaction.

5: Justice in exchange, reciprocity in accordance with proportion.

Some think that *reciprocity*[21] is without qualification just, as the Pythagoreans[22] said; for they defined justice without qualification as reciprocity. Now 'reciprocity' fits neither distributive nor rectificatory justice—yet people *want* even the justice of Rhadamanthus[23] to mean this:

> Should a man suffer what he did, right justice would be done

—for in many cases reciprocity and rectificatory justice are not in accord; e.g., (1) if an official has inflicted a wound, he should not be wounded in return, and if someone has wounded an official, he ought not to be wounded only but punished in addition. Further (2) there is a great difference between a voluntary and an involuntary act. But in associations for exchange this sort of justice does hold men together—reciprocity in accordance with a proportion and not on the basis of precisely equal return. For it is by proportionate requital that the city holds together. Men seek to return either evil for evil—and if they cannot do so, think their position mere slavery—or good for good—and if they cannot do so there is no exchange, but it is by exchange that they hold together. This is why they give a prominent place to the temple of the Graces[24]—to promote the requital of services; for this is characteristic of grace[25]—we should serve in return one who has shown grace to us, and should another time take the initiative in showing it.

Now proportionate return is secured by cross-conjunction. Let A be a builder, B a shoemaker, C a house, D a shoe. The builder, then, must get from the shoemaker the latter's work, and must himself give him in return his own. If, then, first there is proportionate equality of goods, and then reciprocal action takes place, the result we mention will be effected. If

---

totle was mistaken if he thought it was).

19 For the example to work, CD must be equal in length to AE. Aristotle would have used a diagram to make this clear.

20 Which must also be equal in length to AE.

21 The Greek term—*antipeponthos*—literally means "suffering in return for one's action."

22 The followers of Pythagoras (c. 570–495 BCE), a philosopher who believed in reincarnation and defended

the view that all of reality could be understood in numerical terms (*harmonia*).

23 A mythical king of the Minoans, said to be the son of Zeus and Europa. He was famous for his uncompromising sense of justice and as a reward he was made immortal and transported to Hades, the Greek afterworld, where he judges the souls of the dead. The quotation on the next line is probably from Hesiod.

24 The three goddesses of joy, charm, and beauty.

25 *Charis*, Greek for "grace," also suggests the notions of "gratitude" and "favor."

not, the bargain is not equal, and does not hold; for there is nothing to prevent the work of the one being better than that of the other; they must therefore be equated. (And this is true of the other arts also; for they would have been destroyed if what the patient suffered had not been just what the agent did, and of the same amount and kind.) For it is not two doctors that associate for exchange, but a doctor and a farmer, or in general people who are different and unequal; but these must be equated. This is why all things that are exchanged must be somehow comparable. It is for this end that money has been introduced, and it becomes in a sense an intermediate; for it measures all things, and therefore the excess and the defect— how many shoes are equal to a house or to a given amount of food. The number of shoes exchanged for a house [or for a given amount of food] must therefore correspond to the ratio of builder to shoemaker. For if this be not so, there will be no exchange and no intercourse. And this proportion will not be effected unless the goods are somehow equal. All goods must therefore be measured by some one thing, as we said before. Now this unit is in truth demand,[26] which holds all things together (for if men did not need one another's goods at all, or did not need them equally, there would be either no exchange or not the same exchange); but money has become by convention a sort of representative of demand; and this is why it has the name 'money' (*nomisma*)—because it exists not by nature but by law (*nomos*) and it is in our power to change it and make it useless. There will, then, be reciprocity when the terms have been equated so that as farmer is to shoemaker, the amount of the shoe-maker's work is to that of the farmer's work for which it exchanges. But we must not bring them into a figure of proportion when they have already exchanged (otherwise one extreme will have both excesses), but when they still have their own goods. Thus they are equals and associates just because this equality can be effected in their case. Let A be a farmer, C food, B a shoemaker, D his product equated to C. If it had not been possible for reciprocity to be thus effected, there would have been no association of the parties. That

demand holds things together as a single unit is shown by the fact that when men do not need one another, i.e., when neither needs the other or one does not need the other, they do not exchange, as we do when some one wants what one has oneself, e.g., when people permit the exportation of corn in exchange for wine. This equation therefore must be established. And for the future exchange—that if we do not need a thing now we shall have it if ever we do need it—money is as it were our surety; for it must be possible for us to get what we want by bringing the money. Now the same thing happens to money itself as to goods—it is not always worth the same; yet it tends to be steadier. This is why all goods must have a price set on them; for then there will always be exchange, and if so, association of man with man. Money, then, acting as a measure, makes goods commensurate and equates them; for neither would there have been association if there were not exchange, nor exchange if there were not equality, nor equality if there were not commen-surability. Now in truth it is impossible that things differing so much should become commensurate, but with reference to demand they may become so suf-ficiently. There must, then, be a unit, and that fixed by agreement (for which reason it is called money); for it is this that makes all things commensurate, since all things are measured by money. Let A be a house, B ten minae,[27] C a bed. A is half of B, if the house is worth five minae or equal to them; the bed, C, is a tenth of B; it is plain, then, how many beds are equal to a house, viz. five. That exchange took place thus before there was money is plain; for it makes no difference whether it is five beds that exchange for a house, or the money value of five beds.

We have now defined the unjust and the just. These having been marked off from each other, it is plain that just action is intermediate between acting unjustly and being unjustly treated; for the one is to have too much and the other to have too little. Justice is a kind of mean, but not in the same way as the other virtues, but because it relates to an intermediate amount, while injustice relates to the extremes. And justice is that in virtue of which the just man is said to be a doer, by

---

26 Greek—*chreia*—often translated as "need" rather than "demand."

27 A unit of currency. One mina was worth 100 ancient drachmae.

choice, of that which is just, and one who will distribute either between himself and another or between two others not so as to give more of what is desirable to himself and less to his neighbour (and conversely with what is harmful), but so as to give what is equal in accordance with proportion; and similarly in distributing between two other persons. Injustice on the other hand is similarly related to the unjust, which is excess and defect, contrary to proportion, of the useful or hurtful. For which reason injustice is excess and defect, viz.

because it is productive of excess and defect—in one's own case excess of what is in its own nature useful and defect of what is hurtful, while in the case of others it is as a whole like what it is in one's own case, but proportion may be violated in either direction. In the unjust act to have too little is to be unjustly treated; to have too much is to act unjustly.

Let this be taken as our account of the nature of justice and injustice, and similarly of the just and the unjust in general.

THOMAS HOBBES
Leviathan

Who Was Thomas Hobbes?

Thomas Hobbes was born, prematurely, in 1588[1] in the village of Westport near the small town of Malmesbury, in the southern English county of Wiltshire. Though several relatives had grown wealthy in the family's cloth-making business, Hobbes's father was a poor, ill-educated country clergyman, who frequently ran into trouble with the church authorities for disobedience and volatility. Young Thomas was apparently a studious, unhealthy, rather melancholy boy, who loved music. Because of his black hair, he was nicknamed "Crow" by his schoolfellows. When Hobbes was 16, his father's long-running feud with a near-

by vicar, whom he had publicly slandered as "a knave and an arrant knave and a drunken knave," came to a head when (probably drunk) he encountered his enemy in the churchyard at Malmesbury and set about him with his fists. Any act of violence in a church or churchyard was an excommunicable offense at that time, and laying hands on a clergyman was an even more serious crime, subject to corporal punishment and imprisonment. Hobbes's father was forced to flee. It is not known whether Thomas ever again saw his father, who died "in obscurity beyond London."

By the time of his father's disappearance, however, young Hobbes had already been plucked out of his family situation and sent off to Oxford (an education paid for by his uncle Francis, a prosperous glover). There, Hobbes attended Magdalen Hall, one of the poorer foundations at Oxford and one which was renowned for its religious Puritanism.[2] He does not

---

1   This was the year that the Catholic monarch of Spain, Philip II, dispatched a massive fleet of ships—the Armada—to invade Protestant England. Hobbes later wrote, in an autobiographical poem, that "hereupon it was my mother dear / Did bring forth twins at once, both me and fear," and used to joke that this explained his timid nature. (In the event, however, the Armada was decisively defeated in the English Channel before it could rendezvous with the Spanish invasion force waiting in the Spanish Netherlands, an area comprising modern Belgium, Luxembourg, and part of northern France.)

---

2   The Puritans were a group of English Protestants who regarded the Protestant Reformation under Elizabeth I (1558–1603) as incomplete. Influenced by Protestant teachings from continental Europe, such as Calvinism, they advocated strict religious discipline and simplification of the ceremonies and creeds of the Church of England.

seem to have been impressed by the quality of the education he received. Later in life he was dismissive of the Aristotelian logic and metaphysics he was taught and claimed that, at the time, he was more interested in reading about explorations of newly-discovered lands and poring over maps of the world and the stars, than in studying traditional philosophy.

As soon as Hobbes completed his BA, in 1608, he was lucky enough to be offered a job as tutor to the eldest son of William Cavendish, a rich and powerful Derbyshire land-owner who owned the great stately home at Chatsworth (and who became the first Earl of Devonshire in 1618). Cavendish's son, also called William, was only a few years younger than Hobbes himself, and Hobbes's position quickly became that of a servant, secretary, and friend, rather than tutor. In 1614, Hobbes and Cavendish toured France and Italy, where they both learned Italian and encountered some of the currents of Italian intellectual thought, including the fiercely anti-Papal writings of several Venetian authors.

William Cavendish succeeded his father as the Earl of Devonshire in 1626, but died of disease just two years later. Hobbes, now 40 years old, signed on as tutor to the son of another rich landowner, Sir Gervase Clifton. During this period, he accompanied his charge on another trip to the continent (France and Switzerland), and it was in Geneva that he picked up a copy of Euclid's *Elements* and fell in love with its method of deductive reasoning. A contemporary biographer wrote of the incident:

> Being in a gentleman's library, Euclid's *Elements* lay open, and 'twas the 47th Prop. of Book I. He read the proposition. "By G—," said he (he would now and then swear, by way of emphasis), "this is impossible!" So he reads the demonstration of it, which referred him back to

such a proposition; which proposition he read. That referred him back to another, which he also read. And so on, until at last he was demonstratively convinced of that truth. This made him in love with geometry.

After his return to England, Hobbes agreed to re-enter the service of the widowed countess of Devonshire as tutor to her 13-year-old son, the third earl. The 1630s were important years for Hobbes's intellectual development. His secure, and relatively undemanding, position allowed him time to develop both the main outlines of his political philosophy and also to pursue his interest in science (especially optics). His connection to a great noble house also gave him contacts with other intellectuals clustered around noble patrons, such as the mathematicians and scientists supported by the earl of Newcastle, and the theologians, lawyers, and poets associated with the Viscount Falkland.

In 1634, Hobbes embarked on another European tour with his pupil, and spent over a year living in Paris where he met French scientists and mathematicians—and especially the influential and well-connected Marin Mersenne—and became finally and fully gripped by the intellectual excitement of the age. "The extreme pleasure I take in study overcomes in me all other appetites," he wrote at this time in a letter. By 1636, when Hobbes had returned to England, he was devoting as much of his energies as possible to philosophical and scientific work: the third earl turned 18 in 1637, so—although Hobbes remained in his service—he was no longer needed as a tutor and his time was largely his own.

His earliest surviving work is a treatise on the science of optics, in part of which Hobbes attacks Descartes' *Discourse on the Method* (published in 1637). Hobbes accused Descartes of inconsistency and of not taking seriously enough his own mechanistic physics. Since perception is caused entirely by physical motions or pressures, then the mind—that which does the perceiving—must also be a physical object, capable of being affected by motion, Hobbes argued.[3] Hobbes, therefore, in his very earliest philosophical writing rejected the dualism of matter and spirit in favor of a purely mechanical view of the world.

Hobbes's philosophical work was pushed in a different direction at the end of the 1630s, as political events unfolded in England. As the country moved towards civil war, during the final years of the so-called "personal rule" of King Charles I,[4] there was an intense public debate about the degree of absoluteness of the power of the sovereign. The main issue was whether there were any limits to the power of the king at all. It was recognized that the monarch could exceed his normal powers during exceptional circumstances—but the king, himself, claimed to be the judge of which circumstances were exceptional, and this essentially allowed him to exceed his "normal" powers whenever he chose. In 1640, after the Scots invaded and occupied northern England, the King recalled Parliament to grant him extra taxes to raise an army. They refused, and what became known as the "Short Parliament" was abruptly dissolved. In the same year, Hobbes wrote and circulated an unabashedly pro-royalist work called *The Elements of Law*, which attempted to justify the nature and extent of sovereign power from philosophical first principles. By the end of that year, facing a backlash from anti-royalist parliamentarians as tensions grew, Hobbes called in all his investments and left England for Paris.

In Paris, Hobbes was quickly reabsorbed into the intellectual life of the great city, and his reputation was established by the 1642 publication of *De Cive*, a remodeled version of *The Elements of Law*. After this, Hobbes returned to the study of scientific philosophy and theology, and spent several years working on a substantial book on logic, metaphysics, and physics, which was eventually published in 1655 as *De Corpore*. However, his work was frequently interrupted, once by a serious illness from which he nearly died (in 1647), and repeatedly by visitors from England, including royalist exiles from the English Civil War (which had erupted in 1642 and dragged on until 1648). In 1646, Hobbes was made mathematical tutor to the young Prince Charles, now in exile in Paris. This turned Hobbes's thoughts back to politics, and—secretively and rapidly—he completed the major work *Leviathan* between the autumn of 1649 and the spring of 1651.

By this time, Hobbes was keen to return to England. The war had been won by the Parliamentarians (Charles I was beheaded in 1649, the monarchy and House of Lords abolished, and a Commonwealth, led by Oliver Cromwell, set up) and *Leviathan*—which Hobbes took care to ensure was published in London—was partly intended to ease his passage back home. Hobbes did not abandon, or even substantially modify, the central arguments of his earlier, royalist writings, but in *Leviathan* he does emphasize that his project is to justify *political authority* generally (and not necessarily just that of a monarch). He also discusses extensively the question—which at that time was of vital interest to the former aristocratic supporters of the old king—of when it is legitimate to shift allegiance from one ruler to another. Hobbes later said he had written *Leviathan* on behalf of "those many and faithful servants and subjects of His Majesty," who had fought on the royalist side and lost, and who were now in the position of negotiating with the new Parliamentary rulers for their old lands and titles. "They that had done their utmost endeavor to perform their obligation to the King, had done all that they could be obliged unto; and were consequently at liberty to seek the safety of their lives and livelihood wheresoever, and without treachery."

---

3   "Since vision is formally and really nothing but motion, it follows that that which sees is also formally and strictly speaking nothing other than that which is moved; for nothing other than a body ... can be moved." (*Tractatus opticus*, p. 207. This translation is by Noel Malcolm.)

4   In 1629, after a series of clashes with Parliament, Charles dissolved the legislative body permanently and began an eleven-year period of ruling alone, as an absolute monarch.

Hobbes probably did not expect his work to cause offense among the court-in-exile of the young Charles II in Paris,[5] and he presented a hand-written copy to the king in 1651. However, because he denied that kings ruled by a divine right handed down directly from God, Hobbes was perceived as turning against the monarchy. Furthermore, the attack on organized religion, and especially Catholicism, that *Leviathan* contained provoked fury among Charles's courtiers. Hobbes was banned from the court, and shortly afterwards the French clergy attempted to have him arrested; Hobbes quickly fled back to England.

There he settled back into the employ of the Earl of Devonshire, and resumed a quiet bachelor life of light secretarial work and intellectual discussion. However, the notoriety of *Leviathan* slowly grew, and—because of its bitter attacks on religion and the universities— Hobbes made enemies of many influential groups. For example, when the Royal Society was formed in 1660, Hobbes was pointedly *not* invited to become a member, partly because his fellow exponents of the new "mechanical philosophy" were highly wary of being associated with atheism and reacted by violently attacking Hobbes's supposedly "atheistic" new worldview. Throughout the 1660s and 1670s, Hobbes and his works were denounced from pulpits all over England for what was said to be his godlessness and denial of objective moral values. There were even rumors that Hobbes—a.k.a. the "Beast of Malmesbury"—was to be charged for heresy (which could, even then, have resulted in his being burned at the stake, though the last people to be executed for heresy in England died in 1612). In contrast with the general public vilification Hobbes faced in his own country, in France and Holland his reputation was soaring and (after the death of acclaimed scientist Pierre Gassendi in 1655) he was widely regarded by French scientists and men of letters as the greatest living philosopher.

Hobbes, though now well into old age (and suffering severely from Parkinson's disease), continued to write prolifically, including several public defenses of *Leviathan*, several treatises on mathematics, a debate with Robert Boyle about the experimental evidence for vacuums, a short book on six problems in physics, a polemical church history in Latin verse, translations of Homer's *Iliad* and *Odyssey* into English verse, and a history of the English civil war entitled *Behemoth*. When Hobbes died, shortly after suffering a severe stroke in December 1679, he was 91 years old.

What Was Hobbes's Overall Philosophical Project?

Hobbes thought of himself as primarily a scientist. Not only was he interested in what we would, today, think of as science (optics, physics, geometry), he was also concerned to place the study of human beings— especially psychology, ethics, and politics—on what he considered a *scientific* footing. Hobbes was deeply conscious that he was living during a period of intellectual revolution—a time when the old Aristotelian assumptions were being stripped away by the new mechanical and mathematical science which Hobbes enthusiastically endorsed—as well as during an era of political and religious revolution. He wanted to play a significant role in both these movements.

Since Hobbes considered himself a scientist, his view of what *constitutes* science is particularly significant. Hobbes's scheme of the sciences changes somewhat throughout his writings, but its most stable core looks something like this. The most fundamental science is what Hobbes (like Aristotle) called "first philosophy," and it consists in "universal definitions"—of *body*, *motion*, *time*, *place*, *cause*, and so on—and their logical consequences. Thus the most basic kind of science, for Hobbes, is more purely rational than it is experimental. After first philosophy, comes geometry, which (for Hobbes) was the science of the simple motions of bodies. For example, Hobbes rejected the view that geometry is the study of abstract objects and their relations, but instead insisted that it concerns itself with the movements of concrete objects in real space. The next step in the ladder of the sciences is mechanics, which investigates the more complex motions due to whole bodies working together, and this is followed by physics, the study of the invisible motions of the parts of bodies (including the effects on the human senses of the motions of external bodies). Then comes moral philosophy, which Hobbes

---

5   Charles II was eventually restored to the throne, by a vote of Parliament, in 1660.

thought of as primarily the investigation of passion and volition, which he considered the internal effects of sensation on the human mind. Finally, civil philosophy—the science of politics—formulates the laws of conduct that will ensure peace and self-preservation for communities of creatures with our particular internal psychological constitution.

A central—and at the time infamous—plank of Hobbes's scientific world-view was his unrelenting *materialism*. According to the new "mechanical" philosophy which had caught Hobbes up in its sweep across the thinkers of Europe, all physical phenomena are ultimately to be explained in terms of the motions and interactions of large numbers of tiny, material bodies. Hobbes enthusiastically accepted this view, and was one of the earliest thinkers to extend it to phenomena his peers generally did not think of as "physical." In particular, Hobbes declared that *mental* phenomena ought to be just as susceptible to mechanical explanation as anything else in nature. For Hobbes, then, the natural world did not contain both matter and spirit (minds): it was entirely made up of material bodies, and human beings were to be viewed as nothing more than very complex material objects, like sophisticated robots or automata.

Along similar lines, Hobbes was very skeptical of claims to religious knowledge, and this was one among several reasons why he devoted so much energy to attacks on the authority of the church. According to Hobbes's theory of language, words have meaning only if they express thoughts, and thoughts are nothing more than the residue in our minds of sensations produced by the action of external objects upon our bodies. Since God is supposed to be an infinite, transcendent being, beyond our powers to perceive, Hobbes—although it is not at all clear that he was actually an atheist—was led to assert we can have no meaningful thoughts about God, and thus can say nothing positive about him. Furthermore, according to Hobbes's materialism, the notion of an "incorporeal substance" is simply incoherent, and so, if God exists at all, he must exist as a *material* body (which Hobbes claimed, in fact, to believe).

Like Descartes, Hobbes saw himself as developing the foundations for a completely new and radical philosophy which was to decisively change the way his contemporaries saw the world. Furthermore, Hobbes did not see moral and political philosophy as a purely intellectual exercise. He firmly believed the great and tragic upheaval of the English Civil War was directly caused by the promulgation of false and dangerous moral ideas, and could have been avoided by proper appreciation of the moral truth. In *Leviathan*, then, Hobbes's project was to place social and political philosophy on a *scientific* basis for the first time (and he thought doing so would be of immense service to humanity). His model for this was geometry: he begins with a sequence of axiomatic definitions—such as "justice," "obligation," "right of nature," and "law of nature"—and then tries to show that his philosophical results are rationally derivable from these basic assumptions. His goal was to derive and prove universal political laws—rather like the laws of physics—from which infallible judgments about particular cases can be made.[6]

What Is the Structure of This Reading?

Leviathan is divided into four parts: "Of Man," which deals primarily with human psychology and the state of nature; "Of Commonwealth," which discusses the formation of political states and the powers of their sovereigns; "Of a Christian Commonwealth," which examines the relationship between secular and religious law; and "Of the Kingdom of Darkness," which is a vitriolic attack on certain kinds of organized religion, and especially Catholicism. The excerpts given here come from Parts I and II.

First, there is a sequence of three chapters which come nearly at the end of Part I. In these Hobbes describes the unhappy "state of nature" for human beings and argues that several (nineteen) moral "laws of nature" or "theorems" arise as "convenient articles of peace upon which men may be drawn to agreement." Included in this discussion, at the end of Chap-

---

6   On the other hand, it is important to note that, unlike physics, politics is a *normative* science. It does not simply describe what people do do, but in some sense prescribes what they *ought* to do. In this respect, Hobbes's political science resembles modern economics more than mathematics or experimental science.

ter XIV, is an examination of the way in which natural rights can be transferred or renounced (through contracts, covenants, or free gifts). There is also (near the beginning of Chapter XV) a lengthy discussion of the nature of justice, *"that men perform their covenants made."* Then we jump to the first two chapters of "Of Commonwealth," in which Hobbes discusses how political states arise and argues that state sovereigns are entitled to almost absolute power over their subjects.

Some Useful Background Information

1. *Leviathan* was published just forty years after the first "King James" English translation of the Bible; hence Hobbes's writing style, dating from the same period, is what, today, we might think of as "biblical." This makes Hobbes all the more interesting to read, but can impose something of a barrier for modern audiences. Here is a short glossary of some words in the reading which might be unfamiliar or used in an unfamiliar or archaic way.

   Acception: Favoritism, corrupt preference for one person over another.

   Anticipate: To forestall—to prevent someone else's action by acting first.

   Asperity: Roughness, difficulty.

   Attainted (of): Convicted or condemned for something (especially treason).

   Beholding (to): Bound to, under obligation to.

   But: Only.

   Caution: Security, confident lack of anxiety.

   Commodious: Convenient, pleasant. (Hence, an *incommodity* is an inconvenience.)

   Commonwealth: An autonomous community or nation—especially a republic—in which supreme political power is derived from the people.

   Concord: Agreement, harmony.

   Conduce: To lead or contribute to (some result).

   Confederacy: An alliance or league formed for the purpose of joint action or mutual support.

   Conform: To mold together, bring into agreement, regulate.

   Consent (in): To agree to.

   Consequent: A thing that follows or is the result of something.

   Constitute: To enact, set up, establish.

   Contemn: To treat with contempt, scorn, or disdain.

   Contumely: Insolent insult or rudeness.

   Defect: Lack.

   Delectation: Delight, pleasure.

   Despoil: To rob or plunder.

   Detain: To hold or keep back (especially something that is due).

   Diffidence: Distrust (as opposed to the more modern sense, timidity).

   Dissociate: To separate.

   Distracted: Pulled in different directions.

   Dominion: The right to control or possess something.

   Emergent: Unexpectedly arising.

   Emulation: Ambitious rivalry for power or honor, the desire to excel over another.

   Endamage: Injure, cause harm to.

   Except: Unless.

   Froward: Perverse, difficult to deal with.

   Husbandry: Farming, or the careful management of one's resources.

   Ignominy: Disgrace, dishonor.

   Incommunicable: Not capable of being shared.

   Industry: Diligence or energy.

   Iniquity: Wickedness.

   Invention: Discovery.

   Irregular: Unregulated.

   List: To desire, to wish.

   Lust: Desire, pleasure, relish.

   Machination: The act of plotting or scheming.

   Manner: Customary mode of behavior.

   Moment: Importance, significance.

   Obnoxious (to): Exposed to, liable to.

   Original: The origin or source of something; coming first, or preceding all others in time.

   Own: To recognize or claim as one's own.

   Partiality: Bias or prejudice.

   Patience: Forbearance.

   Peradventure: Perhaps.

   Perfect: Complete, lacking nothing.

   Plurality: Majority.

   Presently: Immediately.

Pressure: Burden, weight.

Pretend: To lay claim to or profess (not necessarily deceitfully).

Propriety: Property, ownership (as opposed to the modern sense, suitableness).

Rapine: Plunder, taking the property of others by force.

Redound (to): Make a large contribution to, or have a great effect on, someone's reputation or advantage.

Restrain: Restrict.

Sensible: Readily perceived or appreciated.

Sentence: Judgment.

Several: Separate.

Soever: To any extent, in any way (e.g., "how great soever it may be").

Specious: Misleadingly attractive or plausible.

Translation: Transfer.

Want: Need, lack.

Wit: Intelligence.

Withal: With.

2. The fundamental political problem for Hobbes, and the issue *Leviathan* primarily sets out to address, was the following: How can any political system unambiguously and indisputably determine the answer to the question *What is the law?* How can universally, uncontroversially acceptable rules of conduct by which the citizens of a state must lead their public lives be determined? A precondition, Hobbes thought, was for there to be only a *single* source of law, and for that source to be *absolute* in the sense that whatever the legislator declared as law *was* law. Any other kind of political system, Hobbes believed, would descend inevitably into factionalism, insecurity, and civil war.

3. Hobbes was quite self-conscious in rejecting the Aristotelian view of *human nature* which had been passed down to his day. For Aristotle, human beings are naturally social animals, our natural situation is as active members of a political community, and our highest good is the sort of happiness, or flourishing, for which our biological species is best suited. Furthermore, according to Aristotle, there is a natural hierarchy among human beings, with some people being inherently more noble than others. These inequalities are not *created* by society, on the Aristotelian picture, but ideally should be *mirrored* in the social order.

For Hobbes, by contrast, human beings are *not* naturally social animals, and furthermore there is no single conception of happiness tied to the human 'essence.' Instead, according to Hobbes, human happiness is a matter of the continual satisfaction of desires or appetites, and since individual human beings differ in their particular desires, so too will what makes people happy. Because people's desires often come into conflict—especially when several people compete for the same scarce resource, such as land, money, or honor—human beings are naturally *anti*-social. Furthermore, even when civil society has been established, according to Hobbes, most of its citizens will not, and should not, be active participants in political life, but will simply lead private lives, out of the public sphere, within the constraints of their obedience to the commands of the sovereign. Finally, it was Hobbes's view that human beings, in the state of nature, are in a state of radical equality, where no one is substantially any better (or worse) than anyone else; similarly, in civil society, although there will be gradations of honor among men, everyone is fundamentally equal under the sovereign.

4. Like Aristotle, however, Hobbes sees justice, and morality generally, as applying to character traits—what Hobbes calls "manners"—rather than primarily to states of affairs or types of action. For Hobbes, moral virtues are those habits which it is rational for all people to praise; that is, they are those dispositions which contribute to the preservation, not merely of the individual, but of *everyone* in the community by contributing to peace and stable society.

Some Common Misconceptions

1. When Hobbes talks about "the state of nature" he is referring *neither* to a particular historical period in human history (such as the age

of hunter-gatherers) *nor* to a mere theoretical possibility (a time that never actually occurred). What Hobbes has in mind is any situation, at any time or place, where there is no effective government capable of imposing order on the local population. Thus primitive or prehistoric societies may (or may not) be in the state of nature; but so may modern societies locked in a civil war, destroyed by conflict with other countries, or simply experiencing a constitutional crisis. Likewise, the international community of nations (then, as now) is in a state of nature, lacking any overarching world government capable of determining and enforcing international law. (Hence, as he points out in the text, when Hobbes describes the state of nature as being "a condition of war" he does not mean it will necessarily involve constant fighting and bloodshed, but rather that no one can feel *secure* against the threat of force.)

2. Hobbes is not the "immoralist" he is sometimes taken to be. Far from arguing *against* the existence of universal moral principles, Hobbes is concerned to *combat* the kind of moral relativism which holds that all laws, including moral laws, are mere matters of arbitrary human convention. Hobbes adopts the assumption of the moral skeptic that the only fundamental, universal moral principle is self-interest, but he then argues that, from the skeptic's *own assumption*, certain "natural" laws of justice follow deductively. In this way, he tries to show there can be laws without a lawgiver: moral principles based, not in divine or human command, but in human nature itself. (On the other hand, Hobbes does stress, we are bound by these laws only if we can be sure others will obey them too—that is, on the whole, only once we have agreed to form a civil society. To that extent, at least, the principles of justice remain, for Hobbes, a matter of *convention*.)

3. A mainspring of Hobbes's political philosophy is the claim that human beings seek their own self-preservation. There is textual evidence that Hobbes saw this desire for self-preservation not as merely a non-rational desire, even one which all human beings naturally share, but as actually being a *primary goal of reason*. That is, one of the dictates *of rationality*, for Hobbes, is that we should take all measures necessary for our self-preservation, and so the ethical laws Hobbes generates out of this principle are not merely *hypothetical* commands ("Do this if you care more about your self-preservation than anything else") but are dictates that all rational creatures should recognize as binding.

4. Though Hobbes is, legitimately, often said to be rather pessimistic about human nature, this can be overstated. His view, essentially, is not that *everyone* is selfish, but that *enough* people are fundamentally selfish that it would be unwise to construct a civil society on the assumption that people are generally benevolent. According to Hobbes, children are born concerned only with themselves and, though they can learn to care for others, this can be brought about only with proper moral education. Unfortunately, he believed not very many children are actually brought up in this way, and so most of the citizens of a commonwealth will, in fact, care primarily for themselves and their families and not be much moved by the interests of strangers.

5. Hobbes did not think that people *in fact* always act to preserve themselves: his claim is not that people always behave in a way which is optimal in avoiding hardship or death for themselves—on the contrary, Hobbes was convinced that people are often rash and vainglorious and prone to irrational quarrels—but that it is always *reasonable* or *rational* for people to seek self-preservation, and furthermore that this fact is so universally recognized by human beings that it is capable of serving as a solid basis for civil society. (Contrary to popular belief, then, Hobbes is not quite what is technically called a "psychological egoist": someone who believes that all people, as a matter of psychological necessity, always act only in their own self-interest.)

6. Although Hobbes is frequently thought of as a *social contract theorist*, he actually does not

see the foundation of the state as involving a contract or covenant between *all* members of that society, but instead as a kind of *free gift* by the citizens to their sovereign. That is, people in the state of nature (covenant together to) freely turn over their right of nature to a sovereign power, in the hope that this sovereign will protect them and allow them to live in greater security. (Importantly, this means the sovereign cannot *break a covenant* if he or she fails to protect her subjects, though she does come to be bound by the law of nature prohibiting ingratitude, and so must "endeavour that he which giveth [a gift] have no reasonable cause to repent him of his good will.")

7. Hobbes thought that his new political science could conclusively demonstrate that all states need a sovereign (an absolute dispenser of law). He did not, however, insist that this sovereign must be a *monarch*; he was quite ready to recognize that a republic, led by an assembly of senators for example, could be an equally effective form of government.

How Important and Influential Is This Passage?

Hobbes's *Leviathan* is arguably the most important work of political philosophy in English before the twentieth century, even though the work's *conclusions* have been widely rejected from Hobbes's day to this. The project of justifying and delimiting the extent of the state's power over its subjects, without appeal to such supernatural mechanisms as the divine right of kings, is an immensely important one, and it can be said that Hobbes gave this question its first great answer in modern times. The selections reprinted here include several themes for which Hobbes is most notorious: the doctrine that life in a state of nature is "solitary, poor, nasty, brutish, and short"; the attempt to ground universal principles of justice in the essential selfishness of human nature; the notion that the institution of a political state consists in a kind of "contract" between its members; and the claim that the power of a sovereign is absolute.

Suggestions for Critical Reflection

1. Hobbes argues that, in the state of nature, everybody is fundamentally equal in ability and in rights. Is he right about this? If he is, does this mean all *social* inequalities are based on nothing more than convention?

2. Hobbes argues that human beings, in the state of nature, are in a continual state of "war of every one against every one." How good are his arguments for this claim? Are there any real-world examples of groups of people who are in the state of nature (as Hobbes defines it) but *not* at war with each other? If Hobbes incorrectly equates the state of nature with a condition of warfare, how seriously does this affect his subsequent arguments?

3. "By *liberty* is understood, according to the proper signification of the word, the absence of external impediments." Is this a fully adequate definition? Is Hobbes's view of liberty significant for the political theory that he develops? (For example, would someone who took a different view of freedom be happy with Hobbes's view of sovereign power?)

4. At one point, Hobbes suggests injustice is a kind of absurdity or inconsistency, and thus to be unjust is simply to be irrational. Is Hobbes right (in the terms of his own theory)? If so, does this show something about Hobbes's *definition* of injustice? Is injustice really nothing more or less than "*the not performance of covenant*"?

5. "Of the voluntary acts of every man, the object is some *good to himself*." Is this true? Is it a realistic assumption, or is Hobbes being excessively pessimistic about human nature? (Taken in the wider context of this reading, does it seem that Hobbes means to describe how human beings invariably *do* behave, or to state how people *should* behave if they are being rational? Does the way his claim is understood make a difference to Hobbes's argument?)

6. Hobbes argues that, in the state of nature, there is no justice. If Hobbes is right about this, does it follow that all human beings are *immoral* by nature?

7. Does Hobbes reconcile morality and self-interest? That is, does he successfully show that they are *the same thing*? (Is this, in fact, what he is trying to do?)

8. Hobbes formulates his principles of justice, in part, as a reaction to Aristotle's moral theory. If you have read the previous selection, you might want to think about the differences and similarities between, and the relative merits of, Hobbes and Aristotle.

9. "Whatsoever is done to a man, conformable to his own will signified to the doer, is not injury to him." Does this follow logically from Hobbes's assumptions? If it does, is this a problem for those assumptions?

10. Since there is no mechanism for enforcing agreements in the state of nature, how can people in that state first contract together to form a commonwealth? How can this first crucial covenant be made *before* there exists a power to enforce covenants?

11. "The power of the mighty hath no foundation but in the opinion and belief of the people.... If men know not their duty, what is there that can force them to obey the laws? An army, you will say? But what shall force the army?" (Hobbes, *Behemoth*). Since this is the case, and since the absolute authority of sovereigns rests on their power to protect their subjects and enforce covenants between them, then how can people in a state of nature agree to set up a sovereign? How can some single individual simply be *given* absolute power?

12. Hobbes argues that, once a commonwealth has been set up, every member of the commonwealth must treat the sovereign's actions as being *their own* actions—must "*authorize* all the actions and judgments of that man, or assembly of men, in the same manner as if they were his own"—even if those actions cause them personal hardship. (So, for example, if the state puts you in prison it is no different than if you had voluntarily locked yourself up.) Does this seem reasonable? Is it a crucial part of Hobbes's political theory, or could he have adopted a weaker position on this point?

13. What view do you think Hobbes would take of the notion of *democratically elected* government? What would be his view of civil disobedience or protest movements?

Suggestions for Further Reading

Various editions of Hobbes's *Leviathan* are available. The edition by Edwin Curley (Hackett, 1994), includes a useful introduction and some entertaining biographical material, including Hobbes's verse autobiography. There is also a Penguin edition (1982), edited and with an introduction by C.B. Macpherson; an edition with an introduction by Richard Tuck (Cambridge University Press, 1996); and a Norton Critical Edition, edited by Flathman and Johnson, which includes a great selection of background and interpretive material (W.W. Norton, 1996). It is also well worth looking at Hobbes's *De Cive*, which Hobbes, himself, thought of as his most "scientific" statement of his political philosophy. It is available, edited by Bernard Gert, from Hackett (1991).

Useful books on the political background to Hobbes's work are Quentin Skinner's *The Foundations of Modern Political Thought* (Cambridge University Press, 1978) and David Wootton's *Divine Right and Democracy* (Penguin, 1986). An entertaining account of the hostile contemporary reaction to Hobbes's philosophy is by Samuel Mintz, *The Hunting of Leviathan* (Cambridge University Press, 1962); and a fascinating book on one of Hobbes's forays into experimental science is Shapin and Schaffer's *Leviathan and the Air-Pump* (Princeton University Press, 1985).

Three books which describe Hobbes's philosophy as a whole are R.S. Peters, *Hobbes* (Penguin, 1956), Tom Sorrell, *Hobbes* (Routledge, 1986), and Richard Tuck, *Hobbes* (Oxford University Press, 1989). There are also many books specifically on Hobbes's political philosophy; some of the best are: Deborah Baumgold, *Hobbes's Political Theory* (Cambridge University Press, 1988); David Gauthier, *The Logic of Leviathan* (Oxford University Press, 1969); Jean Hampton, *Hobbes and the Social Contract Tradition* (Cambridge University Press, 1986); David Johnston, *The Rhetoric of Leviathan* (Princeton University Press, 1986); Gregory Kavka, *Hobbesian Moral and Political Theory* (Princeton University

Press, 1986); S.A. Lloyd, *Ideals as Interests in Hobbes's Leviathan* (Cambridge University Press, 1992); A.P. Martinich, *The Two Gods of Leviathan* (Cambridge University Press, 1992); Michael Oakeshott, *Hobbes on Civil Association* (Oxford University Press, 1975); Johann Sommerville, *Thomas Hobbes: Political Ideas in Historical Context* (Palgrave, 1992); Leo Strauss, *The Political Philosophy of Thomas Hobbes* (University of Chicago Press, 1952); and Howard Warrender, *The Political Philosophy of Hobbes* (Oxford University Press, 1957).

Three useful collections of articles on Hobbes are Mary Dietz (ed.), *Thomas Hobbes and Political Theory* (University Press of Kansas, 1990); G.A.J. Rogers and A. Ryan (eds.), *Perspectives on Thomas Hobbes* (Oxford University Press, 1991); and Tom Sorrell (ed.), *The Cambridge Companion to Hobbes* (Cambridge University Press, 1996). There is also *A Hobbes Dictionary* by A.P. Martinich (Blackwell, 1995).

from *Leviathan*[7]

Part I: Of Man

Chapter XIII: Of the Natural Condition of Mankind as Concerning their Felicity and Misery

Nature hath made men so equal in the faculties of body and mind as that, though there be found one man sometimes manifestly stronger in body or of quicker mind than another, yet when all is reckoned together the difference between man and man is not so considerable as that one man can thereupon claim to himself any benefit to which another may not pretend as well as he. For as to the strength of body, the weakest has strength enough to kill the strongest, either by secret machination or by confederacy with others that are in the same danger with himself.

---

7   *Leviathan* was first published, in London, in 1651; the excerpts reprinted here are from that edition (with modernized spelling, and partly modernized punctuation). As well as his English version, Hobbes also prepared an edition in Latin (much of which was probably written before the English version), first published in Amsterdam in 1681.

And as to the faculties of the mind—setting aside the arts grounded upon words, and especially that skill of proceeding upon general and infallible rules, called science, which very few have and but in few things, as being not a native faculty born with us, nor attained, as prudence, while we look after somewhat else—I find yet a greater equality amongst men than that of strength. For prudence is but experience, which equal time equally bestows on all men in those things they equally apply themselves unto. That which may perhaps make such equality incredible is but a vain conceit of one's own wisdom, which almost all men think they have in a greater degree than the vulgar; that is, than all men but themselves, and a few others, whom by fame, or for concurring with themselves, they approve. For such is the nature of men that howsoever they may acknowledge many others to be more witty, or more eloquent, or more learned, yet they will hardly believe there be many so wise as themselves; for they see their own wit at hand, and other men's at a distance. But this proveth rather that men are in that point equal, than unequal. For there is not ordinarily a greater sign of the equal distribution of anything than that every man is contented with his share.

From this equality of ability ariseth equality of hope in the attaining of our ends. And therefore if any two men desire the same thing, which nevertheless they cannot both enjoy, they become enemies; and in the way to their end (which is principally their own conservation, and sometimes their delectation only) endeavour to destroy or subdue one another. And from hence it comes to pass that where an invader hath no more to fear than another man's single power, if one plant, sow, build, or possess a convenient seat, others may probably be expected to come prepared with forces united to dispossess and deprive him, not only of the fruit of his labour, but also of his life or liberty. And the invader again is in the like danger of another.

And from this diffidence of one another, there is no way for any man to secure himself so reasonable as anticipation; that is, by force, or wiles, to master the persons of all men he can so long till he see no other power great enough to endanger him: and this is no more than his own conservation requireth, and is generally allowed. Also, because there be some that, taking pleasure in contemplating their own power in the acts of conquest, which they pursue farther than their security requires, if others (that otherwise would be glad to be at ease within modest bounds) should not by invasion increase their power, they would not be able, long time, by standing only on their defence, to subsist. And by consequence, such augmentation of dominion over men being necessary to a man's conservation, it ought to be allowed him.

Again, men have no pleasure (but on the contrary a great deal of grief) in keeping company where there is no power able to overawe them all. For every man looketh that his companion should value him at the same rate he sets upon himself, and upon all signs of contempt or undervaluing naturally endeavours, as far as he dares (which amongst them that have no common power to keep them in quiet is far enough to make them destroy each other), to extort a greater value from his contemners, by damage; and from others, by the example.

So that in the nature of man, we find three principal causes of quarrel. First, competition; secondly, diffidence; thirdly, glory.

The first maketh men invade for gain; the second, for safety; and the third, for reputation. The first use violence, to make themselves masters of other men's persons, wives, children, and cattle; the second, to defend them; the third, for trifles, as a word, a smile, a different opinion, and any other sign of undervalue, either direct in their persons or by reflection in their kindred, their friends, their nation, their profession, or their name.

Hereby it is manifest that during the time men live without a common power to keep them all in awe, they are in that condition which is called war; and such a war as is of every man against every man. For war consisteth not in battle only, or the act of fighting, but in a tract of time, wherein the will to contend by battle is sufficiently known: and therefore the notion of *time* is to be considered in the nature of war, as it is in the nature of weather. For as the nature of foul weather lieth not in a shower or two of rain, but in an inclination thereto of many days together: so the nature of war consisteth not in actual fighting, but in the known disposition thereto during all the time there is no assurance to the contrary. All other time is peace.

Whatsoever therefore is consequent to a time of war, where every man is enemy to every man, the same consequent to the time wherein men live without other security than what their own strength and their own invention shall furnish them withal. In such condition there is no place for industry, because the fruit thereof is uncertain: and consequently no culture of the earth; no navigation, nor use of the commodities that may be imported by sea; no commodious building; no instruments of moving and removing such things as require much force; no knowledge of the face of the earth; no account of time; no arts; no letters; no society; and which is worst of all, continual fear, and danger of violent death; and the life of man, solitary, poor, nasty, brutish, and short.

It may seem strange to some man that has not well weighed these things that Nature should thus dissociate and render men apt to invade and destroy one another: and he may therefore, not trusting to this inference, made from the passions, desire perhaps to have the same confirmed by experience. Let him therefore consider with himself: when taking a journey, he arms himself and seeks to go well accompanied; when going to sleep, he locks his doors; when even in his house he locks his chests; and this when he knows there be laws and public officers, armed, to revenge all injuries shall be done him; what opinion he has of his fellow subjects, when he rides armed; of his fellow citizens, when he locks his doors; and of his children, and servants, when he locks his chests. Does he not there as much accuse mankind by his actions as I do by my words? But neither of us accuse man's nature in it. The desires, and other passions of man, are in themselves no sin. No more are the actions that proceed from those passions till they know a law that forbids them; which till laws be made they cannot know, nor can any law be made till they have agreed upon the person that shall make it.

It may peradventure be thought there was never such a time nor condition of war as this; and I believe it was never generally so, over all the world: but there are many places where they live so now. For the savage people in many places of *America* (except the government of small families, the concord whereof dependeth on natural lust) have no government at all, and live at this day in that brutish manner, as I said before. Howsoever, it may be perceived what manner of life there would be, where there were no common power to fear, by the manner of life which men that have formerly lived under a peaceful government use to degenerate into, in a civil war.

But though there had never been any time wherein particular men were in a condition of war one against another, yet in all times kings and persons of sovereign authority, because of their independency, are in continual jealousies, and in the state and posture of gladiators, having their weapons pointing, and their eyes fixed on one another; that is, their forts, garrisons, and guns upon the frontiers of their kingdoms, and continual spies upon their neighbours, which is a posture of war. But because they uphold thereby the industry of their subjects, there does not follow from it that misery which accompanies the liberty of particular men.

To this war of every man against every man, this also is consequent; that nothing can be unjust. The notions of right and wrong, justice and injustice, have there no place. Where there is no common power, there is no law; where no law, no injustice. Force and fraud are in war the two cardinal virtues. Justice and injustice are none of the faculties neither of the body nor mind. If they were, they might be in a man that were alone in the world, as well as[8] his senses and passions. They are qualities that relate to men in society, not in solitude. It is consequent also to the same condition that there be no propriety, no dominion, no *mine* and *thine* distinct; but only that to be every man's that he can get, and for so long as he can keep it. And thus much for the ill condition which man by mere nature is actually placed in; though with a possibility to come out of it, consisting partly in the passions, partly in his reason.

The passions that incline men to peace are: fear of death; desire of such things as are necessary to commodious living; and a hope by their industry to obtain them. And reason suggesteth convenient articles of peace upon which men may be drawn to agreement. These articles are they which otherwise are called the laws of nature, whereof I shall speak more particularly in the two following chapters.

Chapter XIV: Of the First and Second Natural Laws, and of Contracts

The *right of nature*, which writers commonly call *jus naturale*,[9] is the liberty each man hath to use his own power as he will himself for the preservation of his own nature; that is to say, of his own life; and consequently, of doing anything which, in his own judgement and reason, he shall conceive to be the aptest means thereunto.

By *liberty* is understood, according to the proper signification of the word, the absence of external impediments; which impediments may oft take away part of a man's power to do what he would, but cannot hinder him from using the power left him according as his judgement and reason shall dictate to him.

A *law of nature*, *lex naturalis*, is a precept, or general rule, found out by reason, by which a man is forbidden to do that which is destructive of his life, or taketh away the means of preserving the same, and to omit that by which he thinketh it may be best preserved. For though they that speak of this subject use to confound *jus* and *lex*, *right* and *law*, yet they ought to be distinguished, because *right* consisteth in liberty to do, or to forbear; whereas *law* determineth and bindeth to one of them: so that law and right differ as much as obligation and liberty, which in one and the same matter are inconsistent.

And because the condition of man (as hath been declared in the precedent chapter) is a condition of war of every one against every one, in which case every one is governed by his own reason, and there is nothing he can make use of that may not be a help unto him in preserving his life against his enemies; it followeth that in such a condition every man has a right to every thing, even to one another's body. And therefore, as long as this natural right of every man to every thing endureth, there can be no security to any man, how strong or wise soever he be, of living out the time which nature ordinarily alloweth men to live. And consequently it is a precept, or general rule of reason: *that every man ought to endeavour peace, as far as he has hope of obtaining it; and when he cannot obtain it, that he may seek and use all helps and advantages of war.* The first branch of which rule

---

8   Just as much as.

9   Natural right.

containeth the first and fundamental law of nature, which is: *to seek peace and follow it*. The second, the sum of the right of nature, which is: *by all means we can to defend ourselves*.

From this fundamental law of nature, by which men are commanded to endeavour peace, is derived this second law: *that a man be willing, when others are so too, as far forth as for peace and defence of himself he shall think it necessary, to lay down*[10] *this right to all things; and be contented with so much liberty against other men as he would allow other men against himself.* For as long as every man holdeth this right, of doing anything he liketh; so long are all men in the condition of war. But if other men will not lay down their right, as well as he, then there is no reason for anyone to divest himself of his: for that were to expose himself to prey, which no man is bound to, rather than to dispose himself to peace. This is that law of the Gospel: Whatsoever you require that others should do to you, that do ye to them. And that law of all men, *quod tibi fieri non vis, alteri ne feceris*.[11]

To *lay down* a man's *right* to anything is to divest himself of the *liberty* of hindering another of the benefit of his own right to the same. For he that renounceth or passeth away his right giveth not to any other man a right which he had not before, because there is nothing to which every man had not right by nature, but only standeth out of his way that he may enjoy his own original right without hindrance from him, not without hindrance from another. So that the effect which redoundeth to one man by another man's defect of right is but so much diminution of impediments to the use of his own right original.

Right is laid aside, either by simply renouncing it, or by transferring it to another. By *simply* renouncing, when he cares not to whom the benefit thereof redoundeth. By transferring, when he intendeth the benefit thereof to some certain person or persons. And when a man hath in either manner abandoned or granted away his right, then is he said to be *obliged*, or *bound*, not to hinder those to whom such right is granted, or abandoned, from the benefit of it: and

that he *ought*, and it is his *duty*, not to make void that voluntary act of his own: and that such hindrance is *injustice*, and *injury*, as being *sine jure*;[12] the right being before renounced or transferred. So that *injury* or *injustice*, in the controversies of the world, is somewhat like to that which in the disputations of scholars is called absurdity. For as it is there called an *absurdity* to contradict what one maintained in the beginning; so in the world it is called injustice and injury voluntarily to undo that which from the beginning he had voluntarily done. The way by which a man either simply renounceth or transferreth his right is a declaration, or signification, by some voluntary and sufficient sign, or signs, that he doth so renounce or transfer, or hath so renounced or transferred the same, to him that accepteth it. And these signs are either words only, or actions only; or, as it happeneth most often, both words and actions. And the same are the *bonds*, by which men are bound and obliged: bonds that have their strength, not from their own nature (for nothing is more easily broken than a man's word), but from fear of some evil consequence upon the rupture.

Whensoever a man transferreth his right, or renounceth it, it is either in consideration of some right reciprocally transferred to himself, or for some other good he hopeth for thereby. For it is a voluntary act: and of the voluntary acts of every man, the object is some *good to himself.* And therefore there be some rights which no man can be understood by any words, or other signs, to have abandoned or transferred. As, first, a man cannot lay down the right of resisting them that assault him by force to take away his life, because he cannot be understood to aim thereby at any good to himself. The same may be said of wounds, and chains, and imprisonment, both because there is no benefit consequent to such patience, as there is to the patience of suffering another to be wounded or imprisoned, as also because a man cannot tell when he seeth men proceed against him by violence whether they intend his death or not. And lastly the motive and end for which this renouncing and transferring of right is introduced is nothing else but the security of a man's person, in his life, and in the means of so preserving life as not to be weary of it. And therefore if a man

---

10   To give up.

11   "Do not do to others what you would not want done to yourself."

---

12   Without right.

by words, or other signs, seem to despoil himself of the end for which those signs were intended, he is not to be understood as if he meant it, or that it was his will, but that he was ignorant of how such words and actions were to be interpreted.

The mutual transferring of right is that which men call *contract*.

There is difference between transferring of right to the thing, and transferring or tradition,[13] that is, delivery of the thing itself. For the thing may be delivered together with the translation of the right (as in buying and selling with ready money, or exchange of goods or lands), and it may be delivered some time after.

Again, one of the contractors may deliver the thing contracted for on his part, and leave the other to perform his part at some determinate time after, and in the meantime be trusted; and then the contract on his part is called *pact*, or *covenant*: or both parts[14] may contract now to perform hereafter, in which cases he that is to perform in time to come, being trusted, his performance is called *keeping of promise*, or *faith*, and the failing of performance, if it be voluntary, *violation of faith*.

When the transferring of right is not mutual, but one of the parties transferreth in hope to gain thereby friendship or service from another, or from his friends; or in hope to gain the reputation of charity, or magnanimity; or to deliver his mind from the pain of compassion; or in hope of reward in heaven; this is not contract, but *gift*, *free-gift*, *grace*: which words signify one and the same thing.

...

If a covenant be made wherein neither of the parties perform presently, but trust one another, in the condition of mere nature (which is a condition of war of every man against every man) upon any reasonable suspicion, it is void: but if there be a common power set over them both, with right and force sufficient to compel performance, it is not void. For he that performeth first has no assurance the other will perform after, because the bonds of words are too weak

---

13 As a legal term, "tradition" means the formal delivery of property to another person.

14 Parties (to the covenant).

to bridle men's ambition, avarice, anger, and other passions, without the fear of some coercive power; which in the condition of mere nature, where all men are equal, and judges of the justness of their own fears, cannot possibly be supposed. And therefore he which performeth first does but betray himself to his enemy, contrary to the right he can never abandon of defending his life and means of living.

But in a civil estate, where there is a power set up to constrain those that would otherwise violate their faith, that fear is no more reasonable; and for that cause, he which by the covenant is to perform first is obliged so to do.

The cause of fear, which maketh such a covenant invalid, must be always something arising after the covenant made, as some new fact or other sign of the will not to perform, else it cannot make the covenant void. For that which could not hinder a man from promising ought not to be admitted as a hindrance of performing....

Chapter XV: Of Other Laws of Nature

From that law of nature by which we are obliged to transfer to another such rights as, being retained, hinder the peace of mankind, there followeth a third; which is this: *that men perform their covenants made*; without which covenants are in vain, and but empty words; and the right of all men to all things remaining, we are still in the condition of war.

And in this law of nature consisteth the fountain and original of *justice*. For where no covenant hath preceded, there hath no right been transferred, and every man has right to everything and consequently, no action can be unjust. But when a covenant is made, then to break it is *unjust* and the definition of *injustice* is no other than *the not performance of covenant*. And whatsoever is not unjust is *just*.

But because covenants of mutual trust, where there is a fear of not performance on either part (as hath been said in the former chapter), are invalid, though the original of justice be the making of covenants, yet injustice actually there can be none till the cause of such fear be taken away; which, while men are in the natural condition of war, cannot be done. Therefore before the names of just and unjust can have place, there must be some coercive power to compel men equally to the performance of their covenants, by the terror of some punishment greater than the benefit they expect by the breach of their covenant, and to make good that propriety which by mutual contract men acquire in recompense of the universal right they abandon: and such power there is none before the erection of a commonwealth. And this is also to be gathered out of the ordinary definition of justice in the Schools,[15] for they say that *justice is the constant will of giving to every man his own*. And therefore where there is no *own*, that is, no propriety, there is no injustice; and where there is no coercive power erected, that is, where there is no commonwealth, there is no propriety, all men having right to all things: therefore where there is no commonwealth, there nothing is unjust. So that the nature of justice consisteth in keeping of valid covenants, but the validity of covenants begins not but with the constitution of a civil power sufficient to compel men to keep them: and then it is also that propriety begins.

The fool hath said in his heart, there is no such thing as justice,[16] and sometimes also with his tongue, seriously alleging that: every man's conservation and contentment being committed to his own care, there could be no reason why every man might not do what he thought conduced thereunto: and therefore also to make, or not make, keep, or not keep, covenants was not against reason when it conduced to one's benefit. He does not therein deny that there be covenants; and that they are sometimes broken, sometimes kept; and that such breach of them may be called injustice, and the observance of them justice: but he questioneth whether injustice, taking away the fear of God (for the same fool hath said in his heart there is no God), not sometimes stand with that reason which dictateth to every man his own good; and particularly then, when it conduceth to such a benefit as shall put a man in a condition to neglect not only the dispraise and revilings, but also the power of other men. The kingdom of God is gotten by violence:[17] but what if it could be gotten by unjust violence? Were it against reason so to get it, when it is impossible to receive hurt by it? And if it be not against reason, it is not against justice: or else justice is not to be approved for good. From such reasoning as this, successful wickedness hath obtained the name of virtue: and some that in all other things have disallowed the violation of faith, yet have allowed it when it is for the getting of a kingdom. And the heathen that believed that *Saturn* was deposed by his son *Jupiter*[18] believed nevertheless the same *Jupiter* to be the avenger of injustice, somewhat like to a piece of law in *Coke's* Commentaries on *Littleton*;[19] where he says if the right heir of the crown be attainted of treason, yet the crown shall descend to him, and *eo instante*[20] the attainder[21] be void: from which instances a man will be very prone to infer that when the heir apparent[22] of a kingdom shall kill him that is in possession, though his father, you may call it injustice, or by what other name you will; yet it can never be against reason, seeing all the voluntary actions of men tend to the benefit of themselves; and those actions are most reasonable that conduce most to their ends. This specious reasoning is nevertheless false.

For the question is not of promises mutual, where there is no security of performance on either side, as when there is no civil power erected over the parties

---

15   The universities or their teachings, the traditional "scholastic" syllabus handed down from the Middle Ages.

16   A paraphrase from Psalm 14 (and Psalm 53) of the Bible: "The Fool has said in his heart, there is no God."

17   Hobbes's fool alludes to a verse in the Gospel of Matthew (11:12): "And from the days of John the Baptist until now, the kingdom of heaven suffereth violence, and the violent take it by force."

18   Saturn was the Roman equivalent of the ancient Greek god Cronus. Jupiter was the chief Roman god, often identified with the Greek Zeus.

19   *The First Part of the Institutes of the Laws of England*, by Edward Coke (1629). It includes Coke's commentary on Thomas Littleton's *Tenures* (1490), the first treatise to be written on English law and a standard text on English property law until the nineteenth century.

20   Immediately.

21   An old legal term for the forfeiture of property and rights suffered as a consequence of being sentenced to death for treason or felony.

22   The person first in line for succession to the throne.

promising; for such promises are no covenants: but either where one of the parties has performed already, or where there is a power to make him perform, there is the question whether it be against reason; that is, against the benefit of the other to perform, or not. And I say it is not against reason. For the manifestation whereof we are to consider: first, that when a man doth a thing which, notwithstanding anything can be foreseen and reckoned on, tendeth to his own destruction (howsoever some accident, which he could not expect, arriving may turn it to his benefit); yet such events do not make it reasonably or wisely done. Secondly, that in a condition of war, wherein every man to every man, for want of a common power to keep them all in awe, is an enemy, there is no man can hope by his own strength, or wit, to defend himself from destruction without the help of confederates (where every one expects the same defence by the confederation that any one else does); and therefore he which declares he thinks it reason to deceive those that help him can in reason expect no other means of safety than what can be had from his own single power. He, therefore, that breaketh his covenant, and consequently declareth that he thinks he may with reason do so, cannot be received into any society that unite themselves for peace and defence but by the error of them that receive him; nor when he is received be retained in it without seeing the danger of their error; which errors a man cannot reasonably reckon upon as the means of his security: and therefore if he be left or cast out of society, he perisheth; and if he live in society, it is by the errors of other men, which he could not foresee nor reckon upon, and consequently against the reason of his preservation; and so, as all men that contribute not to his destruction forbear him only out of ignorance of what is good for themselves.

As for the instance of gaining the secure and perpetual felicity of heaven by any way, it is frivolous; there being but one way imaginable, and that is not breaking, but keeping of covenant.

And for the other instance of attaining sovereignty by rebellion; it is manifest that, though the event follow, yet because it cannot reasonably be expected, but rather the contrary, and because by gaining it so, others are taught to gain the same in like manner, the attempt thereof is against reason. Justice therefore, that is to say, keeping of covenant, is a rule of reason by which we are forbidden to do anything destructive to our life, and consequently a law of nature.

There be some that proceed further and will not have the law of nature to be those rules which conduce to the preservation of man's life on earth, but to the attaining of an eternal felicity after death; to which they think the breach of covenant may conduce, and consequently be just and reasonable; such are they that think it a work of merit to kill, or depose, or rebel against the sovereign power constituted over them by their own consent. But because there is no natural knowledge of man's estate after death, much less of the reward that is then to be given to breach of faith, but only a belief grounded upon other men's saying that they know it supernaturally or that they know those that knew them that knew others that knew it supernaturally, breach of faith cannot be called a precept of reason or nature.

Others, that allow for a law of nature the keeping of faith, do nevertheless make exception of certain persons—as heretics, and such as use not to perform their covenant to others—and this also is against reason. For if any fault of a man be sufficient to discharge our covenant made, the same ought in reason to have been sufficient to have hindered the making of it.

The names of just and unjust when they are attributed to men, signify one thing, and when they are attributed to actions, another. When they are attributed to men, they signify conformity or inconformity of manners to reason. But when they are attributed to action they signify the conformity or inconformity to reason, not of manners, or manner of life, but of particular actions. A just man therefore is he that taketh all the care he can that his actions may be all just; and an unjust man is he that neglecteth it. And such men are more often in our language styled by the names of righteous and unrighteous than just and unjust though the meaning be the same. Therefore a righteous man does not lose that title by one or a few unjust actions that proceed from sudden passion, or mistake of things or persons, nor does an unrighteous man lose his character for such actions as he does, or forbears to do, for fear; because his will is not framed by the justice, but by the apparent benefit of what he is to do. That which gives to human actions the relish of justice is a certain nobleness or gallantness of courage, rarely found, by which a man scorns to be beholding for the contentment of his life to fraud, or breach of promise. This justice of the manners is that which is meant where justice is called a virtue; and injustice, a vice.

But the justice of actions denominates men, not just, but *guiltless*: and the injustice of the same (which is also called injury) gives them but the name of *guilty*.

Again, the injustice of manners is the disposition or aptitude to do injury, and is injustice before it proceed to act, and without supposing any individual person injured. But the injustice of an action (that is to say, injury) supposeth an individual person injured; namely him to whom the covenant was made: and therefore many times the injury is received by one man when the damage redoundeth to another. As when the master commandeth his servant to give money to a stranger; if it be not done, the injury is done to the master, whom he had before covenanted to obey; but the damage redoundeth to the stranger, to whom he had no obligation, and therefore could not injure him. And so also in commonwealths private men may remit to one another their debts, but not robberies or other violences, whereby they are endamaged; because the detaining of debt is an injury to themselves, but robbery and violence are injuries to the person of the commonwealth.

Whatsoever is done to a man, conformable to his own will signified to the doer, is not injury to him. For if he that doeth it hath not passed away his original right to do what he please by some antecedent covenant, there is no breach of covenant, and therefore no injury done him. And if he have, then his will to have it done, being signified, is a release of that covenant, and so again there is no injury done him.

Justice of actions is by writers[23] divided into *commutative* and *distributive*: and the former they say consisteth in proportion arithmetical; the latter in proportion geometrical. Commutative, therefore, they place in the equality of value of the things contracted for; and distributive, in the distribution of equal benefit to men of equal merit. As if it were injustice to sell dearer than we buy, or to give more to a man than he merits. The value of all things contracted for is measured by the appetite of the contractors, and therefore the just value is that which they be contented to give. And merit (besides that which is by covenant, where the performance on one part meriteth the performance of the other part, and falls under justice commutative, not distributive) is not due by justice, but is rewarded of grace only. And therefore this distinction, in the sense wherein it useth to be expounded, is not right. To speak properly, commutative justice is the justice of a contractor; that is, a performance of covenant in buying and selling, hiring and letting to hire, lending and borrowing, exchanging, bartering, and other acts of contract.

And distributive justice, the justice of an arbitrator; that is to say, the act of defining what is just. Wherein, being trusted by them that make him arbitrator, if he perform his trust, he is said to distribute to every man his own: and this is indeed just distribution, and may be called, though improperly, distributive justice, but more properly equity, which also is a law of nature, as shall be shown in due place.

As justice dependeth on antecedent covenant; so does *gratitude* depend on antecedent grace; that is to say, antecedent free-gift; and is the fourth law of nature, which may be conceived in this form: *that a man which receiveth benefit from another of mere grace endeavour that he which giveth it have no reasonable cause to repent him of his good will.* For no man giveth but with intention of good to himself, because gift is voluntary; and of all voluntary acts, the object is to every man his own good; of which if men see they shall be frustrated, there will be no beginning of benevolence or trust, nor consequently of mutual help, nor of reconciliation of one man to another; and therefore they are to remain still in the condition of war, which is contrary to the first and fundamental law of nature which commandeth men to *seek peace*. The breach of this law is called *ingratitude*, and hath the same relation to grace that injustice hath to obligation by covenant.

A fifth law of nature is *complaisance*; that is to say, *that every man strive to accommodate himself to the*

---

23 See the selection from Aristotle in this chapter. A similar distinction would also have been known to Hobbes from Thomas Aquinas's *Summa Theologiae* (the second part of Part II, question 61).

rest. For the understanding whereof we may consider that there is in men's aptness to society a diversity of nature, rising from their diversity of affections, not unlike to that we see in stones brought together for building of an edifice. For as that stone which by the asperity and irregularity of figure takes more room from others than itself fills, and for hardness cannot be easily made plain,[24] and thereby hindereth the building, is by the builders cast away as unprofitable and troublesome: so also, a man that by asperity of nature will strive to retain those things which to himself are superfluous, and to others necessary, and for the stubbornness of his passions cannot be corrected, is to be left or cast out of society as cumbersome thereunto. For seeing every man, not only by right, but also by necessity of nature, is supposed to endeavour all he can to obtain that which is necessary for his conservation, he that shall oppose himself against it for things superfluous is guilty of the war that thereupon is to follow, and therefore doth that which is contrary to the fundamental law of nature, which commandeth to *seek peace*. The observers of this law may be called *sociable* (the Latins call them *commodi*); the contrary, *stubborn*, *insociable*, *froward*, *intractable*.

A sixth law of nature is this: *that upon caution of the future time, a man ought to pardon the offences past of them that, repenting, desire it*. For *pardon* is nothing but granting of peace; which though granted to them that persevere in their hostility, be not peace, but fear; yet not granted to them that give caution of the future time is sign of an aversion to peace, and therefore contrary to the law of nature.

A seventh is: *that in revenges* (that is, retribution of evil for evil), *men look not at the greatness of the evil past, but the greatness of the good to follow*. Whereby we are forbidden to inflict punishment with any other design than for correction of the offender, or direction of others. For this law is consequent to the next before it, that commandeth pardon upon security of the future time. Besides, revenge without respect to the example and profit to come is a triumph, or glorying in the hurt of another, tending to no end (for the end is always somewhat to come); and glorying to no end is vain-glory, and contrary to reason; and to

_____

24 Smooth.

hurt without reason tendeth to the introduction of war, which is against the law of nature, and is commonly styled by the name of *cruelty*.

And because all signs of hatred, or contempt, provoke to fight; insomuch as most men choose rather to hazard their life than not to be revenged, we may in the eighth place, for a law of nature, set down this precept: *that no man by deed, word, countenance, or gesture, declare hatred or contempt of another*. The breach of which law is commonly called *contumely*.

The question who is the better man has no place in the condition of mere nature, where (as has been shown before) all men are equal. The inequality that now is has been introduced by the laws civil. I know that *Aristotle* in the first book of his Politics, for a foundation of his doctrine, maketh men by nature, some more worthy to command, meaning the wiser sort, such as he thought himself to be for his philosophy; others to serve, meaning those that had strong bodies, but were not philosophers as he; as master and servant were not introduced by consent of men, but by difference of wit: which is not only against reason, but also against experience. For there are very few so foolish that had not rather govern themselves than be governed by others: nor when the wise, in their own conceit, contend by force with them who distrust their own wisdom, do they always, or often, or almost at any time, get the victory. If nature therefore have made men equal, that equality is to be acknowledged: or if nature have made men unequal, yet because men that think themselves equal will not enter into conditions of peace, but upon equal terms, such equality must be admitted. And therefore for the ninth law of nature, I put this: *that every man acknowledge another for his equal by nature*. The breach of this precept is *pride*.

On this law dependeth another: *that at the entrance into conditions of peace, no man require to reserve to himself any right which he is not content should be reserved to every one of the rest*. As it is necessary for all men that seek peace to lay down certain rights of nature; that is to say, not to have liberty to do all they list, so is it necessary for man's life to retain some: as right to govern their own bodies; enjoy air, water, motion, ways to go from place to place; and all things else without which a man cannot live, or not live well. If in this case, at the making of peace, men require for themselves that which they would not have to be granted to others, they do contrary to the precedent law that commandeth the acknowledgement of natural equality, and therefore also against the law of nature. The observers of this law are those we call *modest*, and the breakers *arrogant* men. The Greeks call the violation of this law *pleonexia*; that is, a desire of more than their share.

Also, *if a man be trusted to judge between man and man*, it is a precept of the law of nature that *he deal equally between them*. For without that, the controversies of men cannot be determined but by war. He therefore that is partial in judgement, doth what in him lies to deter men from the use of judges and arbitrators, and consequently, against the fundamental law of nature, is the cause of war.

The observance of this law, from the equal distribution to each man of that which in reason belongeth to him, is called *equity*, and (as I have said before) distributive justice: the violation, *acception of persons* (*prosopolepsia*).

And from this followeth another law: *that such things as cannot be divided be enjoyed in common, if it can be; and if the quantity of the thing permit, without stint; otherwise proportionably to the number of them that have right.* For otherwise the distribution is unequal, and contrary to equity.

But some things there be that can neither be divided nor enjoyed in common. Then, the law of nature which prescribeth equity requireth: *that the entire right, or else (making the use alternate) the first possession, be determined by lot.*[25] For equal distribution is of the law of nature; and other means of equal distribution cannot be imagined.

Of *lots* there be two sorts, *arbitrary* and *natural*. Arbitrary is that which is agreed on by the competitors; natural is either *primogeniture*[26] (which the Greek calls *kleronomia*, which signifies, *given by lot*), or *first seizure*.

And therefore those things which cannot be enjoyed in common, nor divided, ought to be adjudged to the first possessor; and in some cases to the first born, as acquired by lot.

It is also a law of nature: *that all men that mediate peace be allowed safe conduct.* For the law that commandeth peace, as the *end*, commandeth intercession, as the *means*; and to intercession the means is safe conduct.

And because, though men be never so willing to observe these laws, there may nevertheless arise questions concerning a man's action—first, whether it were done, or not done; secondly, if done, whether against the law, or not against the law; the former whereof is called a question *of fact*, the latter a question *of right*—therefore unless the parties to the question covenant mutually to stand to the sentence of another, they are as far from peace as ever. This other, to whose sentence they submit, is called an *arbitrator*. And therefore it is of the law of nature *that they that are at controversy submit their right to the judgement of an arbitrator*.

And seeing every man is presumed to do all things in order to his own benefit, *no man is a fit arbitrator in his own cause*: and if he were never so fit, yet equity allowing to each party equal benefit, if one be admitted to be judge, the other is to be admitted also; and so the controversy, that is, the cause of war, remains, against the law of nature.

For the same reason no man in any cause ought to be received for arbitrator to whom greater profit, or honour, or pleasure apparently ariseth out of the victory of one party than of the other: for he hath taken, though an unavoidable bribe, yet a bribe; and no man can be obliged to trust him. And thus also the controversy and the condition of war remaineth, contrary to the law of nature.

And in a controversy of *fact*, the judge (being to give no more credit to one than to the other, if there be no other arguments) must give credit to a third;[27] or to a third and fourth; or more: for else the question is undecided, and left to force, contrary to the law of nature.

These are the laws of nature, dictating peace, for a means of the conservation of men in multitudes; and which only concern the doctrine of civil society.

---

25 By chance.

26 Rights of inheritance or succession derived from being first-born.

27 Must listen to a neutral witness.

There be other things tending to the destruction of particular men; as drunkenness, and all other parts of intemperance, which may therefore also be reckoned amongst those things which the law of nature hath forbidden, but are not necessary to be mentioned, nor are pertinent enough to this place.

And though this may seem too subtle a deduction of the laws of nature to be taken notice of by all men, whereof the most part are too busy in getting food, and the rest too negligent to understand; yet to leave all men inexcusable, they have been contracted into one easy sum, intelligible even to the meanest capacity; and that is: *Do not that to another which thou wouldest not have done to thyself*, which showeth him that he has no more to do in learning the laws of nature but, when weighing the actions of other men with his own they seem too heavy, to put them into the other part of the balance, and his own into their place, that his own passions and self-love may add nothing to the weight; and then there is none of these laws of nature that will not appear unto him very reasonable.

The laws of nature oblige *in foro interno*;[28] that is to say, they bind to a desire they should take place: but *in foro externo*;[29] that is, to the putting them in act, not always. For he that should be modest and tractable, and perform all he promises in such time and place where no man else should do so, should but make himself a prey to others, and procure his own certain ruin, contrary to the ground of all laws of nature which tend to nature's preservation. And again, he that having sufficient security that others shall observe the same laws towards him, observes them not himself, seeketh not peace, but war, and consequently the destruction of his nature by violence.

And whatsoever laws bind *in foro interno* may be broken, not only by a fact contrary to the law, but also by a fact according to it, in case a man think it contrary. For though his action in this case be according to the law, yet his purpose was against the law; which, where the obligation is *in foro interno*, is a breach.

The laws of nature are immutable and eternal; for injustice, ingratitude, arrogance, pride, iniquity,

acception of persons, and the rest can never be made lawful. For it can never be that war shall preserve life, and peace destroy it.

The same laws, because they oblige only to a desire and endeavour (I mean an unfeigned and constant endeavour) are easy to be observed. For in that they require nothing but endeavour, he that endeavoureth their performance fulfilleth them; and he that fulfilleth the law is just.

And the science of them is the true and only moral philosophy. For moral philosophy is nothing else but the science of what is *good* and *evil* in the conversation and society of mankind. *Good* and *evil* are names that signify our appetites and aversions, which in different tempers, customs, and doctrines of men are different: and diverse men differ not only in their judgement on the senses of what is pleasant and unpleasant to the taste, smell, hearing, touch, and sight; but also of what is conformable or disagreeable to reason in the actions of common life. Nay, the same man, in diverse times, differs from himself; and one time praiseth, that is, calleth good, what another time he dispraiseth, and calleth evil: from whence arise disputes, controversies, and at last war. And therefore so long as a man is in the condition of mere nature, which is a condition of war, private appetite is the measure of good and evil: and consequently all men agree on this, that peace is good, and therefore also the way or means of peace, which (as I have shown before) are *justice, gratitude, modesty, equity, mercy*, and the rest of the laws of nature, are good; that is to say, *moral virtues*; and their contrary vices, evil. Now the science of virtue and vice is moral philosophy; and therefore the true doctrine of the laws of nature is the true moral philosophy. But the writers of moral philosophy, though they acknowledge the same virtues and vices; yet, not seeing wherein consisted their goodness, nor that they come to be praised as the means of peaceable, sociable, and comfortable living, place them in a mediocrity[30] of passions: as if not the cause, but the degree of daring, made fortitude; or not the cause, but the quantity of a gift, made liberality.

These dictates of reason men used to call by the name of laws, but improperly: for they are but con-

---

28   In the internal domain (literally, the "inner marketplace").

29   In the external domain.

30   A moderate amount, a mean.

clusions or theorems concerning what conduceth to the conservation and defence of themselves; whereas law, properly, is the word of him that by right hath command over others. But yet if we consider the same theorems as delivered in the word of God that by right commandeth all things, then are they properly called laws.

…

Part II: Of Commonwealth

Chapter XVII: Of the Causes, Generation, and Definition of a Commonwealth

The final cause, end, or design of men (who naturally love liberty, and dominion over others) in the introduction of that restraint upon themselves, in which we see them live in commonwealths, is the foresight of their own preservation, and of a more contented life thereby; that is to say, of getting themselves out from that miserable condition of war which is necessarily consequent, as hath been shown, to the natural passions of men when there is no visible power to keep them in awe, and tie them by fear of punishment to the performance of their covenants, and observation of those laws of nature set down in the fourteenth and fifteenth chapters.

For the laws of nature—as *justice*, *equity*, *modesty*, *mercy*, and, in sum, *doing to others as we would be done to*—of themselves, without the terror of some power to cause them to be observed, are contrary to our natural passions, that carry us to partiality, pride, revenge, and the like. And covenants, without the sword, are but words and of no strength to secure a man at all. Therefore, notwithstanding the laws of nature (which every one hath then kept, when he has the will to keep them, when he can do it safely), if there be no power erected, or not great enough for our security, every man will and may lawfully rely on his own strength and art for caution against all other men. And in all places, where men have lived by small families, to rob and spoil one another has been a trade, and so far from being reputed against the law of nature that the greater spoils they gained, the greater was their honour; and men observed no other laws therein but the laws of honour; that is, to

abstain from cruelty, leaving to men their lives and instruments of husbandry. And as small families did then; so now do cities and kingdoms, which are but greater families (for their own security), enlarge their dominions upon all pretences of danger, and fear of invasion, or assistance that may be given to invaders; endeavour as much as they can to subdue or weaken their neighbours by open force, and secret arts, for want of other caution, justly; and are remembered for it in after ages with honour.

Nor is it the joining together of a small number of men that gives them this security; because in small numbers, small additions on the one side or the other make the advantage of strength so great as is sufficient to carry the victory, and therefore gives encouragement to an invasion. The multitude sufficient to confide in for our security is not determined by any certain number, but by comparison with the enemy we fear; and is then sufficient when the odds of the enemy[31] is not of so visible and conspicuous moment to determine the event of war, as to move him to attempt.

And be there never so great a multitude; yet if their actions be directed according to their particular judgements, and particular appetites, they can expect thereby no defence, nor protection, neither against a common enemy, nor against the injuries of one another. For being distracted in opinions concerning the best use and application of their strength, they do not help, but hinder one another, and reduce their strength by mutual opposition to nothing: whereby they are easily, not only subdued by a very few that agree together, but also, when there is no common enemy, they make war upon each other for their particular interests. For if we could suppose a great multitude of men to consent in the observation of justice, and other laws of nature, without a common power to keep them all in awe, we might as well suppose all mankind to do the same; and then there neither would be, nor need to be, any civil government or commonwealth at all, because there would be peace without subjection.

---

31 The ratio of the enemy's strength to that of the defenders'.

Nor is it enough for the security, which men desire should last all the time of their life, that they be governed and directed by one judgement for a limited time; as in one battle, or one war. For though they obtain a victory by their unanimous endeavour against a foreign enemy, yet afterwards, when either they have no common enemy, or he that by one part is held for an enemy is by another part held for a friend, they must needs by the difference of their interests dissolve, and fall again into a war amongst themselves.

It is true that certain living creatures, as bees and ants, live sociably one with another (which are therefore by *Aristotle* numbered amongst political creatures[32]), and yet have no other direction than their particular judgements and appetites; nor speech, whereby one of them can signify to another what he thinks expedient for the common benefit: and therefore some man may perhaps desire to know why mankind cannot do the same. To which I answer,

First, that men are continually in competition for honour and dignity, which these creatures are not; and consequently amongst men there ariseth on that ground, envy, and hatred, and finally war; but amongst these not so.

Secondly, that amongst these creatures the common good differeth not from the private; and being by nature inclined to their private, they procure thereby the common benefit. But man, whose joy consisteth in comparing himself with other men, can relish nothing but what is eminent.

Thirdly, that these creatures, having not, as man, the use of reason, do not see, nor think they see, any fault in the administration of their common business: whereas amongst men there are very many that think themselves wiser and abler to govern the public better than the rest, and these strive to reform and innovate, one this way, another that way; and thereby bring it into distraction and civil war.

Fourthly, that these creatures, though they have some use of voice in making known to one another their desires and other affections, yet they want that art of words by which some men can represent to others that which is good in the likeness of evil; and evil, in the likeness of good; and augment or diminish the apparent greatness of good and evil, discontenting men and troubling their peace at their pleasure.

Fifthly, irrational creatures cannot distinguish between *injury* and *damage*; and therefore as long as they be at ease, they are not offended with their fellows: whereas man is then most troublesome when he is most at ease; for then it is that he loves to show his wisdom, and control the actions of them that govern the commonwealth.

Lastly, the agreement of these creatures is natural; that of men is by covenant only, which is artificial: and therefore it is no wonder if there be somewhat else required, besides covenant, to make their agreement constant and lasting; which is a common power to keep them in awe and to direct their actions to the common benefit.

The only way to erect such a common power, as may be able to defend them from the invasion of foreigners, and the injuries of one another, and thereby to secure them in such sort as that by their own industry and by the fruits of the earth they may nourish themselves and live contentedly, is to confer all their power and strength upon one man, or upon one assembly of men, that may reduce all their wills, by plurality of voices, unto one will: which is as much as to say, to appoint one man, or assembly of men, to bear their person; and every one to own and acknowledge himself to be author of whatsoever he that so beareth their person shall act, or cause to be acted, in those things which concern the common peace and safety; and therein to submit their wills, every one to his will, and their judgements to his judgement. This is more than consent, or concord; it is a real unity of them all in one and the same person, made by covenant of every man with every man, in such manner as if every man should say to every man: *I authorise and give up my right of governing myself to this man, or to this assembly of men, on this condition; that thou give up, thy right to him, and authorise all his actions in like manner.* This done, the multitude so united in

---

32   See Aristotle's *History of Animals* (Book I, section 1). In fact, Aristotle, though he considered such creatures *social* animals, did not think them *political* in the proper sense of the word (as it applies to human beings). His reasons for this distinction were rather similar to those Hobbes goes on to give.

one person is called a *commonwealth*; in Latin, *civitas*. This is the generation of that great *Leviathan*,[33] or rather, to speak more reverently, of that *Mortal God* to which we owe, under the *Immortal God*, our peace and defence. For by this authority, given him by every particular man in the commonwealth, he hath the use of so much power and strength conferred on him that, by terror thereof, he is enabled to form the wills of them all, to peace at home, and mutual aid against their enemies abroad. And in him consisteth the essence of the commonwealth; which, to define it, is: *one person, of whose acts a great multitude, by mutual covenants one with another, have made themselves every one the author, to the end he may use the strength and means of them all as he shall think expedient for their peace and common defence.*

And he that carryeth this person is called sovereign, and said to have *sovereign power*; and every one besides, his subject.

The attaining to this sovereign power is by two ways. One, by natural force: as when a man maketh his children to submit themselves, and their children, to his government, as being able to destroy them if they refuse; or by war subdueth his enemies to his will, giving them their lives on that condition. The other, is when men agree amongst themselves to sub-

mit to some man, or assembly of men, voluntarily, on confidence to be protected by him against all others. This latter may be called a political commonwealth, or commonwealth by *institution*; and the former, a commonwealth by *acquisition*. And first, I shall speak of a commonwealth by institution.

Chapter XVIII: Of the Rights of Sovereigns by Institution

A *commonwealth* is said to be *instituted* when a *multitude* of men do agree, and *covenant, every one with every one*, that to whatsoever *man*, or *assembly of men*, shall be given by the major part the *right* to *present* the person of them all, that is to say, to be their *representative*; every one, as well he that *voted for it* as he that *voted against it*, shall *authorize* all the actions and judgements of that man, or assembly of men, in the same manner as if they were his own, to the end to live peaceably amongst themselves, and be protected against other men.

From this institution of a commonwealth are derived all the *rights* and *faculties* of him, or them, on whom the sovereign power is conferred by the consent of the people assembled.

First, because they covenant, it is to be understood they are not obliged by former covenant to anything repugnant hereunto. And consequently they that have already instituted a commonwealth, being thereby bound by covenant to own the actions and judgements of one, cannot lawfully make a new covenant amongst themselves to be obedient to any other, in anything whatsoever, without his permission. And therefore, they that are subjects to a monarch cannot without his leave cast off monarchy and return to the confusion of a disunited multitude; nor transfer their person from him that beareth it to another man, or other assembly of men: for they are bound, every man to every man, to own and be reputed author of all that he that already is their sovereign shall do and judge fit to be done; so that any one man dissenting, all the rest should break their covenant made to that man, which is injustice: and they have also every man given the sovereignty to him that beareth their person; and therefore if they depose him, they take from him that which is his own, and so again it is injustice. Besides, if he that attempteth to depose his sovereign be killed or pun-

---

33 This is an allusion to the Old Testament book of Job, where Leviathan is described as a fearsome, fire-breathing, many-headed sea monster. Leviathan's symbolic meaning in the Bible is obscure, but it was sometimes associated with the devil by biblical commentators (such as Aquinas). In the book of Revelation, it is written that God's final victory over Leviathan will herald the end of the world. Why Hobbes chose this controversy-inducing label for the state, and even made it the title of his work, is obscure. However, in a later passage (at the end of Chapter XXVIII) Hobbes quotes from Job: "There is nothing on earth to be compared with him. He is made so as not to be afraid. He seeth every high thing below him, and is king of all the children of pride" (Job 41: 33–34). Yet, Hobbes points out, Leviathan "is mortal and subject to decay, as all other earthly creatures are, and … there is that in heaven (though not on earth) that he should stand in fear of, and whose laws he ought to obey."

ished by him for such attempt, he is author of his own punishment, as being, by the institution, author of all his sovereign shall do; and because it is injustice for a man to do anything for which he may be punished by his own authority, he is also upon that title unjust. And whereas some men have pretended for their disobedience to their sovereign a new covenant, made, not with men but with God, this also is unjust: for there is no covenant with God but by mediation of somebody that representeth God's person, which none doth but God's lieutenant who hath the sovereignty under God. But this pretence of covenant with God is so evident a lie, even in the pretenders' own consciences, that it is not only an act of an unjust, but also of a vile and unmanly disposition.

Secondly, because the right of bearing the person of them all is given to him they make sovereign, by covenant only of one to another, and not of him to any of them, there can happen no breach of covenant on the part of the sovereign; and consequently none of his subjects, by any pretence of forfeiture, can be freed from his subjection. That he which is made sovereign maketh no covenant with his subjects beforehand is manifest; because either he must make it with the whole multitude, as one party to the covenant, or he must make a several covenant with every man. With the whole, as one party, it is impossible, because as yet they are not one person: and if he make so many several covenants as there be men, those covenants after he hath the sovereignty are void; because what act soever can be pretended by any one of them for breach thereof is the act both of himself, and of all the rest, because done in the person and by the right of every one of them in particular. Besides, if any one or more of them pretend a breach of the covenant made by the sovereign at his institution, and others or one other of his subjects, or himself alone, pretend there was no such breach, there is in this case no judge to decide the controversy: it returns therefore to the sword again; and every man recovereth the right of protecting himself by his own strength, contrary to the design they had in the institution. It is therefore in vain to grant sovereignty by way of precedent covenant. The opinion that any monarch receiveth his power by covenant, that is to say, on condition, proceedeth from want of understanding this easy truth: that covenants

being but words, and breath, have no force to oblige, contain, constrain, or protect any man, but what it has from the public sword; that is, from the untied hands of that man, or assembly of men, that hath the sovereignty, and whose actions are avouched by them all, and performed by the strength of them all, in him united. But when an assembly of men is made sovereign, then no man imagineth any such covenant to have passed in the institution: for no man is so dull as to say, for example, the people of *Rome* made a covenant with the Romans to hold the sovereignty on such or such conditions; which not performed, the Romans might lawfully depose the Roman people. That men see not the reason to be alike in a monarchy and in a popular government proceedeth from the ambition of some that are kinder to the government of an assembly, whereof they may hope to participate, than of monarchy, which they despair to enjoy.

Thirdly, because the major part hath by consenting voices declared a sovereign, he that dissented must now consent with the rest; that is, be contented to avow all the actions he shall do, or else justly be destroyed by the rest. For if he voluntarily entered into the congregation of them that were assembled, he sufficiently declared thereby his will, and therefore tacitly covenanted, to stand to what the major part should ordain: and therefore if he refuse to stand thereto, or make protestation against any of their decrees, he does contrary to his covenant, and therefore unjustly. And whether he be of the congregation or not, and whether his consent be asked or not, he must either submit to their decrees or be left in the condition of war he was in before; wherein he might without injustice be destroyed by any man whatsoever.

Fourthly, because every subject is by this institution author of all the actions and judgements of the sovereign instituted, it follows that whatsoever he doth, can be no injury to any of his subjects; nor ought he to be by any of them accused of injustice. For he that doth anything by authority from another doth therein no injury to him by whose authority he acteth: but by this institution of a commonwealth every particular man is author of all the sovereign doth; and consequently he that complaineth of injury from his sovereign complaineth of that whereof he himself is author, and therefore ought not to accuse any man but himself; no, nor himself of injury, because to do injury to oneself is impossible. It is true that they that have sovereign power may commit iniquity, but not injustice or injury in the proper signification.

Fifthly, and consequently to that which was said last, no man that hath sovereign power can justly be put to death, or otherwise in any manner by his subjects punished. For seeing every subject is author of the actions of his sovereign, he punisheth another for the actions committed by himself.

And because the end of this institution is the peace and defence of them all, and whosoever has right to the end has right to the means, it belongeth of right to whatsoever man or assembly that hath the sovereignty to be judge both of the means of peace and defence, and also of the hindrances and disturbances of the same; and to do whatsoever he shall think necessary to be done, both beforehand (for the preserving of peace and security, by prevention of discord at home, and hostility from abroad) and when peace and security are lost, for the recovery of the same. And therefore,

Sixthly, it is annexed to the sovereignty to be judge of what opinions and doctrines are averse, and what conducing, to peace; and consequently, on what occasions, how far, and what men are to be trusted withal in speaking to multitudes of people; and who shall examine the doctrines of all books before they be published. For the actions of men proceed from their opinions, and in the well-governing of opinions consisteth the well-governing of men's actions in order to their peace and concord. And though in matter of doctrine nothing ought to be regarded but the truth, yet this is not repugnant to regulating of the same by peace. For doctrine repugnant to peace can no more be true, than peace and concord can be against the law of nature. It is true that in a commonwealth, where—by the negligence or unskilfulness of governors and teachers—false doctrines are by time generally received, the contrary truths may be generally offensive: yet the most sudden and rough bustling in of a new truth that can be does never break the peace, but only sometimes awake the war. For those men that are so remissly governed that they dare take up arms to defend or introduce an opinion are still in war; and their condition, not peace, but only a cessation of arms for fear of one another; and they live, as it were, in the precincts of battle continually. It belongeth therefore to him that hath the sovereign power to be judge (or constitute all judges) of opinions and doctrines, as a thing necessary to peace; thereby to prevent discord and civil war.

Seventhly, is annexed to the sovereignty the whole power of prescribing the rules whereby every man may know what goods he may enjoy, and what actions he may do, without being molested by any of his fellow subjects: and this is it men call *propriety*. For before constitution of sovereign power, as hath already been shown, all men had right to all things, which necessarily causeth war: and therefore this propriety, being necessary to peace, and depending on sovereign power, is the act of that power, in order to the public peace. These rules of propriety (or *meum* and *tuum*[34]) and of *good*, *evil*, *lawful*, and *unlawful* in the actions of subjects are the civil laws; that is to say, the laws of each commonwealth in particular; though the name of civil law be now restrained to the ancient civil laws of the city of *Rome*; which being the head of a great part of the world, her laws at that time were in these parts the civil law.

Eighthly, is annexed to the sovereignty the right of *judicature*; that is to say, of hearing and deciding all controversies which may arise concerning law, either civil or natural, or concerning fact. For without the decision of controversies, there is no protection of one subject against the injuries of another; the laws concerning *meum* and *tuum* are in vain, and to every man remaineth, from the natural and necessary appetite of his own conservation, the right of protecting himself by his private strength, which is the condition of war, and contrary to the end for which every commonwealth is instituted.

Ninthly, is annexed to the sovereignty the right of making war and peace with other nations and commonwealths; that is to say, of judging when it is for the public good, and how great forces are to be assembled, armed, and paid for that end, and to levy money upon the subjects to defray the expenses thereof. For the power by which the people are to be defended consisteth in their armies, and the strength of an army in the union of their strength under one

---

34   Mine and yours.

command; which command the sovereign instituted therefore hath, because the command of the *militia*, without other institution, maketh him that hath it sovereign. And therefore, whosoever is made general of an army, he that hath the sovereign power is always generalissimo.[35]

Tenthly, is annexed to the sovereignty the choosing of all counsellors, ministers, magistrates, and officers, both in peace and war. For seeing the sovereign is charged with the end, which is the common peace and defence, he is understood to have power to use such means as he shall think most fit for his discharge.

Eleventhly, to the sovereign is committed the power of rewarding with riches or honour; and of punishing with corporal or pecuniary punishment, or with ignominy, every subject according to the law he hath formerly made; or if there be no law made, according as he shall judge most to conduce to the encouraging of men to serve the commonwealth, or deterring of them from doing disservice to the same.

Lastly, considering what values men are naturally apt to set upon themselves, what respect they look for from others, and how little they value other men; from whence continually arise amongst them, emulation, quarrels, factions, and at last war, to the destroying of one another, and diminution of their strength against a common enemy; it is necessary that there be laws of honour, and a public rate of the worth of such men as have deserved or are able to deserve well of the commonwealth, and that there be force in the hands of some or other to put those laws in execution. But it hath already been shown that not only the whole *militia*, or forces of the commonwealth, but also the judicature of all controversies, is annexed to the sovereignty. To the sovereign therefore it belongeth also to give titles of honour, and to appoint what order of place and dignity each man shall hold, and what signs of respect in public or private meetings they shall give to one another.

These are the rights which make the essence of sovereignty, and which are the marks whereby a man may discern in what man, or assembly of men, the sovereign power is placed and resideth. For these are incommunicable and inseparable. The power to coin money, to dispose of the estate and persons of infant heirs, to have preemption in markets,[36] and all other statute prerogatives may be transferred by the sovereign, and yet the power to protect his subjects be retained. But if he transfer the *militia*, he retains the judicature in vain, for want of execution of the laws; or if he grant away the power of raising money, the *militia* is in vain; or if he give away the government of doctrines, men will be frighted into rebellion with the fear of spirits. And so if we consider any one of the said rights, we shall presently see that the holding of all the rest will produce no effect in the conservation of peace and justice, the end for which all commonwealths are instituted. And this division is it whereof it is said, *a kingdom divided in itself cannot stand*:[37] for unless this division precede, division into opposite armies can never happen. If there had not first been an opinion received of the greatest part of *England* that these powers were divided between the King and the Lords and the House of Commons, the people had never been divided and fallen into this Civil War;[38] first between those that disagreed in politics, and after between the dissenters about the liberty of religion, which have so instructed men in this point of sovereign right that there be few now in *England* that do not see that these rights are inseparable, and will be so generally acknowledged at the next return of peace; and so continue, till their miseries are forgotten, and no longer, except the vulgar be better taught than they have hitherto been.

And because they are essential and inseparable rights, it follows necessarily that in whatsoever words any of them seem to be granted away, yet if the sovereign power itself be not in direct terms renounced and the name of sovereign no more given by the grantees to him that grants them, the grant is void: for when he has granted all he can, if we grant back the sovereignty, all is restored, as inseparably annexed thereunto.

---

35 Supreme commander.

36 The right to make a purchase or appropriation before any one else can.

37 A biblical quote, see Matthew 12:25, Mark 3:24, and Luke 11:17.

38 The English Civil War (1642–1648) between the Parliamentarians and the Royalists.

This great authority being indivisible, and inseparably annexed to the sovereignty, there is little ground for the opinion of them that say of sovereign kings, though they be *singulis majores*,[39] of greater power than every one of their subjects, yet they be *universis minores*,[40] of less power than them all together. For if by *all together*, they mean not the collective body as one person, then *all together* and *every one* signify the same; and the speech is absurd. But if by *all together*, they understand them as one person (which person the sovereign bears), then the power of all together is the same with the sovereign's power; and so again the speech is absurd: which absurdity they see well enough when the sovereignty is in an assembly of the people; but in a monarch they see it not; and yet the power of sovereignty is the same in whomsoever it be placed.

And as the power, so also the honour of the sovereign, ought to be greater than that of any or all the subjects. For in the sovereignty is the fountain of honour. The dignities of lord, earl, duke, and prince are his creatures. As in the presence of the master, the servants are equal, and without any honour at all; so are the subjects, in the presence of the sovereign. And though they shine some more, some less, when they are out of his sight; yet in his presence, they shine no more than the stars in presence of the sun.

But a man may here object that the condition of subjects is very miserable, as being obnoxious to the lusts and other irregular passions of him or them that have so unlimited a power in their hands. And commonly they that live under a monarch think it the fault of monarchy; and they that live under the government of democracy, or other sovereign assembly, attribute all the inconvenience to that form of commonwealth; whereas the power in all forms, if they be perfect enough to protect them, is the same: not considering that the estate of man can never be without some incommodity or other; and that the greatest that in any form of government can possibly happen to the people in general is scarce sensible, in respect of the miseries and horrible calamities that accompany a civil war, or that dissolute condition of masterless men without subjection to laws and a coercive power to tie their hands from rapine and revenge: nor considering that the greatest pressure of sovereign governors proceedeth, not from any delight or profit they can expect in the damage weakening of their subjects, in whose vigour consisteth their own strength and glory, but in the restiveness of themselves that, unwillingly contributing to their own defence, make it necessary for their governors to draw from them what they can in time of peace that they may have means on any emergent occasion, or sudden need, to resist or take advantage on their enemies. For all men are by nature provided of notable multiplying glasses[41] (that is their passions and self-love) through which every little payment appeareth a great grievance, but are destitute of those prospective glasses[42] (namely moral and civil science) to see afar off the miseries that hang over them and cannot without such payments be avoided.

---

39 Greater than the individual.
40 Less than the collective.
41 Magnifying glasses.
42 Telescopes.

JOHN STUART MILL

On Liberty

For some information on Mill's life and his overall philosophical project, please see the notes on Mill in Chapter 7.

What Is the Structure of This Reading?

On Liberty is a short five-chapter book, the first, second, and fourth chapters of which are reprinted here. Mill's topic is the extent to which the state, and society in general, ought to have authority over the lives of individuals. He begins by introducing this issue and distinguishing two forms of the problem, one historical and the other more modern. The problem of setting limits to society's claims upon the individual, Mill asserts, is "the principal question in human affairs" but, he laments, its solution has not yet been put on a properly rational footing. Mill seeks to address this by formulating "one very simple principle"—sometimes today known as the "harm principle"—that should "govern absolutely the dealings of society with the individual in the way of compulsion and control." After some clarificatory remarks about this principle, Mill argues in defense of it beginning, in Chapter II, with the particular case of liberty of thought and discussion.

Mill's argument for the freedom of thought has three parts. He considers, first, the possibility that the received opinions might be false and the heretical ones true; second, the possibility that the received views are completely true and the heresy false; and lastly, a situation where dogma and heresy both contain only a part of the truth. In each case, Mill argues, allowing complete freedom of thought and discussion provides much greater value than harm to society.

In Chapter III (not included here) Mill discusses the importance of individuality to human well-being, describing it as a valuable component of personal happiness and an essential motor of social progress. In Chapter IV, therefore, he goes on to consider the question of the proper borderline between personal individuality and social authority, and uses his "harm principle" to show how this border should be drawn. The final chapter (not included) describes some illustrative applications of the principle to detailed sample cases, such as trade regulation, liquor taxation, and marriage laws.

Some Common Misconceptions

1. In arguing for the freedom of thought and discussion, Mill asserts we can never be *completely sure* that views which oppose our own, and which we might want to suppress, are not true (and thus we can never be completely sure that our own views are not false). However, he stresses that he does not mean that we should never feel certain of our own views, or that we should never act on them, or even that we should not attempt to persuade others of their truth. Mill is by no means a skeptic about the possibility of human knowledge and certainty. Rather, Mill argues that we should not *force* others to adopt our views by preventing them from hearing or thinking about alternative positions.

2. In arguing for firm limits on the authority of society over the individual, Mill is not arguing for the kind of a *laissez-faire* system in which everyone is assumed to be fundamentally self-interested, and where individuals are thought to have no moral duties towards their fellow-citizens except those arising from their own self-interest. On the contrary, he claims "[h]uman beings owe to each other help to distinguish the better from the worse, and encouragement to choose the former and avoid the latter," and he thought it was very much society's role to provide opportunities and incentives for self-improvement to its citizens.

Similarly, Mill is not simply claiming that society should interfere with individuals as little as possible—that, for example, the coercion of individuals by the state is always a bad thing and should be resorted to only when necessary. By contrast, he thinks there is a sphere in which society should not interfere with its members but also a sphere in which it *ought* to do so: individuals do have duties to the other members of the societies of which they are a part, and society has the right to force people to perform those duties.

How Important and Influential Is This Passage?

Mill's *On Liberty* has been a 'classic' since it was first published. To his great satisfaction, it immediately inspired intense debate between fervent supporters of the views expressed in the book and sharp critics of them, and—though many of the ideas it contains have now become quite familiar—the work is still the focus of substantial controversy today. *On Liberty* is generally considered to be one of the central statements of classical liberalism, and one of the finest defenses of individualism and freedom of thought ever written.

Suggestions for Critical Reflection

1. Mill suggests that, in modern democratic societies, the question of individual liberty requires "a different and more fundamental treatment" than it has historically been given, since in the past people were governed by an independent ruler while in a democracy it is "the people" themselves who exercise power. What exactly is the difference that democracy makes to the question of individual liberty, according to Mill? Do you think Mill might say—or should have said—that the rise of democracy, ironically, makes it *harder* for individuals to be free of illegitimate social interference?

2. Mill asserts (famously) that "the only purpose for which power can be rightfully exercised over any member of a civilized community,

against his will, is to prevent harm to others." Given this principle, it is obviously crucial to specify what constitutes "harm." Does Mill ever do so adequately? What is the best way of cashing out this crucial concept? Will it require drawing a distinction between *real* harms and what people merely *perceive* to be a harm to them (such as, say, witnessing a homosexual couple kissing)? If so, how can these 'real' harms be distinguished from the merely apparent ones? *Is* there a way of doing so that supports all the conclusions Mill wants to draw?

3. Before he begins his defense of his "harm principle," Mill notes that "I regard utility as the ultimate appeal on all ethical questions." If you have read the selection from Mill's *Utilitarianism* in Chapter 7, you might want to consider how much of his subsequent reasoning is rooted in utilitarianism … or indeed, whether the principle he defends in *On Liberty* is even *consistent* with Mill's utilitarian theory. What do you think Mill means by "utility in the largest sense, grounded on the permanent interests of man as a progressive being"?

4 "The only freedom which deserves the name, is that of pursuing our own good in our own way…." Is this true, or might there be a deeper, more valuable kind of freedom? What if someone's conception of their own good is importantly limited in some way, or is fallacious (even though it causes no harm to other people)? For example, what if I choose to spend my entire life in a basement watching TV, eating pizza, and growing and smoking (but not buying or selling) marijuana—could this really be an example of "the only freedom which deserves the name"? Further, what if I live this way, not through deliberate choice, but simply because it is how I grew up and is all I have ever experienced, and suppose I would, in fact, be much happier if some social authority were empowered to force me to get out more and make some friends. Must Mill still say I am free *only* if society leaves me alone? If so, is he right about that?

5. Part of Mill's argument in Chapter II involves the claim that "[c]omplete liberty of contradicting and disproving our opinion, is the very condition which justifies us in assuming its truth for purposes of action; and on no other terms can a being with human faculties have any rational assurance of being right." Does Mill really mean that we can have *no* "rational assurance" of being right about anything unless there is *complete* freedom of thought on the issue? If so, does he show that this is a plausible claim? Is there a less black-and-white version of this claim which seems more plausible (and which Mill might really have meant)? If so, does this less extreme version adequately support Mill's conclusions about the value of complete freedom of thought?

6. Mill argues believing something merely on the basis of authority, even if it is true, "is not the way in which truth ought to be held by a rational being." That is, he seems to suggest, believing some claim to be true without first having considered all the available arguments for and against that claim is mere vacant "superstition" and not genuine knowledge. Do Mill's arguments make this claim seem plausible, or does it strike you as too extreme? If he is right, how much of what most people believe could count as genuine knowledge? Is there a less contentious intermediate position? If so, would this weaker claim still support Mill's conclusions about the value of complete freedom of thought?

7. Should people be free to express *any* opinion, whatsoever? Imagine the most morally offensive view you can (involving, for example, the horrible torture of innocent toddlers or the most bizarre and uncomfortable kind of sexual act): should society allow people to, for example, make and distribute movies advocating this view? What if, to your horror, these movies prove highly popular and lots of people start watching them: should they still be allowed? Where, if anywhere, should the line be drawn, and does Mill get this line right?

8. Mill begins Chapter IV by stating "every one who receives the protection of society owes a return for the benefit, and the fact of living in society renders it indispensable that each should be bound to observe a certain line of conduct towards the rest." This, according to Mill, is what justifies society in placing at least *some* limits on the freedom of the individual. Does Mill have an argument for this principle, or it is just an assumption he makes? How philosophically significant is this assumption? For example, do you agree (and does Mill mean) that you have duties to your fellow citizens—such as (according to Mill) the duty to serve in the army in times of war, or to perform jury duty when called upon, or to rescue someone who has fallen into an icy river—*merely* in virtue of your living in a society?

9. Mill tries to distinguish between the "natural" social penalties of having a poor and foolish character, and penalties that might be deliberately inflicted on stupid people to punish them for their stupidity. According to Mill, the former kind of harm is an inevitable and acceptable consequence of one's own choices, while the latter constitutes morally unacceptable social interference. Is the crucial distinction between "natural" and punitive social harms an entirely clear one? (For example, what about repeatedly passing someone over for promotion or preventing them from attending a social organization such as a club or educational institution? Would these be "natural" consequences of someone's unpopularity, or a way of punishing them for being unpopular?) If this distinction is unclear, how serious a problem is this for Mill's position?

10. Mill also distinguishes between "self-regarding" and "social" virtues and vices, and claims only the latter are, properly speaking, *moral* virtues and vices, and that only these are properly within the ambit of social control. Again, is this an entirely clear distinction? For example, is it clear which of your character traits affect only you, personally, and which affect other people as well? If this kind of distinction is unclear or

unworkable, how serious a blow is this for Mill's account of individual liberty?

Suggestions for Further Reading

Mill's works, and much of the secondary literature on his political and ethical writings, are described in the Suggestions for Further Reading for the Mill selection in Chapter 7. There are many editions of Mill's *On Liberty* available: two good ones are edited by Edward Alexander (published by Broadview Press, 1999) and Stefan Collini (published by Cambridge University Press, 1989). Alexis de Toqueville's 1840 book *Democracy in America* (trans. Delba Winthrop, University of Chicago Press, 2000) heavily influenced Mill, and is useful for understanding the concerns that led to his writing of *On Liberty*. A fascinating snapshot of the debate Mill unleashed with the publication of *On Liberty* can be found in Andrew Pyle (ed.), *Liberty: Contemporary Responses to John Stuart Mill* (Thoemmes Press, 1994).

In addition to works listed in Chapter 7, there are several helpful books which are specifically about Mill's *On Liberty*, including John Gray, *Mill on Liberty: A Defence* (Routledge, 1996); John C. Rees, *John Stuart Mill's "On Liberty"* (Oxford University Press, 1985); Jonathan Riley, *The Routledge Philosophy Guidebook to Mill On Liberty* (Routledge, 1998); and C.L. Ten, *Mill on Liberty* (Oxford University Press, 1980). Three collections of articles about the book are: Gerald Dworkin (ed.), *Mill's "On Liberty"* (Rowman & Littlefield, 1997); Gray and Smith (eds.), *J.S. Mill's On Liberty In Focus* (Routledge, 1991); and Peter Radcliffe (ed.), *Limits of Liberty: Studies of Mill's On Liberty* (Wadsworth, 1966).

More general books containing valuable discussions relevant to Mill's concerns in *On Liberty* include Isaiah Berlin, *Four Essays on Liberty* (Oxford University Press, 1969); Joel Feinberg, *Harm to Others: Moral Limits of Criminal Law*, Volume 1 (Oxford University Press, 1984); and Rolf Sartorius, *Individual Conduct and Social Norms* (Wadsworth, 1975).

Finally, of the many articles written about *On Liberty*, the following are recommended: D.G. Brown, "Mill on Harm to Others' Interests," *Political Studies* 26 (1978); Richard Freedman, "A New Exploration of Mill's Essay *On Liberty*," *Political Studies* 14 (1966); Ted Honderich, "The Worth of J.S. Mill on Liberty," *Political Studies* 22 (1974); Ted Honderich, "*On Liberty* and Morality—Dependent Harms," *Political Studies* 30 (1982); Jonathan Riley, "One Very Simple Principle," *Utilitas* 3 (1991); Mark Strasser, "Mill and the Utility of Liberty," *Philosophical Quarterly* 34 (1984); Jeremy Waldron, "Mill and the Value of Moral Distress," *Political Studies* 35 (1987); Geraint Williams, "Mill's Principle of Liberty," *Political Studies* 24 (1976); and Richard Wollheim, "John Stuart Mill and the Limits of State Action," *Social Research* 40 (1973).

from *On Liberty*[1]

Chapter I: Introductory

The subject of this Essay is not the so-called Liberty of the Will, so unfortunately opposed to the misnamed doctrine of Philosophical Necessity, but Civil, or Social Liberty: the nature and limits of the power which can be legitimately exercised by society over the individual. A question seldom stated, and hardly ever discussed, in general terms, but which profoundly influences the practical controversies of the age by its latent presence, and is likely soon to make itself recognized as the vital question of the future. It is so far from being new, that, in a certain sense, it has divided mankind, almost from the remotest ages, but in the stage of progress into which the more civilized portions of the species have now entered, it presents itself under new conditions, and requires a different and more fundamental treatment.

The struggle between Liberty and Authority is the most conspicuous feature in the portions of history with which we are earliest familiar, particularly in that of Greece, Rome, and England. But in old times this contest was between subjects, or some classes of subjects, and the government. By liberty, was meant protection against the tyranny of the political rulers. The rulers were conceived (except in some of the popular governments of Greece) as in a necessarily antagonistic position to the people whom they ruled. They consisted of a governing One, or a govern-

---

1   *On Liberty* was first published in London in 1859.

ing tribe or caste, who derived their authority from inheritance or conquest; who, at all events, did not hold it at the pleasure of the governed, and whose supremacy men did not venture, perhaps did not desire, to contest, whatever precautions might be taken against its oppressive exercise. Their power was regarded as necessary, but also as highly dangerous; as a weapon which they would attempt to use against their subjects, no less than against external enemies. To prevent the weaker members of the community from being preyed upon by innumerable vultures, it was needful that there should be an animal of prey stronger than the rest, commissioned to keep them down. But as the king of the vultures would be no less bent upon preying upon the flock than any of the minor harpies, it was indispensable to be in a perpetual attitude of defence against his beak and claws. The aim, therefore, of patriots, was to set limits to the power which the ruler should be suffered to exercise over the community; and this limitation was what they meant by liberty. It was attempted in two ways. First, by obtaining a recognition of certain immunities, called political liberties or rights, which it was to be regarded as a breach of duty in the ruler to infringe, and which, if he did infringe, specific resistance, or general rebellion, was held to be justifiable. A second, and generally a later expedient, was the establishment of constitutional checks; by which the consent of the community, or of a body of some sort supposed to represent its interests, was made a necessary condition to some of the more important acts of the governing power. To the first of these modes of limitation, the ruling power, in most European countries, was compelled, more or less, to submit. It was not so with the second; and to attain this, or when already in some degree possessed, to attain it more completely, became everywhere the principal object of the lovers of liberty. And so long as mankind were content to combat one enemy by another, and to be ruled by a master, on condition of being guaranteed more or less efficaciously against his tyranny, they did not carry their aspirations beyond this point.

A time, however, came in the progress of human affairs, when men ceased to think it a necessity of nature that their governors should be an independent power, opposed in interest to themselves. It appeared to them much better that the various magistrates of the State should be their tenants or delegates, revocable at their pleasure. In that way alone, it seemed, could they have complete security that the powers of government would never be abused to their disadvantage. By degrees, this new demand for elective and temporary rulers became the prominent object of the exertions of the popular party, wherever any such party existed; and superseded, to a considerable extent, the previous efforts to limit the power of rulers. As the struggle proceeded for making the ruling power emanate from the periodical choice of the ruled, some persons began to think that too much importance had been attached to the limitation of the power itself. That (it might seem) was a resource against rulers whose interests were habitually opposed to those of the people. What was now wanted was, that the rulers should be identified with the people; that their interest and will should be the interest and will of the nation. The nation did not need to be protected against its own will. There was no fear of its tyrannizing over itself. Let the rulers be effectually responsible to it, promptly removable by it, and it could afford to trust them with power of which it could itself dictate the use to be made. Their power was but the nation's own power, concentrated, and in a form convenient for exercise. This mode of thought, or rather perhaps of feeling, was common among the last generation of European liberalism, in the Continental section of which, it still apparently predominates. Those who admit any limit to what a government may do, except in the case of such governments as they think ought not to exist, stand out as brilliant exceptions among the political thinkers of the Continent. A similar tone of sentiment might by this time have been prevalent in our own country, if the circumstances which for a time encouraged it had continued unaltered.

But, in political and philosophical theories, as well as in persons, success discloses faults and infirmities which failure might have concealed from observation. The notion, that the people have no need to limit their power over themselves, might seem axiomatic, when popular government was a thing only dreamed about, or read of as having existed at some distant period of the past. Neither was that notion necessarily disturbed by such temporary aberrations as those of the French

Revolution,[2] the worst of which were the work of an usurping few, and which, in any case, belonged, not to the permanent working of popular institutions, but to a sudden and convulsive outbreak against monarchical and aristocratic despotism. In time, however, a democratic republic[3] came to occupy a large portion of the earth's surface, and made itself felt as one of the most powerful members of the community of nations; and elective and responsible government became subject to the observations and criticisms which wait upon a great existing fact. It was now perceived that such phrases as "self-government," and "the power of the people over themselves," do not express the true state of the case. The "people" who exercise the power, are not always the same people with those over whom it is exercised, and the "self-government" spoken of, is not the government of each by himself, but of each by all the rest. The will of the people, moreover, practically means, the will of the most numerous or the most active *part* of the people; the majority, or those who succeed in making themselves accepted as the majority; the people, consequently, *may* desire to oppress a part of their number; and precautions are as much needed against this, as against any other abuse of power. The limitation, therefore, of the power of government over individuals, loses none of its importance when the holders of power are regularly accountable to the community, that is, to the strongest party therein. This view of things, recommending itself equally to the intelligence of thinkers and to the inclination of those important classes in European society to whose real or supposed interests democracy is adverse, has had no difficulty in establishing itself; and in political speculations "the tyranny of the majority" is now generally included among the evils against which society requires to be on its guard.

---

2   The French Revolution, which began with the storming of the Bastille prison in 1789, toppled the Bourbon monarchy—King Louis XVI was executed in 1793—but failed to produce a stable form of republican government and, after a period of ruthless extremism known as the Reign of Terror (1793–1794), was eventually replaced by Napoleon Bonaparte's imperial reign in 1799.

3   The United States of America.

Like other tyrannies, the tyranny of the majority was at first, and is still vulgarly,[4] held in dread, chiefly as operating through the acts of the public authorities. But reflecting persons perceived that when society is itself the tyrant—society collectively, over the separate individuals who compose it—its means of tyrannizing are not restricted to the acts which it may do by the hands of its political functionaries. Society can and does execute its own mandates: and if it issues wrong mandates instead of right, or any mandates at all in things with which it ought not to meddle, it practises a social tyranny more formidable than many kinds of political oppression, since, though not usually upheld by such extreme penalties, it leaves fewer means of escape, penetrating much more deeply into the details of life, and enslaving the soul itself. Protection, therefore, against the tyranny of the magistrate is not enough; there needs protection also against the tyranny of the prevailing opinion and feeling; against the tendency of society to impose, by other means than civil penalties, its own ideas and practices as rules of conduct on those who dissent from them; to fetter the development, and, if possible, prevent the formation, of any individuality not in harmony with its ways, and compel all characters to fashion themselves upon the model of its own. There is a limit to the legitimate interference of collective opinion with individual independence; and to find that limit, and maintain it against encroachment, is as indispensable to a good condition of human affairs, as protection against political despotism.

But though this proposition is not likely to be contested in general terms, the practical question, where to place the limit—how to make the fitting adjustment between individual independence and social control—is a subject on which nearly everything remains to be done. All that makes existence valuable to any one, depends on the enforcement of restraints upon the actions of other people. Some rules of conduct, therefore, must be imposed, by law in the first place, and by opinion on many things which are not fit subjects for the operation of law. What these rules should be, is the principal question in human affairs; but if we except a few of the most obvious

---

4   Commonly, popularly.

cases, it is one of those which least progress has been made in resolving. No two ages, and scarcely any two countries, have decided it alike; and the decision of one age or country is a wonder to another. Yet the people of any given age and country no more suspect any difficulty in it, than if it were a subject on which mankind had always been agreed. The rules which obtain among themselves appear to them self-evident and self-justifying. This all but universal illusion is one of the examples of the magical influence of custom, which is not only, as the proverb says a second nature, but is continually mistaken for the first. The effect of custom, in preventing any misgiving respecting the rules of conduct which mankind impose on one another, is all the more complete because the subject is one on which it is not generally considered necessary that reasons should be given, either by one person to others, or by each to himself. People are accustomed to believe and have been encouraged in the belief by some who aspire to the character of philosophers, that their feelings, on subjects of this nature, are better than reasons, and render reasons unnecessary. The practical principle which guides them to their opinions on the regulation of human conduct, is the feeling in each person's mind that everybody should be required to act as he, and those with whom he sympathizes, would like them to act. No one, indeed, acknowledges to himself that his standard of judgment is his own liking; but an opinion on a point of conduct, not supported by reasons, can only count as one person's preference; and if the reasons, when given, are a mere appeal to a similar preference felt by other people, it is still only many people's liking instead of one. To an ordinary man, however, his own preference, thus supported, is not only a perfectly satisfactory reason, but the only one he generally has for any of his notions of morality, taste, or propriety, which are not expressly written in his religious creed; and his chief guide in the interpretation even of that. Men's opinions, accordingly, on what is laudable or blameable, are affected by all the multifarious causes which influence their wishes in regard to the conduct of others, and which are as numerous as those which determine their wishes on any other subject. Sometimes their reason—at other times their prejudices or superstitions: often their social affections, not seldom

their anti-social ones, their envy or jealousy, their arrogance or contemptuousness: but most commonly, their desires or fears for themselves—their legitimate or illegitimate self-interest. Wherever there is an ascendant class, a large portion of the morality of the country emanates from its class interests, and its feelings of class superiority. The morality between Spartans and Helots,[5] between planters and negroes, between princes and subjects, between nobles and roturiers,[6] between men and women, has been for the most part the creation of these class interests and feelings: and the sentiments thus generated, react in turn upon the moral feelings of the members of the ascendant class, in their relations among themselves. Where, on the other hand, a class, formerly ascendant, has lost its ascendancy, or where its ascendancy is unpopular, the prevailing moral sentiments frequently bear the impress of an impatient dislike of superiority. Another grand determining principle of the rules of conduct, both in act and forbearance which have been enforced by law or opinion, has been the servility of mankind towards the supposed preferences or aversions of their temporal masters, or of their gods. This servility though essentially selfish, is not hypocrisy; it gives rise to perfectly genuine sentiments of abhorrence; it made men burn magicians and heretics. Among so many baser influences, the general and obvious interests of society have of course had a share, and a large one, in the direction of the moral sentiments: less, however, as a matter of reason, and on their own account, than as a consequence of the sympathies and antipathies which grew out of them: and sympathies and antipathies which had little or nothing to do with the interests of society, have made themselves felt in the establishment of moralities with quite as great force.

The likings and dislikings of society, or of some powerful portion of it, are thus the main thing which has practically determined the rules laid down for gen-

5 Sparta, a city-state in ancient Greece, was renowned for its militarism and social and political rigidity. Helots were a class of Spartan serfs, a rank that came between slaves and free citizens.

6 Roturiers are commoners, people of no aristocratic rank, holding land through the payment of rent.

eral observance, under the penalties of law or opinion. And in general, those who have been in advance of society in thought and feeling, have left this condition of things unassailed in principle, however they may have come into conflict with it in some of its details. They have occupied themselves rather in inquiring what things society ought to like or dislike, than in questioning whether its likings or dislikings should be a law to individuals. They preferred endeavouring to alter the feelings of mankind on the particular points on which they were themselves heretical, rather than make common cause in defence of freedom, with heretics generally. The only case in which the higher ground has been taken on principle and maintained with consistency, by any but an individual here and there, is that of religious belief: a case instructive in many ways, and not least so as forming a most striking instance of the fallibility of what is called the moral sense: for the *odium theologicum*,[7] in a sincere bigot, is one of the most unequivocal cases of moral feeling. Those who first broke the yoke of what called itself the Universal Church,[8] were in general as little willing to permit difference of religious opinion as that church itself. But when the heat of the conflict was over, without giving a complete victory to any party, and each church or sect was reduced to limit its hopes to retaining possession of the ground it already occupied; minorities, seeing that they had no chance of becoming majorities, were under the necessity of pleading to those whom they could not convert, for permission to differ. It is accordingly on this battle-field, almost solely, that the rights of the individual against society have been asserted on broad grounds of principle, and the claim of society to exercise authority over dissentients[9] openly controverted. The great writers to whom the world owes what religious liberty it possesses, have mostly asserted freedom of conscience as an indefeasible right, and denied absolutely that a human being is accountable to others for his religious belief. Yet so natural to mankind is intolerance in whatever they really care about, that

religious freedom has hardly anywhere been practically realized, except where religious indifference, which dislikes to have its peace disturbed by theological quarrels, has added its weight to the scale. In the minds of almost all religious persons, even in the most tolerant countries, the duty of toleration is admitted with tacit reserves. One person will bear with dissent in matters of church government, but not of dogma; another can tolerate everybody, short of a Papist[10] or an Unitarian;[11] another, every one who believes in revealed religion;[12] a few extend their charity a little further, but stop at the belief in a God and in a future state.[13] Wherever the sentiment of the majority is still genuine and intense, it is found to have abated little of its claim to be obeyed.

In England, from the peculiar circumstances of our political history, though the yoke of opinion is perhaps heavier, that of law is lighter, than in most other countries of Europe; and there is considerable jealousy of[14] direct interference, by the legislative or the executive power with private conduct; not so much from any just regard for the independence of the individual, as from the still subsisting habit of looking on the government as representing an opposite interest to the public. The majority have not yet learnt to feel the power of the government their power, or its opinions their opinions. When they do so, individual liberty will probably be as much exposed to invasion from the government, as it already is from public opinion. But, as yet, there is a considerable amount of feeling ready to be called forth against any attempt of the law to control individuals in things in which they have not hitherto been accustomed to be controlled by it; and

---

7   Animosity or prejudice generated by religious differences.

8   Catholicism (from the Greek *katholikos*—"universal").

9   Those who dissent, who disagree with a majority view.

10   A Roman Catholic, i.e., a follower of the Pope. (The term is generally considered offensive today.)

11   Unitarianism is a form of Christianity that rejects the doctrines of the Trinity—holding that God is an undivided unity—and thus denies the divinity of Jesus Christ. Unitarians, typically, also reject such doctrines as original sin and eternal punishment.

12   Religion based primarily on the revelations of God to humankind, as in a set of holy scriptures.

13   An afterlife in which people will be rewarded or punished for their behavior on earth.

14   Suspicion or resentment of.

this with very little discrimination as to whether the matter is, or is not, within the legitimate sphere of legal control; insomuch that the feeling, highly salutary on the whole, is perhaps quite as often misplaced as well grounded in the particular instances of its application. There is, in fact, no recognized principle by which the propriety or impropriety of government interference is customarily tested. People decide according to their personal preferences. Some, whenever they see any good to be done, or evil to be remedied, would willingly instigate the government to undertake the business; while others prefer to bear almost any amount of social evil, rather than add one to the departments of human interests amenable to governmental control. And men range themselves on one or the other side in any particular case, according to this general direction of their sentiments; or according to the degree of interest which they feel in the particular thing which it is proposed that the government should do; or according to the belief they entertain that the government would, or would not, do it in the manner they prefer; but very rarely on account of any opinion to which they consistently adhere, as to what things are fit to be done by a government. And it seems to me that, in consequence of this absence of rule or principle, one side is at present as often wrong as the other; the interference of government is, with about equal frequency, improperly invoked and improperly condemned.

The object of this Essay is to assert one very simple principle, as entitled to govern absolutely the dealings of society with the individual in the way of compulsion and control, whether the means used be physical force in the form of legal penalties, or the moral coercion of public opinion. That principle is, that the sole end for which mankind are warranted, individually or collectively in interfering with the liberty of action of any of their number, is self-protection. That the only purpose for which power can be rightfully exercised over any member of a civilized community, against his will, is to prevent harm to others. His own good, either physical or moral, is not a sufficient warrant. He cannot rightfully be compelled to do or forbear because it will be better for him to do so, because it will make him happier, because, in the opinions of others, to do so would be wise, or even right. These

are good reasons for remonstrating with him, or reasoning with him, or persuading him, or entreating him, but not for compelling him, or visiting him with any evil, in case he do otherwise. To justify that, the conduct from which it is desired to deter him must be calculated to produce evil to some one else. The only part of the conduct of any one, for which he is amenable to society, is that which concerns others. In the part which merely concerns himself, his independence is, of right, absolute. Over himself, over his own body and mind, the individual is sovereign.

It is, perhaps, hardly necessary to say that this doctrine is meant to apply only to human beings in the maturity of their faculties. We are not speaking of children, or of young persons below the age which the law may fix as that of manhood or womanhood. Those who are still in a state to require being taken care of by others, must be protected against their own actions as well as against external injury. For the same reason, we may leave out of consideration those backward states of society in which the race itself may be considered as in its nonage.[15] The early difficulties in the way of spontaneous progress are so great, that there is seldom any choice of means for overcoming them; and a ruler full of the spirit of improvement is warranted in the use of any expedients that will attain an end, perhaps otherwise unattainable. Despotism is a legitimate mode of government in dealing with barbarians, provided the end be their improvement, and the means justified by actually effecting that end. Liberty, as a principle, has no application to any state of things anterior to the time when mankind have become capable of being improved by free and equal discussion. Until then, there is nothing for them but implicit obedience to an Akbar or a Charlemagne,[16]

---

15 A period of immaturity, being underage.

16 Akbar the Great was Mogul emperor of northern India from 1556 until 1605. He is generally considered the founder of the Mogul empire, and was famous for implementing an effective administrative system, imposing religious tolerance, and making his court a center for art and literature. Charlemagne ("Charles the Great") was king of the Franks from 768 until 814. His armies conquered much of central and western Europe—including parts of Spain, Italy, Saxony, Bavaria,

if they are so fortunate as to find one. But as soon as mankind have attained the capacity of being guided to their own improvement by conviction or persuasion (a period long since reached in all nations with whom we need here concern ourselves), compulsion, either in the direct form or in that of pains and penalties for non-compliance, is no longer admissible as a means to their own good, and justifiable only for the security of others.

It is proper to state that I forego any advantage which could be derived to my argument from the idea of abstract right as a thing independent of utility. I regard utility as the ultimate appeal on all ethical questions; but it must be utility in the largest sense, grounded on the permanent interests of man as a progressive being. Those interests, I contend, authorize the subjection of individual spontaneity to external control, only in respect to those actions of each, which concern the interest of other people. If any one does an act hurtful to others, there is a *prima facie*[17] case for punishing him, by law, or, where legal penalties are not safely applicable, by general disapprobation.[18] There are also many positive acts for the benefit of others, which he may rightfully be compelled to perform; such as, to give evidence in a court of justice; to bear his fair share in the common defence, or in any other joint work necessary to the interest of the society of which he enjoys the protection; and to perform certain acts of individual beneficence, such as saving a fellow-creature's life, or interposing to protect the defenceless against ill-usage, things which whenever it is obviously a man's duty to do, he may rightfully be made responsible to society for not doing. A person may cause evil to others not only by his actions but by his inaction, and in either case he is justly accountable to them for the injury. The latter case, it is true, requires a much more cautious exercise of compulsion

than the former. To make any one answerable for doing evil to others, is the rule; to make him answerable for not preventing evil, is, comparatively speaking, the exception. Yet there are many cases clear enough and grave enough to justify that exception. In all things which regard the external relations of the individual, he is *de jure*[19] amenable to those whose interests are concerned, and if need be, to society as their protector. There are often good reasons for not holding him to the responsibility; but these reasons must arise from the special expediencies of the case: either because it is a kind of case in which he is on the whole likely to act better, when left to his own discretion, than when controlled in any way in which society have it in their power to control him; or because the attempt to exercise control would produce other evils, greater than those which it would prevent. When such reasons as these preclude the enforcement of responsibility, the conscience of the agent himself should step into the vacant judgment-seat, and protect those interests of others which have no external protection; judging himself all the more rigidly, because the case does not admit of his being made accountable to the judgment of his fellow-creatures.

But there is a sphere of action in which society, as distinguished from the individual, has, if any, only an indirect interest; comprehending all that portion of a person's life and conduct which affects only himself, or, if it also affects others, only with their free, voluntary, and undeceived consent and participation. When I say only himself, I mean directly, and in the first instance: for whatever affects himself, may affect others through himself; and the objection which may be grounded on this contingency, will receive consideration in the sequel. This, then, is the appropriate region of human liberty. It comprises, first, the inward domain of consciousness; demanding liberty of conscience, in the most comprehensive sense; liberty of thought and feeling; absolute freedom of opinion and sentiment on all subjects, practical or speculative, scientific, moral, or theological. The liberty of expressing and publishing opinions may seem to fall under a different principle, since it belongs to that part of the conduct of an individual which concerns other

Austria, and Hungary—and, in 800, he was anointed the first Holy Roman Emperor by Pope Leo III. Like Akbar, Charlemagne is known for making his court a great center of culture and scholarship, and for imposing an effective legal and administrative structure on his dominions.

17   At first sight, on first impression.

18   Strong (moral) disapproval.

19   By law, rightfully.

people; but, being almost of as much importance as the liberty of thought itself, and resting in great part on the same reasons, is practically inseparable from it. Secondly, the principle requires liberty of tastes and pursuits; of framing the plan of our life to suit our own character; of doing as we like, subject to such consequences as may follow; without impediment from our fellow-creatures, so long as what we do does not harm them even though they should think our conduct foolish, perverse, or wrong. Thirdly, from this liberty of each individual, follows the liberty, within the same limits, of combination among individuals; freedom to unite, for any purpose not involving harm to others: the persons combining being supposed to be of full age, and not forced or deceived.

No society in which these liberties are not, on the whole, respected, is free, whatever may be its form of government; and none is completely free in which they do not exist absolute and unqualified. The only freedom which deserves the name, is that of pursuing our own good in our own way, so long as we do not attempt to deprive others of theirs, or impede their efforts to obtain it. Each is the proper guardian of his own health, whether bodily, or mental or spiritual. Mankind are greater gainers by suffering each other to live as seems good to themselves, than by compelling each to live as seems good to the rest.

Though this doctrine is anything but new, and, to some persons, may have the air of a truism, there is no doctrine which stands more directly opposed to the general tendency of existing opinion and practice. Society has expended fully as much effort in the attempt (according to its lights) to compel people to conform to its notions of personal, as of social excellence. The ancient commonwealths thought themselves entitled to practise, and the ancient philosophers countenanced, the regulation of every part of private conduct by public authority, on the ground that the State had a deep interest in the whole bodily and mental discipline of every one of its citizens, a mode of thinking which may have been admissible in small republics surrounded by powerful enemies, in constant peril of being subverted by foreign attack or internal commotion, and to which even a short interval of relaxed energy and self-command might so easily be fatal, that they could not afford to wait

for the salutary permanent effects of freedom. In the modern world, the greater size of political communities, and above all, the separation between the spiritual and temporal authority (which placed the direction of men's consciences in other hands than those which controlled their worldly affairs), prevented so great an interference by law in the details of private life; but the engines of moral repression have been wielded more strenuously against divergence from the reigning opinion in self-regarding, than even in social matters; religion, the most powerful of the elements which have entered into the formation of moral feeling, having almost always been governed either by the ambition of a hierarchy, seeking control over every department of human conduct, or by the spirit of Puritanism. And some of those modern reformers who have placed themselves in strongest opposition to the religions of the past, have been noway behind either churches or sects in their assertion of the right of spiritual domination: M. Comte, in particular, whose social system, as unfolded in his *Système de Politique Positive*,[20] aims at establishing (though by moral more than by legal appliances) a despotism of society over the individual, surpassing anything contemplated in the political ideal of the most rigid disciplinarian among the ancient philosophers.

Apart from the peculiar tenets of individual thinkers, there is also in the world at large an increasing inclination to stretch unduly the powers of society over the individual, both by the force of opinion and even by that of legislation: and as the tendency of all the changes taking place in the world is to strengthen society, and diminish the power of the individual, this encroachment is not one of the evils which tend spontaneously to disappear, but, on the contrary, to grow more and more formidable. The disposition of mankind, whether as rulers or as fellow-citizens, to impose their own opinions and inclinations as a rule of conduct on others, is so energetically supported by some of the best and by some of the worst feelings

---

20 Auguste Comte (1789–1857), a French philosopher, social theorist, and founder of positivism, published *Système de Politique Positive* [*The System of Positive Polity*] in 1851–54. Mill later wrote a book on his work, *Auguste Comte and Positivism* (1865).

incident to human nature, that it is hardly ever kept under restraint by anything but want of power; and as the power is not declining, but growing, unless a strong barrier of moral conviction can be raised against the mischief, we must expect, in the present circumstances of the world, to see it increase.

It will be convenient for the argument, if, instead of at once entering upon the general thesis, we confine ourselves in the first instance to a single branch of it, on which the principle here stated is, if not fully, yet to a certain point, recognized by the current opinions. This one branch is the Liberty of Thought: from which it is impossible to separate the cognate liberty of speaking and of writing. Although these liberties, to some considerable amount, form part of the political morality of all countries which profess religious toleration and free institutions, the grounds, both philosophical and practical, on which they rest, are perhaps not so familiar to the general mind, nor so thoroughly appreciated by many even of the leaders of opinion, as might have been expected. Those grounds, when rightly understood, are of much wider application than to only one division of the subject, and a thorough consideration of this part of the question will be found the best introduction to the remainder. Those to whom nothing which I am about to say will be new, may therefore, I hope, excuse me, if on a subject which for now three centuries has been so often discussed, I venture on one discussion more.

Chapter II: Of the Liberty of Thought and Discussion

The time, it is to be hoped, is gone by when any defence would be necessary of the "liberty of the press" as one of the securities against corrupt or tyrannical government. No argument, we may suppose, can now be needed, against permitting a legislature or an executive, not identified in interest with the people, to prescribe opinions to them, and determine what doctrines or what arguments they shall be allowed to hear. This aspect of the question, besides, has been so often and so triumphantly enforced by preceding writers, that it needs not be specially insisted on in this place. Though the law of England, on the subject of the press, is as servile to this day as it was in the time of the Tudors,[21] there is little danger of its being actually put in force against political discussion, except during some temporary panic, when fear of insurrection drives ministers and judges from their propriety;[22] and, speaking generally, it is not, in constitutional

---

21 The royal dynasty ruling England from 1485 to 1603 (Henry VII–Elizabeth I).

22 [Author's note] These words had scarcely been written, when, as if to give them an emphatic contradiction, occurred the Government Press Prosecutions of 1858. That ill-judged interference with the liberty of public discussion has not, however, induced me to alter a single word in the text, nor has it at all weakened my conviction that, moments of panic excepted, the era of pains and penalties for political discussion has, in our own country, passed away. For, in the first place, the prosecutions were not persisted in; and in the second, they were never, properly speaking, political prosecutions. The offence charged was not that of criticizing institutions, or the acts or persons of rulers, but of circulating what was deemed an immoral doctrine, the lawfulness of Tyrannicide.

If the arguments of the present chapter are of any validity, there ought to exist the fullest liberty of professing and discussing, as a matter of ethical conviction, any doctrine, however immoral it may be considered. It would, therefore, be irrelevant and out of place to examine here, whether the doctrine of Tyrannicide deserves that title. I shall content myself with saying, that the subject has been at all times one of the open questions of morals, that the act of a private citizen in striking down a criminal, who, by raising himself above the law, has placed himself beyond the reach of legal punishment or control, has been accounted by whole nations, and by some of the best and wisest of men, not a crime, but an act of exalted virtue and that, right or wrong, it is not of the nature of assassination but of civil war. As such, I hold that the instigation to it, in a specific case, may be a proper subject of punishment, but only if an overt act has followed, and at least a probable connection can be established between the act and the instigation. Even then it is not a foreign government, but the very government assailed, which alone, in the exercise of self-defence, can legitimately punish attacks directed against its own existence.

countries, to be apprehended that the government, whether completely responsible to the people or not, will often attempt to control the expression of opinion, except when in doing so it makes itself the organ of the general intolerance of the public. Let us suppose, therefore, that the government is entirely at one with the people, and never thinks of exerting any power of coercion unless in agreement with what it conceives to be their voice. But I deny the right of the people to exercise such coercion, either by themselves or by their government. The power itself is illegitimate. The best government has no more title to it than the worst. It is as noxious, or more noxious, when exerted in accordance with public opinion, than when in opposition to it. If all mankind minus one, were of one opinion, and only one person were of the contrary opinion, mankind would be no more justified in silencing that one person, than he, if he had the power, would be justified in silencing mankind. Were an opinion a personal possession of no value except to the owner; if to be obstructed in the enjoyment of it were simply a private injury, it would make some difference whether the injury was inflicted only on a few persons or on many. But the peculiar evil of silencing the expression of an opinion is, that it is robbing the human race; posterity as well as the existing generation; those who dissent from the opinion, still more than those who hold it. If the opinion is right, they are deprived of the opportunity of exchanging error for truth: if wrong, they lose, what is almost as great a benefit, the clearer perception and livelier impression of truth, produced by its collision with error.

It is necessary to consider separately these two hypotheses, each of which has a distinct branch of the argument corresponding to it. We can never be sure that the opinion we are endeavouring to stifle is a false opinion; and if we were sure, stifling it would be an evil still.

First: the opinion which it is attempted to suppress by authority may possibly be true. Those who desire to suppress it, of course deny its truth; but they are not infallible. They have no authority to decide the question for all mankind, and exclude every other person from the means of judging. To refuse a hearing to an opinion, because they are sure that it is false, is to assume that *their* certainty is the same thing as *absolute* certainty. All silencing of discussion is an assumption of infallibility. Its condemnation may be allowed to rest on this common argument, not the worse for being common.

Unfortunately for the good sense of mankind, the fact of their fallibility is far from carrying the weight in their practical judgment, which is always allowed to it in theory; for while every one well knows himself to be fallible, few think it necessary to take any precautions against their own fallibility, or admit the supposition that any opinion of which they feel very certain, may be one of the examples of the error to which they acknowledge themselves to be liable. Absolute princes, or others who are accustomed to unlimited deference, usually feel this complete confidence in their own opinions on nearly all subjects. People more happily situated, who sometimes hear their opinions disputed, and are not wholly unused to be set right when they are wrong, place the same unbounded reliance only on such of their opinions as are shared by all who surround them, or to whom they habitually defer: for in proportion to a man's want of confidence in his own solitary judgment, does he usually repose, with implicit trust, on the infallibility of "the world" in general. And the world, to each individual, means the part of it with which he comes in contact; his party, his sect, his church, his class of society: the man may be called, by comparison, almost liberal and large-minded to whom it means anything so comprehensive as his own country or his own age. Nor is his faith in this collective authority at all shaken by his being aware that other ages, countries, sects, churches, classes, and parties have thought, and even now think, the exact reverse. He devolves upon his own world the responsibility of being in the right against the dissentient worlds of other people; and it never troubles him that mere accident has decided which of these numerous worlds is the object of his reliance, and that the same causes which make him a Churchman in London, would have made him a Buddhist or a Confucian in Pekin.[23] Yet it is as evident in itself as any amount of argument can make it, that ages are no more infallible than individuals; every age having held many opinions which subsequent

---

23   Peking (today called Beijing), the capital of China.

ages have deemed not only false but absurd; and it is as certain that many opinions, now general, will be rejected by future ages, as it is that many, once general, are rejected by the present.

The objection likely to be made to this argument, would probably take some such form as the following. There is no greater assumption of infallibility in forbidding the propagation of error, than in any other thing which is done by public authority on its own judgment and responsibility. Judgment is given to men that they may use it. Because it may be used erroneously, are men to be told that they ought not to use it at all? To prohibit what they think pernicious, is not claiming exemption from error, but fulfilling the duty incumbent on them, although fallible, of acting on their conscientious conviction. If we were never to act on our opinions, because those opinions may be wrong, we should leave all our interests uncared for, and all our duties unperformed. An objection which applies to all conduct can be no valid objection to any conduct in particular. It is the duty of governments, and of individuals, to form the truest opinions they can; to form them carefully, and never impose them upon others unless they are quite sure of being right. But when they are sure (such reasoners may say), it is not conscientiousness but cowardice to shrink from acting on their opinions, and allow doctrines which they honestly think dangerous to the welfare of mankind, either in this life or in another, to be scattered abroad without restraint, because other people, in less enlightened times, have persecuted opinions now believed to be true. Let us take care, it may be said, not to make the same mistake: but governments and nations have made mistakes in other things, which are not denied to be fit subjects for the exercise of authority: they have laid on bad taxes, made unjust wars. Ought we therefore to lay on no taxes, and, under whatever provocation, make no wars? Men, and governments, must act to the best of their ability. There is no such thing as absolute certainty, but there is assurance sufficient for the purposes of human life. We may, and must, assume our opinion to be true for the guidance of our own conduct: and it is assuming no more when we forbid bad men to pervert society by the propagation of opinions which we regard as false and pernicious.

I answer, that it is assuming very much more. There is the greatest difference between presuming an opinion to be true, because, with every opportunity for contesting it, it has not been refuted, and assuming its truth for the purpose of not permitting its refutation. Complete liberty of contradicting and disproving our opinion, is the very condition which justifies us in assuming its truth for purposes of action; and on no other terms can a being with human faculties have any rational assurance of being right.

When we consider either the history of opinion, or the ordinary conduct of human life, to what is it to be ascribed that the one and the other are no worse than they are? Not certainly to the inherent force of the human understanding; for, on any matter not self-evident, there are ninety-nine persons totally incapable of judging of it, for one who is capable; and the capacity of the hundredth person is only comparative; for the majority of the eminent men of every past generation held many opinions now known to be erroneous, and did or approved numerous things which no one will now justify. Why is it, then, that there is on the whole a preponderance among mankind of rational opinions and rational conduct? If there really is this preponderance—which there must be, unless human affairs are, and have always been, in an almost desperate state—it is owing to a quality of the human mind, the source of everything respectable in man, either as an intellectual or as a moral being, namely, that his errors are corrigible.[24] He is capable of rectifying his mistakes by discussion and experience. Not by experience alone. There must be discussion, to show how experience is to be interpreted. Wrong opinions and practices gradually yield to fact and argument: but facts and arguments, to produce any effect on the mind, must be brought before it. Very few facts are able to tell their own story, without comments to bring out their meaning. The whole strength and value, then, of human judgment, depending on the one property, that it can be set right when it is wrong, reliance can be placed on it only when the means of setting it right are kept constantly at hand. In the case of any person whose judgment is really deserving of confidence, how has it become so? Because he has kept his mind open to

24 Correctable.

criticism of his opinions and conduct. Because it has been his practice to listen to all that could be said against him; to profit by as much of it as was just, and expound to himself, and upon occasion to others, the fallacy of what was fallacious. Because he has felt, that the only way in which a human being can make some approach to knowing the whole of a subject, is by hearing what can be said about it by persons of every variety of opinion, and studying all modes in which it can be looked at by every character of mind. No wise man ever acquired his wisdom in any mode but this; nor is it in the nature of human intellect to become wise in any other manner. The steady habit of correcting and completing his own opinion by collating it with those of others, so far from causing doubt and hesitation in carrying it into practice, is the only stable foundation for a just reliance on it: for, being cognizant of all that can, at least obviously, be said against him, and having taken up his position against all gainsayers knowing that he has sought for objections and difficulties, instead of avoiding them, and has shut out no light which can be thrown upon the subject from any quarter—he has a right to think his judgment better than that of any person, or any multitude, who have not gone through a similar process.

It is not too much to require that what the wisest of mankind, those who are best entitled to trust their own judgment, find necessary to warrant their relying on it, should be submitted to by that miscellaneous collection of a few wise and many foolish individuals, called the public. The most intolerant of churches, the Roman Catholic Church, even at the canonization of a saint, admits, and listens patiently to, a "devil's advocate." The holiest of men, it appears, cannot be admitted to posthumous honours, until all that the devil could say against him is known and weighed. If even the Newtonian philosophy were not permitted to be questioned, mankind could not feel as complete assurance of its truth as they now do. The beliefs which we have most warrant for, have no safeguard to rest on, but a standing invitation to the whole world to prove them unfounded. If the challenge is not accepted, or is accepted and the attempt fails, we are far enough from certainty still; but we have done the best that the existing state of human reason admits of; we have neglected nothing that could give the truth

a chance of reaching us: if the lists[25] are kept open, we may hope that if there be a better truth, it will be found when the human mind is capable of receiving it; and in the meantime we may rely on having attained such approach to truth, as is possible in our own day. This is the amount of certainty attainable by a fallible being, and this the sole way of attaining it.

Strange it is, that men should admit the validity of the arguments for free discussion, but object to their being "pushed to an extreme;" not seeing that unless the reasons are good for an extreme case, they are not good for any case. Strange that they should imagine that they are not assuming infallibility when they acknowledge that there should be free discussion on all subjects which can possibly be doubtful, but think that some particular principle or doctrine should be forbidden to be questioned because it is so *certain*, that is, because *they are certain* that it is certain. To call any proposition certain, while there is any one who would deny its certainty if permitted, but who is not permitted, is to assume that we ourselves, and those who agree with us, are the judges of certainty, and judges without hearing the other side.

In the present age—which has been described as "destitute of faith, but terrified at scepticism"[26]—in which people feel sure, not so much that their opinions are true, as that they should not know what to do without them—the claims of an opinion to be protected from public attack are rested not so much on its truth, as on its importance to society. There are, it is alleged, certain beliefs, so useful, not to say indispensable to well-being, that it is as much the duty of governments to uphold those beliefs, as to protect any other of the interests of society. In a case of such necessity, and so directly in the line of their duty, something less than infallibility may, it is maintained, warrant, and even bind, governments, to act on their own opinion, confirmed by the general opinion of mankind. It is also often argued, and still oftener thought, that none but bad men would desire

---

25 An arena for jousting and other tournaments and thus, metaphorically, an area of controversy.

26 Mill is quoting the contemporary essayist Thomas Carlyle (from his "Memoirs of the Life of Scott," *London and Westminster Review*, January 1838).

to weaken these salutary beliefs; and there can be nothing wrong, it is thought, in restraining bad men, and prohibiting what only such men would wish to practise. This mode of thinking makes the justification of restraints on discussion not a question of the truth of doctrines, but of their usefulness; and flatters itself by that means to escape the responsibility of claiming to be an infallible judge of opinions. But those who thus satisfy themselves, do not perceive that the assumption of infallibility is merely shifted from one point to another. The usefulness of an opinion is itself matter of opinion: as disputable, as open to discussion and requiring discussion as much, as the opinion itself. There is the same need of an infallible judge of opinions to decide an opinion to be noxious, as to decide it to be false, unless the opinion condemned has full opportunity of defending itself. And it will not do to say that the heretic may be allowed to maintain the utility or harmlessness of his opinion, though forbidden to maintain its truth. The truth of an opinion is part of its utility. If we would know whether or not it is desirable that a proposition should be believed, is it possible to exclude the consideration of whether or not it is true? In the opinion, not of bad men, but of the best men, no belief which is contrary to truth can be really useful: and can you prevent such men from urging that plea, when they are charged with culpability for denying some doctrine which they are told is useful, but which they believe to be false? Those who are on the side of received opinions, never fail to take all possible advantage of this plea; you do not find *them* handling the question of utility as if it could be completely abstracted from that of truth: on the contrary, it is, above all, because their doctrine is "the truth," that the knowledge or the belief of it is held to be so indispensable. There can be no fair discussion of the question of usefulness, when an argument so vital may be employed on one side, but not on the other. And in point of fact, when law or public feeling do not permit the truth of an opinion to be disputed, they are just as little tolerant of a denial of its usefulness. The utmost they allow is an extenuation of its absolute necessity or of the positive guilt of rejecting it.

In order more fully to illustrate the mischief of denying a hearing to opinions because we, in our own judgment, have condemned them, it will be desirable to fix down the discussion to a concrete case; and I choose, by preference, the cases which are least favourable to me—in which the argument against freedom of opinion, both on the score of truth and on that of utility, is considered the strongest. Let the opinions impugned be the belief in a God and in a future state, or any of the commonly received doctrines of morality. To fight the battle on such ground, gives a great advantage to an unfair antagonist; since he will be sure to say (and many who have no desire to be unfair will say it internally), Are these the doctrines which you do not deem sufficiently certain to be taken under the protection of law? Is the belief in a God one of the opinions, to feel sure of which, you hold to be assuming infallibility? But I must be permitted to observe, that it is not the feeling sure of a doctrine (be it what it may) which I call an assumption of infallibility. It is the undertaking to decide that question *for others*, without allowing them to hear what can be said on the contrary side. And I denounce and reprobate this pretension not the less, if put forth on the side of my most solemn convictions. However positive any one's persuasion may be, not only of the falsity, but of the pernicious consequences—not only of the pernicious consequences, but (to adopt expressions which I altogether condemn) the immorality and impiety of an opinion; yet if, in pursuance of that private judgment, though backed by the public judgment of his country or his contemporaries, he prevents the opinion from being heard in its defence, he assumes infallibility. And so far from the assumption being less objectionable or less dangerous because the opinion is called immoral or impious, this is the case of all others in which it is most fatal. These are exactly the occasions on which the men of one generation commit those dreadful mistakes which excite the astonishment and horror of posterity. It is among such that we find the instances memorable in history, when the arm of the law has been employed to root out the best men and the noblest doctrines; with deplorable success as to the men, though some of the doctrines have survived to be (as if in mockery) invoked, in defence of similar conduct towards those who dissent from *them*, or from their received interpretation.

Mankind can hardly be too often reminded, that there was once a man named Socrates, between whom and the legal authorities and public opinion of his time, there took place a memorable collision. Born in an age and country abounding in individual greatness,[27] this man has been handed down to us by those who best knew both him and the age, as the most virtuous man in it; while we know him as the head and prototype of all subsequent teachers of virtue, the source equally of the lofty inspiration of Plato and the judicious utilitarianism of Aristotle, "*i maestri di color che sanno*,"[28] the two headsprings of ethical as of all other philosophy. This acknowledged master of all the eminent thinkers who have since lived—whose fame, still growing after more than two thousand years, all but outweighs the whole remainder of the names which make his native city illustrious—was put to death by his countrymen, after a judicial conviction, for impiety and immorality. Impiety, in denying the gods recognized by the State; indeed his accuser asserted (see the "Apologia"[29]) that he believed in no gods at all. Immorality, in being, by his doctrines and instructions, a "corrupter of youth." Of these charges the tribunal, there is every ground for believing, honestly found him guilty, and condemned the man who probably of all then born had deserved best of mankind, to be put to death as a criminal.

To pass from this to the only other instance of judicial iniquity, the mention of which, after the condemnation of Socrates, would not be an anti-climax: the event which took place on Calvary[30] rather more than eighteen hundred years ago. The man who left on the memory of those who witnessed his life and conversation, such an impression of his moral grandeur, that eighteen subsequent centuries have done homage to him as the Almighty in person, was ignominiously put to death, as what? As a blasphemer. Men did not merely mistake their benefactor; they mistook him

for the exact contrary of what he was, and treated him as that prodigy of impiety, which they themselves are now held to be, for their treatment of him. The feelings with which mankind now regard these lamentable transactions, especially the latter of the two, render them extremely unjust in their judgment of the unhappy actors. These were, to all appearance, not bad men—not worse than men most commonly are, but rather the contrary; men who possessed in a full, or somewhat more than a full measure, the religious, moral, and patriotic feelings of their time and people: the very kind of men who, in all times, our own included, have every chance of passing through life blameless and respected. The high-priest who rent his garments when the words were pronounced,[31] which, according to all the ideas of his country, constituted the blackest guilt, was in all probability quite as sincere in his horror and indignation, as the generality of respectable and pious men now are in the religious and moral sentiments they profess; and most of those who now shudder at his conduct, if they had lived in his time and been born Jews, would have acted precisely as he did. Orthodox Christians who are tempted to think that those who stoned to death the first martyrs must have been worse men than they themselves are, ought to remember that one of those persecutors was Saint Paul.

Let us add one more example, the most striking of all, if the impressiveness of an error is measured by the wisdom and virtue of him who falls into it. If ever any one, possessed of power, had grounds for thinking himself the best and most enlightened among his contemporaries, it was the Emperor Marcus Aurelius.[32] Absolute monarch of the whole civilized world, he preserved through life not only the most unblemished justice, but what was less to be expected from his Stoical breeding, the tenderest heart. The few failings which are attributed to him, were all on the side

27 Socrates lived in the Greek city-state of Athens in the fifth century BCE.

28 "The masters of those who know," an adaptation of a line from Dante's *Inferno* (Canto IV, 131), where Dante refers, in the singular, to Aristotle.

29 A dialogue by Plato—*The Apology*—which describes Socrates' trial.

30 The crucifixion of Jesus Christ; Calvary is the name of the hill outside Jerusalem where this took place.

31 Caiaphas. This scene is described in Matthew 26:65.

32 Marcus Aurelius (121–180 CE) was a Stoic philosopher and emperor of Rome from 161 to 180. His *Meditations* were an important formulation of Stoicism, a deterministic, rationalistic philosophy which held that the four main virtues are wisdom, courage, justice, and temperance.

of indulgence: while his writings, the highest ethical product of the ancient mind, differ scarcely perceptibly, if they differ at all, from the most characteristic teachings of Christ. This man, a better Christian in all but the dogmatic sense of the word, than almost any of the ostensibly Christian sovereigns who have since reigned, persecuted Christianity. Placed at the summit of all the previous attainments of humanity, with an open, unfettered intellect, and a character which led him of himself to embody in his moral writings the Christian ideal, he yet failed to see that Christianity was to be a good and not an evil to the world, with his duties to which he was so deeply penetrated. Existing society he knew to be in a deplorable state. But such as it was, he saw or thought he saw, that it was held together and prevented from being worse, by belief and reverence of the received divinities. As a ruler of mankind, he deemed it his duty not to suffer society to fall in pieces; and saw not how, if its existing ties were removed, any others could be formed which could again knit it together. The new religion openly aimed at dissolving these ties: unless, therefore, it was his duty to adopt that religion, it seemed to be his duty to put it down. Inasmuch then as the theology of Christianity did not appear to him true or of divine origin; inasmuch as this strange history of a crucified God was not credible to him, and a system which purported to rest entirely upon a foundation to him so wholly unbelievable, could not be foreseen by him to be that renovating agency which, after all abatements, it has in fact proved to be; the gentlest and most amiable of philosophers and rulers, under a solemn sense of duty, authorized the persecution of Christianity. To my mind this is one of the most tragical facts in all history. It is a bitter thought, how different a thing the Christianity of the world might have been, if the Christian faith had been adopted as the religion of the empire under the auspices of Marcus Aurelius instead of those of Constantine.[33] But it would be equally unjust to him and false to truth, to deny, that no one plea which can be urged for punishing anti-Christian teaching, was

wanting to Marcus Aurelius for punishing, as he did, the propagation of Christianity. No Christian more firmly believes that Atheism is false, and tends to the dissolution of society, than Marcus Aurelius believed the same things of Christianity; he who, of all men then living, might have been thought the most capable of appreciating it. Unless any one who approves of punishment for the promulgation of opinions, flatters himself that he is a wiser and better man than Marcus Aurelius—more deeply versed in the wisdom of his time, more elevated in his intellect above it—more earnest in his search for truth, or more single-minded in his devotion to it when found;—let him abstain from that assumption of the joint infallibility of himself and the multitude, which the great Antoninus[34] made with so unfortunate a result.

Aware of the impossibility of defending the use of punishment for restraining irreligious opinions, by any argument which will not justify Marcus Antoninus, the enemies of religious freedom, when hard pressed, occasionally accept this consequence, and say, with Dr. Johnson, that the persecutors of Christianity were in the right;[35] that persecution is an ordeal through which truth ought to pass, and always passes successfully, legal penalties being, in the end, powerless against truth, though sometimes beneficially effective against mischievous errors. This is a form of the argument for religious intolerance, sufficiently remarkable not to be passed without notice.

A theory which maintains that truth may justifiably be persecuted because persecution cannot possibly do it any harm, cannot be charged with being intentionally hostile to the reception of new truths; but we cannot commend the generosity of its dealing with the persons to whom mankind are indebted for them. To discover to[36] the world something which deeply concerns it, and of which it was previously ignorant; to prove to it that it had been mistaken on some vital point of temporal or spiritual interest, is as important a service as a human being can render to his fellow-

---

33   Constantine I, emperor of Rome from 306 to 337, adopted the Christian faith (because he thought it brought him victory in a battle) and suspended the persecution of Christians in 313.

34   Antoninus was Marcus Aurelius's family name.

35   This sentiment of writer and lexicographer Samuel Johnson can be found recorded in James Boswell's *Life of Johnson* (1791), Volume II, entry for May 7, 1773.

36   Expose, reveal to.

creatures, and in certain cases, as in those of the early Christians and of the Reformers,[37] those who think with Dr. Johnson believe it to have been the most precious gift which could be bestowed on mankind. That the authors of such splendid benefits should be requited by martyrdom; that their reward should be to be dealt with as the vilest of criminals, is not, upon this theory, a deplorable error and misfortune, for which humanity should mourn in sackcloth and ashes, but the normal and justifiable state of things. The propounder of a new truth, according to this doctrine, should stand, as stood, in the legislation of the Locrians,[38] the proposer of a new law, with a halter round his neck, to be instantly tightened if the public assembly did not, on hearing his reasons, then and there adopt his proposition.

People who defend this mode of treating benefactors, can not be supposed to set much value on the benefit; and I believe this view of the subject is mostly confined to the sort of persons who think that new truths may have been desirable once, but that we have had enough of them now.

But, indeed, the dictum that truth always triumphs over persecution, is one of those pleasant falsehoods which men repeat after one another till they pass into commonplaces, but which all experience refutes. History teems with instances of truth put down by persecution. If not suppressed forever, it may be thrown back for centuries. To speak only of religious opinions: the Reformation broke out at least twenty times before Luther,[39] and was put down. Arnold of Brescia was put down. Fra Dolcino was put down. Savonarola was put down. The Albigeois were put down. The Vaudois were put down. The Lollards were put down. The Hussites were put down.[40] Even after the era of Luther, wherever persecution was persisted in, it was successful. In Spain, Italy, Flanders, the Austrian empire, Protestantism was rooted out; and, most likely, would have been so in England, had Queen Mary lived, or Queen Elizabeth died. Persecution has always succeeded, save where the heretics were too strong a party to be effectually persecuted. No reasonable person can doubt that Christianity might have been extirpated in the Roman empire. It spread, and became predominant, because the persecutions were only occasional, lasting but a short time, and separated by long intervals of almost undisturbed propagandism. It is a piece of idle sentimentality that truth, merely as truth, has any inherent power denied to error, of prevailing against the dungeon and the stake. Men are not more zealous for truth than they often are for error, and a sufficient application of legal or even of social penalties will generally succeed in stopping the propagation of either. The real advantage which truth has, consists in this, that when an opinion is true, it may be extinguished once, twice, or many times, but in the course of ages there will generally be found persons to rediscover it, until some one of its reappearances falls on a time when from favourable circumstances it escapes persecution until it has made such head as to withstand all subsequent attempts to suppress it.

It will be said, that we do not now put to death the introducers of new opinions: we are not like our fathers who slew the prophets, we even build sep-

---

37 Protestant Reformers, such as Martin Luther and John Calvin, who challenged the doctrines and authority of the Catholic Church in the sixteenth century.

38 Locris was a minor state in ancient Greece, and among the first to adopt a written code of law (in about 660 BCE). Its regulations were severe: in addition to the principle mentioned in the text, it also enshrined the *lex talionis*, the law of retaliation (of taking an eye for an eye, a tooth for a tooth).

39 Martin Luther (1483–1546) was a German theologian who initiated the Protestant Reformation in 1517.

40 Arnold of Brescia was executed as a heretic in 1155; Fra Dolcino of Novara was tortured to death in 1307; Savonarola Girolamo was burned to death in 1498. The Albigeois, or Albigenses, tried to establish a church independent of Roman Catholicism and were exterminated by the Inquisition in the thirteenth century. The Vaudois, or Waldenses, also attempted to break free of Catholicism in the late twelfth century and, though greatly weakened by the oppression of the Inquisition, survived to join the Calvinist movement in the sixteenth century. The Lollards were followers of John Wycliffe (1320–1384) and the Hussites of John Huss (1369–1415). Both movements revolted against the authority of the Church, and both were vigorously suppressed.

ulchres to them. It is true we no longer put heretics to death; and the amount of penal infliction which modern feeling would probably tolerate, even against the most obnoxious opinions, is not sufficient to extirpate them. But let us not flatter ourselves that we are yet free from the stain even of legal persecution. Penalties for opinion, or at least for its expression, still exist by law; and their enforcement is not, even in these times, so unexampled as to make it at all incredible that they may some day be revived in full force. In the year 1857, at the summer assizes of the county of Cornwall, an unfortunate man,[41] said to be of unexceptionable conduct in all relations of life, was sentenced to twenty-one months imprisonment, for uttering, and writing on a gate, some offensive words concerning Christianity. Within a month of the same time, at the Old Bailey, two persons, on two separate occasions,[42] were rejected as jurymen, and one of them grossly insulted by the judge and one of the counsel, because they honestly declared that they had no theological belief; and a third, a foreigner,[43] for the same reason, was denied justice against a thief. This refusal of redress took place in virtue of the legal doctrine, that no person can be allowed to give evidence in a court of justice, who does not profess belief in a God (any god is sufficient) and in a future state; which is equivalent to declaring such persons to be outlaws, excluded from the protection of the tribunals; who may not only be robbed or assaulted with impunity, if no one but themselves, or persons of similar opinions, be present, but any one else may be robbed or assaulted with impunity, if the proof of the fact depends on their evidence. The assumption on which this is grounded, is that the oath is worthless, of a person who does not believe in a future state; a proposition which betokens much ignorance of history in those who assent to it (since it is historically true that a large proportion of infidels in all ages have been

persons of distinguished integrity and honour); and would be maintained by no one who had the smallest conception how many of the persons in greatest repute with the world, both for virtues and for attainments, are well known, at least to their intimates, to be unbelievers. The rule, besides, is suicidal, and cuts away its own foundation. Under pretence that atheists must be liars, it admits the testimony of all atheists who are willing to lie, and rejects only those who brave the obloquy[44] of publicly confessing a detested creed rather than affirm a falsehood. A rule thus self-convicted of absurdity so far as regards its professed purpose, can be kept in force only as a badge of hatred, a relic of persecution; a persecution, too, having the peculiarity that the qualification for undergoing it is the being clearly proved not to deserve it. The rule, and the theory it implies, are hardly less insulting to believers than to infidels. For if he who does not believe in a future state necessarily lies, it follows that they who do believe are only prevented from lying, if prevented they are, by the fear of hell. We will not do the authors and abettors of the rule the injury of supposing, that the conception which they have formed of Christian virtue is drawn from their own consciousness.

These, indeed, are but rags and remnants of persecution, and may be thought to be not so much an indication of the wish to persecute, as an example of that very frequent infirmity of English minds, which makes them take a preposterous pleasure in the assertion of a bad principle, when they are no longer bad enough to desire to carry it really into practice. But unhappily there is no security in the state of the public mind, that the suspension of worse forms of legal persecution, which has lasted for about the space of a generation, will continue. In this age the quiet surface of routine is as often ruffled by attempts to resuscitate past evils, as to introduce new benefits. What is boasted of at the present time as the revival of religion, is always, in narrow and uncultivated minds, at least as much the revival of bigotry; and where there is the strongest permanent leaven[45] of intolerance in

---

41   [Author's note] Thomas Pooley, Bodmin Assizes, July 31, 1857. In December following, he received a free pardon from the Crown.

42   [Author's note] George Jacob Holyoake, August 17, 1857; Edward Truelove, July, 1857.

43   [Author's note] Baron de Gleichen, Marlborough Street Police Court, August 4, 1857.

44   Disgrace, the state of being generally ill-spoken of or abused.

45   A pervasive element that works subtly to modify a whole.

the feelings of a people, which at all times abides in the middle classes of this country, it needs but little to provoke them into actively persecuting those whom they have never ceased to think proper objects of persecution.[46] For it is this—it is the opinions men entertain, and the feelings they cherish, respecting those who disown the beliefs they deem important, which makes this country not a place of mental freedom. For a long time past, the chief mischief of the legal penalties is that they strengthen the social stigma. It is that stigma which is really effective, and so effective is it, that the

---

46 [Author's note] Ample warning may be drawn from the large infusion of the passions of a persecutor, which mingled with the general display of the worst parts of our national character on the occasion of the Sepoy insurrection. The ravings of fanatics or charlatans from the pulpit may be unworthy of notice; but the heads of the Evangelical party have announced as their principle, for the government of Hindoos and Mahomedans, that no schools be supported by public money in which the Bible is not taught, and by necessary consequence that no public employment be given to any but real or pretended Christians. An Under-Secretary of State, in a speech delivered to his constituents on the 12th of November, 1857, is reported to have said: "Toleration of their faith" (the faith of a hundred millions of British subjects), "the superstition which they called religion, by the British Government, had had the effect of retarding the ascendency of the British name, and preventing the salutary growth of Christianity.... Toleration was the great corner-stone of the religious liberties of this country; but do not let them abuse that precious word toleration. As he understood it, it meant the complete liberty to all, freedom of worship, *among Christians, who worshipped upon the same foundation.* It meant toleration of all sects and denominations *of Christians* who believed in the one mediation." I desire to call attention to the fact, that a man who has been deemed fit to fill a high office in the government of this country, under a liberal Ministry, maintains the doctrine that all who do not believe in the divinity of Christ are beyond the pale of toleration. Who, after this imbecile display, can indulge the illusion that religious persecution has passed away, never to return?

profession of opinions which are under the ban of society is much less common in England, than is, in many other countries, the avowal of those which incur risk of judicial punishment. In respect to all persons but those whose pecuniary[47] circumstances make them independent of the good will of other people, opinion, on this subject, is as efficacious as law; men might as well be imprisoned, as excluded from the means of earning their bread. Those whose bread is already secured, and who desire no favours from men in power, or from bodies of men, or from the public, have nothing to fear from the open avowal of any opinions, but to be ill-thought of and ill-spoken of, and this it ought not to require a very heroic mould to enable them to bear. There is no room for any appeal *ad misericordiam*[48] in behalf of such persons. But though we do not now inflict so much evil on those who think differently from us, as it was formerly our custom to do, it may be that we do ourselves as much evil as ever by our treatment of them. Socrates was put to death, but the Socratic philosophy rose like the sun in heaven, and spread its illumination over the whole intellectual firmament. Christians were cast to the lions, but the Christian Church grew up a stately and spreading tree, overtopping the older and less vigorous growths, and stifling them by its shade. Our merely social intolerance, kills no one, roots out no opinions, but induces men to disguise them, or to abstain from any active effort for their diffusion. With us, heretical opinions do not perceptibly gain or even lose, ground in each decade or generation; they never blaze out far and wide, but continue to smoulder in the narrow circles of thinking and studious persons among whom they originate, without ever lighting up the general affairs of mankind with either a true or a deceptive light. And thus is kept up a state of things very satisfactory to some minds, because, without the unpleasant process of fining or imprisoning anybody, it maintains all prevailing opinions outwardly undisturbed, while it does not absolutely interdict[49] the exercise of reason by

---

47 Financial.

48 To pity.

49 Forbid.

dissentients afflicted with the malady of thought. A convenient plan for having peace in the intellectual world, and keeping all things going on therein very much as they do already. But the price paid for this sort of intellectual pacification, is the sacrifice of the entire moral courage of the human mind. A state of things in which a large portion of the most active and inquiring intellects find it advisable to keep the genuine principles and grounds of their convictions within their own breasts, and attempt, in what they address to the public, to fit as much as they can of their own conclusions to premises which they have internally renounced, cannot send forth the open, fearless characters, and logical, consistent intellects who once adorned the thinking world. The sort of men who can be looked for under it, are either mere conformers to commonplace, or time-servers for truth whose arguments on all great subjects are meant for their hearers, and are not those which have convinced themselves. Those who avoid this alternative, do so by narrowing their thoughts and interests to things which can be spoken of without venturing within the region of principles, that is, to small practical matters, which would come right of themselves, if but the minds of mankind were strengthened and enlarged, and which will never be made effectually right until then; while that which would strengthen and enlarge men's minds, free and daring speculation on the highest subjects, is abandoned.

Those in whose eyes this reticence on the part of heretics is no evil, should consider in the first place, that in consequence of it there is never any fair and thorough discussion of heretical opinions; and that such of them as could not stand such a discussion, though they may be prevented from spreading, do not disappear. But it is not the minds of heretics that are deteriorated most, by the ban placed on all inquiry which does not end in the orthodox conclusions. The greatest harm done is to those who are not heretics, and whose whole mental development is cramped, and their reason cowed, by the fear of heresy. Who can compute what the world loses in the multitude of promising intellects combined with timid characters, who dare not follow out any bold, vigorous, independent train of thought, lest it

should land them in something which would admit of being considered irreligious or immoral? Among them we may occasionally see some man of deep conscientiousness, and subtile[50] and refined understanding, who spends a life in sophisticating with an intellect which he cannot silence, and exhausts the resources of ingenuity in attempting to reconcile the promptings of his conscience and reason with orthodoxy, which yet he does not, perhaps, to the end succeed in doing. No one can be a great thinker who does not recognize, that as a thinker it is his first duty to follow his intellect to whatever conclusions it may lead. Truth gains more even by the errors of one who, with due study and preparation, thinks for himself, than by the true opinions of those who only hold them because they do not suffer themselves to think. Not that it is solely, or chiefly, to form great thinkers, that freedom of thinking is required. On the contrary, it is as much, and even more indispensable, to enable average human beings to attain the mental stature which they are capable of. There have been, and may again be, great individual thinkers, in a general atmosphere of mental slavery. But there never has been, nor ever will be, in that atmosphere, an intellectually active people. Where any people has made a temporary approach to such a character, it has been because the dread of heterodox speculation was for a time suspended. Where there is a tacit convention that principles are not to be disputed; where the discussion of the greatest questions which can occupy humanity is considered to be closed, we cannot hope to find that generally high scale of mental activity which has made some periods of history so remarkable. Never when controversy avoided the subjects which are large and important enough to kindle enthusiasm, was the mind of a people stirred up from its foundations, and the impulse given which raised even persons of the most ordinary intellect to something of the dignity of thinking beings. Of such we have had an example in the condition of Europe during the times immediately following the Reformation; another, though limited to the Continent and to a more cultivated class, in the speculative movement of the

---

50 Subtle.

latter half of the eighteenth century;[51] and a third, of still briefer duration, in the intellectual fermentation of Germany during the Goethian and Fichtean period.[52] These periods differed widely in the particular opinions which they developed; but were alike in this, that during all three the yoke of authority was broken. In each, an old mental despotism had been thrown off, and no new one had yet taken its place. The impulse given at these three periods has made Europe what it now is. Every single improvement which has taken place either in the human mind or in institutions, may be traced distinctly to one or other of them. Appearances have for some time indicated that all three impulses are well-nigh spent; and we can expect no fresh start, until we again assert our mental freedom.

Let us now pass to the second division of the argument, and dismissing the supposition that any of the received opinions may be false, let us assume them to be true, and examine into the worth of the manner in which they are likely to be held, when their truth is not freely and openly canvassed. However unwillingly a person who has a strong opinion may admit the possibility that his opinion may be false, he ought to be moved by the consideration that however true it may be, if it is not fully, frequently, and fearlessly discussed, it will be held as a dead dogma, not a living truth.

There is a class of persons (happily not quite so numerous as formerly) who think it enough if a person assents undoubtingly to what they think true, though he has no knowledge whatever of the grounds of the opinion, and could not make a tenable defence of it against the most superficial objections. Such persons, if they can once get their creed taught from authority, naturally think that no good, and some harm, comes of its being allowed to

be questioned. Where their influence prevails, they make it nearly impossible for the received opinion to be rejected wisely and considerately, though it may still be rejected rashly and ignorantly; for to shut out discussion entirely is seldom possible, and when it once gets in, beliefs not grounded on conviction are apt to give way before the slightest semblance of an argument. Waiving, however, this possibility—assuming that the true opinion abides in the mind, but abides as a prejudice, a belief independent of, and proof against, argument—this is not the way in which truth ought to be held by a rational being. This is not knowing the truth. Truth, thus held, is but one superstition the more, accidentally clinging to the words which enunciate a truth.

If the intellect and judgment of mankind ought to be cultivated, a thing which Protestants at least do not deny, on what can these faculties be more appropriately exercised by any one, than on the things which concern him so much that it is considered necessary for him to hold opinions on them? If the cultivation of the understanding consists in one thing more than in another, it is surely in learning the grounds of one's own opinions. Whatever people believe, on subjects on which it is of the first importance to believe rightly, they ought to be able to defend against at least the common objections. But, some one may say, "Let them be *taught* the grounds of their opinions. It does not follow that opinions must be merely parroted because they are never heard controverted. Persons who learn geometry do not simply commit the theorems to memory, but understand and learn likewise the demonstrations; and it would be absurd to say that they remain ignorant of the grounds of geometrical truths, because they never hear any one deny, and attempt to disprove them." Undoubtedly: and such teaching suffices on a subject like mathematics, where there is nothing at all to be said on the wrong side of the question. The peculiarity of the evidence of mathematical truths is, that all the argument is on one side. There are no objections, and no answers to objections. But on every subject on which difference of opinion is possible, the truth depends on a balance to be struck between two sets of conflicting reasons. Even in natural philosophy, there is always some other explanation possible of the same facts; some geocentric theory

---

51   The Enlightenment, a philosophical and cultural movement that emphasized individualism and the use of reason to question previously accepted doctrines.

52   Johann Wolfgang von Goethe (1749–1832) was a writer, poet, and philosopher-scientist. Johann Gottlieb Fichte (1762–1814) was an influential idealist philosopher. Both figures were important in sparking the Romantic movement of the late eighteenth century.

instead of heliocentric,[53] some phlogiston[54] instead of oxygen; and it has to be shown why that other theory cannot be the true one: and until this is shown and until we know how it is shown, we do not understand the grounds of our opinion. But when we turn to subjects infinitely more complicated, to morals, religion, politics, social relations, and the business of life, three-fourths of the arguments for every disputed opinion consist in dispelling the appearances which favour some opinion different from it. The greatest orator, save one, of antiquity,[55] has left it on record that he always studied his adversary's case with as great, if not with still greater, intensity than even his own. What Cicero practised as the means of forensic[56] success, requires to be imitated by all who study any subject in order to arrive at the truth. He who knows only his own side of the case, knows little of that. His reasons may be good, and no one may have been able to refute them. But if he is equally unable to refute the reasons on the opposite side; if he does not so much as know what they are, he has no ground for preferring either opinion. The rational position for him would be suspension of judgment, and unless he contents himself with that, he is either led by authority, or adopts, like the generality of the world, the side to which he feels most inclination. Nor is it enough that he should hear the arguments of adversaries from his own teachers, presented as they state them, and accompanied by what they offer as refutations. This is not the way to do justice to the arguments, or bring them into real contact with his own mind. He must be able to hear them from persons who actually believe them; who defend them in earnest, and do their very utmost for them. He must know them in their most plausible and persuasive form; he must feel the whole force of the difficulty which the true view of the subject has to encounter and dispose of, else he will never really possess himself of the portion of truth which meets and removes that difficulty. Ninety-nine in a hundred of what are called educated men are in this condition, even of those who can argue fluently for their opinions. Their conclusion may be true, but it might be false for anything they know: they have never thrown themselves into the mental position of those who think differently from them, and considered what such persons may have to say; and consequently they do not, in any proper sense of the word, know the doctrine which they themselves profess. They do not know those parts of it which explain and justify the remainder; the considerations which show that a fact which seemingly conflicts with another is reconcilable with it, or that, of two apparently strong reasons, one and not the other ought to be preferred. All that part of the truth which turns the scale, and decides the judgment of a completely informed mind, they are strangers to; nor is it ever really known, but to those who have attended equally and impartially to both sides, and endeavoured to see the reasons of both in the strongest light. So essential is this discipline to a real understanding of moral and human subjects, that if opponents of all important truths do not exist, it is indispensable to imagine them and supply them with the strongest arguments which the most skilful devil's advocate can conjure up.

To abate the force of these considerations, an enemy of free discussion may be supposed to say, that there is no necessity for mankind in general to know and understand all that can be said against or for their opinions by philosophers and theologians. That it is not needful for common men to be able to expose all the misstatements or fallacies of an ingenious opponent. That it is enough if there is always somebody capable of answering them, so that nothing likely to mislead uninstructed persons remains unrefuted. That simple minds, having been taught the obvious grounds of the truths inculcated on them, may trust to authority for the rest, and being aware that they have neither knowledge nor talent to resolve every difficulty which can be raised, may repose in the assurance that all

---

53 On the geocentric theory, the sun, planets, and other heavenly bodies circle the Earth. According to heliocentric accounts, the planets orbit the Sun.

54 Phlogiston is a mythical substance, once thought to be a volatile constituent of all combustible substances, released as flame in combustion. It is now known that combustion is, in general, a chemical interaction with oxygen.

55 The greatest orator of antiquity was said to be Demosthenes, and the second greatest was Cicero.

56 Relating to debate or argument, especially in a court of law or public discussion.

those which have been raised have been or can be answered, by those who are specially trained to the task.

Conceding to this view of the subject the utmost that can be claimed for it by those most easily satisfied with the amount of understanding of truth which ought to accompany the belief of it; even so, the argument for free discussion is no way weakened. For even this doctrine acknowledges that mankind ought to have a rational assurance that all objections have been satisfactorily answered; and how are they to be answered if that which requires to be answered is not spoken? or how can the answer be known to be satisfactory, if the objectors have no opportunity of showing that it is unsatisfactory? If not the public, at least the philosophers and theologians who are to resolve the difficulties, must make themselves familiar with those difficulties in their most puzzling form; and this cannot be accomplished unless they are freely stated, and placed in the most advantageous light which they admit of. The Catholic Church has its own way of dealing with this embarrassing problem. It makes a broad separation between those who can be permitted to receive its doctrines on conviction, and those who must accept them on trust. Neither, indeed, are allowed any choice as to what they will accept; but the clergy, such at least as can be fully confided in, may admissibly and meritoriously make themselves acquainted with the arguments of opponents, in order to answer them, and may, therefore, read heretical books; the laity, not unless by special permission, hard to be obtained. This discipline recognizes a knowledge of the enemy's case as beneficial to the teachers, but finds means, consistent with this, of denying it to the rest of the world: thus giving to the elite more mental culture, though not more mental freedom, than it allows to the mass. By this device it succeeds in obtaining the kind of mental superiority which its purposes require; for though culture without freedom never made a large and liberal mind, it can make a clever *nisi prius*[57] advocate of a cause. But in

countries professing Protestantism, this resource is denied; since Protestants hold, at least in theory, that the responsibility for the choice of a religion must be borne by each for himself, and cannot be thrown off upon teachers. Besides, in the present state of the world, it is practically impossible that writings which are read by the instructed can be kept from the uninstructed. If the teachers of mankind are to be cognizant of all that they ought to know, everything must be free to be written and published without restraint.

If, however, the mischievous operation of the absence of free discussion, when the received opinions are true, were confined to leaving men ignorant of the grounds of those opinions, it might be thought that this, if an intellectual, is no moral evil, and does not affect the worth of the opinions, regarded in their influence on the character. The fact, however, is, that not only the grounds of the opinion are forgotten in the absence of discussion, but too often the meaning of the opinion itself. The words which convey it, cease to suggest ideas, or suggest only a small portion of those they were originally employed to communicate. Instead of a vivid conception and a living belief, there remain only a few phrases retained by rote; or, if any part, the shell and husk only of the meaning is retained, the finer essence being lost. The great chapter in human history which this fact occupies and fills, cannot be too earnestly studied and meditated on.

It is illustrated in the experience of almost all ethical doctrines and religious creeds. They are all full of meaning and vitality to those who originate them, and to the direct disciples of the originators. Their meaning continues to be felt in undiminished strength, and is perhaps brought out into even fuller consciousness, so long as the struggle lasts to give the doctrine or creed an ascendancy over other creeds. At last it either prevails, and becomes the general opinion, or its progress stops; it keeps possession of the ground it has gained, but ceases to spread further. When either of these results has become apparent, controversy on the subject flags, and gradually dies away. The doctrine has taken its place, if not as a received opinion, as one of the admitted sects or divisions of opinion: those

57   Latin for "unless previously," most commonly a legal term for a type of court. However, by a "*nisi prius* advocate" Mill probably means someone who can make a case for something only by refuting all potential objections to it—someone who argues on the grounds that a position is sound unless shown to be unsound.

who hold it have generally inherited, not adopted it; and conversion from one of these doctrines to another, being now an exceptional fact, occupies little place in the thoughts of their professors. Instead of being, as at first, constantly on the alert either to defend themselves against the world, or to bring the world over to them, they have subsided into acquiescence, and neither listen, when they can help it, to arguments against their creed, nor trouble dissentients (if there be such) with arguments in its favour. From this time may usually be dated the decline in the living power of the doctrine. We often hear the teachers of all creeds lamenting the difficulty of keeping up in the minds of believers a lively apprehension of the truth which they nominally recognize, so that it may penetrate the feelings, and acquire a real mastery over the conduct. No such difficulty is complained of while the creed is still fighting for its existence: even the weaker combatants then know and feel what they are fighting for, and the difference between it and other doctrines; and in that period of every creed's existence, not a few persons may be found, who have realized its fundamental principles in all the forms of thought, have weighed and considered them in all their important bearings, and have experienced the full effect on the character, which belief in that creed ought to produce in a mind thoroughly imbued with it. But when it has come to be an hereditary creed, and to be received passively, not actively—when the mind is no longer compelled, in the same degree as at first, to exercise its vital powers on the questions which its belief presents to it, there is a progressive tendency to forget all of the belief except the formularies, or to give it a dull and torpid assent, as if accepting it on trust dispensed with the necessity of realizing it in consciousness, or testing it by personal experience; until it almost ceases to connect itself at all with the inner life of the human being. Then are seen the cases, so frequent in this age of the world as almost to form the majority, in which the creed remains as it were outside the mind, encrusting and petrifying it against all other influences addressed to the higher parts of our nature; manifesting its power by not suffering any fresh and living conviction to get in, but itself doing nothing for the mind or heart, except standing sentinel over them to keep them vacant.

To what an extent doctrines intrinsically fitted to make the deepest impression upon the mind may remain in it as dead beliefs, without being ever realized in the imagination, the feelings, or the understanding, is exemplified by the manner in which the majority of believers hold the doctrines of Christianity. By Christianity I here mean what is accounted such by all churches and sects—the maxims and precepts contained in the New Testament. These are considered sacred, and accepted as laws, by all professing Christians. Yet it is scarcely too much to say that not one Christian in a thousand guides or tests his individual conduct by reference to those laws. The standard to which he does refer it, is the custom of his nation, his class, or his religious profession. He has thus, on the one hand, a collection of ethical maxims, which he believes to have been vouchsafed to him by infallible wisdom as rules for his government; and on the other, a set of every-day judgments and practices, which go a certain length with some of those maxims, not so great a length with others, stand in direct opposition to some, and are, on the whole, a compromise between the Christian creed and the interests and suggestions of worldly life. To the first of these standards he gives his homage; to the other his real allegiance. All Christians believe that the blessed are the poor and humble, and those who are ill-used by the world; that it is easier for a camel to pass through the eye of a needle than for a rich man to enter the kingdom of heaven; that they should judge not, lest they be judged; that they should swear not at all; that they should love their neighbour as themselves; that if one take their cloak, they should give him their coat also; that they should take no thought for the morrow; that if they would be perfect, they should sell all that they have and give it to the poor.[58] They are not insincere when they say that they believe these things. They do believe them, as people believe what they have always heard lauded and never discussed. But in the sense of that living belief which regulates conduct, they believe these doctrines just up to the point to which it is usual to act upon them. The doctrines in their integrity are serviceable to pelt adversaries with; and it is understood

---

58   All these principles appear in the Gospel of Matthew, except the first, which appears in Luke.

that they are to be put forward (when possible) as the reasons for whatever people do that they think laudable. But any one who reminded them that the maxims require an infinity of things which they never even think of doing would gain nothing but to be classed among those very unpopular characters who affect to be better than other people. The doctrines have no hold on ordinary believers—are not a power in their minds. They have an habitual respect for the sound of them, but no feeling which spreads from the words to the things signified, and forces the mind to take them in, and make them conform to the formula. Whenever conduct is concerned, they look round for Mr. A and B to direct them how far to go in obeying Christ.

Now we may be well assured that the case was not thus, but far otherwise, with the early Christians. Had it been thus, Christianity never would have expanded from an obscure sect of the despised Hebrews into the religion of the Roman empire. When their enemies said, "See how these Christians love one another"[59] (a remark not likely to be made by anybody now), they assuredly had a much livelier feeling of the meaning of their creed than they have ever had since. And to this cause, probably, it is chiefly owing that Christianity now makes so little progress in extending its domain, and after eighteen centuries, is still nearly confined to Europeans and the descendants of Europeans. Even with the strictly religious, who are much in earnest about their doctrines, and attach a greater amount of meaning to many of them than people in general, it commonly happens that the part which is thus comparatively active in their minds is that which was made by Calvin, or Knox,[60] or some such person much nearer in character to themselves. The sayings of Christ coexist passively in their minds, producing hardly any effect beyond what is caused by mere listening to words so amiable and bland. There are

---

59   Said by Tertullian, a Roman lawyer who converted to Christianity in about 195 and was one of the first Christian theologians to write in Latin. The quote comes from his *Apologeticus* (written in 197).

60   John Calvin (1509–1564), a French-born Swiss Protestant reformer; John Knox (1505–1572), a Scottish religious reformer. Both were important in the foundation of Presbyterianism.

many reasons, doubtless, why doctrines which are the badge of a sect retain more of their vitality than those common to all recognized sects, and why more pains are taken by teachers to keep their meaning alive; but one reason certainly is, that the peculiar doctrines are more questioned, and have to be oftener defended against open gainsayers. Both teachers and learners go to sleep at their post, as soon as there is no enemy in the field.

The same thing holds true, generally speaking, of all traditional doctrines—those of prudence and knowledge of life, as well as of morals or religion. All languages and literatures are full of general observations on life, both as to what it is, and how to conduct oneself in it; observations which everybody knows, which everybody repeats, or hears with acquiescence, which are received as truisms, yet of which most people first truly learn the meaning, when experience, generally of a painful kind, has made it a reality to them. How often, when smarting under some unforeseen misfortune or disappointment, does a person call to mind some proverb or common saying familiar to him all his life, the meaning of which, if he had ever before felt it as he does now, would have saved him from the calamity. There are indeed reasons for this, other than the absence of discussion: there are many truths of which the full meaning *cannot* be realized, until personal experience has brought it home. But much more of the meaning even of these would have been understood, and what was understood would have been far more deeply impressed on the mind, if the man had been accustomed to hear it argued *pro* and *con* by people who did understand it. The fatal tendency of mankind to leave off thinking about a thing when it is no longer doubtful, is the cause of half their errors. A contemporary author has well spoken of "the deep slumber of a decided opinion."[61]

But what! (it may be asked) Is the absence of unanimity an indispensable condition of true knowledge? Is it necessary that some part of mankind should persist in error, to enable any to realize the truth? Does a belief cease to be real and vital as soon as it is generally received—and is a proposition never thoroughly

---

61   Sir Arthur Helps, in *Thoughts in the Cloister and the Crowd* (1835).

understood and felt unless some doubt of it remains? As soon as mankind have unanimously accepted a truth, does the truth perish within them? The highest aim and best result of improved intelligence, it has hitherto been thought, is to unite mankind more and more in the acknowledgment of all important truths: and does the intelligence only last as long as it has not achieved its object? Do the fruits of conquest perish by the very completeness of the victory?

I affirm no such thing. As mankind improve, the number of doctrines which are no longer disputed or doubted will be constantly on the increase: and the well-being of mankind may almost be measured by the number and gravity of the truths which have reached the point of being uncontested. The cessation, on one question after another, of serious controversy, is one of the necessary incidents of the consolidation of opinion; a consolidation as salutary in the case of true opinions, as it is dangerous and noxious when the opinions are erroneous. But though this gradual narrowing of the bounds of diversity of opinion is necessary in both senses of the term, being at once inevitable and indispensable, we are not therefore obliged to conclude that all its consequences must be beneficial. The loss of so important an aid to the intelligent and living apprehension of a truth, as is afforded by the necessity of explaining it to, or defending it against, opponents, though not sufficient to outweigh, is no trifling drawback from, the benefit of its universal recognition. Where this advantage can no longer be had, I confess I should like to see the teachers of mankind endeavouring to provide a substitute for it; some contrivance for making the difficulties of the question as present to the learner's consciousness, as if they were pressed upon him by a dissentient champion, eager for his conversion.

But instead of seeking contrivances for this purpose, they have lost those they formerly had. The Socratic dialectics, so magnificently exemplified in the dialogues of Plato, were a contrivance of this description. They were essentially a negative discussion of the great questions of philosophy and life, directed with consummate skill to the purpose of convincing any one who had merely adopted the commonplaces of received opinion, that he did not understand the subject—that he as yet attached no definite meaning to the doctrines he professed; in order that, becoming aware of his ignorance, he might be put in the way to attain a stable belief, resting on a clear apprehension both of the meaning of doctrines and of their evidence. The school disputations of the Middle Ages had a somewhat similar object. They were intended to make sure that the pupil understood his own opinion, and (by necessary correlation) the opinion opposed to it, and could enforce the grounds of the one and confute those of the other. These last-mentioned contests had indeed the incurable defect, that the premises appealed to were taken from authority, not from reason; and, as a discipline to the mind, they were in every respect inferior to the powerful dialectics which formed the intellects of the "Socratici viri":[62] but the modern mind owes far more to both than it is generally willing to admit, and the present modes of education contain nothing which in the smallest degree supplies the place either of the one or of the other. A person who derives all his instruction from teachers or books, even if he escape the besetting temptation of contenting himself with cram,[63] is under no compulsion to hear both sides; accordingly it is far from a frequent accomplishment, even among thinkers, to know both sides; and the weakest part of what everybody says in defence of his opinion, is what he intends as a reply to antagonists. It is the fashion of the present time to disparage negative logic—that which points out weaknesses in theory or errors in practice, without establishing positive truths. Such negative criticism would indeed be poor enough as an ultimate result; but as a means to attaining any positive knowledge or conviction worthy the name, it cannot be valued too highly; and until people are again systematically trained to it, there will be few great thinkers, and a low general average of intellect, in any but the mathematical and physical departments of speculation. On any other subject no one's opinions deserve the name of knowledge, except so far as he has either had forced upon him by others, or gone through of himself, the same mental process which would have been required of him in carrying on an active controversy with op-

---

62 The disciples of Socrates.

63 With hasty memorization, rather than true study and understanding.

ponents. That, therefore, which when absent, it is so indispensable, but so difficult, to create, how worse than absurd is it to forego, when spontaneously offering itself! If there are any persons who contest a received opinion, or who will do so if law or opinion will let them, let us thank them for it, open our minds to listen to them, and rejoice that there is some one to do for us what we otherwise ought, if we have any regard for either the certainty or the vitality of our convictions, to do with much greater labour for ourselves.

It still remains to speak of one of the principal causes which make diversity of opinion advantageous, and will continue to do so until mankind shall have entered a stage of intellectual advancement which at present seems at an incalculable distance. We have hitherto considered only two possibilities: that the received opinion may be false, and some other opinion, consequently, true; or that, the received opinion being true, a conflict with the opposite error is essential to a clear apprehension and deep feeling of its truth. But there is a commoner case than either of these; when the conflicting doctrines, instead of being one true and the other false, share the truth between them; and the nonconforming opinion is needed to supply the remainder of the truth, of which the received doctrine embodies only a part. Popular opinions, on subjects not palpable to sense, are often true, but seldom or never the whole truth. They are a part of the truth; sometimes a greater, sometimes a smaller part, but exaggerated, distorted, and disjoined from the truths by which they ought to be accompanied and limited. Heretical opinions, on the other hand, are generally some of these suppressed and neglected truths, bursting the bonds which kept them down, and either seeking reconciliation with the truth contained in the common opinion, or fronting it as enemies, and setting themselves up, with similar exclusiveness, as the whole truth. The latter case is hitherto the most frequent, as, in the human mind, one-sidedness has always been the rule, and many-sidedness the exception. Hence, even in revolutions of opinion, one part of the truth usually sets while another rises. Even progress, which ought to superadd, for the most part only substitutes one partial and incomplete truth for another; improvement consisting chiefly in this, that the new fragment of truth is more wanted, more adapted to the needs of the time, than that which it displaces. Such being the partial character of prevailing opinions, even when resting on a true foundation; every opinion which embodies somewhat of the portion of truth which the common opinion omits, ought to be considered precious, with whatever amount of error and confusion that truth may be blended. No sober judge of human affairs will feel bound to be indignant because those who force on our notice truths which we should otherwise have overlooked, overlook some of those which we see. Rather, he will think that so long as popular truth is one-sided, it is more desirable than otherwise that unpopular truth should have one-sided asserters too; such being usually the most energetic, and the most likely to compel reluctant attention to the fragment of wisdom which they proclaim as if it were the whole.

Thus, in the eighteenth century, when nearly all the instructed, and all those of the uninstructed who were led by them, were lost in admiration of what is called civilization, and of the marvels of modern science, literature, and philosophy, and while greatly overrating the amount of unlikeness between the men of modern and those of ancient times, indulged the belief that the whole of the difference was in their own favour; with what a salutary shock did the paradoxes of Rousseau[64] explode like bombshells in the midst, dislocating the compact mass of one-sided opinion, and forcing its elements to recombine in a better form and with additional ingredients. Not that the current opinions were on the whole farther from the truth than Rousseau's were; on the contrary, they were nearer to it; they contained more of positive truth, and very much less of error. Nevertheless there lay in Rousseau's doctrine, and has floated down the stream of opinion along with it, a considerable amount of exactly those

---

64 Jean-Jacques Rousseau (1712–1778), a very influential Swiss-born philosopher, argued that the troubles of the human condition derive from the distorting effects of human society and civilization, and that human beings in their natural state are free, independent, innocent, happy, and intuitively wise. His most famous work is *The Social Contract* (1762), which helped lay the ideological groundwork for the French Revolution.

truths which the popular opinion wanted;[65] and these are the deposit which was left behind when the flood subsided. The superior worth of simplicity of life, the enervating and demoralizing effect of the trammels and hypocrisies of artificial society, are ideas which have never been entirely absent from cultivated minds since Rousseau wrote; and they will in time produce their due effect, though at present needing to be asserted as much as ever, and to be asserted by deeds, for words, on this subject, have nearly exhausted their power.

In politics, again, it is almost a commonplace, that a party of order or stability, and a party of progress or reform, are both necessary elements of a healthy state of political life; until the one or the other shall have so enlarged its mental grasp as to be a party equally of order and of progress, knowing and distinguishing what is fit to be preserved from what ought to be swept away. Each of these modes of thinking derives its utility from the deficiencies of the other; but it is in a great measure the opposition of the other that keeps each within the limits of reason and sanity. Unless opinions favourable to democracy and to aristocracy, to property and to equality, to co-operation and to competition, to luxury and to abstinence, to sociality and individuality, to liberty and discipline, and all the other standing antagonisms of practical life, are expressed with equal freedom, and enforced and defended with equal talent and energy, there is no chance of both elements obtaining their due; one scale is sure to go up, and the other down. Truth, in the great practical concerns of life, is so much a question of the reconciling and combining of opposites, that very few have minds sufficiently capacious and impartial to make the adjustment with an approach to correctness, and it has to be made by the rough process of a struggle between combatants fighting under hostile banners. On any of the great open questions just enumerated, if either of the two opinions has a better claim than the other, not merely to be tolerated, but to be encouraged and countenanced, it is the one which happens at the particular time and place to be in a minority. That is the opinion which, for the time being, represents the neglected interests, the side of

human well-being which is in danger of obtaining less than its share. I am aware that there is not, in this country, any intolerance of differences of opinion on most of these topics. They are adduced to show, by admitted and multiplied examples, the universality of the fact, that only through diversity of opinion is there, in the existing state of human intellect, a chance of fair play to all sides of the truth. When there are persons to be found, who form an exception to the apparent unanimity of the world on any subject, even if the world is in the right, it is always probable that dissentients have something worth hearing to say for themselves, and that truth would lose something by their silence.

It may be objected, "But *some* received principles, especially on the highest and most vital subjects, are more than half-truths. The Christian morality, for instance, is the whole truth on that subject and if any one teaches a morality which varies from it, he is wholly in error." As this is of all cases the most important in practice, none can be fitter to test the general maxim. But before pronouncing what Christian morality is or is not, it would be desirable to decide what is meant by Christian morality. If it means the morality of the New Testament, I wonder that any one who derives his knowledge of this from the book itself, can suppose that it was announced, or intended, as a complete doctrine of morals. The Gospel always refers to a pre-existing morality, and confines its precepts to the particulars in which that morality was to be corrected, or superseded by a wider and higher; expressing itself, moreover, in terms most general, often impossible to be interpreted literally, and possessing rather the impressiveness of poetry or eloquence than the precision of legislation. To extract from it a body of ethical doctrine, has never been possible without eking it out from the Old Testament, that is, from a system elaborate indeed, but in many respects barbarous, and intended only for a barbarous people. St. Paul, a declared enemy to this Judaical mode of interpreting the doctrine and filling up the scheme of his Master, equally assumes a pre-existing morality, namely, that of the Greeks and Romans; and his advice to Christians is in a great measure a system of accommodation to that; even to the extent of giving an apparent sanction to slavery. What is called Christian,

---

65   Needed, lacked.

but should rather be termed theological, morality, was not the work of Christ or the Apostles, but is of much later origin, having been gradually built up by the Catholic Church of the first five centuries, and though not implicitly adopted by moderns and Protestants, has been much less modified by them than might have been expected. For the most part, indeed, they have contented themselves with cutting off the additions which had been made to it in the Middle Ages, each sect supplying the place by fresh additions, adapted to its own character and tendencies. That mankind owe a great debt to this morality, and to its early teachers, I should be the last person to deny; but I do not scruple to say of it, that it is, in many important points, incomplete and one-sided, and that unless ideas and feelings, not sanctioned by it, had contributed to the formation of European life and character, human affairs would have been in a worse condition than they now are. Christian morality (so called) has all the characters of a reaction; it is, in great part, a protest against Paganism. Its ideal is negative rather than positive; passive rather than active; Innocence rather than Nobleness; Abstinence from Evil, rather than energetic Pursuit of Good: in its precepts (as has been well said) "thou shalt not" predominates unduly over "thou shalt." In its horror of sensuality, it made an idol of asceticism, which has been gradually compromised away into one of legality. It holds out the hope of heaven and the threat of hell, as the appointed and appropriate motives to a virtuous life: in this falling far below the best of the ancients, and doing what lies in it to give to human morality an essentially selfish character, by disconnecting each man's feelings of duty from the interests of his fellow-creatures, except so far as a self-interested inducement is offered to him for consulting them. It is essentially a doctrine of passive obedience; it inculcates submission to all authorities found established; who indeed are not to be actively obeyed when they command what religion forbids, but who are not to be resisted, far less rebelled against, for any amount of wrong to ourselves. And while, in the morality of the best Pagan nations, duty to the State holds even a disproportionate place, infringing on the just liberty of the individual; in purely Christian ethics that grand department of duty is scarcely noticed or acknowledged. It is in the Koran, not the New Testament, that we read the maxim—"A ruler who appoints any man to an office, when there is in his dominions another man better qualified for it, sins against God and against the State." What little recognition the idea of obligation to the public obtains in modern morality, is derived from Greek and Roman sources, not from Christian; as, even in the morality of private life, whatever exists of magnanimity, high-mindedness, personal dignity, even the sense of honour, is derived from the purely human, not the religious part of our education, and never could have grown out of a standard of ethics in which the only worth, professedly recognized, is that of obedience.

I am as far as any one from pretending that these defects are necessarily inherent in the Christian ethics, in every manner in which it can be conceived, or that the many requisites of a complete moral doctrine which it does not contain, do not admit of being reconciled with it. Far less would I insinuate this of the doctrines and precepts of Christ himself. I believe that the sayings of Christ are all, that I can see any evidence of their having been intended to be; that they are irreconcilable with nothing which a comprehensive morality requires; that everything which is excellent in ethics may be brought within them, with no greater violence to their language than has been done to it by all who have attempted to deduce from them any practical system of conduct whatever. But it is quite consistent with this, to believe that they contain and were meant to contain, only a part of the truth; that many essential elements of the highest morality are among the things which are not provided for, nor intended to be provided for, in the recorded deliverances of the Founder of Christianity, and which have been entirely thrown aside in the system of ethics erected on the basis of those deliverances by the Christian Church. And this being so, I think it a great error to persist in attempting to find in the Christian doctrine that complete rule for our guidance, which its author intended it to sanction and enforce, but only partially to provide. I believe, too, that this narrow theory is becoming a grave practical evil, detracting greatly from the value of the moral training and instruction, which so many well-meaning persons are now at length exerting themselves to promote. I much fear that by attempting to form the mind and feelings on an exclusively religious type, and discarding those secular standards (as for want of a better name they may be called) which heretofore coexisted with and supplemented the Christian ethics, receiving some of its spirit, and infusing into it some of theirs, there will result, and is even now resulting, a low, abject, servile type of character, which, submit itself as it may to what it deems the Supreme Will, is incapable of rising to or sympathizing in the conception of Supreme Goodness. I believe that other ethics than any one which can be evolved from exclusively Christian sources, must exist side by side with Christian ethics to produce the moral regeneration of mankind; and that the Christian system is no exception to the rule that in an imperfect state of the human mind, the interests of truth require a diversity of opinions. It is not necessary that in ceasing to ignore the moral truths not contained in Christianity, men should ignore any of those which it does contain. Such prejudice, or oversight, when it occurs, is altogether an evil; but it is one from which we cannot hope to be always exempt, and must be regarded as the price paid for an inestimable good. The exclusive pretension made by a part of the truth to be the whole, must and ought to be protested against, and if a reactionary impulse should make the protestors unjust in their turn, this one-sidedness, like the other, may be lamented, but must be tolerated. If Christians would teach infidels to be just to Christianity, they should themselves be just to infidelity. It can do truth no service to blink the fact, known to all who have the most ordinary acquaintance with literary history, that a large portion of the noblest and most valuable moral teaching has been the work, not only of men who did not know, but of men who knew and rejected, the Christian faith.

I do not pretend that the most unlimited use of the freedom of enunciating all possible opinions would put an end to the evils of religious or philosophical sectarianism. Every truth which men of narrow capacity are in earnest about, is sure to be asserted, inculcated, and in many ways even acted on, as if no other truth existed in the world, or at all events none that could limit or qualify the first. I acknowledge that the tendency of all opinions to become sectarian is not cured by the freest discussion, but is often heightened and exacerbated thereby; the truth which ought to have been, but was not, seen, being rejected all the more violently because proclaimed by persons regarded as opponents. But it is not on the impassioned partisan, it is on the calmer and more disinterested bystander, that this collision of opinions works its salutary effect. Not the violent conflict between parts of the truth, but the quiet suppression of half of it, is the formidable evil: there is always hope when people are forced to listen to both sides; it is when they attend only to one that errors harden into prejudices, and truth itself ceases to have the effect of truth, by being exaggerated into falsehood. And since there are few mental attributes more rare than that judicial faculty which can sit in intelligent judgment between two sides of a question, of which only one is represented by an advocate before it, truth has no chance but in proportion as every side of it, every opinion which embodies any fraction of the truth, not only finds advocates, but is so advocated as to be listened to.

We have now recognized the necessity to the mental well-being of mankind (on which all their other well-being depends) of freedom of opinion, and freedom of the expression of opinion, on four distinct grounds; which we will now briefly recapitulate.

First, if any opinion is compelled to silence, that opinion may, for aught we can certainly know, be true. To deny this is to assume our own infallibility.

Secondly, though the silenced opinion be an error, it may, and very commonly does, contain a portion of truth; and since the general or prevailing opinion on any object is rarely or never the whole truth, it is only by the collision of adverse opinions that the remainder of the truth has any chance of being supplied.

Thirdly, even if the received opinion be not only true, but the whole truth; unless it is suffered to be, and actually is, vigorously and earnestly contested, it will, by most of those who receive it, be held in the manner of a prejudice, with little comprehension or feeling of its rational grounds. And not only this, but, fourthly, the meaning of the doctrine itself will be in danger of being lost, or enfeebled, and deprived of its vital effect on the character and conduct: the dogma becoming a mere formal profession, inefficacious for good, but cumbering the ground, and preventing the growth of any real and heartfelt conviction, from reason or personal experience.

Before quitting the subject of freedom of opinion, it is fit to take notice of those who say, that the free expression of all opinions should be permitted, on condition that the manner be temperate, and do not pass the bounds of fair discussion. Much might be said on the impossibility of fixing where these supposed bounds are to be placed; for if the test be offence to those whose opinion is attacked, I think experience testifies that this offence is given whenever the attack is telling and powerful, and that every opponent who pushes them hard, and whom they find it difficult to answer, appears to them, if he shows any strong feeling on the subject, an intemperate opponent. But this, though an important consideration in a practical point of view, merges in a more fundamental objection. Undoubtedly the manner of asserting an opinion, even though it be a true one, may be very objectionable, and may justly incur severe censure. But the principal offences of the kind are such as it is mostly impossible, unless by accidental self-betrayal, to bring home to conviction. The gravest of them is, to argue sophistically,[66] to suppress facts or arguments, to misstate the elements of the case, or misrepresent the opposite opinion. But all this, even to the most aggravated degree, is so continually done in perfect good faith, by persons who are not considered, and in many other respects may not deserve to be considered, ignorant or incompetent, that it is rarely possible on adequate grounds conscientiously to stamp the misrepresentation as morally culpable; and still less could law presume to interfere with this kind of controversial misconduct. With regard to what is commonly meant by intemperate discussion, namely, invective, sarcasm, personality, and the like, the denunciation of these weapons would deserve more sympathy if it were ever proposed to interdict them equally to both sides; but it is only desired to restrain the employment of them against the prevailing opinion: against the unprevailing they may not only be used without general disapproval, but will be likely to obtain for him who uses them the praise of honest zeal and righteous indignation. Yet whatever mischief arises from their use, is greatest when they are employed against the comparatively defenceless;

and whatever unfair advantage can be derived by any opinion from this mode of asserting it, accrues almost exclusively to received opinions. The worst offence of this kind which can be committed by a polemic, is to stigmatize those who hold the contrary opinion as bad and immoral men. To calumny of this sort, those who hold any unpopular opinion are peculiarly exposed, because they are in general few and uninfluential, and nobody but themselves feels much interest in seeing justice done them; but this weapon is, from the nature of the case, denied to those who attack a prevailing opinion: they can neither use it with safety to themselves, nor if they could, would it do anything but recoil on their own cause. In general, opinions contrary to those commonly received can only obtain a hearing by studied moderation of language, and the most cautious avoidance of unnecessary offence, from which they hardly ever deviate even in a slight degree without losing ground: while unmeasured vituperation[67] employed on the side of the prevailing opinion, really does deter people from professing contrary opinions, and from listening to those who profess them. For the interest, therefore, of truth and justice, it is far more important to restrain this employment of vituperative language than the other; and, for example, if it were necessary to choose, there would be much more need to discourage offensive attacks on infidelity, than on religion. It is, however, obvious that law and authority have no business with restraining either, while opinion ought, in every instance, to determine its verdict by the circumstances of the individual case; condemning every one, on whichever side of the argument he places himself, in whose mode of advocacy either want of candour, or malignity, bigotry or intolerance of feeling manifest themselves, but not inferring these vices from the side which a person takes, though it be the contrary side of the question to our own; and giving merited honour to every one, whatever opinion he may hold, who has calmness to see and honesty to state what his opponents and their opinions really are, exaggerating nothing to their discredit, keeping nothing back which tells, or can be supposed to tell, in their favour. This is the real morality of public discussion; and if often violated, I am happy to think that

---

66 Plausibly but fallaciously.

67 Harsh abuse.

there are many controversialists who to a great extent observe it, and a still greater number who conscientiously strive towards it.

…

Chapter IV: Of the Limits to the Authority of Society over the Individual

What, then, is the rightful limit to the sovereignty of the individual over himself? Where does the authority of society begin? How much of human life should be assigned to individuality, and how much to society?

Each will receive its proper share, if each has that which more particularly concerns it. To individuality should belong the part of life in which it is chiefly the individual that is interested; to society, the part which chiefly interests society.

Though society is not founded on a contract, and though no good purpose is answered by inventing a contract in order to deduce social obligations from it, every one who receives the protection of society owes a return for the benefit, and the fact of living in society renders it indispensable that each should be bound to observe a certain line of conduct towards the rest. This conduct consists, first, in not injuring the interests of one another; or rather certain interests, which, either by express legal provision or by tacit understanding, ought to be considered as rights; and secondly, in each person's bearing his share (to be fixed on some equitable principle) of the labours and sacrifices incurred for defending the society or its members from injury and molestation. These conditions society is justified in enforcing, at all costs to those who endeavour to withhold fulfilment. Nor is this all that society may do. The acts of an individual may be hurtful to others, or wanting in due consideration for their welfare, without going the length of violating any of their constituted rights. The offender may then be justly punished by opinion, though not by law. As soon as any part of a person's conduct affects prejudicially the interests of others, society has jurisdiction over it, and the question whether the general welfare will or will not be promoted by interfering with it, becomes open to discussion. But there is no room for entertaining any such question when a person's conduct affects the interests of no persons besides himself, or needs not affect them unless they like (all the persons concerned

being of full age, and the ordinary amount of understanding). In all such cases there should be perfect freedom, legal and social, to do the action and stand the consequences.

It would be a great misunderstanding of this doctrine, to suppose that it is one of selfish indifference, which pretends that human beings have no business with each other's conduct in life, and that they should not concern themselves about the well-doing or well-being of one another, unless their own interest is involved. Instead of any diminution, there is need of a great increase of disinterested exertion to promote the good of others. But disinterested benevolence can find other instruments to persuade people to their good, than whips and scourges, either of the literal or the metaphorical sort. I am the last person to undervalue the self-regarding virtues; they are only second in importance, if even second, to the social. It is equally the business of education to cultivate both. But even education works by conviction and persuasion as well as by compulsion, and it is by the former only that, when the period of education is past, the self-regarding virtues should be inculcated. Human beings owe to each other help to distinguish the better from the worse, and encouragement to choose the former and avoid the latter. They should be forever stimulating each other to increased exercise of their higher faculties, and increased direction of their feelings and aims towards wise instead of foolish, elevating instead of degrading, objects and contemplations. But neither one person, nor any number of persons, is warranted in saying to another human creature of ripe years, that he shall not do with his life for his own benefit what he chooses to do with it. He is the person most interested in his own well-being, the interest which any other person, except in cases of strong personal attachment, can have in it, is trifling, compared with that which he himself has; the interest which society has in him individually (except as to his conduct to others) is fractional, and altogether indirect: while, with respect to his own feelings and circumstances, the most ordinary man or woman has means of knowledge immeasurably surpassing those that can be possessed by any one else. The interference of society to overrule his judgment and purposes in what only regards himself, must be grounded on general presumptions;

which may be altogether wrong, and even if right, are as likely as not to be misapplied to individual cases, by persons no better acquainted with the circumstances of such cases than those are who look at them merely from without. In this department, therefore, of human affairs, Individuality has its proper field of action. In the conduct of human beings towards one another, it is necessary that general rules should for the most part be observed, in order that people may know what they have to expect; but in each person's own concerns, his individual spontaneity is entitled to free exercise. Considerations to aid his judgment, exhortations to strengthen his will, may be offered to him, even obtruded on him, by others; but he, himself, is the final judge. All errors which he is likely to commit against advice and warning, are far outweighed by the evil of allowing others to constrain him to what they deem his good.

I do not mean that the feelings with which a person is regarded by others, ought not to be in any way affected by his self-regarding qualities or deficiencies. This is neither possible nor desirable. If he is eminent in any of the qualities which conduce to his own good, he is, so far, a proper object of admiration. He is so much the nearer to the ideal perfection of human nature. If he is grossly deficient in those qualities, a sentiment the opposite of admiration will follow. There is a degree of folly, and a degree of what may be called (though the phrase is not unobjectionable) lowness or depravation of taste, which, though it cannot justify doing harm to the person who manifests it, renders him necessarily and properly a subject of distaste, or, in extreme cases, even of contempt: a person could not have the opposite qualities in due strength without entertaining these feelings. Though doing no wrong to any one, a person may so act as to compel us to judge him, and feel to him, as a fool, or as a being of an inferior order: and since this judgment and feeling are a fact which he would prefer to avoid, it is doing him a service to warn him of it beforehand, as of any other disagreeable consequence to which he exposes himself. It would be well, indeed, if this good office were much more freely rendered than the common notions of politeness at present permit, and if one person could honestly point out to another that he thinks him in fault, without being considered unman-

nerly or presuming. We have a right, also, in various ways, to act upon our unfavourable opinion of any one, not to the oppression of his individuality, but in the exercise of ours. We are not bound, for example, to seek his society; we have a right to avoid it (though not to parade the avoidance), for we have a right to choose the society most acceptable to us. We have a right, and it may be our duty, to caution others against him, if we think his example or conversation likely to have a pernicious effect on those with whom he associates. We may give others a preference over him in optional good offices, except those which tend to his improvement. In these various modes a person may suffer very severe penalties at the hands of others, for faults which directly concern only himself; but he suffers these penalties only in so far as they are the natural, and, as it were, the spontaneous consequences of the faults themselves, not because they are purposely inflicted on him for the sake of punishment. A person who shows rashness, obstinacy, self-conceit—who cannot live within moderate means—who cannot restrain himself from hurtful indulgences—who pursues animal pleasures at the expense of those of feeling and intellect—must expect to be lowered in the opinion of others, and to have a less share of their favourable sentiments, but of this he has no right to complain, unless he has merited their favour by special excellence in his social relations, and has thus established a title to their good offices, which is not affected by his demerits towards himself.

What I contend for is, that the inconveniences which are strictly inseparable from the unfavourable judgment of others, are the only ones to which a person should ever be subjected for that portion of his conduct and character which concerns his own good, but which does not affect the interests of others in their relations with him. Acts injurious to others require a totally different treatment. Encroachment on their rights; infliction on them of any loss or damage not justified by his own rights; falsehood or duplicity in dealing with them; unfair or ungenerous use of advantages over them; even selfish abstinence from defending them against injury—these are fit objects of moral reprobation, and, in grave cases, of moral retribution and punishment. And not only these acts, but the dispositions which lead to them, are properly immoral, and fit subjects of disapprobation which may rise to abhorrence. Cruelty of disposition; malice and ill-nature; that most anti-social and odious of all passions, envy; dissimulation and insincerity, irascibility on insufficient cause, and resentment disproportioned to the provocation; the love of domineering over others; the desire to engross more than one's share of advantages (the πλεονεξία[68] of the Greeks); the pride which derives gratification from the abasement of others; the egotism which thinks self and its concerns more important than everything else, and decides all doubtful questions in his own favour;—these are moral vices, and constitute a bad and odious moral character: unlike the self-regarding faults previously mentioned, which are not properly immoralities, and to whatever pitch they may be carried, do not constitute wickedness. They may be proofs of any amount of folly, or want of personal dignity and self-respect; but they are only a subject of moral reprobation when they involve a breach of duty to others, for whose sake the individual is bound to have care for himself. What are called duties to ourselves are not socially obligatory, unless circumstances render them at the same time duties to others. The term duty to oneself, when it means anything more than prudence, means self-respect or self-development; and for none of these is any one accountable to his fellow-creatures, because for none of them is it for the good of mankind that he be held accountable to them.

The distinction between the loss of consideration which a person may rightly incur by defect of prudence or of personal dignity, and the reprobation which is due to him for an offence against the rights of others, is not a merely nominal distinction. It makes a vast difference both in our feelings and in our conduct towards him, whether he displeases us in things in which we think we have a right to control him, or in things in which we know that we have not. If he displeases us, we may express our distaste, and we may stand aloof from a person as well as from a thing that displeases us; but we shall not therefore feel called on to make his life uncomfortable. We shall reflect that he already bears, or will bear, the whole penalty of his error; if he spoils his life by mismanagement, we

shall not, for that reason, desire to spoil it still further: instead of wishing to punish him, we shall rather endeavour to alleviate his punishment, by showing him how he may avoid or cure the evils his conduct tends to bring upon him. He may be to us an object of pity, perhaps of dislike, but not of anger or resentment; we shall not treat him like an enemy of society: the worst we shall think ourselves justified in doing is leaving him to himself, if we do not interfere benevolently by showing interest or concern for him. It is far otherwise if he has infringed the rules necessary for the protection of his fellow-creatures, individually or collectively. The evil consequences of his acts do not then fall on himself, but on others; and society, as the protector of all its members, must retaliate on him; must inflict pain on him for the express purpose of punishment, and must take care that it be sufficiently severe. In the one case, he is an offender at our bar,[69] and we are called on not only to sit in judgment on him, but, in one shape or another, to execute our own sentence: in the other case, it is not our part to inflict any suffering on him, except what may incidentally follow from our using the same liberty in the regulation of our own affairs, which we allow to him in his.

The distinction here pointed out between the part of a person's life which concerns only himself, and that which concerns others, many persons will refuse to admit. How (it may be asked) can any part of the conduct of a member of society be a matter of indifference to the other members? No person is an entirely isolated being; it is impossible for a person to do anything seriously or permanently hurtful to himself, without mischief reaching at least to his near connections, and often far beyond them. If he injures his property, he does harm to those who directly or indirectly derived support from it, and usually diminishes, by a greater or less amount, the general resources of the community. If he deteriorates his bodily or mental faculties, he not only brings evil upon all who depended on him for any portion of their happiness, but disqualifies himself for rendering the services which he owes to his fellow-creatures generally; perhaps becomes a burthen[70] on their affection or

---

68 *Pleonexia*—greediness, graspingness.

69 Tribunal, place of judgment.

70 Burden.

benevolence; and if such conduct were very frequent, hardly any offence that is committed would detract more from the general sum of good. Finally, if by his vices or follies a person does no direct harm to others, he is nevertheless (it may be said) injurious by his example; and ought to be compelled to control himself, for the sake of those whom the sight or knowledge of his conduct might corrupt or mislead.

And even (it will be added) if the consequences of misconduct could be confined to the vicious or thoughtless individual, ought society to abandon to their own guidance those who are manifestly unfit for it? If protection against themselves is confessedly due to children and persons under age, is not society equally bound to afford it to persons of mature years who are equally incapable of self-government? If gambling, or drunkenness, or incontinence,[71] or idleness, or uncleanliness, are as injurious to happiness, and as great a hindrance to improvement, as many or most of the acts prohibited by law, why (it may be asked) should not law, so far as is consistent with practicability and social convenience, endeavour to repress these also? And as a supplement to the unavoidable imperfections of law, ought not opinion at least to organize a powerful police against these vices, and visit rigidly with social penalties those who are known to practise them? There is no question here (it may be said) about restricting individuality, or impeding the trial of new and original experiments in living. The only things it is sought to prevent are things which have been tried and condemned from the beginning of the world until now; things which experience has shown not to be useful or suitable to any person's individuality. There must be some length of time and amount of experience, after which a moral or prudential truth may be regarded as established, and it is merely desired to prevent generation after generation from falling over the same precipice which has been fatal to their predecessors.

I fully admit that the mischief which a person does to himself, may seriously affect, both through their sympathies and their interests, those nearly connected with him, and in a minor degree, society at large. When, by conduct of this sort, a person is led to violate a distinct and assignable obligation to any other person or persons, the case is taken out of the self-regarding class, and becomes amenable to moral disapprobation in the proper sense of the term. If, for example, a man, through intemperance or extravagance, becomes unable to pay his debts, or, having undertaken the moral responsibility of a family, becomes from the same cause incapable of supporting or educating them, he is deservedly reprobated, and might be justly punished; but it is for the breach of duty to his family or creditors, not for the extravagance. If the resources which ought to have been devoted to them, had been diverted from them for the most prudent investment, the moral culpability would have been the same. George Barnwell murdered his uncle to get money for his mistress, but if he had done it to set himself up in business, he would equally have been hanged.[72] Again, in the frequent case of a man who causes grief to his family by addiction to bad habits, he deserves reproach for his unkindness or ingratitude; but so he may for cultivating habits not in themselves vicious, if they are painful to those with whom he passes his life, or who from personal ties are dependent on him for their comfort. Whoever fails in the consideration generally due to the interests and feelings of others, not being compelled by some more imperative duty, or justified by allowable self-preference, is a subject of moral disapprobation for that failure, but not for the cause of it, nor for the errors, merely personal to himself, which may have remotely led to it. In like manner, when a person disables himself, by conduct purely self-regarding, from the performance of some definite duty incumbent on him to the public, he is guilty of a social offence. No person ought to be punished simply for being drunk; but a soldier or a policeman should be punished for being drunk on duty. Whenever, in

---

71 Lack of self-control.

72 This tale was featured in the popular seventeenth-century ballad "George Barnwell," and later formed the subject matter of a play by George Lillo, *The London Merchant, or, the History of George Barnwell* (1731), which was one of the first prose works of domestic tragedy in English. It is the story of a young apprentice's downfall caused by his love for a beautiful, but unfeeling, prostitute.

short, there is a definite damage, or a definite risk of damage, either to an individual or to the public, the case is taken out of the province of liberty, and placed in that of morality or law.

But with regard to the merely contingent or, as it may be called, constructive injury which a person causes to society, by conduct which neither violates any specific duty to the public, nor occasions perceptible hurt to any assignable individual except himself; the inconvenience is one which society can afford to bear, for the sake of the greater good of human freedom. If grown persons are to be punished for not taking proper care of themselves, I would rather it were for their own sake, than under pretence of preventing them from impairing their capacity of rendering to society benefits which society does not pretend it has a right to exact. But I cannot consent to argue the point as if society had no means of bringing its weaker members up to its ordinary standard of rational conduct, except waiting till they do something irrational, and then punishing them, legally or morally, for it. Society has had absolute power over them during all the early portion of their existence: it has had the whole period of childhood and nonage in which to try whether it could make them capable of rational conduct in life. The existing generation is master both of the training and the entire circumstances of the generation to come; it cannot indeed make them perfectly wise and good, because it is itself so lamentably deficient in goodness and wisdom; and its best efforts are not always, in individual cases, its most successful ones; but it is perfectly well able to make the rising generation, as a whole, as good as, and a little better than, itself. If society lets any considerable number of its members grow up mere children, incapable of being acted on by rational consideration of distant motives, society has itself to blame for the consequences. Armed not only with all the powers of education, but with the ascendancy which the authority of a received opinion always exercises over the minds who are least fitted to judge for themselves; and aided by the *natural* penalties which cannot be prevented from falling on those who incur the distaste or the contempt of those who know them; let not society pretend that it needs, besides all this, the power to issue commands and enforce obedience in the personal concerns of individuals, in which, on all principles of justice and policy, the decision ought to rest with those who are to abide the consequences. Nor is there anything which tends more to discredit and frustrate the better means of influencing conduct, than a resort to the worse. If there be among those whom it is attempted to coerce into prudence or temperance, any of the material of which vigorous and independent characters are made, they will infallibly rebel against the yoke. No such person will ever feel that others have a right to control him in his concerns, such as they have to prevent him from injuring them in theirs; and it easily comes to be considered a mark of spirit and courage to fly in the face of such usurped authority, and do with ostentation the exact opposite of what it enjoins; as in the fashion of grossness which succeeded, in the time of Charles II,[73] to the fanatical moral intolerance of the Puritans. With respect to what is said of the necessity of protecting society from the bad example set to others by the vicious or the self-indulgent; it is true that bad example may have a pernicious effect, especially the example of doing wrong to others with impunity to the wrong-doer. But we are now speaking of conduct which, while it does no wrong to others, is supposed to do great harm to the agent himself: and I do not see how those who believe this, can think otherwise than that the example, on the whole, must be more salutary than hurtful, since, if it displays the misconduct, it displays also the painful or degrading consequences which, if the conduct is justly censured, must be supposed to be in all or most cases attendant on it.

But the strongest of all the arguments against the interference of the public with purely personal conduct, is that when it does interfere, the odds are that it interferes wrongly, and in the wrong place. On questions of social morality, of duty to others, the opinion of the public, that is, of an overruling majority, though often wrong, is likely to be still oftener right; because on such questions they are only required to judge of their own interests; of the manner in which some mode of conduct, if allowed to be practised, would affect themselves. But the opinion of a similar majority, imposed

---

73   Charles II was King of England (1660–1685) immediately following the Restoration of the monarchy after its overthrow during the English Civil War.

as a law on the minority, on questions of self-regarding conduct, is quite as likely to be wrong as right; for in these cases public opinion means, at the best, some people's opinion of what is good or bad for other people; while very often it does not even mean that; the public, with the most perfect indifference, passing over the pleasure or convenience of those whose conduct they censure, and considering only their own preference. There are many who consider as an injury to themselves any conduct which they have a distaste for, and resent it as an outrage to their feelings; as a religious bigot, when charged with disregarding the religious feelings of others, has been known to retort that they disregard his feelings, by persisting in their abominable worship or creed. But there is no parity between the feeling of a person for his own opinion, and the feeling of another who is offended at his holding it; no more than between the desire of a thief to take a purse, and the desire of the right owner to keep it. And a person's taste is as much his own peculiar concern as his opinion or his purse. It is easy for any one to imagine an ideal public, which leaves the freedom and choice of individuals in all uncertain matters undisturbed, and only requires them to abstain from modes of conduct which universal experience has condemned. But where has there been seen a public which set any such limit to its censorship? or when does the public trouble itself about universal experience? In its interferences with personal conduct it is seldom thinking of anything but the enormity of acting or feeling differently from itself; and this standard of judgment, thinly disguised, is held up to mankind as the dictate of religion and philosophy, by nine tenths of all moralists and speculative writers. These teach that things are right because they are right; because we feel them to be so. They tell us to search in our own minds and hearts for laws of conduct binding on ourselves and on all others. What can the poor public do but apply these instructions, and make their own personal feelings of good and evil, if they are tolerably unanimous in them, obligatory on all the world?

The evil here pointed out is not one which exists only in theory; and it may perhaps be expected that I should specify the instances in which the public of this age and country improperly invests its own preferences with the character of moral laws. I am not writing an essay on the aberrations of existing moral feeling. That is too weighty a subject to be discussed parenthetically, and by way of illustration. Yet examples are necessary, to show that the principle I maintain is of serious and practical moment, and that I am not endeavouring to erect a barrier against imaginary evils. And it is not difficult to show, by abundant instances, that to extend the bounds of what may be called moral police, until it encroaches on the most unquestionably legitimate liberty of the individual, is one of the most universal of all human propensities.

As a first instance, consider the antipathies which men cherish on no better grounds than that persons whose religious opinions are different from theirs, do not practise their religious observances, especially their religious abstinences. To cite a rather trivial example, nothing in the creed or practice of Christians does more to envenom the hatred of Mahomedans[74] against them, than the fact of their eating pork. There are few acts which Christians and Europeans regard with more unaffected disgust, than Mussulmans[75] regard this particular mode of satisfying hunger. It is, in the first place, an offence against their religion; but this circumstance by no means explains either the degree or the kind of their repugnance; for wine also is forbidden by their religion, and to partake of it is by all Mussulmans accounted wrong, but not disgusting. Their aversion to the flesh of the "unclean beast" is, on the contrary, of that peculiar character, resembling an instinctive antipathy, which the idea of uncleanness, when once it thoroughly sinks into the feelings, seems always to excite even in those whose personal habits are anything but scrupulously cleanly and of which the sentiment of religious impurity, so intense in the Hindoos, is a remarkable example. Suppose now that in a people, of whom the majority were Mussulmans, that majority should insist upon not permitting pork to be eaten within the limits of the country. This would be nothing new in Mahomedan countries.[76] Would

---

74 Muslims.

75 Also Muslims (archaic form).

76 [Author's note] The case of the Bombay Parsees is a curious instance in point. When this industrious and enterprising tribe, the descendants of the Persian fire-worshippers, flying from their native country before

822 SOCIAL/POLITICAL PHILOSOPHY

it be a legitimate exercise of the moral authority of public opinion? and if not, why not? The practice is really revolting to such a public. They also sincerely think that it is forbidden and abhorred by the Deity. Neither could the prohibition be censured as religious persecution. It might be religious in its origin, but it would not be persecution for religion, since nobody's religion makes it a duty to eat pork. The only tenable ground of condemnation would be, that with the personal tastes and self-regarding concerns of individuals the public has no business to interfere.

To come somewhat nearer home: the majority of Spaniards consider it a gross impiety, offensive in the highest degree to the Supreme Being, to worship him in any other manner than the Roman Catholic; and no other public worship is lawful on Spanish soil. The people of all Southern Europe look upon a married clergy as not only irreligious, but unchaste, indecent, gross, disgusting. What do Protestants think of these perfectly sincere feelings, and of the attempt to enforce them against non-Catholics? Yet, if mankind are justified in interfering with each other's liberty in things which do not concern the interests of others, on what principle is it possible consistently to exclude these cases? or who can blame people for desiring to suppress what they regard as a scandal in the sight of God and man? No stronger case can be shown for prohibiting anything which is regarded as a personal immorality, than is made out for suppressing these practices in the eyes of those who regard them as impieties; and unless we are willing to adopt the logic of persecutors, and to say that we may persecute others because we are right, and that they must not persecute us because they are wrong, we must beware

---

the Caliphs, arrived in Western India, they were admitted to toleration by the Hindoo sovereigns, on condition of not eating beef. When those regions afterwards fell under the dominion of Mahomedan conquerors, the Parsees obtained from them a continuance of indulgence, on condition of refraining from pork. What was at first obedience to authority became a second nature, and the Parsees to this day abstain both from beef and pork. Though not required by their religion, the double abstinence has had time to grow into a custom of their tribe; and custom, in the East, is a religion.

of admitting a principle of which we should resent as a gross injustice the application to ourselves.

The preceding instances may be objected to, although unreasonably, as drawn from contingencies impossible among us: opinion, in this country, not being likely to enforce abstinence from meats, or to interfere with people for worshipping, and for either marrying or not marrying, according to their creed or inclination. The next example, however, shall be taken from an interference with liberty which we have by no means passed all danger of. Wherever the Puritans have been sufficiently powerful, as in New England, and in Great Britain at the time of the Commonwealth, they have endeavoured, with considerable success, to put down all public, and nearly all private, amusements: especially music, dancing, public games, or other assemblages for purposes of diversion, and the theatre. There are still in this country large bodies of persons by whose notions of morality and religion these recreations are condemned; and those persons belonging chiefly to the middle class, who are the ascendant power in the present social and political condition of the kingdom, it is by no means impossible that persons of these sentiments may at some time or other command a majority in Parliament. How will the remaining portion of the community like to have the amusements that shall be permitted to them regulated by the religious and moral sentiments of the stricter Calvinists and Methodists? Would they not, with considerable peremptoriness, desire these intrusively pious members of society to mind their own business? This is precisely what should be said to every government and every public, who have the pretension that no person shall enjoy any pleasure which they think wrong. But if the principle of the pretension be admitted, no one can reasonably object to its being acted on in the sense of the majority, or other preponderating power in the country; and all persons must be ready to conform to the idea of a Christian commonwealth, as understood by the early settlers in New England, if a religious profession similar to theirs should ever succeed in regaining its lost ground, as religions supposed to be declining have so often been known to do.

To imagine another contingency, perhaps more likely to be realized than the one last mentioned. There is confessedly a strong tendency in the modern world towards a democratic constitution of society, accompanied or not by popular political institutions. It is affirmed that in the country where this tendency is most completely realized—where both society and the government are most democratic—the United States—the feeling of the majority, to whom any appearance of a more showy or costly style of living than they can hope to rival is disagreeable, operates as a tolerably effectual sumptuary law,[77] and that in many parts of the Union it is really difficult for a person possessing a very large income, to find any mode of spending it, which will not incur popular disapprobation. Though such statements as these are doubtless much exaggerated as a representation of existing facts, the state of things they describe is not only a conceivable and possible, but a probable result of democratic feeling, combined with the notion that the public has a right to a veto on the manner in which individuals shall spend their incomes. We have only further to suppose a considerable diffusion of Socialist opinions, and it may become infamous in the eyes of the majority to possess more property than some very small amount, or any income not earned by manual labour. Opinions similar in principle to these, already prevail widely among the artisan class, and weigh oppressively on those who are amenable to[78] the opinion chiefly of that class, namely, its own members. It is known that the bad workmen who form the majority of the operatives in many branches of industry, are decidedly of opinion that bad workmen ought to receive the same wages as good, and that no one ought to be allowed, through piecework or otherwise, to earn by superior skill or industry more than others can without it. And they employ a moral police, which occasionally becomes a physical one, to deter skilful workmen from receiving, and employers from giving, a larger remuneration for a more useful service. If the public have any jurisdiction over private concerns, I cannot see that these people are in fault, or that any individual's particular

public can be blamed for asserting the same authority over his individual conduct, which the general public asserts over people in general.

But, without dwelling upon supposititious cases, there are, in our own day, gross usurpations upon the liberty of private life actually practised, and still greater ones threatened with some expectation of success, and opinions proposed which assert an unlimited right in the public not only to prohibit by law everything which it thinks wrong, but in order to get at what it thinks wrong, to prohibit any number of things which it admits to be innocent.

Under the name of preventing intemperance the people of one English colony, and of nearly half the United States,[79] have been interdicted by law from making any use whatever of fermented drinks, except for medical purposes: for prohibition of their sale is in fact, as it is intended to be, prohibition of their use. And though the impracticability of executing the law has caused its repeal in several of the States which had adopted it, including the one from which it derives its name,[80] an attempt has notwithstanding been commenced, and is prosecuted with considerable zeal by many of the professed philanthropists, to agitate for a similar law in this country. The association, or "Alliance" as it terms itself,[81] which has been formed for this purpose, has acquired some notoriety through the publicity given to a correspondence between its Secretary and one of the very few English public men[82] who hold that a politician's opinions ought

---

77 A law regulating or limiting personal expenditures, especially one forbidding great displays of wealth (e.g., building excessively large houses) or expenditures which are judged immoral (e.g., gambling).

78 Accountable to, judged by.

79 New Brunswick (then an English colony; it became one of the four founding provinces of the Dominion of Canada in 1867) and thirteen of the American states.

80 Maine: "Maine Law" was a popular term for prohibition in this period.

81 The "United Kingdom Alliance for the Legislative Suppression of the Sale of Intoxicating Liquors," founded in 1853. This organization energetically continued its fight into the early decades of the twentieth century.

82 Edward John Stanley, a Whig (Liberal) politician who was president of the Board of Trade from 1855 until 1858. In the later years of the nineteenth century the temperance movement became generally associated with the Liberal Party, while the Conservative Party tended to defend the interests of the drink trade.

to be founded on principles. Lord Stanley's share in this correspondence is calculated to strengthen the hopes already built on him, by those who know how rare such qualities as are manifested in some of his public appearances, unhappily, are among those who figure in political life. The organ of the Alliance, who would "deeply deplore the recognition of any principle which could be wrested to justify bigotry and persecution," undertakes to point out the "broad and impassable barrier" which divides such principles from those of the association. "All matters relating to thought, opinion, conscience, appear to me," he says, "to be without the sphere of legislation; all pertaining to social act, habit, relation, subject only to a discretionary power vested in the State itself, and not in the individual, to be within it." No mention is made of a third class, different from either of these, viz., acts and habits which are not social, but individual; although it is to this class, surely, that the act of drinking fermented liquors belongs. Selling fermented liquors, however, is trading, and trading is a social act. But the infringement complained of is not on the liberty of the seller, but on that of the buyer and consumer; since the State might just as well forbid him to drink wine, as purposely make it impossible for him to obtain it. The Secretary, however, says, "I claim, as a citizen, a right to legislate whenever my social rights are invaded by the social act of another." And now for the definition of these "social rights." "If anything invades my social rights, certainly the traffic in strong drink does. It destroys my primary right of security, by constantly creating and stimulating social disorder. It invades my right of equality, by deriving a profit from the creation of a misery I am taxed to support. It impedes my right to free moral and intellectual development, by surrounding my path with dangers, and by weakening and demoralizing society, from which I have a right to claim mutual aid and intercourse." A theory of "social rights," the like of which probably never before found its way into distinct language—being nothing short of this—that it is the absolute social right of every individual, that every other individual shall act in every respect exactly as he ought; that whosoever fails thereof in the smallest particular, violates my social right, and entitles me to demand from the legislature the removal of the grievance. So

monstrous a principle is far more dangerous than any single interference with liberty; there is no violation of liberty which it would not justify; it acknowledges no right to any freedom whatever, except perhaps to that of holding opinions in secret, without ever disclosing them; for the moment an opinion which I consider noxious, passes any one's lips, it invades all the "social rights" attributed to me by the Alliance. The doctrine ascribes to all mankind a vested interest in each other's moral, intellectual, and even physical perfection, to be defined by each claimant according to his own standard.

Another important example of illegitimate interference with the rightful liberty of the individual, not simply threatened, but long since carried into triumphant effect, is Sabbatarian legislation.[83] Without doubt, abstinence on one day in the week, so far as the exigencies of life permit, from the usual daily occupation, though in no respect religiously binding on any except Jews,[84] is a highly beneficial custom. And inasmuch as this custom cannot be observed without a general consent to that effect among the industrious classes, therefore, in so far as some persons by working may impose the same necessity on others, it may be allowable and right that the law should guarantee to each, the observance by others of the custom, by suspending the greater operations of industry on a particular day. But this justification, grounded on the direct interest which others have in each individual's observance of the practice, does not apply to the self-chosen occupations in which a person may think fit to employ his leisure; nor does it hold good, in the smallest degree, for legal restrictions on amusements. It is true that the amusement of some is the day's work of others; but the pleasure, not to say the useful recreation, of many, is worth the labour of a few, provided the occupation is freely chosen, and can be freely resigned. The operatives are perfectly right in thinking that

83 Legislation making it unlawful to work or perform other activities on the Sabbath (which, for most Christians, is Sunday).

84 Orthodox Jews are prohibited from work and travel during their Sabbath (sundown Friday until sundown Saturday).

if all worked on Sunday, seven days' work would have to be given for six days' wages: but so long as the great mass of employments are suspended, the small number who for the enjoyment of others must still work, obtain a proportional increase of earnings; and they are not obliged to follow those occupations, if they prefer leisure to emolument.[85] If a further remedy is sought, it might be found in the establishment by custom of a holiday on some other day of the week for those particular classes of persons. The only ground, therefore, on which restrictions on Sunday amusements can be defended, must be that they are religiously wrong; a motive of legislation which never can be too earnestly protested against. "Deorum injuriae Diis curae."[86] It remains to be proved that society or any of its officers holds a commission from on high to avenge any supposed offence to Omnipotence, which is not also a wrong to our fellow-creatures. The notion that it is one man's duty that another should be religious, was the foundation of all the religious persecutions ever perpetrated, and if admitted, would fully justify them. Though the feeling which breaks out in the repeated attempts to stop railway travelling on Sunday, in the resistance to the opening of Museums, and the like, has not the cruelty of the old persecutors, the state of mind indicated by it is fundamentally the same. It is a determination not to tolerate others in doing what is permitted by their religion, because it is not permitted by the persecutor's religion. It is a belief that God not only abominates the act of the misbeliever, but will not hold us guiltless if we leave him unmolested.

I cannot refrain from adding to these examples of the little account commonly made of human liberty, the language of downright persecution which breaks out from the press of this country, whenever it feels called on to notice the remarkable phenomenon of Mormonism. Much might be said on the unexpected and instructive fact, that an alleged new revelation, and a religion, founded on it, the product of palpable imposture,[87] not even supported by the *prestige* of extraordinary qualities in its founder, is believed by hundreds of thousands, and has been made the foundation of a society, in the age of newspapers, railways, and the electric telegraph. What here concerns us is, that this religion, like other and better religions, has its martyrs; that its prophet and founder was, for his teaching, put to death by a mob; that others of its adherents lost their lives by the same lawless violence; that they were forcibly expelled, in a body, from the country in which they first grew up; while, now that they have been chased into a solitary recess in the midst of a desert,[88] many in this country openly declare that it would be right (only that it is not convenient) to send an expedition against them, and compel them by force to conform to the opinions of other people. The article of the Mormonite doctrine which is the chief provocative to the antipathy which thus breaks through the ordinary restraints of religious tolerance, is its sanction of polygamy;[89] which, though permitted to Mahomedans, and Hindoos, and Chinese, seems to excite unquenchable animosity when practised by persons who speak English, and profess to be a kind of Christians. No one has a deeper disapprobation than I have of this Mormon institution; both for other reasons, and because, far from being in any way countenanced by the principle of liberty, it is a direct infraction of that principle, being a mere riveting of

---

85 Compensation, payment.

86 "The gods can avenge their own wrongs"—from the *Annals* (c. 116 CE) of Tacitus, a Roman historian.

87 Obvious deception. The Mormon religion, officially known as the Church of Jesus Christ of Latter-Day Saints, was founded in 1830 in Palmyra, New York by Joseph Smith. He based the religion on the *Book of Mormon*, which he claimed was revealed to him by an angel in 1827. This was a translation of a golden book written in a mysterious hieroglyphic script, buried in a nearby hill, and accessible only through the angel's intervention. The religion has more than eight million members today.

88 Now Salt Lake City, in Utah. The Mormons were this inhospitable area's first permanent, Western settlers. Utah did not become a part of the United States until 1896.

89 Having more than one spouse at the same time: in the case of the Mormons, one man may have several wives.

the chains of one half of the community, and an emancipation of the other from reciprocity of obligation towards them. Still, it must be remembered that this relation is as much voluntary on the part of the women concerned in it, and who may be deemed the sufferers by it, as is the case with any other form of the marriage institution; and however surprising this fact may appear, it has its explanation in the common ideas and customs of the world, which teaching women to think marriage the one thing needful, make it intelligible that many a woman should prefer being one of several wives, to not being a wife at all. Other countries are not asked to recognize such unions, or release any portion of their inhabitants from their own laws on the score of Mormonite opinions. But when the dissentients have conceded to the hostile sentiments of others, far more than could justly be demanded; when they have left the countries to which their doctrines were unacceptable, and established themselves in a remote corner of the earth, which they have been the first to render habitable to human beings; it is difficult to see on what principles but those of tyranny they can be prevented from living there under what laws they please, provided they commit no aggression on other nations, and allow perfect freedom of departure to those who are dissatisfied with their ways. A recent writer, in some respects of considerable merit, proposes (to use his own words,) not a crusade, but a *civilizade*, against this polygamous community, to put an end to what seems to him a retrograde step in civilization. It also appears so to me, but I am not aware that any community has a right to force another to be civilized. So long as the sufferers by the bad law do not invoke assistance from other communities, I cannot admit that persons entirely unconnected with them ought to step in and require that a condition of things with which all who are directly interested appear to be satisfied, should be put an end to because it is a scandal to persons some thousands of miles distant, who have no part or concern in it. Let them send missionaries, if they please, to preach against it; and let them, by any fair means, (of which silencing the teachers is not one,) oppose the progress of similar doctrines among their own people. If civilization has got the better of barbarism when barbarism had the world to itself, it is too much to profess to be afraid lest barbarism, after having been fairly got under, should revive and conquer civilization. A civilization that can thus succumb to its vanquished enemy must first have become so degenerate, that neither its appointed priests and teachers, nor anybody else, has the capacity, or will take the trouble, to stand up for it. If this be so, the sooner such a civilization receives notice to quit, the better. It can only go on from bad to worse, until destroyed and regenerated (like the Western Empire[90]) by energetic barbarians.

---

90   The western part of the Roman Empire, which was broken up by barbarian invaders during the fifth century.

KARL MARX AND FRIEDRICH ENGELS
The Communist Manifesto

The philosophers have only *interpreted* the
world in different ways; the point is to *change* it.
(Karl Marx, *Theses on Feuerbach*)

Who Were Karl Marx and Friedrich Engels?

Karl Heinrich Marx was born in 1818 in the town of
Trier in the Rhineland, formerly a region of Prussia lying next to the French border that is today part of
Germany. Both his parents were Jewish, descended
from a long line of rabbis and Jewish intellectuals.
They were part of the first generation of German
Jews to enjoy equal legal status with Christians and
to be granted free choice of residence and profession. The Rhineland had been ruled by the French
during the Napoleonic period, from 1792 until 1815,
and Marx's father Heinrich had benefited from the
relatively enlightened French regime, using the op-

portunity to forge a successful career as a respected
lawyer. However, after Prussian power was restored
in Trier in 1815, Marx's father felt obliged to convert
himself and his family to Lutheranism in order to
protect his career, and so Karl was not brought up
as a Jew.

Karl's father wanted him to become a lawyer, but
Karl was a rowdy, rebellious child and, as a young
man, chose to spend his time studying philosophy
and history, dueling, and writing romantic verses to
his childhood sweetheart, the daughter of his neighbor, Jenny von Westphalen (whom he married in
1843). From 1835 to 1841 Marx studied at the universities of Bonn (where he spent a year studying
law) and Berlin, where he was exposed to, and heavily influenced by, the idealist philosophy of G.W.F.
Hegel. Marx's early writings show his preoccupation
with the notion of human self-realization through
the struggle for freedom and a view of the nature of
reality as turbulently chang-
ing, themes which find reso-
nance in Hegel. However, like
many contemporary "Young
Hegelians," Marx found the
Hegelian system, as it was
then taught in the Prussian
universities, to be politically
and religiously much too
conservative.

In 1841 Marx success-
fully submitted a doctoral
dissertation (on Greek philosophy) to the university of
Jena, but—because his po-
litical radicalism made him
effectively unhireable in the
contemporary political climate—he quickly gave up
any prospect of an academic

Karl Marx

Friedrich Engels

career. Instead, he wrote for a liberal newspaper in Cologne, the *Rheinische Zeitung*, and in short order became its editor. Under Marx, the paper went from cautious criticism of the government to a more radical critique of prevailing conditions, especially issues of economic justice. Inevitably, the paper was first heavily censored and then, in 1843, shut down by the Prussian authorities. At this point Marx and his new wife left for the more bohemian city of Paris, where Marx worked as a journalist for another radical publication, the *Deutsch-Französische Jahrbücher* [*German-French Annals*]. Realizing that he knew little about the economic issues which he saw as so politically significant, Marx threw himself into the study of political economy. Even before these studies began, however, Marx was already—like many of his compatriots—politically left-wing in a way that could loosely be called "communist." He was convinced of the need for "cooperative" rather than individual control of economic resources, and was ferociously concerned about the need to alleviate the living conditions of the swelling numbers of urban poor.

In 1845, pressure from the Prussian government caused Marx to be expelled from France and he and his family moved to Brussels. There he developed a close friendship, begun in France, with Friedrich Engels, the man who was to be Marx's most important intellectual collaborator, supporter, and friend (indeed, the only lasting friend Marx ever had).

Engels was born in 1820 in Barmen, near Düsseldorf. His family were wealthy mill owners in the rapidly-industrializing northwest German Ruhr valley, and although Engels had hoped for a career in literature, his father insisted that he leave school at 17 to work for the family firm. He worked first in a local factory, then in an export office in the port city of Bremen, and finally as an accountant for the English branch of the firm Ermen and Engels. Thus, from the time he was a young man, Engels saw first-hand the profound social changes brought about by the introduction of new methods of production in the textile industry. Although he never formally attended university, he did sit in on lectures at Berlin university during his spell of compulsory military service and, through his exposure to the radical democratic movement, acquired a working knowledge of Hegel-

ian philosophy. He worked for the *Rheinische Zeitung* while Marx was its editor, writing articles from Manchester, England, where, employed by the family firm, he was appalled to witness the living conditions of the English working class. In 1844 he wrote the impassioned *Condition of the Working Classes in England*. He also wrote a critical study of the standard positions in political economy—a work that greatly impressed Marx, and directly intersected with his interests at the time. After Engels's return to Germany in 1844, the two began collaborating on writings, speeches, and debates intended to spread their radical ideas among workers and intellectuals. Their most important publication of this period was the *Communist Manifesto*.

1848, the year the *Communist Manifesto* was published, was a year of revolution in Europe. Most of the countries of Europe, except Britain, Belgium, and Russia, underwent a spasm of social upheaval in which old, aristocratic regimes fell and were replaced (briefly) by bold, new republican governments. Marx and Engels, in their different ways, attempted to play a role in this revolutionary process. Marx, now expelled from Belgium for his activism, returned to Cologne and started up a new radical broadsheet, the *Neue Reinische Zeitung*, his goal being to inspire and educate the revolutionary leaders (along the lines of the *Communist Manifesto*). Meanwhile, Engels was an officer in a short-lived military uprising in the German region of Baden. Within a matter of months, however, the European upheaval was over and, everywhere except France, the new democratic, republican regimes began to collapse and the old order reasserted itself. Marx and his associates were tried in a Cologne court for charges of inciting revolt and, although Marx successfully defended himself in court, he was nevertheless exiled from Prussian territory in 1849. As a result, Marx and Engels emigrated permanently to England: Marx, to live and write in London, and Engels to work for his family firm in Manchester.

Conditions were extremely hard for the Marx family, especially for the first decade of their lives in London. Marx was unwilling to take work that would interfere with his writing, and when he did seek stable employment he was unable to get it. (At one point he applied for a job as a railway clerk, but was unsuccessful because of the—now notorious—illegibility of his handwriting.) He and his family—his wife, her servant, and six children—subsisted on financial gifts from family and friends and on the income from Marx's occasional freelance journalism (mostly as a European correspondent for the *New York Tribune*, which paid £1 per article). Their main financial benefactor was Engels, who sent them grants and allowances taken from his own income and the money from his investments. Nevertheless, the Marx household lived in relative poverty for many years, enduring poor housing and bad food. Three of Marx's children died young, in part because of these hard conditions, and his own health suffered a collapse from which it never fully recovered.[1]

Meanwhile, Marx single-mindedly devoted his life to the cause of ending what he saw as the serious, and increasing, inequalities and exploitation inherent in capitalist society. His role, he thought, was to formulate the theoretical framework that would reveal the true state of things to the masses of workers and, by doing so, would both incite and guide the impending revolutionary replacement of capitalism by communism. He saw himself mainly as an 'ideas man' and a publicist for the communist movement, rather than an organizer or leader (and indeed, during his lifetime, his personal political influence was quite small). He spent ten hours a day, most days, in the Reading Room of the British Museum, conducting research and writing; after returning home, he would often continue to write late into the night. His main work during these years, a massive, wide-ranging, detailed analysis of capitalist society and what Marx saw as the tensions intrinsic to it, was eventually published in three substantial volumes as *Das Kapital* or *Capital*.[2]

Engels, meanwhile, ran his family's cotton mills in Lancashire and became a respected figure in Man-

chester society. He rode two days a week with the aristocratic Cheshire Hunt (valuable training, he claimed, for a future leader of the armies of the revolution), but at heart, Engels was unquestionably a devoted revolutionary, sincerely committed to the cause of communism, and he did his best to support Marx's work. He lived with an Irish factory girl called Mary Burns, and when she died he took in, and eventually married, her sister Lizzie.

In 1864 the International Working Men's Association (otherwise known as the First International) was formed. This was a watershed in the history of the working class movement, and for the next eight years the organization was highly influential in European left-wing politics. Marx was one of its main leaders, and was heavily engaged with its internal politics. By the 1870s he had become the leading theoretician for the radical movement in Europe, especially in Germany, and had become notorious across the continent as the "Red Doctor Marx."

Marx died, of chronic respiratory disease, in London in 1883. (Despite Engels's best efforts: he took him on a tour of France, Switzerland, and Algiers in the hope that a change of climate might help his condition.) He is buried next to his wife in Highgate Cemetery.

After 1870, Engels—who retired at fifty, an independently wealthy man—had devoted all of his time to helping Marx with his research, and after Marx's death he continued the writing of *Capital* from Marx's notes, completing it in 1894, a year before his own death.

In a speech given at Marx's graveside, Engels said

…Marx was above all else a revolutionist. His real mission in life was to contribute, in one way or another, to the overthrow of capitalist society and of the state institutions which it had brought into being, to contribute to the liberation of the modern proletariat, which *he* was the first to make conscious of its own position and needs, conscious of the conditions of its emancipation. Fighting was his element. And he fought with a passion, a tenacity and a success such as few could rival.

1   Despite these hardships, however, Marx's marriage was apparently a very happy one, and he was a devoted husband and father.

2   Marx's mother is said to have commented that it was a shame that her boy merely wrote about capital and never acquired any.

What Was Marx's Overall Philosophical Project?

In 1852, Marx summarized his three most important political ideas in the following way:

1. That social classes are not permanent features of society, but instead are phases in the historical development of the relations of economic production.
2. That the struggle between these classes will necessarily lead to the "dictatorship of the proletariat," in which the working people will forcibly take over political power from the property-owners.
3. That the dictatorship of the proletariat is not an end in itself, but a transition period before the advent of a classless communist society devoted to the free development and flourishing of individuals.

What does Marx mean by these three claims? The first is best approached through Marx's analysis of capitalism. A large proportion of his writing was devoted to this analysis, and it provides the clearest example of how he thought social class divisions were produced and perpetuated by a particular type of economic system.

A society is capitalist, according to Marx, if the production of goods is dominated by the use of wage-labor: that is, by the use of labor power sold, as their only way to make a living, by people who have no significant control over means of production (the proletariat), and bought by other people who do have control over means of production such as raw materials, capital, and machinery (the bourgeoisie). The bourgeoisie make their money mostly by combining the purchased labor power with the means of production they own, and selling the commodities thus produced. Marx held that the relationship between these two classes, bourgeoisie and proletariat, was intrinsically and inescapably *antagonistic*, and he attempted to explain all the main institutional features of capitalist society in terms of this relation. Since, in Marx's view, the main institutions of a capitalist society have the function of preserving the interests of the bourgeoisie, and since these interests are opposed to those of the proletarians, capitalist society is therefore a kind of class rule, or oppression, of the majority by the minority.

Furthermore, for Marx, social structures, such as capitalism, that are based on the oppression of one class by another give rise to what he called *ideologies*. An ideology is a (socially influential) system of beliefs or assumptions that reflects a false perception of reality—a perception of reality distorted by the social forces involved in class oppression. Central examples, for Marx, were systems of religious belief and the capitalist doctrine of the "free market." The dominance of a ruling class, whose members usually make up only a tiny minority of society, cannot be preserved through physical coercion alone: it can only survive as long as most people believe (falsely) that the social status quo is in their own interests, or that there is no realistic alternative to the current system, or in a situation where the oppressed classes are divided against each other (e.g., by nationalism, racism, or sexism) and fail to see their own common interest.

Considerations like these give rise to one of the best-known components of Marx's philosophical system, *historical materialism*: "[t]he mode of production of material life conditions the social, political, and intellectual life-process in general." This is the view that the foundation or "base" of society is its economic structure, which is defined by historical facts about the means of production (for example, facts about the level of agricultural sophistication, industrial technology, trade and transportation networks, and so on). As productive forces change, economic adjustments—changes to the relations of production—give rise to revolutions in society's "superstructure": the political, legal, moral, religious, and philosophical components of culture. In other words, political and social changes do not cause economic change, but the other way around: political and social systems are determined by their economic basis.

Marx's second main political-philosophical idea, in his 1852 summary, was the view that capitalism contains internal tensions which, in time, will inevitably produce the revolutionary overthrow of the bourgeoisie by the workers and usher in a "dictatorship of the proletariat." This view is, in part, the heritage of Marx's early influence by, and reaction to, the philosophical system of Hegel. For Hegel, history is a "dialectical" movement in which a thesis—a principle or idea—is challenged by its antithesis, and from this conflict there emerges a synthesis of the two, a new principle. In time this new principle meets *its* antithesis, and so on (until the ideal, final synthesis is achieved). Thus Hegel was an *idealist*, in the sense that for him the engine of world change was the clash of *Ideas*.[3] In Engels's words, Marx turned the Hegelian system on its head: instead of conflicts between ideas (in the shape of political structures) driving change, Marx held that the world contains its own internal conflicts and that political ideas actually spring up *from* this conflict rather than causing it. These built-in conflicts, the mainspring of historical change, are *economic* in nature, generated by people's attempts to satisfy their material needs—for food, clothing, shelter and so on—and their subsequent pursuit of personal wealth, within the context of their society's particular level of economic development. (Thus, Marx's system is often called *dialectical materialism*, though Marx himself never used this label.)

Marx's diagnosis of the economic conflicts driving capitalism towards revolution is complex and many-faceted. One of its central notions is that of *alienation*, which in turn arises from two other fundamental ideas in Marx's system: his theory of human nature and his "labor theory of value." According to Marx, human beings are essentially *active* and *creative* beings. Human flourishing consists in the continual transformation of one's inherent creative power into objective products, the constant *realization* of one's "subjectivity." Thus, productive activity—that is, work—is an essential component of human well-being. Marx's concern for the poor was never merely concern for their basic "material needs," such as food and housing, but was part of his view of human flourishing as being a matter of "free self-activity," of true self-expression in a social context.

The institution of private property, in Marx's view, stifles the flourishing of the human spirit. Since private property represents the products of labor as if

they were mere *things*, it alienates labor—and thus, human nature—from itself. Workers in a modern economy typically do not experience the economic goods they spend their lives producing as expressions of *themselves*, but merely as things to be sold. Furthermore, capitalism intensifies this process of alienation by treating *labor itself* as a commodity, to be bought and sold. Not only is the product of your creative activity alienated from you, but that very activity, work itself, is alienated—it is no longer *yours*, once you have sold it to an employer.

Furthermore, on Marx's analysis, the capitalist sale of goods for profit is inherently exploitative. According to the labor theory of value, which Marx took over from British economists Adam Smith (1723–1790) and David Ricardo (1772–1823) and developed into his own economic theory, the fair value of anything in a free market is determined by the amount of labor required to produce it. This has two major implications. First it means, according to Marx, that *capital* adds no value to goods over and above the labor taken to produce them, and thus the capitalist, after recompensing his workers for the value of the labor they have expended in his factories, simply appropriates the "surplus value" which is generated as profits. Although not economically "unfair," in Marx's view, this is nevertheless a form of exploitation. Second, when the labor theory of value is applied to a free market for *labor itself*, it has the implication that the working classes will necessarily (and not "unjustly," by the lights of capitalism) be forced into permanent poverty. This is because the labor-value of labor itself is simply the amount necessary to keep the worker healthy and ready to work each day—that is, the minimum amount of food and shelter necessary to sustain the worker. This therefore, no more and no less, is the labor wage in a free capitalist market, and this produces a huge class of workers with no security, no prospects, no savings, no interest in preserving the current social conditions—in short, "nothing to lose but their chains."

Finally, there is the third part of Marx's 1852 summary: communism. Marx actually had relatively little to say about the nature of a future communist society, but it is clear that he saw it as a society in which the tensions inherent in capitalism have annihilated

---

3   This is, of necessity, rather a caricature of Hegel's philosophical system. A good first introduction to Hegel's work is Charles Taylor's *Hegel* (Cambridge University Press, 1977).

themselves and produced an economic system that—because there is no private property or capital—does not generate alienation and exploitation but instead allows for genuine human flourishing as active, creative individuals, self-determined and self-sufficient within a community of other self-determined human beings.

What Is the Structure of This Reading?

The *Communist Manifesto* was written to be a statement of the ideals and aims of the Communist League. The Communist League, an umbrella organization linking the main centers of communist activity in London, Paris, Brussels, and Cologne was formed in June 1847, largely at the instigation of Marx and Engels, and was descended from a shadowy Parisian 'secret society' called the League of the Just. Most of its (few) members were German émigrés, and included several tailors, a few students, a typesetter, a cobbler, a watchmaker, a painter of miniatures, a disgraced Prussian officer, and Marx's aristocratic brother-in-law. A Congress of the League was held in London in November of 1847. To quote the eminent British historian A.J.P. Taylor:

> Marx attended in person. He listened impatiently while the worthy tailors lamented the wickedness of capitalism and preached universal brotherhood. He rose and denounced brotherhood in the name of class war. The tailors were entranced. Where they relied on sentiment, a learned man explained to them how society worked and placed the key to the future in their hands. They invited Marx to write a declaration of principles for them. He agreed.

Engels wrote a first draft—a question-and-answer brief on the main principles of communism—which was then completely rewritten by Marx (who was less than 30 years old at the time) in the space of less than six weeks.

The *Manifesto* has four sections. The first part is a history of society from the Middle Ages to the present day, presented as a succession of class struggles, and predicting the imminent victory of the proletariat over the present ruling class, the bourgeoisie. Part II

describes the position of communists with respect to the proletarian class and then goes on to reject a sequence of bourgeois objections to communism. This is followed by a brief characterization of the nature of the forthcoming communist revolution. The third part, not included here, contains an extended criticism of other forms of socialism: reactionary, bourgeois, and utopian. The final section provides a short description of communist tactics toward opposition parties and culminates with a call for proletarian unity.

Some Useful Background Information

For Marx, no external force or random accident is required to topple capitalism. He believed the overthrow of capitalism by socialism was inescapable, that it would come about because of the very nature of capitalism itself. An accurate grasp of the forces that sustain almost all social systems throughout history, Marx thought, would show that they must inevitably, as a result of internal processes, decline and be replaced by a radically different social system. However, *inevitably* does not mean *spontaneously*: the actual overthrow of existing society must be performed by a band of determined revolutionaries, joining the already existing, day-to-day class struggles and introducing revolutionary ideas to combat the ruling ideology, emphasizing the need for unity among the oppressed, and, when the time is ripe, boldly leading the revolution. The key is to follow the course of history *knowingly* by controlling the circumstances that generate it.

Some Common Misconceptions

1. Although Marx believed all the main institutions of society function to preserve the interests of the ruling class, he was not a conspiracy theorist. He did not believe, for example, that leading political figures receive covert orders from the business community. Instead, he held that institutional mechanisms press the actions of successful political figures into reflecting the long-term interests of the bourgeoisie (including the need for social and economic stability

and the suppression of revolution). One especially important mechanism for this, according to Marx, is national debt: governments depend on capitalists to renew huge but routine loans, and these financiers could throw national finances into chaos if their interests are too directly threatened. Another major influence is the pace of investment: if capitalists are displeased, the rate of investment slows and this has serious repercussions for employment rates and income levels. A third major factor is bourgeois ownership of the media (in Marx's time, mass-circulation newspapers), and their consequent ability to manipulate and mould public opinion.

2. Marx's philosophy, as it is found in his writings, is not exactly the same thing as the ideological system often called "Marxism" today. His thought has been built on and interpreted by many other writers, starting with Engels and including several prominent Russian thinkers such as Georgy Plekhanov (1856–1918) and Vladimir Ilich Lenin (1870–1924) who formulated an 'orthodox,' systematic Soviet version of Marxism, and the so-called Western Marxists such as Georg Lukács (1885–1971), Theodor Adorno (1903–1969), and Louis Althusser (1918–1990). Nor is it quite the same thing as communism. The notion of the abolition of private property dates back at least to the early Christians, and was proposed during the French Revolution by a few fringe groups whom even the revolutionaries considered beyond the pale. And of course, the modern association of Communism with the political and economic structures of China and the Soviet Union is a development which occurred after Marx's death (and it is highly unlikely that Marx would have unconditionally approved of those regimes).

How Important and Influential Is This Passage?

The *Communist Manifesto* is the most successful political pamphlet of all time: for a substantial period of the twentieth century, roughly a third of the human race was ruled by governments that claimed allegiance to the ideas expressed in it. Practically, Marx's thought is the chief inspiration for all modern forms of social radicalism. Intellectually, according to the *Blackwell Encyclopedia of Political Thought*, "[o]ver the whole range of the social sciences, Marx has proved probably the most influential figure of the twentieth century." Marx's central ideas—"historical materialism," the labor theory of value, the notion of class struggle—have had an inestimable influence on the development of contemporary economics, history, and sociology, even when they are not widely accepted by most Western intellectuals today.

Suggestions for Critical Reflection

1. "The history of all hitherto existing society is the history of class struggles." What role does this resounding phrase have in Marx's argument? Is it a *true* claim? (How easy would it be for professional historians to show it to be either true or false?) If its historical truth is open to question, how serious a problem is this for Marx's views?

2. Marx's critique of the bourgeoisie has both positive and negative elements. For example, he notes that they have "accomplished wonders far surpassing ... Gothic cathedrals," but also claims the bourgeois have reduced the family to "a mere money relation." What is Marx's overall judgment of the bourgeoisie? How far do you agree with it?

3. "The executive of the modern State is but a committee for managing the common affairs of the whole bourgeoisie." How does Marx support this claim? What, exactly, do you think he means by it? What implications does it have, if true?

4. Marx suggests modern bourgeois society contains within it the seeds of its own self-destruction (as did feudal society before it). How compelling are his arguments for this claim?

5. Marx says that, for the proletariat, "[l]aw, morality, religion, are to him so many bourgeois prejudices, behind which lurk in ambush just as many bourgeois interests." What are the im-

plications of this statement? Why do you think Marx says it, and do you think he is justified in doing so?

6. Marx addresses the criticism of communism which says that, if private property and personal wealth are abolished, people will have no incentive to be productive at all "and universal laziness will overtake us." How adequately do you think Marx handles this objection?

7. What do you make of Marx's list of ten components for the dictatorship of the proletariat? How radical or unreasonable do they seem today? How likely would they be to result in the elimination of private property and the emancipation of the proletariat?

8. What, if anything, do historical developments since Marx's death—in particular, the rise and fall of the Soviet Union, and the failure of capitalism to end in revolution in the democratic West—show about the validity of his philosophical thought?

Suggestions for Further Reading

Marx's theoretical masterwork is *Capital*, a massive, detailed and rigorous critical study of the capitalist form of life, a project which involves Marx in descriptions of his views of science, culture, art, religion, and knowledge. (A single-volume version, abridged by David McLellan, is available from Oxford University Press, 2000.) Two shorter works, *Wage-Labour and Capital* and *Value, Price and Profit* were written as lectures to workers and present Marx's critique of capitalist society in simpler terms, while his *Contribution to a Critique of Political Economy* includes a succinct statement of historical materialism in the Preface. Marx's main political writings include *The Eighteenth Brumaire of Louis Napoleon* and *The Civil War in France*, while perhaps his most purely "philosophical" book is *The German Ideology*, though it is not a particularly accessible work for modern readers. A good way to approach Marx's voluminous writings is to use an edited volume of selections from his works. Three of the best such anthologies are *Karl Marx: Selected Writings*, ed. David McLellan (Oxford University Press, 2000), *The Marx-Engels Reader*, ed. Robert Tucker (W.W. Norton,

1978), and *Karl Marx: Selected Writings*, ed. Lawrence Simon (Hackett, 1994).

There are several available editions of *The Communist Manifesto*. The Penguin edition, edited by A.J.P. Taylor (Penguin, 1967), contains a valuable, and entertainingly astringent, introduction. *The Communist Manifesto* edited by John Toews (Bedford/St. Martin's, 1999), contains lots of interesting and useful background material, and there is also a Norton Critical Edition of the *Manifesto*, edited by Frederic Bender (W.W. Norton, 1988).

A good short biography of Marx is Werner Blumenberg's *Karl Marx: An Illustrated Biography* (Verso, 1998); worthwhile longer studies include Isaiah Berlin, *Karl Marx: His Life and Environment* (Oxford University Press, 1978) and David McLellan, *Karl Marx: His Life and Thought* (Harper & Row, 1977).

As one might expect, given Marx's historical importance, there are huge numbers of books about his thought. The reader needs to be somewhat judicious in choosing secondary material, however, as a significant number of works are of relatively low philosophical quality or merely uncritical Marxian apologetics. Though encompassing diverse philosophical viewpoints, the following books are all reliable and valuable: Shlomo Avineri, *The Social and Political Thought of Karl Marx* (Cambridge University Press, 1970); Ball and Farr (eds.), *After Marx* (Cambridge University Press, 1984); Allen Buchanan, *Marx and Justice* (Rowman & Littlefield, 1982); Terrell Carver, *Marx's Social Theory* (Oxford University Press, 1982); G.A. Cohen, *Karl Marx's Theory of History: A Defense* (Princeton University Press, 1978); Jon Elster, *Making Sense of Marx* (Cambridge University Press, 1985); Jon Elster, *An Introduction to Karl Marx* (Cambridge University Press, 1986); Michael Evans, *Karl Marx* (Allen & Unwin, 1975); Richard Heilbroner, *Marxism: For and Against* (Norton, 1980); George Lichtheim, *Marxism: An Historical and Critical Study* (Praeger, 1967); Steven Lukes, *Marxism and Morality* (Oxford University Press, 1984); David McLellan, *The Thought of Karl Marx: An Introduction* (Pan Books, 1995); Richard Miller, *Analyzing Marx: Morality, Power and History* (Princeton University Press, 1984); R.G. Peffer, *Marxism, Morality, and Social Justice* (Princeton University Press, 1990); John Plamenatz, *Karl Marx's Philosophy of Man* (Oxford University Press,

1975); John Roemer (ed.), *Analytical Marxism* (Cambridge University Press, 1986); Richard Schmitt, *Introduction to Marx and Engels* (Westview Press, 1997); Robert Paul Wolff, *Understanding Marx* (Princeton University Press, 1984); and Allen Wood, *Karl Marx* (Routledge & Kegan Paul, 1981).

from *The Communist Manifesto*[4]

A spectre is haunting Europe—the spectre of Communism. All the Powers of old Europe have entered into a holy alliance to exorcise this spectre: Pope and Tsar, Metternich and Guizot,[5] French Radicals and German police-spies.

Where is the party in opposition that has not been decried as Communistic by its opponents in power? Where the Opposition that has not hurled back the branding reproach of Communism, against the more advanced opposition parties, as well as against its reactionary adversaries?

Two things result from this fact:

I.   Communism is already acknowledged by all European Powers to be itself a Power.

II. It is high time that Communists should openly, in the face of the whole world, publish their views, their aims, their tendencies, and meet this nursery tale of the Spectre of Communism with a Manifesto of the party itself.

To this end, Communists of various nationalities have assembled in London and sketched the follow-

ing Manifesto, to be published in the English, French, German, Italian, Flemish and Danish languages.[6]

I. Bourgeois and Proletarians[7]

The history of all hitherto existing society[8] is the history of class struggles.

Freeman and slave, patrician and plebeian, lord and serf, guild-master[9] and journeyman,[10] in a word, op-

---

4   *Manifest der Kommunistischen Partei* was first published, in German, in London in 1848. The text reprinted here is the English translation made in 1888 by Samuel Moore, which was edited and authorized by Friedrich Engels. The author's notes in the text are those made by Engels in 1888.

5   Prince Klemens Metternich (1773–1859) was the conservative chancellor of the Austrian empire; he was the dominant figure in European politics at this time, but was soon to be driven from power by the Revolutions of 1848. François Guizot (1787–1874) was the liberal moderate premier of France until he also was overthrown in the political turbulence of 1848.

6   In the event, only one translation—into Swedish—was published in 1848–49, and widespread translation and reprinting of the *Manifesto* did not begin until after 1870.

7   [Author's note] By bourgeoisie is meant the class of modern Capitalists, owners of the means of social production and employers of wage-labour. By proletariat, the class of modern wage-labourers who, having no means of production of their own, are reduced to selling their labour-power in order to live.

8   [Author's note] That is, all *written* history. In 1847, the pre-history of society, the social organization existing previous to recorded history, was all but unknown. Since then, [August von] Haxthausen discovered common ownership of land in Russia, [Georg Ludwig von] Maurer proved it to be the social foundation from which all Teutonic races started in history, and by and by village communities were found to be, or to have been the primitive form of society everywhere from India to Ireland. The inner organization of this primitive Communistic society was laid bare, in its typical form, by [Lewis Henry] Morgan's crowning discovery of the true nature of the *gens* and its relation to the *tribe*. With the dissolution of these primaeval communities society begins to be differentiated into separate and finally antagonistic classes. I have attempted to retrace this dissolution in *Der Ursprung der Familie, des Privateigenthums und des Staats* [*The Origins of the Family, Private Property and the State*], second edition, Stuttgart, 1886.

9   [Author's note] Guild-master, that is, a full member of a guild, a master within, not a head of a guild.

10 A patrician was a member of one of the noble families of the ancient Roman republic, while plebeians were the common people of Rome. The terminology was also used in later ages (e.g., in the medieval free cities of Italy and Germany) to mark a similar distinction. A

pressor and oppressed, stood in constant opposition to one another, carried on an uninterrupted, now hidden, now open fight, a fight that each time ended, either in a revolutionary re-constitution of society at large, or in the common ruin of the contending classes.

In the earlier epochs of history, we find almost everywhere a complicated arrangement of society into various orders, a manifold gradation of social rank. In ancient Rome we have patricians, knights, plebeians, slaves; in the Middle Ages, feudal lords, vassals,[11] guild-masters, journeymen, apprentices, serfs; in almost all of these classes, again, subordinate gradations.

The modern bourgeois society that has sprouted from the ruins of feudal society has not done away with class antagonisms. It has but established new classes, new conditions of oppression, new forms of struggle in place of the old ones.

Our epoch, the epoch of the bourgeoisie, possesses, however, this distinctive feature: it has simplified class antagonisms. Society as a whole is more and more splitting up into two great hostile camps, into two great classes directly facing each other: Bourgeoisie and Proletariat.

From the serfs of the Middle Ages sprang the chartered burghers[12] of the earliest towns. From these burgesses the first elements of the bourgeoisie were developed.

The discovery of America, the rounding of the Cape,[13] opened up fresh ground for the rising bourgeoisie. The East-Indian and Chinese markets, the colonisation of America, trade with the colonies, the increase in the means of exchange and in commodities generally, gave to commerce, to navigation, to industry, an impulse never before known, and thereby, to the revolutionary element in the tottering feudal society, a rapid development.

The feudal system of industry, under which industrial production was monopolized by closed guilds, now no longer sufficed for the growing wants of the new markets. The manufacturing system took its place. The guild-masters were pushed on one side by the manufacturing middle class; division of labour between the different corporate guilds vanished in the face of division of labour in each single workshop.

Meantime the markets kept ever growing, the demand ever rising. Even manufacture no longer sufficed. Thereupon, steam and machinery revolutionized industrial production. The place of manufacture was taken by the giant, Modern Industry, the place of the industrial middle class, by industrial millionaires, the leaders of whole industrial armies, the modern bourgeois.

Modern industry has established the world market, for which the discovery of America paved the way. This market has given an immense development to commerce, to navigation, to communication by land. This development has, in its turn, reacted on the extension of industry; and in proportion as industry, commerce, navigation, railways extended, in the same proportion the bourgeoisie developed, increased its capital, and pushed into the background every class handed down from the Middle Ages.

We see, therefore, how the modern bourgeoisie is itself the product of a long course of development, of a series of revolutions in the modes of production and of exchange.

Each step in the development of the bourgeoisie was accompanied by a corresponding political advance in that class. An oppressed class under the sway of the feudal nobility, an armed and self-governing association in the medieval commune;[14] here inde-

---

serf was a member of a particular feudal class of people in Europe, those bound by law to a particular piece of land and, like the land, owned by a lord. A journeyman is a craftsman who has completed his apprenticeship and is employed at a fixed wage by a master artisan, but who is not yet allowed (by his guild) to work for himself.

11   A vassal received land and protection from a feudal lord, in return for homage and allegiance.

12   Someone who is a citizen of a town in virtue of being a full member of a legally chartered trade association or guild.

13   The Cape of Good Hope, at the southern tip of Africa.

---

14   [Author's note] "Commune" was the name taken, in France, by the nascent towns even before they had conquered from their feudal lords and masters local self-government and political rights as the "Third Estate." Generally speaking, for the economical development

pendent urban republic (as in Italy and Germany), there taxable "third estate" of the monarchy (as in France), afterwards, in the period of manufacture proper, serving either the semi-feudal or the absolute monarchy as a counterpoise against the nobility, and, in fact, cornerstone of the great monarchies in general, the bourgeoisie has at last, since the establishment of Modern Industry and of the world market, conquered for itself, in the modern representative State,[15] exclusive political sway. The executive of the modern State is but a committee for managing the common affairs of the whole bourgeoisie.

The bourgeoisie, historically, has played a most revolutionary part.

The bourgeoisie, wherever it has got the upper hand, has put an end to all feudal, patriarchal, idyllic relations. It has pitilessly torn asunder the motley feudal ties that bound man to his "natural superiors," and has left no other nexus between man and man than naked self-interest, than callous "cash payment." It has drowned out the most heavenly ecstasies of religious fervour, of chivalrous enthusiasm, of philistine sentimentalism, in the icy water of egotistical calculation. It has resolved personal worth into exchange value, and in place of the numberless indefeasible chartered freedoms, has set up that single, unconscionable freedom—Free Trade. In one word, for exploitation, veiled by religious and political illusions, it has substituted naked, shameless, direct, brutal exploitation.

The bourgeoisie has stripped of its halo every occupation hitherto honoured and looked up to with reverent awe. It has converted the physician, the lawyer, the priest, the poet, the man of science, into its paid wage-labourers.

The bourgeoisie has torn away from the family its sentimental veil, and has reduced the family relation to a mere money relation.

The bourgeoisie has disclosed how it came to pass that the brutal display of vigour in the Middle Ages, which Reactionists so much admire, found its fitting complement in the most slothful indolence. It has been the first to show what man's activity can bring about. It has accomplished wonders far surpassing Egyptian pyramids, Roman aqueducts, and Gothic cathedrals; it has conducted expeditions that put in the shade all former Exoduses of nations and crusades.

The bourgeoisie cannot exist without constantly revolutionizing the instruments of production, and thereby the relations of production, and with them the whole relations of society. Conservation of the old modes of production in unaltered form, was, on the contrary, the first condition of existence for all earlier industrial classes. Constant revolutionizing of production, uninterrupted disturbance of all social conditions, everlasting uncertainty and agitation distinguish the bourgeois epoch from all earlier ones. All fixed, fast-frozen relations, with their train of ancient and venerable prejudices and opinions, are swept away, all new-formed ones become antiquated before they can ossify. All that is solid melts into air, all that is holy is profaned, and man is at last compelled to face with sober senses, his real condition of life and his relations with his kind.

The need of a constantly expanding market for its products chases the bourgeoisie over the entire surface of the globe. It must nestle everywhere, settle everywhere, establish connections everywhere.

The bourgeoisie has, through its exploitation of the world market, given a cosmopolitan character to production and consumption in every country. To the great chagrin of Reactionists, it has drawn from under the feet of industry the national ground on which it stood. All old-established national industries have been destroyed or are daily being destroyed. They are dislodged by new industries, whose introduction becomes a life and death question for all civilized nations, by industries that no longer work up indigenous raw material, but raw material drawn from the remotest zones; industries whose products are consumed, not only at home, but in every quarter of the globe. In place of the old wants, satisfied by the production of the country, we find new wants, requiring for their satisfaction the products of distant lands and climes.

---

of the bourgeoisie, England is here taken as the typical country; for its political development, France.

15 A modern, rather than a feudal, state: one whose institutions are based on the political representation of *individuals*, rather than of social corporations (such as towns or guilds) or estates (such as the nobility or the clergy).

In place of the old local and national seclusion and self-sufficiency, we have intercourse in every direction, universal inter-dependence of nations. And as in material, so also in intellectual production. The intellectual creations of individual nations become common property. National one-sidedness and narrow-mindedness become more and more impossible, and from the numerous national and local literatures, there arises a world literature.

The bourgeoisie, by the rapid improvement of all instruments of production, by the immensely facilitated means of communication, draws all, even the most barbarian, nations into civilization. The cheap prices of its commodities are the heavy artillery with which it batters down all Chinese walls, with which it forces the barbarians' intensely obstinate hatred of foreigners to capitulate.[16] It compels all nations, on pain of extinction, to adopt the bourgeois mode of production; it compels them to introduce what it calls civilization into their midst, *i.e.*, to become bourgeois themselves. In one word, it creates a world after its own image.

The bourgeoisie has subjected the country to the rule of the towns. It has created enormous cities, has greatly increased the urban population as compared with the rural, and has thus rescued a considerable part of the population from the idiocy of rural life. Just as it has made the country dependent on the towns, so it has made barbarian and semi-barbarian countries dependent on the civilized ones, nations of peasants on nations of bourgeois, the East on the West.

The bourgeoisie keeps more and more doing away with the scattered state of the population, of the means of production, and of property. It has agglomerated population, centralized means of production, and has concentrated property in a few hands. The necessary consequence of this was political centralization. Independent, or but loosely connected provinces with separate interests, laws, governments and systems of taxation, became lumped together into one nation, with one government, one code of laws, one national class-interest, one frontier, and one customs-tariff.

The bourgeoisie, during its rule of scarce one hundred years, has created more massive and more colossal productive forces than have all preceding generations together. Subjection of Nature's forces to man, machinery, application of chemistry to industry and agriculture, steam-navigation, railways, electric telegraphs, clearing of whole continents for cultivation, canalization of rivers, whole populations conjured out of the ground—what earlier century had even a presentiment that such productive forces slumbered in the lap of social labour?

We see then: the means of production and of exchange, on whose foundation the bourgeoisie built itself up, were generated in feudal society. At a certain stage in the development of these means of production and of exchange, the conditions under which feudal society produced and exchanged, the feudal organization of agriculture and manufacturing industry, in one word, the feudal relations of property became no longer compatible with the already developed productive forces; they became so many fetters. They had to be burst asunder; they were burst asunder.

Into their place stepped free competition, accompanied by a social and political constitution adapted in it, and the economical and political sway of the bourgeois class.

A similar movement is going on before our own eyes. Modern bourgeois society, with its relations of production, of exchange and of property, a society that has conjured up such gigantic means of production and of exchange, is like the sorcerer who is no longer able to control the powers of the nether world whom he has called up by his spells. For many a decade past the history of industry and commerce is but the history of the revolt of modern productive forces against modern conditions of production, against the property relations that are the conditions for the existence of the bourgeois and of its rule. It is enough to mention the commercial crises that by their periodical return put on its trial, each time more threateningly, the existence of the entire bourgeois society. In these crises a great part not only of the existing products, but also of the previously created productive forces, are periodically destroyed. In these crises there breaks

---

16   A reference to the first Opium War in China (1839–1843), which forced the Chinese to cede Hong Kong to the British and to open five of their ports to foreign trade.

out an epidemic that, in all earlier epochs, would have seemed an absurdity—the epidemic of over-production.[17] Society suddenly finds itself put back into a state of momentary barbarism; it appears as if a famine, a universal war of devastation had cut off the supply of every means of subsistence; industry and commerce seem to be destroyed; and why? Because there is too much civilization, too much means of subsistence, too much industry, too much commerce. The productive forces at the disposal of society no longer tend to further the development of the conditions of bourgeois property; on the contrary, they have become too powerful for these conditions, by which they are fettered, and so soon as they overcome these fetters, they bring disorder into the whole of bourgeois society, endanger the existence of bourgeois property. The conditions of bourgeois society are too narrow to comprise the wealth created by them. And how does the bourgeoisie get over these crises? On the one hand by enforced destruction of a mass of productive forces; on the other, by the conquest of new markets, and by the more thorough exploitation of the old ones. That is to say, by paving the way for more extensive and more destructive crises, and by diminishing the means whereby crises are prevented.

The weapons with which the bourgeoisie felled feudalism to the ground are now turned against the bourgeoisie itself.

But not only has the bourgeoisie forged the weapons that bring death to itself; it has also called into existence the men who are to wield those weapons—the modern working class—the proletarians.

In proportion as the bourgeoisie, *i.e.*, capital, is developed, in the same proportion is the proletariat, the modern working class, developed—a class of labourers, who live only so long as they find work, and who find work only so long as their labour increases capital. These labourers, who must sell themselves piecemeal, are a commodity, like every other article of commerce, and are consequently exposed to all the vicissitudes of competition, to all the fluctuations of the market.

Owing to the extensive use of machinery and to division of labour, the work of the proletarians has lost all individual character, and, consequently, all charm for the workman. He becomes an appendage of the machine, and it is only the most simple, most monotonous, and most easily acquired knack, that is required of him. Hence, the cost of production of a workman is restricted, almost entirely, to the means of subsistence that he requires for maintenance, and for the propagation of his race. But the price of a commodity, and therefore also of labour, is equal to its cost of production. In proportion, therefore, as the repulsiveness of the work increases, the wage decreases. Nay more, in proportion as the use of machinery and division of labour increases, in the same proportion the burden of toil also increases, whether by prolongation of the working hours, by the increase of the work exacted in a given time, or by increased speed of the machinery, etc.

Modern industry has converted the little workshop of the patriarchal master into the great factory of the industrial capitalist. Masses of labourers, crowded into the factory, are organized like soldiers. As privates of the industrial army they are placed under the command of a perfect hierarchy of officers and sergeants. Not only are they slaves of the bourgeois class, and of the bourgeois State; they are daily and hourly enslaved by the machine, by the overlooker, and, above all, by the individual bourgeois manufacturer himself. The more openly this despotism proclaims gain to be its end and aim, the more petty, the more hateful and the more embittering it is.

The less the skill and exertion of strength implied in manual labour, in other words, the more modern

---

17   Such crises occurred regularly in advanced capitalist economies from 1825 until 1939. Periodically, as more and more companies joined a particular industry, firms found themselves facing a glut of their products on the market. This over-supply depressed prices below expected profit levels, and so companies suddenly began to cut back production. Each time, these cutbacks started a vicious chain reaction, as suppliers were also forced to make cutbacks, which increased the unemployment rate, which reduced consumer spending and so increased over-supply, which depressed prices still further, and so on. At the height of the Great Depression of the 1930s, the worst such crisis, unemployment reached 25% in the United States. Marx provided a sophisticated analysis of such crises in *Capital*.

industry becomes developed, the more is the labour of men superseded by that of women. Differences of age and sex have no longer any distinctive social validity for the working class. All are instruments of labour, more or less expensive to use, according to their age and sex.

No sooner is the exploitation of the labourer by the manufacturer, so far, at an end, and he receives his wages in cash, than he is set upon by the other portions of the bourgeoisie, the landlord, the shopkeeper, the pawnbroker, etc.

The lower strata of the middle class—the small tradespeople, shopkeepers, and retired tradesmen generally, the handicraftsmen and peasants—all these sink gradually into the proletariat, partly because their diminutive capital does not suffice for the scale on which Modern Industry is carried on, and is swamped in the competition with the large capitalists, partly because their specialized skill is rendered worthless by new methods of production. Thus, the proletariat is recruited from all classes of the population.

The proletariat goes through various stages of development. With its birth begins its struggle with the bourgeoisie. At first, the contest is carried on by individual labourers, then by the workpeople of a factory, then by the operatives of one trade, in one locality, against the individual bourgeois who directly exploits them. They direct their attacks not against the bourgeois condition of production, but against the instruments of production themselves; they destroy imported wares that compete with their labour, they smash to pieces machinery, they set factories ablaze, they seek to restore by force the vanished status of the workman of the Middle Ages.

At this stage the labourers still form an incoherent mass scattered over the whole country, and broken up by their mutual competition. If anywhere they unite to form more compact bodies, this is not yet the consequence of their own active union, but of the union of the bourgeoisie, which class, in order to attain its own political ends, is compelled to set the whole proletariat in motion, and is moreover yet, for a time, able to do so. At this stage, therefore, the proletarians do not fight their enemies, but the enemies of their enemies, the remnants of absolute monarchy, the landowners,

the non-industrial bourgeois, the petty bourgeoisie.[18] Thus, the whole historical movement is concentrated in the hands of the bourgeoisie; every victory so obtained is a victory for the bourgeoisie.

But with the development of industry, the proletariat not only increases in number; it becomes concentrated in greater masses, its strength grows, and it feels that strength more. The various interests and conditions of life within the ranks of the proletariat are more and more equalized, in proportion as machinery obliterates all distinctions of labour, and nearly everywhere reduces wages to the same low level. The growing competition among the bourgeois, and the resulting commercial crises, make the wages of the workers ever more fluctuating. The increasing improvement of machinery, ever more rapidly developing, makes their livelihood more and more precarious; the collisions between individual workmen and individual bourgeois take more and more the character of collisions between two classes. Thereupon, the workers begin to form combinations (Trades' Unions) against the bourgeois; they club together in order to keep up the rate of wages; they found permanent associations in order to make provision beforehand for these occasional revolts. Here and there the contest breaks out into riots.

Now and then the workers are victorious, but only for a time. The real fruit of their battles lies, not in the immediate result, but in the ever expanding union of the workers. This union is helped on by the improved means of communication that are created by modern industry and that place the workers of different localities in contact with one another. It was just this contact that was needed to centralize the numerous local struggles, all of the same character, into one national struggle between classes. But every class struggle is a political struggle. And that union, to attain which the burghers of the Middle Ages, with their miserable highways, required centuries, the modern proletarian, thanks to railways, achieve in a few years.

18　The petty bourgeoisie, for Marx, are those who control means of production (like the bourgeoisie) but work them with their own labor (like the proletariat): for example, independent shopkeepers or small farmers.

This organization of the proletarians into a class, and consequently into a political party, is continually being upset again by the competition between the workers themselves. But it ever rises up again, stronger, firmer, mightier. It compels legislative recognition of particular interests of the workers, by taking advantage of the divisions among the bourgeoisie itself. Thus, the ten-hours' bill in England was carried.[19]

Altogether collisions between the classes of the old society further, in many ways, the course of development of the proletariat. The bourgeoisie finds itself involved in a constant battle. At first with the aristocracy; later on, with those portions of the bourgeoisie itself, whose interests have become antagonistic to the progress of industry; at all times, with the bourgeoisie of foreign countries. In all these battles it sees itself compelled to appeal to the proletariat, to ask for its help, and thus, to drag it into the political arena. The bourgeoisie itself, therefore, supplies the proletariat with its own elements of political and general education, in other words, it furnishes the proletariat with weapons for fighting the bourgeoisie.

Further, as we have already seen, entire sections of the ruling class are, by the advance of industry, precipitated into the proletariat, or are at least threatened in their conditions of existence. These also supply the proletariat with fresh elements of enlightenment and progress.

Finally, in times when the class struggle nears the decisive hour, the progress of dissolution going on within the ruling class, in fact within the whole range of old society, assumes such a violent, glaring character, that a small section of the ruling class cuts itself adrift, and joins the revolutionary class, the class that holds the future in its hands. Just as, therefore, at an earlier period, a section of the nobility went over to the bourgeoisie, so now a portion of the bourgeoisie goes over to the proletariat, and in particular, a portion of the bourgeois ideologists, who have raised themselves to the level of comprehending theoretically the historical movement as a whole.

Of all the classes that stand face to face with the bourgeoisie today, the proletariat alone is a genuinely revolutionary class. The other classes decay and finally disappear in the face of Modern Industry; the proletariat is its special and essential product.

The lower middle class, the small manufacturer, the shopkeeper, the artisan, the peasant, all these fight against the bourgeoisie, to save from extinction their existence as fractions of the middle class. They are therefore not revolutionary, but conservative. Nay more, they are reactionary, for they try to roll back the wheel of history. If by chance they are revolutionary, they are only so in view of their impending transfer into the proletariat, they thus defend not their present, but their future interests, they desert their own standpoint to place themselves at that of the proletariat.

The "dangerous class," the social scum,[20] that passively rotting mass thrown off by the lowest layers of the old society may, here and there, be swept into the movement by a proletarian revolution; its conditions of life, however, prepare it far more for the part of a bribed tool of reactionary intrigue.

In the condition of the proletariat, those of old society at large are already virtually swamped. The proletarian is without property; his relation to his wife and children has no longer anything in common with the bourgeois family relations; modern industrial labour, modern subjection to capital, the same in England as in France, in America as in Germany, has stripped him of every trace of national character. Law, morality, religion, are to him so many bourgeois prejudices, behind which lurk in ambush just as many bourgeois interests.

All the preceding classes that got the upper hand sought to fortify their already acquired status by subjecting society at large to their conditions of appropriation. The proletarians cannot become masters of the productive forces of society, except by abolishing their own previous mode of appropriation, and thereby also every other previous mode of appropriation. They

---

19 This law—part of the 1847 Factory Act—limited the daily working hours of women and children to 58 hours a week. It was highly controversial, and was passed by Parliament only because conservative "Old England" landowners opposed the interests of the ever-more-powerful industrialists and mill owners.

20 The original German word here is *Lumpenproletariat*, literally, "proletariat in rags."

have nothing of their own to secure and to fortify; their mission is to destroy all previous securities for, and insurances of, individual property.

All previous historical movements were movements of minorities, or in the interest of minorities. The proletarian movement is the self-conscious, independent movement of the immense majority, in the interest of the immense majority. The proletariat, the lowest stratum of our present society, cannot stir, cannot raise itself up, without the whole superincumbent strata of official society being sprung into the air.

Though not in substance, yet in form, the struggle of the proletariat with the bourgeoisie is at first a national struggle. The proletariat of each country must, of course, first of all settle matters with its own bourgeoisie.

In depicting the most general phases of the development of the proletariat, we traced the more or less veiled civil war, raging within existing society, up to the point where that war breaks out into open revolution, and where the violent overthrow of the bourgeoisie lays the foundation for the sway of the proletariat.

Hitherto, every form of society has been based, as we have already seen, on the antagonism of oppressing and oppressed classes. But in order to oppress a class, certain conditions must be assured to it under which it can, at least, continue its slavish existence. The serf, in the period of serfdom, raised himself to membership in the commune, just as the petty bourgeois, under the yoke of the feudal absolutism, managed to develop into a bourgeois. The modern labourer, on the contrary, instead of rising with the progress of industry, sinks deeper and deeper below the conditions of existence of his own class. He becomes a pauper, and pauperism develops more rapidly than population and wealth. And here it becomes evident that the bourgeoisie is unfit any longer to be the ruling class in society, and to impose its conditions of existence upon society as an over-riding law. It is unfit to rule because it is incompetent to assure an existence to its slave within his slavery, because it cannot help letting him sink into such a state, that it has to feed him, instead of being fed by him. Society can no longer live under this bourgeoisie, in other words, its existence is no longer compatible with society.

The essential condition for the existence, and for the sway of the bourgeois class, is the formation and augmentation of capital; the condition for capital is wage-labour. Wage-labour rests exclusively on competition between the labourers. The advance of industry, whose involuntary promoter is the bourgeoisie, replaces the isolation of the labourers, due to competition, by their revolutionary combination, due to association. The development of Modern Industry, therefore, cuts from under its feet the very foundation on which the bourgeoisie produces and appropriates products. What the bourgeoisie, therefore, produces, above all, is its own grave-diggers. Its fall and the victory of the proletariat are equally inevitable.

II. Proletarians and Communists

In what relation do the Communists stand to the proletarians as a whole?

The Communists do not form a separate party opposed to the other working-class parties.

They have no interests separate and apart from those of the proletariat as a whole.

They do not set up any sectarian principles of their own, by which to shape and mold the proletarian movement.

The Communists are distinguished from the other working-class parties by this only: (1) In the national struggles of the proletarians of the different countries, they point out and bring to the front the common interests of the entire proletariat, independently of all nationality. (2) In the various stages of development which the struggle of the working class against the bourgeoisie has to pass through, they always and everywhere represent the interests of the movement as a whole.

The Communists, therefore, are on the one hand, practically, the most advanced and resolute section of the working-class parties of every country, that section which pushes forward all others; on the other hand, theoretically, they have over the great mass of the proletariat the advantage of clearly understanding the line of march, the conditions, and the ultimate general results of the proletarian movement.

The immediate aim of the Communists is the same as that of all other proletarian parties: formation of the proletariat into a class, overthrow of the bourgeois supremacy, conquest of political power by the proletariat.

The theoretical conclusions of the Communists are in no way based on ideas or principles that have been invented, or discovered, by this or that would-be universal reformer.

They merely express, in general terms, actual relations springing from an existing class struggle, from a historical movement going on under our very eyes. The abolition of existing property relations is not at all a distinctive feature of Communism.

All property relations in the past have continually been subject to historical change consequent upon the change in historical conditions.

The French Revolution, for example, abolished feudal property in favour of bourgeois property.

The distinguishing feature of Communism is not the abolition of property generally, but the abolition of bourgeois property. But modern bourgeois private property is the final and most complete expression of the system of producing and appropriating products, that is based on class antagonisms, on the exploitation of the many by the few.

In this sense, the theory of the Communists may be summed up in the single sentence: Abolition of private property.

We Communists have been reproached with the desire of abolishing the right of personally acquiring property as the fruit of a man's own labour, which property is alleged to be the groundwork of all personal freedom, activity and independence.

Hard-won, self-acquired, self-earned property! Do you mean the property of the petty artisan and of the small peasant, a form of property that preceded the bourgeois form? There is no need to abolish that; the development of industry has to a great extent already destroyed it, and is still destroying it daily.

Or do you mean the modern bourgeois private property?

But does wage-labour create any property for the labourer? Not a bit. It creates capital, *i.e.*, that kind of property which exploits wage-labour, and which cannot increase except upon conditions of begetting a new supply of wage-labour for fresh exploitation. Property, in its present form, is based on the antago-

nism of capital and wage-labour. Let us examine both sides of this antagonism.

To be a capitalist, is to have not only a purely personal, but a social *status* in production. Capital is a collective product, and only by the united action of many members, nay, in the last resort, only by the united action of all members of society, can it be set in motion.

Capital is, therefore, not a personal, it is a social power.

When, therefore, capital is converted into common property, into the property of all members of society, personal property is not thereby transformed into social property. It is only the social character of the property that is changed. It loses its class character.

Let us now take wage-labour.

The average price of wage-labour is the minimum wage, *i.e.*, that quantum of the means of subsistence, which is absolutely requisite to keep the labourer in bare existence as a labourer. What, therefore, the wage-labourer appropriates by means of his labour, merely suffices to prolong and reproduce a bare existence. We by no means intend to abolish this personal appropriation of the products of labour, an appropriation that is made for the maintenance and reproduction of human life, and that leaves no surplus wherewith to command the labour of others. All that we want to do away with is the miserable character of this appropriation, under which the labourer lives merely to increase capital, and is allowed to live only in so far as the interest of the ruling class requires it.

In bourgeois society, living labour is but a means to increase accumulated labour. In Communist society, accumulated labour is but a means to widen, to enrich, to promote the existence of the labourer.

In bourgeois society, therefore, the past dominates the present; in Communist society, the present dominates the past. In bourgeois society capital is independent and has individuality, while the living person is dependent and has no individuality.

And the abolition of this state of things is called by the bourgeois abolition of individuality and freedom! And rightly so. The abolition of bourgeois individuality, bourgeois independence, and bourgeois freedom is undoubtedly aimed at.

By freedom is meant, under the present bourgeois conditions of production, free trade, free selling and buying.

But if selling and buying disappears, free selling and buying disappears also. This talk about free selling and buying, and all the other "brave words" of our bourgeoisie about freedom in general, have a meaning, if any, only in contrast with restricted selling and buying, with the fettered traders of the Middle Ages, but have no meaning when opposed to the Communistic abolition of buying and selling, or the bourgeois conditions of production, and of the bourgeoisie itself.

You are horrified at our intending to do away with private property. But in your existing society, private property is already done away with for nine-tenths of the population; its existence for the few is solely due to its non-existence in the hands of those nine-tenths. You reproach us, therefore, with intending to do away with a form of property, the necessary condition for whose existence is the non-existence of any property for the immense majority of society.

In one word, you reproach us with intending to do away with your property. Precisely so; that is just what we intend.

From the moment when labour can no longer be converted into capital, money, or rent, into a social power capable of being monopolized, *i.e.*, from the moment when individual property can no longer be transformed into bourgeois property, into capital, from that moment, you say, individuality vanishes.

You must, therefore, confess that by "individual" you mean no other person than the bourgeois, than the middle-class owner of property. This person must, indeed, be swept out of the way, and made impossible.

Communism deprives no man of the power to appropriate the products of society; all that it does is to deprive him of the power to subjugate the labour of others by means of such appropriation.

It has been objected that upon the abolition of private property all work will cease, and universal laziness will overtake us.

According to this, bourgeois society ought long ago to have gone to the dogs through sheer idleness; for those who work, acquire nothing, and those who acquire anything, do not work. The whole of this objection is but another expression of the tautology: that there can no longer be any wage-labour when there is no longer any capital.

All objections urged against the Communistic mode of producing and appropriating material products, have, in the same way, been urged against the Communistic mode of producing and appropriating intellectual products. Just as, to the bourgeois, the disappearance of class property is the disappearance of production itself, so the disappearance of class culture is to him identical with the disappearance of all culture.

That culture, the loss of which he laments, is, for the enormous majority, a mere training to act as a machine.

But don't wrangle with us so long as you apply, to our intended abolition of bourgeois property, the standard of your bourgeois notions of freedom, culture, law, etc. Your very ideas are but the outgrowth of the conditions of your bourgeois production and bourgeois property, just as your jurisprudence is but the will of your class made into a law for all, a will, whose essential character and direction are determined by the economical conditions of existence of your class.

The selfish misconception that induces you to transform into eternal laws of nature and of reason, the social forms springing from your present mode of production and form of property—historical relations that rise and disappear in the progress of production—this misconception you share with every ruling class that has preceded you. What you see clearly in the case of ancient property, what you admit in the case of feudal property, you are of course forbidden to admit in the case of your own bourgeois form of property.

Abolition of the family! Even the most radical flare up at this infamous proposal of the Communists.

On what foundation is the present family, the bourgeois family, based? On capital, on private gain. In its completely developed form this family exists only among the bourgeoisie. But this state of things finds its complement in the practical absence of the family among proletarians, and in public prostitution.

The bourgeois family will vanish as a matter of course when its complement vanishes, and both will vanish with the vanishing of capital.

Do you charge us with wanting to stop the exploitation of children by their parents? To this crime we plead guilty.

But, you will say, we destroy the most hallowed of relations, when we replace home education by social.

And your education! Is not that also social, and determined by the social conditions under which you educate, by the intervention, direct or indirect, of society, by means of schools, etc.? The Communists have not invented the intervention of society in education; they do but seek to alter the character of that intervention, and to rescue education from the influence of the ruling class.

The bourgeois clap-trap about the family and education, about the hallowed co-relation of parent and child, becomes all the more disgusting, the more, by the action of Modern Industry, all family ties among the proletarians are torn asunder, and their children transformed into simple articles of commerce and instruments of labour.

But you Communists would introduce community of women, screams the bourgeoisie in chorus.

The bourgeois sees his wife a mere instrument of production. He hears that the instruments of production are to be exploited in common, and, naturally, can come to no other conclusion that the lot of being common to all will likewise fall to the women.

He has not even a suspicion that the real point aimed at is to do away with the status of women as mere instruments of production.

For the rest, nothing is more ridiculous than the virtuous indignation of our bourgeois at the community of women which, they pretend, is to be openly and officially established by the Communists. The Communists have no need to introduce community of women; it has existed almost from time immemorial.

Our bourgeois, not content with having the wives and daughters of their proletarians at their disposal, not to speak of common prostitutes, take the greatest pleasure in seducing each other's wives.

Bourgeois marriage is in reality a system of wives in common and thus, at the most, what the Communists might possibly be reproached with is that they desire to introduce, in substitution for a hypocritically concealed, an openly legalized community of women. For the rest, it is self-evident that the abolition of the present system of production must bring with it the abolition of the community of women springing from that system, *i.e.*, of prostitution both public and private.

The Communists are further reproached with desiring to abolish countries and nationality.

The workers have no country. We cannot take from them what they have not got. Since the proletariat must first of all acquire political supremacy, must rise to be the leading class of the nation, must constitute itself *the* nation, it is so far, itself national, though not in the bourgeois sense of the word.

National differences and antagonism between peoples are daily more and more vanishing, owing to the development of the bourgeoisie, to freedom of commerce, to the world market, to uniformity in the mode of production and in the conditions of life corresponding thereto.

The supremacy of the proletariat will cause them to vanish still faster. United action, of the leading civilized countries at least, is one of the first conditions for the emancipation of the proletariat.

In proportion as the exploitation of one individual by another is put an end to, the exploitation of one nation by another will also be put an end to. In proportion as the antagonism between classes within the nation vanishes, the hostility of one nation to another will come to an end.

The charges against Communism made from a religious, a philosophical, and, generally, from an ideological standpoint, are not deserving of serious examination.

Does it require deep intuition to comprehend that man's ideas, views, and conception, in one word, man's consciousness, changes with every change in the conditions of his material existence, in his social relations and in his social life?

What else does the history of ideas prove, than that intellectual production changes its character in proportion as material production is changed? The ruling ideas of each age have ever been the ideas of its ruling class.

When people speak of ideas that revolutionize society, they do but express that fact, that within the old society, the elements of a new one have been created, and that the dissolution of the old ideas keeps even pace with the dissolution of the old conditions of existence.

When the ancient world was in its last throes, the ancient religions were overcome by Christianity. When Christian ideas succumbed in the eighteenth century to rationalist ideas, feudal society fought its death battle with the then revolutionary bourgeoisie. The ideas of religious liberty and freedom of conscience merely gave expression to the sway of free competition within the domain of knowledge.

"Undoubtedly," it will be said, "religious, moral, philosophical, and juridical ideas have been modified in the course of historical development. But religion, morality, philosophy, political science, and law, constantly survived this change.

"There are, besides, eternal truths, such as Freedom, Justice, etc., that are common to all states of society. But Communism abolishes eternal truths, it abolishes all religion and all morality, instead of constituting them on a new basis; it therefore acts in contradiction to all past historical experience."

What does this accusation reduce itself to? The history of all past society has consisted in the development of class antagonisms, antagonisms that assumed different forms at different epochs.

But whatever form they may have taken, one fact is common to all past ages, *viz.*, the exploitation of one part of society by the other. No wonder, then, that the social consciousness of past ages, despite all the multiplicity and variety it displays, moves within certain common forms, or general ideas, which cannot completely vanish except with the total disappearance of class antagonisms.

The Communist revolution is the most radical rupture with traditional relations; no wonder that its development involved the most radical rupture with traditional ideas.

But let us have done with the bourgeois objections to Communism.

We have seen above, that the first step in the revolution by the working class is to raise the proletariat to the position of ruling class, to win the battle of democracy.

The proletariat will use its political supremacy to wrest, by degrees, all capital from the bourgeoisie, to centralize all instruments of production in the hands of the State, *i.e.*, of the proletariat organized as the ruling class; and to increase the total productive forces as rapidly as possible.

Of course, in the beginning, this cannot be effected except by means of despotic inroads on the rights of property, and on the conditions of bourgeois production; by means of measures, therefore, which appear economically insufficient and untenable, but which, in the course of the movement, outstrip themselves, necessitate further inroads upon the old social order, and are unavoidable as a means of entirely revolutionizing the mode of production.

These measures will, of course, be different in different countries.

Nevertheless in most advanced countries, the following will be pretty generally applicable:

1. Abolition of property in land and application of all rents of land to public purposes.

2. A heavy progressive or graduated income tax.

3. Abolition of all right of inheritance.

4. Confiscation of the property of all emigrants and rebels.

5. Centralization of credit in the banks of the State, by means of a national bank with State capital and an exclusive monopoly.

6. Centralization of the means of communication and transport in the hands of the State.

7. Extension of factories and instruments of production owned by the State; the bringing into cultivation of waste-lands, and the improvement of the soil generally in accordance with a common plan.

8. Equal liability of all to labour. Establishment of industrial armies, especially for agriculture.

9. Combination of agriculture with manufacturing industries; gradual abolition of all the distinction between town and country by a more equable distribution of the population over the country.

10. Free education for all children in public schools. Abolition of children's factory labour in its present form. Combination of education with industrial production, etc., etc.

When, in the course of development, class distinctions have disappeared, and all production has been concentrated in the hands of a vast association of the whole nation, the public power will lose its political character. Political power, properly so called, is merely the organized power of one class for oppressing another. If the proletariat during its contest with the bourgeoisie is compelled, by the force of circumstances, to organize itself as a class, if, by means of a revolution, it makes itself the ruling class, and, as such, sweeps away by force the old conditions of production, then it will, along with these conditions, have swept away the conditions for the existence of class antagonisms and of classes generally, and will thereby have abolished its own supremacy as a class.

In place of the old bourgeois society, with its classes and class antagonisms, we shall have an association, in which the free development of each is the condition for the free development of all.

…

IV. Position of the Communists in Relation to the Various Existing Opposition Parties

Section II has made clear the relations of the Communists to the existing working-class parties, such as the Chartists in England and the Agrarian Reformers in America.[21]

The Communists fight for the attainment of the immediate aims, for the enforcement of the momentary interests of the working class; but in the movement of the present, they also represent and take care of the future of that movement. In France the Communists ally with the Social Democrats,[22] against the conservative

and radical bourgeoisie, reserving, however, the right to take up a critical position in regard to phases and illusions traditionally handed down from the great Revolution.

In Switzerland, they support the Radicals, without losing sight of the fact that this party consists of antagonistic elements, partly of Democratic Socialists, in the French sense, partly of radical bourgeois.

In Poland, they support the party that insists on an agrarian revolution as the prime condition for national emancipation, that party which fomented the insurrection of Kraków in 1846.[23]

In Germany, they fight with the bourgeoisie whenever it acts in a revolutionary way, against the absolute monarchy, the feudal squirearchy,[24] and the petty bourgeoisie.

But they never cease, for a single instant, to instil into the working class the clearest possible recognition of the hostile antagonism between bourgeoisie and proletariat, in order that the German workers may straightway use, as so many weapons against the bourgeoisie, the social and political conditions that the bourgeoisie must necessarily introduce along with its supremacy, and in order that, after the fall of the reactionary classes in Germany, the fight against the bourgeoisie itself may immediately begin.

The Communists turn their attention chiefly to Germany, because that country is on the eve of a bourgeois revolution that is bound to be carried out under more advanced conditions of European civilization, and with a much more developed proletariat, than that of England was in the seventeenth, and France in the eighteenth century, and because the bourgeois revolution in Germany will be but the prelude to an immediately following proletarian revolution.

In short, the Communists everywhere support every revolutionary movement against the existing social and political order of things.

21   Chartism was a popular reformist movement that lasted from 1837 to 1848. Among its demands (outlined in an 1837 "People's Charter") were universal male suffrage, equal electoral districts, abolition of the property qualification for running for Parliament, and annual parliaments. The National Reform Association was founded in 1844 to campaign for free settlement of the landless on public lands, a moratorium on seizure of family farms for non-payment of debt, and establishment of a 160-acre ceiling on land ownership to ensure there would be enough small-holdings to go around.

22   [Author's note] The party then represented in Parliament by Ledru-Rollin, in literature by Louis Blanc, in the daily press by the *Réforme*. The name of Social-Democracy signified, with these its inventors, a section of the Democratic or Republican Party more or less tinged with Socialism.

23   A nationalist, republican uprising in southern Poland against the Russians, Prussians, and Austrians who had jointly occupied it since the collapse of Napoleon's empire in 1815. The rebellion was crushed, and Kraków incorporated into the Austrian empire.

24   Landed gentry.

In all these movements they bring to the front, as the leading question in each, the property question, no matter what its degree of development at the time.

Finally, they labour everywhere for the union and agreement of the democratic parties of all countries.

The Communists disdain to conceal their views and aims. They openly declare that their ends can be attained only by the forcible overthrow of all existing social conditions. Let the ruling classes tremble at a Communist revolution. The proletarians have nothing to lose but their chains. They have a world to win.

WORKING MEN OF ALL COUNTRIES, UNITE!

SIMONE DE BEAUVOIR

"Introduction" to *The Second Sex*

Who Was Simone de Beauvoir?

Born in Paris in 1908, Simone de Beauvoir had become such an important figure in France by the time of her death in 1986 that her funeral was attended by 5000 people, including four former ministers of the Mitterrand government. A headline announcing her death read "Women, you owe her everything!"

De Beauvoir was the eldest of two daughters in a respectable, conservative bourgeois family, and she spent her formative years heatedly reacting against her parents and their values. She became an atheist while still a teenager, and decided early on to devote her life to writing and studying 'rather than' becoming a wife and mother. She studied philosophy at the ancient Parisian university of the Sorbonne and was the youngest person ever to obtain the *agrégation* (a high-level competitive examination for recruiting teachers in France) in philosophy, in 1929.[1] She was 21. In that same year she met the famous existentialist philosopher Jean-Paul Sartre and began an intense relationship with him—the most important of her life—that lasted until his death in 1980.

De Beauvoir and Sartre became notorious throughout France as a couple who were lovers and soul-mates but who maintained an open relationship; both considered themselves highly sexually 'liberated,' and de Beauvoir was openly bisexual. Sartre made what he called a "pact" with de Beauvoir—they could have affairs with other people, but they were required to tell each other everything—and he proceeded to match his actions to this rule. As he put it to de Beauvoir: "What *we* have is an *essential* love; but it is a good idea for us also to experience *contingent* love affairs."

Despite the rotating cast of lovers, de Beauvoir remained devoted to Sartre all her life and always maintained that he was the most brilliant man she had ever known. Indeed, she once declared that, her many books, literary prizes, and social influence notwithstanding, her greatest achievement in life was her relationship with Sartre.

Between 1932 and 1943 de Beauvoir was a high school teacher of philosophy in Rouen, in northwestern France. There, she was subject to official reprimands for her protests about male chauvinism and for her pacifism; finally, a parental complaint made against her for 'corrupting' one of her female students caused her dismissal. For the rest of her life, de Beauvoir lived in Paris and made her living from her writing. At the end of World War II, de Beauvoir became an editor at *Les Temps Modernes*, a new political journal founded by Sartre and other French

---

1   When the university *agrégation* results came out, Sartre was ranked first in the year and de Beauvoir second. Also, incidentally, 1929 was the year de Beauvoir acquired her lifelong nickname, *le Castor* (the French for beaver, because of the resemblance of her surname to "beaver").

intellectuals. She used this journal to promote her own work, and several excerpts from *The Second Sex* were first published in it.

Interestingly, part of the impetus to write *The Second Sex* came to her as she gradually realized that, unlike some of her female friends, she did *not* at first feel any sense that she was disadvantaged as a woman, but that this feeling of personal satisfaction and of independence resulted primarily from her relationship with a well-known, influential man—Sartre. When she reflected on this relationship, she realized with astonishment that she was fundamentally different from Sartre "because he was a man and I was only a woman." As she put it, "In writing *The Second Sex* I became aware, for the first time, that I myself was leading a false life, or rather, that I was profiting from this male-oriented society without even knowing it."

She was also influenced by what she saw in America, during a visit in 1947, of the experience of blacks in a segregated society. For example, she was friends with the black American short story writer and novelist Richard Wright, who, with his white wife Ellen, was a tireless advocate for black equality. For de Beauvoir, feminism was part of a larger project of social justice and human rights. From the late 1940s until the 1960s she was a very public left-wing political activist and a vocal supporter of communism (and critic of American-style capitalism).

The Second Sex is an extended examination of the problems women have encountered throughout history and of the possibilities left open to them. After the Introduction (reprinted here), the book is broken into two halves: Book One is a historical overview of "Facts and Myths" about women, and Book Two deals with "Women's Life Today." Book One is

divided into sections describing the "Destiny" of women according to theories of biology, psychoanalysis and Marxist historical materialism; the "History" of women from prehistoric times to the granting of the vote to women in France in 1947; and "Myths" about women in literature. Book Two is more personal, and talks about women in childhood, adolescence, sexual initiation, various forms of mature loving and sexual relationships, and old age. The conclusion of the book is positive and optimistic, as de Beauvoir tries to set out a model of life and action for future generations of women.

Some Useful Background Information

1. The first words of Book Two of *The Second Sex* are "One is not born, but rather becomes, a woman. No biological, psychological or economic fate determines the figure that the human female presents in society; it is civilization as a whole that determines this creature." This is how de Beauvoir most famously expresses an influential central thesis of the book: that 'woman,' as a biological category, is separable from 'feminine,' as a social construction—or more generally, that sex is not the same thing as gender. Thus, woman's status under the patriarchy as the Other is a contingent, socially constructed fact rather than an essential truth about the female gender.

It is important to appreciate that de Beauvoir is not denying that there are biological differences between men and women, nor does she insist that these biological differences must be simply ignored in a properly constituted society. Rather, she is arguing that our *biologi-*

cal constitutions do not determine our *gender* characteristics: such things as 'femininity' or 'masculinity,' being 'nurturing' or 'modest' or 'emotional' or 'delicate'—these things are constructed and constrained purely by *social* influences. Under different social conditions women and men might naturally and freely behave in ways radically different from contemporary social norms.

Thus, according to de Beauvoir, gender is more something we *do*—a way we live—than something we *are*. Gender is constrained by social pressures in large part because social pressures constrain how we can legitimately behave. A woman in, say, Canada in the 1950s could not just decide as an individual to behave like a man—or like someone who is neither masculine nor feminine—and in this way change her gender unilaterally. Even if she were brave enough to attempt the experiment, according to de Beauvoir—and the other existentialists—one cannot possess a certain trait, such as being masculine, unless others recognize one as doing so.

2. This emphasis on the social construction of gender, race, and other aspects of the reality we experience in our day-to-day lives is related to de Beauvoir's commitment to *existentialism*. Central to existentialism is the doctrine that *existence precedes essence*: humans have no pre-given purpose or essence determined for them by God or by biology. According to existentialism, each consciousness faces the world as an isolated individual, and inevitably creates itself—gives itself determinate form—by making choices. These choices are forced by the need to respond to the things around us, including both passive natural objects and other consciousnesses.

De Beauvoir and Sartre see the meeting of one consciousness with another as profoundly disturbing: faced with the gaze of an Other, we recognize a point of view which is necessarily different from our own and so we are required to concede our own incompleteness; furthermore, the opposing consciousness must treat us as an Other, which we feel as a threat to destroy us by turning us into an object.

De Beauvoir's feminism can be seen as a development of this idea: in response to the threat posed by other consciousnesses, according to existentialism, one might retaliate by objectifying and dominating the Other, to be able to control it without destroying it and thus be able to withstand its gaze. Thus, according to de Beauvoir, men have objectified and dominated women as the Other, and succumbing to all-pervasive social pressures women have allowed themselves to be dominated.

3. Towards the end of this essay, de Beauvoir mentions the contrast between being *en-soi* (in-itself) and being *pour-soi* (for-itself). Being for-itself is a mode of existence that is purposive and, as it were, constituted by its own activity; being in-itself, by contrast, is a less fully human kind of existence that is more like being a 'thing'—self-sufficient, non-purposive, driven by merely contingent current conditions.

How Important and Influential Is This Passage?

The Second Sex is often considered the founding work of twentieth-century feminism. It has been called "one of the most important and far-reaching books on women ever published" (Terry Keefe) and "the best book about women ever written" (*The Guardian*, 1999). From the day it was published it was both popular and controversial: twenty-two thousand copies of the first volume were sold in France in the first week, and de Beauvoir received large quantities of hate mail including some from "very active members of the First Sex." "How courageous you are.... You're going to lose a lot of friends!" one of her friends wrote to her. She was accused of writing a pornographic book (because of *The Second Sex*'s discussion of female sexuality), and the Vatican put it on the Index of prohibited books. "Once," de Beauvoir reported in her autobiography, "during an entire dinner at Nos Provinces on the Boulevard Montparnasse, a table of people nearby stared at me and giggled; I didn't like dragging [her lover, Nelson] Algren into a scene, but as I left I gave them a piece of my mind." On the other hand, some of the contemporary reviews were glowing: *The New Yorker* called it "more than a work of scholarship; it is a work of art, with the salt of reckless-ness that makes art sting."

After the initial furor died down, the book was criti-cized by scholars and critics as having too much of a middle-class, distorted viewpoint—as having been written by someone who had no cause to actually feel the pressures that give life to feminism. The poet Stevie Smith wrote, in 1953: "She has written an enor-mous book about women and it is soon clear that she does not like them, nor does she like being a woman." This debate continues today, and arguably it is only recently that *The Second Sex* has come to be appreci-ated seriously as a work of philosophy that stands on its own merits, rather than read solely in terms of de Beauvoir's "biography, relationship with ... Sartre, psy-che, or feminist credentials" (*TLS*, 2005).

De Beauvoir is a pivotal figure in the history of feminist thought from the Renaissance to the twen-ty-first century. In the Renaissance and early mod-ern period, writers that we would today think of as feminist [such as Christine de Pizan (1365–c. 1430) and Mary Astell (1666–1731)] tended to focus on the social asymmetries between women and men. They argued that women have similar innate abil-ities to men and should be granted opportunities equivalent to those their male counterparts enjoyed in certain key areas, especially education, the family, and sometimes work and politics. The eighteenth and nineteenth centuries [in work by writers such as Olympe de Gouges (1745–93), Mary Wollstonecraft (1759–97), Sojourner Truth (1797–1883), John Stuart Mill (1806–73), and Harriet Taylor (1807–58)] saw a greater accumulation of forceful writings against the oppression of women, combined with more explicit (but only gradually successful) political campaigns to have women's equal status with men enshrined in law. It was at the end of the nineteenth century—in France, during the 1890s—that the term 'feminism' first appeared.

Up to this point, feminism can be usefully—albeit simplistically—understood as characterized by a de-mand for equal rights with men. Once women are educated as extensively as men, are given the oppor-tunity to vote, are not forbidden from joining certain professions, and so on, then it was assumed that their innate capacities—in many (though perhaps not all) respects equal to, or even superior to, those of the male sex—would flourish free from oppression. That is, pre-twentieth-century feminism tended to focus on the suppression and distortion of woman's nature by contingent social structures such as laws and institu-tions. De Beauvoir's writings marked a significant shift and deepening in the nature of feminist thought. She denied that there is an inborn 'female nature' that just awaits the opportunity to break free from male op-pression, and insisted that women are dominated by men in *all* aspects of their lives—that their very con-sciousness, the very shape of their minds, is formed by the patriarchal society of which they are a part. Fem-inism cannot aspire simply to change the laws and in-stitutions of a country; this will leave the subordinate position of women essentially untouched. Feminists must fight for much more thoroughgoing change to the basic practices and assumptions of the whole society.

Later twentieth-century feminism, often known as *second-wave feminism* [representatives of which include Susan Moller Okin (1946–2004), Catharine MacKinnon (1946–), Martha Nussbaum (1947–), and Iris Young (1949–)], took up this emphasis on the deep and subtle nature of patriarchal dominance (though often without a very self-conscious sense of the debt to de Beauvoir). The distinction between sex and gender—the notion of gender as a social construct—proved especially significant in making this case. For many feminists, this has evolved into a critique of standards that are taken to have an object-ive and universal status—such as 'rational,' 'true,' and 'right'—but which, feminists argue, in fact reflect par-ticular gender interests. Thus, for example, to argue— as Wollstonecraft did—that women are 'equally rational' as men is to succumb to, rather than combat, one of the hidden patriarchal structures that oppress women.

The so-called *third-wave* (or sometimes, *postmod-ern*) feminism that began in the 1980s can also be seen as having roots in the work of de Beauvoir. Third-wave feminism emphasizes the claim that gender is a social, contingent, rather than a natural category, and adopts an 'anti-essentialist' stance about women: that is, there is nothing that can be usefully said about woman 'as such,' and instead we must focus in an explicitly un-unified way on different conceptions of femininity in particular ethnic, religious, and social groups.

Suggestions for Critical Reflection

1. De Beauvoir begins her book by asking "What is a woman?" How do you think she answers this question?
2. De Beauvoir claims that the terms *masculine* and *feminine* are not symmetrical opposites. What do you make of this claim? How does de Beauvoir develop it? What is its importance?
3. "Throughout history [women] have always been subordinated to men, and hence their dependency is not the result of a historical event or a social change—it was not something that *occurred*." Does this claim seem plausible? How important is it to de Beauvoir's argument?
4. De Beauvoir suggests that for women to renounce their status as an Other would be to abandon "all the advantages conferred upon them by their alliance with the superior caste." What does she mean by this? Is she right? How serious a difficulty is this for feminism?
5. "[T]he dominant class bases its argument on a state of affairs that it has itself created." Does this ring true? How important is it for the social activist, including the feminist, to notice this? How much does this explain the behavior towards women by even well-intentioned men?
6. "We are no longer like our partisan elders; by and large we have won the game." Is de Beauvoir right about this? Is this claim consistent with her general theory of the oppression of women in society?
7. "One is not born, but rather becomes, a woman." Some commentators have argued that, in making this central claim, de Beauvoir herself falls victim to the patriarchal mindset she is criticizing—that she is tacitly assuming that "femaleness is indeed optional and subhuman, and maleness the slipped-from standard." Does

this criticism strike you as plausible? Does it suggest a fundamental problem with de Beauvoir's project, or with the way she carries it out?

Suggestions for Further Reading

De Beauvoir's two most important works of philosophy are *The Second Sex* (1949) and *The Ethics of Ambiguity* (1947; it was translated into English by Bernard Frechtman and published by Citadel Press in 1949). The latter is an excellent introduction to existentialism. De Beauvoir also published four philosophical novels between 1943 and 1954, and in her later years she published several volumes of autobiography and biography, especially exploring her relationship with Sartre and the phenomenon of old age.

There are several biographies of de Beauvoir, including Deirdre Bair, *Simone de Beauvoir: A Biography* (Summit Books, 1990), and Toril Moi, *Simone de Beauvoir: The Making of an Intellectual Woman* (Blackwell, 1994). Useful secondary sources include: Nancy Bauer, *Simone de Beauvoir, Philosophy and Feminism* (Columbia University Press, 2001); Debra Bergoffen, *The Philosophy of Simone de Beauvoir: Gendered Phenomenologies, Erotic Generosities* (SUNY Press, 1996); Claudia Card, ed., *The Cambridge Companion to Simone de Beauvoir* (Cambridge University Press, 2003); Ruth Evans, ed., *Simone de Beauvoir's the Second Sex: New Interdisciplinary Essays* (St. Martin's, 1998); Elizabeth Fallaize, ed., *Simone de Beauvoir: A Critical Reader* (Routledge, 1998); Lori Jo Marso and Patricia Moynagh, eds., *Simone de Beauvoir's Political Thinking* (University of Illinois Press, 2006); Toril Moi, *Feminist Theory and Simone de Beauvoir* (Blackwell, 1990); Fredrika Scarth, *The Other Within* (Rowman & Littlefield, 2004); Margaret Simons, ed., *Feminist Interpretations of Simone de Beauvoir* (Pennsylvania State University Press, 1995); Margaret Simons, *Beauvoir and the Second Sex: Feminism, Race, and the Origins of Existentialism* (Rowman & Littlefield, 1999); and Karen Vintges, *Philosophy as Passion: The Thinking of Simone de Beauvoir* (translated by Anne Lavelle, Indiana University Press, 1996). Volume 72 of *Yale French Studies* (1986) is devoted to articles on Simone de Beauvoir, several of which are valuable.

"Introduction" to *The Second Sex*[2]

For a long time I have hesitated to write a book on woman. The subject is irritating, especially to women; and it is not new. Enough ink has been spilled in the quarreling over feminism, now practically over, and perhaps we should say no more about it. It is still talked about, however, for the voluminous nonsense uttered during the last century seems to have done little to illuminate the problem. After all, is there a problem? And if so, what is it? Are there women, really? Most assuredly the theory of the eternal feminine still has its adherents who will whisper in your ear: "Even in Russia[3] women still are *women*"; and other erudite persons—sometimes the very same—say with a sigh: "Woman is losing her way, woman is lost." One wonders if women still exist, if they will always exist, whether or not it is desirable that they should, what place they occupy in this world, what their place should be. "What has become of women?" was asked recently in an ephemeral magazine.[4]

But first we must ask: what is a woman? "*Tota mulier in utero*,"[5] says one, "woman is a womb." But in speaking of certain women, connoisseurs declare that they are not women, although they are equipped with a uterus like the rest. All agree in recognizing the fact that females exist in the human species; today as always they make up about one half of humanity. And yet we are told that femininity is in danger; we are exhorted to be women, remain women, become women. It would appear, then, that every female human being is not necessarily a woman; to be so considered she must

share in that mysterious and threatened reality known as femininity. Is this attribute something secreted by the ovaries? Or is it a Platonic essence, a product of the philosophic imagination? Is a rustling petticoat enough to bring it down to earth? Although some women try zealously to incarnate this essence, it is hardly patentable. It is frequently described in vague and dazzling terms that seem to have been borrowed from the vocabulary of the seers, and indeed in the times of St. Thomas[6] it was considered an essence as certainly defined as the somniferous virtue[7] of the poppy.

But conceptualism has lost ground. The biological and social sciences no longer admit the existence of unchangeably fixed entities that determine given characteristics, such as those ascribed to woman, the Jew, or the Negro. Science regards any characteristic as a reaction dependent in part upon a *situation*. If today femininity no longer exists, then it never existed. But does the word *woman*, then, have no specific content? This is stoutly affirmed by those who hold to the philosophy of the enlightenment, of rationalism, of nominalism;[8] women, to them, are merely the human beings arbitrarily designated by the word *woman*. Many American women particularly are prepared to think that there is no longer any place for woman as such; if a backward individual still takes herself for a woman, her friends advise her to be psychoanalyzed and thus get rid of this obsession. In regard to a work, *Modern Woman: The Lost Sex*,[9] which in other respects has its irritating features, Dorothy Parker[10] has written: "I cannot be just to books which treat of woman as woman.... My idea is that all of us, men as

---

2   This is the Introduction to *The Second Sex* by Simone de Beauvoir, translated by H.M. Parshley, copyright 1952 and renewed 1980 by Alfred A. Knopf Inc. (It was first published in French in 1949.) Used by permission of Alfred A. Knopf, a division of Random House, Inc.

3   That is, even after the reorganization of society in Russia after the Communist revolution of 1917 (and the upheaval of World War II).

4   [Author's note] *Franchise*, dead today.

5   "The whole woman is in her uterus," or, more snappily, "Woman is a womb." This aphorism dates back to medieval scholastic theology.

6   Aquinas.

7   "Power to induce sleep."

8   Nominalism is the view that only particular things exist, and 'abstract' things—*universals*—such as beauty, redness, or species-membership, are not real. Conceptualism (mentioned above) is the view that abstractions do exist as mental concepts.

9   By Ferdinand Lundberg and Marynia F. Farnham, published in 1947. Among other things, this book proposed that laws be adopted prohibiting single women from working, thus forcing them into marriage.

10 Parker (1893–1967) was an American critic, satirical poet, and short-story writer, famous for her acerbic wit.

well as women, should be regarded as human beings." But nominalism is a rather inadequate doctrine, and the antifemininists have had no trouble in showing that women simply *are not* men. Surely woman is, like man, a human being; but such a declaration is abstract. The fact is that every concrete human being is always a singular, separate individual. To decline to accept such notions as the eternal feminine, the black soul, the Jewish character, is not to deny that Jews, Negroes, women exist today—this denial does not represent a liberation for those concerned, but rather a flight from reality. Some years ago a well-known woman writer refused to permit her portrait to appear in a series of photographs especially devoted to women writers; she wished to be counted among the men. But in order to gain this privilege she made use of her husband's influence! Women who assert that they are men lay claim none the less to masculine consideration and respect. I recall also a young Trotskyite standing on a platform at a boisterous meeting and getting ready to use her fists, in spite of her evident fragility. She was denying her feminine weakness; but it was for love of a militant male whose equal she wished to be. The attitude of defiance of many American women proves that they are haunted by a sense of their femininity. In truth, to go for a walk with one's eyes open is enough to demonstrate that humanity is divided into two classes of individuals whose clothes, faces, bodies, smiles, gaits, interests, and occupations are manifestly different. Perhaps these differences are superficial, perhaps they are destined to disappear. What is certain is that right now they do most obviously exist.

If her functioning as a female is not enough to define woman, if we decline also to explain her through "the eternal feminine," and if nevertheless we admit, provisionally, that women do exist, then we must face the question: what is a woman?

To state the question is, to me, to suggest, at once, a preliminary answer. The fact that I ask it is in itself significant. A man would never get the notion of writing a book on the peculiar situation of the human male.[11] But if I wish to define myself, I must first of all say: "I am a woman"; on this truth must be based all further discussion. A man never begins by presenting himself as an individual of a certain sex; it goes without saying that he is a man. The terms *masculine* and *feminine* are used symmetrically only as a matter of form, as on legal papers. In actuality the relation of the two sexes is not quite like that of two electrical poles, for man represents both the positive and the neutral, as is indicated by the common use of *man* to designate human beings in general; whereas woman represents only the negative, defined by limiting criteria, without reciprocity. In the midst of an abstract discussion it is vexing to hear a man say: "You think thus and so because you are a woman"; but I know that my only defense is to reply: "I think thus and so because it is true," thereby removing my subjective self from the argument. It would be out of the question to reply: "And you think the contrary because you are a man," for it is understood that the fact of being a man is no peculiarity. A man is in the right in being a man; it is the woman who is in the wrong. It amounts to this: just as for the ancients there was an absolute vertical with reference to which the oblique was defined, so there is an absolute human type, the masculine. Woman has ovaries, a uterus; these peculiarities imprison her in her subjectivity, circumscribe her within the limits of her own nature. It is often said that she thinks with her glands. Man superbly ignores the fact that his anatomy also includes glands, such as the testicles, and that they secrete hormones. He thinks of his body as a direct and normal connection with the world, which he believes he apprehends objectively, whereas he regards the body of woman as a hindrance, a prison, weighed down by everything peculiar to it. "The female is a female by virtue of a certain *lack* of qualities," said Aristotle; "we should regard the female nature as afflicted with a natural defectiveness." And St. Thomas for his part pronounced woman to be an "imperfect man," an "incidental" being. This is symbolized in Genesis where Eve is depicted as

---

11 [Author's note] The Kinsey Report [Alfred C. Kinsey and others: *Sexual Behavior in the Human Male* (W.B. Saunders Co., 1948)] is no exception, for it is limited to describing the sexual characteristics of American men, which is quite a different matter.

made from what Bossuet called "a supernumerary bone" of Adam.[12]

Thus humanity is male and man defines woman not in herself but as relative to him; she is not regarded as an autonomous being. Michelet writes: "Woman, the relative being...." And Benda is most positive in his *Rapport d'Uriel*: "The body of man makes sense in itself quite apart from that of woman, whereas the latter seems wanting in significance by itself.... Man can think of himself without woman. She cannot think of herself without man."[13] And she is simply what man decrees; thus she is called "the sex," by which is meant that she appears essentially to the male as a sexual being. For him she is sex—absolute sex, no less. She is defined and differentiated with reference to man and not he with reference to her; she is the incidental, the inessential as opposed to the essential. He is the Subject, he is the Absolute—she is the Other.[14]

The category of the *Other* is as primordial as consciousness itself. In the most primitive societies, in the most ancient mythologies, one finds the expression of a duality—that of the Self and the Other. This duality was not originally attached to the division of the sexes; it was not dependent upon any empirical facts. It is revealed in such works as that of Granet on Chinese thought and those of Dumézil on the East Indies and Rome.[15] The feminine element was at first no more involved in such pairs as Varuna-Mitra, Uranus-Zeus,[16] Sun-Moon, and Day-Night than it was in the contrasts between Good and Evil, lucky and unlucky auspices, right and left, God and Lucifer. Otherness is a fundamental category of human thought.

Thus it is that no group ever sets itself up as the One without at once setting up the Other over against itself. If three travelers chance to occupy the same compartment, that is enough to make vaguely hostile "others" out of all the rest of the passengers on the train. In small-town eyes all persons not belonging to the village are "strangers" and suspect; to the native of a country all who inhabit other countries are "foreigners"; Jews are "different" for the anti-Semite, Negroes are "inferior" for American racists, aborigines are "natives" for colonists, proletarians are the "lower class" for the privileged.

Lévi-Strauss,[17] at the end of a profound work on the various forms of primitive societies, reaches the

---

12   Jacques-Bénigne Bossuet (1627–1704) was a French bishop famous for his brilliant sermons. *Supernumerary* means "superfluous," "exceeding the required number."

13   Jules Michelet (1798–1874) was a French historian. Julien Benda (1867–1956) was a French novelist and critic; *Le rapport d'Uriel* was published in 1946.

14   [Author's note] E. Lévinas expresses this idea most explicitly in his essay *Temps et l'Autre*. "Is there not a case in which otherness, alterity [*altérité*], unquestionably marks the nature of a being, as its essence, an instance of otherness not consisting purely and simply in the opposition of two species of the same genus? I think that the feminine represents the contrary in its absolute sense, this contrariness being in no wise affected by any relation between it and its correlative and thus remaining absolutely other. Sex is not a certain specific difference ... no more is the sexual difference a mere contradiction.... Nor does this difference lie in the duality of two complementary terms, for two complementary terms imply a pre-existing whole.... Otherness reaches its full flowering in the feminine, a term of the same rank as consciousness but of opposite meaning."

I suppose that Lévinas does not forget that woman, too, is aware of her own consciousness, or ego. But it is striking that he deliberately takes a man's point of view, disregarding the reciprocity of subject and object. When he writes that woman is mystery, he implies that she is mystery for man. Thus his description, which is intended to be objective, is in fact an assertion of masculine privilege.

15   Marcel Granet (1884–1940) was a French sociologist, and Georges Dumézil (1898–1986) was a philologist and historian of religions.

16   Varuna and Mitra are Hindu gods (both concerned with upholding law and order), and Uranus and Zeus were Greek gods. One of Dumézil's classic books is *Mitra-Varuna: An Essay on Two Indo-European Representations of Sovereignty* (1948).

17   Claude Lévi-Strauss (1908–2009) was a French anthropologist, famous for developing structuralism as a method of understanding human society and culture (e.g., the structures of kinship systems).

following conclusion: "Passage from the state of Nature to the state of Culture is marked by man's ability to view biological relations as a series of contrasts; duality, alternation, opposition, and symmetry, whether under definite or vague forms, constitute not so much phenomena to be explained as fundamental and immediately given data of social reality."[18] These phenomena would be incomprehensible if in fact human society were simply a *Mitsein*[19] or fellowship based on solidarity and friendliness. Things become clear, on the contrary, if, following Hegel, we find in consciousness itself a fundamental hostility toward every other consciousness; the subject can be posed only in being opposed—he sets himself up as the essential, as opposed to the other, the inessential, the object.

But the other consciousness, the other ego, sets up a reciprocal claim. The native traveling abroad is shocked to find himself in turn regarded as a "stranger" by the natives of neighboring countries. As a matter of fact, wars, festivals, trading, treaties, and contests among tribes, nations, and classes tend to deprive the concept *Other* of its absolute sense and to make manifest its relativity; willy-nilly, individuals and groups are forced to realize the reciprocity of their relations. How is it, then, that this reciprocity has not been recognized between the sexes, that one of the contrasting terms is set up as the sole essential, denying any relativity in regard to its correlative and defining the latter as pure otherness? Why is it that women do not dispute male sovereignty? No subject will readily volunteer to become the object, the inessential; it is not the Other who, in defining himself as the Other, establishes the One. The Other is posed as such by the One in defining himself as the One. But if the Other is not to regain the status of being the One, he must be submissive enough to accept this alien point of view. Whence comes this submission in the case of woman?

There are, to be sure, other cases in which a certain category has been able to dominate another completely for a time. Very often this privilege depends upon inequality of numbers—the majority imposes its rule upon the minority or persecutes it. But women are not a minority, like the American Negroes or the Jews; there are as many women as men on earth. Again, the two groups concerned have often been originally independent; they may have been formerly unaware of each other's existence, or perhaps they recognized each other's autonomy. But a historical event has resulted in the subjugation of the weaker by the stronger. The scattering of the Jews, the introduction of slavery into America, the conquests of imperialism are examples in point. In these cases the oppressed retained at least the memory of former days; they possessed in common a past, a tradition, sometimes a religion or a culture.

The parallel drawn by Bebel[20] between women and the proletariat is valid in that neither ever formed a minority or a separate collective unit of mankind. And instead of a single historical event it is in both cases a historical development that explains their status as a class and accounts for the membership of *particular individuals* in that class. But proletarians have not always existed, whereas there have always been women. They are women in virtue of their anatomy and physiology. Throughout history they have always been subordinated to men, and hence their dependency is not the result of a historical event or a social change—it was not something that *occurred*. The reason why otherness in this case seems to be an absolute is in part that it lacks the contingent or incidental nature of historical facts. A condition brought about at a certain time can be abolished at some other time, as the Negroes of Haiti and others have proved; but it might seem that a natural condition is beyond the possibility of change. In truth, however, the nature

---

18   [Author's note] See C. Lévi-Strauss: *Les Structures élémentaires de la parenté* [1949]. My thanks are due to C. Lévi-Strauss for his kindness in furnishing me with the proofs of his work, which, among others, I have used liberally in Part II.

19   A Hegelian term, literally meaning "being with."

20   August Bebel (1840–1913) was a German Marxist revolutionary. In *Woman and Socialism*, first published in 1879, he argued that the social emancipation of women was a crucial precursor to the overthrow of capitalism. In Marxist theory the proletariat is the lower class of society that does not have ownership of the means of production and must instead work for wages.

of things is no more immutably given, once for all, than is historical reality. If woman seems to be the inessential which never becomes the essential, it is because she herself fails to bring about this change. Proletarians say "We"; Negroes also. Regarding themselves as subjects, they transform the bourgeois, the whites, into "others." But women do not say "We," except at some congress of feminists or similar formal demonstration; men say "women," and women use the same word in referring to themselves. They do not authentically assume a subjective attitude. The proletarians have accomplished the revolution in Russia, the Negroes in Haiti, the Indo-Chinese are battling for it in Indo-China; but the women's effort has never been anything more than a symbolic agitation. They have gained only what men have been willing to grant; they have taken nothing, they have only received.[21]

The reason for this is that women lack concrete means for organizing themselves into a unit which can stand face to face with the correlative unit. They have no past, no history, no religion of their own; and they have no such solidarity of work and interest as that of the proletariat. They are not even promiscuously herded together in the way that creates community feeling among the American Negroes, the ghetto Jews, the workers of Saint-Denis,[22] or the factory hands of Renault. They live dispersed among the males, attached through residence, housework, economic condition, and social standing to certain men—fathers or husbands—more firmly than they are to other women. If they belong to the bourgeoisie, they feel solidarity with men of that class, not with proletarian women; if they are white, their allegiance is to white men, not to Negro women. The proletariat can propose to massacre the ruling class, and a sufficiently fanatical Jew or Negro might dream of getting sole possession of the atomic bomb and making humanity wholly Jewish or black; but woman cannot

even dream of exterminating the males. The bond that unites her to her oppressors is not comparable to any other. The division of the sexes is a biological fact, not an event in human history. Male and female stand opposed within a primordial *Mitsein*, and woman has not broken it. The couple is a fundamental unity with its two halves riveted together, and the cleavage of society along the line of sex is impossible. Here is to be found the basic trait of woman: she is the Other in a totality of which the two components are necessary to one another.

One could suppose that this reciprocity might have facilitated the liberation of woman. When Hercules sat at the feet of Omphale[23] and helped her with her spinning, his desire for her held him captive; but why did she fail to gain a lasting power? To revenge herself on Jason, Medea killed their children;[24] and this grim legend would seem to suggest that she might have obtained a formidable influence over him through his love for his offspring. In *Lysistrata*[25] Aristophanes gaily depicts a band of women who joined

---

21   [Author's note] See Part II, ch. viii [not reprinted here].

22.   Saint-Denis is a region including the northern suburbs of Paris and has been the scene of several significant worker uprisings and strikes, including the revolt of 1848 (and others as recently as 2003). Saint-Ouen, in Saint-Denis, was one of the first cities where a factory worker was elected mayor.

23   A queen of Lydia, an ancient kingdom in the region that is today Turkey, who is said to have owned Hercules as her slave for three years. (Hercules was being punished for the murder of his friend Iphitus. The story goes that during his time as a slave he became so weak that he wore women's clothes and did 'women's work,' while the queen wore his lion skin and carried his club.)

24   Medea was a powerful sorceress, the daughter of King Aeëtes of Colchis (at the eastern end of the Black Sea), and the granddaughter of Helios, the sun god. When Jason and the crew of the Argo arrived at Colchis seeking the Golden Fleece, Medea fell in love with Jason and used her magic to help him, in return for Jason's promise to marry her. When Jason later deserted her and married the daughter of Creon, the king of Corinth, Medea took her revenge by killing the new bride with a poisoned robe and crown which burned the flesh from her body (and killed King Creon as well when he tried to embrace his dying daughter), and also murdering the two children she had with Jason.

25   A play, written in about 411 BCE, in which the women of Hellas (ancient Greece) agree to withhold sex from their men folk until they agree to end the long-running war between Athens and Sparta.

forces to gain social ends through the sexual needs of their men; but this is only a play. In the legend of the Sabine women, the latter soon abandoned their plan of remaining sterile to punish their ravishers.[26] In truth woman has not been socially emancipated through man's need—sexual desire and the desire for offspring—which makes the male dependent for satisfaction upon the female.

Master and slave, also, are united by a reciprocal need, in this case economic, which does not liberate the slave. In the relation of master to slave the master does not make a point of the need that he has for the other; he has in his grasp the power of satisfying this need through his own action; whereas the slave, in his dependent condition, his hope and fear, is quite conscious of the need he has for his master. Even if the need is at bottom equally urgent for both, it always works in favor of the oppressor and against the oppressed. That is why the liberation of the working class, for example, has been slow.

Now, woman has always been man's dependent, if not his slave; the two sexes have never shared the world in equality. And even today woman is heavily handicapped, though her situation is beginning to change. Almost nowhere is her legal status the same as man's, and frequently it is much to her disadvantage. Even when her rights are legally recognized in the abstract, long-standing custom prevents their full expression in the mores.[27] In the economic sphere men and women can almost be said to make up two castes; other things being equal, the former hold the better jobs, get higher wages, and have more opportunity for success than their new competitors. In industry and politics men have a great many more positions and they monopolize the most important posts. In addition to all this, they enjoy a traditional prestige that the education of children tends in every way to support, for the present enshrines the past—and in the past all history has been made by men. At the present time, when women are beginning to take part in the affairs of the world, it is still a world that belongs to men—they have no doubt of it at all and women have scarcely any. To decline to be the Other, to refuse to be a party to the deal—this would be for women to renounce all the advantages conferred upon them by their alliance with the superior caste. Man-the-sovereign will provide woman-the-liege with material protection and will undertake the moral justification of her existence; thus she can evade at once both economic risk and the metaphysical risk of a liberty in which ends and aims must be contrived without assistance. Indeed, along with the ethical urge of each individual to affirm his subjective existence, there is also the temptation to forgo liberty and become a thing. This is an inauspicious road, for he who takes it—passive, lost, ruined—becomes henceforth the creature of another's will, frustrated in his transcendence and deprived of every value. But it is an easy road; on it one avoids the strain involved in undertaking an authentic existence. When man makes of woman the *Other*, he may, then, expect her to manifest deep-seated tendencies toward complicity. Thus, woman may fail to lay claim to the status of subject because she lacks definite resources, because she feels the necessary bond that ties her to man regardless of reciprocity, and because she is often very well pleased with her role as the *Other*.

But it will be asked at once: how did all this begin? It is easy to see that the duality of the sexes, like any duality, gives rise to conflict. And doubtless the winner will assume the status of absolute. But why should man have won from the start? It seems possible that women could have won the victory; or that

---

26   At the beginning of Roman history, according to myth, the newly founded city of Rome needed to increase its population quickly in order to defend itself against its neighbors, but they did not have enough women to sustain their numbers. The Romans therefore invited the neighboring community of the Sabines to a religious celebration in honour of Neptune, and during the party the younger Roman men kidnapped the Sabine women and raped them. The Sabines—some months later!—returned with an army to bring back their women by force, but discovered (according to legend) that their erstwhile wives and daughters had reconciled with their new Roman husbands, and borne their children. The women stopped the battle before it started by placing themselves between the two armies; the Romans and the Sabines made peace, and Rome continued to grow.

---

27   "Prevailing manners or habits."

the outcome of the conflict might never have been decided. How is it that this world has always belonged to the men and that things have begun to change only recently? Is this change a good thing? Will it bring about an equal sharing of the world between men and women?

These questions are not new, and they have often been answered. But the very fact that woman *is the Other* tends to cast suspicion upon all the justifications that men have ever been able to provide for it. These have all too evidently been dictated by men's interest. A little-known feminist of the seventeenth century, Poulain de la Barre,[28] put it this way: "All that has been written about women by men should be suspect, for the men are at once judge and party to the lawsuit." Everywhere, at all times, the males have displayed their satisfaction in feeling that they are the lords of creation. "Blessed be God ... that He did not make me a woman," say the Jews in their morning prayers, while their wives pray on a note of resignation: "Blessed be the Lord, who created me according to His will." The first among the blessings for which Plato thanked the gods was that he had been created free, not enslaved; the second, a man, not a woman. But the males could not enjoy this privilege fully unless they believed it to be founded on the absolute and the eternal; they sought to make the fact of their supremacy into a right. "Being men, those who have made and compiled the laws have favored their own sex, and jurists have elevated these laws into principles," to quote Poulain de la Barre once more.

Legislators, priests, philosophers, writers, and scientists have striven to show that the subordinate position of woman is willed in heaven and advantageous on earth. The religions invented by men reflect this wish for domination. In the legends of Eve and Pandora men have taken up arms against women. They have made use of philosophy and theology, as the quotations from Aristotle and St. Thomas have shown. Since ancient times satirists and moralists have delighted in showing up the weaknesses of women. We are familiar with the savage indictments hurled against women throughout French literature. Montherlant, for example, follows the tradition of Jean de Meung,[29] though with less gusto. This hostility may at times be well founded, often it is gratuitous; but in truth it more or less successfully conceals a desire for self-justification. As Montaigne[30] says, "It is easier to accuse one sex than to excuse the other." Sometimes what is going on is clear enough. For instance, the Roman law limiting the rights of woman cited "the imbecility, the instability of the sex" just when the weakening of family ties seemed to threaten the interests of male heirs. And in the effort to keep the married woman under guardianship, appeal was made in the sixteenth century to the authority of St. Augustine, who declared that "woman is a creature neither decisive nor constant," at a time when the single woman was thought capable of managing her property. Montaigne understood clearly how arbitrary and unjust was woman's appointed lot: "Women are not in the wrong when they decline to accept the rules laid down for them, since the men make these rules without consulting them. No wonder intrigue and strife abound." But he did not go so far as to champion their cause.

28 François Poulain de la Barre, a French Catholic village priest, published three pamphlets urging the equality of the sexes, including "De l'égalité des deux sexes" (1671) from which this quote is taken.

29 Henri de Montherlant (1896–1972) was a French writer, soldier, athlete and bullfighter whose novels glorify force and masculinity. Jean de Meung (c. 1240–c. 1305) was a French poet and alchemist known for his continuation of the *Roman de la rose* (Romance of the Rose), an allegorical poem in the courtly love tradition begun by Guillaume de Lorris in about 1230. His section of the poem is particularly noted for its controversial digressions on a variety of topics, including a quatrain vilifying womankind. (For this offense, it is said, he was cornered by the ladies of the court of Charles VI who tried to have him stripped naked and whipped; only his impish eloquence allowed him to escape.)

30 Michel de Montaigne (1533–1592) was a French courtier and the author of *Essais*, which established, as a new literary form, the essay (a short piece dealing with the author's personal thoughts about a particular subject).

It was only later, in the eighteenth century, that genuinely democratic men began to view the matter objectively. Diderot,[31] among others, strove to show that woman is, like man, a human being. Later John Stuart Mill came fervently to her defense. But these philosophers displayed unusual impartiality. In the nineteenth century the feminist quarrel became again a quarrel of partisans. One of the consequences of the industrial revolution was the entrance of women into productive labor, and it was just here that the claims of the feminists emerged from the realm of theory and acquired an economic basis, while their opponents became the more aggressive. Although landed property lost power to some extent, the bourgeoisie clung to the old morality that found the guarantee of private property in the solidity of the family. Woman was ordered back into the home the more harshly as her emancipation became a real menace. Even within the working class the men endeavored to restrain woman's liberation, because they began to see the women as dangerous competitors—the more so because they were accustomed to work for lower wages.[32]

In proving woman's inferiority, the antifeminists then began to draw not only upon religion, philosophy, and theology, as before, but also upon science—biology, experimental psychology, etc. At most they were willing to grant "equality in difference" to the *other* sex. That profitable formula is most significant; it is precisely like the "equal but separate" formula of the Jim Crow laws[33] aimed at

the North American Negroes. As is well known, this so-called equalitarian segregation has resulted only in the most extreme discrimination. The similarity just noted is in no way due to chance, for whether it is a race, a caste, a class, or a sex that is reduced to a position of inferiority, the methods of justification are the same. "The eternal feminine" corresponds to "the black soul" and to "the Jewish character." True, the Jewish problem is on the whole very different from the other two—to the anti-Semite the Jew is not so much an inferior as he is an enemy for whom there is to be granted no place on earth, for whom annihilation is the fate desired. But there are deep similarities between the situation of woman and that of the Negro. Both are being emancipated today from a like paternalism, and the former master class wishes to "keep them in their place"—that is, the place chosen for them. In both cases the former masters lavish more or less sincere eulogies, either on the virtues of "the good Negro" with his dormant, childish, merry soul—the submissive Negro—or on the merits of the woman who is "truly feminine"—that is, frivolous, infantile, irresponsible—the submissive woman. In both cases the dominant class bases its argument on a state of affairs that it has itself created. As George Bernard Shaw[34] puts it, in substance, "The American white relegates the black to the rank of shoeshine boy; and he concludes from this that the black is good for nothing but shining shoes." This vicious circle is met with in all analogous circumstances; when an individual (or a group of individuals) is kept in a situation of inferiority, the fact is that he *is* inferior. But the significance of the verb *to be* must be rightly understood here; it is in bad faith to give it a static value when it really has the dynamic Hegelian sense of "to have become." Yes, women on the whole *are* today inferior to men; that is, their situation affords them fewer possibilities. The question is: should that state of affairs continue?

31 Denis Diderot (1713–1784) was a French philosopher best known as the chief editor of *L'Encyclopédie*. Arguably the supreme literary creation of the Age of Enlightenment, *L'Encyclopédie* attempted to present all the achievements of human learning in a single (28 volume) work.

32 [Author's note] See Part II, pp. 115–117 [not reprinted here].

33 From the 1880s until, in many cases, the 1960s, more than half of the US states passed "Jim Crow" laws (so-called after a black character in minstrel shows) to enforce segregation, imposing legal punishments on people for consorting with members of another race. For example, business owners and public institutions were often ordered to keep their black and white clientele separated.

34 Shaw (1856–1950) was an Irish playwright and critic, awarded the Nobel Prize in Literature in 1925. In addition to his plays, he is also the author of *The Intelligent Woman's Guide to Socialism and Capitalism* (1928).

Many men hope that it will continue; not all have given up the battle. The conservative bourgeoisie still see in the emancipation of women a menace to their morality and their interests. Some men dread feminine competition. Recently a male student wrote in the *Hebdo-Latin*:[35] "Every woman student who goes into medicine or law robs us of a job." He never questioned his rights in this world. And economic interests are not the only ones concerned. One of the benefits that oppression confers upon the oppressors is that the most humble among them is made to *feel* superior; thus, a "poor white" in the South can console himself with the thought that he is not a "dirty nigger"—and the more prosperous whites cleverly exploit this pride.

Similarly, the most mediocre of males feels himself a demigod as compared with women. It was much easier for M. de Montherlant to think himself a hero when he faced women (and women chosen for his purpose) than when he was obliged to act the man among men—something many women have done better than he, for that matter. And in September 1948, in one of his articles in the *Figaro littéraire*, Claude Mauriac—whose great originality is admired by all—could[36] write regarding woman: "*We* listen on a tone [*sic!*] of polite indifference ... to the most brilliant among them, well knowing that her wit reflects more or less luminously ideas that come from *us*."[37] Evidently the speaker referred to is not reflecting the ideas of Mauriac himself, for no one knows of his having any. It may be that she reflects ideas originating with men, but then, even among men there are those who have been known to appropriate ideas not their own; and one can well ask whether Claude Mauriac might

not find more interesting a conversation reflecting Descartes, Marx, or Gide[38] rather than himself. What is really remarkable is that by using the questionable *we* he identifies himself with St. Paul, Hegel, Lenin, and Nietzsche, and from the lofty eminence of their grandeur looks down disdainfully upon the bevy of women who make bold to converse with him on a footing of equality. In truth, I know of more than one woman who would refuse to suffer with patience Mauriac's "tone of polite indifference."

I have lingered on this example because the masculine attitude is here displayed with disarming ingenuousness. But men profit in many more subtle ways from the otherness, the alterity[39] of woman. Here is miraculous balm for those afflicted with an inferiority complex, and indeed no one is more arrogant toward women, more aggressive or scornful, than the man who is anxious about his virility. Those who are not fear-ridden in the presence of their fellow men are much more disposed to recognize a fellow creature in woman; but even to these the myth of Woman, the Other, is precious for many reasons.[40] They cannot be blamed for not cheerfully relinquishing all the benefits they derive from the myth, for they realize what they

---

35 Like *Franchise*, another ephemeral magazine of the era.

36 [Author's note] Or at least he thought he could.

37 Claude Mauriac (1914–1996) was a French journalist, critic, and avant-garde novelist. Several of his experimental novels (published in the late 1950s and early 1960s) focus on the exploits of a cold-hearted, womanizing egoist named Bertrand Carnéjoux. *Figaro littéraire* is the literary supplement of the French daily newspaper *Le Figaro* (which has been in operation since 1866).

38 André Gide (1869–1951), a French novelist, intellectual, literary critic, and social crusader (for, especially, homosexual rights). He received the Nobel Prize for Literature in 1947.

39 *Alterity* is the state of being different, especially lack of identification with some part of one's personality or community. It has come to be a technical, philosophical term for the principle of exchanging one's own perspective for that of the Other.

40 [Author's note] A significant article on this theme by Michel Carrouges appeared in No. 292 of the *Cahiers du Sud*. He writes indignantly: "Would that there were no woman-myth at all but only a cohort of cooks, matrons, prostitutes, and bluestockings serving functions of pleasure or usefulness!" That is to say, in his view woman has no existence in and for herself; he thinks only of her *function* in the male world. Her reason for existence lies in man. But then, in fact, her poetic "function" as a myth might be more valued than any other. The real problem is precisely to find out why woman should be defined with relation to man.

would lose in relinquishing woman as they fancy her to be, while they fail to realize what they have to gain from the woman of tomorrow. Refusal to pose oneself as the Subject, unique and absolute, requires great self-denial. Furthermore, the vast majority of men make no such claim explicitly. They do not *postulate* woman as inferior, for today they are too thoroughly imbued with the ideal of democracy not to recognize all human beings as equals.

In the bosom of the family, woman seems in the eyes of childhood and youth to be clothed in the same social dignity as the adult males. Later on, the young man, desiring and loving, experiences the resistance, the independence of the woman desired and loved; in marriage, he respects woman as wife and mother, and in the concrete events of conjugal life she stands there before him as a free being. He can therefore feel that social subordination as between the sexes no longer exists and that on the whole, in spite of differences, woman is an equal. As, however, he observes some points of inferiority—the most important being unfitness for the professions—he attributes these to natural causes. When he is in a co-operative and benevolent relation with woman, his theme is the principle of abstract equality, and he does not base his attitude upon such inequality as may exist. But when he is in conflict with her, the situation is reversed: his theme will be the existing inequality, and he will even take it as justification for denying abstract equality.[41]

So it is that many men will affirm as if in good faith that women *are* the equals of man and that they have nothing to clamor for, while *at the same time* they will say that women can never be the equals of man and that their demands are in vain. It is, in point of fact, a difficult matter for man to realize the extreme importance of social discriminations which seem outwardly insignificant but which produce in woman moral and intellectual effects so profound

that they appear to spring from her original nature.[42] The most sympathetic of men never fully comprehend woman's concrete situation. And there is no reason to put much trust in the men when they rush to the defense of privileges whose full extent they can hardly measure. We shall not, then, permit ourselves to be intimidated by the number and violence of the attacks launched against women, nor to be entrapped by the self-seeking eulogies bestowed on the "true woman," nor to profit by the enthusiasm for woman's destiny manifested by men who would not for the world have any part of it.

We should consider the arguments of the feminists with no less suspicion, however, for very often their controversial aim deprives them of all real value. If the "woman question" seems trivial, it is because masculine arrogance has made of it a "quarrel"; and when quarreling one no longer reasons well. People have tirelessly sought to prove that woman is superior, inferior, or equal to man. Some say that, having been created after Adam, she is evidently a secondary being; others say on the contrary that Adam was only a rough draft and that God succeeded in producing the human being in perfection when He created Eve. Woman's brain is smaller; yes, but it is relatively larger. Christ was made a man; yes, but perhaps for his greater humility. Each argument at once suggests its opposite, and both are often fallacious. If we are to gain understanding, we must get out of these ruts; we must discard the vague notions of superiority, inferiority, equality which have hitherto corrupted every discussion of the subject and start afresh.

Very well, but just how shall we pose the question? And, to begin with, who are we to propound it at all? Man is at once judge and party to the case; but so is woman. What we need is an angel—neither man nor woman—but where shall we find one? Still, the angel would be poorly qualified to speak, for an angel is ignorant of all the basic facts involved in the problem. With a hermaphrodite we should be no better off, for here the situation is most peculiar; the hermaphrodite is not really the combination of a whole man and a whole woman, but consists of parts

---

41   [Author's note] For example, a man will say that he considers his wife in no wise degraded because she has no gainful occupation. The profession of housewife is just as lofty, and so on. But when the first quarrel comes he will exclaim: "Why, you couldn't make your living without me!"

42   [Author's note] The specific purpose of Book II of this study is to describe this process.

of each and thus is neither. It looks to me as if there are, after all, certain women who are best qualified to elucidate the situation of woman. Let us not be misled by the sophism that because Epimenides was a Cretan he was necessarily a liar;[43] it is not a mysterious essence that compels men and women to act in good or in bad faith, it is their situation that inclines them more or less toward the search for truth. Many of today's women, fortunate in the restoration of all the privileges pertaining to the estate of the human being, can afford the luxury of impartiality—we even recognize its necessity. We are no longer like our partisan elders; by and large we have won the game. In recent debates on the status of women the United Nations has persistently maintained that the equality of the sexes is now becoming a reality, and already some of us have never had to sense in our femininity an inconvenience or an obstacle. Many problems appear to us to be more pressing than those which concern us in particular, and this detachment even allows us to hope that our attitude will be objective. Still, we know the feminine world more intimately than do the men because we have our roots in it, we grasp more immediately than do men what it means to a human being to be feminine; and we are more concerned with such knowledge. I have said that there are more pressing problems, but this does not prevent us from seeing some importance in asking how the fact of being women will affect our lives. What opportunities precisely have been given us and what withheld? What fate awaits our younger sisters, and what directions should they take? It is significant that books by women on women are in general animated in our day less by a wish to demand our rights than by an effort toward clarity and understanding. As we emerge from an era of excessive controversy, this book is offered as one attempt among others to confirm that statement.

But it is doubtless impossible to approach any human problem with a mind free from bias. The way in which questions are put, the points of view assumed, presuppose a relativity of interest; all characteristics imply values, and every objective description, so called, implies an ethical background. Rather than attempt to conceal principles more or less definitely implied, it is better to state them openly at the beginning. This will make it unnecessary to specify on every page in just what sense one uses such words as *superior*, *inferior*, *better*, *worse*, *progress*, *reaction*, and the like. If we survey some of the works on woman, we note that one of the points of view most frequently adopted is that of the public good, the general interest; and one always means by this the benefit of society as one wishes it to be maintained or established. For our part, we hold that the only public good is that which assures the private good of the citizens; we shall pass judgment on institutions according to their effectiveness in giving concrete opportunities to individuals. But we do not confuse the idea of private interest with that of happiness, although that is another common point of view. Are not women of the harem[44] more happy than women voters? Is not the housekeeper happier than the working-woman? It is not too clear just what the word *happy* really means and still less what true values it may mask. There is no possibility of measuring the happiness of others, and it is always easy to describe as happy the situation in which one wishes to place them.

In particular those who are condemned to stagnation are often pronounced happy on the pretext that happiness consists in being at rest. This notion we reject, for our perspective is that of existentialist ethics. Every subject plays his part as such specifically through exploits or projects that serve as a mode of transcendence; he achieves liberty only through a continual reaching out toward other liberties. There is no justification for present existence other than its expansion into an indefinitely open future. Every time transcendence falls back into immanence, stagnation, there is a degradation of existence into the "*en-soi*"— the brutish life of subjection to given conditions—and

---

43 The Cretan philosopher Epimenides of Knossos (who lived around 600 BCE) invented a famous logical paradox by asserting, "Cretans, always liars." That is, since Epimenides himself was a Cretan, if this sentence is true then it must be false; a bit less obviously, if it is false then (arguably) it is true since it says of itself that it is false, which is true.

---

44 The private part of an Arab household, traditionally forbidden to male strangers.

of liberty into constraint and contingence. This downfall represents a moral fault if the subject consents to it; if it is inflicted upon him, it spells frustration and oppression. In both cases it is an absolute evil. Every individual concerned to justify his existence feels that his existence involves an undefined need to transcend himself, to engage in freely chosen projects.

Now, what peculiarly signalizes the situation of woman is that she—a free and autonomous being like all human creatures—nevertheless finds herself living in a world where men compel her to assume the status of the Other. They propose to stabilize her as object and to doom her to immanence since her transcendence is to be overshadowed and forever transcended by another ego (*conscience*) which is essential and sovereign. The drama of woman lies in this conflict between the fundamental aspirations of every subject (ego)—who always regards the self as the essential—and the compulsions of a situation in which she is the inessential. How can a human being in woman's situation attain fulfillment? What roads are open to her? Which are blocked? How can

independence be recovered in a state of dependency? What circumstances limit woman's liberty and how can they be overcome? These are the fundamental questions on which I would fain throw some light. This means that I am interested in the fortunes of the individual as defined not in terms of happiness but in terms of liberty.

Quite evidently this problem would be without significance if we were to believe that woman's destiny is inevitably determined by physiological, psychological, or economic forces. Hence I shall discuss first of all the light in which woman is viewed by biology, psychoanalysis, and historical materialism. Next I shall try to show exactly how the concept of the "truly feminine" has been fashioned—why woman has been defined as the Other—and what have been the consequences from man's point of view. Then from woman's point of view I shall describe the world in which women must live; and thus we shall be able to envisage the difficulties in their way as, endeavoring to make their escape from the sphere hitherto assigned them, they aspire to full membership in the human race.

JOHN RAWLS

Justice as Fairness: A Restatement

Who Is John Rawls?

John Borden Rawls was, until his death in 2002, perhaps the world's most important contemporary political philosopher, and his 1971 book *A Theory of Justice* is generally regarded as the most significant work of political theory published in the twentieth century. Born in 1921 in Baltimore to an upper-class southern family, Rawls's father was a successful tax lawyer and constitutional expert while his mother was the feminist president of the local League of Women Voters. As a boy, Rawls was sent to Kent, a renowned Episcopalian preparatory school in Connecticut, and then went

on to Princeton for his undergraduate degree. In 1943, he joined the US infantry and served in New Guinea, the Philippines, and Japan (where he witnessed firsthand the aftermath of the atomic bombing of Hiroshima). He turned down the opportunity to become an officer, and left the army as a private in 1946, returning to Princeton to pursue his PhD in philosophy.

After completing the doctorate, he taught at Princeton for two years, visited Oxford University for a year on a Fulbright Fellowship, and was then employed as a professor at Cornell. In 1964 Rawls moved to Harvard University, where he was appointed James Bryant Conant Professor of Philosophy in 1979.

Throughout the eighties and early nineties Rawls was an omnipresent figure in political philosophy, and exerted a great influence on the discipline through his teaching and mentoring of younger academics as well as his writings. Unfortunately, in 1995, Rawls suffered the first of several strokes that seriously impeded his ability to continue working.

Though Rawls was always much more the reclusive academic than a campaigning public figure, his work was nevertheless guided by a deep personal commitment to combating injustice. Because of his family's origins in the American south, one of Rawls's earliest moral concerns was the injustice of black slavery. He was interested in formulating a moral theory that not only showed slavery to be unjust, but described its injustice *in the right way*. For Rawls, the immorality of slavery does not lie merely in the fact that benefits for slaveowners were outweighed by harms done to slaves—rather, slavery is the kind of thing that should *never* be imposed on any human being, no matter what overall benefits or efficiencies it might bring about. Thus, Rawls found himself opposed to the then-dominant political morality of utilitarianism, and seeking a new foundation for social justice in the work of Immanuel Kant and social contract theorists such as John Locke and Jean-Jacques Rousseau.[1]

Two guiding assumptions behind Rawls's neo-Kantian project (he calls it "Kantian constructivism") have been, first, that there is such a thing as moral truth—that at least some fundamental moral questions have objectively correct answers, even if it is difficult to discover them—and second, that "the right"

is separate from and prior to "the good." This latter claim is the idea (which is found in Kant) that the morally right thing to do cannot be defined as, and will not always be the same thing as, the maximization of some moral good, such as happiness or equality. There are certain constraints on how people can be treated which always take precedence over the general welfare.

The central doctrine which has informed the resulting political morality is what Rawls calls "justice as fairness." This is the view that social institutions should not confer morally arbitrary long-term advantages on some persons at the expense of others. According to Rawls, one's prospects and opportunities in life are strongly influenced by the circumstances of one's birth—one's place in the social, political, and economic structure defined by the basic institutions of one's society. For example, one might have been born to slaveowners or to slaves, to a wealthy political dynasty in New England or to a poor family in a Philadelphia ghetto, to an Anglophone or to a Francophone family in 1950s Montréal. These important differences are morally arbitrary—a mere matter of luck—not something for which people deserve to be either rewarded or punished. According to Rawls, therefore, the fundamental problem of social justice is to ensure that the basic institutions of our society are set up in such a way that they do not generate and perpetuate morally arbitrary inequalities.

The upshot of this, in Rawls's view, includes the radical result that inequalities in wealth, income, and other "primary social goods" are justified *only* if they are to the advantage of the least well off in society. Rawls's work has thus been widely seen (and criticized) as the philosophical foundation for a particularly egalitarian and left-wing version of the modern welfare state, and also—because of his emphasis

1   See Chapter 7 for readings on utilitarianism and Kant's moral theory. Social contract theory is represented by the Hobbes reading in this chapter.

on a set of universal, indefeasible basic rights and liberties—as an important successor to the rich tradition of liberal political thought.

What Is the Structure of This Reading?

The selection reprinted here comes from Rawls's recent book *Justice as Fairness*. In it he sets out to re-present, in their final form, the ideas first laid out in his seminal 1971 work *A Theory of Justice*. The heart of his substantive theory is the so-called "two principles of justice," and his description of these (though not his extended argument for their adequacy) is included here.

In Part I of *Justice as Fairness* Rawls lays out the fundamental ideas underlying his political theory, including the important notion of society as a fair system of co-operation, and the main concepts involved in arguing for his theory of justice as being justified by a "contract" made in the "original position." Some of these basic notions are briefly described in "Some Useful Background Information," below. Part II of the book presents his two principles of justice, and the first two sections of it are reprinted here. In the first section, Rawls summarizes three basic points which inform and constrain his reasoning, and in the second he describes the two principles themselves. In the rest of Part II (not included) he provides more details about the two principles, and in Part III he lays out the argument from the original position. In Part IV he describes some of the institutions of a just basic structure, and finally in Part V he address questions about the political stability of such a society.

Some Useful Background Information

1. Rawls believes democratic societies are always characterized by what he calls "the fact of reasonable pluralism." By this he means "the fact of profound and irreconcilable differences in citizens' reasonable comprehensive religious and philosophical conceptions of the world, and in their views of the moral and aesthetic values to be sought in human life." A consequence of this reasonable pluralism, Rawls believes, is that a democratic society can never genuinely be a *community*—a collection of persons united in affirming and pursuing the same conception of the good life. Rawls therefore proposes that we adopt—in fact, tacitly already have adopted—a different view of contemporary society: one that sees it as *a fair system of co-operation between free and equal citizens*. The task of a theory of justice then becomes one of specifying the fair terms of co-operation (and doing so in a way that is acceptable—that seems fair—even to citizens who have widely divergent conceptions of the good).

2. Rawls assumes the primary subject of this kind of theory of justice will be what he calls the *basic structure* of society. "[T]he basic structure of society is the way in which the main political and social institutions of society fit together into one system of social co-operation, and the way they assign basic rights and duties and regulate the division of advantages that arises from social co-operation over time.... The basic structure is the background social framework within which the activities of associations and individuals take place." Examples of components of the basic structure include the political constitution, the relationship between the judiciary and the government, the structure of the economic system, and the social institution of the family. The kinds of things *not* included in the basic structure—and thus affected only indirectly by Rawls's theory of justice—are the internal arrangements of associations such as churches and universities, particular pieces of non-constitutional legislation or legal decisions, and social relationships between individual citizens.

3. If justice consists in the fair terms of co-operation for society viewed as a system of co-operation, then the question becomes: how are these fair terms of co-operation arrived at? Since the fact of reasonable pluralism precludes appeal to any kind of shared moral authority or outlook, Rawls concludes that the free terms of co-operation must be "settled by an agreement reached by free and equal citizens engaged in co-operation, and made in view of what they

regard as their reciprocal advantage." Furthermore this contract, like any agreement, must be made under conditions which are fair to all the parties involved. Rawls's attempt to specify the circumstances in which agreement on the basic structure of society would be fair is called the *original position*.

In the original position, the parties to the contract are placed behind what Rawls calls a *veil of ignorance*: they are not allowed to know their social positions; their particular comprehensive doctrines of the good; their race, sex, or ethnic group; or their genetic endowments of such things as strength and intelligence. In other words, knowledge of all the contingent or arbitrary aspects of one's place in actual society are removed. On the other hand, the parties in the original position are assumed to be well-informed about such things as economic and political theory and human psychology, and to be rational. In this way, all information which would—in Rawls's view—introduce unfair distortions into the social contract is excluded from the original position and only the data needed to make a fair decision are allowed in: thus, for example, there could be no question of rich people trying to establish a basic social structure which protects their wealth by disadvantaging the poor, since nobody in the original position knows whether they are rich or poor.

Rawls's idea is that whatever contract would be agreed to by representatives in the original position must be a fair one, one that any reasonable citizen could accept no matter what their place in society or their conception of the good. This contract is, of course, merely hypothetical (there was never actually any original position). Rawls's point is not that citizens are actually bound by a historical social contract, but that the thought-experiment of making a contract in the original position is a device for showing what principles of justice *we should accept if we are reasonable*. And, Rawls argues, the principles that would be rationally arrived at in the original position will not be, say, utili-

tarian, or non-egalitarian, but will be something very much like his two principles of justice.

Suggestions for Critical Reflection

1. Rawls restricts the application of his theory of justice to democratic societies. Why do you think he makes this restriction? Is it appropriate to stipulate such preconditions for a philosophical theory of social justice? Could his theory of justice as fairness be recast to apply to *all* kinds of societies, and not just democracies?

2. Rawls argues "the fact of reasonable pluralism" in democratic societies gives rise to a problem of political legitimacy, and offers what he calls a "liberal" solution to that problem via a "political" conception of justice. How plausible is it that democracies really do face the deep problem of political legitimacy which Rawls describes? How adequate and attractive do you find his proposed solution? Is the kind of political conception of justice Rawls describes even *available* in contemporary liberal democratic societies?

3. Rawls appeals several times to "our firmest considered convictions" to help us decide what the basic structure of a just society should look like. Is this kind of appeal to intuition legitimate—or avoidable—in political philosophy?

4. Rawls's theory of justice as fairness is encapsulated in his two principles. How plausible and attractive are they? How radical are they? What kind of implications might they have, if any, which could be controversial? What changes would we have to make to bring our society into accord with these principles (in particular with the second principle, which deals with distributive justice)?

5. The "difference principle" makes a crucial reference to the "least-advantaged members of society." Who exactly is Rawls thinking of here? What difference does it make?

6. The first part of the second principle stipulates "fair equality of opportunity." What does Rawls seem to have in mind? How different is Rawls's idea of fair equality of opportunity from what

one might think of as the "free market" view of equal opportunity?

7. Rawls emphasizes that the question of the justice of social inequalities arises, for his theory, only *after* basic equal liberties and fair equality of opportunity have been secured. Why does he prioritize his principles in this way? Is he right to do so? Does this "lexical ordering" of the principles mean substantial social inequalities could, in fact, be justified in a Rawlsian society?

8. Why does Rawls not consider the second principle of justice a "constitutional essential"? What is the significance of this?

9. Rawls suggests the notion of democratic equality "involves reciprocity at the deepest level," and that this in turn requires "something like the difference principle." Is he right? What kind of argument might he have in mind?

Suggestions for Further Reading

Rawls's main work, and the first place to turn when delving further into Rawls, is *A Theory of Justice* (1971, revised edition Harvard University Press, 1999). Many of these themes are further developed and defended in his book *Political Liberalism* (Columbia University Press, 1995). *Justice as Fairness: A Restatement* (Harvard University Press, 2001) is a useful and accessible presentation of Rawls's mature view. *The Law of Peoples* (Harvard University Press, 1999) applies the Rawlsian outlook to international politics, while his *Collected Papers* (Harvard University Press, 1999) and a series of *Lectures on the History of Moral Philosophy* (Harvard University Press, 2000) have also recently been published.

Some significant critiques and developments of Rawls's justice as fairness are found in: Roberto Alejandro, *The Limits of Rawlsian Justice* (Johns Hopkins University Press, 1998); Brian Barry, *The Liberal Theory of Justice* (Oxford University Press, 1973) and *Theories of Justice* (University of California Press, 1991); Daniel Dombrowski, *Rawls and Religion* (State University of New York Press, 2001); Kukathas and Pettit, *Rawls* (Stanford University Press, 1990); Rex Martin, *Rawls and Rights* (University Press of Kansas, 1985); Robert Nozick, *Anarchy, State, and Utopia* (Basic Books, 1974); A. Pampapathy Rao, *Distributive Justice* (International

Scholars Publications, 1998); Thomas Pogge, *Realizing Rawls* (Cornell University Press, 1989); Michael Sandel, *Liberalism and the Limits of Justice* (Cambridge University Press, 1998); David Lewis Schaefer, *Justice or Tyranny?* (Associated Faculty Press, 1979); and Robert Paul Wolff, *Understanding Rawls* (Princeton University Press, 1977).

Collections of articles on Rawls's philosophy include J. Angelo Corlett (ed.), *Equality and Liberty* (Palgrave, 1991); Norman Daniels (ed.), *Reading Rawls* (Stanford University Press, 1989); and Mulhall and Swift, *Liberals and Communitarians* (Blackwell, 1996). Finally, an excellent overview of the relevant philosophical terrain is Will Kymlicka's *Contemporary Political Philosophy* (Oxford University Press, 2001).

Justice as Fairness: A Restatement[2]
Part II: Principles of Justice, §§ 12–13

§12. Three Basic Points

12.1. In Part II we discuss the content of the two principles of justice that apply to the basic structure, as well as various grounds in favor of them and replies to a number of objections. A more formal and organized argument for these principles is presented in Part III, where we discuss the reasoning that moves the parties in the original position. In that argument the original position serves to keep track of all our assumptions and to bring out their combined force by uniting them into one framework so that we can more easily see their implications.

I begin with three basic points which review some matters discussed in Part I and introduce others we are about to examine. Recall first that justice as fairness is framed for a democratic society. Its principles are meant to answer the question: once we view a demo-

---

2   Reprinted with permission of the publisher from "Three Basic Points" and "Two Principles of Justice" in *Justice as Fairness: A Restatement* by John Rawls, edited by Erin Kelly, pp. 39–50, Cambridge: Mass.: The Belknap Press of Harvard University Press. Copyright © 2001 by the President and Fellows of Harvard College.

cratic society as a fair system of social cooperation between citizens regarded as free and equal, what principles are most appropriate to it? Alternatively: which principles are most appropriate for a democratic society that not only professes but wants to take seriously the idea that citizens are free and equal, and tries to realize that idea in its main institutions? The question of whether a constitutional regime is to be preferred to majoritarian democracy, we postpone until later (Part IV, §44).[3]

12.2. The second point is that justice as fairness takes the primary subject of political justice to be the basic structure of society, that is, its main political and social institutions and how they fit together into one unified system of cooperation (§4). We suppose that citizens are born into society and will normally spend their whole lives within its basic institutions. The nature and role of the basic structure importantly influence social and economic inequalities and enter into determining the appropriate principles of justice.

In particular, let us suppose that the fundamental social and economic inequalities are the differences in citizens' life-prospects (their prospects over a complete life) as these are affected by such things as their social class of origin, their native endowments, their opportunities for education, and their good or ill fortune over the course of life (§16). We ask: by what principles are differences of that kind—differences in life-prospects—made legitimate and consistent with the idea of free and equal citizenship in society seen as a fair system of cooperation?

12.3. The third point is that justice as fairness is a form of political liberalism: it tries to articulate a family of highly significant (moral) values that characteristi-

cally apply to the political and social institutions of the basic structure. It gives an account of these values in the light of certain special features of the political relationship as distinct from other relationships, associational, familial, and personal.

> (a) It is a relationship of persons within the basic structure of society, a structure we enter only by birth and exit only by death (or so we may assume for the moment). Political society is closed, as it were; and we do not, and indeed cannot, enter or leave it voluntarily.
>
> (b) Political power is always coercive power applied by the state and its apparatus of enforcement; but in a constitutional regime political power is at the same time the power of free and equal citizens as a collective body. Thus political power is citizens' power, which they impose on themselves and one another as free and equal.

The idea of political liberalism arises as follows. We start from two facts: first, from the fact of reasonable pluralism, the fact that a diversity of reasonable comprehensive doctrines is a permanent feature of a democratic society; and second, from the fact that in a democratic regime political power is regarded as the power of free and equal citizens as a collective body. These two points give rise to a problem of political legitimacy. For if the fact of reasonable pluralism always characterizes democratic societies and if political power is indeed the power of free and equal citizens, in the light of what reasons and values—of what kind of a conception of justice—can citizens legitimately exercise that coercive power over one another?

Political liberalism answers that the conception of justice must be a political conception, as defined in §9.1.[4] Such a conception when satisfied allows us

---

3   In that section, Rawls explains that "[a] constitutional regime is one in which laws and statutes must be consistent with certain fundamental rights and liberties…. There is in effect a constitution (not necessarily written) with a bill of rights specifying those freedoms and interpreted by the courts as constitutional limits on legislation." By contrast, there are no constitutional limits on legislation in a majoritarian democracy, and whatever the majority decides (according to the proper procedures) is law.

4   According to Rawls, a conception of justice is *political* if, a) it applies only to the basic structure of society (and not directly to particular groups of people within those societies); b) it does not presuppose any particular comprehensive conception of the good life; and c) it is formulated, as far as possible, from ideas already implicit in the public political culture of a democratic society.

to say: political power is legitimate only when it is exercised in accordance with a constitution (written or unwritten) the essentials of which all citizens, as reasonable and rational, can endorse in the light of their common human reason. This is the liberal principle of legitimacy. It is a further desideratum[5] that all legislative questions that concern or border on these essentials, or are highly divisive, should also be settled, so far as possible, by guidelines and values that can be similarly endorsed.

In matters of constitutional essentials, as well as on questions of basic justice, we try to appeal only to principles and values each citizen can endorse. A political conception of justice hopes to formulate these values: its shared principles and values make reason public, while freedom of speech and thought in a constitutional regime make it free. In providing a public basis of justification, a political conception of justice provides the framework for the liberal idea of political legitimacy. As noted in §9.4, however, and discussed further in §26, we do not say that a political conception formulates political values that can settle all legislative questions. This is neither possible nor desirable. There are many questions legislatures must consider that can only be settled by voting that is properly influenced by nonpolitical values. Yet at least on constitutional essentials and matters of basic justice we do try for an agreed basis; so long as there is at least rough agreement here, fair social cooperation among citizens can, we hope, be maintained.[6]

12.4. Given these three points, our question is: viewing society as a fair system of cooperation between citizens regarded as free and equal, what principles of justice are most appropriate to specify basic rights and liberties, and to regulate social and economic in-

equalities in citizens' prospects over a complete life? These inequalities are our primary concern.

To find a principle to regulate these inequalities, we look to our firmest considered convictions about equal basic rights and liberties, the fair value of the political liberties as well as fair equality of opportunity. We look outside the sphere of distributive justice more narrowly construed to see whether an appropriate distributive principle is singled out by those firmest convictions once their essential elements are represented in the original position as a device of representation (§6). This device is to assist us in working out which principle, or principles, the representatives of free and equal citizens would select to regulate social and economic inequalities in these prospects over a complete life when they assume that the equal basic liberties and fair opportunities are already secured.

The idea here is to use our firmest considered convictions about the nature of a democratic society as a fair system of cooperation between free and equal citizens—as modeled in the original position—to see whether the combined assertion of those convictions so expressed will help us to identify an appropriate distributive principle for the basic structure with its economic and social inequalities in citizens' life-prospects. Our convictions about principles regulating those inequalities are much less firm and assured; so we look to our firmest convictions for guidance where assurance is lacking and guidance is needed (*Theory*, §§4, 20).

§13. Two Principles of Justice

13.1. To try to answer our question, let us turn to a revised statement of the two principles of justice discussed in *Theory*, §§11–14. They should now read:[7]

---

5   Something which is needed or considered highly desirable.

6   [Author's note] It is not always clear whether a question involves a constitutional essential, as will be mentioned in due course. If there is doubt about this and the question is highly divisive, then citizens have a duty of civility to try to articulate their claims on one another by reference to political values, if that is possible.

7   [Author's note] This section summarizes some points from "The Basic Liberties and Their Priority," *Tanner Lectures on Human Values*, vol. 3, ed. Sterling McMurrin (Salt Lake City: University of Utah Press, 1982), §I, reprinted in *Political Liberalism*. In that essay I try to reply to what I believe are two of the more serious objections to my account of liberty in *Theory* raised by H.L.A. Hart in his splendid critical review essay, "Rawls on Liberty and Its Priority," *University of Chicago Law Review* 40 (Spring 1975): 551–555, re-

(a) Each person has the same indefeasible[8] claim to a fully adequate scheme of equal basic liberties, which scheme is compatible with the same scheme of liberties for all; and

(b) Social and economic inequalities are to satisfy two conditions: first, they are to be attached to offices and positions open to all under conditions of fair equality of opportunity; and second, they are to be to the greatest benefit of the least-advantaged members of society (the difference principle).[9]

As I explain below, the first principle is prior to the second; also, in the second principle fair equality of opportunity is prior to the difference principle. This priority means that in applying a principle (or checking it against test cases) we assume that the prior principles are fully satisfied. We seek a principle of distribution (in the narrower sense) that holds within the setting of background institutions that secure the basic equal liberties (including the fair value of the political liberties)[10] as well as fair equality of opportunity. How far that principle holds outside that setting is a separate question we shall not consider.[11]

13.2. The revisions in the second principle are merely stylistic. But before noting the revisions in the first principle, which are significant,[12] we should attend to the meaning of fair equality of opportunity. This is a difficult and not altogether clear idea; its role is perhaps best gathered from why it is introduced: namely, to correct the defects of formal equality of opportunity—careers open to talents—in the system of natural liberty, so-called (*Theory*, §12: 62ff.; §14).[13] To this end, fair equality of opportunity is said to require not merely that public offices and social positions be open in the formal sense, but that all should have a fair chance to attain them. To specify the idea of a fair chance we say: supposing that there is a distribution of native endowments, those who have the same level

---

printed in his *Essays in Jurisprudence and Philosophy* (Oxford: Oxford University Press, 1983). No changes made in justice as fairness in this restatement are more significant than those forced by Hart's review.

8 One which cannot, under any circumstances, be annulled.

9 [Author's note] Instead of "the difference principle," many writers prefer the term "the maximin principle," or simply "maximin justice," or some such locution. See, for example, Joshua Cohen's very full and accurate account of the difference principle in "Democratic Equality," *Ethics* 99 (July 1989): 727–751. But I still use the term "difference principle" to emphasize first, that this principle and the maximin rule for decision under uncertainty (§28.1) are two very distinct things; and second, that in arguing for the difference principle over other distributive principles (say a restricted principle of (average) utility, which includes a social minimum), there is no appeal at all to the maximin rule for decision under uncertainty. The widespread idea that the argument for the difference principle depends on extreme aversion to uncertainty is a mistake, although a mistake unhappily encouraged by the faults of exposition in *Theory*, faults to be corrected in Part III of this restatement.

10 [Author's note] See *Theory*, §36: 197–199.

11 [Author's note] Some have found this kind of restriction objectionable; they think a political conception should be framed to cover all logically possible cases, or all conceivable cases, and not restricted to cases that can arise only within a specified institutional context. See for example Brian Barry, *The Liberal Theory of Justice* (Oxford: Oxford University Press, 1973), p. 112. In contrast, we seek a principle to govern social and economic inequalities in democratic regimes as we know them, and so we are concerned with inequalities in citizens' life-prospects that may actually arise, given our understanding of how certain institutions work.

12 Rawls's original, 1971 formulation was: "Each person is to have an equal right to the most extensive total system of equal basic liberties compatible with a similar system of liberty for all."

13 The "system of natural liberty," in Rawls's terminology, is one which assumes that, in an economically efficient free market economy, a basic structure "in which positions are open to those able and willing to strive for them will lead to a just distribution" (*A Theory of Justice*, §12), but which makes no effort to correct for arbitrary inequalities in the initial social conditions of the competitors.

of talent and ability and the same willingness to use these gifts should have the same prospects of success regardless of their social class of origin, the class into which they are born and develop until the age of reason. In all parts of society there are to be roughly the same prospects of culture and achievement for those similarly motivated and endowed.

Fair equality of opportunity here means liberal equality. To accomplish its aims, certain requirements must be imposed on the basic structure beyond those of the system of natural liberty. A free market system must be set within a framework of political and legal institutions that adjust the long-run trend of economic forces so as to prevent excessive concentrations of property and wealth, especially those likely to lead to political domination. Society must also establish, among other things, equal opportunities of education for all regardless of family income (§15).[14]

13.3. Consider now the reasons for revising the first principle.[15] One is that the equal basic liberties in this principle are specified by a list as follows: freedom of thought and liberty of conscience; political liberties (for example, the right to vote and to participate in politics) and freedom of association, as well as the rights and liberties specified by the liberty and integrity (physical and psychological) of the person; and finally, the rights and liberties covered by the rule of law. That the basic liberties are specified by a list is quite clear from *Theory*, §11: 61 (1st ed.); but the use of the singular term "basic liberty" in the statement of the principle in *Theory*, §11: 60 (1st ed.), obscures this important feature of these liberties.

This revision brings out that no priority is assigned to liberty as such, as if the exercise of something called "liberty" had a preeminent value and were the main, if not the sole, end of political and social justice. While there is a general presumption against imposing legal and other restrictions on conduct without a sufficient reason, this presumption creates no special priority for any particular liberty. Throughout the history of democratic thought the focus has been on achieving certain specific rights and liberties as well as specific constitutional guarantees, as found, for example, in various bills of rights and declarations of the rights of man. Justice as fairness follows this traditional view.

13.4. A list of basic liberties can be drawn up in two ways. One is historical: we survey various democratic regimes and assemble a list of rights and liberties that seem basic and are securely protected in what seem to be historically the more successful regimes. Of course, the veil of ignorance means that this kind of particular information is not available to the parties in the original position, but it is available to you and me in setting up justice as fairness.[16] We are perfectly free to use it to specify the principles of justice we make available to the parties.

A second way of drawing up a list of basic rights and liberties is analytical: we consider what liberties provide the political and social conditions essential for the adequate development and full exercise of the two moral powers of free and equal persons (§7.1).[17]

---

14   [Author's note] These remarks are the merest sketch of a difficult idea. We come back to it from time to time.

15   [Author's note] This principle may be preceded by a lexically prior principle requiring that basic needs be met, as least insofar as their being met is a necessary condition for citizens to understand and to be able fruitfully to exercise the basic rights and liberties. For a statement of such a principle with further discussion, see R.G. Peffer, *Marxism, Morality, and Social Justice* (Princeton: Princeton University Press, 1990), p.14.

16   [Author's note] Here I should mention that there are three points of view in justice as fairness that it is essential to distinguish: the point of view of the parties in the original position, the point of view of citizens in a well-ordered society, and the point of view of you and me who are setting up justice as fairness as a political conception and trying to use it to organize into one coherent view our considered judgments at all levels of generality. Keep in mind that the parties are, as it were, artificial persons who are part of a procedure of construction that we frame for our philosophical purposes. We may know many things that we keep from them. For these three points of view, see *Political Liberalism*, p. 28.

17   These moral powers are a) the capacity to understand, apply, and act from the principles of political justice,

Following this we say: first, that the equal political liberties and freedom of thought enable citizens to develop and to exercise these powers in judging the justice of the basic structure of society and its social policies; and second, that liberty of conscience and freedom of association enable citizens to develop and exercise their moral powers in forming and revising and in rationally pursuing (individually or, more often, in association with others) their conceptions of the good.

Those basic rights and liberties protect and secure the scope required for the exercise of the two moral powers in the two fundamental cases just mentioned: that is to say, the first fundamental case is the exercise of those powers in judging the justice of basic institutions and social policies; while the second fundamental case is the exercise of those powers in pursuing our conception of the good. To exercise our powers in these ways is essential to us as free and equal citizens.

13.5. Observe that the first principle of justice applies not only to the basic structure (both principles do this) but more specifically to what we think of as the constitution, whether written or unwritten. Observe also that some of these liberties, especially the equal political liberties and freedom of thought and association, are to be guaranteed by a constitution (*Theory*, chap. IV). What we may call "constituent power," as opposed to "ordinary power,"[18] is to be suitably institutionalized in the form of a regime: in the right to vote and to hold office, and in so-called bills of rights, as well as in the procedures for amending the constitution, for example.

These matters belong to the so-called constitutional essentials, these essentials being those crucial matters about which, given the fact of pluralism, working political agreement is most urgent (§9.4). In view of the fundamental nature of the basic rights and liberties, explained in part by the fundamental interests they protect, and given that the power of the people to constitute the form of government is a superior power (distinct from the ordinary power exercised routinely by officers of a regime), the first principle is assigned priority.

This priority means (as we have said) that the second principle (which includes the difference principle as one part) is always to be applied within a setting of background institutions that satisfy the requirements of the first principle (including the requirement of securing the fair value of the political liberties), as by definition they will in a well-ordered society.[19, 20] The fair value of the political liberties ensures that citizens similarly gifted and motivated have roughly an equal chance of influencing the government's policy and of attaining positions of authority irrespective of their economic and social class.[21] To explain the priority of the first principle over the second: this priority rules out exchanges ("trade-offs," as economists say)

---

19 [Author's note] It is sometimes objected to the difference principle as a principle of distributive justice that it contains no restrictions on the overall nature of permissible distributions. It is concerned, the objection runs, solely with the least advantaged. But this objection is incorrect: it overlooks the fact that the parts of the two principles of justice are designed to work in tandem and apply as a unit. The requirements of the prior principles have important distributive effects. Consider the effects of fair equality of opportunity as applied to education, say, or the distributive effects of the fair value of the political liberties. We cannot possibly take the difference principle seriously so long as we think of it by itself, apart from its setting within prior principles.

20 By "well-ordered society," Rawls means a society in which the following are true: a) all citizens accept the same political conception of justice, b) its basic structure is publicly known to satisfy those shared principles of justice, and c) citizens have an "effective sense of justice," i.e., they understand and act in accordance with those principles of justice.

21 [Author's note] See *Political Liberalism*, p. 358.

---

and b) the capacity to have, revise, and rationally pursue a conception of the good (i.e., what is of value in human life).

18 [Author's note] This distinction is derived from Locke, who speaks of the people's power to constitute the legislative as the first and fundamental law of all commonwealths. John Locke, *Second Treatise of Government*, §§134, 141, 149.

between the basic rights and liberties covered by the first principle and the social and economic advantages regulated by the difference principle. For example, the equal political liberties cannot be denied to certain groups on the grounds that their having these liberties may enable them to block policies needed for economic growth and efficiency.

Nor can we justify a selective service act that grants educational deferments or exemptions to some on the grounds that doing this is a socially efficient way both to maintain the armed forces and to provide incentives to those otherwise subject to conscription to acquire valuable skills by continuing their education. Since conscription is a drastic interference with the basic liberties of equal citizenship, it cannot be justified by any needs less compelling than those of the defense of these equal liberties themselves (*Theory*, §58: 333f.).

A further point about priority: in asserting the priority of the basic rights and liberties, we suppose reasonably favorable conditions to obtain. That is, we suppose historical, economic and social conditions to be such that, provided the political will exists, effective political institutions can be established to give adequate scope for the exercise of those freedoms. These conditions mean that the barriers to constitutional government (if such there are) spring largely from the political culture and existing effective interests, and not from, for instance, a lack of economic means, or education, or the many skills needed to run a democratic regime.[22]

13.6. It is important to note a distinction between the first and second principles of justice. The first principle, as explained by its interpretation, covers the constitutional essentials. The second principle requires fair equality of opportunity and that social and economic inequalities be governed by the difference principle, which we discuss in §§17–19. While some principle of opportunity is a constitutional essential—for example, a principle requiring an open society, one with careers open to talents (to use the eighteenth-century phrase)—fair equality of opportunity requires more than that, and is not counted a constitutional essential. Similarly, although a social minimum providing for the basic needs of all citizens is also a constitutional essential (§38.3–4; §49.5), the difference principle is more demanding and is not so regarded.

The basis for the distinction between the two principles is not that the first expresses political values while the second does not. Both principles express political values. Rather, we see the basic structure of society as having two coordinate roles, the first principle applying to one, the second principle to the other (*Theory*, §11: 53). In one role the basic structure specifies and secures citizens' equal basic liberties (including the fair value of the political liberties (§45)) and establishes a just constitutional regime. In the other role it provides the background institutions of social and economic justice in the form most appropriate to citizens seen as free and equal. The questions involved in the first role concern the acquisition and the exercise of political power. To fulfill the liberal principle of legitimacy (§12.3), we hope to settle at least these questions by appeal to the political values that constitute the basis of free public reason (§26).[23]

The principles of justice are adopted and applied in a four-stage sequence.[24] In the first stage, the parties adopt the principles of justice behind a veil of ignorance. Limitations on knowledge available to the parties are progressively relaxed in the next three stages: the stage of the constitutional convention, the legislative stage in which laws are enacted as the constitution allows and as the principles of justice require and permit, and the final stage in which the

---

22 [Author's note] The priority (or the primacy) of the basic equal liberties does not, contrary to much opinion, presuppose a high level of wealth and income. See Amartya Sen and Jean Dreze, *Hunger and Public Action* (Oxford: Oxford University Press, 1989), chap. 13; and Partha Dasgupta, *An Inquiry into Well-Being and Destitution* (Oxford: Oxford University Press, 1999), chaps. 1–2, 5 and passim.

23 By "free public reason," Rawls means the principles of reasoning and the rules of evidence which are accepted by all the citizens of a well-ordered society (irrespective of their differing conceptions of the good).

24 [Author's note] See *Theory*, §31: 172–176, and *Political Liberalism* pp. 397–398.

rules are applied by administrators and followed by citizens generally and the constitution and laws are interpreted by members of the judiciary. At this last stage, everyone has complete access to all the facts. The first principle applies at the stage of the constitutional convention, and whether the constitutional essentials are assured is more or less visible on the face of the constitution and in its political arrangements and the way these work in practice. By contrast the second principle applies at the legislative stage and it bears on all kinds of social and economic legislation, and on the many kinds of issues arising at this point (*Theory*, §31: 172–176). Whether the aims of the second principle are realized is far more difficult to ascertain. To some degree these matters are always open to reasonable differences of opinion; they depend on inference and judgment in assessing complex social and economic information. Also, we can expect more agreement on constitutional essentials than on issues of distributive justice in the narrower sense.

Thus the grounds for distinguishing the constitutional essentials covered by the first principle and the institutions of distributive justice covered by the second are not that the first principle expresses political values and the second does not. Rather, the grounds of the distinction are four:

> (a) The two principles apply to different stages in the application of principles and identify two distinct roles of the basic structure;
> (b) It is more urgent to settle the constitutional essentials;
> (c) It is far easier to tell whether those essentials are realized; and
> (d) It seems possible to gain agreement on what those essentials should be, not in every detail, of course, but in the main outlines.

13.7. One way to see the point of the idea of constitutional essentials is to connect it with the idea of loyal opposition, itself an essential idea of a constitutional regime. The government and its loyal opposition agree on these constitutional essentials. Their so agreeing makes the government legitimate in intention and the opposition loyal in its opposition. Where the loyalty of both is firm and their agreement mutually recognized, a constitutional regime is secure. Differences about

the most appropriate principles of distributive justice in the narrower sense, and the ideals that underlie them, can be adjudicated, though not always properly, within the existing political framework.

While the difference principle does not fall under the constitutional essentials, it is nevertheless important to try to identify the idea of equality most appropriate to citizens viewed as free and equal, and as normally and fully cooperating members of society over a complete life. I believe this idea involves reciprocity[25] at the deepest level and thus democratic equality properly understood requires something like the difference principle. (I say "something like," for there may be various nearby possibilities.) The remaining sections of this part (§§14–22) try to clarify the content of this principle and to clear up a number of difficulties.

---

25 [Author's note] As understood in justice as fairness, reciprocity is a relation between citizens expressed by principles of justice that regulate a social world in which all who are engaged in cooperation and do their part as the rules and procedures require are to benefit in an appropriate way as assessed by a suitable benchmark of comparison. The two principles of justice, including the difference principle with its implicit reference to equal division as a benchmark, formulate an idea of reciprocity between citizens. For a fuller discussion of the idea of reciprocity, see *Political Liberalism*, pp. 16–17, and the introduction to the paperback edition, pp. xliv, xlvi, li. The idea of reciprocity also plays an important part in "The Idea of Public Reason Revisited," *University of Chicago Law Review*, 64 (Summer 1997): 765–807, reprinted in *The Law of Peoples* (Cambridge, Mass.: Harvard University Press, 1999) and *Collected Papers*.

ROBERT NOZICK
Anarchy, State, and Utopia

Who Was Robert Nozick?

Robert Nozick was born in 1938 and grew up in Brooklyn, New York. He took his undergraduate degree at Columbia College and his PhD, on theories of rational decision-making, at Princeton. He taught at Princeton from 1962 until 1965, Harvard from 1965 to 1967, Rockefeller University from 1967 until 1969, and then returned to Harvard, a full professor of philosophy, at the tender age of 30. Already well-known in philosophical circles, Nozick's first book, *Anarchy, State, and Utopia* (1974) propelled him into the public eye with its controversial but intellectually dazzling defense of political libertarianism. It won the National Book Award and was named by *The Times Literary Supplement* as one of "The Hundred Most Influential Books Since the War." In 1998, Nozick was made Joseph Pellegrino University Professor at Harvard. Sadly he died of stomach cancer in 2002, at the relatively young age of 63.

As a young man, Nozick was a radical left-winger; he was converted to libertarianism—the view that individual rights should be maximized and the role of the state minimized—as a graduate student, largely through reading *laissez-faire* economists like F.A. Hayek and Milton Friedman. However, he was never fully comfortable with his public reputation as a right-wing ideologue. In a 1978 article in *The New York Times Magazine*, he said, "right-wing people like the pro-free-market argument, but don't like the arguments for individual liberty in cases like gay rights—although I view them as an interconnecting whole."

In the same article, Nozick also described his fresh and lively approach to philosophical writing, noting, "[i]t is as though what philosophers want is a way of saying something that will leave the person they're talking to no escape. Well, why should they be bludgeoning people like that? It's not a nice way to behave."

Nozick's philosophical interests were notably broad. Best known for his work in political philosophy, he also made important contributions to epistemology (especially his notion of knowledge as a kind of "truth tracking"), metaphysics (with his "closest continuer" theory of personal identity), and decision theory (particularly through his introduction of Newcomb's problem to the philosophical literature).

What Is the Structure of This Reading?

In Part I of *Anarchy, State, and Utopia*, Nozick argues that a minimal state is justified; then, in Part II, that no state more powerful or extensive than a minimal state is morally justified. In Part III he argues this is not an unfortunate result, that rather, the minimal state is "a framework for utopia" and "inspiring as well as right." The material reprinted here is from the first section of the first chapter of Part II, where Nozick argues that considerations of distributive justice do not require going beyond the minimal state, and, in fact, on the contrary, a proper account of distributive justice shows that state interference in distributive patterns must violate the rights of individuals.

Nozick first outlines what he considers the correct theory of distributive justice. He calls this the *entitlement theory of justice in holdings*, and presents it as made up of exactly three principles of justice. Nozick goes on to contrast what he calls *historical* theories of justice with *end-state* principles, and explains that the entitlement theory belongs to the former—in his view more plausible—type. He then distinguishes between two possible varieties of historical principles of justice—*patterned* or *non-patterned*—and claims that his entitlement theory belongs to the latter class. In the next section, Nozick argues that all end-state or patterned theories of distributive justice are inconsistent with liberty—i.e., they are committed to the repeated violation of the rights of individuals.

The final two sections deal with what Nozick calls the principle of justice in acquisition. He begins by critiquing John Locke's seventeenth-century theory of just acquisition, but preserves a version of the Lockean proviso that an acquisition is just only if it leaves "enough and as good left in common for others." He then spells out details and implications of such a proviso, including some of the constraints its "historical shadow" places on just transfers of holdings.

Some Useful Background Information

Nozick argues in *Anarchy, State, and Utopia* that only a minimal "night-watchman" state is consistent with individual liberty. A minimal state has a monopoly on the use of force within its boundaries (except for force used in immediate self-defense), and it uses this monopoly to guard its citizens against violence, theft, and fraud, and to enforce compliance with legally-made contracts. Beyond this, however, the minimal state has no legitimate function. For example, in the minimal state there can be no central bank or other form of economic regulation, no department of public works, no public education system, no welfare provisions or state pensions, no social healthcare system, no environmental protection regulations or agencies, and so on.

A Common Misconception

Nozick does not believe it is actually *immoral* to help the poor (or preserve the environment, or provide universal healthcare, or foster the arts …). He argues that it is immoral to *force* people to do these things—

in other words, that we have no legally enforceable *duty* to do them—but it is perfectly consistent to believe that it would be *morally good* if we were (voluntarily) to contribute to these ends.

Suggestions for Critical Reflection

1. What does Nozick mean when he claims that "[t]he term 'distributive justice' is not a neutral one"? Is the terminology he introduces instead any more "neutral"? What is the significance of this issue (if any) for the arguments that follow?

2. "Whatever arises from a just situation by just steps is itself just." Is this apparently straightforward claim *really* true? Can you think of any reasons to doubt it—for example, can you come up with any plausible counter-examples to this general claim? How significant a part of Nozick's general argument is this assertion? If we accept it, might we then be forced to accept a version of libertarianism, or is there a way of making it consistent with a more extensive state?

3. How plausible do you find Nozick's sketch of a principle of rectification of injustice? Is the goal of such rectifications to return injured parties (such as former slaves or their present-day children) to the position they would have been in had the injustice not occurred, or do we normally think there is more (or less) to it than that?

4. Is the distinction between historical and end-state principles of justice as clear-cut as Nozick presents it? Are most—or even many—theories of justice pure forms of one or the other? How comfortably, if at all, can historical and end-state views of justice be combined in a single theory (for example, an egalitarian theory)?

5. "People want their society to be and to look just. But must the look of justice reside in a resulting pattern rather than in the underlying generating principles?" This is a crucial question for Nozick, and the plausibility of his theory depends upon our willingness to answer, "No." But what if the entitlement theory generates distributive patterns which many people intui-

tively find *unjust*, such as very wide inequalities in wealth, educational opportunities, access to health care, and so on? Would we then want to say that distributive justice *does* place constraints on appropriate patterns of distribution for social goods? If so, what implications would this have for Nozick's theory of justice?

6. What do you think of Nozick's Wilt Chamberlain argument? If it is sound, what are its implications? If you think it is not sound, what, exactly, is wrong with it (bearing in mind that it's not enough to simply disagree with its conclusion)?

7. Nozick argues that distributional patterns "cannot be continuously realized without continuous interference with people's lives." Does this, in itself, show that no adequate principles of justice can be patterned? What ethical assumptions might Nozick be making here? Are these assumptions justified?

8. Does Nozick's "weaker" version of the Lockean proviso seem adequate as an account of justice in acquisition? Are you persuaded by his suggestion that the institution of private property is consistent with such a proviso? How substantial is the "baseline" problem he identifies?

9. How acceptable is Nozick's assertion that "[a] medical researcher who synthesizes a new substance that effectively treats a certain disease and who refuses to sell except on his terms" does not behave unjustly? Does Nozick's principle of justice in acquisition commit him to this position?

10. Nozick claims that the unfettered operations of a free market will be perfectly consistent with his Lockean proviso on justice. Do you agree? What justification might there be for such a claim?

Suggestions for Further Reading

Nozick's books cover a wide philosophical terrain, and each one is a stimulating read. They include: *Anarchy, State, and Utopia* (Basic Books, 1974); *Philosophical Explanations* (Harvard University Press, 1981); *The Examined Life* (Touchstone Books, 1990); *The Nature of Rationality* (Princeton University Press, 1993); *So-*

cratic Puzzles (Harvard University Press, 1997); and *Invariances: The Structure of the Objective World* (Harvard University Press, 2001). Five useful books explaining and critiquing Nozick's philosophy are: Jeffrey Paul (ed.), *Reading Nozick: Essays on 'Anarchy, State, and Utopia'* (Rowman & Littlefield, 1981); Jonathan Wolff, *Robert Nozick: Property, Justice, and the Minimal State* (Stanford University Press, 1991); Simon Hailwood, *Exploring Nozick: Beyond Anarchy, State, and Utopia* (Avebury, 1996); A.R. Lacey, *Robert Nozick* (Princeton University Press, 2001); and David Schmidtz (ed.), *Robert Nozick* (Cambridge University Press, 2002). Finally, two good sources for exploring libertarianism are David Boaz (ed.), *The Libertarian Reader* (Free Press, 1998) and Jan Narveson, *The Libertarian Idea* (Broadview Press, 2001).

from *Anarchy, State, and Utopia*[1]

The minimal state is the most extensive state that can be justified. Any state more extensive violates people's rights. Yet many persons have put forth reasons purporting to justify a more extensive state. It is impossible within the compass of this book to examine all the reasons that have been put forth. Therefore, I shall focus upon those generally acknowledged to be most weighty and influential, to see precisely wherein they fail. In this chapter we consider the claim that a more extensive state is justified, because necessary (or the best instrument) to achieve distributive justice; in the next chapter we shall take up diverse other claims.

The term "distributive justice" is not a neutral one. Hearing the term "distribution," most people presume that some thing or mechanism uses some principle or criterion to give out a supply of things. Into this process of distributing shares some error may have crept. So it is an open question, at least, whether *re*distribution should take place; whether we should do again what has already been done once,

---

1 From Chapter 7, "Distributive Justice," of *Anarchy, State, and Utopia* by Robert Nozick (New York: Basic Books, 1974), 149–164, 174–182. Copyright © 1974 by Basic Books, Inc. Reprinted by permission of Basic Books, a member of the Perseus Books Group.

though poorly. However, we are not in the position of children who have been given portions of pie by someone who now makes last minute adjustments to rectify careless cutting. There is no *central* distribution, no person or group entitled to control all the resources, jointly deciding how they are to be doled out. What each person gets, he gets from others who give to him in exchange for something, or as a gift. In a free society, diverse persons control different resources, and new holdings arise out of the voluntary exchanges and actions of persons. There is no more a distributing or distribution of shares than there is a distributing of mates in a society in which persons choose whom they shall marry. The total result is the product of many individual decisions which the different individuals involved are entitled to make. Some uses of the term "distribution," it is true, do not imply a previous distributing appropriately judged by some criterion (for example, "probability distribution"); nevertheless, despite the title of this chapter, it would be best to use a terminology that clearly is neutral. We shall speak of people's holdings; a principle of justice in holdings describes (part of) what justice tells us (requires) about holdings. I shall state first what I take to be the correct view about justice in holdings, and then turn to the discussion of alternate views.[2]

Section I:

The Entitlement Theory

The subject of justice in holdings consists of three major topics. The first is the *original acquisition of holdings*, the appropriation of unheld things. This includes the issues of how unheld things may come to be held, the process, or processes, by which unheld things may come to be held, the things that may come to be held by these processes, the extent of what comes to be held by a particular process, and so on. We shall refer to the complicated truth about this topic, which we shall not formulate here, as the principle of justice in acquisition. The second topic concerns the *transfer of holdings* from one person to another. By what processes may a person transfer holdings to another? How may a person acquire a holding from another who holds it? Under this topic come general descriptions of voluntary exchange, and gift and (on the other hand) fraud, as well as reference to particular conventional details fixed upon in a given society. The complicated truth about this subject (with placeholders for conventional details) we shall call the principle of justice in transfer. (And we shall suppose it also includes principles governing how a person may divest himself of a holding, passing it into an unheld state.)

If the world were wholly just, the following inductive definition would exhaustively cover the subject of justice in holdings.

1. A person who acquires a holding in accordance with the principle of justice in acquisition is entitled to that holding.
2. A person who acquires a holding in accordance with the principle of justice in transfer, from someone else entitled to the holding, is entitled to the holding.
3. No one is entitled to a holding except by (repeated) applications of 1 and 2.

The complete principle of distributive justice would say simply that a distribution is just if everyone is entitled to the holdings they possess under the distribution.

A distribution is just if it arises from another just distribution by legitimate means. The legitimate means of moving from one distribution to another are specified by the principle of justice in transfer. The legitimate first "moves" are specified by the principle of justice in acquisition.[3] Whatever arises

---

2   [Author's note] The reader who has looked ahead and seen that the second part of this chapter discusses Rawls' theory mistakenly may think that every remark or argument in the first part against alternative theories of justice is meant to apply to, or anticipate, a criticism of Rawls' theory. This is not so; there are other theories also worth criticizing.

---

3   [Author's note] Applications of the principle of justice in acquisition may also occur as part of the move from one distribution to another. You may find an unheld thing now and appropriate it. Acquisitions also are to be understood as included when, to simplify, I speak only of transitions by transfers.

from a just situation by just steps is itself just. The means of change specified by the principle of justice in transfer preserve justice. As correct rules of inference are truth-preserving, and any conclusion deduced via repeated application of such rules from only true premises is itself true, so the means of transition from one situation to another specified by the principle of justice in transfer are justice-preserving, and any situation actually arising from repeated transitions in accordance with the principle from a just situation is itself just. The parallel between justice-preserving transformations and truth-preserving transformations illuminates where it fails as well as where it holds. That a conclusion could have been deduced by truth-preserving means from premises that are true suffices to show its truth. That from a just situation a situation *could* have arisen via justice-preserving means does *not* suffice to show its justice. The fact that a thief's victims voluntarily *could* have presented him with gifts does not entitle the thief to his ill-gotten gains. Justice in holdings is historical; it depends upon what actually has happened. We shall return to this point later.

Not all actual situations are generated in accordance with the two principles of justice in holdings: the principle of justice in acquisition and the principle of justice in transfer. Some people steal from others, or defraud them, or enslave them, seizing their product and preventing them from living as they choose, or forcibly exclude others from competing in exchanges. None of these are permissible modes of transition from one situation to another. And some persons acquire holdings by means not sanctioned by the principle of justice in acquisition. The existence of past injustice (previous violations of the first two principles of justice in holdings) raises the third major topic under justice in holdings: the rectification of injustice in holdings. If past injustice has shaped present holdings in various ways, some identifiable and some not, what now, if anything, ought to be done to rectify these injustices? What obligations do the performers of injustice have toward those whose position is worse than it would have been had the injustice not been done? Or, than it would have been had compensation been paid promptly? How, if at all, do things

change if the beneficiaries and those made worse off are not the direct parties in the act of injustice, but, for example, their descendants? Is an injustice done to someone whose holding was itself based upon an unrectified injustice? How far back must one go in wiping clean the historical slate of injustices? What may victims of injustice permissibly do in order to rectify the injustices being done to them, including the many injustices done by persons acting through their government? I do not know of a thorough or theoretically sophisticated treatment of such issues.[4] Idealizing greatly, let us suppose theoretical investigation will produce a principle of rectification. This principle uses historical information about previous situations and injustices done in them (as defined by the first two principles of justice and rights against interference), and information about the actual course of events that flowed from these injustices, until the present, and it yields a description (or descriptions) of holdings in the society. The principle of rectification presumably will make use of its best estimate of subjunctive information[5] about what would have occurred (or a probability distribution[6] over what might have occurred, using the expected value) if the injustice had not taken place. If the actual description of holdings turns out not to be one of the descriptions yielded by the principle, then one of the descriptions yielded must be realized.[7]

---

4   [Author's note] See, however, the useful book by Boris Bittker, *The Case for Black Reparations* (New York: Random House, 1973).

5   Information about a hypothetical, non-actual situation.

6   A specification of all possible values of a variable along with the probability that each will occur.

7   [Author's note] If the principle of rectification of violations of the first two principles yields more than one description of holdings, then some choice must be made as to which of these is to be realized. Perhaps the sort of considerations about distributive justice and equality that I argue against play a legitimate role in *this* subsidiary choice. Similarly, there may be room for such considerations in deciding which otherwise arbitrary features a statute will embody, when such features are unavoidable because other considerations do not specify a precise line; yet a line must be drawn.

The general outlines of the theory of justice in holdings are that the holdings of a person are just if he is entitled to them by the principles of justice in acquisition and transfer, or by the principle of rectification of injustice (as specified by the first two principles). If each person's holdings are just, then the total set (distribution) of holdings is just. To turn these general outlines into a specific theory we would have to specify the details of each of the three principles of justice in holdings: the principle of acquisition of holdings, the principle of transfer of holdings, and the principle of rectification of violations of the first two principles. I shall not attempt that task here. (Locke's principle of justice in acquisition is discussed below.)

Historical Principles and the End-Result Principle

The general outlines of the entitlement theory illuminate the nature and defects of other conceptions of distributive justice. The entitlement theory of justice in distribution is *historical*; whether a distribution is just depends upon how it came about. In contrast, *current time-slice principles* of justice hold that the justice of a distribution is determined by how things are distributed (who has what) as judged by some *structural* principle(s) of just distribution. A utilitarian who judges between any two distributions by seeing which has the greater sum of utility and, if the sums tie, applies some fixed equality criterion to choose the more equal distribution, would hold a current time-slice principle of justice. As would someone who had a fixed schedule of trade-offs between the sum of happiness and equality. According to a current time-slice principle, all that needs to be looked at, in judging the justice of a distribution, is who ends up with what; in comparing any two distributions one need look only at the matrix presenting the distributions. No further information need be fed into a principle of justice. It is a consequence of such principles of justice that any two structurally identical distributions are equally just. (Two distributions are structurally identical if they present the same profile, but perhaps have different persons occupying the particular slots. My having ten and your having five, and my having five and your having ten are structurally identical distributions.) Welfare economics is the theory of current time-

slice principles of justice. The subject is conceived as operating on matrices representing only current information about distribution. This, as well as some of the usual conditions (for example, the choice of distribution is invariant under relabeling of columns), guarantees that welfare economics will be a current time-slice theory, with all of its inadequacies.

Most persons do not accept current time-slice principles as constituting the whole story about distributive shares. They think it relevant in assessing the justice of a situation to consider not only the distribution it embodies, but also how that distribution came about. If some persons are in prison for murder or war crimes, we do not say that to assess the justice of the distribution in the society we must look only at what this person has, and that person has, and that person has, … at the current time. We think it relevant to ask whether someone did something so that he *deserved* to be punished, deserved to have a lower share. Most will agree to the relevance of further information with regard to punishments and penalties. Consider also desired things. One traditional socialist view is that workers are entitled to the product and full fruits of their labor; they have earned it; a distribution is unjust if it does not give the workers what they are entitled to. Such entitlements are based upon some past history. No socialist holding this view would find it comforting to be told that because the actual distribution *A* happens to coincide structurally with the one he desires *D*, *A* therefore is no less just than *D*; it differs only in that the "parasitic" owners of capital receive under *A* what the workers are entitled to under *D*, and the workers receive under *A* what the owners are entitled to under *D*, namely very little. This socialist rightly, in my view, holds onto the notions of earning, producing, entitlement, desert, and so forth, and he rejects current time-slice principles that look only to the structure of the resulting set of holdings. (The set of holdings resulting from what? Isn't it implausible that how holdings are produced and come to exist has no effect at all on who should hold what?) His mistake lies in his view of what entitlements arise out of what sorts of productive processes.

We construe the position we discuss too narrowly by speaking of *current* time-slice principles. Nothing is changed if structural principles operate upon a time sequence of current time-slice profiles and, for example, give someone more now to counterbalance the less he has had earlier. A utilitarian or an egalitarian or any mixture of the two over time will inherit the difficulties of his more myopic comrades. He is not helped by the fact that *some* of the information others consider relevant in assessing a distribution is reflected, unrecoverably, in past matrices. Henceforth, we shall refer to such unhistorical principles of distributive justice, including the current time-slice principles, as *end-result principles* or *end-state principles*.

In contrast to end-result principles of justice, *historical principles* of justice hold that past circumstances or actions of people can create differential entitlements or differential deserts to things. An injustice can be worked by moving from one distribution to another structurally identical one, for the second, in profile the same, may violate people's entitlements or deserts; it may not fit the actual history.

Patterning

The entitlement principles of justice in holdings that we have sketched are historical principles of justice. To better understand their precise character, we shall distinguish them from another subclass of the historical principles. Consider, as an example, the principle of distribution according to moral merit. This principle requires that total distributive shares vary directly with moral merit; no person should have a greater share than anyone whose moral merit is greater. (If moral merit could be not merely ordered but measured on an interval or ratio scale, stronger principles could be formulated.) Or consider the principle that results by substituting "usefulness to society" for "moral merit" in the previous principle. Or instead of "distribute according to moral merit," or "distribute according to usefulness to society," we might consider "distribute according to the weighted sum[8] of moral merit, usefulness to society, and need," with the weights of the different dimensions equal. Let us call a principle of distribution *patterned* if it specifies that a distribu-

tion is to vary along with some natural dimension, weighted sum of natural dimensions, or lexicographic ordering[9] of natural dimensions. And let us say a distribution is patterned if it accords with some patterned principle. (I speak of natural dimensions, admittedly without a general criterion for them, because for any set of holdings some artificial dimensions can be gimmicked up to vary along with the distribution of the set.) The principle of distribution in accordance with moral merit is a patterned historical principle, which specifies a patterned distribution. "Distribute according to I.Q." is a patterned principle that looks to information not contained in distributional matrices. It is not historical, however, in that it does not look to any past actions creating differential entitlements to evaluate a distribution; it requires only distributional matrices whose columns are labeled by I.Q. scores. The distribution in a society, however, may be composed of such simple patterned distributions, without itself being simply patterned. Different sectors may operate different patterns, or some combination of patterns may operate in different proportions across a society. A distribution composed in this manner, from a small number of patterned distributions, we also shall term "patterned." And we extend the use of "pattern" to include the overall designs put forth by combinations of end-state principles.

Almost every suggested principle of distributive justice is patterned: to each according to his moral merit, or needs, or marginal product,[10] or how hard

---

8   A weighted sum is obtained by adding terms, each of which is given a certain value (weight) by using a multiplier which reflects their relative importance.

9   Strictly speaking, this means sorting a group of items in the order they would appear if they were listed in a dictionary (i.e., roughly, alphabetically), but listing first all the words made up of only *one* letter, then all the words made up of *two* letters, then all those with *three* letters, and so on. (The main idea here is to impose a useful *order* on an infinite sequence of formulae.) In the philosophical literature on justice, however, the phrase is generally used to mean a strict *prioritizing* of principles: first principle A must be satisfied, and only then should we worry about principle B; only when both A and B are satisfied can we apply principle C; and so on.

10   The contribution that each additional worker makes to total output. Thus, to be rewarded according to one's

he tries, or the weighted sum of the foregoing, and so on. The principle of entitlement we have sketched is not patterned.[11] There is no one natural dimension or weighted sum or combination of a small number of natural dimensions that yields the distributions generated in accordance with the principle of entitlement. The set of holdings that results when some persons receive their marginal products, others win at gambling, others receive a share of their mate's income, others receive gifts from foundations, others receive interest on loans, others receive gifts from admirers, others receive returns on investment, others make for themselves much of what they have, others find things, and so on, will not be patterned. Heavy strands of patterns will run through it; significant portions of the variance in holdings will be accounted for by pattern-variables. If most people most of the time choose to transfer some of their entitlements to others only in exchange for something from them, then a large part of what many people hold will vary with what they held that others wanted. More details are provided by the theory of marginal productivity. But gifts to relatives, charitable donations, bequests to children, and the like, are not best conceived, in the first instance, in this manner. Ignoring the strands of pattern, let us suppose for the moment that a distribution actually arrived at by the operation of the principle of entitlement is random with respect to any pattern. Though the resulting set of holdings will be unpatterned, it will not be incomprehensible, for it can be seen as arising from the operation of a small number of principles. These principles specify how an initial distribution may arise (the principle of acquisition of holdings) and how distributions may be transformed into others (the principle of transfer of holdings). The process whereby the set of holdings is generated will be intelligible, though the set of holdings itself that results from this process will be unpatterned.

The writings of F.A. Hayek[12] focus less than is usually done upon what patterning distributive justice requires. Hayek argues that we cannot know enough about each person's situation to distribute to each according to his moral merit (but would justice demand we do so if we did have this knowledge?); and he goes on to say, "our objection is against all attempts to impress upon society a deliberately chosen pattern of distribution, whether it be an order of equality or of inequality."[13] However, Hayek concludes that in a free society there will be distribution in accordance with value rather than moral merit; that is, in accordance with the perceived value of a person's actions and services to others. Despite his rejection of a patterned conception of distributive justice, Hayek himself suggests a pattern he thinks justifiable: distribution in accordance with the perceived benefits given to others, leaving room for the complaint that a free society does not

---

marginal product is to be paid in proportion to the amount that your contribution has increased output over what it would have been if you hadn't been employed.

11   [Author's note] One might try to squeeze a patterned conception of distributive justice into the framework of the entitlement conception, by formulating a gimmicky obligatory "principle of transfer" that would lead to the pattern. For example, the principle that if one has more than the mean income one must transfer everything one holds above the mean to persons below the mean so as to bring them up to (but not over) the mean. We can formulate a criterion for a "principle of transfer" to rule out such obligatory transfers, or we can say that no correct principle of transfer, no principle of transfer in a free society will be like this. The former is probably the better course, though the latter also is true.

Alternatively, one might think to make the entitlement conception instantiate a pattern, by using matrix entries that express the relative strength of a person's entitlements as measured by some real-valued function. But even if the limitation to natural dimensions failed to exclude this function, the resulting edifice would *not* capture our system of entitlements to *particular* things.

12   Friedrich August Hayek (1899–1992) was an Austrian-British economist and political philosopher best known for his critique of socialism and the welfare state, and defense of extreme *laissez-faire* economic individualism.

13   [Author's note] F.A. Hayek, *The Constitution of Liberty* (Chicago: University of Chicago Press, 1960), p. 87.

realize exactly this pattern. Stating this patterned strand of a free capitalist society more precisely, we get "To each according to how much he benefits others who have the resources for benefiting those who benefit them." This will seem arbitrary unless some acceptable initial set of holdings is specified, or unless it is held that the operation of the system over time washes out any significant effects from the initial set of holdings. As an example of the latter, if almost anyone would have bought a car from Henry Ford, the supposition that it was an arbitrary matter who held the money then (and so bought) would not place Henry Ford's earnings under a cloud. In any event, *his* coming to hold it is not arbitrary. Distribution according to benefits to others *is* a major patterned strand in a free capitalist society, as Hayek correctly points out, but it is only a strand and does not constitute the whole pattern of a system of entitlements (namely, inheritance, gifts for arbitrary reasons, charity, and so on) or a standard that one should insist a society fit. Will people tolerate for long a system yielding distributions that they believe are unpatterned?[14] No doubt people will not long accept a distribution they believe is *unjust*. People want their society to be and to look just. But must the look of justice reside in a resulting pattern rather than in the underlying generating principles? We are in no position to conclude that the inhabitants of a society embodying an entitlement conception of justice in holdings will find it unacceptable. Still, it must be granted that were people's reasons for transferring some of their holdings to others always irrational or arbitrary, we would find this disturbing. (Suppose people always determined what holdings they would transfer, and to whom, by using a random device.) We feel more comfortable upholding the justice of an entitlement system if most of the transfers under it are done for reasons. This does not mean necessarily that all deserve what holdings they receive. It means only that there is a purpose or point to someone's transferring a holding to one person rather than to another; that usually we can see what the transferrer thinks he's gaining, what cause he thinks he's serving, what goals he thinks he's helping to achieve, and so forth. Since in a capitalist society people often transfer holdings to others in accordance with how much they perceive these others benefiting them, the fabric constituted by the individual transactions and transfers is largely reasonable and intelligible.[15] (Gifts to loved ones, bequests to children, charity to the needy also are nonarbitrary components of the fabric.) In stressing the large strand of distribution in accordance with benefit to others, Hayek shows the point of many transfers, and so shows that the system of transfer of entitlements is not just spinning its gears aimlessly. The system of entitlements is defensible when constituted by the individual aims of individual transactions. No overarching aim is needed, no distributional pattern is required.

To think that the task of a theory of distributive justice is to fill in the blank in "to each according to

---

14   [Author's note] This question does not imply that they will tolerate any and every patterned distribution. In discussing Hayek's views, Irving Kristol has recently speculated that people will not long tolerate a system that yields distributions patterned in accordance with value rather than merit. ("'When Virtue Loses All Her Loveliness'—Some Reflections on Capitalism and 'The Free Society,'" *The Public Interest*, Fall 1970, pp. 3–15.) Kristol, following some remarks of Hayek's, equates the merit system with justice. Since some case can be made for the external standard of distribution in accordance with benefit to others, we ask about a weaker (and therefore more plausible) hypothesis.

15   [Author's note] We certainly benefit because great economic incentives operate to get others to spend much time and energy to figure out how to serve us by providing things we will want to pay for. It is not mere paradox mongering to wonder whether capitalism should be criticized for most rewarding and hence encouraging, not individualists like Thoreau who go about their own lives, but people who are occupied with serving others and winning them as customers. But to defend capitalism one need not think businessmen are the finest human types. (I do not mean to join here the general maligning of businessmen, either.) Those who think the finest should acquire the most can try to convince their fellows to transfer resources in accordance with *that* principle.

his _____ " is to be predisposed to search for a pattern; and the separate treatment of "from each according to his _____ " treats production and distribution as two separate and independent issues. On an entitlement view these are *not* two separate questions. Whoever makes something, having bought or contracted for all other held resources used in the process (transferring some of his holdings for these cooperating factors), is entitled to it. The situation is *not* one of something's getting made, and there being an open question of who is to get it. Things come into the world already attached to people having entitlements over them. From the point of view of the historical entitlement conception of justice in holdings, those who start afresh to complete "to each according to his _____ " treat objects as if they appeared from nowhere, out of nothing. A complete theory of justice might cover this limit case as well; perhaps here is a use for the usual conceptions of distributive justice.[16]

So entrenched are maxims of the usual form that perhaps we should present the entitlement conception as a competitor. Ignoring acquisition and rectification, we might say:

> From each according to what he chooses to do, to each according to what he makes for himself (perhaps with the contracted aid of others) and what others choose to do for him and choose to give him of what they've been given previously (under this maxim) and haven't yet expended or transferred.

This, the discerning reader will have noticed, has its defects as a slogan. So as a summary and great simplification (and not as a maxim with any independent meaning) we have:

> *From each as they choose, to each as they are chosen.*

---

16 [Author's note] Varying situations continuously from that limit situation to our own would force us to make explicit the underlying rationale of entitlements and to consider whether entitlement considerations lexicographically precede the considerations of the usual theories of distributive justice, so that the *slightest* strand of entitlement outweighs the considerations of the usual theories of distributive justice.

How Liberty Upsets Patterns

It is not clear how those holding alternative conceptions of distributive justice can reject the entitlement conception of justice in holdings. For suppose a distribution favored by one of these non-entitlement conceptions is realized. Let us suppose it is your favorite one and let us call this distribution D_1; perhaps everyone has an equal share, perhaps shares vary in accordance with some dimension you treasure. Now suppose that Wilt Chamberlain[17] is greatly in demand by basketball teams, being a great gate attraction. (Also suppose contracts run only for a year, with players being free agents.) He signs the following sort of contract with a team: In each home game, twenty-five cents from the price of each ticket of admission goes to him. (We ignore the question of whether he is "gouging" the owners, letting them look out for themselves.) The season starts, and people cheerfully attend his team's games; they buy their tickets, each time dropping a separate twenty-five cents of their admission price into a special box with Chamberlain's name on it. They are excited about seeing him play; it is worth the total admission price to them. Let us suppose that in one season one million persons attend his home games, and Wilt Chamberlain winds up with $250,000, a much larger sum than the average income and larger even than anyone else has.[18] Is he entitled to this income? Is this new distribution D_2, unjust? If so, why? There is *no* question about whether each of the people was entitled to the control over the resources they held in D_1; because that was the distribution (your favorite) that (for the purposes of argument) we assumed was acceptable. Each of these persons *chose* to give twenty-five cents of their money to Chamberlain. They could have spent it on going to the movies, or on candy bars, or on copies of *Dissent* magazine, or of *Monthly Review*. But they all, at least one million of them, converged on giving it to Wilt Chamberlain in exchange for watching him play

---

17 Wilt Chamberlain was a well-known American basketball player during the 1960s. He was seven-time consecutive winner of the National Basketball Association scoring title from 1960 to 1966, and in 1962 he scored a record 100 points in a single game.

18 In 1974, the U.S. average (mean) income was $5,672.

basketball. If D_1 was a just distribution, and people voluntarily moved from it to D_2, transferring parts of their shares they were given under D_1 (what was it for if not to do something with?), isn't D_2 also just? If the people were entitled to dispose of the resources to which they were entitled (under D_1), didn't this include their being entitled to give it to, or exchange it with, Wilt Chamberlain? Can anyone else complain on grounds of justice? Each other person already has his legitimate share under D_1. Under D_1, there is nothing that anyone has that anyone else has a claim of justice against. After someone transfers something to Wilt Chamberlain, third parties *still* have their legitimate shares; *their* shares are not changed. By what process could such a transfer among two persons give rise to a legitimate claim of distributive justice on a portion of what was transferred, by a third party who had no claim of justice on any holding of the others *before* the transfer?[19] To cut off objections irrelevant here, we might imagine the exchanges occurring in a socialist society, after hours. After playing whatever basketball he does in his daily work, or doing whatever other daily work he does, Wilt Chamberlain decides to put in *overtime* to earn additional money. (First his work quota is set; he works time over that.) Or imagine it is a skilled juggler people like to see, who puts on shows after hours.

Why might someone work overtime in a society in which it is assumed their needs are satisfied? Perhaps because they care about things other than needs. I like to write in books that I read, and to have easy access to books for browsing at odd hours. It would be very pleasant and convenient to have the resources of Widener Library[20] in my back yard. No society, I assume, will provide such resources close to each person who would like them as part of his regular allotment (under D_1). Thus, persons either must do without some extra things that they want, or be allowed to do something extra to get some of these things. On what basis could the inequalities that would eventuate be forbidden? Notice also that small factories would spring up in a socialist society, unless forbidden. I melt down some of my personal possessions (under D_1) and build a machine out of the material. I offer you, and others, a philosophy lecture once a week in exchange for your cranking the handle on my machine, whose products I exchange for yet other things, and so on. (The raw materials used by the machine are given to me by others who possess them under D_1, in exchange for hearing lectures.) Each person might participate to gain things over and above their allotment under D_1. Some persons even might want to leave their job in socialist industry and work full time in this private sector. I shall say something more about these issues in the next chapter. Here I wish merely to note how private property even in means of production would occur in a socialist society that did not forbid people to use as they wished some of the resources they are given under the socialist distribution D_1.[21] The social-

---

19   [Author's note] Might not a transfer have instrumental effects on a third party, changing his feasible options? (But what if the two parties to the transfer independently had used their holdings in this fashion?) I discuss this question below, but note here that this question concedes the point for distributions of ultimate intrinsic noninstrumental goods (pure utility experiences, so to speak) that are transferrable. It also might be objected that the transfer might make a third party more envious because it worsens his position relative to someone else. I find it incomprehensible how this can be thought to involve a claim of justice. On envy, see Chapter 8 [of *Anarchy, State and Utopia*].

Here and elsewhere in this chapter, a theory which incorporates elements of pure procedural justice might find what I say acceptable, *if* kept in its proper place; that is, if background institutions exist to ensure the satisfaction of certain conditions on distributive shares. But if these institutions are not themselves the sum or invisible-hand result of people's voluntary (nonaggressive) actions, the constraints they impose require justification. At no point does *our* argument assume any background institutions more extensive than those of the minimal night-watchman state, a state limited to protecting persons against murder, assault, theft, fraud, and so forth.

20   Harvard University's library.

21   [Author's note] See the selection from John Henry MacKay's novel, *The Anarchists*, reprinted in Leonard Krimmerman and Lewis Perry, eds., *Patterns of Anarchy* (New York: Doubleday Anchor Books, 1966), in

ist society would have to forbid capitalist acts between consenting adults.

The general point illustrated by the Wilt Chamberlain example and the example of the entrepreneur in a socialist society is that no end-state principle or distributional patterned principle of justice can be continuously realized without continuous interference with people's lives. Any favored pattern would be transformed into one unfavored by the principle, by people choosing to act in various ways; for example, by people exchanging goods and services with other people, or giving things to other people, things the transferrers are entitled to under the favored distributional pattern. To maintain a pattern one must either continually interfere to stop people from transferring resources as they wish to, or continually (or periodically) interfere to take from some persons resources

---

which an individualist anarchist presses upon a communist anarchist the following question: "Would you, in the system of society which you call 'free Communism' prevent individuals from exchanging their labour among themselves by means of their own medium of exchange? And further: Would you prevent them from occupying land for the purpose of personal use?" The novel continues: "[the] question was not to be escaped. If he answered 'Yes!' he admitted that society had the right of control over the individual and threw overboard the autonomy of the individual which he had always zealously defended; if on the other hand, he answered 'No!' he admitted the right of private property which he had just denied so emphatically.... Then he answered 'In Anarchy any number of men must have the right of forming a voluntary association, and so realizing their ideas in practice. Nor can I understand how any one could justly be driven from the land and house which he uses and occupies ... every serious man must declare himself: for Socialism, and thereby for force and against liberty, or for Anarchism, and thereby for liberty and against force.'" In contrast, we find Noam Chomsky writing, "Any consistent anarchist must oppose private ownership of the means of production," "the consistent anarchist then ... will be a socialist ... of a particular sort." Introduction to Daniel Guerin, *Anarchism: From Theory to Practice* (New York: Monthly Review Press, 1970), pages xiii, xv.

---

that others for some reason chose to transfer to them. (But if some time limit is to be set on how long people may keep resources others voluntarily transfer to them, why let them keep these resources for *any* period of time? Why not have immediate confiscation?) It might be objected that all persons voluntarily will choose to refrain from actions which would upset the pattern. This presupposes unrealistically (1) that all will most want to maintain the pattern (are those who don't, to be "reeducated" or forced to undergo "self-criticism"?), (2) that each can gather enough information about his own actions and the ongoing activities of others to discover which of his actions will upset the pattern, and (3) that diverse and far-flung persons can coordinate their actions to dovetail into the pattern. Compare the manner in which the market is neutral among persons' desires, as it reflects and transmits widely scattered information via prices, and coordinates persons' activities.

It puts things perhaps a bit too strongly to say that every patterned (or end-state) principle is liable to be thwarted by the voluntary actions of the individual parties transferring some of their shares they receive under the principle. For perhaps some *very* weak patterns are not so thwarted.[22] Any distributional pattern

---

22 [Author's note] Is the patterned principle stable that requires merely that a distribution be Pareto-optimal? One person might give another a gift or bequest that the second could exchange with a third to their mutual benefit. Before the second makes this exchange, there is not Pareto-optimality. Is a stable pattern presented by a principle choosing that among the Pareto-optimal positions that satisfies some further condition C? It may seem that there cannot be a counter-example, for won't any voluntary exchange made away from a situation show that the first situation wasn't Pareto-optimal? (Ignore the implausibility of this last claim for the case of bequests.) But principles are to be satisfied over time, during which new possibilities arise. A distribution that at one time satisfies the criterion of Pareto-optimality might not do so when some new possibilities arise (Wilt Chamberlain grows up and starts playing basketball); and though people's activities will tend to move then to a new Pareto-optimal position, *this* new one need not satisfy the contentful condition

with any egalitarian component is overturnable by the voluntary actions of individual persons over time; as is every patterned condition with sufficient content so as actually to have been proposed as presenting the central core of distributive justice. Still, given the possibility that some weak conditions or patterns may not be unstable in this way, it would be better to formulate an explicit description of the kind of interesting and contentful patterns under discussion, and to prove a theorem about their instability. Since the weaker the patterning, the more likely it is that the entitlement system itself satisfies it, a plausible conjecture is that any patterning either is unstable or is satisfied by the entitlement system.

…

Locke's Theory of Acquisition

Before we turn to consider other theories of justice in detail, we must introduce an additional bit of complexity into the structure of the entitlement theory: This is best approached by considering Locke's[23] attempt to specify a principle of justice in acquisition. Locke views property rights in an unowned object as originating through someone's mixing his labor with it. This gives rise to many questions. What are the boundaries of what labor is mixed with? If a private astronaut clears a place on Mars, has he mixed his labor with (so that he comes to own) the whole planet, the whole uninhabited universe, or just a particular plot? Which plot does an act bring under ownership? The minimal (possibly disconnected) area such that an act decreases entropy in that area, and not elsewhere? Can virgin land (for the purposes of ecological investigation by high-flying airplane) come under ownership by a Lockean process? Building a fence around a territory presumably would make one the owner of only the fence (and the land immediately underneath it).

Why does mixing one's labor with something make one the owner of it? Perhaps because one owns one's labor, and so one comes to own a previously unowned thing that becomes permeated with what one owns. Ownership seeps over into the rest. But why isn't mixing what I own with what I don't own a way of losing what I own rather than a way of gaining what I don't? If I own a can of tomato juice and spill it in the sea so that its molecules (made radioactive, so I can check this) mingle evenly throughout the sea, do I thereby come to own the sea, or have I foolishly dissipated my tomato juice? Perhaps the idea, instead, is that laboring on something improves it and makes it more valuable; and anyone is entitled to own a thing whose value he has created. (Reinforcing this, perhaps, is the view that laboring is unpleasant. If some people made things effortlessly, as the cartoon characters in *The Yellow Submarine*[24] trail flowers in their wake, would they have lesser claim to their own products whose making didn't *cost* them anything?) Ignore the fact that laboring on something may make it less valuable (spraying pink enamel paint on a piece of driftwood that you have found). Why should one's entitlement extend to the whole object rather than just to the *added value* one's labor has produced? (Such reference to value might also serve to delimit the extent of ownership; for example, substitute "increases the value of" for "decreases entropy in" in the above entropy criterion.) No workable or coherent value-added property scheme has yet been devised, and any such scheme presumably would fall to objections (similar to those) that fell to the theory of Henry George.[25]

It will be implausible to view improving an object as giving full ownership to it, if the stock of unowned objects that might be improved is limited. For an object's coming under one person's ownership changes the situation of all others. Whereas previously they

---

C. Continual interference will be needed to insure the continual satisfaction of C. (The theoretical possibility of a pattern's being maintained by some invisible-hand process that brings it back to an equilibrium that fits the pattern when deviations occur should be investigated.)

23   English philosopher John Locke (1632–1704). Nozick is referring specifically to Locke's *Two Treatises on Government* (1690).

24   A 1968 animated film by the *Beatles*.

25   Henry George (1839–1897) was a US social philosopher and economist who argued that the economic boom in the American West, brought about by the advent of the railroads, was actually making most people poorer, and only a few richer, and proposed controversial tax reforms (shifting the tax burden from buildings to land) in order to rectify this situation.

were at liberty (in Hohfeld's sense[26]) to use the object, they now no longer are. This change in the situation of others (by removing their liberty to act on a previously unowned object) need not worsen their situation. If I appropriate a grain of sand from Coney Island, no one else may now do as they will with *that* grain of sand. But there are plenty of other grains of sand left for them to do the same with. Or if not grains of sand, then other things. Alternatively, the things I do with the grain of sand I appropriate might improve the position of others, counterbalancing their loss of the liberty to use that grain. The crucial point is whether appropriation of an unowned object worsens the situation of others.

Locke's proviso that there be "enough and as good left in common for others" (sect. 27) is meant to ensure that the situation of others is not worsened. (If this proviso is met is there any motivation for his further condition of nonwaste?) It is often said that this proviso once held but now no longer does. But there appears to be an argument for the conclusion that if the proviso no longer holds, then it cannot ever have held so as to yield permanent and inheritable property rights. Consider the first person Z for whom there is not enough and as good left to appropriate. The last person Y to appropriate left Z without his previous liberty to act on an object, and so worsened Z's situation. So Y's appropriation is not allowed under Locke's proviso. Therefore the next to last person X to appropriate left Y in a worse position, for X's act ended permissible appropriation. Therefore X's appropriation wasn't permissible. But then the appropriator two from last, W, ended permissible appropriation and so, since it worsened X's position, W's appropriation wasn't permissible. And so on back to the first person A to appropriate a permanent property right.

This argument, however, proceeds too quickly. Someone may be made worse off by another's appropriation in two ways: first, by losing the opportunity

to improve his situation by a particular appropriation or any one; and second, by no longer being able to use freely (without appropriation) what he previously could. A *stringent* requirement that another not be made worse off by an appropriation would exclude the first way if nothing else counterbalances the diminution in opportunity, as well as the second. A *weaker* requirement would exclude the second way, though not the first. With the weaker requirement, we cannot zip back so quickly from Z to A, as in the above argument; for though person Z can no longer *appropriate*, there may remain some for him to *use* as before. In this case Y's appropriation would not violate the weaker Lockean condition. (With less remaining that people are at liberty to use, users might face more inconvenience, crowding, and so on; in that way the situation of others might be worsened, unless appropriation stopped far short of such a point.) It is arguable that no one legitimately can complain if the weaker provision is satisfied. However, since this is less clear than in the case of the more stringent proviso, Locke may have intended this stringent proviso by "enough and as good" remaining, and perhaps he meant the nonwaste condition to delay the end point from which the argument zips back.

Is the situation of persons who are unable to appropriate (there being no more accessible and useful unowned objects) worsened by a system allowing appropriation and permanent property? Here enter the various familiar social considerations favoring private property: it increases the social product by putting means of production in the hands of those who can use them most efficiently (profitably); experimentation is encouraged, because with separate persons controlling resources, there is no one person or small group whom someone with a new idea must convince to try it out; private property enables people to decide on the pattern and types of risks they wish to bear, leading to specialized types of risk bearing; private property protects future persons by leading some to hold back resources from current consumption for future markets; it provides alternate sources of employment for unpopular persons who don't have to convince any one person or small group to hire them, and so on. These considerations enter a Lockean theory to support the claim that appropriation of private property

---

26   Wesley Newcomb Hohfeld (1879–1918) was an American law professor, best remembered for his influential analysis of a number of basic legal notions, especially the idea of a legal and moral right. Hohfeld's definition of a legal liberty (or privilege) is that one can do X when one does not have a duty (to Y) *not* to do X.

satisfies the intent behind the "enough and as good left over" proviso, *not* as a utilitarian justification of property. They enter to rebut the claim that because the proviso is violated no natural right to private property can arise by a Lockean process. The difficulty in working such an argument to show that the proviso is satisfied is in fixing the appropriate base line for comparison. Lockean appropriation makes people no worse off than they would be *how*?[27] This question of fixing the baseline needs more detailed investigation than we are able to give it here. It would be desirable to have an estimate of the general economic importance of original appropriation in order to see how much leeway there is for differing theories of appropriation and of the location of the baseline. Perhaps this importance can be measured by the percentage of all income that is based upon untransformed raw materials and given resources (rather than upon human actions), mainly rental income representing the unimproved value of land, and the price of raw material *in situ*,[28] and by the percentage of current wealth which represents such income in the past.[29]

We should note that it is not only persons favoring *private* property who need a theory of how property rights legitimately originate. Those believing in collective property, for example those believing that a group of persons living in an area jointly own the territory, or its mineral resources, also must provide a theory of how such property rights arise; they must show why the persons living there have rights to determine what is done with the land and resources there that persons living elsewhere don't have (with regard to the same land and resources).

The Proviso

Whether or not Locke's particular theory of appropriation can be spelled out so as to handle various difficulties, I assume that any adequate theory of justice in acquisition will contain a proviso similar to the weaker of the ones we have attributed to Locke. A process normally giving rise to a permanent bequeathable property right in a previously unowned thing will not do so if the position of others no longer at liberty to use the thing is thereby worsened. It is important to specify *this* particular mode of worsening the situation of others, for the proviso does not encompass other modes. It does not include the worsening due to more limited opportunities to appropriate (the first way above, corresponding to the more stringent condition), and it does not include how I "worsen" a seller's position if I appropriate materials to make some of what he is selling, and then enter into competition with him. Someone whose appropriation otherwise would violate the proviso still may appropriate provided he compensates the others so that their situation is not thereby worsened; unless he does compensate these others, his appropriation will violate the proviso of the principle of justice in acquisition and will be an illegitimate one.[30] A theory of appropriation incorporating this Lockean proviso will handle correctly the cases (objections to the theory lacking the proviso) where

---

27   [Author's note] Compare this with Robert Paul Wolff's "A Refutation of Rawls' Theorem on Justice," *Journal of Philosophy*, March 31, 1966, sect. 2. Wolff's criticism does not apply to Rawls' conception under which the baseline is fixed by the difference principle.

28   In its original position, i.e., not yet extracted or harvested.

29   [Author's note] I have not seen a precise estimate. David Friedman, *The Machinery of Freedom* (N.Y.: Harper & Row, 1973), pp. xiv, xv, discusses this issue and suggests 5 percent of U.S. national income as an upper limit for the first two factors mentioned. However he does not attempt to estimate the percentage of current wealth which is based upon such income in the past. (The vague notion of "based upon" merely indicates a topic needing investigation.)

30   [Author's note] [Charles] Fourier [1772–1837] held that since the process of civilization had deprived the members of society of certain liberties (to gather, pasture, engage in the chase), a socially guaranteed minimum provision for persons was justified as compensation for the loss (Alexander Gray, *The Socialist Tradition* (New York: Harper & Row, 1968), p. 188). But this puts the point too strongly. This compensation would be due those persons, if any, for whom the process of civilization was a *net loss*, for whom the benefits of civilization did not counterbalance being deprived of these particular liberties.

someone appropriates the total supply of something necessary for life.[31]

A theory which includes this proviso in its principle of justice in acquisition must also contain a more complex principle of justice in transfer. Some reflection of the proviso about appropriation constrains later actions. If my appropriating all of a certain substance violates the Lockean proviso, then so does my appropriating some and purchasing all the rest from others who obtained it without otherwise violating the Lockean proviso. If the proviso excludes someone's appropriating all the drinkable water in the world, it also excludes his purchasing it all. (More weakly, and messily, it may exclude his charging certain prices for some of his supply.) This proviso (almost?) never will come into effect; the more someone acquires of a scarce substance which others want, the higher the price of the rest will go, and the more difficult it will become for him to acquire it all. But still, we can imagine, at least, that something like this occurs: someone makes simultaneous secret bids to the separate owners of a substance, each of whom sells assuming he can easily purchase more from the other owners; or some natural catastrophe destroys all of the supply of something except that in one person's possession. The total supply could not be permissibly appropriated by one person at the beginning. His later acquisition of it all does not show that the original appropriation violated the proviso (even by a reverse argument similar to the one above that tried to zip back from *Z* to *A*). Rather, it is the combination of the original appropriation *plus* all the later transfers and actions that violates the Lockean proviso.

Each owner's title to his holding includes the historical shadow of the Lockean proviso on appropriation. This excludes his transferring it into an agglomeration that does violate the Lockean proviso and excludes his using it in a way, in coordination with others or independently of them, so as to violate the proviso by making the situation of others worse than their baseline situation. Once it is known that someone's ownership runs afoul of the Lockean proviso, there are stringent limits on what he may do with (what it is difficult any longer unreservedly to call) "his property." Thus a person may not appropriate the only water hole in a desert and charge what he will. Nor may he charge what he will if he possesses one, and unfortunately it happens that all the water holes in the desert dry up, except for his. This unfortunate circumstance, admittedly no fault of his, brings into operation the Lockean proviso and limits his property rights.[32] Similarly, an owner's property right in the only island in an area does not allow him to order a castaway from a shipwreck off his island as a trespasser, for this would violate the Lockean proviso.

Notice that the theory does not say that owners do have these rights, but that the rights are overridden

---

31 [Author's note] For example, Rashdall's case of someone who comes upon the only water in the desert several miles ahead of others who also will come to it and appropriates it all. Hastings Rashdall, "The Philosophical Theory of Property," in *Property, Its Duties and Rights* (London: MacMillan, 1915).

We should note Ayn Rand's theory of property rights ("Man's Rights" in *The Virtue of Selfishness* (New York: New American Library, 1964), p. 94), wherein these follow from the right to life, since people need physical things to live. But a right to life is not a right to whatever one needs to live; other people may have rights over these other things (see Chapter 3 of this book). At most, a right to life would be a right to have or strive for whatever one needs to live, provided that having it does not violate anyone else's rights. With regard to material things, the question is whether having it does violate any right of others. (Would appropriation of all unowned things do so? Would appropriating the water hole in Rashdall's example?) Since special considerations (such as the Lockean proviso) may enter with regard to material property, one *first* needs a theory of property rights before one can apply any supposed right to life (as amended above). Therefore the right to life cannot provide the foundation for a theory of property rights.

32 [Author's note] The situation would be different if his water hole didn't dry up, due to special precautions he took to prevent this. Compare our discussion of the case in the text with Hayek, *The Constitution of Liberty*, p. 136; and also with Ronald Hamowy, "Hayek's Concept of Freedom; A Critique," *New Individualist Review*, April 1961, pp. 28–31.

to avoid some catastrophe. (Overridden rights do not disappear; they leave a trace of a sort absent in the cases under discussion.)[33] There is no such external (and *ad hoc*?) overriding. Considerations internal to the theory of property itself, to its theory of acquisition and appropriation, provide the means for handling such cases. The results, however, may be coextensive with some condition about catastrophe, since the baseline for comparison is so low as compared to the productiveness of a society with private appropriation that the question of the Lockean proviso being violated arises only in the case of catastrophe (or a desert-island situation).

The fact that someone owns the total supply of something necessary for others to stay alive does *not* entail that his (or anyone's) appropriation of anything left some people (immediately or later) in a situation worse than the baseline one. A medical researcher who synthesizes a new substance that effectively treats a certain disease and who refuses to sell except on his terms does not worsen the situation of others by depriving them of whatever he has appropriated. The others easily can possess the same materials he appropriated; the researcher's appropriation or purchase of chemicals didn't make those chemicals scarce in a way so as to violate the Lockean proviso. Nor would someone else's purchasing the total supply of the synthesized substance from the medical researcher. The fact that the medical researcher uses easily available chemicals to synthesize the drug no more violates the Lockean proviso than does the fact that the only surgeon able to perform a particular operation eats easily obtainable food in order to stay alive and to have the energy to work. This shows that the Lockean proviso is not an "end-state principle"; it focuses on a particular way that appropriative actions affect others, and not on the structure of the situation that results.[34]

Intermediate between someone who takes all of the public supply and someone who makes the total supply out of easily obtainable substances is someone who appropriates the total supply of something in a way that does not deprive the others of it. For example, someone finds a new substance in an out-of-the-way place. He discovers that it effectively treats a certain disease and appropriates the total supply. He does not worsen the situation of others; if he did not stumble upon the substance no one else would have, and the others would remain without it. However, as time passes, the likelihood increases that others would have come across the substance; upon this fact might be based a limit to his property right in the substance so that others are not below their baseline position; for example, its bequest might be limited. The theme of someone worsening another's situation by depriving him of something he otherwise would possess may also illuminate the example of patents. An inventor's patent does not deprive others of an object which would not exist if not for the inventor. Yet patents would have this effect on others who independently invent the object. Therefore, these independent inventors, upon whom the burden of proving independent discovery may rest, should not be excluded from utilizing their own invention as they wish (including selling it to others). Furthermore, a known inventor drastically lessens the chances of actual independent invention. For persons who know of an invention usually will not try to reinvent it, and the notion of independent discovery here would be murky at best. Yet we may assume that in the absence of the original invention, sometime later someone else would have come up with it. This suggests placing a time limit on patents, as a rough rule of thumb to approximate how long it would have taken, in the absence of knowledge of the invention, for independent discovery.

---

33   [Author's note] I discuss overriding and its moral traces in "Moral Complications and Moral Structures," *Natural Law Forum*, 1968, p. 1–50.

34   [Author's note] Does the principle of compensation (Chapter 4) introduce patterning considerations? Though it requires compensation for the disadvantages imposed by those seeking security from risks, it is not a patterned principle. For it seeks to remove only those disadvantages which prohibitions inflict on those who might present risks to others, not all disadvantages. It specifies an obligation on those who impose the prohibition, which stems from their own particular acts, to remove a particular complaint those prohibited may make against them.

I believe that the free operation of a market system will not actually run afoul of the Lockean proviso. (Recall that crucial to our story in Part I of how a protective agency becomes dominant and a *de facto* monopoly is the fact that it wields force in situations of conflict, and is not merely in competition, with other agencies. A similar tale cannot be told about other businesses.) If this is correct, the proviso will not play a very important role in the activities of protective agencies and will not provide a significant opportunity for future state action. Indeed, were it not for the effects of previous illegitimate state action, people would not think the possibility of the proviso's being violated as of more interest than any other logical possibility. (Here I make an empirical historical claim; as does someone who disagrees with this.) This completes our indication of the complication in the entitlement theory introduced by the Lockean proviso.

SUSAN MOLLER OKIN
"Justice and Gender"

Who Was Susan Moller Okin?

Susan Moller Okin, "perhaps the best feminist political philosopher in the world,"[1] was born in 1946 in Auckland, New Zealand, and died in 2004 at the age of only 57. At the time of her death she was a professor of political science at Stanford University, and she had previously taught at Auckland, Vassar, Brandeis, and Harvard. Her doctorate, which she received in 1975, was from Harvard.

Okin's main importance as a political philosopher lay in her insistence that gender—the status and position of women—is an issue that lies at the heart of political theory, and is not merely a fringe topic that can be addressed after the main principles of justice have been laid down. As the article reprinted here makes clear, at the time that Okin began writing—in the 1970s—this was a radical view:

one which, it seems fair to say, had not even occurred to the (male) writers who were mainly responsible for carrying on the liberal political tradition. Okin formulated careful and forceful arguments that, in particular, the role and structure of the family—the so-called 'domestic sphere,' that shaped, and still shapes, the opportunities available to women in society—were crucial to any adequate account of social justice. These arguments brought about a sea change in political philosophy, carrying issues surrounding gender roles and the family to the center of the discipline.

Towards the end of her career, Okin's interests shifted towards the situation of women in less developed countries, and she worked on the complex tangle of issues raised by the interaction between gender issues, poverty, and multiculturalism. Once again, she was among the first to identify an issue that at the time was barely on the radar and has since become a main theme in political thought: the potential for conflict between the aim of gender

---

1   Debra Satz, a Stanford philosopher, quoted in Okin's obituary in the *Stanford Report*, March 9, 2004.

equality, and sensitivity to the customs of other cultures and religions. Okin's own view was a provocative defense of the liberal egalitarian position that all citizens in a state should have equal rights and privileges and that this trumps certain oppressive cultural practices, such as forced marriage, polygamy, or female genital mutilation. She became a highly visible supporter of the Global Fund for Women, an international foundation devoted to the support of women's human rights.

Probably Okin's best-known work is the book *Justice, Gender and the Family*, published in 1989. She also wrote two other very influential books—*Women in Western Political Thought* (1979), and *Is Multiculturalism Bad for Women?* (1999)—and many widely-read articles.

What Is the Structure of This Reading?

After introducing the topic "how just is gender?", Okin begins by outlining the role of gender in justifying inequality in the western tradition of political thought, including that of Aristotle, Rousseau, Kant, Hegel, and Bentham. She then asks whether modern political theory fares any better on this front— whether modern theorists are more sensitive to the problem of gender-based inequalities in society— and examines two representative leading writers: John Rawls, the most prominent liberal ideologist; and Michael Walzer, a leading communitarian. Okin concludes that insufficient attention is still being devoted to gender. She argues that, although Walzer appears on the surface to be more sympathetic to feminist concerns, in fact it is the Rawlsian tradition that is best able to accommodate feminism. However, she concludes by suggesting that full consideration of the problem of gender in a theory of social justice will require not only modifying contemporary liberal theory but also, potentially, a radical alteration of gender itself.

Some Useful Background Information

1. In her article, Okin deliberately focuses on a leading representative of liberalism (Rawls) and a leading communitarian (Walzer). Liberalism,

as a political ideology, focuses on the rights of the individual, as against the government or other social institutions, and tends to hold that such rights—such as the right to freedom of expression, equality of respect, freedom of religion, and so on—are universally applicable. Communitarianism, by contrast, stresses the manner in which individual self-identity is embedded in, even created by, social ties of kinship, tradition, and common purpose, and hence rejects liberal individualism.

Some Common Misconceptions

1. Although Okin, in this article and elsewhere in her work, attacks liberalism for its historical bias against women, she nevertheless does not reject liberal political theory. On the contrary, her view is that liberalism is an emancipatory doctrine that simply has not been taken far enough. The basic idea of freedom and equality for all citizens is the right one—but in order to apply fully to women (and, indeed, to men), these liberal principles must be applied to the family as well as to the public spheres of government and economics.

Questions for Further Thought

1. Okin writes that, "[i]n one way or another, liberals have assumed that the 'individual' who is the basic subject of their theories is the male head of a patriarchal household." Consider the works from this tradition that you might have read: is Okin right in her judgment? What implications does she draw from this?

2. Is there a difference between the way we should understand justice and equity within families as opposed to in society at large? Does Okin think there should be? Do you?

3. "For the family with its gender structure, female parenting in particular, is clearly a crucial determinant in the different socialization of the two sexes—in how men and women 'get to be what they are.'" Is Okin right about this? What implications does it have?

4. Okin quotes Rawls as apparently assuming "that family institutions are just," and then proceeds to argue that, by Rawls's own lights, the institution of the family cannot be considered just. Does Okin mean by this that it must be considered *unjust*? How effective are Okin's arguments on this point? Do they apply only to Rawls, or do they have wider application?

5. Okin asserts that "a much larger proportion of women's than men's labor is unpaid, and is often not even acknowledged to be labor." What are the implications of this claim for social justice?

6. In her discussion of Walzer, Okin compares gender inequality with hierarchies of caste that exist, or have existed, in some societies (such as nineteenth-century India). How plausible is this comparison? How does Okin use it to critique Walzer? What implication does this comparison have for the place of gender in modern political theory?

7. "The danger of [Walzer's] conception of justice is that what is just depends heavily on what people are persuaded of." What is your assessment of this important criticism by Okin?

8. In the final section of her paper, Okin "raises the question whether, in fact, sex *is* a morally irrelevant and contingent human characteristic, in a society structured by gender." What is the significance of this question? How does Okin answer it?

9. Okin concludes that "gender [is] incompatible with a just society." What does she mean by this? How radical a claim is this? Do you think it is warranted?

10. This article was published in 1987. In your view, has there been any significant change to the attitudes that Okin describes concerning the relevance of gender to justice, or the place of principles of justice within the family?

Suggestions for Further Reading

Okin wrote three books that mark the main stages of the progression of her feminist critique of political science. In *Women in Western Political Thought* (Princeton University Press, 1979) she argues that unquestioned assumptions about the 'natural' form of the family have excluded women from public political life throughout western history. Then in *Justice, Gender and the Family* (Basic Books, 1989) Okin applies this critique to contemporary political theorists. *Is Multiculturalism Bad for Women?* (Princeton University Press, 1999) collects together Okin's titular essay with responses from a range of different critical commentators, and a reply from Okin.

Two review essays are useful starting points for critical responses to Okin's views on the family: Joshua Cohen, "Okin on Justice, Gender, and the Family," *The Canadian Journal of Philosophy* 22 (1992), pp. 263–86; and Will Kymlicka, "Rethinking the Family," *Philosophy and Public Affairs* 20 (1991), pp. 77–97.

"Justice and Gender"[2,3]

Theories of justice are centrally concerned with whether, how, and why persons should be treated differently from each other. Which initial or acquired characteristics or positions in society, they ask, legitimize differential treatment of persons by social institutions, laws, and customs? In particular, how should beginnings affect outcomes? The division of humanity into two sexes would seem to provide an obvious subject for such inquiries. We live in a society in whose past the innate characteristic of sex has been regarded as one of the clearest legitimizers of different rights and

2 From *Philosophy and Public Affairs*, Vol. 16, No. 1 (Winter, 1987), 42–72. Reproduced by permission of Wiley-Blackwell Inc.

3 [Author's note] An earlier version of this article was presented at the 80th Annual Meeting of the American Political Science Association, August 30–September 2, 1984 in Washington, D.C. I gratefully acknowledge the helpful comments of the following people: Robert Amdur, Peter Euben, Robert Goodin, Anne Harper, Robert Keohane, Carole Pateman, John Rawls, Nancy Rosenblum, Robert Simon, Quentin Skinner, Michael Walzer, Iris Young and the Editors of *Philosophy & Public Affairs*. Thanks also to Lisa Carisella and Elaine Herrmann for typing the manuscript.

restrictions, both formal and informal. While the legal sanctions that uphold male dominance have been to some extent eroded within the past century, and more rapidly in the last twenty years, the heavy weight of tradition, combined with the effects of socialization broadly defined, still work powerfully to reinforce roles for the two sexes that are commonly regarded as of unequal prestige and worth.[4] The sexual division of labor within the family, in particular, is not only a fundamental part of the marriage contract, but so deeply influences us in our most formative years that feminists of both sexes who try to reject it find themselves struggling against it with varying degrees of ambivalence. Based on this linchpin, the deeply entrenched social institutionalization of sex difference, which I will refer to as "the gender system" or simply "gender," still permeates our society.

This gender system has rarely been subjected to the tests of justice. When we turn to the great tradition of Western political thought with questions about the justice of gender in mind, it is to little avail. Bold feminists like Mary Astell, Mary Wollstonecraft, Harriet Taylor, and George Bernard Shaw have occasionally challenged the tradition,[5] often using its own premises and arguments to overturn its justification of the un-

equal treatment of women. But John Stuart Mill is a rare exception to the rule that those who hold central positions in the tradition almost never questioned the justice of the subordination and oppression of women. This phenomenon is undoubtedly due in part to the fact that Aristotle, whose theory of justice has been so influential, relegated women and slaves to a realm of "household justice," whose participants are not fundamentally equal to the free men who participate in political justice, but inferiors whose natural function is to serve those who are more fully human. The liberal tradition, despite its supposed foundation of individual rights and human equality, is more Aristotelian in this respect than is generally acknowledged.[6] In one way or another, liberals have assumed that the "individual" who is the basic subject of their theories is the male head of a patriarchal household.[7] Thus the application of principles of justice to relations between the sexes, or within the household, has frequently been ruled out from the start.

Other assumptions, too, contribute to the widespread belief that neither women nor the family are appropriate subjects for discussions of justice. One is that women, whether because of their essential disorderliness, their enslavement to nature, their private and particularist inclinations, or their oedipal development,[8] are incapable of developing a sense

---

4   [Author's note] On the history of the legal enforcement of traditional sex roles and recent changes therein, see Leo Kanowitz, *Sex Roles in Law and Society* (Albuquerque: University of New Mexico Press, 1973, and 1974 Supplement), esp. pts. 2, 4, 5; also Kenneth M. Davidson, Ruth Bader Ginsburg and Henna Hill Kay, *Sex-Based Discrimination* (St. Paul: West Publishing Co., 1974, and 1978 Supplement by Wendy Williams), esp. chap. 2.

5   Mary Astell (1666–1731) wrote *A Serious Proposal to the Ladies, for the Advancement of Their True and Greatest Interest* (1694) and fought for more equal educational opportunities for women; Mary Wollstonecraft (1759–1797) was the author of *A Vindication of the Rights of Woman* (1792); Harriet Taylor (1807–1858) worked with John Stuart Mill (her second husband) as a key contributor to *On Liberty* (1859); George Bernard Shaw (1856–1950), the playwright, was a prominent socialist and author of *The Intelligent Woman's Guide to Socialism and Capitalism* (1928).

6   [Author's note] See Judith Hicks Stiehm, "The Unit of Political Analysis: Our Aristotelian Hangover," in Sandra Harding and Merrill B. Hintikka, eds., *Discovering Reality: Feminist Perspectives on Epistemology, Metaphysics, Methodology, and Philosophy of Science* (Dordrecht: Reidel, 1983), pp. 31–43.

7   [Author's note] See Carole Pateman and Theresa Brennan, "'Mere Auxiliaries to the Commonwealth'; Women and the Origins of Liberalism," *Political Studies* 27, no. 2 (June 1979): 183–200; also Susan Moller Okin, "Women and the Making of the Sentimental Family," *Philosophy & Public Affairs* 11, no. 1 (Winter 1982): 65–88.

8   That is, according to Freudian psychoanalytic theory, the psychosexual development of children, passing through a period during which they develop the unconscious desire to possess the parent of the opposite sex and eliminate the parent of the same sex. This has

of justice. This notion can be found—sometimes briefly suggested, sometimes developed at greater length—in the works of theorists from Plato to Freud, including Bodin, John Knox,[9] Rousseau, Kant, Hegel and Bentham.[10] The frequent implication is that those who do not possess the qualifications for fully ethical reasoning or action need not have principles of justice applied to them. Finally, in Rousseau (as so often, original) we find the unique claim that woman, being "made to submit to man and even to put up with his injustice," is imbued innately with a capacity to tolerate the unjust treatment with which she is likely to meet.[11]

For those who are not satisfied with these reasons for excluding women and gender from the subject matter of justice, the great tradition has little to offer, directly at least, to our inquiry. When we turn to contemporary theories of justice, however, we can expect to find more illuminating and positive contributions to the subject of gender and justice. I turn to two such theories, John Rawls's *A Theory* of *Justice* and Michael Walzer's *Spheres of Justice,* to

see what they say or imply in response to the question "How just is gender?"[12]

Justice as Fairness

An ambiguity runs throughout John Rawls's *A Theory of Justice,* continually noticeable to anyone reading it from a feminist perspective. On the one hand, as I shall argue below, a consistent and wholehearted application of Rawls's liberal principles can lead us to challenge fundamentally the gender system of our society. On the other hand, in his own account of his theory, this challenge is barely hinted at, much less developed. The major reason is that throughout most of the argument, it is assumed (as throughout almost the entire liberal tradition) that the appropriate subjects of political theories are heads of families. As a result, although Rawls indicates on several occasions that a person's sex is a morally arbitrary and contingent characteristic, and although he states explicitly that the family itself is one of those basic social institutions to which the principles of justice must apply, his theory of justice fails to develop either of these convictions.

Rawls, like almost all political theorists until very recent years, employs supposedly generic male terms of reference. "Men," "mankind," "he" and "his" are interspersed with nonsexist terms of reference such as "individual" and "moral person." Examples of intergenerational concern are worded in terms of "fathers" and "sons," and the difference principle[13] is said to correspond to "the principle of fraternity."[14] This linguistic usage would perhaps be less significant if it were not for the fact that Rawls is self-consciously a member of a long tradition of moral and political philosophy that has used in its arguments either such

become known as the Oedipus complex.

9   Jean Bodin (1530–1596) was a French legal theorist who argued for the absolute authority of the sovereign; John Knox (c. 1510–1572) was the leading Protestant reformer in Scotland, and author of *The First Blast of the Trumpet Against the Monstrous Regiment of Women* (1558).

10   [Author's note] See Nannerl O. Keohane, "Female Citizenship: The Monstrous Regiment of Women," presented at the Annual Meeting of the Conference for the Study of Political Thought, April 6–8, 1979, on Bodin, John Knox and Rousseau; Carole Pateman, "'The Disorder of Women'; Women, Love, and The Sense of Justice," *Ethics* 81, no. 1 (October 1980): 20–34, on Rousseau and Freud; Susan Moller Okin, "Thinking like a Woman," unpublished ms., 1984, on Plato and Hegel; Terence Ball, "Utilitarianism, Feminism and the Franchise: James Mill and his Critics," *History of Political Thought* 1, no. 1 (Spring 1980): 91–115, on Bentham.

11   [Author's note] Jean-Jacques Rousseau, *Émile*, in *Oeuvres Complètes* 4 (Paris: Pléiade, 1969), pp. 734–35, 750.

12   [Author's note] John Rawls, *A Theory of Justice* (Cambridge, MA: Harvard University Press, 1971), hereafter referred to as *Theory*; Michael L. Walzer, *Spheres of Justice* (New York: Basic Books, 1983), hereafter referred to as *Spheres*.

13   The principle, developed by Rawls, that inequalities in the distribution of goods are justified only if those inequalities benefit the worst-off members of society.

14   [Author's note] *Theory*, pp. 105–106, 208–209, 288–289.

supposedly generic masculine terms, or even more inclusive terms of reference ("human beings," "persons," "all rational beings as such"), only to exclude women from the scope of the conclusions reached. Kant is a clear example.[15] But when Rawls refers to the generality and universality of Kant's ethics, and when he compares the principles chosen in his own original position to those regulative of Kant's kingdom of ends, "acting from [which] expresses our nature as free and equal rational persons,"[16] he does not mention the fact that women were not included in that category of "free and equal rational persons," to which Kant meant his moral theory to apply. Again, in a brief discussion of Freud's account of moral development, Rawls presents Freud's theory of the formation of the male super-ego in largely gender-neutral terms, without mentioning that Freud considered women's moral development to be sadly deficient, on account of their incomplete resolution of the Oedipus complex.[17] Thus there is a certain blindness to the sexism of the tradition in which Rawls is a participant, which tends to render his terms of reference even more ambiguous than they might otherwise be. A feminist reader finds it difficult not to keep asking: "Does this theory of justice apply to women, or not?"

This question is not answered in the important passages that list the characteristics that persons in the original position[18] are not to know about themselves, in order to formulate impartial principles of justice. In a subsequent article, Rawls has made it clear that sex is one of those morally irrelevant contingencies that is to be hidden by the veil of ignorance.[19] But throughout

A Theory of Justice, while the list of things unknown by a person in the original position includes

> his place in society, his class position or social status, ... his fortune in the distribution of natural assets and abilities, his intelligence and strength, and the like, ... his conception of the good, the particulars of his rational plan of life, [and] even the special features of his psychology...[20]

"his" sex is not mentioned. Since the parties also "know the general facts about human society,"[21] presumably including the fact that it is structured along the lines of gender both by custom and by law, one might think that whether or not they knew their sex might matter enough to be mentioned. Perhaps Rawls means to cover it by his phrase "and the like," but it is also possible that he did not consider it significant.

The ambiguity is exacerbated by Rawls's statement that those free and equal moral persons in the original position who formulate the principles of justice are to be thought of not as "single individuals" but as "heads of families" or "representatives of families."[22] He says that it is not necessary to think of the parties as heads of families, but that he will generally do so. The reason he does this, he explains, is to ensure that each person in the original position cares about the well-being of some persons in the next generation. These "ties of sentiment" between generations, which Rawls regards as important in the establishment of his just savings principle, would otherwise constitute a problem, because of the general assumption that the parties in the original position are mutually disinterested. In spite of the ties of sentiment *within* families, then, "as representatives of families their interests are opposed as the circumstances of justice imply."[23]

The head of a family need not necessarily, of course, be a man. The very fact, however, that in com-

---

15   [Author's note] See Okin, "Women and the Making of the Sentimental Family," pp. 78–82.

16   [Author's note] *Theory*, pp. 251, 256.

17   [Author's note] Ibid., p. 459.

18   A hypothetical situation in which people are deprived of all knowledge of their personal and historical circumstances that are irrelevant to justice—they are behind "the veil of ignorance"—in order to ensure that any judgments they make about the proper structure of society will be appopriately impartial.

19   [Author's note] "Fairness to Goodness," *Philosophical Review* 84 (1975): 537. He says: "That we have one conception of the good rather than another is not

relevant from a moral standpoint. In acquiring it we are influenced by the same sort of contingencies that lead us to rule out a knowledge of our sex and class."

20   [Author's note] *Theory*, p. 137; see also p. 12.

21   [Author's note] Ibid., p. 137.

22   [Author's note] Ibid., pp. 128, 146.

23   [Author's note] Ibid., p. 128; see also p. 292.

mon usage the term "female-headed households" is used *only* in reference to households without resident adult males, tends to suggest that it is assumed that any present male adult takes precedence over a female as the household or family head. Rawls does nothing to dispel this impression when he says of those in the original position that "imagining themselves to be fathers, say, they are to ascertain how much they should set aside for their sons by noting what they would believe themselves entitled to claim of their fathers."[24] He makes the "heads of families" assumption only in order to address the problem of savings between generations, and presumably does not intend it to be a sexist assumption. Nevertheless, Rawls is effectively trapped by this assumption into the traditional mode of thinking that life within the family and relations between the sexes are not properly to be regarded as part of the subject matter of a theory of social justice.

Before I go on to argue this, I must first point out that Rawls states at the outset of his theory that the family *is* part of the subject matter of social justice. "For us" he says,

> the primary subject of justice is the basic structure of society, or more exactly, the way in which the major social institutions distribute fundamental rights and duties and determine the division of advantages from social cooperation.[25]

He goes on to specify "the monogamous family" as an example of such major social institutions, together with the political constitution, the legal protection of essential freedoms, competitive markets, and private property. The reason that Rawls makes such institutions the primary subject of his theory of social justice is that they have such profound effects on people's lives from the start, depending on where they find themselves placed in relation to them. He explicitly distinguishes between these major institutions and other "private associations," "less comprehensive social groups," and "various informal conventions and customs of everyday life,"[26] for which the principles

of justice satisfactory for the basic structure might be less appropriate or relevant. There is no doubt, then, that in his initial definition of the sphere of social justice, the family is included.[27] The two principles of justice that Rawls defends in Part I, the principle of equal basic liberty, and the difference principle combined with the requirement of fair equality of opportunity, are intended to apply to the basic structure of society. They are "to govern the assignment of rights and duties and to regulate the distribution of social and economic advantages."[28] Whenever in these basic institutions there are differences in authority, in responsibility, in the distribution of resources such as wealth or leisure, these differences must be both to the greatest benefit of the least advantaged, and attached to positions accessible to all under conditions of fair equality of opportunity.

In Part II, Rawls discusses at some length the application of his principles of justice to almost all of the major social institutions listed at the beginning of the book. The legal protection of freedom of thought and liberty of conscience is defended, as are just democratic constitutional institutions and procedures; competitive markets feature prominently in the discussion of the just distribution of income; the issue of the private or public ownership of the means of production is explicitly left open, since Rawls argues that justice as fairness might be compatible with certain versions of either. But throughout these discussions, the question of whether the monogamous family, in either its traditional or any other form, is a just social institution, is never raised. When Rawls announces that "the sketch of the system of institutions that satisfy the two principles of justice is now complete,"[29] he has still paid no attention at all to the internal justice of the family. The family, in fact, apart from passing references, appears in *A Theory*

---

24 [Author's note] Ibid., p. 289.

25 [Author's note] Ibid., p. 8.

26 [Author's note] Ibid., p. 7.

27 [Author's note] It is interesting to note that in a subsequent paper on the question why the basic structure of society is the primary subject of justice, Rawls does not mention the family as part of the basic structure. "The Basic Structure as Subject," *American Philosophical Quarterly* 14, no. 2 (April 1977): 159.

28 [Author's note] Theory, p. 61.

29 [Author's note] Ibid., p. 303.

of Justice in only three contexts: as the link between generations necessary for the savings principle, as a possible obstacle to fair equality of opportunity—on account of inequalities amongst families—and as the first school of moral development. It is in the third of these contexts that Rawls first specifically mentions the family as a just institution. He mentions it, however, not to *consider* whether or not the family "in some form" is a just institution, but to *assume* it. Clearly regarding it as important, Rawls states as part of his first psychological law of moral development: "given that family institutions are just...."[30]

Clearly, however, by Rawls's own reasoning about the social justice of major institutions, this assumption is unwarranted. For the central tenet of the theory is that justice characterizes institutions whose members could hypothetically have agreed to their structure and rules from a position in which they did not know which place in the structure they were to occupy. The argument of the book is designed to show that the two principles of justice as fairness are those that individuals in such a hypothetical situation would indeed agree upon. But since those in the original position are the heads or representatives of families, they are *not in a position to determine questions of justice within families*.[31] As far as children are concerned, Rawls makes a convincing argument from paternalism for their temporary inequality. But wives (or whichever adult member[s] of a family are *not* its "head") go completely unrepresented in the original position. If

families are just, as Rawls assumes, then they must *get* to be just in some different way (unspecified by Rawls) than other institutions, for it is impossible to see how the viewpoint of their less advantaged members ever gets to be heard.

There are two occasions where Rawls seems either to depart from his assumption that those in the original position are "family heads" or to assume that a "head of a family" is equally likely to be a woman as a man. In the assumption of the basic rights of citizenship, Rawls argues, favoring men over women is "justified by the difference principle ... only if it is to the advantage of women and acceptable from their standpoint."[32] Later, he seems to imply that the injustice and irrationality of racist doctrines are also characteristic of sexist ones.[33] But in spite of these passages, which appear to challenge formal sex discrimination, the discussions of institutions in Part II implicitly rely, in a number of respects, on the assumption that the parties formulating just institutions are (male) heads of (fairly traditional) families, and are therefore not concerned with issues of just distribution within the family. Thus the "head of family" assumption, far from being neutral or innocent, has the effect of banishing a large sphere of human life—and a particularly large sphere of most women's lives—from the scope of the theory.

First, Rawls's discussion of the distribution of wealth seems to assume that all the parties in the original position expect to be, once the veil of ignorance is removed, participants in the paid labor market. Distributive shares are discussed in terms of household income, but reference to "individuals" is interspersed into this discussion as if there were no difference between the advantage or welfare of a household and that of an individual.[34] This confusion obscures the fact that wages are paid to those in the labor force but that in societies characterized by a gender system (all current societies) a much larger proportion of women's than men's labor is unpaid, and is often not even acknowledged to be labor. It obscures the fact that such resulting disparities and the

---

30 [Author's note] *Theory*, p. 490. See Deborah Kearns, "A Theory of Justice—and Love; Rawls on the Family," *Politics* (Australasian Political Studies Association Journal) 18, no. 2 (November 1983): 30–40 for an interesting discussion of the significance of Rawls's failure to address the justice of the family for his theory of moral development.

31 [Author's note] As Jane English says, in a paper that is more centrally concerned with the problems of establishing Rawls's savings principle than with justice within the family *per se*: "By making the parties in the original position heads of families rather than individuals, Rawls makes the family opaque to claims of justice." "Justice between Generations," *Philosophical Studies* 31 (1977): 95.

32 [Author's note] *Theory*, p. 99.

33 [Author's note] Ibid., p. 149.

34 [Author's note] Ibid., pp. 270–274, 304–309.

economic dependence of women on men are likely to affect power relations within the household, as well as access to leisure, prestige, political office, and so on amongst its adult members. Any discussion of justice *within* the family would have to address these issues.

Later, too, in his discussion of the obligations of citizens, Rawls's assumption that justice is the result of agreement amongst heads of families in the original position seems to prevent him from considering an issue of crucial importance to women as citizens—their exemption from the draft. He concludes that military conscription is justifiable in the case of defense against an unjust attack on liberty, so long as institutions "try to make sure that the risks of suffering from these imposed misfortunes are more or less evenly shared by all members of society over the course of their life, and that there is no avoidable *class* bias in selecting those who are called for duty."[35] However, the issue of the exemption of women from this major interference with the basic liberties of equal citizenship is not even mentioned.

In spite of two explicit rejections of the justice of formal sex discrimination in Part I, then, Rawls seems in Part II to be so heavily influenced by his "family heads" assumption that he fails to consider as part of the basic structure of society the greater economic dependence of women and the sexual division of labor within the typical family, or any of the broader social repercussions of this basic gender structure. Moreover, in Part III, where Rawls *assumes* the justice of the family "in some form" as a given, although he has not discussed any alternative forms, he sounds very much as though he is thinking in terms of traditional, gendered family structure. The family, he says, is "a small association, normally characterized by a definite hierarchy, in which each member has certain rights and duties."[36] The family's role as moral teacher is achieved partly through parental expectations of "the virtues of a good son or a good daughter."[37] In the family and in other associations such as schools, neighborhoods, and peer groups, Rawls continues, one learns various moral virtues and ideals, leading

to those adopted in the various statuses, occupations, and family positions of later life. "The content of these ideals is given by the various conceptions of a good wife and husband, a good friend and citizen, and so on."[38] It seems likely, given these unusual departures from the supposedly generic male terms of reference used throughout the rest of the book, that Rawls means to imply that the goodness of daughters is distinct from the goodness of sons, and that of wives from that of husbands. A fairly traditional gender system seems to be assumed.

However, despite this, not only does Rawls, as noted above, "assume that the basic structure of a well-ordered society includes the family *in some form*." He adds to this the comment that "in a broader inquiry the institution of the family might be questioned, and other arrangements might indeed prove to be preferable."[39] But why should it require a broader inquiry than that engaged in *A Theory of Justice,* to ask questions about the institution of the family? Surely Rawls is right at the outset when he names it as one of those basic social institutions that most affects the life chances of individuals. The family is not a private association like a church or a university, which vary considerably in type, and which one can join and leave voluntarily. For although one has some choice (albeit highly constrained) about marrying into a gender-structured family, one has no choice at all about being born into one. Given this, Rawls's failure to subject the structure of the family to his principles of justice is particularly serious in the light of his belief that a theory of justice must take account of "how [individuals] get to be what they are" and "cannot take their final aims and interests, their attitudes to themselves and their life, as given."[40] For the family with its gender structure, female parenting in particular, is clearly a crucial determinant in the different socialization of the two sexes—in how men and women "get to be what they are."

If Rawls were to assume throughout the construction of his theory that all human adults are to be par-

35   [Author's note] Ibid., pp. 380–381 (emphasis added).
36   [Author's note] Ibid., p. 467.
37   [Author's note] Ibid., p. 468.
38   [Author's note] Ibid.
39   [Author's note] Ibid., pp. 462–63 (emphasis added).
40   [Author's note] "The Basic Structure as Subject," p. 160.

ticipants in what goes on behind the veil of ignorance, he would have no option but to require that the family, as a major social institution affecting the life chances of individuals, be constructed in accordance with the two principles of justice. I will develop this conclusion in the final section of the paper. But first I will turn to another recent theory of justice which is argued very differently from Rawls's, and poses another set of problems from a feminist point of view.

Justice In Its Separate Spheres

Michael Walzer's *Spheres of Justice* is remarkable amongst contemporary theories of justice for the attention that its author pays to sex- and gender-related issues.[41] From its largely non-sexist language to its insistence that the family constitutes a significant "sphere of justice" and its specific references to power imbalances between the sexes and discrimination, Walzer's theory stands out in contrast to most moral and political philosophers' continued indifference to feminist issues. Viewing the book through the prism of gender, however, accentuates both its strengths and its weaknesses. The theoretical framework of separate spheres that, in a just society, must allow for different inequalities to exist side by side without creating a situation of domination, has considerable force as a tool for feminist criticism. But I will argue that, to the extent that this criticism is developed and emphasized, it calls into question the cultural relativism that is so essential a part of Walzer's theory of justice. And to the extent that the relativism flourishes, it seriously blunts the impact of the theory's feminist potential.

At the beginning of *Spheres of Justice,* Walzer sets out the aims of his theory:

> I want to argue ... that the principles of justice are themselves pluralistic in form; that differ-

ent social goods ought to be distributed for different reasons, in accordance with different procedures, by different agents; and that all these differences derive from different understandings of the social goods themselves—the inevitable product of historical and cultural particularism.[42]

Within this brief summary are contained two criteria for justice, criteria that, I will argue, are not only quite distinct but in serious tension with each other. I will first summarize Walzer's "separate spheres" argument and his relativist or particularist position, and will then show how the conflict between them is readily apparent in the context of issues of gender and their justice or injustice.

It is one of Walzer's fundamental theses that justice does not require the equal distribution of social goods within their respective spheres but, rather, that these spheres of distribution be kept autonomous, in the sense that the inequality that exists within each should not be allowed to translate itself into inequalities within the others. In principle, both the monopoly by one or a few persons of a social good or goods within a single sphere, and the dominance of a good over the command of other goods outside of its sphere, are threats to social justice. But because of his conviction that monopoly is impossible to eliminate without continual state intervention,[43] Walzer concerns himself primarily with the elimination of dominance. His critique of dominance leads to the adoption of the distributive principle that "no social good x should be distributed to men and women who possess some other good y merely because they possess y and without regard to the meaning of x."[44] The result of the adoption of this principle would be a society whose justice consisted in the distribution of "different goods to different companies of men and women for different reasons and in accordance with different procedures."[45]

---

41   Michael Walzer (1935–) is professor emeritus at the Institute for Advanced Study in Princeton. He is a leading representative of the 'communitarian' position in political theory, which holds—in contrast to liberalism—that theories of justice must be grounded in the traditions and culture of particular societies (and hence that no abstract, universal account of justice is possible or desirable).

---

42   [Author's note] *Spheres*, p. 6.
43   [Author's note] Ibid., pp. 14–17.
44   [Author's note] Ibid., p. 20.
45   [Author's note] Ibid., p. 26.

This conception of justice as depending on the autonomy of the various spheres of distribution is presented by Walzer as "a critical principle—indeed, ... a radical principle."[46] A number of his specific applications of the principle—notably to the issue of worker ownership and control of all but small-scale enterprises[47]—confirm this view, and when we turn to the feminist implications of the separate spheres criterion of justice, we shall see that they, too, can be interpreted as establishing the need for radical social change. Walzer says that the standards for distribution that the criterion establishes

> are often violated, the goods usurped, the spheres invaded, by powerful men and women.
> In fact, the violations are systematic.... For all the complexity of their distributive arrangements, most societies are organized on what we might think of as a social version of the gold standard: one good or one set of goods is dominant and determinative of value in all the spheres of distribution. And that good or set of goods is commonly monopolized, its value upheld by the strength and cohesion of its owners.[48]

Having thus indicated the extent to which the "spheres of justice" criterion is commonly violated, Walzer goes on to show how ideology is used to legitimate such violations. Operating in the service of a group's claim to monopolize a dominant good, "its standard form is to connect legitimate possession with some set of personal qualities through the medium of a philosophical principle."[49] But Walzer regards ideologies, like conceptions of justice, as pluralistic. In his view, groups using different ideological principles to justify their dominance "compete with one another, struggling for supremacy. One group wins, and then a different one; or coalitions are worked out, and supremacy is uneasily shared. There is no final victory, nor should there be."[50] If this is an accurate depiction of the past and present situation in our society, it softens the critical impact of Walzer's first criterion of justice, for it is difficult to see how the dominance and monopoly that he finds characteristic of most societies could coexist with genuinely competing pluralistic ideologies. But before examining it further, we must turn to his second criterion.

Walzer asserts clearly from the start that his theory of justice is highly relativist or, as he puts it, "radically particularist."[51] Beyond rights to life and liberty, he argues, men's and women's rights "do not follow from our common humanity; they follow from shared conceptions of social goods; they are local and particular in character."[52] "Justice" he says, "is relative to social meanings.... A given society is just if its substantive life is lived ... in a way faithful to the shared understandings of the members."[53] And since "social meanings are historical in character, ... distributions, and just and unjust distributions, change over time."[54]

In the course of establishing and emphasizing the cultural relativism of his theory of justice, Walzer takes issue with philosophers who "leave the city [to] fashion ... an objective and universal standpoint."[55] In particular, he argues with Rawls's development of a theory of justice that is not tied to a particular culture, that does not issue from the shared understandings or agreements of actual historical human beings with full knowledge of who they are and where they are situated in society. While he seems not to disagree that things would be decided by rational subjects behind the veil of ignorance much as Rawls concludes, he is unconvinced of the significance or force of the principles of justice agreed upon in such a situation for those same human beings once they are transformed into "ordinary people, with a firm sense of their own identity, with their own goods in their hands, caught up in everyday troubles." Would they "reiterate their hypothetical choice or even recognize it as their own [?]"[56] If conclusions about justice are to have

46 [Author's note] Ibid., p. 10.
47 [Author's note] Ibid., pp. 291–303.
48 [Author's note] Ibid., p. 10.
49 [Author's note] Ibid., p. 12.
50 [Author's note] Ibid.
51 [Author's note] Ibid., p. xiv.
52 [Author's note] Ibid., p. xv.
53 [Author's note] Ibid., p. 312–313.
54 [Author's note] Ibid., p. 9.
55 [Author's note] Ibid., p. xiv.
56 [Author's note] Ibid., p. 5; see also p. 79.

"force," they must be principles chosen not in some such hypothetical situation, but in answer to the question:

> What would individuals like us choose, who are situated as we are, who share a culture and are determined to go on sharing it? And this is a question that is readily transformed into, What choices have we already made in the course of our common life? What understandings do we (really) share?[57]

A distinct lack of critical perspective seems to be embodied in this highly relativist criterion for the justice of social arrangements and distributions. If all that Walzer were to mean by a conclusion's or a system's having "force" were that they were more readily *enforceable,* he would undoubtedly be right to reject Rawls's method. But he clearly means more than this. For he says that Rawls's formula for deciding principles of justice behind the veil of ignorance "doesn't help very much in determining what choices people will make, *or what choices they should make,* once they know who and where they are."[58] He means, then, that the principles of justice chosen in a Rawlsian manner do not have any particular *moral* force. To the contrary, it is only "when philosophers ... write out of a respect for the understandings they share with their fellow citizens [that] they pursue justice justly."[59]

A multitude of complexities, however, is contained within Walzer's reliance on "shared understandings." For he does not want to construct a theory of justice that is completely uncritical of whatever distributions take place and are justified within any given society. He says that the social vision he seeks is "*latent* already ... in our shared understandings of social goods," and that "the goal ... is a reflection of a special kind, which picks up *those deeper understandings* of social goods which are not necessarily mirrored in the everyday practice of dominance and monopoly."[60] But how is it to be determined which understandings

we "(really) share," deep, latent, and not necessarily mirrored in our practices?

Walzer's reliance on two distinct criteria for justice—"the separate spheres" standard and the "shared understandings" or "social meanings" standard—creates considerable tension within his theory. There seems to be only one way of preventing the two criteria from yielding different conclusions about what is just, and that is to argue that our shared social understandings about issues of justice do in fact satisfy the criterion of "separate spheres." In spite of passages such as that quoted on p. 54 above, Walzer at times appears to believe this to be the case. He says that if a just or egalitarian society "isn't already here—hidden, as it were, in our concepts and categories—we will never know it concretely or realize it in fact," and adds that "our conceptions ... do tend steadily to proscribe the use of things for the purposes of domination."[61]

Walzer's two criteria for justice are subjected to most strain in relation to each other in the case of fundamentally hierarchical societies, those in which "dominance and monopoly are not violations but enactments of meaning, where social goods are conceived in hierarchical terms." He chooses feudal and caste societies, particularly the latter, in order to explore the challenge posed by such societies to his assumption that "social meanings call for the autonomy, or the relative autonomy, of distributive spheres."[62] Such systems, he says, are

> constituted by an extraordinary integration of meanings. Prestige, wealth, knowledge, office, occupation, food, clothing, even the social good of conversation: all are subject to the intellectual as well as to the physical discipline of hierarchy.[63]

The hierarchy itself is determined by a single value—in the case of the caste system, ritual purity, dominated by birth and blood—which dominates over the distribution of all other goods, so that "social meanings overlap and cohere,"[64] losing their autonomy.

---

57 [Author's note] Ibid., p. 5.

58 [Author's note] Ibid., p. 79 (emphasis added).

59 [Author's note] Ibid., p. 320.

60 [Author's note] Ibid., pp. xiv, 26 (emphasis added).

61 [Author's note] Ibid., pp. xiv–xv.

62 [Author's note] Ibid., p. 26.

63 [Author's note] Ibid., p. 27.

64 [Author's note] Ibid.

In such systems, Walzer says, the more perfect the coherence of social meanings, "the less possible it is even to think about complex equality" and "justice will come to the aid of inequality."[65] Nevertheless, as he must in measuring them against his "shared understandings" or "social meanings" criterion for justice, he asserts unambiguously that such societies can meet "(internal) standards of justice."[66] By this criterion, indeed, there are no grounds for concluding that caste societies are any less just than societies that do not discriminate on the basis of inborn status or characteristics.

Walzer writes of caste societies, with their undifferentiated social meanings, as if they were distant from anything that characterizes our culture. It is only on this assumption that he is able to perceive his two criteria for a just society as not seriously in conflict in the contemporary context. But when we read his description of caste society, in which an inborn characteristic determines dominant or subordinate status in relation to social goods over the whole range of spheres, it can be seen to bear strong resemblances to the gender system that our society has only begun to shed formally within the last century, and that it still perpetuates to a large extent through the force of its economic structure and custom, and the ideology inherited from its highly patriarchal past. There seem, in fact, to be only two significant differences between caste and gender hierarchies: one is that women have not been physically segregated from men; the other is that, whereas Walzer says that "political power seems always to have escaped the laws of caste,"[67] it has only rarely escaped the laws of gender. Like the caste hierarchy, the gender hierarchy is determined by a single value—sex—with maleness taking the place of ritual purity. Like the hierarchy of caste, that of gender ascribes roles, responsibilities, rights, and other social goods in accordance with an inborn characteristic that is imbued with tremendous significance. All the social goods listed in Walzer's description of a caste society have been, and many still are, differentially distributed to the members of the two sexes. In the cases of prestige, wealth, knowledge, office, and occupation, this statement is fairly obviously true, although the disparities between the sexes have begun to decline in some of them in recent years. Better and greater amounts of food are often reserved for men in poor classes and cultures, women's clothing has been and still is to a large extent designed either to constrict their movements or to appeal to men rather than for their own comfort and convenience, and women have been excluded from men's conversation in numerous social contexts, from ancient Greece to nineteenth- and twentieth-century after-dinner conversations and men's clubs.[68]

As in caste societies, ideology has played a crucial part in perpetuating the legitimacy of patriarchy. Though Walzer says in the context of caste society that "we should not assume that men and women are ever entirely content with radical inequality,"[69] ideology helps us to comprehend the extent to which they often have been and are content. Taking the gender system as an example, if the family is founded in law and custom on male dominance and female subordination and dependence, if religion inculcates the same hierarchy and enhances it with the mystical and sacred significance of a male god, and if the educational system not only excludes women from its higher reaches but establishes as truth and reason the same intellectual foundations of patriarchy, the opportunity for a competing ideology about sex and gender to arise is seriously limited. In fact, the ideology that is embodied in what has recently been termed "male-stream" thought is undoubtedly one of the most

---

65   [Author's note] Ibid., pp. 27, 313.

66   [Author's note] Ibid., p. 315.

67   [Author's note] Ibid., p. 27.

68   [Author's note] In a passage in which his nonsexist language strains credibility, Walzer says that "in different historical periods," dominant goods such as "physical strength, familial reputation, religious or political office, landed wealth, capital, technical knowledge" have each been "monopolized by some group of men and women" (*Spheres*, p. 11). In fact, men have monopolized these goods to the exclusion of women (and still monopolize some of the most important ones) to at least as great an extent as any group of men and women has monopolized them to the exclusion of any other group.

69   [Author's note] *Spheres*, p. 27.

all-encompassing and pervasive examples of ideology in history.[70]

Walzer relies, for the possibility of social change in general, on the flourishing of dissent. In most societies, even if

> the ideology that justifies the seizure [of social goods] is widely believed to be true, ... resentment and resistance are (almost) as pervasive as belief. There are always some people, and after a time there are a great many, who think the seizure is not justice but usurpation.[71]

But the closer the social system is to a caste system, in which social meanings "overlap and cohere," the less likely is the appearance or development of such dissent. The more thoroughgoing the dominance, and the more pervasive its ideology across the various spheres, the less chance there is that the whole prevailing structure will be questioned or resisted. By arguing that such a system can meet "(internal) standards of justice" if it is really accepted by its members, Walzer admits the paradox that the more *unjust* a system is by one of his criteria (in that dominance is all-pervasive within it) the more likely it is to be able to enshrine the ideology of the ruling group and hence to meet his other criterion (that it is in accord with shared understandings). The danger of his conception of justice is that what is just depends heavily on what people are persuaded of.[72]

Even if the social meanings in a fundamentally hierarchical society were shared, we should surely be wary of concluding, as Walzer clearly does, that the hierarchy was rendered just by the agreement or lack of dissent.[73] But what if the oppressors and the oppressed disagree fundamentally? What if the oppressors claim, as they often have, that aristocrats, or Brahmins,[74] or men are fully human in a way that serfs, or untouchables, or women are not, and that while the rulers institutionalize equal justice amongst themselves, it is just for them to require the other categories of people to perform functions supportive of the fully human existence of those capable of it? And what if the serfs or untouchables or women somehow actually do become convinced (against all the odds) that they too are fully human and that whatever principles of justice apply amongst their oppressors should rightfully be extended to them too? With disagreements this basic, rather than a meaningful debate being joined, there would seem to be two irreconcilable theories of justice. There would be no shared meanings on the most fundamental of questions.

This problem is rendered even more complex if there are fundamental disagreements not only between the oppressors and the oppressed, but even *within* the ranks of the oppressed. Contemporary views about the gender system are a clear example of such disagreement. As studies of feminism and antifeminism have shown, women themselves are deeply divided on the subject of the gender system, with antifeminist women not rejecting it as unjust, but regarding the continued economic dependence of women and the dominance of the world outside the home by men as natural and inevitable, given women's special reproductive functions.[75] Even amongst feminists, there has grown

---

70   [Author's note] This phrase was coined by Mary O'Brien in *The Politics of Reproduction* (London: Routledge and Kegan Paul, 1981).

71   [Author's note] *Spheres*, p. 12.

72   [Author's note] See Bernard Williams, "The Idea of Equality," in *Philosophy, Politics and Society* (Second Series), ed. Peter Laslett and W.G. Runciman (Oxford: Basil Blackwell, 1962), pp. 119–120, for a succinct discussion of social conditioning and the justification of hierarchical societies, critical of a position such as Walzer takes. Norman Daniels has recently criticized Walzer on this issue in a review of *Spheres of Justice,* in *The Philosophical Review* XCIV, no. 1 (January 1985): 145–146.

73   [Author's note] See Ronald Dworkin's review of *Spheres of Justice,* in *New York Review of Books* (April 14, 1983), pp. 4–5, and Walzer's response in *New York Review of Books* (July 21, 1983).

74   The highest caste in Hinduism: the class of educators, lawmakers, scholars, and preachers.

75   [Author's note] For a recent analysis of such attitudes, see Kristin Luker, *Abortion and the Politics of Motherhood* (Berkeley: University of California Press, 1984), esp. chap. 8. Feminists tend to attribute such attitudes in part at least to the influence of patriarchal ideology; it is clear that religion is an important factor. Such an

a rift in recent years between those who see the gender system itself as the problem and look forward to an androgynous society, and those who, celebrating women's unique nature and traditional roles, consider the problem to be not the *existence* of these roles but the *devaluation* of women's qualities and activities by a male-dominated culture.[76] These opposite poles of opinion about the very nature of sex difference and its appropriate social repercussions seem to provide no shared intellectual structure in which to debate distributions. And Walzer's theory of justice provides no criterion for adjudicating between them, aside from an appeal to some deeper, latent understandings which all supposedly hold, beneath their disagreements.

As I pointed out above, the coherence of Walzer's theory of justice depends on the compatibility of his two criteria of justice, which in turn depends upon whether the shared understandings of a society call for the autonomy of different distributive spheres. I have also suggested that contemporary society is still sufficiently pervaded by the caste-like gender system that fully characterized its past that it does not fulfill this condition.

While at times Walzer seems forgetful of our patriarchal history,[77] he sometimes shows clear awareness of its current manifestations. At the beginning of his chapter on recognition, for example, he states that the argument to follow applies only in part to women.

The extent to which women are still designated and defined by their position within the family, he says, is symbolized by the continued use of the titles "Miss" and "Mrs.": "the absence of a universal title suggests the continued exclusion of women, or of many women, from the social universe, the sphere of recognition as it is currently constituted."[78] But this point—that the argument applies only in part to women, or to a few women—is equally applicable to almost all of the other spheres of justice discussed in the book. Political power and office, hard work, money and commodities, security—is any of these things evenly distributed between the two sexes? Surely in each case, the explicit or implicit assignment of women to the functional role of actual or potential wife and mother and, as primary nurturer, to basic dependence upon a man, has a great deal to do with the fact that women are, in general, less benefited by the benefits and more burdened by the burdens, in the distribution of most social goods. While Walzer occasionally extends the feminist perspective he displays in the argument on recognition, and develops briefly a section entitled "The Woman Question," he frequently overlooks its implications.

Introducing his discussion of the oppression of women, Walzer argues that "the real domination of women has less to do with their familial place than with their exclusion from all other places." The family disfavors women by imposing sex-roles upon many activities "to which sex is entirely irrelevant." Liberation from this "political and economic misogyny" begins outside of the family. The market must set "no internal bar to the participation of women."[79] But, as he seems to imply, in the context of the example of nineteenth-century China, it cannot *end* outside: "The family itself must be reformed so that its power no longer reaches into the sphere of office" (or any of the other spheres of distribution, we might add).[80] On a number of occasions, both within his section

---

antifeminist posture becomes increasingly difficult to maintain consistently, once feminist reforms are instituted. For then, female proponents of it are faced with the problem of how they are to be successful in reversing political change while maintaining what they believe to be their proper, politically powerless role.

76   [Author's note] For a fair and lucid account of this division, see Iris Marion Young, "Humanism, Gynocentrism and Feminist Politics," *Hypatia: A Journal of Feminist Philosophy* no. 3, a special issue of *Women's Studies International Forum* 8, no. 3 (1985): 173–83. Gynocentric feminism faces a similar problem to that faced by antifeminism: How *can* women's work, concerns and perspectives come to be properly valued, unless women seek and attain power in the predominant, male realm?

77   [Author's note] See note [68] above.

78   [Author's note] *Spheres*, p. 252. See also William Safire, "On Language," and the Editors' response, *New York Times Magazine*, Sunday, August 5, 1984, pp. 8–10. In 1986, the *New York Times* finally agreed to use the term "Ms." in certain circumstances.

79   [Author's note] *Spheres*, pp. 240–241.

80   [Author's note] Ibid., p. 240.

on "The Woman Question" and elsewhere, Walzer criticizes the operation of the gender system outside of the family. But he pays almost no attention to its continued operation within.

This lacuna is certainly not attributable to a belief that justice is not an appropriate moral virtue for families. For Walzer, although he perceives the family as "a sphere of special relationships,"[81] also asserts plainly that "the sphere of personal relations, domestic life, reproduction, and child-rearing remains ... the focus of enormously important distributions,"[82] and where there are distributions, whether of responsibilities, rights, favors or goods, there is potential for justice and injustice. He does not, however, give this important sphere of distribution the attention it would seem to warrant. While all kinds of hard (undesirable but necessary) work done for wages are discussed at some length, virtually no attention is paid to all the unpaid work, much of it "hard" by his definition, that is done by women at home, and he refers only briefly to the immensely time-consuming activity of child care. If his argument were not in so many respects egalitarian, one might suppose that he accepted, as a less egalitarian thinker might, paid domestic labor for those who could afford it as the solution to these demands on wives and/or mothers who chose to work, to seek recognition, political power or office, and so on, in the outside world. But this is clearly not an acceptable solution, since he regards families with live-in servants as "inevitably ... little tyrann[ies]," and considers domestic service of any sort to be "degraded" work.[83] In an egalitarian society, at any rate, he considers that the market will raise the wages of unskilled workers much closer to those of skilled ones than at present, with the desirable result that workers will be much less likely to take on such degraded work.[84] To compound the problems of working couples with children, he disapproves of the communal care of young children as "likely to result in a great loss of love," except in a small, close-knit society such as the kibbutz.[85] This is reiterated in a passage in which he talks of children being "abandoned to bureaucratic rearing."[86]

How, then, is the unpaid work that is currently done almost entirely by women within the household to be done in a society that regards the family, and relations between the sexes in particular, as an appropriate sphere for the operations of justice? Walzer's answers to this question are so rapidly whisked over, in a clause and a footnote respectively, that they are easily missed. In the chapter on hard work—which is mostly concerned with hard wage work (also, as he points out, largely done by women)—he suggests that the only answer to hard, and particularly to dirty, work in a society of equals is that "at least in some partial and symbolic sense, we will all have to do it."[87] Otherwise, those who do it will be degraded by it and will never be equal members of the political community. "What is required, then, is a kind of domestic *corvée*,[88] not only in households—though it is especially important there—but also in communes, factories, offices, and schools."[89] Thus in a society of equals, "at least in some partial and symbolic sense," housework will be shared, regardless of sex. And, while child care is a different matter, since it hardly meets his negative definition of "hard work" (at least, most of the time), Walzer suggests the same solution. Parenthetically, in a footnote, he asks "(why can't the parents share in social *re*production?)"[90]

---

81   [Author's note] Ibid., p. 229.
82   [Author's note] Ibid., p. 242.
83   [Author's note] Ibid., p. 52.
84   [Author's note] Ibid., pp. 179–180.

85   [Author's note] Ibid., p. 233n.
86   [Author's note] Ibid., p. 238.
87   [Author's note] Ibid., p. 174.
88   *Corvée* is labor that someone can be compelled to perform unless this obligation is commuted in some way (such as by a cash payment). For example, the vassal of a medieval feudal lord might be obliged to work for a certain number of days plowing or harvesting his lord's land, or a nobleman might have to fight for the monarch in a time of war.
89   [Author's note] Ibid., p. 175.
90   [Author's note] Ibid., p. 233n. The importance of shared childrearing for justice between the sexes is not due to its being undesirable work, for in favorable circumstances it can be immensely challenging and pleasurable. It is the immensely time-consuming nature

With one important proviso,[91] I would affirm that these solutions (if the sharing is real and complete rather than symbolic) represent the only way in which the injustices inherent in the traditional gender-structured family can be done away with. Until the unpaid and largely unrecognized work of the household is shared equally by its adult members, women will not have equal opportunities with men either within the family or in any of the other spheres of distribution—from politics to free time, from recognition to security to money. This sharing is necessary if Walzer's separate spheres criterion for justice is to be met—if a society of equal men and women is to distribute its social goods in such a way that what happens within the family is not to dominate over, to invade, all the other spheres of justice. But, on the other hand (and perhaps this is why it is so rapidly brushed past in the argument),

---

of childrearing, and the everpresence of its demands, that make its just distribution essential. While Walzer asserts that free time is not readily convertible into other social goods (p. 184), I would strongly dissent. The kind of free time that one does *not* have when primarily or solely responsible for small children is translatable into many things, including education, career advancement and recognition, the pursuit of political office and wealth, as well as just plain leisure. On the other hand, those who do not share in parenting to a substantial extent could be said to suffer injustice in the sense that they miss out on its own special social rewards, the experiences of intimacy with and nurturing love for a child.

91 [Author's note] Walzer is too quick to dismiss day care for small children as a partial solution. Even a "mass society" does not have to provide "mass" day care. It can provide small-scale, loving day care for all if it cares enough and is prepared to subsidize the full costs for parents unable to afford them. Good day care, besides being a positive experience for the child, also helps to solve two other problems: without it, the shared parenting solution is of no help at all to single parents, of whom there are increasing numbers, mainly women; and good, subsidized day care can help to alleviate the obstacle that the inequality of family situation poses for equality of opportunity.

this solution constitutes a radical break not only from prevailing patterns of behavior but also from widely, though not completely, shared understandings of our society about the social meanings of sex and gender. It constitutes no less than the abolition of gender in its most entrenched bastion, with likely reverberations throughout all social spheres. Only if it could be argued that deep or latent in our shared current understandings lies the justification for the total abolition of gender could Walzer claim that his solution to sex inequality is just by his relativist criterion.

Thus the paradox of Walzer's theory of justice is strikingly exemplified by the theory's feminist implications. Insofar as the reduction of domination requires a thoroughgoing feminism that undermines the very roots of our gendered institutions, it is in considerable tension with the relativist requirement that a just society is one that abides by its shared understandings. And insofar as the latter criterion is applied, the feminist implications of the theory lose their force, on account of the deeply rooted attitudes about sex differences that we have inherited from our past and continue to imbibe from many aspects of our culture.

Women and Justice in Theory and Practice

I have argued that Walzer's requirement that justice be relative to "shared understandings" or "social meanings" tends to conflict with his "separate spheres" criterion of justice. It is also inadequate as a foundation for a moral theory. On some important issues in contemporary society—gender in particular—there are no fully shared understandings. To the extent that understandings are in fact shared in this or any existing society, their influence may be due to the past or present hegemony of certain groups over others. Moreover, divisions between conservative and radical standpoints on such issues may be so deep that they provide little foundation from which the different parties, *situated as they actually are,* can come to any conclusions about what is just. The significance of Rawls's central, brilliant idea of the original position, in which one's characteristics and position in society are not known, is that it forces one to question shared understandings from all points of view, and ensures that the principles of justice chosen are acceptable to everyone, regardless of what position he ends up in.

The problem for a feminist reader of Rawls's theory as stated by Rawls himself however, is encapsulated in that ambiguous "he." As I have shown above, while Rawls briefly rules out formal, legal discrimination on the grounds of sex (as on other grounds that he regards as "morally irrelevant"), he fails entirely to address the justice of the gender system, which—with its roots in the sex roles of the family and with its branches extending into virtually every corner of our lives—is one of the fundamental structures of our society. If, however, we read Rawls taking seriously both the notion that those behind the veil of ignorance are sexless persons, and the requirement that the family and the gender system—as basic social institutions—are to be subject to scrutiny, constructive feminist criticism of these contemporary institutions follows. So, also, do hidden difficulties for a Rawlsian theory of justice in a gendered society.

I will explain each of these points in turn. But first, both the critical perspective and the incipient problems of a feminist reading of Rawls can perhaps be illuminated by a description of a cartoon I saw a few years ago. Three elderly, robed male justices are depicted, looking down with astonishment at their very pregnant bellies. One says to the others, without further elaboration: "Perhaps we'd better reconsider that decision." This illustration points to several things. First, it graphically demonstrates the importance, in thinking about justice, of a concept like Rawls's original position, which makes us put ourselves into the positions of others—especially positions that we ourselves can never be in. Second, it suggests that those thinking in such a way might well conclude that more than formal legal equality of the sexes is required if justice is to be done. As we have seen in recent years, it is quite possible to institutionalize the formal legal equality of the sexes and at the same time to enact laws concerning pregnancy, abortion, maternity leave, and so on, that in effect discriminate against women, not as women *per se,* but as "pregnant persons." The U.S. Supreme Court decided in 1976, for example, that "an exclusion of pregnancy from a disability benefits plan ... providing general coverage

is not a gender-based discrimination at all."[92] One of the virtues of the cartoon is its suggestion that one's thinking on such matters is likely to be affected by the knowledge that one might become a "pregnant person." Finally, however, the illustration suggests the limits of what is possible, in terms of thinking ourselves into the original position, as long as we live in a gender-structured society. While the elderly male justices can, in a sense, imagine *themselves* pregnant, what is much more doubtful is whether, in constructing principles of justice, they can imagine themselves *women.* This raises the question whether, in fact, sex *is* a morally irrelevant and contingent human characteristic, in a society structured by gender.

Let us first assume that sex is contingent in this way, though I will later question this assumption. Let us suppose that it is possible, as Rawls clearly considers that it is, to hypothesize the moral thinking of representative human beings, ignorant of their sex and of all the other things that are hidden by the veil of ignorance. It seems clear that, while Rawls does not do this, we must consistently take the relevant positions of both sexes into account in formulating principles of justice. In particular, those in the original position must take special account of the perspective of women, since their knowledge of "the general facts about human society"[93] must include the knowledge that women have been and continue to be the less advantaged sex in a number of respects. In considering the basic institutions of society, they are more likely to pay special attention to the family than virtually to ignore it, since its unequal assigning of responsibilities and privileges to the two sexes and its socialization of children into sex roles make it, in its current form, a crucial institution for the preservation of sex inequality.

It is impossible to discuss here all the ways in which the principles of justice that Rawls arrives at are inconsistent with a gender-structured society. A general explanation of this point and three examples to illustrate it will have to suffice. The critical impact of a feminist reading of Rawls comes chiefly from his

92 [Author's note] *General Electric* vs. *Gilbert,* 429, U.S. 125 (1976).
93 [Author's note] *Theory,* p. 137.

second principle, which requires that inequalities be "to the greatest benefit of the least advantaged" and "attached to offices and positions open to all."[94] This means that if any roles or positions analogous to our current sex roles, including those of husband and wife, mother and father, were to survive the demands of the first requirement, the second requirement would disallow any linkage between these roles and sex. Gender, as I have defined it in this article, with its ascriptive designation of positions and expectations of behavior in accordance with the inborn characteristic of sex, could no longer form a legitimate part of the social structure, whether inside or outside the family. Three illustrations will help to link this conclusion with specific major requirements that Rawls makes of a just or well-ordered society.

First, after the basic political liberties, one of the most essential liberties is "the important liberty of free choice of occupation."[95] It is not difficult to see that this liberty is compromised by the assumption and customary expectation, central to our gender system, that women take far greater responsibility than men for housework and child care, whether or not they also work for wages outside the home. In fact, both the assigning of these responsibilities to women—resulting in their asymmetrical economic dependency on men—and also the related responsibility of husbands to support their wives, compromise the liberty of choice of occupation of both sexes. While Rawls has no objection to some aspects of the division of labor, he asserts that, in a well-ordered society, "no one need be servilely dependent on others and made to choose between monotonous and routine occupations which are deadening to human thought and sensibility" but that work can be "meaningful for all."[96] These conditions are far more likely to be met in a society which does not assign family responsibilities in a way that makes women into a marginal sector of the paid work force and renders likely their economic dependence upon men.

Second, the abolition of gender seems essential for the fulfillment of Rawls's criteria for political

justice. For he argues that not only would equal formal political liberties be espoused by those in the original position, but that any inequalities in the *worth* of these liberties (for example, the effects on them of factors like poverty and ignorance) must be justified by the difference principle. Indeed, "the constitutional process should preserve the equal representation of the original position to the degree that this is practicable."[97] While Rawls discusses this requirement in the context of *class* differences, stating that those who devote themselves to politics should be "drawn more or less equally from all sectors of society,"[98] it is just as clearly applicable to sex differences. And the equal political representation of women and men, especially if they are parents, is clearly inconsistent with our gender system.

Finally, Rawls argues that the rational moral persons in the original position would place a great deal of emphasis on the securing of self-respect or self-esteem. They "would wish to avoid at almost any cost the social conditions that undermine self-respect," which is "perhaps the most important" of all the primary goods.[99] In the interests of this primary value, if those in the original position did not know whether they were to be men or women, they would surely be concerned to establish a thoroughgoing social and economic equality between the sexes that would preserve either from the need to pander to or servilely provide for the pleasures of the other. They would be highly motivated, for example, to find a means of regulating pornography that did not seriously compromise freedom of speech. In general, they would be unlikely to tolerate basic social institutions that asymmetrically either forced or gave strong incentives to members of one sex to become sex objects for the other.

There is, then, implicit in Rawls's theory of justice a potential critique of gender-structured social institutions, which can be made explicit by taking seriously the fact that those formulating the principles of justice

---

94 [Author's note] Ibid., p. 302.

95 [Author's note] Ibid., p. 274.

96 [Author's note] Ibid., p. 529.

97 [Author's note] Ibid., p. 222; see also pp. 202–205, 221–228.

98 [Author's note] Ibid., p. 228.

99 [Author's note] Ibid., pp. 440, 396; see also pp. 178–179.

do not know their sex. At the beginning of my brief discussion of this feminist critique, however, I made an assumption that I said would later be questioned— that a person's sex is, as Rawls at times indicates, a contingent and morally irrelevant characteristic, such that human beings can hypothesize ignorance of this fact about them, imagining themselves as *sexless,* free and equal, rational, moral persons. First, I will explain why, unless this assumption is a reasonable one, there are likely to be further feminist ramifications for a Rawlsian theory of justice, as well as those I have just sketched out. I will then argue that the assumption is very probably not plausible in any society that is structured along the lines of gender. The conclusion I reach is that not only is the disappearance of gender necessary if social justice is to be enjoyed in practice by members of both sexes, but that the disappearance of gender is a prerequisite for the *complete* development of a nonsexist, fully human *theory* of justice.

Although Rawls is clearly aware of the effects on individuals of their different places in the social system, he regards it as possible to hypothesize free and rational moral persons in the original position who, freed from the contingencies of actual characteristics and social circumstances, will adopt the viewpoint of the "representative human being." He is under no illusions about the difficulty of this task, which requires "a great shift in perspective" from the way we think about fairness in everyday life. But with the help of the veil of ignorance, he believes that we can "take up a point of view that everyone can adopt on an equal footing," so that "we share a common standpoint along with others and do not make our judgments from a personal slant."[100] The result of this rational impartiality or objectivity, Rawls argues, is that, all being convinced by the same arguments, agreement about the basic principles of justice will be unanimous.[101] He does not mean that those in the original position will agree about *all* moral or social issues, but that complete agreement will be reached on all basic principles, or "essential understandings."[102] It is a crucial assumption of this argument for una-

nimity, however, that all the parties have similar motivations and psychologies (he assumes mutually disinterested rationality and an absence of envy), and that they have experienced similar patterns of moral development (they are presumed capable of a sense of justice). Rawls regards these assumptions as the kind of "weak stipulations" on which a general theory can safely be founded.[103]

The coherence of Rawls's hypothetical original position, with its unanimity of representative human beings, however, is placed in doubt if the kinds of human beings we actually become in society not only differ in respect of interests, superficial opinions, prejudices, and points of view that we can discard for the purpose of formulating principles of justice, but also differ in their basic psychologies, conceptions of self in relation to others, and experiences of moral development. A number of feminist scholars have argued in recent years that, in a gender-structured society, women's and men's different life experiences in fact affect their respective psychologies, modes of thinking, and patterns of moral development in significant ways.[104] Special attention has been paid to the effects on the psychological and moral development of both sexes of the fact, fundamental to our gendered

---

100 [Author's note] Ibid., pp. 516–517.

101 [Author's note] Ibid., pp. 139–141.

102 [Author's note] Ibid., pp. 516–517.

103 [Author's note] Ibid., p. 149.

104 [Author's note] Major works contributing to this thesis are Jean Baker Miller, *Toward a New Psychology of Women* (Boston: Beacon Press, 1976); Dorothy Dinnerstein, *The Mermaid and the Minotaur* (New York: Harper and Row, 1977); Nancy Chodorow, *The Reproduction of Mothering* (Berkeley: University of California Press, 1978); Carol Gilligan, *In a Different Voice* (Cambridge, MA: Harvard University Press, 1982); Nancy Hartsock, *Money, Sex, and Power* (New York: Longmans, 1983). Two of the more important individual papers are Jane Flax, "The Conflict between Nurturance and Autonomy in Mother-Daughter Relationships and within Feminism," *Feminist Studies* 4, no. 2 (Summer 1978); Sara Ruddick, "Maternal Thinking," *Feminist Studies* 6, no. 2 (Summer 1980). A good summary and discussion of "women's standpoint" is presented in Alison Jaggar, *Feminist Politics and Human Nature* (Totowa, NJ: Rowman and Allanheld, 1983), chap. 11.

society, that children of both sexes are primarily reared by women. It has been argued that the experience of individuation—of separating oneself from the nurturer with whom one is originally psychologically fused—is a very different experience for girls than for boys, leaving the members of each sex with a different perception of themselves and of their relations with others. In addition, it has been argued that the experience of *being* primary nurturers (and of growing up with this expectation) also affects the psychological and moral perspective of women, as does the experience of growing up in a society in which members of one's sex are in many respects subordinate to the other. Feminist theorists' scrutiny and analysis of the different experiences that we encounter as we develop, from our actual lived lives to our absorption of their ideological underpinnings, have in valuable ways filled out de Beauvoir's claim that "one is not born, but rather becomes, a woman."[105]

What is already clearly indicated by these studies, despite their incompleteness so far, is that in a gender-structured society there is such a thing as the distinct standpoint of women, and that this standpoint cannot be adequately taken into account by male philosophers doing the theoretical equivalent of the elderly male justices in the cartoon. The formative influence on small children of female parenting, especially, seems to suggest that sex difference is more likely to affect one's moral psychology, and therefore one's thinking about justice, in a gendered society than, for example, racial difference in a society in which race has social significance or class difference in a class society. The notion of the standpoint of women, while not without its own problems, suggests that a fully human moral theory can be developed only when there is full participation by both sexes in the dialogue that is moral and political philosophy. This will not come to pass until women take their place with men in the enterprise in approximately equal numbers and in positions of comparable influence. In a society structured along the lines of gender, this is most unlikely to happen.

In itself, moreover, it is insufficient for the complete development of a fully human theory of justice. For if principles of justice are to be adopted unanimously by representative human beings ignorant of their particular characteristics and positions in society, they must be persons whose psychological and moral development is in all essentials identical. This means that the social factors influencing the differences presently found between the sexes—from female parenting to all the manifestations of female subordination and dependence—would have to be replaced by genderless institutions and customs. Only when men participate equally in what has been principally women's realm of meeting the daily material and psychological needs of those close to them, and when women participate equally in what have been principally men's realms of larger scale production, government, and intellectual and creative life, will members of both sexes develop a more complete *human* personality than has hitherto been possible. Whereas Rawls and most other philosophers have assumed that human psychology, rationality, moral development and so on are completely represented by the males of the species, this assumption itself is revealed as a part of the male-dominated ideology of our gendered society.

It is not feasible to indicate here at any length what effect the consideration of women's standpoint might have on a theory of justice. I would suggest, however, that in the case of Rawls's theory, it might place in doubt some assumptions and conclusions, while reinforcing others. For example, Rawls's discussion of rational plans of life and primary goods might be focused more on relationships and less exclusively on the complex activities that his "Aristotelian principle" values most highly, if it were to encompass the traditionally more female parts of life.[106] On the other hand, those aspects of Rawls's theory, such as the difference principle, that seem to require a greater capacity to identify with others than is normally characteristic of liberalism, might be strengthened

---

105 [Author's note] Simone de Beauvoir, *The Second Sex* (1949; reprinted., London: New English Library, 1969), p. 9.

106 [Author's note] Brian Barry has made a similar, though more general, criticism of the Aristotelian principle in *The Liberal Theory of Justice* (Oxford: Oxford University Press, 1973), pp. 27–30.

by reference to conceptions of relations between self and others that seem in a gendered society to be more predominantly female.

In the earlier stages of working on this article, I thought mainly in terms of what justice has to say about gender, rather than about the effects of gender on justice. I looked at two recent theories of justice from this perspective, and found that although Walzer's focused far more attention on women's place in society, it was in fact Rawls's that could more consistently yield feminist principles of justice when the standpoint of women was taken into account. But, given the reliance of this latter theory on the agreement of representative human beings about the basic moral principles that are to govern their lives, I conclude that, while we can use it along the way to critique existing inequalities, we cannot complete such a theory of justice until the life experiences of the two sexes become as similar as their biological differences permit. Such a theory, and the society that puts it into practice, will be fundamentally influenced by the participation of both women and men in all spheres of human life. Not only is gender incompatible with a just society but the disappearance of gender is likely to lead in turn to important changes in the theory and practices of justice.

APPENDIX 1

Philosophical Puzzles and Paradoxes

INTRODUCTION

Paradoxes and puzzles have played an important role in philosophy since the beginning of philosophical thought. They make us question our beliefs and pre-suppositions—often very basic ones. They don't always make us reject what we had taken for granted, but they do always subject it to scrutiny from a new and fascinating direction.

A paradox is an argument that appears to derive an absurd or obviously false conclusion by entirely valid reasoning from clearly acceptable premises. Sometimes philosophers argue that a premise is, despite appearances, actually false, or that the reasoning is actually invalid. Sometimes they argue that the premises and reasoning are fine, but the conclusion is true. Sometimes philosophers simply don't know what to do about a paradox. Any of these reactions is surprising, and may be of deep philosophical importance.

Puzzles are questions that seem like they ought to have a satisfying answer—but apparently do not. Philosophical reactions here include arguments for an (unobvious) solution, claims that there's something wrong with the unanswerable question in the first place, or, again, just puzzlement. Again, any of these reactions is surprising and can be instructive.

The puzzles and paradoxes presented here are almost all very well-known and widely discussed in the philosophical literature. We'll often include a brief indication of how, in general, philosophers have reacted. We have not included very much discussion of philosophical reactions, or bibliographies, but you won't have any trouble finding these on the Internet. We have also little to say about philosophical implications. What we aim at here is to give you enough of an introduction to each puzzle or paradox to stimulate your own philosophical intelligence—to get you to think about these brain-twisters on your own—and

we're confident you'll often find this engaging, enlightening, and fun.

BARBER PARADOX

Imagine a town in which there's a (male) barber who shaves all the men who don't shave themselves, and only those men. Does he shave himself? The answer can't be yes—because he doesn't shave men who shave themselves. The answer can't be no—because he does shave all the men who don't shave themselves. This paradox is resolved by concluding that there can't be a town with a barber who is the way we're trying to imagine.

BERTRAND'S BOX PARADOX

Imagine three boxes, each containing two drawers. In one box, both drawers contain a gold coin. (Call this box GG.) In another box, both drawers contain a silver coin. (Call this box SS.) In the third box, one drawer has a gold coin, the other has a silver. (Call this box GS.) You pick a box at random, open one drawer, and find a gold coin. What's the probability the other drawer in that box contains a silver coin? (Stop now and try to answer.)

Here's how most people reason. You've got a gold coin, so that means that the box you picked isn't SS. It's equally likely—50%—to be GG or GS. So the likelihood that the other coin is silver is 50%.

But that's wrong. What you've got might be (1) drawer G of GS; (2) drawer G1 of GG; (3) drawer G2 of GG. The probability of each of these is equal:

33%. So the probability the other drawer has a silver coin is the probability of outcome (1): 33%.

BLACKMAIL PARADOX

It's neither illegal nor immoral to ask somebody for money. It's neither illegal nor immoral to threaten to expose somebody's theft. But it's both illegal and immoral to ask somebody for money, threatening that if you don't get the money, you'll expose their theft.

This is a paradox only if you accept the principle that if it's not illegal (or immoral) to do X, and it's not illegal (or immoral) to do Y, then it's not illegal (immoral) to do X and Y. But that's clearly a false principle. There are plenty of counter-examples. It's not illegal (or immoral) for example to drink, or to drive, but it is illegal to drink-and-drive (and probably immoral too, because of the increased risk of a damaging accident).

What is illegal (and immoral) in the blackmail case is not merely doing both actions—I might threaten to expose your theft, and also, unconnectedly, ask you for money—but to do both with a particular connection between them. What connection? What's the general principle here?

BURIDAN'S ASS

Imagine an ass (come on now, we mean a donkey) who is very hungry and very thirsty, and is placed equidistant between equal quantities of hay and water. If we assume that the ass is determined to choose by a variety of factors (more hungry or thirsty?; which hunger/thirst remover is nearer?; which is larger?), since all these are equal, nothing would cause the ass to go to one or the other; so it would stay stuck in the middle and starve to death.

Some philosophers argue that because this could never happen, decisions (even from an ass) cannot be fully determined in this fashion: there must be an arbitrary—free—element that's at least capable of resolving ties. (This free element is supposedly of primary importance in human decisions.) Others argue, however, that this sort of paralysis between equally attractive options could happen, but rarely does because such perfect equality is so uncommon.

THE CIRCLE THAT'S A STRAIGHT LINE

As the radius of a circle gets larger and larger, the curvature of the circle gets less and less. A circle with infinite radius would thus be a straight line!

Sometimes it's said that we should accept this odd result, and that it's just one of the odd things that happen when infinite magnitudes are imagined. (See, for example, the St. Petersburg Paradox, below.) Others point out that this would be true only if space is Euclidian—which it isn't, in fact.

CURRY'S PARADOX

Consider this sentence, which we'll call 'S':

If S is true, then Santa Claus exists.

Is S true? Well, suppose for the moment it is. Now we have the antecedent of the true conditional statement S, so the consequent follows: Santa Claus exists. When we assume S is true we derive Santa Claus exists, and this is the standard way to prove the truth of a conditional statement. So we've just proven If S is true then Santa Claus exists. But this is Statement S; so it follows that Santa Claus exists.

What's wrong here is not a matter of whether you're a Santa-believer or not. It's that this kind of reasoning can be used to prove any arbitrary proposition. What has gone wrong? Briefly, we can see the problem here as one of many odd consequences of allowing self-referential statements. (Statement S mentions itself.) See also, among others, Grelling's Paradox and The Liar Paradox.

DETERRENCE PARADOX

Think back to when the cold war between the US and the USSR was raging. Both countries had hundreds of nuclear warheads aimed at each other's cities. Each warned the other that the other's first strike would result in massive retaliation, in which hundreds of cities would be devastated and millions of innocent civilians killed and injured.

The aim here on both sides was preventing war, and in hindsight it seems we can say it was an astoundingly successful strategy. It's hard to find any other instances in history in which a face-off between powerful armed enemies did not result in major war.

But there are other moral considerations to raise here besides the morally laudable aim of preventing war. When one side threatens retaliation, it is announcing its intention to commit an absolutely horrible act. Is an intention to commit a hugely immoral act under certain circumstances itself immoral, even though—thankfully—those circumstances never come about?

Imagine that back then accidentally or on purpose the USSR bombed one or more US cities. Then what? The US would have had to choose whether to go forward with its threatened massive and unspeakably horrible retaliation on the USSR. That would have been in itself hugely immoral—it would have made things much worse than they already were, and would have been completely without any possible good effect. (At that point, nobody would have been deterred from anything.) If the US government had had any shred of morality left at that point, it would not have retaliated.

But surely the Soviet planners knew that the US people would have been thinking this way, and in fact would not have retaliated. (And vice versa: the US planners knew this about the Soviets.) If so, everyone would have known that all the threats of retaliation were empty.

To give retaliation-threats some force, in a situation like this, there would have to be some mechanism that unleashed retaliation automatically, no matter what the attacked side wanted to do then. (This is the "Doomsday Machine" imagined in the great movie *Doctor Strangelove*.) But then, having suffered a first strike from side B, horrible, useless, immoral retaliation would be unavoidable, whatever side A did—and they set it up to be this way!

GRELLING'S PARADOX

A couple of definitions:

- an adjective is homological if it describes itself.
- an adjective is heterological if it doesn't.

The adjective 'short' is homological because it's short. The adjective 'German' is heterological: it's not German—it's English.

Now consider the adjective 'heterological.' Which category does it go into? Is it heterological? If it is, then it doesn't describe itself; but if 'heterological' doesn't describe it, then it isn't heterological. So if it is heterological, then it isn't.

Is it then homological? If it is, then it does describe itself, but if 'heterological' describes itself, then it isn't homological. So if it is homological, then it isn't.

Either way, we get a self-contradiction. Another paradox resulting from self-reference; this one was formulated in 1908 by German mathematician Kurt Grelling. (See Russell's Paradox, below, which is analogous.)

GRUE (GOODMAN'S NEW RIDDLE OF INDUCTION)

Definitions:

- Time T is midnight on New Year's Eve at the end of the year 2020.
- X is grue provided that (a) it's T or earlier, and X is green; or (b) it's later than T, and X is blue.
- X is bleen provided that (a) it's T or earlier, and X is blue; or (b) it's later than T, and X is green.

All the emeralds we've seen so far have been green, so (because it's not yet T), they've also been grue. Ordinary scientific reasoning predicts the future on the basis of past observation, so we predict that after T, emeralds will still be green. But this sort of reasoning also predicts that after T emeralds will still be grue. But after T, something that's still green won't be grue any longer—it will have turned bleen overnight! It order to stay grue, it would have to turn blue.

A common reaction to this problem is to try to explain why 'grue' and 'bleen' are illegitimate properties to do science with. But what's wrong with them? The way we have defined them, they seem unlike regular color properties, in that their definitions include mention of time. Scientists who wanted to see whether things stayed grue around time T would have to keep checking their watches. But note that this is just a matter of the way we've been putting things. We could just as well have taken 'grue' and 'bleen' as the real color properties, and defined 'blue' and 'green' in terms of these, plus time T. (See if you can produce these definitions.) And a grue/bleen perceiving scientist would look at an emerald at time T, and might say, without consulting a watch, 'Yep, it stayed grue okay!' or 'Jeez! It suddenly turned bleen!'

HARMING THE DEAD

Imagine your best friend gives you a shirt which you hate, but you wear occasionally when you see her, so as not to insult. If she knew you hated it, she'd be upset, and you don't want that. But now your friend has died. You still think very kindly of her memory, but is it okay to throw away that awful shirt now? The answer seems to be yes. After all, the only morally relevant thing here is that you not hurt her feelings. That would be harming her. But after death, people can't be harmed.

But now consider other things that might be done to "harm the dead." Suppose you maliciously do what you can to destroy the good reputation of someone now dead. A lot of people think that there's something wrong with this. But what? Sometimes it's thought that the morality of actions regarding others isn't all a

matter of helping or harming them, because this never applies to the dead. So what other moral considerations are relevant for "dealing with" dead people? and why?

HERACLITUS' PARADOX

The paradox associated with this ancient Greek philosopher is the claim that you can't step into the same river twice. Why not? Because at every instant, the water that makes up this section of the river (or the river as a whole, for that matter), changes.

What this shows, of course, is that identical water is not the basis for the same river. What then is? Note that the same sort of question might be raised with regard to the "same" anything, which (almost) always changes, to some small or large degree, over time.

HOTEL INFINITY
(HILBERT'S HOTEL)

David Hilbert was a pioneer in the mathematical treatment of infinity. He illustrated one way that notion introduces strange results by asking us to imagine a hotel with an infinite number of rooms, all completely booked for the night. A traveler arrives, asking for a room—a request that would be denied by an ordinary completely-booked hotel—but in Hilbert's Hotel, matters are easily solved: the guests in room 1 are asked to move to room 2, while those in room 2, move to room 3, and those in 3 to room 4, and so on. This leaves room 1 empty for the arrivals.

HYPOTHETICAL DESIRE
PARADOX

If you're right-handed, you'd probably assent to this:

If I have to lose an arm, I want to lose my left arm.

Now imagine that, unfortunately, the antecedent of this conditional (hypothetical statement) becomes true: you have to lose one arm. Given the truth of the conditional, it follows by very elementary logic that You want to lose your left arm. But wait! That's hardly true. You don't want to lose either arm! Is this a counter-example to the very basic logical principle called modus ponens: If P then Q; P; therefore Q?

Instead of rejecting modus ponens, it has been suggested, we might understand that original proposition not as "If P then I want X," but rather, "I want: (If P then X)." From P and the latter, X does not follow. But now we need a logic to distinguish hypothetical desires from desires for hypotheticals.

LIAR PARADOX

(EPIMENIDES' PARADOX)

Suppose Fred says, "I'm lying right now." Is he telling the truth? Well, telling the truth isn't lying, so he isn't lying. But what he says is that he is lying, so if he's telling the truth he is lying. On the other hand, if he's not telling the truth, then ... well the same kind of self-negating puzzle emerges. Turns out both the assumption that Fred's statement is true and that it's false both imply self-contradictions.

There are many versions of this sort of paradox. Another one frequently seen is the Postcard Paradox: on one side of a postcard, it says, "What's written on the other side is false." On the other side, it says, "What's written on the other side is true." See if you can work out how there isn't any way to assign truth and falsity here.

And another variant is this book title:

There Are Two Errors in the
the Title of this Book

The Liar Paradox is one of the most basic and oldest versions of a self-referential paradox. It's sometimes called the Epimenides' Paradox, after the ancient Cretan philosopher who wrote that all Cretans (probably intending to exclude himself) were liars. There has been a great deal written ever since in the attempt

to try to cope with self-reference. One major tack has been to try to find a way in principle to rule out self-reference (without making arbitrary restrictions).

LOTTERY PARADOX

Imagine a lottery that will randomly draw one winning ticket from a million tickets. It's unreasonable to believe that the ticket you hold—number 439,664—will win, and you believe it won't win. But it's also unreasonable to believe that number 439,665 will win, and to believe that 439,666 will win, and so on, for every one of the million tickets. So for each of the tickets, you completely reasonably believe it won't win. But you also believe, completely reasonably again, that one of the million will win. So your set of a million and one completely reasonable beliefs is inconsistent.

One sort of reply points out that ground-floor inconsistency of belief requires a belief that P and a belief that not-P; but that's not what we have here, unless we believe a principle of agglomeration: that if you believe Q and you believe R, then you do (or should) believe (Q and R). Some sort of principle of this type is very attractive, but perhaps needs to yield here.

MONTY HALL PARADOX

Loosely based on the TV gameshow of which Monty Hall was the emcee, the question is this:

You're presented with three doors, and told that one hides a valuable car, the other two each a worthless goat. You pick a door at random. Then Monty, the emcee, knowing what's behind the other two, picks one that hides a goat, and opens it, revealing the contents. Now he asks you: do you want to stick to your door or switch to the contents of the remaining closed door?

This widely-publicized problem got wrong answers from a huge variety of people including many mathematicians. They reasoned: you've picked (say) Door A: Door C is opened to reveal a goat. Now it's 50/50 whether the car is behind your door or behind door B. If there's any advantage to sticking to door A (e.g., you're offered $100 to stay put) you should do so; but otherwise there's no reason to stay put or switch.

The correct (but widely disbelieved) answer is this: there's 1/3 probability that Door A, the one you picked first, has the car, thus 2/3 that the car is behind one of Door B or Door C. Monty knows what's back there, and he picks one of (or the only) door hiding a goat (say Door C) and opens it. But there's still a 2/3 chance that a door you haven't picked—only Door B now—has the car; and a 1/3 chance that Door A has it. So you'll double your chances by switching.

(See also the related Bertrand's Box Paradox, above.)

MORAL LUCK

Fred and Barney are both at a party at Wilma's house, and both of them are drinking way more than they should, given that each will be driving himself home. When the booze runs out and Wilma kicks both of them out, they each get in their cars, and attempt to drive to their homes. They're barely capable of steering effectively, and both frequently swerve onto the wrong side of the road. Fred is stopped by the police half-way home, and is charged (and eventually convicted) of driving under the influence. He pays a large fine, and has his license suspended for a year. Barney is unlucky, however: while driving on the opposite side of the road, his car collides head-on with one coming the other way, killing its driver. Barney is convicted of second-degree murder, and is sentenced to a very long jail term.

What Fred and Barney did was significantly similar. Both drank far too much at the party, given that they intended to drive themselves home. Both drove themselves, at great risk, despite knowing that they had drunk too much. Both were swerving all over the road. The difference was merely a matter of luck: Fred didn't crash into anything, and the property and persons of others were unharmed, but unluckily for Barney, an oncoming car just happened to be there just where he swerved off of his side of the road.

Everyone feels that Barney's more to blame than Fred is, and that his much more severe legal punishment was entirely justified. But the difference between his case and Fred's was entirely out of either's control: one was comparatively lucky, the other wasn't. How can we distribute moral blame and judicial punishment differently on the basis of this sort of luck (or un-luck)? But we do it all the time.

NEWCOMB'S PARADOX

Imagine a really smart computer, able to predict people's responses almost perfectly having been fed information about their personality and background. This computer presents you with a choice involving two boxes, Box A and Box B. You can choose to take either the contents of Box B alone, or else what's in Box A plus what's in Box B. In Box A there is $10,000, and it's transparent, so you can see the big pile of $100 notes sitting inside. The contents of Box B, you're told, however, depends on the computer's prediction of what you're going to do. If it has predicted that you'll take Box B alone, it has already put $1 million in Box B. If it has predicted that you'll take Box A plus Box B, it has put nothing into Box B. Should you take what's in Box B alone, or what's in both boxes? There are two lines of reasoning that attempt to answer this question.

(1) At the time you must decide, the computer has already set up what's in Box B—maybe nothing or maybe $1 million. Anyway, your decision won't cause a change in what's in there. You can take whatever's in Box B alone, or else that plus the $10,000 in Box A. Maybe there's a million in Box B, maybe nothing; either way, you'd get $10,000 more by taking both boxes, so do it.

(2) The computer, remember, is almost always right in its predictions. That means that if you take both boxes, it almost certainly has predicted that, and put nothing in Box B, and you'll get $10,000. But if you take just Box B, it almost certainly has predicted that, and put $1 million in Box B, so you'll get a million. Go with the probabilities. Take just Box B.

This interesting problem has resulted in a lot of response. Reactions are divided between advocating strategy (1) and advocating strategy (2), and there are interesting implications for decision theory about which strategy might be the right one.

OMNISCIENCE PROOF OF GOD'S EXISTENCE

God is often conceived of as omniscient—that is, all-knowing. That means that He knows everything that's the case. Maybe we'd like to express that fact this way:

> For all propositions P (P is true if and only if God knows that P).

The trouble is that this seems to presuppose the existence of God, so atheists wouldn't accept it. Let's reformulate it more neutrally:

> For all propositions P (P is true if and only if, if God existed, God would know that P).

That sounds unexceptionable. Now, if that's true for all propositions, it's true in particular for the proposition, God exists. So we can infer:

> 'God exists' is true if and only if, if God existed, God would know that he exists.

Consider the second part of that sentence:

> if God existed, God would know that he exists.

Nobody, it seems—atheist or believer—could deny this. After all, if anybody exists, he'd know that he exists, right?

But when you have a true sentence made of two parts connected by 'if and only if,' and when one of those parts is true, it follows that the other is true. So from the truth of the second part of that sentence, we can validly infer the truth of the first part:

> 'God exists' is true.

Or, putting the same thing more briefly,

> God exists.

The reason there has to be something wrong in this reasoning is not that there isn't any God. The reason is that we appear to be pulling a proof of God's existence out of thin air—something atheists and believers alike should be suspicious of. What, exactly, has gone wrong here?

THE PREFACE

If you find out that what you say or believe is inconsistent, you shouldn't rationally continue to say or believe that: you should try to fix it, right? It's irrational to allow to stand what you know is an inconsistent set of statements one makes or beliefs one has, right? Wrong and wrong. Here's why.

Often one finds in the preface of a book the modest statement that the book surely contains errors, but that these are the fault of the author, not of the numerous people thanked for help in writing the book.

Now consider the set of sentences consisting of everything stated in book B, including the statement in its preface, "There's at least one error in here." It's logically impossible that this whole set is true. Here's why. If the preface-statement is true, then there's at least one false statement elsewhere in the set. But if the preface is false, then again the whole set isn't true. That set is what logicians call a logically inconsistent set: one such that it's logically impossible that everything in it is true.

Never mind about books and their prefaces. Everyone who is a clear thinker and who doesn't have inappropriately and ridiculously inflated views about his own omniscience knows that some of his many beliefs—one hopes not many, but some anyway—must be false. This is a rational thing to believe. Rational, but rendering one's whole belief set logically inconsistent.

PRISONER'S DILEMMA

You and your buddy are arrested for a major crime; the police know you both did it, but have evidence only good enough for convictions on a rather trivial charge. So they put you two in separate cells, and offer you a deal: your sentence will depend on whether or not you confess, implicating yourself and the other guy, and on what your buddy does when offered the same deal. The following chart summarizes how this works, specifies the years in jail you will serve under all four eventualities.

	He confesses	He stays silent
You confess	7 years	1 year
You stay silent	10 years	3 years

The best outcome for you is confession—if he stays silent. But he's offered the same deal, so his best deal is confession, while you stay silent. And if both of you confess, you'll both be badly off.

It seems that what's best for both of you would be to both keep quiet; you'd each get your second-best possible outcome, but you'd both avoid other possible disasters. If there were a way of making an enforceable and effective deal that both of you would keep silent, this would be good. But there isn't.

Under the circumstances, then, it seems that the most rational thing for you to do is to confess. Whatever he does, you'll come out better than if you stayed silent. This, however, is the most rational choice for the other guy as well. So if both of you do what's rational, both will get seven years in jail—next to the worst of the four possibilities. It seems that there's something irrational about doing what's most rational.

This little story can be taken as a simplified model for a wide range of social situations: competition vs. cooperation between individuals, and between nations. Psychologists and social and ethical philosophers have had a lot to say about it.

PROTAGORAS' PARADOX

The famous ancient Greek philosopher Protagoras taught law to Euathlus, with the agreement that Euathlus would pay Protagoras tuition fees if he won his first case; but if he lost, he wouldn't have to pay. Euathlus finishes his education, sets himself up as a lawyer, but for some reason takes on no cases. Finally, Protagoras gets fed up, and sues Euathlus for the money.

Protagoras points out that he's suing for the fees, so if he wins, Euthalus would have to pay, and if he loses, Euthalus wouldn't have to. But Euathlus reminds the court of the contract for payment: if he wins his first case, he pays the tuition; if he loses he doesn't. And this, of course, is his first case.

So who is right?

(Also called The Lawyer, Euathlus, the Paradox of the Court.)

THE QUESTION PARADOX

An angel visits the Annual Meetings of the American Philosophical Association, and tells the philosophers there that they will be given the gift of asking God exactly one question, and that God in His omniscience will answer it.

There is a good deal of debate about what is the one question to ask. "What is the meaning of life?" is ruled out as too vague, and as very likely to have an unsatisfying answer. "How do you best remove red wine stains from a light-colored carpet?" is a question whose answer many philosophers have an interest in, but in the end it's thought too trivial for such a great opportunity. There's some enthusiasm for asking "What is the most important question we could ask, and what is its answer?" but there's a worry this might be counted as two questions. A logician suggests they avoid this potential difficulty by converting this to one question: "What is the ordered pair consisting of (a) the most important question that could be asked and (b) the answer to that question?"

The angel appears, is asked this question, and five minutes later returns with God's answer: "The most important question you could ask is 'What is the ordered pair consisting of (a) the most important question that could be asked and (b) the answer to that question?' and the answer to that question is what I'm saying now."

RAVEN PARADOX

This famous paradox challenges two seemingly obvious assumptions: (1) that scientific generalizations are confirmed by observation of instances of them (e.g., that 'All ravens are black' is confirmed a little every time an additional black raven is observed); and (2) that if some observation O confirms generalization G, and G is logically equivalent to H, then O must also confirm H (because, after all, when two statements are logically equivalent, they say the same thing—anything that makes one true (or false) does the same to the other).

G: All non-black things are non-ravens is logically equivalent to H: All ravens are black. The observation of a yellow pencil confirms G, but it surely does not seem to confirm H. (Otherwise H would be confirmed by the uncountable number of observations of non-black non-ravens everyone makes all the time.)

Maybe, on the other hand, you might want to insist that that pencil does confirm (to an extremely tiny degree) the raven generalization. Or else, you might want to explore the idea that scientific confirmation is not at all merely a simple matter of observations of instances of a generalization.

RUSSELL'S PARADOX

Think of a class in the technical sense involved here as a collection of things that share a common attribute. Some classes are not members of themselves: the class of poodles, for example, is not itself a poodle.

Call these classes non-self-inclusive. Some classes are members of themselves: examples are the class of non-poodles (which is itself not a poodle), or the class of things with more than five members, which itself has more than five members. Call these classes self-inclusive.

Now consider the class of non-self-inclusive classes. It contains poodles, planets, and so on, but is it a member of itself? Try two answers:

YES: but since it's the class of non-self-inclusive classes, if it's a member of itself, then it's non-self-inclusive, so it doesn't include itself.

NO: but if it's not in there, it must be in the class of self-inclusive classes; so it does include itself.

Bertrand Russell discovered this paradox in 1901, and shortly thereafter told the great logician Frege about it. Frege realized that this paradox showed that two very basic axioms used in his book on formal logic, about to be published, were inconsistent. There has been a great deal of consideration about the implications of Russell's Paradox ever since. (See Grelling's Paradox, above, which is analogous.)

RUSSELL'S PROOF OF
GOD'S EXISTENCE

The next time you're driving around, take a look at the first license plate number you see: it's EJR 036 (or whatever). What are the odds against seeing exactly that license plate number, out of all the possible ones, just then? They're minuscule, one out of several million or more. It's a miracle! God must exist.

This "proof" was cooked up by Bertrand Russell, who was a well-known atheist and of course had his tongue firmly planted in his cheek. Of course this goes no way toward proving God's existence. But the interesting question it raises is: why exactly is seeing that license plate not a hugely unlikely—almost miraculous—event?

SAYING WHAT YOU MEAN

Can you say, "Gloob! Gloob! Gloob!" but mean, It's snowing in Tibet? No? Why not?

SHIP OF THESEUS

According to ancient Greek legend, Theseus kept repairing the ship of which he was captain while at sea, replacing, one at a time, old rotten planks with new sound ones. When this process was complete, there was not a single bit of the ship that was there at the start of the voyage. Is the ship Theseus returned in the same one as the one he started out in? If yes, then how come? If no, then what happened to the old one?

In the seventeenth century, Thomas Hobbes added a wrinkle to this story by imagining further that Theseus kept all the old rotten lumber, and eventually a (pretty useless) ship was constructed out of this. At that point there are two ships: the one made of new, sound lumber, and the one made of rotten old planks. Which is the one Theseus began his voyage in?

SIMPSON'S PARADOX

In basketball, you get two points for a basket shot from closer in, 3 points from further out. The following table lists successes/attempts at 2- and 3-point shots made during a season by two players, Wilt Jordan and Michael Chamberlain:

	Jordan	Chamberlain
2 pt	200 / 400: 50%	440 / 950: 46.3%
3 pt	80 / 320: 25%	30 / 190: 15.8%

As you can see, Jordan's average is better at scoring on attempted 2-point shots and 3-point shots. That implies that Jordan is better at making shots altogether, right? Wrong. Here are the totals:

Jordan	Chamberlain
280 / 720: 38.9%	470 / 1140: 41.2%

Check the arithmetic yourself: there's no trick here. This sort of counterintuitive result is quite common in statistics. It was brought to wide attention by a mathematician named E.H. Simpson.

SORITES' PARADOX

A person 7 feet high is definitely tall. Subtract a ¼ inch from this, and consider a person 6 feet 11¾ inches high: that person is definitely tall too. Now imagine a series of subtractions, each of ¼ inch; is there a height H in this series such that a person of height H is tall, but a person of height (H–¼") is not tall? It seems not. If you think there is, try to specify that height, and see if you can get anyone to agree with you. But if there is no such H, then we can keep subtracting ¼", and still have the height of a tall person; so reach the obviously false conclusion that a person 3 feet high is tall. What has gone wrong here?

There are practical (mis)applications of this fallacious reasoning. Someone considering one more little sip of beer before driving home can believe correctly that one more little sip won't make any difference in his driving ability. But this is true of each little sip in a series in which, at some point, the drinker has become completely disabled.

A lot of thought has been given to how to rethink matters to locate and fix the mistake in reasoning of this sort.

'Sorites', pronounced so-RIGHT-eez, is Greek for heap (another traditional name for this paradox); a very early version imagined starting with one grain of sand—clearly not a heap—and reasoning that adding one additional grain never transformed a non-heap into a heap. Another traditional example reasons that removal of just one hair from a head cannot transform a non-bald head into a bald one.

THE SPECIOUS PRESENT

Your third birthday party does not exist—now. Nothing in the past exists. Neither does anything in the future. All that exists is the present.

Now consider apparently present facts: the cat is on the mat, Cleveland is in Ohio, Jupiter is the largest planet. Each of these has a time span, with a past and (we'd expect) a future component. But the past and future components, as we've seen, don't exist. Well, what about the present component? How long does that last? If it has any non-zero duration, then part of it is non-existent, in the past or in the future. Anything that's completely present must have a zero duration. But here's the problem: something that lasts for zero time is nothing at all. So the supposedly zero-duration present doesn't exist either. It apparently follows that nothing exists.

Obviously this reasoning is mistaken. But it's no easy job to figure out exactly where. In the process of considering this, in any case, we can get clearer on some things we would never otherwise consider, some basic presuppositions about duration and existence.

ST. PETERSBURG PARADOX

When you're playing a game of chance, a fair bet is the amount of money you should pay to play, expecting to come out even in the long run. (Of course, casinos never offer a fair bet in this sense—they need to make a profit on you.)

You calculate a fair bet by summing the products of multiplying the probability of each outcome times the payoff given that outcome. Imagine a coin flip that would pay you $1 for heads, $2 for tails. Each outcome has a probability of .5, so the fair bet is $(.5 \times \$1) + (.5 \times \$2)$. This equals $1.50.

Now consider the St. Petersburg Game. You flip a fair coin counting the number of flips till it comes up tails, when the game ends. Call the number of flips in a finished game n; the payoff is then $\$2^n$. (A run of three heads then a tails would thus have $n = 4$, and a payoff of $16.)

What's the fair bet for St. Petersburg? The probability that $n = 1$ is 1/2; its payoff is $2. The probability that $n = 2$ is 1/4; its payoff is $4. The probability that $n = 3$ is 1/8; its payoff is $8. And so on. You can see where this is going. The sum of $(1/2 \times \$2) + (1/4 \times \$4) + (1/8 \times \$8)$ and so on equals $1 + $1 + $1 + $1 and so on. The fair bet is an infinite amount of money! In other words, any finite amount you pay to play each game will be smaller than your eventual winnings, if you play long enough.

Of course, you'd probably run out of money to bet before you had an enormous win; or the casino would close, or you'd die. This is not a practical plan. But it does, probability theorists think, raise important theoretical questions about the ideas taken for granted in thinking about fair bets on chance events.

THE THOMSON LAMP

This is an imaginary light-fixture. You push a button to turn it on, and in ½ of a minute, it turns itself off; then after another ¼ of a minute, it turns back on again, then after another ⅛ of a minute, it turns back off, and so on. Imagine (contrary, perhaps, to the laws of physics) that it can do this switching an infinite number of times. It doesn't take a great deal of mathematical skill to sum this series, and determine that the whole series will finish exactly one minute after you start it. The question is: at the end of this minute, will the lamp be on or off? (or, bizarrely, neither or both?)

This kind of peculiar event has been treated extensively in the literature, where it's sometimes called a supertask.

THE TIME AND THE PLACE

OF A MURDER

On December 2, 2002, Bob is visiting a tourist attraction, the Four Corners Monument, located at the only point in the US where four states come together and you can stand with one foot overlapping all four states (should that sound exciting to you). Bob notices his enemy Bart standing nearby, pulls out his gun, and shoots Bart in the foot. Police apprehend Bob, and Bart is taken to hospital, and eventually dies of his wound.

Bob is guilty of murder, but where did it take place? Bob was standing in Arizona when he shot Bart, but about eighteen inches of his right arm, with the gun in hand, extended east into New Mexico. Bart was standing north of Bob, in Utah, but his foot, when it was shot, was slightly over the state line, and was in Colorado. Did the murder take place where Bob was? And was that in Arizona or New Mexico (or both)? Or did it take place where Bart was? And was that in Utah or Colorado (or both)? Or maybe the murder took place in all four states?

Bart's medical condition deteriorated despite treatment, and he died in hospital in early January. This raises questions about timing. Did the murder take place when Bart was shot, in December, or when he died, the following January? Or maybe it was a spread-out event, taking about a month to happen? Imagine you're the police officer at the press conference in December, following Bob's apprehension. You're asked, "Was that murder?" What's the answer: "Not yet!" because Bart was still alive? But when he dies in January, does that retroactively transform the shooting, done the previous month, into murder? Or was it murder all along, though given Bart's survival through December, nobody knew it yet?

How these questions are answered may have practical bearing: the location questions if the laws regarding murder are different in each of the four states; the timing question if there's a change in law to take place on January 1. A court may have to decide these answers. Notice however that there don't seem to be any facts that could be discovered that would determine the right answers. We already know all the relevant facts, and they don't add up to any answers. Would the answers to these questions then be a matter of totally arbitrary decision?

TIME TRAVEL

The main paradox involved here involves the question about whether a time traveler could change the past. For example, could you, on Tuesday, go back to Monday, and move that coffee cup away from the edge of the table, so that it didn't get knocked off and break? This is hard to understand. We start by supposing that it's Tuesday, and the coffee cup did break on Monday. Then, supposedly, you go back and prevent this; but then does it happen that on Tuesday that the coffee cup didn't break earlier? Do those pieces of coffee-cup in the trash suddenly disappear? Or were they never there in the first place?

This sort of science-fiction story is familiar: Fred goes back 60 years, finds his grandfather aged 15, and tries to kill him. If Fred succeeds, then he wouldn't have been born, but then who went back in time and killed grandpa? Some philosophers argue that this doesn't show that time travel is inherently self-contradictory, but rather that no matter what else you accomplish when going back in time, you won't kill your grandfather when he was a teenager, because—simply put—it didn't happen!

TRAGEDY OF THE COMMONS

A commons is a piece of land in the center of a town which traditionally was publicly owned and reserved for shared use. Sometimes all the livestock owners in the town were allowed to graze their animals on this land. When grazed by too many animals, however, the grass could not grow back, and the land was ruined for this use.

The problem here is that it's clearly to each individual herder's self-interest to graze as many animals as he could on the commons. It would be highly unlikely that putting just his few animals there would overload an otherwise sustainable grass crop; if the land was already overloaded by general use, and the grass crop was headed for extinction, it would still be to each herder's interest to get as much as he could out of it, before it became useless.

The generalized problem illustrated here is that in many situations, when individuals act in their own undoubted rational self-interest, a shared general resource will ultimately be depleted, contrary to anyone's interest. What's at issue here is very much like the problem raised, above, by the Prisoner's Dilemma.

TREASURE-HUNTER PARADOX

Years ago, the CBC interviewed a historian who was researching treasure-hunting in Nova Scotia, where the numerous islands and hidden coves gave pirates an ideal place to bury their treasure. Of the many attempts to find buried treasure, a few had actually found it; the historian reported that a very large proportion of successful diggers had deepened holes made by previous searchers. The earlier searches had stopped just short of success. So the interviewer asked the historian what advice to give future treasure-hunters, on the basis of this information. The historian hesitated for a moment, then replied that he guessed that they should dig a little deeper than they do.

TRISTRAM SHANDY

This is the name of the hero of the novel bearing his name. In the novel, he has undertaken to write his autobiography, but he writes so slowly that he takes a year to cover only one day of his life. That means, as time goes on, he'll fall more and more behind. Bertrand Russell, however, pointed out in an influential study of infinity, that paradoxically if Shandy would live for an infinite length of time, despite falling further and further behind at any moment, he'd nevertheless be able to finish his work. One of the many paradoxes of infinity.

TROLLEY PROBLEM

You're standing next to trolley tracks, and see an out-of-control trolley fast approaching. Five people are tied to the tracks farther down, and would die when the trolley gets there; but you can throw a switch which would steer the trolley instead on to another track where only one person would die.

Some philosophers react to this story (introduced by Philippa Foot and widely discussed) that one is not morally permitted to throw the switch, because that would amount to killing the one person on the alternate track; one must, then, accept the (nevertheless horrible) outcome of the death of the five, because that's not the result of your wrongdoing. Killing is wrong; allowing to die is under some circumstances permitted.

Other philosophers, however, have the strong reaction that all that's relevant here is that you have the choice of five dying, or just one; so you must throw the switch: they deny that the difference between acting and refraining from acting has any moral significance.

TWO ENVELOPES PARADOX

You're presented with two sealed envelopes, a red and a blue one, and told that one contains twice the amount of money as the other; but you can't tell which is which. You pick the red one, at random. But before opening it, you're offered the option of swapping it for the blue one. Should you take that option?

At first glance, it seems that it's a matter of indifference whether you swap or not. But consider this reasoning: Call the amount of money in the red envelope (whatever that is) M. It's 50% probable that the blue envelope contains $\frac{1}{2} \times$ M, and 50% probable it contains $2 \times$ M. So it's equiprobable that swapping would increase your payoff by M, or decrease it by $\frac{1}{2}$ M. Swapping is a good bet. It's probably advantageous for you to swap.

Now, imagine that the reasoning convinces you, and you agree to swap, and exchange envelopes. Now you hold the blue envelope. But now you're offered the option of swapping again, back to the red one. You reason this way: Call the amount of money in the blue envelope (whatever that is) N. It's 50% probable that the red envelope contains ½ × N, and 50% probable it contains 2 × N. So it's equiprobable that swapping would increase your payoff by N, or decrease it by ½ N. Swapping is a good bet. It's probably advantageous for you to swap. So you swap again.

But it's clear that something has gone wrong here. It's impossible that this could go on and on, with your reasoning telling you that every time that each swap adds to your advantage. That can't be. Okay, it's clear that somewhere there's a mistake in your reasoning: but where?

There's a variant of the Two-Envelopes Paradox called the Two-Wallet Game. Here's how this works. You and a friend are drinking in a bar, and he suggests this game. You both put your wallets on the table, and whoever's wallet has less money in it gets the money that's in the other's wallet. (Neither of you has any idea of how much is in the others' wallet, or in your own.)

You reason: Call the amount of money in my wallet (whatever it is) A, and call the amount of money in Buddy's wallet B. It's equally likely that A is less than B, or more. So there's a 50% probability that A is more than B, and I'd lose A. But it's 50% probability that I'd win B—if B was larger than A. So if I won, what I'd win is more than what I'd lose if I lost. The game is favorable to me.

Buddy, of course, is reasoning the same way. It can't be that this game is favorable to both players. Both of you have made a mistake, and maybe you have the feeling that it's the same sort of mistake that showed up in the reasoning about the envelope switch.

UNEXPECTED (SURPRISE) HANGING (OR EXAM) PARADOX

On Friday, your algebra teacher announces that there will be a surprise quiz during one of the classes next week—'surprise' meaning that you won't be able to figure out when it will take place before the class starts in which it is given.

You reason: there are classes on Monday, Wednesday, and Friday. If the test were on Friday, we'd know that in advance—after class on Wednesday—because there was no test on Monday or Wednesday, and it had to be on one of those three days. So a Friday quiz wouldn't be a surprise. It can't be on Friday.

So it must be on Monday or Wednesday. But if it were on Wednesday, we'd know that in advance—after class on Monday; as we've already figured out, so since it wasn't on Monday, it would have to be on Wednesday. So a Wednesday quiz wouldn't be a surprise. It can't be on Wednesday.

So it must be on Monday, the only remaining possibility. But we can figure that out—know already that it has to be Monday. But that wouldn't be a surprise then.

So a surprise quiz under these conditions is impossible.

This is a very perplexing paradox because it's perfectly clear that there can be a surprise quiz, and so there has to be an error in the reasoning above. But philosophers have had some trouble finding a persuasive account of what has gone wrong.

Does this addition to the story help you figure out what's wrong? Having done all the reasoning above, you show up in Monday's algebra class, and the teacher hands out the quiz. "But!" you object, "But! But!" The teacher says, "Surprise!!"

(A nastier version of the same story involves the surprise timing of the hanging of a condemned man.)

UNINTERESTING NUMBERS

Consider what we'll call interesting numbers—positive integers with special facts or associations attached to them. 1 is surely an interesting number: it's the number of gods believed in by many religions, the smallest prime number, etc. 2 is also interesting: it's the smallest even number. 3 is the number of blind mice, of little pigs, of bears Goldilocks met, etc. 4 is the July date celebrated as the US national holiday. 5 is the number of fingers on one hand. Probably you can think of something that sets apart 6, 7, 8, 9, 10, and more, and makes them interesting. What then is the smallest uninteresting number? Hard to say, but let's suppose that it's 2,693, a number associated with no facts whatsoever. Oh but wait: there is something that makes this number stand out: it's the smallest uninteresting number, so it's interesting after all. (A contradiction?) Okay, anyway, let's keep looking. How about 2,694 then? If that's the smallest uninteresting number, that's an interesting fact about it. And so on, as high as you care to go. So we've proven that every number is interesting, right?

What's foolish about this reasoning?

VOTER'S PARADOX (1)

In the most common sort of election, the candidate wins who receives more votes than the others; and there are special procedures in the regulations concerning ties.

Voters often want to see their candidate get a large number of votes, win or lose, but we'll ignore this for our purposes, and consider only what's by far the chief motivation for voting: you want your candidate to win. Regarding this motivation, your vote can make a difference if, without it, your candidate would be tied for first place, or if your vote creates a tie.

Now, consider the chances of either of these happening in an election with more than a handful of voters. A statistics professor estimates that a tied congressional election might be expected to occur in the US once approximately every 400 years. It is overwhelmingly unlikely that your vote will make a difference in this and in almost every other sort of election.

So why vote? Your chances of being hit by lightning on the way to the polling station are probably greater than the chance of making a difference.

VOTER'S PARADOX (2)

Confusingly sometimes known by the same name as the one just considered, this one shows that under certain circumstances, voting is not a way to produce a rational general will out of individual preferences.

Consider this simple case: There are three candidates for a position, A, B, and C, and three voters, 1, 2, and 3. The three voters each have preferences among the candidates, in this order:

voter 1: prefers A to B, and B to C

voter 2: prefers B to C, and C to A

voter 3: prefers C to A, and A to B

A simple vote in which each voted for his/her preferred candidate would result in a tie: one vote for each of A, B, and C, and no decision.

Let's try a series of votes to see in general what preferences the voters have when considering only two of the three. Vote first on A and B: 1 and 3 prefer A to B; only 2 disagrees. Good so far. Now let's compare B and C: 1 and 2 prefer B to C.

So now we have majority votes preferring A to B, and B to C. Does that mean that the general will is best served by ranking them in the order A, B, C, giving the victory to A, with C coming in third? To make sure, let's compare A and C: 2 and 3 both prefer A to C. Whoops.

ZENO'S PARADOXES

Zeno of Elea was a fifth-century BCE Greek philosopher who is now known for having created a number of paradoxes involving motion, plurality, and change. Nine of these are known today, on the basis of quotation or discussion by other philosophers; we'll briefly look at the three best-known of them.

On the surface, Zeno's paradoxes seem like silly denials of the obvious, but really they are, in Russell's words, "immeasurably subtle and profound" explorations of problems involved in our presuppositions about time, space, motion, and so on.

Achilles and the Tortoise is the most famous of Zeno's paradoxes. Suppose speedy Achilles is in a race with a tortoise. Achilles can run much faster than the tortoise, so the latter is given a head start, beginning farther down the track than Achilles. The race begins, and Achilles very soon runs to the place the tortoise started from; but by then the tortoise has run (or waddled) on to a point a little further on. So then Achilles continues running till he gets to this second point, but by then the tortoise has gone on to a third point. And so on. No matter how many times Achilles catches up to where the tortoise just left, he hasn't caught up with him. Conclusion: he can never catch up.

This conclusion is obviously false, and modern mathematics (given the figures for the speed of each, and the head-start distance) can tell us exactly when Achilles will catch up—and pass—the tortoise. But then what has gone bad in this reasoning? This is a hard question to answer. (Note, by the way, the connection between this item and what's discussed above in the Thomson Lamp section.)

The Racecourse is closely related to the first Achilles paradox. Here Zeno concentrates simply on Achilles' run down the racecourse, ignoring the tortoise. Can Achilles reach the end of the course? To do so, he must first reach the half-way point; then, having gotten there, he must travel half of the remaining portion, arriving at the point ¾ of the way down the field; then he must again cover half the remaining distance, arriving at the ⅞ point; and so on and so on. There's an endless series of smaller and smaller runs he must make, and at the end of each run in the series there's still some distance to go. So he can never get to the end of the field. (This paradox is also often called The Dichotomy.)

The Arrow. Consider an arrow flying through the air. At any one moment—a dimensionless point in time, with zero duration—it's in exactly one well-defined space, which is not moving. At another moment, it's in another motionless space, not moving. There isn't any moment during its flight when this is not true. So how can it be moving?

APPENDIX 2

Philosophical Lexicon

INTRODUCTION

Philosophy, having been around the longest of any academic discipline, has accumulated what may be the longest list of technical jargon terms. These are useful shorthand for philosophers already familiar with these words, but they can provide stumbling-blocks for students. We've included here a rather minimal dictionary of the more common philosophical terms, including some that occur in the readings in this volume, and others that don't.

This is a revised and severely shortened version of a much more inclusive philosophical lexicon: *The Philosopher's Dictionary*, by Robert M. Martin (Broadview Press).

LEXICON

abstract / concrete entities / ideas Abstract entities are supposed not to be locatable in space or time, not perceptible, without causes or effects, necessarily existing. Putative examples are properties, universals, sets, geometrical figures, and numbers. Something is, by contrast, concrete when it is particular and spatially and temporally locatable—perhaps material. There's a long history of philosophical argument about the reality of certain abstracta. Clearly some of them aren't real, for example, the average American family, with its 2.6 children. Reification is mistakenly taking something to be real that's merely abstract; this sort of reasoning is known as the fallacy of misplaced concreteness.

There's a good deal of historical debate about whether we can even have abstract ideas at all. We experience only particulars, so abstract ideas were a problem for the classical empiricists, who thought that every idea was a copy of an experience. Plato and others argued that we must have innate abstract ideas, not originating with sensation, in order to be able to classify the particulars.

act / agent moralities Some moral philosophers think that the basic sort of thing ethics evaluates is the worth of actions people do (act morality); others think that what's basic to moral theory is the worth of the person who acts (agent morality). Kant argued that good actions were those done by people with the right sort of motives, so his ethical theory is one species of agent morality; another species is virtue ethics. The utilitarians held that the basic kind of ethical reasoning evaluates actions (via their consequences), whatever the motives or moral worth of the people who do them, so their ethics is a variety of act morality.

action at a distance The effect that one thing can have on another that it is not touching and to which it is not connected by something in-between. Gravitation is an example. Some philosophers and scientists—e.g., Leibniz—thought that this was impossible. One way they tried to explain gravitation is to suppose that bodies that gravitationally attract each other are connected by some intervening invisible thing that fills the space between them and transfers the gravitational force.

action theory The branch of philosophy that considers questions about action. Examples of these are: What differentiates an action from other movements? Can there be actions that are refrainings from acting? Where does an action end and its consequences begin? What sort of explanation is suitable for actions?

Moral questions (about, for example, acts / omissions) and the questions of free will and responsibility are sometimes included in action theory.

acts / omissions An act is doing something, by contrast with an omission (or refraining), which is merely failing to do something. Some philosophers think that there can be a moral difference between these even when they have the same motives and outcome.

a fortiori (Latin: "from what is stronger") Means 'with even stronger reason', 'even more so'. "You owe thanks to someone who lets you use his car for a day. So a fortiori, you should really be grateful to Fred, who let you have his car for a whole month."

agent An agent is one who can perform a genuine intentional action, and who is thus morally responsible for what he/she does. This excludes people, for example, who are unable to perceive relevant facts, or who can't reason about consequences.

agent / event causation Often it is thought that causes and effects must be events. But if our actions are caused by other events, then how can we be responsible for them? It's sometimes argued that the cause of an action is not an event but rather the agent who did it.

agnosticism is in general the position that one does not, maybe cannot, know the truth or falsity of statements in some area—that there is insufficient reason to believe either. This term is used most frequently regarding religion, to contrast with theism and atheism (which are confident that we know that God does / doesn't exist).

alienation Estrangement, separation. Hegel discussed the possibility of human estrangement from the natural world. The existentialists thought that our alienation from nature and from each other was an important and inevitable part of the human condition. In Marx, 'alienation' means the separation from the products of our labor (as employees, we don't own what we produce) as well as from society and from ourselves.

altruism 1. Generosity. 2. The philosophical position that one ought to act for the benefit of others; contrast with egoism.

analogy / disanalogy An analogy is a similarity of two things. Reasoning from (or by) analogy—'analogical argument'—concludes that because two things share one or more characteristics, they share another; e.g., that because others show external behavior similar to one's own, others must have a similar internal life. A disanalogy is a difference between compared things; disanalogies between things reduce the strength of an argument from analogy.

analysis Some things are capable of being understood in terms of their component parts; analysis takes them apart into their simpler elements. Some twentieth century anglophone philosophers took analysis of concepts to be the job of philosophy. What is to be analyzed is called the analysandum, and what provides the analysis is called the analysans.

analytic / synthetic Kant called a judgment analytic when the "predicate was contained in the subject"; thus, for example, the judgment that all bachelors are unmarried is analytic because the subject ('bachelors') "contains" the predicate ('unmarried'). Later philosophers preferred to make this distinction in terms of sentences and meanings: a sentence is analytic when the meaning of the subject of that sentence contains the meaning of the predicate: 'unmarried' is part of the definition of 'bachelor'. So an analytic sentence is one that is true merely because of the meanings of the words. 'It's snowing or it's not snowing' is true merely because of the meaning of the words 'or' and 'not', so perhaps we should count this as analytic too. But since the relevant words in this case are "logical" words, this sentence is more particularly known as a logical truth. A synthetic truth is a sentence that is true, but not merely because of the meaning of the words. 'Pigs don't fly' is true partially because of the meaning of the words, of course: if 'pigs' meant 'woodpeckers', then that sentence would be false. But since the definition of 'pig' tells us nothing about flying, this sentence is not true merely because of the meaning of the words. One can speak also about analytically false sentences, for example, 'There exists a married bachelor'. Analytic sentences are necessarily true, and may (sometimes) be known a priori; but Kant argued that there are also synthetic a priori statements. Quine argued that the analytic / synthetic distinction is not a good one, because one cannot distinguish between matters of meaning of the words of a sentence and matters of fact.

ancient philosophy Ancient philosophy began in primitive form, we suppose, in prehistory; the earliest Western philosopher of whose work we have a historical account is Thales (c. 580 BCE.). The end of this period is often marked by the beginning of medieval philosophy, with the work of Augustine (about 400 CE).

antecedent conditions The events or states of affairs that come before a given event and that cause it, or are necessary or sufficient (See necessary / sufficient conditions) for it to happen.

a priori / a posteriori Two different ways in which something might be known to be true (or false). It can be known a priori if it can be known before—that is, or independently of—sense-experience of the fact in question. It can be known a posteriori if it can be known after—that is, on the basis of—sense-experience of the fact. One can know that all bachelors are unmarried a priori; one doesn't need to observe even one bachelor to know this is true. In this case (but perhaps not in all cases) a priori knowledge is possible because what's known is a conceptual truth or because the sentence that expresses this truth is analytic or logically true. Kant argued that certain a priori truths (for example, that every event has a cause) were not conceptual or analytic.

argument An argument in ordinary talk is a debate, especially a heated one. But in philosophical usage, an argument is one or more statements (called 'premises'; singular 'premise' or 'premiss') advanced in order to support another statement (the conclusion). Thus philosophers need not get angry when they argue. Premises actually support a conclusion only when there is the appropriate sort of logical connection between the premises and the conclusion. In deductive arguments, the conclusion must be true given the truth of the premises; in an inductive argument, the truth of the premises makes the conclusion more probable. Any deductive argument in which the premises really do have the appropriate logical connection with the conclusion is called a 'valid' argument; in invalid arguments, this connection is lacking. A valid argument may, however, fail to support its conclusion because one or more of its premises is false—for example: All pigs fly. All flying things are lighter than air. Therefore all pigs are lighter than air. This argument is valid, but it fails to convince because both of its premises are false. An argument with at least one false premise is called 'unsound'; a sound argument is a valid argument all of whose premises are true. A sound argument provides a proof of its conclusion (though in logic it's often said that a proof is provided merely when the argument is valid).

argument from illusion / hallucination The argument (against naïve realisms) that the existence of perceptual illusions and hallucinations shows that we really directly perceive only sense-data and not an independent world.

artificial intelligence An area of study in computer science and psychology that involves building (or imagining) machines, or programming computers, to mimic certain complex intelligent human activities. The creation of a program that can play chess at a high level is one of its successes. Artificial intelligence might shed light on what human mentality is like, and its successes and failures enter into arguments about materialism.

artificial / natural language A natural language is one used by some actual group of people, that has developed on its own, culturally and historically. An artificial language is one developed for some purpose—examples are computer languages and symbolic logic.

association of ideas One thought produces another: when you think about shoes, maybe this drags along the thought of socks. Associationism was the view that this sort of thing is at the core of our mental life, and that its laws constitute a scientific cognitive psychology.

atheism Atheists believe that God doesn't exist, and (sometimes) that religious practice is foolish, or that the morality fostered by religion is wrong. Because atheism has been so unpopular, atheistic philosophers have sometimes disguised their views. Lucretius and Hume were probably atheists. Russell was open about his atheism, and got into trouble for it. Not every religion includes the belief in God—Buddhism, for example, is sometimes said to be an atheistic religion. Atheism contrasts with theism, the view that God does exist, and with agnosticism, the view that there isn't any good reason to believe either that God exists or that He doesn't.

atomism The view that things are composed of elementary basic parts. From ancient times onward physics was often atomistic (though what's now called an 'atom' is no longer regarded as a basic component—contemporary physicists think that much smaller parts might be basic).

automata These are (arguably) mindless devices that imitate the intelligent and goal-directed actions of people—robots, for example. Descartes thought that animals were automata—merely physical "mechanisms" without mind.

autonomy / heteronomy Autonomy is self-governance—the ability or right to determine one's own actions and beliefs. Some ethical theories see the respect for autonomy as a central ethical principle. Heteronomy is its opposite: dependence on others.

average / total utilitarianism Utilitarianism needs to specify how to understand the greatest good for the greatest number of people. Is the measure of the worth of a society the average utility of its members, or the total utility?

axiom / postulate / posit An axiom is a statement regarded as obviously true, used as a starting point for deriving other statements. An axiomatic theory is one that is based on axioms. Non-axiomatic theories don't have such basic statements. 'Postulate' (as a noun) is often used to mean the same thing, though sometimes it refers only to such statements within a particular theory, while axioms are basic and obvious statements common to many theories (for example, the basic laws of logic). The verb 'to postulate' means the act of postulation—assumption, often of the existence of something, for theoretical purposes. A posit is an assumption, especially some thing assumed to exist; to posit something is to assume it.

basic statement The truth or falsity of some statements is determined by appeal to some others (by means of logic or scientific method, for example), but some philosophers think that there must be a starting point: basic statements. Whether there are basic statements, what they are, and why they are acceptable, are all controversial questions.

behaviorism Early in the twentieth century, many psychologists decided that introspection was not a good basis for the science of the mind; instead they advocated reliance on subjects' external, observable behavior. Methodological (psychological) behaviorism is the view that only external behavior should be investigated by science. Metaphysical or analytical behaviorism is the philosophical view that public behavior is all there is—that this is what we're talking about when we refer to mental events or characteristics in others, and even in ourselves. This is a form of materialism.

best of all possible worlds A phrase associated with Leibniz, who believed that God, being perfectly good, knowing, and powerful, could not have created anything less than perfect; thus this world (despite how it sometimes appears) is the best of all possible worlds.

bioethics The ethics involved in various sorts of biology-related activities, mostly centering on medical matters, where subjects for debate include, for example, abortion, genetic control, euthanasia, and in vitro fertilization.

biting the bullet What philosophers are said to do when they choose to accept the unlikely counterintuitive consequences of their position, rather than taking them as counterexamples. The phrase supposedly arose because biting down on something would help with the pain of surgery without anaesthetic.

bodily interchange This is what would happen if the same person existed at one time in one body and at another time in another body, for example, through reincarnation, or through a variety of science-fiction techniques such as brain or memory transplant. The topic is important in religious contexts and in thought experiments about personal identity.

bourgeoisie / proletariat Names of the two social /economic classes important in Marx's analysis. The former is the capitalist class—employers, financiers, landlords, etc., though more generally now the bourgeoisie is taken to include middle class wage earners as well. The latter is the working class.

bundle theory In general, the view of classical empiricists who argued that things are nothing more than bundles of properties, and that there is no need to think of substrata (underlying substance). The phrase most often refers to Hume's bundle theory of personal identity: we don't perceive a continuing self, so our self-idea must refer to an introspectible continuously changing "bundle" of different mental events.

burden of proof When there is a disagreement, it's sometimes the case that one side has the burden of proof, that is, it is expected to prove its case, and if it can't, the other wins by default. It may be the side with the position that is surprising, or unorthodox, or that runs counter to other well-accepted beliefs.

calculus An abstract system of symbols, aimed at calculating something. One can call each symbol-system of symbolic logic a 'calculus': for example, the sentential and quantifier calculi. The system for calculating probabilities is called the 'probability calculus'. Some philosophers think of the various sciences as interpreted calculi; a calculus is interpreted (given a "valuation") when its symbols are given meaning by relating them to things in the real world; uninterpreted, it is just a bunch of symbols with syntax but no semantics. 'The calculus' names a branch of mathematics independently developed by Leibniz and Newton during the late seventeenth century.

casuistry The determination of right and wrong by reasoning involving general principles applied to particular cases. Because religious casuists sometimes reasoned in overly complex ways to silly conclusions, this word has come to have disparaging overtones.

categorical / hypothetical imperative Kant's distinction. An imperative is a command. 'Categorical' means absolute—not dependent on particular aims or circumstances; 'hypothetical' means relative to, depending on, particular aims or circumstances. Thus, 'Tell the truth' is a categorical imperative, but 'If it is to everyone's benefit, tell the truth' and 'If you want others to trust you, tell the truth' are hypothetical imperatives. Kant argued that hypothetical imperatives could give useful practical advice, but do not express the standards of morality, which are expressed only by categorical imperatives. He argued further that there is one command central to all morality—the categorical imperative: Act in a way such that the general rule behind your action could consistently be willed to be a universal law. He argued that this was equivalent to saying that others should be treated as ends, never as means only.

category mistake A claim that's absurd because it makes an ascription completely inappropriate to the category of the object in question. To claim that the number 7 is faster than the number 8 is to assert this kind of absurdity. Gilbert Ryle introduced this term arguing that the standard Cartesian view of mind/body dualism committed this kind of mistake.

causal theories A variety of theories that make the notion of cause basic in some way. The causal theory of knowledge proposes, as a condition of 'P knows that x', that P's belief be causally connected in some appropriate way to the fact that x. The causal theory of perception points out that a "blue sensation" is one normally caused by a blue thing, and tries to avoid sense-data by explaining that what is happening when there is no blue thing there is that the sensation is one that would have been caused by a blue thing, were the situation normal. Functionalism is a causal theory of mind. The causal theory of meaning / reference makes the meaning / reference of terms a matter of the causal connections their uses have with the external world.

causation The relation that holds between a cause and its effect. Also called 'causality'. Longstanding philosophical problems are concerned with the nature of cause, and how we find out about it. Hume skeptically argued that we perceive no "power" in causal connections, and that when we say that x causes y, we're only saying that things of x-sort regularly precede things of y-sort. Critics object that this fails to distinguish between causal connections and mere accidental but universal regularities.

cause-of-itself (Latin: causa sui) Narrowly, a thing that causes itself to exist (or to be the way it is). God is commonly thought to be the only thing that is capable of this. But because causes are supposed to precede their effects, a cause-of-itself would (problematically) have to precede its own existence. Thinking of cause in an older way, as explanation, perhaps avoids this difficulty, but has its own problems: how can something provide the explanation for its own existence?

certainty A belief is called 'certain' in ordinary talk when it is believed very strongly, or when one is unable to think, or even imagine, that it might be false. Philosophers often don't want to rely on a subjective and psychological test for certainty, and demand proof that some belief really is beyond rational doubt. Some philosophers think that all our knowledge must have a certain foundation. 'Moral certainty' means sufficiently warranted to justify action; 'metaphysical certainty' means warranted not merely by fallible perception of particulars, but rather by some presumably more reliable reasoning about all being; 'logical certainty' is the extremely strong warrant we get for a proposition which is in some sense a truth of logic.

ceteris paribus (Latin: "other things being equal") This is used in comparing two things while assuming they differ only in the one characteristic under consideration. For example, it could be said that, ceteris paribus, a simple theory is better than a complicated one; though if everything else is not equal—if, for example, the simpler theory has fewer true predictions—then it might not be better.

circular reasoning / definition A definition is (viciously) circular (and thus useless) when the term to be defined, or a version of it, occurs in the definition; for example, the definition of 'free action' as 'action that is freely done'. (Viciously) circular reasoning defends some statement by assuming the truth of that statement; e.g.: "Why do you think what the Bible says is true?" "Because the Bible is the Word of God." "How do you know that it is the Word of God?" "Because it says so in the Bible, and everything there is true." Some philosophers argue that not all circles are vicious, and that some sorts of circular reasoning are acceptable—"virtuously circular"—for example, when the circle is wide enough. A dictionary, for example, must be circular, defining words in terms of other words; but this is okay. Circular reasoning is also known as 'begging the question'. Careless speakers sometimes think that this means 'raising the question'; it doesn't. Begging the question is sometimes called by its Latin name, 'petitio principii'.

cognitive / emotive meaning The former is what a sentence states—what makes it true or false. The latter is its "expressive" content—the speaker's feelings that it communicates, rather than any beliefs. Some theories of ethical statements hold that they have emotive, but no cognitive, meaning.

cognition The operations of the mind; sometimes particularly believing and awareness; sometimes, more particularly, the mental process by which we get knowledge.

cognitive science A recently-developed discipline combining philosophers, psychologists, and computer scientists, devoted to providing theories of cognition.

cognitivism / noncognitivism Cognitivism is the position that something can be known. Ethical cognitivism is the view that ethical statements are statements about (supposed) facts and thus are true or false, and might be known to be true or false. This is opposed to the noncognitivist position that ethical statements are not knowable. A species of ethical noncognitivism is emotivism, which argues that ethical statements are expressions of approval or disapproval (like 'Hooray for that!'), or invitations to action (like 'Please do that!') and are thus neither true nor false, and not knowable.

coherence / incoherence A set of beliefs or sentences is coherent when it fits together in a logical way—that is, when everything in the set is consistent, or when the items in it confirm others in it. A set in which one item would be false, or probably false, given the truth of others is not coherent (is incoherent).

collectively / distributively What applies to a group collectively applies to it as a whole only, i.e., not to its individual members (not distributively). The atoms that constitute a pig collectively, but not distributively, outweigh a fly.

collective responsibility The controversial idea that a group or nation or culture can bear responsibility as a whole for bad acts: for example, the whole German nation for Nazi atrocities.

commensurability / incommensurability Different things are commensurable when they can be measured on the same scale. Utilitarians sometimes assume that different people's different pleasures are commensurable on a common scale of utiles; but it has been argued that there's no way to make sensible quantity comparisons. Another example of supposed incommensurability is in the comparison of science and religion: some philosophers think that it's foolish to criticize religious statements using the criteria of scientific adequacy.

common sense 1. Until the eighteenth century or so, this term named the supposed mental faculty which combined input from different senses to give us a unified idea of an external object, combining, for example, the smell, taste, look and feel of a peach. 2. More recently, it has come to mean the mental faculty which all people are supposed to possess "in common," for knowledge of basic everyday truths. This is sometimes taken to answer skeptical doubts about the obvious truths that there exists an external world, other minds, etc. The eighteenth-century Scottish "common sense philosophers" relied heavily on this notion as a vindication of ordinary views and a refutation of skepticism.

communitarianism Advocates the position in social philosophy that the rights of individuals are not basic—that groups, or society as a whole, can have rights that are not constituted by or based on the individual rights of the members of those groups, and that these group rights may override claims to individual rights. Fascism is a rather extreme example of communitarianism. Communitarianism is a form of holism in social theory; the contrast is with individualism.

compatibilism Any philosophical position that claims that two things are compatible (they can both exist at once), most referring to the view that free will and determinism are compatible—that is, that people's actions are (sometimes) free even though they are fully causally determined. Compatibilists argue that we're not free when we're acting under compulsion (that is, forced to act), but that this is a different thing from the action's being determined or caused.

compulsion An action is said to be done under compulsion (also known as 'constraint' or 'coercion') when it is "forced" by internal or external circumstances, and thus the doer of that action can't be held morally responsible for doing it. If you steal something, for example, because someone is forcing you to do it at gunpoint, or because you are a kleptomaniac, that doesn't make your action any better, but it does mean that you're not to blame. Compatibilists about free will argue that compulsion makes one unfree and not responsible, but that ordinary actions are causally determined but not compelled in this sense.

concept May refer to the ability to categorize things; thus to say that someone has the concept of duck is to say that that person can sort things correctly into ducks and non-ducks. A concept is sometimes distinguished from a percept, which is a particular mental item had while sensing a particular thing. A concept, then, may be thought to be a generalization or abstraction from one or many percepts. Thus a percept is sometimes considered a particular idea, and a concept a general or abstract idea.

conceptual scheme The most general framework of someone's view of the world—a structured system of concepts that divide that person's world into kinds of things. It has sometimes been supposed that two people's conceptual schemes might differ so much that one would never be able to understand or translate what the other said.

conceptual truth A statement that is true merely because of the nature of the concepts that make it up. The fact that all bachelors are unmarried is a conceptual truth, because the concept of being a bachelor involves being unmarried. Compare: snow is white is not a conceptual truth, because being white, despite being true of snow, is not part of the concept of snow. We can imagine, consistent with our concept of snow, that snow is always green. (Substitute 'word' for 'concept' in this definition, and it turns into the definition of 'analytic truth'.)

confirmation / disconfirmation / verification / falsification Confirmation is the collection of evidence for a statement. Because there might be some evidence for a false statement, a statement might be confirmed though false. Collecting evidence that a statement is false is called 'disconfirmation'. 'Verification' means 'confirmation' and 'falsification' means 'disconfirmation', though one tends to speak of a statement as having been verified (or falsified) only if the statement is really true (or false), and has been shown to be so by the evidence. Confirmation theory is the attempt to give a general account of what counts as confirmation.

conscience This is the sense of right and wrong that is sometimes supposed to be a way of knowing moral facts, perhaps through a reliable internal "voice" or moral sense-perception, or a faculty of moral intuition.

consciousness 1. The state that we are in when awake: mental events are going on. 2. Awareness of something. (You aren't usually conscious of the position of your tongue.) 3. = mind (though it might be that the mind exists even while we are asleep or not aware of anything). The fact that we are conscious is supposed by some to distinguish people from machines and other non-living things, and perhaps from (at least the lower) animals.

consequentialism The position that people's actions are right or wrong because of their consequences (their results). This sort of ethical theory also called 'teleological', is contrasted with deontological theories—those that hold that results of actions are morally irrelevant. Thus, for example, a deontologist might think that lying is always wrong just in itself, whereas a consequentialist might think that lying is morally permissible in those circumstances in which the lie results in good consequences overall.

consistency A set of statements is consistent if it is logically possible that all the statements in that set are true. It is inconsistent if this is not possible—if one statement contradicts another, or if a contradiction results from reasoning from the set. The set consisting of this one statement 'It's raining and it's not raining' is inconsistent, because this statement is self-contradictory.

contingency To say that a statement is contingent is to say that it is neither necessary nor impossible. Metaphysical contingency is contrasted with what must be true or false; logical contingency is contrasted with logical truth / falsity.

contra-causal freedom It's sometime argued that a free action—one we're responsible for—could only be one that is not caused by previous events. Libertarians believe that some of our actions are free because contra-causal.

contradiction / contrary Two statements are contradictories when the truth of one logically requires the falsity of the other, and the falsity of one requires the truth of the other—in other words, when it is impossible that both are true, and it is impossible that both are false. 'It's raining' and 'It's not raining' are contradictory: exactly one of them must be true. Two statements are contraries when it is impossible that they are both true, though they might both be false. 'No pigs fly' and 'All pigs fly' are contraries, not contradictories. It is logically impossible that both of them are true, though they both might be false (were it the case that some, but not all, pigs fly). One can also call a self-contradiction a 'contradiction'.

cosmological argument for God's existence Given that every natural event has a cause, an apparently unacceptable infinite chain of past events would follow—unless there were an initial uncaused (supernatural) cause, identified with God. A very commonly encountered argument, with versions dating back at least to Plato. It's also commonly known as the first-cause argument.

counterexample An example intended to show that some general claim is false. Reasoning by counterexample is frequently a useful philosophical tactic for arguing against some position. (Also called 'counterinstance'.)

counterfactual A counterfactual (also called a 'counterfactual conditional' or a 'contrary-to-fact conditional') is a conditional statement whose antecedent is false. The subjunctive is used in English counterfactuals: 'If Fred were here, you wouldn't be doing that'. (This is

properly said only when Fred isn't here.) One important and controversial area in modern logic is concerned with the truth-conditions for counterfactuals. A powerful and widely accepted way of understanding counterfactuals uses the notion of possible worlds: a counterfactual is true when the consequent is true in the nearest possible world (i.e., a world as much as possible like ours) in which the antecedent is true.

covering law A general law applying to a particular instance. The covering law theory (or "model") of explanation (also called the 'Deductive-Nomological' or 'D-N' theory) says that a particular event is explained by providing one or more covering laws that, together with particular facts, imply the event. For example, we can explain why a piece of metal rusted by appealing to the covering law that iron rusts when exposed to air and moisture, and the facts that the metal is iron, and was exposed to air and moisture.

criterion A test or standard for the presence of a property, or for the applicability of a word, or for the truth or falsity of a proposition. This word is singular; its plural is 'criteria'.

crucial experiment This is an experiment whose outcome would provide a central or conclusive test for the truth or falsity of some position or scientific hypothesis. Sometimes called, in Latin, 'experimentum crucis'.

decision theory The largely mathematical theory of decision-making. Generally includes some way of evaluating desirability of outcomes and their probabilities when not certain.

deconstructionism A skeptical and frequently anti-intellectual postmodern movement which seeks to interpret texts and the positions held in them by "deconstructing" them—showing their incoherence, the hidden and often contradictory presuppositions, prejudices, motives, and political aims behind them.

de dicto / de re (Latin: "about what's said" / "about a thing") A de re belief is a belief considered with respect to the actual thing that it's about. Thus, if someone mistakenly thinks that the moving thing in the sky he's looking at is a satellite, whereas it's actually a meteor, then he has the de re belief that a meteor is moving in the sky—more clearly: about that meteor, he believes it's moving in the sky above him. But he has the de dicto belief that a satellite is moving in the sky above him. Philosophers speak also of a distinction between de dicto and de re necessity. It is de re necessary of the number of planets that it is larger than five (because nine is necessarily larger than five); but it is de dicto contingent, because there might have been only three planets.

deduction / induction 1. In an outdated way of speaking, deduction is reasoning from the general to the particular, and induction is reasoning from the particular to the general. 2. Nowadays, this distinction between kinds of reasoning is made as follows: correct ("valid") deductive reasoning is reasoning of the sort that if the premises are true, the conclusion must be true; whereas correct inductive reasoning supports the conclusion by showing only that it's more probably true. Examples:

Deduction: No pigs fly; Porky is a pig; therefore, Porky doesn't fly.
Induction: Porky, Petunia, and all the other pigs observed in a wide variety of circumstances don't fly; therefore no pigs fly.

These examples in fact fit definition 1; but here are examples of deduction according to definition 2 that do not fit definition 1:

No pigs fly; therefore all pigs are non-flying things.
Porky doesn't fly; Porky is a pig; therefore not all pigs fly.

A common form of induction works by enumeration: as support for the conclusion that all A's are B's, one lists many examples of A's that are B's.

defeasible Means 'defeatible', in the sense of 'capable of being overruled'. A driver's license confers a defeasible right to drive, for example, because under certain circumstances (e.g., when he is drunk) the holder of a valid license would nevertheless not be allowed to drive. A defeasible proposition is one that can be overturned by future evidence.

definiens / definiendum A definiendum (Latin: "to be defined") is a word or phrase to be defined, and the definition is the definiens (Latin: "defining thing").

degrees of perfection argument for God's existence One of many different forms of this argument: Comparative terms describe degrees of approximation to superlative terms. Nothing would count as falling short of the superlative unless the superlative thing existed. Ordinary things are less than perfect, so there must be something completely perfect; and what is completely perfect is God. Objection: Comparative terms do not imply the existence of a superlative instance. For example, the existence of people who are more or less stupid does not imply that someone exists who is maximally, completely, perfectly stupid.

deism A form of religious belief especially popular during the Enlightenment. Deists practice "natural religion"—that is, they rely on reason, distrusting faith, revelation, and the institutional churches. They believe that God produced the universe with its laws of nature, but then left it alone to operate solely by these laws. Deism seems incompatible with some aspects of conventional religion, for example, with the notion of a loving God, or with the practice of prayer.

denotation / connotation The denotation or reference of a word is what that word refers to—the thing in the world that it "names." The connotation or sense of a word is, by contrast, its meaning. Synonymous with 'extension / intension'. A word can have connotation but no denotation: 'unicorn' has meaning but no reference. Note that the philosophical use of 'connotation' is different from the ordinary one, in which it refers not to what a word means, but to more or less distant associations it has; for example, the word 'roses' may carry the connotation of romance to many people. A connotative definition is one that gives the characteristics shared by all and only the objects to which the term refers; often a definition by genus / species. A denotative definition defines by identifying the denotation—for example, by pointing out or listing several things to which the word applies.

deontic Means 'having to do with obligation'. Deontic logic is that branch of modal logic dealing with connections of sentences saying what one ought to do, must do, is permitted to do, etc.

derivation A method for proving deductive validity, in which one moves from premises to succeeding steps using accepted rules of inference, eventuating at the conclusion. There are other methods of proof; for example, in sentential logic, the truth table.

determinism The view that every event is necessitated by previous causes, so that given its causes, each event must have existed in the form it does. There is some debate about how (and whether) this view can be justified. The view that at least some events are not fully caused is called 'indeterminism'. Determinism is often taken to be a presupposition of science; Kant thought it was necessary; but quantum physics says that it is false. One of the main areas of concern about determinism arises when it is considered in connection with free will.

deterrence A motive for punishment: that threatening punishment can prevent future occurrences of undesirable acts. (Other competing theories of punishment attempt to justify it as retribution or rehabilitation.) So one may try to justify jailing criminals by claiming that the threat of similar jailing will discourage them and others from future crime. One may even successfully deter crime by framing the innocent. Deterrence as a national defense policy attempts to prevent other nations' aggression by threatening them with massive (perhaps nuclear) retaliation. The moral status of deterrence is controversial. Preventing war is of course a good thing, but is threatening deterrence justified when it involves the willingness to go through with really horrible retaliation?

dialectic Sometimes this word refers to a style of philosophical discourse most famously due to Plato, involving dialogue: claims, counterclaims, and logical argument. (A contrasting style is rhetoric.) In Kant, dialectical reasoning fallaciously attributes external existence to objects internal to our minds. In Hegel, Marx, and other Continental philosophers, the Dialectic is the interplay of contradictory forces supposed to be a central principle of metaphysical and social existence and change.

divine command theory The ethical theory which explains morality as what is commanded by God. It is often argued that this has things backwards: God commands it because it is right, not vice versa.

double effect The doctrine of double effect holds that, although it is always wrong to use a bad means to a good end, one may act to bring about a good result when also knowingly bringing about bad results, under the following conditions: 1) The bad result is not caused by the good result—both are caused by the action (thus 'double effect'); (2) there's no way of getting the good result without the bad; 3) the good result is so good that it's worth accepting the bad one.

For example, a dentist is allowed to drill, and thus cause some pain (the bad result) for the sake of dental improvements (the good result), since these conditions hold—most notably (1): the pain doesn't cause the improvement; both are results of the drilling.

This principle is associated with Catholic morality, and has been applied most frequently in contexts of medical ethics. It is disputed by some philosophers, who sometimes argue that the distinction between double effect and bad means / good end is artificial and not morally relevant.

doxastic Means 'pertaining to belief', as in 'doxastic state', 'doxastic principle' (for justifying beliefs).

dualism Dualists hold that there are two sorts of things that exist, neither of which can be understood in terms of the other—often, in particular, mental and physical. Other sorts of dualism distinguish the visible and invisible, the actual and the possible, God and the universe, etc. The contrast here is with monism.

egalitarianism The view that people are equal—that they are entitled to equal rights and treatment in society, or to equal possessions or satisfactions.

egoism, ethical / psychological Psychological egoism is the position that people in fact act only in their own interests. It's sometimes argued that even the most generous act is done for the doer's own satisfaction; but this might simply be a way of saying that even the most generous act is motivated—something nobody would deny. Ethical egoism is the position that I (or people in general) ought to act only in my (their) own interests.

emotivism A position in meta-ethics that holds that ethical utterances are to be understood not as statements of fact that are either true or false, but rather as expressions of approval or disapproval, and invitations to the listener to have the same reactions and to act accordingly. Thus emotivists emphasize the "emotive meaning" of ethical utterances, denying that they have cognitive meaning. Emotivists can nevertheless agree that evaluative utterances have some "descriptive content": when I say this is a good apple, I express my approval, but also describe it as having certain characteristics on which my approval rests: that it is, for example, not worm-infested.

empirical This means having to do with sense-experience and experiment. Empirical knowledge is knowledge we get through experience of the world; thus it is a posteriori. An empirical concept is one that is not innate; it can be developed only through experience.

empiricism The position (usually contrasted with rationalism) that all our concepts and substantive knowledge come from sense experience. Empiricists deny that there are innate concepts. While they grant that certain kinds of trivial knowledge (of conceptual, analytic, and logical truths) can be gained by reason alone, independently of experience, they deny the existence of the synthetic a priori.

end in itself 1. Something sought for its own sake; an intrinsic good. 2. Someone is seen as an end in him / herself when that person's aims are seen as having value just because they are that person's aims. Treating people as ends in themselves is respecting their aims, and refraining from thinking of, or using, that person merely as a means to your aims.

ends / means A long-standing controversy in ethics is whether one might be permitted to use bad means to a good end: does the end justify the means? For example, is it permitted to lie to someone if everyone will be better off in the long run as a result? Extreme opponents of consequentialism sometimes hold that no action that is bad in itself is ever permitted no matter how good the consequences. Notice that this means that telling a little lie would not be justified even if it would prevent the destruction of the earth. A more moderate view merely warns against actions which are so bad in themselves that the good consequences do not overwhelm this badness.

Enlightenment The Enlightenment was a cultural and philosophical movement of the seventeenth and eighteenth centuries whose chief features were a belief in rationality and scientific method, and a tendency to reject conventional religion and other traditions. The Age of Enlightenment is also known as the 'Age of Reason'.

enthymeme An argument with some steps left unstated but understood. All pigs are sloppy eaters, so Porky is a sloppy eater is an enthymeme, leaving unsaid Porky is a pig.

epiphenomenalism A variety of dualism in which mental events are just "by-products" of physical ones: physical events cause mental ones, but not vice versa. Analogy: the noise your car makes is caused by the mechanical goings-on inside, but it has no effect on them.

epistemic Having to do with knowledge. Epistemic logic is that branch of modal logic dealing with relations between sentences involving 'knows', 'believes', etc.

epistemology Theory of knowledge: one of the main branches of philosophy. Among the central questions studied here are: What is the difference between knowledge and mere belief? Is all (or any) knowledge based on sense-perception? How, in general, are our knowledge-claims justified?

essence / accident The essential characteristics of something are the ones that it must have in order to be what it is, or the kind of thing it is. It is essential, for example, for a tree to be a plant—if something was not a plant, it could not be a tree. By contrast, a tree that in fact is thirty-three meters high could still be a tree if it weren't that height; thus this characteristic is accidental. (Note that 'accident' and 'accidental' don't have their ordinary meanings in this philosophical use.) Some philosophers think that the essence / accident distinction does not concern the real characteristics of something, but is only a consequence of the words we apply to them: being a plant is said to be an essential characteristic of a tree only because it's part of the definition of 'tree'. But essentialist philosophers believe in real, objective essences.

ethics The general philosophical study of what makes things good or bad, right or wrong. Often the following areas of study are distinguished within ethics: (1) Descriptive ethics: the discovery of what ethical views particular societies in fact have; and speculative anthropological theorizing about the origin and function of these views; (2) Normative ethics: theorizing about what the basic principles are that might serve systematically to distinguish right from wrong. (3) Applied ethics: the normative ethics of particular areas or disciplines: medical ethics, business ethics, computer ethics ... . (4) Meta-ethics: the study of the meaning of moral language and the possibility of ethical knowledge.

'Morality' and 'ethics' (and 'moral' and 'ethical') are usually used as synonyms, though 'ethics' is more frequently generally used as the name of the philosophical study of these matters. Philosophers usually avoid the tendency in ordinary talk to restrict the word 'ethics' to an official code of acceptable behavior in some area (as in 'professional ethics').

ethnocentric Someone is ethnocentric who regards the views or characteristics of his / her own race or culture as the only correct or important ones. Other "-centric" words have arisen by analogy: eurocentric, logocentric, phallocentric for example.

euthanasia Mercy killing, the intentional bringing-about or hastening the death of someone, presumably for his own good, when his life is judged not to be worth continuing, typically when that person is suffering from an untreatable, fatal illness causing horrible unavoidable pain or suffering. Voluntary euthanasia is done at the expressed wish of that person; this wish is not expressed in the case of involuntary euthanasia (for example, when the person has mentally deteriorated beyond the point of being able to express, or perhaps even to have, coherent wishes). Passive euthanasia involves refraining from providing life-prolonging treatment to someone suffering from a fatal condition; active euthanasia is killing, for example, by administering a fatal injection. Ethical opinion is deeply divided concerning euthanasia. Some who argue in favor of its permissibility would accept it only when voluntary, and/or only when passive.

expected utility / value The expected utility (or expected value) of an action is calculated by multiplying the utility (or value) of each possible result of that action by its probability, and adding up the results. For example, consider this betting game: you get $10 if a random draw from a deck of cards is a spade; and you pay $4 if it's any other suit. Assuming the utility of each dollar is 1, to calculate the expected utility of this game we add: [.25 (probability of a spade) x 10 (the utility if it's a spade)] + [.75

(the probability of a non-spade) x -4 (the util-ity of a non-spade)]. Since (.25 x 10) + (.75 x -4) = 2.5 - 3 = -.5, the game thus has an expect-ed utility of -.5, so you'll average 50 cents loss per play in the long run. One (controversial) theory for rational decision-making advocates maximizing expected utility, so you should not play this game. (But if you enjoy gambling, this has to be figured in too, and might make it worthwhile.)

explanans / explanandum An explanandum (Lat-in: "to be explained") is something that is be-ing explained: what does the explaining is the explanans (Latin: "explaining thing").

explanation An explanation answers the question 'Why?' and provides understanding; some-times it also provides us with the abilities to control, and to predict (and retrodict) the world. This is fairly vague, and philosophers have tried to provide theories of explanation—to give a general account of how explanations work, and what makes some good and some bad. One important account is the covering law model. One (but only one) sort of explana-tion is causal: we explain something by saying what its causes are. Sometimes, instead, we explain by telling what something is made of, or by giving reasons for human actions, as in some explanations in history.

externalism / internalism A variety of related doc-trines. Meta-ethical externalism holds that the fact that something is good does not by itself automatically supply the motivation for some-one to do it; in addition, motivation ("exter-nal" to the mere belief about goodness) must be supplied; internalism is the view that the judgment that something is good itself guar-antees or includes the motivation to do it. As a theory of mind, externalism is the view that to specify the "content" of a belief one must refer to the external facts or objects that the belief is about.

fallacy An argument of a type that may seem cor-rect but in fact is not. (Thus, not just any mis-taken argument should be called 'fallacious'.) Formal fallacies are mistakes in reasoning that spring from mistakes in logical form; their per-suasiveness springs from their similarity, on first glance, to valid forms. Informal fallacies spring instead from ambiguities in meaning or grammar, or from psychological tendencies to be convinced by reasons that are not good reasons.

fatalism The position that our futures are inevitable, whatever we do—that events are "fated" to happen. It's important to distinguish this from determinism, which claims merely that our fu-tures are determined. A determinist who is not a fatalist thinks that our futures are not inevi-table—they depend on what we do.

feminism The name of various philosophical—es-pecially ethical, social, and political—theories and social movements that see elements of our society as unjust to and exploitative of women. Feminists often advocate equality under the law and equal economic status for women; but many go further, arguing in favor of prefer-ential treatment for women to counteract past injustices. Sometimes they find male bias and male patterns of thought in many areas of our personal, social, and intellectual lives. Recent developments are feminist theories of the self, of knowledge, and of science.

formal In philosophy this means pertaining to struc-ture (as opposed to content); or rigorous and rule-governed.

foundationalism The position that there is a par-ticular sort of statement (sometimes thought to be indubitable) from which all other state-ments comprising a system of belief should be derived. There are foundationalist theories of knowledge, of ethics, etc.

free will To say that we have free will (or freedom) is to say that our decisions and actions are sometimes entirely (or at least partially) "up to us"—not forced or determined by anything internal or external to us. We can then either do or not do—we have alternatives. It seems that this is necessary for responsibility for our actions. But if determinism is true, then our actions and "decisions" are determined by previous causes, themselves determined by still earlier causes, and ultimately whatever we decide or do is determined by events that happened a long time ago, and that are not up to us. Thus, it seems that determinism is incompatible with free will. There are three main responses to this apparent problem: (1) Hard determinists accept determinism, which they take to rule out free will. (2) Libertarians accept free will. They think that this means determinism is false, at least for some human events. Both libertarianism and hard determinism are incompatibilist; that is, they hold that the freedom of an act is incompatible with its being determined. (3) Soft determinists are compatibilists, in that they attack the reasoning above, and argue that our actions might be determined, but also free in some sense—that a determined action might nevertheless be up to the doer, and one that the doer is morally responsible for—when it's determined but not compelled.

functional A functional definition defines by giving the typical use of the kind of thing, or its typical cause-and-effect relations with other things; a functional explanation explains something by its function, for example, telling what use the pancreas is in the body, or a social ritual in a particular society. A functional kind is defined by causes and effects (and not, for example, by shape or physical make-up). Functionalism centrally argues that a kind of thing is a functional kind. In philosophy of mind, functionalists argue that mental kinds are functional kinds.

generalization A statement about a group of things, or about everything in a particular category (contrasted with a 'particular statement / proposition'); or the process of reasoning that arrives at one of these. Inductive logic studies the principles of deriving them from particular instances; the rule in deductive logic for deriving one is called universal generalization. An ethical generalization is a rule everyone should follow; Kant argued that the right action was the one whose maxim could be generalized.

general will What is desired by, or desirable for, society as a whole; sometimes taken to be the appropriate justification for government policy. This notion can be problematic when it is taken to mean something other than what's revealed by majority vote or unanimity.

hedonism The advocacy of pleasure as the basic good; philosophical hedonists often distinguish between the "higher" (sometimes = mental or spiritual) and the "lower" pleasures (the merely sensual), making the former more important. Psychological hedonism claims that people in fact seek only pleasure; ethical hedonism claims that people ought to seek pleasure (or only pleasure).

holism / individualism In philosophical use, holism involves the claim that certain sorts of things are more than merely the sum of their parts—that they can be understood only by examining them as a whole; contrasted with individualism. In social science and history, for example, holists argue that one can't explain events on the basis of individual people's actions, because these get their significance only in a society. Semantic holism insists that words and sentences get their meaning only through their relationships with all other words and sentences. Holism about living things refuses to see them merely as the sum of their non-living parts. Methodological individualism is the method in sociology of investigating social facts by discovering facts about individual people. Individualism in ethics emphasizes individual rights and freedoms, contrasting with communitarianism.

hypothesis A tentative suggestion that may be merely a guess or a hunch, or may be based on some sort of reasoning; in any case it needs further evidence to be rationally acceptable as true. Some philosophers think that all scientific enquiry begins with hypotheses.

idea / impression An "idea" is, in general, any thought or perception in the mind. Platonic forms are sometimes called 'ideas'. In Hume, ideas are the faint imprint left on the mind by impressions, which are the mental events one has as the immediate result of, and while, using one's senses (= sense-data); ideas may be called up later in the absence of sensation. Empiricists believe that all ideas are copies of impressions.

idealism In the philosophical sense of this word, it's the view that only minds and their contents really or basically exist. Its competitors are materialism and dualism.

ideal observer theory A theory of ethics that attempts to explain what is really good as what would be chosen by an ideal observer—that is, someone who would have all the relevant information, and who would not be misled by particular interests or biases.

identity 1. Your identity is what you are—what's important about you, or what makes you different from everyone else. 2. Two different things might be said to be 'identical' when they are exactly alike in some characteristics; this is sometimes called qualitative identity. 3. Object a and object b are said to be (strictly or numerically or quantitatively) identical when a and b are in fact the same thing—when 'a' and 'b' are two different names or ways of referring to exactly the same object. 4. Identity (over time) is the relation between something at one time and that same thing at another time: they are said to be two temporal stages (or time-slices) of the same continuing thing.

identity theory of mind The view that each mental state is really a physical state, probably of the brain. Often identity theorists believe in addition in the type-identity of mental and physical states.

illusion / hallucination / delusion Illusions and hallucinations are "false" perceptual experiences—ones that lead, or could lead, to mistakes about what is out there. A hallucination is the apparent perception of something that does not exist at all (as in dreaming, mirages, drug-induced states). An illusion is the incorrect perception of something that does exist. A delusion is a perception that actually results in a false belief; illusions and hallucinations can delude, but often do not. The argument from illusion draws epistemological conclusions from the existence of these things.

imagination Sometimes philosophers have used this word to refer to the faculty of having images—mental pictures.

immaterialism 1. The view that some things exist that are not material: that are not made of ordinary physical stuff, but of mental or spiritual—immaterial stuff instead. This is the denial of materialism. The most extreme form of immaterialism is the view that no material things exist: this is idealism. 2. The view that objects are merely collections of qualities, without a substratum to hold them together. If one thinks of qualities as essentially mental perceptions, then this is a species of immaterialism in sense 1.

immediate / mediate In its more technical philosophical sense 'immediate' means 'without mediation'—that is, 'directly'. In this sense, for example, philosophers ask whether external things are sensed immediately, or mediated by the sensing of internal images. An immediate inference is one performed in one step, needing only a single use of only one rule, for example, when Q is inferred from (P and Q).

immorality / amorality The first means 'contrary to morality'; the second, 'without morality'. Someone who knows about moral rules but intentionally disobeys them or rejects them is immoral; someone who doesn't know or think about morality is amoral. Amorality is typical of small children; immorality of adults.

incorrigibility / corrigibility 'Corrigibility' means 'correctibility'. Something is incorrigible when it is impossible to correct it, or when it is guaranteed correct. Some philosophers have thought that our beliefs about our own mental states are incorrigible. For example, if you sincerely believe that you are now feeling a pain, how could you be wrong?

indubitability / dubitability 'Dubitable' means 'doubtable'. Dubitable statements are not just ones we are psychologically capable of doubting, but ones about which even highly fanciful and unlikely doubts might be raised, doubts that no one in his/her right mind would seriously have. Thus Descartes thought that because our senses might be fooled, information from them was dubitable. He then went on to try to discover what sort of belief was really indubitable: about which it could be proven that no doubt can be raised.

inference / implication / entailment 1. Implication (also known as entailment) is a logical relation that holds between two statements when the second follows deductively from the first. The first is then said to 'imply' (or 'entail') the second. Be careful not to confuse these with 'inference', which is something that people do, when they reason from one statement to another. A rule of inference is an acceptable procedure for reasoning from one set of statements of a particular form to another statement. 2. Sometimes a sentence 'implies' what it doesn't literally state. For example, if I said "Fred is now not robbing banks," I imply that at one time he was robbing banks. This is sometimes called conversational or contextual implicature, or pragmatic implication, to distinguish it from logical implicature.

infinite regress A sequence (of definition, explanation, justification, cause, etc.) that must continue backwards endlessly. For example, if every event must have a cause, then a present event must be caused by some past event; and this event by another still earlier, and so on infinitely. Sometimes the fact that reasoning leads to an infinite regress shows that it is faulty. One then calls it a vicious regress.

informal / formal logic The latter is that kind of logic that relies heavily on symbols and rigorous procedures much like those in mathematics; it concentrates on reasoning that is correct because of syntax. Only a small fraction of the ordinary sorts of reasoning we do can be explained this way, and there is a vast scope for informal logic, which analyzes good and bad arguments semantically, and relies less heavily on symbols and mathematics-style procedures.

informed consent Agreement based on sufficient knowledge of relevant information; relevant especially to medical ethics. It's widely agreed that informed consent by the patient is necessary for all medical procedures, but problems arise here: how much information is enough? What should be done when the patient is unable to understand the information or to make a rational choice?

innateness A belief, concept, or characteristic is innate when it is inborn—when it doesn't come from experience or education—though experience may be thought necessary to make conscious or actualize something that is given innately. An argument for the innateness of something is that experience is not sufficient to produce it in us.

in principle Contrasted with 'in fact' or 'in practice'. Philosophers talk about things we can do in principle, meaning that we could do them if we had the time or technology, or if other merely practical difficulties did not stand in the way. For example, we can verify the statement 'There is a red pebble lying on the north pole of Mars' in principle, though at the moment we can't test this by observation. In principle, we can count to one trillion, because we know the rules for doing it, though in fact we lack the patience and wouldn't live long enough anyway.

intentionality Sometimes this refers to what's true of things done on purpose—intentionally. But in contemporary usage in philosophy of mind, it usually refers to aboutness—the power of referring to or meaning real or imagined external objects. It's sometimes argued that this is a necessary, unique, and essential characteristic of mental states.

interactionism A form of mind / body dualism. It holds that mind and body can interact—that is, that mental events can cause physical events (e.g., when your decision to touch something causes your physical hand movement) and that physical events can cause mental events (e.g., when a physical stimulation to your body causes a mental feeling of pain). A standard objection to this commonsense position is that it's hard to see how this sort of causal interaction could take place, since the mental and the physical work according to their own laws: how could an electrical impulse in a (physical) nerve cell cause a non-physical pain in a mind?

intrinsic / inherent / instrumental / extrinsic Something has intrinsic value when it is valuable for its own sake and not merely as a means to something else. Pleasure, for example, is intrinsically valuable. Something by contrast has instrumental value when it is valuable as a means to some other end. The value of money is primarily instrumental. An intrinsic or inherent or natural right is one people have permanently or essentially, because of the very nature of a person. An extrinsic right is one people have only temporarily, or one they don't have unless they are granted it.

introspection The capacity for finding things out about oneself by "looking inward"—by direct awareness of one's own mental states. You might find out that you have a headache, for example, by introspection. This is contrasted with the way someone else might find this out, by observing your outward behavior—your groaning, holding your head, etc. Sometimes called 'reflection'.

intuition A belief that comes immediately, without reasoning, argument, evidence; before analysis (thus 'preanalytic'). Some philosophers think that certain intuitions are the reliable, rational basis for knowledge of certain sorts. Some beliefs that arise immediately when we perceive are the basis of our knowledge of the outside world (though perceptual intuitions are not always reliable). Our ethical intuitions are sometimes taken to be the basis and the test of ethical theories. Intuitionism is any theory that holds that intuition is a valid source of knowledge.

is / ought problem Clearly what is is sometimes different from what ought to be; but can one infer the latter from the former? Some philosophers hold that you can't: no matter how detailed an account you have of how things are, they don't imply how things ought to be. But ethical naturalists and other objectivists typically claim that they do, because ethical facts are facts too. The supposed is / ought gap is also known as the fact-value gap.

lawlike statements Statements which have the logical form of laws whether they are true or not. Part of the philosophy of science is the attempt to specify the logic of lawlike statements.

law of the indiscernibility of identicals The supposed law of metaphysics (associated with Leibniz, thus also called 'Leibniz's law') that says that if x and y are identical—that is, if x is y—then x and y are indiscernible (share all the same properties). Distinguish this from its reverse, the law of the identity of indiscernibles: if x and y are indiscernible, then they are identical. Imagine two things that are alike in every detail: they even occupy the same space at the same time. Why then think of them as two? Wouldn't there really be only one thing?

libertarianism 1. The position that some of our actions are free in the sense of not being caused. 2. The political position that people have a strong right to political liberty. Thus libertarians tend to object to restrictive laws, taxes, the welfare state, and state economic control. A more specific variety of (traditional) liberalism, though nowadays this position tends to be espoused by some of those who are called 'conservatives'.

logic Loosely speaking, logic is the process of correct reasoning, and something is logical when it makes sense. Philosophers often reserve this word for reasoning norms covered by various particular theories of inference, justification, and proof. Traditional logic was fairly narrowly restricted, concentrating on the syllogism. Nowadays, symbolic deductive and inductive logics cover a much wider area, but far from the totality of reasoning.

logical form The form of a sentence is its general structure, ignoring the particular content it has. For example, If it's Tuesday, then I'm late for class and If Peru is in Asia, then Porky is a frog have the same overall logical form (if P then Q). The sort of logic that works by exhibiting, often in symbolic notation, the logical form of sentences is called 'formal logic'.

logical positivism A school of philosophy (also known as "logical empiricism"), subscribed to by many twentieth-century English-speaking philosophers. Impressed by empiricism and by the success and rigor of science, the logical positivists advocated that philosophers avoid speculation about matters only science and experience could settle; if a sentence was not scientifically verifiable or a matter of logical truth or conceptual truth, it was nonsense and should be discarded (the verifiability criterion). Ethical statements were thought not verifiable, so without literal meaning: they were sometimes thought merely to be expressions of feelings of approval or disapproval.

logical truth / falsity A sentence is logically true (or false) when it is true (or false) merely because of its logical structure. Examples: All ducks are ducks. Either it's raining or it's not raining. These should be distinguished from analytic truths / falsehoods, which are true / false merely because of the meaning of their words: for example, All fathers are male. Logical truths / falsehoods are also called logically necessary / impossible sentences, but these should also be distinguished from (metaphysically) necessary truths / falsehoods (see necessary / contingent truth): those that must be true or false. 'Tautology' is sometimes used as a synonym for 'logical truth', though in ordinary talk a tautology is something that says the same thing twice. Thus, It's raining and it's raining is a tautology in the ordinary sense, though not in the philosophers' sense (since it might be false). Sentences that are neither logically true nor logically false—that are merely true or false—are said to be logically contingent (or logically indeterminate).

materialism As a philosophical term, this refers to the position that all that exists is physical. (Synonym: physicalism.) Materialists about mind sometimes argue that apparently non-physical things like the soul or mind or thoughts are actually material things. Central-state materialists identify mental events with physical events central in the body (i.e., in the nervous system). Eliminative materialists, however, think that categorizing things as mental is altogether a mistake (like believing in ghosts).

matter of fact / relation of ideas Hume's distinction. He seems to have meant that a matter of fact is a contingent state of affairs, to be discovered a posteriori; a relation of ideas is a conceptual or analytic or logical truth, which can be known a priori.

medieval philosophy The dividing lines between ancient, medieval, and modern philosophy are rough, but it's often said that medieval philosophy starts with Augustine (c. 400), and ends just before Descartes (c. 1600).

meta- This prefix often means 'beyond', or 'about', so thinking about meta-x is (sometimes) thinking about the structure or nature of x. Examples of its use are 'meta-language' and 'meta-ethics'; it is used differently, however, in 'metaphysics'.

metaphysics One of the main branches of philosophy, having to do with the ultimate components of reality, the types of things that exist, the nature of causation, change, time, God, free will.

mind-body problem What is the relation between mental and physical events? Is one sort of event reducible to the other? Are mental events merely a sort of bodily event? Or are they distinct? If so, how are they connected?

modal statements are (roughly speaking) the ones that are not straightforward assertions, and have complexities involved in the logic of their relations (studied in modal logic), their confirmation, etc. The basic kind of modal statements are those affirming necessity and possibility; but also considered in this category are belief, tense, moral, counterfactual, causal, and lawlike statements.

modern philosophy The borderline between medieval philosophy and modern philosophy is rough, but it is usually said that Descartes was the first modern philosopher (around 1600). The era of modern philosophy can be said to extend through the present, though it's often taken to end around the beginning of the nineteenth century, or later with the advent of postmodernism.

monism A monistic metaphysics is the belief that there is one basic kind of thing in existence. Monists about mind deny dualism (belief in two irreducible substances, mind and matter). Nowadays most monists are materialists, but historically, many were idealists (believing that this one kind of stuff was basically mental).

monotheism / polytheism / pantheism Monotheism is the belief in one (and only one) God. Polytheism is the belief in many gods. Pantheism is the belief that God somehow exists in everything, or that everything is God.

moral argument for God's existence One version of this argument: There is a real objective difference between right and wrong, but the only way to make sense of this is to think of it as arising from a divine moral order. So the existence of morality shows that God exists.

moral realism The view that there are real, objective, knowable moral facts.

moral sense theory The idea that we have a way of "sensing" the objective moral properties, on the analogy of the way we can sense the property of redness using our eyes. Moral sensation would clearly be a very different kind of sensation, however; what is the sense organ involved? Is it at all reliable?

mutatis mutandis (Latin: "having changed the things that were to be changed") Philosophers say things like "This case is, mutatis mutandis, like the other," meaning that the two cases are alike except for certain details—that one can derive one case from the other by making the appropriate substitutions or changes.

mutually exclusive / jointly exhaustive Mutually exclusive sets do not overlap each other in membership. For example, each of these sets: mammals, birds, fish, reptiles, amphibians, is exclusive of the others, since nothing belongs to more than one of them. The list is jointly exhaustive of vertebrates, since every vertebrate is included in these categories. It is mutually exclusive and jointly exhaustive because every vertebrate is included in exactly one of these categories.

mystical experience argument for God's existence The existence and nature of the mystical experiences some people have are sometimes taken to show God's existence. One criticism of this argument is that even though having this experience sometimes provides a compelling motivation for belief, it's not reliable evidence.

mysticism A variety of religious practice that relies on direct experience which is often taken to be a union with God or with the divine ground of all being. The content of these experiences is often taken to be ineffable, but we are told that they produce enlightenment or bliss. Mystics often advocate exercises or rituals designed to induce the abnormal psychological states in which these experiences occur.

naïve realism What's supposed to be the ordinary view about perception: that it (usually) reveals external objects to us directly, the way they really are. The implication is that this "naïve" view is overturned by philosophical sophistication. Also called common-sense realism or direct realism.

naturalism This term names the view that everything is a natural entity, and thus to be studied by the usual methods of natural science. Naturalistic or "naturalizing" theories in philosophy try to apply ordinary scientific categories and methods to philosophical problems. Philosophers have proposed naturalized epistemology, philosophy of mind, and ethics.

natural kind Some philosophers think that some of the ways we divide the world into kinds correspond to the way nature really is divided—they "cut nature at the joints." Classically, a natural kind is a kind that things belong to necessarily: thus, human being is a natural kind because Fred is necessarily human; but living within fifty miles of the Empire State Building is not: Fred might move further away; or, if he doesn't he might have. Some contemporary thinkers hold that natural kinds are the ones that support certain modal implications needed in science; but others argue that there are no natural kinds—all kinds are artificial human creations.

natural law There are several philosophically relevant senses of this phrase: 1. A law of nature—i.e., a formulation of a regularity found in the natural world, the sort of thing science discovers. 2. A principle of proper human action or conduct, taken to be God-given, or to be a consequence of "human nature"—our structure or function. In this sense, there are "natural law" theories in ethics and in political philosophy. 3. The view that the validity of the laws of a legal system depends on their coherence with God-given or otherwise objective morality.

necessary / contingent truth A necessary truth is one that could not possibly be false; a contingent truth could be false but isn't, just as a matter of fact. Some philosophers think that the necessity or contingency of some fact is a metaphysical matter—is a matter of the way the external world is—but others hold that this difference is merely a matter of the way we think or talk about the world—that a truth taken to be necessary is merely a conceptual or logical or analytic truth. A necessary truth is also called a necessity, a contingent truth a contingency, and a necessary falsehood an impossibility.

necessary / sufficient condition x is a sufficient condition for y when: if x is true, then y must also be true—that x can't exist without y. This is the same as saying: x can't be without y. x is a necessary condition for y when: if y is true, then x must also be true. In other words, y can't be without x. If you can't have either without the other, then x and y are both necessary and sufficient for each other.

nomic Means 'having to do with law'. A nomic regularity is distinguished from a mere (accidental) regularity or coincidence, in that the first represents a law of nature. One way this difference is explained is by saying that a nomic regularity supports counterfactuals: it's not only the case that all A's are B's, but it's also the case that if something were an A, it would be a B. [synonym: 'nomological']

norm / normative A norm is a standard. 'Normative' means prescribing a norm. When somebody says, "We think abortion is wrong," that statement may be descriptive—informing you what a group's views are, or normative—morally condemning abortion.

obligation Generally, something one morally must do, a synonym for 'duty'. What one must do is perhaps not all there is to morality. Some good things are supererogatory—above and beyond the call of duty—great if you do them, but nobody would blame you if you didn't.

omni- Many (not all) religious thinkers take God to be omnibenevolent—totally, perfectly good; omnipotent—all-powerful, able to do anything; omnipresent—everywhere at once, or influential in everything; and omniscient—all-knowing.

ontological argument for God's existence A variety of arguments that rely on the concept of God to prove His existence. In the best-known version it is supposed that part of the concept of God is that He is perfect: since something would not be perfect if it did not exist, it follows that God exists.

ontology The philosophical study of existence or being. Typical questions are: What basic sorts of things exist? What are the basic things out of which others are composed, and the basic relations between things?

operational definition Defines by giving an account of the procedures or measurements used to apply the word. For example, one might describe weighing procedures and outcomes to define 'weight'.

operationalism / instrumentalism Operationalism is the view that scientific concepts should have operational definitions, and that any terms not definable in this way should be eliminated from science as meaningless. Instrumentalists are operationalists who are explicitly anti-realists about theoretical entities. They say that electrons, for example, don't really exist; electron-talk is about nothing but what's observable.

ordinary language philosophy A branch of twentieth-century philosophy that held that philosophical problems arose because of confusions about, or complexities in, ordinary language, and might be solved (or dissolved) by attention to the subtleties of actual talk.

overdetermination An event is overdetermined when two or more events have happened, each of which is individually a sufficient condition for it. Thus someone's death is overdetermined when he is given a fatal dose of poison and then shot through the heart.

parallelism Because of the difficulties in interactionism some philosophers were led to the belief that mind and body events don't cause each other, but just run along independently; they are coordinated, however, perhaps inexplicably, or maybe because God sets them up in advance (occasionalism) to run in parallel, like two clocks set in advance to chime the hour simultaneously.

Pascal's wager is Blaise Pascal's famous argument for belief in God: Belief in God might result in infinite benefit—eternal salvation—if He exists, while we risk only a little—wasting some time, and foregoing some pleasures forbidden to believers—if He doesn't. Conversely, disbelief might result in infinite harm—eternal damnation—if He exists, or could provide a tiny benefit if we were right. So even if there isn't any evidence one way or the other, it's a very good bet to believe.

paternalism Paternalistic action provides for what is taken to be someone's good, without giving that person responsibility for determining his/ her own aims or actions. It arises from a sort of benevolence plus lack of trust in people's ability to decide what's to their own benefit or to act for their own real long-range good. Some critics of paternalism argue that the only way to determine someone's good is to see what that person chooses. Some argue that respect for individual autonomy means that we shouldn't interfere even when someone is

choosing badly. This issue arises most importantly in political theory and medical ethics, since governments and physicians often act paternalistically.

patriarchy Societal and familial institutions are patriarchal when they systematically embody male dominance over women: when they arrange things so that men hold power and women do not. Feminists emphasize the widespread incidence of patriarchal institutions in historical and contemporary families and societies.

perception In its broadest use, this means any sort of mental awareness, but it's more often used to refer to the awareness we get when using the senses.

person Philosophers sometimes use this word in such a way that persons do not necessarily coincide with living human organisms. The idea here is that a person is anything that has special rights (for example, the right to life, or to self-determination) or special dignity or worth. Sometimes it's held that some humans (e.g., those in a permanent coma) are not persons in this sense, or that some higher animals are.

personal identity 1. What makes you you. Is it your body, your mind, your personality, your memories, or something else? 2. What makes this person now the same person as that one, earlier. Is it a continuing body, or mind, or personality, or that this later stage remembers the experiences that happened to the earlier one?

phenomenalism Phenomenalists believe (on the basis, for example, of the argument from illusion) that all we're ever aware of is appearances or sense-data, the mental events we have when using our senses. Accepting the empiricist rule that we're entitled to believe in only what's given by our senses, they deny the existence of external objects independent of perception. Ordinary "objects" like tables and chairs are thus thought to be collections of these appearances—actual and perhaps possible ones.

phenomena / noumena Philosophers sometimes use 'phenomenon' in the ordinary sense, referring merely to something that happens, but often it's used in a more technical way, referring to a way things seem to us—to something as we perceive it. Noumena are, by contrast, things-in-themselves—things as they really are. These are unavailable to the senses, but perhaps rationally comprehensible; though Kant argued that they are unknowable.

pluralism Pluralist theories argue for a multiplicity of basic kinds. To be a pluralist about value is to believe that there are many incompatible, but equally valid, value systems.

positivism The philosophy associated with Auguste Comte, which holds that scientific knowledge is the only valid kind of knowledge, and that anything else is idle speculation. Sometimes this term is loosely used to refer to logical positivism, which is a twentieth-century outgrowth of more general nineteenth-century positivism.

possible worlds This world—the collection of all facts—is the actual world. The set of possible worlds includes the actual world plus non-actual worlds—ones in which one or more things are not as they actually are, but might have been.

postmodernism Various late twentieth-century movements, in general characterized by a rejection of foundationalism, an interest in textual interpretation and deconstruction, antagonism to analytic philosophy, rejection of the goals of the Enlightenment, tendency to perspectivism, denial of the applicability of the concepts of reality, objectivity, truth.

poststructuralism A postmodern view, thought of as a successor to structuralism. Holds in general that the meaning of words is their relation to other words (in a "text"), not their relation to reality; that human activity is not lawlike, but understood through its relations to power and the unconscious.

pragmatism A largely American school of philosophers who emphasized the relevance of the practical application of things, their connections to our lives, our activities and values, demanding instrumental definitions of philosophically relevant terms, and urged that we judge beliefs on the basis of their benefit to the believer.

pre-Socratics The ancient Greek philosophers before Socrates, that is, of the sixth and fifth centuries BCE. Their thought is the earliest recorded Western philosophy.

presupposition A necessary condition for the truth of a statement, assumed beforehand by the speaker, but not itself stated. The speaker of 'The present king of France is bald' assumes that there is a present king of France. Because there isn't, the statement is not true, but is it false, or rather inappropriate and lacking a truth value?

prima facie (Latin: "at first appearance") Based on the first impression: what would be true, or seem to be true in general, before we have additional information about a particular case. Prima facie duties are what we're in general obliged to do, but that might not turn out to be obligatory in particular cases. Prima facie evidence can be overridden by contrary considerations.

primary / secondary qualities Locke (and others) argued that some characteristics we perceive are really as perceived in external objects (the primary qualities), whereas others (the secondary qualities) don't exist as perceived in the real world, but are just powers of external objects to produce ideas in us which don't resemble what's out there. Something's dimensions are supposed to be primary, but its color secondary.

privileged access Supposedly a special way you alone can find out about the contents of your mind. Other people need to infer what's in your mind from your external behavior, but you can discover your mental states directly.

problem of evil A problem for religious believers: God is supposed to be all-powerful, benevolent, and all-knowing. Evil is what is bad for us, so God must eliminate all evil. But there clearly is evil. So a God with all of these features does not exist.

problem of induction Everyone believes that the basic regularities we have observed in the past will continue into the future; this principle is called the principle of induction or the principle of the uniformity of nature. Note however that it would be circular to justify this principle by our past experience. How then to justify it?

problem of other minds If only your mind and its contents can be "perceived" directly only by you, this raises the problem of what ground (if any) you have for thinking that anyone else has a mind, and is not, for example, just a body with external appearance and behavior much like yours.

proposition This term has been used in a confusing variety of ways. Sometimes it means merely a sentence or a statement. Perhaps the most common modern use is the one in which a proposition is what is expressed by a (declarative) sentence: an English sentence and its French translation express the same proposition, and so do Seymour is Marvin's father and Marvin's male parent is Seymour.

propositional attitudes These are our mental states which are, so to speak, directed at propositions. For example, toward the proposition It will snow on Christmas, one can have the propositional attitude of wishing (I wish that it would snow on Christmas), believing, fearing, and so on. Compare these with mental states which are not directed at propositions: feeling happy, enjoying an ice cream, remembering Mama.

punishment Must punishment be unpleasant? Then a judicial sentence of not-unpleasant corrective therapy wouldn't be punishment. Must punishment be given in response to a previous bad act? Then a jail sentence given to an innocent person, either by mistake or to set an example for future wrongdoers, wouldn't count as punishment.

A continuing philosophical problem is the attempt to justify the existence of punishment. The deterrence and rehabilitation theories claim punishments are justified when they have good effects: for example, the prevention of future bad acts through the deterrent threat of punishment to others, or the reform of the wrongdoer. Retributivists claim that such uses of punishment are immoral, and that punishment is justified for wrongdoers merely because wrongdoing demands it—because it's justice—or a restoration of the moral order—to inflict punishment on wrongdoers.

pure reason 1. Pure reason is often taken to be reason working on its own, as contrasted with practical reason which connects facts with desires and yields conclusions about what we ought to do. 2. Pure reason is sometimes spoken of in contrast to empirical reason; thus it's a priori reasoning, supposedly independent of what we get from the senses.

qua (Latin: as) Means considered as (such and such). Usage example: "He is investigating hip hop qua social phenomenon, not qua music."

qualia 1. = characteristics (old-fashioned use). 2. = sense-data. 3. The characteristics of sensations (of sense-data), distinguished from characteristics of things sensed; for example, the flavor of an apple, as tasted, or the feel of a headache. The existence of qualia is sometimes supposed to be a problem for functionalism.

quality / attribute / property These words are synonyms. They each mean a characteristic of something. Some philosophers argue that a thing cannot be composed entirely of qualities; there must be something else, the thing itself, which these are qualities of, in which these qualities are said to "inhere".

rationalism Broadly, any philosophical position which makes reasoning or rationality extra-important. More particularly the view, contrasted with empiricism, that reason alone, unaided by sense experience, is capable of reliable and substantive knowledge; rationalists also tend to believe in innate ideas. Sometimes by "the rationalists" one means the modern continental rationalists, notably Descartes, Leibniz, and Spinoza.

rational self-interest Acting from self-interest is seeking one's own benefit. Some philosophers have sometimes argued that sometimes one can achieve this only by fulfilling some interests of others too; so they argue that rational self-interest often involves more than narrow selfishness.

realism / antirealism Realists hold views (in a variety of philosophical areas) that some sort of entity has external existence, independent of the mind; anti-realists think that that sort of entity is only a product of our thought.

reasons / causes You sometimes have reasons for doing something, but is this to be understood causally? That is, does that mean that there is a special sort of cause for your action? One reason to think that reasons are not causes is that talk about reasons often mentions the future, but a cause of x must occur before x does.

recursive Something (for example, a definition or a function) is recursive when it is to be applied over and over again to its own previous product. For example, one can define 'integer' by saying that 0 is an integer, and if x is an integer, then x + 1 is an integer. Thus, applying the second part of this definition to the first, 1 is an integer, applying the second part to this result, 2 is an integer, and so on.

reduction To reduce some notion is to define (or analyze) it in terms of others, and thus to eliminate it from the list of basic entities in the field under discussion. Reductionism about some notion is the idea that that notion can be reduced—can be given a reductive analysis.

reflective equilibrium A goal sometimes thought to guide the construction of theories. A theory is in reflective equilibrium when the basic general principles of the theory square with the particular facts the theory is supposed to explain. We start with beliefs about particulars, and construct some general principles to explain these. Alterations might then be made in other beliefs about particulars when they conflict with the principles, or in the principles when they conflict with beliefs about particulars.

reification The mistaken way of thinking about some abstract notion as if it were a real thing.

relational / intrinsic properties A property is intrinsic if things have that property in themselves, rather than in relation to other things.

Thus being 100 meters tall is an intrinsic property, but being the tallest building in town is a relational property, because this is relative to the heights of other buildings in town.

relativism / absolutism Relativists argue that when certain views vary among individual people and among cultures (cultural relativism) there is no universal truth: there is instead, only "true for me (or us); false for you (or them)." This contrasts with absolutism (sometimes called objectivism): the position that there is an objectively right view. The most common relativist views concern morality (ethical relativism).

Renaissance The period (fourteenth through sixteenth century) characterized by the diminution of the authority of the Church in favor of a new humanism, and the rapid growth of science.

representationalism Theories that hold that mental contents—thoughts, perceptions, etc.—represent reality. If these representations are the only thing directly available to the mind, how do we know that the external world is actually being represented—and what it is really like?

retrocausation "Backward" causation, in which the effect occurs before the cause. The possibility of retrocausation is debatable.

retrodiction Means 'prediction backwards'—"prediction" of the past. A historian might retrodict, for example, on the basis of certain historical documents, that a battle took place centuries ago at a certain location. This retrodiction can be confirmed by present evidence, for example, by artifacts of war dug up at that site.

rights You are said to have a right to do or have something when it is thought that nobody should be allowed to keep you from it. Thus, we can speak of a right to property, or to vote, or to life. Having a right to do something doesn't mean you must or even ought to do it, but merely that you're allowed to do it if you want. Utilitarians might be able to justify according certain rights, but usually rights-theorists insist that a right is independent of utility:

that someone morally can exercise a genuine right even if it is contrary to the general welfare. An inalienable right is a right that one cannot give up or get rid of. A civil right is a right that is (or ought to be) guaranteed and enforced by government. Conventional rights are rights produced or guaranteed by society (by government or agreement, or just by custom). Natural rights, on the other hand, are rights we are supposed to have just because we are human (perhaps because they are God-given).

rigid designator A rigid designator is a term that refers to the same thing in every other possible world in which it exists. It's often thought that proper names are rigid designators, but definite descriptions aren't—they're non-rigid.

self-consciousness In philosophical use, this may mean the sort of knowledge one has of one's self that one gets by adopting the perspective that others might have of one; or else the sort of self-awareness one gets by introspection.

self-contradiction A statement is self-contradictory when it asserts and denies the same thing (It's raining and it's not raining), or when it's logically false. An inconsistent set is self-contradictory. Sometimes (more loosely) a statement that is analytically false is called a self-contradiction.

semantics / syntax / pragmatics These terms name aspects of language and the study of these aspects. Semantics is that part of language which has to do with meaning and reference. Syntax has to do with grammar or logical form. Syntax, then, can tell you whether a sentence is formed correctly (for example, 'Is the on but but' is not formed correctly), but cannot tell you what a correctly formed sentence means, or what conditions would make it true. Pragmatics concerns the relations between bits of language and their uses by language-users.

sense-data The data of the senses—what they give us: the internal event or picture or representation we get when perceiving external objects—or sometimes, as when we dream or hallucinate, even in their absence. A straight stick half under water looks bent; we then have a bent sense-datum, the same sort of internal picture we would have if we saw a bent stick out of water. The argument from illusion is supposed to show that all we really directly (immediately) perceive are sense-data, and that we only infer external objects from these.

simple / complex ideas A complex idea is one that can be analyzed into simpler ideas. Brother, for example, names a complex idea that is "composed" of the ideas of male and sibling; but green perhaps names a simple idea.

skepticism The view that knowledge in some area is not possible. The Skeptics were a group of (skeptical!) Greek philosophers. Skeptics often don't really doubt the truth of the belief about which they are skeptical: their central claim is that we don't have justification for that belief.

slippery slope A form of moral reasoning in which it is argued that some act or practice is undesirable not because it's bad in itself, but because its acceptance will or might lead to a series of other acts that differ from each other in small ways, and eventuate in something clearly bad. It might be argued, for example, that a city's allowing street vendors on one corner isn't in itself bad, but this might gradually lead to more and more permissiveness, resulting eventually in the clogging of city sidewalks by all sorts of undesirables.

social contract A way of justifying the legitimacy of a ruler or government, or the restrictions imposed by government or by moral rules, on the basis of an agreement (whether explicit or tacit or merely hypothetical) of the people involved. It is supposed that people agree (or would agree) to these restrictions because of the resulting long-range benefits to everyone. This agreement is called a 'social contract'. Thinking about this social contract is usually intended (by contractarians) to provide not an actual history of the origin of these rules, but rather a justification of their existence and of their binding force.

solipsism The position that the self is the only thing that can be known, or, more extremely, that one's own mind is the only thing that exists in the universe. Nobody sane ever believed this latter view, but it is philosophically interesting to try to refute it.

state of nature The condition of human societies—typically but not invariably thought to be unpleasant—before the invention of governmental or conventional rules regulating conduct, typically held to justify such invention.

Stoicism The views of the Stoics, an ancient Greek and Roman school. They held that virtue is the highest good, and stressed control of the passions and indifference to pleasure and pain (thus the ordinary use of 'stoic').

straw man Straw man argument or reasoning (or "setting up a straw man") is a bad form of reasoning in which one argues against some position by producing and refuting a false and stupid version of that position.

structuralism Wide-ranging and controversial largely French twentieth-century philosophical school of thought. Its central idea is that cultural phenomena should be understood as manifesting unchanging and universal abstract structures or forms; their meaning can be understood only when these forms are revealed.

subjective / objective Whether something is objective—a feature of the real external mind-independent world, or subjective—in our minds only—is a perennial and pervasive topic in all areas of philosophy. Examples: ethical subjectivism, for example, holds that our ethical "judgments" reflect our own feelings only, not facts about externals. Aesthetic subjectivism puts beauty (and other aesthetic properties) in the eye of the beholder.

substance Any basic, independently existing entity or subject; the stuff of which things are made. Thought sometimes to be unavailable to our senses, but conceptually necessary as that which "underlies" or "supports" characteristics we can sense, and as that which is responsible for things existing through time despite changes in characteristics. Dualists believe there are two substances: (1) physical (material, corporeal, or extended substance), making up physical things, that to which material qualities (size and shape, weight or mass, etc.) apply; (2) mental (immaterial or incorporeal), what mental or spiritual things are made of, and to which characteristics such as thinking, feeling, desiring apply.

supervenience Things of kind A supervene on things of kind B (the 'supervenience base') when the presence or absence of things of kind A is completely determined by the presence or absence of things of kind B; there can be no difference of sort A without a difference in sort B (though there may be differences in B without differences in A). A clear example is the supervenience of the biological on the microphysical: things have biological properties in virtue of their microphysical properties, and there can be no biological difference without a microphysical difference. It is sometimes thought that ethical properties, and mental properties, supervene on the physical.

tabula rasa (Latin: "blank slate") The term is associated with Locke; he and others opposed to innateness think that at birth our minds have no concepts or beliefs in them—they are "blank slates" that will get things "written" on them only after, and by, sense experience.

teleological argument for God's existence Arguments based on the apparent goal-directedness of things in nature. A common version: Living things are adapted to their environment—they are built in complex and clever ways to function well in their surroundings. This could not have happened merely by the random and mechanical processes of nature. They must have been constructed this way, with their functions in mind, by a creator much more clever and powerful than humans; thus they are evidence for God's existence. The usual reply to this argument is that Darwinian evolutionary theory provides a scientific account of how these things arose merely by the mechanical processes of nature, so one need not posit something unseen and supernatural to account for them.

teleology The study of aims, purposes, or functions. Much ancient philosophical and scientific thought saw teleology as a central principle of things, and a very important basis for explanation. Teleology is much less important in contemporary thought, but philosophers are still interested in what teleology remains (for example, scientific talk about what the pancreas is for, or about the function of individual species in the ecosystem). Teleological ethics sees the aim of actions—good results—as the basic concept, from which the notions of right action and good person can be derived.

theism Belief in the existence of at least one god; often, however, more narrowly monotheism—the belief in just one God. The contrast here is with atheism.

theory Scientists and philosophers do not mean "just a guess" by the word theory. A theory here is a system of interrelated statements designed to explain a variety of phenomena. Sometimes a theory is distinguished from a law or set of laws insofar as a theory postulates the existence of unseen theoretical entities.

thought experiment A state of affairs or story we are asked to imagine to raise a philosophical question, or to illustrate or test some philosophical point. For example, imagine that the brains of two people were interchanged; what you would then say about the location of the two might have implications for the principles of personal identity. (Sometimes encountered in its German translation, *Gedankenexperiment*.)

transcendental The most general philosophical usage of this term applies to any idea or system that goes beyond some supposed limit. The word is most often encountered, however, in connection with transcendental idealism, the name of Kant's system; he produced transcendental arguments that were supposed to show truths beyond the evidence of our senses, as necessary presuppositions of any rational experience or thought.

twin-earth An imaginary planet almost exactly like our Earth, commonly referred to in philosophical thought-experiments. Suppose, for example, that rivers and oceans on twin-earth are filled with XYZ, not H_2O, though the two are (except by chemists) indistinguishable. Then when on twin-earth Twin-John asks for "water" in his scotch, does this mean the same as in English?

type / token Two different things that are both of a certain sort are said to be two tokens of one type. Thus, in the sentence 'The cat is on the mat' there are six word tokens, but only five word types. Token physicalism is the view that each particular mental event is identical with (the same thing as) a particular physical event (e.g., a brain event). Type physicalism (sometimes known as the type-type identity theory) adds that each kind of mental event is also a kind of physical event. Functionalists tend to be token physicalists but not type physicalists. Identity theorists tend to be type physicalists. Anomalous monism admits token identity, but denies type identity.

underdetermination Something is underdetermined by a set of conditions if these conditions don't determine how (or that) it will exist. Thus, the striking of a match underdetermines its lighting because it's not sufficient. Language behavior underdetermines a translation manual when different equally adequate translation manuals can be constructed for that behavior. Scientific theory is underdetermined by empirical evidence when two rival hypotheses are both consistent with all the evidence.

universalizability True of a particular action when it can be universalized—that is, when the rule behind it can consistently or reasonably be conceived of as a universal law (one that could apply to everyone). The test of consistent rational universalizability is roughly what Kant thought to be the test of ethically right action. The test of practical universalizability (not Kant's test) is perhaps what we apply when we think morally about some action by evaluating the consequences if everyone were to do that sort of thing.

universals These are "abstract" things—beauty, courage, redness, etc. The problem of universals is whether these exist in the external world. Thus, one may be a realist or anti-realist about universals. Plato's theory of forms is an early and well-known realism about universals; the empiricists are associated with anti-realism. Nominalism is a variety of anti-realism that claims that only particulars exist, and that such abstractions are merely the result of the way we talk.

utilitarianism Utilitarians think that the moral worth of any action can be measured by the extent to which it provides valued results—usually pleasure or happiness—to the greatest number of people. Thus, their general moral principle is the principle of utility, also known as the 'greatest happiness principle': "Act so as to produce the greatest happiness for the greatest number of people." Act utilitarians hold that moral thinking evaluates each act, in context, separately; rule utilitarians argue that morality is concerned with general rules for action, and that a particular action is right if it is permitted or recommended by a moral code whose acceptance in the agent's society would maximize utility, even if that act in particular does not.

utility In utilitarianism, this means the quantity of value or desirability something has. Often it is thought that the utility of something can be given a number (the quantity of "utiles" it possesses), and utilities can be compared or added.

vacuous Means 'empty'. In logic, the statement All A's are B's is understood to be equivalent to For all x, if x is an A then x is a B. Suppose there aren't any A's at all. Then it's always false that any x is an A: but this makes the conditional, if x is an A then x is a B true. It follows, then, that if there aren't any A's, all statements of the form All A's are B's are true. So, for example, because there aren't any unicorns, the statement All unicorns are mammals is true, and so is All unicorns are non-mammals. This strange kind of truth is called vacuous truth.

vagueness In a technical logician's sense, a term is vague whose application involves borderline cases: thus, 'tall' is vague, because there are some people who are clearly tall, some clearly not tall, and some who are in a borderline area, and are not clearly tall or not tall.

verifiability A statement is verifiable when there exist (at least in principle) procedures that would show that it is true or false. 'In principle' is added here because there do not need to be procedures actually available now or ever, as long as we can imagine what they are. So, for example, the statement There is a planet on a star seven million light years from here is unverifiable given our current (and perhaps future) technology, but because we can imagine what would be evidence for its truth or falsity, it is verifiable in principle.

virtue Moral excellence or uprightness; the state of character of a morally worthwhile person. The virtues are those character traits that make for a good person. Some philosophers think that virtue, not good states of affairs or right action, is the central notion in ethics: thus virtue ethics.

zombies These are, of course, the walking dead of horror movies, starring also in the problem of absent qualia which haunts functionalism. In this thought experiment, we are to imagine that zombies show normal stimulus-response connections, but no qualia—no consciousness. The functionalist would have to grant them mentality; this is supposed to show what's wrong with functionalism.

IMAGE CREDITS

Line drawing portraits by Rose McNeil:

A.J. Ayer
Nelson Goodman
Carl Hempel
Thomas Kuhn
J.L. Mackie
Mary Midgley
G.E. Moore
Karl Popper
Gilbert Ryle
Wesley Salmon

Author images contributed by their respective authors:

David Chalmers
Lorraine Code
Daniel Dennett
Edmund Gettier
Virginia Held
Frank Jackson
Thomas Nagel
Alvin Plantinga
Hilary Putnam
J.J.C. Smart

ACKNOWLEDGMENTS

The publisher has made every attempt to locate the authors of the copyrighted material or their heirs and assigns, and would be grateful for information that would allow correction of any errors or omissions in subsequent editions of the work.

Anselm of Canterbury, St. From *Anselm of Canterbury: The Major Works*. Edited by Brian Davies and G.R. Evans, Oxford World's Classics, 1998; pp. 82–83; 87–89; 105–122. By permission of Oxford University Press.

Aquinas, St. Thomas. From *Basic Writings of Saint Thomas Aquinas*, Volume I, Anton C. Pegis, editor. Hackett Publishing Company, 1997; pp. 18–24. Reprinted by permission of Hackett Publishing Company, Inc. All rights reserved.

Aristotle. *Aristotle: The Nicomachean Ethics*, translated with an Introduction by David Ross [aka W.D. Ross], revised by J.O. Urmson and J.L. Ackrill. Oxford World's Classics, 1998; pp. 1–3; 11–15; 35–47; 106–122; 261–269. By permission of Oxford University Press.

Ayer, A.J. "Freedom and Necessity." From *Philosophical Essays*, published in New York by St. Martin's Press, 1969; pp. 271–284. Reproduced with permission of Palgrave Macmillan.

Berkeley, George. *Three Dialogues Between Hylas and Philonous.* 3rd edition (revised), 1734.

Campbell, C.A. From Chapter IX, "Has the Self Free Will?" From *On Selfhood and Godhood*. London: HarperCollins Publishers Ltd., pp. 158–179. Originally published by George Allen & Unwin, 1957. Copyright © C.A. Campbell, 1957. Reproduced by permission of Taylor & Francis Books UK.

Chalmers, David. "The Puzzle of Conscious Experience." *Scientific American*, December 1995, pp. 80–86. Reprinted by permission of the author.

Churchland, Paul M. "Eliminative Materialism and the Propositional Attitudes." *The Journal of Philosophy* Volume 78, Number 2, February, 1981; pp. 67–90. Reprinted by permission of *The Journal of Philosophy* and Paul Churchland.

Code, Lorraine. "Is the Sex of the Knower Epistemologically Significant?" Chapter 1 of *What Can She Know?: Feminist Theory and the Construction of Knowledge*; pp. 1–26. Copyright © 1991 by Cornell University. Used by permission of the publisher, Cornell University Press.

de Beauvoir, Simone. "Introduction" translated by H.M. Parshley, from *The Second Sex* by Simone de Beauvoir, pp. xix–xxxv, copyright © 1952 and renewed 1980 by Alfred A. Knopf, a division of Random House, Inc. Used by permission of Alfred A. Knopf, a division of Random House, Inc.

Dennett, Daniel. *Brainstorms: Philosophical Essays on Mind and Psychology*, pp. 286–299. Copyright © 1981, Massachusetts Institute of Technology, by permission of The MIT Press.

Descartes, René. *Meditations on First Philosophy*, 1641. Translated and edited by John Cottingham. Copyright © 1996 Cambridge University Press; pp. 9–62. Reprinted with the permission of Cambridge University Press.

Gettier, Edmund. "Is Justified True Belief Knowledge?" *Analysis* 23, June 1963; pp. 121–123. By permission of Oxford University Press.

Goodman, Nelson. "The New Riddle of Induction" reprinted by permission of the publisher from *Fact,*

Fiction, and Forecast by Nelson Goodman, pp. 59–83, Cambridge, MA: Harvard University Press. Copyright © 1979, 1983 by Nelson Goodman.

Held, Virginia. "Feminist Transformations of Moral Theory." *Philosophy and Phenomenological Research*, Volume 50, Supplement, Autumn 1990; pp. 321–344. Reproduced with permission of Wiley-Blackwell Inc.

Hempel, Carl G. "Scientific Inquiry: Invention and Test." From *Philosophy of Natural Science*, 1st Edition, © 1967; pp. 10–15. Reprinted by permission of Pearson Education, Inc., Upper Saddle River, NJ.

Hobbes, Thomas. *Leviathan*. London, 1651.

Hume, David. *Dialogues Concerning Natural Religion*. 1779.

Hume, David. *Enquiry Concerning Human Understanding*. 1748; 1777.

Jackson, Frank. "Epiphenomenal Qualia." *The Philosophical Quarterly* Volume 32, Number 127, April 1982; pp. 127–130 and pp. 133–136. Reproduced with permission of Wiley-Blackwell Inc.

Jackson, Frank. "What Mary Didn't Know." *The Journal of Philosophy* 83, May 1986; pp. 291–295 (excerpt).

James, William. "The Will to Believe." From *The Will to Believe, and Other Essays in Popular Philosophy*. Longmans, Green & Co., 1897, pp. 1–31.

Kant, Immanuel. *Critique of Pure Reason*. Translated by Norman Kemp Smith, 1929, Basingstoke, Hants: Palgrave, pp. 41–62. Copyright © 1929; revised edition 1933. Reproduced with permission of Palgrave Macmillan.

Kant, Immanuel. "Groundwork for the Metaphysics of Morals." Translated by Thomas K. Abbott with revisions by Lara Denis. Broadview Press, 2005, pp. 55–95.

Kuhn, Thomas. "Objectivity, Value Judgment and Theory Choice." From *The Essential Tension: Selected Studies in Scientific Tradition and Change*. University of Chicago Press, 1977; pp. 320–339. Copyright © University of Chicago 1977.

Leibniz, Gottfried. "Theodicy: Abridgement of the Argument Reduced to Syllogistic Form." From *The Philosophical Works of Leibnitz*, translated by George M. Duncan. Tuttle, Morehouse & Taylor, 1890.

Locke, John. *An Essay Concerning Human Understanding* was first published in 1690. The excerpts given here are from the sixth edition of 1710.

Longino, Helen. "Can There Be a Feminist Science?" *Hypatia* Volume 2, Issue 3, 1987; pp. 51–64.

Mackie, J.L. "Evil and Omnipotence." *Mind* (New Series), Vol. 64, Issue 254, April 1955; pp. 200–212. By permission of Oxford University Press.

Marx, Karl and Engels, Friedrich. *The Communist Manifesto*. Translated by Samuel Moore and edited by Friedrich Engels, 1888.

Midgley, Mary. "Is a Dolphin a Person?" From *In Defence of Animals*. Edited by Peter Singer. Oxford: Basil Blackwell, copyright © 1985; pp. 52–62. Reproduced with permission of Wiley-Blackwell Inc.

Mill, John Stuart. *On Liberty*. London: John W. Parker & Son, London, 1859.

Mill, John Stuart. *Utilitarianism*, 4th edition. London: Longmans, Green, Reader, and Dyer, 1871.

Moore, G.E. "Proof of an External World." *Proceedings of the British Academy*. Volume 25, 1939; pp. 273–300. Reprinted with the kind permission of Dr. Thomas Baldwin, Literary Executor to G.E. Moore.

Nagel, Thomas. "What Is It Like to Be a Bat?" *The Philosophical Review*, Volume 83, Issue 4, October 1974; pp. 435–450. Published by Duke University Press.

Nietzsche, Friedrich. From *Beyond Good and Evil.* Translated by Marion Faber. Oxford World's Classics, 1998, pp. 152–158. By permission of Oxford University Press.

Nozick, Robert. Excerpt from Chapter 7, "Distributive Justice," of *Anarchy, State and Utopia* (New York: Basic Books, 1974), pp. 149–164, 174–182. Copyright © 1974 by Basic Books, Inc. Reprinted by permission of Basic Books, a member of the Perseus Books Group.

Okin, Susan Moller. "Justice and Gender." *Philosophy and Public Affairs* 16, 1987; pp. 42–72. Reproduced with permission of Wiley-Blackwell Inc.

Peirce, C.S. "The Fixation of Belief." From *Illustrations of the Logic of Science, Popular Science Monthly* 12, November 1877; pp. 1–15.

Plantinga, Alvin. "Is Belief in God Properly Basic?" *Noûs* 15, 1981; pp. 41–51. Reproduced with permission of Wiley-Blackwell Inc.

Plato. Book II (357a-367e), of the *Republic.* Translated by G.M.A. Grube and revised by C.D.C. Reeve. Hackett Publishing Company, 1992; pp. 33–42. Reprinted by permission of Hackett Publishing Company, Inc. All rights reserved.

Popper, Karl. "Science: Conjectures and Refutations." Chapter 1 of *Conjectures and Refutations: The Growth of Scientific Knowledge*, 5th revised edition. London: Routledge, 1989, pp. 33–59. Copyright © University of Klagenfurt/Karl Popper Library.

Putnam, Hilary. "The Nature of Mental States." Originally published as "Psychological Predicates" in *Art, Mind, and Religion*, edited by W.H. Capitan and D.D. Merrill, © 1967. Reprinted by permission of the University of Pittsburgh Press.

Rawls, John. "Three Basic Points" and "Two Principles of Justice" reprinted by permission of the publisher from *Justice as Fairness: A Restatement* by John Rawls, edited by Erin Kelly, pp. 39–50, Cambridge, MA: The Belknap Press of Harvard University Press, copyright © 2001 by the President and Fellows of Harvard College.

Rée, Paul. "The Illusion of Free Will." *Die Illusion der Willensfreiheit.* Translated by Stefan Bauer-Mengelberg; edited by Paul Edwards and Arthur Pap, 1973. Reprinted with the kind permission of Dr. Tim Madigan, Literary Executor to Paul Edwards.

Russell, Bertrand. From Chapters 1 to 3 of *The Problems of Philosophy.* © Bertrand Russell, 1967. By permission of Oxford University Press.

Ryle, Gilbert. "Descartes' Myth." From *The Concept of Mind*, copyright © 1984, London: Routledge and Chicago: The University of Chicago Press. Reproduced by permission of Taylor & Francis Books UK and with permission of the Principal, Fellows, and Scholars of Hertford College in the University of Oxford.

Salmon, Wesley. "Unfinished Business: The Problem of Induction." *Philosophical Studies* Volume 33, Number 1, January 1978; pp. 1–19. With kind permission from Springer Science+Business Media.

Searle, John R. "Minds, Brains, and Programs." *Behavioral and Brain Sciences.* Volume 3, Issue 3, September 1980; pp. 417–424. Copyright © 1990 Cambridge University Press. Reprinted with the permission of Cambridge University Press.

Smart, J.J.C. "Sensations and Brain Processes." *The Philosophical Review*, Volume 68, Issue 2, April 1959; pp. 141–156. Published by Duke University Press.

Williams, B.A.O. and Nagel, Thomas. "Moral Luck," *Proceedings of the Aristotelian Society, Supplementary Volumes.* Volume 50, 1976; pp. 115–135 and pp. 137–151. Reprinted by courtesy of the Editor of the Aristotelian Society: © 1976.

SOURCES FOR QUOTATIONS

CHAPTER 1

Plato, *Apology*. In Plato, *Complete Works*, ed. John M. Cooper (Indianapolis: Hackett, 1997), 33.

Immanuel Kant, "An Answer to the Question: What is Enlightenment?" In Kant, *Practical Philosophy*, ed. Mary J. Gregor (Cambridge: Cambridge University Press, 1996), 17.

Bertrand Russell, *The Problems of Philosophy* (Oxford: Oxford University Press, 1912), 93–94.

CHAPTER 2

Anselm

Max Charlesworth, "Introduction" to *St. Anselm's Proslogion* (Oxford: Clarendon Press, 1965), 17.

Eadmer, *The Life of St. Anselm*, ed. R.W. Southern (Oxford: Clarendon Press, 1962), 142.

Hume

David Hume, "The Life of David Hume, Esq. Written by Himself," reprinted in *The Cambridge Companion to Hume*, ed. David Fate Norton (Cambridge: Cambridge University Press, 1993), 351, 352, 356.

David Hume, *An Enquiry Concerning Human Understanding*, ed. Selby-Bigge and Nidditch (Oxford: Clarendon Press, 1975), 165.

David Hume, letter of 8th June 1776, which can be found in *The Letters of David Hume*, ed. J.Y.T. Greig (Oxford: Clarendon Press, 1935).

Leibniz

Gottfried Leibniz, letter to Remond of 10th January 1714, which can be found in *Die philosophischen Schriften von Gottfried Wilhelm Leibniz*, ed. C.I. Gerhardt (Berlin), Volume III, 60.

Gottfried Leibniz, letter to Bourget of 22nd March 1714, which can be found in *Die philosophischen Schriften von Gottfried Wilhelm Leibniz*, ed. C.I. Gerhardt (Berlin), Volume III, 567.

Gottfried Leibniz, *Reflections on the Advancement of True Metaphysics and Particularly on the Nature of Substance Explained by Force* (1694), section 4.

James

William James, "Diary" for April 30th, 1870, in *The Letters of William James*, ed. Henry James, Jr. (Boston: Atlantic Monthly Press, 1920), Volume I, 147–148.

William James, *The Varieties of Religious Experience* (1902), Lectures VI and VII. In *William James, The Essential Writings*, ed. Bruce Wilshire (Albany: State University of New York Press, 1984), 232.

William James, *Pragmatism*. In the Harvard edition (Cambridge, MA: Harvard University Press, 1975), 29.

CHAPTER 3

Descartes

René Descartes, *Discourse on the Method*, Part 1. In *The Philosophical Writings of Descartes*, ed. Cottingham, Stoothoff and Murdoch (Cambridge: Cambridge University Press, 1985) the quote is in Volume I, page 115.

René Descartes, *Rules for the Direction of the Mind*, Rule Four. In *The Philosophical Writings of Descartes*, *ibid.*, the quote is in Volume I, page 19.

René Descartes, *Principles of Philosophy*, Part 64. In *The Philosophical Writings of Descartes*, *ibid.*, the quote is in Volume I, page 247.

René Descartes, *Principles of Philosophy*, Part 51. In *The Philosophical Writings of Descartes*, *ibid.*, the quote is in Volume I, page 210.

Bernard Williams, "Introduction" to Descartes' *Meditations on First Philosophy*, trans. John Cottingham (Cambridge: Cambridge University Press, 1996), vii.

John Cottingham, *The Cambridge Companion to Descartes*, ed. John Cottingham (Cambridge: Cambridge University Press, 1992), 1.

David Hume, *An Enquiry Concerning Human Understanding*, ed. Selby-Bigge and Nidditch (Oxford: Clarendon Press, 1975), 153.

Elizabeth Anscombe, "The First Person," in S. Guttenplan (ed.) *Mind and Language: Wolfson College Lectures 1974* (Oxford: Oxford University Press, 1975), 45–65.

Locke
P.H. Nidditch, "Introduction" to *An Essay Concerning Human Understanding* (Oxford: Oxford University Press, 1975), vii.

Kant
Immanuel Kant, *Critique of Practical Reason*, ed. Mary Gregor (Cambridge: Cambridge University Press, 1997), 133.

Immanuel Kant, *Critique of Pure Reason*, ed. Norman Kemp Smith (New York: Palgrave, 192), 24–25.

Russell
Bertrand Russell, *Autobiography* (London: George Allen & Unwin, 1967), Volume I, 145.

Moore
Gilbert Ryle, "G.E. Moore," in his *Collected Papers* (London: Hutchinson, 1971), Volume I, 270–271.

CHAPTER 4
Hume
Bertrand Russell, "The Metaphysician's Nightmare" in *Nightmares of Eminent Persons* (London: Simon & Schuster, 1955).

Goodman
Hilary Putnam, "Preface," to *Fact, Fiction, and Forecast* (Cambridge, MA: Harvard University Press, 1983), vii.

Hempel
Richard Jeffrey, "Preface," to Hempel's *Selected Philosophical Essays*, ed. Jeffrey (Cambridge: Cambridge University Press, 2000), ix.

Popper
Peter Medawar, BBC Radio 3, 28 July 1972.

John Eccles, *Facing Reality* (New York: Springer-Verlag, 1970).

Peirce
Peirce, "How to Make Our Ideas Clear" (1878). In *The Essential Peirce*, ed. Houser and Kloesel (Bloomington: Indiana University Press, 1992) the quote is on page 132.

CHAPTER 5
Smart
J.J.C. Smart, "A Philosophical Self-Portrait," in the *Penguin Dictionary of Philosophy*, ed. Thomas Mautner (London: Penguin Books, 1996), 523–524.

Churchland
Paul Churchland, "Preface" to revised edition of *Matter and Consciousness* (Cambridge, MA: MIT Press, 1988), ix.

Nagel
Thomas Nagel, *The View from Nowhere* (Oxford: Oxford University Press, 1986), 3.

CHAPTER 6
Rée
Walter Kaufmann, *Nietzsche: Philosopher, Psychologist, Antichrist* (Princeton: Princeton University Press, 1978), 48.

Campbell
H.D. Lewis, "Obituary of C.A. Campbell," *The (London) Times* March 19, 1974.

CHAPTER 7
Plato
Plato, *Seventh Letter*, translated by C.D.C. Reeves in his "Introduction" to Plato's *Republic*, trans. G.M.A. Grube, revised by C.D.C. Reeve (Indianapolis: Hackett, 1992), ix–x. A later fragmentary quote is from the translation of the *Seventh Letter* by Glen R. Morrow, in *Plato: Complete Works*, ed. John M. Cooper and D.S. Hutchinson (Indianapolis: Hackett, 1997), 1648.

Alfred North Whitehead, *Process and Reality*, corrected edition, ed. D.R. Griffin and D.W. Sherburne (New York: Free Press, 1978), 39.

Aristotle

Jonathan Barnes, "Introduction" to *Aristotle: Ethics*, trans. J.A.K. Thomson, revised by Hugh Tredennick (London: Penguin, 1976), 24.

J.L. Ackrill, *Aristotle the Philosopher* (Oxford: Oxford University Press, 1981), 8.

Kant

Immanuel Kant, *Critique of Practical Reason*, Preface, note 5. This translation is by Mary Gregor.

H.J. Paton, "Preface" to his translation of *The Moral Law, or Kant's Groundwork of the Metaphysics of Morals* (London: Hutchinson University Library, 1949), 7.

G.W.F. Hegel, *Philosophy of Right*, trans. T.M. Knox (Oxford: Oxford University Press, 1967), 90.

Mill

J.S. Mill, *Autobiography* (London: Penguin Books, 1989), 27, 112, 117, 68. The passage from an early draft of his autobiography, deleted before publication, can be found in *The Early Draft of John Stuart Mill's "Autobiography,"* edited by Jack Stillinger (Urbana: University of Illinois Press, 1961), 184. The quote from *Auguste Comte and Positivism* is from page 337 of Vol. 10 of the *Collected Works of J.S. Mill* (Toronto: The University of Toronto Press, 1979).

Henry Sidgwick, in a May 1873 letter to C.H. Pearson; he is quoted in Stefan Collini, *Public Moralists, Political Thought and Intellectual Life in Great Britain 1850–1930* (Oxford: Oxford University Press, 1991), 178.

Arthur James Balfour, *Theism and Humanism* (London: Hodder and Stoughton, 1915), 138.

John Skorupski, "Introduction: The Fortunes of Liberal Naturalism," in John Skorupski, ed., *The Cambridge Companion to Mill* (Cambridge: Cambridge University Press, 1998), 1–34.

John Stuart Mill, *On Liberty*, ed. Edward Alexander (Peterborough, ON: Broadview Press, 1999), 51–52.

Roger Crisp, "Editor's Introduction" to *J.S. Mill: Utilitarianism* (Oxford: Oxford University Press, 1998), 23.

G.E. Moore, *Principia Ethica* (Cambridge: Cambridge University Press, 1903), 67.

Nietzsche

Friedrich Nietzsche, *Nachlass* [Nietzsche's previously unpublished notebooks], Division VIII, Volume 3, Nietzsche's *Werke Kritische Gesamtausgabe*, ed. Colli and Montinari (Berlin: de Gruyter, 1967), 412. This translation is by Tracy Strong.

Friedrich Nietzsche, *Beyond Good and Evil*, section 5. The next quotation is from section 26, and a third from section 46. (These translations are by Marion Faber.)

Friedrich Nietzsche, quoted from a letter to Peter Gast dated June 8, 1887. (Printed in *Friedrich Nietzsche's Briefe an Peter Gast*, published in Leipzig in 1908, and cited by, for example, Walter Kaufmann in the preface to his translation of *Beyond Good and Evil* (New York: Random House, 1996), xi.)

Friedrich Nietzsche, *The Antichrist*, section 57. (This translation is by Walter Kaufmann.)

Friedrich Nietzsche, *Daybreak*, section 101. (This translation is by Maudemarie Clark.)

Walter Kaufmann, "Translator's Preface" to *Beyond Good and Evil* (New York: Random House, 1996), xvii.

Midgley

Andrew Brown, "Mary, Mary, quite contrary," *The Guardian*, Saturday, January 13, 2001.

CHAPTER 8

Hobbes

Thomas Hobbes, *Verse Autobiography* (1670), lines 27–28. This poem is reprinted in the Curley edition of *Leviathan* (Indianapolis: Hackett, 1994), liv–lxiv.

John Aubrey, *Brief Lives, Chiefly of Contemporaries, Set Down by John Aubrey, Between the Years 1669 & 1696*, ed. A. Clark (Oxford: Oxford University Press, 1898), Volume 1, 387.

Thomas Hobbes, Letter 21 in Volume 4 of *The Clarendon Edition of the Works of Thomas*

Hobbes, ed. H. Warender, et al. (Oxford: Oxford University Press, 1983).

Thomas Hobbes, "Tractatus opticus: prima edizione integrale," ed. F. Alessio, *Revista Critica di Storia dela Filosofia* 18 (1963), 147–188.

Thomas Hobbes, *Behemoth*, ed. Stephen Holmes (University of Chicago Press, 1990), 16, 59.

Marx

Karl Marx, *Theses on Feuerbach*, Thesis 11.

Karl Marx, *Early Writings*, trans. Livingstone and Benton (Harmondsworth: Penguin Books and New Left Review, 1975), 425.

A.J.P. Taylor, "Introduction" to Marx and Engels, *The Communist Manifesto* (Harmondsworth: Penguin Books, 1967), 22.

Friedrich Engels, from Marx and Engels, *Collected Works*, Volume 24 (New York: International Publishers, 1989), 468–9.

David McLellan in Miller, et al. (eds.), *The Blackwell Encyclopedia of Political Thought* (Oxford: Blackwell, 1987), 322.

de Beauvoir

The quote from a friend of de Beauvoir is from a letter by Claudine Chonez and is mentioned by de Beauvoir in her autobiography *Force of Circumstances* (1963, translated by Richard Howard and published by Penguin in 1968), from which the quote about the scene at the restaurant also comes. The quote about de Beauvoir realizing she was 'only a woman' compared to Sartre is cited by Deirdre Bair in her introduction to the 1989 Vintage edition of *The Second Sex*, and comes from interviews Bair conducted with de Beauvoir in the 1980s. The subsequent quote is from an interview with de Beauvoir published in *Society*, February 1976. Praise of the book as one of the most important on women ever published comes from Terry Keefe, *Simone de Beauvoir: A Study of Her Writings*, Barnes & Noble Books, 1983 (p. 111), and Maureen Freely, *The Guardian*, June 6, 1999. The quote from Smith is from her review of the book published in *The Spectator*, November 20, 1953, and the quote from *The New Yorker* is from a review by Brendan Gill, February 28, 1953. The *Times Literary Supplement* quote is by Alison Fell, December 9, 2005. The quotation in Suggestions for Critical Reflection 7 is from Jane O'Grady, writing in the *Oxford Companion to Philosophy* (first edition, 1995, p. 179).

Rawls

John Rawls, *Justice as Fairness: A Restatement* (Cambridge, MA: Harvard University Press, 2001), 3, 10, 15.